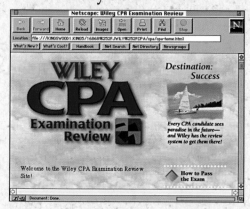

•••••••••••••••••••••• **Special Offer Coupon** ••••••••••••••••••••••

Yes, please send me:

Wiley CPA Examination Review, 25E 1998-1999
- ☐ **2-VOLUME SET** (1-24706-5) ~~$92.00~~ $82.80
- ☐ **Outlines and Study Guides** (1-24707-3) $46.00
- ☐ **Problems and Solutions** (1-24708-1) $46.00

Wiley CPA Examination Review 3.0 for Windows®
- ☐ **Complete Set: CD-ROM** (1-19525-1) ~~$319.00~~ $287.10
- ☐ **Complete Set: Diskettes** (1-24574-7) ~~$319.00~~ $287.10
- ☐ **Accounting and Reporting—Diskette** (1-19556-1) $85.00
- ☐ **Auditing—Diskette** (1-19559-6) $85.00
- ☐ **Business Law—Diskette** (1-19561-8) $85.00
- ☐ **Fin. Acc. and Reporting—Diskette** (1-19558-8) $89.00

Wiley CPA Examination Review, Audio Cassette Program
- ☐ **4-MODULE SET** (1-84275-3) ~~$460.00~~ $414.00
- ☐ **Accounting and Reporting 98** (1-28343-6) $115.00
- ☐ **Auditing** (1-24021-4) $115.00
- ☐ **Business Law** (1-14808-3) $115.00
- ☐ **Financial Accounting and Reporting 98** (1-28344-4) $115.00

Wiley CPA Examination Review, Focus Notes
- ☐ **4-VOLUME SET** (1-32235-0) ~~$127.80~~ $115.00
- ☐ **Accounting and Reporting** (1-19847-1) $31.95
- ☐ **Auditing** (1-19845-5) $31.95
- ☐ **Business Law** (1-19846-3) $31.95
- ☐ **Fin. Acc. and Reporting** (1-19848-X) $31.95

Wiley GAAS 99
- ☐ **Book** (1-19394-1) $62.00
- ☐ **Disk** (avail. 1/99) (1-29855-7) $69.00
- ☐ **CD-ROM** (avail. 1/99) (1-19532-4) $69.00
- ☐ **Book/Disk Set** (avail. 1/99) (1-19535-9) $131.00
- ☐ **Book/CD-ROM Set** (avail. 1/99) (1-32052-8) $131.00

Wiley IAS 99
- ☐ **Book** (1-29626-0) $65.00
- ☐ **Disk** (avail. 2/99) (1-31633-4) $69.00
- ☐ **CD-ROM** (avail. 2/99) (1-31632-6) $69.00
- ☐ **Book/Disk Set** (avail. 2/99) (1-31667-9) $134.00
- ☐ **Book/CD-ROM Set** (avail. 2/99) (1-31666-0) $134.00

Wiley GAAP 99
- ☐ **Book** (1-29639-2) $62.00
- ☐ **Disk** (avail. 1/99) (1-31665-2) $69.00
- ☐ **CD-ROM** (avail. 1/99) (1-31662-8) $69.00
- ☐ **Book/Disk Set** (avail. 1/99) (1-31664-4) $131.00
- ☐ **Book/CD-ROM Set** (avail. 1/99) (1-31663-6) $131.00

10% OFF ON ALL COMPLETE SETS!

Wiley GAAP for Governments 99
- ☐ **Book** (avail. 2/99) (1-29588-4) $65.00
- ☐ **Disk** (avail. 4/99) (1-19540-5) $69.00

Wiley Not-for-Profit GAAP 99
- ☐ **Book** (avail. 2/99) (1-29596-5) $65.00
- ☐ **Disk** (avail. 3/99) (1-31630-X) $69.00

- ☐ **Wiley GAAP Quarterly Update Service** (1094-9976) $96.00/year

(Please type or print clearly.) SOFTWARE AND P.O. BOX ORDERS MUST BE PREPAID.

Name _____

Title _____

Firm _____

Address _____

City_____ State/Zip _____

Telephone _____

Payment: $ _____ plus tax. Total: $ _____

Method of ☐ Bill me ☐ Bill firm VISA MasterCard AMERICAN EXPRESS DISCOVER
Payment: ☐ Check enclosed ☐ ☐ ☐ ☐

All orders include a charge for shipping, applicable sales tax and a handling charge of $4.00 for orders totalling less than $40.00, $6.00 for orders totalling $40.01 to $75.00, and $8.00 for orders totalling $75.01 and above. Orders on approval have a credit limit of $150.00.

Card No. _____ Expiration date _____ / _____

SIGN HERE _____
Credit card orders invalid if not signed. Prices valid in the continental U.S.A., Alaska, Hawaii, and slightly higher in Canada. Prices may change without notice.

613   Promo Code #9-8006   CPA 4-VOL 99

WILEY
Publishers Since 1807

 RUSH!

BUSINESS REPLY MAIL
FIRST-CLASS MAIL   PERMIT NO. 2277   NEW YORK, NY

POSTAGE WILL BE PAID BY ADDRESSEE

JOHN WILEY & SONS INC
DEPT S613
PO BOX 6793
SOMERSET NJ 08875-9977

 WILEY
Publishers Since 1807

 RUSH!

NO POSTAGE
NECESSARY
IF MAILED
IN THE
UNITED STATES

BUSINESS REPLY MAIL
FIRST-CLASS MAIL   PERMIT NO. 2277   NEW YORK, NY

POSTAGE WILL BE PAID BY ADDRESSEE

JOHN WILEY & SONS INC
DEPT S613
PO BOX 6793
SOMERSET NJ 08875-9977

The material included in this manual provides an excellent supplement for the following courses:

COLLEGE/UNIVERSITY COURSE	DELANEY MODULES
Intermediate Financial Accounting	22–30
Advanced Financial Accounting	31–33

IF FOUND, please notify and arrange return to owner. This text is important for the owner's preparation for the Uniform Certified Public Accountant Examination.

Name of CPA Candidate   _____

Address   _____

City, State, Zip   _____

Telephone   (___) _____

Additional texts are available at your local bookstore or directly from John Wiley & Sons, Inc.

Wiley CPA Examination Review

December 1998

Dear Candidate:

Did you know that you can pass all four parts of the CPA Exam on the very first try? *You can.* In fact, over 50% of my students do. You see, in my classroom I employ a rigorous, in-depth, organized, and time-tested approach to preparing for the CPA Exam. This approach can help you pass the CPA Exam on the first try, too. Just as I do in my classroom, *The Wiley CPA Examination Review System* (books, audio-cassettes, and software) leads you step-by-step through each phase of preparation, stresses key concepts, and provides all the pointers and tips you need to succeed.

The CPA Exam is one of the toughest exams to pass. Over 80% of first-time takers fail at least one part. *You* do not have to be one of those people. You *can* pass all four sections of the CPA Exam on your first try. To do so, you'll need a study plan, the right set of tools, and a serious commitment. *The Wiley CPA Examination Review System* provides both a proven study plan and the best study tools available anywhere. But, as I tell my students, you must supply the commitment. Over the next several months you must dedicate yourself to your preparation. It will not be easy. But, if you follow our guidance and focus on your goal, you will be thrilled with the results.

Best of luck,

Pat Delaney

Pat Delaney

SEE ENCLOSED INFORMATION ON SOFTWARE AND AUDIO LECTURES

Examination Review

1999

Financial Accounting and Reporting
BUSINESS ENTERPRISES

Patrick R. Delaney

John Wiley & Sons, Inc.
New York • Chichester • Weinheim • Brisbane • Singapore • Toronto

PERMISSIONS

The following items copyright © by the American Institute of Certified Public Accountants, Inc., are reprinted with permission:

1. Material from *Uniform CPA Examination Questions and Answers*, 1978 through 1998.

2. *Information for CPA Candidates* Board of Examiners, 1998.

Reproduction and adaption of pronouncements, copyright © Financial Accounting Standards Board, Norwalk, Connecticut 06856-5116, with permission.

This text is printed on acid-free paper.

ISBN 0-471-29591-4

Printed in the United States of America

10 9 8 7 6 5 4 3 2 1

PREFACE

The objectives of this review text are to provide study outlines of Financial Accounting and Reporting: Business Enterprises as it is tested on the Uniform CPA Examination, to provide CPA candidates with recent examination questions organized by topic, and to explain the AICPA unofficial answers to the questions included in this text.

This review manual is organized into 12 manageable study units (modules) to assist candidates in organizing their study programs. The clear concise phraseology of the study outlines is supplemented by brief examples and illustrations designed to help candidates quickly understand and retain the material. The multiple-choice questions and other objective format questions in this book are an effective means of studying the material tested on past exams; however, it is also necessary to develop the solutions approach for solving CPA essay questions and problems efficiently. To assist candidates in developing a solutions approach and to assist them in reviewing material tested, we have included a detailed solution guide for each accounting problem and outlines of the unofficial answers to the essay questions published by the AICPA are provided. The coverage in this manual is based on the AICPA's Content Specification Outlines for the Uniform Certified Public Accountant Examination. A Sample Examination is included in Appendix A at the end of this book.

This book has been updated and revised to include new authoritative pronouncements through October 1998. The CPA exam became nondisclosed in May 1996. We are now developing our own questions for new standards as they are issued.

In October 1998, the AICPA released some questions for each section of the November 1997 May 1998 exams. We have included these questions and unofficial answers along with our answer explanations and outlines in Appendix B at the end of this book.

The multiple-choice questions are grouped into topical categories which correspond to the sequencing of the text material as it appears within each of the corresponding modules in this manual.

The author is indebted to the American Institute of Certified Public Accountants for permission to reproduce and adapt examination materials from past certification examinations.

I deeply appreciate the enthusiastic and dedicated attitude of the many CPA candidates with whom I have had the pleasure to work. As always, I welcome any comments concerning materials contained in or omitted from this text. Please send them to Patrick R. Delaney, c/o John Wiley & Sons, Inc., 155 N. 3rd Street, Suite 502, DeKalb, Illinois, 60115 before September 1, 1999.

Please read Chapter 1 carefully, especially "Attributes of Examination Success" and "Purpose and Organization of This Review Textbook."

Good Luck on the Exam,

Patrick R. Delaney
November 1, 1998

ABOUT THE AUTHOR

Patrick R. Delaney is the Arthur Andersen LLP Alumni Professor of Accountancy and Department Chair at Northern Illinois University. He received his PhD in Accountancy from the University of Illinois. He has public accounting experience with Arthur Andersen LLP and is coauthor of *GAAP: Interpretation and Application*, also published by John Wiley & Sons, Inc. He served as Vice President and a member of the Board of Directors, Illinois CPA Society and Chairman of its Accounting Principles Committee; is a past president of the Rockford Chapter, Institute of Management Accountants; and has served on numerous other professional committees. He is a member of the American Accounting Association, American Institute of Certified Public Accountants, and Institute of Accountants. Professor Delaney has published in *The Accounting Review* and is a recipient of the Illinois CPA Society's Outstanding Educator Award, NIU's Excellence in Teaching Award, and Lewis University's Distinguished Alumnus Award. He has been involved in NIU's CPA Review Course as director and instructor.

ABOUT THE CONTRIBUTING AUTHORS

Richard E. Baker, PhD, CPA, is the Ernst and Young Professor of Accountancy and University Presidential Teaching Professor at Northern Illinois University and teaches in the NIU CPA Review Course. Professor Baker prepared the Business Combinations and Consolidations Module. He has received several teaching awards at NIU.

John C. Borke, MAS, CPA, is an Associate Professor of Accounting at the University of Wisconsin-Platteville. He received the UW-Platteville Excellence in Teaching Award, and has worked as a staff auditor with KPMG Peat Marwick. Professor Borke prepared several other sections in Financial Accounting including the section in Chapter 5 on the Conceptual Framework.

John McDougald, MAS, CPA, is an Instructor in the College of Business at Northern Illinois University. He has extensive industry experience having spent 28 years in management positions with Ameritech. Mr. McDougald prepared the Derivatives section of Module 32.

W. Max Rexroad, PhD, CPA, is Professor of Accounting at Illinois State University. He has received the Distinguished Teaching Award from the College of Business at ISU as well as other teaching awards. He has taught numerous CPE courses for the Illinois CPA Society and other state societies. He prepared a revision of the Pensions section in Module 26.

John R. Simon, PhD, CPA, is the Coopers and Lybrand LLP Professor of Accountancy and a Presidential Teaching Professor at Northern Illinois University. He has taught in NIU's CPA Review Course for the past 22 years and was the director of the course for 10 years. He is a recipient of NIU's Excellence in Teaching Award. Professor Simon prepared the Earnings Per Share section of the Stockholders' Equity Module, the Foreign Currency Translation Module, and expanded topical coverage in several other modules in Chapter 5.

Susan Smith, MA, CAS (English), CPA. Ms. Smith has taught rhetoric and technical writing at Northern Illinois University. Ms. Smith prepared material on "Improving Your Writing" in Chapter 3.

CONTENTS

*As explained in Chapter 1, this book is organized into 12 modules (manageable study units). The numbering of the modules commences with number 22 to correspond with the numbering system used in our two-volume set.

ACKNOWLEDGEMENTS

Writing an annualized text is always a publishing event and a rejuvenating human experience. The author is most grateful to the many users of previous editions, both instructors and students who have so generously shared with me their satisfaction with my work and their suggestions for changes and improvements. I hope that this will continue for I have benefited from those communications.

This work continues to be a "community effort." In addition to those colleagues cited as contributors above, I would like to acknowledge and thank those many friends who gave me so many devoted hours to bring this edition to you: Brenda Bannon, Lydia Gage, Margy Miller, Pam Miller, Kay Poormehr, and Toni Simmons.

OTHER CONTRIBUTORS AND REVIEWERS

The following individuals assisted in the preparation of this volume by drafting and reviewing answer explanations for the questions from the Financial Accounting and Reporting Examination.

Kathleen Duff, MAS, CPA, is employed with Sikich Gardner and Co., LLP.

Kendra Schoenholz, MAS, just finished a MAS degree at Northern Illinois University.

Shannon Somers, BS, is working on a MAS degree at Northern Illinois University.

BEGINNING YOUR CPA REVIEW PROGRAM

To maximize the efficiency of your review program, begin by studying (not merely reading) this chapter and the next three chapters of this volume. They have been carefully organized and written to provide you with important information to assist you in successfully completing the Financial Accounting and Reporting section of the CPA exam. Beyond providing a comprehensive outline to help you organize the material tested on the Financial Accounting and Reporting section of the exam, Chapter 1 will assist you in organizing a study program to prepare for the Financial Accounting and Reporting portion. Self-discipline is essential.

GENERAL COMMENTS ON THE EXAMINATION

Successful completion of the Uniform CPA Examination in Financial Accounting and Reporting is an attainable goal. Keep this point foremost in your mind as you study the first four chapters in this volume and develop your study plan.

Purpose of the Examination*

The CPA examination is designed to measure basic technical competence, including

1. Technical knowledge and application of such knowledge
2. Exercise of good judgment
3. Understanding of professional responsibilities

The CPA examination is one of many screening devices to assure the competence of those licensed to perform the attest function and to render professional accounting services. Other screening devices include educational requirements, ethics examinations, etc.

The examination appears to test the material covered in accounting programs of the better business schools. It also appears to be based upon the body of knowledge essential for the practice of public accounting and, perhaps specifically, the audit of a medium-sized client. Since the examination is primarily a textbook or academic examination, you should plan on taking it as soon as possible after completing your undergraduate accounting education.

Examination Content

Guidance concerning topical content of the Financial Accounting and Reporting part of the CPA exam can be found in a document prepared by the Board of Examiners of the AICPA entitled *Content Specification Outlines for the Uniform Certified Public Accountant Examination*. These are incorporated into *Information for CPA Candidates*.

The Board's objective in preparing this detailed listing of topics tested on the exam is to help "in assuring the continuing validity and reliability of the Uniform CPA Examination." These outlines are an excellent source of guidance concerning the areas and the emphasis to be given each area on future exams.

We have included the content outlines for Financial Accounting and Reporting in Chapter 5. Although the exam is now nondisclosed, these outlines should be used as an indication of the topics' relative importance on past exams.

The AICPA Board of Examiners issued revised Content Specification Outlines in December 1997. These are provided to each candidate in *Information for CPA Candidates* when s/he applies to sit for the exam.

New accounting and auditing pronouncements, including those in the governmental and not-for-profit areas, are tested 6 months after the pronouncement's *effective* date. If early application is per-

---

* *The following general comments are largely adapted from **Information for CPA Candidates**, published by the American Institute of Certified Public Accountants. **Information for CPA Candidates** is usually sent to CPA candidates by their State Board of Accountancy as they apply to sit for the CPA examination. If you will not be immediately applying to your State Board of Accountancy to sit for the exam, you may wish to request a complimentary copy from your board or the AICPA. (Write to AICPA, Examination Division, 201 Plaza III Center, Jersey City, NJ 07311-3881.)*

mitted, a pronouncement is tested 6 months after the *issuance* date; candidates are also responsible for the old pronouncement until it is superseded. The exam covers the Internal Revenue Code and federal tax regulations in effect 6 months before the date of the exam. For the Business Law and Professional Responsibilities section, federal laws are tested 6 months following their *effective* date and of uniform acts 1 year after their adoption by a simple majority of jurisdictions.

Nondisclosure of Examination Questions and Answers

As of May 1996, the Uniform CPA Examination became nondisclosed. Candidates will not be allowed to retain or receive their question booklets after the exam. Questions and unofficial answers will no longer be published; however, the AICPA will continue to update and publish *Selected Questions and Unofficial Answers*. This book contains items that are no longer used on actual exams, but they are representative of questions appearing on future exams. Candidates are required to sign a statement that stipulates that they will not reveal the questions and answers after the exam is administered.

Schedule of Examinations

The 2-day Uniform Certified Public Accountant Examination is given twice a year, usually on the first consecutive Wednesday-Thursday in May and November. The subject and time schedules are

CPA EXAM SCHEDULE AND FORMAT

SECTION	*TIME PERIOD*	*MC*	*FORMAT* *OOAF*	*FRE/P*
Business Law and Professional Responsibilities	Wed. 9:00 - Noon	50-60%	20-30%	20-30%
Auditing	Wed. 1:30 - 6:00	50-60%	20-30%	20-30%
Accounting and Reporting (Taxation; Managerial; and Governmental and Not-for-Profit Organizations)	Thur. 8:30 - Noon	50-60%	40-50%	--
Financial Accounting and Reporting (Business Enterprises)	Thurs. 1:30 - 6:00	50-60%	20-30%	20-30%
TOTAL	15.5 hours			
MC = Multiple-Choice; OOAF = Other Objective Answer Formats; FRE/P = Free Response Essay/Problem				

The exact number of multiple-choice questions, other objective format questions, problems, and essay questions that will appear on the exam is unknown. Therefore, it is very important that candidates are aware of the suggested time limits for each question to avoid the possibility of running out of time.

The AICPA began testing with other objective formats on the May 1992 examination. **Note that this is a change in __form__ only. The exam continues to test the same __concepts__.** The other objective questions are included in this book in the modules to which they pertain. A listing of all question material in this book can be found on the first page of Chapter 5.

You will receive one score for the Financial Accounting and Reporting examination. A score of 75 or greater is considered passing. Rules for partial credit on the examination vary from state to state (see "State Boards of Accountancy" section).

The dates for future CPA examinations are

1999	May 5, 6	2000	May 3, 4
	November 3, 4		November 1, 2

Essay questions in the Auditing, Business Law and Professional Responsibilities, and Financial Accounting and Reporting parts of the exam are graded for writing skills. Five percent of the points available on each of these sections is allocated to writing skills. Candidates are graded according to the following six characteristics:

1. Coherent organization
2. Conciseness
3. Clarity

4. Use of standard English
5. Responsiveness to the requirement of the question
6. Appropriateness for the reader

State Boards of Accountancy

The right to practice public accounting as a CPA is governed by individual state statutes. While some rules regarding the practice of public accounting vary from state to state, all State Boards of Accountancy use the Uniform CPA Examination and AICPA advisory grading service as one of the requirements to practice public accounting. Every candidate should inquire of his/her State Board of Accountancy to determine the requirements to sit for the exam (e.g., education, filing dates, references, and fees). A frequent problem candidates encounter is failure to apply by the deadline. APPLY TO SIT FOR THE EXAMINATION EARLY. ALSO, YOU SHOULD USE EXTREME CARE IN FILLING OUT THE APPLICATION AND MAILING THE REQUIRED MATERIALS TO YOUR STATE BOARD OF ACCOUNTANCY. If possible, have a friend review your completed application before mailing with check, photo, etc. Too many candidates are turned down for sitting for a particular CPA examination simply because of minor technical details that were overlooked (checks not signed, photos not enclosed, question not answered on application, etc.). BECAUSE OF THE VERY HIGH VOLUME OF APPLICATIONS RECEIVED IN THE MORE POPULOUS STATES, THE ADMINISTRATIVE STAFF DOES NOT HAVE TIME TO CALL OR WRITE TO CORRECT MINOR DETAILS AND WILL SIMPLY REJECT YOUR APPLICATION. This can be extremely disappointing particularly after spending many hours preparing to sit for a particular exam.

The various state boards, their addresses, and telephone numbers are listed on the following page. Be sure to inquire to your state board for specific and current requirements.

It is possible for candidates to sit for the examination in another state as an out-of-state candidate. Candidates desiring to do so should contact the State Board of Accountancy in their home state.

ATTRIBUTES OF EXAMINATION SUCCESS

Your primary objective in preparing for the Financial Accounting and Reporting part of the CPA exam is to pass. Other objectives such as learning new and reviewing old material should be considered secondary. The six attributes of examination success discussed below are **essential**. You should study the attributes and work toward achieving/developing each of them **before** taking the examination.

	STATE BOARD ADDRESS	TELEPHONE #
AK	Dept. of Comm. and Econ. Dev. Div. of Occ. Licensing • P.O. Box 110806 • Juneau, AK • 99811-0806	(907) 465-2580
AL	RSA Plaza • 770 Washington Avenue• STE 236 • Montgomery, AL • 36130	(334) 242-5700
AR	101 E. Capitol • STE 430 • Little Rock, AR • 72201	(501) 682-1520
AZ	3877 N. 7th St. • STE 106 • Phoenix, AZ • 85014	(602) 255-3648
CA	2000 Evergreen St.• STE 250 • Sacramento, CA • 95815-3832	(916) 263-3680
CO	1560 Broadway • STE 1370 • Denver, CO • 80202	(303) 894-7800
CT	Secretary of State • 30 Trinity Street • PO Box 150470 • Hartford, CT • 06115	(860) 566-7835
DC	614 H Street, N.W. • P.O. Box 37200 • Washington, DC • 20013	(202) 727-7473
DE	Cannon Bldg. • STE 203 • P.O. Box 1401 • Dover, DE • 19903	(302) 739-4522
FL	2610 N.W. 43rd St. • STE 1A • Gainesville, FL • 32606	(352) 955-2165
GA	166 Pryor Street, S.W. • Atlanta, GA • 30303	(404) 656-2281
GU	P.O. Box 5753 • Agana, Guam • 96932	(671) 646-5044
HI	P.O. Box 3469 • Honolulu, HI • 96801	(808) 586-2694
IA	1918 S.E. Hulsizer Ave. • Ankeny, IA • 50021	(515) 281-4126
ID	P.O. Box 83720 • Boise, ID • 83720-0002	(208) 334-2490
IL	505 E. Green St. • STE 216 • Urbana, IL • 61820	(217) 333-1565
IN	302 W. Washington St. Rm E034 • Indianapolis, IN • 46204	(317) 232-5987
KS	900 S.W. Jackson Street • STE 556 • Topeka, KS • 66612-1239	(913) 296-2162
KY	332 W. Broadway • STE 310 • Louisville, KY • 40202	(502) 595-3037
LA	Pan-American Life Center • 601 Poydras St. • STE 1770 • New Orleans, LA • 70130	(504) 566-1244
MA	Saltonstall Bldg. • 100 Cambridge St. • Room 1315 • Boston, MA • 02202	(617) 727-1806
MD	500 N. Calvert St. • Room 308 • Baltimore, MD • 21202	(410) 333-6322
ME	Dept. of Prof.-Fin. Reg. • State House Station 35 • Augusta, ME • 04333	(207) 624-8603
MI	Dept. of Consumer & Industry Services • P.O. Box 30018 • Lansing, MI • 48909	(517) 373-0682
MN	85 E. 7th Pl.• STE 125 • St. Paul, MN • 55101	(612) 296-7937
MO	P.O. Box 613 • Jefferson City, MO • 65102	(573) 751-0012
MS	653 N. State St. • Jackson, MS • 39202	(601) 354-7320
MT	Arcade Bldg, Lower Level • 111 N. Jackson • P.O. Box 200513 • Helena, MT • 59620-0513	(406) 444-3739
NC	1101 Oberlin Rd. • STE 104 • P.O. Box 12827 • Raleigh, NC • 27605	(919) 733-4222
ND	2701 S. Columbia Rd. • Grand Forks, ND • 58201	(800) 532-5904
NE	P.O. Box 94725 • Lincoln, NE • 68509	(402) 471-3595
NH	57 Regional Dr. • Concord, NH • 03301	(603) 271-3286
NJ	P.O. Box 45000• Newark, NJ • 07101	(201) 504-6380
NM	1650 University N.E. • STE 400A • Albuquerque, NM • 87102	(505) 841-9108
NV	200 S. Virginia St. • STE 670 • Reno, NV • 89501	(702) 786-0231
NY	Cultural Ed. Center • Room 3013 • Albany, NY • 12230	(518) 474-3836
OH	77 S. High St. • 18th Flr. • Columbus, OH • 43266-0301	(614) 466-4135
OK	4545 Lincoln Blvd. • STE 165 • Oklahoma City, OK • 73105-3413	(405) 521-2397
OR	3218 Pringle Rd SE • Salem, OR • 97302	(503) 378-4181
PA	116 Pine Street • Harrisburg, PA • 17101	(717) 783-1404
PR	Box 3271 • Old San Juan Station • San Juan, Puerto Rico • 00902	(787) 722-4816
RI	Dept. of Bus. Reg. • 233 Richmond St. • STE 236 • Providence, RI • 02903	(401) 277-3185
SC	P.O. Box 11329 • Columbia, SC • 29211	(803) 896-4494
SD	301 E. 14th St. • STE 200 • Sioux Falls, SD • 57104	(605) 367-5770
TN	500 James Robertson Prkwy. • 2nd Flr. • Nashville, TN • 37243-1141	(615) 741-2550
TX	333 Guadalupe Tower 3• STE 900 • Austin, TX • 78701	(512) 305-7800
UT	160 E. 300 South • Box 45805 • Salt Lake City, UT • 84145	(801) 530-6720
VA	3600 West Broad Street • Richmond, VA • 23230-4917	(804) 367-8505
VI	P.O. Box 3016 • No. 1A Gallows Bay Mkt. Pla. • Christiansted • St. Croix, VI • 00822	(809) 773-4305
VT	Redstone Bldg. • 26 Terrace St. • Montpelier, VT • 05609	(802) 828-2837
WA	210 E. Union Street • STE H • Box 9131 • Olympia, WA • 98507-9131	(360) 753-2585
WI	1400 E. Washington Ave. • P.O. Box 8935 • Madison, WI • 53708	(608) 266-1397
WV	200 L & S Bldg • 812 Quarrier St. • STE 2000 • Charleston, WV • 25301	(304) 558-3557
WY	First Bank Building • 2020 Carey Ave. • Cheyenne, WY • 82002	(307) 777-7551

NOTE: The publisher does not assume responsibility for errors in the above information. You should request information concerning requirements in your state at least 6 months in advance of the exam dates.

1. Knowledge of Material

Two points are relevant to "knowledge of material" as an attribute of examination success. **First**, there is a distinct difference between being familiar with material and knowing the material. Frequently we (you) confuse familiarity with knowledge. Can you remember when you just could not answer an examination question or did poorly on an examination, but maintained to yourself or your instructor that you knew the material? You probably were only familiar with the material. On the CPA examination, familiarity is insufficient; you must know the material. For example, you may be familiar with the concepts in accounting for leases (SFAS 13), but can you compute the present value of an annuity due under a lease agreement and record entries for the lessee and lessor? Once again, a major concern must be to know the material rather than just being familiar with it. Knowledgeable discussion of the material is required on the CPA examination. **Second**, the Uniform Certified Public Accountant Examination in Financial Accounting and Reporting tests a literally overwhelming amount of material at a rigorous level. From an undergraduate point of view, the CPA examination in Financial Accounting and Reporting includes material from the following courses.

> Intermediate Financial
> Advanced Financial

Furthermore, as noted earlier, the CPA exam tests new material in all of these areas. In other words, you are not only responsible for material in the above courses, but also for all new developments in each of these areas.

This text contains outlines of accounting topics from FASB pronouncements, financial accounting courses, etc. Return to the original material (e.g., FASB, your accounting textbooks, etc.) when the outlines less than reinforce material you already know.

2. Commitment to Exam Preparation

Your preparation for the CPA exam should begin at least 3 months prior to your scheduled exam date. Over the course of your preparation, you will experience many peaks and valleys. There will be days when you feel completely prepared and there will also be days when you feel totally overwhelmed. This is not unusual and, in fact, should be expected.

The CPA exam is a very difficult and challenging exam. How many times in your college career did you study months for an exam? Probably not too many. Therefore, candidates need to remain focused on the objective--succeeding on the CPA exam.

Develop a personal study program so that you are reviewing material daily. Of course, you should schedule an occasional study break to help you relax, but don't schedule too many breaks. Candidates who dedicate themselves to studying for the exam have a much greater chance of only going through this process once. On the other hand, a lack of focus and piecemeal preparation will only extend the process over several exams.

3. Solutions Approach

The solutions approach is a systematic approach to solving the problems found on the CPA examination. Many candidates know the material fairly well when they sit for the CPA exam, but they do not know how to take the examination. Candidates generally neither work nor answer problems efficiently in terms of time or grades. The solutions approach permits you to avoid drawing "blanks" on CPA exam problems; using the solutions approach coupled with grader orientation (see below) allows you to pick up a sizable number of points on questions testing material with which you are not familiar. Chapter 3 outlines the solutions approach for problem/essay questions, multiple-choice questions, and other objective questions. Example problems are worked as well as explained.

4.   Grader Orientation

Your score on each section of the exam is determined by the sum of points assigned to individual questions. Thus, you must attempt to maximize your points on each individual question. The name of the game is to satisfy the grader, as s/he is the one who awards you points. Your answer and the grading guide (which conforms closely to the unofficial answer) are the basis for the assignment of points.

This text helps you develop grader orientation by analyzing AICPA grading procedures and grading guides (this is explained further in Chapter 2). The author believes that the solutions approach and grader orientation, properly developed, are worth at least 10 to 15 points on each section to most candidates.

5.   Examination Strategy

Prior to sitting for the examination, it is important to develop an examination strategy (i.e., a preliminary inventory of the questions, the order in which to work questions, etc.). Your ability to cope successfully with the 4 1/2 hours of examination in Financial Accounting and Reporting can be improved by

   a.   Recognizing the importance and usefulness of an examination strategy
   b.   Using Chapter 4 "Taking the Examination" and previous examination experience to develop a "personal strategy" for the exam
   c.   Testing your "personal strategy" on recent CPA questions under examination conditions (using no reference material and with a time limit)

6.   Examination Confidence

You need confidence to endure the physical and mental demands of 4 1/2 hours of problem solving under tremendous pressure. Examination confidence results from proper preparation for the exam, which includes mastering the first five attributes of examination success. Examination confidence is necessary to enable you to overcome the initial frustration with problems for which you may not be specifically prepared.

This study manual, properly used, should contribute to your examination confidence. The systematic outlines herein will provide you with a sense of organization so that as you sit for the examination you will feel reasonably prepared (it is impossible to be completely prepared).

Reasons for Failure

The Uniform Certified Public Accountant Examination is a formidable hurdle in your accounting career. Candidates, generally with a college degree and an accounting major, face about a 30% pass rate nationally on each section of the exam. About 20% of all candidates (first-time and re-exam) sitting for each examination successfully complete that examination. The cumulative pass rate on the exam is about 70-75%; that is, nearly three fourths of first-time candidates eventually pass the exam. The rate is even higher for serious candidates (80%-90%) because a significant number of candidates "drop out" after failing the exam the first time.

Attempt to identify and correct your weaknesses before you sit for the examination based on your experience with undergraduate and previous CPA examinations. Also, analyze the contributing factors to incomplete or incorrect solutions to CPA problems prepared during your study program. The more common reasons for failure are

1. Failure to understand the requirements
2. Misunderstanding the text of the problem
3. Lack of knowledge of material tested
4. Inability to apply the solutions approach
5. Lack of an exam strategy (e.g., time budgeting)
6. Sloppiness, computational errors, etc.
7. Failure to proofread and edit

The above are not mutually exclusive categories. Some candidates get in such a hurry that they misread the requirements and the problem text, fail to use a solutions approach, make computational errors, and omit proofreading and editing.

PURPOSE AND ORGANIZATION OF THIS REVIEW TEXTBOOK

This book is designed to help you prepare adequately for the Financial Accounting and Reporting examination. There is no easy approach to prepare for the successful completion of the CPA Examination; however, through the use of this manual, your approach will be systematic and logical.

The objective of this book is to provide study materials supportive to CPA candidates. While no guarantees are made concerning the success of those using this text, this book promotes efficient preparation by

1. Explaining how to **"satisfy the grader"** through analysis of examination grading and illustration of the solutions approach.

2. **Defining areas tested previously** through the use of the content specification outlines described earlier. Note that predictions of future exams are not made. You should prepare yourself for all possible topics rather than gambling on the appearance of certain questions.

3. **Organizing your study program** by comprehensively outlining all of the subject matter tested on the examination in 12 easy-to-use study modules. Each study module is a manageable task which facilitates your exam preparation. Turn to the TABLE OF CONTENTS and peruse it to get a feel for the organization of this book.

4. **Providing CPA candidates with previous examination problems** organized by topic (e.g., consolidations, inventory, etc.)

5. **Explaining the AICPA unofficial answers** to the examination problems included in this text. The AICPA publishes unofficial answers to all past CPA examinations; however, no explanation is made of the approach that should have been applied to the examination problems to obtain these unofficial answers. Relatedly, the AICPA unofficial answers to multiple-choice and other objective questions provide no justification and/or explanation.

A significant feature of this manual is the grouping of textual material and multiple-choice questions into study sets within the 44 study modules. These distinct study sets are numerically sequenced after each textual set and before the related multiple-choice questions. The Wiley CPA logo ⌗ divides each study set. For example, the end of study set two's review material in the textual material would be marked by [🔖 2]. This number corresponds to multiple-choice problem set [🔖 2] found in the following multiple-choice section. The study sets include a smaller amount of related material than the study modules which provides greater flexibility in the individual candidate's study strategy. It may be helpful to place a marker in the pages on which the multiple-choice question set begins and in the companion answer explanation section to avoid continually flipping through the manual to regain one's spot. The answer explanations for the multiple-choice questions also include headings which provide cross references to the text material. For example, in Module 24, Fixed Assets, the heading "F. Depreciation" appears above the answers to those questions dealing with depreciation. The topical coverage of depreciation can then be found by referring to the corresponding heading within Module 24.

As you read the next few paragraphs which describe the contents of this book, flip through the chapters to gain a general familiarity with the book's organization and contents.

Chapters 2, 3, and 4 are to help you "satisfy the grader."

Chapter 2   Examination Grading and Grader Orientation
Chapter 3   The Solutions Approach
Chapter 4   Taking the Examination

Chapters 2, 3, and 4 contain material that should be kept in mind throughout your study program. Refer back to them frequently. Reread them for a final time just before you sit for the exam.

Chapter 5, Financial Accounting and Reporting, outlines and discusses the coverage of the Financial Accounting and Reporting section of the CPA examination. It also contains the AICPA Content Specification Outlines for all the Financial Accounting and Reporting topics tested in this part of the exam.

Chapter 5 (Financial Accounting and Reporting Modules) contains:

1. AICPA Content Specification Outlines of the material tested on the Financial Accounting and Reporting part of the exam
2. Multiple-choice questions
3. Other objective questions
4. Practice problems and/or essay questions
5. AICPA unofficial answers with the author's explanations for the multiple-choice questions
6. AICPA unofficial answers with the author's explanations for the other objective questions
7. AICPA unofficial answers prefaced by the author's solution guides for the problems
8. AICPA unofficial answers prefaced by the author's answer outlines for the essay questions

Also included at the end of this text are two complete Sample Financial Accounting and Reporting CPA Examinations. We have included two in this volume because of the wide scope of this section of the exam. The sample exams are included to enable candidates to gain experience in taking a "realistic" exam. While studying the modules, the candidate can become accustomed to concentrating on fairly narrow topics. By working through the sample examination near the end of their study programs, candidates will be better prepared for taking the actual examination. The selection of multiple-choice and essay questions/practice problems was based on a statistical analysis of recent exams.

Other Textbooks

This text is a comprehensive compilation of study guides and outlines; it should not be necessary to supplement them with accounting textbooks and other materials for most topics. You probably already have some of these texts or earlier editions of them. In such a case, you must make the decision whether to replace them and trade familiarity (including notes therein, etc.), with the cost and inconvenience of obtaining the newer texts containing a more updated presentation.

Before spending time and money acquiring new texts, begin your study program with *CPA EXAMINATION REVIEW: FINANCIAL ACCOUNTING AND REPORTING* to determine your need for supplemental texts.

Ordering Other Textual Materials

You probably already have intermediate and advanced texts for financial accounting and reporting. If you cannot order desired texts through a local bookstore, write the publisher directly.

The pervasive need of candidates will be AICPA materials. Candidates should locate an AICPA educator member to order their materials, since educator members are entitled to a 30% discount and may place telephone orders. The backlog at the order department is substantial; telephone orders decrease delivery time.

Telephone: (800) 862-4272   Address: Order Department
                                                       American Institute of Certified
                                                       Public Accountants
                                                       P.O. Box 2209
                                                       Jersey City, NJ 07303-2209

Working CPA Questions

The AICPA Content Outlines, study outlines, etc., will be used to acquire and assimilate the knowledge tested on the examination. This, however, should be only **one half** of your preparation program. The other half should be spent practicing how to work problems. Some candidates probably spend over 90% of their time reviewing material tested on the CPA exam. Much more time should be allocated to working old examination problems **under exam conditions**. Working old examination problems (including essay questions) serves two functions. First, it helps you develop a solutions approach as well as solutions that will satisfy the grader. Second, it provides the best test of your knowledge of the material.

At a minimum, candidates should work one of the more complex and difficult problems (e.g., pensions, statement of cash flows, consolidated financial statement worksheet) in each area or module.

The multiple-choice questions and answers can be used in many ways. First, they may be used as a diagnostic evaluation of your knowledge. For example, before beginning to review deferred taxes you may wish to answer 10 to 15 multiple-choice questions to determine your ability to answer CPA examination questions on deferred taxes. The apparent difficulty of the questions and the correctness of your answers will allow you to determine the necessary breadth and depth of your review. Additionally, exposure to examination questions prior to review and study of the material should provide motivation. You will develop a feel for your level of proficiency and an understanding of the scope and difficulty of past examination questions. Moreover, your review materials will explain concepts encountered in the diagnostic multiple-choice questions.

Second, the multiple-choice questions can be used as a poststudy or postreview evaluation. You should attempt to understand all concepts mentioned (even in incorrect answers) as you answer the questions. Refer to the explanation of the answer for discussion of the alternatives even though you selected the correct response. Thus, you should read the explanation of the unofficial answer unless you completely understand the question and all of the alternative answers.

Third, you may wish to use the multiple-choice questions as a primary study vehicle. This is probably the quickest but least thorough approach in preparing for the exam. Make a sincere effort to understand the question and to select the correct response before referring to the unofficial answer and explanation. In many cases, the explanations will appear inadequate because of your unfamiliarity with the topic. Always refer back to an appropriate study source, such as the outlines and text in this volume, your accounting textbooks, FASB pronouncements, etc.

The multiple-choice questions outnumber the essay questions/practice problems by greater than 10 to 1 in this book. This is similar to recent CPA exams. One problem with so many multiple-choice questions is that you may overemphasize them. Candidates generally prefer to work multiple-choice questions because they are

1. Shorter and less time consuming
2. Solvable with less effort
3. Less frustrating than essay questions and practice problems

Another problem with the large number of multiple-choice questions is that you may tend to become overly familiar with the questions. The result may be that you begin reading the facts and assumptions of previously studied questions into the questions on your examination. Guard against this potential problem by reading each multiple-choice question with **extra** care.

Beginning with the May 1992 examination, the AICPA began testing with other objective formats. The other objective format questions that were given on previous exams and others prepared by the author are incorporated in the modules to which they pertain. (See the listing of question and problem material at the beginning of Chapter 5.)

Essay questions require the ability to organize and compose a solution, as well as knowledge of the subject matter. Remember, working essay questions/practice problems is just as important as, if not more important than, working multiple-choice questions. The essay questions and unofficial answers may also be used for study purposes without preparation of answers. Before turning to the unofficial answers, study the question and outline the solution (either mentally or in the margin of the book). Look at our answer outline preceding the unofficial answer for each question and compare it to your own. Next, read the unofficial answer, underlining keywords and phrases. The underlining should reinforce your study of the answer's content and also assist you in learning how to structure your solutions. Answer outlines representing the major concepts found in the unofficial answer are provided for each Financial Accounting and Reporting question. These will facilitate your study of essay questions.

REMEMBER! The AICPA does **not** accept solutions in outline form. THE AICPA EXPECTS THE GRADING CONCEPTS TO BE EXPLAINED IN CLEAR, CONCISE, WELL-ORGANIZED SENTENCES.

However, you may prepare answers in list form as long as the listed items complete a sentence that begins with a lead-in phrase.

The questions and solutions in this volume provide you with an opportunity to diagnose and correct any exam-taking weaknesses prior to sitting for the examination. Continually analyze your incorrect solutions to determine the cause of the error(s) during your preparation for the exam. Treat each incorrect solution as a mistake that will not be repeated (especially on the examination). Also attempt to generalize your weaknesses so that you may change, reinforce, or develop new approaches to exam preparation and exam taking.

After you have finished reviewing for the Financial Accounting and Reporting exam, work the two complete sample exams provided in the Appendix.

SELF-STUDY PROGRAM

The following suggestions will assist you in developing a **systematic**, **comprehensive**, and **successful** self-study program to help you complete the Financial Accounting and Reporting exam.

CPA candidates generally find it difficult to organize and to complete their own self-study programs. A major problem is determining **what** and **how** to study. Another major problem is developing the self-discipline to stick to a study program. Relatedly, it is often difficult for CPA candidates to determine how much to study (i.e., determining when they are sufficiently prepared). The following self-study suggestions will address these and other problems that you face in preparing for the Financial Accounting and Reporting exam. Remember that these are only suggestions. You should modify them to suit your personality, available study time, and other constraints. Some of the suggestions may appear trivial, but CPA candidates generally need all the assistance they can get to systemize their study programs.

Study Facilities and Available Time

Locate study facilities that will be conducive to concentrated study. Factors that you should consider include

1. Noise distraction
2. Interruptions
3. Lighting
4. Availability (e.g., a local library is not available at 5:00 A.M.)
5. Accessibility (e.g., your kitchen table vs. your local library)
6. Desk or table space

You will probably find different study facilities optimal for different times (e.g., your kitchen table during early morning hours and local libraries during early evening hours).

Next review your personal and professional commitments from now until the exam to determine regularly available study time. Formalize a schedule to which you can reasonably commit yourself. In the appendix to this chapter, you will find a detailed approach to managing your time available for the exam preparation program.

Self-Evaluation

The *CPA EXAMINATION REVIEW: FINANCIAL ACCOUNTING AND REPORTING* self-study program is partitioned into 12 topics or modules. Since each module is clearly defined and should be studied separately, you have the task of preparing for the Financial Accounting and Reporting section of the CPA exam by tackling 12 manageable tasks. Partitioning the overall project into 12 modules makes preparation psychologically easier, since you sense yourself completing one small step at a time rather than seemingly never completing one or a few large steps.

By completing the following "Preliminary Estimate of Your Knowledge of Subject" inventory, organized by the 12 modules in this program, you will tabulate your strong and weak areas at the beginning of your study program. This will help you budget your limited study time. Note that you should begin studying the material in each module by answering up to 1/4 of the total multiple-choice questions covering that module's topics (see instruction 4.A. in the next section). This "mini-exam" should constitute a diagnostic evaluation as to the amount of review and study you need.

PRELIMINARY ESTIMATE OF YOUR PRESENT KNOWLEDGE OF SUBJECT*

No.	Module	Proficient	Fairly proficient	Generally familiar	Not familiar
22	Basic Theory and Financial Reporting				
23	Inventory				
24	Fixed Assets				
25	Monetary Current Assets and Current Liabilities				
26	Present Value				
27	Deferred Taxes				
28	Stockholders' Equity				
29	Investments				
30	Statement of Cash Flows				
31	Business Combinations and Consolidations				
32	Foreign Currency Translation				
33	Miscellaneous				

*The number of modules in this text commences with number 22 to correspond with the numbering system used in our two-volume set.

Time Allocation

The study program below entails an average of 80 hours (Step 5. below) of study time. The breakdown of total hours is indicated in the left margin.

[2 1/2 hrs.]   1. Study Chapters 2-4 in this volume. These chapters are essential to your efficient preparation program.

Time estimate includes candidate's review of the examples of the solutions approach in Chapters 2 and 3.

[1/2 hr.]   2. Begin FINANCIAL ACCOUNTING AND REPORTING by studying Chapter 5.

3. Study one module at a time. The modules are listed above in the self-evaluation section.

4. For each module

[10 hrs.]   A. Work 1/4 of the multiple-choice questions (e.g., if there are 40 multiple-choice questions in a module, you should work every 4th question). Score yourself.

This diagnostic routine will provide you with an index of your proficiency and familiarity with the type and difficulty of questions.

Time estimate: 3 minutes each, not to exceed 1 hour total.

[20 hrs.]   B. Study the outlines and illustrations. Refer to outlines of authoritative pronouncements per instructions. Also refer to your accounting textbooks and original authoritative pronouncements (this will occur more frequently for topics in which you have a weak background).

Time estimate: 1 hour minimum per module, with more time devoted to topics less familiar to you.

[20 hrs.]   C. Work the remaining multiple-choice questions. Study the explanations of the multiple-choice questions you missed or had trouble answering.

Time estimate: 3 minutes to answer each question and 2 minutes to study the answer explanation of each question missed.

[5 hrs.]   D. Work the other objective format questions.

Time estimate: 20 minutes for each other objective question and 10 minutes to study the answer explanations for each item missed.

[16 hrs.]   E. Under exam conditions, work at least 2 essay questions and/or practice problems. Work additional essay/problems as time permits.

Time estimate: 20 minutes for each essay question, 45 minutes for each practice problem, and 10 minutes to review the unofficial answer and solution guide for each problem worked.

[6 hrs.]   F. Work through the sample CPA examination presented at the end of this text. The exam should be taken in one sitting.

Take the examination under simulated exam conditions (i.e., in a strange place with other people present [e.g., your local municipal library]). Apply your solutions approach to each problem and your exam strategy to the overall exam.

You should limit yourself to the allotted exam times, and spend time afterwards grading your work and reviewing your effort. It might be helpful to do this with other CPA candidates. Another person looking over your exam might be more objective and notice things such as clarity of essays, logic of problem presentations, etc.

Time estimate: 5-6 hours to take the exam and review it later.

5. The total suggested time of 80 hours is only an average. Allocation of time will vary candidate by candidate. Time requirements vary due to the diverse backgrounds and abilities of CPA candidates.

Allocate your time so you gain the most proficiency in the least time. Remember that while 80 hours will be required, you should break the overall project down into 12 more manageable tasks. Do not study more than one module during each study session.

Using Notecards

Below are one candidate's notecards on financial accounting and reporting topics which illustrate how key definitions, formulas, lists, etc. can be summarized on index cards for quick review. Since candidates can take these anywhere they go, they are a very efficient review tool.

<table>
<tr><td colspan="4"><u>Business Combinations</u></td></tr>
<tr><td><u>Purchase:</u></td><td colspan="3">FMV, differential may have goodwill CNI from date of combination</td></tr>
<tr><td><u>Pooling:</u></td><td colspan="3">BV, capital mix
<u>no</u> goodwill
CNI as if combination took place at beginning of year</td></tr>
</table>

<u>Accounting Changes</u>

	Cum. effect	Pro forma	Restate FS
Δ in estimate	n	n	n
Δ in principle	y	y	n
Δ in reporting entity	n	n	y

Prepared by Greg Graber, CPA, former student, Northern Illinois University

Using Calculators on the Exam

Candidates are provided with calculators at the examination sites for use on the Financial Accounting and Reporting section of the exam. The calculators will have keys for the four primary functions (add, subtract, multiply, and divide) as well as function keys for square root, percentage, and memory. Candidates, however, should only need to use the primary functions. Test calculations are printed in the examination booklet.

The AICPA has stated that "the purpose of providing calculators is to save the time candidates spend on performing and rechecking manual calculations; it is not intended to allow for more difficult and complex calculations and problems."*

It is very important that candidates test their calculators before the start of the Financial Accounting and Reporting section of the exam. **IT IS THE CANDIDATE'S RESPONSIBILITY TO NOTIFY ONE OF THE PROCTORS IMMEDIATELY IN THE EVENT OF A MALFUNCTION. REPLACEMENT CALCULATORS WILL BE AVAILABLE.**

Levels of Proficiency Required

What level of proficiency must you develop with respect to each of the topics to pass the exam? You should work toward a minimum correct rate on the multiple-choice questions of 80% in Financial Accounting and Reporting. Working towards these correct rates or higher ones for Financial Accounting and Reporting will allow for a margin.

Warning: Disproportional study time devoted to multiple-choice and other objective questions (relative to essay questions/problems) can be disastrous on the exam. You should work a substantial number of essay questions and problems under exam conditions, even though multiple-choice questions are easier to work and

---

* *Information for CPA Candidates*, AICPA 14th Edition, p. 50.

are used to gauge your proficiency. The author believes that a serious effort on essay questions and problems will also improve your proficiency on the multiple-choice questions.

Multiple-Choice Feedback

One of the benefits of working through previous exam questions is that it helps you to identify your weak areas. Once you have graded your answers, your strong areas and weak areas should be clearly evident. Yet, the important point here is that you should not stop at a simple percentage evaluation. The percentage only provides general feedback about your knowledge of the material contained within that particular module. The percentage **does not** give you any specific feedback regarding the concepts which were tested. In order to get this feedback, you should look at the questions missed on an individual basis because this will help you gain a better understanding of **why** you missed the question.

This feedback process has been facilitated by the fact that within each module where the multiple-choice answer key appears, two blank lines have been inserted next to the multiple-choice answers. As you grade the multiple-choice questions, mark those questions which you have missed. However, instead of just marking the questions right and wrong, you should now focus on marking the questions in a manner which identifies **why** you missed the question. As an example, a candidate could mark the questions in the following manner: ✓ for math mistakes, x for conceptual mistakes, and ? for areas which the candidate was unfamiliar with. The candidate should then correct these mistakes by reworking through the marked questions.

The objective of this marking technique is to help you identify your weak areas and thus, the concepts which you should be focusing on. While it is still important for you to get between 75% and 80% correct when working multiple-choice questions, it is more important for you to understand the concepts. This understanding applies to both the questions answered correctly and those answered incorrectly. Remember, most of the questions on the CPA exam will be different from the questions in the book, however, the concepts will be the same. Therefore, your preparation should focus on understanding concepts, not just getting the correct answer.

Conditional Candidates

If you have received conditional status on the examination, you must concentrate on the remaining part(s). Unfortunately, many candidates do not study after conditioning the exam, relying on luck to get them through the remaining part(s). Conditional candidates will find that material contained in Chapters 1-4 and the information contained in the appropriate modules will benefit them in preparing for the remaining part(s) of the examination.

PLANNING FOR THE EXAMINATION

Overall Strategy

An overriding concern should be an orderly, systematic approach toward both your preparation program and your examination strategy. A major objective should be to avoid any surprises or anything else that would rattle you during the examination. In other words, you want to be in complete control as much as possible. Control is of paramount importance from both positive and negative viewpoints. The presence of control on your part will add to your confidence and your ability to prepare for and take the exam. Moreover, the presence of control will make your preparation program more enjoyable (or at least less distasteful). On the other hand, a lack of organization will result in inefficiency in preparing and taking the examination, with a highly predictable outcome. Likewise, distractions during the examination (e.g., inadequate lodging, long drive) are generally disastrous.

In summary, establishing a systematic, orderly approach to taking the examination is of paramount importance.

1. Develop an overall strategy at the beginning of your preparation program (see below)
2. Supplement your overall strategy with outlines of material tested on the Financial Accounting and Reporting exam (see Chapter 5)
3. Supplement your overall strategy with an explicitly stated set of problem-solving procedures--the solutions approach
4. Supplement your overall strategy with an explicitly stated approach to each examination session (see Chapter 4)
5. Evaluate your preparation progress on a regular basis and prepare lists of things "to do" (see Weekly Review of Preparation Program Progress on following page)
6. RELAX: You can pass the exam. About 10,000 candidates successfully complete the exam each sitting. You will be one of them if you complete an efficient preparation program and execute well (i.e., use your solutions approach and exam strategy) while writing the exam.

The following outline is designed to provide you with a general framework of the tasks before you. You should tailor the outline to your needs by adding specific items and comments.

A. Preparation Program (refer to Self-Study Program discussed previously)

1. Obtain and organize study materials
2. Locate facilities conducive for studying and block out study time
3. Develop your solutions approach (including solving essay questions and practice problems as well as multiple-choice questions)
4. Prepare an examination strategy
5. Study the material tested recently and prepare answers to actual exam questions on these topics under examination conditions
6. Periodically evaluate your progress

B. Physical Arrangements

1. Apply to and obtain acceptance from your State Board
2. Reserve lodging for examination nights

C. Taking the Examination (covered in detail in Chapter 4)

1. Become familiar with exam facilities and procedures
2. Implement examination strategies and the solutions approach

Weekly Review of Preparation Program Progress

The following pages contain a hypothetical weekly review of program progress. You should prepare a similar progress chart. This procedure, which takes only about 5 minutes per week, will help you proceed through a more efficient, complete preparation program.

Make notes of materials and topics

1. That you have studied
2. That you have completed
3. That need additional study

Weeks To Go	Comments on progress, "to do" items, etc.
12	1) Read Basic Theory and Financial Reporting Module 2) Made notecards 3) Worked the MC and other objective questions 4) Need to work problems using the solutions approach
11	1) Read Fixed Assets and Stockholders' Equity Modules 2) Made notecards 3) Read the SFAS and APB outlines that correspond to these topics 4) Briefly looked over the MC for both modules
10	1) Read Monetary Current Assets and Current Liabilities Module 2) Made notecards 3) Read the corresponding SFAS/APB outlines 4) Worked the MC and other objective questions for Fixed Assets, Stockholders' Equity, and Monetary CA/CL
9	1) Read the Inventory and Statement of Cash Flows Modules 2) Made notecards 3) Skimmed the SFAS and APB outlines, taking notes of important areas 4) Worked the MC and other objective questions
8	1) Read the Present Value Module 2) Made notecards 3) Studied the SFASs and APBs on leases and pensions 4) Completed the MC and other objective questions 5) Need to work problems for leases and pensions
7	1) Read Deferred Taxes Module 2) Made notecards 3) Read the corresponding SFAS and APB outlines 4) Worked the MC and other objective questions 5) Worked some essays/problems for all modules studied thus far

6
1) Read the Foreign Currency Translation and Miscellaneous Modules
2) Made notecards
3) Read the corresponding SFAS and APB outlines
4) Worked the MC and problems for these modules
5) Confident with these mods; only need a quick review

5
1) Read Investments Module
2) Made notecards
3) Read the corresponding SFAS and APB outlines
4) Worked the MC and other objective questions

4
1) Read the Business Combinations and Consolidations Module
2) Reviewed consolidations in an advanced accounting textbook
3) Made notecards
4) Worked the MC and other objective questions

3
1) Worked some essays/problems for all modules studied in weeks 6-4
2) Took Financial Accounting and Reporting Sample Exam
3) Worked lease, pension, and purchase and pooling problems. Am now confident in those areas.

2
1) Reviewed all prior topics, picking out a few MC for each topic and working them out
2) Did a statement of cash flows
3) Completed all essays/problems

1
1) Reviewed notecards and SFAS and APB outlines
2) Worked MC from Deferred Taxes and Stockholders' Equity Modules

0
1) Tried to relax and review topics

Time Management of Your Preparation

As you begin your CPA exam preparation, you obviously realize that there is a large amount of material to cover over the course of the next 3 to 4 months. Therefore, it is very important for you to organize your calendar, and maybe even your daily routine, so that you can allocate sufficient time to studying. An organized approach to your preparation is much more effective than a last week cram session. An organized approach also builds up the confidence necessary to succeed on the CPA exam.

An approach which we have already suggested, is to develop weekly "to do" lists. This technique helps you to establish intermediate objectives and goals as you progress through your study plan. You can then focus your efforts on small tasks and not feel overwhelmed by the entire process. And as you accomplish these tasks you will see yourself moving one step closer to realizing the overall goal, succeeding on the CPA exam.

Note, however, that the underlying assumption of this approach is that you have found the time during the week to study and thus accomplish the different tasks. Although this is an obvious step, it is still a very important step. Your exam preparation should be of a continuous nature and not one that jumps around the calendar. Therefore, you should strive to find available study time within your daily schedule, which can be utilized on a consistent basis. For example, everyone has certain hours of the day which are already committed for activities such as jobs, classes, and, of course, sleep. There is also going to be the time you spend relaxing because CPA candidates should try to maintain some balance in their lives. Sometimes too much studying can be counterproductive. But there will be some time available to you for studying and working through the questions. Block off this available time and use it only for exam prep. Use the time to accomplish your weekly tasks and to keep yourself committed to the process. After awhile your preparation will develop into a habit and the preparation will not seem as overwhelming as it once did.

**NOW IS THE TIME
TO MAKE YOUR COMMITMENT**

EXAMINATION GRADING AND GRADER ORIENTATION

All State Boards of Accountancy use the AICPA advisory grading service. As your grade is to be determined by this process, it is very important that you understand the AICPA grading process and its **implications for your preparation program and for the solution techniques you will use during the examination.**

The AICPA has a full-time staff of CPA examination personnel whose responsibilities include

1. Preparing questions for the examination
2. Working with outside consultants who prepare questions
3. Preparing grading guides and unofficial answers
4. Supervising and reviewing the work of examination graders

The AICPA examination staff is under the supervision of the AICPA Board of Examiners, which has the responsibility for the CPA examination.

This chapter contains a description of the AICPA grading process based on the description of AICPA grading in *Information for CPA Candidates.*

The AICPA Grading Process

The AICPA exercises very tight control over all of the examination papers during the grading process and prior to their return to individual State Boards of Accountancy.

Multiple-choice and other objective questions are graded electronically. Only the candidates' responses are graded. No consideration is given to any comments or explanations. **The AICPA has begun to pretest multiple-choice questions on the exam; there are approximately 10% of these questions in each section of the exam that are not included in the candidate's grade.** Essay and problem answers are graded individually on the basis of grading guides. Grading guides consist of **grading concepts**, which are ideas, constructs, principles, etc., that can be clearly defined.

While tentative grading guides (answers) are prepared prior to the examination, the final grading guides are based upon a test grading of samples of actual examinations. Objective questions are analyzed to determine whether a significant number of candidates selected an answer other than the one identified as the best answer by the AICPA. If an alternative answer is determined to be valid, the Grading Subcommittee may accept both answers. Other acceptable concepts may be added to the grading guide as a result of the test grading process. Additionally alternative interpretations and approaches to essay and problem solutions may result in changes in the grading guides. Once grading guides are fully developed, "production graders" perform the first grading of the examination. The "production graders" are practicing CPAs, university professors, attorneys, etc., commissioned by the AICPA on a per diem basis to grade the examination. These graders specialize in a single essay or problem answer, and grade answers to that question for about 6 weeks.

In this process examination papers move from grader to grader. Attached to each essay/problem is a grading guide similar to the "Hypothetical Grading Guide" on page 25. The objective at this stage is to separate candidates' papers into three categories: obvious pass, marginal, and obvious failures.

A **first review** is performed by highly experienced graders. Essay or problem answers that receive this review fall in the 65-74 range. Quality control is obtained in this process because the reviewer examines the work of individual graders to make sure that the grading guides are being applied correctly. Grading errors are corrected in this process.

Upon completion of the first review for all sections of the exam, a **second review** is done by a grading supervisor or a reviewer who did not perform the first review. To qualify for a second review the candidates' papers must earn grades from 73 through 74 on the sections of the exam failed. According to the *Information for CPA Candidates*, as amended, the second review consists of

1. Manual verification of the accuracy of the objective answer grade.
2. Independent verification of the accuracy of the essay and problem grading by a reviewer who did not perform the first review.

Based on this review, candidate grades are adjusted to reflect any scoring inconsistencies. Second reviews are also given to failing papers of candidates who need to meet a minimum grade requirement in their state in order to condition the exam.

The examination grades are returned to the individual state boards several weeks prior to the official grade release date. The grade release date is usually at the beginning of February for the November exam, and at the beginning of August for the May exam.

Multiple-Choice Grading

Each multiple-choice question is worth one point and grades are based on an overall curve using a combined difficulty adjustment for all types of questions for the Financial Accounting and Reporting section of the exam. Thus, candidates should do their best regardless of the difficulty of the questions. Perfect and use the "multiple-choice question solutions approach" discussed in Chapter 3. If you are unsure about a particular question, you should make an educated guess (i.e., pick the "best" answer). Your grade will be based on your total correct answers since no penalty exists for incorrect answers. The grading procedure for multiple-choice questions is explained in the instructions at the beginning of each section of the exam. As mentioned earlier, up to 10% of the multiple-choice questions are pretest items that are not included in the candidate's grade. The importance of carefully reading and following these and all other instructions cannot be overemphasized.

Other Objective Question Grading

These questions are also graded electronically. The weight for each item will depend on the number of points assigned to the question. For example, if a question that has been assigned 10 points contains 13 items, each correct response would be worth .77 (10/13) of a point. Again, do not be discouraged by your performance; the Financial Accounting and Reporting section is curved on an overall basis.

Essay Grading

To illustrate the grading of essay questions, we have included question Number 5 from the May 1993 Theory examination (now Financial Accounting and Reporting). Following the question are the AICPA Unofficial Answer and a hypothetical grading guide.

Number 5 (Estimated time--15 to 25 minutes)

At December 31, 1999, Niki Co. reviewed the following situations to consider their impact on its 1999 financial statements:

- In December 1999, Niki became aware of a safety hazard related to one of its products. Estimates of the probable costs resulting from the hazard include highest, most likely, and lowest amounts.
- During 1999, Niki received a note for goods sold to a customer. The note was sold to a bank with recourse. The customer filed for bankruptcy in December 1999, before the note's 2000 due date.
- In 1995, Niki moved and assigned the remaining 10 years of its old lease to Pro Co., an unrelated third party. Pro agreed to make all payments due on the assigned lease, but Niki has prime responsibility for the lease to the lessor. At December 31, 1999, it is reasonably possible that Pro will be unable to make all payments due on the assigned lease.
- On November 30, 1999, Niki received goods with a cost denominated in pounds. During December 1999, the dollar's value declined relative to the pound. Niki believes that the original exchange rate will be restored by the time payment is due in 2000.

Required:

For each of the following occurrences, state how Niki should report the impact, if any, on its 1999 financial statements, and explain why the reporting is appropriate.

a. The safety hazard.

b. The customer's filing for bankruptcy.

c. Pro's reasonably possible inability to make all payments due on the assigned lease.

d. Changes in the exchange rate of the dollar and the pound.

UNOFFICIAL ANSWER
Number 5

a. For the safety hazard, Niki should accrue for a loss and a liability equal to the most likely cost. The most likely loss is the best estimate of the expected loss. Accrual of a loss is appropriate because the loss is both probable and can be reasonably estimated. In addition, Niki should separately disclose in the notes to the 1999 financial statements the nature of the hazard and the range of possible loss.

b. Niki should accrue for a loss and a liability for the note sold to a bank. The accrual should equal the amount due on the note plus related costs and less any expected settlement from the bankruptcy. Accrual is appropriate because it is probable that a loss has occurred, as evidenced by the bankruptcy filing, even though this note is not yet due.

c. Niki should disclose the possible loss on the assigned lease in notes to the 1999 financial statements. Disclosures should include details of the assigned lease and the amounts due, estimates of any revenues that might be earned on the property, and any amounts recoverable from Pro. Although disclosure is appropriate for the financial statements not to be misleading, accrual of a loss is inappropriate because the loss is only reasonably possible.

d. Niki should report a foreign exchange loss on its 1999 income statement, and an increase in the account payable to reflect the exchange rate at December 31, 1999. Reporting a foreign exchange loss is appropriate because, consistent with accrual accounting, the exchange rate on December 31, 1999, should be used to value the contract. Niki's beliefs as to future exchange movements are excluded from the financial statements.

Essay questions are generally graded based on the number of **grading concepts** in the candidate's solution. The grading guide is a list of the grading concepts and raw point(s) assigned to each concept. The total raw points listed may be in excess of the maximum points which a candidate may earn on the question. However, for most questions it is necessary for candidates to identify all concepts listed in the AICPA Unofficial Answer to receive all 10 points. A hypothetical grading guide for the preceding accounting theory question appears below. Note that there are 17 grading concepts. The maximum points for the entire question is 10 points.

Sometimes candidates answer one requirement elsewhere than required (i.e., the answer to requirement **a.** may be written as part of the answer to requirement **b.**). Frequently, the grading guides permit cross-grading (i.e., giving credit in one part of the answer for a correct response in another part of the answer). To assure full credit, however, candidates should be very careful to organize their answers to meet the question requirements; you should answer requirement **a.** in answer **a.**, answer requirement **b.** in answer **b.**, etc. Additionally, the efficient use of time is of the utmost importance. If you have included grading concepts in one part of a question that are applicable to another part of the same question, **do not repeat them**. Simply refer the grader to your previous answer.

Two common misconceptions about the AICPA grading of essay questions have cost candidates points in recent years. First, answers should **not** consist of a listing (or outline) of **keywords**. Answers should be set forth in short, concise sentences, organized per the requirements of the question. Second, a candidate should **not** answer only one or two parts of a question very thoroughly and leave the remaining parts blank.

The examiners will grade two samples from essay questions (e.g., requirement c. from one essay and requirement b. from another essay) in the Financial Accounting and Reporting section for writing skills. 5% of the points available on this section is allocated to writing skills. The samples are graded according to the following characteristics:

1. Coherent organization
2. Conciseness
3. Clarity
4. Use of standard English
5. Responsiveness to the requirements of the question
6. Appropriateness for the reader

The "holistic" grading process will provide for the same graders who grade for content to assign 0-5 points based on their overall evaluation of the six characteristics as follows:

0	1	2	3	4	5
	Less than competent		Competent		More than competent

Prior to the actual grading, writing consultants will grade a sample of papers and assign points as shown above. The content graders then use the consultants' evaluations as a guide.

MAY 1993 THEORY, NUMBER 5
HYPOTHETICAL GRADING GUIDE*

Grading Concepts	*Grading Concepts Mentioned*
a. Probable that liability incurred	◯
Amount of loss can be reasonably estimated	◯
Accrue most likely amount (best estimate)	◯
Disclose nature of hazard	◯
Disclose range of possible loss in FS notes	◯
b. Probable that liability incurred	◯
Amount of loss can be reasonably estimated	◯
Accrue amount equal to amount due on note plus related	
costs minus any expected settlement	◯
c. Loss only reasonably possible--no accrual	◯
Disclose possible loss in notes to FS	◯
Include:	
Details of assigned lease	◯
Estimates of revenue that may be earned	◯
Amounts recoverable from Pro	◯
d. Report foreign exchange loss on IS	◯
Report increase in AP	◯
Spot rate should be used to value contract	◯
Consistent with accrual accounting	◯
Grading Concepts Mentioned	═══

The conversion scale below converts the number of concepts mentioned to the grade on the question.

CONVERSION SCALE

Concepts Mentioned	17	16	15	14	13	12	11	10	9	8	7	6	5	4	3	2	1	0
Grade	10	9.4	8.9	8.3	7.7	7.1	6.5	5.9	5.3	4.7	4.1	3.5	3	2.4	1.8	1.2	.6	0

The grading guide might be thought of as a brief outline on the unofficial answer. Note the similarities between the grading guide and the unofficial answer shown with question Number 5. In the above grading guide, note that each grading concept is summarized in a **keyword**. Graders undoubtedly scan for these **keywords** during the first grading. Note that if one of the writing samples, worth 2 points, were taken from the above essay then each concept would be worth .47 points (8 ÷ 17). However, the number of points allocated to writing skills will not be specified in the candidate's grade.

Problem Grading

Problem grading guides are more structured than the grading guides for essay questions, because essay questions have an open-ended nature. Although some alternative calculations may be acceptable for problems, relatively little latitude is available in the problem solutions. Problem grading guides consist of check

---

* *The AICPA Board of Examiners does not release the grading guides used for scoring essay questions and practice problems. The grading guide above was prepared by the author to illustrate the manner in which points are allocated to grading concepts.*

figures from throughout the unofficial answer. The grading of a practice problem is illustrated in the next chapter, The Solutions Approach.

Overall Grade

A hypothetical example appears below to indicate how a candidate's grade is determined for the Financial Accounting and Reporting section of the exam. The example presents one possibility for the format and point assignment on this section of the exam. Candidates should remember that the point distribution of the exam has consisted of 60% multiple-choice, 20% other objective format, and 20% essay/problem.

Type Question	Question Number	Points Allocated	Earned Points
Multiple-Choice	1	60*	43.1
Other Objective Answer Format	2	10	5.3
	3	10	7.2
Essay/Problem	4	10	6.8**
	5	10	8.2**
		100	70.6
Rounding adjustment***			.4
			71.0
Difficulty adjustment			7.0
Grade reported to candidate			78.0

   * *Excluding pretested questions*
  ** *Including writing skill points*
 *** *Rounded up*

Allocation of Points to Questions

Information for CPA Candidates states that the "maximum point values for each question are approximately proportional to the minutes allotted to the question in the suggested time budget printed in the examination booklet." Candidates should be concerned with point allocations for the purpose of allocating their time on the exam.

Grading Implications for CPA Candidates

Analysis of the grading process helps you to understand what graders are looking for and how you can present solutions to "satisfy the grader." Before turning to Chapter 3 for a discussion of how to prepare solutions, consider the following conclusions derived from the foregoing grading analysis.

1. Your solutions should be presented in a neat and organized fashion. Even though the candidate does not receive points solely on the basis of neatness, this is still an important concern. If the candidate's paper must go through a second or third review, the grader will undoubtedly look more favorably upon an organized paper than a sloppy, disorganized paper.
2. Allocate your time based on AICPA minimum suggested times
3. Do your best on every question, no matter how difficult

   a. Remember that the exam is graded on a relative basis
   b. If a question is difficult for you, it probably is difficult for others also
   c. Develop a "solutions approach" to assist you

4. No supporting notes or computations are required for the multiple-choice questions; however, you may use scratch paper to perform computations, etc. The multiple-choice answers are machine-graded, and any related work on scratch paper is ignored.

   a. Conversely, supplementary computation sheets should be prepared for problems for submission to the grader

5. Essay solutions should be numbered and organized according to the problem requirements (e.g., a., b.1., b.2., c.1., c.2., c.3.).

    a. Label your solutions parallel to the requirements
    b. Emphasize keywords
    c. Separate grading concepts into individual sentences or short paragraphs

        (1) Do not bury grading concepts in lengthy paragraphs that might be missed by the grader. Include as many **sensible** grading concepts as possible.
        (2) Use short, uncomplicated sentence structure
        (3) DO NOT PRESENT YOUR ANSWER IN OUTLINE FORMAT

    d. Do not omit any requirements

6. Problem solutions should also be numbered and organized according to the requirements of the problem

    a. Solutions should be complete because of the finite number of grading concepts
    b. Label solutions neatly to help the grader find the required grading concepts (check figures)

        (1) Headings should be prepared for all schedules and statements
        (2) Assumptions should be briefly stated indicating knowledge of alternative treatments

    c. All supporting calculations should be prepared on answer sheets or computational sheets

        (1) Reasonable abbreviations are fine (e.g., AP for accounts payable)
        (2) All such supporting calculations and schedules should be labeled
        (3) In your answer, you should use references such as "See sched. A" or simply place numbers in parentheses alongside the amounts that correspond to subschedules of the required FS or main schedules

In summary, SATISFY THE GRADER. You need neat, readable solutions organized according to the requirements, which will also be the organization of the grading guides. Remember that a legible, well-organized solution gives a professional appearance. Additionally, recognize the plight of the grader having to decipher one mess after another, day after day. Give him/her a break with a neat, orderly solution. The "halo" effect will be rewarded by additional consideration (and hopefully points!).

Candidate Diagnostic Report

The Financial Accounting and Reporting section of this report appears in the space below.

JURISDICTION ILLINOIS		CANDIDATE NUMBER 1-09-000426			EXAMINATION DATE MAY 1996				
SECTION	GRADE	CONTENT AREAS AND PERCENT COVERAGE			PERCENTAGE OF AREA EARNED				
					≤50	51-60	61-70	71-80	81-90	>90
FARE	91	I	Concepts and Standards for Financial Statements	20%					*	
		II	Typical Items in Financial Statements	40%					*	
		III	Specific Transactions and Events in Financial Statements	40%				*		
				100%						

AUTHOR'S NOTE: The above percentages were earned by one of the top 120 candidates in the nation.

If you need to take the Financial Accounting and Reporting section of the exam again, you can use it to help plan your preparation for the next exam. In using your percentage performance in each of the four content areas, remember that they are based on responses to relatively few questions.

NOW IS THE TIME

TO MAKE YOUR COMMITMENT

THE SOLUTIONS APPROACH **3**

The solutions approach is a systematic problem-solving methodology. The purpose is to assure efficient, complete solutions to CPA exam problems, some of which are complex and confusing relative to most under-graduate accounting problems. Unfortunately, there appears to be a widespread lack of emphasis on problem-solving techniques in accounting courses. Most accounting books and courses merely provide solutions to specific types of problems. Memorization of these solutions for examinations and preparation of homework problems from examples is "cookbooking." "Cookbooking" is perhaps a necessary step in the learning process, but it is certainly not sufficient training for the complexities of the business world. Professional accountants need to be adaptive to a rapidly changing, complex environment. For example, CPAs have been called on to interpret and issue reports on new concepts such as price controls, energy allocations, and new taxes. These CPAs rely on their problem-solving expertise to understand these problems and to formulate solutions to them.

The steps outlined below represent only one of many possible series of solution steps. Admittedly, the procedures suggested are **very** structured; thus, you should adapt the suggestions to your needs. You may find that some steps are occasionally unnecessary, or that certain additional procedures increase your problem-solving efficiency. Whatever the case, substantial time should be allocated to developing an efficient solutions approach before taking the examination. You should develop your solutions approach by working old CPA problems.

Note that the steps below relate to any specific question or problem; overall examination strategies are discussed in Chapter 4.

Multiple-Choice Questions Solutions Approach Algorithm

1. **Work individual questions in order.**

   a. If a question appears lengthy or difficult, skip it until you can determine that extra time is available. Put a big question mark in the margin to remind you to return to questions you have skipped or need to review.

2. **Cover the choices before reading each question.**

   a. The answers are sometimes misleading and may cause you to misread or misinterpret the question.

3. **Read each question <u>carefully</u> to determine the topical area.**

   a. Study the requirements **first** so you know which data are important.
   b. Underline keywords and important data.
   c. Identify pertinent information with notations in the margin of the exam.
   d. Be especially careful to note when the requirement is an **exception** (e.g., "Which of the following is **not** an accounting change handled by the cumulative effect method?").
   e. If a set of data is the basis for two or more questions, read the requirements of each of the questions before beginning to work the first question (sometimes it is more efficient to work the questions out of order or simultaneously).
   f. Be alert to read questions as they are, not as you would like them to be. You may encounter a familiar looking item; don't jump to the conclusion that you know what the answer is without reading the question completely.
   g. For comprehensive questions, prepare intermediary solutions as you read the question.

4. **Anticipate the answer before looking at the alternative answers.**

   a. Recall the applicable principle (e.g., change in estimate) or the applicable model (e.g., net present value).
   b. If a question deals with a complex area like earnings per share, set up full-blown diagrams on scratch paper, if necessary, using abbreviations that enable you to follow your work (remember that these questions are machine-graded).

5. **Read the answers and select the <u>best</u> alternative.**

   a. If the answer you have computed is not among the choices, quickly check your math and the logic of your solution. If you don't arrive at one of the given answers in the allotted time, make an educated guess.

6. **Mark the correct answer (or your educated guess) on the examination booklet itself.**

7. **After completing all of the individual questions in an overall question, transfer the answers to the machine gradable answer sheet with extreme care.**

   a. Be very careful not to fall out of sequence with the answer sheet. A mistake would cause most of your answers to be wrong. SINCE THE AICPA USES ANSWER SHEETS WITH VARYING FORMATS, IT WOULD BE VERY EASY TO GO ACROSS THE SHEET INSTEAD OF DOWN OR VICE VERSA. Note the format of your answer sheet carefully!
   b. Review to check that you have transferred the answers correctly.
   c. Do not leave this step until the end of the exam as you may find yourself with too little time to transfer your answers to the answer sheet. THE EXAM PROCTORS ARE NOT PERMITTED TO GIVE YOU EXTRA TIME TO TRANSFER YOUR ANSWERS.

Multiple-Choice Question Solutions Approach Example

A good example of the multiple-choice solutions approach follows, using multiple-choice question number 45 from the November 1994 Financial Accounting and Reporting.

Step 3:

Topical area? Bad debt expense

Step 4A:

Principle? Recognize that uncollectible accounts are debited to the allowance account

Inge Co. determined that the net value of its accounts receivable at December 31, 1999, based on an aging of the receivables, was $325,000. Additional information is as follows:

Allowance for uncollectible accounts--1/1/99	$ 30,000
Uncollectible accounts written off during 1999	18,000
Uncollectible accounts recovered during 1999	2,000
Accounts receivable at 12/31/99	350,000

For 1999, what would be Inge's uncollectible accounts expense?

a. $ 5,000
b. $11,000
c. $15,000
d. $21,000

Currently, all multiple-choice questions are scored based on the number correct (i.e., there is no penalty for guessing). The rationale is that a "good guess" indicates knowledge. Thus, you should answer all multiple-choice questions.

Other Objective Questions Solutions Approach Algorithm

The following types of other objective questions have been tested previously on the Financial Accounting and Reporting section:

a)   Matching
b)   Yes/No or True/False
c)   Numerical computations
d)   Fill-in-the-numbers

The following solutions approach is suggested for answering other objective questions:

1. **Glance over the entire problem.** Scan the problem in order to get a feel for the topical area and related concepts that are being tested. Even though the format of the question may vary, the exam continues to test your understanding of applicable principles or concepts. Relax, take a deep breath, and determine your strategy for conquering the problem.

2. **Identify the requirements of the problem.** This step will help you focus in more quickly on the solution(s) without wasting time reading irrelevant material.

3. **Study the items to be answered.** As you do this and become familiar with the topical area being tested, you should review the concepts of that area. This will help you organize your thoughts so that you can relate logically the requirements of the question with the applicable concepts.

4. **Answer each item one at a time.** The type of OOAF question determines how the candidate should accomplish this step. For instance, when the answer choices are presented in a matching question, the candidate must first understand how the answer choices apply to the question items. The candidate will then be able to differentiate among the answer choices in order to select the appropriate answer for each question. On the other hand, there are questions where the candidate is not presented with

the answer choices (e.g., fill-in-the-numbers). For these questions, the candidate should focus on understanding the question requirements and then applying the correct concepts to compute the answer. You may want to work backwards from the answers to the questions. Don't be afraid to answer questions out of order. Just be careful to place your selected answer next to the appropriate item number in your question booklet.

5. **Use journal entries, T-accounts, time lines, schedules, etc. as appropriate.** The use of these items helps to lay out the information in a logical manner to avoid silly mistakes.

6. **Mark your selected answer on the examination booklet itself.** Once the candidate has selected an answer it should be clearly marked on the examination booklet before moving on to the next question.

7. **After completing all of the items, carefully transfer the answers to the answer sheet.** Be careful to follow the instructions given for the correct placement of zeros. It is very important that all items be recorded on the objective answer sheet, as they cannot be graded if they are not.

Other Objective Questions Solutions Approach Example

Question Number 4(a) consists of 5 items. Use a No. 2 pencil to indicate your answers on the Objective Answer Sheet. These items require numerical answers and selection of the proper cash flow category. For the numerical answers, you are to both write your numerical answer in the boxes and blacken the corresponding oval below each box. **These items cannot be graded if you fail to blacken the ovals.** Write zeros in any blank boxes preceding your numerical answer. If there is a discrepancy between the amount written in the boxes and the amount indicated by the blackened ovals, the amount indicated by the blackened ovals will prevail. **Answer all items.** Your grade will be based on the total number of correct answers.

Following are selected balance sheet accounts of Zach Corp. at December 31, 2000 and 1999, and the increases or decreases in each account from 1999 to 2000. Also presented is selected income statement information for the year ended December 31, 2000, and additional information.

Selected balance sheet accounts	2000	1999	Increase (Decrease)
Assets			
Op. Accounts receivable	$ 34,000	$ 24,000	$10,000
Inv. { Property, plant, and equipment	277,000	247,000	30,000
Accumulated depreciation	(178,000)	(167,000)	(11,000)
Liabilities and stockholders' equity			
{ Bonds payable	49,000	46,000	3,000
Dividends payable	8,000	5,000	3,000
Fin. { Common stock, $1 par	22,000	19,000	3,000
Additional paid-in capital	9,000	3,000	6,000
Retained earnings	104,000	91,000	13,000
Selected income statement information for the year ended December 31, 2000			
Op. Sales revenue	$155,000		
{ Depreciation	33,000		
Inv. { Gain on sale of equipment	13,000		
Net income	28,000		

Additional information

Jnv. • During 2000, equipment costing $40,000 was sold for cash.

Op. • Accounts receivable relate to sales of merchandise.

Fin. • During 2000, $20,000 of bonds payable were issued in exchange for property, plant, and equipment. There was no amortization of bond discount or premium.

AD	?
Cash	?
Equipment	40,000
Gain	13,000

PPE	20,000
BP	20,000

Noncash

Required:

Items 61 through 65 represent activities that will be reported in Zach's statement of cash flows for the year ended December 31, 2000. The following two responses are required for each item:

• Determine the amount that should be reported in Zach's 2000 statement of cash flows. To record your answer, write the number in the boxes on the Objective Answer Sheet and blacken the corresponding oval below each box. These items cannot be graded if you fail to blacken the ovals.
• Using the list below, determine the category in which the amount should be reported in the statement of cash flows and blacken the corresponding oval on the Objective Answer Sheet.

    O. Operating activity
    I. Investing activity
    F. Financing activity

Example

The following is an example of the manner in which the Objective Answer Sheet should be marked. **Zeros have already been marked on the Objective Answer Sheet for the ones, tens, and hundreds columns.**

Item

99. Proceeds from sale of common stock.

Answer Sheet

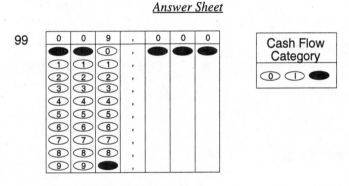

Items to be answered

Op. **61.** Cash collections from customers (direct method).
Jnv. **62.** Payments for purchase of property, plant, and equipment.
Jnv. **63.** Proceeds from sale of equipment.
Fin. **64.** Cash dividends paid.
Fin. **65.** Redemption of bonds payable .

AR		
Beg.	24	x = collections
Sales	155	
End	34	

ANSWER NUMBER 4(a)

61. ($145,000, O) The solutions approach is to set up a T-account for accounts receivable.

PPE		
Beg.	247	40 sold
Exch.	20	
Purch. =	x	
End	277	

	Accounts receivable		
12/31/99	24,000		
Sales revenue	155,000	?	Collections
12/31/00	34,000		

Collections = $ 24,000 + $155,000 - $34,000
        = $145,000

Per SFAS 95, operating activities generally involve delivering or producing goods for sale and providing services. Cash collections from customers are specifically identified as an operating activity.

62.   **($50,000, I)**   The solutions approach is to prepare a T-account for property, plant, and equipment.

	Property, plant & equipment		
12/31/99	247,000		
Equipment from exchange of B/P	20,000		
Payments for purchase of PP&E	?	40,000	Equipment sold
12/31/00	277,000		

Payments = $277,000 + $40,000 - $247,000 - $20,000
        = $50,000

SFAS 95 states that investing activities include the acquisition and disposition of long-term productive assets. Accordingly, the purchase of property, plant, and equipment is an investing activity. Note that the acquisition of property, plant, and equipment in exchange for bonds payable would be disclosed as a noncash investing and financing activity.

63.   **($31,000, I)**   The solutions approach is to set up a T-account for accumulated depreciation.

	Accumulated depreciation		
		167,000	12/31/99
		33,000	Depreciation expense
Equipment sold	?		
		178,000	12/31/00

Accumulated depreciation on equipment sold = $167,000 + $33,000 - $178,000
        = $ 22,000

The entry to reflect the sale of equipment is:

Cash (proceeds from sale of equipment)	31,000 (plug)	
Accumulated depreciation	22,000	
Property, plant, and equipment		40,000 (given)
Gain on sale of equipment		13,000

The proceeds from the sale of equipment of $31,000 is considered an investing activity. Investing activities include the acquisition and disposition of long-term productive assets.

64.   **($12,000, F)**   The cash dividends paid can be determined by analyzing T-accounts for retained earnings and dividends payable.

	Retained earnings		
		91,000	12/31/99
Dividends declared	?	28,000	Net income
		104,000	12/31/00

Dividends declared = $91,000 + $28,000 - $104,000
        = $15,000

	Dividends payable	
	5,000	12/31/99
	15,000	Dividends declared
Cash dividends paid ?		
	8,000	12/31/00

Cash dividends paid = $ 5,000 + $15,000 - $8,000
              = $12,000

Financing activities include all cash flows involving liabilities and equity other than operating items. Payment of cash dividends is thus a financing activity.

65. **($17,000, F)**   The redemption of bonds payable amount is determined by setting up a T-account.

	Bonds payable	
	46,000	12/31/99
	20,000	Issuance of B/P for PP&E
Redemption of B/P ?		
	49,000	12/31/00

The problem states that there was no amortization of bond premium or discount, thus, the redemption of bonds payable is the only change not accounted for.

Redemption of bonds payable = $46,000 + $20,000 - $49,000
                = $17,000

Financing activities include all cash flows involving liabilities and equity other than operating items. Therefore, redemption of bonds payable is considered a financing activity.

Problem 2   (15 to 25 minutes)

This question consists of 12 items. Select the **best** answer for each item. Use a No. 2 pencil to blacken the appropriate ovals on the Objective Answer Sheet to indicate your answers. **Answer all items.** Your grade will be based on the total number of correct answers.

Edge Co., a toy manufacturer, is in the process of preparing its financial statements for the year ended December 31, 1999. Edge expects to issue its 1999 financial statements on March 1, 2000.

Required: *Step 2:*

Items 1 through 12 represent various information that has not been reflected in the financial statements. For each item, the following two responses are required:

a. Determine if an adjustment is required and select the appropriate amount, if any, from the list below.

b. Determine (Y/N) if additional disclosure is **required**, either on the face of the financial statements or in the notes to the financial statements.

Blacken the corresponding ovals on the Objective Answer Sheet.

Adjustment amounts	
A. No adjustment is required	D. $250,000
B. $100,000	E. $400,000
C. $150,000	F. $500,000

Items to be answered   *Step 4:*   *Step 6:*

1. Edge owns a small warehouse located on the banks of a river, in which it stores inventory worth approximately $500,000. Edge is not insured against flood losses. The river last overflowed its banks 20 years ago. *A, n*
   No impairment or liability incurred.

2. During 1999, Edge began offering certain health care benefits to its eligible retired employees. Edge's actuaries have determined that the discounted expected cost of these benefits for current employees is $150,000. *C, y*
   Probable and reasonably estimable = Accrue, disclose details in notes.

Step 4:   *Step 6:*

3. Edge offers an unconditional warranty on its toys. Based on past experience, Edge estimates its warranty expense
    to be 1% of sales. Sales during 1999 were $10,000,000. *Probable & Reasonably estimable*   *B, N*
    $10,000,000 x .01 = $100,000.   *No additional disclosure*

4. On October 30, 1999, a safety hazard related to one of Edge's toy products was discovered. It is considered prob-
    able that Edge will be liable for an amount in the range of $100,000 to $500,000.
    Probable and reasonably estimable — Accrue low amount; disclose high   *B, 4*

5. On November 22, 1999, Edge initiated a lawsuit seeking $250,000 in damages from patent infringement.
    Gain contingency   *A, N*

6. On December 17, 1999, a former employee filed a lawsuit seeking $100,000 for unlawful dismissal. Edge's attor-
    neys believe the suit is without merit. No court date has been set.
    Remote   *A, N*

7. On December 15, 1999, Edge guaranteed a bank loan of $100,000 for its president's personal use.   *A, 4*
    Guarantee of indebtedness of others

8. On December 31, 1999, Edge's board of directors voted to discontinue the operations of its computer games divi-
    sion and sell all the assets of the division. The division was sold on February 15, 2000. On December 31, 1999,
    Edge estimated that losses from operations, net of tax, for the period January 1, 2000, through February 15, 2000,
    would be $400,000 and that the gain from the sale of the division's assets, net of tax, would be $250,000 These
    estimates were materially correct. *400,000 — 250,000 = 150,000. Disclose plan*   *C, 4*
    Measurement date

9. On January 5, 2000, a warehouse containing a substantial portion of Edge's inventory was destroyed by fire. Edge
    expects to recover the entire loss, except for a $250,000 deductible, from insurance.   *A, 4*
    Subsequent event——Condition did not exist at balance sheet date = Disclose

10. On January 24, 2000, inventory purchased FOB shipping point from a foreign country was detained at that coun-
    try's border because of political unrest. The shipment is valued at $150,000. Edge's attorneys have stated that it is
    probable that Edge will be able to obtain the shipment.
    Possibility of loss is remote   *A, N*

11. On January 30, 2000, Edge issued $10,000,000 bonds at a premium of $500,000.
    Subsequent event —— Did not exist at balance sheet date = Disclose   *A, 4*

12. On February 4, 2000, the IRS assessed Edge an additional $400,000 for the 1998 tax year. Edge's tax attorneys and
    tax accountants have stated that it is likely that the IRS will agree to a $100,000 settlement.   *B, 4*
    Subsequent event about conditions which existed at balance sheet date = Adjustment, use best estimate Disclose range

Problem 2

1. **(A, N)** This situation is a nonevent. In other words, there has been no impairment of an asset or incurrence of
a liability (i.e., no flood has occurred). Therefore, no adjustment or disclosure is required.

2. **(C, Y)** In this situation, the contingency is probable and reasonably estimable. Therefore, an adjustment of
$150,000 is required to the financial statements. The detail of the postretirement benefit and actuarial assumptions would
be required in notes to the financial statements.

3. **(B, N)** Per SFAS 5, a loss contingency should be accrued if it is probable that a liability has been incurred at
the balance sheet date and the amount of the loss is reasonably estimable. In this situation, the warranty liability is probable and reasonably estimable. Therefore, $100,000 (10,000,000 x 1%) should be accrued for warranty liability. No ad-
ditional disclosure is required.

4. **(B, Y)** In this situation, the loss is both probable and reasonably estimable. FASB Interpretation 14 requires
that when some amount within an estimated range is a better estimate than any other amount in the range, that amount is
accrued. Therefore, a loss of $100,000 should be accrued. If no amount within the range is a better estimate than any
other amount, the amount at the low end of the range is accrued and the amount at the high end is disclosed.

5. **(A, N)** This situation involves a gain contingency. According to SFAS 5, contingencies that might result in
gains usually are not reflected in the accounts since to do so might be to recognize revenue prior to its realization. Therefore, no adjustment is required. SFAS 5 also states that adequate disclosure shall be made of contingencies that might

result in gains, but care should be exercised to avoid misleading implications as to the likelihood of realization. Consequently, unless the probability of collection is **extremely high**, it is not necessary to disclose the gain contingency.

6.   (A, N)   In this situation, the possibility of loss is **remote.** Accordingly, no adjustment or disclosure is required.

7.   (A, Y)   Per SFAS 5, contingencies such as the guarantee of indebtedness of others should be disclosed in the financial statements even though the possibility of loss may be remote. Therefore, no adjustment is required but disclosure is required.

8.   (C, Y)   This situation is the disposal of a segment of a business. According to APB 30, December 31, 1999, is considered the measurement date since on that date management committed itself to a formal plan to dispose of a segment of a business. The estimated loss from operating the discontinued segment, $400,000, is combined with the estimated gain from the sale of the division, $250,000, and the net loss, $150,000, is the required adjustment at December 31, 1999. Since the financial statements are not issued until March 1, 2000, a final adjustment of the December 31 estimated amounts would be made when the division was sold on February 15, 2000 if the estimated amounts differed materially from the actual amounts. In this case no additional adjustment is required. In addition, the plan of disposal would be disclosed. Note that if the gain from the sale of the division was greater than the operating loss, no adjustment would be made at December 31, 1999, but disclosure would still be required.

9.   (A, Y)   In this situation, the fire loss is a subsequent event. Subsequent events can be defined as events or transactions having a material effect on the financial statements that occur subsequent to the balance-sheet date, but prior to issuance of the financial statements and auditor's report. There are two types of subsequent events.

   a.   **Type 1 subsequent events**--those events that provide additional evidence about **conditions that existed** at the date of the balance sheet and affect the estimates used in preparing financial statements.
   b.   **Type 2 subsequent events**--those events that provide evidence with respect to **conditions that did not exist** at the date of the balance sheet being reported on, but arose after that date.

Type I subsequent events require an adjustment to the financial statements. Type II subsequent events require disclosure in notes to the financial statements. Since the fire loss was not a condition which existed at the balance sheet date, it is a type II subsequent event which only requires disclosure.

10.   (A, N)   In this situation, the possibility of loss is **remote.** Therefore, no adjustment or disclosure is required.

11.   (A, Y)   This event is a type II subsequent event. Therefore, no adjustment is required but disclosure is required.

12.   (B, Y)   Since this condition existed at the date of the financial statements, it is a Type I subsequent event which requires an adjustment to the financial statements. FASB Interpretation 14 requires that when some amount within an estimated range is a better estimate than any other amount in the range, that amount is accrued. In this situation, the $100,000 would be accrued since it is the best estimate. Disclosure of the range is required.

Problem Solutions Approach Algorithm

1.   **Glance over the problem.** Only scan the problem. Get a feel for the type or category of problem. Do not read it. Until you understand the requirements, you cannot discriminate important data from irrelevant data.

2.   **Study the requirements.** "Study" as differentiated from "read." Candidates continually lose points due to misunderstanding the requirements. Underline key phrases and words.

2a. **Visualize the solution format.** Determine the expected format of the required solution. Develop an awareness of "schedule and statement format." Put headings on the required statements and schedules. Often a single requirement will require two or more statements, schedules, etc. A common example is a question followed by "why" or "explain." Explicitly recognize multiple requirements by numbering or lettering them on your examination booklet, expanding on the letters already assigned to problem parts.

3.   **Outline the required procedures mentally.** Interrelate any data (e.g., a trial balance or comparative balance sheets) given in the problem to the expected solution format, mentally formulating a "to do" list. Determine what it is you are going to do before you begin doing it. You should usually work through the requirements in order. However, be watchful for problems with interrelated requirements (e.g., each paragraph of information given in the problem is needed to solve more than one requirement). An alternative solutions approach for these types of problems is to make all required compu-

tations for each item of information at one time. By using this time-saving approach, you will solve a part of each requirement as each item of information is covered, but not necessarily in the same order as given on the exam.

3a. **Review applicable principles, knowledge.** Before immersing yourself in the details of the problem, quickly (30-60 seconds) review and organize your knowledge of the principles applicable to the problem. Jot down any acronyms, formulas, or other memory aids relevant to the topic of the question. Otherwise, the details of the problem may confuse and overshadow your previous knowledge of the applicable principles.

4. **Study the text of the problem.** Read the problem carefully. With the requirements in mind, you can now begin to sort relevant data from irrelevant data. Underline and circle important data. The data necessary for answering each requirement may be scattered throughout the problem. As you study the text, use arrows, etc. to connect data pertaining to a common requirement. List the requirements (a., b., etc.) in the margin alongside the data to which they pertain. Use a bright colored pen to mark up the problem. Heavy colored underlining and comments are attention-getting and give you confidence.

4a. **Prepare intermediary solutions as you study the problem.** For example, calculate goodwill, reconstruct accounts, prepare time diagrams, etc. You are able to perceive these required intermediary solutions because you already understand the problem requirements. These intermediary solutions, along with your underlining and your notes in the text of the problem, will drastically decrease re-reading time.

5. **Prepare the solution.** You now are in a position to write a neat, complete, organized, labeled solution. Label computations, intermediary solutions, assumptions made, etc., on your scratch sheets and turn them in with your solution.

6. **Proofread and edit.** Do not underestimate the utility of this step. Just recall all of the "silly" mistakes you made on undergraduate examinations. Corrections of errors and completion of oversights during this step can easily make the difference between passing and failing.

7. **Review the requirements.** Assure yourself that you have answered them all.

Schedule layout. Many candidates are concerned with how to "lay out" schedules and "set up" problems. As you visualize the solution formats, prepare the statement and schedule headings. This will help you understand the requirements and develop the necessary intermediary solutions, analyses, etc. Put the headed answer sheets aside until you have worked through the entire problem and are ready to write up your final solution.

In preparation for the examination, you should continually be concerned with schedule and statement formats. As you study topics (e.g., consolidations, leases, inventory, etc.) and work recent CPA exam problems, always note the schedule and statement formats. To assist you, numerous formats are illustrated throughout this text. Recognize that there generally are several acceptable formats for most presentations. Become comfortable with the alternate presentations by comparing and contrasting unfamiliar formats to the format(s) with which you are familiar.

It is not necessary to memorize the format to be able to solve many financial accounting problems because the necessary components are often listed in the requirements. For example, assume a problem has the following requirement:

a.   Prepare a schedule analyzing the changes in each of the plant asset accounts during 1999. This
     schedule should include columns for beginning balances, increase, decrease and ending balances for
     each of the plant asset accounts.

Analysis: The requirement is to prepare a schedule with four columns as follows:

Cord Company

ANALYSIS OF CHANGES IN PLANT ASSETS
For the Year Ended December 31, 1999

Balance 12/31/98	*Increase*	*Decrease*	*Balance 12/31/99*

Diagrams are very important to help you understand interrelationships within a problem setting. You
should practice using diagrams to analyze problems. For example, if the Sterling Company has investments
in Turner, Grotex, and Scott Companies, this may be diagramed as:

A very important form of diagram is the time diagram or time line as shown below. Time diagrams are
frequently helpful to sort out a series of transactions occurring over several time periods.

Diagrams are recommended for three reasons. First, diagrams help to organize your analysis of the information in the problem. Second, diagrams create a firmer impression in your mind so as to prevent confusion while you are working the problem. A simple diagram, such as 0 ————➤ S indicating that Operating Corp. invested in Service Corp., will often aid your solution. Third, time diagrams promote preparation of
solutions in chronological order, which tends to make them more orderly and complete.

T-accounts (representing ledger accounts) are extremely useful to reconstruct account balances and to
depict the flow of information from account to account. One example of information flows is drawn from
revenue recognition when the installment sales method is used. The gross profit on the installment sales is
deferred to future periods and then recognized proportionately to collection of the receivables.

An example of T-account analysis to reconstruct ledger accounts is inherent in the solution to the
multiple-choice question below:

With certain products, Hite Foods, Inc., includes coupons having no expiration date which are redeemable in merchandise. In the Company's experience, 40% of such coupons are redeemed. The liability for unredeemed coupons at December 31, 1998, was $9,000. During 1999, coupons worth $18,000 were issued and merchandise worth $8,000 was distributed in exchange for coupons redeemed. The December 31, 1999 balance sheet should include a liability of

    a. $ 7,600.
    b. $ 8,200. (correct per the T-account below)
    c. $ 9,800.
    d. $13,000.

	Liability	
Beginning		9,000
40% of Issued		7,200
Redeemed	8,000	
Ending		8,200

Journal Entries. Journal entries are often a "solutions approach" in themselves. When you do not understand a transaction (e.g., amount of profit on a combined sale-financing lease), prepare the journal entries. Furthermore, journal entries can constitute a solutions approach even though they are not explicitly required in the solution, as in the preparation of consolidated worksheets. Many candidates have trouble with journal entries. When you come upon a seemingly difficult entry, diagram the economic event that occurred. Most economic events are transactions with third parties. Therefore, ask yourself, "What did we give up?" and "What did we receive?" Also, always start with the easy elements of a journal entry. If we sold something for cash, debit cash and then worry about the credit. This is particularly important with compound/complex entries.

Problem Solutions Approach Example

We have selected a problem from a previous CPA exam (FARE,1194,Number 4)to demonstrate the solutions approach. It appears on the following pages. Following this solution guide is the AICPA Unofficial Answer.

First, glance over the problem noting that it consists of three related parts requiring various computations and schedules for property, plant, and equipment.

Second, study the requirements. Part a. is essentially two subrequirements requiring a schedule showing depreciation and amortization expense (requirement a.1.) for the year ended 12/31/99 and a schedule showing accumulated depreciation and amortization (requirement a.2.) at 12/31/99 for the depreciable assets.

Part b. requires the computation of gain or loss from disposal of assets that would appear in Blake's income statement for the year ended 12/31/99.

The requirement in part c. is the preparation of the property, plant, and equipment section of the 12/31/99 balance sheet.

Third, determine the steps to your solution. The standard solutions approach for most problems is to complete each requirement in order before moving on to the next requirement. This approach will, of course, work for this problem. However, you may wish to modify your solutions approach for problems of this type in which the requirements are interrelated. This alternative solutions approach is to prepare time lines for each depreciable asset, make all computations for each asset at one time, and label each computation according to the requirement to which it relates. For example, if a number or computation relates to requirement b., it can be labeled "b." Numbers can be added to designate subrequirements contained in each lettered requirement (e.g., a1., a2.). Using this approach, the candidate will solve a part of each requirement as each asset is covered, but not necessarily in the same order as given on the exam. Once you have worked through all the information given, the formal required schedules can be prepared.

Fourth, study the text of the problem, preparing intermediary solutions as you proceed. Go through the problem using a felt tip pen to make marginal notes setting out key information (e.g., useful life is 5 years, salvage value of the depreciable assets is immaterial). Set up time lines for each depreciable asset and transfer data from the text of the problem to the time lines.

Number 4 (Estimated time -- 30 to 40 minutes)

The following condensed trial balance of Probe Co., a publicly held company, has been adjusted except for income tax expense.

Probe Co.
CONDENSED TRIAL BALANCE*

	12/31/99 Balances Dr. (Cr.)	12/31/98 Balances Dr. (Cr.)	Net change Dr. (Cr.)
Cash	$ 473,000	$ 817,000	$(344,000)
Accounts receivable, net	670,000	610,000	60,000
Property, plant, and equipment	1,070,000	995,000	75,000
Accumulated depreciation	(345,000)	(280,000)	(65,000)
Dividends payable	(25,000)	(10,000)	(15,000)
Income taxes payable	35,000	(150,000)	185,000
Deferred income tax liability	(42,000)	(42,000)	--
Bonds payable	(500,000)	(1,000,000)	500,000
Unamortized premium on bonds	(71,000)	(150,000)	79,000
Common stock	(350,000)	(150,000)	(200,000)
Additional paid-in capital	(430,000)	(375,000)	(55,000)
Retained earnings	(185,000)	(265,000)	80,000
Sales	(2,420,000)		
Cost of sales	1,863,000		
Selling and administrative expenses	220,000		
Interest income	(14,000)		
Interest expense	46,000	*Other income/Expense*
Depreciation	88,000		
Loss on sale of equipment	7,000		
Gain on extinguishment of bonds	(90,000)		
	$ 0	$ 0	$300,000

Extraordinary --Show net of tax

---

* *The reason that this problem contains comparative trial balances with net changes is because Number 3 on the same FARE Exam (11/94), which was a SCF, OOAF format, used the same information (see Module 30, "Other Objective Questions" Problem 1.)*

Additional information

- During 1999 equipment with an original cost of $50,000 was sold for cash, and equipment costing $125,000 was purchased. → *Loss of $7,000. Given*
- On January 1, 1999, bonds with a par value of $500,000 and related premium of $75,000 were redeemed. The $1,000 face value, 10% par bonds had been issued on January 1, 1989, to yield 8%. Interest is payable annually every December 31 through 2008. *Net gain = [$90,000 – ($90,000 x 30%)]* ←
- Probe's tax payments during 1999 were debited to Income Taxes Payable. For the year ended December 31, 1998, Probe had recorded a deferred income tax liability of $42,000 based on temporary differences of $120,000 and an enacted tax rate of 35%. Probe's 1999 financial statement income before income taxes was greater than its 1999 taxable income, due entirely to temporary differences, by $60,000. Probe's cumulative net taxable temporary differences at December 31, 1999, were $180,000. Probe's enacted tax rate for the current and future years is 30%.
- 60,000 shares of common stock, $2.50 par, were outstanding on December 31, 1998. Probe issued an additional 80,000 shares on April 1, 1999. *60,000 sh. o/s 3 months,   140,000 sh. o/s 9 months*
- There were no changes to retained earnings other than dividends declared.

Required:

Prepare Probe Co.'s multiple-step income statement for the year ended December 31, 1999, with earnings per share information and supporting computations for current and deferred income tax expense.

SOLUTION
Number 4

1. The requirement is to prepare a multiple-step income statement with earnings per share information and all components of income tax appropriately shown.

2. The basic outline for a formal multiple-step income statement is presented below:

   Net sales
   − Cost of sales
   Gross profit
   − Operating expenses
   Operating income
   ± Other income (expense)
   Income from continuing operations before income taxes
   − Income taxes
   Income from continuing operations
   ± Discontinued operations (net of tax)
   Income before extraordinary items and cumulative effect of accounting change
   ± Extraordinary items (net of tax)
   ± Cumulative effect of change in accounting principle (net of tax)
   Net income
   Per share data

3. Once the revenue and expense items have been identified on the trial balance, the top half of the income statement can be prepared. Probe had no unusual or infrequent items during 1999.

3.1 The sales, cost of sales, and operating expense figures are given in the problem. Operating income equals $249,000, calculated as:

Sales	$2,420,000
CGS	(1,863,000)
S&A exp.	(220,000)
Depr. exp.	(88,000)
Operating inc.	$ 249,000

3.2 Interest income and interest expense are not related to the principal operations of the firm and should be reported as other income (expense). Likewise, the $7,000 loss on sale of equipment (given) is reported as other expense.

Operating inc.	$249,000
Interest inc.	14,000
Interest exp.	(46,000)
Loss on sale of equipment	(7,000)
Income before income tax and extraordinary item	$210,000

4. The only item to be shown net of tax on Probe's income statement is the gain on extinguishment of debt, which is an extraordinary item. Thus two sections of the income statement will disclose income tax expense. Additionally, income taxes on income before income tax and extraordinary item will consist of both current and deferred taxes.

4.1 Since pretax financial statement income exceeded taxable income by $60,000 (given), this amount is subtracted from income before income tax and extraordinary item to determine the amount of income subject to tax. ($210,000 – $60,000 = $150,000 taxable income.) The $60,000 represents temporary differences (no permanent differences occurred in 1999). The current portion of income tax expense equals 30% of taxable income ($150,000 x 30% = $45,000 current tax expense).

4.2 The amount of deferred income tax expense to be reported in 1999 equals the change in Probe's deferred tax liability during the year. Probe's cumulative temporary differences as of 12/31/99 ($180,000, given) multiplied by Probe's tax rate in 1999 (30%) yields the deferred tax liability at year end ($180,000 x 30% = $54,000 deferred tax liability). Subtracting from this the deferred tax liability as of 12/31/98 ($42,000, given) results in the deferred tax expense for 1999 ($54,000 – $42,000 = $12,000 deferred tax expense).

5. In 1999, Probe realized a $90,000 gain on extinguishment of debt. Per SFAS 4, gains and losses from debt extinguishment are classified as extraordinary items to be reported separately and net of tax. Thus, Probe's gain is reported after income before extraordinary item at $63,000 [$90,000 – ($90,000 x 30%)].

6. Earnings per share data must be presented on the face of the income statement because Probe is a publicly held company.

6.1 The weighted-average number of shares outstanding for 1999 must be calculated. 60,000 common shares were outstanding for the first 3 months of the year, and 140,000 (60,000 + 80,000 newly issued) for the remaining 9 months. Thus, weighted-average shares are calculated as:

$$\frac{(60,000 \times 3) + (140,000 \times 9)}{12} = 120,000$$

6.2 Earnings per share information must be shown on the face of the income statement for the following items:

- Income before extraordinary item(s)
- Net income

Reporting a gain or loss per share due to extraordinary items may appear on the face of the statement or in the footnotes.. The three earnings per share amounts are calculated by dividing the respective income amounts by the weighted-average common shares outstanding. Income before extraordinary item equals $153,000 [$210,000 – ($45,000 current + $12,000 deferred tax)], or $1.275 per share. $0.525 per share was earned on the $63,000 extraordinary gain. Net income equals $216,000 ($153,000 + $63,000 extraordinary gain), or $1.80 per share.

Fifth, prepare the solution (see following pages). Place your lettered computations in the appropriate schedule. All schedules should have a heading which includes the name of the company, schedule title, and period covered. Supporting schedules should be appropriately titled and referenced (e.g., "See Schedule 1").

Sixth, proofread and edit.

Seventh, review later if time permits.

UNOFFICIAL ANSWER
Number 4

Probe Co.
INCOME STATEMENT
For the Year Ended December 31, 1999

Sales		$2,420,000
Cost of sales		1,863,000
Gross profit		557,000
Selling and administrative expenses	$220,000	
Depreciation	88,000	308,000
Operating income		249,000
Other income (expenses):		
Interest income	14,000	
Interest expense	(46,000)	
Loss on sale of equipment	(7,000)	(39,000)
Income before income tax and extraordinary item		210,000
Income tax:		
Current	45,000 [1]	
Deferred	12,000 [2]	57,000

Income before extraordinary item	153,000
Extraordinary item:	
Gain on extinguishment of debt, net of income taxes of $27,000	63,000
Net income	$ 216,000

Earnings per share		
Earnings before extraordinary item	$1.275	[3]
Extraordinary item	.525	
Net income	$1.800	

[1]　Current income tax expense:

Income before income tax and extraordinary item	$ 210,000
Differences between financial statement and taxable income	(60,000)
Income subject to tax	150,000
Income tax rate	x 30%
Income tax excluding extraordinary item	$ 45,000

[2]　Deferred income tax expense:

Cumulative temporary differences--12/31/99	$ 180,000
Income tax rate	x 30%
Deferred tax liability--12/31/99	54,000
Deferred tax liability--12/31/98	42,000
Deferred tax expense for 1999	$ 12,000

[3]　Earnings per share:

Weighted-average number of shares outstanding for 1999:

January thru March	60,000 x 3	180,000
April thru December	140,000 x 9	1,260,000
Total		1,440,000
		÷ 12
		120,000

Income before extraordinary item		153,000
Earnings per share	(153,000 ÷ 120,000)	1.275

The hypothetical grading guide below is a schedule of key solution figures showing the "raw" grading points assigned to these key figures.

November 1994 FARE, Number 4　　　　　*Grading concepts*
Hypothetical Grading Guide*　　　　　　　*mentioned*

Probe Co.
INCOME STATEMENT
For the Year Ended December 31, 1999

			Grading
Sales		$2,420,000	◯
Cost of sales		1,863,000	◯
Gross profit		557,000	◯
Selling and administrative expenses	$220,000		◯
Depreciation	88,000	308,000	◯
Operating income		249,000	◯
Other income (expenses):			◯
Interest income	14,000		◯
Interest expense	(46,000)		◯
Loss on sale of equipment	(7,000)	(39,000)	◯
Income before income tax and extraordinary item		210,000	◯

---

* *The AICPA Board of Examiners does not release the grading guides used for scoring essay questions and problems. The grading guide above was prepared by the author to illustrate to candidates the manner in which points are allocated to grading concepts.*

Income tax:

Current   45,000

Deferred   12,000   57,000

Income before extraordinary item   153,000

Extraordinary item:

Gain on extinguishment of debt, net of income taxes of $27,000   63,000

Net income $ 216,000

Earnings per share

Earnings before extraordinary item $1.275

Extraordinary item   .525   Optional

Net income $1.800

Grade for the Problem

Grade = # of concepts mentioned x .33 (10 points ÷ 30 concepts) per concept

NOTE: Credit would be given for aggregate numbers listed for each category such as for other income (expense) even if only two of the three items were listed. For items like deferred income taxes partial credit would be given on a second grading.

Essay Question Solutions Approach Algorithm

1. **Glance over the question.** Scan the question to get a feel for the topical area addressed. Do not read it. Until you understand the requirements, you cannot discriminate important data from irrelevant data.

2. **Study the requirements.** "Study" as differentiated from "read." Candidates continually lose points due to misunderstanding the requirements. Underline key phrases and words.

2a. **Visualize the solution format.** Determine the expected format of the required solution. As you would expect, the usual format for the solution to essay questions will be the paragraph format. However, there will be occasions where the requirements of the question may be answered by a list of items. Also, a single question may contain two or more requirements. Explicitly recognize multiple requirements by numbering or lettering them on your examination booklet, expanding on the letters already assigned to the question.

3. **Outline the required procedures mentally.** Interrelate the background data given in the question to the expected solution format, mentally noting a "to do" list. Determine what it is you are going to do before you begin doing it. You should work through the requirements in order but be alert for questions with interrelated requirements.

3a. **Review applicable principles, knowledge.** Before immersing yourself in the details of the essay, quickly (30-60 seconds) review and organize your knowledge of the principles applicable to the question. Jot down any acronyms, formulas, or other memory aids relevant to the topics of the question. Otherwise, the details of the question may confuse and overshadow your previous knowledge of the applicable principles.

4. **Study the text of the question.** Read the question carefully. With the requirements in mind, you can now begin to sort out relevant from irrelevant data. Underline and circle important data. The data necessary for answering each requirement may be scattered throughout the question. List the requirements in the margin alongside the data to which they pertain. Remember--this is your exam and you should use whatever technique you find effective to highlight important data and concepts.

4a. **Write down keywords (concepts).** Jot down a list of keywords (grading concepts) in the margin of the examination or on the lined paper.

4b. **Organize the keywords into a solution outline.** After you have noted all of the grading concepts that relate to the requirements, reorganize the outline for the entire answer. Make sure that you respond to each requirement and do not preempt answers to other requirements.

5. **Prepare the solution.** You are now in a position to write a neat, complete, and organized solution. Remember that 5% of your score on each section comes from the grading of your writing skills. Therefore, it is very important that you write something for each requirement of the question and take the time to develop a clear and organized essay for the reader/grader.

6. **Proofread and edit.** Do not underestimate the benefits of this step. Just recall all of the "silly" mistakes you made on undergraduate exams. Corrections of errors and completion of oversights during this step can easily be the difference between passing and failing.

7. **Review the requirements.** Assure yourself that you have answered them all.

Turn back to the essay question, unofficial answer, and hypothetical grading guide presented in Chapter 2. You should read this section and then practice the solutions approach on the essay question provided in Chapter 2. The major difference between the solutions approach for problems and the one for essay questions is the use of a **keyword** outline. The **keyword** outline in the essay solutions approach takes the place of the intermediary solution in the problem solutions approach.

Highlights of the Solutions Approach to Essay Questions

After studying the requirements and visualizing the format of the unofficial answer, study the text of the question, making notes and preparing a **keyword** outline. After the keyword outline has been prepared, a basic distinction must be made as to the type of essay question presented. The first type of essay question contains one fact situation from which two or more requirements cover the **same** or similar accounting rules. The proper method of answering this type of question is to handle the requirements simultaneously. In other words, apply each step in the solutions approach to all of the requirements before moving on to the next step.

The second type of essay question contains one fact situation from which two or more requirements cover **different** topics or rules. The proper method of answering this type of question is to handle the requirements independently, following each step of the solutions approach separately for each requirement. Thus, after the first requirement is completed, repeat the solutions approach for each remaining requirement. The benefit to handling the requirements independently lies in keeping the different topics or rules separate in your mind, which allows you to complete one requirement before moving on to another requirement and mentally "changing gears."

When you have identified the type of question involved, reorganize the keyword outline for the entire answer. Make sure that you have answered each requirement completely, but be careful not to preempt an answer to another requirement. The **keyword** outline for the example question should be similar to the grading guide in Chapter 2. Next, write your solution and edit as needed. Revisions may be made in the margin of your answer sheet, or, you might use only 3/4 of each page to write your solution. The remaining 1/4 can then be used to add material or to make revisions which can be keyed to the text with asterisks. Alternatively, write on every other line. The solution will thus be easier for the grader to read, and also easier for you to proofread and edit. Remember, there is no limit on the number of answer sheets you may use. If you have time later, review your solution again.

NOTE: You **must** write out the answers to the essay questions. **Keyword** outlines are not sufficient. The AICPA requires you to show an understanding of the grading concepts, not merely a listing of grading concepts. However, you may prepare answers in list form as long as the listed items are in sentence format. Prepare brief paragraphs consisting of several concise sentences about each grading concept. The paragraphs may be numbered in an outline format similar to that of the unofficial answers.

The examiners grade candidates on their writing skills. Two samples will be taken from each section of the exam (e.g., requirement **c.** from one essay and requirement **b.** from another essay). Candidates will not be told which responses will be evaluated. Writing skills will be assessed by the same individuals who grade the essay responses for technical content. Five percent of the total points available on each section above will be based on writing skills; however, the number of points allocated to writing skills will not be specified in the final grades.

Candidates' writing skills will be graded according to the following six characteristics:

1. **Coherent organization**

    Candidates should organize their responses in a manner that is logical and easy to follow. Jumbled paragraphs and disorderly sentences will only confuse the grader and make his/her job more difficult. The following techniques will help improve written coherence.*

    - Use short paragraphs composed of short sentences
    - Indent paragraphs to set off lists, equations, key ideas, etc. when appropriate
    - Maintain coherence **within** paragraphs
        - Use a topic sentence at the beginning of each paragraph
        - Develop and support this topic throughout the rest of the paragraph
        - Present old or given information before discussing new information
        - Discuss ideas in chronological order
        - Use parallel grammatical structure
        - Be consistent in person, verb tense, and number
        - Substitute pronouns or synonyms for previously used key words
        - Use transitions (e.g., therefore, finally)
    - Maintain coherence **between** paragraphs
        - Repeat keywords from previous paragraph
        - Use transitions

    As discussed above, candidates are strongly advised to keyword outline their responses **before** writing their essays. This technique helps the candidate to focus on the flow of ideas s/he wants to convey before starting the actual writing task.

2. **Conciseness**

    Candidates should express themselves in as few words as possible. Complex, wordy sentences are hard to understand. Conciseness can be improved using the following guidelines.

    - Write in short sentences
    - Use a simple word instead of a long word if it serves the same purpose
    - Avoid passive constructions (e.g., **was** evaluated)

---

* *Adapted from **Writing for Accountants** by Aletha S. Hendrickson (Cincinnati, OH: Southwestern Publishing Co., 1993) pp.128-209.*

- Use words instead of phrases
- Combine sentences, if possible
- Avoid empty fillers (e.g., **it is** apparent; **there seems to be**)
- Avoid multiple negatives (e.g., **no** reason for **not** using)

3. **Clarity**

Written responses should leave no doubt in the reader's mind as to the meaning intended. Clarity can be improved as follows:

- Do **not** use abbreviations
- Use correct terminology
- Use words with specific and precise meanings
- Write in short, well-constructed sentences
- Make sure subjects and verbs agree in number
- Make sure pronouns and their antecedents agree in number (e.g., the partnership must decide how **it** (not **they**) wants to split profits.)
- Avoid unclear reference to a pronoun's antecedent (e.g., the comptroller should inform the staff accountant that **he** must compute depreciation. -- Who does "he" refer to?)

4. **Use of standard English**

Spelling, punctuation, and word usage should follow the norm used in most books, newspapers, and magazines. Note the following common mistakes:

- Confusion of its/it's
  *The firm issued **its** stock.*
  ***It's** (it is) the stock of that firm.*

- Confusion of there/their/they're
  ***There** will be a dividend declaration.*
  ***Their** dividend was declared last week.*
  ***They're** (they are) declaring a dividend.*

- Spelling errors
  *Separate **not** seperate*
  *Receivable **not** recievable*

5. **Responsiveness to the question's requirements**

Candidates should respond directly to the question being asked. No more information should be given than necessary. Broad expositions on the general topic demonstrate an inability to focus and organize writing to fulfill a specific purpose. Avoid irrelevance by following your keyword outline.

6. **Appropriateness for the reader**

Essay questions may ask the candidate to prepare a document for a certain reader (e.g., a memorandum for a client). Writing that is appropriate for the reader will take into account the reader's background, knowledge of the subject, interests, and concerns. (When the intended reader is not specified, the candidate should write for a knowledgeable CPA.)

Intended readers may include those who are unfamiliar with most terms and concepts, and who seek financial information because of self-interest (i.e., clients, stockholders). Try the following techniques for these readers:

- Avoid jargon, if possible (i.e., GAAP, etc.)

- Use parenthetical definitions

  - *unearned revenues (advance payments by customers)*
  - *marketable equity securities (short-term investments in stock)*

- Set off definitions as appositives

  For example: The lag, the time between the receipt and deposit of cash, needs to be shortened.

- Incorporate a "you" attitude

The requirement of a question may also specify that the response should be directed to professionals who are knowledgeable of most terms and concepts. Employ the following techniques with these readers:

- Use jargon
- Refer to authoritative sources (i.e., FASB pronouncements)
- Incorporate a "we" attitude

Again, preparing a keyword outline will assist you in meeting many of these requirements. You should also reread each written answer in its entirety. Writing errors are common during the exam, so it is well worth your time to edit your answers.

Methods for Improving Your Writing Skills

1. **Organization**

   In preparing to answer a CPA exam essay, read the question carefully, determining the exact requirements of the question. Reread the question, underlining main points and noting them in the margin of your exam booklet. (This is the keyword approach.) Once you have identified the keywords, take a few minutes to organize these ideas in a logical manner.

   For example, if the question requires a discussion of the equity and cost adjusted for fair value methods of accounting for an investment in another company, you might consider these main points: recording of the investment, recognition of income, recognition of dividends, and disposition of the investment. This question lends itself to comparison/contrast type development. Thus, you would arrange your keywords to reflect that type of organization. Your first body paragraph(s) might discuss how to account for an investment under the cost adjusted for fair value method, detailing how the investment is first recorded, how dividends are treated, and how the investment is taken off the books when it is disposed of. Your next paragraph(s) would discuss the above points as they relate to the equity method.

   Sometimes, a long narrative is provided prior to the actual questions. This narrative exists to facilitate your answer; it provides data to work with so that you do not have to make up all your own examples. If this type of narrative exists, read through it, searching for accounting issues and examples; these will come in handy when actually writing your response.

2. **Development**

Frequently, the CPA exam essays merely require you to recite a list of main points in an essay format. The graders are looking more for how many points you have covered than the depth with which you covered any one of them. Unfortunately, putting together a number of semi-related facts into a coherent essay may prove to be a more difficult task than coming up with the facts to begin with.

In this situation, try to see if you can group your points into categories. These categories may be thematic, chronological, or descriptive. If you are able to group the points, then each category can be discussed in one paragraph. If not, you may have to unify your answer with a topic sentence that indicates the many facets of the problem about which you are writing. This type of sentence sets up your essay for listing these facets.

Regardless of how you begin, do not simply list your points--this becomes monotonous. Rather, list, explain, and provide an example. Move from general to specific: provide the general concept, explain it in more specific terms, and provide a very pointed example. In addition, do not forget to use sequential connectors such as "first," "second," "next," etc.

3. **Syntax, grammar, and style**

By the time you sit for the CPA exam, you have at your disposal various grammatical constructs from which you may form sentences. Believe it or not, you know quite a bit of English grammar; if you did not, you would never have made it this far in your studies. So in terms of your grammar, relax! You already know it.

A frequent problem with writing occurs with the syntactic structure of sentences. Although the Board of Examiners does not expect the rhetoric of Cicero, it does expect to read and understand your answer. The way in which the graders will assess writing skills further indicates that they are looking more for writing skills at the micro level (sentence level) than at the macro level (organizational level).

a. Basic syntactic structure (transitive and intransitive action verbs)

Most English sentences are based on this simple dynamic: that someone or something (the subject) does some action (the predicate). These sentences involve action verbs and are grouped in the following categories:

(1)   Subject-Verb

The CONSTRUCTION COMPANY WAITED until the contract was complete to record any revenue.

(2)   Subject-Verb-Direct Object (The object receives the action of the verb.)

The ACCOUNTANT CALCULATED an AGING SCHEDULE.

(3)   Subject-Verb-Indirect Object-Direct Object (The direct object receives the action of the verb, but the indirect object is also affected by this action, though not in the same way as the direct object.)

The INVESTEE GAVE US our DIVIDEND soon after the date of declaration.

b. Syntactic structure (linking verbs)

Linking verbs are verbs which, rather than expressing action, say something about the subject's state of being. In sentences with linking verbs, the subject is linked to a word which describes it or renames it.

(1)   Subject-Linking Verb-Nominative (The nominative renames the subject.)

In the field of Accounting, the FASB IS the standard-setting BOARD.

(2)   Subject-Linking Verb-Adjective (The adjective describes the subject.)

An amortization SCHEDULE IS always HELPFUL in determining interest payments.

c.   Subordinate clauses

(1)   Adverbial clauses (subordinating connector + sentence). These clauses modify the action of the main clause.

When a related-party transaction occurs, it must be disclosed in the footnotes to the financial statements.

(2)   Noun clauses (nominal connectors + sentence). These clauses function as nouns in the main sentence.

In pension accounting, we know that excessive unrecognized gains and losses must be amortized.

(3)   Adjective clauses [relative pronoun + verb + (object/nominative/adjective)]. These clauses function as noun modifiers.

The depreciation methods which show the greatest amount of depreciation in the first year are the accelerated methods.

d.   The above are patterns which form basic clauses (both dependent and independent). In addition, numerous phrases may function as modifiers of the basic sentence elements.

(1)   Prepositional (a preposition + an object)

of the FASB
on the data
about a new type of depreciation

(2)   Verbal

(a)   Verb + ing + a modifier (noun, verb, adverb, prepositional phrase)

i]   Used as an adjective

the discount requiring amortization
the option maximizing operating income

ii]   Used as a noun (gerund)

Consolidating the balance sheets of an entity's subsidiaries is difficult and time consuming.

(b)   Verb + ed + modifier (noun, adverb, prepositional phrase)

i]   Used as an adjective

The method of depreciation used to depreciate a group of assets as a single unit is the composite method.

(c)   Infinitive (to + verb + object)

i]   Used as a noun

The company needs to depreciate that asset over 5 years.

4. **Sentence clarity**

   a. When constructing your sentences, do not separate basic sentence elements with too many phrases:

      The amortization of unrecognized gains and losses falling outside of a predetermined corridor value is another component of pension cost.

      Better

      One component of pension cost is the amortization of unrecognized gains and losses which fall outside a predetermined corridor value.

   b. Refrain from lumping prepositional and infinitive phrases together:

      The exposure draft by the FASB on the accounting for the restructuring of an entity due to troubled debt is very recent.

      Better

      Accounting for troubled debt restructuring is the topic of the most recent FASB exposure draft.

   c. Make sure that your pronouns have a clear and obvious referent.

      When accountants prepare notes to the financial statements, they serve a special function.

      Better

      The notes to the financial statements serve a special function.

   d. Make sure that any adjectival verbal phrase clearly modifies a noun stated in the sentence.

      To reach this decision, each investment's market value was compared to its purchase price.

      Better

      To reach this decision, we compared each investment's market value to its purchase price.

Time Requirements for the Solutions Approach

Many candidates bypass the solutions approach because they feel it is too time-consuming. Actually, the solutions approach is a time-saver, and more importantly, it helps you prepare better solutions to all problems.

Without committing yourself to using the solutions approach, try it step-by-step on several essay questions and problems. After you conscientiously go through the step-by-step routine a few times, you will begin to adopt and modify aspects of the technique which will benefit you. Subsequent usage will become subconscious and painless. The important point is that you must try the solutions approach several times to accrue any benefits.

Efficiency of the Solutions Approach

The mark of an inefficient solution is one wherein the candidate immediately begins to write an essay/ problem solution. Remember, the final solution is one of the last steps in the solutions approach. You should have the solution under complete control (with the **keyword** outline or intermediary solutions) before you begin your final solution.

While the large amount of intermediary work in the solutions approach may appear burdensome and time-consuming, this technique results in more complete solutions in less time than do haphazard approaches. Moreover, the solutions approach really allows you to work out problems that you feel unfamiliar with at first reading. The solutions approach, however, must be mastered prior to sitting for the CPA examination. In other words, the candidate must be willing to invest a reasonable amount of time into perfecting his/her own solutions approach.

In summary, the solutions approach may appear foreign and somewhat cumbersome. At the same time, if you have worked through the material in this chapter, you should have some appreciation for it. Develop the solutions approach by writing down the seven steps in the solutions approach algorithm at the beginning of this chapter, and keep them before you as you work recent CPA exam problems. Remember that even though the suggested procedures appear **very structured** and **time-consuming**, integration of these procedures into your own style of problem solving will help improve **your** solutions approach. The next chapter discusses strategies for the overall examination.

**NOW IS THE TIME
TO MAKE YOUR COMMITMENT**

TAKING THE EXAMINATION 4

This chapter is concerned with developing an examination strategy (e.g., how to cope with the environment at the examination site, the order in which to work problems, etc.).

EXAMINATION STRATEGIES

Your performance during the 2-day examination is final and not subject to revision. While you may sit for the examination again if you are unsuccessful, the majority of your preparation will have to be repeated, requiring substantial, additional amounts of time. Thus, examination strategies (discussed in this chapter) which maximize your exam-taking efficiency are very important.

Getting "Psyched Up"

The CPA exam is quite challenging and worthy of your best effort. Explicitly develop your own psychological strategy to get yourself "up" for the exam. Pace your study program such that you will be able to operate at peak performance when you are actually taking the exam. Many candidates give up because they have a bad day or encounter a rough problem. Do the best you can; the other candidates are probably no better prepared than you.

Examination Supplies

The AICPA recommends that candidates prepare their solutions in pencil. As you practice your solutions approach, experiment with pencils, lead types, erasers, etc., that are comfortable to use and that also result in good copy for the grader.

In addition to an adequate supply of pencils and erasers, it is very important to take a watch to the examination. Also, take refreshments (as permitted), which are conducive to your exam efficiency. Finally, dress to assure your comfort during the exam. Layered clothing is recommended for possible variations in temperature at the examination site.

Do **not** take study materials to the examination room. You will not be able to use them. They will only muddle your mind and get you "uptight." Finally, DO NOT carry notes or crib sheets upon your person--this can only result in the gravest of problems. If you choose to bring study materials to the examination site, you are only permitted to review these materials before or after the examination session, **not** during the session.

Lodging, Meals, Exercise

Make advance reservations for comfortable lodging convenient to the examination facilities. Do not stay with friends, relatives, etc. Both uninterrupted sleep and total concentration on the exam are a must. Consider the following in making your lodging plans:

1. Proximity to exam facilities
2. Lodging and exam parking facilities
3. Availability of meals and snacks
4. Recreational facilities

Plan your meal schedule to provide maximum energy and alertness during the day and maximum rest at night.

Do not experiment with new foods, drinks, etc., during the examination time period. Within reasonable limits, observe your normal eating and drinking habits. Recognize that overconsumption of coffee during the exam could lead to a hyperactive state and disaster. Likewise, overindulgence in alcohol to overcome nervousness and to induce sleep the night before might contribute to other difficulties the following morning.

Tenseness should be expected before and during the examination. Rely on a regular exercise program to unwind at the end of the day. As you select your lodging for the examination, try to accommodate your exercise pleasure (e.g., running, swimming, etc.). Continue to indulge in your exercise program on the days of the examination.

To relieve tension or stress while studying, try breathing or stretching exercises. Use these exercises before and during the examination to start and to keep your adrenaline flowing. Do not hesitate to attract attention by doing pushups, jumping jacks, etc., in a lobby outside of the examination room if it will improve your exam efficiency. Remain determined not to go through another examination to obtain your certificate.

A problem you will probably experience during the exam related to general fatigue and tenseness is writer's cramp. Experiment with alternate methods of holding your pencil, rubbing your hand, etc., during your preparation program.

In summary, the examination is likely to be both rigorous and fatiguing. Expect it and prepare for it by getting in shape, planning methods of relaxation during the exam and exam evenings, and finally building the confidence and competence to successfully complete the exam.

Examination Facilities and Procedures

Visit the examination facilities at least the evening before the examination to assure knowledge of the location. Remember: no surprises. Having a general familiarity with the facilities will lessen anxiety prior to the examination.

Talking to a recent veteran of the examination will give you background for the general examination procedures, such as

1. Procedure for distributing exam booklets, papers, etc.
2. Accessibility of restrooms
3. Availability of coffee and snacks at exam location
4. Admissibility of coffee and snacks in the exam room
5. Peculiar problems of exam facilities (e.g., noise, lighting, temperature, etc.)
6. Permissibility of early departure from exam
7. His/her experience in taking the exam
8. Any other suggestions s/he might make

As you can see, it is important to talk with someone who recently sat for the examination at the same location where you intend to sit. The objective is to reduce your anxiety just prior to the examination and to minimize any possible distractions. Finally, if you have any remaining questions regarding examination procedure, call or write your state board.

On a related point, do not be distracted by other candidates who show up at the examination completely relaxed and greet others with confidence. These are most likely candidates who have been there before. Probably the only thing they are confident of is a few days' vacation from work. Also, do not become distracted when they leave early; some candidates may leave after signing in for that session.

Arrive at the Examination Early

On the day of the exam, be sure to get to the examination site at least 30 minutes early to reduce tension and to get yourself situated. Most states have assigned seating. If this is the case, you will be seated by your candidate ID number. However, if you have a choice, it is probably wise to sit away from the door and the administration table to avoid being distracted by candidates who arrive late, leave early, ask questions, etc., and by proctors who occasionally converse. AVOID ALL POSSIBLE DISTRACTIONS. **Stay away from friends**. Find a seat that will be comfortable; consider sunlight, interior lighting, heating/air conditioning, pedestrian traffic, etc.

Usually the proctors open the sealed boxes of exams and distribute the Examination Question Booklets to candidates 10 minutes before the scheduled beginning of the examination. Shown below are the cover sheets for the Examination Question Booklet and the Examination Answer Booklet from the November 1995 Financial Accounting and Reporting exam, the last disclosed exam. Record your 7-digit candidate number in the boxes provided at the upper right-hand corner of the front cover of the Examination Question Booklet. You are not permitted to open the booklet until the starting signal is given, but you should study the instructions printed on the front cover. The instructions generally explain

EXAMINATION QUESTIONS

CANDIDATE NUMBER

Record your 7-digit candidate number in the boxes.

Print your STATE name here.

FARE (DO NOT PROVIDED)

UNIFORM CERTIFIED PUBLIC ACCOUNTANT EXAMINATION
Financial Accounting & Reporting—Business Enterprises

November 2, 1995; 1:30 P.M. to 6:00 P.M.

The point values for each question, and estimated time allotments based primarily on point value, are as follows:

	Point Value	Estimated Minutes	
		Minimum	Maximum
No. 1	60	130	140
No. 2	10	15	25
No. 3	10	15	25
No. 4	10	30	40
No. 5	10	30	40
Totals	100	220	270

INSTRUCTIONS TO CANDIDATES *Failure to follow these instructions may have an adverse effect on your Examination grade.*

1. Do not break the seal around the *Examination Questions* (pages 3 through 26) until you are told to do so.

2. Question Numbers 1, 2, and 3 should be answered on the *Objective Answer Sheet*, which is pages 35 and 36. You should attempt to answer all objective items. There is no penalty for incorrect responses. Work space to solve the objective questions is provided in the *Examination Questions* on pages 5 through 21. Since the objective items are computer-graded, your comments and calculations associated with them are not considered. Be certain that you have entered your answers on the *Objective Answer Sheet* before the examination time is up. The objective portion of your examination will not be graded if you fail to record your answers on the *Objective Answer Sheet*. You will not be given additional time to record your answers.

3. Question Numbers 4 and 5 should be answered beginning on page 27. Support all answers with properly labeled and legible calculations that can be identified as sources of amounts used to derive your final answer. If you have not completed answering a question on a page, fill in the appropriate spaces in the wording on the bottom of the page "QUESTION NUMBER ____ CONTINUES ON PAGE ____ ." If you have completed

answering a question, fill in the appropriate space in the wording on the bottom of the page "QUESTION NUMBER ____ ENDS ON THIS PAGE." Always begin the start of an answer to a question on the top of a new page (which may be the reverse side of a sheet of paper). Use the entire width of the page to answer requirements of a noncomputational nature. To answer requirements of a computational nature, you may wish to use the three vertical columns provided on the right side of each page.

4. Although the primary purpose of the examination is to test your knowledge and application of the subject matter, selected essay responses will be graded for writing skills.

5. You are required to turn in by the end of each session:
   a. Attendance Record and Calculator Sign-off Record Form, page 1;
   b. *Examination Questions*, pages 3 through 26;
   c. *Essay Ruled Paper*, pages 27 through 34;
   d. *Objective Answer Sheet*, pages 35 and 36;
   e. Calculator; and
   f. All unused examination materials.

Your examination will not be graded unless the above listed items are handed in before leaving the examination room.

Prepared by the Board of Examiners of the American Institute of Certified Public Accountants and adopted by the examining boards of all states, the District of Columbia, Guam, Puerto Rico, and the Virgin Islands of the United States.

Copyright © 1995 by the American Institute of Certified Public Accountants, Inc.

Examination Questions Booklet No.

3 07331 Q

over

3

EXAMINATION QUESTION AND ANSWER BOOKLET

ATTENDANCE RECORD
(To Be Retained by State Board)

CANDIDATE NUMBER

Record your 7-digit candidate number in the boxes.

Print your STATE name here.

Name *(please print)*

Home Address

City _____ State _____ Zip Code

I hereby certify that the calculator I received was tested by me and performed all test functions accurately.

Signature _____ Date _____

CALCULATOR SIGN-OFF RECORD
Test Calculations

Keystroke			Display
CA	53000	+	100600
CA	125000	−	26700
CA	5000	×	8335
CA	39000	÷	30

	47600			
	98300			
	1.667			
	1300			

FARE
VERSION 2

UNIFORM CERTIFIED PUBLIC ACCOUNTANT EXAMINATION
Financial Accounting & Reporting—Business Enterprises

November 2, 1995; 1:30 P.M. to 6:00 P.M.

INSTRUCTIONS TO CANDIDATES

(This *Examination Question and Answer Booklet* contains an *Attendance Record and Calculator Sign-Off Record, Examination Questions, Essay Ruled Paper*, and *Objective Answer Sheet*)

1. Do not begin writing on this *Booklet* until you are told to do so.

2. Complete the *Attendance Record and Calculator Sign-off Record*, and your 7-digit candidate number above. Detach the page at the perforation so it can be collected and retained by the State Board.

3. Test your calculator and sign the *Calculator Sign-off Record*. Press CA once to turn the calculator on. The display will read "0." Perform the *test calculations*. The calculator automatically turns itself off approximately 8 minutes after the last entry. Instructions on

how to use the calculator are on pages 2 and 4.

4. Turn the *Booklet* over and record your 7-digit candidate number and state on the *Objective Answer Sheet*.

5. The *Objective Answer Sheet* is on pages 35 and 36. The objective portion of your examination will not be graded unless you fail to record your answers on the *Objective Answer Sheet*.

6. In order to grade your *Objective Answer Sheet* and essay answers, the Booklet No. above must be identical to the Booklet Nos. on pages 3, 27, and 36.

over

1

307331 S

Attendance Record Booklet No.

1. How to turn in examination papers
2. Handling of

    a. Examination Question Booklet
    b. Examination Answer Booklet

3. Examiners' consideration of the candidate's ability to express him/herself in acceptable written language

You will be given an Examination Answer Booklet in addition to the Examination Question Booklet. Carefully read the instructions on the Examination Answer Booklet. You should not begin writing on the answer booklet until told to do so.

The Examination Answer Booklet is divided into three sections:

1. An Attendance Record
2. An Objective Answer Sheet
3. Essay/Problem Answer Ruled/Columnar Paper

Prior to the start of the exam, you will be instructed to complete and detach the Attendance Record, which will be retained by the State Boards of Accountancy. You should record your 7-digit candidate number on this record and on all other papers you submit. You are also permitted to record your 7-digit candidate number in the upper right-hand corner and blacken the corresponding oval below each box on the front and back covers of your answer booklet.

The Objective Answer Sheet contained on the back cover of the answer booklet will be used to record answers to both the multiple-choice section of the exam and other objective format questions. In some states, you will be asked to detach the Objective Answer Sheet and turn it in separately; however, in other states the Objective Answer Sheet is to remain attached to the answer booklet. Follow the instructions of your State Board. Also, record your candidate number where indicated. Two different versions of the Objective Answer Sheet from the November 1995 Financial Accounting and Reporting Exam are shown below. **Candidates should be aware that different versions of the answer sheet have different arrangements for the multiple-choice questions. The answer sheet may be organized vertically, horizontally, or a combination of the two. The candidate, therefore, must be sure to correctly transfer his/her answers to the answer sheet.**

The essay/problem answer ruled/columnar paper will be used for answering the essay questions/problems. Record your candidate number on the ruled paper where indicated. As you proceed through the exam, you will indicate the essay question or problem number which is being answered. Always begin the start of an answer to a question on top of a new page. Additional ruled/columnar paper is available if needed and should be enclosed in the answer booklet when turning it in.

Inventory of the Examination Content

When you receive your question booklet, carefully read the instructions. The objective is to review the standard instructions and to note any new or special instructions. Read the instructions carefully in order to comply with the examination procedures. After reviewing the instructions on the front of your question booklet, make note of the number of questions/problems and the time allocated to each. Immediately after

receiving permission to open the question booklet, glance over each of the questions sufficiently and jot down the topics next to the question number on the front of the question booklet. This will give you an overview of the ensuing 4 1/2 hours of work. You may find it to your advantage to write down keywords, acronyms, etc. on the front of the question booklet **before** you forget them, but only **after** you have been told to begin the examination.

Allocation of Time

Budget your time. Time should be carefully allocated in your attempt to maximize your points. Remember that the maximum number of points available on each question is proportional to the suggested time allotments on the front of each exam booklet. Theoretically, time should be allocated so that you maximize points per minute.

While you must develop your own strategy with respect to time allocation, some suggestions may be useful. First, consider the Financial Accounting and Reporting examination, which is 270 minutes long. Allocate 5 minutes to reading the instructions and to taking an inventory, jotting the topics tested by question on the front cover. Write the topic next to the time allotment. Assuming 60 individual multiple-choice and 4 essay/other objective questions, you should spend about 10 minutes **keyword** outlining each of the 2 or 3 essay questions.

Budget your time based on the points allocated to each question. The FARE exam is a 4 1/2 hour (270 minutes) exam which would have points allocated as follows:

Hypothetical Time Budget (4 1/2 hour exam)

Question	*Type*	*Point Value*	*Calculated Maximum Time*
No. 1	Multiple-Choice	60	60/100 x 270 min. = 160 min.
No. 2	OOAF	10	10/100 x 270 min. = 27 min.
No. 3	OOAF	10	10/100 x 270 min. = 27 min.
No. 4	Essay	10	10/100 x 270 min. = 27 min.
No. 5	Essay	10	10/100 x 270 min. = 27 min.
Total pts.		100	268 min.

Note that this budget can be done easily with a calculator, which is provided for the FARE exam. It is your responsibility to be ready at the start of the session and to stop writing when told to do so. Therefore, take control of the exam from the very start.

Then, plan on spending about 2 to 2 1/2 minutes working each of the individual multiple-choice questions. Next, work the other objective answer format questions. (Do not prepare the final solutions to the essay questions until you work all of the objective questions. Frequently, objective questions will jog your memory about additional grading concepts for the essays.) Then complete the objective question answer sheet by CAREFULLY transferring your answers from the question booklet to the machine gradable form. This should take about 5 minutes. The answers must be transferred before the exam session ends. THE PROCTORS ARE NOT ALLOWED TO GIVE YOU EXTRA TIME TO DO THIS.

After completing these tasks, you now have spent 3 1/3 to 3 2/3 hours and have substantially completed both the objective questions and essay questions. Revise the **keyword** outline and prepare the final solutions of the essay questions one at a time. Allocate about 15 minutes to each solution. Recognize that you can write all the grader will care to read in 15 minutes from a well-developed outline. This time should include proofreading and editing.

Techniques for Time Management

Note that the FARE exam has historically had 60 multiple-choice questions. Referring to the above hypothetical time budget, note that the maximum time you should take to complete a group of 10 questions is about 25 minutes per group. Remember that you alone control watching your progress towards successfully completing this exam. One possible way of monitoring your progress is to write down your start time of each question before you start reading and answering the questions. For example, when you begin the multiple-choice questions in FARE, write the start time of 1:30 p.m. Monitor your time by either blocks of questions (40 to 50 minutes per 20 questions) or by realizing you must have completed the multiple-choice questions by 4:00 p.m. If you complete the multiple-choice questions at 3:30, you have successfully banked 30 minutes to use in answering OOAFs and Essays.

Order of Working Questions/Problems

Select the question/problem that you are going to work first from the notes you made on the front of your examination. Some will select the question/problem that appears easiest to get started and build confidence. Others will begin with the question/problem they feel is most difficult to get it out of the way. Objective questions generally should not be worked first on the Financial Accounting and Reporting exam, since each question may contain 4 or 5 grading concepts (for possible inclusion in your essay solutions) as alternate answers. You should therefore work through the objective questions only after you have **keyword** outlined all of the essay questions (but before you write your final solutions). This way, when doing the objective questions, you may pick up a grading concept or keyword which you had not included in your initial keyword outline.

Once you select a question/problem, you should apply the solutions approach. Comprehensive problems should be worked through to the final stage, and all calculations and schedules should be labeled before leaving the problem. If you start another problem before completing one, you will have to rework (or at a minimum, waste time becoming familiar again with) the unfinished problem.

You should, however, leave a problem if you get stuck, rather than just "spinning your wheels." Later, when you come back and retool the problem, you may be able to think of a new approach to "unlock" the solution. Likewise, proofreading and editing should be undertaken after working on one or more other problems, so you have a fresh perspective as you evaluate your own solution.

On the other hand, essay questions should be worked only through the **keyword** outline prior to moving on to the next question. Recall that essay questions are generally graded with an open-ended grading guide. Thus, you want to include as many grading concepts as possible in your solution. Waiting to write your essay solution until after all other questions have been dealt with will force you to take a fresh look at the question.

As a result, additional grading concepts are often found. As you recognize grading concepts applicable to other questions, turn to the respective question and jot down the **keywords** (remember that the **keyword** outlines should be prepared in the margin of your exam booklet).

Candidates should allocate more time to the questions/problems which are troublesome. The natural tendency is to write on and on for questions/problems with which you are conversant. Remember to do the opposite--spend more time where more points are available (i.e., you may already have earned the maximum allowable on the question/problem familiar to you).

Never, but never, leave a question blank, as this almost certainly precludes a passing grade on that section. Some candidates talk about "giving certain types of questions to the AICPA," (i.e., no answer). The only thing being given to the AICPA is grading time since the grader will not have to read a solution. Expect a couple of "far out" or seemingly insurmountable questions/problems. Apply the solutions approach--imagine yourself having to make a similar decision, computation, explanation, etc., in an actual situation--and come up with as much as possible to answer the question.

Calculator Use

Candidates are provided with calculators at the examination sites for use on the Accounting and Reporting--taxation, managerial, and governmental and not-for-profit organizations and Financial Accounting and Reporting sections.

Candidates should only need to use the calculators' four primary functions--add, subtract, multiply, and divide. However, the calculators also have function keys for square root, percentage, and memory. Candidates are given an opportunity to test the calculators to ensure that the calculators are functioning properly. It is the candidate's responsibility to notify one of the proctors immediately in the event of a malfunction. Replacement calculators are available. Test calculations are printed in the examination booklets.

To turn the calculator on press ⟨CA⟩. Display will read "0." The calculator automatically turns itself off approximately 8 minutes after the last entry. All data in the calculator will be lost once the calculator is off. We recommend that when you press ⟨=⟩, you press ⟨CA⟩ before beginning a new calculation. The basic key descriptions are as follows:

⟨CA⟩　　　　**On and Clear**--Clears the calculator of all entries, including entries in memory, once calculator is on.

⟨C.CE⟩　　　**Clear Calculation**--Clears the Display.

⟨0⟩ ... ⟨9⟩　**Numericals**--Inputs that number.

⟨·⟩　　　　　**Decimal**--Indicates that all numbers to follow are decimals.

⟨+/-⟩　　　　**Change sign**--Changes plus (minus) to minus (plus).

⟨+⟩ & ⟨-⟩　**Add & Subtract**--Adds the next number entered to, or subtracts the next number entered from, the displayed number.

⟨x⟩ & ⟨÷⟩　**Multiply & Divide**--Multiplies or divides the displayed number by the next number entered.

⟨=⟩　　　　　**Equal**--Displays the results of all previously entered operations.

⟨√⟩　　　　　**Square Root**--Calculates the square root of the displayed number. It is unlikely that you will need to use this key during the exam.

(%)   **Percentage**--Converts the displayed number to a percentage (i.e., divides it by 100) and completes all previously entered operations. It is unlikely that you will need to use this key during the exam.

(M+)   **Memory Add**--Adds the displayed number to the balance in memory.

(M--)   **Memory Subtract**--Subtracts the displayed number from the balance in memory.

(R.CM)   **Recall Memory**--Pressed once, displays the balance in memory. Pressed twice in a row, eliminates the balance in memory but not the displayed number.

Since each Sharp calculator provided has these basic functions, the only difference between calculators is in the placement of the keys. While it may be helpful to have the exact calculator that you are familiar with, this is not essential to your examination success.

Test Calculations

Keystroke								*Display*
(CA)	53000		(+)	47600		(=)		100600
(CA)	125000		(--)	98300		(=)		26700
(CA)	5000		(x)	1.667		(=)		8335
(CA)	39000		(÷)	1300		(=)		30

Pitfalls of Calculator Use

The use of calculators is designed to save candidates time on performing and verifying manual calculations. However, there are some pitfalls that the candidate must remain aware of throughout the entire exam. For instance, how many times have you simply hit the wrong key (e.g., a six instead of a nine)? Or, how many times have you forgotten to clear the calculator before beginning a new calculation? Both of these mistakes are simple errors that everyone makes at one time or another. Yet, these simple mistakes could be the difference between a candidate receiving a passing grade or a failing grade. In order to guard against these errors, candidates should avoid rushing through the questions. Accuracy is just as important, if not more so, as speed. Candidates should work each section of the exam with a time budget in mind to avoid any last-minute panic attacks. There are no points given for finishing first, and so, candidates should concentrate on working accurately, by using the calculator carefully to ensure such accuracy.

The candidate should also guard against using the calculator as a crutch. For example, there should be no need to multiply an amount by 10%. This calculation simply distracts the candidate from the real issue of solving the problem.

In addition, candidates should avoid the urge to overcalculate. While the calculator may give you some extra time, there is no benefit to number crunching all the different possibilities. The focus of the exam remains understanding and applying the basic concepts of accounting. A candidate will not be able to successfully pass the exam simply by using the calculator to back into the answer.

Postmortem of Your Performance

DON'T DO IT and especially don't do it until Thursday evening. Do not speak to other candidates about the exam after completing sections on Wednesday noon, Wednesday evening, and Thursday noon. Exam postmortem will only upset, confuse, and frustrate you. Besides, the other candidates probably will not be as well prepared as you, and they certainly cannot influence your grade. Often, those candidates who seem very confident have overlooked an important requirement(s) or fact(s). As you leave the exam room after each session, think only ahead to achieve the best possible performance on each of the remaining sections. In addition, past candidates felt they had failed all four parts; yet they actually had passed the exam.

AICPA GENERAL RULES
GOVERNING EXAMINATION*

Rules for Examination Day

The examination is a closed-book examination and no reference materials are permitted to be taken to an examination site. Candidates are not permitted to bring calculators, computers, or other electronic data storage devices into the examination room.

At the examination site, candidates are provided with Examination Question Booklets and Examination Answer Booklets for each section they are taking. In addition, for the Accounting & Reporting--taxation, managerial, and governmental and not-for-profit organizations and Financial Accounting & Reporting sections, candidates are provided with calculators identified for the specific examination. Candidates should bring adequate supplies of Number 2 pencils and erasers.

The general candidate instructions are as follows:

1. Prior to the start of the examination, you will be required to sign a *Statement of Confidentiality* which states:

    I hereby attest that I will not divulge the nature or content of any question or answer to any individual or entity, and I will report to the board of accountancy any solicitations and disclosures of which I become aware. I will not remove, or attempt to remove, any Uniform CPA Examination materials, notes, or other unauthorized materials from the examination room. I understand that failure to comply with this attestation may result in invalidation of my grades, disqualification from future examinations, and possible civil and criminal penalties.

2. The only aids you are allowed to take to the examination tables are pens, pencils, and erasers.

3. You will receive a prenumbered identification card (or admission notice) with your 7-digit candidate number on it. The prenumbered identification card must be available for inspection by the proctors throughout the examination.

4. Any reference during the examination to books or other materials or the exchange of information with other persons shall be considered misconduct sufficient to bar you from further participation in the examination.

Penalties will be imposed on any candidate who is caught cheating before or during the examination. These penalties may include expulsion from the examination and denial of applications for future examinations.

5. You must observe the fixed time for each session. It is your responsibility to be ready at the start of the session and to stop writing when told to do so.

6. The following is an example of point values for each question as it might appear in the *Examination Questions* portion of the *Examination Question and Answer Booklet* (*Booklet*). For each question, the point values are as follows:

	Point value
No. 1	60
No. 2	10
No. 3	10
No. 4	10
No. 5	<u>10</u>
Totals	<u>100</u>

    When answering each question, you should allocate the total examination time in proportion to the question's point value.

7. The *Booklet* will be distributed shortly before each session begins. Do not break the seal around the *Examination Questions* portion of the *Booklet* until you are told to do so.

---

* *Information for CPA Candidates*, Fourteenth Edition, AICPA, 1998, p. 45.

Prior to the start of the examination, you are permitted to complete page 1 of the *Booklet* by recording your 7-digit candidate number in the boxes provided in the upper right-hand corner of the page and by filling out and signing the *Attendance Record*. You are also permitted to turn the *Booklet* over and record your 7-digit candidate number and State on the *Objective Answer Sheet* portion of the *Booklet*.

You must also check the booklet numbers on the *Attendance Record*, *Examination Questions*, *Objective Answer Sheet*, and *Essay Paper*. Notify the proctor if any of these numbers do not match.

You must also review the *Examination Questions* (after you are told to break the seal), *Objective Answer Sheet*, and *Essay Paper* for any possible defects, such as missing pages, blurred printing, or stray marks (*Objective Answer Sheet* only). If any defects are found, request an entirely new *Examination Question and Answer Booklet* from a proctor before you answer any questions.

8. For the Business Law and Professional Responsibilities (LPR), Auditing (AUDIT), and Financial Accounting and Reporting (FARE) sections, your answers to the essay questions or problems must be written on the paper provided in the *Essay Paper* portion of the *Booklet*. After the start of the examination, you should record your 7-digit candidate number, State, and question number on the first page of the *Essay Paper* portion of the *Booklet* and on the other pages where indicated.

9. For the ARE and FARE examination sections, you will be given a calculator. You should test the calculator in accordance with the instructions on the cover page of the *Booklet*. Inform your proctor if your calculator is defective. Calculators will not be provided for the LPR and AUDIT examination sections because the number of questions requiring calculations is minimal and the calculations are simple.

10. All amounts given in objective items or essay questions/problems are to be considered material unless otherwise stated.

11. Answer all objective items on the *Objective Answer Sheet* provided. Use a No. 2 pencil only. You should attempt to answer all objective items, as there is no penalty for incorrect responses. Since the objective items are computer-graded, your comments and calculations associated with them are not considered.

You should blacken the ovals as darkly as possible and erase clearly any marks you wish to change. You should make no stray marks. Approximately 10% of the multiple-choice items are included for pretesting only and are not included in your grade.

12. The *Objective Answer Sheet* may vary for each section of the examination. It is important to pay strict attention to the manner in which your *Objective Answer Sheet* is structured. As you proceed with the examination, be certain that you blacken the oval that corresponds exactly with the item number in the *Examination Questions* portion of your *Booklet*. If you mark your answers in the *Examination Questions* portion of your *Booklet*, be certain that you transfer them to the *Objective Answer Sheet* before the session ends. Your examination paper will not be graded if you fail to record your answers on the *Objective Answer* Sheet. You will not be given additional time to record your answers.

13. If an objective item requires you to record a numerical answer, blacken the ovals on the *Objective Answer Sheet*. If zeros precede your numerical answer, blacken the zeros in the ovals preceding your answer. You cannot receive credit for your answers if you fail to blacken an oval in each column. You may write the numbers in the boxes provided to facilitate blackening the ovals; however, the numbers written in the boxes will not be graded.

14. Answer all essay questions and problems on the *Essay Paper* provided. Always begin the start of an answer to a question on the top of a new page (which may be the reverse side of a sheet of paper). Cross out anything that you do not want graded.

15. Selected essay responses will be graded for writing skills.

16. Include all computations to the problems in the FARE section. This may assist the graders in understanding your answers.

17. You may not leave the examination room with any examination materials, nor may you take notes about the examination with you from the examination room. You are required to turn in by the end of each session:

a. *Attendance Record* and *Statement of Confidentiality*

b. *Examination Questions*

c. *Essay Paper* (for LPR, AUDIT, and FARE). Do not remove unused paper.

d. *Objective Answer Sheet*

e. Calculator (for ARE and FARE)

f. All unused examination materials

g. Prenumbered Identification Card (or Admission Notice) at the last examination section for which you sit (if required by your examining jurisdiction)

Your examination will not be graded unless you hand in the above-listed items before you leave the examination room.

18. If you believe one or more questions contain errors and want your concerns evaluated, you must fax to the AICPA your comments, including the precise nature of any defect; your rationale; and, if possible, references. The fax should include your 7-digit candidate number and must be received by the AICPA within 4 days of the completion of the examination administration. Comments should be faxed to (201) 938-3443. This will ensure that all comments are reviewed before the grading bases for the Uniform CPA Examination are confirmed. Although the AICPA cannot respond directly to each fax, it will investigate all comments received within the 4-day period.

19. Examination question booklets will be destroyed by the AICPA 30 days after the examination section is administered.

20. Contact your board of accountancy for information regarding any other applicable rules.

In addition to the above general rules, oral instructions will be given by the examination supervisor shortly before the start of each session. They should include the location and/or rules concerning

    a. Storage of briefcases, handbags, books, personal belongings, etc.
    b. Food and beverages
    c. Smoking
    d. Rest rooms
    e. Telephone calls and messages
    f. Requirements (if any) that candidates must take all parts not previously passed each time they sit for the examination. Minimum grades (if any) needed on parts failed to get credit on parts passed.
    g. Official clock, if any
    h. Additional supplies
    i. Assembly, turn-in, inspection, and stapling of solutions

The next section provides a detailed listing (mind-jogger) of things to do for your last-minute preparation. It also contains a list of strategies for the exam.

CPA EXAM CHECKLIST

One week before exam

___ 1. Look over major topical areas, concentrating on schedule formats and the information flow of the formats.
For example:
Accounting Changes and Error Correction
Income Statement Format
Long-Term Construction Accounting
Inventory Methods
Cost Adjusted for Fair Value vs. Equity
  Method Investments
Lessee-Lessor Accounting
EPS Calculations
Purchase, Pooling, Consolidation Methods

___ 2. If time permits, work through a few questions in your weakest areas so that techniques/concepts are fresh in your mind.

___ 3. Assemble notecards and key outlines of major topical areas into a manageable "last review" notebook to be taken with you to the exam.

What to bring

___ 1. *Registration material*--for the CPA exam. You will save time at the examination site by filling out ahead of time the survey that you received with your registration materials.

___ 2. *Hotel confirmation.*

___ 3. *Cash*--payment for anything by personal check is rarely accepted.

___ 4. *Major credit card*--American Express, Master Card, Visa, etc.

___ 5. *Alarm clock*--this is too important an event to trust to a hotel wake-up call that might be overlooked.

___ 6. *Food*--candidates should carefully review the instructions provided by their State Board Examiners regarding policies about food at the exam.

___ 7. *Clothing*--should be comfortable and layered to suit the temperature range over the 2-day period and the examination room conditions.

___ 8. *Watch*--it is imperative that you be aware of the time remaining for each session.

___ 9. *Earplugs*--even though an examination is being given, there is constant activity in the examination room (e.g., proctors walking around, rustling of paper, people coughing, etc.). The use of earplugs may block out some of this distraction and help you concentrate better.

__ 10. *Other*--"last review" materials, pencils, erasers, leads, sharpeners, pens, paperclips, etc.

While waiting for the exam to begin

1. Put your ID card on the table for ready reference to your number. The front page of your Examination Answer Booklet contains an Attendance Record. When told to do so, fill out the Attendance Record that the proctor will pick up prior to the start of the exam.

2. Realize that proctors will be constantly circulating throughout each exam session. You need only raise your hand to receive more paper at any time or paper will be available at nearby tables.

3. Take a few deep breaths and compose yourself. Resolve to do your very best and to go after every point you can get!

Before leaving for exam each day

1. Put your ID card in your wallet, purse, or on your person for entry to take the exam. This is your official entrance permit that allows you to participate in all sections of the exam.

2. Remember your hotel room key.

3. Pack snack items and lunch (optional).

4. Limit consumption of liquids.

5. Realize that on Thursday morning you must check out and arrange for storage of your luggage (most hotels have such a service) PRIOR TO departing for the exam to prevent late charges on your hotel bill.

Evenings before exams

1. Reviewing the evenings before the exams could earn you the extra points needed to pass a section. Just keep this last-minute effort in perspective and do NOT panic yourself into staying up all night trying to cover every possible point. This could lead to disaster by sapping your body of the endurance needed to attack questions creatively during the next 7-8 hour day.

2. Before the Financial Accounting and Reporting session, scan the general schedule formats to imprint the *flow* of information on your mind (e.g., income statement and EPS formats, lease formats, etc.).

3. Read over KEY notecards or the most important outlines on topics in which you feel deficient.

4. Go over mnemonics and acronyms you have developed as study aids. Test yourself by writing out the letters on paper while verbally giving a brief explanation of what the letters stand for.

5. Scan outlines of SFAC 1, 2, 5, 6 and any other notes pertinent to answering conceptual questions to imprint keywords.

6. Avoid postmortems during the examination period. Nothing you can do will affect your grade on sections of the exam you have already completed. Concentrate only on the work ahead in remaining sections.

7. GET A GOOD NIGHT'S REST! Being well rested will permit you to meet each day's challenge with a fresh burst of creative energy.

Exam taking strategy

1. Open the exam booklet, noting the number of objective questions and the areas they cover.

2. Scan the "required" sections of all problems to get a feel for the nature of the topics covered, making a mental note of the time allotted to each section (exam point allotments parallel time allocation). Also note whether the problems require schedules or FS or numerical responses for selected items that are to be blackened into ovals on an objective question answer sheet. Remember to divide allotted time per question proportionately over ALL parts of a question (parts are often unrelated, so don't forget that if 40-50 minutes are allowed for Problem 5, that much time must be divided among all required parts). Knowing the nature of these problems that you will tackle later allows your subconscious to sort out needed facts for solving them as you work the objective questions.

3. Reconcile the problem numbers with the questions listed on the front of the exam booklet and check consecutive page numbers in your booklet to reassure yourself that it is complete, that no pages are stuck together, etc.

4. Recognize that you may be feeling a little "burned out" by Thursday afternoon, so fight to stay sharp and go after the available points!

5. Begin working the objective questions, noting the time begun at the start of each set. Realize that you have approximately 2 to 2 1/2 minutes per computational-type multiple-choice question and approximately 1 2/3 minutes per concept-type multiple-choice question. Use the area marked "work space" in the Examination Question Booklet for the computations. If you need more room to develop minischedules, time lines, etc. use some of the columnar paper in the Answer Booklet. Do not

waste time labeling computations because the grader will not use objective question computation sheets. It is wise to number your computations for your own use if you wish to come back to a question, however.

6. Read each question **carefully!** Dates are extremely important! (For example, a long-term contract problem using the percentage-of-completion method may give information for a contract begun in 19**X8** but ask for income recognized for the year ended Dec. 31, 19**X9**.)

7. If you are struggling with problems beyond your time limit, use the strategy of dividing objective questions into two categories

    a. Questions for which you **know** you lack knowledge to answer: Drawing from any resources you have, narrow answers down to as few as possible; then make an EDUCATED GUESS.

    b. Questions for which you feel you should be getting correct answer: Put "?" by objective question number on your Examination Question Booklet and label computational sheet so you can return to it later. Your mental block may clear, or you may spot a simple math error that now can be corrected, thus giving you extra points.

8. Remember: NEVER change a first impulse objective question answer later unless you are **absolutely certain** you are right. It is a proven fact that your subconscious often guides you to the correct answer.

9. Work problems that you consider easiest first, noting time begun and time allotted. Your goal is to pick up extra time to allocate to problems you are weaker on.

10. Read the "required" section, underlining and noting EVERY requirement that you are asked for.

11. Read the information given, underlining key facts, circling percentages and interest rates that you plan to use, crossing out extraneous information, etc.

12. Draw time lines, visualize schedule headings, schedule formats, etc., that will help you respond to requirements. Do not forget to put a heading on each schedule or statement.

13. Computations should be made on columnar paper contained in your Examination Answer Booklet which WILL be used by the grader as an "audit trail" to support your work. Label and cross-reference to schedules and work sheets as necessary. (For example, when asked to show comparative balance sheets for 19X8 and 19X9 with the correct valuation of Investment in Subsidiary, show supporting computations by stating "See Schedule A on page ....")

14. Write legibly; be neat and organized. Leave space on schedules, etc., to add information that you might think of later. Remember: A legible, well-organized, grammatically correct answer--containing as many buzzwords as possible--gives a professional appearance.

15. For essays/problems, format, organization, technique, disclosure, etc., are of critical importance.

16. Constantly compare your progress with the time remaining. NEVER spend more than the maximum time on any problem until **ALL** problems are answered and time remains. Fight the urge to **complete** one problem at the expense of another problem. Remember that there are more gradable points in the **beginning** stages of problems than toward the end (the law of diminishing returns applies!). Ten points is the maximum you can earn, so once you feel you have answered sufficiently, **move on!**

17. As each problem is completed, quickly reread the "required" section again to make sure you have responded to each requirement. Organize any additional pages used to answer each question and set them aside for final assembly before handing in.

18. Each test will include a problem or question for which you may feel unprepared. Accept the challenge and go after the points! Draw from all your resources. Ask yourself how GAAP would be applied to similar situations, scan the objective questions for clues, look for relationships in **all** the available information given in the problem, try "backing into" the problem from another angle, etc. Every problem (no matter how impossible it may look at first glance) contains some points that are yours for the taking. Make your best effort. You may be on the right track and not even know it!

19. The cardinal rule is NEVER, but NEVER, leave an answer blank.

20. When you see alternate routes to take in problem solving, explain to the grader any assumptions you are making and why. Should you run out of time on a problem that you know how to complete, write a note to the grader briefly describing what you would have done had time permitted.

21. The most important technique to use for **ALL** essay questions is to constantly remind yourself that the grader assumes you know nothing (s/he cannot read your mind) and you, as a candidate for a professional designation, must convince him/her of your knowledge of the subject matter under question. **NEVER OMIT THE OBVIOUS!**

22. If time permits, go back to any objective question that you "guessed" on.

23. Double check to make certain you have answered ALL parts of EVERY problem to the best of your ability. You've come too far to end the exam early, just because it's the last part and you feel you've written enough. Stick it out until they call for the exams.

24. Transfer objective question answers to the form provided in your Examination Answer Booklet. Be especially careful to follow the numbers exactly, because number patterns differ on each answer form! Don't wait until it's too late. The proctors are not authorized to give you extra time for this.

25. Assemble any additional answer sheets in the correct order.

26. Take your Examination Question Booklet and Examination Answer Booklet to the front of the exam room. Staple the additional answer sheets in the Examination Answer Booklet.

**HAVE YOU MADE YOUR
COMMITMENT?**

FINANCIAL ACCOUNTING AND REPORTING

Module 22/Basic Theory and Financial Reporting (TREP)

Module 23/Inventory (INVY)

Module 24/Fixed Assets (FA)

Module 25/Monetary Current Assets and Current Liabilities (CACL)

Module 26/Present Value (PV)

Module 27/Deferred Taxes (DETX)

Module 28/Stockholders' Equity (STK)

Module 29/Investments (IVES)

Sample Examination

AICPA November 1997 and May 1998 Released Questions

INTRODUCTION

This chapter is written to help you review intermediate and advanced accounting (financial accounting) for the Financial Accounting and Reporting section of the exam. The AICPA Content Specification Outline of financial accounting coverage appears on the following page.

Although the time devoted to financial accounting on the CPA exam since May 1994 is only 55% of the time previously devoted to this area, the scope of coverage has not been reduced. Additionally, the depth of coverage has not changed under reduced coverage.

The chapter is organized along the lines of the traditional intermediate and advanced accounting texts. The topics are arranged per the twelve financial modules (on the previous pages). The objective is to provide you with the basic concepts, journal entries, and formulas for each topic and subtopic. Hopefully you will be able to expand, adapt, and apply the basics to specific problem situations as presented in multiple-choice questions, other objective-type questions, essay questions, and problems appearing on the exam. Keep in mind the importance of working all four types of questions under exam conditions as you study the basics set forth in this chapter. Refer to the multiple-choice questions, other objective-type questions, essay questions, and problems on each of the financial accounting topics.

As you work through this chapter, remember that there are many possible series of journal entries and account titles that can be used in accounting for a specific type of economic transaction (e.g., long-term construction contracts). Reconcile the approach illustrated in the chapter with the approach you studied as an undergraduate per your intermediate or advanced text.

In this chapter, you will be referred frequently to the outlines of authoritative pronouncements at the end of the financial accounting modules in this chapter on the particular topic being discussed. These outlines can be located easily by referring to the headings identifying the pronouncements which appear at the top of each page at the end of this chapter. At first consideration, the presentation might appear more comprehensive if the outlines of APB, SFAS, etc., were integrated in this chapter rather than presented separately. Separate presentation, however, allows separate study of the pronouncements which is particularly beneficial as a last minute review. Please note that you **do not need to know** the numbers of these pronouncements for the exam.

AICPA Content Specification Outline

The AICPA Content Specification Outline of the coverage of Financial Accounting and Reporting appears on the following page. This outline was issued by the AICPA, effective for May 1998.

AICPA CONTENT SPECIFICATION OUTLINE: FINANCIAL ACCOUNTING AND REPORTING

I. Concepts and Standards for Financial Statements (**20%**)

  A. Financial Accounting Concepts

  B. Financial Accounting Standards for Presentation and Disclosure in General Purpose Financial Statements

    1. Consolidated and Combined Financial Statements

    2. Balance Sheet

    3. Statement(s) of Income, Comprehensive Income, and Changes in Equity Accounts

    4. Statement of Cash Flows

    5. Accounting Policies and Other Notes to Financial Statements

  C. Other Presentations of Financial Data

    1. Financial Statements Prepared in Conformity With Comprehensive Bases of Accounting Other Than Generally Accepted Accounting Principles

    2. Personal Financial Statements

    3. Prospective Financial Information

  D. Financial Statement Analysis

II. Recognition, Measurement, Valuation, and Presentation of Typical Items in Financial Statements in Conformity With Generally Accepted Accounting Principles (**40%**)

  A. Cash, Cash Equivalents, and Marketable Securities

  B. Receivables

  C. Inventories

D. Property, Plant, and Equipment
E. Investments
F. Intangible and Other Assets
G. Payables and Accruals
H. Deferred Revenues
I. Notes and Bonds Payable
J. Other Liabilities
K. Equity Accounts
L. Revenue, Cost, and Expense Accounts

III. Recognition, Measurement, Valuation, and Presentation of Specific Types of Transactions and Events in Financial Statements in Conformity With Generally Accepted Accounting Principles (**40%**)

A. Accounting Changes and Corrections of Errors
B. Business Combinations
C. Cash Flow Components--Financing, Investing, and Operating

D. Contingent Liabilities and Commitments
E. Discontinued Operations
F. Earnings Per Share
G. Employee Benefits
H. Extraordinary Items
I. Financial Instruments
J. Foreign Currency Transactions and Translation
K. Income Taxes
L. Interest Costs
M. Interim Financial Reporting
N. Leases
O. Nonmonetary Transactions
P. Quasi Reorganizations, Reorganizations, and Changes in Entity
Q. Related Parties
R. Research and Development Costs
S. Segment Reporting

PREPARING FOR FINANCIAL ACCOUNTING AND REPORTING

This section of the exam includes financial accounting theory and its practical application (problem-solving). Candidates can expect to see multiple-choice questions (both concept and computational), other objective format questions, essays, and problems. Therefore, in order to be thoroughly prepared for this section of the exam, candidates will need to master the material covered in Modules 22-33.

First, candidates' preparation should emphasize an understanding of the basic principles and objectives underlying accounting (e.g., revenue and expense recognition rules, etc.). By focusing in on the key concepts, candidates will be able to develop a solution for whatever question format is tested.

Candidates should then evaluate their competence by working 10 to 20 multiple-choice questions from each of the Modules (22-33) in this volume. This diagnostic routine will acquaint you with the specific nature of the questions tested on each topic as well as indicate the amount of study required per topic. You should work toward a 75-80% correct response rate as a minimum on each topic.

Third, work actual CPA practice problems and essay questions from recent exams under examination conditions. **This is a critical step that candidates should not overlook**. It is not enough to just work multiple-choice and other objective-type questions. CPA problems are more involved and longer than typical problems found on undergraduate accounting examinations. CPA problems require special skills that are usually not developed in undergraduate accounting programs. You must develop these skills **before** the examination by applying the methodology described in Chapter 3 on "live" CPA problems. Similarly, most CPA candidates have little experience with accounting essay questions; undergraduate accounting examinations generally consist of problems. You should write out complete solutions to essay questions. Do not wait until the examination to develop answering techniques. Selected essays or portions thereof are graded for writing skills. Candidates should also recognize the value of the keyword outline (prepared in the exam margin or on the ruled paper). Practice it while answering old examination questions, and perhaps more importantly, orient your study habits to the keyword outline approach. As you review material, think of it in "outline" or "list" form. While you should use the keyword outline to organize your answer, your answer must be written out for the grader. LISTS OF KEYWORDS, EVEN IN OUTLINE FORM, ARE NOT ACCEPTABLE TO THE AICPA. Finally, get yourself in good physical and mental condition. Commit yourself to stay and to work until the end of the session. It is very easy to get up and leave an hour early.

BASIC THEORY AND FINANCIAL REPORTING

A. Basic Concepts

This module includes the basic financial statements except the Statement of Cash Flows. It also includes revenue and expense recognition rules, accounting changes, and error correction. **The relevant accounting pronouncements are indicated in the discussion, complete with cross-references to outlines of the pronouncements at the end of this chapter**. (Note these outlines appear in the following sequence: ARB, APB, SFAS, and SFAC. The page headers in the outlines identify the sources of the pronouncements outlined on those pages.) Turn to each outline as directed and study the outline while reviewing the related journal entries, computations, etc.

1. Basic Accounting Theory

The foundation of financial accounting is generally accepted accounting principles (GAAP). In practice, GAAP has come to include SFAS, FASB Interpretations, APB Opinions, ARB and SEC releases. These are the pronouncements to which practitioners look when determining if financial statements fairly present financial position, results of operations, and changes in cash flows.

Per SAS 69 (AU 411), for business enterprises the following hierarchy applies. If the accountant/ auditor cannot find a specified accounting treatment in category (A), s/he would proceed to the next lowest category.

- **Category (A),** officially established accounting principles, consists of Financial Accounting Standards Board (FASB) Statements of Financial Accounting Standards and Interpretations, Accounting Principles Board (APB) Opinions, and AICPA Accounting Research Bulletins.
- **Category (B)** consists of FASB Technical Bulletins and, if cleared by the FASB, AICPA Industry Audit and Accounting Guides and AICPA Statements of Position.
- **Category (C)** consists of AICPA Accounting Standards Executive Committee (AcSEC) Practice Bulletins that have been cleared by the FASB and consensus positions of the FASB Emerging Issues Task Force.
- **Category (D)** includes AICPA accounting interpretations and implementation guides ("Qs and As") published by the FASB staff, and practices that are widely recognized and prevalent either generally or in the industry.

Although GAAP is the current basis for financial reporting, it does not constitute a cohesive body of accounting theory. Generally, SFAS and the other authoritative pronouncements have been the result of a problem-by-problem approach. The pronouncements have dealt with specific problems as they occur and are not predicated on an underlying body of theory.

Theory can be defined as a coherent set of hypothetical, conceptual, and pragmatic principles forming a general frame of reference for a field of inquiry; thus, accounting theory should be the basic principles of accounting rather than its practice (which GAAP describes or dictates). Accounting has a definite need for conceptual theoretical structure. Such a structure is necessary if an authoritative body such as the FASB is to promulgate consistent standards. A body of accounting theory should be the foundation of the standard-setting process and should provide guidance where no authoritative GAAP exists.

There have been efforts to develop such a frame of reference. The most recent attempt to develop accounting theory led to the establishment of the Statements of Financial Accounting Concepts, of which six have been issued. The purpose of this series is "to set forth fundamentals on which financial accounting and reporting standards will be based." In other words, the SFAC attempt to organize a framework that can serve as a reference point in formulating SFAS.

Financial Reporting. "Financial reporting includes not only financial statements but also other means of communicating information that relates, directly or indirectly, to the information provided by a business enterprise's accounting system--that is, information about an enterprise's resources, obligations, earnings, etc." (SFAC 1). It is important to note that not all informational needs are met by accounting or financial reporting. The following diagram from SFAC 5 describes the information spectrum.

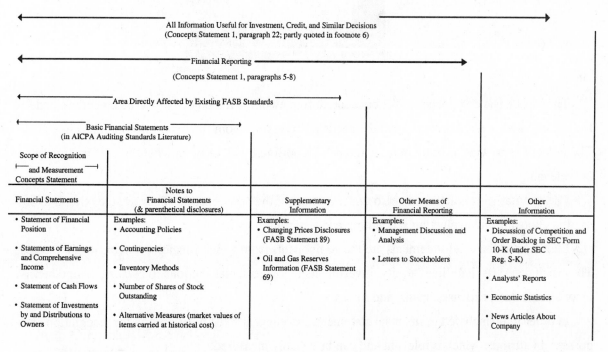

Components of the Conceptual Framework. The components of the conceptual framework for financial accounting and reporting include objectives, qualitative characteristics, elements, recognition, measurement, financial statements, earnings, funds flow, and liquidity. The relationship between these components is illustrated in the following diagram, from *Financial Statements and Other Means of Financial Reporting*, a FASB Invitation to Comment.

In the diagram below, components to the left are more basic and those to the right depend on components to their left. Components are closely related to those above or below them.

Conceptual Framework
For Financial Accounting and Reporting

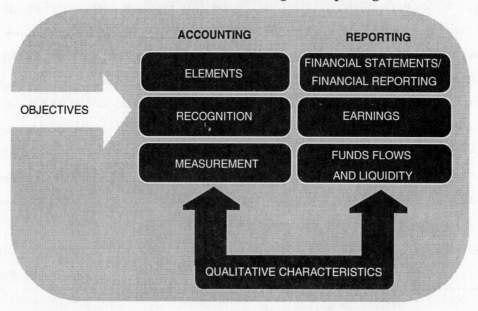

The most basic component of the conceptual framework is the objectives. The objectives underlie the other phases and are derived from the needs of those for whom financial information is intended. The objectives provide a focal point for financial reporting by identifying what types of information are relevant.

The qualitative characteristics also underlie most of the other phases. They are the criteria to be used in choosing and evaluating accounting and reporting policies.

Elements of financial statements are the components from which financial statements are created. They include assets, liabilities, equity, investments by owners, distributions to owners, comprehensive income, revenues, expenses, gains, and losses.

In order to be included in financial statements, an element must meet criteria for recognition and possess an attribute which is relevant and can be reliably measured.

Finally, reporting and display considerations are concerned with what information should be provided, who should provide it, and where it should be displayed. How the financial statements (financial position, earnings, and cash flow) are presented is the focal point of this part of the conceptual framework project.

Objectives of Financial Reporting. (See outline of SFAC 1.) Remember, objectives of financial reporting underlie the conceptual framework. They are the basis upon which a body of theory is established. The objectives described in SFAC 1 have not been verified by an empirical process, but they are an attempt by the FASB to provide a foundation for a cohesive set of interrelated concepts.

The objectives focus on users of financial information. They are derived from "the needs of external users who lack the authority to prescribe the information they want and must rely on information management communicates to them." The external users who are emphasized in the objectives are actual and potential investors and creditors. These users are particularly interested in the amounts, timing, and relative uncertainty of future cash flows, whether they be return of capital, interest, dividends, etc.

Three basic objectives are listed in SFAC 1. The objectives state that financial reporting should provide (1) information useful in investment and credit decisions, (2) information useful in assessing cash flow prospects (amount, timing, and uncertainty), and (3) information about enterprise resources, claims to those resources, and changes therein. A focal point in SFAC 1 is information about earnings and earning power. Earnings are a major cause of changes in resources. Despite the emphasis on cash flows, earnings are to be computed on the accrual basis, because accrual accounting "provides a better indication of an enterprise's present and continuing ability to generate favorable cash flows than information limited to the financial effects of cash receipts and payments."

Qualitative Characteristics. (See outline of SFAC 2.) The qualitative characteristics also underlie the conceptual framework, but in a different way. While the objectives provide an overall basis, the qualitative characteristics establish criteria for selecting and evaluating accounting alternatives which will meet the objectives. In other words, information must possess the qualitative characteristics if that information is to fulfill the objectives.

SFAC 2 views these characteristics as a hierarchy of accounting qualities, as represented in the diagram below.

The diagram reveals many important relationships. At the top and bottom are constraints. If information falls outside these constraints, it would not be reported although it may possess some qualitative characteristics. Thus, information is not disclosed if the costs of disclosure outweigh the benefits or if the information is not material enough to influence users.

The first two qualities in the hierarchy (understandability and decision usefulness) are not qualities relating solely to information. They also depend on qualities of particular decision makers. The usefulness and understandability of information depends on the knowledge and ability of those using it. SFAC 1 states that "financial information is a tool, and like most tools, cannot be of direct help to those who are unable or unwilling to use it or who misuse it."

The primary qualities that accounting information should possess are relevance and reliability. As the chart indicates, each of these is broken down into three components. Comparability is a secondary quality which interacts with relevance and reliability to enhance usefulness of information.

A HIERARCHY OF ACCOUNTING QUALITIES

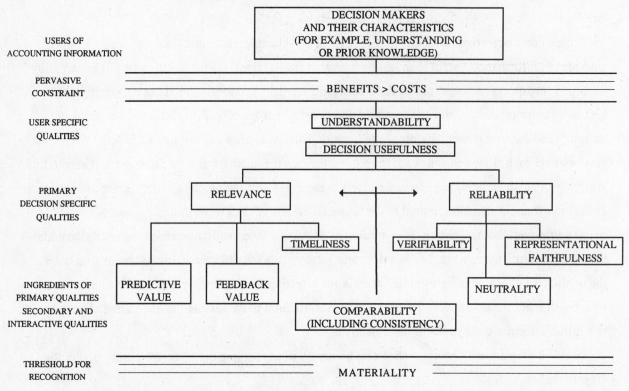

Accounting information is relevant if it has the "capacity to make a difference" in a decision. To be relevant in an investment or credit decision, information must help users form predictions about future cash flows (refer to objectives). This can occur through predictive value (improving capacity to predict) or feedback value (confirmation or correction of prior predictions). Of course, to be relevant, information must be available before it loses its capacity to affect decisions (timeliness).

Information is reliable if it is reasonably free from error and bias, and faithfully represents what it claims to represent. Reliability consists of verifiability, representational faithfulness, and neutrality.

The secondary qualities of comparability and consistency become important when assessing cash flows of different enterprises or of the same enterprises over different periods. Comparability of information enables users to identify similarities in and differences between two enterprises, while consistency (unchanging policies and procedures from period to period) does the same between periods for each enterprise.

Basic Elements. (See outline of SFAC 6.) Elements of financial statements are the ten basic building blocks from which financial statements are constructed. These definitions are based upon the objectives of SFAC 1. They are intended to assure that users will receive decision-useful information about enterprise resources (assets), claims to those resources (liabilities and equity), and changes therein (the other seven elements). In order to be included in the statements, an item must qualify as an element, meet recognition criteria, and be measurable.

The meaning of financial statement elements depends on the conceptual view of earnings which is adopted. Two basic views are the asset-liability view and the revenue-expense view. Under the asset-liability view, earnings are measured by the change (other than investments or withdrawals) in the net economic resources of an enterprise during a period. Therefore, definitions of assets and liabilities are the key under this view, and definitions of revenues, expenses, gains, and losses are secondary and are based on assets and liabilities.

The revenue-expense view holds that earnings are a measure of an enterprise's effectiveness in using its inputs to obtain and sell outputs. Thus, definitions of revenues and expenses are basic to this view, and definitions of assets, liabilities, and other elements are derived from revenues and expenses.

The definitions of all ten elements are contained in the outline of SFAC 6. Let us examine one definition in more detail. "Assets are probable future economic benefits obtained or controlled by a particular entity as a result of past transactions or events." This definition is based on the objectives and qualities of SFAC 1 and 2. The overall thrust of the objectives--predicting and evaluating future cash flows--is reflected in the phrase "probable future economic benefits." "Control by a particular entity" is crucial if reporting an item as an asset is to have decision usefulness (or relevance). The quality of reliability is assured by the phrase "as a result of past transactions." Information is more verifiable, valid, and neutral (the components of reliability) if based on past transactions. A similar analysis can be applied to liabilities, equity, investments by owners, distributions to owners, compre- hensive income, revenues, expenses, gains and losses.

SFAC 6 also defines some other concepts in addition to the ten elements. Especially important among these 11 additional concepts are accrual accounting, realization, recognition, and matching. Realization and recognition are addressed by the FASB in SFAC 5. The definition of accrual account- ing is important because SFAC 1 stated that accrual accounting should be used since it provides a bet- ter indication of future cash flows than the cash basis. This is true because accrual accounting records transactions with cash consequences (involving future cash flows) as they occur, not when the cash actually moves. Matching is referred to in most accounting literature as a principle, or fundamental law, of accounting.

Recognition and Measurement. (See outline of SFAC 5.) Recognition principles establish crite- ria concerning when an element should be included in the statements, while measurement principles govern the valuation of those elements.

SFAC 5 established four fundamental recognition criteria: definitions, measurability, relevance, and reliability. If an item meets the definition of an element, can be reliably measured, is capable of making a difference in user decisions, and is verifiable, neutral, and representationally faithful, it should be included in the financial statements.

Five different attributes are used to measure assets and liabilities in present practice. These are discussed below in an excerpt from SFAC 5.

a. ***Historical cost (historical proceeds).*** Property, plant, and equipment and most inventories are reported at their historical cost, which is the amount of cash, or its equivalent, paid to acquire an asset, commonly adjusted after acquisition for amortization or other allocations. Liabilities that involve obligations to provide goods or services to customers are generally reported at historical proceeds, which is the amount of cash, or its equivalent, received when the obligation was incurred and may be adjusted after acquisition for amortization or other allocations.

b. **Current cost.** Some inventories are reported at their current (replacement) cost, which is the amount of cash, or its equivalent, that would have to be paid if the same or an equivalent asset were acquired currently.

c. **Current market value.** Some investments in marketable securities are reported at their current market value, which is the amount of cash or its equivalent, that could be obtained by selling an asset in orderly liquidation. Current market value is also generally used for assets expected to be sold at prices lower than previous carrying amounts. Some liabilities that involve marketable commodities and securities, for example, the obligations of writers of options or sellers of common shares who do not own the underlying commodities or securities, are reported at current market value.

d. **Net realizable (settlement) value.** Short-term receivables and some inventories are reported at their net realizable value, which is the nondiscounted amount of cash, or its equivalent, into which an asset is expected to be converted in due course of business less direct costs, if any, necessary to make that conversion. Liabilities that involve known or estimated amounts of money payable at unknown future dates, for example, trade payables or warranty obligations, generally are reported at their net settlement value, which is the nondiscounted amount of cash, or its equivalent, expected to be paid to liquidate an obligation in the due course of business, including direct costs, if any, necessary to make that payment.

e. **Present (or discounted) value of future cash flows.** Long-term receivables are reported at their present or discounted value (discounted at the implicit or historical rate), which is the present value of future cash inflows into which an asset is expected to be converted in due course of business less present values of cash outflows necessary to obtain those inflows. Long-term payables are similarly reported at their present or discounted value (discounted at the implicit or historical rate), which is the present or discounted value of future cash outflows expected to be required to satisfy the liability in due course of business.

SFAC 5 states that each of these attributes is appropriate in different situations and that all five attributes will continue to be used in the future.

Similarly, SFAC 5 states that nominal units of money will continue to be the measurement unit. However, if inflation increases to a level where the FASB feels that financial statements become too distorted, another unit (such as units of constant purchasing power) could be adopted.

SFAC 5 is based on the concept of financial capital maintenance. Two basic concepts of capital maintenance (financial and physical) can be used to separate return **on** capital (earnings) from return **of** capital (capital recovery). Remember, any capital which is "used up" during a period must be returned before earnings can be recognized. In other words, earnings is the amount an entity can distribute to its owners and be as well-off at the end of the year as at the beginning.

One way "well-offness" can be measured is in terms of financial capital. This concept of capital maintenance holds that the capital to be maintained is measured by the amount of cash (possibly restated into constant dollars) invested by owners. Earnings may not be recognized until the dollar investment in net assets, measured in units of money or purchasing power, is returned. The financial capital maintenance concept is the traditional view which is reflected in most present financial statements.

An alternative definition of "well-offness" is expressed in terms of physical capital. This concept holds that the capital to be maintained is the physical productive capacity of the enterprise. Earnings may not be recognized until the current replacement costs of assets with the same productive capabilities of the assets used up are returned. The physical capital maintenance concept supports current cost accounting. Again, the physical productive capacity may be measured in nominal or constant dollars.

A simple example can further clarify the two capital maintenance concepts. Suppose an enterprise invests $10 in an inventory item. At year end, the enterprise sells the item for $15. In order to replace the item at year end, they would have to pay $12 rather than $10. To further simplify, assume the increase in replacement cost is due to specific price changes, and there is no general inflation.

The financial capital concept would maintain that the firm is as well-off once the dollar investment ($10) is returned. At that point, the financial capital is maintained and the remaining $5 is a return **on** capital, or income. The physical capital concept maintains that the firm is not as well-off until the physical capacity (a similar inventory item) is returned. Therefore, the firm must reinvest $12 to be as well-off. Then physical capital is maintained, and only the remaining $3 is a return **on** capital or income.

SFAC 5 also gives specific guidance as to recognition of revenues and gains, and expenses and losses, as indicated below.

Revenues	When realized or realizable (when related assets received or held are readily convertible to known amounts of cash or claims to cash) and earned
Gains	When realized or realizable
Expenses	When economic benefits are consumed in revenue-earning activities, or when future economic benefits are reduced or eliminated
Losses	When future economic benefits are reduced or eliminated

When economic benefits are consumed during a period, the expense may be recognized by matching (such as cost of goods sold), immediate recognition (such as selling and administrative salaries), or systematic and rational allocation (such as depreciation).

Revenues, expenses, gains, and losses are used to compute **earnings**. Earnings is the extent to which revenues and gains associated with cash-to-cash cycles substantially completed during the period exceed expenses and losses directly or indirectly associated with those cycles. Earnings adjusted for cumulative accounting adjustments and other nonowner changes in equity (such as foreign currency translation adjustments) is **comprehensive income**. Per SFAC 5, comprehensive income would reflect all changes in the equity of an entity during a period, except investments by owners and distributions to owners. SFAS 130, covered in Section D.3. of this module, only goes part way in implementing this concept.

2. **Income Determination** (See outlines of SFAC 1, 2, 5, and 6)

The primary objective of accounting is to measure income. Income is a measure of management's efficiency in combining the factors of production into desired goods and services.

Efficient firms with prospects of increased efficiency (higher profits) have greater access to financial capital and at lower costs. Their stock usually sells at a higher price-earnings ratio than the stock of a company with less enthusiastic prospects. The credit rating of the prospectively efficient company is probably higher than the prospectively less efficient company. Thus, the "cost of capital" will be lower for the company with the brighter outlook (i.e., lower stock dividend yield rates and/or lower interest rates).

The entire process of acquiring the factors of production, processing them, and selling the resulting goods and services produces revenue. The acquisition of raw materials is part of the revenue-producing process, as is providing warranty protection.

Under the accrual basis of accounting, revenue is generally recognized at the point of sale (ARB 43, chap 1A, Rule 1) or as service is performed. The point of sale is when title passes: generally when shipped (i.e., FOB shipping point) or when received (i.e., FOB destination).

Three exceptions exist to the general revenue recognition rule: during production, at the point where production is complete, and at the point of cash collection. The table below identifies the criteria applicable to each basis, the appropriate accounting method, and the reasons for using that basis.

Recognition basis/ source of GAAP	*Accounting method*	*Criteria for use of basis*	*Reasons(s) for departing from sale basis*
• **Point of sale ARB 43 (Ch 1A, Rule 1)**	• Transactions approach (sales basis)	• Exchange has taken place • Earnings process is (virtually) complete	
• **During production basis ARB 45 and AICPA Contractors Guide**	• Percentage-of-completion	• Long-term construction,* property, or service contract • Dependable estimates of extent of progress and cost to complete • Reasonable assurance of collectibility of contract price	• Availability of evidence of ultimate proceeds • Better measure of periodic income • Avoidance of fluctuations in revenues, expenses, and income
• **Completion-of-production basis ARB 43 (Ch 4, St 9)**	• Net realizable value	• Immediate marketability at quoted prices • Unit interchangeability • Difficulty of determining costs	• Known or determinable revenues • Inability to determine costs and thereby defer expense recognition until sale
• **Cash collection basis APB 10**	• Installment and cost recovery methods	• Absence of a reasonable basis for estimating degree of collectibility	• Level of uncertainty with respect to collection of the receivable precludes recognition of gross profit before cash is received

*Note that the "completed contract" method for construction contracts is not a departure from the sale basis.

Source: Adapted from Henry R. Jaenicke, *Survey of Present Practices in Recognizing Revenues, Expenses, Gains, and Losses*, FASB, 1981.

Under accrual accounting, expenses are recognized as related revenues are recognized, that is, (product) expenses are matched with revenues. Some (period) expenses, however, cannot be associated with particular revenues. These expenses are recognized as incurred.

(1) Product costs are those which can be associated with particular sales (e.g., cost of sales). Product costs attach to a unit of product and become an expense only when the unit to which they attach is sold. This is known as associating "cause and effect."

(2) Period costs are not particularly or conveniently assignable to a product. They become expenses due to the passage of time by

(a) Immediate recognition if the future benefit cannot be measured (e.g., advertising)

(b) Systematic and rational allocation if benefits are produced in certain future periods (e.g., asset depreciation)

Thus, income is the net effect of inflows of revenue and outflows of expense during a period of time. The period in which revenues and expenses are taken to the income statement (recognized) is determined by the above criteria.

Cash basis accounting, in contrast to accrual basis accounting, recognizes income when cash is received and expenses when cash is disbursed. Cash basis accounting is subject to manipulation (i.e., cash receipts and expenses can be switched from 1 year to another by management). Another reason for adopting accrual basis accounting is that economic transactions have become more involved and multiperiod. An expenditure for a fixed asset may produce revenue for years and years.

3. **Accruals and Deferrals**

Accrual--accrual basis recognition precedes (leads to) cash receipt/expenditure

> Revenue--recognition of revenue earned, but not received
> Expense--recognition of expense incurred, but not paid

Deferral--cash receipt/expenditure precedes (leads to) accrual basis recognition

> Revenue--postponement of recognition of revenue; cash is received,
>   but revenue is not earned
> Expense--postponement of recognition of expense; cash is paid,
>   but expense is not incurred

A deferral postpones recognition of revenue or expense by placing the amount in liability or asset accounts. Two methods are possible for deferring revenues and expenses depending on whether real or nominal accounts are originally used to record the cash transaction.

BOOKKEEPING METHODS
Deferrals of Expense

	Expense method			*Asset method*		
When paid	Insurance expense	xx		Prepaid insurance	xx	
	Cash		xx	Cash		xx
Year end	Prepaid insurance	xx		Insurance expense	xx	
	Insurance expense		xx	Prepaid insurance		xx
Reverse	Yes			No		

Deferrals of Revenue

	Revenue method			*Liability method*		
When received	Cash	xx		Cash	xx	
	Rent revenue		xx	Unearned rent		xx
Year end	Rent revenue	xx		Unearned rent	xx	
	Unearned rent		xx	Rent revenue		xx
Reverse	Yes			No		

Accruals

	Expense			*Revenue*		
Adjustment	Wages expense	xx		Interest receivable	xx	
	Wages payable		xx	Interest revenue		xx
Reverse	Yes			Yes		

Entries are reversed for bookkeeping expediency. If accruals are reversed, the subsequent cash transaction is reflected in the associated nominal account. If accruals are not reversed, the subsequent cash transaction must be apportioned between a nominal and real account.

Cash	(amount received)
Revenue	(earned in current period)
Revenue receivable	(accrual at last year end)

Accruals do not have two methods, but can be complicated by failure to reverse adjusting entries (also true for deferrals initially recorded in nominal accounts).

4. **Cash to Accrual**

Many smaller companies use the **cash basis** of accounting, where revenues are recorded when cash is received and expenses are recorded when cash is paid (except for purchases of fixed assets, which are capitalized and depreciated). Often the accountant is called upon to convert cash basis accounting records to the accrual basis. This type of problem is also found on the CPA examination.

When making journal entries to adjust from the cash basis to the accrual basis, it is important to identify two types of amounts: the **current balance** in the given account (cash basis) and the **correct balance** in the account (accrual basis). The journal entries must adjust the account balances from their current amounts to the correct amounts.

It is also important to understand relationships between balance sheet accounts and income statement accounts. When adjusting a balance sheet account from the cash basis to the accrual basis, the other half of the entry will generally be to the related income statement account. Thus, when adjusting accounts receivable, the related account is sales; for accounts payable, purchases; for prepaid rent, rent expense; and so on.

For example, assume a company adjusts to the accrual basis every 12/31; during the year, they use the cash basis. The 12/31/99 balance in accounts receivable, after adjustment, is $17,000. During 2000, whenever cash is collected, the company debits cash and credits sales. Therefore, the 12/31/00 balance in accounts receivable **before adjustment** is still $17,000. Suppose the **correct** 12/31/00 balance in accounts receivable is $28,000. The necessary entry is

Accounts receivable	11,000	
Sales		11,000

This entry not only corrects the accounts receivable account, but also increases sales since unrecorded receivables means that there are also unrecorded sales. On the other hand, suppose the **correct** 12/31/00 balance of accounts receivable is $12,500. The necessary entry is

Sales	4,500	
Accounts receivable		4,500

Sales is debited because during 2000, $4,500 more cash was collected on account than should be reported as sales. When cash is received on account the transaction is recorded as a credit to sales, not accounts receivable. This overstates the sales account.

Some problems do not require journal entries, but instead a computation of accrual amounts from cash basis amounts, as in the example below.

	12/31/99	*12/31/00*	*2000*
Rent payable	*$4,000*	*$6,000*	
Prepaid rent	*8,000*	*4,500*	
Cash paid for rent			*$27,000*

The rent expense can be computed using either T-accounts or a formula.

T-accounts are shown below.

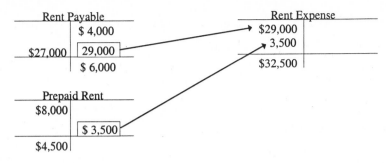

The use of a formula is illustrated next.

Payments	+	Beginning prepaid	+	Ending payable	–	Ending prepaid	–	Beginning payable	=	Expense
$27,000	+	8,000	+	6,000	–	4,500	–	4,000	=	$32,500

Formulas for conversion of various income statement amounts from the cash basis to the accrual basis are summarized in the following table.

Cash basis		Additions		Deductions		Accrual basis
Collections from sales	+	Ending AR (a) (AR written off (b))	–	Beginning AR (c)		= Sales
Collections from other revenues	+	⎛Beginning unearned revenue (d)⎞ ⎝Ending revenue receivable (e)⎠	–	⎛Beginning unearned revenue (f)⎞ ⎝Ending revenue receivable (g)⎠		= Other revenues

Cash basis		Additions		Deductions		Accrual basis
Payments for purchases	+	Beginning inventory (h) (Ending AP (i))	–	Ending inventory (j) (Beginning AP (k))		= Cost of goods sold
Payments for expenses	+	⎛Beginning prepaid expenses (l)⎞ ⎜Ending accrued expenses⎟ ⎝ payable (m)⎠	–	⎛Ending prepaid expenses (n)⎞ ⎜Beginning accrued expenses⎟ ⎝ payable (o)⎠		= Operating expenses*

*Provision must also be made for depreciation expense and similar write-offs and bad debt expense.

(a) Ending AR and related sales have not yet been recorded
(b) AR written off reduced AR but did not result in cash collected
(c) Beginning AR was collected and recorded as sale during the period but was sale of the prior period
(d) Beginning unearned revenue was collected and recorded as revenue in the prior period but was earned in the current period
(e) Ending revenue receivable was earned during the period but has not yet been recorded because it has not been collected
(f) Ending unearned revenue was recorded upon collection as revenue but has not yet been earned
(g) Beginning revenue receivable was recorded during the current period upon collection as revenue but was earned last period
(h) Beginning inventory was sold during the period
(i) Ending AP and related purchases have not yet been recorded
(j) Ending inventory must be excluded from cost of goods sold
(k) Beginning AP reflects purchases last period which were not paid for or recorded until the current period
(l) Beginning prepaid expenses were recorded as expenses when paid in a prior period but are expenses of the current period
(m) Ending accrued expenses payable have not yet been recorded
(n) Ending prepaid expenses were recorded as expenses when paid this period but are expenses of future periods
(o) Beginning accrued expenses payable were recorded currently as expenses when paid but are expenses of the prior period

Since the accrual basis numbers can be derived with T-accounts, you should not have to memorize the formulas.

5. **Installment Sales**

Revenue is recognized as cash is collected. Thus, revenue recognition takes place at the point of cash collection rather than the point of sale. Installment sales accounting can only be used where "collection of the sale price is not reasonably assured" (APB 10, para 12).

Under the installment sales method, gross profit is deferred to future periods and recognized proportionately to collection of the receivables. Installment receivables and deferred gross profit accounts must be kept separate by year, because the gross profit rate usually varies from year to year.

EXAMPLE:

| | | | Collections of | |
Year	Sales	Cost of sales	Year 1	Year 3
1	300,000	225,000 *	80,000	--
2	--	--	120,000	--
3	200,000	160,000 **	100,000	100,000

*25% gross profit rate
**20% gross profit rate

To record sale	Year 1		Year 2		Year 3	
Install AR-1	300,000		--		--	
Install AR-3	--		--		200,000	
Install sales		300,000		--		200,000
To record cash receipt						
Cash	80,000		120,000		200,000	
Install AR-1		80,000		120,000		100,000
Install AR-3		--		--		100,000
To record CGS						
Install cost of sales	225,000		--		160,000	
Inventory (or Purchases)		225,000		--		160,000
To defer gross profit						
Install sales	300,000		--		200,000	
Install cost of sales		225,000		--		160,000
Deferred install GP-1		75,000		--		--
Deferred install GP-3		--		--		40,000
To recognize gross profit						
Deferred install GP-1	20,000 [a]		30,000 [b]		25,000 [c]	
Deferred install GP-3	--		--		20,000 [d]	
GP realized on install method		20,000		30,000		45,000

[a](25% x 80,000)   [c](25% x 100,000)

[b](25% x 120,000)   [d](20% x 100,000)

**Summary of Accounts Used in
Installment Sales Accounting**

BALANCE SHEET

Cash		Installment AR--Year 1		Installment AR--Year 2	
(B)		Ending balance from year 1 sales	(B)	(A)	(B)

Inventory (or Purchases)		Deferred Gross Profit--Year 1		Deferred Gross Profit--Year 2	
	(C)	(E)	Ending balance from year 1 installment sales	(E)	(D)

INCOME STATEMENT

Cost of Installment Sales			Installment Sales	
(C)	(D)		(D)	(A)

Realized Gross Profit on Installment Sales			Income Summary	
(F)	(E)			(F)

Explanation of Journal Entries made in Year 2

(A) To record installment sales
(B) To record cash collected from year 1 and year 2 installment receivables
(C) To record cost of goods sold (perpetual or periodic)
(D) To close installment sales and cost of installment sales accounts
(E) To remove gross profit realized through collections from the deferred gross profit account

  (Gross profit rate for year 1 x Cash collections from year 1 receivables)
  (Gross profit rate for year 2 x Cash collections from year 2 receivables)

(F) To close realized gross profit at year end

6. **Cost Recovery Method**

   The cost recovery method is similar to the installment sales method in that gross profit on the sale is deferred. The difference is that no profit is recognized until the cumulative receipts exceed the cost of the asset sold. For example, in the installment sales example, the entire profit from year 1 sales ($75,000) would be recognized in year 3. Profit on year 3 sales will be recognized in year 4 to the extent that in year 4 cash collections on year 3 sales exceed the $60,000 ($160,000 cost – $100,000 cash collected) unrecovered cost on year 3 sales. If interest revenue was to be earned by the seller, it would likewise be deferred until the entire cost was recovered. The cost recovery method is used when the uncertainty of collection is so great that even use of the installment method is precluded.

7. **Franchise Agreements**

   SFAS 45 (see outline) provides that the initial franchise fee be recognized as revenue by the franchisor **only** upon substantial performance of their initial service obligation. The amount and timing of revenue recognized depends upon whether the contract contains bargain purchase agreements, tangible property, and whether the continuing franchise fees are reasonable in relation to future service obligations. Direct franchise costs are deferred until the related revenue is recognized.

8. **Real Estate Transactions**

   Accounting treatment for real estate sales is provided by SFAS 66. Due to the variety of methods of financing real estate transactions, determining when the risks and rewards of ownership have been clearly transferred and when revenue should be recognized becomes very complex.

   Profit from real estate sales may be recognized in full, provided the profit is determinable and the earnings process is virtually complete. Additionally, the following four criteria must be met to recognize profit in full at the point of sale:

   1. A sale is consummated.
   2. The buyer's initial and continuing investments are adequate to demonstrate a commitment to pay for the property.
   3. The seller's receivable is not subject to future subordination.

4. The seller has transferred to the buyer the usual risks and rewards of ownership in a transaction that is, in substance, a sale and does not have a substantial continuing involvement in the property.

Depending on which combination of criteria is met, the real estate sales will be recorded using one of the following methods:

1. Deposit
2. Cost recovery
3. Installment
4. Reduced profit
5. Percentage-of-completion
6. Full accrual

The deposit and reduced profit methods require explanation. In accordance with the deposit method, payments received are recorded as a liability until the contract is canceled or a sale is achieved. Under the reduced profit method, the seller recognizes a portion of profit at the time of sale with the remaining portion recognized in future periods. Profit recognized at the time of sale is determined by calculating the present value of the buyer's receivable applying a formula. The reduced profit recognized at the time of sale is the gross profit less the present value of the receivable as determined above. The remaining profit is recognized in future periods. See the outline of SFAS 66.

9. **Software Revenue Recognition**

Statement of Position 97-2 provides guidance on recognizing revenue for software transactions. Software products that require significant production, modification, or customization should be accounted for using ARB 45, *Long-Term Construction-Type Contracts*. Software products that don't require significant production, modification, or customization should recognize revenue when all of the following criteria are met:

a. Persuasive evidence of an arrangement exists.
b. Delivery has occurred.
c. Vendor's fee is fixed or determinable.
d. Collectibility is probable.

10. **Sales Basis Criteria for Selected Transactions**

Under GAAP, specific rules have been developed which are stated in the form of conditions which must be met before it is acceptable to recognize profit from "a sale in the ordinary course of business." Unfortunately, these rules represent a patchwork set of criteria for applying the sales basis of revenue recognition. This patchwork set of criteria contains many inconsistencies either in the results obtained or in the rationale justifying the criteria. The table below summarizes the criteria which have been devised for applying the sales basis to selected transactions involving the sale of assets.

Recognition issue/ source of GAAP	Factors to be considered before recognizing revenue on the sale basis	Conditions that cause recognition to be delayed beyond time of sale
• **Sale with a right of return** SFAS 48	• Whether economic substance of the transaction is a sale or a financing arrangement • Determination of sales price • Probability of collection of sales price • Seller's future obligations • Predictability of returns	• Sales price not fixed or determinable • Payment excused until product is sold • Payment excused if property stolen or damaged • Buyer without separate economic substance • Seller's obligation to bring about resale of the property • Inability to predict future returns
• **Product financing arrangement** SFAS 49	• Whether risks and rewards of ownership are transferred	• Agreement requires repurchase at specified prices or provides compensation for losses
• **Real estate sale** SFAS 66	• Probability of collection • Seller's continued involvement • Whether economic substance of the transaction is a sale of real estate or another type of transaction such as a service contract	• Inadequate buyer investment in the property • Seller's continuing obligations, such as participation in future losses, responsibility to obtain financing, construct buildings, or initiate or support operations
• **Sales-type lease** SFAS 13	• Transfer of benefits and risks of ownership • Probability of collection • Predictability of future unreimbursable costs	• Inability to meet conditions specified above for real estate sales • Inability to meet specified conditions (four criteria) indicating transfer of benefits and risks of ownership • Collectibility not predictable • Uncertainty about future unreimbursable costs
• **Sale of receivables with recourse** SFAS 125	• Isolation of transferred assets • Right to pledge or exchange transferred assets • Control of receivables	• Transferred assets can be reached by transferor or its creditors • Transferee's inability to pledge or exchange transferred assets • Control of receivables not surrendered due to repurchase or redemption agreement
• **Nonmonetary exchange** APB 29	• Completion of earning process	• Exchanges of similar inventory or productive assets
• **Sale-leaseback transaction** SFAS 13	• Substance of the transaction • Portion of property leased back • Length of leaseback period	• All sale-leaseback transactions are financing transactions and not sales transactions unless leaseback covers only a small part of the property or is for a short period of time

Source: Adapted from Henry R. Jaenicke, *Survey of Present Practices in Recognizing Revenues, Expenses, Gains, and Losses,* FASB, 1981.

MULTIPLE-CHOICE QUESTIONS (1-64)

1. What are the Statements of Financial Accounting Concepts intended to establish?
   a. Generally accepted accounting principles in financial reporting by business enterprises.
   b. The meaning of "Present fairly in accordance with generally accepted accounting principles."
   c. The objectives and concepts for use in developing standards of financial accounting and reporting.
   d. The hierarchy of sources of generally accepted accounting principles.

2. According to the FASB conceptual framework, the objectives of financial reporting for business enterprises are based on
   a. Generally accepted accounting principles.
   b. Reporting on management's stewardship.
   c. The need for conservatism.
   d. The needs of the users of the information.

3. According to the FASB conceptual framework, the usefulness of providing information in financial statements is subject to the constraint of
   a. Consistency.
   b. Cost-benefit.
   c. Reliability.
   d. Representational faithfulness.

4. During a period when an enterprise is under the direction of a particular management, its financial statements will directly provide information about
   a. Both enterprise performance and management performance.
   b. Management performance but **not** directly provide information about enterprise performance.
   c. Enterprise performance but **not** directly provide information about management performance.
   d. Neither enterprise performance nor management performance.

5. According to Statements of Financial Accounting Concepts, neutrality is an ingredient of

	Reliability	*Relevance*
a.	Yes	Yes
b.	Yes	No
c.	No	Yes
d.	No	No

6. According to the FASB conceptual framework, which of the following relates to both relevance and reliability?
   a. Comparability.
   b. Feedback value.
   c. Verifiability.
   d. Timeliness.

7. According to the FASB conceptual framework, the process of reporting an item in the financial statements of an entity is
   a. Allocation.
   b. Matching.

   c. Realization.
   d. Recognition.

8. Under FASB Statement of Financial Accounting Concepts 5, which of the following items would cause earnings to differ from comprehensive income for an enterprise in an industry **not** having specialized accounting principles?
   a. Unrealized loss on investments classified as available-for-sale securities.
   b. Unrealized loss on investments classified as trading securities.
   c. Loss on exchange of similar assets.
   d. Loss on exchange of dissimilar assets.

9. Under FASB Statement of Financial Accounting Concepts 5, comprehensive income excludes changes in equity resulting from which of the following?
   a. Loss from discontinued operations.
   b. Prior period error correction.
   c. Dividends paid to stockholders.
   d. Unrealized loss on securities classified as available-for-sale.

10. According to the FASB conceptual framework, which of the following situations violates the concept of reliability?
   a. Data on segments having the same expected risks and growth rates are reported to analysts estimating future profits.
   b. Financial statements are issued 9 months late.
   c. Management reports to stockholders regularly refer to new projects undertaken, but the financial statements never report project results.
   d. Financial statements include property with a carrying amount increased to management's estimate of market value.

11. According to the FASB conceptual framework, which of the following statements conforms to the realization concept?
   a. Equipment depreciation was assigned to a production department and then to product unit costs.
   b. Depreciated equipment was sold in exchange for a note receivable.
   c. Cash was collected on accounts receivable.
   d. Product unit costs were assigned to cost of goods sold when the units were sold.

12. What is the underlying concept that supports the immediate recognition of a contingent loss?
   a. Substance over form.
   b. Consistency.
   c. Matching.
   d. Conservatism.

13. What is the underlying concept governing the generally accepted accounting principles pertaining to recording gain contingencies?
   a. Conservatism.
   b. Relevance.
   c. Consistency.
   d. Reliability.

14. FASB's conceptual framework explains both financial and physical capital maintenance concepts. Which capital maintenance concept is applied to currently reported net income, and which is applied to comprehensive income?

	Currently reported net income	Comprehensive income
a.	Financial capital	Physical capital
b.	Physical capital	Physical capital
c.	Financial capital	Financial capital
d.	Physical capital	Financial capital

15. According to the FASB conceptual framework, an entity's revenue may result from
    a.   A decrease in an asset from primary operations.
    b.   An increase in an asset from incidental transactions.
    c.   An increase in a liability from incidental transactions.
    d.   A decrease in a liability from primary operations.

16. According to the FASB conceptual framework, which of the following is an essential characteristic of an asset?
    a.   The claims to an asset's benefits are legally enforceable.
    b.   An asset is tangible.
    c.   An asset is obtained at a cost.
    d.   An asset provides future benefits.

17. According to the FASB conceptual framework, which of the following attributes would **not** be used to measure inventory?
    a.   Historical cost.
    b.   Replacement cost.
    c.   Net realizable value.
    d.   Present value of future cash flows.

18. On December 31, 1999, Brooks Co. decided to end operations and dispose of its assets within 3 months. At December 31, 1999, the net realizable value of the equipment was below historical cost. What is the appropriate measurement basis for equipment included in Brooks' December 31, 1999 balance sheet?
    a.   Historical cost.
    b.   Current reproduction cost.
    c.   Net realizable value.
    d.   Current replacement cost.

19. In the hierarchy of generally accepted accounting principles, APB Opinions have the same authority as AICPA
    a.   Statements of Position.
    b.   Industry Audit and Accounting Guides.
    c.   Issues Papers.
    d.   Accounting Research Bulletins.

 2

20. On October 1, 1999, Acme Fuel Co. sold 100,000 gallons of heating oil to Karn Co. at $3 per gallon. Fifty thousand gallons were delivered on December 15, 1999, and the remaining 50,000 gallons were delivered on January 15, 2000. Payment terms were: 50% due on October 1, 1999, 25% due on first delivery, and the remaining 25% due on second delivery. What amount of revenue should Acme recognize from this sale during 1999?
    a. $ 75,000
    b. $150,000
    c. $225,000
    d. $300,000

21. Amar Farms produced 300,000 pounds of cotton during the 1999 season. Amar sells all of its cotton to Brye Co., which has agreed to purchase Amar's entire production at the prevailing market price. Recent legislation assures that the market price will not fall below $.70 per pound during the next 2 years. Amar's costs of selling and distributing the cotton are immaterial and can be reasonably estimated. Amar reports its inventory at expected exit value. During 1999, Amar sold and delivered to Brye 200,000 pounds at the market price of $.70. Amar sold the remaining 100,000 pounds during 2000 at the market price of $.72. What amount of revenue should Amar recognize in 1999?
    a. $140,000
    b. $144,000
    c. $210,000
    d. $216,000

22. Lin Co., a distributor of machinery, bought a machine from the manufacturer in November 1999 for $10,000. On December 30, 1999, Lin sold this machine to Zee Hardware for $15,000, under the following terms: 2% discount if paid within 30 days, 1% discount if paid after 30 days but within 60 days, or payable in full within 90 days if not paid within the discount periods. However, Zee had the right to return this machine to Lin if Zee was unable to resell the machine before expiration of the 90-day payment period, in which case Zee's obligation to Lin would be canceled. In Lin's net sales for the year ended December 31, 1999, how much should be included for the sale of this machine to Zee?
    a. $0
    b. $14,700
    c. $14,850
    d. $15,000

23. Under a royalty agreement with another company, Wand Co. will pay royalties for the assignment of a patent for 3 years. The royalties paid should be reported as expense
    a.   In the period paid.
    b.   In the period incurred.
    c.   At the date the royalty agreement began.
    d.   At the date the royalty agreement expired.

24. Clark Co.'s advertising expense account had a balance of $146,000 at December 31, 1999, before any necessary year-end adjustment relating to the following:

- Included in the $146,000 is the $15,000 cost of printing catalogs for a sales promotional campaign in January 2000. −15

- Radio advertisements broadcast during December 1999 were billed to Clark on January 2, 2000. Clark paid the $9,000 invoice on January 11, 2000. +9

What amount should Clark report as advertising expense in its income statement for the year ended December 31, 1999?

- a. $122,000
- b. $131,000
- c. $140,000
- d. $155,000

25. An analysis of Thrift Corp.'s unadjusted prepaid expense account at December 31, 1999, revealed the following:

- An opening balance of $1,500 for Thrift's comprehensive insurance policy. Thrift had paid an annual premium of $3,000 on July 1, 1998.
- A $3,200 annual insurance premium payment made July 1, 1999.
- A $2,000 advance rental payment for a warehouse Thrift leased for 1 year beginning January 1, 2000.

In its December 31, 1999 balance sheet, what amount should Thrift report as prepaid expenses?

- a. $5,200
- b. $3,600
- c. $2,000
- d. $1,600

26. Roro, Inc. paid $7,200 to renew its only insurance policy for 3 years on March 1, 1999, the effective date of the policy. At March 31, 1999, Roro's unadjusted trial balance showed a balance of $300 for prepaid insurance and $7,200 for insurance expense. What amounts should be reported for prepaid insurance and insurance expense in Roro's financial statements for the 3 months ended March 31, 1999?

	Prepaid insurance	Insurance expense
a.	$7,000	$300
b.	$7,000	$500
c.	$7,200	$300
d.	$7,300	$200

27. Aneen's Video Mart sells 1- and 2-year mail order subscriptions for its video-of-the-month business. Subscriptions are collected in advance and credited to sales. An analysis of the recorded sales activity revealed the following:

	1998	1999
Sales	$420,000	$500,000
Less cancellations	20,000	30,000
Net sales	$400,000	$470,000

Subscriptions expirations:		
1998	$120,000	
1999	155,000	$130,000
2000	125,000	200,000
2001		140,000
	$400,000	$470,000

In Aneen's December 31, 1999 balance sheet, the balance for unearned subscription revenue should be

- a. $495,000
- b. $470,000

- c. $465,000
- d. $340,000

28. Regal Department Store sells gift certificates, redeemable for store merchandise, that expire 1 year after their issuance. Regal has the following information pertaining to its gift certificates sales and redemptions:

Unredeemed at 12/31/98	$ 75,000
1999 sales	250,000
1999 redemptions of prior year sales	25,000
1999 redemptions of current year sales	175,000

Regal's experience indicates that 10% of gift certificates sold will not be redeemed. In its December 31, 1999 balance sheet, what amount should Regal report as unearned revenue?

- a. $125,000
- b. $112,500
- c. $100,000
- d. $ 50,000

29. Wren Corp.'s trademark was licensed to Mont Co. for royalties of 15% of sales of the trademarked items. Royalties are payable semi-annually on March 15 for sales in July through December of the prior year, and on September 15 for sales in January through June of the same year. Wren received the following royalties from Mont:

	March 15	September 15
1998	$10,000	$15,000
1999	12,000	17,000

Mont estimated that sales of the trademarked items would total $60,000 for July through December 1999. In Wren's 1999 income statement, the royalty revenue should be

- a. $26,000
- b. $29,000
- c. $38,000
- d. $41,000

30. In 1998, Super Comics Corp. sold a comic strip to Fantasy, Inc. and will receive royalties of 20% of future revenues associated with the comic strip. At December 31, 1999, Super reported royalties receivable of $75,000 from Fantasy. During 2000, Super received royalty payments of $200,000. Fantasy reported revenues of $1,500,000 in 2000 from the comic strip. In its 2000 income statement, what amount should Super report as royalty revenue?

- a. $125,000
- b. $175,000
- c. $200,000
- d. $300,000

31. Rill Co. owns a 20% royalty interest in an oil well. Rill receives royalty payments on January 31 for the oil sold between the previous June 1 and November 30, and on July 31 for oil sold between December 1 and May 31. Production reports show the following oil sales:

June 1, 1998---November 30, 1998	$300,000
December 1, 1998--December 31, 1998	50,000
December 1, 1998--May 31, 1999	$400,000
June 1, 1999--November 30, 1999	325,000
December 1, 1999--December 31, 1999	70,000

What amount should Rill report as royalty revenue for 1999?

- a. $140,000
- b. $144,000
- c. $149,000
- d. $159,000

32. Decker Company assigns some of its patents to other enterprises under a variety of licensing agreements. In some instances advance royalties are received when the agreements are signed, and in others, royalties are remitted within 60 days after each license year end. The following data are included in Decker's December 31 balance sheet:

	1998	1999
Royalties receivable	$90,000	$85,000
Unearned royalties	60,000	40,000

During 1999 Decker received royalty remittances of $200,000. In its income statement for the year ended December 31, 1999, Decker should report royalty income of

- a. $195,000
- b. $215,000
- c. $220,000
- d. $225,000

33. Cooke Company acquires patent rights from other enterprises and pays advance royalties in some cases, and in others, royalties are paid within 90 days after year end. The following data are included in Cooke's December 31 balance sheets:

	1998	1999
Prepaid royalties	$55,000	$45,000
Royalties payable	80,000	75,000

During 1999 Cooke remitted royalties of $300,000. In its income statement for the year ended December 31, 1999, Cooke should report royalty expense of

- a. $295,000
- b. $305,000
- c. $310,000
- d. $330,000

34. The premium on a 3-year insurance policy expiring on December 31, 2001, was paid in total on January 1, 1999. The original payment was initially debited to a prepaid asset account. The appropriate journal entry has been recorded on December 31, 1999. The balance in the prepaid asset account on December 31, 1999, should be

- a. Zero.
- b. The same as it would have been if the original payment had been debited initially to an expense account.
- c. The same as the original payment.
- d. Higher than if the original payment had been debited initially to an expense account.

35. On January 1, 1999, Sip Co. signed a 5-year contract enabling it to use a patented manufacturing process beginning in 1999. A royalty is payable for each product produced, subject to a minimum annual fee. Any royalties in excess of the minimum will be paid annually. On the contract date, Sip prepaid a sum equal to 2 years' minimum annual fees. In 1999, only minimum fees were incurred. The royalty prepayment should be reported in Sip's December 31, 1999 financial statements as

- a. An expense only.
- b. A current asset and an expense.
- c. A current asset and noncurrent asset.
- d. A noncurrent asset.

36. A retail store received cash and issued gift certificates that are redeemable in merchandise. The gift certificates lapse 1 year after they are issued. How would the deferred revenue account be affected by each of the following transactions?

	Redemption of certificates	Lapse of certificates
a.	No effect	Decrease
b.	Decrease	Decrease
c.	Decrease	No effect
d.	No effect	No effect

37. Jersey, Inc. is a retailer of home appliances and offers a service contract on each appliance sold. Jersey sells appliances on installment contracts, but all service contracts must be paid in full at the time of sale. Collections received for service contracts should be recorded as an increase in a

- a. Deferred revenue account.
- b. Sales contracts receivable valuation account.
- c. Stockholders' valuation account.
- d. Service revenue account.

38. Ward, a consultant, keeps her accounting records on a cash basis. During 1999, Ward collected $200,000 in fees from clients. At December 31, 1998, Ward had accounts receivable of $40,000. At December 31, 1999, Ward had accounts receivable of $60,000, and unearned fees of $5,000. On an accrual basis, what was Ward's service revenue for 1999?

- a. $175,000
- b. $180,000
- c. $215,000
- d. $225,000

39. Zeta Co. reported sales revenue of $4,600,000 in its income statement for the year ended December 31, 1999. Additional information is as follows:

	12/31/98	12/31/99
Accounts receivable	$1,000,000	$1,300,000
Allowance for uncollectible accounts	(60,000)	(110,000)

Zeta wrote off uncollectible accounts totaling $20,000 during 1999. Under the cash basis of accounting, Zeta would have reported 1999 sales of

- a. $4,900,000
- b. $4,350,000

c. $4,300,000
d. $4,280,000

40. Marr Corp. reported rental revenue of $2,210,000 in its cash basis federal income tax return for the year ended November 30, 1999. Additional information is as follows:

Rents receivable	
--November 30, 1999	$1,060,000
Rents receivable	
--November 30, 1998	800,000
Uncollectible rents written off	
during the fiscal year	30,000

Under the accrual basis, Marr should report rental revenue of

   a. $1,920,000
   b. $1,980,000
   c. $2,440,000
   d. $2,500,000

41. The following information pertains to Eagle Co.'s 1999 sales:

Cash sales	
Gross	$ 80,000
Returns and allowances	4,000
Credit sales	
Gross	120,000
Discounts	6,000

On January 1, 1999, customers owed Eagle $40,000. On December 31, 1999, customers owed Eagle $30,000. Eagle uses the direct writeoff method for bad debts. No bad debts were recorded in 1999. Under the cash basis of accounting, what amount of net revenue should Eagle report for 1999?

   a. $ 76,000
   b. $170,000
   c. $190,000
   d. $200,000

42. The following balances were reported by Mall Co. at December 31, 1999 and 1998:

	12/31/99	*12/31/98*
Inventory	$260,000	$290,000
Accounts payable	75,000	50,000

Mall paid suppliers $490,000 during the year ended December 31, 1999. What amount should Mall report for cost of goods sold in 1999?

   a. $545,000
   b. $495,000
   c. $485,000
   d. $435,000

43. Class Corp. maintains its accounting records on the cash basis but restates its financial statements to the accrual method of accounting. Class had $60,000 in cash-basis pretax income for 1999. The following information pertains to Class's operations for the years ended December 31, 1999 and 1998:

	1999	*1998*
Accounts receivable	$40,000	$20,000
Accounts payable	15,000	30,000

Under the accrual method, what amount of income before taxes should Class report in its December 31, 1999 income statement?

   a. $25,000
   b. $55,000
   c. $65,000
   d. $95,000

44. On February 1, 1999, Tory began a service proprietorship with an initial cash investment of $2,000. The proprietorship provided $5,000 of services in February and received full payment in March. The proprietorship incurred expenses of $3,000 in February, which were paid in April. During March, Tory drew $1,000 against the capital account. In the proprietorship's financial statements for the 2 months ended March 31, 1999, prepared under the cash basis method of accounting, what amount should be reported as capital?

   a. $1,000
   b. $3,000
   c. $6,000
   d. $7,000

45. Compared to the accrual basis of accounting, the cash basis of accounting understates income by the net decrease during the accounting period of

	Accounts receivable	*Accrued expenses*
a.	Yes	Yes
b.	Yes	No
c.	No	No
d.	No	Yes

46. White Co. wants to convert its 1999 financial statements from the accrual basis of accounting to the cash basis. Both supplies inventory and office salaries payable increased between January 1, 1999, and December 31, 1999. To obtain 1999 cash basis net income, how should these increases be added to or deducted from accrual basis net income?

	Supplies inventory	*Office salaries payable*
a.	Deducted	Deducted
b.	Deducted	Added
c.	Added	Deducted
d.	Added	Added

47. Before 1999, Droit Co. used the cash basis of accounting. As of December 31, 1999, Droit changed to the accrual basis. Droit cannot determine the beginning balance of supplies inventory. What is the effect of Droit's inability to determine beginning supplies inventory on its 1999 accrual basis net income and December 31, 1999 accrual-basis owners' equity?

	1999 net income	*12/31/99 owners' equity*
a.	No effect	No effect
b.	No effect	Overstated
c.	Overstated	No effect
d.	Overstated	Overstated

48. Gant Co., which began operations on January 1, 1999, appropriately uses the installment method of accounting. The following information pertains to Gant's operations for the year 1999:

Installment sales	$500,000
Regular sales	300,000
Cost of installment sales	250,000
Cost of regular sales	150,000
General and administrative expenses	50,000
Collections on installment sales	100,000

In its December 31, 1999 balance sheet, what amount should Gant report as deferred gross profit?

a. $250,000
b. $200,000
c. $160,000
d. $ 75,000

49. Since there is no reasonable basis for estimating the degree of collectibility, Astor Co. uses the installment method of revenue recognition for the following sales:

	1999	1998
Sales	$900,000	$600,000
Collections from:		
1998 sales	100,000	200,000
1999 sales	300,000	----
Accounts written off:		
1998 sales	150,000	50,000
1999 sales	50,000	----
Gross profit percentage	40%	30%

What amount should Astor report as deferred gross profit in its December 31, 1999 balance sheet for the 1998 and 1999 sales?

a. $150,000
b. $160,000
c. $225,000
d. $250,000

50. Luge Co., which began operations on January 2, 1999, appropriately uses the installment sales method of accounting. The following information is available for 1999:

Installment accounts receivable, December 31, 1999	$800,000
Deferred gross profit, December 31, 1999 (before recognition of realized gross profit for 1999)	560,000
Gross profit on sales	40%

For the year ended December 31, 1999, cash collections and realized gross profit on sales should be

	Cash collections	Realized gross profit
a.	$400,000	$320,000
b.	$400,000	$240,000
c.	$600,000	$320,000
d.	$600,000	$240,000

51. Dolce Co., which began operations on January 1, 1998, appropriately uses the installment method of accounting to record revenues. The following information is available for the years ended December 31, 1998 and 1999:

	1998	1999
Sales	$1,000,000	$2,000,000
Gross profit realized on sales made in:		
1998	150,000	90,000
1999	--	200,000
Gross profit percentages	30%	40%

What amount of installment accounts receivable should Dolce report in its December 31, 1999 balance sheet?

a. $1,225,000
b. $1,300,000
c. $1,700,000
d. $1,775,000

52. On December 31, 1998, Mill Co. sold construction equipment to Drew, Inc. for $1,800,000. The equipment had a carrying amount of $1,200,000. Drew paid $300,000 cash on December 31, 1998, and signed a $1,500,000 note bearing interest at 10%, payable in five annual installments of $300,000. Mill appropriately accounts for the sale under the installment method. On December 31, 1999, Drew paid $300,000 principal and $150,000 interest. For the year ended December 31, 1999, what total amount of revenue should Mill recognize from the construction equipment sale and financing?

a. $250,000
b. $150,000
c. $120,000
d. $100,000

53. On January 2, 1998, Blake Co. sold a used machine to Cooper, Inc. for $900,000, resulting in a gain of $270,000. On that date, Cooper paid $150,000 cash and signed a $750,000 note bearing interest at 10%. The note was payable in three annual installments of $250,000 beginning January 2, 1999. Blake appropriately accounted for the sale under the installment method. Cooper made a timely payment of the first installment on January 2, 1999, of $325,000, which included accrued interest of $75,000. What amount of deferred gross profit should Blake report at December 31, 1999?

a. $150,000
b. $172,500
c. $180,000
d. $225,000

54. For financial statement purposes, the installment method of accounting may be used if the

a.   Collection period extends over more than 12 months.
b.   Installments are due in different years.
c.   Ultimate amount collectible is indeterminate.
d.   Percentage-of-completion method is inappropriate.

55. According to the installment method of accounting, gross profit on an installment sale is recognized in income

a.   On the date of sale.
b.   On the date the final cash collection is received.
c.   In proportion to the cash collection.

d. After cash collections equal to the cost of sales have been received.

56. Income recognized using the installment method of accounting generally equals cash collected multiplied by the
  a. Net operating profit percentage.
  b. Net operating profit percentage adjusted for expected uncollectible accounts.
  c. Gross profit percentage.
  d. Gross profit percentage adjusted for expected uncollectible accounts.

57. It is proper to recognize revenue prior to the sale of merchandise when

I. The revenue will be reported as an installment sale.
II. The revenue will be reported under the cost recovery method.

  a. I only.
  b. II only.
  c. Both I and II.
  d. Neither I nor II.

58. The following information pertains to a sale of real estate by Ryan Co. to Sud Co. on December 31, 1998:

Carrying amount		$2,000,000
Sales price:		
Cash	$ 300,000	
Purchase money		
mortgage	2,700,000	3,000,000

The mortgage is payable in nine annual installments of $300,000 beginning December 31, 1999, plus interest of 10%. The December 31, 1999, installment was paid as scheduled, together with interest of $270,000. Ryan uses the cost recovery method to account for the sale. What amount of income should Ryan recognize in 1999 from the real estate sale and its financing?
  a. $570,000
  b. $370,000
  c. $270,000
  d. $0

59. Wren Co. sells equipment on installment contracts. Which of the following statements best justifies Wren's use of the cost recovery method of revenue recognition to account for these installment sales?
  a. The sales contract provides that title to the equipment only passes to the purchaser when all payments have been made.
  b. No cash payments are due until 1 year from the date of sale.
  c. Sales are subject to a high rate of return.
  d. There is **no** reasonable basis for estimating collectibility.

60. According to the cost recovery method of accounting, gross profit on an installment sale is recognized in income
  a. After cash collections equal to the cost of sales have been received.
  b. In proportion to the cash collections.
  c. On the date the final cash collection is received.
  d. On the date of sale.

61. On December 31, 1999, Rice, Inc. authorized Graf to operate as a franchisee for an initial franchise fee of $150,000. Of this amount, $60,000 was received upon signing the agreement and the balance, represented by a note, is due in three annual payments of $30,000 each beginning December 31, 2000. The present value on December 31, 1999, of the three annual payments appropriately discounted is $72,000. According to the agreement, the nonrefundable down payment represents a fair measure of the services already performed by Rice; however, substantial future services are required of Rice. Collectibility of the note is reasonably certain. In Rice's December 31, 1999 balance sheet, unearned franchise fees from Graf's franchise should be reported as
  a. $132,000
  b. $100,000
  c. $ 90,000
  d. $ 72,000

62. Each of Potter Pie Co.'s 21 new franchisees contracted to pay an initial franchise fee of $30,000. By December 31, 1999, each franchisee had paid a nonrefundable $10,000 fee and signed a note to pay $10,000 principal plus the market rate of interest on December 31, 2000, and December 31, 2001. Experience indicates that one franchisee will default on the additional payments. Services for the initial fee will be performed in 2000. What amount of net unearned franchise fees would Potter report at December 31, 1999?
  a. $400,000
  b. $600,000
  c. $610,000
  d. $630,000

63. In which of the following examples of real estate transactions would the seller not transfer the usual risks and rewards of ownership?

I. The buyer can compel the seller to repurchase the property.
II. The seller guarantees the return of the buyer's investment.
III. The seller is required to support operations of the buyer and will be reimbursed on a cost plus 5% basis.

  a. I.
  b. II.
  c. III.
  d. I and II.

64. Esker Inc. specializes in real estate transactions other than retail land sales. On January 1, 1999, Esker consummated a sale of property to Kame Ltd. The amount of profit on the sale is determinable and Esker is not obligated to perform any additional activities to earn the profit. Kame's initial and continuing investments were adequate to demonstrate a commitment to pay for the property under SFAS 66. However, Esker's receivable may be subject to future subordination. Esker should account for the sale using the
  a. Deposit method.
  b. Reduced recovery method.
  c. Cost recovery method.
  d. Full accrual method.

OTHER OBJECTIVE QUESTIONS

Problem 1 (15 to 25 minutes)

This question consists of 10 items which represent descriptions or definitions of the various elements of the FASB's *Statements of Financial Accounting Concepts*.

Required:

Select the **best** answer for each item from the terms listed in A - L. A term may be used once, more than once, or not at all.

Concept statement definitions	*Terms*
1. Component of relevance.	A. Recognition
2. Increases in net assets from incidental or peripheral transactions affecting an entity.	B. Comprehensive Income
3. The process of converting noncash resources and rights into cash or claims to cash.	C. Representational Faithfulness
4. Ingredient of relevance **and** reliability.	D. Revenues
5. The process of formally recording an item in the financial statements of an entity after it has met existing criteria and been subject to cost-benefit constraints and materiality thresholds.	E. Predictive Value
6. All changes in net assets of an entity during a period except those resulting from investments by owners and distributions to owners.	F. Consistency
7. Inflows or other enhancements of assets of an entity or settlements of its liabilities from delivering or producing goods, rendering services, or other activities that constitute the entity's ongoing operations.	G. Gains
8. The amount of cash, or its equivalent, that could be obtained by selling an asset in orderly liquidation.	H. Net Income
9. The quality of information that helps users to increase the likelihood of correctly forecasting the outcome of past or present events.	I. Earnings
10. A performance measure concerned primarily with cash-to-cash cycles.	J. Realization
	K. Replacement Cost
	L. Current Market Value

PROBLEM

Problem 1   (30 to 40 minutes)

The following information pertains to Baron Flowers, a calendar-year sole proprietorship, which maintained its books on the cash basis during the year.

Baron Flowers
TRIAL BALANCE
December 31, 1999

	Dr.	Cr.
Cash	$ 25,600	
Accounts receivable, 12/31/98	16,200	
Inventory, 12/31/98	62,000	
Furniture & fixtures	118,200	
Land improvements	45,000	
Accumulated depreciation, 12/31/98		$ 32,400
Accounts payable, 12/31/98		17,000
Baron, Drawings		
Baron, Capital, 12/31/98		124,600
Sales		653,000
Purchases	305,100	
Salaries	174,000	
Payroll taxes	12,400	
Insurance	8,700	
Rent	34,200	
Utilities	12,600	
Living expenses	13,000	
	$827,000	$827,000

Baron has developed plans to expand into the wholesale flower market and is in the process of negotiating a bank loan to finance the expansion. The bank is requesting 1999 financial statements prepared on the accrual basis of accounting from Baron. During the course of a review engagement, Muir, Baron's accountant, obtained the following additional information.

1.   Amounts due from customers totaled $32,000 at December 31, 1999.

2.   An analysis of the above receivables revealed that an allowance for uncollectible accounts of $3,800 should be provided.

3.   Unpaid invoices for flower purchases totaled $30,500 and $17,000, at December 31, 1999, and December 31, 1998, respectively.

4.   The inventory totaled $72,800 based on a physical count of the goods at December 31, 1999. The inventory was priced at cost, which approximates market value.

5.   On May 1, 1999, Baron paid $8,700 to renew its comprehensive insurance coverage for 1 year. The premium on the previous policy, which expired on April 30, 1999, was $7,800.

6.   On January 2, 1999, Baron entered into a 25-year operating lease for the vacant lot adjacent to Baron's retail store for use as a parking lot. As agreed in the lease, Baron paved and fenced in the lot at a cost of $45,000. The improvements were completed on April 1, 1999, and have an estimated useful life of 15 years. No provision for depreciation or amortization has been recorded. Depreciation on furniture and fixtures was $12,000 for 1999.

7.   Accrued expenses at December 31, 1998 and 1999, were as follows:

	1998	*1999*
Utilities	$ 900	$1,500
Payroll taxes	1,100	1,600
	$2,000	$3,100

8.   Baron is being sued for $400,000. The coverage under the comprehensive insurance policy is limited to $250,000. Baron's attorney believes that an unfavorable outcome is probable and that a reasonable estimate of the settlement is $300,000.

9.   The salaries account includes $4,000 per month paid to the proprietor. Baron also receives $250 per week for living expenses.

Required:

a.   Using the worksheet on the following page, prepare the adjustments necessary to convert the trial balance of Baron Flowers to the accrual basis of accounting for the year ended December 31, 1999. Formal journal entries are not required to support your adjustments. However, use the numbers given with the additional information to cross-reference the postings in the adjustment columns on the worksheet.

b.   Write a brief memo to Baron explaining why the bank would require financial statements prepared on the accrual basis instead of the cash basis.

Baron Flowers
WORKSHEET TO CONVERT TRIAL BALANCE TO ACCRUAL BASIS
DECEMBER 31, 1999

Account title	Cash basis		Adjustments		Accrual basis*	
	Dr.	Cr.	Dr.	Cr.	Dr.*	Cr.*
Cash	25,600					
Accounts receivable	16,200					
Inventory	62,000					
Furniture & fixtures	118,200					
Land improvements	45,000					
Accumulated depreciation & amortization		32,400				
Accounts payable		17,000				
Baron, Drawings						
Baron, Capital		124,600				
Sales		653,000				
Purchases	305,100					
Salaries	174,000					
Payroll taxes	12,400					
Insurance	8,700					
Rent	34,200					
Utilities	12,600					
Living expenses	13,000					
	827,000	827,000				

---

* *Completion of these columns is not required.*

Problem 2   (30 to 40 minutes)

Wyatt, CPA, is meeting with Brown, the controller of Emco, a wholesaler, to discuss the accounting issues regarding two unrelated items:

- Emco is considering offering its customers the right to return its products for a full refund within 1 year of purchase. Emco expects its sales to increase as a result, but is unable to estimate the amount of future returns.

- Brown is aware that Statement of Financial Accounting Standards (SFAS) 106, *Employers' Accounting for Postretirement Benefits Other Than Pensions*, is effective for years beginning after December 15, 1992. Brown is uncertain about the benefits and beneficiaries covered by this Statement. Brown believes that, regardless of SFAS 106, no estimate of postretirement obligation can be reasonable because it would be based on too many assumptions. For this reason, Brown wishes to continue to account for the postretirement benefits that Emco pays to its retirees on the pay-as-you-go (cash) basis.

Brown has asked Wyatt to write a brief memo to Brown that Brown can use to explain these issues to Emco's president.

Required:

Write a brief advisory memo from Wyatt to Brown to:

a. Explain the general principle of revenue recognition, the method of revenue recognition when right to return exists, and the impact of offering a right to return on Emco's ability to recognize revenue, if any.

b. State the principal benefit covered by SFAS 106 and give an example of other benefits covered by SFAS 106. Explain the reasoning given in SFAS 106 for requiring accruals based on estimates. Indicate the primary recipients of postretirement benefits other than pensions.[*]

---

[*] *This requirement should not be completed until you have done Module 26D, Present Value: Pensions. A cross-reference in the Module 26D problem material will direct you to return to it.*

MULTIPLE-CHOICE ANSWERS[*]

1. c __ __	15. d __ __	29. a __ __	43. d __ __	57. d __ __
2. d __ __	16. d __ __	30. d __ __	44. c __ __	58. d __ __
3. b __ __	17. d __ __	31. c __ __	45. d __ __	59. d __ __
4. c __ __	18. c __ __	32. b __ __	46. b __ __	60. a __ __
5. b __ __	19. d __ __	33. b __ __	47. c __ __	61. d __ __
6. a __ __	20. b __ __	34. b __ __	48. b __ __	62. c __ __
7. d __ __	21. c __ __	35. b __ __	49. d __ __	63. d __ __
8. a __ __	22. a __ __	36. b __ __	50. d __ __	64. c __ __
9. c __ __	23. b __ __	37. a __ __	51. c __ __	
10. d __ __	24. c __ __	38. c __ __	52. a __ __	
11. b __ __	25. b __ __	39. d __ __	53. a __ __	
12. d __ __	26. b __ __	40. d __ __	54. c __ __	
13. a __ __	27. c __ __	41. d __ __	55. c __ __	1st: __/64 = __%
14. c __ __	28. d __ __	42. a __ __	56. c __ __	2nd: __/64 = __%

MULTIPLE-CHOICE ANSWER EXPLANATIONS

A.1. Basic Accounting Theory

1.   (c)   The Statements of Financial Accounting Concepts were issued to establish a framework from which financial accounting and reporting standards could be developed. The six SFAC provide the theory behind accounting and reporting and provide guidance when no GAAP exists. Answers (a), (b), and (d) are incorrect because these items were derived from the SFAC.

2.   (d)   Per SFAC 1, the objectives of financial reporting focus on providing present and potential investors with information useful in making investment decisions. Financial statement users do not have the authority to prescribe the data they desire. Therefore, they must rely on external financial reporting to satisfy their information needs, and the objectives must be based on the needs of those users [answer (d)].

3.   (b)   The FASB conceptual framework has identified two constraints to the usefulness of providing information in financial statements, cost benefit [answer (b)] and materiality. Information is **not** disclosed if the costs of disclosure outweigh the benefits or if the information is not material enough to influence users. Consistency [answer (a)] is a secondary quality of accounting information; reliability [answer (c)] is a primary quality of accounting information; and representational faithfulness [answer (d)] is a component of reliability.

4.   (c)   Per SFAC 1, para 43, the primary focus of financial reporting is to provide information about an enterprise's performance. SFAC 1 para 53, states that financial reporting does not directly provide information about the performance of a particular management for the period since actions of past management may also affect the current period earnings. Answers (a), (b), and (d) are incorrect because financial reporting primarily focuses on the enterprise's performance and management performance would only be indirectly illustrated.

5.   (b)   SFAC 2 defines neutrality as the quality of information which requires freedom from bias toward a predetermined result. Since unbiased information would always be more reliable than biased information, this quality contributes to reliability. Other components of reliability include verifiability and representational faithfulness. Neutrality is not an ingredient of relevance because relevance refers to the usefulness of information, characterized by its predictive value, feedback value, and timeliness. Therefore, answer (b) is correct because neutrality is a component of reliability but not of relevance.

6.   (a)   Per SFAC 2, comparability is a secondary quality which relates to **both** of the primary qualities of relevance and reliability. Therefore, answer (a) is correct. Answers (b) and (d) are incorrect because both feedback value and timeliness are described by SFAC 2 as ingredients only of relevance. They are not considered ingredients of reliability. Answer (c) is incorrect because verifiability is described as an ingredient only of reliability.

7.   (d)   Per SFAC 5, para 6, recognition is the process of formally recording or incorporating an item into the financial statements as an asset, liability, revenue, expense, or the like and thus, answer (d) is correct. Answer (a) is incorrect because according to SFAC 6, para 142, allocation is the process of assigning or distributing an amount according to a plan or formula. Answer (b) is also incorrect because per SFAC 6, matching is the simultaneous recognition of revenues with expenses which are related directly or jointly to the same transactions or events. Answer (c) is incorrect because according to SFAC 6, para 143, realization is the process of converting noncash resources and rights into money.

8.   (a)   Per SFAC 5, para 42, earnings and comprehensive income have the same broad components--revenues, expenses, gains, and losses--but are not the same because certain classes of gains and losses are excluded from earnings. Changes in market values of investments in market-

---

[*] *Explanation of how to use this performance record appears on p. 16.*

able equity securities classified as available-for-sale securities are included in comprehensive income, but are excluded from earnings until realized. Therefore, answer (a) is correct. Answers (b), (c), and (d) are incorrect because they would be included in both earnings and comprehensive income. Note that unrealized gains and losses on marketable equity securities classified as trading securities are included in earnings. This treatment is in accordance with SFAS 115.

9.   (c)   Per para 70 of SFAC 6, comprehensive income includes all changes in equity during a period except those resulting from investments by owners and distributions to owners. Answer (c), dividends paid to stockholders, is a change in equity resulting from a distribution to owners, so it is excluded from comprehensive income. Answers (a), (b), and (d) are all included in comprehensive income because they **are** changes in equity, but are **not** investments by, or distributions to, owners.

Under SFAS 130, prior period error corrections would also be excluded from comprehensive income. This standard addresses only the display of unrealized gains (losses) on foreign currency items, available-for-sale marketable securities, and the minimum pension liability adjustment. Other changes suggested in SFAC 5 and 6 will be addressed in future SFAS.

10.   (d)   Reliability has three subcomponents, as defined in SFAC 2: neutrality, representational faithfulness, and verifiability. **Neutrality** means that information should **not** be prepared or reported in such a way as to obtain a predetermined result, and **should** be free from bias. **Representational faithfulness** is defined as the correspondence between a measure and what it purports to represent. **Verifiability** means that two or more individuals who are independent of each other would arrive at a similar conclusion based on an examination of the same evidence. Answer (d) violates verifiability because different individuals would come up with different estimates of market value. Answer (a) is incorrect because reporting data to analysts does not violate reliability. Answers (b) and (c) are incorrect because they are examples of violations of relevance, not reliability. Answer (b) violates the relevance subcomponent of **timeliness**, while answer (c) violates the relevance subcomponent of **feedback value.**

11.   (b)   According to SFAC 6, realization is the process of converting noncash resources and rights into money through the sale of assets for cash or claims to cash. When equipment is sold for a note receivable, money is realized since a note qualifies as a claim to cash. Therefore, answer (b) is correct. Answers (a) and (d) relate to cost allocation. Answer (c) is incorrect because AR represents a claim to cash realization occurs at the time of sale rather than when cash is collected.

12.   (d)   A loss contingency is accrued by a charge to expense if it is reasonably estimable and it is **probable that a liability has been incurred** as of the balance sheet date. The **cause of the liability must have occurred on or before the date of the financial statements** if the liability is to be accrued, because the intention is to recognize the loss

in the same period that the underlying cause took place. Therefore, some authorities would say that matching is the underlying concept supporting the immediate recognition of a contingent loss. A larger number, however, would mention conservatism as the more pervasive underlying concept underlying immediate recognition of these losses. Thus, answer (d) is correct.

13.   (a)   Conservatism means that when in doubt, accountants should choose the procedure that will be least likely to overstate assets and income. This concept underlies the GAAP pertaining to recording gain contingencies. In an effort to not overstate assets or income, gain contingencies are not recorded until they are no longer contingencies, and are disclosed only when probabilities are high that a gain contingency will become reality.

14.   (c)   Per SFAC 6, paras 70-72, the major difference between financial and physical capital maintenance is related to the effects of price changes on assets held and liabilities owed during a period. The financial capital concept is applied in current GAAP. Under this concept, the effects of the price changes described above are considered "holding gains and losses," and are included in computing return on capital. Comprehensive income which is described in SFAC 5, para 39, is "the change in equity of a business enterprise during a period from transactions and other events and circumstances from nonowner sources." It is also a measure of return on **financial** capital. Therefore, answer (c) is correct. The concept of physical capital maintenance seeks to measure the effects of price changes which are not currently captured under GAAP (e.g., replacement costs of nonmonetary assets). Under this concept, holding gains and losses are considered "capital maintenance adjustments" which would be included directly in equity and excluded from return on capital. Therefore, answers (a), (b), and (d) are incorrect.

15.   (d)   Per SFAC 6, para 78, revenues are inflows of assets or settlements of liabilities, or both, during a period as a result of an entity's major or primary operations. Two essential characteristics of revenues are that revenues (1) arise from a company's primary earnings activities and (2) are recurring or continuing in nature. Therefore, answer (d) is correct because it meets the above criteria. Answers (b) and (c) are incorrect because they result from incidental transactions. Answer (a) is incorrect because a decrease of an asset is not a revenue.

16.   (d)   Per SFAC 6, para 28, the common quality shared by all assets is "service potential" or "future economic benefit." Therefore, answer (d) is correct. Per SFAC 6, para 26, assets commonly have other distinguishing features, such as being legally enforceable, tangible or acquired at a cost. These features, however, are not essential characteristics of assets. Therefore, answers (a), (b), and (c) are incorrect.

17.   (d)   Per SFAC 5, five different attributes are used to measure assets and liabilities in present practice: historical cost, current (replacement) cost, current market value, net realizable value, and present value of future cash flows. Three of these (historical cost, replacement cost, and net realizable value) are used in measuring inventory at lower of cost or market. Present value of future cash flows [answer (d)] is not used to measure inventory.

18.   (c)   APB 30, para 15, provides guidance on the determination of gain or loss on disposal of a segment of a business. According to this guidance, such determination should be based on estimates of the net realizable value of the segment. Since Brooks Co. plans to discontinue its entire operations, the appropriate measurement basis for its equipment is net realizable value, and answer (c) is correct. Historical cost and current reproduction and replacement costs are not appropriate measurement bases for assets once an entity has decided to discontinue its operations because these amounts do not reflect the entity's probable future benefit, which is a characteristic of assets per SFAC 6, para 26.

19.   (d)   Per AU 411, there are four primary levels of authority and an "Other" category in the hierarchy of generally accepted accounting principles. The most authoritative level includes FASB Statements and Interpretations, APB Opinions, and AICPA Accounting Research Bulletins. Therefore, answer (d) is correct. Answers (a), (b), and (c) are incorrect because Statements of Opinion, Industry Audit and Accounting Guides, and Issues Papers are all sources of support for accounting principles but are lesser in authority.

A.2.   Income Determination

20.   (b)   Generally, sales revenue is recognized at the date of delivery, because that generally is the time at which a sale has occurred. At that point the two criteria for revenue recognition were met; the revenue is (1) realized or realizable and (2) it is earned (SFAC 6, para 83). Therefore, the amount of sales revenue recognized in 1999 is $150,000 (50,000 x $3 = $150,000).

21.   (c)   Per ARB 43, Chapter 4, para 16, income generally accrues only at the time of sale, and gains may not be anticipated by reflecting assets at their **current** sales prices. Exception to this general rule is granted, however, for agricultural products which are homogenous and have an immediate marketability at quoted prices (such as the cotton in this problem). When these inventories are stated at sales prices, they should be reduced by expenditures to be incurred in disposal. Amar Farms should, therefore, recognize revenue on the entire 300,000 pound crop in 1999 at the guaranteed (and prevailing) market price of $.70 per pound. This amounts to $210,000 (300,000 pounds x $.70 per pound = $210,000). Note that the additional $.02 per pound for the cotton sold in 2000 would be recognized in 2000, since its selling price exceeded the current (1999) market price.

22.   (a)   Per SFAS 48, para 6, revenue from the sale of a product may be recognized at the time of sale only if **all** of the following conditions are met:

1.   The seller's price is fixed or readily determinable.

2.   The buyer has paid the seller or is obligated to pay the seller, the obligation not being contingent on resale of the product.
3.   The buyer's obligation to the seller remains unchanged in the event of damage or destruction of the product.
4.   The buyer is independent from the seller.
5.   The seller does not have any significant obligations regarding resale of the product by the buyer.
6.   The amount of future returns can be reasonably estimated.

Because the buyer, Zee, has the right to return the machine to the seller, Lin, condition (2) above has not been met. Therefore, the recognition of sales revenue and cost of sales is not allowable for this transaction and answer (a) is correct.

A.3.   Accruals and Deferrals

23.   (b)   Under accrual accounting, events that change an entity's financial position are recorded in the period in which the events occur. This means revenues are recognized when earned rather than when cash is received, and expenses are recognized when incurred rather than when cash is paid. Therefore, when the royalties are paid, Wand should debit an asset account (prepaid royalties) rather than an expense account. The royalties paid should be reported as expense in the period incurred (by debiting royalty expense and crediting prepaid royalties).

24.   (c)   The balance in the advertising expense account on 12/31/99 before adjustment is $146,000. Since the sales promotional campaign is to be conducted in January, any associated costs are an expense of 2000. Thus, the $15,000 cost of printing catalogs should be removed from the advertising expense account and recorded as a prepaid expense as of 12/31/99. In addition, advertising expense must be increased by the $9,000 cost of December's radio advertisements, which are an expense of 1999 even though they were not billed to Clark or paid until 2000. The $9,000 must be accrued as an expense and a liability at 12/31/99. Therefore, 1999 advertising expense should total $140,000 ($146,000 – $15,000 + $9,000), and answer (c) is correct.

25.   (b)   The opening balance in prepaid expenses ($1,500) results from a 1-year insurance premium paid on 7/1/98. Since this policy would have expired by 12/31/99, no part of the $1,500 is included in 12/31/99 prepaid expenses. The insurance premium paid on 7/1/99 ($3,200) would be partially expired (6/12) by 12/31/99. The remainder (6/12 x $3,200 = $1,600) would be a prepaid expense at year end. The entire advance rental payment ($2,000) is a prepaid expense at 12/31/99 because it applies to 2000. Therefore, total 12/31/99 prepaid expenses are $3,600.

Prepaid insurance ($3,200 x 6/12)	$1,600
Prepaid rent	2,000
Total prepaid expenses	$3,600

26.   (b)   Apparently Roro records policy payments as charges to insurance expense and records prepaid insurance at the end of the quarter through an adjusting entry. The unadjusted trial balance amounts at 3/31/99 must represent the final 2 months of the old policy ($300 of prepaid insurance) and the cost of the new policy ($7,200 of insurance expense). An adjusting entry must be prepared to reflect the correct 3/31/99 balances. Since the new policy has been in force 1 month (3/1 through 3/31), 35 months remain unexpired. Therefore, the balance in prepaid insurance should be $7,000 ($7,200 x 35/36). Insurance expense should include the cost of the last 2 months of the old policy and the first month of the new policy [$300 + ($7,200 x 1/36) = $500]. Roro's adjusting entry would transfer $6,700 from insurance expense to prepaid insurance to result in the correct balances.

27. (c)   At 12/31/99, the liability account unearned subscription revenue should have a balance which reflects all unexpired subscriptions. Of the 1998 sales, $125,000 expires during 2000 and would still be a liability at 12/31/99. Of the 1999 sales, $340,000 ($200,000 + $140,000) expires during 2000 and 2001, and therefore is a liability at 12/31/99. Therefore, the total liability is $465,000 ($125,000 + $340,000). This amount would have to be removed from the sales account and recorded as a liability in a 12/31/99 adjusting entry.

28. (d)   Regal's unredeemed gift certificates at 12/31/97 are $75,000. During 1999, these certificates are either redeemed ($25,000) or expire by 12/31/99 ($75,000 – $25,000 = $50,000). Therefore, none of the $75,000 affects the 12/31/99 unearned revenue amount. During 1999, additional certificates totalling $250,000 were sold. Of this amount, $225,000 is expected to be redeemed in the future [$250,000 – (10% x $250,000)]. Since $175,000 of 1999 certificates were redeemed in 1999, 12/31/99 unearned revenue is $50,000 ($225,000 – $175,000).

29. (a)   The requirement is to calculate Wren's royalty revenue for 1999. The 3/15/99 royalty receipt ($12,000) would not affect 1999 revenue because this amount pertains to revenues earned for July through December of 1998 and would have been accrued as revenue on 12/31/98. On 9/15/99, Wren received $17,000 in royalties for the first half of 1999. Royalties for the second half of 1999 will not be received until 3/15/00. However, the royalty payment to be received for the second 6 months (15% x $60,000 = $9,000) has been earned and should be accrued at 12/31/99. Therefore, 1999 royalty revenue is $26,000 ($17,000 + $9,000) and answer (a) is correct.

30. (d)   The agreement states that Super is to receive royalties of 20% of revenues associated with the comic strip. Since Fantasy's 2000 revenues from the strip were $1,500,000, Super's royalty revenue is $300,000 ($1,500,000 x 20%). The other information in the problem about the receivable and cash payments is not needed to compute revenues. Super's 2000 summary entries would be

Cash	200,000	
Royalties rec.		75,000
Royalty revenue		125,000 ($200,000 – $75,000)
Royalties rec.	175,000	
Royalty revenue		175,000 ($300,000 – $125,000)

31. (c)   Royalty revenues should be recognized when earned, regardless of when the cash is collected. Royalty revenue earned from 12/1/98 to 5/31/99 is $80,000 ($400,000 x 20%). Of this amount, $10,000 ($50,000 x 20%) was earned in December of 1998, so the portion earned in the first 5 months of 1998 is $70,000 ($80,000 – $10,000). Royalty revenue earned from 6/1/99 to 11/30/99 is $65,000 ($325,000 x 20%). The amount earned from 12/1/99 to 12/31/99, which would be accrued at 12/31, is $14,000 ($70,000 x 20%). Therefore, 1998 royalty revenue is $149,000.

1/1/99 - 5/31/99	$70,000
6/1/99 - 11/30/99	65,000
12/1/99 - 12/31/99	14,000
	$149,000

32. (b)   The requirement is to calculate the amount of royalty income to be recognized in 1999. Cash collected for royalties totalled $200,000 in 1999. However, this amount must be adjusted for changes in the related accounts, as follows:

1999 cash received	$200,000
Royalty receivable 12/31/98	(90,000)
Royalty receivable 12/31/99	85,000
Unearned royalty 12/31/98	60,000
Unearned royalty 12/31/99	(40,000)
Royalty income	$215,000

The beginning receivable balance ($90,000) is subtracted because that portion of the cash collected was recognized as revenue last year. The ending receivable balance ($85,000) is added because that amount is 1999 revenue, even though it has not yet been collected. The beginning balance of unearned royalties ($60,000) is added because that amount is assumed to be earned during the year. Finally, the ending balance of unearned royalties ($40,000) is subtracted since this amount was collected, but not earned as revenue, by 12/31/99.

33. (b)   The requirement is to determine the amount of royalty expense to be recognized in 1999. Cash paid for royalties totalled $300,000 in 1999. However, this amount must be adjusted for changes in the related accounts, as follows:

1999 cash paid	$300,000
Royalty payable 12/31/98	(80,000)
Royalty payable 12/31/99	75,000
Prepaid royalty 12/31/98	55,000
Prepaid royalty 12/31/99	(45,000)
	$305,000

The beginning payable balance ($80,000) is subtracted because that portion of the cash paid was recognized as expense during the previous year. The ending payable balance ($75,000) is added because that amount has been accrued as 1999 expense, even though it has not yet been paid. The beginning balance of prepaid royalties ($55,000) is added because that amount is assumed to have expired during the year. Finally, the ending balance of prepaid royalties ($45,000) is subtracted since this amount was paid, but not incurred as an expense, by 12/31/99.

34.   (b)   When the insurance policy was initially purchased, the entire balance was debited to a prepaid asset account (i.e., prepaid insurance). The adjusting entry at December 31, 1999, to recognize the expiration of 1 year of the policy would be:

Insurance expense	(1/3 of original pymt.)
Prepaid insurance	(1/3 of original pymt.)

After the adjusting entry, the prepaid asset account would contain 2/3 of the original payment. If the original payment had instead been debited to an expense account (i.e., insurance expense), then the adjusting entry at December 31, 1999 would be:

Prepaid insurance	(2/3 of original pymt.)
Insurance expense	(2/3 of original pymt.)

This alternate approach would also result in 1/3 of the original payment being expensed in 1999 and 2/3 of the original payment being carried forward as a prepaid asset. Thus, answer (b) is correct. Answer (a) is incorrect because the premium paid was for a 3-year policy, 2/3 of which had not yet expired and would therefore be carried forward in the prepaid asset account. Answer (c) is incorrect because 1/3 of the original payment was already expensed. Answer (d) is incorrect because the amount would be the same as it would have been if the original payment had been debited initially to an expense account (as explained for answer (b) above).

35.   (b)   Per ARB 43, chap 3A, para 4, current assets are identified as resources that are reasonably expected to be realized in cash or sold or **consumed** during the normal operating cycle of the business. These resources include prepaid expenses such as royalties. Since the balance remaining in Sip Co.'s royalty prepayment (the payment relating to 2000 royalties) will be consumed within the next year, it should be reported as a current asset. Additionally, the payment relating to 1999 should be reported as an expense. Therefore, answer (b) is correct.

36.   (b)   At the time the gift certificates were issued, the following entry was made, reflecting the store's future obligation to honor the certificates:

Cash	xx	
Deferred revenue		xx

Upon redemption of the certificates, the obligation recorded in the deferred revenue account becomes satisfied and the revenue is earned. Similarly, as the certificates expire, the store is no longer under any obligation to honor the certificates and the deferred revenue should be taken into income. In both instances, the deferred revenue account must be reduced (debited) to reflect the earning of revenue [answer (b)]. This is done through the following entry:

Deferred revenue	xx	
Revenue		xx

37.   (a)   The revenues from service contracts should be recognized on a pro rata basis over the term of the contract. This treatment allocates the contract revenues to the period(s) in which they are earned. Since the sale of a service contract does not culminate in the completion of the earnings process (i.e., does not represent the seller's performance of the contract), payments received for such a contract should be recorded initially in a deferred revenue account.

A.4.   Cash to Accrual

38.   (c)   The following formula is used to adjust service revenue from the cash basis to the accrual basis:

$$\text{Cash fees collected} + \text{End. AR} - \text{Beg. AR} + \text{Beg. unearned fees} - \text{End. unearned fees} = \text{Accrual basis service revenue}$$

$200,000 + $60,000 - $40,000 + 0 - $5,000 = $215,000

As an alternative, T-accounts can be used:

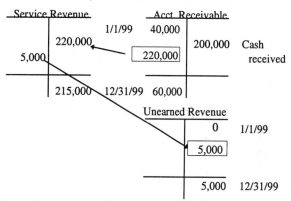

39.   (d)   To determine cash basis revenue, the solutions approach is to prepare a T-account for accounts receivable.

Accounts Receivable			
12/31/98	1,000,000		
Sales	4,600,000	20,000	Write-offs
		?	Collections
12/31/99	1,300,000		

The missing amount for cash collections is $4,280,000. Another approach is to use the following formula:

Sales	+	Decrease (– increase) in AR	–	Write-offs	=	Collections
$4,600,000	–	$300,000	–	$20,000	=	$4,280,000

The increase in receivables ($300,000) means that cash collected during the period was less than sales during the period and therefore is deducted from sales revenue. The write-offs ($20,000) represent recognized sales which will never be collected in cash and therefore must also be deducted to compute collections.

40.   (d)   To determine rental revenue, the solutions approach is to prepare a T-account for rents receivable.

Rents Receivable			
11/30/98	800,000		
Revenue	?	2,210,000	Cash collections
		30,000	Write-offs
11/30/99	1,060,000		

The journal entries resulting in the above postings to rents receivable would be:

Revenue:	Rents receivable	?	
	Rent revenue		?
Collections:	Cash	2,210,000	
	Rents receivable		2,210,000
Write-offs:	Allowance for		
	doubtful accounts	30,000	
	Rents receivable		30,000

The missing amount can be computed as $2,500,000 ($800,000 + ? – $2,210,000 – $30,000 = $1,060,000). The above analysis assumes all revenues were initially recorded as receivables. Even if some were recorded as revenue when cash was received, total revenue would still be $2,500,000.

41.   **(d)**   Under the cash laws of accounting, revenue is recognized as it is collected. Cash sales after returns and allowances totaled $76,000 ($80,000 – $4,000). Net credit sales for 1999 were $114,000 ($120,000 credit sales – $6,000 discounts). As made evident by the T-account below, cash collections from credit sales must equal $124,000 ($40,000 + $114,000 – $30,000), since $10,000 in excess of current credit sales was received and reduced Accounts Receivable by this amount.

	Accounts Receivable		
Bal. 1/1	40,000		
Net credit sales	114,000	?	Collections
Bal. 12/31	30,000		

A summary journal entry would be

Cash	124,000	
Sales discounts	6,000	
Accounts receivable		130,000

Total cash basis revenue for 1999 is $200,000 as shown below.

Cash sales ($80,000 – $4,000)	$ 76,000
Collections of credit sales [($40,000 +	
$120,000 – $30,000) – $6,000]	124,000
Total cash received	$200,000

42.   **(a)**   Cost of goods sold is computed as follows:

Beg. inv. + Net purchases – End. inv. = CGS

Net purchases must be computed from the information given using a T-account or a formula.

	AP		
		50,000	12/31/98
Payments	490,000	?	Purchases
		75,000	12/31/99

The missing amount for purchases is $515,000. Another approach is to use the following formula:

Payments	+	Ending AP	–	Beginning AP	=	Purchases
$490,000	+	$75,000	–	$50,000	=	$515,000

This amount can be used to determine cost of goods sold

Beg. inventory	$290,000
+ Net purchases	515,000
Cost of goods available	805,000
– End. inventory	260,000
Cost of goods sold	$545,000

43.   **(d)**   Cash-basis income of $60,000 must be adjusted for changes in accounts receivable and accounts payable to compute accrual income

Cash-basis income	$ 60,000
12/31/98 AR	(20,000)
12/31/99 AR	40,000
12/31/98 AP	30,000
12/31/99 AP	(15,000)
Accrual income	$ 95,000

The beginning AR ($20,000) is subtracted because although this amount was **collected in 1999**, it is properly accrued as **1998 revenue**. The ending AR is added because although **not collected in 1999**, it should be accrued as **1999 revenue**. The beginning AP is added because although this amount was **paid in 1999**, it is properly accrued as **1998 expense**. The ending AP is subtracted because although **not paid in 1999**, it should be accrued as **1999 expense**.

44.   **(c)**   The ending balance in Tory's capital account on either the accrual or cash basis is computed as follows:

$$\frac{\text{Beginning}}{\text{capital}} + \text{Investments} + \text{Income} - \text{Drawings} = \frac{\text{Ending}}{\text{capital}}$$

Tory's beginning capital is his initial cash investment of $2,000. No other investments were made. Under the cash basis method of accounting, income is the excess of cash revenues ($5,000) over cash expenses ($0, since the expenses were not paid until after March 31). Therefore, cash basis income is $5,000. Drawings are $1,000. Therefore, ending capital is $6,000 ($2,000 + $0 + $5,000 – $1,000).

45.   **(d)**   The requirement of this question is to determine if a decrease in accounts receivable and/or a decrease in accrued expenses would result in **cash-basis income** being **lower** than accrual-basis income.

A decrease in the accounts receivable balance would generally mean that cash was collected. In accordance with the cash basis of accounting when cash is received it is recorded as revenue (Dr. Cash, Cr. Revenue). Whereas under the accrual basis the revenue would have recorded when the receivable was recorded (Dr. AR, Cr. Revenue). Thus, a decreased accounts receivable balance would result in increased revenue/income. Therefore, the answer for this account is No.

A decrease in the accrued expenses account would generally mean cash was paid on some expenses. Under the cash basis, when the cash is paid the expense is recorded (Dr. Expense, Cr. Cash). Whereas under the accrual basis the expense would have been recorded when the accrued expense was recorded (Dr. Expense, Cr. Accrued Expense). Thus, a decreased accrued expenses account would result in increased expenses/lower income for the cash basis. Thus, the answer for this account is Yes.

46.   **(b)**   When a company operates on the accrual basis, supplies are inventoried and expensed as they are used. Under the cash method, however, supplies are expensed as they are paid for. Therefore if White Co. experiences an increase in supplies inventory during the year, this increase must be deducted from accrual income to get to the cash basis, because the cost of the supplies would be expensed at the time of purchase.

Office salaries payable works the opposite way. Under the accrual method, a liability would have been established resulting in additional expense over the amount of cash paid to employees. Under the cash method, no liability is accrued and the unpaid salaries are not expensed. Therefore, the increase must be added to the accrual basis net income.

47. (c)   Prior to 1999, Droit Co. used the cash basis of accounting. Accordingly, Droit would have expensed all purchases of supplies as incurred. In contrast, under the accrual basis of accounting, the cost of unused supplies at each year end would have been carried as an asset and, therefore, excluded from the current year's supplies expense. In 1999, the year Droit adopted the accrual basis of accounting, Droit would have inventoried unused supplies at December 31 and excluded those costs from 1999 net income. Since the cost of 1999's beginning balance of supplies was expensed during 1998, even though the supplies were not used until 1999, Droit's inability to determine the beginning supplies inventory would result in an understatement of supplies expense and overstatement of 1999 net income. However, since Droit properly inventoried supplies at December 31, 1999, its cumulative (inception-to-date) supplies expense would be properly stated. Therefore, Droit's inability to determine 1999's beginning supplies expense would have no impact on Droit's December 31, 1999 retained earnings, and answer (c) is correct.

A.5. Installment Sales

48. (b)   Under the installment method, gross profit is deferred at the time of sale and is recognized by applying the gross profit rate to subsequent cash collections. At the time of sale, gross profit of $250,000 is deferred ($500,000 installment sales less $250,000 cost of installment sales). The gross profit rate is 50% ($250,000 ÷ $500,000). Since 1999 collections on installment sales were $100,000, gross profit of $50,000 (50% x $100,000) is recognized in 1999. This would decrease the deferred gross profit account to a 12/31/99 balance of $200,000 ($250,000 – $50,000). Note that regular sales, cost of regular sales, and general and administrative expenses do not affect the deferred gross profit account.

49. (d)   Under the installment sales method, gross profit is deferred to future periods and recognized proportionately to collection of the receivables. Therefore, at each year-end, deferred gross profit can be computed by multiplying the gross profit percentage by the accounts receivable balance, as indicated below:

	1999	*1998*
Sales	$900,000	$600,000
1998 Collections		(200,000)
1999 Collections	(300,000)	(100,000)
1998 Write-offs		(50,000)
1999 Write-offs	(50,000)	(150,000)
12/31/99 AR	$550,000	$100,000
Gross profit %	x 40%	x 30%
12/31/99 Deferred GP	$220,000	$30,000

Thus, total deferred gross profit at 12/31/99 is $250,000 ($220,000 + $30,000).

50. (d)   Under the installment sales method, gross profit is deferred to future periods and is recognized proportionately as cash is collected. To determine cash collections in this case, first compute the 1999 installment sales by dividing deferred gross profit by the gross profit percentage ($560,000 ÷ 40% = $1,400,000). Then, the 12/31/99 installment accounts receivable is subtracted to determine cash collections ($1,400,000 – $800,000 = $600,000). Realized gross profit is then computed by multiplying cash collections by the gross profit percentage ($600,000 x 40% = $240,000).

51. (c)   When using the installment method, gross profit realized is computed as indicated below:

Cash collections   x   GP%   =   GP realized

This equation can be rearranged as follows:

GP realized   ÷   GP%   =   Cash collections

Therefore, cash collected to date on 1998 sales is $800,000 [($150,000 + $90,000) ÷ 30%], and on 1999 sales is $500,000 ($200,000 ÷ 40%). Installment accounts receivable at 12/31/99 is computed by subtracting cash collections from the original sales amount:

Installment AR - 1998 ($1,000,000 – $800,000)	$ 200,000
Installment AR - 1999 ($2,000,000 – $500,000)	1,500,000
Total 12/31/99 installment AR	$1,700,000

52. (a)   The plant sale is accounted for using the installment method. The gross profit percentage on the sale is 33 1/3% ($600,000 profit ÷ $1,800,000 selling price). Since $300,000 of the sales price is collected in 1999, gross profit of $100,000 is recognized (33 1/3% x $300,000). The **total** revenue recognized is $250,000 ($100,000 gross profit + $150,000 interest revenue).

53. (a)   The machine sale is accounted for using the installment method, where gross profit is deferred and recognized in proportion to cash collected. Initially, the entire $270,000 gain is deferred. In 1998, $150,000 of the sales price was collected, and the gross profit percentage is 30% ($270,000 ÷ $900,000), so gross profit recognized was $45,000 (30% x $150,000). In 1999, $250,000 of the sales price was collected, so gross profit recognized was $75,000 (30% x $250,000). Therefore, at 12/31/99, deferred gross profit is $150,000 ($270,000 – $45,000 – $75,000). As a shortcut, you can compute the 12/31/99 note receivable balance ($750,000 – $250,000 = $500,000), and multiply by the 30% gross profit percentage (30% x $500,000 = $150,000). Note that the **interest** collected ($75,000) does not affect the computation because it is not a collection of sales price.

54. (c)   Per APB 10, para 12, the profit on a sale in the ordinary course of business is considered to be realized at the time of sale unless it is uncertain whether the sale price will be collected. The Board concluded that use of the installment method of accounting is not acceptable unless this uncertainty exists. Therefore, answer (c) is correct. Answers (a), (b), and (d) are incorrect because they do not involve the element of uncertainty regarding the collectibility of the sale price.

55.   (c)   According to the **installment method** of accounting, gross profit on an installment sale is recognized in income in proportion to the cash collection [answer (c)]. The cash collected from a given year's sales is multiplied by that year's gross profit percentage to compute the amount of gross profit to be recognized. Answer (a) describes the **point-of-sale** recognition basis, while answer (d) describes the **cost recovery** method. Answer (b) does not describe any recognition basis currently used.

56.   (c)   Per APB 10, para 12, the installment method of accounting is used when there is a high degree of uncertainty regarding the collectibility of the sale price. Under this method, sales revenues and the related cost of goods sold are recognized in the period of the sale. However, the gross profit is deferred to the periods in which cash is collected. Income recognized in the period of collection is generally computed by multiplying the cash collected by the gross margin percentage. Therefore, answer (c) is correct. Answers (a) and (b) are incorrect because the installment method is based upon deferral of the gross profit, not the net operating profit. Answer (d) is incorrect because APB 10, para 12, states that the installment method is generally only applicable when the reporting company is unable to estimate the amount of uncollectible accounts.

57.   (d)   Under the installment method (case I) revenue (gross profit) is recognized **after** the sale, in proportion to cash collected. Under the cost recovery method (case II), revenue (gross profit) is again recognized **after** the sale, when cumulative receipts exceed the cost of the asset sold. Therefore, revenue is not recognized prior to the sale of merchandise in either case I or case II [answer (d)].

A.6. Cost Recovery Method

58.   (d)   Under the cost recovery method **no profit of any type** is recognized until the cumulative receipts (principal and interest) exceed the cost of the asset sold. This means that the entire gross profit ($3,000,000 – $2,000,000 = $1,000,000) and the 1999 interest received ($270,000) will be deferred until cash collections exceed $2,000,000. Therefore, no income is recognized in 1999.

59.   (d)   The **installment method** is used when collection of the selling price is not reasonably assured. However, when the uncertainty of collection is so great that even the use of the installment method is precluded, then the cost recovery method may be used. Therefore, answer (d) is correct as having no reasonable basis for estimating collectibility would provide a great enough uncertainty to use the cost recovery method. Answers (a), (b), and (c) are incorrect because the situations presented are standard transactions under the installment method. It is important to note that anytime the installment method is used, some risk of

100% collection exists, but the risk must be extreme before the cost recovery method is employed.

60.   (a)   Per APB 10, para 12, installment methods of recognizing revenue are appropriate only when "collection of the sale price is not reasonably assured." Under the cost recovery method, gross profit is deferred and recognized only when the cumulative receipts exceed the cost of the asset sold. Therefore, answer (a) is correct.

A.7. Franchise Agreements

61.   (d)   Per para 5 of SFAS 45, Franchise fee revenue is recognized when all material services have been substantially performed by the franchiser. Substantial performance means the franchiser has performed substantially all of required initial services and has no remaining obligation to refund any cash received. The $60,000 nonrefundable down payment applies to the initial services already performed by Rice. Therefore, the $60,000 may be recognized as revenue in 1999. The three remaining $30,000 installments relate to substantial future services to be performed by Rice. The present value of these payments ($72,000) is recorded as unearned franchise fees and recognized as revenue once substantial performance of the future services has occurred.

Cash	60,000	
Notes receivable	90,000	
Discount on notes receivable		18,000
Franchise revenue		60,000
Unearned franchise fees		72,000

62.   (c)   Initial franchise fees are not recognized as revenue until the franchisor makes substantial performance of the required services, and collection is reasonably assured. Since Potter Pie has not yet performed the required services, the initial franchise fee (21 x $30,000 = $630,000) is reported as **unearned franchise fees** at 12/31/99. The estimated uncollectible amount ($20,000) normally would be recorded as a debit to **bad debt expense** and a credit to **allowance for uncollectible accounts**. However, since no revenue has yet been recognized, it is inappropriate to record bad debt expense. Instead, **unearned franchise fees** is debited, because an unearned revenue should not be recorded when, in effect, no related asset has been received. Therefore, the **net** unearned franchise fees is $610,000 ($630,000 – $20,000).

A.8. Real Estate Transactions

63.   (d)   Items I and II do not transfer the risks and rewards of ownership to the buyer since both scenarios entitle the buyer to a return of his/her initial investment. Thus, the risks of ownership still remain with the seller. The economic substance of such arrangements is that of financing, leasing, or profit-sharing transactions. Item III transfers the risks and rewards of ownership since the seller will be reimbursed for cost plus a 5% profit on the support provided. Therefore, the seller is not required to support operations of the property at its **own** risk.

64.   (c)   Answer (c) is correct because the problem states that the sale has been consummated and that Kame's initial and continuing investments are adequate to demonstrate a commitment to pay for the property. However, the fact that Esker's receivable is subject to future subordination precludes recognition of the profit in full. Instead, the cost recovery method must be used to account for the sale. Answer (a) is incorrect because the deposit method is to be used

(1)   Until the sale is consummated, when all activities necessary for closing have been performed.

(2)   If the buyer's initial and continuing investments are not adequate to demonstrate a commitment to pay for the property and the seller is not reasonably assured of recovering the cost of the property if the buyer defaults.

The problem states that the sale has been consummated and that Kame's initial and continuing investments are adequate. Therefore, the deposit method will not be used to account for the sale. Answer (b) is incorrect. The reduced profit method is used only when the initial investment is adequate to demonstrate a commitment to pay for the property but the continuing investments are not. The continuing investments must also meet certain additional requirements for the reduced profit method to be used. Since Kame's continuing investments are adequate, the reduced profit method will not be used to account for the sale. Answer (d) is incorrect because the full accrual method may be used only if profit on the sale is determinable, the earning process is virtually complete, and all of the following:

1.   A sale is consummated.

2.   The buyer's initial and continuing investments are adequate to demonstrate a commitment to pay for the property.

3.   The seller's receivable is not subject to future subordination.

4.   The seller has transferred to the buyer the usual risks and rewards of ownership in a transaction that is, in substance, a sale and does not have a substantial continuing involvement in the property.

OTHER OBJECTIVE ANSWERS AND ANSWER EXPLANATIONS

Problem 1

1.   **(E)** SFAC 5, para 73, states that "Relevance is a primary qualitative characteristic. To be relevant, information about an item must have feedback value or predictive value (or both) for users and must be timely."

2.   **(G)** SFAC 6, para 82, states that "Gains are increases in equity (net assets) from peripheral or incidental transactions of an entity and from all other transactions and other events and circumstances affecting the entity except those that result from revenues or investments by owners."

3.   **(J)** SFAC 5, para 83(a), states that "Revenues and gains are realized when products (goods or services), merchandise, or other assets are exchanged for cash or claims to cash."

4.   **(F)** SFAC 2, para 33, states that "Comparability, including consistency, is a secondary quality that interacts with relevance and reliability to contribute to the usefulness of information."

5.   **(A)** SFAC 5, para 6, states that "Recognition is the process of formally recording or incorporating an item into the financial statements of an entity as an asset, liability, revenue, expense, or the like." Paragraph 63 continues the recognition concept by stating, "An item and information about it should meet four fundamental recognition criteria to be recognized and should be recognized when the criteria are met, subject to a cost-benefit constraint and a materiality threshold."

6.   **(B)** SFAC 5, para 39, states that "Comprehensive income is a broad measure of the effects of transactions and other events on an entity, comprising all recognized changes in equity (net assets) of the entity during a period from transactions and other events and circumstances except those resulting from investments by owners and distributions to owners."

7.   **(D)** SFAC 6, para 78, defines revenues as "inflows or other enhancements of assets of an entity or settlements of its liabilities (or a combination of both) from delivering or producing goods, rendering services, or other activities that constitute the entity's ongoing major or central operations."

8.   **(L)** SFAC 5, para 67(c), defines current market value as "the amount of cash, or its equivalent, that could be obtained by selling an asset in orderly liquidation."

9.   **(E)** SFAC 2, in its Glossary of Terms, defines predictive value as "the quality of information that helps users to increase the likelihood of correctly forecasting the outcome of past or present events."

10.   **(I)** SFAC 5, para 36, states that "Earnings is a measure of performance during a period that is concerned primarily with the extent to which asset inflows associated with cash-to-cash cycles substantially completed (or completed) during the period exceed (or are less than) asset outflows associated, directly or indirectly, with the same cycles."

SOLUTION GUIDE

Problem 1 Cash to Accrual Worksheet; Comparison of These Bases

a.

1. This problem consists of two related parts. Part (a) requires the entering of adjustments to convert from cash to accrual on the worksheet provided. Part (b) requires a brief memo explaining why the bank would require accrual-basis financial statements.

2. To complete the worksheet provided in part (a), you must refer back to the additional information given (labeled 1 through 9). The solutions approach is to treat each of the nine items as an independent problem.

2.1 Amounts due from customers total $32,000 at 12/31/99. The balance in the accounts receivable account from the last year-end is $16,200. This account must be debited for $15,800 to bring the balance up to $32,000. The corresponding credit is to Sales, since unrecorded receivables means that there are also unrecorded sales.

2.2 An allowance for doubtful accounts of $3,800 is required at 12/31/99. Since the balance in the allowance account is $0, an adjusting entry for $3,800 is required.

Doubtful accounts expense	3,800	
Allowance for doubtful accounts		3,800

2.3 Unpaid invoices for flower (the company's product) purchases total $30,500 at 12/31/99. The balance in accounts payable from last year is $17,000. This account must be credited for $13,500 to bring the balance up to $30,500. The corresponding debit is to Purchases, since these purchases were never recorded. Accrual basis Purchases for 1999 thus equals $318,600 ($305,100 + $30,500 – $17,000).

2.4 The 12/31/99 inventory is $72,800, but the books now reflect the 12/31/98 inventory of $62,000. The beginning inventory must be removed from the books, and the ending inventory must be recorded.

Income summary	62,000	
Inventory		62,000
Inventory	72,800	
Income summary		72,800

The net adjustment to inventory is $10,800. You may make either both of the above entries or a net entry on the worksheet.

An alternative method of adjusting the inventory and purchases account using a Cost of goods sold account exists. The adjustments to the inventory account could be made to a Cost of goods sold account instead of to Income summary--inventory.

In this case, the appropriate journal entries for information item (4) would be as follows:

Cost of goods sold	62,000	
Inventory (12/31/98)		62,000
Inventory (12/31/99)	72,800	
Cost of goods sold		72,800

An additional entry transferring net purchases to Cost of goods sold is then required to obtain the correct ending balance for that account. This entry should be recorded after the purchases account is adjusted to the correct accrual basis balance of $318,600 calculated in item (3).

Cost of goods sold	318,600	
Purchases		318,600

Although the AICPA Unofficial Answer did not require the balance of Cost of goods sold, accrual basis CGS equals $307,800 ($62,000 BI + $318,600 purch. – $72,800 EI).

If this method were used, the accrual basis ending balances in the debit column of the worksheet as of 12/31/99 for those accounts affected would be as follows:

Inventory	$ 72,800
Purchases	-0-
Cost of Goods Sold	$307,800

2.5 The insurance coverage is paid 1 year in advance. The $8,700 payment made on May 1 was recorded as insurance expense. Therefore, $2,900 (4/12 x 8,700) must be removed from the insurance expense account and recorded as prepaid insurance. An additional entry must be made to record some of the 4/1/98 insurance premium as 1999 expense. The last 4 months of that payment ($7,800 x 4/12 = $2,600) should be expensed in 1999. The credit is to Baron, capital, since the 12/31/98 balance was understated when the total premium was expensed in 1998.

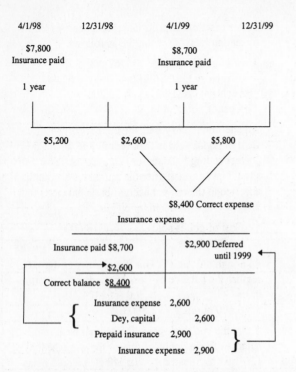

Alternatively, these entries could be netted as is done in the AICPA Unofficial Answer.

2.6   Depreciation on furniture and fixtures is $12,000. In addition, land improvements must be depreciated. The depreciation period is the useful life (15 years), because it is less than the lease term of 25 years. Depreciation on the land improvements is $2,250 ($45,000 x 1/15 x 9/12), and total depreciation is $14,250 ($12,000 + $2,250). The entry is:

| Depreciation expense | 14,250 | |
| Accumulated depreciation | | 14,250 |

2.7   Accrued expenses were unrecorded at both 12/31/98 and 12/31/99. Those unrecorded at 12/31/98 would have been recorded as an expense when paid in 1999. Therefore, those amounts must be removed from the 1999 expense accounts. The corresponding debit is to Baron, capital, since the 12/31/98 balance of that account was overstated when the accrued expenses were not recorded in 1998.

Baron, capital	2,000	
Utilities expense		900
Payroll taxes expense		1,100

The accrued expenses unrecorded at 12/31/99 must be recorded with an adjusting entry to debit the expenses and credit the related liability.

Utilities expense	1,500	
Payroll taxes expense	1,600	
Accrued expenses		3,100

Alternatively, these entries could be netted as is done in the AICPA Unofficial Answer.

2.8   The contingent lawsuit liability must be accrued because it meets the **probable** and **reasonably estimable** criteria. The estimate of the settlement is $300,000, but $250,000 of that amount is covered by insurance. Therefore the net loss and liability of $50,000 ($300,000 – $250,000) must be accrued.

| Lawsuit loss | 50,000 | |
| Lawsuit liability | | 50,000 |

2.9   Baron's "salary" (12 x $4,000 = $48,000) and living expenses ($250 x 52 = $13,000) must be reclassified from expense accounts to the drawing account.

Baron, drawing	61,000	
Salaries		48,000
Living expenses		13,000

Note: With regard to the treatment of Baron's salary, no authoritative pronouncement addresses this issue. However, elementary accounting textbooks treat such salaries as drawings.

b.   Advantages of accrual basis instead of cash basis
  • More complete information regarding earnings, assets, and claims to assets
  • Cannot manipulate earnings via the timing of receipts and payments
  • Events which change financial position are reported in the period of occurrence
  • Revenues and expenses reflect amounts owed or receivable, which is more meaningful than cash payments/receipts

UNOFFICIAL ANSWER

Problem 1 Cash to Accrual Worksheet; Comparison of These Bases

a.

Baron Flowers
WORKSHEET TO CONVERT TRIAL BALANCE TO ACCRUAL BASIS
DECEMBER 31, 1999

Account title	Cash basis Dr.	Cash basis Cr.	Adjustments Dr.	Adjustments Cr.	Accrual basis* Dr.*	Accrual basis* Cr.*
Cash	25,600				25,600	
Accounts receivable	16,200		(1) 15,800		32,000	
Inventory	62,000		(4) 10,800		72,800	
Furniture & fixtures	118,200				118,200	
Land improvements	45,000				45,000	
Accumulated depreciation & amortization		32,400		(6) 14,250		46,650
Accounts payable		17,000		(3) 13,500		30,500
Baron, Drawings			(9) 61,000		61,000	
Baron, Capital		124,600	(7) 2,000	(5) 2,600		125,200
Allowance for uncollectible accounts				(2) 3,800		3,800
Prepaid insurance			(5) 2,900		2,900	
Accrued expenses				(7) 3,100		3,100
Estimated liability from lawsuit				(8) 50,000		50,000
Sales		653,000		(1) 15,800		668,800
Purchases	305,100		(3) 13,500		318,600	
Salaries	174,000			(9) 48,000	126,000	
Payroll taxes	12,400		(7) 500		12,900	
Insurance	8,700			(5) 300	8,400	
Rent	34,200				34,200	
Utilities	12,600		(7) 600		13,200	
Living expenses	13,000			(9) 13,000		
Income summary-- inventory			(4) 62,000	(4) 72,800		10,800
Uncollectible accounts			(2) 3,800		3,800	
Depreciation & amortization			(6) 14,250		14,250	
Estimated loss from lawsuit			(8) 50,000		50,000	
	827,000	827,000	237,150	237,150	938,850	938,850

Explanations of Adjustments

[1] To convert 1999 sales to accrual basis.
Accounts receivable balances:

December 31, 1999	$32,000
December 31, 1998	16,200
Increase in sales	$15,800

[2] To record provision for uncollectible accounts.

[3] To convert 1999 purchases to accrual basis.
Accounts payable balances:

December 31, 1999	$30,500
December 31, 1998	17,000
Increase in purchases	$13,500

[4] To record increase in inventory from 12/31/98 to 12/31/99.
Inventory balances:

December 31, 1999	$72,800
December 31, 1998	62,000
Increase in inventory	$10,800

---

* *Completion of these columns was not required.*

[5] To adjust prepaid insurance.
  Prepaid balances:

December 31, 1999 ($8,700 x 4/12)	$2,900
December 31, 1998 ($7,800 x 4/12)	2,600
Decrease in insurance expense	$ 300

[6] To record 1999 depreciation and amortization expense.

Cost of leasehold improvement	$45,000
Estimated life	15 years
Amortization ($45,000 x 1/15 x 9/12)	2,250
Depreciation expense on fixtures and equipment	12,000
	$14,250

[7] To convert expenses to accrual basis.

	Balances December 31, 1999	1998	Increase in expenses
Utilities	$1,500	$ 900	$ 600
Payroll taxes	1,600	1,100	500
	$3,100	$2,000	$1,100

[8] To record lawsuit liability at 12/31/99.

Attorney's estimate of probable loss	$300,000
Amount covered by insurance	250,000
Baron's estimated liability	$ 50,000

[9] To record Baron's drawings for 1999.

Salary ($4,000 x 12)	$48,000
Living expenses	13,000
	$61,000

b.

To:	Baron Flowers
From:	Muir
Re:	Accrual basis financial statements

You have asked me to explain why the bank would require financial statements prepared on the accrual basis instead of the cash basis. The bank is concerned about your ability to repay the loan. To assess that ability, it wants information about your earnings for the period, total assets, and all claims on those assets. This information about your enterprise's performance and financial position is provided more completely by accrual-basis financial statements than by cash-basis financial statements.

Under the cash basis, revenues are recognized when received and expenses when paid. Earnings can be manipulated by the timing of cash receipts and disbursements. Accrual basis accounting, while grounded in cash flows, reports transactions and other events with cash consequences at the time the transactions and events occur. Revenues and expenses are reported in the accounting period benefited and reflect receivables and payables, not just what the enterprise was able to collect or chose to pay.

ANSWER OUTLINE

Problem 2   Revenue Recognition and Postretirement Benefits Other than Pensions

a.   Revenue recognition
  • Recognized when realized or realizable and earned
  • Sales with right of return:
    • Revenue and cost of sales, net of returns, recognized at time of sale only if specified conditions met
    • Recognition postponed if conditions not met
  • Impact of right of return on Emco:
    • Cannot reasonably estimate returns
    • Emco must defer recognition until either return privilege expires or it can reasonably estimate returns

b.   SFAS 106, *Employers' Accounting for Postretirement Benefits Other Than Pensions*
  • Primary recipients: retired employees, their beneficiaries, and covered dependents
  • Principal benefit is health care
  • Other benefits: tuition assistance, legal services, life insurance benefits, day care, and housing subsidies
  • Accruals based on estimates required because failure to accrue implies that no obligation exists

UNOFFICIAL ANSWER

Problem 2   Revenue Recognition and Postretirement Benefits Other than Pensions

TO:	Brown
FROM:	Wyatt

As we discussed, here is a brief overview of revenue recognition and Statement of Financial Accounting Standards 106.

a.   Revenue recognition

The revenue recognition principle provides that revenue is recognized when it is realized or realizable and it is earned. Accordingly, revenues from the sale of products ordinarily are recognized at the time of sale. Revenue from sales transactions in which the buyer has a right to return the product are recognized at time of sale only if specified conditions are met. If all these conditions are not met, revenue recognition is postponed; if they are met, sales revenue and cost of sales should be reported in the income statement, reduced to reflect estimated returns.

One of the specified conditions is that the amount of future returns can be reasonably estimated. Since Emco cannot reasonably estimate future returns, Emco should defer recognition of sales revenue and cost of sales until the return privilege has substantially expired or it can reasonably estimate returns, whichever occurs first.

b.   Statement of Financial Accounting Standards 106, *Employers' Accounting for Postretirement Benefits Other Than Pensions.*

The primary recipients of postretirement benefits other than pensions are retired employees, their beneficiaries, and covered dependents. The principal benefit covered by SFAS 106 is postretirement health care benefits. Examples of other benefits include tuition assistance, legal services, life insurance benefits, day-care, and housing subsidies.

The reasoning given in SFAS 106 is that accrual of the obligation based on best estimates is superior to implying, by a failure to accrue, that no obligation exists prior to the payment of benefits.

B. Error Correction

Accountants must be in a position to anticipate, locate, and correct errors in their functions of systems and procedures design, controllership, and attestation. Errors which are discovered in the same year that they are made are corrected by

1. Determining the entry that was made
2. Determining the correct entry
3. Analyzing increases or decreases needed in affected accounts
4. Making the correct entry

Errors in classification (e.g., sales expense instead of R&D expense) affect only one period. Nonsystematic errors in adjusting entries (e.g., an error in ending inventory of one period) affect two periods and are known as self-correcting (counterbalancing) errors. For example, overstating ending inventory of 1999 will overstate the income of 1999 and understate that of 2000. Other errors will affect the income of several periods such as misrecording the cost of a long-lived asset (i.e., depreciation will be misstated for all periods).

The chart below shows four examples of counterbalancing errors.

ERRORS WHICH WILL SELF-CORRECT AFTER 2 YEARS

Omitting Accruals

Case #1

	12/31/99	12/31/00	1/1/01
Expense (wages)	Understated	Overstated	Correct
Net income	Overstated	Understated	Correct
Payable (wages)	Understated	Correct	Correct
Retained earnings	Overstated	Correct	Correct

Case #2

	12/31/99	12/31/00	1/1/01
Revenue (interest)	Understated	Overstated	Correct
Net income	Understated	Overstated	Correct
Receivable (interest)	Understated	Correct	Correct
Retained earnings	Understated	Correct	Correct

Omitting Deferrals (Prepaids)

Case #3

	12/31/99	12/31/00	1/1/01
Expense (insurance)	Overstated	Understated	Correct
Net income	Understated	Overstated	Correct
Prepaid asset	Understated	Correct	Correct
Retained earnings	Understated	Correct	Correct

Case#4

	12/31/99	12/31/00	1/1/01
Revenue (unearned)	Overstated	Understated	Correct
Net income	Overstated	Understated	Correct
Liability (un. rev.)	Understated	Correct	Correct
Retained earnings	Overstated	Correct	Correct

Notice that in all four cases the income statement errors have the opposite effect in 1999 and 2000. Also notice that by the end of 2000 the balance sheet accounts are correct. Therefore, even if the error is not discovered, the financial statements will be correct by the beginning of the third year.

When an error is discovered in a period subsequent to the period when the error occurred, an entry must be made to correct the accounts as if the error had not been made. For example, assume the entry to accrue wage expense in the amount of $10,000 is omitted on 12/31/99. The effects that would be caused by such an omission may be categorized as follows:

	1999	*2000*	*2001*
Expense	Understated	Overstated	Correct
Income	Overstated	Understated	Correct
Wages payable	Understated	Correct	Correct
Retained earnings	Overstated	Correct	Correct

If the company follows the policy of reversing adjusting entries for accruals, then correction of the error any time during 2000 will require

| Adjustment to correct error | 10,000 | |
| Wage expense | | 10,000 |

The adjustment account, when closed to retained earnings, will correct for the 1/1/00 overstatement in retained earnings due to the overstatement of 1999 income. The credit to wage expense will reduce the expense account for 2000 to an amount equal to 2000 wages.

If the error was discovered in 2001, no entry would be required since the error self-corrects during 2000. The 2001 balances would be the same with or without the error.

The requirements of error analysis questions vary considerably. When asked for the effect of errors, be careful to determine the effect rather than the correction; they are opposite. The effect of revenue overstatement on income is over or plus; therefore, the correction to income is to subtract. Also distinguish between correcting/adjusting entries (which can be made in the accounts to correct the current period) and "worksheet entries" which adjust amounts reported in prior periods (i.e., journal entries are not recorded to correct nominal accounts of prior periods).

Correction of errors meets the criteria for prior period adjustments (refer to the outline of SFAS 16). They should be reported as adjustments to beginning retained earnings of single-year statements and to retained earnings of each year presented in comparative statements for the error effects prior to each of the years presented. Note that reporting of prior years' errors is required even if a journal entry is not required because the errors have self-corrected. Adjustments to the comparative years should be made to reflect retroactive application of the prior period adjustments to specific accounts affected.

The example below shows the revision of prior years' financial statements, including the format of the retained earnings statement for the $10,000 wage expense discussed above.

EXAMPLE:

Assume $10,000 of wages were not recorded in Year 1; the error was not discovered until Year 3.

Income Statement Effects

	Year 1	*Year 2*	*Year 3*
Wage expense	–$10,000	+$10,000	-0-
Net income	+$10,000	–$10,000	-0-

Comparative Balance Sheets
Issued in Year 3, for Year 2 and Year 3
Balance Sheet Effects

	Year 1	*Year 2*	*Year 3*
Wages payable	–$10,000	-0-	-0-
Retained earnings	+$10,000	-0-	-0-

Comparative Income Statements
Issued in Year 3, for Year 2 and Year 3

	Year 2 (As Restated)	*Year 3*
Wage expense	$ xxx – 10,000	$ xxxx _____
Net income	$ xxx + 10,000	$ xxxx

Comparative Retained Earnings Statement
Issued in Year 3, for Year 2 and Year 3

	Year 2 (As Restated)	*Year 3*
Beginning balance	$ xxxx	$ xxxx
Prior period adjustment--		
Understatement of wages expense	–10,000	--
Beginning balance as restated	$ xxxx	$ xxxx
Net income	xxxx	xxxx
Dividends	(xxxx)	(xxxx)
Ending retained earnings	$ xxxx	$ xxxx

> *NOTE: The restated amounts in year 2 for net income and the prior period adjustment would need to be reported net of tax.*

Inventory errors have an impact on both the balance sheet and the income statement. Inventory errors include a misstatement of the ending inventory balance, which is followed by a misstatement of the beginning balance for the next period, or an inventory error could be a misstatement of purchases for the period. The analysis of inventory errors in a periodic inventory system is facilitated by setting up a statement of cost of goods sold. The statement of cost of goods sold shows the relationship between the inventory and purchases accounts and the impact of incorrect amounts. The four examples shown below use the statement of cost of goods sold to analyze different inventory errors. Items which are correct are identified by an "OK," while items which are incorrect are listed as overstated (over) or understated (under).

INVENTORY ERRORS

	Case #1 (Overstated Inventory Count)		Case #2 (Understated Inventory Count)	
	1999	*2000*	*1999*	*2000*
Beginning inventory	OK	Over	OK	Under
+ Purchases	OK	OK	OK	OK
Goods available for sale	OK	Over	OK	Under
Ending inventory*	Over	OK	Under	OK
Cost of goods sold	Under	Over	Over	Under
Net income	Over	Under	Under	Over
Retained earnings	Over	OK	Under	OK
Accounts payable	OK	OK	OK	OK

Determined by physical count.

	Case #3 (Overstated Purchases**)		Case #4 (Understated Purchases***)	
	1999	*2000*	*1999*	*2000*
Beginning inventory	OK	OK	OK	Under
+ Purchases	Over	Under	Under	Over
Goods available for sale	Over	Under	Under	OK
Ending inventory*	OK	OK	Under	OK
Cost of goods sold	Over	Under	OK	OK
Net income	Under	Over	OK	OK
Retained earnings	Under	OK	OK	OK
Accounts payable	Over	OK	Under	OK

Determined by physical count.
**Goods shipped FOB destination and not received by 12/31, but recorded as purchases and not included in physical inventory count.*
***Goods shipped FOB shipping point prior to 12/31, but not recorded as purchases or included in physical inventory count.*

MULTIPLE-CHOICE QUESTIONS (1-12)

1.   Loeb Corp. frequently borrows from the bank in order to maintain sufficient operating cash. The following loans were at a 12% interest rate, with interest payable at maturity. Loeb repaid each loan on its scheduled maturity date.

Date of loan	Amount	Maturity date	Term of loan
11/1/98	$ 5,000	10/31/99	1 year
2/1/99	15,000	7/31/99	6 months
5/1/99	8,000	1/31/00	9 months

Loeb records interest expense when the loans are repaid. As a result, interest expense of $1,500 was recorded in 1999. If no correction is made, by what amount would 1999 interest expense be understated?

    a. $540
    b. $620
    c. $640
    d. $720

2.   The first examination of Rudd Corp.'s financial statements was made for the year ended December 31, 1999. The auditor found that Rudd had purchased another company in January 1997 and had recorded goodwill of $100,000 in connection with this purchase. It was determined that the goodwill had an estimated useful life of only 5 years because of obsolescence. No amortization of goodwill had ever been recorded. For the December 31, 1999 financial statements, Rudd should debit

	Amortization expense	Retained earnings
a.	$0	$100,000
b.	$20,000	$ 40,000
c.	$33,333	$0
d.	$60,000	$0

3.   During 1999, Paul Company discovered that the ending inventories reported on its financial statements were incorrect by the following amounts:

1997	$60,000 understated
1998	75,000 overstated

Paul uses the periodic inventory system to ascertain yearend quantities that are converted to dollar amounts using the FIFO cost method. Prior to any adjustments for these errors and ignoring income taxes, Paul's retained earnings at January 1, 1999 would be

    a.   Correct.
    b. $ 15,000 overstated.
    c. $ 75,000 overstated.
    d. $135,000 overstated.

4.   Tack, Inc. reported a retained earnings balance of $150,000 at December 31, 1998. In June 1999, Tack discovered that merchandise costing $40,000 had not been included in inventory in its 1998 financial statements. Tack has a 30% tax rate. What amount should Tack report as adjusted beginning retained earnings in its statement of retained earnings at December 31, 1999?

    a. $190,000

    b. $178,000
    c. $150,000
    d. $122,000

5.   Conn Co. reported a retained earnings balance of $400,000 at December 31, 1998. In August 1999, Conn determined that insurance premiums of $60,000 for the 3-year period beginning January 1, 1998, had been paid and fully expensed in 1998. Conn has a 30% income tax rate. What amount should Conn report as adjusted beginning retained earnings in its 1999 statement of retained earnings?

    a. $420,000
    b. $428,000
    c. $440,000
    d. $442,000

6.   Lore Co. changed from the cash basis of accounting to the accrual basis of accounting during 1999. The cumulative effect of this change should be reported in Lore's 1999 financial statements as a

    a.   Prior period adjustment resulting from the correction of an error.
    b.   Prior period adjustment resulting from the change in accounting principle.
    c.   Component of income before extraordinary item.
    d.   Component of income after extraordinary item.

7.   Bren Co.'s beginning inventory at January 1, 1999, was understated by $26,000, and its ending inventory was overstated by $52,000. As a result, Bren's cost of goods sold for 1999 was

    a.   Understated by $26,000.
    b.   Overstated by $26,000.
    c.   Understated by $78,000.
    d.   Overstated by $78,000.

8.   On January 2, 1999, Air, Inc. agreed to pay its former president $300,000 under a deferred compensation arrangement. Air should have recorded this expense in 1998 but did not do so. Air's reported income tax expense would have been $70,000 lower in 1998 had it properly accrued this deferred compensation. In its December 31, 1999 financial statements, Air should adjust the beginning balance of its retained earnings by a

    a. $230,000 credit.
    b. $230,000 debit.
    c. $300,000 credit.
    d. $370,000 debit.

9.   Net income is understated if, in the first year, estimated salvage value is excluded from the depreciation computation when using the

	Straight-line method	Production or use method
a.	Yes	No
b.	Yes	Yes
c.	No	No
d.	No	Yes

10.   At the end of 1998, Ritzcar Co. failed to accrue sales commissions earned during 1998 but paid in 1999. The error was not repeated in 1999. What was the effect of this

error on 1998 ending working capital and on the 1999 ending retained earnings balance?

	1998 ending working capital	*1999 ending retained earnings*
a.	Overstated	Overstated
b.	No effect	Overstated
c.	No effect	No effect
d.	Overstated	No effect

11. On December 31, 1999, special insurance costs, incurred but unpaid, were not recorded. If these insurance costs were related to work in process, what is the effect of the omission on accrued liabilities and retained earnings in the December 31, 1999 balance sheet?

	Accrued liabilities	*Retained earnings*
a.	No effect	No effect
b.	No effect	Overstated
c.	Understated	No effect
d.	Understated	Overstated

12. Which of the following errors could result in an overstatement of both current assets and stockholders' equity?

- a. An understatement of accrued sales expenses.
- b. Noncurrent note receivable principal is misclassified as a current asset.
- c. Annual depreciation on manufacturing machinery is understated.
- d. Holiday pay expense for administrative employees is misclassified as manufacturing overhead.

PROBLEM

Problem 1   (40 to 50 minutes)

Cord Corp., a nonpublic enterprise, requires audited financial statements for credit purposes. After making normal adjusting entries, but before closing the accounting records for the year ended December 31, 1999, Cord's controller prepared the following financial statements for 1999:

Cord Corp.
STATEMENT OF FINANCIAL POSITION
December 31, 1999

Assets

Cash	$1,225,000
Marketable equity securities	125,000
Accounts receivable	460,000
Allowance for doubtful accounts	(55,000)
Inventories	530,000
Property and equipment	620,000
Accumulated depreciation	(280,000)
Total assets	$2,625,000

Liabilities and Stockholders' Equity

Accounts payable and accrued liabilities	$1,685,000
Income tax payable	110,000
Common stock, $20 par	300,000
Additional paid-in capital	75,000
Retained earnings	455,000
Total liabilities and stockholders' equity	$2,625,000

Cord Corp.
STATEMENT OF INCOME
For the Year Ended December 31, 1999

Net sales	$1,700,000
Operating expenses:	
Cost of sales	570,000
Selling and administrative	448,000
Depreciation	42,000
Total operating expenses	1,060,000
Income before income tax	640,000
Income tax expense	192,000
Net income	$ 448,000

Cord's tax rate for all income items was 30% for all affected years, and it made estimated tax payments when due. Cord has been profitable in the past and expects results in the future to be similar to 1999. During the course of the audit, the following additional information (not considered when the above statements were prepared) was obtained:

1.   The investment portfolio consists of short-term investments, classified as available-for-sale, for which total market value equaled cost at December 31, 1998. On February 2, 1999, Cord sold one investment with a carrying value of $100,000 for $130,000. The total of the sale proceeds was credited to the investment account.

2.   At December 31, 1999, the market value of the remaining securities in the portfolio was $142,000.

3.   The $530,000 inventory total, which was based on a physical count at December 31, 1999, was priced at cost. Subsequently, it was determined that the inventory cost was overstated by $66,000. At December 31, 1999, the inventory's market value approximated the adjusted cost.

4.   Pollution control devices costing $48,000, which is high in relation to the cost of the original equipment, were installed on December 29, 1998, and were charged to repairs in 1998.

5.   The original equipment referred to in Item 4, which had a remaining useful life of 6 years on December 20, 1998, is being depreciated by the straight-line method for both financial and tax reporting.

6.   A lawsuit was filed against Cord in October 1999 claiming damages of $250,000. Cord's legal counsel believes that an unfavorable outcome is probable, and a reasonable estimate of the court's award to the plaintiff is $60,000, which will be paid in 2000 if the case is settled.

7.   Cord determined that its accumulated benefits obligation under the pension plan exceeded the fair value of plan assets by $40,000 at December 31, 1999. Cord has unrecognized prior service cost of $50,000 at December 31, 1999. Cord funds the total pension expense each year.

Required:

Prepare journal entries, without explanations, to record the effects of the foregoing data on Cord's accounting records at December 31, 1999. Do **not** prepare corrected financial statements for 1999. The journal entries should be numbered to correspond with the numbers in the additional information. Include as the last entry any necessary adjustments to the 1999 income tax expense, and support your computations for this entry.

1. a __ __	4. b __ __	7. c __ __	10. d __ __	1st: __/12 = __%
2. b __ __	5. b __ __	8. b __ __	11. c __ __	2nd: __/12 = __%
3. c __ __	6. a __ __	9. b __ __	12. d __ __	

MULTIPLE-CHOICE ANSWER EXPLANATIONS

B. Error Correction

1. (a) The correct amount of 1999 interest expense is $2,040, as computed below.

11/1/98 note	
Interest from 1/1/99 to 10/31/99	
($5,000 x 12% x 10/12)	$500
2/1/99 note	
Interest from 2/1/99 to 7/31/99	
($15,000 x 12% x 6/12)	900
5/1/99 note	
Interest from 5/1/99 to 12/31/99	
($8,000 x 12% x 8/12)	640
Total 1999 interest	$2,040

Since interest expense of $1,500 was recorded, 1999 interest expense was understated by $540 ($2,040 – $1,500).

2. (b) The failure to amortize goodwill in prior years (1997 and 1998) is considered an error. The profession requires that a correction of an error be treated as a prior period adjustment, be recorded in the year in which the error was discovered, and be reported in the financial statements as an adjustment to the beginning balance of retained earnings. Therefore, the $40,000 of amortization that was not expensed in 1997 and 1998 [(1/5 x $100,000) + (1/5 x $100,000)] should be debited to retained earnings. The $20,000 amortization expense for the current year (1/5 x $100,000) is considered a current year adjustment and should be expensed. The journal entry would be

Amortization expense	20,000	
Retained earnings, 1/1/98	40,000	
Goodwill		60,000

3. (c) The error in understating the 1997 ending inventory would have reversed by 1/1/99 (1997 income understated by $60,000; 1998 income overstated by $60,000). The error in overstating the 1998 ending inventory would **not** have been reversed by 1/1/99. This error overstates both 1998 income and the 1/1/99 retained earnings balance by $75,000.

4. (b) A correction of an error is treated as a prior period adjustment, recorded in the year the error is discovered, and is reported in the financial statements as an adjustment to the beginning balance of retained earnings. The adjustment is reported net of the related tax effect. In this case the net-of-tax effect is $28,000 [$40,000 – ($30% x $40,000)]. This should **increase** beginning retained earnings because the understatement of 12/31/98 inventory would have resulted in an overstatement of cost of goods sold and therefore an understatement of retained earnings. Thus, the adjustment 1/1/99 retained earnings is $178,000

($150,000 + $28,000). Tack's journal entry to record the adjustment is

Inventory	40,000	
Retained earnings		28,000
Taxes payable		12,000

5. (b) A correction of an error is treated as a prior period adjustment and is reported in the financial statements as an adjustment to the beginning balance of retained earnings in the year the error is discovered. The adjustment is reported net of the related tax effect. In 1998, insurance expense of $60,000 was recorded. The correct 1998 insurance expense was $20,000 ($60,000 x 1/3). Therefore, before taxes, 1/1/99 retained earnings is understated by $40,000. The net of tax effect is $28,000 [$40,000 – (30% x $40,000)], so the adjusted beginning retained earnings is $428,000 ($400,000 + $28,000).

6. (a) A change in accounting principle is a change from one **generally accepted** principle to another **generally accepted** principle. A correction of an error is the correction of a mathematical mistake, a mistake in the application of an accounting principle, an oversight or misuse of existing facts, or **a change from an unacceptable principle to a generally accepted one**. Therefore, a switch from the cash basis (unacceptable) to the accrual basis (acceptable) is a correction of an error reported as a prior period adjustment.

7. (c) The requirement is to determine the effect of inventory errors on cost of goods sold. The effect of the errors on Bren's 1999 cost of goods sold (CGS) is illustrated below.

BI	– $26,000	CGS understated $26,000
+ P		
CGAS		
– EI	(+ $52,000)	CGS understated 52,000
CGS		CGS understated $78,000

Beginning inventory is the starting point for the CGS computation, so BI errors have a direct effect on CGS. The understatement of BI ($26,000) causes an **understatement** of goods available for sale (CGAS) and thus of CGS. Ending inventory is subtracted in the CGS computation, so EI errors have an inverse effect on CGS. The overstatement of EI ($52,000) means that too much was subtracted in the CGS computation, causing another **understatement** of CGS. Therefore, CGS is understated by a total of $78,000.

8. (b) The failure to record the $300,000 of deferred compensation expense in 1998 is considered an error. The profession requires that the correction of an error be treated as a prior period adjustment. Thus, the requirement is to determine the retroactive adjustment which should be made to the beginning balance of the retained earnings for 1999 (**including** any income tax effect). The net adjustment to beginning retained earnings would be a debit for $230,000 ($300,000 less the income tax benefit of $70,000).

9. (b) The depreciable base used to compute depreciation expense under both the straight line and production methods is equal to the cost less estimated salvage value of the asset. Depreciation expense is overstated and net income is, therefore, understated when the estimated salvage value is excluded from the depreciation computation under both of these methods. Therefore, answer (b) is correct.

10. (d) The entry Ritzcar should have made to accrue sales commissions earned but unpaid at the end of its 1998 fiscal year is

| Commission expense | xxx | |
| Commissions payable | | xxx |

Since Commissions payable is a current liability, the 1998 ending working capital is overstated due to Ritzcar's failure to record this entry. Since this error was not repeated at the end of Ritzcar's 1999 fiscal year, the income impact of the 1998 error "self-corrected" during 1999, when Ritzcar recorded both the earned but unpaid 1998 commissions plus the 1999 earned commissions. Therefore, the 1999 ending retained earnings would not be impacted by the error, and answer (d) is correct.

11. (c) A liability is accrued when an obligation to pay or perform services has been incurred. This is the case even if the liability will not be satisfied until a future date. Therefore, accrued liabilities will be understated on the December 31, 1999, balance sheet because the special insurance costs were not recorded. However, there will be no effect on the December 31, 1999, balance of retained earnings because these costs relate to work in process, and work in process does not affect net income currently. Please note that if the special insurance costs related to goods that were sold, cost of goods sold would have been understated which would have caused both net income and retained earnings to be overstated.

12. (d) The classification of holiday pay expense for administrative employees as manufacturing overhead would result in the capitalization of some or all of these costs as a component of ending inventory, while these costs should be expensed as incurred. This error could overstate ending inventory, a current asset. The overstatement of ending inventory also understates the cost of goods sold (Beginning inventories + Net purchases – Ending inventories = Cost of goods sold), and overstates net income and stockholders' equity. Therefore, answer (d) is correct. Answer (a) is incorrect because the understatement of accrued sales expenses would not affect current assets. Answer (b) is incorrect because the misclassification of the noncurrent note receivable principal as a current asset would have no impact on stockholders' equity. Answer (c) is incorrect because the understatement of depreciation on **manufacturing** machinery would understate the overhead added to inventories, a current asset.

SOLUTION GUIDE

Problem 1   Correcting Journal Entries

1.   This problem requires the preparation of correcting journal entries necessary to reflect the effects of seven items of data given in the problem. In addition, an entry to adjust 1999 income tax expense is required. The solutions approach is to simply go through the additional data, preparing the correcting entry for each item as you come to it.

1.1   On the sale of MES, Cord debited **cash** and credited **MES** for $130,000. It should have credited **MES** for the carrying value of $100,000 and also credited **gain on sale** for $30,000 ($130,000 proceeds less $100,000 carrying value). Therefore, the correcting entry must debit **MES** for $30,000 (to offset the additional $30,000 credited to that account) and credit **gain on sale** for the same amount.

1.2   In the balance sheet given, the MES are reported at $125,000. The first correcting entry included a $30,000 debit to MES. Therefore, the adjusted carrying value is $155,000 ($125,000 + $30,000). Since market value is $142,000, an **unrealized loss** of $13,000 ($155,000 – $142,000) must be recorded as a credit to the MES account and a debit to unrealized loss. Because these securities are carried in an available-for-sale portfolio, the unrealized loss is reported as an element of comprehensive income net of tax in the section termed other comprehensive income and part of accumulated other comprehensive income in the stockholders' equity section of the balance sheet.

1.3   Cord overstated the 12/31/99 inventory by $66,000. Therefore, **inventories** must be credited for $66,000. Since ending inventory was used to compute cost of sales (cost of goods available for sale less ending inventory equals cost of sales), the inventory error means **cost of sales** was understated by $66,000, and therefore this account must be debited.

1.4   The pollution control devices (cost of $48,000) should have been recorded as an asset instead of being expensed in 1998. Therefore, **property and equipment** must be debited for $48,000 in the correcting entry. For tax purposes, apparently the entire $48,000 was also expensed. Thus, Kern owes additional taxes for 1998 of $14,400 ($48,000 x 30%). This amount is credited to **income tax payable**. The prior period adjustment, net of the tax effect ($48,000 – $14,400 = $33,600) is credited to **retained earnings**, since a prior year's earnings (1998) was understated by that amount.

1.5   **Depreciation expense** on the pollution control devices must be recorded for 1999, with an offsetting credit to **accumulated depreciation**. 1999 depreciation is $8,000 ($48,000 x 1/6).

1.6   The **lawsuit liability** must be accrued by debiting **loss on lawsuit** and crediting the liability account because it is both **probable** that a liability has been incurred at 12/31/99 and the amount of the liability is **reasonably estimable** ($60,000).

1.7   SFAS 87 states that a minimum liability must be reported for the excess of the accumulated benefit obligation over the fair value of the plan assets. The amount to be **recorded** is the minimum liability required to be **reported** ($40,000 in this case) plus prepaid pension cost or minus accrued pension cost. There is no prepaid/accrued pension cost in this situation because Cord funds the total pension expense each year, so the amount to be recorded is $40,000. When recording the minimum liability, a **pension liability** account is credited. The debit is to the **intangible asset** account and/or the **contra equity** account. The contra equity account must be used if the debit ($40,000) exceeds the unrecognized prior service cost ($50,000). In this case, it does not, so the entire amount is debited to the intangible asset account.

2.   The final entry required is necessary to adjust 1999 income tax expense.

2.1   The first step is to compute the adjustment to income taxes payable and income tax expense. Income before taxes was reported at $640,000. This amount did not include the gain on sale of MES ($30,000), the increase in cost of goods sold ($66,000), or the increase in depreciation expense ($8,000). After adjusting for these items, **taxable income** is $596,000 ($640,000 + $30,000 – $66,000 – $8,000). Note that the unrealized loss on MES ($13,000) and the accrued loss on lawsuit ($60,000) does not affect **taxable** income because it is not deductible on the tax return until realized. The current portion of income tax expense and income taxes payable is therefore $178,800 (30% x $596,000).

2.2   The unrealized loss on MES ($13,000) and the lawsuit loss ($60,000) are both temporary differences which result in future deductible amounts. A **deferred tax asset** and reduction in income tax expense should be recognized for these future deductible amounts. Therefore, the deferred tax asset and reduction in income tax expense is measured using the tax rate of 30% (30% x $73,000 = $21,900). Corrected total income tax expense is $156,900.

2.3   The adjustment to income tax payable is $13,200 ($192,000 originally recorded less the correct amount of $178,800). Note that the balance in the income tax payable account of $110,000 at 12/31/99 is net of payments made during the year.

2.4   The adjustment to get the correct total **income tax expense** can be plugged into the entry now that the adjustments to income tax payable and deferred tax asset have been computed, or it can be computed as follows. Income tax expense was reported at $192,000. The correct 1999 income tax expense is $156,900 ($178,800 current portion of tax expense less the $21,900 reduction from the future deductible amounts). Therefore, income tax expense must be adjusted with a $35,100 credit ($192,000 – $156,900).

UNOFFICIAL ANSWER

Problem 1   Correcting Journal Entries

Cord Corp.
ADJUSTING JOURNAL ENTRIES
December 31, 1999
(Explanations not required)

	Dr.	Cr.
(1)		
Marketable equity securities	$ 30,000	
Realized gain on sale of marketable equity securities		$ 30,000 [a]
(2)		
Unrealized loss on marketable equity securities (other comprehensive income)	13,000	
Adjustment to reduce marketable equity securities to market value		13,000 [b]
(3)		
Cost of sales	66,000	
Inventories		66,000
(4)		
Property and equipment	48,000	
Income tax payable		14,400 [c]
Retained earnings		33,600 [c]
(5)		
Depreciation	8,000	
Accumulated depreciation		8,000 [d]
(6)		
Estimated loss from lawsuit	60,000	
Estimated liability from lawsuit		60,000
(7)		
Deferred pension cost	40,000	
Additional pension liability		40,000
(8)		
Deferred tax asset	21,900 [i]	
Income tax payable	13,200 [ii]	
Income tax expense		35,100 [iii]

Supporting Computations for Number 8

Corrected total income tax expense for 1999		
Income before income tax, as reported		$640,000
Add adjustment increasing income		
Realized gain on sale of securities		30,000 [1]
		670,000
Deduct adjustments decreasing income		
Increase cost of sales for inventory overstatement	$66,000	
Depreciation on pollution control devices	8,000	74,000
Adjusted taxable income before income tax		$596,000
Corrected current portion income tax expense and income taxes payable		
($596,000 x 30%)		$178,800
Deferred income tax benefits--based on following temporary differences:		
Lawsuit expected to be settled in 2000	$60,000 [6]	
Unrealized loss on short-term marketable equity securities	13,000 [2]	
Total future deductible amounts	$73,000	

[i]	Deferred tax benefit of future deductible amounts ($73,000 x 30%)	21,900
	Corrected total income tax expense	$156,900
[ii]	Income tax expense as reported (all current, no deferred)	$192,000
	Corrected income tax payable and income tax expense	178,800
		$ 13,200
[iii]	Income tax expense, as reported	$192,000
	Corrected total income tax expense	156,900
		$ 35,100

Explanations of Amounts

[a]	Gain on sale of marketable equity securities	
	Selling price	$130,000
	Cost	100,000
	Gain	$ 30,000

[b]	Adjustment to reduce marketable equity securities to market value	
	Marketable equity securities, at cost	
	Balance, 2/2/99 as reported	$125,000
	Adjustment for recording error	30,000
	Adjusted balance, 12/31/99	155,000
	Market valuation, 12/31/99	142,000
	Adjustment required, 12/31/99	$ 13,000

[c]	Prior year adjustment for pollution control devices	
	Cost of installation, 12/29/98	$ 48,000
	Deduct income tax effect ($48,000 x 30%)	14,400
	Credit adjustment to retained earnings, 1/1/99	$ 33,600

[d]	Depreciation for 1999 on pollution control devices	
	Cost of the installation on 12/29/98	$ 48,000
	Depreciation for 1999 ($48,000 ÷ 6 years)	$ 8,000

C. Accounting Changes

1. Changes in Accounting Principle

One type of accounting change which may occur is a change in accounting principle. A change in accounting principle occurs when there is a change from one generally accepted accounting principle to another. A change from an accounting principle that is not generally accepted to a generally accepted method is a correction of an error not a change in principle.

Changes in accounting principles (or the method of applying them) must be justified by management unless they are made in order to comply with a FASB pronouncement. Presumption exists that, once adopted, accounting principles should not be changed for events and transactions of a similar type. Changes in accounting principle may be treated as a retroactive or as a cumulative adjustment to the financial statements. Study the outline of APB 20.

a.   Retroactive effect type changes in accounting principle

A retroactive change in accounting principle is determined by computing the effect on beginning retained earnings of applying the new principle to affected prior years and reporting the amount net of tax in the retained earnings statement as an adjustment to the beginning balance. Additionally, financial statements from earlier periods that are presented with the current period's FS must be retroactively restated. Retroactive restatement means redoing all statements presented as if they had originally been prepared using the new accounting principle. Any part of the cumulative effect which is attributed to financial statements of prior years that are not being presented in the current period should be an adjustment of retained earnings of the earliest period being presented.

There are five special changes that require retroactive restatement of all periods presented as if the new method had been used in all prior periods. These five special changes are

(1) Change from LIFO to another inventory method
(2) Change in method of accounting for long-term contracts
(3) Change to or from the full cost method of accounting for exploration costs in the extractive industries
(4) Any change made by a company first issuing financial statements to the public for the purpose of obtaining additional equity capital or effecting a business combination or registering securities (APB 20, para 29)
(5) Change for which the retroactive approach is mandated by an authoritative pronouncement

When a retroactive restatement is made, the reasons for the change must be disclosed. The effects on net income and earnings per share should also be disclosed for each period presented.

b.   Cumulative effect type changes in accounting principle

All other changes in principle are accounted for as current changes in accordance with the cumulative effect method. When a change in accounting principle is accounted for as a current change, then the entire cumulative effect of the change is reported in the current period's financial statements. The entire cumulative effect would be recorded as an adjustment to an income statement account, and reported as a special item displayed after extraordinary items on the income statement. The cumulative effect should be reported net of tax. The following steps summarize the procedures to account for an accounting change under the cumulative effect method:

1.   **Compute** the prior years' effect of the change on retained earnings at the beginning of the year in which the change is made.
2.   **Use** the new principle in determining the current year's net income.

3. **Report** the effect of the new method on beginning retained earnings less tax effects as "cumulative effect on prior years of new accounting method (described), net of tax" to be displayed after extraordinary items and before net income on the income statement.

4. **Present** comparative years' data as previously reported (no restatement).

It is important to note that under the cumulative effect method there is no restatement of the prior year's financial statements. Instead, "pro forma" (as if) data concerning EPS and net income must be presented as supplementary information for all past years being reported upon. These pro forma data are presented as if the new accounting method had been used in the determination of prior years' EPS and net incomes. The retroactive methodology described above would be used to determine pro forma amounts. Thus, the face of the income statement must disclose the net income and EPS under both the retroactive and cumulative methods. The disclosure of the effects of both methods is intended to provide supplementary information to the users of the financial statements. The following illustrates the pro forma disclosure:

PRO FORMA AMOUNTS ASSUMING RETROACTIVE APPLICATION OF NEW METHOD

	19X9	*19X8*
Income from continuing operations	$xxx	$xxx
Basic earnings per share	x	x
Diluted earnings per share	x	x
Net income	$xxx	xxx
Basic earnings per share	x	x
Diluted earnings per share	x	x

There are two exceptions to be considered when using the cumulative effect method.

(1) Changes in inventory method **to** LIFO, because the cumulative effect is usually not determinable. For changes to LIFO, no recognition is given to any cumulative effect associated with the change. The base year inventory for all subsequent LIFO calculations is the opening inventory under the old method in the year LIFO is adopted.

(2) The application of a depreciation method to **newly** acquired assets that is different than the method that has been applied to existing assets. No cumulative effect results from this type of change.

The following example is adapted from paras 42 and 43 of APB 20. Assume a change in 1999 from accelerated to straight-line depreciation. It describes the

a. Depreciation effect per year (decrease in expense, increase in income)
b. Depreciation effect, net of tax (constant 40%)

Year	Excess of accelerated depreciation over straight-line depreciation	Excess less tax effect
Prior to 1995	$ 20,000	$ 12,000
1995	80,000	48,000
1996	70,000	42,000
1997	50,000	30,000
1998	30,000	18,000
Total at beginning of 1999	$250,000	$150,000

Example income statements, EPS disclosures, and pro forma retroactive disclosures are presented below for 1999 and 1998. (Assume 1,000,000 shares outstanding.)

	1999	*1998*
Income before extraordinary item and cumulative effect of a change in accounting principle	$1,200,000	$1,100,000
Extraordinary item (description)	(40,000)	100,000
Cumulative effect on prior years (to December 31, 1998) of changing to a different depreciation method (net of tax $100,000)	150,000	
Net income	$1,310,000	$1,200,000
Earnings per common share		
Income before extraordinary item and cumulative effect of a change in accounting principle	$ 1.20	$1.10
Extraordinary item	(0.04)	0.10
Cumulative effect on prior years (to December 31, 1998) of changing to a different depreciation method	0.15	
Net income	$ 1.31	$1.20
Pro forma amounts assuming the new depreciation method is applied retroactively--		
Income before extraordinary item	$1,200,000	$1,118,000
Earnings per common share	$1.20	$1.12 (rounded)
Net income	$1,160,000	$1,218,000
Earnings per common share	$1.16	$1.22 (rounded)

Special points to note about the preceding example include

    a. The 1999 income before extraordinary items of $1,200,000 is the same as pro forma income for that year, because the new accounting method was used in 1999.

    b. The 1999 net income is different from the 1999 pro forma net income because the pro forma amount does not include the cumulative effect. The amounts that comprise the cumulative effect are reported as pro forma amounts in the years to which they pertain.

    c. In 1998, both incomes in the income statement differ from those in the pro forma data by $18,000 (depreciation less tax effects).

    d. If this company had a complex capital structure, all EPS amounts, actual and pro forma, would have to be reported as both basic EPS and diluted EPS.

2. **Changes in Accounting Estimates**

    A change in estimate occurs when, based upon new information or experience, a better estimate may be made. Some examples that may require a change in estimate are changes in estimates of useful lives, salvage value, collectibility of receivables, etc. Changes in estimates should be treated prospectively--that is, no retroactive restatement. For example, if the useful life of an asset is increased from 10 years to 15 years during year 6, the remaining depreciable cost is amortized over the years 6 through 15.

    Sometimes an event may have characteristics of both a change in accounting principle and a change in estimate; in these cases the change should be treated as a change in estimate.

3. **Change in Reporting Entity**

    The final type of accounting change which may occur is a change in reporting entity. A change in reporting entity occurs when a change in the structure of the organization is made which results in financial statements that represent a different or changed entity. Some examples of a change in reporting entity include presenting consolidated statements in place of individual statements, a pooling of interests, a change in subsidiaries, or a change in the use of the equity method for an investment.

A change in reporting entity should be disclosed by retroactively restating all of the prior period financial statements presented. A disclosure of the type of change and the reasons for the change should be added to the financial statements in the year of the change. The disclosure should also include the effect of the change on the net income before extraordinary items, net income, and earnings per share.

The following chart summarizes the three types of accounting changes and the related financial statement treatment and disclosure requirements:

TYPES OF ACCOUNTING CHANGES

Type of accounting change	Definition	Financial statement treatment	Financial statement disclosure
1. Change in Accounting Principle	Change from the use of one generally accepted accounting principle to another generally accepted accounting principle	**Cumulative:** Required for all items not requiring retroactive treatment. Record the entire effects of the change net of tax in the current period. Record after extraordinary items on the income statement. No prior period restatement occurs.	Income statement must disclose pro forma net income and EPS for all periods presented, as if the retroactive method had been used.
		Retroactive: Required for 5 special changes listed in module. Restatement of all prior period financial statements presented is required.	Disclose the effect of the change on prior net incomes and EPS presented in the year of the change.
2. Change in Estimate	Change of estimated FS amount based on new information or experience	**Prospective:** Report the current period's financial statements in accordance with the new method. No restatement of prior period information is required.	Disclose the effect on income before extraordinary items, net income, and related per share amounts if the change affects several future periods.
3. Change in Reporting Entity	Change that results in the financial statements representing a different entity	**Retroactive:** Restate all prior periods presented.	Disclose the type of change and the reasons for the change and the related effects on net income and EPS for all prior periods presented.

MULTIPLE-CHOICE QUESTIONS (1-22)

1. On January 1, 1997, Bray Company purchased for $240,000 a machine with a useful life of 10 years and no salvage value. The machine was depreciated by the double-declining balance method and the carrying amount of the machine was $153,600 on December 31, 1998. Bray changed retroactively to the straight-line method on January 1, 1999. Bray can justify the change. What should be the depreciation expense on this machine for the year ended December 31, 1999?

    a. $15,360
    b. $19,200
    c. $24,000
    d. $30,720

Items 2 and 3 are based on the following:

On January 1, 1997, Warren Co. purchased a $600,000 machine, with a 5-year useful life and no salvage value. The machine was depreciated by an accelerated method for book and tax purposes. The machine's carrying amount was $240,000 on December 31, 1998. On January 1, 1999, Warren changed retroactively to the straight-line method for financial statement purposes. Warren can justify the change. Warren's income tax rate is 30%.

2. In its 1999 income statement, what amount should Warren report as the cumulative effect of this change?

    a. $120,000
    b. $ 84,000
    c. $ 36,000
    d. $0

3. On January 1, 1999, what amount should Warren report as deferred income tax liability as a result of the change?

    a. $120,000
    b. $ 72,000
    c. $ 36,000
    d. $0

4. On January 2, 1999, to better reflect the variable use of its only machine, Holly, Inc. elected to change its method of depreciation from the straight-line method to the units of production method. The original cost of the machine on January 2, 1997, was $50,000, and its estimated life was 10 years. Holly estimates that the machine's total life is 50,000 machine hours.

Machine hours usage was 8,500 during 1997 and 3,500 during 1998.

Holly's income tax rate is 30%. Holly should report the accounting change in its 1999 financial statements as a(n)

    a.   Cumulative effect of a change in accounting principle of $2,000 in its income statement. *correct*
    b.   Adjustment to beginning retained earnings of $2,000.
    c.   Cumulative effect of a change in accounting principle of $1,400 in its income statement.
    d.   Adjustment to beginning retained earnings of $1,400. *retro*

5. The cumulative effect of a change in accounting principle should be recorded separately as a component of income after continuing operations, when the change is from the

    a.   Cash basis of accounting for vacation pay to the accrual basis.
    b.   Straight-line method of depreciation for previously recorded assets to the double declining balance method.
    c.   Presentation of statements of individual companies to their inclusion in consolidated statements.
    d.   Completed-contract method of accounting for long-term construction-type contracts to the percentage-of-completion method.

6. When a company changes from the straight-line method of depreciation for previously recorded assets to the double-declining balance method, which of the following should be reported?

	Cumulative effects of change in accounting principle	Pro forma effects of retroactive application
a.	No	No
b.	No	Yes
c.	Yes	Yes
d.	Yes	No

Items 7 and 8 are based on the following:

During 1999, Orca Corp. decided to change from the FIFO method of inventory valuation to the weighted-average method. Inventory balances under each method were as follows:

	FIFO	Weighted-average
January 1, 1999	$71,000	$77,000
December 31, 1999	79,000	83,000

Orca's income tax rate is 30%.

7. In its 1999 financial statements, what amount should Orca report as the cumulative effect of this accounting change?

    a. $2,800
    b. $4,000
    c. $4,200
    d. $6,000

8. Orca should report the cumulative effect of this accounting change as a(n)

    a.   Prior period adjustment.
    b.   Component of income from continuing operations.
    c.   Extraordinary item.
    d.   Component of income after extraordinary items.

9. On January 1, 1999, Roem Corp. changed its inventory *retro* method to FIFO from LIFO for both financial and income tax reporting purposes. The change resulted in a $500,000 increase in the January 1, 1999 inventory. Assume that the income tax rate for all years is 30%. The cumulative effect of the accounting change should be reported by Roem in its 1999

    a.   Retained earnings statement as a $350,000 addition to the beginning balance.
    b.   Income statement as a $350,000 cumulative effect of accounting change.

c. Retained earnings statement as a $500,000 addition to the beginning balance.

d. Income statement as a $500,000 cumulative effect of accounting change.

10. Is the cumulative effect of an inventory pricing change on prior years earnings reported separately between extraordinary items and net income for a change from

	LIFO to weighted-average?	FIFO to weighted-average?
a.	Yes	Yes√
b.	Yes	No
c.	No	No
d.	No	Yes

11. On August 31, 1999, Harvey Co. decided to change from the FIFO periodic inventory system to the weighted-average periodic inventory system. Harvey is on a calendar year basis. The cumulative effect of the change is determined

a. As of January 1, 1999.

b. As of August 31, 1999.

c. During the 8 months ending August 31, 1999, by a weighted-average of the purchases.

d. During 1999 by a weighted-average of the purchases.

12. In 1999, Brighton Co. changed from the individual item approach to the aggregate approach in applying the lower of FIFO cost or market to inventories. The cumulative effect of this change should be reported in Brighton's financial statements as a

a. Prior period adjustment, with separate disclosure.

b. Component of income from continuing operations, with separate disclosure.

c. Component of income from continuing operations, without separate disclosure.

d. Component of income after continuing operations, with separate disclosure.

13. On January 1, 1999, Poe Construction, Inc. changed to the percentage-of-completion method of income recognition for financial statement reporting but not for income tax reporting. Poe can justify this change in accounting principle. As of December 31, 1998, Poe compiled data showing that income under the completed-contract method aggregated $700,000. If the percentage-of-completion method had been used, the accumulated income through December 31, 1998, would have been $880,000. Assuming an income tax rate of 40% for all years, the cumulative effect of this accounting change should be reported by Poe in the 1999

a. Retained earnings statement as a $180,000 credit adjustment to the beginning balance.

b. Income statement as a $180,000 credit.

c. Retained earnings statement as a $108,000 credit adjustment to the beginning balance.

d. Income statement as a $108,000 credit.

14. On January 1, 1996, Taft Co. purchased a patent for $714,000. The patent is being amortized over its remaining legal life of 15 years expiring on January 1, 2011. During 1999, Taft determined that the economic benefits of the patent would not last longer than 10 years from the date of ac-

quisition. What amount should be reported in the balance sheet for the patent, net of accumulated amortization, at December 31, 1999?

a. $428,400

b. $489,600

c. $504,000

d. $523,600

15. On January 1, 1996, Flax Co. purchased a machine for $528,000 and depreciated it by the straight-line method using an estimated useful life of 8 years with no salvage value. On January 1, 1999, Flax determined that the machine had a useful life of 6 years from the date of acquisition and will have a salvage value of $48,000. An accounting change was made in 1999 to reflect these additional data. The accumulated depreciation for this machine should have a balance at December 31, 1999 of

a. $292,000

b. $308,000

c. $320,000

d. $352,000

16. How should the effect of a change in accounting estimate be accounted for?

a. By restating amounts reported in financial statements of prior periods.

b. By reporting pro forma amounts for prior periods.

c. As a prior period adjustment to beginning retained earnings.

d. In the period of change and future periods if the change affects both.

17. During 1999, Krey Co. increased the estimated quantity of copper recoverable from its mine. Krey uses the units of production depletion method. As a result of the change, which of the following should be reported in Krey's 1999 financial statements?

	Cumulative effect of a change in accounting principle	Pro forma effects of retroactive application of new depletion base
a.	Yes	Yes
b.	Yes	No
c.	No	No
d.	No	Yes

18. Oak Co. offers a 3-year warranty on its products. Oak previously estimated warranty costs to be 2% of sales. Due to a technological advance in production at the beginning of 1999, Oak now believes 1% of sales to be a better estimate of warranty costs. Warranty costs of $80,000 and $96,000 were reported in 1997 and 1998, respectively. Sales for 1999 were $5,000,000. What amount should be disclosed in Oak's 1999 financial statements as warranty expense?

a. $ 50,000

b. $ 88,000

c. $100,000

d. $138,000

19. For 1998, Pac Co. estimated its 2-year equipment warranty costs based on $100 per unit sold in 1995. Experience during 1999 indicated that the estimate should have been based on $110 per unit. The effect of this $10 difference from the estimate is reported

   a.   In 1999 income from continuing operations.

   b.   As an accounting change, net of tax, below 1999 income from continuing operations.

   c.   As an accounting change requiring 1998 financial statements to be restated.

   d.   As a correction of an error requiring 1998 financial statements to be restated.

20. The effect of a change in accounting principle that is inseparable from the effect of a change in accounting estimate should be reported

   a.   By restating the financial statements of all prior periods presented.

   b.   As a correction of an error.

   c.   As a component of <u>income</u> from continuing operations, in the period of change and future periods if the change affects both.

   d.   As a separate disclosure after income from continuing operations, in the period of change and future periods if the change affects both.

21. A company has included in its consolidated financial statements this year a subsidiary acquired several years ago that was appropriately excluded from consolidation last year. This results in

   a.   An accounting change that should be reported prospectively.

   b.   An accounting change that should be reported by restating the financial statements of all prior periods presented.

   c.   A correction of an error.

   d.   Neither an accounting change nor a correction of an error.

22. Which of the following statements is correct regarding accounting changes that result in financial statements that are, in effect, the statements of a different reporting entity?

   a.   Cumulative-effect adjustments should be reported as separate items on the financial statements pertaining to the year of change.

   b.   No restatements or adjustments are required if the changes involve consolidated methods of accounting for subsidiaries.

   c.   No restatements or adjustments are required if the changes involve the cost or equity methods of accounting for investments.

   d.   The financial statements of all prior periods presented should be restated.

OTHER OBJECTIVE QUESTIONS

Problem 1   (15 to 25 minutes)

This question consists of 10 items. Select the **best** answer for each item. Use a No. 2 pencil to blacken the appropriate ovals on the Objective Answer Sheet to indicate your answers. **Answer all items**. Your grade will be based on the total number of correct answers.

On January 2, 1999, Quo, Inc. hired Reed to be its controller. During the year, Reed, working closely with Quo's president and outside accountants, made changes in accounting policies, corrected several errors dating from 1998and before, and instituted new accounting policies.

Quo's 1999 financial statements will be presented in comparative form with its 1998 financial statements.

Required:

Items 1 through 10 represent Quo's transactions. List A represents possible classifications of these transactions as: a change in accounting principle, a change in accounting estimate, a correction of an error in previously presented financial statements, or neither an accounting change nor an accounting error.

List B represents the general accounting treatment for these transactions. These treatments are:

• Cumulative effect approach--Include the cumulative effect of the adjustment resulting from the accounting change or error correction in the 1999 financial statements, and do **not** restate the 1998 financial statements.

• Retroactive restatement approach--Restate the 1998 financial statements and adjust 1998 beginning retained earnings if the error or change affects a period prior to 1998.

• Prospective approach--Report 1999 and future financial statements on the new basis, but do **not** restate 1998 financial statements.

For each item, select one from List A and one from List B and blacken the corresponding ovals on the Objective Answer Sheet.

List A (Select one)	*List B (Select one)*
A. Change in accounting principle.	X. Cumulative effect approach.
B. Change in accounting estimate.	Y. Retroactive restatement approach.
C. Correction of an error in previously presented financial statements.	Z. Prospective approach.
D. Neither an accounting change nor an accounting error.	

Items to be answered

1. Quo manufactures heavy equipment to customer specifications on a contract basis. On the basis that it is preferable, accounting for these long-term contracts was switched from the completed-contract method to the percentage-of-completion method.

2. As a result of a production breakthrough, Quo determined that manufacturing equipment previously depreciated over 15 years should be depreciated over 20 years.

3. The equipment that Quo manufactures is sold with a 5-year warranty. Because of a production breakthrough, Quo reduced its computation of warranty costs from 3% of sales to 1% of sales.

4. Quo changed from LIFO to FIFO to account for its finished goods inventory.

5. Quo changed from FIFO to average cost to account for its raw materials and work in process inventories.

6. Quo sells extended service contracts on its products. Because related services are performed over several years, in 1999 Quo changed from the cash method to the accrual method of recognizing income from these service contracts.

7. During 1999, Quo determined that an insurance premium paid and entirely expensed in 1998 was for the period January 1, 1998, through January 1, 2000.

8. Quo changed its method of depreciating office equipment from an accelerated method to the straight-line method to more closely reflect costs in later years.

9. Quo instituted a pension plan for all employees in 1999 and adopted Statement of Financial Accounting Standards 87, *Employers' Accounting for Pensions*. Quo had not previously had a pension plan.

10. During 1999, Quo increased its investment in Worth, Inc. from a 10% interest, purchased in 1998, to 30%, and acquired a seat on Worth's board of directors. As a result of its increased investment, Quo changed its method of accounting for investment in subsidiary from the cost adjusted for fair value method to the equity method.

PROBLEM

Problem 1   (15 to 25 minutes)

Boulder Company appropriately changed its depreciation method for its production machinery from the double-declining balance method to the production method effective January 1, 1999.

In addition, effective January 1, 1999, Boulder appropriately changed the salvage values used in computing depreciation for its office equipment.

On December 31, 1999, Boulder appropriately changed the specific subsidiaries constituting the group of companies for which consolidated financial statements are presented.

Required:

a.   Identify any accounting changes in the three situations described above. For each accounting change identified, indicate whether Boulder should show:

   •   The cumulative effect of a change in accounting principle in net income of the period of change.
   •   Pro forma effects of retroactive application for all prior periods presented currently.
   •   Restatement of the financial statements of all prior periods presented currently.

b.   **1.**   Why are accounting principles, once adopted, normally continued?
   2.   What is the rationale for disclosure of a change from one generally accepted accounting principle to another generally accepted accounting principle?

Problem 2   (15 to 25 minutes)

On January 1, 1999, Windsor Corp. made the following changes in its accounting policies:

   •   Changed from the LIFO inventory method to the FIFO inventory method.
   •   Adopted the straight-line depreciation method for all future machinery acquisitions, but continued to use sum-of-the-years' digits depreciation method for all machinery purchased before 1999.
   •   Changed from the cash to the accrual basis of accounting for accumulated vacation pay.

Windsor prepares 2-year comparative financial statements.

Required:

a.   What type of accounting change is the change from the LIFO to the FIFO inventory costing method? How should Windsor report this change in its 1999 comparative financial statements?

b.   What type of accounting change is Windsor's change from the sum-of-the-years' digits to the straight-line depreciation method for all machinery purchased after 1998? How should Windsor report this change?

c.   What type of change occurs when recognition of vacation pay expense is changed from the cash basis to the accrual basis? How should Windsor report this change?

MULTIPLE-CHOICE ANSWERS

1. c __ __	7. c __ __	12. d __ __	17. c __ __	21. b __ __
2. b __ __	8. d __ __	13. c __ __	18. a __ __	22. d __ __
3. c __ __	9. a __ __	14. b __ __	19. a __ __	
4. c __ __	10. d __ __	15. a __ __	20. c __ __	
5. b __ __	11. a __ __	16. d __ __		1st: __/22 = __%
6. c __ __				2nd: __/22 = __%

MULTIPLE-CHOICE ANSWER EXPLANATIONS

C.1. Changes in Accounting Principles

1. (c) Per APB 20, when a change in principle is made, generally the current or catch-up approach is used. The cumulative effect of the adjustment of prior years is reported in the current income statement, and the new method is used in the current year. Do not be misled by the statement in the question that says Bray changed retroactively. The term retroactive is being used in this question to refer to the way in which the catch-up or cumulative amount is computed, not the manner of reporting it. In comparative financial statements, no changes are made to the previously published financial statements for catch-up adjustments as an accounted for catch-up or cumulative type change. In this case the cumulative effect is $38,400 ($86,400 double declining balance accumulated depreciation – $48,000 straight-line accumulated depreciation). The journal entry to reflect this cumulative effect would be

Accumulated depreciation	38,400	
Cumulative effect		38,400

In 1999, depreciation expense would be computed using straight-line depreciation, computed as follows:

Depreciation exp. is $24,000 ($240,000 ÷ 10).

Depreciation expense	24,000	
Accumulated depreciation		24,000

2. (b) Per APB 20, a change in principle is generally recorded using the current approach. The cumulative effect of the adjustment on prior years is reported in the current income statement net of the related tax effect. In this case, the accumulated depreciation account must be decreased by $120,000 [$360,000 – ($600,000 x 2/5)], the excess of accelerated depreciation over straight-line. The tax effect is $36,000 (30% x $120,000), so the cumulative effect reported is $84,000 ($120,000 – $36,000). The journal entry is

Accum. depr.	120,000	
Cum. eff.		84,000
Def. tax liability		36,000

3. (c) Per APB 20, a change in principle is generally recorded using the current approach. The cumulative effect of the adjustment on prior years is reported in the current income statement net of the related tax effect. The cause of the tax effect is that while **before the change**, the tax basis and accounting book value of the asset were both $240,000, and **after the change**, the tax basis remains at $240,000 but the accounting book value is now $360,000 [$600,000 – (2/5 x $600,000)]. When the book value of an asset is greater than its tax basis due to a temporary difference, the result is future taxable amounts for which a deferred tax liability must be recorded. The deferred tax liability is the future tax rate times the future taxable amounts [$30% x ($360,000 – $240,000) = $36,000]

4. (c) Per APB 20, when a change in principle is made, generally, the **current** approach is used. The cumulative effect of the change on prior years, net of tax, is reported in the current income statement, and the new method is used in the current year. Depreciation recorded in the prior years (1996-97) using the straight-line method totaled $10,000 [($50,000 x 1/10) x 2]. If the units of production method had been used, depreciation would have been $12,000 [($50,000/50,000) x (8,500 + 3,500)]. Therefore, the cumulative effect on prior years before taxes is $2,000 ($12,000 – $10,000), and the net-of-tax effect is $1,400 [$2,000 – (30% x $2,000)]. Using the current approach, this amount is recorded as a cumulative effect in the income statement rather than as an adjustment to the beginning balance of retained earnings.

5. (b) The requirement is to determine which accounting change should be reported as the cumulative effect of a change in accounting principle. Per APB 20, a change from straight-line depreciation to the double declining balance method should be reported as a cumulative effect of a change in accounting principle after income from continuing operations. Therefore, answer (b) is correct. Answer (a) is incorrect because a change from the cash basis to the accrual basis of accounting is a change from non GAAP to GAAP accounted for as the correction of an error. Answer (c) is incorrect because a change in reporting entity requires restatement of the financial statements of all prior periods presented in order to show financial information for the new reporting entity for all periods (APB 20, para 34). Answer (d) is incorrect because a change in the method of accounting for long-term contracts qualifies as a "special" change under APB 20, para 27, requiring restatement of prior periods as if the new method had been used.

6. (c) The requirement is to determine whether a change in depreciation method from straight-line to double-declining balance should be reported as a cumulative effect of a change in accounting principle and if the pro forma effects of retroactive application should also be reported. Answer (c) is correct because APB 20, paras 20 and 21, requires the presentation of the cumulative effect of the change and the pro forma effects of retroactive application (for a change in accounting principle). Additionally, the pro forma effects of retroactive application are to be shown on the face of the income statement in a separate section, below earnings per share. Answers (a), (b), and (d) are incorrect.

7.   (c)   The cumulative effect of a change in accounting principle is the cumulative effect on prior years' income as if the new method had been used in those prior years. For the years prior to 1999, beginning inventory would be the same for both methods ($0 inventory at the formation of the firm), and ending inventory would be $71,000 (FIFO) or $77,000 (WA). Therefore, the cumulative effect on prior years' income, before taxes, would be $6,000 ($77,000 – $71,000). Since APB 20 requires that a cumulative effect be recorded net of the related tax effect, Orca should report a cumulative effect of $4,200 [$6,000 – (30% x $6,000)].

8.   (d)   Per APB 20, a change in accounting principle generally should be recognized by including in the net income of the period of change the cumulative effect, based on retroactive computation, of changing to the new accounting principle. The cumulative effect is to be reported as a special item after extraordinary items [answer (d)]. Only retroactive-type accounting changes (not cumulative effect-type) and error corrections are reported as prior period adjustments [answer (a)]. Answer (b) is incorrect because the cumulative effect is reported separately after income from continuing operations. Answer (c) is incorrect because extraordinary items are a separate category distinct from cumulative effect of change in accounting principle, and are defined as unusual and infrequent nonrecurring events which have material effects.

9.   (a)   APB 20 states that a change in inventory methods from LIFO is one of the exceptions requiring the use of the **retroactive** approach rather than the **current** approach. The cumulative effect at the beginning of the period of change is entered directly to retained earnings as a prior period adjustment, and the prior year statements are retroactively restated. The cumulative effect is recorded net of the related tax effect. In this case, the cumulative effect is $350,000 [$500,000 – (30% x $500,000)].

The journal entry is

Inventory	500,000	
Retained earnings		350,000
Deferred tax liability		150,000

Answer (c) is incorrect because the amount is not net of tax. Answers (b) and (d) are incorrect because the **current** approach is used [and (d) is not net of tax].

10.   (d)   Per APB 20, para 27, certain "special" changes in accounting principle are reported by retroactively applying the new method in restatements of prior periods including reporting the cumulative effect of the change as an adjustment to the beginning balance of retained earnings. A change from the LIFO method of inventory pricing to another method is designated as such a change. In contrast, per para 20, a change from FIFO to weighted-average should be accounted for by presenting the cumulative effect of the change in the income statement between the captions "extraordinary items" and "net income." Therefore, answer (d) is correct and answers (a), (b), and (c) are incorrect.

11.   (a)   Per APB 20, para 20, the amount shown in the income statement for the cumulative effect of changing to a new accounting principle is the difference between (a) the amount of retained earnings **at the beginning of the period** of a change and (b) the amount of retained earnings that would have been reported at that date if the new accounting principle had been applied retroactively for all prior periods which would have been affected and by recognizing only the direct effects of the change and related income tax effect. Therefore, answer (a) is correct.

12.   (d)   Per APB 20, para 7, a change in accounting principle includes both accounting principles and practices and the methods of applying them. Such a change should be recognized by including the cumulative effect, based on retroactive computation, of changing to the new accounting principle in the net income of the period of the change. The effect of adopting the new accounting principle on income before extraordinary items (if any) and net income of the period of the change should be disclosed. Therefore, answer (d) is correct. Answers (b) and (c) are incorrect because the cumulative effect of the change is **excluded** from income from continuing operations due to the unique nature of this component of net income. Answer (a) is incorrect because corrections of errors, not accounting changes, are treated as prior period adjustments.

13.   (c)   The requirement is to indicate how a change in accounting principle from the completed-contract method to the percentage-of-completion method should be reported. Per para 27 of APB 20, a change in the method of accounting for long-term contracts is one of the exceptions requiring the use of the **retroactive**, rather than the **current**, approach. The cumulative effect at the beginning of the period of change is entered directly to retained earnings as a prior period adjustment, and prior year statements are retroactively restated. The cumulative effect is recorded net of the related tax effect. In this case, the cumulative effect is $108,000 [($880,000 – $700,000) x (1 – .40)]. The journal entry is as follows:

Construction-in-progress	180,000	
Deferred taxes		72,000
Retained earnings		108,000

Answer (a) is incorrect because the effect is not shown net of tax. Answers (b) and (d) are incorrect because they apply the current approach instead of the retroactive approach.

C.2.   Change in Accounting Estimates

14.   (b)   This situation is a change in accounting estimate and should be accounted for currently and prospectively. From 1/1/96 to 12/31/98, patent amortization was recorded using a 15-year life. Yearly amortization was $47,600 ($714,000 ÷ 15), accumulated amortization at 12/31/98 was $142,800 ($47,600 x 3), and the book value of the patent at 12/31/98 was $571,200 ($714,000 – $142,800). Beginning in 1999, this book value must be amortized over its remaining useful life of 7 years (10 years – 3 years). Therefore, 1999 amortization is $81,600 ($571,200 ÷ 7) and the 12/31/99 book value is $489,600 ($571,200 – $81,600).

15.   (a)   From 1/1/96 to 12/31/98, depreciation was recorded using an 8-year life. Yearly depreciation was $66,000 ($528,000 ÷ 8), and accumulated depreciation at 12/31/98 was $198,000 (3 x $66,000). In 1999, the estimated useful life was changed to 6 years total with a salvage value of $48,000. Therefore, the 12/31/98 book value ($528,000 – $198,000 = $330,000) is depreciated down to the $48,000 salvage value over a remaining useful life of 3 years (6 years total – 3 years already recorded). 1999 depreciation expense is $94,000 [($330,000 – $48,000) ÷ 3], increasing accumulated depreciation to $292,000 ($198,000 + $94,000).

16. (d) Para 31 of APB 20 states that changes in accounting estimate are to be accounted for in the period of change and in future periods if the change affects both (i.e., **prospectively**). Therefore, answer (d) is correct. Answer (b) is incorrect because pro forma amounts are presented for changes in accounting principle accounted for using the **current** (cumulative effect) approach. Answers (a) and (c) are incorrect because they apply to **retroactive**-type changes in principle and error correction, respectively.

17. (c) APB 20, para 10, provides examples of items for which estimates are required to prepare financial statements. Recoverable mineral reserves is one of the provided examples. Paragraph 31 of APB 20 states that the effect of a change in accounting estimate should be accounted for in (a) the period of change if the change affects that period only, or (b) the period of change and future periods if the change affects both. Paragraph 31 further states that a change in an estimate should not be accounted for by restating amounts reported in financial statements of prior periods or by reporting pro forma amounts for prior periods. Therefore, answer (c) is correct.

18. (a) A change in estimated warranty costs due to technological advances in production qualifies as a change in accounting estimate. Changes in estimate are treated prospectively; there is no retroactive restatement, and the new estimate is used in current and future years. Therefore, in 1999, Oak should use the new estimate of 1% and report warranty expense of $50,000 ($5,000,000 x 1%).

19. (a) A change in equipment warranty costs based on additional information obtained through experience qualifies as a change in accounting estimate. Changes in estimate should be accounted for in the period of change as a component of income from continuing operations and in future periods if necessary. Therefore, answer (a) is correct. Answer (b) is incorrect because accounting changes reported net of tax below income from continuing operations are cumulative effects of changes in accounting principle. Answers (c) and (d) are incorrect because no restatement is required for a change in estimate.

20. (c) Per APB 20, para 11, the effect of a change in accounting principle which is inseparable from the effect of a change in accounting estimate should be accounted for as a change in accounting estimate. Answer (c) is correct and answer (d) is incorrect because changes in estimate should be accounted for in the period of change and also in any affected future periods as a component of income from continuing operations (APB 20, para 31). Answer (a) is incorrect because financial statements are only restated for "special" changes in accounting principle, changes in entity,

and changes due to an error. Answer (b) is incorrect because errors include mathematical mistakes, mistakes in applying accounting principles, oversights or misuse of available facts, and changes from unacceptable accounting principles to GAAP (APB 20, para 13). The situation described in this question does not meet the description of an error.

C.3. Change in Reporting Entity

21. (b) The requirement is the determination of the consequences of including a subsidiary in the current year's statements when it was appropriately excluded in last year's. Per APB 20, para 12, when (1) consolidated or combined statements are presented in place of individual statements; (2) there is a change in the group of subsidiaries for which consolidated statements are prepared [answer (b)]; (3) there is a change in companies included in combined statements; or (4) there is a business combination accounted for as a pooling of interests, then a change in the reporting entity has occurred. Such changes should be reported by restating the financial statements of all prior periods presented to show financial information for the new reporting entity for all periods (APB 20, para 34). Answer (a) is incorrect because retroactive restatement is required. Answer (c) is incorrect since errors consist of correcting mathematical mistakes, mistakes in applying principles, oversights or misuse of avoidable facts, and changes from unacceptable to acceptable GAAP. Answer (d) is incorrect since a change in reporting entity is an accounting change.

22. (d) An accounting change that results in financial statements that are, in effect, the statements of a different reporting entity is treated as a change in reporting entity. Per APB 20, when a change in reporting entity occurs, it should be reported by restating the financial statements of all prior periods presented to show financial information for the new reporting entity for all periods [answer (d)]. Answer (a) is incorrect because cumulative effect adjustments are not reported when the retroactive approach is used. Answers (b) and (c) are incorrect because a change in entity **does** require restatement.

OTHER OBJECTIVE ANSWERS AND ANSWER EXPLANATIONS

Problem 1

1. (A,Y)   This situation represents a change in the method of accounting for long-term construction-type contracts and requires retroactive restatement of past financial statements.

2.   (B,Z)   This situation is not a change in accounting principle but is a change in an estimate and should be handled prospectively.

3.   (B,Z)   This situation is a change in an estimate. The change in the percentage of warranty costs is not a change in accounting principle. Changes in estimate are handled prospectively.

4. (A,Y)   This situation is a change from one acceptable accounting principle to another and requires retroactive restatement.

5. (A,X)   This situation is a change from one acceptable accounting method to another and requires the cumulative effect approach.

6. (C,Y)   The use of the cash method is considered an error since that method is generally **not** acceptable. The switch to an acceptable method (accrual) is considered the correction of an error and requires the retroactive restatement approach.

7. (C,Y)   The write-off of the insurance premium was an error. Since comparative financial statements are prepared, past years must be corrected using the retroactive restatement approach even though this error is self-correcting after 2 years.

8. (A,X)   This situation is a change in method which is considered a change in principle and requires the cumulative effect approach.

9. (D,Z)   Since the company did not previously account for pensions this situation is simply the adoption of an appropriate accounting principle for pensions. No change in principle occurs.

10.   (D,Y)   Quo's increase in ownership interest (10% to 30%) and its acquisition of a seat on Worth's board of directors has given Quo the ability to exercise significant influence in the operating decisions of Worth. Therefore, according to APB 18, Quo should adopt the equity method to account for its investment in Worth. The cost adjusted for fair value method is no longer applicable due to the change in Quo's investment in Worth. However, the change from the cost adjusted for fair value method to the equity method is not a change in accounting principle. A change in accounting principle occurs when an accounting principle different from the one used previously for reporting purposes is adopted. For a change to occur, a choice between two or more accounting principles must exist (APB 20, para 8). In this case, the change in Quo's situation dictates that the equity method be used to account for the investment. Quo's current economic situation is clearly different and this necessitates the adoption of a different accounting principle (APB 20, para 8). Consequently, this is not an accounting change. However, APB 18 requires that the investment account be retroactively restated to reflect balances as if the equity method had always been used.

ACCOUNTING CHANGES

ANSWER OUTLINE

Problem 1   Types of Accounting Changes

a.   Changes in depreciation method is change in accounting principle
   Show cumulative effect of change in accounting principle in net income of period of change
   Show pro forma effects of retroactive application for all prior periods presented currently
   Do not restate FS of all prior periods presented currently
   Change in salvage values is change in accounting estimate
   Do not report cumulative effect
   Do not report pro forma effects
   Do not restate prior period FS
   Change in subsidiaries constituting group of companies for consolidated FS is change in reporting entity
   Do not report cumulative effect
   Do not report pro forma effects
   Restate FS of prior periods presented currently

b.   1.   Accounting principles normally continued
      Consistency enhances comparability of accounting information across accounting periods
      Consistency increases usefulness of FS
   2.   Disclosure of change in accounting principle
      Avoids misleading FS users
      Presumption exists that once adopted, accounting principle should not be changed
      For events and transactions of similar type

UNOFFICIAL ANSWER

Problem 1   Types of Accounting Changes

a.   Boulder's change in depreciation method is a change in accounting principle. This change in accounting principle should show the cumulative effect of a change in accounting principle in net income of the period of change, and the pro forma effects of retroactive application for all prior periods presented currently. Financial statements of prior periods should not be restated.

Boulder's change in salvage values is a change in accounting estimate. Boulder would not report a cumulative effect, nor pro forma effects, nor would prior period financial statements be restated.

Boulder's change in the specific subsidiaries constituting the group of companies for which consolidated financial statements are presented is a change in reporting entity. Neither the cumulative effect nor the pro forma effects of the change should be reported. However, financial statements of prior periods presented currently should be restated.

b.   1.   Consistent use of accounting principles from one accounting period to another enhances the comparability of accounting information across accounting periods, and thus increases the usefulness of financial statements.

2.   If a change in accounting principle occurs, the nature and effect of a change in accounting principle should be disclosed to avoid misleading financial statement users. Disclosure is required because there is a presumption that an accounting principle once adopted should not be changed in accounting for events and transactions of a similar type.

ANSWER OUTLINE

Problem 2   Types of Accounting Changes

a.   Change from LIFO to FIFO
   Change in accounting principle
   Restate 1998 FS
      Adjust for effect on 1/1/98 RE
   Disclosures
      For 1999
         Nature and justification for change
      For all periods presented
         Effects on IS components

b.   Change from sum-of-the-years' digits
   Change in accounting principle
   1998 FS unaffected
   No cumulative effect in 1999
      Because change not being applied to existing assets
   Disclosures for 1999
      Nature and justification for change
      Effect on 1999 income components

c.   Change from cash basis to accrual basis
   Error correction
      Change from non GAAP to GAAP
   Restate 1998 FS
      Adjust for effect on 1/1/95 RE
   Disclosures for 1999
      Nature and details of corrections

UNOFFICIAL ANSWER

Problem 2   Types of Accounting Changes

a.   A change from the LIFO inventory method to the FIFO inventory method is a change in accounting principle. Windsor should restate the 1998 financial statements, including adjustment for the effect on January 1, 1998, retained earnings, as if the FIFO method had been adopted at the beginning of 1998. The nature and justification for the change in inventory method should be disclosed in the notes to the 1999 financial statements. The effects of the change on income statement components should be disclosed for all periods presented.

b.   Windsor's change from sum-of-the-years' digits depreciation method for all future machinery acquisitions is a change in accounting principle. The nature and justification for the change in depreciation methods should be disclosed in the notes to the 1999 comparative financial statements. The 1998 financial statements are unaffected by the change, but the effects of the change on 1999 income components should be disclosed.

c.   A change from the cash basis of vacation pay expense recognition to the accrual basis is a change from an accounting principle that is not generally accepted to one that is generally accepted. Such a change is considered an error correction. Windsor should restate the 1998 financial statements, including adjustment for the effect on January 1, 1998 retained earnings, to correct prior errors. Windsor should disclose the nature and details of the corrections in notes to the 1999 financial statements.

D. Financial Statements

1. Income and Retained Earnings Statement Formats

Review the outlines of APB 9, APB 30, and SFAS 130 before proceeding. Income statements may be prepared using a multiple-step or single-step form. The income (earnings) and comprehensive income statement illustrated below for Totman Company includes separate categories for continuing operations, discontinued operations, extraordinary items, and changes in accounting principles. The other comprehensive income is required per SFAS 130. The purpose of these separate categories is to enable users to assess future cash flows. The Totman Co. statement is a combined statement of income and comprehensive income.

Totman Company
STATEMENT OF EARNINGS AND COMPREHENSIVE INCOME
For the Year Ended December 31, 1999

Sales		$2,677
Cost of goods sold		1,489
Gross margin on sales		1,188
Operating expenses		
Selling expenses	$ 220	
Administrative expenses	255	475
Operating income		713
Other revenues and gains		
Interest revenue	$ 5	
Equity in Huskie Co. earnings	15	
Gain on sale of available-for-sale securities	45	65
Other expenses and losses		
Interest expense	(60)	
Loss from permanent impairment of value of manufacturing facilities	(120)	(180)
Income from continuing operations before provision for income taxes		598
Provision for income taxes		
Current	$ 189	
Deferred	50	239
Income from continuing operations		359(a)
Discontinued operations:		
Loss from operations of discontinued Division Z (less applicable taxes of $466)	(699)	
Loss on disposal of Division Z including operating losses during phase-out period (less applicable taxes of $67)	(100)	(799)(b)
Income (loss) before extraordinary item and cumulative effect of an accounting change		(440)
Extraordinary item: Loss due to earthquake (less applicable income taxes of $30)		(45)(b)
Cumulative effect on prior years of retroactive application of new depreciation method (less applicable income taxes of $80)		(120)(b)
Net earnings (loss)		(605)(a)
Other comprehensive income:		
Foreign currency translation adjustments (less applicable income taxes of $6)		26
Unrealized gains on securities:		
Unrealized holding gains arising during period (less applicable income taxes of $43)	179	
Less: reclassification adjustment (less applicable income taxes of $10) for gain included in net income	(35)	144
Minimum pension liability (less applicable income taxes of $12) taxes		(53)
Other comprehensive income		117
Comprehensive income		$(488)

The bracket to the left of the statement (from "Operating expenses" through "Other expenses and losses") is labeled: **See Note #5 below**

Note:
1. Assumes a tax rate of 40% on applicable items
2. (a) indicates where earnings per share (EPS) amounts would be necessary on the face of the IS. (b) EPS may be shown on the face of the income statement or in the notes. On the CPA exam, rather than memorizing these, simply calculate an EPS number for all numbers starting with income from continuing operations through net earnings.
3. Footnote explanations would also be required for many of the above events and transactions.
4. In the multiple-step format above, the Securities and Exchange Commission (SEC) requires that public companies place impairment losses in operating income instead of under "Other expenses and losses."
5. This is the format for a multiple-step income statement. A single-step income statement would differ only for the portion of the statement shown below. Otherwise, the single-step statement format is the same.

Revenues

Sales	$2,677	
Interest	5	
Gain on sale of available-for-sale securities	45	
Equity in Huskie Co. earnings	15	
Total revenues		$2,742

Expenses

Cost of goods sold	1,489	
Selling expenses	220	
Administrative expenses	255	
Interest expense	60	
Loss from permanent impairment of value of manufacturing facilities	120	
Total expenses		2,144
Income from continuing operations before provision for income taxes		598

If the retained earnings statement had been presented, it would begin with prior period adjustments (as shown in Module 22B). The following chart summarizes the various category definitions and their placement on the income statement and retained earnings statement. These categories are all discussed in various parts of this module.

INCOME STATEMENT AND RETAINED EARNINGS STATEMENT CATEGORIES

Description	*Definition*	*Placement on income statement or retained earnings statement*
1. **Unusual or Infrequent Items**	An unusual or infrequent event considered to be material that does not qualify as extraordinary	Placed as part of income from continuing operations after normal recurring revenues and expenses
2. **Discontinued Operations**	Results from disposal of a business segment or a line of business	Placed as a separate category after income from continuing operations
3. **Extraordinary Items**	An unusual and infrequent nonrecurring event which has material effects	Placed as a separate category after discontinued operations
4. **Change in Accounting Principle:**		
Cumulative effect:	Change from one generally accepted accounting principle to another	Placed as a separate category after extraordinary items
Restatement:	Change which requires restatement of all prior periods presented	Placed as a separate category in retained earnings
5. **Correction of an Error**	A correction of a material error from a prior period	Placed as a separate category in retained earnings

2. **Discontinued Operations**

As shown on the Totman Co. income statement, the "Discontinued operations" section consists of two components. The first one, "Income (loss) from operations," is disclosed for the current year only if the decision to discontinue operations is made after the beginning of the fiscal year for which the financials are being prepared. In the diagram below, the "Income (loss) from operations" component is determined for the time period designated by "A"--the period from the beginning of the year to the date the decision is made to discontinue a segment's operations (measurement date). The second component, "Gain (loss) on disposal" may consist of two elements.

    a. Income (loss) from operations during the phase-out period (the period between the measurement date and disposal date), and

    b. Gain (loss) from disposal of segment assets

The "Gain (loss) on disposal" component is determined for the time period designated "B" in the diagram below.

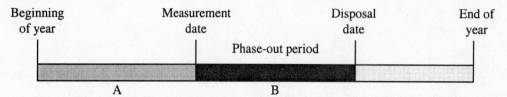

There are special rules for situations in which the disposal date occurs in the year after the measurement date. The problem is one of estimating the unrealized "Gain (loss) on disposal" for that part of the phase-out period which is in the following year and comparing it to the actual "Gain (loss) on disposal" that has already been realized at the end of the preceding year for which the financials are being prepared. Two rules apply to this situation.

a. A realized "Loss on disposal" may be increased by an estimated loss or it may be reduced by an estimated gain (but only to zero), or on the CPA exam, questions will ask for the amount of gain (loss) for "discontinued operations" or for the gain (loss) for one of the two components. You must know these FS headings and what is included under each.

b. A realized "Gain on disposal" may be reduced by an estimated loss but cannot be increased due to an estimated gain.

The diagram below depicts the relationships discussed above.

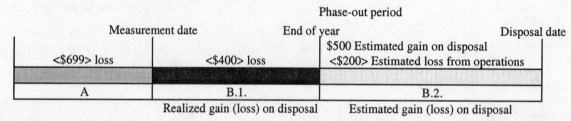

EXAMPLE:

Facts	*Analysis*
A. *Loss from Operations from beginning of year to the measurement date, $699, net of taxes of $466*	*Reported as first component of discontinued operations*
B. 1. *Realized loss from operations from measurement date to end of current year, $400, net of taxes of $267.*	*Reported as second component of discontinued operations: $400 loss realized during phase-out period minus the $300 estimated **net** gain to be realized in the next period (estimated gain on disposal less the estimated loss from operations)*
2. *Estimated loss from operations from year end to disposal date, $200, net of taxes of $133. Estimated gain from disposal of assets during next year, $500, net of taxes of $333.*	

The presentation of this case in the financials is shown in the combined statement of income and comprehensive income illustrated in the Totman Company example.

When "discontinued operations" are disclosed in a comparative income statement, the income statement presented for each previous year must be adjusted retroactively to enhance comparability with the current year's income statement. Accordingly, the revenues, cost of goods sold, and operating expenses (including income taxes) for the discontinued segment are removed from the revenues, cost of goods sold, and operating expenses of continuing operations and are netted into one figure, that is, "Income (loss) from operations." The following excerpt from a comparative income statement shows the proper disclosure (1998 figures assumed).

	1999	*1998*
Discontinued operations:		
Loss from operations of discontinued Division Z net of applicable taxes	$699	$820
Loss on disposal of assets of discontinued Division Z, including loss during phase-out period, net of applicable taxes	$100	--

3. **Comprehensive Income**

Reporting. Comprehensive income is the sum of net earnings (loss) and other comprehensive income. Refer to the outline of SFAS 130. This standard goes part way in implementing the concept of comprehensive income per SFAC 5 and 6. These two concept statements would require reporting all transactions other than those with owners in comprehensive income. However, SFAS 130 leaves prior period adjustments in retained earnings. It requires disclosure of **changes during a period** of the following components of other comprehensive income: unrealized gains and losses on available-for-sale investments and foreign currency items, including any reclassification adjustments and the minimum pension liability adjustment. These are shown after net income on a statement entitled "statement of earnings and comprehensive income" (as in the statement shown at the beginning of this submodule 22 [D.1.]), in a separate "statement of comprehensive income," or in the statement of changes in stockholders' equity. The first two alternatives are preferred by the FASB. If either the second or third one is used, it is necessary to begin with net earnings so that net earnings would be reconciled to comprehensive income as it is in the single statement. The new standard continues the required disclosure of the **accumulated** amounts of these components in the stockholders' equity section of the balance sheet, in a statement of changes in stockholders' equity, or in the notes to financial statements. (See the balance sheet on the following page and the statement of changes in stockholders' equity at the beginning of Module 28.)

Recycling. In the statement of income and comprehensive income shown earlier note the treatment of reclassified (recycled) items. Once unrealized items recorded and reported in the current or prior periods are recognized as realized and reported in net income it is necessary to reverse them out of other comprehensive income. The reclassification adjustment of $35 is to avoid double counting. Assume the adjustment was $45 before tax and the tax effect was $10. Since the $45 was realized in the current period, a realized gain of $45 was reported in the income from continuing operations before income taxes of $598, the last item under other revenue. The $10 of income tax on the $45 is reported in the current income tax expense of $189.

Bookkeeping. When an entity has components of other comprehensive income, the total of these is closed to the balance sheet account entitled **accumulated other comprehensive income**, not retained earnings.

4. **Balance Sheets (Statements of Financial Position)**

Balance sheets or statements of financial position present assets, liabilities, and stockholders' equity. The balance sheet reports the effect of transactions at a point in time, whereas the statement of earnings (income) and comprehensive income, statement of retained earnings, and statement of cash flows report the effect of transactions over a period of time.

An example of balance sheet classification and presentation is illustrated by the comprehensive balance sheet on the following page.

Distinction between current and noncurrent assets and liabilities is almost universal.

Current assets--"cash and other assets or resources commonly identified as those which are reasonably expected to be realized in cash or sold or consumed during the normal operating cycle of the business."   (ARB 43, chap 3A, para 4)

Current liabilities--"obligations whose liquidation is reasonably expected to require the use of existing resources properly classifiable as current assets or the creation of other current liabilities" (during the normal operating cycle of the business).

(ARB 43, chap 3A, para 7)

Note current assets include those expected to be

   a. Realized in cash
   b. Sold
   c. Consumed

Current liabilities are those expected to

   a. Use current assets
   b. Create other current liabilities

The operating cycle is the average time between acquisition of materials and final cash realization. Review the outline of ARB 43, chap 3A.

5. **Other Financial Statement Concepts**

   a. **Disclosures.** Related party disclosures are covered by SFAS 57 (refer to that outline). Additional disclosures required for specific situations are specified at the end of most pronouncements (e.g., APB and SFAS). Study these disclosure requirements by assuming you are a financial analyst analyzing the statements: "What would you want disclosed? Note any required disclosures that are not 'common sense'." It is not necessary to memorize them for the exam.

   b. **Accounting policies** must be set forth as the initial footnote to the statements. Disclosures are required of

     (1) Accounting principles used when alternatives exist
     (2) Principles peculiar to a particular industry
     (3) Unusual or innovative applications of accounting principles

   Turn to the outline of APB 22.

   c. **Development stage enterprise accounting** should be per generally accepted accounting principles. The only additional disclosure required is that cumulative amounts from inception of losses, revenues, expenses, and cash flows should be shown in the income statement and statement of cash flows. Furthermore, the stockholders' equity section of the balance sheet should include cumulative net losses termed "deficit accumulated during development stage." These statements should be identified as those of a development stage enterprise. (More detailed coverage appears in Module 24.)

   d. **Constant dollar accounting.** SFAS 89 encourages, but does not require, a business enterprise that prepares its financial statements in US dollars and in accordance with US generally accepted accounting principles to disclose supplementary information on the effects of changing prices. This statement presents requirements to be followed by enterprises that voluntarily elect to disclose this information.

     Constant dollar accounting is a method of reporting financial statement elements in dollars which have the same purchasing power. This method is often described as accounting in units of current purchasing power.

     Purchasing power indicates the ability of a dollar to command goods and services. If the inflation rate during a given year for a group of items is 10%, then 110 end-of-year dollars are needed to purchase the same group of items which cost $100 at the beginning of the year. Similarly, a machine purchased at the beginning of that year for $1,000 would be presented in a year-end constant dollar balance sheet at a restated cost of $1,100. This represents the basic thrust of constant dollar accounting: the adjustment of historical data (nominal dollars) for changes in the general price level.

Totman Company
BALANCE SHEET
December 31, 1999

Assets			Liabilities and Stockholders' Equity		
Current assets:			*Current liabilities:*		
Cash and bank deposits:			Commercial paper and other short-term notes	$xxx	
Restricted to current bond maturity	$xxx		Accounts payable	xxx	
Unrestricted	xxx	$xxx	Salaries, wages, and commissions	xxx	
Short-term investments:			Taxes withheld from employees	xxx	
Marketable securities (Trading)		xxx	Income taxes payable	xxx	
Refundable income taxes		xxx	Dividends payable	xxx	
Receivables from affiliates		xxx	Rent revenue collected in advance	xxx	
Accounts receivable	xxx		Other advances from customers	xxx	
Less allowance for doubtful accounts	(xxx)	xxx	Current portion of long-term debt	xxx	
Notes receivable due in 2000		xxx	Current obligations under capital leases	xxx	
Installment notes due in 2000		xxx	Deferred tax liability	xxx	
Interest receivable		xxx	Short-term portion of accrued warranty	xxx	
Creditors' accounts with debit balances		xxx	Other accrued liabilities	xxx	
Advances to employees		xxx	Total current liabilities		$xxx
Inventories (carried at lower of cost or market by					
FIFO)			*Noncurrent liabilities:*		
Finished goods	xxx		Notes payable due after 1999	$xxx	
Work in process	xxx		Plus unamortized note premium	xxx	$xxx
Raw materials	xxx	xxx	Long-term bonds:		
Prepaid expenses:			10% debentures due 2011	xxx	
Prepaid rent	xxx		9-1/2% collateralized obligations maturing		
Prepaid insurance	xxx	xxx	serially to 2002	xxx	
			8% convertible subordinated debentures due		
Total current assets		$xxx	2016	xxx	
			Less unamortized discounts net of premiums	(xxx)	xxx
Long-term investments:			Accrued pension cost		xxx
Investments in marketable securities (available-for-			Obligations under capital leases		xxx
sale)	xxx		Deferred tax liability		xxx
Investments in bonds (held-to-maturity)	xxx		Long-term portion of accrued warranty		xxx
Investments in unused land	xxx		Total noncurrent liabilities		$xxx
Cash surrender value of officers' life insurance			Total liabilities		$xxx
policies	xxx				
Sinking fund for bond retirement	xxx		*Capital stock:*		
Plant expansion fund	xxx		$12.50 convertible preferred stock, $100 stated		
Total long-term investments		$xxx	value, 200,000 shares authorized, 175,000		
			outstanding	$xxx	
Property, plant, and equipment:			12% cumulative preferred stock, $100 stated value,		
Land	$xxx		callable at $115, 100,000 shares authorized and		
Buildings	xxx		outstanding	xxx	
Machinery and equipment	xxx		Common stock, $10 stated value, 500,000 shares		
Furniture and fixtures	xxx		authorized, 450,000 issued, 15,000 held in		
Leasehold improvements	xxx		treasury	xxx	
Leased assets	xxx		Common stock subscribed 10,000 shares	xxx	
Less accumulated depreciation and amortization			Less: Subscriptions receivable	(xxx)	$xxx
	(xxx)				
Total property, plant, and equipment		$xxx	*Additional paid-in capital:*		
			From 12% cumulative preferred	xxx	
Intangible assets net of amortization:			From common stock	xxx	
Excess of cost over net assets of acquired busi-			From treasury stock transactions	xxx	
nesses	$xxx		From stock dividends	xxx	
Patents	xxx		From expiration of stock options	xxx	
Trademarks	xxx		Warrants outstanding	xxx	xxx
Organization costs	xxx				
Total intangible assets, net		$xxx	*Retained earnings:*		
			Appropriated for bond indebtedness	xxx	
Other assets:			Free and unappropriated	xxx	xxx
Installment notes due after 1999	$xxx				
Unamortized bond issue costs	xxx		*Accumulated other comprehensive income:*		xxx*
Equipment to be disposed of	xxx		Total stockholders' equity		$xxx
Total other noncurrent assets		$xxx	Less: Treasury stock at cost		(xxx)
Total assets		$xxx	Total liabilities and stockholders' equity		$xxx

*Assumes components thereof are disclosed either in a statement of changes in stockholders' equity or in the notes to FS.

The adjustment of nominal dollar data is facilitated by the use of the Consumer Price Index, which reflects the average change in the retail prices of a wide variety of consumer goods. The adjustment is made by multiplying historical cost by the TO/FROM ratio.

Historical cost (nominal dollars) $\times$ $\dfrac{\text{Price level adjusting to}}{\text{Price level adjusting from}}$ = Restated historical cost (constant dollar)

For example, an asset was purchased on 12/31/99 for $20,000 and the Consumer Price Index was 100 on 12/31/99, 110 on 12/31/00, and 120 on 12/31/01. Restatement for end-of-year balance sheets would be

$$12/31/99 \quad \$20,000 \quad \times \quad \frac{100}{100} \quad = \quad \$20,000$$

$$12/31/00 \quad \$20,000 \quad \times \quad \frac{110}{100} \quad = \quad \$22,000$$

$$12/31/01 \quad \$20,000 \quad \times \quad \frac{120}{100} \quad = \quad \$24,000$$

or

$$\$22,000 \quad \times \quad \frac{120}{110} \quad = \quad \$24,000$$

The preparation of constant dollar financial statements requires the classification of balance sheet items as either monetary or nonmonetary. Items are monetary if their amounts are fixed by statute or contract in terms of numbers of dollars. Examples include cash, accounts and notes receivable, accounts and notes payable, and bonds payable. By contract or statute, these items are already stated in current dollars and require no restatement. Nonmonetary items, on the other hand, do require restatement to current dollars. Inventory, property, plant, and equipment, and unearned service revenue are examples of nonmonetary items. Under some increasingly popular loan arrangements, when the repayment of loan principal is adjusted by an index, the receivable/payable is classified as a nonmonetary item.

The holding of a nonmonetary asset such as land during a period of inflation need not result in a loss of purchasing power because the value of that land can "flow" with the price level (hence, the need for restatement). However, if a monetary asset such as cash is held during a period of inflation with no interest, purchasing power is lost because the cash will be able to purchase less goods and services at year end than at the beginning of the year. This type of loss is simply called a "purchasing power loss." Holding a monetary liability has the opposite effect. Therefore, if a firm's balance sheet included more monetary liabilities than monetary assets throughout a given year, a purchasing power **gain** would result, since the firm could pay its liabilities using cash which is "worth less" than the cash they borrowed.

A simple example can illustrate both the restatement process and the effect of holding monetary assets. Assume that the Static Company has the following balance sheet at the beginning of period 1:

Static Co.
Beginning of Period 1
Consumer Price Index = 100

Cash	$1,000	Common Stock	$2,000
Land	1,000		
	$2,000		$2,000

If the index increases to 110 by the end of year 1 and no transactions have taken place, both the land and common stock would be restated to end-of-year dollars. But in order to maintain the same level of purchasing power that was present at the beginning of the year, Static Co. should also have cash of $1,100 at year end. The fact that the company held $1,000 cash throughout the year has resulted in a $100 purchasing power loss. The balance sheet at the end of period 1 would, therefore, be

Static Co.
End of Period 1
Consumer Price Index = 110

Cash	$1,000	Common Stock	$2,200[b]
Land	1,100[a]	Retained Earnings	(100)[c]
	$2,100		$2,100

[a]$1,000 $\times \dfrac{110}{100}$ [b]$2,000 $\times \dfrac{110}{100}$ [c]Purchasing power loss $1,000 - ($1,000 $\times \dfrac{110}{100})$

e. **Current cost accounting** is a method of valuing and reporting assets, liabilities, revenues, and expenses at their current cost at the balance sheet date or at the date of their use or sale.

It is important to distinguish between constant dollar and current cost accounting. Constant dollar accounting is concerned only with changes in the unit of measure--from nominal dollars to units of general purchasing power. Current cost accounting discards historical cost as a reporting model.

Preparation of a current cost income statement requires an understanding of certain basic current cost concepts. **Current cost income from continuing operations** is sales revenue less expenses on a current cost basis. **Realized holding gains** (the difference between current cost and historical cost of assets consumed) are then added to arrive at **realized income**, which will always be equal to historical cost net income. Finally, **unrealized holding gains** (increases in the current cost of assets held throughout the year) are included to result in **current cost net income**.

An example should help clarify these terms. Bell Co. went into business on 1/1/99. 1999 sales revenue was $200,000 and purchases totaled $150,000. Inventory with a historical cost of $100,000 was sold when its current cost was $160,000. Ending inventory (historical cost, $50,000) had a year-end current cost of $80,000. No other revenue was realized or expenses incurred during 1999. Historical and current cost income statements for 1999 are presented below.

Bell Company
INCOME STATEMENTS

Historical cost		*Current cost*	
Sales	$200,000	Sales	$200,000
Less CGS	(100,000)	Less CGS	(160,000)
		Cur. cost income from cont. oper.	40,000
		Realized holding gains (160,000 – 100,000)	60,000
Net income	$100,000	Realized income	100,000
		Unrealized holding gains (80,000 – 50,000)	30,000
		Current cost net income	$130,000

1999 journal entries for Bell Company in current cost system would be as follows:

a) Inventory   150,000
        Cash   150,000

b) Inventory   90,000
        Realizable
        holding gain   90,000

c) Cash   200,000
        Sales revenue   200,000

d) Cost of goods sold   160,000
        Inventory   160,000

e) Realizable holding gain   90,000
        Realized holding gain   60,000
        Unrealized holding gain   30,000

In general, sales and some expense amounts (salaries, rent, etc.) will be the same under historical and current cost systems. However, whenever an expense represents the use or consumption of an asset whose current cost has changed since its acquisition (as with the inventory in the Bell Co. example), that expense must be expressed at the current cost of the asset when used. Realized holding gains are computed by comparing the current cost of assets when used or consumed with their historical cost. Unrealized holding gains for the period are determined by identifying changes in the current cost of assets held throughout the year (not used or consumed). Notice that the holding gains do not reflect changes in the general purchasing power. In other words, the holding gains are not reported net of general inflation when the reporting model is current cost/nominal dollar.

f. **Risks and Uncertainties.** AICPA Statement of Position 94-6 *Disclosure of Certain Significant Risks and Uncertainties* requires disclosure in financial statements about the risks and uncertainties existing as of the date of those statements. The four areas of disclosure are

(1) Nature of operations

   (a) Major products/services and principal markets served
   (b) Industries operating within and relative importance of each industry, including basis of determination (assets, revenue or earnings).

   NOTE: Quantification not required and words such as predominantly, equally, major, or other may be used.

(2) Use of estimates in preparation of financial statements

   (a) This fact must be disclosed by an explanation that management must use estimates
   (b) Purpose is to alert users clearly to pervasiveness of estimates

(3) Certain significant estimates

   (a) Potential impact of estimates to value assets, liabilities, gains or losses when

      1] Reasonably possible the estimate will change in the near term
      2] Effect of change would be material to financial statements

      NOTE: Near term is defined as not to exceed 1 year from date of financial statements.

   (b) This is not a change in SFAS 5, *Accounting for Contingencies*
   (c) Disclosure of factors causing the estimate to be sensitive to change is encouraged, but not required
   (d) Materiality is measured by the effect that using a different estimate would have on the financial statements

(4) Current vulnerability due to concentrations

   (a) Before issuance of financial statements, management knows that concentrations

      1] Exist at balance sheet date
      2] Make entity vulnerable to risk of near term severe impact
      3] Reasonably possible events could cause severe impact in near future

      NOTE: Severe impact is defined as higher than materiality and would have a significant financially disruptive effect on the normal functioning of the entity.

   (b) Examples are concentrations in

      1] Volume of business transacted with a particular customer, supplier, lender, grantor, or contributor
      2] Revenue from particular products, services, or fund-raising events
      3] Available sources of supply of materials, labor, or services, or of licenses or other rights used in the entity's operations
      4] Market or geographical area in which an entity conducts its operations

   (c) Disclose the percentage of labor covered by a collective bargaining agreement and the percentage covered whose agreement expires within 1 year
   (d) Describe for operations outside of home country, the carrying value of net assets and location

6. **Comparative Financial Statements**

   The Totman Company balance sheet and income statement illustrated in this module are presented for a single year. Most companies present comparative financial statements. Comparative financial statements present not only the current year's information, but prior periods also. The purpose of comparative financial statements is to enable users to evaluate trends which may reveal information about the company's future performance. The SEC requires that a 2-year comparative balance sheet and a 3-year comparative income statement and statement of cash flows be presented.

7. **Other Comprehensive Bases of Accounting**

   Financial statements may be prepared in conformity with a comprehensive basis of accounting other than Generally Accepted Accounting Principles. Other comprehensive bases are illustrated in the chart below.

Accounting method	*Characteristics*
1. Cash basis (pure)	Fixed assets would be expensed in the period paid for
2. Income tax bases	
• Modified cash basis--hybrid method of IRS	Reflects use of accrual basis for inventories, cost of goods sold, sales, and depreciation if these are significant
• Accrual basis--IRS	Use accruals and deferrals with several exceptions (e.g., prepaid income, warranty expense)
3. Prescribed basis by regulatory agency	Determined by regulatory agency

   Guidance for preparing these statements is found in the AICPA publication entitled *Preparing and Reporting on Cash- and Tax-Basis Financial Statements*. When financial statements are prepared on an income tax basis the financial statements should not simply repeat items and amounts reported in the tax return. Thus, items such as nontaxable municipal interest and the nondeductible portion of travel and entertainment expense should be **fully** reflected in the income statement on the basis used for tax purposes (cash or accrual) with footnote disclosure of the differences between the amounts reported in the income statement and tax return.

8. **Prospective Financial Information**

   This area was added to the AICPA Content Specification Outlines for the May 1998 exam. We have included the key points from the AICPA Accounting and Auditing Guide below.

   • Definitions:
     • Prospective financial information--any financial information about the future
     • Responsible party--person(s), usually management, who are responsible for assumptions underlying the information
     • Users of prospective financial information:
       • General--use of FS by parties with whom responsible party is not negotiating directly
       • Limited use--use of prospective financial information by the responsible party only or by responsible party and third parties with whom responsible party is negotiating directly

   • Financial forecast--prospective FS that present the knowledge and belief of responsible party in terms of expected financial position, results of operations, and cash flows
       • May be prepared for **general or limited** use
       • Monetary amounts are expressed as a single-point estimate of results or range

- Financial projection--prospective FS that present the knowledge and belief of responsible party, based on one or more **hypothetical** assumptions, the enterprise's financial position, results of operations, and cash flows
    - Assumptions **not necessarily** expected to occur
    - May contain a single-point estimate of results or a range of dollars
    - May be prepared only for **limited** use
- Reasons for preparation:
    - Needed to obtain external financing
    - Consider change in accounting or operations
    - Prepare budget
- Process for preparing forecasts and projections may consist of any of the following:
    - Formal system
    - Carrying out a work program that outlines steps followed in preparation
    - Documented procedures, methods, and practices used in preparation
- Financial forecasts and projections should reflect **a reasonably objective basis** as a result of preparing them:
    - In good faith
    - With due care by qualified personnel
    - In accordance with GAAP
    - With the highest quality information that is reasonably available
    - Using information that is in accordance with plans of the entity
    - Identifying key factors as basis for assumptions
        - Key factors are important matters for which outcomes are expected to depend
    - Using appropriate assumptions
        - Quality of these is crucial
        - **Hypothetical** assumptions used in projections do **not** need to meet a strict reasonableness test; they must, however, be appropriate in light of the purpose of the projection's purpose
    - Providing ways to determine relative effect of variations in main assumptions (i.e., sensitivity analysis)
    - Documenting forecast/projection and process used
    - Providing for comparison of forecast/projection with attained results
    - Providing adequate review of the responsible party at appropriate levels of authority in the organization

MULTIPLE-CHOICE QUESTIONS (1-62)

1. In Baer Food Co.'s 1999 single-step income statement, the section titled "Revenues" consisted of the following:

Net sales revenue		$187,000
Results from discontinued operations:		
Loss from operations of segment (net of $1,200 tax effect)	$ (2,400)	
Gain on disposal of segment (net of $7,200 tax effect)	14,400	12,000
Interest revenue		10,200
Gain on sale of equipment		4,700
Cumulative change in 1997 and 1998 income due to change in depreciation method (net of $750 tax effect)		1,500
Total revenues		$215,400

In the revenues section of the 1999 income statement, Baer Food should have reported total revenues of

- a. $216,300
- b. $215,400
- c. $203,700
- d. $201,900

Items 2 and 3 are based on the following:

Vane Co.'s trial balance of income statement accounts for the year ended December 31, 1999, included the following:

	Debit	Credit
Sales		$575,000
Cost of sales	$240,000	
Administrative expenses	70,000	
Loss on sale of equipment	10,000	
Sales commissions	50,000	
Interest revenue		25,000
Freight out	15,000	
Loss on early retirement of long-term debt	20,000	
Uncollectible accounts expense	15,000	
Totals	$420,000	$600,000

Other information
Finished goods inventory:

January 1, 1999	$400,000
December 31, 1999	360,000

Vane's income tax rate is 30%. In Vane's 1999 multiple-step income statement,

2. What amount should Vane report as the cost of goods manufactured?

- a. $200,000
- b. $215,000
- c. $280,000
- d. $295,000

3. What amount should Vane report as income after income taxes from continuing operations?

- a. $126,000
- b. $129,500
- c. $140,000
- d. $147,000

4. Brock Corp. reports operating expenses in two categories: (1) selling, and (2) general and administrative. The adjusted trial balance at December 31, 1999, included the following expense and loss accounts:

Accounting and legal fees	$120,000
Advertising	150,000
Freight-out	80,000
Interest	70,000
Loss on sale of long-term investment	30,000
Officers' salaries	225,000
Rent for office space	220,000
Sales salaries and commissions	140,000

One-half of the rented premises is occupied by the sales department.

Brock's total selling expenses for 1999 are

- a. $480,000
- b. $400,000
- c. $370,000
- d. $360,000

5. The following costs were incurred by Griff Co., a manufacturer, during 1999:

Accounting and legal fees	$ 25,000
Freight-in	175,000
Freight-out	160,000
Officers salaries	150,000
Insurance	85,000
Sales representatives salaries	215,000

What amount of these costs should be reported as general and administrative expenses for 1999?

- a. $260,000
- b. $550,000
- c. $635,000
- d. $810,000

6. Which of the following should be included in general and administrative expenses?

	Interest	Advertising
a.	Yes	Yes
b.	Yes	No
c.	No	Yes
d.	No	No

7. In Yew Co.'s 1999 annual report, Yew described its social awareness expenditures during the year as follows:

> "The Company contributed $250,000 in cash to youth and educational programs. The Company also gave $140,000 to health and human service organizations, of which $80,000 was contributed by employees through payroll deductions. In addition, consistent with the Company's commitment to the environment, the Company spent $100,000 to redesign product packaging."

What amount of the above should be included in Yew's income statement as charitable contributions expense?

- a. $310,000
- b. $390,000
- c. $410,000
- d. $490,000

8. During 1999 both Raim Co. and Cane Co. suffered losses due to the flooding of the Mississippi River. Raim is located 2 miles from the river and sustains flood losses every 2 to 3 years. Cane, which has been located 50 miles from the river for the past 20 years, has never before had flood losses. How should the flood losses be reported in each company's 1999 income statement?

	Raim	Cane
a.	As a component of income from continuing operations	As an extraordinary item
b.	As a component of income from continuing operations	As a component of income from continuing operations
c.	As an extraordinary item	As a component of income from continuing operations
d.	As an extraordinary item	As an extraordinary item

9. Witt Co. incurred the following infrequent losses during 1999:

- $175,000 from a major strike by employees.
- $150,000 from an early extinguishment of debt.
- $125,000 from the abandonment of equipment used in the business.

In Witt's 1999 income statement, the total amount of infrequent losses **not** considered extraordinary should be
- a. $275,000
- b. $300,000
- c. $325,000
- d. $450,000

10. Kent Co. incurred the following infrequent losses during 1999:

- A $300,000 loss was incurred on disposal of one of four dissimilar factories.
- A major currency devaluation caused a $120,000 exchange loss on an amount remitted by a foreign customer.
- Inventory valued at $190,000 was made worthless by a competitor's unexpected product innovation.

In its 1999 income statement, what amount should Kent report as losses that are **not** considered extraordinary?
- a. $610,000
- b. $490,000
- c. $420,000
- d. $310,000

11. Midway Co. had the following transactions during 1999:

- $1,200,000 pretax loss on foreign currency exchange due to a major unexpected devaluation by the foreign government.
- $500,000 pretax loss from discontinued operations of a division.
- $800,000 pretax loss on equipment damaged by a hurricane. This was the first hurricane ever to strike in Midway's area. Midway also received $1,000,000 from its insurance company to replace a building, with a carrying value of $300,000, that had been destroyed by the hurricane.

What amount should Midway report in its 1999 income statement as extraordinary loss before income taxes?

- a. $ 100,000
- b. $1,300,000
- c. $1,800,000
- d. $2,500,000

12. Ocean Corp.'s comprehensive insurance policy allows its assets to be replaced at current value. The policy has a $50,000 deductible clause. One of Ocean's waterfront warehouses was destroyed in a winter storm. Such storms occur approximately every 4 years. Ocean incurred $20,000 of costs in dismantling the warehouse and plans to replace it. The following data relate to the warehouse:

Current carrying amount	$ 300,000
Replacement cost	1,100,000

What amount of gain should Ocean report as a separate component of income before extraordinary items?
- a. $1,030,000
- b. $ 780,000
- c. $ 730,000
- d. $0

13. Purl Corporation's income statement for the year ended December 31, 1999, shows the following:

Income before income tax and extraordinary item	$900,000
Gain on life insurance coverage-- included in the above $900,000 income amount	100,000
Extraordinary item--loss due to earthquake damage	300,000

Purl's tax rate for 1999 is 40%. How much should be reported as the provision for income tax in Purl's 1999 income statement?
- a. $200,000
- b. $240,000
- c. $320,000
- d. $360,000

14. Thorpe Co.'s income statement for the year ended December 31, 1999, reported net income of $74,100. The auditor raised questions about the following amounts that had been included in net income:

Unrealized loss on decline in market value of noncurrent in vestments in stock classified as available-for-sale	$(5,400)
Gain on early retirement of bonds payable (net of $11,000 tax effect)	22,000
Adjustment to profits of prior years for errors in depreciation (net of $3,750 tax effect)	(7,500)
Loss from fire (net of $7,000 tax effect)	(14,000)

The loss from the fire was an infrequent but not unusual occurrence in Thorpe's line of business. Thorpe's December 31, 1999 income statement should report net income of
- a. $65,000
- b. $66,100
- c. $81,600
- d. $87,000

15. On January 1, 1999, Brecon Co. installed cabinets to display its merchandise in customers' stores. Brecon expects to use these cabinets for 5 years. Brecon's 1999 multi-step income statement should include

    a. One-fifth of the cabinet costs in cost of goods sold.

    b. One-fifth of the cabinet costs in selling, general, and administrative expenses.

    c. All of the cabinet costs in cost of good sold.

    d. All of the cabinet costs in selling, general, and administrative expenses.

16. A material loss should be presented separately as a component of income from continuing operations when it is

    a. An extraordinary item.

    b. A cumulative-effect-type change in accounting principle.

    c. Unusual in nature and infrequent in occurrence.

    d. Not unusual in nature but infrequent in occurrence.

17. During 1999, Peg Construction Co. recognized substantial gains from:

    • An increase in value of a foreign customer's remittance caused by a major foreign currency revaluation.

    • A court-ordered increase in a completed long-term construction contract's price due to design changes.

Should these gains be included in continuing operations or reported as an extraordinary item in Peg's 1999 income statement?

	Gain from major currency revaluation	Gain from increase in contract's price
a.	Continuing operations	Continuing operations
b.	Extraordinary item	Continuing operations
c.	Extraordinary item	Extraordinary item
d.	Continuing operations	Extraordinary item

18. An extraordinary item should be reported separately on the income statement as a component of income

	Net of income taxes	Before discontinued operations of a segment of a business
a.	Yes ✓	Yes
b.	Yes ✓	No ✓
c.	No	No
d.	No	Yes

19. In 1999, hail damaged several of Toncan Co.'s vans. Hailstorms had frequently inflicted similar damage to Toncan's vans. Over the years, Toncan had saved money by not buying hail insurance and either paying for repairs, or selling damaged vans and then replacing them. In 1999, the damaged vans were sold for less than their carrying amount. How should the hail damage cost be reported in Toncan's 1999 financial statements?

    a. The actual 1999 hail damage loss as an extraordinary loss, net of income taxes.

    b. The actual 1999 hail damage loss in continuing operations, with **no** separate disclosure.

    c. The expected average hail damage loss in continuing operations, with **no** separate disclosure.

    d. The expected average hail damage loss in continuing operations, with separate disclosure.

20. A transaction that is unusual in nature and infrequent in occurrence should be reported separately as a component of income

    a. After cumulative effect of accounting changes and before discontinued operations of a segment of a business.

    b. After cumulative effect of accounting changes and after discontinued operations of a segment of a business.

    c. Before cumulative effect of accounting changes and before discontinued operations of a segment of a business.

    d. Before cumulative effect of accounting changes and after discontinued operations of a segment of a business.

21. In 1999, Teller Co. incurred losses arising from its guilty plea in its first antitrust action, and from a substantial increase in production costs caused when a major supplier's workers went on strike. Which of these losses should be reported as an extraordinary item?

	Antitrust action	Production costs
a.	No	No
b.	No	Yes
c.	Yes	No
d.	Yes	Yes

22. In open market transactions, Gold Corp. simultaneously sold its long-term investment in Iron Corp. bonds and purchased its own outstanding bonds. The broker remitted the net cash from the two transactions. Gold's gain on the purchase of its own bonds exceeded its loss on the sale of the Iron bonds. Gold should report the

    a. Net effect of the two transactions as an extraordinary gain.

    b. Net effect of the two transactions in income before extraordinary items.

    c. Effect of its own bond transaction gain in income before extraordinary items, and report the Iron bond transaction as an extraordinary loss.

    d. Effect of its own bond transaction as an extraordinary gain, and report the Iron bond transaction loss in income before extraordinary items.

23. Under SFAS 130, *Reporting Comprehensive Income,* corrections of errors are reported in

    a. Other comprehensive income.

    b. Other income/(expense).

    c. Retained earnings.

    d. Stockholders' equity

24. On April 30, 1999, Deer Corp. approved a plan to dispose of a segment of its business. For the period January 1 through April 30, 1999, the segment had revenues of $500,000 and expenses of $800,000. The assets of the segment were sold on October 15, 1999, at a loss for which no tax benefit is available. In its income statement for the year ended December 31, 1999, how should Deer report the segment's operations from January 1 to April 30, 1999?

    a. $500,000 and $800,000 should be included with revenues and expenses, respectively, as part of continuing operations.

  b. $300,000 should be reported as part of the loss on disposal of a segment.

  c. $300,000 should be reported as an extraordinary loss.

  d. $300,000 should be reported as a loss from operations of a discontinued segment.

25. On October 1, 1998, Host Co. approved a plan to dispose of a segment of its business. Host expected that the sale would occur on April 1, 1999, at an estimated gain of $350,000. The segment had actual and estimated operating losses as follows:

1/1/98 to 9/30/98	$(300,000)
10/1/98 to 12/31/98	(200,000)
1/1/99 to 3/31/99	(400,000)

In its 1998 income statement, what should Host report as a loss on disposal of the segment before income taxes?
  a. $200,000
  b. $250,000
  c. $500,000
  d. $600,000

26. During January 1998, Doe Corp. agreed to sell the assets and product line of its Hart division. The sale was completed on January 15, 1999, and resulted in a gain on disposal of $900,000. Hart's operating losses were $600,000 for 1998 and $50,000 for the period January 1 through January 15, 1999. Disregarding income taxes, what amount of net gain (loss) should be reported in Doe's comparative 1999 and 1998 income statements?

	1999	*1998*
a.	$0	$ 250,000
b.	$250,000	$ 0
c.	$850,000	$(600,000)
d.	$900,000	$(650,000)

27. On December 31, 1998, Greer Co. entered into an agreement to sell its Hart segment's assets. On that date, Greer estimated the gain from the disposition of the assets in 1999 would be $700,000 and Hart's 1999 operating losses would be $200,000. Hart's actual operating losses were $300,000 in both 1998 and 1999, and the actual gain on disposition of Hart's assets in 1999 was $650,000. Disregarding income taxes, what net gain (loss) should be reported for discontinued operations in Greer's comparative 1999 and 1998 income statements?

	1999	*1998*
a.	$ 50,000	$(300,000)
b.	$0	$ 50,000
c.	$ 350,000	$(300,000)
d.	$(150,000)	$ 200,000

28. A segment of Ace, Inc. was discontinued during 1999. Ace's loss on disposal should
  a. Exclude employee relocation costs associated with the decision to dispose.
  b. Exclude operating losses during the phase-out period.
  c. Include additional pension costs associated with the decision to dispose.

  d. Include operating losses of the current period up to the measurement date.

29. When a segment of a business has been discontinued during the year, this segment's operating losses of the current period up to the measurement date should be included in the
  a. Income statement as part of the income (loss) from operations of the discontinued segment.
  b. Income statement as part of the loss on disposal of the discontinued segment.
  c. Income statement as part of the income (loss) from continuing operations.
  d. Retained earnings statement as a direct decrease in retained earnings.

30. When a segment of a business has been discontinued during the year, the loss on disposal should
  a. Exclude operating losses of the current period up to the measurement date.
  b. Exclude operating losses during the phase-out period.
  c. Be an extraordinary item.
  d. Be an operating item.

31. On December 1, 1999, Shine Co. agreed to sell a business segment on March 1, 2000. Throughout 1999 the segment had operating losses that were expected to continue until the segment's disposition. However, the gain on disposition was expected to exceed the segment's total operating losses in 1999 and 2000. The amount of estimated net gain from disposal recognized in 1999 equals
  a. Zero.
  b. The entire estimated net gain.
  c. All of the segment's 1999 operating losses.
  d. The segment's December 1999 operating losses.

32. What is the purpose of reporting comprehensive income?
  a. To report changes in equity due to transactions with owners.
  b. To report a measure of overall enterprise performance.
  c. To replace net income with a better measure.
  d. To combine income from continuing operations with income from discontinued operations and extraordinary items.

33. What amount of comprehensive income should Searles Corporation report on its statement of income and comprehensive income given the following net of tax figures which represent changes during a period?

Minimum pension liability	$ (3,000)
Unrealized gain on available-for-sale securities	15,000
Reclassification adjustment, for securities gain included in net income	(2,500)
Stock warrants outstanding	4,000
Net income	77,000

  a. $86,500
  b. $89,000
  c. $89,500
  d. $90,500

34. If ($2,450) net of tax is the reclassification adjustment under comprehensive income in the year the securities are sold, what is the gain (loss) that is included in income from continuing operations before income taxes? Assume a 30% tax rate.

    a. ($2,450)
    b. ($3,500)
    c. $2,450
    d. $3,500

35. Which of the following is true?

    a. Separate EPS amounts must be presented for both other comprehensive income and comprehensive income.
    b. Separate EPS amounts must be presented for other comprehensive income but not for comprehensive income.
    c. Separate EPS amounts must be presented for comprehensive income but not for other comprehensive income.
    d. Separate EPS amounts are not required to be presented for either other comprehensive income or comprehensive income.

Items 36 through 38 are based on the following:

The following trial balance of Mint Corp. at December 31, 1999, has been adjusted except for income tax expense.

	Dr.	Cr.
Cash	$ 600,000	
Accounts receivable, net	3,500,000	
Cost in excess of billings on long-term contracts	1,600,000	
Billings in excess of costs on long-term contracts		$ 700,000
Prepaid taxes	450,000	
Property, plant, and equipment, net	1,480,000	
Note payable--noncurrent		1,620,000
Common stock		750,000
Additional paid-in capital		2,000,000
Retained earnings-- unappropriated		900,000
Retained earnings--restricted for note payable		160,000
Earnings from long-term contracts		6,680,000
Costs and expenses	5,180,000	
	$12,810,000	$12,810,000

Other financial data for the year ended December 31, 1999, are:

• Mint uses the percentage-of-completion method to account for long-term construction contracts for financial statement and income tax purposes. All receivables on these contracts are considered to be collectible within 12 months.

• During 1999, estimated tax payments of $450,000 were charged to prepaid taxes. Mint has not recorded income tax expense. There were no temporary or permanent differences, and Mint's tax rate is 30%.

In Mint's December 31, 1999 balance sheet, what amount should be reported as:

36. Total retained earnings?

    a. $1,950,000
    b. $2,110,000
    c. $2,400,000
    d. $2,560,000

37. Total noncurrent liabilities?

    a. $1,620,000
    b. $1,780,000
    c. $2,320,000
    d. $2,480,000

38. Total current assets?

    a. $5,000,000
    b. $5,450,000
    c. $5,700,000
    d. $6,150,000

39. Mirr, Inc. was incorporated on January 1, 1999, with proceeds from the issuance of $750,000 in stock and borrowed funds of $110,000. During the first year of operations, revenues from sales and consulting amounted to $82,000, and operating costs and expenses totaled $64,000. On December 15, Mirr declared a $3,000 cash dividend, payable to stockholders on January 15, 2000. No additional activities affected owners' equity in 1999. Mirr's liabilities increased to $120,000 by December 31, 1999. On Mirr's December 31, 1999 balance sheet, total assets should be reported at

    a. $885,000
    b. $882,000
    c. $878,000
    d. $875,000

40. The following changes in Vel Corp.'s account balances occurred during 1999:

	Increase
Assets	$89,000
Liabilities	27,000
Capital stock	60,000
Additional paid-in capital	6,000

Except for a $13,000 dividend payment and the year's earnings, there were no changes in retained earnings for 1999. What was Vel's net income for 1999?

    a. $ 4,000
    b. $ 9,000
    c. $13,000
    d. $17,000

41. When preparing a draft of its 1999 balance sheet, Mont, Inc. reported net assets totaling $875,000. Included in the asset section of the balance sheet were the following:

Treasury stock of Mont, Inc. at cost, which approximates market value on December 31	$24,000
Idle machinery	11,200
Cash surrender value of life insurance on corporate executives	13,700
Allowance for decline in market value of noncurrent equity investments	8,400

At what amount should Mont's net assets be reported in the December 31, 1999 balance sheet?

a. $851,000
b. $850,100
c. $842,600
d. $834,500

42. In analyzing a company's financial statements, which financial statement would a potential investor primarily use to assess the company's liquidity and financial flexibility?

    a. Balance sheet.
    b. Income statement.
    c. Statement of retained earnings.
    d. Statement of cash flows.

43. During 1999, Jones Company engaged in the following transactions:

• Salary expense to key employees who are also principal owners	$100,000
• Sales to affiliated enterprises	250,000

Which of the two transactions would be disclosed as related-party transactions in Jones' 1999 financial statements?

    a. Neither transaction.
    b. The $100,000 transaction only.
    c. The $250,000 transaction only.
    d. Both transactions.

44. Dean Co. acquired 100% of Morey Corp. prior to 1999. During 1999, the individual companies included in their financial statements the following:

	Dean	Morey
Officers' salaries	$ 75,000	$ 50,000
Officers' expenses	20,000	10,000
Loans to officers	125,000	50,000
Intercompany sales	150,000	--

What amount should be reported as related-party disclosures in the notes to Dean's 1999 consolidated financial statements?

    a. $150,000
    b. $155,000
    c. $175,000
    d. $330,000

45. For which type of material related-party transactions does Statement of Financial Accounting Standard 57, *Related-Party Disclosures*, require disclosure?

    a. Only those not reported in the body of the financial statements.
    b. Only those that receive accounting recognition.
    c. Those that contain possible illegal acts.
    d. All those other than compensation arrangements, expense allowances, and other similar items in the ordinary course of business.

46. Financial statements shall include disclosures of material transactions between related parties except

    a. Nonmonetary exchanges by affiliates.
    b. Sales of inventory by a subsidiary to its parent.
    c. Expense allowance for executives which exceed normal business practice.
    d. A company's agreement to act as surety for a loan to its chief executive officer.

47. What is the purpose of information presented in notes to the financial statements?

    a. To provide disclosures required by generally accepted accounting principles.
    b. To correct improper presentation in the financial statements.
    c. To provide recognition of amounts **not** included in the totals of the financial statements.
    d. To present management's responses to auditor comments.

48. Which of the following information should be included in Melay, Inc.'s 1999 summary of significant accounting policies?

    a. Property, plant, and equipment is recorded at cost with depreciation computed principally by the straight-line method.
    b. During 1999, the Delay Segment was sold.
    c. Business segment 1999 sales are Alay $1M, Belay $2M, and Celay $3M.
    d. Future common share dividends are expected to approximate 60% of earnings.

49. Which of the following information should be disclosed in the summary of significant accounting policies?

    a. Refinancing of debt subsequent to the balance sheet date.
    b. Guarantees of indebtedness of others.
    c. Criteria for determining which investments are treated as cash equivalents.
    d. Adequacy of pension plan assets relative to vested benefits.

50. A company that wishes to disclose information about the effect of changing prices in accordance with Statement of Financial Accounting Standards 89, *Financial Accounting and Changing Prices*, should report this information in

    a. The body of the financial statements.
    b. The notes to the financial statements.
    c. Supplementary information to the financial statements.
    d. Management's report to shareholders.

51. Lewis Company was formed on January 1, 1998. Selected balances from the historical cost balance sheet at December 31, 1999, were as follows:

Land (purchased in 1998)	$120,000
Investment in nonconvertible bonds (purchased in 1998, and expected to be held to maturity)	60,000
Long-term debt	80,000

The average Consumer Price Index was 100 for 1998, and 110 for 1999. In a supplementary constant dollar balance sheet (adjusted for changing prices) at December 31, 1999, these selected account balances should be shown at

	Land	Investment	Long-term debt
a.	$120,000	$60,000	$88,000
b.	$120,000	$66,000	$88,000
c.	$132,000	$60,000	$80,000
d.	$132,000	$66,000	$80,000

52. The following items were among those that appeared on Rubi Co.'s books at the end of 1999:

Merchandise inventory	$600,000
Loans to employees	20,000

What amount should Rubi classify as monetary assets in preparing constant dollar financial statements?

a. $0
b. $ 20,000
c. $600,000
d. $620,000

53. In its financial statements, Hila Co. discloses supplemental information on the effects of changing prices in accordance with Statement of Financial Accounting Standards 89, *Financial Reporting and Changing Prices*. Hila computed the increase in current cost of inventory as follows:

Increase in current cost (nominal dollars)	$15,000
Increase in current cost (constant dollars)	$12,000

What amount should Hila disclose as the inflation component of the increase in current cost of inventories?

a. $ 3,000
b. $12,000
c. $15,000
d. $27,000

54. When computing purchasing power gain or loss on net monetary items, which of the following accounts is classified as nonmonetary?

a. Advances to unconsolidated subsidiaries.
b. Allowance for uncollectible accounts.
c. Unamortized premium on bonds payable.
d. Accumulated depreciation of equipment.

55. During a period of inflation in which a liability account balance remains constant, which of the following occurs?

a. A purchasing power gain, if the item is a nonmonetary liability.
b. A purchasing power gain, if the item is a monetary liability.
c. A purchasing power loss, if the item is a nonmonetary liability.
d. A purchasing power loss, if the item is a monetary liability.

56. The following information pertains to each unit of merchandise purchased for resale by Vend Co.:

March 1, 1999

Purchase price	$ 8
Selling price	$12
Price level index	110

December 31, 1999

Replacement cost	$10
Selling price	$15
Price level index	121

Under current cost accounting, what is the amount of Vend's holding gain on each unit of this merchandise?

a. $0
b. $0.80
c. $1.20
d. $2.00

57. Kerr Company purchased a machine for $115,000 on January 1, 1999, the company's first day of operations. At the end of the year, the current cost of the machine was $125,000. The machine has no salvage value, a 5-year life, and is depreciated by the straight-line method. For the year ended December 31, 1999, the amount of the current cost depreciation expense which would appear in supplementary current cost financial statements is

a. $14,000
b. $23,000
c. $24,000
d. $25,000

58. At December 31, 1999, Jannis Corp. owned two assets as follows:

	Equipment	*Inventory*
Current cost	$100,000	$80,000
Recoverable amount	$ 95,000	$90,000

Jannis voluntarily disclosed supplementary information about current cost at December 31, 1999. In such a disclosure, at what amount would Jannis report total assets?

a. $175,000
b. $180,000
c. $185,000
d. $190,000

59. Could current cost financial statements report holding gains for goods sold during the period and holding gains on inventory at the end of the period?

	Goods sold	*Inventory*
a.	Yes	Yes
b.	Yes	No
c.	No	Yes
d.	No	No

60. Manhof Co. prepares supplementary reports on income from continuing operations on a current cost basis in accordance with FASB Statement 89, *Financial Reporting and Changing Prices*. How should Manhof compute cost of goods sold on a current cost basis?

a. Number of units sold times average current cost of units during the year.
b. Number of units sold times current cost of units at year end.
c. Number of units sold times current cost of units at the beginning of the year.
d. Beginning inventory at current cost plus cost of goods purchased less ending inventory at current cost.

61. Which of the following accounting bases may be used to prepare financial statements in conformity with a comprehensive basis of accounting other than generally accepted accounting principles?

I. Basis of accounting used by an entity to file its income tax return.
II. Cash receipts and disbursements basis of accounting.

a. I only.
b. II only.
c. Both I and II.
d. Neither I nor II.

62. In financial statements prepared on the income-tax basis, how should the nondeductible portion of expenses such as meals and entertainment be reported?

   a. Included in the expense category in the determination of income.
   b. Included in a separate category in the determination of income.
   c. Excluded from the determination of income but included in the determination of retained earnings.
   d. Excluded from the financial statements.

OTHER OBJECTIVE QUESTIONS

Problem 1 (15 to 25 minutes)

The illustrations below represent accounting transactions that affect the recognition of income for an accounting period. Their classification is the subject of this objective format matching question.

Required:

For each of the 10 illustrations below, select the best classification from those listed A-I below. A classification may be used once, more than once, or not at all.

Illustration

1. Newly acquired assets are depreciated using the sum-of-the-years' digits method; previously recorded assets are depreciated using the straight-line method.
2. Accounting for a pooling of interests.
3. Reported as a prior period adjustment on the Retained Earnings Statement.
4. Write-down of inventory due to obsolescence.
5. Gains or losses on the disposal of the net assets of a segment are included in this calculation.
6. Changing from the gross profit method for determining year-end inventory balances to dollar value LIFO.
7. Accounting for existing construction contracts is changed from completed contract to percentage-of-completion.
8. The effects of a change in estimate and a change in principle are inseparable for the same event.
9. The excess of cash paid over the carrying value to extinguish bonds.
10. Income or loss from the measurement date to the disposal date (the phase-out period) is included in this calculation.

Classification

A. Change in Reporting Entity.
B. Correction of an Error.
C. Change in Accounting Principle.
D. Change in Estimate.
E. Extraordinary Item.
F. Discontinued Operations--Gain or loss from Operations.
G. Not an accounting change.
H. Unusual or Infrequent Item.
I. Discontinued Operations--Gain or loss on disposal.

Problem 2* (9 to 15 minutes)

This question consists of 8 items. Select the **best** answer for each item. Use a No. 2 pencil to blacken the appropriate ovals on the Objective Answer Sheet to indicate your answer. **Answer all items**. Your grade will be based on the total number of correct answers.

Items 1 through 8 are based on the following:

Pucket Corp. is in the process of preparing its financial statements for the year ended December 31, 1999. Items 1 through 8 represent various transactions or situations that occurred during 1999.

Required:

For items 1 through 8, select from the list of financial statement categories below the category in which the item should be presented, and blacken the corresponding oval on the Objective Answer Sheet. A financial statement category may be selected once, more than once, or not at all.

Financial Statement Categories
A. Income from continuing operations, with **no** separate disclosure.
B. Income from continuing operations, with separate disclosure (either on the face of statement or in the notes).
C. Other comprehensive income for the period.
D. Extraordinary items.
E. Separate component of stockholders' equity.
F. None of the above categories include this item.

Example

The following is an example of the manner in which the answer sheet should be marked.

Item

99. Recording of annual depreciation expense.

Answer Sheet

Item	Financial Statement Categories (select one)
99	(A) ● (C) (D) (E) (F)

---

* *The other 5 items in this question deal with topics now tested on the ARE exam. That portion of Problem 2 appears in Module 36.*

Items to be Answered

1. An increase in the unrealized excess of cost over market value of marketable equity securities classified as trading type securities.
2. The accumulated amount of the unrealized excess of cost over market value of available-for-sale marketable equity securities.
3. Income from operations of a discontinued segment in the segment's disposal year, but before the measurement date.
4. A gain on remeasuring a foreign subsidiary's financial statements from the local currency into the functional currency.
5. A loss on translating a foreign subsidiary's financial statements from the functional local currency into the reporting currency during this period.
6. A loss caused by a major earthquake in an area previously considered to be subject to only minor tremors.
7. The probable receipt of $1,000,000 from a pending lawsuit.
8. The purchase of research and development services. There were **no** other research and development activities.

Problem 3   (15 to 20 minutes)

You have been asked to assist the chief accountant of the Baker Corporation in the preparation of a balance sheet. The outline presented below represents the various classifications suggested by the chief accountant for the balance sheet.

Assets	_Liabilities and capital_
A. Current	G. Current
B. Investments	H. Long-term
C. Plant and equipment	I. Other liabilities
D. Intangibles	J. Preferred stock
E. Deferred charges	K. Common stock
F. Other assets	L. Paid-in capital excess of par
	M. Retained earnings
	N. Items excluded from the balance sheet.
	X. Contra valuation account

Required:

Items 1 through 18: Items 1 through 18 represent accounts of the Baker Corporation. Determine how each account would be classified from the list above and blacken the corresponding oval on the Objective Answer Sheet. If the account is a contra or valuation account, mark "X" before the letter. For example: "Allowance for Doubtful Accounts" would be "X-A."

Items to be answered

1. Dividend payable (on Baker's preferred stock).
2. Plant construction in progress by the company.
3. Factory building (retired from use and held for sale).
4. Land (held for possible future building site).
5. Merchandise inventory (held by Baker corporation on consignment).
6. Stock dividend distributable (in common stock to common stockholders and to be issued at par).
7. Office supplies inventory.
8. Sinking fund cash (First National Bank, Trustee).
9. Installment sales accounts receivable (average collection period 18 months). All sales are installment sales.
10. Temporary decline in inventory value.
11. Advances to officers (indefinite repayment date).
12. Estimated warranty costs. The warranty costs are for a 1-year warranty on parts and labor.
13. Inventory of small tools used in the business.
14. Treasury stock under par value method.
15. Common stock subscribed (Baker Corporation's stock).
16. Convertible bonds.
17. Securities held as collateral.
18. Bank overdraft (only account with bank).

PROBLEMS*

Problem 1   (15 to 25 minutes)

Hillside Company had a loss during the year ended December 31, 1999, that is properly reported as an extraordinary item.

On July 1, 1999, Hillside committed itself to a formal plan for sale of a business segment. A loss is expect-ed from the proposed sale. Segment operating losses were incurred continuously throughout 1999, and were expected to continue until final disposition in 2000. Costs were incurred in 1999 to relocate segment employees.

Required:

a. How should Hillside report the extraordinary item in its income statement? Why?

b. How should Hillside report the effect of the discontinued operations in its 1999 income statement?

c. How should Hillside report the costs that were incurred to relocate employees of the discontinued segment? Why?

Do not discuss earnings per share requirements.

Problem 2   (40 to 50 minutes)

The following condensed trial balance of Powell Corp., a publicly owned company, has been adjusted except for income tax expense:

Powell Corp.
CONDENSED TRIAL BALANCE
June 30, 1999

	Debit	Credit
Total assets	$25,080,000	
Total liabilities		$9,900,000
5% cumulative preferred stock		2,000,000
Common stock		10,000,000
Retained earnings		2,900,000
Machine sales		750,000
Service revenues		250,000
Interest revenue		10,000
Gain on sale of factory		250,000
Cost of sales--machines	425,000	
Cost of services	100,000	
Administrative expenses	300,000	
Research and development expenses	110,000	
Interest expense	5,000	
Loss from asset disposal	40,000	
	$26,060,000	$26,060,000

Other information and financial data for the year ended June 30, 1999, follows:

• The weighted-average number of common shares outstanding during 1999 was 200,000. The potential dilution from the exercise of stock options held by Powell's officers and directors was not material.

• There were no dividends-in-arrears on Powell's preferred stock at July 1, 1998. On May 1, 1999, Powell's directors declared a 5% preferred stock dividend to be paid in August 1999.

• During 1999, one of Powell's foreign factories was expropriated by the foreign government, and Powell received a $900,000 payment from the foreign government in settlement. The carrying value of the plant was $650,000. Powell has never disposed of a factory.

• Administrative expenses includes a $5,000 premium payment for a $1,000,000 life insurance policy on Powell's president, of which the corporation is the beneficiary.

• Powell depreciates its assets using the straight-line method for financial reporting purposes and an accelerated method for tax purposes. The differences between book and tax depreciation are as follows:

June 30	Financial statements over (under) tax depreciation
1998	$(15,000)
1999	10,000
2000	5,000

There were no other temporary differences.

• Powell's enacted tax rate for the current and future years is 30%.

Required:

a. Using the single-step format, prepare Powell's income statement for the year ended June 30, 1999.

b. Prepare a schedule reconciling Powell's financial statement net income to taxable income for the year ended June 30, 1999.

Problem 3   (45 to 55 minutes)

Presented below is the unaudited balance sheet as of December 31, 1999, prepared by the bookkeeper of Zues Manufacturing Corp.

Zues Manufacturing Corp.
BALANCE SHEET
For the Year Ended December 31, 1999

Assets	
Cash	$ 225,000
Accounts receivable (net)	345,700
Inventories	560,000
Prepaid income taxes	40,000
Investments	57,700
Land	450,000
Building	1,750,000
Machinery and equipment	1,964,000
Goodwill	37,000
Total assets	$5,429,400

---

* The Financial Accounting and Reporting Exam format (FARE) will consist of 20% - 30% essays/problems; thus, it is important that candidates work as many problems as possible so as to be prepared for them. Additionally, the experience of doing them will give candidates a better comprehension of the concepts in preparation for the multiple-choice and other objective type questions. At this point you may want to peruse the FARE Sample Exam in the Appendix of this volume, noting the format of the exam.

Liabilities & Stockholders' Equity

Accounts payable	$ 133,800
Mortgage payable	900,000
Notes payable	500,000
Lawsuit liability	80,000
Income taxes payable	61,200
Deferred tax liability	28,000
Accumulated depreciation	420,000
Total liabilities	$2,123,000
Common stock, $50 par; 40,000	
shares issued	2,231,000
Retained earnings	1,075,400
Total stockholders' equity	$3,306,400
Total liabilities and	
stockholders' equity	$5,429,400

Your firm has been engaged to perform an audit, during which the following data are found:

• Checks totaling $14,000 in payment of accounts payable were mailed on December 30, 1999, but were not recorded until 2000. Late in December 1999, the bank returned a customer's $2,000 check, marked "NSF," but no entry was made. Cash includes $100,000 restricted for building purposes.

• Included in accounts receivable is a $30,000 note due on December 31, 2002, from Zues' president.

• During 1999, Zues purchased 500 shares of common stock of a major corporation that supplies Zues with raw materials. Total cost of this stock was $51,300, and market value on December 31, 1999, was $47,000. The decline in market value is considered temporary. Zues plans to hold these shares indefinitely.

• Treasury stock was recorded at cost when Zues purchased 200 of its own shares for $32 per share in May 1999. This amount is included in investments.

• On December 30, 1999, Zues borrowed $500,000 from a bank in exchange for a 10% note payable, maturing December 30, 2004. Equal principal payments are due December 30 of each year, beginning in 2000. This note is collateralized by a $250,000 tract of land acquired as a potential future building site, which is included in land.

• The mortgage payable requires $50,000 principal payments, plus interest, at the end of each month. Payments were made on January 31 and February 28, 2000. The balance of this mortgage was due June 30, 2001. On March 1, 2000, prior to issuance of the audited financial statements, Zues consummated a noncancelable agreement with the lender to refinance this mortgage. The new terms require $100,000 annual principal payments, plus interest, on February 28 of each year, beginning in 2001. The final payment is due February 28, 2008.

• The lawsuit liability will be paid in 2000.

• The following is an analysis of the deferred tax liability at December 31, 1999:

Deferred taxes related to	
depreciation	$48,000
Deferred taxes related to	
a lawsuit liability	(20,000)
Net deferred tax liability	$28,000

• The current income tax expense reported in Zues' 1999 income statement was $61,200.

• The company was authorized to issue 100,000 shares of $50 par value common stock.

Required:

Prepare a corrected classified balance sheet as of December 31, 1999. This financial statement should include a proper heading, format, and necessary descriptions.

Problem 4   (15 to 25 minutes)

SFAS 130 requires enterprises to disclose comprehensive income.

Required:

a. Define comprehensive income, **other** comprehensive income, and **accumulated** other comprehensive income. You **do not** need to list specific items of other comprehensive income.

b. How shall comprehensive income be reported in the financial statements?

c. Explain the purpose of reclassification adjustments in measuring comprehensive income. How should they be reported?

d. What earnings per share disclosures are required for other comprehensive income items and comprehensive income for public companies?

Problem 5

This problem is covered in Chapter 3 under "Problem Solutions Approach Example."

MULTIPLE-CHOICE ANSWERS

1.	d	__ __	16.	d	__ __	31.	a	__ __	46.	b	__ __	61.	c	__ __
2.	a	__ __	17.	a	__ __	32	b	__ __	47.	a	__ __	62.	a	__ __
3.	c	__ __	18.	b	__ __	33	a.	__ __	48.	a	__ __			
4.	a	__ __	19.	b	__ __	34	d	__ __	49.	c	__ __			
5.	a	__ __	20.	d	__ __	35	d	__ __	50.	c	__ __			
6.	d	__ __	21.	c	__ __	36	b	__ __	51.	c	__ __			
7.	a	__ __	22.	d	__ __	37	a	__ __	52.	b	__ __			
8.	a	__ __	23.	c	__ __	38	c	__ __	53.	a	__ __			
9.	b	__ __	24.	d	__ __	39	a	__ __	54.	d	__ __			
10.	a	__ __	25.	b	__ __	40.	b	__ __	55.	b	__ __			
11.	a	__ __	26.	b	__ __	41.	a	__ __	56.	d	__ __			
12.	c	__ __	27.	c	__ __	42.	a	__ __	57.	c	__ __			
13.	c	__ __	28.	c	__ __	43.	c	__ __	58.	a	__ __			
14.	d	__ __	29.	a	__ __	44.	c	__ __	59.	a	__ __	1st:	__/62 = __%	
15.	b	__ __	30.	a	__ __	45.	d	__ __	60.	a	__ __	2nd:	__/62 = __%	

MULTIPLE-CHOICE ANSWER EXPLANATIONS

D.1. Income and Retained Earnings Statements

1. (d) Baer Food's 1999 revenues should include net sales revenue ($187,000), interest revenue ($10,200), and gain on sale of equipment ($4,700), for a total of $201,900. Discontinued operations ($12,000) and the change in accounting principle ($1,500) are both special items which should be reported as separate components of income, after **income from continuing operations**. Therefore, these items should **not** be included in the revenues section of the income statement (which is placed **before** income from continuing operations).

2. (a) To directly compute cost of goods manufactured (CGM), the formula is:

Beginning work in process
+ Direct materials used
+ Direct labor
+ Factory overhead
– Ending work in process
Cost of goods manufactured

However, none of these elements are given in this problem, so CGM must be computed indirectly, using the cost of sales formula

	Beginning finished goods	$400,000
+	Cost of goods manufactured	+ CGM
–	Ending finished goods	–360,000
	Cost of sales	$240,000

Solving for the missing amount, CGM is $200,000.

3. (c) All of the revenues, gains, expenses, and losses given in this problem are components of income from continuing operations except for the loss on early retirement of long-term debt, which is an extraordinary item. Per SFAS 4, material gains and losses from extinguishment of debt should be reported as an extraordinary item even if these gains or losses do not meet the criteria of infrequent and unusual. Income before income taxes is $200,000, as computed below.

Revenues ($575,000 + $25,000)	$600,000
Expenses and losses ($240,000 + $70,000 + $10,000 + $50,000 + $15,000 + $15,000)	400,000
Income before income taxes	$200,000

To compute income from continuing operations (after taxes), income taxes ($200,000 x 30% = $60,000) must also be deducted ($200,000 – $60,000 = $140,000).

4. (a) The requirement is to compute the amount of expenses to be included in selling expenses for 1999. Advertising ($150,000) and sales salaries and commissions ($140,000) are clearly selling expenses, as is the rent for the office space occupied by the sales department ($220,000 x 1/2 = $110,000). Additionally, freight-out ($80,000) is a selling expense because shipping the goods **from** the point of sale to the customer is the final effort in the selling process. The total selling expense is, therefore, $480,000 ($150,000 + $140,000 + $110,000 + $80,000). The remaining expenses given are general and administrative expenses, except for interest and the loss on sale of long-term investment, which are nonoperating items (other expenses and losses).

5. (a) Operating expenses are usually divided into two categories, **selling expenses** and **general and administrative (G&A) expenses**. Selling expenses are related to the sale of a company's products, while G&A expenses are related to the company's general operations. Therefore, Griff should include the following costs in G&A expense:

Accounting and legal fees	$ 25,000
Officers' salaries	150,000
Insurance	85,000
G&A expense	$260,000

Freight-in ($175,000) is an inventoriable cost which should be reflected in cost of goods sold and ending inventory. Freight-out, the cost of delivering goods to customers ($160,000), is included in selling expenses. Sales representatives salaries ($215,000) is also a selling expense.

6. (d) Interest expense is generally considered to be a nonoperating item and is therefore included in **other expenses and losses**. Operating expenses are usually divided into two categories, **selling expenses** and **general and ad-**

ministrative expenses. Since advertising expense is directly related to the sale of the company's products, it is included in selling expenses. Therefore, neither of the expenses given are general and administrative expenses.

7.   (a)   Charitable contributions expense should include all expenses incurred in 1999 by Yew Co. which involve charitable contributions to other entities. The total charitable contributions expense is $310,000, consisting of the $250,000 donated to youth and educational programs and the $60,000 ($140,000 – $80,000) donated to health and human service organizations. The other $80,000 was given to these organizations **by the employees**, with the company merely acting as an agent collecting that amount through payroll deductions and forwarding it on to the organizations. The expenditure for redesigning product packaging ($100,000) would be properly classified as research and development expense.

8.   (a)   Per APB 30, extraordinary items are material gains or losses which are both **unusual** in nature and **infrequent** in occurrence. For Raim Co., which sustains flood losses every 2-3 years, the 1999 flood loss is not infrequent, and should be recognized as a component of income from continuing operations. For Cane Co., the 1999 flood loss is both unusual and infrequent, so it should be recognized as an extraordinary item.

9.   (b)   Per APB 30, extraordinary items are material items which are **both unusual** in nature and **infrequent** in occurrence. Para 23 of APB 30 specifically states that the effect of a strike ($175,000) and a gain or loss from sale or abandonment of equipment ($125,000) are **not** considered extraordinary. However, para 8 of SFAS 4 states that gains and losses from extinguishment of debt are to be classified as extraordinary even if they do not meet the **unusual** and **infrequent** criteria. Therefore the $150,000 loss is extraordinary, and the total amount of infrequent losses **not** considered extraordinary is $300,000 ($175,000 + $125,000).

10.   (a)   Per APB 30, para 30, extraordinary items are material items which are **both unusual** in nature and **infrequent** in occurrence. Disposals of plant assets, foreign currency losses, and inventory losses are not considered to be unusual in nature, and thus are not extraordinary. Items which may qualify as extraordinary items include some casualties, expropriations, prohibitions under a new law, and extinguishment of debt. In Kent Co.'s 1999 income statement, losses not considered extraordinary amount to $610,000. The factory disposal ($300,000) is classified as discontinued operations because the operations carried on there are dissimilar from operations carried on at the other factories. The $120,000 foreign currency loss and $190,000 inventory loss are not extraordinary because they are not unusual in nature. Therefore, answer (a) is correct.

11.   (a)   Per APB 30, para 30, extraordinary items are material gains or losses which are both **unusual** in nature and **infrequent** in occurrence. Foreign currency losses ($1,200,000) and losses due to discontinued operations ($500,000) are not considered to be unusual in nature and thus are not extraordinary. Items which may qualify as extraordinary include some casualties, expropriations, prohibitions under a new law, and extinguishment of debt. Mid-

way's casualty loss appears to be extraordinary because the hurricane was the first ever to strike in Midway's area. The net pretax loss was $100,000 [$800,000 equipment loss – $700,000 building gain ($1,000,000 – $300,000)].

12.   (c)   A gain (loss) must be recognized when a nonmonetary asset is involuntarily converted into monetary assets even if the company reinvests the monetary assets in replacement nonmonetary assets. The gain or loss is the difference between the insurance proceeds ($1,100,000 replacement cost – $50,000 deductible = $1,050,000) and the carrying amount of the assets destroyed or used up as a result of the casualty loss. The warehouse (carrying amount of $300,000) was destroyed, and cash of $20,000 was used to cover removal costs. Therefore, the gain is $730,000 [$1,050,000 – ($300,000 + $20,000)]. It is **not** an extraordinary item because storms similar to the one which destroyed the warehouse occur frequently (every 4 years).

13.   (c)   In this situation, the provision for income tax (income tax expense) will be the amount of the tax liability to the government determined without including the extraordinary loss. This amount is determined by applying the 40% tax rate to pretax accounting income before extraordinary items adjusted for any permanent differences. Accounting income before taxes is $900,000, but that amount includes a gain on life insurance coverage ($100,000). A gain on life insurance coverage is a **permanent** difference because it is included in accounting income but will **never** be included in taxable income. Therefore, the amount of accounting income which will be subject to taxes is $800,000 ($900,000 – $100,000), and the provision for income taxes is $320,000 ($800,000 x 40%). The tax savings from the extraordinary loss ($300,000 x 40% = $120,000) will not affect the provision for income taxes because the extraordinary item must be reported together with its tax effect (extraordinary loss of $180,000; net of tax).

14.   (d)   Net income as reported ($74,100) properly included the gain on early retirement of bonds payable ($22,000) and the loss from fire ($14,000). Note that the gain should be reported net of tax as an extraordinary item, while the loss should be reported at its gross amount ($21,000) as an operating loss. The fact that the loss was reported net of taxes in the income statement was incorrect, but does not cause the net income amount to be in error. However, the other two items should **not** be reported in the income statement at all. An unrealized loss on **noncurrent** investments in stock ($5,400) is reported as a **direct** reduction of stockholders' equity, bypassing the income statement. A correction of an error ($7,500) is treated as a prior period adjustment. It is reported in the financial statements as an adjustment to the beginning balance of retained earnings, rather than in the income statement. Since both of these items were subtracted in the computation of reported net income, they must be added back to compute the correct net income of $87,000 ($74,100 + $5,400 + $7,500).

15.   (b)   In 1999, Brecon Co. would report one fifth of the cabinet costs as depreciation expense in selling, general, and administrative expenses. Four fifths of the cabinet cost would remain capitalized as fixed assets at the end of 1999. Therefore, answer (d) is incorrect. Answers (a) and (c) are incorrect because the cabinets are considered fixed assets and not a part of cost of goods sold.

16. (d)   Para 26 of APB 30 states that a material gain or loss that is unusual in nature or infrequent in occurrence, but not both, should be presented as a separate component of income or loss from continuing operations. Therefore, answer (d) is correct. Answers (a) and (b) are incorrect because both extraordinary items and cumulative effect type changes in accounting principle are reported separately **after** income from continuing operations. Answer (c) is incorrect because it is simply the definition of an extraordinary item.

17. (a)   Per APB 30, for an item to qualify as an extraordinary item it must be **both** unusual in nature and infrequent in occurrence. The above criteria must take into account the environment in which the entity operates. An entity with sales in different countries will experience foreign currency revaluations on a regular basis, so a currency revaluation would not be infrequent in occurrence and it is not an extraordinary item. Gains from increases in contract prices are neither infrequent nor unusual, so they cannot qualify as extraordinary items. Therefore, answer (a) is correct.

18. (b)   Per APB 30, extraordinary items are reported **net of income taxes** as a separate component of income **after** discontinued operations but before cumulative effect of a change in accounting principle.

19. (b)   Per APB 30, para 20, extraordinary items are events and transactions that are distinguished by both their unusual nature and the infrequency of their occurrence. Since losses of this type are both common and frequent for Toncan, answer (a) is incorrect, and answer (b) is correct. Answers (c) and (d) are incorrect because per SFAS 5, estimates of the losses would not be presented in the financial statements. No amount is recorded until a loss actually occurs.

20. (d)   Per para 20 of APB 30, a transaction that is unusual in nature and infrequent in occurrence is considered an extraordinary item. An extraordinary item is reported **after** discontinued operations but **before** cumulative effect of accounting changes. Therefore, answer (d) is correct.

21. (c)   Per APB 30, para 20, extraordinary items are events and transactions that are distinguished by both their unusual nature and the infrequency of their occurrence. Teller Co.'s loss arising from its **first** antitrust action meets both of these criteria (particularly since they pleaded guilty) and should therefore be reported as an extraordinary item. The strike against Teller's major supplier, however, should not be reported as an extraordinary item because it is usual in nature but may be expected to recur as a consequence of customary and continuing business activities. Therefore, answer (c) is correct and answers (a), (b), and (d) are incorrect.

22. (d)   Per APB 30, extraordinary items are material items which are **both unusual** in nature and **infrequent** in occurrence. Therefore, the loss on sale of a bond investment is not extraordinary. However, para 8 of SFAS 4 states that gains and losses from extinguishment of debt are to be clas-

sified as extraordinary even if they do not meet the **unusual** and **infrequent** criteria. Thus, Gold's gain on the retirement of its own bonds is reported as an extraordinary item.

23. (c)   SFAS 130 does not completely operationalize the concept of comprehensive income per SFAC 5 and 6 which state all transactions and events other than those with owners should be reported in comprehensive income. Under SFAS 130, corrections of errors shall continue to be reported net of tax in retained earnings as an adjustment of the beginning balance.

D.2. Discontinued Operations

24. (d)   Amounts reported as discontinued operations are classified as either **income (loss) from operations of discontinued segment** (results prior to the measurement date of April 30) or **gain (loss) from disposal** [results after the measurement date including gain (loss) on sale].

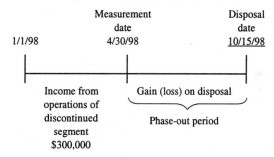

The operating loss of $300,000 ($500,000 revenues less $800,000 expenses) relates to a discontinued segment, so it is part of discontinued operations, **not** continuing operations [answer (a)]. The loss occurred prior to the measurement date, so it is a loss from operations of discontinued segment [answer (d)], **not** loss on disposal of segment [answer (b)]. Answer (c) is incorrect because **discontinued operations** is a category distinct from **extraordinary items**.

25. (b)   The information can be diagrammed as follows:

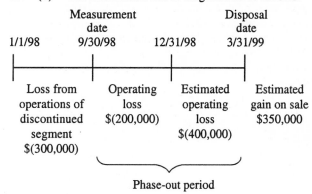

Generally, the estimated gain (loss) is recognized in the current year because its cause is the decision to dispose of the segment, which occurred in the current year. If there was an estimated net **gain**, it could only be recognized to the extent that it offset a current year realized operating loss. Therefore, Host would recognize two components of discontinued operations: loss from operations of discontinued segment, $300,000; and loss on disposal, $250,000 [$200,000 + ($400,000 – $350,000)].

26. (b) Amounts reported as discontinued operations are classified as either **income (loss) from operations of discontinued segment** (results prior to the measurement date in January 1998) or **gain (loss) from disposal** [results after measurement date including gain (loss) on sale].

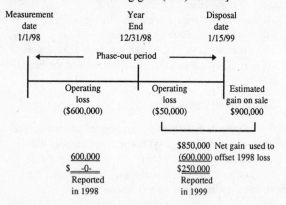

In this case, all amounts given occur after the measurement date and therefore are all part of the gain (loss) from disposal. If the phaseout period extends over more than one reporting period, as in this case, APB 30 requires that the realized loss from operations of the discontinued segment during the phaseout period included in the current reporting period be reduced by any net gain on disposal estimated for the following period. Thus, the $600,000 loss from operations in 1998 would be reduced to $0 by the net gain of $850,000 estimated for 1999 ($900,000 gain on sale less $50,000 loss from operations). This leaves a remaining gain of $250,000 ($850,000 – $600,000) to be recognized in 1999.

27. (c) Amounts reported as discontinued operations are classified as either **income (loss) from operations of discontinued segment** (results prior to measurement date of 12/31/98) or **gain (loss) from disposal** [results after measurement date including gain (loss) on sale]. The loss from operation of the discontinued segment in 1998 is $300,000. The **estimated** gain on disposal ($700,000 – $200,000 = $500,000) cannot be accrued at 12/31/98 because there is no loss on disposal against which it can be offset in 1998 (because the measurement date was 12/31/98). Therefore, the actual gain recognized in 1999 is $350,000 ($650,000 – $300,000).

28. (c) Per APB 30, para 17, costs and expenses directly associated with the decision to dispose include items such as severance pay, additional pension costs [answer (c)], employee relocation expenses, and future rentals on long-term leases to the extent they are not offset by sublease rentals. Answer (a) is incorrect because employee relocation costs should be included in the decision to dispose. Answer (b) is incorrect because operating losses are included in the phase-out period. Answer (d) is incorrect because the loss on disposal does not include operating losses of the current period up to the measurement date. It includes operating losses after the measurement date.

29. (a) The requirement is to determine how a discontinued segment's operating losses for the current period up to the measurement date should be classified in the financial statements. Answer (a) is correct because according to

APB 30, the "income (loss) from operations" is calculated from the beginning of the period to the measurement date. The income (loss) from operations is shown as a separate line item under discontinued operations on the income statement. Answer (b) is incorrect because it is not combined with the loss on disposal. Answer (c) is incorrect because discontinued operations is shown separately from income (loss) from continuing operations. Answer (d) is incorrect because discontinued operations is included on the income statement, **not** on the retained earnings statement.

30. (a) Per APB 30, para 13, gains or losses from the operation of a discontinued business segment realized from the beginning of the year to the measurement date are separately disclosed, net of tax, in the discontinued operations section of the income statement under the heading "Income (loss) from operations of discontinued division." Thus, answer (a) is correct. Answer (b) is incorrect because operating losses during the phase-out period are included in the loss on disposal of business segment. Answers (c) and (d) are incorrect because the loss on disposal of a business segment should be shown separately on the income statement in the discontinued operations section, after income from continuing operations and before extraordinary items.

31. (a) Per APB 30, para 15, the determination of whether a gain or loss results from the disposal of a segment of a business should be made at the measurement date (the date on which the company's management commits to dispose of a segment of a business). At that date the gain or loss should be based on estimates of the net realizable value of the segment after giving consideration to any estimated costs and expenses directly associated with the disposal and to any estimated income or losses from operations between the measurement date and the disposal date (i.e., during the phase-out period). If it is expected that net losses from operations will be incurred during the phase-out period, as in this case, the computation of the gain or loss on disposal should also include an estimate of such amounts. When a gain is expected on the sale, it should generally be recognized when realized, which ordinarily is the disposal date. Therefore, answer (b) is incorrect. In this case, the anticipated losses from operations of the segment during the phase-out period should be offset by the anticipated gain on the disposal of the segment, and the net gain should be reported in 2000, upon disposal. The **net** gain from disposal to be recognized in 1999 is therefore zero. Thus, answer (a) is correct. Answer (c) is incorrect because, per para 16, the gain or loss from the disposal should not include the results of operations of the segment prior to measurement date. Answer (d) is incorrect because the segment's December 1999 operating loss is only a component of the net gain from disposal which should not be recognized until 2000.

D.3. Comprehensive Income

32. (b) Per SFAS 130, the purpose of reporting comprehensive income is to report a measure of overall enterprise performance by displaying all changes in equity of an enterprise that result from recognized transactions and other economic events of the period other than transactions with owners in their capacity as owners. An enterprise should continue to display an amount for net income with equal prominence to the comprehensive income amount displayed. Therefore, answer (b) is correct.

33. **(a)** Per SFAS 130, comprehensive income is computed as follows:

Net income		77,000
Other comprehensive income net of tax:		
Unrealized gain on securities	15,000	
Less: reclassification adjustment	(2,500)	12,500
Minimum pension liability adjustment		(3,000)
Other comprehensive income		9,500
Comprehensive income		86,500

Notice that stock warrants outstanding are not included as part of comprehensive income. Thus, answer (a) is correct.

34. **(d)** If $2,450 (net of tax) is being deducted from other comprehensive income as a reclassification adjustment, $2,450 must be the amount of unrealized gains (net of tax) that have been recognized in other comprehensive income. The realized gains will then be recognized in income from continuing operations before tax. The gains before tax effects are $3,500 ($2,450 ÷ 70%). Answer (a) is incorrect because what is added or subtracted to compute net income should not be net of tax. Also, a realized gain has occurred so the amount should be added to arrive at net income. Answer (b) is incorrect because $3,500 should be added, not deducted. Answer (c) is incorrect because the amount should not be net of tax.

35. **(d)** Separate EPS calculations are not required for other comprehensive income or comprehensive income according to SFAS 130. Answer (a) is incorrect because separate EPS calculations are not required for either other comprehensive income or comprehensive income. Answer (b) is incorrect because separate EPS calculations are not required for other comprehensive income. Answer (c) is incorrect because separate EPS calculations are not required for comprehensive income.

D.4. Balance Sheets

36. **(b)** Total retained earnings includes both unappropriated retained earnings and restricted retained earnings. Therefore, before closing entries, total retained earnings is $1,060,000 ($900,000 + $160,000). Before computing 1998 net income, tax expense must be recorded. Earnings ($6,680,000) less costs and expenses ($5,180,000) result in pretax income of $1,500,000. Since the tax rate is 30%, tax expense is $450,000 (30% x $1,500,000). Therefore, an adjustment is necessary to debit **income tax expense** and credit **prepaid taxes** for $450,000. After the adjustment, net income is $1,050,000 ($6,680,000 − $5,180,000 − $450,000). After closing entries, total retained earnings is $2,110,000 ($1,060,000 + $1,050,000).

37. **(a)** The only liabilities included in the trial balance are billings in excess of costs on long-term contracts ($700,000) and note payable-noncurrent ($1,620,000). Only the note is noncurrent. Billings in excess of costs on long-term contracts is similar to unearned revenue and is always reported as a current liability.

38. **(c)** Current assets listed in the trial balance are cash ($600,000), accounts receivable ($3,500,000), cost in excess of billings on long-term contracts ($1,600,000) and prepaid taxes ($450,000). However, income tax expense has not yet been recorded. Earnings ($6,680,000) less costs and expenses ($5,180,000) result in pretax income of $1,500,000. Since the tax rate is 30%, tax expense is $450,000 (30% x $1,500,000). Therefore, an adjustment is necessary to debit **income tax expense** and credit **prepaid taxes** for $450,000. Total current assets, after this adjustment, are $5,700,000.

Cash	$ 600,000
Accounts receivable	3,500,000
Cost in excess of billings	1,600,000
	$5,700,000

39. **(a)** Mirr began operations on 1/1/99 with the following balance sheet elements:

Assets	=	Liabilities	+	Owners' equity
$860,000	=	$110,000	+	$750,000

During 1999, liabilities increased to $120,000, and owners' equity increased to $765,000 [$750,000 beginning balance + $18,000 net income ($82,000 revenues − $64,000 expenses) − $3,000 dividends declared]. Therefore, 12/31/99 assets must be $885,000.

Assets	=	Liabilities	+	Owners' equity
Assets	=	$120,000	+	$765,000
Assets	=	$885,000		

40. **(b)** The requirement is to determine the net income for 1999 by analyzing changes in the balance sheet. Recall the accounting equation: Assets − Liabilities = Stockholders' equity. By inserting the changes given into this formula, we find an increase of $62,000 exists in the entire stockholders' equity section ($89,000 − $27,000 = $62,000). Stockholders' equity is composed of capital stock, additional paid-in capital and retained earnings. Because increases in the other two balances are given that total $66,000 ($60,000 + $6,000), the retained earnings balance must have decreased by $4,000 ($66,000 − $62,000). When dividends are paid, this reduces retained earnings, while Vel Corp. net income increases the balance of retained earnings. For the equation to balance, the changes in retained earnings account must reduce total stockholders' equity by $4,000. Therefore, if $13,000 in dividends are paid, which reduce retained earnings, and total retained earnings are to be reduced by $4,000, then net income, which increases retained earnings, must be $9,000. This creates the $4,000 difference needed to make the equation balance ($89,000 − $27,000 = $66,000 − $4,000). The following shows the analysis of the retained earnings account:

Retained earnings (beg.)	$ xxx
Net income (plug)	**9,000**
Dividends	(13,000)
Retained earnings (decrease)	($ 4,000)

41. **(a)** Idle machinery ($11,200) and cash surrender value of life insurance ($13,700) are both assets. The allowance for decline in market value of noncurrent marketable equity securities ($8,400) is a contra asset which is properly included in the asset section of the balance sheet (as a deduction). The only item listed which should **not** be included in the asset section of the balance sheet is the treasury stock ($24,000). Although the treasury stock account has a debit balance, it is not an asset; instead, it is reported as a contra equity account. Therefore, the $24,000 must be excluded from the asset section, reducing the net asset amount to $851,000 ($875,000 – $24,000).

42. (a)   Although the statement of cash flows provides information about liquidity, solvency, and financial flexibility, a potential investor would **primarily** use the balance sheet to assess liquidity and financial flexibility. Thus, answer (a) is correct. The balance sheet helps users analyze the company's ability to use current assets to pay current liabilities (liquidity) and the company's ability to alter the amounts and timing of future cash flows to adapt to unexpected needs or to take advantage of opportunities (flexibility).

D.5.a. Disclosures

43. (c)   SFAS 57, para 2, requires that financial statements include disclosures of material transactions between related parties. Compensation arrangements in the ordinary course of business, however, are specifically excluded from this disclosure requirement. Therefore, only the $250,000 sale to affiliated enterprises must be disclosed, and answer (c) is correct.

44. (c)   SFAS 57 requires disclosure of material transactions between related parties except: (1) compensation agreements, expense allowances, and other similar items in the ordinary course of business, and (2) transactions which are eliminated in the preparation of consolidated or combined financial statements. The officers' salaries and officers' expenses fall into category (1), while the intercompany sales fall into category (2). Therefore, only the loans to officers ($125,000 + $50,000 = $175,000) are reported as related-party disclosures.

45. (d)   SFAS 57 requires disclosure of material transactions between related parties except: (1) compensation agreements, expense allowances, and other similar items in the ordinary course of business [answer (d)], and (2) transactions eliminated in the preparation of consolidated or combined financial statements.

46. (b)   Answer (b) is correct because SFAS 57, para 2, requires disclosure of any material related-party transactions except

   (1) Compensation agreements, expense allowances, and similar items in the ordinary course of business.
   (2) Transactions which are eliminated in the preparation of consolidated or combined financial statements.

Since sales of inventory between subsidiary and parent are eliminated in preparing consolidated financial statements, such sales need not be disclosed as a related-party transaction. Answer (a) is incorrect because nonmonetary exchanges by affiliates are not specifically exempted from disclosure by SFAS 57, and therefore must be disclosed as related-party transactions. Answer (c) is incorrect because SFAS 57, para 2, states that compensation arrangements, expense allowances, and similar items in the ordinary course of business need not be disclosed as related-party transac-

tions. However, in this case the allowances are in excess of normal business practice and therefore must be disclosed. Answer (d) is incorrect because surety and guaranty agreements between related parties are not specifically exempted from disclosure by SFAS 57, and therefore must be disclosed as related-party transactions.

47. (a)   The users of the information are the focus of financial reporting. GAAP requires disclosures in the notes to facilitate the users' understanding of the financial statements. Answer (b) is incorrect because the financial statements should be properly presented in accordance with GAAP; thus no improper presentation should exist. Answer (c) is incorrect because the totals of the financial statements should include all items; thus, no items would be excluded. Answer (d) is incorrect because management's responses to the auditor's comments would be contained in the management letter, which is a separate report typically presented to the audit committee or the board of directors.

D.5.b. Accounting Policies

48. (a)   The requirement is to determine which information should be included in the summary of significant accounting policies. Per APB 22, para 12, disclosure of accounting policies should identify and describe the accounting principles followed by the reporting entity and methods of applying those principles. Answer (a) is correct because the method of recording and depreciating assets is an example of such a required disclosure. Answers (b) and (c) are incorrect because both represent detail presented elsewhere in the financial statements. Answer (d) is incorrect because it is an estimate of earnings rather than an accounting policy.

49. (c)   Per para 12 of APB 22, disclosure of accounting policies should identify and describe the accounting principles followed by the reporting entity and methods of applying those principles. Answer (c) is correct because the criteria for determining which investments are treated as cash equivalents is an example of how the entity applies accounting principles. Para 14 of the same opinion states that these disclosures should not duplicate details presented elsewhere as part of the financial statements. Answers (a), (b), and (d) are not disclosures of accounting **policies**, and also would be presented elsewhere in the financial statements.

D.5.d. Constant Dollar Accounting

50. (c)   SFAS 89 encourages, but does not require, business enterprises to disclose **supplementary information** on the effects of changing prices. The statement presents requirements to be followed by enterprises that voluntarily elect to disclose this information. Answers (a) and (b) are incorrect because the information is not reported in the body of the financial statements or in the notes to the financial statements. Answer (d) is incorrect because management's report to shareholders identifies management's responsibilities, including responsibilities for the internal control system, and would not include information about changing prices.

51. (c)   The requirement is to determine the amounts to be reported for three balance sheet accounts in a supplementary **constant dollar** balance sheet. In a constant dollar balance sheet, **nonmonetary** items are restated to the current price level, while monetary items are **not** restated because they are already stated in current dollars. The investment in bonds and the long-term debt are monetary items since their amounts are fixed by contract in terms of number of dollars. Therefore, these items are not restated and are reported at $60,000 and $80,000, respectively. The land, however, is a nonmonetary item and its cost ($120,000) must be restated to current dollars by using the TO/FROM ratio (110/100), resulting in an adjusted amount of $132,000 ($120,000 x 110/100). Reference to SFAS 89, paras 96-108, will provide guidance on monetary/nonmonetary classifications.

52. **(b)** According to SFAS 89, para 96, "loans to employees" is a monetary asset account since its payment amount is fixed at some point in the future. Conversely, merchandise inventory is considered a nonmonetary asset account since its value will change based on relative price levels in the future. The total value of monetary assets is the balance of the loans to employees account, or $20,000.

53. **(a)** The increase in current cost (nominal dollars) of $15,000 is the **total** increase in current cost, including any increase caused by inflation. The effect of changes in the general price level is **not** separated from the effect of changes in specific value. The increase in current cost (constant dollars) of $12,000 is the increase in current cost after eliminating any increase caused by inflation. Therefore, the inflation component of the increase in current cost of inventories is $3,000 ($15,000 – $12,000).

54. **(d)** The requirement is to determine which item is classified as nonmonetary when computing the purchasing power gain or loss on net monetary items. SFAS 89, para 44, defines a monetary item as one that is fixed or determinable without reference to future prices. Accumulated depreciation is not a monetary item. Therefore, answer (d) is correct. Answers (a), (b), and (c) are incorrect because advances to unconsolidated subsidiaries, allowance for doubtful accounts, and unamortized premium on bonds payable are all monetary items.

55. **(b)** Per SFAS 89, a purchasing power gain or loss is the net gain or loss determined by restating in units of constant purchasing power the opening and closing balances of, and transactions in, **monetary** assets and liabilities. Therefore, answers (a) and (c) are incorrect. During a period of rising prices, monetary liabilities give rise to purchasing power gains because they will be settled with cash which can be used to purchase relatively fewer goods or services at a future time. Therefore, answer (b) is correct and answer (d) is incorrect.

D.5.e. Current Cost Accounting

56. **(d)** Current cost accounting is a method of valuing and reporting assets, liabilities, revenues, and expenses at their current cost at the balance sheet date or at the date of their use or sale. A holding gain is recorded as an increase in an item's value. At December 31, 1999, Vend Co. is holding merchandise which is currently valued at $10 per unit (replacement cost), while the original recorded value of the merchandise was $8 per unit (purchase price). There-

fore, the holding gain is $2 per unit and answer (d) is correct.

57. **(c)** The requirement is to calculate the amount of current cost depreciation expense which would appear in supplementary current cost financial statements. Per para 52b of SFAS 89, depreciation is to be measured based on the **average** current cost of the asset during the period of use. The average current cost of this machine during 1999 is $120,000 [($115,000 + $125,000) ÷ 2]. Therefore, 1999 depreciation expense is $24,000 ($120,000 ÷ 5-year useful life).

58. **(a)** SFAS 89 requires that current cost for inventories and equipment be measured at the lower of current cost or recoverable amount. For equipment, recoverable amount ($95,000) is lower than current cost; for inventory, current cost ($80,000) is lower than recoverable amount. Therefore, the total amount to be reported for these assets is $175,000 ($95,000 + $80,000).

59. **(a)** Per SFAS 89, para 34, increases or decreases in the current cost of inventory result from the difference between the measures of assets at their entry dates (beginning of year or purchase date) and measures of assets at their exit dates (end of year or date of use/sale). Based on this definition, holding gains would be reported both when inventory is sold during the year (realized gains), and when inventory is held at the end of the year (unrealized gains). Therefore, answer (a) is correct.

60. **(a)** SFAS 89, para 61, illustrates the computation of cost of goods sold under the current cost method. According to that paragraph, the current cost of goods sold is computed by multiplying the average cost of units produced or purchased during the year times the number of units sold. Therefore, answer (a) is correct.

D.5.g.7. Other Comprehensive Bases of Accounting

61. **(c)** Other than generally accepted accounting principles, the only other bases which may be used to prepare financial statements in conformity with a comprehensive basis of accounting are the **cash basis** and a **basis of accounting used to file an income tax return.**

62. **(a)** In financial statements prepared on the income-tax basis, the nondeductible portion of meals and entertainment expense should be included with the deductible portion as a total amount of travel and entertainment expense. Additionally, the nondeductible portion should be footnoted. Answer (a) is the best answer among the alternatives given, although it does not indicate that a footnote is required. The answer to this question is found in an AICPA practice publication entitled *Preparing and Reporting on Cash- and Tax-basis Financial Statements* that gives guidance to practitioners on preparing financial statements on other comprehensive bases of accounting.

AUTHOR'S NOTE: Candidates should not worry about preparing for such questions.

OTHER OBJECTIVE ANSWERS AND ANSWER EXPLANATIONS

Problem 1

1.   (G) The acquisition of assets does not necessitate that the same method of depreciation be used for the newly acquired assets as for the existing assets. Therefore, no change in accounting principle has occurred because the previously recorded assets will continue to be depreciated using the straight-line method.

2.   (A) Accounting for a pooling of interests is properly accounted for as a change in reporting entity.

3.   (B) According to SFAS 16, all corrections of errors should be treated as prior period adjustments. This requires prompt recording of the error in the year in which the error was discovered, and reporting the effects of the error in the financial statements as an adjustment to the beginning balance of retained earnings.

4.   (H) According to APB Opinion 30, for an item to qualify as an extraordinary item it must be both unusual in nature and infrequent in occurrence. Clearly, the write-down of inventory due to obsolescence does not qualify for extraordinary treatment; therefore, it should be disclosed separately in the income statement as an unusual or infrequent item.

5.   (I) Gains or losses on the disposal of net assets is included in the calculation of gain or loss on disposal of discontinued operations. Therefore, the total gain or loss on disposal should consist of the following two calculations: the net asset gain or loss mentioned above and the income or loss from operations from the measurement date to the disposal date (the phase-out period).

6.   (B) The use of the gross profit method to determine year-end inventory balances is not proper GAAP. Therefore, if a situation such as this existed, it should be treated as a correction of an error.

7.   (C) The change from one generally accepted accounting principle to another is considered a change in accounting principle. Since both the completed contract method and the percentage-of-completion methods are recognized GAAP, the change from one to the other is properly accounted for as a change in accounting principle.

8.   (D) According to APB 20, para 11, when it is impossible to determine whether a change in accounting principle or a change in estimate has occurred, the change should be considered as a change in estimate.

9.   (E) According to SFAS 4, "Reporting Gains and Losses From Extinguishment of Debt," the extinguishment of debt is always treated as an extraordinary item. In this illustration, where the cash paid to extinguish the debt is greater than its carrying value, the proper accounting treatment would be recognition of an extraordinary loss on extinguishment of debt.

10.   (I) Income or loss from operations during the phase-out period (from the measurement date to the disposal date) is properly included in the calculation of the gain or loss on the disposal of discontinued operations. Therefore, this calculation includes both the income or loss from operations during the phase-out period and the gain or loss on the disposal of net assets.

Problem 2

1.   (B) Per SFAS 115, changes in the market value of (trading type) marketable securities shall be included in the determination of income from continuing operations of the period in which the change in market value occurs.

2.   (E) Per SFAS 130, the accumulated changes in the valuation (unrealized excess of cost over market value) of **available-for-sale** marketable equity securities shall be reported as accumulated other comprehensive income.

3.   (F) Per APB 30, para 8, results of operations of a segment that has been or will be discontinued should be reported **separately** as a component of income, after income from continuing operations but before extraordinary items and the cumulative effect of accounting changes.

4.   (B) Per SFAS 52, a foreign subsidiary must **remeasure** its financial statements when its functional currency (the currency of the primary economic environment in which the entity operates) is different from its local currency (the currency currently used by the entity). The effect of the remeasurement process (gain or loss) should be recognized currently in income. Aggregate gain or loss for the period should also be disclosed either in the financial statements or in the notes.

5.   (C) Per SFAS 52, when translating a foreign subsidiary's financial statements from functional currency to reporting currency, a translation adjustment will result. The translation adjustment is not included in net income but is reported as a component of comprehensive income and called other comprehensive income.

6.   (D) Per APB 30, para 30, extraordinary items are events and transactions that are **both** unusual and infrequent. The earthquake in this problem occurred in an area previously considered subject to only minor tremors. Therefore, the earthquake would be considered an extraordinary event. Per APB 30, para 11, extraordinary items should be shown separately on the income statement, after income from continuing operations.

7.   (F) The question indicates that it is probable that Pucket Corp. will **receive** $1,000,000 from a pending lawsuit. Thus, the $1,000,000 is a **gain** contingency. Per SFAS 5, para 5, contingencies that may result in **gains** are not reflected in the accounts, as doing so might result in the recognition of revenue before its realization. Adequate disclosure of the gain contingency should be made, but care should be taken to avoid misleading implications as to the likelihood of realization.

8. (B) Per SFAS 2, paras 11-13, the cost of research and development services performed by others on behalf of the enterprise are included in R&D costs. R&D costs are charged to expense when incurred and thus are included in income from continuing operations of that period. In addition, separate disclosure of the total R&D costs for the period should be made either in the financial statements or in the notes.

Problem 3

1. (G) When a corporation declares a cash or property dividend, the amount to be paid becomes a liability of the corporation. The dividends payable amount would be classified as a current liability on the balance sheet. It is important to note that dividends payable represent the amount distributed to stockholders as a return on their investment. Dividends are not expenses.

2. (C) When an item of property, plant, or equipment is being constructed by the company that intends to use it, all of the relevant costs related to the construction should be included in the asset. The asset would be classified as plant and equipment.

3. (F) A factory building which has been retired from use and held for sale should be classified as an **other asset** rather than as property, plant and equipment. The property, plant and equipment account should include only those tangible assets which are being used in operations.

4. (B) Land which is held for speculative or investment purposes should be classified as an investment rather than as property, plant, and equipment. The property, plant, and equipment account should represent only those assets being used in current operations.

5. (N) Consigned inventory is excluded from the balance sheet because it is not owned by Baker. Consigned inventory represents an arrangement whereby the owner of the goods transfers physical possession to an agent (Baker). The agent (consignee) will attempt to sell the goods on the owner's behalf. The inventory remains an asset of its owner.

6. (K) A stock dividend distributable represents a dividend to be distributed to shareholders in the form of additional shares of the corporation's stock. Each shareholder will receive a proportional share of additional stock. The declaration of a stock dividend does not result in a liability, as it does not result in any of the corporation's assets being paid. Thus, a stock dividend distributable would be classified as an addition in the stockholders' equity section in the common stock account.

7. (A) Current assets represent cash or other assets which are expected to be used within the operating cycle. Office supplies inventory represents an asset which could be expected to be used within the operating cycle.

8. (B) Generally, a fund is a group of assets set aside for a future nonoperating purpose. A sinking fund contains assets to be used in the future to retire bonds. These assets are generally invested while waiting to be used and are noncurrent.

9. (A) An installment sales accounts receivable results when the corporation makes a sale to a customer and does not receive payment in full on the date of sale. Since this company normally sells on the installment basis, its operating cycle becomes 18 months. Its receivables are current assets because their average life falls within the operating cycle.

10. (N) Temporary decline in inventory value is a loss and appears on the income statement.

11. (F) Advances to officers are considered nontrade receivables. These types of receivables should be reported separately on the balance sheet as other assets.

12. (G) A warranty is a guarantee made by the seller to the purchaser against defects in the product's quality. Estimated warranty expense for a given period can be estimated as a percentage of sales. The percentage is based on past warranty experience. The estimated warranty cost represents the warranty expenditures in the future for past sales and is a current liability.

13. (C) Property, plant, and equipment consists of items used in the normal operations of a business. The inventory of small tools represents tools **used** in the business and are not for sale.

14. (X-K) Treasury stock is a corporation's own stock which has been issued and reacquired by the corporation. Treasury stock may be accounted for under the cost or par value method. When the par value method is used, treasury stock would be recorded on the balance sheet as a reduction or contra to the common stock account.

15. (K) Common stock subscribed represents stock subscriptions that have not been fully paid. The stock is not considered to be issued until the full price is paid. This account should be classified as an increase in the common stock and it is offset in stockholders' equity by a contra account for the balance of the subscription due.

16. (H) A convertible bond is a bond which may be converted to another form of the corporation's securities during a specified time frame. A bond is typically classified as a long-term liability on the balance sheet.

17. (N) Corporations do not own securities they hold as collateral. The corporation will retain the securities only in the event of a default on the receivable the securities are collateralizing. Thus, the securities are excluded from the balance sheet of Baker and they appear on the balance sheets of their owners.

18. (G) A bank overdraft occurs when a check is written for a greater amount than the balance in the bank account. A bank overdraft should be classified as a current liability. It should not be offset against other cash account balances unless the cash account is in the same bank.

ANSWER OUTLINE

Problem 1   Discontinued Operations and Extraordinary Items

a.   Report extraordinary item after continuing operations and discontinued operations
     Net of tax
Presentation required to enable users to assess future cash flows

b.   Report discontinued operations in separate section after continuing operations
     Present as 2 components
       Loss from operations of discontinued segment (net of tax)
         Beg. of yr. ⟶ Meas. date
       Loss on disposal of discontinued segment (net of tax)
         Includes
           Operating losses:
             Meas. date ⟶ Disposal date
           Loss on sale of assets plus direct costs associated with disposal

c.   Report relocation costs as part of "loss on disposal" component
Reason for treating as part of "loss on disposal" component is that they directly relate to decision to dispose

UNOFFICIAL ANSWER

Problem 1   Discontinued Operations and X/O Items

a.   Hillside should report the extraordinary item separately, net of applicable income taxes, below the continuing operations section in the income statement. Exclusion of extraordinary items from the results of continuing operations is intended to produce a measure of income from continuing operations that is useful in projecting future operating cash flows.

b.   Hillside should report the discontinued operations separately in the 1999 income statement immediately below income from continuing operations. Discontinued operations should be comprised of two categories, with each category reported net of income taxes:

   •   Loss from operations of the discontinued segment from the beginning of the year to the measurement date.
   •   Loss on disposal of the discontinued segment, including the provision of operating losses during the phase-out period.

c.   Hillside should include the costs incurred to relocate employees in the loss on disposal of the discontinued segment in its 1999 income statement. These costs are a direct result of the commitment to dispose of its segment.

SOLUTION GUIDE

Problem 2   Prepare Single-Step IS; Reconcile Net Income to Taxable Income

1.   This problem consists of two related parts requiring a single-step income statement and a schedule reconciling net income to taxable income.

2.   Part a. requires preparation of a single-step income statement. In a single-step income statement, total expenses and losses are subtracted from total revenues and gains to compute income. There are no "steps" resulting in subtotals such as gross profit, income from operations, etc. For any format income statement, however, nonrecurring items such as extraordinary items, discontinued operations, and cumulative effect of change in accounting principle are reported separately.

2.1   Revenues and gains listed in the trial balance include machine sales, service revenues, interest revenue, and gain on sale of factory. The gain is not listed in the revenues and gains section because it is an extraordinary item. The gain is extraordinary because it is unusual, infrequent and results from an expropriation. APB 30 specifies expropriations as an example of an extraordinary item.

2.2   Expenses and losses listed in the trial balance include cost of sales, cost of services, administrative expenses, research and development expenses, interest expense, and loss from asset disposal.

2.3   One expense **not** listed in the trial balance is income tax expense, which has not yet been recorded. To compute the current portion of income tax expense on ordinary income, first the expenses and losses listed in 2.1 are subtracted from the revenues (excluding the extraordinary item) listed in 2.2. The difference of $30,000 is income before income tax and extraordinary item. The amount must be adjusted for permanent and temporary differences to compute taxable income (excluding extraordinary item). The $5,000 life insurance premium payment must be added back because it was deducted to compute accounting income, but is not deductible for tax purposes, (permanent difference). The $15,000 excess tax depreciation (temporary difference) must be subtracted. Therefore, taxable income, excluding the extraordinary item, is $20,000 ($30,000 + $5,000 − $15,000). Since the tax rate is 30%, the current portion of income tax expense is $6,000 ($20,000 x 30%).

2.4   The deferred portion of income tax expense is computed by multiplying the future taxable amounts ($10,000 + $5,000 = $15,000) by the future enacted tax rate of 30% (30% x $15,000 = $4,500).

2.5   After computing tax expense, other revenues ($1,010,000) less total expenses ($990,500) equals income before extraordinary item ($19,500). Note that the two components of income taxes could have been disclosed after "income before income taxes and extraordinary item," which would be $30,000 (see 2.3).

2.6   As discussed in 2.1, the gain from the expropriation of the factory ($250,000) is an extraordinary item. Per APB 30, extraordinary items must be reported separately, and net of their tax effect. Since the

$250,000 gain is taxable, the gain must be reported at $175,000 ($250,000 less tax effect of 30% x $250,000). Therefore, net income is $194,500 ($19,500 + $175,000).

2.7 Earnings per share (EPS) must be reported on income before extraordinary items and on net income, in accordance with SFAS 128. EPS on the extraordinary gain may be shown either on the face of the IS or in the notes to the FS. The 1999 cumulative preferred dividends ($2,000,000 x 5% = $100,000) must be subtracted from the income amounts to determine the amount available to common stockholders. This result is then divided by the weighted-average number of common shares outstanding. For example, earnings per share on net income is:

$$\frac{(\$194,500 \text{ net income}) - (\$100,000 \text{ pref. dividends})}{200,000 \text{ weighted-average shares}} = \$\underline{.47}$$

3. Part b. requires the preparation of a schedule reconciling net income to taxable income.

3.1 Net income from part a. is $194,500. This must be adjusted for any items which affect net income but not taxable income, or vice versa.

3.2 Income taxes (current, deferred, and on the extraordinary item) decrease net income, but do not affect taxable income. Therefore, these amounts ($6,000; $4,500; $75,000) must be added back to net income.

3.3 The officer's life insurance expense ($5,000) also reduces net income, but is not deductible for tax purposes. Therefore, it, too, must be added back to net income.

3.4 The excess tax depreciation ($15,000) is deductible on the tax return but is not an expense on the income statement. This item must be deducted to reconcile to taxable income.

3.5 The resulting taxable income ($270,000) can be computed directly to check its correctness as follows:

Revenues and gains		
Machine sales		$750,000
Service revenues		250,000
Interest revenue		10,000
Gain on sale of factory		250,000
		1,260,000
Expenses and losses		
Cost of sales ($425,000 + $15,000)*	$440,000	
Cost of services	100,000	
Administrative expenses ($300,000 – $5,000)	295,000	
Research and development expense	110,000	
Interest expense	5,000	
Loss from asset disposal	40,000	990,000
Taxable income		$ 270,000

*assumes depreciation is included in cost of sales

Note that taxable income times the tax rate results in taxes currently payable of $81,000 ($270,000 x 30%), which corresponds to **income tax expense-current** ($6,000) plus the tax expense applicable to the extraordinary item ($75,000).

UNOFFICIAL ANSWER

Problem 2 Prepare Single-Step IS; Reconcile Net Income to Taxable Income

a.
Powell Corp.
INCOME STATEMENT
For the Year Ended June 30, 1999

Revenues:

Machine sales	$750,000	
Service revenues	250,000	
Interest revenue	10,000	
Total revenues		$1,010,000

Expenses:

Cost of sales--machines	425,000	
Cost of services	100,000	
Administrative expenses	300,000	
Research and development expenses	110,000	
Interest expense	5,000	
Loss from asset disposal	40,000	
Current income tax expense	6,000	
Deferred income tax expense	4,500	
Total expenses and losses		990,500
Income before extraordinary gain		19,500
Extraordinary gain, net of income taxes of $75,000		175,000
Net income		$ 194,500

Earnings (loss) per share:

Income before extraordinary gain	.87 −0.40
Extraordinary gain	($0.40) .87
Net income	$0.47

b.

Net income	$ 194,500
Add:	
Taxes on extraordinary gain	75,000
Provision for income taxes	10,500
Financial statement income before income taxes	280,000
Permanent difference--officer's life insurance	5,000
Temporary difference--excess of tax over financial statement depreciation	(15,000)
Taxable income	$ 270,000

SOLUTION GUIDE

Problem 3 Prepare Balance Sheet

1. In this problem, a corrected, classified 12/31/99 balance sheet with proper format and necessary descriptions must be prepared. The solutions approach is to first write the correct statement heading on paper. Second, skim the incorrect balance sheet provided, then go through the additional data to determine the necessary adjustments and disclosures. As you do this, label each item CA, CL, investment, etc.

2. The unrecorded payment on accounts payable should be recorded at 12/30/99, resulting in a $14,000 decrease in cash and accounts payable.

2.1 No entry was made for the customer's NSF check ($2,000), which should be recorded as a decrease in cash and an increase in accounts receivable (since the customer still owes Zues $2,000).

2.2   Cash restricted for building purposes ($100,000) must be reported separately from unrestricted cash. Restricted cash is classified either as current or long-term depending on the expected date of disbursement. In this case, since the cash is restricted for future **building purposes**, it is classified as long-term.

2.3   The $30,000 note receivable from Zues' president should be reported separately from accounts receivable, reducing AR by the same amount. The note should be classified as long-term since it is not due until 12/31/02.

2.4   Current assets should include cash ($225,000 – $14,000 – $2,000 – $100,000 = $109,000), accounts receivable, net ($345,700 + $2,000 – $30,000 = $317,700) and inventories ($560,000). The restricted cash ($100,000) and notes receivable ($30,000) are reported as other assets.

3.   The next two items of additional data concern the investments account, which is reported in the bookkeeper's balance sheet at $57,700 [$51,300 cost of investment plus $6,400 cost of treasury stock (200 x $32)].

3.1   The cost of treasury stock ($6,400) should be removed from the investments account and reported as a separate reduction of stockholders' equity. This brings the investment account down to a balance of $51,300 ($57,700 – $6,400), which is the cost of the investment.

3.2   The remaining investment consists of shares of stock of a **major** corporation, which indicates that these are **marketable** equity securities (MES), which should be reported at market. Since cost is $51,300 and market value is $47,000, an unrealized loss should be recorded at $4,300 ($51,300 – $47,000). The unrealized loss is reported as a separate component of stockholders' equity because these MES should be classified as "available-for-sale." Additionally, the investment account should be reduced by $4,300.

3.3   The land held as a potential future building site ($250,000) is shown under "other assets" in the AICPA answer. It would also be acceptable to classify the land as an investment.

4.   None of the additional data gives any information on the amounts reported as land, building, machinery, and equipment, or accumulated depreciation, except for the information about the land held as a potential future plant site (see 3.3 above).

4.1   Property, plant, and equipment consists of land ($450,000 – $250,000 = $200,000), building ($1,750,000), and machinery and equipment ($1,964,000). Accumulated depreciation ($420,000) is subtracted from the building, machinery, and equipment.

4.2   Goodwill ($37,000) is reported as an intangible asset.

5.   The next few items of additional information involve liabilities. The main concern is determining classification as current or long-term.

5.1   The notes payable ($500,000) are classified as $100,000 current (for the installment due 12/30/99) and $400,000 long-term (for the remaining four installments).

5.2   The mortgage payable would generally be reported as $600,000 current (12 x $50,000) and the remaining $300,000 long-term ($900,000 – $600,000). However, after two $50,000 installments were paid, the remaining $800,000 was refinanced on a long-term basis. Per SFAS 6, a short-term obligation can be reclassified as long-term if the enterprise intends to refinance the obligation on a long-term basis **and** the intent is supported by the ability to refinance. Zues demonstrated its intent and ability to refinance $800,000 of the mortgage when it actually refinanced that amount on 3/1/00, before the 12/31/99 financial statements were issued. Therefore, in the 12/31/99 balance sheet, $100,000 of the mortgage should be classified as current and $800,000 as long-term.

5.3   The lawsuit liability ($80,000) is classified as current since it will be paid in 2000.

5.4   Income taxes payable ($61,200) is the amount recorded as the current portion of income tax expense in the 1999 income statement. Zues also has recorded $40,000 of prepaid income taxes, which apparently represents estimated tax payments made during 1999. Therefore, the net income taxes payable to be reported as a current liability at 12/31/99 is $21,200 ($61,200 – $40,000).

5.5   The classification of deferred tax liabilities and assets is a two-step process. First, all deferred tax liabilities and assets are classified as current or long-term. Once classified, all current items are netted to determine either a current asset or liability, and all long-term items are similarly netted. In this case, a noncurrent DT liability of $48,000 exists due to the depreciation difference and a current DT asset of $20,000 exists due to the lawsuit liability difference. These should not be netted. A $20,000 current deferred tax asset is reported. In addition, there is a long-term deferred tax liability of $48,000 caused by the depreciation difference.

5.6   Accounts payable is reported as a current liability at $119,800 ($133,800 less the $14,000 adjustment discussed in item 2 above).

6.   In the stockholders' equity section common stock is reported at the par value of the shares issued ($40,000 x $50 = $2,000,000). Additional disclosures for the common stock are the number of shares authorized, issued, and outstanding, and the par value per share.

6.1   Paid-in capital in excess of par is the excess of the issue price of the stock (the $2,231,000 balance reported in the bookkeeper's balance sheet) over the par value of $2,000,000 ($2,231,000 – $2,000,000 = $231,000).

6.2   The other stockholders' equity items are retained earnings (given at $1,075,400) and the two items discussed earlier: treasury stock (see 3.1 above) and the unrealized loss (see 3.2 above).

6.3   Once you have identified where each element should go in the BS, prepare the statement.

UNOFFICIAL ANSWER

Problem 3   Prepare Balance Sheet

Zues Manufacturing Corp.
BALANCE SHEET
December 31, 1999

Assets

	Current Assets			
[1]*	Cash		$ 109,000	
[2]	Accounts receivable (net)		317,700	
	Inventories		560,000	
	Deferred tax asset		$ 20,000	
	Total current assets			$1,006,700
[3]	Long-term investment, at cost			47,000
	Property, plant, and equipment, at cost			
[4]	Land		200,000	
	Building	$1,750,000		
	Machinery and equipment	1,964,000		
	Total	3,714,000		
	Less accumulated depreciation	420,000	3,294,000	
	Total property, plant, and equipment			3,494,000
	Intangible asset			
	Goodwill			37,000
	Other assets			
[1]	Cash restricted for building purposes		100,000	
[2]	Officer's note receivable		30,000	
[4]	Land held for future building site		250,000	380,000
	Total assets			$4,964,700

Numbers in brackets are keyed to explanations of amounts.

Liabilities and Stockholders' Equity

	Current Liabilities			
[5]	Accounts payable		$ 119,800	
[6&7]	Current installments of long-term debt		200,000	
	Lawsuit liability		80,000	
[8]	Income taxes payable		21,200	
	Total current liabilities			$ 421,000
	Long-term debt			
[6]	Mortgage payable		800,000	
[7]	Note payable		400,000	
	Deferred tax liability		48,000	
	Total long-term debt			1,248,000
	Stockholders' equity			
[9]	Common stock, authorized 100,000 shares of $50 par value; issued 40,000 shares; outstanding 39,800 shares		2,000,000	
[9]	Additional paid-in capital		231,000	
	Total paid-in capital		2,231,000	
	Retained earnings		1,075,400	
	Accumulated other comprehensive income:			
	Unrealized loss on long-term investment		(4,300)	
	Total		3,302,100	

---

* *Numbers in brackets are keyed to explanations of amounts.*

[3]	Less: Cost of treasury stock	($6,400)	
	Total stockholders' equity		3,295,700
	Total liabilities and stockholders' equity		$4,964,700

Explanations of Amounts

[1]	Cash, per unaudited balance sheet	$ 225,000
	Less: Unrecorded checks in payment of accounts payable	(14,000)
	NSF check not recorded	(2,000)
	Cash restricted for rebuilding purposes (reported in other assets)	(100,000)
	Corrected balance	$109,000

[2]	Accounts receivable (net), per unaudited balance sheet	$345,700
	Add charge-back for NSF check (see [1])	2,000
	Less officer's note receivable (reported in other assets)	(30,000)
	Corrected balance	$317,700

[3]	Investments, per unaudited balance sheet	$ 57,700
	Less: Long-term investment (reported separately)	(47,000)
	Write-down of investment to market	(4,300)
	Treasury stock (reported in stockholders' equity)	(6,400)
	Corrected balance	$ 0

[4]	Land, per unaudited balance sheet	$ 450,000
	Less land acquired for future building site (reported in other assets)	(250,000)
	Correct balance	$ 200,000

[5]	Accounts payable, per unaudited balance sheet	$ 133,800
	Less unrecorded payments (see [1])	(14,000)
	Corrected balance	$ 119,800

[6]	Mortgage payable, per unaudited balance sheet	$ 900,000
	Less current portion ($50,000 x 2)	(100,000)
	Refinanced as long-term mortgage payable	$ 800,000

[7]	Note payable, per unaudited balance sheet	$ 500,000
	Less current portion	(100,000)
	Long-term note payable	$ 400,000

[8]	Income taxes payable, per unaudited balance sheet	$ 61,200
	Less prepaid income taxes	(40,000)
	Corrected balance	$21,200

[9]	Common stock, per unaudited balance sheet	$2,231,000
	Less additional paid-in capital in excess of par value	(231,000)
	Corrected balance	$2,000,000

ANSWER OUTLINE

Problem 4   Comprehensive Income

a.   Comprehensive income (CI) = Net income + Other comprehensive income (OCI)

OCI = Rev., gains, exp., loss not included in NI under GAAP

AOCI = Cumulative BS amounts vs. single period OCI items

b.   Alternatives for reporting comprehensive income

- Continuation of IS, or
- Separate FS starting with NI, or
- Statement of Δs in SE

Reported net of tax or total tax effect for all items with detail in notes.

c.   Reclassification adjustments

Avoid double counting for items realized in net income of current period

Shown as increases or decreases to related items in OCI except for min. pen. liability

Reported net of tax in other comprehensive income or total tax effect for all items with detail in notes.

d.   EPS not required for CI or OCI components

UNOFFICIAL ANSWER

Problem 4   Comprehensive Income

a.   Comprehensive income as used in SFAS 130 includes the total of all items of comprehensive income of which net income is a part. Additional items are called other comprehensive income and include revenues, gains, expenses, and losses that are not included in net income under generally accepted accounting principles. Accumulated other comprehensive income represents cumulative amounts on the stockholders' equity section of the balance sheet, whereas other comprehensive income components are single period amounts.

b.   Comprehensive income may be reported in the financial statements under one of three alternatives.

- At the bottom of the income statement, continue from net income to arrive at a **comprehensive income** figure, or

- In a separate comprehensive income statement that starts with net income, or

- In the statement of changes in stockholders' equity; the first two are preferred by the FASB.

All components shall be shown net of tax or a total tax expense may be shown with the detail for each component disclosed in the notes.

c.   Reclassification adjustments are necessary to avoid double counting of items recognized as realized in net income of the current period that were recognized as unrealized in other comprehensive income in the current or prior period. The adjustment are shown as additions or subtractions from each item adjusted, except for those relating to

the minimum pension liability which shall be shown net of adjustment for the period.

d.   Disclosure of earnings per share is not required for other comprehensive income items or for comprehensive income.

INVENTORY

Inventory is defined in ARB 43 (see outline) as tangible personal property (1) held for sale in the ordinary course of business, (2) in the process of production for such sale, or (3) to be used currently in the production of items for sale.

Inventory is tested on the Financial Accounting and Reporting section of the exam. The primary topics covered by questions on the exam are

1. **Ownership of goods**: the determination of which items are to be included in inventory.
2. **Cost**: the determination of which costs are to be assigned to inventory.
3. **Cost flow assumptions**: the determination of costs assigned to cost of goods sold and inventory under the various cost flow methods.
4. **Valuation**: the determination of how and when inventories should reflect their market values.

ARB 43, chap 4 is the primary authoritative pronouncement regarding the accounting for inventories. You should review the outline before continuing your study of this module.

A. **Determining Inventory and Cost of Goods Sold**

Inventory cost is a function of two variables

1. The number of units included in inventory, and
2. The costs attached to those units

The units to be included in inventory are those which the firm owns; ownership is usually determined by legal title.

The costs to be included in inventory include all costs necessary to prepare the goods for sale. For a manufacturing entity this would include direct materials, direct labor, and both direct and indirect factory overhead. These costs are then allocated to the work in process and finished goods inventory accounts.

For a merchandising concern, the costs to be included in inventory include the purchase price of the goods, freight-in, insurance, warehousing, and any other costs incurred in the preparation of these goods for sale. The amount used as a purchase price for the goods will vary depending upon whether the gross or net method is used in the recording of purchases. If the gross method is used to record the purchases, then any subsequent discount taken is shown as purchase discount which is netted against the purchases account in determining cost of goods sold. If the net method is used to record purchases, then any purchase discounts offered are assumed taken and the purchase account reflects the net price. If subsequent to the recording of the purchases the discount is not taken (i.e., payment is tendered after the discount period has elapsed), a purchase discounts lost account is debited. The balance in the purchase discounts lost account does **not** enter into the determination of cost of goods sold; this amount is treated as a period expense. Note that regardless of the method used, purchases are always recorded net of any allowable trade discounts. These are discounts that are allowed to the entity because of its being a wholesaler, a good customer, or merely the fact that the item is on sale at a reduced price. Also note that interest paid to vendors is not included in the cost of inventory.

The determination of cost of goods sold and inventory under each of the cost flow assumptions depends upon the method used to record the inventory: periodic or perpetual.

Periodic system: inventory is counted periodically and then priced. The ending inventory is usually recorded in the cost of goods sold (CGS) entry.

Ending inventory (EI)	xx	
CGS	(plug)	
Beginning inventory (BI)		xx
Purchases		xx

CGS = Purchases - (the change in inventory). For example, if ending inventory decreases, all of the purchases and some of the beginning inventory have been sold. If ending inventory increases, not all of the purchases have been sold.

Perpetual system: a running total is kept of the units on hand (and possibly their value) by recording all increases and decreases as they occur. When inventory is purchased, the inventory account, rather than purchases, is debited. As inventory is sold, the following entry is recorded.

CGS	(cost)	
Inventory		(cost)

B. **Inventory Valuation and Cost-Flow Methods**

1. Specific identification
2. Weighted-average
3. Simple average
4. Moving average
5. Lower of cost or market
6. Losses on purchase commitments
7. First-in, first-out (FIFO)
8. Last-in, first-out (LIFO)
9. Dollar-value LIFO
10. Retail method
11. Retail dollar-value LIFO
12. Gross profit
13. Standard costs
14. Direct costing
15. Market
16. Cost apportionment by relative sales value

1. **Specific Identification**

The seller determines which item is sold. For example, a seller has for sale four identical machines costing $260, $230, $180, and $110. Since the machines are identical, a purchaser will have no preference as to which machine s/he receives when purchased. Note that the seller is able to manipulate income as s/he can sell any machine (and charge the appropriate amount to CGS). Significant dollar value items are frequently accounted for by specific identification. The use of the specific identification method is appropriate when there is a relatively small number of significant dollar value items in inventory.

2. **Weighted-Average**

The seller averages the cost of all items on hand and purchased during the period. The units in ending inventory and units sold (CGS) are costed at this average cost. For example

	Cost	*Units*	
Beginning inventory	$200	100	($2.00 unit)
Purchase 1	315	150	($2.10 unit)
Purchase 2	85	50	($1.70 unit)
	$600	300	

Weighted-average cost $600/300 = $2.00 unit

3. **Simple Average**

The seller does not weight the average for units purchased or in beginning inventory (e.g., the above $2.00, $2.10, and $1.70 unit costs would be averaged to $1.93). The method is fairly accurate if all purchases, production runs, and beginning inventory quantities are equal.

4. **Moving Average**

The average cost of goods on hand must be recalculated any time additional inventory is purchased at a unit cost different from the previously calculated average cost of goods on hand. For example

	Dollar cost of units on hand	÷	Units on hand	=	Inventory unit cost
Beginning inventory	$200		100		$2.00
Sale of 50 units @ $2.00 = $100	100		50		2.00
Purchase of 150 units for $320	420		200		2.10
Sale of 50 units @ $2.10 = $105	315		150		2.10
Purchase of 50 units for $109	424		200		2.12

Note that sales do not change the unit price because they are taken out of inventory at the average price. Moving average may only be used with perpetual systems which account for changes in value with each change in inventory (and not with perpetual systems only accounting for changes in the number of units).

5. **Lower of Cost or Market**

"A departure from the cost basis of pricing the inventory is required when the utility of the goods is no longer as great as its cost." (ARB 43, chap 4, para 8)

The following steps should be used to apply the lower of cost or market rule given in chapter 4 of ARB 43.

a. Determine market
   Market is replacement cost limited to

   (1) **Ceiling**--which is net realizable value (selling price less selling costs and costs to complete).
   (2) **Floor**--which is net realizable value less normal profit.

   Note that if replacement cost is greater than net realizable value, market equals net realizable value. Likewise, market equals net realizable value minus normal profit if replacement cost is less than net realizable value minus normal profit.

b. Determine cost
   Note that the floor and ceiling have nothing to do with cost

c. Select the lower of cost or market either for each individual item or for inventory as a whole (compute total market and total cost, and select lower)

LOWER OF COST OR MARKET EXAMPLE

Item	Cost	Replacement cost	Selling price	Selling cost	Normal profit
A	$10.50	$10.25	$15.00	$2.50	$2.50
B	5.75	5.25	8.00	1.50	1.00
C	4.25	4.75	5.50	1.00	1.50

Item	Replacement cost	NRV (ceiling)	NRV-Profit (floor)	Designated market value	Cost	LCM
A	$10.25	$12.50	$10.00	$10.25	$10.50	$10.25
B	5.25	6.50	5.50	5.50	5.75	5.50
C	4.75	4.50	3.00	4.50	4.25	4.25

Item A--Market is replacement cost, $10.25, because it is between the floor ($10.00) and the ceiling ($12.50). Lower of cost or market is $10.25.

Item B--Market is limited to the floor, $5.50 ($8.00 – $1.50 – $1.00) because the $5.25 replacement cost is beneath the floor. Lower of cost or market is $5.50.

Item C--Market is limited to the ceiling, $4.50 ($5.50 – $1.00) because the $4.75 replacement cost is above the ceiling. Lower of cost or market is $4.25.

Observations about the ARB 43 rule

(1) The floor limitation on market prevents recognition of more than normal profit in future periods (if market is less than cost).
(2) The ceiling limitation on market prevents recognition of a loss in future periods (if market is less than cost).
(3) Cost or market applied to individual items will always be as low as, and usually lower than, cost or market applied to the inventory as a whole. They will be the same when all items at market or all items at cost are lower.
(4) Once inventory has been written down there can be no recovery from the write-down until the units are sold. Recall that this differs from marketable securities where recoveries of prior write-downs are required to be taken into the income stream.

Methods of recording the write-down

If market is less than cost at the end of any period, there are two methods available to record the market decline. The entry to establish the ending inventory can be made using the market figure. The difficulty with this procedure is that it forces the loss to be included in the cost of goods sold, thus overstating the cost of goods sold by the amount of the loss. Note that under this method the loss is not separately disclosed.

An alternative treatment is to debit the inventory account for the actual cost (not market) of goods on hand, and then to make the following entry to give separate recognition to the market decline.

Loss due to market decline	xx	
Inventory		xx

6. **Losses on Purchase Commitments**

Purchase commitments (PC) result from legally enforceable contracts to purchase specific quantities of goods at fixed prices in the future. When there is a decline in market value below the contract price at the balance sheet date and the contracts are noncancellable, an unrealized loss has occurred and, if material, should be recorded in the period of decline.

Estimated loss on PC ~state	(excess of PC over mkt.)	
Accrued loss on PC B/S	(excess of PC over mkt.)	

If further declines in market value are estimated to occur before delivery is made, the amount of the loss to be accrued should be increased to include this additional decline in market value per SFAS 5. The loss is taken to the income statement; the accrued loss on PC is a liability account and shown on the balance sheet.

When the goods are subsequently received

Purchases	xx	
Accrued loss on PC	xx	
Cash		xx

If a partial or full recovery occurs before the inventory is received, the accrued loss account would be reduced by the amount of the recovery. Likewise, an income statement account, "Recovery on Loss of PC," would be credited.

7. **First-In, First-Out (FIFO)**

The goods from beginning inventory and the earliest purchases are assumed to be the goods sold first. In a period of rising prices, cost of goods sold is made up of the earlier, lower-priced goods resulting in a larger profit (relative to LIFO). The ending inventory is made up of more recent purchases and thus represents a more current value (relative to LIFO) on the balance sheet. It should be noted that this cost-flow assumption may be used even when it does not match the physical flow of goods. Whenever the FIFO method is used, the results of inventory and cost of goods sold are the same at the end of the period under either a perpetual or a periodic system.

8. **Last-In, First-Out (LIFO)**

Under this cost-flow method, the most recent purchases are assumed to be the first goods sold; thus, ending inventory is assumed to be composed of the oldest goods. Therefore, the cost of goods sold contains relatively current costs (resulting in the matching of current costs with sales). Again, this cost-flow assumption usually does not parallel the physical flow of goods.

LIFO is widely adopted because it is acceptable for tax purposes and because in periods of rising prices it reduces tax liability due to the lower reported income (resulting from the higher cost of goods sold). LIFO smoothes out fluctuations in the income stream relative to FIFO because it matches current costs with current revenues. A primary disadvantage of LIFO is that it results in large profits if inventory decreases because earlier, lower valued layers are included in the cost of goods sold. This is generally known as a LIFO liquidation. Another disadvantage is the cost involved in maintaining separate LIFO records for each item in inventory. If LIFO is used for tax purposes, it must be used for financial reporting purposes. This is known as the LIFO conformity rule. Under current tax law, inventory layers may be added using the (1) earliest acquisition costs, (2) weighted-average unit cost for the period, or (3) latest acquisition costs. In solving questions on the CPA Exam, use the earliest acquisition costs unless you are instructed to use one of the other alternatives.

When a company uses LIFO for external reporting purposes and another inventory method for internal purposes, a **LIFO Reserve** account is used to reduce inventory from the internal valuation to the LIFO valuation. LIFO Reserve is a contra account to inventory, and is adjusted up or down at year end with a corresponding increase or decrease to **Cost of Goods Sold**.

9. **Dollar-Value LIFO**

Dollar-value LIFO is LIFO applied to **pools** of inventory items rather than to **individual** items. Thus, the cost of keeping inventory records is less under dollar-value LIFO than under unit LIFO. Because the LIFO conformity rule (if LIFO is used for tax, it must also be used for external financial statements) also applies to dollar-value LIFO, companies using dollar-value LIFO define their LIFO pools so as to conform with IRS regulations. Under these regulations, a LIFO pool can contain all of the inventory items for a natural business unit, or a multiple pool approach can be elected whereby a business can group similarly used inventory items into several groups or pools.

The advantage of using inventory pools is that an involuntary liquidation of LIFO layers is less likely to occur because of the increased number of items in the pool (if the level of one item decreases it can be offset by increases in the levels of other items), and because the pools can be adjusted for changes in product composition or product mix.

Like unit LIFO, dollar-value LIFO is a layering method. Unlike unit LIFO, dollar-value LIFO determines increases or decreases in ending inventory in terms of dollars of the same purchasing power rather than in terms of units. Dollar-value LIFO seeks to determine the real dollar change in inventory. Therefore, ending inventory is deflated to base-year cost by dividing ending inventory by the current year's conversion price index and comparing the resulting amount with the beginning inventory, which has also been stated in base-year dollars.

The difference represents the layer which, after conversion, must be added or subtracted to arrive at the appropriate value of ending inventory. Always remember that the individual layers in a dollar-value LIFO inventory are valued as follows:

$$\begin{array}{ccc} \$ \\ \text{value} & = & \text{Inventory at} \\ \text{LIFO} & & \text{base-year prices} \end{array} \quad \text{x} \quad \begin{array}{c} \text{Conversion} \\ \text{price index} \end{array}$$

In applying dollar-value LIFO, manufacturers develop their own indexes while retailers and wholesalers use published figures. In computing the conversion price index, the **double-extension technique** is used, named so because each year the ending inventory is extended at both base-year prices and current-year prices. The index, computed as follows, measures the change in the inventory prices since the base year.

$$\frac{\text{EI at end-of-year prices}}{\text{EI at base-year prices}} = \begin{array}{c} \text{Conversion} \\ \text{price index} \end{array}$$

To illustrate the computation of the index, assume that the base-year price of products A and B is $3 and $5, respectively, and at the end of the year, the price of product A is $3.20 and B, $5.75, with 2,000 and 800 units on hand, respectively. The index for the year is 110%, computed as follows:

	EI at end-of-year prices	÷	EI at base-year prices	=	Conversion price index
Product A	2,000 @ $3.20 = $ 6,400		2,000 @ $3 = $ 6,000		
Product B	800 @ $5.75 = $ 4,600		800 @ $5 = $ 4,000		
	$11,000	÷	$10,000	=	1.10 (or 110%)

Steps in dollar-value LIFO

| | *Manufacturers* |
| | |

Manufacturers

1. Compute the conversion price index

2. Compare BI at base-year prices to EI at base-year prices to determine the
   a) New inventory layer added, or
   b) Old inventory layer removed (LIFO liquidation)

3. If there is an increase at base-year prices, value this new layer by multiplying the layer (stated in base-year dollars) by the conversion price index. If there is a decrease at base-year prices, the remaining layers are valued at the index in effect when the layer was first added.

Retailers and wholesalers

1. Determine index from appropriate published source

2. Divide EI by conversion price index to restate to base-year prices

3. Same as "2." opposite

4. Same as "3." opposite

For example, assume the following:

	EI at end-of-year prices	÷	Conversion price index	=	EI at base-year prices		Change as measured in base-year dollars
Year 1 (base)	$100,000		1.00		$100,000		
Year 2	121,000		1.10		110,000	>	$10,000
Year 3	150,000		1.20		125,000	>	15,000
Year 4	135,000		1.25		108,000	>	(17,000)

In both year 2 and year 3, ending inventory in terms of base-year dollars increased 10,000 and 15,000 base-year dollars, respectively. Since layers are added every year that ending inventory at base-year prices is greater than the previous year's ending inventory at base-year prices, the ending inventory for year 3 would be computed as follows:

Ending inventory, Year 3

	Base-year prices	x	Index	=	EI at dollar-value LIFO cost
Year 1 (base)	$100,000		1.00		$100,000
Year 2 layer	10,000		1.10		11,000
Year 3 layer	15,000		1.20		18,000
Ending inventory	$125,000				$129,000

Note that each layer added is multiplied by the conversion price index in effect when the layer was added. Thus, the year 2 layer is multiplied by the year 2 index of 1.10 and the year 3 layer is multiplied by the year 3 index of 1.20.

In year 4, ending inventory decreased by 17,000 base-year dollars. Therefore, a LIFO liquidation has occurred whereby 17,000 base-year dollars will have to be removed from the previous year's ending inventory. Because LIFO is being used, the liquidation affects the most recently added layer first and then, if necessary, the next most recently added layer(s). Ending inventory in year 4 is composed of

	Base-year prices	x	Index =	EI at dollar-value LIFO cost
Year 1 (base)	$100,000		1.00	$100,000
Year 2 layer	8,000		1.10	8,800
Ending inventory	$108,000			$108,800

Note that the liquidation of 17,000 base year dollars in year 4 caused the entire year 3 layer of 15,000 base-year dollars to be liquidated as well as 2,000 base-year dollars from year 2. Also note that the remaining 8,000 base-year dollars in the year 2 layer is still multiplied by the year 2 index of 1.10.

Link-chain technique. The computations for application of the double-extension technique can become very arduous even if only a few items exist in the inventory. Also, consider the problems that arise when there is a constant change in the inventory mix or in situations in which the breadth of the inventory is large.

The link-chain method was originally developed for (and limited to) those companies that wanted to use LIFO but, because of a substantial change in product lines over time, were unable to recreate or keep the historical records necessary to make accurate use of the double-extension method.

The link-chain method is the process of developing a single cumulative index. Technological change is allowed for by the method used to calculate each current year index. The index is derived by double extending a representative sample (generally thought to be between 50% and 75% of the dollar value of the pool) at both beginning-of-year prices and end-of-year prices. This annual index is then applied (multiplied) to the previous period's cumulative index to arrive at the new current year cumulative index.

The brief example below illustrates how the links and cumulative index are computed.

End of period	Ratio of end of period prices to beginning prices*	Cumulative index number**
0	--	1.000
1	1.10	1.100
2	1.05	1.155
3	1.07	1.236

* $\dfrac{\text{End of period prices}}{\text{Beginning of period prices}}$ = Index number for **this period only**

** *Multiply the cumulative index number at the beginning of the period by the ratio computed with the formula shown above.*

The ending inventory is divided by the cumulative index number to derive the ending inventory at base period prices. An increase (layer) in base period dollars for the period is priced using the newly derived index number.

10. **Retail Method**

Inventory is counted at retail value and then reduced to cost by a COST/RETAIL ratio. A "conservative" retail method adds markups, but not markdowns, in determining the COST/RETAIL ratio, for example

	Cost	Retail
Beginning inventory	x	x
+ Purchases	x	x
+ Markups	-	x
Goods available	z	zz
– Sales		x
– Markdowns		x
Ending inventory		x

EI at retail x $\dfrac{\text{COST}}{\text{RETAIL}}$ ratio = EI at cost

The goods available ratio (z/zz) provides the COST/RETAIL ratio. The retail inventory method can be calculated to approximate FIFO, FIFO LCM, average, average LCM, LIFO, or LIFO LCM inventory methods. LIFO LCM is not acceptable for tax purposes.

The approximation obtained depends upon the figures which are used to calculate the COST/RETAIL ratio. To obtain valuations at cost, the goods available at retail should include both markups and markdowns in the calculation of the COST/RETAIL ratio. To obtain LCM valuations, markdowns are excluded from the goods available at retail, thus inflating the denominator of the ratio and making the ratio smaller or more conservative.

The average cost ratio includes the BI in the ratio, while FIFO ratio ignores the BI and includes only the purchases in the calculation. The FIFO and average ratios may be dichotomized as shown below.

	Include BI	*Exclude BI*
Include markups and markdowns	Average cost	FIFO cost
Include markups but exclude markdowns	Average LCM	FIFO LCM

The FIFO or average retail EI is the EI at retail multiplied by the respective COST/RETAIL percentages. Remember that the average LCM calculation is frequently referred to as the **conventional** retail inventory method.

The LIFO calculation also uses the FIFO percentages if the inventory is increasing. The percentage is used to calculate the value of the incremental layer only--not the value of the whole inventory. The value of the incremental layer is added to the BI at cost to establish the EI at LIFO. If the EI at retail is less than the BI at retail, then the reduction in the LIFO inventory takes place at the COST/RETAIL ratio of the BI.

The following example, which assumes no additional markups or markdowns, illustrates the LIFO calculations.

	Cost	*Retail*
BI	$20	$ 40
Purchases	30	90
		$130
Sales		80
EI at retail		$ 50

Since the EI at retail has increased, the BI is still unused under a LIFO assumption and a new layer of $10 at retail has been added to the inventory. Since the layer was established from purchases of the current period, the FIFO percentage of 30/90 is used to convert the $10 retail layer to the new cost layer of $3.33. The EI at LIFO will be $20 + $3.33, or $23.33.

If the EI at retail had been $30, not $50, then the EI at cost would have been $30 x (20/40), or $15. The purchases of the current period would be irrelevant since it is assumed they are all sold and cannot be in inventory.

11. **Retail Dollar-Value LIFO**

This method couples the retail method with dollar-value LIFO. The dollar-value LIFO records are counted and maintained at retail with the conversion to cost by a COST/RETAIL ratio being made as a final step.

Retail dollar-value LIFO involves the following five steps:

a. Count the EI at current retail price and convert it to base-year retail prices by dividing by the current year's conversion price index

b. Determine the BI (previous year's ending inventory) at base-year retail prices

c. Compare b. with a. to determine the real change in inventory measured in terms of base-year retail prices

d. If the inventory has increased, convert the real change in inventory at base year's retail prices to the real change in inventory at current year's retail prices by multiplying the quantity in c. by the conversion price index

e. Determine the cost of the new layer by multiplying the quantity in d. by the COST/RETAIL ratio for the current year

Any increase will form a layer which will be added to the BI at cost to establish the EI at cost. The following example illustrates these steps.

Assume the following information:

		Cost	*Retail*	*COST/RETAIL %*	*Conversion price index*
1)	*BI*	*$24,000*	*$40,000*	*60%*	*1.00*
2)	*EI--counted at ending retail prices = $44,100*				
3)	*COST/RETAIL ratio on current year purchases = 80%*				
4)	*The price level has increased from 100 to 105 during the year*				

The previously described steps are as follows for the above data:

	Inventory at retail prices	÷	*Conversion price index*	=	*Inventory at base-year retail prices*		*Change as measured in base-year retail dollars*
BI	*$40,000*		*1.00*		*$40,000*		
EI	*44,100*		*1.05*		*42,000*	*>*	*$2,000*

Ending inventory at cost:

	Base-year retail dollars	x	*Conversion price index*	x	*COST/ RETAIL %*	=	*Extension*
BI layer	*$40,000*		*1.00*		*60%*		*$24,000*
EI layer	*2,000*		*1.05*		*80%*		*1,680*
							$25,680 EI at cost

If the EI counted at retail prices had been $31,500 and all other data remained unchanged, the ending inventory would be computed as follows:

	Inventory at retail prices	÷	*Conversion price index*	=	*Inventory at base-year retail prices*		*Change as measured in base-year retail dollars*
BI	*$40,000*		*1.00*		*$40,000*		
EI	*31,500*		*1.05*		*30,000*	*>*	*$(10,000)*

Ending inventory:

	Base-year retail dollars	x	*Conversion price index*	x	*COST/ RETAIL %*	=	*Extension*
	$30,000		*1.00*		*60%*		*$18,000*

Thus, a LIFO liquidation has occurred, and part of the base-year layer has been removed. The remaining portion of the base-year layer is multiplied by the price index in effect when the layer was established and also by the COST/RETAIL ratio in effect when the layer was first established to arrive at the appropriate EI figure.

12. **Gross Profit**

Ending inventory is estimated by using the gross profit (GP) percentage to convert sales to cost of goods presumed sold. Since ending inventory is only estimated, the gross method is not acceptable for either tax or annual financial reporting purposes. Its major uses are to estimate ending inventory for internal use, for use in interim financial statements, and for establishing the amount of loss due to the destruction of inventory by fire, flood, or other catastrophes.

As an example, suppose the inventory of the Luckless Company has been destroyed by fire and the following information is available from duplicate records stored at a separate facility: beginning inventory of $30,000, purchases for the period of $40,000, sales of $60,000, and an average GP percentage of 25%. The cost of the inventory destroyed is computed as follows:

Beginning inventory	$30,000
+ Purchases	40,000
Goods available	70,000
− Cost of goods sold	45,000*
Inventory destroyed	$25,000

Cost of goods sold is computed as (1) sales of $60,000 – ($60,000 x 25%) or (2) sales of $60,000 x 75%.

If you need to convert a GP rate on cost to a markup (MU) rate on the selling price, divide the GP rate on cost by 1 **plus** the GP rate on cost, that is, if the GP rate on cost is 50%, then .50/(1 + .50) = 33 1/3% is the MU rate on the selling price. If you need to convert a MU rate on the selling price to a GP rate on cost, divide the MU rate on the selling price by 1 **minus** the MU rate on the selling price, that is, if the MU rate on the selling price is 20%, then .20/(1 – .20) = 25% GP rate on cost. Always be cautious about gross profit rates (on cost or the selling price).

13. **Standard Costs**

Standard costs are predetermined costs in a cost accounting system, generally used for control purposes. Inventory may be costed at standard only if variances are reasonable (i.e., not large). Large debit (unfavorable) variances would indicate inventory (and cost of sales) were undervalued, whereas large credit (favorable) variances would indicate inventory is overvalued.

14. **Direct (Variable) Costing**

Direct costing is not an acceptable method for valuing inventory (ARB 43, chap 4, para 5). Direct costing considers only variable costs as product costs and fixed production costs as period costs. In contrast, absorption costing considers both variable and fixed manufacturing costs as product costs.

15. **Market**

Inventory is usually valued at market value when market is lower than cost. However, occasionally, inventory will be valued at market even if it is above cost. This usually occurs with

a. Precious metals with a fixed market value
b. Industries such as meatpacking where costs cannot be allocated and

   (1) Quoted market prices exist
   (2) Goods are interchangeable (e.g., agricultural commodities)

16. **Cost Apportionment By Relative Sales Value**

Basket purchases and similar situations require cost allocation based on relative value. For example, a developer may spend $400,000 to acquire land, survey, curb and gutter, pave streets, etc. for a subdivision. Due to location and size, the lots may vary in selling price. If the total of all selling prices were $600,000, the developer could cost each lot at 2/3 (400/600; COST/RETAIL ratio) of its selling price.

C. **Items to Include in Inventory**

Goods shipped FOB shipping point which are in transit should be included in the inventory of the buyer since title passes to the buyer when the carrier receives the goods. Goods shipped FOB destination should be included in the inventory of the seller until the goods are received by the buyer since title passes to the buyer when the goods are received at their final destination. The more complicated UCC rules concerning transfer of title should be used for the law portion, not the financial accounting and reporting portion, of the exam.

D. **Consignments**

Consignors consign their goods to consignees who are sales agents of the consignors. Consigned goods remain the property of the consignor until sold. Therefore, any unsold goods (including a proportionate share of freight costs incurred in shipping the goods to the consignee) must be included in the consignor's inventory.

Consignment sales revenue should be recognized by the consignor when the consignee sells the consigned goods to the ultimate customer. Therefore, no revenue is recognized at the time the consignor ships the goods to the consignee. Note that sales commission made by the consignee would be reported as a selling expense by the consignor and would **not** be netted against the sales revenue recognized by the consignor. The UCC rules concerning consignments should be used for the law portion, not the financial accounting and reporting portion, of the exam.

E. **Ratios**

The two ratios below relate to inventory:

1. **Inventory turnover**--Measures the number of times inventory was sold and reflects inventory order and investment policies

$$\frac{\text{Cost of goods sold}}{\text{Average inventory}}$$

2. **Number of days' supply in average inventory**--number of days inventory is held before sale; reflects on efficiency of inventory policies

$$\frac{365}{\text{Inventory turnover}}$$

F. **Long-Term Construction Contracts**

The outline of ARB 45 should be reviewed before continuing to study long-term construction contracts. This section also reflects the treatment of these contracts in the AICPA's *Construction Contractors Audit and Accounting Guide.*

Long-term contracts are accounted for by two methods: completed-contract method and percentage-of-completion method.

1. Completed-contract method--recognition of contract revenue and profit at contract completion. All related costs are deferred until completion and then matched to revenues.
2. Percentage-of-completion--recognition of contract revenue and profit during construction based on expected total profit and estimated progress towards completion in the current period. All related costs are recognized in the period in which they occur.

The use of the percentage-of-completion method depends on the ability to make reasonably dependable estimates of contract revenues, contract costs, and the extent of progress toward completion. For entities which customarily operate under contractual arrangements and for whom contracting represents a significant part of their operations, the **presumption** is that they have the ability to make estimates that are sufficiently dependable to justify the use of the percentage-of-completion method of accounting.

In Statement of Position 81-1, the Accounting Standards Division states that the percentage-of-completion method is **preferable** in circumstances in which reasonably dependable estimates can be made and in which all of the following conditions exist:

*   Contracts executed by the parties normally include provisions that clearly specify the enforceable rights regarding goods or services to be provided and received by the parties, the consideration to be exchanged, and the manner and terms of settlement.
*   The buyer can be expected to satisfy obligations under the contract.
*   The contractor can be expected to perform contractual obligation.

The completed-contract method is **preferable** in circumstances in which estimates cannot meet the criteria for reasonable dependability or one of the above conditions does not exist.

The advantage of percentage-of-completion is periodic recognition of income, and the disadvantage is dependence on estimates. The advantage of the completed-contract method is that it is based on results, not estimates, and the disadvantage is that current performance is not reflected and income recognition may be irregular.

In practice, various procedures are used to measure the extent of progress toward completion under the percentage-of-completion method, but the most widely used one is **cost-to-cost** which is based on the assumed relationship between a unit of input and productivity. Under cost-to-cost, either revenue and/or profit to be recognized in the current period can be determined by the following formula.

$$\text{Revenue (profit)} = \left(\frac{\text{Cost to date}}{\substack{\text{Total expected} \\ \text{cost based on} \\ \text{latest estimate}}} \times \substack{\text{Contract price} \\ \text{(Expected profit)}} \right) - \substack{\text{Revenue (profit)} \\ \text{recognized in} \\ \text{previous periods}}$$

It is important to note that revenue and profit are two different terms. Profit is calculated by subtracting construction expenses from revenue. Revenue is the contract price. Therefore, pay particular attention to what item the CPA exam asks you to calculate.

The ledger account titles used in the following discussion are unique to long-term construction contracts. In practice, there are numerous account titles for the same item (e.g., "billings on LT contracts" vs. "partial billings on construction in progress") and various methodologies for journalizing the same transactions (e.g., separate revenue and expense control accounts in lieu of an "income on LT contracts" account). The following example has been simplified to highlight the main concepts.

EXAMPLE: Assume a 3-year contract at a contract price of $500,000 as well as the following data:

	Year 1	*Year 2*	*Year 3*
Cost incurred this year	$135,000	$225,000	$ 45,000
Prior years' costs	-0-	135,000	360,000
Estimated costs to complete	$315,000	40,000	-0-
Total costs	$450,000	400,000	$405,000
Progress billings made during the year	$200,000	$200,000	$100,000
Collection of billings each year	$175,000	$200,000	$125,000

From the above information, the following may be determined.

Percent of completion *(costs to date/total costs)*
Year 1: $135,000/$450,000 = 30%
Year 2: $360,000/$400,000 = 90%
Year 3: $405,000/$405,000 = 100%

	Year 1	*Year 2*	*Year 3*
Total revenue	$500,000	$500,000	$500,000
x percent of completion	x 30%	x 90%	x 100%
Total revenue to be recognized by end of year	$150,000	$450,000	$500,000
− Revenue recognized in prior periods	-0-	(150,000)	(450,000)
Current year's revenue (to be recognized)	$150,000	$300,000	$ 50,000
Contract price	$500,000	$500,000	500,000
− Total estimated costs	(450,000)	(400,000)	(405,000)
Estimated profit	$ 50,000	$100,000	$ 95,000
x percent of completion	x 30%	x 90%	x 100%
Total profit to be recognized by end of year	$ 15,000	$ 90,000	$ 95,000
− Profit recognized in prior periods	-0-	(15,000)	(90,000)
Current year's profit (to be recognized)	$ 15,000	$ 75,000	$ 5,000

		Percentage-of-completion		Completed-contract	
Year 1 Costs	Construction in progress	135,000		135,000	
	Cash		135,000		135,000
Year 1 Progress billings	Accounts receivable	200,000		200,000	
	Billings on LT contracts		200,000		200,000
Year 1 Cash collected	Cash	175,000		175,000	
	Accounts receivable		175,000		175,000
Year 1 Profit recognition	Construction expenses	135,000		none	
	Construction in progress	15,000			
	Construction revenue		150,000		
Year 2 Costs	Construction in progress	225,000		225,000	
	Cash		225,000		225,000
Year 2 Progress billings	Accounts receivable	200,000		200,000	
	Billings on LT contracts		200,000		200,000
Year 2 Cash collected	Cash	200,000		200,000	
	Accounts receivable		200,000		200,000
Year 2 Profit recognition	Construction expenses	225,000		none	
	Construction in progress	75,000			
	Construction revenue		300,000		

Year 3 Costs	Construction in progress	45,000		45,000	
	Cash		45,000		45,000
Year 3 Progress billings	Accounts receivable	100,000		100,000	
	Billings on LT contracts		100,000		100,000
Year 3 Cash collected	Cash	125,000		125,000	
	Accounts receivable		125,000		125,000
Year 3 Profit recognition and closing of special accounts	Construction expenses	45,000			
	Construction in progress	5,000			
	Construction revenue		50,000		
	Billings on LT contracts	500,000			
	Const. in progress		500,000		
	Construction expenses			405,000	
	Const. in progress				405,000
	Billings on LT contracts			500,000	
	Construction revenue				500,000

The "construction in progress" (CIP) account is a cost accumulation account similar to "work in process" for job-order costing, except that the percentage-of-completion method includes interim profits in the account. The "billings on LT contracts" account is similar to an unearned revenue account. At each financial statement date, the "construction in progress" account should be netted against the "billings on LT contracts" account on a project-by-project basis, resulting in a net current asset and/or a net current liability. Under the percentage-of-completion method in the above example, a net current asset of $50,000 [($135,000 + $15,000 + $225,000 + $75,000) – ($200,000 + $200,000)] would be reported at the end of year 2. A net current liability of $40,000 would result under the completed-contract method [($200,000 + $200,000) – ($135,000 + $225,000)] for the same year.

SUMMARY OF ACCOUNTS USED IN CONSTRUCTION ACCOUNTING
(NO LOSS EXPECTED OR INCURRED)

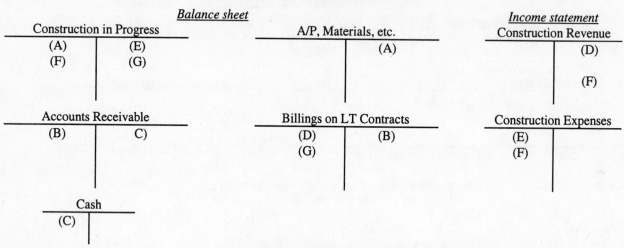

Explanation of Journal Entries

Both methods
(A) To record accumulated costs
(B) To record progress billings
(C) To record cash collections

Completed-contract method
(D) To record revenue upon completion and to close billings account
(E) To record expenses upon completion and to close construction in progress account

Percentage-of-completion method
(F) To record recognition of interim revenue and expense
(G) To close construction-in-progress and billings accounts at project completion

Balance Sheet Classification*

Current asset	*Current liability*
Projects where CIP at year end** > Billings	Projects where billings > CIP at year end** Estimated loss on uncompleted contract***

* *Evaluate and classify on a project-by-project basis.*
** *Construction in progress including income (when percentage-of-completion method is used) or loss recognized.*
*** *When recognizing and reporting losses, it is necessary to use a current liability account instead of reducing CIP in those cases in which a contract's billings exceed its accumulated costs.*

Contract Losses. In any year when a **percentage-of-completion** contract has an expected loss on the entire contract, the amount of the loss reported in that year is the total expected loss on the entire contract **plus** all profit previously recognized. For example, if the expected costs yet to be incurred at the end of year 2 were $147,000, the total expected loss is $7,000 [$500,000 – ($135,000 + $225,000 + $147,000)] and the total loss reported in year 2 would be $22,000 ($7,000 + $15,000). Similarly, under the **completed-contract** method, total expected losses on the entire contract are recognized as soon as they are estimated. The loss recognized is similar to that for percentage-of-completion except the amount is for the expected loss on the entire contract. In the aforementioned example, the loss to be recognized is only $7,000 (the entire loss on the contract expected in year 2) because interim profits have not been recorded. Journal entries and a schedule for profit or loss recognized on the contract under the percentage-of-completion method follow:

Journal entry at end of year 2	*Percentage-of-completion*	*Completed-contract*
Construction expenses	227,000*	
Construction in progress (loss)	22,000	
Construction revenue	205,000**	
Loss on uncompleted LT contracts		7,000
Construction in progress (loss)		7,000

Supporting Calculations:

* Year 2 costs		$225,000
Loss attributable to year 3:		
Year 3 revenue ($500,000 –		
$150,000 – $205,000)	$145,000	
Year 3 costs (expected)	147,000	2,000
Total		$227,000

** *($360,000/$507,000) (Costs to date/Total estimated costs) = 71% (rounded); (71% x $500,000) – $150,000 = $205,000*

PERCENTAGE-OF-COMPLETION METHOD

	Year 1	*Year 2*	*Year 3*
Contract price:	$500,000	$500,000	$500,000
Estimated total costs:			
Costs incurred this year	$135,000	$225,000	$144,000***
Prior year's costs	--	135,000	360,000
Estimated cost yet to be incurred	315,000	147,000	--
Estimated total costs for the 3-year period, actual for year 3	$450,000	$507,000	$504,000
Estimated total income (loss) for 3-year period, actual for year 3	$ 15,000	$ (7,000)	$ (4,000)
Income (loss) on entire contract previously recognized	--	15,000	(7,000)
Amount of estimated income (loss) recognized in the current period, actual for year 3	$ 15,000	$(22,000)	$ 3,000

***Assumed

MULTIPLE-CHOICE QUESTIONS (1-57)

1. The following information applied to Fenn, Inc. for 1999:

Merchandise purchased for resale	$400,000
Freight-in	↑ 10,000
Freight-out	5,000
Purchase returns	2,000

Fenn's 1999 inventoriable cost was
- a. $400,000
- b. $403,000
- c. $408,000
- d. $413,000

2. On December 28, 1999, Kerr Manufacturing Co. purchased goods costing $50,000. The terms were FOB destination. Some of the costs incurred in connection with the sale and delivery of the goods were as follows:

Packaging for shipment	$1,000
Shipping	1,500
Special handling charges	2,000

These goods were received on December 31, 1999. In Kerr's December 31, 1999 balance sheet, what amount of cost for these goods should be included in inventory?
- a. $54,500
- b. $53,500
- c. $52,000
- d. $50,000

3. On June 1, 1999, Pitt Corp. sold merchandise with a list price of $5,000 to Burr on account. Pitt allowed trade discounts of 30% and 20%. Credit terms were 2/15, n/40 and the sale was made FOB shipping point. Pitt prepaid $200 of delivery costs for Burr as an accommodation. On June 12, 1999, Pitt received from Burr a remittance in full payment amounting to
- a. $2,744
- b. $2,940
- c. $2,944
- d. $3,140

4. The following information was taken from Cody Co.'s accounting records for the year ended December 31, 1999:

Decrease in raw materials inventory	$ 15,000
Increase in finished goods inventory	35,000
Raw material purchased	430,000
Direct labor payroll	200,000
Factory overhead	300,000
⊣ Freight-out	45,000

There was no work in process inventory at the beginning or end of the year. Cody's 1999 cost of goods sold is
- a. $895,000
- b. $910,000
- c. $950,000
- d. $955,000

5. The following information pertains to Deal Corp.'s 1999 cost of goods sold:

Inventory, 12/31/98	$ 90,000
1999 purchases	124,000
1999 write-off of obsolete inventory	34,000
Inventory, 12/31/99	30,000

The inventory written off became obsolete due to an unexpected and unusual technological advance by a competitor. In its 1999 income statement, what amount should Deal report as cost of goods sold?
- a. $218,000
- b. $184,000
- c. $150,000
- d. $124,000

6. How should the following costs affect a retailer's inventory?

	Freight-in	Interest on inventory loan
a.	Increase	No effect
b.	Increase	Increase
c.	No effect	Increase
d.	No effect	No effect

7. According to the net method, which of the following items should be included in the cost of inventory?

	Freight costs	Purchase discounts not taken
a.	Yes	No
b.	Yes	Yes
c.	No	Yes
d.	No	No

8. The weighted-average for the year inventory cost flow method is applicable to which of the following inventory systems?

	Periodic	Perpetual
a.	Yes	Yes
b.	Yes	No
c.	No	Yes
d.	No	No

9. During January 1999, Metro Co., which maintains a perpetual inventory system, recorded the following information pertaining to its inventory:

	Units	Unit cost	Total cost	Units on hand
Balance on 1/1/99	1,000	$1	$1,000	1,000
Purchased on 1/7/99	600	3	1,800	1,600
Sold on 1/20/99	900			700
Purchased on 1/25/99	400	5	2,000	1,100

Under the moving-average method, what amount should Metro report as inventory at January 31, 1999?
- a. $2,640
- b. $3,225
- c. $3,300
- d. $3,900

10. Moss Co. has determined its December 31, 1999, inventory on a FIFO basis to be $400,000. Information pertaining to that inventory follows:

Estimated selling price	$408,000
Estimated cost of disposal	20,000
Normal profit margin	60,000
Current replacement cost	360,000

Moss records losses that result from applying the lower of cost or market rule. At December 31, 1999, what should be the net carrying value of Moss' inventory?

a. $400,000
b. $388,000
c. $360,000
d. $328,000

11. Based on a physical inventory taken on December 31, 1999, Chewy Co. determined its chocolate inventory on a FIFO basis at $26,000 with a replacement cost of $20,000. Chewy estimated that, after further processing costs of $12,000, the chocolate could be sold as finished candy bars for $40,000. Chewy's normal profit margin is 10% of sales. Under the lower of cost or market rule, what amount should Chewy report as chocolate inventory in its December 31, 1999 balance sheet?

a. $28,000
b. $26,000
c. $24,000
d. $20,000

12. Reporting inventory at the lower of cost or market is a departure from the accounting principle of

a. Historical cost.
b. Consistency.
c. Conservatism.
d. Full disclosure.

13. The original cost of an inventory item is below both replacement cost and net realizable value. The net realizable value less normal profit margin is below the original cost. Under the lower of cost or market method, the inventory item should be valued at

a. Replacement cost.
b. Net realizable value.
c. Net realizable value less normal profit margin.
d. Original cost.

14. Which of the following statements are correct when a company applying the lower of cost or market method reports its inventory at replacement cost?

I. The original cost is less than replacement cost.
II. The net realizable value is greater than replacement cost.

a. I only.
b. II only.
c. Both I and II.
d. Neither I nor II.

15. The original cost of an inventory item is above the replacement cost and the net realizable value. The replacement cost is below the net realizable value less the normal profit margin. As a result, under the lower of cost or market method, the inventory item should be reported at the

a. Net realizable value.
b. Net realizable value less the normal profit margin.
c. Replacement cost.
d. Original cost.

16. On January 1, 1999, Card Corp. signed a 3-year noncancelable purchase contract, which allows Card to purchase up to 500,000 units of a computer part annually from Hart

Supply Co. at $.10 per unit and guarantees a minimum annual purchase of 100,000 units. During 1999, the part unexpectedly became obsolete. Card had 250,000 units of this inventory at December 31, 1999, and believes these parts can be sold as scrap for $.02 per unit. What amount of probable loss from the purchase commitment should Card report in its 1999 income statement?

a. $24,000
b. $20,000
c. $16,000
d. $ 8,000

17. Thread Co. is selecting its inventory system in preparation for its first year of operations. Thread intends to use either the periodic weighted-average method or the perpetual moving average method, and to apply the lower of cost or market rule either to individual items or to the total inventory. Inventory prices are expected to generally increase throughout 1999, although a few individual prices will decrease. What inventory system should Thread select if it wants to maximize the inventory carrying amount at December 31, 1999?

	Inventory method	Cost or market application
a.	Perpetual	Total inventory
b.	Perpetual	Individual item
c.	Periodic	Total inventory
d.	Periodic	Individual item

18. Marsh Company had 150 units of product A on hand at January 1, 1999, costing $21 each. Purchases of product A during the month of January were as follows:

	Units	Unit cost
Jan. 10	200	$22
18	250	23
28	100	24

A physical count on January 31, 1999, shows 250 units of product A on hand. The cost of the inventory at January 31, 1999, under the LIFO method is

a. $5,850
b. $5,550
c. $5,350
d. $5,250

19. During January 1999, Metro Co., which maintains a perpetual inventory system, recorded the following information pertaining to its inventory:

	Units	Unit Cost	Total Cost	Units on hand
Balance on 1/1/99	1,000	$1	$1,000	1,000
Purchased on 1/7/99	600	3	1,800	1,600
Sold on 1/20/99	900			700
Purchased on 1/25/99	400	5	2,000	1,100

Under the LIFO method, what amount should Metro report as inventory at January 31, 1999?

a. $1,300
b. $2,700
c. $3,900
d. $4,100

20. Drew Co. uses the average cost inventory method for internal reporting purposes and LIFO for financial statement and income tax reporting. At December 31, 1999, the inventory was $375,000 using average cost and $320,000 using LIFO. The unadjusted credit balance in the LIFO Reserve account on December 31, 1999, was $35,000. What adjusting entry should Drew record to adjust from average cost to LIFO at December 31, 1999?

		Debit	Credit
a.	Cost of goods sold	$55,000	
	Inventory		$55,000
b.	Cost of goods sold	$55,000	
	LIFO reserve		$55,000
c.	Cost of goods sold	$20,000	
	Inventory		$20,000
d.	Cost of goods sold	$20,000	
	LIFO reserve		$20,000

21. A company decided to change its inventory valuation method from FIFO to LIFO in a period of rising prices. What was the result of the change on ending inventory and net income in the year of the change?

	Ending inventory	Net income
a.	Increase	Increase
b.	Increase	Decrease
c.	Decrease	Decrease
d.	Decrease	Increase

22. Generally, which inventory costing method approximates most closely the current cost for each of the following?

	Cost of goods sold	Ending inventory
a.	LIFO	FIFO
b.	LIFO	LIFO
c.	FIFO	FIFO
d.	FIFO	LIFO

23. During periods of rising prices, a perpetual inventory system would result in the same dollar amount of ending inventory as a periodic inventory system under which of the following inventory cost flow methods?

	FIFO	LIFO
a.	Yes	No
b.	Yes	Yes
c.	No	Yes
d.	No	No

24. On January 1, 1998, Poe Company adopted the dollar-value LIFO inventory method. Poe's entire inventory constitutes a single pool. Inventory data for 1998 and 1999 are as follows:

Date	Inventory at current year cost	Inventory at base year cost	Relevant price index
1/1/98	$150,000	$150,000	1.00
12/31/98	220,000	200,000	1.10
12/31/99	276,000	230,000	1.20

Poe's LIFO inventory value at December 31, 1999, is
- a. $230,000
- b. $236,000
- c. $241,000
- d. $246,000

25. Brock Co. adopted the dollar-value LIFO inventory method as of January 1, 1998. A single inventory pool and an internally computed price index are used to compute Brock's LIFO inventory layers. Information about Brock's dollar-value inventory follows:

	Inventory		
Date	At base year cost	At current year cost	At dollar value LIFO
1/1/98	$40,000	$40,000	$40,000
1998 layer	5,000	14,000	6,000
12/31/98	45,000	54,000	46,000
1999 layer	15,000	26,000	?
12/31/99	$60,000	$80,000	?

What was Brock's dollar-value LIFO inventory at December 31, 1999?
- a. $80,000
- b. $74,000
- c. $66,000
- d. $60,000

26. Estimates of price-level changes for specific inventories are required for which of the following inventory methods?
- a. Conventional retail.
- b. Dollar-value LIFO.
- c. Weighted-average cost.
- d. Average cost retail.

27. When the double-extension approach to the dollar-value LIFO inventory method is used, the inventory layer added in the current year is multiplied by an index number. Which of the following correctly states how components are used in the calculation of this index number?
- a. In the numerator, the average of the ending inventory at base year cost and at current year cost.
- b. In the numerator, the ending inventory at current year cost, and, in the denominator, the ending inventory at base year cost.
- c. In the numerator, the ending inventory at base year cost, and, the denominator, the ending inventory at current year cost.
- d. In the denominator, the average of the ending inventory at base year cost and at current year cost.

28. Jones Wholesalers stocks a changing variety of products. Which inventory costing method will be most likely to give Jones the lowest ending inventory when its product lines are subject to specific price increases?
- a. Specific identification.
- b. Weighted-average.
- c. Dollar-value LIFO.
- d. FIFO periodic.

29. Dean Company uses the retail inventory method to estimate its inventory for interim statement purposes. Data relating to the computation of the inventory at July 31, 1999, are as follows:

	Cost	Retail
Inventory, 2/1/99	$ 180,000	$ 250,000
Purchases	1,020,000	1,575,000
Markups, net		175,000
Sales		1,705,000
Estimated normal shop-lifting losses		20,000
Markdowns, net		125,000

Under the approximate lower of average cost or market retail method (conventional), Dean's estimated inventory at July 31, 1999, is

- a. $ 90,000
- b. $ 96,000
- c. $102,000
- d. $150,000

30. The retail inventory method includes which of the following in the calculation of both cost and retail amounts of goods available for sale?

- a. Purchase returns.
- b. Sales returns.
- c. Net markups.
- d. Freight-in. ✓

31. On December 31, 1998, Jason Company adopted the dollar-value LIFO retail inventory method. Inventory data for 1999 are as follows:

	LIFO cost	Retail
Inventory, 12/31/98	$360,000	$500,000
Inventory, 12/31/99	?	660,000
Increase in price, level for 1999		10%
Cost to retail ratio for 1999		70%

Under the LIFO retail method, Jason's inventory at December 31, 1999, should be

- a. $437,000
- b. $462,000
- c. $472,000
- d. $483,200

32. Dart Company's accounting records indicated the following information:

Inventory, 1/1/99	$ 500,000
Purchases during 1999	2,500,000
Sales during 1999	3,200,000

A physical inventory taken on December 31, 1999, resulted in an ending inventory of $575,000. Dart's gross profit on sales has remained constant at 25% in recent years. Dart suspects some inventory may have been taken by a new employee. At December 31, 1999, what is the estimated cost of missing inventory?

- a. $ 25,000
- b. $100,000
- c. $175,000
- d. $225,000

33. On July 1, 1999, Casa Development Co. purchased a tract of land for $1,200,000. Casa incurred additional cost of $300,000 during the remainder of 1999 in preparing the land for sale. The tract was subdivided into residential lots as follows:

Lot class	Number of lots	Sales price per lot
A	100	$24,000
B	100	16,000
C	200	10,000

Using the relative sales value method, what amount of costs should be allocated to the Class A lots?

- a. $300,000
- b. $375,000
- c. $600,000
- d. $720,000

 2

34. Herc Co.'s inventory at December 31, 1999, was $1,500,000 based on a physical count priced at cost, and before any necessary adjustment for the following:

- Merchandise costing $90,000, shipped FOB shipping point from a vendor on December 30, 1999, was received and recorded on January 5, 2000.
- Goods in the shipping area were excluded from inventory although shipment was not made until January 4, 2000. The goods, billed to the customer FOB shipping point on December 30, 1999, had a cost of $120,000.

What amount should Herc report as inventory in its December 31, 1999 balance sheet?

- a. $1,500,000
- b. $1,590,000
- c. $1,620,000
- d. $1,710,000

35. Kew Co.'s accounts payable balance at December 31, 1999, was $2,200,000 before considering the following data:

- Goods shipped to Kew FOB shipping point on December 22, 1999, were lost in transit. The invoice cost of $40,000 was not recorded by Kew. On January 7, 2000, Kew filed a $40,000 claim against the common carrier.
- On December 27, 1999, a vendor authorized Kew to return, for full credit, goods shipped and billed at $70,000 on December 3, 1999. The returned goods were shipped by Kew on December 28, 1999. A $70,000 credit memo was received and recorded by Kew on January 5, 2000.
- Goods shipped to Kew FOB destination on December 20, 1999, were received on January 6, 2000. The invoice cost was $50,000.

What amount should Kew report as accounts payable in its December 31, 1999 balance sheet?

- a. $2,170,000
- b. $2,180,000
- c. $2,230,000
- d. $2,280,000

36. Lewis Company's usual sales terms are net 60 days, FOB shipping point. Sales, net of returns and allowances, totaled $2,300,000 for the year ended December 31, 1999, before year-end adjustments. Additional data are as follows:

- On December 27, 1999, Lewis authorized a customer to return, for full credit, goods shipped and billed at

$50,000 on December 15, 1999. The returned goods were received by Lewis on January 4, 2000, and a $50,000 credit memo was issued and recorded on the same date.

• Goods with an invoice amount of $80,000 were billed and recorded on January 3, 2000. The goods were shipped on December 30, 1999.

• Goods with an invoice amount of $100,000 were billed and recorded on December 30, 1999. The goods were shipped on January 3, 2000.

Lewis' adjusted net sales for 1999 should be
- a. $2,330,000
- b. $2,280,000
- c. $2,250,000
- d. $2,230,000

37. On January 1, 1999, Dell, Inc. contracted with the city of Little to provide custom built desks for the city schools. The contract made Dell the city's sole supplier and required Dell to supply no less than 4,000 desks and no more than 5,500 desks per year for 2 years. In turn, Little agreed to pay a fixed price of $110 per desk. During 1999, Dell produced 5,000 desks for Little. At December 31, 1999, 500 of these desks were segregated from the regular inventory and were accepted and awaiting pickup by Little. Little paid Dell $450,000 during 1999. What amount should Dell recognize as contract revenue in 1999?
- a. $450,000
- b. $495,000
- c. $550,000
- d. $605,000

38. On October 20, 1999, Grimm Co. consigned 40 freezers to Holden Co. for sale at $1,000 each and paid $800 in transportation costs. On December 30, 1999, Holden reported the sale of 10 freezers and remitted $8,500. The remittance was net of the agreed 15% commission. What amount should Grimm recognize as consignment sales revenue for 1999?
- a. $ 7,700
- b. $ 8,500
- c. $ 9,800
- d. $10,000

39. The following items were included in Opal Co.'s inventory account at December 31, 1999:

Merchandise out on consignment, at sales price, including 40% markup on selling price	$40,000
Goods purchased, in transit, shipped FOB shipping point	36,000
Goods held on consignment by Opal	27,000

By what amount should Opal's inventory account at December 31, 1999, be reduced?
- a. $103,000
- b. $ 67,000
- c. $ 51,000
- d. $ 43,000

40. On December 1, 1999, Alt Department Store received 505 sweaters on consignment from Todd. Todd's cost for the sweaters was $80 each, and they were priced to sell at $100. Alt's commission on consigned goods is 10%. At December 31, 1999, five sweaters remained. In its Decem-

ber 31, 1999 balance sheet, what amount should Alt report as payable for consigned goods?
- a. $49,000
- b. $45,400
- c. $45,000
- d. $40,400

41. Southgate Co. paid the in-transit insurance premium for consignment goods shipped to Hendon Co., the consignee. In addition, Southgate advanced part of the commissions that will be due when Hendon sells the goods. Should Southgate include the in-transit insurance premium and the advanced commissions in inventory costs?

	Insurance premium	*Advanced commissions*
a.	Yes	Yes
b.	No	No
c.	Yes	No
d.	No	Yes

42. Jel Co., a consignee, paid the freight costs for goods shipped from Dale Co., a consignor. These freight costs are to be deducted from Jel's payment to Dale when the consignment goods are sold. Until Jel sells the goods, the freight costs should be included in Jel's
- a. Cost of goods sold.
- b. Freight-out costs.
- c. Selling expenses.
- d. Accounts receivable.

43. Heath Co.'s current ratio is 4:1. Which of the following transactions would normally increase its current ratio?
- a. Purchasing inventory on account.
- b. Selling inventory on account.
- c. Collecting an account receivable.
- d. Purchasing machinery for cash.

44. During 1999, Rand Co. purchased $960,000 of inventory. The cost of goods sold for 1999 was $900,000, and the ending inventory at December 31, 1999, was $180,000. What was the inventory turnover for 1999?
- a. 6.4
- b. 6.0
- c. 5.3
- d. 5.0

45. In a comparison of 1999 to 1998, Neir Co.'s inventory turnover ratio increased substantially although sales and inventory amounts were essentially unchanged. Which of the following statements explains the increased inventory turnover ratio?
- a. Cost of goods sold decreased.
- b. Accounts receivable turnover increased.
- c. Total asset turnover increased.
- d. Gross profit percentage decreased.

46. Selected data pertaining to Lore Co. for the calendar year 1999 is as follows:

Net cash sales	$ 3,000
Cost of goods sold	18,000
Inventory at beginning of year	6,000
Purchases	24,000
Accounts receivable at beginning of year	20,000
Accounts receivable at end of year	22,000

Lore would use which of the following to determine the average days' sales in inventory?

	Numerator	Denominator
a.	365	Average inventory
b.	365	Inventory turnover
c.	Average inventory	Sales divided by 365
d.	Sales divided by 365	Inventory turnover

47. Cord Builders, Inc. has consistently used the percentage-of-completion method of accounting for construction-type contracts. During 1998 Cord started work on a $9,000,000 fixed-price construction contract that was completed in 2000. Cord's accounting records disclosed the following:

	December 31	
	1998	*1999*
Cumulative contract costs incurred	$3,900,000	$6,300,000
Estimated total cost at completion	7,800,000	8,100,000

How much income would Cord have recognized on this contract for the year ended December 31, 1999?

a. $100,000
b. $300,000
c. $600,000
d. $700,000

48. State Co. recognizes construction revenue and expenses using the percentage-of-completion method. During 1998, a single long-term project was begun, which continued through 1999. Information on the project follows:

	1998	*1999*
Accounts receivable from construction contract	$100,000	$300,000
Construction expenses	105,000	192,000
Construction in progress	122,000	364,000
Partial billings on contract	100,000	420,000

Profit recognized from the long-term construction contract in 1999 should be

a. $ 50,000
b. $108,000
c. $128,000
d. $228,000

49. Lake Construction Company has consistently used the percentage-of-completion method of recognizing income. During 1998 Lake entered into a fixed-price contract to construct an office building for $10,000,000. Information relating to the contract is as follows:

	At December 31,	
	1998	*1999*
Percentage of completion	20%	60%
Estimated total cost at completion	$7,500,000	$8,000,000
Income recognized (cumulative)	500,000	1,200,000

Contract costs incurred during 1999 were

a. $3,200,000
b. $3,300,000

c. $3,500,000
d. $4,800,000

50. Hansen Construction, Inc. has consistently used the percentage-of-completion method of recognizing income. During 1999 Hansen started work on a $3,000,000 fixed-price construction contract. The accounting records disclosed the following data for the year ended December 31, 1999:

Costs incurred	$ 930,000
Estimated cost to complete	2,170,000
Progress billings	1,100,000
Collections	700,000

How much loss should Hansen have recognized in 1999?
a. $230,000
b. $100,000
c. $ 30,000
d. $0

Items 51 and 52 are based on the following data pertaining to Pell Co.'s construction jobs, which commenced during 1999:

	Project 1	*Project 2*
Contract price	$420,000	$300,000
Costs incurred during 1999	240,000	280,000
Estimated costs to complete	120,000	40,000
Billed to customers during 1999	150,000	270,000
Received from customers during 1999	90,000	250,000

51. If Pell used the completed contract method, what amount of gross profit (loss) would Pell report in its 1999 income statement?
a. $(20,000)
b. $ 0
c. $ 340,000
d. $ 420,000

52. If Pell used the percentage-of-completion method, what amount of gross profit (loss) would Pell report in its 1999 income statement?
a. $(20,000)
b. $ 20,000
c. $ 22,500
d. $ 40,000

53. Which of the following is used in calculating the income recognized in the fourth and final year of a contract accounted for by the percentage-of-completion method?

	Actual total costs	Income previously recognized
a.	Yes	Yes
b.	Yes	No
c.	No	Yes
d.	No	No

54. A company used the percentage-of-completion method of accounting for a 5-year construction contract. Which of the following items will the company use to calculate the income recognized in the third year?

	Progress billings to date	Income previously recognized
a.	Yes	No
b.	No	Yes
c.	No	No
d.	Yes	Yes

55. The calculation of the income recognized in the third year of a 5-year construction contract accounted for using the percentage-of-completion method includes the ratio of

    a.   Total costs incurred to date to total estimated costs.

    b.   Total costs incurred to date to total billings to date.

    c.   Cost incurred in year 3 to total estimated costs.

    d.   Costs incurred in year 3 to total billings to date.

56. When should an anticipated loss on a long-term contract be recognized under the percentage-of-completion method and the completed-contract method, respectively?

	Percentage-of-completion	Completed-contract
a.	Over life of project	Contract complete
b.	Immediately	Contract complete
c.	Over life of project	Immediately
d.	Immediately	Immediately

57. In accounting for a long-term construction contract using the percentage-of-completion method, the progress billings on contracts account is a

    a.   Contra current asset account.

    b.   Contra noncurrent asset account.

    c.   Noncurrent liability account.

    d.   Revenue account.

OTHER OBJECTIVE QUESTIONS

Problem 1   (15 to 25 minutes)

Items 1 through 15 represent True or False statements concerning inventory accounting methods.

Required:

For **items 1 through 15,** respond to each statement as either True or False. On the CPA Exam, you would be required to fill in the corresponding oval for each True ⟨T⟩ or False ⟨F⟩ response.

Items to be answered

1. The gross margin method uses historical sales margins to estimate the cost of inventory.

2. The conventional retail method computes an ending inventory value which approximates the lower of cost or market.

3. The dollar-value LIFO method preserves old inventory costs by charging current costs to cost of goods sold.

4. Inventory should be reported at the lower of cost or market and it may be based on the values of individual items, categories, or the total inventory.

5. A loss on a purchase commitment should be recorded when the contract price is greater than the market and it is anticipated that a loss will occur when the contract is completed.

6. The conventional retail method requires that net markups and net markdowns be subtracted in the calculation of the cost percentage.

7. Under the dollar-value LIFO method, increases and decreases in a layer would be measured based upon the change in the total dollar value of the layer.

8. The link-chain method uses a cumulative index to value the base cost of ending inventory.

9. The price index for dollar-value LIFO is a measure of changes in price levels between the current year and the base year.

10. Under the LIFO method, an inventory liquidation will result in higher profits in a period of rising prices.

11. A holding gain results from holding an item while the market value experiences a decline.

12. During a period of rising prices, the LIFO cost flow assumption results in a higher net income as compared to FIFO.

13. In a period of rising prices, when a company changes from FIFO to LIFO the net income will tend to decline as will working capital.

14. The use of LIFO for book and tax purposes will result in a lower tax payment in a period of rising prices.

15. Under the LIFO method, the cost of goods sold balance would be the same whether a perpetual or periodic inventory system is used.

PROBLEMS

Problem 1   (15 to 25 minutes)

Happlia Co. imports expensive household appliances. Each model has many variations and each unit has an identification number. Happlia pays all costs for getting the goods from the port to its central warehouse in Des Moines. After repackaging, the goods are consigned to retailers. A retailer makes a sale, simultaneously buys the appliance from Happlia, and pays the balance due within 1 week.

To alleviate the overstocking of refrigerators at a Minneapolis retailer, some were reshipped to a Kansas City retailer where they were still held in inventory at December 31, 1999. Happlia paid the costs of this reshipment.

Happlia uses the specific identification inventory costing method.

Required:

a. In regard to the specific identification inventory costing method
1. Describe its key elements.
2. Discuss why it is appropriate for Happlia to use this method.

b. 1. What general criteria should Happlia use to determine inventory carrying amounts at December 31, 1999? Ignore lower of cost or market considerations.
2. Give four examples of costs included in these inventory carrying amounts.

c. What costs should be reported in Happlia's 1999 income statement? Ignore lower of cost or market considerations.

Problem 2   (15 to 25 minutes)

Blaedon Co. makes ongoing design refinements to lawnmowers that are produced for it by contractors. Blaedon stores the lawnmowers in its own warehouse and sells them at list price, directly to retailers. Blaedon uses the FIFO inventory method. Approximately two-thirds of new lawnmower sales involve trade-ins. For each used lawnmower traded in and returned to Blaedon, retailers receive a $40 allowance regardless of whether the trade-in was associated with a sale of a 1999 or 2000 model. Blaedon's net realizable value on a used lawnmower averages $25.

At December 31, 1999, Blaedon's inventory of new lawnmowers includes both 1999 and 2000 models. When the 2000 model was introduced in September 1999, the list price of the remaining 1999 model lawnmowers was reduced below cost. Blaedon is experiencing rising costs.

Required:

a. At December 31, 1999, how should Blaedon determine the carrying amounts assigned to its lawnmower inventory of
1. 2000 models?
2. 1999 models?

b. Considering only the 2000 model lawnmower, explain the impact of the FIFO cost flow assumptions on Blaedon's 1999

1. Income statement amounts.
2. Balance sheet amounts.

Problem 3   (30 to 40 minutes)

York Co. sells one product, which it purchases from various suppliers. York's trial balance at December 31, 1999, included the following accounts:

Sales (33,000 units @ $16)	$528,000
Sales discounts	7,500
Purchases	368,900
Purchase discounts	18,000
Freight-in	5,000
Freight-out	11,000

York Co.'s inventory purchases during 1999 were as follows:

	Units	Cost per unit	Total cost
Beginning inventory, January 1	8,000	$8.20	$ 65,600
Purchases, quarter ended March 31	12,000	8.25	99,000
Purchases, quarter ended June 30	15,000	7.90	118,500
Purchases, quarter ended September 30	13,000	7.50	97,500
Purchases, quarter ended December 31	7,000	7.70	53,900
	55,000		$434,500

Additional information

York's accounting policy is to report inventory in its financial statements at the lower of cost or market, applied to total inventory. Cost is determined under the last-in, first-out (LIFO) method.

York has determined that, at December 31, 1999, the replacement cost of its inventory was $8 per unit and the net realizable value was $8.80 per unit. York's normal profit margin is $1.05 per unit.

Required:

a. Prepare York's schedule of cost of goods sold, with a supporting schedule of ending inventory. York uses the direct method of reporting losses from market decline of inventory.

b. Explain the rule of lower of cost or market and its application in this situation.

Problem 4   (20 to 25 minutes)

On January 1, 1997, Silver Industries, Inc. adopted the dollar-value LIFO method of determining inventory costs for financial and income tax reporting. The following information relates to this change:

• Silver has continued to use the FIFO method, which approximates current costs, for internal reporting purposes. Silver's FIFO inventories at December 31, 1997,

1998, and 1999 were $100,000, $137,500, and $195,000, respectively.

- The FIFO inventory amounts are converted to dollar-value LIFO amounts using a single inventory pool and cost indices developed using the link-chain method. Silver estimated that the current year cost change indices, which measure year-to-year cost changes, were 1.25 for 1998 and 1.20 for 1999.

Required:

Prepare a schedule showing the computation of Silver's dollar-value LIFO inventory at December 31, 1998 and 1999. Show all calculations.

Problem 5   (15 to 25 minutes)

On July 1, 1998, Bow Construction Co. commenced operations and began constructing a building for Crecy under a fixed price contract. Anticipated completion date was June 15, 2000. Bow projects a large profit because it purchased most of the contract materials at exceptionally low prices in August 1998.

At the end of each month, Crecy is billed for completed work, for which it pays within 30 days. On December 31, 1999, all costs incurred exceed billings on the contract.

For the Crecy contract, Bow uses the percentage-of-completion (cost-to-cost) method for financial statement purposes. For income tax purposes, Bow qualifies for and uses the completed-contract method. Bow has no other contracts and no other differences between financial statement and income tax reporting.

Required:

a.   How should Bow determine that the percentage-of-completion method is appropriate for the Crecy contract?

b.   How should Bow calculate its 1999 income to be recognized on the Crecy contract? Explain any special treatment of unused material costs and why it is required.

c.   Ignoring income tax effects, specify how the accounts related to the Crecy contract should be reported on Bow's December 31, 1999 balance sheet.

d.   What are the income tax effects of the Crecy contract on Bow's 1999 balance sheet and income statement?*

* This requirement should not be completed until you have done Module 27, Deferred Taxes. A cross-reference in the Module 27 problem material will direct you to return to it.

Problem 6   (40 to 50 minutes)

London, Inc. began operation of its construction division on October 1, 1998, and entered into contracts for two separate projects. The Beta project contract price was $600,000 and provided for penalties of $10,000 per week for late completion. Although during 1999 the Beta project had been on schedule for timely completion, it was completed 4 weeks late in August 2000. The Gamma project's original contract price was $800,000. Change orders during 2000 added $40,000 to the original contract price.

The following data pertains to the separate long-term construction projects in progress:

	Beta	Gamma
As of September 30, 1999:	600,000	800,000
Costs incurred to date	$360,000	$410,000
Estimated costs to complete	40,000	410,000
Billings	315,000	440,000
Cash collections	275,000	365,000
As of September 30, 2000:		
Costs incurred to date	450,000	720,000
Estimated costs to complete	--	180,000
Billings	560,000	710,000
Cash collections	560,000	625,000

Additional information

- London accounts for its long-term construction contracts using the percentage-of-completion method for financial reporting purposes and the completed-contract method for income tax purposes.
- Enacted income tax rates are 25% for 1999 and 30% for future years.
- London's income before income taxes from all divisions, before considering revenues from long-term construction projects, was $300,000 for the year ended September 30, 1999. There were no other temporary or permanent differences.

Required:

a.   Prepare a schedule showing London's gross profit (loss) recognized for the years ended September 30, 1999, and 2000, under the percentage-of-completion method.

b.   Prepare a schedule showing London's balances in the following accounts at September 30, 1999, under the percentage-of-completion method:

- Accounts receivable
- Costs and estimated earnings in excess of billings
- Billings in excess of costs and estimated earnings

c.   Prepare a schedule reconciling London's financial statement income and taxable income for the year ended September 30, 1999, and showing all components of taxes payable and current and deferred income tax expense for the year then ended. Do not consider estimated tax requirements.*

*This requirement should not be completed until you have done Module 27, Deferred Taxes. A cross-reference in the Module 27 problem material will direct you to return to it.

MULTIPLE-CHOICE ANSWERS

1. c __ __	13. d __ __	25. c __ __	37. c __ __	49. b __ __
2. d __ __	14. b __ __	26. b __ __	38. d __ __	50. b __ __
3. c __ __	15. b __ __	27. b __ __	39. d __ __	51. a __ __
4. b __ __	16. c __ __	28. c __ __	40. c __ __	52. b __ __
5. c __ __	17. a __ __	29. a __ __	41. c __ __	53. a __ __
6. a __ __	18. c __ __	30. a __ __	42. d __ __	54. b __ __
7. a __ __	19. b __ __	31. a __ __	43. b __ __	55. a __ __
8. b __ __	20. d __ __	32. a __ __	44. b __ __	56. d __ __
9. b __ __	21. c __ __	33. c __ __	45. d __ __	57. a __ __
10. c __ __	22. a __ __	34. d __ __	46. b __ __	
11. c __ __	23. a __ __	35. a __ __	47. a __ __	1st: __/57 = __%
12. a __ __	24. c __ __	36. d __ __	48. a __ __	2nd: __/57 = __%

MULTIPLE-CHOICE ANSWER EXPLANATIONS

A. Determining Inventory and Cost of Goods Sold

1. (c) Inventoriable costs include all costs necessary to prepare goods for sale. For a merchandising concern these costs include the purchase price of the goods, freight-in, insurance, warehousing, and any costs necessary to get the goods to the point of sale (except interest on any loans obtained to purchase the goods). In this problem, inventoriable costs total $408,000.

Purchase price less returns	
($400,000 – $2,000)	$398,000
Freight-in	10,000
	$408,000

Note that freight-out is a **selling expense**, not an inventoriable cost, as the diagram below indicates.

2. (d) When the shipping terms are FOB destination the seller bears **all** costs of transporting the goods to the buyer. Therefore, the seller is responsible for the payment of packaging costs ($1,000), shipping costs ($1,500), and the special handling charges ($2,000). The only amount to be included as the buyer's cost of the inventory purchased is the purchase price ($50,000).

3. (c) Purchases are always recorded net of trade discounts. When more than one trade discount is applied to a list price, it is called a chain discount. Chain discounts are applied in steps; each discount applies to the previously discounted price. The cost, net of trade discounts, is $2,800 [$5,000 – (30% x $5,000) = $3,500; and $3,500 – (20% x $3,500) = $2,800]. Payment was made within the discount period, so the net purchase price is $2,744 [$2,800 – (2% x $2,800)]. The remittance from Burr would also include reimbursement of the $200 of delivery costs. Since the terms were FOB shipping point, Burr is responsible for paying this amount, and must reimburse Pitt, who prepaid the freight. Thus, the total remittance is $2,944 ($2,744 + $200).

4. (b) Three computations must be performed: raw materials used, cost of goods manufactured, and cost of goods sold.

(1)	Raw materials purchased	$430,000
	Decrease in RM inventory	15,000
	Raw materials used	$445,000

(2)	Beginning WIP	$ -0-
	RM used (from above)	445,000
	Direct labor	200,000
	Factory overhead	300,000
	Cost to account for	945,000
	Ending WIP	-0-
	Cost of goods manuf.	$945,000

(3)	Cost of goods manuf.	$945,000
	Increase in FG inventory	35,000
	Cost of goods sold	$910,000

The decrease in RM inventory is added when computing RM used because RM were used in excess of those purchased. The increase in FG inventory is deducted when computing cost of goods sold because it represents the portion of goods manufactured which were not sold. The freight-out is irrelevant for this question because freight-out is a selling expense and therefore does not affect cost of goods sold.

5. (c) To compute cost of goods sold, the solutions approach is to set up a T-account for inventory:

	Inventory		
12/31/98	90,000		
Purchases	124,000	34,000	Write-off
		?	Cost of goods sold
12/31/99	30,000		

Purchases increase inventory, while the write-off and cost of goods sold decrease inventory. Cost of goods sold can be computed as $150,000 using the T-account. An alternate solutions approach is to use the CGS computation:

BI	$ 90,000
+Purchases	124,000
CGAS	214,000
- EI	30,000
	$184,000

Cost of goods available for sale
$ 34,000 recognized as invy. loss*
$150,000 recognized as CGS

Theoretically correct treatment.

6.   (a)   Per ARB 43, chap 4, para 4, the cost of inventory should include all expenditures (direct and indirect) incurred to bring an item to its existing condition and location. Freight-in charges are thus appropriately included in inventory costs. Per SFAS 34, para 34, interest cost shall not be capitalized for assets that are in use or ready for their intended use in the earnings activities of the enterprise. Thus, interest on an inventory loan should not be included in inventory (it should be expensed as incurred). Therefore, answer (a) is correct.

7.   (a)   Per ARB 43, chap 4, para 4, the cost of inventory should include all expenditures (direct and indirect) incurred to bring an item to its existing condition and location. Freight charges are thus appropriately included in inventory costs. Under the net purchase method, purchase discounts not taken are recorded in a Purchase Discounts Lost account. When this method is used, purchase discounts lost are considered a financial (i.e., "other") expense, and are thus excluded from the cost of inventory. Therefore, answer (a) is correct, and answers (b), (c), and (d) are incorrect.

B.2.   Weighted-Average

8.   (b)   The requirement is to determine whether the weighted-average inventory method is applicable to a periodic and/or a perpetual inventory system. The weighted-average method computes a weighted-average unit cost of inventory for the entire period and is used with periodic records. The moving average method requires that a new unit of cost be computed each time new goods are purchased and is used with perpetual records. Therefore, answers (a), (c), and (d) are incorrect.

B.4.   Moving Average

9.   (b)   The moving average method requires that a new unit cost be computed each time goods are purchased. The new unit cost is used to cost all sales of inventory until the next purchase. After the 1/7/99 purchase, Metro owns 1,600 units (1,000 + 600) at a total cost of $2,800 ($1,000 + $1,800). Therefore, the moving average unit cost at that time is $1.75 ($2,800 ÷ 1,600 units). After the 1/20/99 sale of 900 units (at a unit of cost of $1.75), Metro owns 700 units at a unit cost of $1.75 (700 x $1.75 = $1,225). The 1/25/99 purchase of 400 units at a total cost of $2,000 increases inventory to its 1/31/99 balance of $3,225 ($1,225 + $2,000). The new unit cost (not required) is $2.93 ($3,225 ÷ 1,100).

B.5.   Lower of Cost or Market

10.   (c)   ARB 43, chap 4, para 8, requires the use of lower of cost or market (LCM) for financial reporting of inventories. The market value of inventory is defined as the replacement cost (RC), as long as it is less than the ceiling (net realizable value, or NRV) and more than the floor (NRV less a normal profit, or NRV − NP). In this case, the amounts are:

Ceiling: NRV = $408,000 est. sell. price −
                    $20,000 dep. cost =   <u>$388,000</u>
Replacement cost   <u>$360,000</u>
Floor: NRV − NP = $388,000 − $60,000 =   <u>$328,000</u>

The designated market value is the replacement cost of $360,000 because it falls between the floor and the ceiling. Once market value is designated, LCM can be determined by simply picking the lower of cost ($400,000) or market ($360,000). Thus, the inventory should be reported at market and answer (c) is correct.

11.   (c)   ARB 43 requires the use of lower of cost or market (LCM) for financial reporting of inventories. The market value of inventory is defined as the replacement cost (RC), as long as it is less than the ceiling (net realizable value, or NRV) and more than the floor (NRV less a normal profit, or NRV − NP). In this case, the amounts are:

Ceiling: NRV = $40,000 est. sell. price
                   − $12,000 disp. cost =   <u>$28,000</u>
Floor: NRV − NP = $28,000 − (10% x $40,000)   <u>$24,000</u>
RC: <u>$20,000</u>

Since RC falls below the floor, the floor (NRV − NP) is the designated market value. Once market value is designated, LCM can be determined by simply determining the lower of cost ($26,000) or market ($24,000). Therefore, inventory is reported at $24,000.

12.   (a)   SFAC 5, para 67, establishes five different attributes on which assets can be measured. The attribute used should be determined by the nature of the item and the relevance and reliability of the attribute measured. The five attributes are historical cost, current cost, current market value, net realizable value, and present value. Historical cost is defined as the amount of cash, or its equivalent, paid to acquire an asset. Reporting inventory at lower of cost or market is a departure from the historical cost principle as the inventory could potentially be carried at the market value if lower. Although, reporting inventory at lower of cost or market does not create a departure from conservatism as this method carries at inventory the lowest or most conservative value. The use of LCM does not violate the principle of consistency either, as it would be reported on this basis continually. Finally the use of LCM would not violate the principle of full disclosure as its use would be discussed in the footnotes.

13.   (d)   According to ARB 43, chap 4, paras 8 and 9, inventory is to be valued at the lower of cost or market. Under this method, market is replacement cost provided that replacement cost is lower than net realizable value (ceiling) and higher than net realizable value less the normal profit margin (floor). The question does not specify whether replacement cost is above or below net realizable value, but since the original cost is below **both** of these values, that information is irrelevant.

Either NRV or RC will be designated as the market value of the inventory, and since the original cost is below **both** of these values, the inventory will be valued at its original cost.

Therefore, answer (d) is correct. Answer (c) is incorrect because NRV-NP represents the market floor. Answers (a) and (b) are incorrect because they are both **above** the original cost.

14.   (b)   ARB 43 requires the use of lower of cost or market (LCM) for financial reporting of inventories. The market value of inventory is defined as the replacement cost (RC) as long as it is less than the ceiling (net realizable value, or NRV) and more than the floor (NRV less a normal profit, or NRV – NP). Therefore, if inventory is reported at RC, RC must be less than original cost (meaning statement I is **not** correct), and RC must be less than NRV (meaning statement II **is** correct) and greater than NRV – NP.

15.   (b)   ARB 43, chap 4, requires the pricing of inventory at market when market value is less than cost. Market value is defined as current replacement cost, subject to a ceiling of net realizable value (NRV) and a floor of net realizable value minus a normal profit margin.

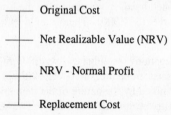

Original Cost

Net Realizable Value (NRV)

NRV - Normal Profit

Replacement Cost

In this situation, replacement cost lies outside of (below) the floor and ceiling limitations. Therefore, NRV less a normal profit margin (the floor), will be used as the market to determine LCM. Since original cost is greater than market, market will be used to price the inventory for the period. Therefore, answer (b) is correct.

16.   (c)   The requirement is to determine the amount of probable loss from the purchase commitment that Card should report in its 1999 income statement. When there is a decline in market value below the contract price at the balance sheet date and the contract is noncancelable, an unrealized loss should be recorded in the period of decline and reported in the income statement. In this case, Card has a contract to purchase a minimum of 100,000 units both in 2000 and 2001 at $.10 per unit. The $20,000 loss (200,000 x $.10) on these obsolete units should be reduced by the amount Card believes is unrealizable from the sale of these units. Therefore, the loss on **purchase commitment** is $16,000 [$20,000 – (200,000 x .02)]. Additionally, Card Corp. would need to record a loss of $20,000 ($.08 x 250,000) from **inventory obsolescence.**

17.   (a)   Answer (a) is correct because to maximize its inventory carrying amount at December 31, 1999, Thread should use the perpetual moving average method with the lower of cost or market rule applied to the total inventory. First, when using the perpetual moving average method, the cost of sales throughout the year are determined using the average cost of purchases up to the time of the sale. On the other hand, under the periodic weighted-average method, the cost of each item is the weighted-average of **all** units purchased during the year. During a period of rising prices, the perpetual moving average method results in a lower cost of

goods sold and a higher ending inventory because the cost of items sold throughout the year is the average of the earlier, lower prices. Second, the application of the lower of cost or market rule to the total inventory will result in a higher ending inventory because market values lower than cost are offset against market values higher than cost. Therefore, answers (b), (c), and (d) are incorrect.

B.7. & B.8.   First-In, First-Out (FIFO), and Last-In, First-Out (LIFO)

18.   (c)   The requirement is to determine the cost of the 1/31/99 inventory, using the LIFO method. LIFO stands for last-in, first-out; this means that the cost of the units purchased most recently are included in cost of goods sold. Therefore, the 1/31/99 inventory consists of the 250 units which were purchased at the earliest date(s). Thus, the 1/31/99 inventory would consist of the 150 units on hand at 1/1/99 (150 x $21 = $3,150) plus an additional 100 units purchased at the earliest purchase date in January (January 10; 100 x $22 = $2,200). The total value of the inventory at 1/31/99 would be $5,350 ($3,150 + $2,200).

19.   (b)   LIFO stands for last-in, first-out; this means that it is assumed that any units sold are the units most recently purchased. In a perpetual system, LIFO is applied at the time of each sale rather than once a year as in a periodic system. Using LIFO, the 900 units sold on 1/20/99 would consist of the 600 units purchased on 1/7/99 and 300 of the 1,000 units in the 1/1/99 balance. This would leave in inventory 700 units from the 1/1/99 balance. After the 1/25/99 purchase, inventory included those 700 units plus the 400 units purchased on 1/25/99. Therefore, ending inventory is $2,700 [(700 x $1) + (400 x $5)].

20.   (d)   When a company uses LIFO for external reporting purposes and another inventory method for internal purposes, a **LIFO Reserve** account is used to reduce inventory from the internal valuation to the LIFO valuation. LIFO Reserve is a contra account to inventory, and is adjusted up or down at year end with a corresponding increase or decrease to **Cost of Goods Sold**. In this case, the LIFO Reserve account must be adjusted from a balance of $35,000 to a balance of $55,000 ($375,000 – $320,000). Therefore, LIFO Reserve is credited for $20,000 ($55,000 – $35,000) with a corresponding debit to Cost of Goods Sold.

21.   (c)   In a change **to** LIFO, no recognition is given to any cumulative effect associated with the change because it is usually not determinable. Thus, the effect on ending inventory and net income is the result solely of current year effects. In a period of rising prices, LIFO will result in a **lower ending inventory** amount than FIFO because the earlier lower costs are assumed to remain in ending inventory. LIFO will also result in a **lower net income** because the more recent higher costs are assigned to cost of goods sold.

22.   (a)   The inventory costing method which most closely approximates the current cost for cost of goods sold is LIFO, while the method which more accurately reflects ending inventory is FIFO. Under LIFO, the most recent purchases are assumed to be the first goods sold; thus, cost of goods sold contains relatively current costs. On the other hand, since FIFO assumes that the goods from beginning inventory and the earliest purchases are sold first, the ending inventory is made up of more recent purchases and thus represents a more current value. Therefore, answer (a) is correct and answers (b), (c), and (d) are incorrect.

23. **(a)** Under the FIFO method, the first goods purchased are considered to be the first goods used or sold. Ending inventory is thus made up of the latest (most recent) purchases. Whenever the FIFO method is used, the ending inventory is the same whether a perpetual or periodic system is used. This is true even during periods of rising or falling prices because the inventory flow is always in chronological order. Under the LIFO method, the latest (most recent) purchases are considered to be the first goods used or sold. Ending inventory is thus made up of the first (oldest) purchases. When a periodic method is used, the first/last purchase determination is made only at the end of the year, based upon the actual chronological order of all purchases. When a perpetual method is used, however, the first/last purchase determination is made continuously throughout the year. When inventory levels get low under the perpetual method, early purchase costs will often be assigned to goods sold, a situation which is much less likely to occur in a periodic system. Therefore, in times of either rising or falling prices, LIFO ending inventory is usually different under a periodic system than under a perpetual system, and answer (a) is correct.

B.9.   Dollar-Value LIFO

24. **(c)** When using dollar-value LIFO, the ending inventory at current year cost must first be converted to base year cost. This amount is given at 12/31/99 ($230,000), but it could be computed as follows: $276,000 ÷ 1.20 = $230,000. The next step is to determine the incremental LIFO layers at base year cost. The 1/1/98 (base year) layer is $150,000, the 1998 layer is $50,000 ($200,000 – $150,000), and the 1999 layer is $30,000 ($230,000 – $200,000). Finally, the LIFO layers are restated using the price index in effect at the time each layer was added:

	Base cost		Ending inventory at DV LIFO cost
1/1/98 layer	150,000	x 1.00 =	$150,000
1998 layer	50,000	x 1.10 =	55,000
1999 layer	30,000	x 1.20 =	36,000
	$230,000		$241,000

25. **(c)** When using dollar-value LIFO, the ending inventory at current year cost must first be converted to base year cost. The 12/31/99 inventory at base year cost is given as $60,000. Since the 12/31/98 inventory at base year cost was $45,000 ($40,000 base layer and $5,000 1998 layer), a new layer of $15,000 was added in 1999 ($60,000 – $45,000). This layer must be restated using the 1999 price index. The 1999 price index is computed using the double-extension technique, as illustrated below:

$$\frac{\text{EI at year end prices}}{\text{EI at base-year prices}} = \frac{\$80,000}{\$60,000} = \underline{1.33}$$

Therefore, the 12/31/99 inventory using dollar-value LIFO is $66,000 as computed below:

	Base cost		DV LIFO
Base layer	$40,000		$40,000
1998 layer	5,000		6,000
1999 layer	15,000	x 1.33	20,000
			$66,000

26. **(b)** The requirement is to determine which inventory method requires estimates of price level changes for specific inventories. In accordance with the dollar-value LIFO method, the ending inventory is first converted to the base year cost so that the incremental layers can be determined. The incremental layers are then restated using the price index which was in effect at the time each of the layers were added to the inventory. Thus, the specific layers of the ending inventory are adjusted to the current price level. Therefore, answer (b) is correct. Answers (a), (c), and (d) are incorrect because these methods do not specifically adjust for price level changes.

27. **(b)** The requirement is to determine the appropriate use of ending inventory at current year cost and ending inventory at base year cost in calculating the dollar-value LIFO index. Answer (b) is correct because according to ARB 43, chap 4, the index number used to convert the current year's inventory layer is calculated as follows:

$$\text{Index} = \frac{\text{Ending inventory at current year cost}}{\text{Ending inventory at base year cost}}$$

This index indicates the relationship between current and base year prices as a percentage, and when multiplied by the new layer (which is the increase in inventory in base year dollars), it will convert the layer to current dollars. Therefore, answers (a), (c), and (d) are incorrect.

28. **(c)** During periods of rising prices, the inventory costing methods which will give Jones the lowest ending inventory balance are LIFO methods, because inventory items that were purchased at the earliest date (when prices were lower) will remain in inventory and the most recently purchased and more expensive items will be expensed through cost of goods sold. Therefore, answer (c) is correct. Answer (d) is incorrect because any FIFO method will produce a higher ending inventory balance during inflation since the items purchased earliest (at lower prices) will be expensed through COGS, while the more expensive items remain in inventory. Answers (a) and (b) are incorrect because neither will give Jones a lower ending inventory balance than dollar-value LIFO, particularly as Jones' inventory changes (because dollar-value LIFO allows the LIFO "layers" to be made up of similar, not necessarily identical, items).

B.10.   Retail Method

29. **(a)** Under the retail method, inventory is determined at retail and then reduced to cost by a cost-to-retail ratio. To approximate **lower of cost or market**, markups are included in the denominator of the cost/retail ratio, while markdowns are not. Beginning inventory is included in the computations of the ratio because the **average cost** basis is being used. The first step is to construct a cost and retail table.

	Cost	Retail
2/1/99 Inventory	$ 180,000	$ 250,000
Purchases	1,020,000	1,575,000
Net markups		175,000
Cost/retail ratio totals	$1,200,000	2,000,000
Sales		(1,705,000)
Net markdowns		(125,000)
Estimated normal shop-lifting losses		(20,000)
Ending inventory at retail		$ 150,000

Normal shoplifting losses are deducted because the goods shoplifted are no longer in inventory. If the shoplifting losses were **abnormal**, they would be subtracted from both the cost and retail columns **before** the cost/retail totals so the cost/retail ratio would not be distorted. The second step is to compute the cost/retail ratio.

$1,200,000/$2,000,000 = 60%

The final step is to determine the ending inventory at cost by multiplying the cost/retail ratio by the ending inventory at retail.

$150,000 x 60% = $90,000

30. **(a)** Purchase returns and allowances are ordinarily considered both as an adjustment of the cost price and the retail price. Sales returns [answer (b)] and net mark-ups [answer (c)] are adjustments to the retail price. Freight charges [answer (d)] are an additional cost incurred for goods available for sale.

B.11.   Retail Dollar-Value LIFO

31. **(a)** The requirement is to calculate the 12/31/99 inventory using the LIFO retail method. The 12/31/99 inventory at retail is $660,000. This amount at base year prices is $600,000 ($660,000 ÷ 1.10). This means that ending inventory at retail, in terms of base year prices, increased by $100,000 ($600,000 − $500,000). Thus, the 12/31/99 inventory consists of two layers: the 12/31/98 LIFO base layer ($500,000) and the 1999 layer ($100,000 at base year prices). These two layers must be priced using the appropriate price indexes and cost-to-retail ratios, resulting in a 12/31/99 inventory at cost of $437,000, as indicated below.

	Base-year retail	Index	Retail	Cost-to retail ratio	LIFO cost
12/31/98 layer	$500,000 x 1.00 =	$500,000 x	72% =	$360,000
1999 layer	100,000 x 1.10 =	110,000 x	70% =	77,000
					$437,000

B.12.   Gross Profit

32. **(a)** The gross profit method can be used to estimate the cost of missing inventory. The first step is to compute the cost of goods available for sale.

Beginning inventory	$ 500,000
Purchases	2,500,000
Cost of goods available for sale	$3,000,000

The second step is to estimate cost of goods sold based on the gross profit percentage.

Sales		$3,200,000
Estimated gross profit ($3,200,000 x 25%)		(800,000)
Cost of goods sold ($3,200,000 x 75%)		$2,400,000

Note that a shortcut is to realize that if gross profit is 25% of sales, cost of goods sold must be 75% of sales. The third step is to compute estimated ending inventory.

Cost of goods available for sale	$ 3,000,000
Estimated cost of goods sold	(2,400,000)
Estimated ending inventory	$ 600,000

Since the actual count of ending inventory at December 31 was only $575,000, the estimated shortage in inventory is $25,000 ($600,000 − $575,000).

B.16.   Cost Apportionment by Relative Sales Value

33. **(c)** The total cost of acquiring the land and preparing it for sale ($1,200,000 + $300,000 = $1,500,000) should be allocated to the residential lots based on their relative sales value, as computed below:

Lot class	# of lots		Sales price		Total sales value
A	100	x	$24,000	=	$2,400,000
B	100	x	16,000	=	1,600,000
C	200	x	10,000	=	2,000,000
					$6,000,000

Total cost		Fraction allocated to Class A		Allocated cost
$1,500,000	x	($2,400/$6,000)	=	$600,000

C. Items to Include in Inventory

34. **(d)** Before adjustment, the inventory based on a physical count was $1,500,000. The $90,000 of merchandise shipped FOB shipping point by a vendor on 12/30/99 should also be included in Herc's 12/31/99 inventory because Herc, the buyer, owns the goods while in transit under these terms. The goods in the shipping area (cost, $120,000) are also owned by Herc because they were not shipped until 2000 and Herc still retains the risks of ownership until that point. Therefore, 12/31/99 inventory is $1,710,000 ($1,500,000 + $90,000 + $120,000).

35. **(a)** Before adjustment, the balance in the Accounts Payable account is $2,200,000. The $40,000 of goods lost in transit from a vendor were shipped FOB **shipping point**. This means the buyer owns the goods while they were in transit; therefore, Kew should record the purchase and accounts payable in 1999. Kew, not the vendor, is ultimately responsible for the lost goods (note that Kew, not the vendor, is suing the common carrier). The $70,000 return which was recorded on 1/5/00 should have been recorded in 1999 when the return was authorized (December 27, 1999). Therefore, Kew should reduce 12/31/99 Accounts Payable by $70,000. The $50,000 of goods received on 1/6/00 were properly recorded in 2000, since the terms were FOB destination (the buyer does not own the goods until they are physically received). Therefore, no adjustment is necessary for this amount. Kew should report 12/31/99 Accounts Payable at $2,170,000 ($2,200,000 + $40,000 – $70,000).

36.   (d)   Net sales is $2,300,000, subject to three possible adjustments. The goods returned ($50,000) should be recorded as a return in 1999, when Lewis authorized the return. Since this return was not recorded until 2000, 1999 sales must be adjusted downward. The goods shipped on 12/30/96 ($80,000) were recorded as a sale in 2000. Since the terms were FOB shipping point, the sale must be recorded in 1999 when the goods were shipped; therefore, 1999 sales must be adjusted upward. The goods shipped on 1/3/00 ($100,000) should not be recorded as a sale until 2000. Since the sale was recorded in 1999, 1999 sales must be adjusted downward. Therefore, adjusted net sales for 1999 should be $2,230,000 ($2,300,000 – $50,000 + $80,000 – $100,000).

37.   (c)   Generally, goods are considered sold when legal title to the goods passes to the buyer. In certain situations, however, the transfer of title criteria does not reflect the underlying economics of the situation. In this situation, although transfer of legal title may not have occurred for the 500 segregated desks, the economic substance of the transaction is that the seller no longer retains the risks of ownership. Therefore, all 5,000 desks (including the 500 segregated and accepted desks) are considered sold in 1999, and revenue of $550,000 is recognized (5,000 x $110). Note that the amount of cash collected ($450,000) does not affect the amount of revenue recognized in this case.

D. Consignments

38.   (d)   A consignor recognizes sales revenue from consignments when the consignee sells the consigned goods to the ultimate customer. Sales commissions earned by the consignee ($10,000 x 15% = $1,500) are reported as a selling expense by the consignor and are **not** netted against sales revenue. Therefore, sales revenue is reported at the total selling price of $10,000 (10 x $1,000). Note that the transportation costs ($800) do not affect sales either; one-fourth (10/40) is reflected in cost of goods sold and three-fourths (30/40) is included in ending inventory.

39.   (d)   No adjustment is necessary for the goods in transit ($36,000). The goods were shipped **FOB shipping point**, which means the buyer (Opal) owns the goods while in transit. Therefore, Opal properly included these goods in 12/31/99 inventory. The merchandise **out** on consignment is owned by the consignor (Opal) and should be included in Opal's inventory **at cost** [$40,000 – (40% x $40,000) = $24,000]. Therefore, inventory must be reduced by $16,000 for this item ($40,000 – $24,000). The goods **held** on consignment ($27,000) are owned by the consignor, not Opal; therefore, inventory must be reduced $27,000 for this item. The total reduction in inventory is $43,000 ($16,000 + $27,000).

40.   (c)   Alt sold 500 of the consigned sweaters (505 – 5) at $100 each, resulting in total sales of $50,000 (500 x $100). Alt must report a payable to Todd for this amount, less Alt's commission [$50,000 – (10% x $50,000) =

$45,000]. Alt does not owe Todd anything for the unsold sweaters until they are sold.

41.   (c)   Inventoriable costs include all costs necessary to prepare goods for sale. These costs include the purchase price or manufacturing cost of the goods, freight, and any other costs necessary to get the goods to the point of sale. The in-transit insurance premium would therefore be included in inventory costs. Commissions paid to the consignee are selling expenses in the period the consigned goods are sold which are not required to ready the goods for sale. These costs, therefore, are not included in inventory, and answer (c) is correct.

42.   (d)   In a consignment, the manufacturer or wholesaler is referred to as the consignor and the dealer or retailer is referred to as the consignee. In such an arrangement, title to the goods remains with the consignor until they are sold to a third party. Jel's payment of reimbursable freight costs results in an account receivable from Dale, which Jel will subtract from the sale proceeds it remits to Dale. Therefore, answer (d) is correct. Answers (a), (b), and (c) are incorrect because the consignee, Jel, generally does not bear any costs associated with the sale of consigned goods.

E. Ratios

43.   (b)   The formula to compute the current ratio is:

$$\text{Current ratio} = \frac{\text{Current assets}}{\text{Current liabilities}}$$

The following entries would be recorded when inventory is sold on account:

Accounts receivable Sales	} Sales price of merchandise
Cost of goods sold Inventory	} Cost of merchandise

Since the selling price (increase to AR) is normally higher than the cost of the merchandise sold (decrease to merchandise inventory) the sale would normally cause a net increase in current assets, and therefore, a net increase in the current ratio. Therefore, answer (b) is correct. Answer (a) is incorrect because when the existing current ratio is greater than one, increases of equal amounts to the numerator (inventory, a component of current assets) and denominator (accounts payable, a component of current liabilities) will reduce the ratio. Answer (c) is incorrect because when an account receivable is collected, cash (a current asset) is increased by the same amount that accounts receivable (another current asset) is decreased. Thus, the transaction has no impact on the current ratio. Answer (d) is incorrect because when machinery (a noncurrent asset) is purchased for cash (a current asset), there is a **decrease** in the current ratio.

44.   (b)   The formula for inventory turnover is:

$$\frac{\text{Cost of goods sold}}{\text{Average inventory}}$$

Average inventory is equal to beginning inventory plus ending inventory, divided by 2. Since beginning inventory is not given, it must be computed using the cost of goods sold relationship:

Cost of goods sold	$ 900,000
+ Ending inventory	180,000
Cost of goods available for sale	$1,080,000
– Purchases	– 960,000
Beginning inventory	$ 120,000

Therefore, average inventory is $150,000 [($120,000 + $180,000) ÷ 2], and inventory turnover is 6.0 times ($900,000 ÷ 150,000).

45. (d)   The solutions approach is to create a numerical example that conforms to the facts given in the question. The inventory turnover ratio is calculated as follows:

$$\frac{\text{Cost of goods sold}}{\text{Average inventory}}$$

If we assume that cost of goods sold has increased from 100 to 150 and average inventory has remained unchanged at 50 then the following ratios result:

$$\frac{\text{Cost of goods sold}}{\text{Average inventory}} \qquad \frac{100}{50} = 2 \qquad \frac{150}{50} = 3$$

Thus, if cost of goods sold increases while inventory remains unchanged, then the inventory turnover ratio will increase.

In addition, we must examine the effects of the increase in cost of goods sold on the gross profit percentage when sales remain constant. Assuming the same facts as above, and sales of $200, we get the following results:

Sales	200	200
– Cost of goods sales	– 100	– 150
Gross profit	100	50

Thus, as cost of goods sold increases the gross profit and the gross profit percentage will decrease.

Therefore answer (d) is correct. Answer (a) is incorrect because a decrease in cost of goods sold will cause the inventory ratio to increase. Answers (b) and (c) are incorrect because they are not related to inventory turnover.

46. (b)   Average days' sales in inventory measures the number of days inventory is held before sale; it reflects on efficiency of inventory policies. It is computed using the following formula:

$$\frac{365}{\text{Inventory turnover}}$$

F. Long-Term Construction Contracts

47. (a)   The total expected income on the contract at 12/31/99 is $900,000 ($9,000,000 – $8,100,000). The formula for recognizing profit under the percentage-of-completion method is:

$$\frac{\text{Costs to date}}{\text{Total expected costs}} \times \frac{\text{Expected}}{\text{profit}} = \frac{\text{Profit recog-}}{\text{nized to date}}$$

$$\frac{\$6,300,000}{\$8,100,000} \times \$900,000 = \underline{\$700,000}$$

This result is the **total** profit on the contract in 1998 and 1999. The 1998 profit recognized must be subtracted from $700,000 to determine the 1999 profit. At 12/31/98, the total expected income on the contract was $1,200,000

($9,000,000 – $7,800,000). The income recognized in 1995 was $600,000, as computed below:

$$\frac{\$3,900,000}{\$7,800,000} \times \$1,200,000 = \underline{\$600,000}$$

Therefore, 1999 income is $700,000 less $600,000, or $100,000.

48. (a)   Profit to be recognized using the percentage-of-completion method is generally computed as follows:

$$\left(\frac{\text{Cost to date}}{\text{Total expected cost}} \times \frac{\text{Expected}}{\text{profit}}\right) - \frac{\text{Profit recognized}}{\text{in previous periods}}$$

Not enough information is given in this problem to perform this computation, so 1999 profit must be computed indirectly. Since only construction expenses and profit are debited to the construction-in-progress (CIP account), 1998 profit must have been $17,000 ($122,000 CIP less $105,000 const. exp.). Cumulative profit recognized by the end of 1999 must be $67,000 [$364,000 CIP less $297,000 cumulative const. exp. ($105,000 + $192,000)]. Therefore, 1999 profit was $50,000 ($67,000 – $17,000).

	CIP	
1998 Exp.	105,000	
1998 Profit	?	1998 Profit = $17,000
1998 End. bal.	122,000	
1999 Exp.	192,000	
1999 Profit	?	1999 Profit = $50,000
1999 End. bal.	364,000	

49. (b)   Based on the information given, it must be assumed that costs incurred are used to measure the extent of progress toward project completion. At 12/31/98, the project was 20% complete and total estimated costs were $7,500,000. Therefore, costs incurred as of 12/31/98 were 20% of $7,500,000, or $1,500,000. At 12/31/99, the project was 60% complete and total estimated costs were $8,000,000. Therefore, costs incurred as of 12/31/99 are 60% of $8,000,000 or $4,800,000. The costs incurred during 1999 were $4,800,000 less $1,500,000, or $3,300,000.

50. (b)   The requirement is to determine the amount of loss to recognize in 1999 on a long-term, fixed-price construction contract. Under both the percentage-of-completion method and the completed-contract method, an expected **loss** on a contract must be recognized in **full** in the period in which the expected loss is discovered. Therefore, Hanson must recognize a loss of $100,000 in 1999.

Expected contract revenue	$3,000,000
Expected contract costs ($930,000 + $2,170,000)	3,100,000
Expected loss	$ (100,000)

51. (a)   The expected income on project 1 [$420,000 – ($240,000 + $120,000) = $60,000] is **not** recognized until the project is completed under the completed contract method. However, under the completed contract method, an expected **loss** on a contract must be recognized in full in the period in which it is discovered. Project 2 has an expected loss of ($20,000) [$300,000 – ($280,000 + $40,000)] which must be recognized immediately in 1999. Thus, answer (a) is correct.

52. **(b)** Construction companies that use the percentage-of-completion method in accounting for long-term construction contracts usually recognize gross profit according to the cost-to-cost method:

$$\frac{\text{Costs to date}}{\text{Total estimated costs}} \times \text{Estimated profit} = \text{Gross profit to date}$$

Pell would recognize gross profit of $40,000 on project 1:

$$\frac{\$240,000}{\$240,000 + \$120,000} \times [\$420,000 - (\$240,000 + \$120,000)] = \underline{\$40,000}$$

Note that prior years' gross profit need not be subtracted from $40,000 because the project commenced during 1999. Under both the percentage-of-completion method and the completed-contract method, an expected **loss** must be recognized in full in the period in which the expected loss is discovered. Project 2 has an expected loss of ($20,000) [$300,000 – ($280,000 + $40,000)] which must be recognized in full in 1999. The net gross profit recognized on the two projects is $20,000 ($40,000 profit less ($20,000) loss).

53. **(a)** In the **final year** of a contract accounted for by the percentage-of-completion method, the percentage of completion is 100%, since costs to date equal total costs. Therefore, the formula to calculate income to be recognized in the final year is simply:

$$\underbrace{(\text{Contract price} - \text{Actual total costs}) - \left(\begin{array}{c}\text{Income previously} \\ \text{recognized}\end{array}\right)}_{\text{Actual income}}$$

Therefore both **actual total costs** and **income previously recognized** are used in calculating income [answer (a)].

54. **(b)** Under the percentage-of-completion method of accounting for long-term contracts, the cost-to-cost formula is used to compute the amount of income to be recognized in a particular year. The formula to calculate current income is as follows:

$$\left(\frac{\text{Cost to date}}{\text{Total expected cost}} \times \begin{array}{c}\text{Expected} \\ \text{profit}\end{array}\right) - \begin{array}{c}\text{Profit recognized} \\ \text{in prior years}\end{array}$$

Progress billings do not impact the amount of income recognized. Therefore, answer (b) is correct.

55. **(a)** The requirement is to determine the ratio to be used to calculate income in the third year using the percentage-of-completion method. ARB 45, para 4, suggests that income be recognized on a cost-to-cost basis when the percentage-of-completion method is used.

$$\left(\frac{\text{Cost to date}}{\text{Total expected cost}} \times \begin{array}{c}\text{Expected} \\ \text{income}\end{array}\right) - \begin{array}{c}\text{Profit recognized} \\ \text{in previous years}\end{array}$$

Therefore, answer (a) is correct. Answers (b) and (d) are incorrect because billings to date are not used as a basis for recognizing revenues. Answer (c) is incorrect as the cost-to-cost calculation requires a cumulative calculation so changes in expected costs and expected income can be adjusted for; thus, costs incurred in year 3 would be an incorrect basis for recognition of income.

56. **(d)** Per ARB 45, paras 6 and 11, an anticipated loss on a long-term contract should be recognized immediately under **both** the percentage-of-completion and the completed-contract methods. Therefore, answer (d) is correct.

57. **(a)** The requirement is to determine the proper classification for the progress billings on contracts account under the percentage-of-completion method. In the construction industry, operating cycles for construction contracts generally exceed 1 year. Therefore, the predominant practice is to classify all contract-related assets and liabilities as current. On the balance sheet, the Construction in Progress (CIP) account is netted with the contra account, progress billings. If CIP exceeds billings, the excess is reported as a current asset [answer (a)]. If billings exceed CIP, the excess is reported as a current liability. Answers (b) and (c) are incorrect because the accounts related to construction contracts are classified as current. Answer (d) is incorrect because progress billings is not used as a basis for recognizing revenues.

OTHER OBJECTIVE ANSWERS AND ANSWER EXPLANATIONS

Problem 1

1.   **(T)**   The gross margin method uses historical margins on sales to estimate the cost of inventory. This method is typically used for interim reporting only because it may not be precise enough for the year end financial statements.

2.   **(T)**   The conventional retail method includes markups and markup cancellations in the cost percentage. This method produces a conservative percentage which will approximate the lower of cost or market for the inventory balance.

3.   **(T)**   The dollar-value LIFO method groups inventory into layers and charges the most recent items to cost of goods sold before using older layers which have older inventory costs.

4.   **(T)**   Inventory should be carried at the lower of cost or market. In determining the lower of cost or market it may be based on the values of individual items, item categories, or even total inventory.

5.   **(T)**   When the market price of a contract to purchase goods falls below the contract price and it is foreseeable that the contract will result in a loss, then a loss on the purchase commitment should be recorded.

6.   **(F)**   The conventional retail method includes net markups but **excludes net markdowns** in the calculation of the cost percentage.

7.   **(T)**   The dollar-value LIFO method measures changes in inventory layers based upon the total dollar value change in the layer.

8.   **(T)**   The link-chain method uses a cumulative index to compute the base cost of inventory. The cumulative index is equal to the current year's prices divided by the prior year's prices, multiplied by the prior year's cumulative index. The link-chain method is only used in limited circumstances.

9.   **(T)**   A price index provides a measure of the changes in price between base year and the current year. The price index is generally used to compute changes in inventory levels.

10.   **(T)**   In a period of rising prices, a liquidation of older inventory, which carries lower costs, will result in a decline in the cost of goods sold and higher profits.

11.   **(F)**   A holding gain results from holding an item while the market value **increases**. Thus, the holding gain would be equal to the current market value less the value on the books.

12.   **(F)**   During a period of rising prices, the LIFO method will result in higher priced items being charged to cost of goods sold, thus lowering net income. It is the FIFO method which would produce a higher net income because the cost of goods sold would reflect the older or lower cost goods.

13.   **(T)**   A change from FIFO to LIFO will tend to result in a decrease in net income and working capital. This is because the LIFO method will put the more recent/higher priced items on the income statement (last in) and the older/less expensive goods will be carried in inventory. Thus, net income will be lower due to higher cost of goods sold, and working capital will be lower due to the lower inventory asset balance.

14.   **(T)**   The LIFO method results in the most recently purchased inventory items being expensed first. In a period of rising prices this would result in a lower net income and thus a lower taxes payable. The IRS allows the use of LIFO for tax only if it is also used for external reporting purposes as well.

15.   **(F)**   The cost of goods sold would be different because a periodic system will compute the cost of goods sold based on the total goods sold and total purchases for a period whereas a perpetual will match each good sold with the most recent purchase on an ongoing basis.

ANSWER OUTLINE

Problem 1 Specific Identific. Method, LCM, and Inventoriable Costs

a. 1. Specific identification method (SIM)
Each unit distinguished from similar units
Cost flows identical to physical flows
Recording of costs to each unit is not burdensome
If similar units have different costs, CGS influenced by units sold
   2. SIM appropriate because
Units are costly,
Identifiable by # and description, and
Good records exist
Inventory at retailers not subject to CGS manipulation by Happlia

b. 1. General criteria for cost inclusion
Include all necessary and reasonable costs to get units in place for sale
     Allocate common or joint costs
   2. Costs included in inventory
Invoice costs
Des Moines Freight
Insurance costs
Repackaging costs

c. 1999 IS
Report as CGS all costs attached to units sold in 1999
Deduct reshipment costs in finding operating income

UNOFFICIAL ANSWER

Problem 1 Specific Identific. Method, LCM, and Inventoriable Costs

a. 1. The specific identification method requires **each unit to be clearly distinguished** from similar units either by description, identification number, location, or other characteristic. Costs are accumulated for specific units and expensed as the units are sold. Thus, the specific identification method results in recognized **cost flows being identical to actual physical flows**. Ideally, each unit is relatively expensive and the number of such units relatively few so that **recording of costs is not burdensome**. Under the specific identification method, if similar items have different costs, cost of goods sold is influenced by the specific units sold.

   2. It is appropriate for Happlia to use the specific identification method because each appliance is expensive, and easily identified by number and description. The specific identification method is feasible because Happlia already maintains records of its units held by individual retailers. Management's ability to manipulate cost of goods sold is minimized because once the inventory is in retailers' hands Happlia's management cannot influence the units selected for sale.

b. 1. Happlia should include in inventory carrying amounts all necessary and reasonable costs to get an appliance into a useful condition and place for sale. Common (or joint) costs should be allocated to individual units. Such costs exclude the excess costs incurred in transporting refrigerators to Minneapolis and their reshipment to Kansas City. These units' costs should only include normal freight costs from Des Moines to Kansas City. In addition, costs incurred to provide time utility to the goods (i.e., ensuring that they are available when required) will also be included in inventory carrying amounts.

   2. Examples of inventoriable costs include the unit invoice price, plus an allocated proportion of the port handling fees, import duties, freight costs to Des Moines and to retailers, insurance costs, repackaging, and warehousing costs.

c. The 1999 income statement should report in cost of goods sold all inventory costs related to units sold in 1999, regardless of when cash is received from retailers. Excess freight costs incurred for shipping the refrigerators from Minneapolis to Kansas City should be included in determining operating income.

ANSWER OUTLINE

Problem 2 Inventory Costs, LCM, and FIFO FS Effects

a. 1. Costs included in 2000 inventory
All necessary and reasonable costs
Design costs
Purchase price from contractors
Freight-in
Warehousing costs
   2. Carrying amount for 1999 inventory
Reported at net realizable value (NRV)
Net realizable value below original cost
NRV = Current list price – disposition costs – [2/3 ($40 allowance – carrying amount of trade-ins)]
Trade-ins' carrying amount = $25 average NRV – profit margin (if any)

b. 1. Effect of FIFO on income statement when costs are rising
Earliest costs assigned to CGS (CGS lower)
Low costs matched against current revenues
Net income higher than under other inventory methods
   2. Effect of FIFO on balance sheet when costs are rising
Latest costs assigned to EI (EI higher)
EI approximates replacement cost
RE higher than under other inventory methods

UNOFFICIAL ANSWER

Problem 2 Inventory Costs, LCM, and FIFO FS Effects

a. 1. For its 2000 models, Blaedon should include in inventory carrying amounts all necessary and reasonable costs. These costs may include design costs, purchase price from contractors, freight-in, and warehousing costs.

   2. Blaedon's 1999 model inventory should be assigned a carrying amount equal to its net realizable value, which is its current list price reduced by both its disposition costs and two-thirds of the difference between the $40 allowance given and the carrying amount assigned to trade-ins. The trade-ins' carrying amount should equal the $25 average net realizable value less the profit margin, if any, assigned.

b.   1.   Using FIFO, Blaedon would assign the earliest lawnmower costs to cost of goods sold. With rising costs, this would result in matching old, relatively low inventory costs against current revenues. Net income would be higher than that reported using certain other inventory methods.

2.   Blaedon would assign the latest costs to ending inventory. Normally, the carrying amount of Blaedon's FIFO ending inventory would approximate replacement cost at December 31, 1999. Retained earnings would be higher than that reported using certain other inventory methods.

SOLUTION GUIDE

Problem 3   LIFO and LCM

a.

1.   This problem requires preparation of a cost of goods sold (CGS) schedule with a supporting schedule of ending inventory at lower of cost or market (LCM). York uses the direct method for LCM, which means the LCM amount is used directly in the CGS computation with no separate disclosure of any LCM loss.

2.   The cost of goods sold schedule can be prepared first, leaving the last two lines (ending inventory and CGS) blank for now. The computation starts with **beginning inventory** plus **cost of goods purchased** equals **cost of goods available for sale** (cost of goods purchased is **purchases** less **purchase discounts** plus **freight-in**). **Freight-out** is a selling expense which does not affect CGS.

3.   When determining LCM, the market value of inventory is defined as the **replacement cost**, as long as it is less than the ceiling [**net realizable value** (NRV)] and more than the floor (**NRV less a normal profit**).

3.1   There are 22,000 units in ending inventory (55,000 units available less 33,000 units sold). Using LIFO, the earliest units in are assumed to remain in ending inventory. Therefore, ending inventory consists of the 8,000 units from beginning inventory, plus the 12,000 units purchased in the first quarter, plus 2,000 more units from second quarter purchases to get up to the 22,000 unit total. The cost of ending inventory is $180,400 [(8,000 x $8.20) + (12,000 x $8.25) + (2,000 x $7.90)].

3.2   The replacement cost of the inventory is $176,000 (22,000 x $8).

3.3   The ceiling (NRV) is $193,600 (22,000 x $8.80).

3.4   The floor (NRV less a normal profit) is $170,500 [22,000 x ($8.80 – $1.05)].

3.5   Because replacement cost ($176,000) falls between the floor ($170,500) and the ceiling ($193,600), the replacement cost of $176,000 is the designated market value.

3.6   Since the designated market value of $176,000 is less than cost ($180,400), the LCM valuation of ending inventory is $176,000. This amount can be put into

the cost of goods sold schedule, resulting in CGS of $245,500.

b.   Value inventory at LCM
     Market is replacement with limits
          Market must ≤ NRV and
          Market must ≥ NRV – normal profit
     Market is replacement cost in this situation
          Replacement cost ($176,000) falls between above limits
     Inventory reported at market because < cost

UNOFFICIAL ANSWER

Problem 3   LIFO and LCM

a.

York Co.
SCHEDULE OF COST OF GOODS SOLD
For the Year Ended December 31, 1999

Beginning inventory	$ 65,600
Add: Purchases	368,900
Less: Purchase discounts	(18,000)
Add: Freight-in	5,000
Goods available for sale	421,500
Less: Ending inventory	(176,000) [1]
Cost of Goods Sold	$245,500

York Co.
SUPPORTING SCHEDULE OF ENDING INVENTORY
December 31, 1999

Inventory at cost (LIFO):

	Units	Cost per unit	Total cost
Beginning inventory, January 1	8,000	$8.20	$ 65,600
Purchases, quarter ended March 31	12,000	8.25	99,000
Purchases, quarter ended June 30	2,000	7.90	15,800
	22,000		$180,400

Inventory at market:
22,000 units @ $8 = $176,000 [1]

b.   Inventory should be valued at the lower of cost or market. Market means current replacement cost, except that

(1)   Market should not exceed the net realizable value; and

(2)   Market should not be less than net realizable value reduced by an allowance for an approximately normal profit margin.

In this situation, because replacement cost ($8 per unit) is less than net realizable value, but greater than net realizable value reduced by a normal profit margin, replacement cost is used as market. Because inventory valued at market ($176,000) is lower than inventory valued at cost ($180,400), inventory should be reported in the financial statements at market.

SOLUTION GUIDE

Problem 4 Dollar-Value LIFO Using Link-Chain Method

1. This problem requires the preparation of a schedule showing the computation of Silver's dollar-value LIFO inventory at December 31, 1998 and 1999.

2. The solutions approach is to first make the calculations for each year, and then to organize the information into a schedule.

2.1 Under the link-chain method, an index number is computed for **each period**:

$$\frac{\text{End of current period prices}}{\text{Beginning of current period prices}} = \frac{\text{Current year}}{\text{index number}}$$

2.2 The link-chain (cumulative) index number is:

$$\left(\begin{array}{c}\text{Cumulative index number}\\ \text{at beginning of period}\end{array}\right) \text{ x } \left(\begin{array}{c}\text{Current year}\\ \text{index number}\end{array}\right)$$

This link-chain (cumulative) index number is divided into the ending inventory amount to reach ending inventory at base year prices.

2.3 The new layer added is:

$$\left(\begin{array}{c}\text{Ending inventory}\\ \text{at base prices}\end{array} - \begin{array}{c}\text{Beginning inventory}\\ \text{at base prices}\end{array}\right) \text{ x } \begin{array}{c}\text{Link-chain}\\ \text{(cumulative)}\\ \text{index number}\end{array}$$

2.4 Ending dollar-value LIFO inventory is the base layer plus all layers added.

3. Silver's inventory of $100,000 at 12/31/97 constitutes the base layer. The index number for this layer

is 1.00. The current year index number for 1998 is 1.25, so the cumulative index number at 12/31/98 is 1.25 x 1.00 = 1.25

3.1 Ending inventory at 12/31/98 prices was $137,500. This is converted to base prices as $137,500 ÷ 1.25 = $110,000.

3.2 The new 1998 layer is ($110,000 – $100,000) x 1.25 = $12,500.

3.3 Ending dollar-value LIFO inventory at 12/31/98 is:

1997 Base layer	$100,000
1998 Layer added	12,500
	$112,500

4. The cumulative index number at 12/31/98 is 1.25. The current year index number for 1999 is 1.20, so the cumulative index number at 12/31/99 is 1.20 x 1.25 = 1.50.

4.1 Ending inventory at 12/31/99 prices was $195,000, which is converted to base prices as $195,000 ÷ 1.50 = $130,000.

4.2 The new 1999 layer is calculated by subtracting the beginning inventory at base prices ($110,000 from 3.1 above) from $130,000. ($130,000 – $110,000) x 1.50 = $30,000.

4.3 Ending dollar-value LIFO inventory at 12/31/99 is the two layers shown in 3.3 plus the $30,000 layer added in 1999.

UNOFFICIAL ANSWER

Problem 4 Dollar-Value LIFO Using Link-Chain Method

Silver, Inc.
COMPUTATION OF DOLLAR-VALUE INVENTORY
December 31, 1998 and 1999

Year	FIFO inventory	Current year cost change index	Link-chain cost index	Inventory at base-year costs
1997	$100,000	1.00	1.00	$100,000
1998	137,500	1.25	1.25	110,000
1999	195,000	1.20	1.50	130,000

Year	LIFO inventory layers at base-year costs	Link-chain cost index	1998 dollar-value LIFO inventory	1999 dollar-value LIFO inventory
1997	$100,000	1.00	$100,000	$100,000
1998	10,000	1.25	12,500	12,500
1999	20,000	1.50		30,000
	$130,000		$112,500	$142,500

ANSWER OUTLINE

Problem 5 LT Contracts

a. Percentage-of-completion
    Use if 2 conditions met:
        Reasonable estimates of profitability at completion
        Reliable measures of progress toward completion

b. Income recognized in 1999

$$\begin{array}{c}1999\\ \text{Income}\end{array} = \left(\frac{\text{Costs incurred to date - Cost of unused materials}}{\text{Total estimated costs to complete}} \text{ x } \begin{array}{c}\text{Total}\\ \text{profit}\end{array}\right)$$

- Income recognized in 1998

Exclude costs of unused materials
    May cause overstatement of income compared with efforts of period

c. BS reporting
    AR on contract--current asset

Excess of costs + Gross profit > billings--current asset

d.   Income tax effects
   BS

$$\text{Current deferred tax liability} = \text{Total net income reported in 1998 and 1999} \times \text{Enacted 2000 average tax rate}$$

   IS

$$\text{Deferred income tax expense} = \text{Increase in deferred tax liability during 1999}$$

UNOFFICIAL ANSWER

Problem 5   LT Contracts

a.   Bow must have a system that is capable of meeting both of the following conditions for the Crecy contract:

- Reasonable estimates of profitability at completion.
- Reliable measures of progress toward completion.

b.   At December 31, 1999, Bow should calculate the percentage of completion by comparing the costs incurred to date, less costs of unused materials, to the estimated total cost to complete Crecy. Income to date equals the percentage of completion multiplied by the estimated total profit to be earned on the contract. The 1999 income equals the income to be recognized to December 31, 1999, less the income reported under the contract in 1998.

When contract materials are purchased but not used, costs of the unused materials are excluded from income recognition calculations. Otherwise, the early period income reported may be overstated compared with the income earning efforts of that period.

c.   Bow should report a current asset for the Crecy account receivable, and another for the excess of costs incurred plus total profit recognized over contract billings.

d.   Bow should report a current deferred tax liability equal to its total net income reported in 1998 and 1999 multiplied by its enacted 2000 average tax rate. A deferred income tax expense should be recognized for the increase during 1999 in the deferred tax liability balance.

SOLUTION GUIDE

Problem 6   LT Construction Contracts and Deferred Taxes

1.   This problem consists of three related requirements concerning long-term construction contracts. The candidates must compute gross profit recognized for 2 years using the percentage-of-completion method, compute balances in various accounts, and reconcile financial statement income and taxable income.

2.   Using the percentage-of-completion method, gross profit is recognized periodically based on progress toward completion of the project using the following formula.

$$\frac{\text{Costs to date}}{\text{Total estimated costs}} \times \text{Estimated profit} = \text{Gross profit to date}$$

For the Beta project, London would recognize gross profit of $180,000 the first year.

$$\frac{\$360,000}{(\$360,000 + \$40,000)} \times [\$600,000 - (\$360,000 + \$40,000)] = \underline{\$180,000}$$

The estimates available at 9/30/99 are used above.

2.1   By the end of the second year, the Beta project is complete and has resulted in actual gross profit of $110,000 ($560,000 revenues less $450,000 costs). Since gross profit of $180,000 was recognized the first year, a loss of $70,000 must be recognized the second year [$110,000 − $180,000 = $(70,000)]. The loss of $70,000 is in effect an adjustment of the excessive gross profit recognized the first year. Instead of restating the prior period, the prior period misstatement is absorbed in the current period, as is appropriate for a change in estimate.

2.2   Under both the percentage-of-completion method and the completed contract method, for financial accounting purposes, an expected **loss** on a contract must be recognized in full in the period in which the expected loss is discovered. At the end of the first year, London has an expected loss on the Gamma contract [$800,000 − ($410,000 + $410,000) = $(20,000)] which must be recognized immediately.

2.3   By the end of the second year, the expected loss on the Gamma contract has increased to $60,000 [$840,000 − ($720,000 + $180,000)]. Since a loss of $20,000 was recognized the first year, an additional loss of $40,000 must be recognized in the second year to bring the cumulative loss recognized up to the new estimate of $60,000.

3.   Part (b) requires the computation of the 9/30/99 balances of accounts receivable, costs and estimated earnings in excess of billings, and billings in excess of costs and estimated earnings. At 10/1/98, the balances in all three accounts were $0 since the construction division began operations on that date.

3.1   **Accounts receivable** is increased by billings:

Accounts receivable
   Billings on LT contracts

It is decreased by cash collections:

Cash
   Accounts receivable

Therefore, 9/30/99 AR is computed by adding the billings on the two projects ($315,000 + $440,000 = $755,000) and subtracting the collections on the two projects ($275,000 + $365,000 = $640,000). The 9/30/99 balance is $115,000 ($755,000 − $640,000).

3.2   **Construction-in-progress** is debited for costs incurred and profit recognized. **Billings on LT contracts** is credited for billings made. In the balance sheet, the two accounts are netted on a project-by-project basis, resulting in a net current asset and/or a net current liability. At 9/30/99, the costs incurred on the Beta project ($360,000) and the estimated earnings ($180,000 from item 2 of this solution guide) exceed billings ($315,000) by $225,000.

3.3 On the Gamma project billings ($440,000) exceed costs ($410,000) by $30,000. There is no estimated earnings on this project because it is expected, at 9/30/99, to result in a $20,000 loss (see item 2.2 above). This estimated loss does not affect the excess of billings over costs and estimated earnings because it is reported separately as a current liability.

4. Financial statement income consists of income before taxes before considering construction projects ($300,000) plus gross profit from construction contracts [$160,000 from part (a) of the solution], less income tax expense. The **pretax** financial income, therefore, is $460,000 ($300,000 + $160,000). The income not from construction projects will be taxed this year, so current income tax expense is $75,000 ($300,000 x 25%). Because the completed contract method is used for tax purposes, the $160,000 gross profit from construction contracts will not be taxed until future years (note that for **tax** purposes no gross profit or gross **loss** is recognized until completion under the completed contract method). Therefore, deferred tax expense is $48,000 (future enacted rate of 30% times $160,000). Financial statement income is $337,000 [$460,000 – ($75,000 + $48,000)].

4.1 Since the $160,000 gross profit will not be recognized for tax purposes until later years, taxable income is $300,000. To reconcile financial statement income ($337,000 from above) to taxable income, the current and deferred income tax must be added back to compute pretax financial income ($337,000 + $75,000 + $48,000 = $460,000). Then the gross profit not recognized for tax purposes is subtracted to reconcile to taxable income ($460,000 – $160,000 = $300,000).

UNOFFICIAL ANSWER

Problem 6 LT Construction Contracts and Deferred Taxes

a.

London Inc.
SCHEDULE OF GROSS PROFIT (LOSS)

	Beta	Gamma
For the Year Ended September 30, 1999:		
Estimated gross profit (loss):		
Contract price	$600,000	$800,000
Less total costs	400,000	820,000
Estimated gross profit (loss)	$200,000	$ (20,000)
Percent complete:		
Costs incurred to date	$360,000	$410,000
Total costs	400,000	820,000
Percent complete	90%	50%
Gross profit (loss) recognized	$180,000	$ (20,000)
For the Year Ended September 30, 2000:		
Estimated gross profit (loss):		
Contract price	$560,000	$840,000
Less total costs	450,000	900,000
Estimated gross profit (loss)	$110,000	$ (60,000)
Percent complete:		
Costs incurred to date	$450,000	$720,000
Total costs	450,000	900,000
Percent complete	100%	80%
Gross profit (loss) recognized	110,000	(60,000)
Less gross profit (loss) recognized in prior year	180,000	(20,000)
Gross profit (loss) recognized	$ (70,000)	$ (40,000)

b.

London Inc.
SCHEDULE OF SELECTED BALANCE SHEET ACCOUNTS
September 30, 1999

Accounts receivable		$115,000
Costs and estimated earnings in excess of billings:		
Construction in progress	$540,000	
Less: Billings	315,000	
Costs and estimated earnings in excess of billings		225,000
Billings in excess of costs and estimated earnings		30,000
Estimated loss on contract		20,000

c.

London Inc.
SCHEDULE OF INCOME TAXES PAYABLE AND INCOME TAX EXPENSE
September 30, 1999

Financial statement income:		
From other divisions		$300,000
From Beta project		180,000
From Gamma project		(20,000)
Total financial statement income		$460,000
Less temporary differences:		
Beta project income		(180,000)
Gamma project loss		20,000
Total taxable income		$300,000
Taxes payable ($300,000 x 25%)		$ 75,000
Deferred tax liability ($160,000 x 30%)		48,000
Tax expense:		
Current	$ 75,000	
Deferred	48,000	123,000

FIXED ASSETS

A. Acquisition Cost

Fixed assets represent the capitalized amount of expenditures made to acquire tangible property which will be used for a period of more than 1 year. Their cost, therefore, is deferred to future periods in compliance with the matching principle. Tangible property includes land, buildings, equipment, or any other property that physically exists. All of the costs necessary to get the asset to the work site and to prepare it for use are capitalized, including the cost of negotiations, sales taxes, finders' fees, razing an old building, shipment, installation, preliminary testing, and so forth. When capitalizing such costs it is necessary to associate them with the asset which is being prepared for use. Thus, the cost of razing an old building is added to the cost of acquiring the land on which the building stood. Charges for self-constructed fixed assets include direct materials, direct construction labor, variable overhead, and a fair share of fixed overhead. Assets received through donation should be recorded at FMV with a corresponding credit to revenue; if FMV is not determinable, book value should be used (see outline of SFAS 116).

B. Capitalization of Interest

SFAS 34 (see outline) requires the capitalization of interest as part of the cost of certain assets. Only assets which require a period of time to be prepared for use qualify for interest capitalization. These include assets constructed for sale produced as discrete projects (e.g., ships) and assets constructed for a firm's own use, whether by the entity itself or by an outsider. For example, a building purchased by an entity **would not** qualify, but one constructed over a period of time **would**. Other assets that do **not** qualify include those in use or ready for use and ones not being used in the earnings activities of a firm (e.g., idle land). Inventories routinely manufactured or repetitively produced in large quantities do not qualify, even if a long maturation period is involved (e.g., tobacco and whiskey).

The amount of interest to be capitalized is the amount which could have been avoided if the project had not been undertaken. This amount includes amortization of any discount, premium, or issue costs; but, it shall not exceed the actual interest incurred during the period. The amount of "avoidable" interest is computed as

$$\begin{pmatrix} \text{Average accumulated expenditures} \\ \text{during construction} \end{pmatrix} \quad \text{x} \quad (\text{Interest rate}) \quad \text{x} \quad \begin{pmatrix} \text{Construction} \\ \text{period} \end{pmatrix}$$

The interest rate used is the rate on specific borrowings for the asset, or a weighted-average of other borrowings when a specific rate is not available. Capitalized interest should be compounded. This is usually accomplished by including the interest capitalized in a previous period in the calculation of average accumulated expenditures of subsequent periods. Furthermore, noninterest-bearing payables (e.g., trade payables and accruals) are excluded in determining these expenditures. In practice, both the weighted-average interest rate and the average accumulated expenditures have been computed on the following bases: monthly, quarterly, semiannual, and annual. The interest capitalization period begins when, and continues as long as, all three of the following conditions are met:

1) Expenditures for the asset have been made

2) Activities necessary to get the asset ready for its intended use are in progress
3) Interest cost is being incurred

The period ends when the asset is substantially complete. Brief interruptions and delays do not suspend interest capitalization, while suspension of the activities will. In no case should the amount capitalized exceed the interest actually incurred.

EXAMPLE: Interest Capitalization
Assume the company is constructing an asset which qualifies for interest capitalization. By the beginning of July $3,000,000 had been spent on the asset, and an additional $800,000 was spent during July. The following debt was outstanding for the entire month.

1) *A loan of $2,000,000, interest of 1% per month, specifically related to the asset.*
2) *A note payable of $1,500,000, interest of 1.5% per month.*
3) *Bonds payable of $1,000,000, interest of 1% per month.*

The amount of interest to be capitalized is computed below.

Average accumulated expenditures (for the month of July)
($3,000,000 + $3,800,000) ÷ 2 = $3,400,000

Avoidable interest			Actual interest		
$2,000,000 x 1%	=	$20,000	$2,000,000 x 1%	=	$20,000
1,400,000 x 1.3%*	=	18,200	1,500,000 x 1.5%	=	22,500
			1,000,000 x 1%	=	10,000
$3,400,000		$38,200	$4,500,000		$52,500

$38,200 ≤ $52,500
∴ $38,200 is capitalized

Amount of interest to be capitalized is $38,200

Asset	38,200	
Interest expense		38,200

*The average rate on other borrowings is ($22,500 + $10,000) ÷ ($1,500,000 + $1,000,000) = 1.3%. Notice that a specific rate is used to the extent possible and the average rate is used only on any excess. Alternatively, the rate on all debt may be used.

Interest on expenditures made to acquire land on which a building is to be constructed qualifies for interest capitalization. The capitalization period begins when activities necessary to construct the building commence and ends when the building is substantially complete. Interest so capitalized becomes part of the cost of the building. Thus, it is charged to expense as the building is depreciated.

Frequently, the funds borrowed to finance the construction project are temporarily invested until needed. Per SFAS 62, the interest earned on these funds must be recognized as revenue and may not be offset against the interest expense to be capitalized.

The diagram below outlines the requirements pertaining to capitalization of interest.

SUMMARY OF ACCOUNTING FOR INTEREST CAPITALIZATION

> Capitalization of Interest During Construction

Qualifying Assets:
Capitalize means to include an expenditure in an asset's cost.
Interest costs, when material, incurred in acquiring the following types of assets, shall be capitalized

1. Assets constructed or produced for a firm's own use

   a. Including construction by outside contractors requiring progress payments

2. Assets intended for lease or sale that are produced as discrete projects

   a. For example, ships and real estate developments

3. But **not** on

   a. Routinely produced inventories (e.g., widgets)
   b. Assets ready for their intended use when acquired
   c. Assets not being used nor being readied for use (e.g., idle equipment)
   d. Land, unless it is being developed (e.g., as a plant site, real estate development, etc.). Then capitalized interest resulting from land expenditure (cash outlay) is added to building.

When to Capitalize Interest (All three must be met):
1. Expenditures for asset have been made
2. Activities intended to get asset ready are in progress
3. Interest cost is being incurred

Applicable Interest (Net of discounts, premiums, and issue costs):
1. Interest obligations having explicit rates
2. Imputed interest on certain payables/receivables
3. Interest related to capital leases

How Much Interest Cost Is Capitalized?

$$\left(\begin{array}{l}\text{Accumulated expenditures beg. of period (C-I-P bal.)} + \\ \text{Accumulated expenditures end of period (C-I-P bal.)}\end{array}\right) \div 2 \times \text{Portion of year} = \text{Weighted-average accumulated expenditures}$$

$$\text{Weighted-average accumulated expenditures} \times \left(\begin{array}{c}\text{Interest*} \\ \text{rate}\end{array}\right) = \text{Amount capitalized (cannot exceed total interest incurred)}$$

* *AICPA questions have given the specific borrowing rate on debt incurred to finance a project and indicated that expenditures were incurred evenly throughout the year. SFAS 34 requires that the firm's weighted-average borrowing rate be used after the amount of a specific borrowing is exhausted. Alternatively, only the firm's weighted-average borrowing rate may be used on all expenditures.*

Qualifications:
1. Amount of interest to be capitalized cannot exceed total interest costs incurred during the entire reporting period

Rationale for interest capitalization:

a. To reflect asset's acquisition cost
b. To match asset's cost with revenue of periods that benefit from its use

C. Nonmonetary Exchanges

Study the outline of APB 29 and Interpretation 31. The exchange of nonmonetary assets (such as inventory, property, and equipment) for other nonmonetary assets requires special consideration of two amounts:

(1) Gain or loss, if any
(2) Fair market value of the nonmonetary assets received

Gain or loss on a nonmonetary exchange is computed as follows:

Fair value of the asset given – Book value of the asset given = Gain (loss)

If the fair value (FV) of the asset given up cannot be determined, assume it is equal to the fair value of the asset received. If neither fair values are determinable, gain or loss cannot be computed.

The asset received is generally recorded at the fair value of the asset surrendered (or the FV of the asset received if "more clearly evident"). Some exceptions do exist. Remember, however, that the asset given up will always be removed from the books at book value.

The following rules apply in recording nonmonetary exchanges:

* Losses are always recognized (conservatism).
* Gains are recognized when **dissimilar assets** are exchanged (i.e., a machine for a truck).
* Gains are **not** recognized when **similar assets** are exchanged (i.e., a machine for a machine) because the earnings process is **not** considered complete.
* The asset received is recorded at the **fair value** of the asset given up (or the FV of the asset received if "more clearly evident") whenever gains and losses are recognized.
* The asset received is recorded at the **book value** of the asset given up when gains and losses are **not** recognized. Gains and losses are not recognized when (1) the earnings process is not considered complete, and (2) gain or loss cannot be computed.

Exceptions to these rules occur when boot (cash) is involved in the exchange.

The chart on the next page summarizes the process involved in accounting for nonmonetary exchanges. Refer to this chart as you work through the following examples.

Situation 1. FV is not determinable.

EXAMPLE: A company trades a machine (cost, $10,000; accumulated depreciation, $3,000) for land. Neither the FV of the machine or the land is determinable.

Land	7,000	(BV given)
Accumulated depreciation	3,000	
Machine		10,000

Since FV is unknown, no gain can be computed, and the asset received is recorded at the BV of the asset given up ($10,000 – $3,000).

Situation 2. Loss, no boot involved.

EXAMPLE: A company trades a machine with a FV of $5,000 (cost, $10,000; accumulated depreciation, $3,000) for land.

	FV	BV	Gain (loss)
Machine given	$5,000	$7,000	$(2,000)
Land received			

The loss (FV – BV) is recognized immediately and the land is recorded at the FV of the machine given up.

Land	5,000	(FV given)
Accumulated depreciation	3,000	
Loss	2,000	
Machine		10,000

(Note that this transaction would be treated the same way if similar assets had been exchanged.)

ACCOUNTING FOR NONMONETARY EXCHANGES

Concepts Summary

*For tax purposes losses are not recognized on exchanges of similar assets; they are adjustments to the asset's basis as are gains.

EXAMPLE: *A company trades a machine (cost, $10,000; accumulated depreciation, $3,000) for another machine with an FV of $6,000.*

	FV	BV	Gain (loss)
Machine given		*$7,000*	*$(1,000)*
Machine received	*$6,000*		

In this case, the FV of the asset given is unknown. You can substitute the FV of the asset received for FV given when computing gain/loss. The fair value of the asset given is implied in this case.

$6,000		$7,000		$(1,000)
FV given	–	BV given	=	Loss
(assumed or implied)				

Machine	6,000		(FV received)
Accumulated depreciation	3,000		
Loss	1,000		
Machine		10,000	

Situation 3. Loss, boot given.

EXAMPLE: A company trades a machine with a FV of $6,000 (cost, $10,000; accumulated depreciation, $3,000) and $500 cash for land.

	Boot	FV	BV	Gain (loss)
Machine given	$500	$6000	$7,000	$(1000)
Land received				

Gain (loss) still equals FV less BV. Boot given is added to the value of the asset given.

Land	6,500		(FV given + boot given)
Accumulated depreciation	3,000		
Loss	1,000		
Machine		10,000	
Cash		500	

Assume the FV of the machine was unknown, but the FV of the land received was known to be $6,000.

	Boot	FV	BV	Gain (loss)
Machine given	$500		$7,000	$(1,500)
Land received		$6,000		

To compute gain (loss), you can assume FV given is equal to FV received less boot given ($6,000 – $500).

$5,500		$7,000		$(1,500)
FV given	–	BV given	=	Loss
(assumed)				

Land	6,000		(FV received)
Accumulated depreciation	3,000		
Loss	1,500		
Machine		10,000	
Cash		500	

Situation 4. Loss, boot received.

EXAMPLE: A company trades a machine with a FV of $6,000 (cost, $10,000; accumulated depreciation, $3,000) for land and $500 cash.

	Boot	FV	BV	Gain (loss)
Machine given		$6,000	$7,000	$(1,000)
Land received	$500			

Boot received is deducted from the value of the asset given.

Land	5,500		(FV given – boot received)
Accumulated depreciation	3,000		
Cash	500		
Loss	1,000		
Machine		10,000	

Now assume the FV of the machine is unknown but the FV of the land received is known to be $6,000.

	Boot	FV	BV	Gain (loss)
Machine given			$7,000	$(500)
Land received	$500	$6,000		

In this case, you can assume FV given is equal to FV received plus the boot received ($6,000 + $500).

$6,500		$7,000		$(500)
FV given	–	BV given	=	Loss
(assumed)				

Land	6,000	(FV received)
Accumulated depreciation	3,000	
Cash	500	
Loss	500	
Machine		10,000

Situation 5. Gain, dissimilar assets.

EXAMPLE: A company trades a computer with a FV of $12,000 (cost, $11,000; accumulated depreciation, $4,000) for a building.

	FV	BV	Gain (loss)
Computer given	$12,000	$7,000	$5,000
Building received			

Since the assets traded are dissimilar, the earnings process is considered complete and the entire gain is recognized.

Building	12,000	(FV given)
Accumulated depreciation	4,000	
Computer		11,000
Gain		5,000

If boot had been involved, the accounting would be the same as that illustrated in the loss situation.

Situation 6. Gain, similar assets, no boot involved.

EXAMPLE: A company trades equipment with a FV of $12,000 (cost, $11,000; accumulated depreciation, $4,000) for similar equipment.

	FV	BV	Gain (loss)
Equipment given	$12,000	$7,000	$5,000
Equipment received			

Since similar assets have been traded, the earnings process is **not** considered complete and no gain is recognized. The asset received is debited at the book value (**not** fair value) of the asset given.

Equipment	7,000	(BV given)
Accumulated depreciation	4,000	
Equipment		11,000

The unrecognized gain of $5,000 will be deferred; it will be recognized as the equipment received is depreciated (lower depreciation results than if FV had been used) and/or sold or disposed of in a subsequent transaction.

Situation 7. Gain, similar assets, boot given.

EXAMPLE: A company trades a machine (cost, $10,000; accumulated depreciation, $2,000) and $4,000 in cash for a similar machine with a FV of $16,000.

	Boot	FV	BV	Gain (loss)
Machine given	$4,000		$8,000	$4,000
Machine received		$16,000		

As in the loss situation, the FV of the asset given can be assumed equal to the FV received less the boot given ($16,000 – $4,000).

$12,000		$8,000		$4,000
FV given	–	BV given	=	Gain
(assumed)				

Boot given is added to the value of the asset received (in this case, book value). Gain is still unrecognized.

Machine	12,000	(BV given + Boot given)
Accumulated depreciation	2,000	
Machine		10,000
Cash		4,000

Below are alternative ways to calculate the asset received.

FV received	$16,000	BV given	$ 8,000
Gain deferred	(4,000)	Cash paid	4,000
	12,000		12,000

Situation 8. Gain, similar assets, boot received.

An exception to nonrecognition of gain on exchange of similar assets arises when boot is received in the exchange. This type of exchange is treated as a hybrid transaction--part sale and part exchange. The earnings process is assumed complete for the portion related to the boot received (i.e., "sale" portion), but is **not** assumed complete for the portion related to the asset received (i.e., "exchange" portion). Therefore, a gain is recognized only for that portion related to the boot. Gain recognized is computed as follows:

$$\left(\frac{\text{Boot}}{\text{Boot + FV of asset received}}\right) \text{ x Total gain = Gain recognized}$$

If the FV of the asset received is not given, it may be determined by subtracting the boot received from the FV of the asset given up.

EXAMPLE: A company trades a machine with a FV of $12,000 (cost, $9,000; accumulated depreciation, $2,000) for a similar machine and $4,000 cash.

	Boot	*FV*	*BV*	*Gain (loss)*
Machine given		*$12,000*	*$7,000*	*$5,000*
Machine received	*$4,000*			

Since boot was received, the portion of the gain relating to the boot must be recognized.

$$\left(\frac{\$4,000}{\$4,000 + \$8,000*}\right) \text{ x } (\$5,000) = \$1,667$$

*The FV of the asset received ($8,000) was derived by deducting boot received from the FV given.

$12,000		*$4,000*		*$8,000*
FV given	–	*Boot received*	=	*FV received*
				(assumed)

Thus, only $1,667 of the gain will be recognized. The machine received would be recorded at its FV less the gain deferred [$8,000 – (5,000 gain – 1,667 gain recognized)]. Alternatively, the asset received will be debited at BV given less boot received, plus gain recognized ($7,000 – $4,000 + $1,667 = $4,667).

Cash	4,000		
Machine	4,667		$\left(\begin{array}{c}\text{FV received} - \\ \text{Gain deferred}\end{array}\right)$ or $\left(\begin{array}{c}\text{BV given} - \text{Boot received} \\ + \text{Gain recognized}\end{array}\right)$
Accumulated depreciation	2,000		
Machine		9,000	
Gain		1,667	

D. Purchase of Groups of Fixed Assets (Basket purchase)

Cost should be allocated based on relative market value.

$$\text{Cost of all assets acquired x } \frac{\text{Market value of A}}{\text{Market value of all assets acquired}}$$

EXAMPLE: Purchase of Asset 1 with an FMV of $60,000, Asset 2 with a FMV of $120,000, and Asset 3 with a FMV of $20,000 all for $150,000 cash.

	FMV	*Relative FMV*	*x*	*Total cost*	*=*	*Allocated cost*
Asset 1	*$ 60,000*	*60/200*		*$150,000*		*$45,000*
Asset 2	*120,000*	*120/200*		*150,000*		*90,000*
Asset 3	*20,000*	*20/200*		*150,000*		*15,000*
Total FMV	*$200,000*					

Journalized:

Asset 1	$45,000	
Asset 2	90,000	
Asset 3	15,000	
Cash		$150,000

E. Capital vs. Revenue Expenditures

Capital expenditures and revenue expenditures are charges that are incurred after the acquisition cost has been determined and the related fixed asset is in operation.

Capital expenditures are not normal, recurring expenses; they benefit the operations of more than one period. The cost of major rearrangements of assets to increase efficiency is an example of a capital expenditure.

Revenue expenditures are normal recurring expenditures. However, some expenditures that meet the test for capital expenditures are expensed because they are immaterial (e.g., less than $50).

Expenditures to improve the efficiency or extend the asset life should be capitalized and charged to future periods. A subtle distinction is sometimes made between an improvement in efficiency and an extension of the asset life. Some accountants feel improvements in efficiency should be charged to the asset account, and improvements extending the asset life should be charged to the accumulated depreciation account. The rationale is that improvements extending the asset life will need to be depreciated over an extended period of time, requiring revision of depreciation schedules.

The chart on the following page summarizes the appropriate treatment of expenditures related to fixed assets.

F. Depreciation

Depreciation is the annual charge to income for asset use during the period. This is simply a means of spreading asset costs to periods in which the assets produce revenue. Essentially, the "depreciation base" is allocated over the asset's useful life in a rational and systematic manner. The meaning of the key terms is as follows:

Systematic--Formula or plan
Rational--Representational faithfulness (fits with reality)
Allocation--Not a process of valuation

The objective is to match asset cost with revenue produced. The depreciation base is cost less salvage value (except for the declining balance method which ignores salvage value). The cost of an asset will include any reasonable cost incurred in bringing an asset to an enterprise and getting it ready for its intended use. The useful life can be limited by

1) Technological change
2) Normal deterioration
3) Physical usage

COSTS SUBSEQUENT TO ACQUISITION OF PROPERTY, PLANT, AND EQUIPMENT

Type of expenditure	Characteristics	Expense when incurred	Capitalize Debit (credit) to asset	Debit (credit) to accum. deprec.	Other
1. Additions	• Extensions, enlargements, or expansions made to an existing asset		x		
2. Repairs and maintenance					
a. Ordinary	• Recurring, relatively small expenditures				
	1. Maintain normal operating condition	x			
	2. **Do not** add materially to use value	x			
	3. **Do not** extend useful life	x			
b. Extraordinary (major)	• Not recurring, relatively large expenditures				
	1. Primarily increase the quality and/or output of services		x		
	2. Primarily extend the useful life			x	
3. Replacements and improvements	• Major component of asset is removed and replaced with the same type of component with comparable performance capabilities (replacement) or a different type of component having superior performance capabilities (betterment)				
a. Book value of old component is known	• Old component amounts		(x)		• Recognize any proceeds and loss (or gain) on old asset
	• New component outlay		x		
b. Book value of old component is **not** known	• Primarily increases the use value		x		
	• Primarily extends the useful life			x	
4. Reinstallations and rearrangements	• Provide greater efficiency in production or reduce production costs				
	1. Material costs, benefits extend into future accounting periods		x		
	2. No measurable future benefit	x			

The first two indicate depreciation is a function of time whereas the third indicates depreciation is a function of the level of activity. Other depreciation methods include inventory, retirement, replacement, group, composite, etc.

Depreciation methods based on time are

1) Straight-line (SL)
2) Accelerated

    a) Declining balance (DB)

        1] Most common is double-declining balance (DDB)

    b) Sum-of-the-years' digits (SYD)

Straight-line and ***accelerated*** depreciation are illustrated by the following example: $10,000 asset, 4-year life, $2,000 salvage value.

Year	Straight line	DDB	SYD
1	$2,000	$5,000	$3,200
2	$2,000	$2,500	$2,400
3	$2,000	$ 500*	$1,600
4	$2,000	--	$ 800

Straight-line $\dfrac{\$10,000 - \$2,000}{4}$

DDB   Twice the straight-line rate (2 x 25%) times the net book value at beginning of each year, but not below salvage value (salvage value is not deducted for depreciation base).

$10,000 – ($5,000 + 2,500) = $2,500 Book value at beginning of year 3. $2,500 – 2,000 salvage value = $500.

SYD   4/10**, 3/10, 2/10, 1/10 of ($10,000 – $2,000).

$$\frac{**n(n+1)}{2} = \frac{4 \times 5}{2} = 10$$

Physical usage depreciation is based on activity (e.g., machine hours) or output (e.g., finished widgets).

$$\frac{\text{Annual}}{\text{depreciation}} = \frac{\text{Current activity or output}}{\text{Total expected activity or output}} \times \text{Depreciation base}$$

EXAMPLE: A machine costs $60,000. The machine's total output is expected to be 500,000 units. If 100,000 units are produced in the first year, $12,000 of depreciation would be incurred (100/500 x $60,000).

Note that physical usage depreciation results in a varying charge (i.e., not constant). Also physical usage depreciation is based on asset activity rather than expiration of time.

Straight-line and accelerated depreciation methods are illustrated by the following graphs:

Accelerated depreciation is justified by

1) Increased productivity when asset is new
2) Increasing maintenance charges with age
3) Risk of obsolescence

Accelerated depreciation methods result in a better matching of costs and revenues when one or more of these factors are present.

Inventory depreciation is a method typically used in situations where there are many low-cost tangible assets, such as hand tools for a manufacturer or utensils for a restaurant. Using this method, an inventory of the assets is taken at the beginning and the end of the year. Valuation of these assets is based on appraisal value. Depreciation is calculated as follows:

$$\text{Annual depreciation} = \text{Beginning inventory} + \text{Cost of acquisitions} - \text{Ending inventory}$$

The inventory method is advantageous in situations involving such small assets because it is not practical to maintain separate depreciation schedules for them. On the other hand, this method is often criticized because it is not systematic and rational.

Composite (group) depreciation averages the service life of a number of property units and depreciates the group as if it were a single unit. The term "group" is used when the assets are similar; "composite" when they are dissimilar. The depreciation rate is the following ratio:

$$\frac{\text{Sum of annual SL depreciation of individual assets}}{\text{Total asset cost}}$$

Thus, composite depreciation is a weighted-average of a group of assets--usually of a similar nature, expected life, etc.

EXAMPLE: Three types of assets (A, B, and C) are depreciated under the composite method.

Asset type	Asset cost	Salvage value	Depreciation base	Useful life (yrs.)	SL annual depreciation
A	$ 45,000	$15,000	$ 30,000	5	$ 6,000
B	90,000	50,000	40,000	4	10,000
C	145,000	25,000	120,000	3	40,000
	$280,000	$90,000	$190,000		$56,000

$$\text{Depreciation or composite rate} = \frac{\$56,000}{\$280,000} = 20\%$$

Composite life = 3.39 years ($190,000 ÷ $56,000)

Note that the composite life is the depreciation base divided by the annual depreciation. Depreciation is recorded until the book value of the composite group is depreciated to the salvage value of the then remaining assets. As assets are retired the composite group salvage value is reduced. Also note that gains and losses are not recognized on disposal (i.e., gains and losses are netted into accumulated depreciation). This latter practice also affects the length of time required to reduce the book value (cost less accumulated depreciation) to the group salvage value. The entry to record a retirement is

Cash, other consideration	(amount received)
Accumulated depreciation	(plug)
Asset	(original cost)

Changes in Depreciation. The exam tests changes in depreciation due to changes in expected useful life and salvage value. Make the change prospectively from the beginning of the year in which the change in estimate is made. The procedure for straight-line depreciation is

1) Divide the periods remaining (from the beginning of the year of change) into
2) The remaining depreciation base (i.e., undepreciated cost to date less revised salvage value)

Fractional Year Depreciation. Many conventions exist for accounting for depreciation for midyear asset acquisitions. They include

1) A whole year's depreciation in year of acquisition and none in year of disposal
2) One-half year's depreciation in year of acquisition and year of disposal
3) Depreciation to nearest whole month in both year of acquisition and year of disposal

CPA exam questions generally specify the convention to be followed. If not and the question is an essay/problem, select a convention reasonable in the circumstances and provide an explanation to the grader.

G. **Disposals and Impairment of Value** (see the outline of SFAS 121)

The entry to record the disposal (sale) of an asset is

Cash	(amount received)	
Accumulated depreciation	(old asset)	
Old asset		(cost)
Gain or loss	(loss)	(gain)

Do not forget to record depreciation for disposed assets up to the point of disposal.

For example, Jimco, a manufacturer of sports equipment, purchased a machine for $6,000 on 1/1/94. The machine had an 8-year life, a $600 salvage value, and was depreciated using the straight-line method. Thus, depreciation was charged at a rate of $56.25 per month [($6,000 cost – $600 salvage) ÷ (8 yrs x 12 mos/yr)]. If Jimco sells the asset on 9/1/99 for $3,000, the following entries must be made to record 1999 depreciation and to record the sale:

Depreciation expense	*450*	
Accumulated depreciation		*450*
($56.25 x 8 mos)		
Cash	*3,000*	
Accumulated depreciation	*3,825*	
($56.25 x 68 mos)		
Equipment		*6,000*
Gain on sale of equip.		*825*
[$3,000 cash – ($6,000 – $3,825)CV]		

In some cases, assets are intended to be **disposed of** in a future reporting period rather than held for use. Per SFAS 121, if management has adopted such a plan for disposal, a loss is recognized if the fair value minus selling costs (NRV) is less than the recorded carrying value.

Assume that the asset in the above example has not been sold yet. However, management intends to dispose of it in the next year at NRV of $1,500. The entry to record management's intents would be as follows:

*Loss on planned disposition	*675*	
Equipment to be disposed of	*1,500*	
Accumulated depreciation	*3,825*	
Equipment		*6,000*

*[($1,500 – ($6,000 – 3,825) CV]

Fixed assets intended for disposal are not subsequently depreciated. The equipment to be disposed of would be classified as other assets on the balance sheet.

Losses on fixed assets to be disposed of can be recovered due to changes in the fair value or selling costs associated with the asset. This write-up, however, **cannot** exceed the carrying amount prior to recognition of impairment. If the NRV for this asset increases in the next period, the maximum recovery (gain) that could be recognized is $675.

In some cases, the carrying (book) value of fixed assets **intended to be held and used for productive purposes** may have to be reduced due to an **impairment** of value. This means that not all of the asset's cost will be recovered. If one or more factors (see the outline of SFAS 121) indicate that an asset or group of assets might be impaired, it is necessary to do the **recovery** test, which is to compare the undiscounted expected net future cash flows generated by a fixed asset to its carrying amount on the balance sheet. If the cash flows are equal to or greater than the asset's carrying value, the asset's cost will be recovered and no accounting recognition is required. However, if the cash flows are less than the carrying value a loss must be recognized. The subsequent loss is measured by the difference between the carrying value and the **fair value not the undiscounted net cash flows**, at the impairment date. The asset's carrying value is adjusted to reflect its fair value.

*Assume that the asset in the above example is not sold. A test for impairment indicates that the net undiscounted cash flows from the machine are less than its carrying value. Thus, the asset is impaired as of 9/1/99. The machine's actual fair value at this date is $1,400, with **no** salvage value. Therefore, its carrying value is reduced,*

Loss on impairment	*775*	
[($6,000 – $3,825)CV – $1,400 FV]		
Accumulated depreciation		*775*

and it will continue to be depreciated at $50.00 per month for its remaining useful life ($1,400 ÷ 28 mos = $50.00). At 12/31/01, when the asset is fully depreciated, Jimco retires it and writes the machine off with the following entry:

Accumulated depreciation	*6,000*	
Equipment		*6,000*

Note that the entire cost has been depreciated because upon impairment of the asset it was determined that the equipment did not have a salvage value.

Subsequent to the impairment loss, the asset is depreciated based on its new carrying value. **Recoveries of previously recognized impairment losses may not be recognized in subsequent periods.**

H. **Depletion**

Depletion is "depreciation" of natural resources. The depletion base is the total cost of the property providing the natural resources. This includes all development costs such as exploring, drilling, excavating, and other preparatory costs.

The depletion base is usually allocated by the ratio of extracted units over the total expected recoverable units.

$$\frac{\text{Units extracted}}{\text{Total expected recoverable units}} \times (\text{Depletion base})$$

The unit depletion rate is frequently revised due to the uncertainties surrounding the recovery of natural resources. The revised unit rate in any year takes the following form:

$$\frac{\text{Orig. cost} + \text{Add'l. cost incurred} - \text{Resid. value} - \text{Depletion taken in prev. yrs.}}{\text{Units withdrawn currently} + \text{Estimated units recoverable at year end}}$$

Note that the adjustment is being made prospectively (i.e., the remaining undepleted cost is being expensed over the remaining recoverable units).

Depletion on resources extracted during an accounting period is allocated between inventory and cost of goods sold.

I. **Insurance**

Loss Account for Fixed Assets. When an insured loss occurs, an insurance loss account should be set up and charged for all losses. These losses include decreases in asset value, earned insurance premiums, etc. The account should be credited for any payments from the insurance company. The remainder is closed to revenue and expense summary.

Coinsurance. This area is tested on the Business Law and Professional Responsibilities section of the exam.

J. **Intangible Assets (See the outline of APB 17)**

Intangible assets are nonphysical assets. Intangible assets normally include only noncurrent intangibles (e.g., accounts receivable are not considered intangibles). Examples of intangible assets include copyrights, leaseholds, organizational costs, trademarks, franchises, patents, and goodwill. These intangibles may be categorized according to the following characteristics:

1. Identifiability. Separately identifiable or lacking specific identification.
2. Manner of acquisition. Acquired singly, in groups, or in business combinations; or developed internally.
3. Expected period of benefit. Limited by law or contract, related to human or economic factors, or indefinite or indeterminate duration.
4. Separability from enterprise. Rights transferable without title, salable, or inseparable from the entire enterprise.

Acquisition of Intangibles. Purchased intangibles should be recorded at cost, which represents the potential earning power of the intangible at time of acquisition. Internally developed intangibles are written off as research and development expense; an exception is the cost to register a patent. **Goodwill** is recorded only when an entire business is purchased because internally developed goodwill is not specifically identifiable, has an indeterminate life, and is not separable from the enterprise. Purchase of goodwill as part of acquiring a business is discussed in the Investments and Business Combinations and Consolidation modules.

Amortization of Intangibles. Intangible assets are usually amortized by crediting the intangible account directly (ordinarily, contra accounts are not used).

Amortization expense	xx	
Intangible asset		xx

Intangibles are normally amortized on a straight-line basis, although other systematic and rational approaches are acceptable. Amortization is over the intangible's economic life. In no case is the useful life to exceed 40 years. Factors to consider in determining economic life are listed in the outline of APB 17.

Impairment of Assets Acquired With Goodwill. When testing assets for recoverability that were acquired as part of a business combination in which goodwill was associated, each asset grouping should include an allocated amount of goodwill on a pro rata basis using fair values of the net assets acquired at acquisition, unless other evidence of association is more appropriate. A resulting impairment loss will reduce the associated goodwill carrying amount before the carrying amount of the long-lived assets and identifiable intangibles in the group are reduced to fair value.

EXAMPLE OF IMPAIRMENT WITH GOODWILL

Parent Company purchased a wholly-owned Subsidiary Company for $1,300,000 cash. Book value of the equity acquired was $900,000. Assume that as of 12/31/99 several circumstances indicate that operational assets may be impaired. The relevant values at acquisition follow:

	(In 000s)		
	1/1/98		1/1/98
	Book value	Excess	Fair value
Cash	$ 200	---	$ 200
Accounts receivable	200	---	200
Inventory	100	$100	200
Net plant (20-yr. life)	500	100	600
Patents (5-yr. life)	100	100	200
Goodwill (10-yr. life)	___	100	100
Total	$1,100		$1,500
Current liabilities	$ 100	---	$ 100
Long-term debt	100	---	100
Common stock	200	---	---
Paid-in-capital	300	---	---
Retained earnings	400	---	---
Total	$1,100		

Before testing for impairment of the plant and patent using the recoverability test on 12/31/99, goodwill is allocated as indicated below:

	12/31/99 Book values*	Allocated goodwill	Total carrying value 12/31/99	Expected future cash flows	12/31/99 Fair values
Net plant (20-yr. life)	$540	$ 60**	$600	$800	$620
Patents (5-yr. life)	120	20***	140	120	105
Goodwill (10-yr. life)	80	(80)	-0-	-0-	-0-

   * *1/1/98 fair values less depreciation/amortization for 2 years*
  ** *Plant $80 x $600/$800 = $60*
*** *Patent $80 x $200/$800 = $20*

The allocation of goodwill is done in the manner demonstrated in the example. There is no impairment loss recognized on the plant because the expected future undiscounted cash flows ($800) exceed the adjusted carrying value of the plant ($600) on 12/31/99.

The above analysis indicates that the patent's future cash flows ($120) are less than the carrying amount ($140). The amortization policy was reviewed and was found to be satisfactory. The patent's carrying value including the allocated goodwill is $140 ($120 + $20) and the fair value is $105. Thus, a $35 ($140 – $105) loss must be recognized. The adjusting journal entry is:

Impairment loss	35	
Goodwill		20
Patent		15

If the fair value of the patent was $130, the adjusting journal entry would be:

Impairment loss	10	
Goodwill		10

The resulting balances of the patent account and the goodwill account are amortized over the remaining life.

K. **Reporting on the Costs of Start-up Activities**

SOP 98-5 provides guidance on financial reporting of start-up costs and organization costs and requires such costs to be expensed as incurred. Start-up costs are defined as one-time activities related to opening a new facility or new class of customer, initiating a new process in an existing facility or some new operation. These are sometimes referred to as preopening costs, preoperating costs, organization costs, and start-up costs. Routine ongoing efforts to improve existing quality of products, services, or facilities, are not start-up costs.

L. **Research and Development Costs (SFAS 2 and 68)**

SFAS 2 and 68 (see outlines) require R&D costs to be expensed as incurred except for intangibles or fixed assets purchased from others having alternative future uses. These should be capitalized and amortized over their useful life. Thus, the cost of patents and R&D equipment purchased from third parties may be deferred and amortized over the asset's useful life. Internally developed R&D may not be deferred.

Finally, R&D done under contract **for others** is not required to be expensed per SFAS 2. The costs incurred would be matched with revenue using the completed-contract or percentage-of-completion method.

M. **Computer Software Costs**

For sale or lease. SFAS 86 (see outline) establishes the standards for recording internally developed or purchased computer software costs which are to be either sold, leased, or marketed as an individual product or as part of a process. The costs which are incurred internally to create the software should be expensed as research and development until technological feasibility is established. Thereafter, all costs should be capitalized and reported at the lower of unamortized cost or net realizable value. Capitalization should cease when the software is available for general release to customers.

The annual amortization of capitalized computer software costs will be the greater of the ratio of current revenues to anticipated total revenues or the straight-line amortization which is based on the estimated economic life.

Once the software is available for general release to customers, the inventory costs should include costs for duplicating software and for physically packaging the product. The cost of maintenance and customer support should be charged to expense in the period incurred.

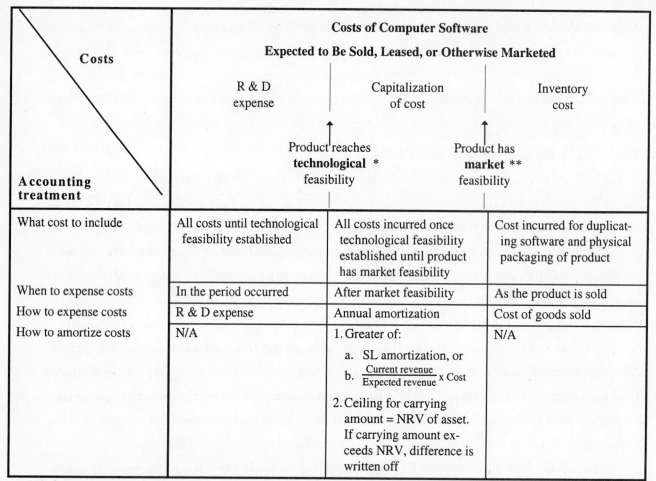

Costs	Costs of Computer Software Expected to Be Sold, Leased, or Otherwise Marketed		
	R & D expense	Capitalization of cost	Inventory cost
		Product reaches **technological** * feasibility	Product has **market** ** feasibility
Accounting treatment			
What cost to include	All costs until technological feasibility established	All costs incurred once technological feasibility established until product has market feasibility	Cost incurred for duplicating software and physical packaging of product
When to expense costs	In the period occurred	After market feasibility	As the product is sold
How to expense costs	R & D expense	Annual amortization	Cost of goods sold
How to amortize costs	N/A	1. Greater of: a. SL amortization, or b. $\frac{\text{Current revenue}}{\text{Expected revenue}} \times \text{Cost}$ 2. Ceiling for carrying amount = NRV of asset. If carrying amount exceeds NRV, difference is written off	N/A

* *Software creation process includes a detail program design.*
** *Product ready for release to customers.*

Software Developed for Internal Use. SOP 98-1 was developed to provide guidance for internally developed software. Software must meet two criteria to be accounted for as internally developed software. First, the software's specifications must be designed or modified to meet the reporting entity's internal needs, including costs to customize purchased software. Second, during the period in which the software is being developed, there can be no plan or intent to market the software externally, although development of the software can be jointly funded by several entities that each plan to use the software internally.

In order to justify capitalization of related costs, it is necessary for management to conclude that it is probable that the project will be completed and that the software will be used as intended. Absent that level of expectation, costs must be expensed currently as research and development costs are required to be. Entities which historically were engaged in both research and development of software for internal use and for sale to others would have to carefully identify costs with one or the other activity, since the former would (if all conditions are met) be subject to capitalization, while the latter might be expensed as research and development costs until technological feasibility had been demonstrated, per SFAS 86.

Under terms of the standard, cost capitalization commences when an entity has completed the conceptual formulation, design, and testing of possible project alternatives, including the process of vendor selection for purchased software, if any. These early-phase costs (referred to as "preliminary project stage" in SOP 98-1) are analogous to research and development costs and must be expensed as incurred. These cannot be later restored to an asset account if the development proves to be successful.

Costs incurred subsequent to the preliminary stage, and which meet the criteria under GAAP as long-lived assets, can be capitalized and amortized over the asset's expected economic life. Capitalization of costs will begin when both of two conditions are met. First, management having the relevant authority authorizes and commits to funding the project and believes that it is probable that it will be completed and that the resulting software will be used as intended. Second, the conceptual formulation, design, and testing of possible software project alternatives (i.e., the preliminary project stage) have been completed.

N. **Development Stage Enterprises (SFAS 7)**

SFAS 7 (see outline) defines a development stage enterprise as one devoting substantially all of its efforts to establishing a new business and (1) planned principal operations have not commenced, or (2) planned principal operations have commenced, but there has been no significant revenue. It is important to note that generally accepted accounting principles are to be followed in preparing the financial statements of a development stage enterprise. Therefore, no special treatment is allowed concerning capitalization or deferral of costs; only costs that may be deferred for an established enterprise may be capitalized by a development stage enterprise. Additionally, the balance sheet should show cumulative losses since inception under stockholders' equity. The income statement and statement of cash flows should include both current period and cumulative amounts, since inception, of revenues, expenses, losses, and cash flows. The financial statements must be identified as those of a development stage enterprise. It should also be noted that the first fiscal year after the development stage, a disclosure is required in the financial statements stating that the entity was previously in the development stage.

MULTIPLE-CHOICE QUESTIONS (1-59)

1. Merry Co. purchased a machine costing $125,000 for its manufacturing operations and paid shipping costs of $20,000. Merry spent an additional $10,000 testing and preparing the machine for use. What amount should Merry record as the cost of the machine?

- a. $155,000
- b. $145,000
- c. $135,000
- d. $125,000

2. On December 1, 1999, Boyd Co. purchased a $400,000 tract of land for a factory site. Boyd razed an old building on the property and sold the materials it salvaged from the demolition. Boyd incurred additional costs and realized salvage proceeds during December 1999 as follows:

Demolition of old building	$50,000
Legal fees for purchase contract and recording ownership	10,000
Title guarantee insurance	12,000
Proceeds from sale of salvaged materials	8,000

In its December 31, 1999 balance sheet, Boyd should report a balance in the land account of

- a. $464,000
- b. $460,000
- c. $442,000
- d. $422,000

3. Cole Co. began constructing a building for its own use in January 1999. During 1999, Cole incurred interest of $50,000 on specific construction debt, and $20,000 on other borrowings. Interest computed on the weighted-average amount of accumulated expenditures for the building during 1999 was $40,000. What amount of interest cost should Cole capitalize?

- a. $20,000
- b. $40,000
- c. $50,000
- d. $70,000

4. Clay Company started construction of a new office building on January 1, 1999, and moved into the finished building on July 1, 2000. Of the building's $2,500,000 total cost, $2,000,000 was incurred in 1999 evenly throughout the year. Clay's incremental borrowing rate was 12% throughout 1999, and the total amount of interest incurred by Clay during 1999 was $102,000. What amount should Clay report as capitalized interest at December 31, 1999?

- a. $102,000
- b. $120,000
- c. $150,000
- d. $240,000

5. During 1999, Bay Co. constructed machinery for its own use and for sale to customers. Bank loans financed these assets both during construction and after construction was complete. How much of the interest incurred should be reported as interest expense in the 1999 income statement?

	Interest incurred for machinery for own use	Interest incurred for machinery held for sale
a.	All interest incurred	All interest incurred
b.	All interest incurred	Interest incurred after completion
c.	Interest incurred after completion	Interest incurred after completion
d.	Interest incurred after completion	All interest incurred

6. On July 1, 1999, Balt Co. exchanged a truck for 25 shares of Ace Corp.'s common stock. On that date, the truck's carrying amount was $2,500, and its fair value was $3,000. Also, the book value of Ace's stock was $60 per share. On December 31, 1999, Ace had 250 shares of common stock outstanding and its book value per share was $50. What amount should Balt report in its December 31, 1999 balance sheet as investment in Ace?

- a. $3,000
- b. $2,500
- c. $1,500
- d. $1,250

7. On March 31, 1999, Winn Company traded in an old machine having a carrying amount of $16,800, and paid a cash difference of $6,000 for a new machine having a total cash price of $20,500. On March 31, 1999, what amount of loss should Winn recognize on this exchange?

- a. $0
- b. $2,300
- c. $3,700
- d. $6,000

8. Amble, Inc. exchanged a truck with a carrying amount of $12,000 and a fair value of $20,000 for a truck and $5,000 cash. The fair value of the truck received was $15,000. At what amount should Amble record the truck received in the exchange?

- a. $ 7,000
- b. $ 9,000
- c. $12,000
- d. $15,000

9. In an exchange of similar assets, Transit Co. received equipment with a fair value equal to the carrying amount of equipment given up. Transit also contributed cash. As a result of the exchange, Transit recognized

- a. A loss equal to the cash given up.
- b. A loss determined by the proportion of cash paid to the total transaction value.
- c. A gain determined by the proportion of cash paid to the total transaction value.
- d. Neither gain **nor** loss.

10. May Co. and Sty Co. exchanged nonmonetary assets. The exchange did not culminate an earning process for either May or Sty. May paid cash to Sty in connection with the exchange. To the extent that the amount of cash exceeds a proportionate share of the carrying amount of the asset surrendered, a realized gain on the exchange should be recognized by

	May	*Sty*
a.	Yes	Yes
b.	Yes	No
c.	No	Yes
d.	No	No

11. Vik Auto and King Clothier exchanged goods, held for resale, with equal fair values. Each will use the other's goods to promote their own products. The retail price of the car that Vik gave up is less than the retail price of the clothes received. What profit should Vik recognize for the nonmonetary exchange?

 a. A profit is **not** recognized.
 b. A profit equal to the difference between the retail prices of the clothes received and the car.
 c. A profit equal to the difference between the retail price and the cost of the car.
 d. A profit equal to the difference between the fair value and the cost of the car.

12. Yola Co. and Zaro Co. are fuel oil distributors. To facilitate the delivery of oil to their customers, Yola and Zaro exchanged ownership of 1,200 barrels of oil without physically moving the oil. Yola paid Zaro $30,000 to compensate for a difference in the grade of oil. On the date of the exchange, cost and market values of the oil were as follows:

	Yola Co.	*Zaro Co.*
Cost	$100,000	$126,000
Market values	120,000	150,000

In Zaro's income statement, what amount of gain should be reported from the exchange of the oil?

 a. $0
 b. $ 4,800
 c. $24,000
 d. $30,000

13. An entity disposes of a nonmonetary asset in a nonreciprocal transfer. A gain or loss should be recognized on the disposition of the asset when the fair value of the asset transferred is determinable and the nonreciprocal transfer is to

	Another entity	*A stockholder of the entity*
a.	No	Yes
b.	No	No
c.	Yes	No
d.	Yes	Yes

14. On July 1, 1999, one of Rudd Co.'s delivery vans was destroyed in an accident. On that date, the van's carrying value was $2,500. On July 15, 1999, Rudd received and recorded a $700 invoice for a new engine installed in the van in May 1999, and another $500 invoice for various repairs. In August, Rudd received $3,500 under its insurance policy on the van, which it plans to use to replace the van. What amount should Rudd report as gain (loss) on disposal of the van in its 1999 income statement?

 a. $1,000
 b. $ 300
 c. $0
 d. $ (200)

15. Lano Corp.'s forest land was condemned for use as a national park. Compensation for the condemnation exceeded the forest land's carrying amount. Lano purchased similar, but larger, replacement forest land for an amount greater than the condemnation award. As a result of the condemnation and replacement, what is the net effect on the carrying amount of forest land reported in Lano's balance sheet?

 a. The amount is increased by the excess of the replacement forest land's cost over the condemned forest land's carrying amount.
 b. The amount is increased by the excess of the replacement forest land's cost over the condemnation award.
 c. The amount is increased by the excess of the condemnation award over the condemned forest land's carrying amount.
 d. No effect, because the condemned forest land's carrying amount is used as the replacement forest land's carrying amount.

16. On July 1, 1999, Town Company purchased for $540,000 a warehouse building and the land on which it is located. The following data were available concerning the property:

	Current appraised value	*Seller's original cost*
Land	$200,000	$140,000
Warehouse building	300,000	280,000
	$500,000	$420,000

Town should record the land at

 a. $140,000
 b. $180,000
 c. $200,000
 d. $216,000

17. During 1999, King Company made the following expenditures relating to its plant building:

Continuing and frequent repairs	$40,000
Repainted the plant building	10,000
Major improvements to the electrical wiring system	32,000
Partial replacement of roof tiles	14,000

How much should be charged to repair and maintenance expense in 1999?

 a. $96,000
 b. $82,000
 c. $64,000
 d. $54,000

18. On June 18, 1999, Dell Printing Co. incurred the following costs for one of its printing presses:

Purchase of collating and stapling attachment	$84,000
Installation of attachment	36,000
Replacement parts for overhaul of press	26,000
Labor and overhead in connection with overhaul	14,000

The overhaul resulted in a significant increase in production. Neither the attachment nor the overhaul increased the estimated useful life of the press. What amount of the above costs should be capitalized?

a. $0
b. $84,000
c. $120,000
d. $160,000

19. A building suffered uninsured fire damage. The damaged portion of the building was refurbished with higher quality materials. The cost and related accumulated depreciation of the damaged portion are identifiable. To account for these events, the owner should

a. Reduce accumulated depreciation equal to the cost of refurbishing.
b. Record a loss in the current period equal to the sum of the cost of refurbishing and the carrying amount of the damaged portion of the building.
c. Capitalize the cost of refurbishing and record a loss in the current period equal to the carrying amount of the damaged portion of the building.
d. Capitalize the cost of refurbishing by adding the cost to the carrying amount of the building.

20. Derby Co. incurred costs to modify its building and to rearrange its production line. As a result, an overall reduction in production costs is expected. However, the modifications did not increase the building's market value, and the rearrangement did not extend the production line's life. Should the building modification costs and the production line rearrangement costs be capitalized?

	Building modification costs	Production line rearrangement costs
a.	Yes	No
b.	Yes	Yes
c.	No	No
d.	No	Yes

21. On January 2, 1999, Lem Corp. bought machinery under a contract that required a down payment of $10,000, plus 24 monthly payments of $5,000 each, for total cash payments of $130,000. The cash equivalent price of the machinery was $110,000. The machinery has an estimated useful life of 10 years and estimated salvage value of $5,000. Lem uses straight-line depreciation. In its 1999 income statement, what amount should Lem report as depreciation for this machinery?

a. $10,500
b. $11,000
c. $12,500
d. $13,000

22. Turtle Co. purchased equipment on January 2, 1997, for $50,000. The equipment had an estimated 5-year service life. Turtle's policy for 5-year assets is to use the 200% double-declining depreciation method for the first 2 years of the asset's life, and then switch to the straight-line depreciation method. In its December 31, 1999 balance sheet, what amount should Turtle report as accumulated depreciation for equipment?

a. $30,000

b. $38,000
c. $39,200
d. $42,000

23. Rago Company takes a full year's depreciation expense in the year of an asset's acquisition, and no depreciation expense in the year of disposition. Data relating to one of Rago's depreciable assets at December 31, 1999, are as follows:

Acquisition year	1997
Cost	$110,000
Residual value	20,000
Accumulated depreciation	72,000
Estimated useful life	5 years

Using the same depreciation method as used in 1997, 1998, and 1999, how much depreciation expense should Rago record in 2000 for this asset?

a. $12,000
b. $18,000
c. $22,000
d. $24,000

24. On January 2, 1996, Union Co. purchased a machine for $264,000 and depreciated it by the straight-line method using an estimated useful life of 8 years with no salvage value. On January 2, 1999, Union determined that the machine had a useful life of 6 years from the date of acquisition and will have a salvage value of $24,000. An accounting change was made in 1999 to reflect the additional data. The accumulated depreciation for this machine should have a balance at December 31, 1999, of

a. $176,000
b. $160,000
c. $154,000
d. $146,000

25. Weir Co. uses straight-line depreciation for its property, plant, and equipment, which, stated at cost, consisted of the following:

	12/31/99	12/31/98
Land	$ 25,000	$ 25,000
Buildings	195,000	195,000
Machinery and equipment	695,000	650,000
	915,000	870,000
Less accumulated depreciation	400,000	370,000
	$515,000	$500,000

Weir's depreciation expense for 1999 and 1998 was $55,000 and $50,000, respectively. What amount was debited to accumulated depreciation during 1999 because of property, plant, and equipment retirements?

a. $40,000
b. $25,000
c. $20,000
d. $10,000

26. On January 1, 1995, Crater, Inc. purchased equipment having an estimated salvage value equal to 20% of its original cost at the end of a 10-year life. The equipment was sold December 31, 1999, for 50% of its original cost. If the

equipment's disposition resulted in a reported loss, which of
the following depreciation methods did Crater use?
- a.   Double-declining balance.
- b.   Sum-of-the-years' digits.
- c.   Straight-line.
- d.   Composite.

27. A depreciable asset has an estimated 15% salvage
value. At the end of its estimated useful life, the accumulated depreciation would equal the original cost of the asset
under which of the following depreciation methods?

	Straight-line	*Productive output*
a.	Yes	No
b.	Yes	Yes
c.	No	Yes
d.	No	No

28. In which of the following situations is the units-of-
production method of depreciation most appropriate?
- a.   An asset's service potential declines with use.
- b.   An asset's service potential declines with the pas-
       sage of time.
- c.   An asset is subject to rapid obsolescence.
- d.   An asset incurs increasing repairs and maintenance
       with use.

29. A machine with a 5-year estimated useful life and an
estimated 10% salvage value was acquired on January 1,
1996. On December 31, 1999, accumulated depreciation,
using the sum-of-the-years' digits method, would be
- a.   (Original cost less salvage value) multiplied by
       1/15.
- b.   (Original cost less salvage value) multiplied by
       14/15.
- c.   Original cost multiplied by 14/15.
- d.   Original cost multiplied by 1/15.

30. The graph below depicts three depreciation expense
patterns over time.

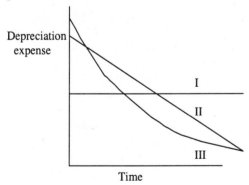

Time

Which depreciation expense pattern corresponds to the sum-
of-the-years' digits method and which corresponds to the
double-declining balance method?

	Sum-of-the-years' digits	*Double-declining balance*
a.	III	II
b.	II	I
c.	I	III
d.	II	III

31. Which of the following uses the straight-line depreciation method?

	Group depreciation	*Composite depreciation*
a.	No	No
b.	Yes	No
c.	Yes	Yes
d.	No	Yes

32. A company using the composite depreciation method
for its fleet of trucks, cars, and campers retired one of its
trucks and received cash from a salvage company. The net
carrying amount of these composite asset accounts would be
decreased by the
- a.   Cash proceeds received and original cost of the
       truck.
- b.   Cash proceeds received.
- c.   Original cost of the truck less the cash proceeds.
- d.   Original cost of the truck.

33. During 1999, the management of West Inc. decided to
dispose of some of its older equipment and machinery. By
year end, December 31, 1999, these assets had not been
sold, although the company was negotiating their sale to
another company. On the December 31, 1999 balance sheet
of West Inc., this equipment and machinery should be reported at
- a.   Fair value.
- b.   Carrying amount.
- c.   The lower of carrying amount or fair value.
- d.   The lower of carrying amount or fair value less
       cost to sell.

34. At December 31, 1999, Matson Inc. was holding long-
lived assets which it intended to sell. The company appropriately recognized a loss in 1999 related to these assets. On
Matson's income statement for the year ended December 31,
1999, this loss should be reported as a(n)
- a.   Extraordinary item.
- b.   Component of income from continuing operations
       before income taxes.
- c.   Separate component of selling or general and ad-
       ministrative expenses, disclosed net of tax benefit.
- d.   Component of the gain (loss) from sale of discon-
       tinued operations, disclosed net of income taxes.

35. Taft Inc. recognized a loss in 1998 related to long-lived
assets which it intended to sell. These assets were not sold
during 1999, and the company estimated, at December 31,
1999, that the loss recognized in 1998 had been more than
recovered. On the December 31, 1999 balance sheet, Taft
should report these long-lived assets at their
- a.   Fair value on December 31, 1998.
- b.   Fair value less cost to sell on December 31, 1998.
- c.   Fair value on December 31, 1999.
- d.   Carrying amount on December 31, 1998.

36. Assets intended to be held and used for productive
purposes may suffer from impairment in each of the following circumstances **except**
- a.   A change in the way the assets are used or physical
       change in the assets.

b. Asset costs incurred exceed the original amounts planned.

c. Discounted expected future cash flows and interest charges are less than the carrying amount of the assets.

d. A significant adverse change in legal factors that might affect the assets' fair value.

37. The provisions of SFAS 121, *Accounting for the Impairment of Long-Lived Assets,* as they relate to assets in use include

	Recognition of loss upon impairment	Restoration of previously recognized impairment losses
a.	Yes	Yes
b.	Yes	No
c.	No	Yes
d.	No	No

38. During December 1999, Bubba Inc. determined that there had been a significant decrease in the market value of its equipment used in its manufacturing process. At December 31, 1999, Bubba compiled the information below.

Original cost of the equipment	$500,000
Accumulated depreciation	300,000
Expected net future cash inflows (undiscounted) related to the continued use and eventual disposal of the equipment	175,000
Fair value of the equipment	125,000

What is the amount of impairment loss that should be reported on Bubba's income statement prepared for the year ended December 31, 1999?

a. $ 75,000
b. $ 25,000
c. $325,000
d. $375,000

39. Marjorie, Inc., acquired a machine for $320,000 on August 31, 1996. The machine has a 5-year life, a $50,000 salvage value, and was depreciated using the straight-line method. On May 31, 1999, a test for recoverability reveals that the expected net future undiscounted cash inflows related to the continued use and eventual disposal of the machine total $150,000. The machine's actual fair value on May 31, 1999, is $135,000, with no salvage value. Assuming a loss on impairment is recognized May 31, 1999, what is Marjorie's depreciation expense for June 1999?

a. $6,352
b. $5,000
c. $4,500
d. $3,148

40. Which of the following statements is(are) correct about the carrying amount of a long-lived asset after an impairment loss has been recognized? Assume the long-lived asset is being held for use in the business and that the asset is depreciable.

I. The reduced carrying amount of the asset may be increased in subsequent years if the impairment loss has been recovered.

II. The reduced carrying amount of the asset represents the amount that should be depreciated over the asset's remaining useful life.

a. I only.
b. II only.
c. I and II.
d. Neither I nor II.

41. In January 1999, Vorst Co. purchased a mineral mine for $2,640,000 with removable ore estimated at 1,200,000 tons. After it has extracted all the ore, Vorst will be required by law to restore the land to its original condition at an estimated cost of $180,000. Vorst believes it will be able to sell the property afterwards for $300,000. During 1999, Vorst incurred $360,000 of development costs preparing the mine for production and removed and sold 60,000 tons of ore. In its 1999 income statement, what amount should Vorst report as depletion?

a. $135,000
b. $144,000
c. $150,000
d. $159,000

 3

42. On January 2, 1999, Judd Co. bought a trademark from Krug Co. for $500,000. Judd retained an independent consultant, who estimated the trademark's remaining life to be 50 years. Its unamortized cost on Krug's accounting records was $380,000. Judd decided to amortize the trademark over the maximum period allowed. In Judd's December 31, 1999 balance sheet, what amount should be reported as accumulated amortization?

a. $ 7,600
b. $ 9,500
c. $10,000
d. $12,500

43. On January 2, 1999, Paye Co. purchased Shef Co. at a cost that resulted in recognition of goodwill of $200,000 having an expected benefit period of 10 years. During the first quarter of 1999, Paye spent an additional $80,000 on expenditures designed to maintain goodwill. Due to these expenditures, at December 31, 1999, Paye estimated that the benefit period of goodwill was 40 years. In its December 31, 1999 balance sheet, what amount should Paye report as goodwill?

a. $180,000
b. $195,000
c. $252,000
d. $273,000

44. On January 2, 1998, Carver Inc. acquired Jones Company in a business combination accounted for under the purchase method. The fair values of the long-lived assets, identifiable intangible assets, and goodwill acquired on January 2, 1998, are disclosed below.

Long-lived assets	$720,000
Identifiable intangibles	180,000
Goodwill (5 year estimated useful life)	50,000

At December 31, 1999, Carver estimated that significant declines had occurred in the market values of the long-lived assets and identifiable intangible assets acquired from Jones. In determining whether or not to report an impairment loss related to these assets for 1999, how should goodwill be allocated to the assets being tested for recoverability?

	Long-lived assets	Identifiable intangibles
a.	$50,000	$0
b.	$40,000	$10,000
c.	$24,000	$ 6,000
d.	$30,000	$0

45. On January 2, 1996, Lava, Inc. purchased a patent for a new consumer product for $90,000. At the time of purchase, the patent was valid for 15 years; however, the patent's useful life was estimated to be only 10 years due to the competitive nature of the product. On December 31, 1999, the product was permanently withdrawn from sale under governmental order because of a potential health hazard in the product. What amount should Lava charge against income during 1999, assuming amortization is recorded at the end of each year?

a. $ 9,000
b. $54,000
c. $63,000
d. $72,000

46. Malden, Inc. has two patents that have allegedly been infringed by competitors. After investigation, legal counsel informed Malden that it had a weak case on patent A34 and a strong case in regard to patent B19. Malden incurred additional legal fees to stop infringement on B19. Both patents have a remaining legal life of 8 years. How should Malden account for these legal costs incurred relating to the two patents?

a. Expense costs for A34 and capitalize costs for B19.
b. Expense costs for both A34 and B19.
c. Capitalize costs for both A34 and B19.
d. Capitalize costs for A34 and expense costs for B19.

47. Which of the following statements concerning patents is correct?

a. Legal costs incurred to successfully defend an internally developed patent should be capitalized and amortized over the patent's remaining economic life.
b. Legal fees and other direct costs incurred in registering a patent should be capitalized and amortized on a straight-line basis over a 5-year period.
c. Research and development contract services purchased from others and used to develop a patented manufacturing process should be capitalized and amortized over the patent's economic life.
d. Research and development costs incurred to develop a patented item should be capitalized and amortized on a straight-line basis over 17 years.

48. On January 1, 1999, Kew Corp. incurred organization costs of $24,000. For financial accounting purposes, Kew is amortizing these costs on the same basis as the maximum allowable for federal income tax purposes. What portion of

the organization costs will Kew defer to years subsequent to 1999?

a. $23,400
b. $19,200
c. $ 4,800
d. $0

49. Cody Corp. incurred the following costs during 1999:

Design of tools, jigs, molds, and dies involving new technology	$125,000
Modification of the formulation of a process	160,000
Troubleshooting in connection with breakdowns during commercial production	100,000
Adaptation of an existing capability to a particular customer's need as part of a continuing commercial activity	110,000

In its 1999 income statement, Cody should report research and development expense of

a. $125,000
b. $160,000
c. $235,000
d. $285,000

50. In 1999, Ball Labs incurred the following costs:

Direct costs of doing contract research and development work for the government to be reimbursed by governmental unit	$400,000

Research and development costs not included above were

Depreciation	$300,000
Salaries	700,000
Indirect costs appropriately allocated	200,000
Materials	180,000

What was Ball's total research and development expense in 1999?

a. $1,080,000
b. $1,380,000
c. $1,580,000
d. $1,780,000

51. West, Inc. made the following expenditures relating to Product Y:

- Legal costs to file a patent on Product Y--$10,000. Production of the finished product would not have been undertaken without the patent.
- Special equipment to be used solely for development of Product Y--$60,000. The equipment has no other use and has an estimated useful life of 4 years.
- Labor and material costs incurred in producing a prototype model--$200,000.
- Cost of testing the prototype--$80,000.

What is the total amount of costs that will be expensed when incurred?

a. $280,000
b. $295,000

c. $340,000
d. $350,000

52. Brill Co. made the following expenditures during 1999:

Costs to develop computer software
for internal use in Brill's general
management information system $100,000
Costs of market research activities   75,000

What amount of these expenditures should Brill report in its 1999 income statement as research and development expenses?

a. $175,000
b. $100,000
c. $ 75,000
d. $0

53. On January 1, 1999, Jambon purchased equipment for use in developing a new product. Jambon uses the straight-line depreciation method. The equipment could provide benefits over a 10-year period. However, the new product development is expected to take 5 years, and the equipment can be used only for this project. Jambon's 1999 expense equals

a.   The total cost of the equipment.
b.   One-fifth of the cost of the equipment.
c.   One-tenth of the cost of the equipment.
d.   Zero.

Items 54 and 55 are based on the following:

During 1999, Pitt Corp. incurred costs to develop and produce a routine, low-risk computer software product, as follows:

Completion of detailed program design $13,000
Costs incurred for coding and testing to
establish technological feasibility   10,000
Other coding costs after establishment of
technological feasibility   24,000
Other testing costs after establishment of
technological feasibility   20,000
Costs of producing product masters for
training materials   15,000
Duplication of computer software and
training materials from product masters
(1,000 units)   25,000
Packaging product (500 units)   9,000

54. In Pitt's December 31, 1999 balance sheet, what amount should be reported in inventory?

a. $25,000
b. $34,000
c. $40,000
d. $49,000

55. In Pitt's December 31, 1999 balance sheet, what amount should be capitalized as software cost, subject to amortization?

a. $54,000
b. $57,000
c. $59,000
d. $69,000

56. On December 31, 1998, Bit Co. had capitalized costs for a new computer software product with an economic life of 5 years. Sales for 1999 were 30% of expected total sales of the software. At December 31, 1999, the software had a net realizable value equal to 90% of the capitalized cost. What percentage of the original capitalized cost should be reported as the net amount on Bit's December 31, 1999 balance sheet?

a.   70%
b.   72%
c.   80%
d.   90%

57. Tanker Oil Co., a development stage enterprise, incurred the following costs during its first year of operations:

Legal fees for incorporation and other
related matters $55,000
Underwriters' fees for initial stock
offering   40,000
Exploration costs and purchases of
mineral rights   60,000

Tanker had no revenue during its first year of operation. What amount may Tanker capitalize as organizational costs?

a. $155,000
b. $115,000
c. $ 95,000
d. $ 55,000

58. Financial reporting by a development stage enterprise differs from financial reporting for an established operating enterprise in regard to footnote disclosures

a.   Only.
b.   And expense recognition principles only.
c.   And revenue recognition principles only.
d.   And revenue and expense recognition principles.

59. A development stage enterprise

a.   Issues an income statement that shows only cumulative amounts from the enterprise's inception.
b.   Issues an income statement that is the same as an established operating enterprise, but does **not** show cumulative amounts from the enterprise's inception as additional information.
c.   Issues an income statement that is the same as an established operating enterprise, and shows cumulative amounts from the enterprise's inception as additional information.
d.   Does **not** issue an income statement.

OTHER OBJECTIVE QUESTIONS

Problem 1   (15 to 25 minutes)

This problem consists of 14 items. Select the **best** answer for each item. Use a No. 2 pencil to blacken the appropriate ovals on the Objective Answer Sheet to indicate your answers. **Answer all items**. Your grade will be based on the total number of correct answers.

Items 1 through 6 represent expenditures for goods held for resale and equipment.

Required:

For **items 1 through 6**, determine for each item whether the expenditure should be capitalized ⒸＣ or expensed as a period cost ⒺＥ and blacken the corresponding oval on the Objective Answer Sheet.

1. Freight charges paid for goods held for resale.

2. In-transit insurance on goods held for resale purchased FOB shipping point.

3. Interest on note payable for goods held for resale.

4. Installation of equipment.

5. Testing of newly purchased equipment.

6. Cost of current year service contract on equipment.

Items 7 through 10 are based on the following 1999 transactions:

- Link Co. purchased an office building and the land on which it is located by paying $800,000 cash and assuming an existing mortgage of $200,000. The property is assessed at $960,000 for realty tax purposes, of which 60% is allocated to the building.
- Link leased construction equipment under a 7-year capital lease requiring annual year-end payments of $100,000. Link's incremental borrowing rate is 9%, while the lessor's implicit rate, which is not known to Link, is 8%. Present value factors for an ordinary annuity for seven periods are 5.21 at 8% and 5.03 at 9%. Fair value of the equipment is $515,000.
- Link paid $50,000 and gave a plot of undeveloped land with a carrying amount of $320,000 and a fair value of $450,000 to Club Co. in exchange for a plot of undeveloped land with a fair value of $500,000. The land was carried on Club's books at $350,000.

Required:

For **items 7 through 10**, calculate the amount to be recorded for each item. To record your answer, write the number in the boxes on the Objective Answer Sheet **and** blacken the corresponding oval below each box. Write zeros in any blank boxes preceding your numerical answer, and blacken the zero in the oval below the box. **You cannot receive credit for your answers if you fail to blacken an oval in each column.**

7. Building.

8. Leased equipment.

9. Land received from Club on Link's books.

10. Land received from Link on Club's books.

Items 11 through 14 are based on the following information:

On January 2, 1998, Half, Inc. purchased a manufacturing machine for $864,000. The machine has an 8-year estimated life and a $144,000 estimated salvage value. Half expects to manufacture 1,800,000 units over the life of the machine. During 1999, Half manufactured 300,000 units.

Required:

Items 11 through 14 represent various depreciation methods. For each item, calculate depreciation expense for 1999 (the second year of ownership) for the machine described above under the method listed. To record your answer, write the number in the boxes on the Objective Answer Sheet **and** blacken the corresponding oval below each box. Write zeros in any blank boxes preceding your numerical answer, and blacken the zero in the oval below the box. **You cannot receive credit for your answers if you fail to blacken an oval in each column.**

11. Straight-line.

12. Double-declining balance.

13. Sum-of-the-years' digits.

14. Units of production.

PROBLEMS

Problem 1   (15 to 25 minutes)

Winter Sports Co. rents winter sports equipment to the public. Snowmobiles are depreciated by the double declining balance method. Before the season began, the estimated lives of several snowmobiles were extended because engines were replaced. Winter was given 30 days to pay for the engines. Winter gave the old engines to a local mechanic who agreed to provide repairs and maintenance service in the next year equal to the fair value of the engines. Rental skis, poles, and boots are capitalized and depreciated according to the inventory (appraisal) method.

Required:

a. How would Winter account for the purchase of the new engines and the transfer of the old engines to the local mechanic if the old engines' costs are
1.   Known?
2.   Unknown?

b. 1.   What are two assumptions underlying use of an accelerated depreciation method?
2.   How should Winter calculate the snowmobiles' depreciation?

c. How should Winter calculate and report the costs of the skis, poles, and boots in its balance sheets and income statements?

Problem 2   (15 to 25 minutes)

Portland Co. uses the straight-line depreciation method for depreciable assets. All assets are depreciated individually except manufacturing machinery, which is depreciated by the composite method.

During the year, Portland exchanged a delivery truck with Maine Co. for a larger delivery truck. It paid cash equal to 10% of the larger truck's value.

Required:

a. What factors should have influenced Portland's selection of the straight-line depreciation method?

b. How should Portland account for and report the truck exchange transaction?

c. 1.   What benefits should Portland derive from using the composite method rather than the individual basis for manufacturing machinery?
2.   How should Portland have calculated the manufacturing machinery's annual depreciation expense in its first year of operation?

Problem 3   (15 to 25 minutes)

Jones Corporation has significant amounts of property, plant, and equipment.

Required:

a. Define what is meant by impairment of an operational asset (e.g., equipment).

b. How is the definition of impairment applied in practice? Include in the answer signs or indicators of impairment, loss determination, and measurement of losses.

c. Describe the accounting and reporting for an impairment loss in current and future periods.

d. How are losses on operational assets that management expects to dispose of measured, accounted for, and reported on the financial statements?

Problem 4   (30 to 40 minutes)

During 1999, Broca Co. had the following transactions:

• On January 2, Broca purchased the net assets of Amp Co. for $360,000. The fair value of Amp's identifiable net assets was $172,000. Broca believes that, due to the popularity of Amp's consumer products, the life of the resulting goodwill is unlimited.

• On February 1, Broca purchased a franchise to operate a ferry service from the state government for $60,000 and an annual fee of 1% of ferry revenues. The franchise expires after 5 years. Ferry revenues were $20,000 during 1999. Broca projects future revenues of $40,000 in 2000, and $60,000 per annum for the 3 years thereafter.

• On April 5, Broca was granted a patent that had been applied for by Amp. During 1999, Broca incurred legal costs of $51,000 to register the patent and an additional $85,000 to successfully prosecute a patent infringement suit against a competitor. Broca estimates the patent's economic life to be 10 years.

Broca's accounting policy is to amortize all intangibles on the straight-line basis over the maximum period permitted by generally accepted accounting principles, taking a full year's amortization in the year of acquisition.

Required:

a. 1.   Describe the characteristics of intangible assets. Discuss the accounting for the purchase or internal development of intangible assets with an indeterminable life, such as goodwill.
2.   Over what period should intangible assets be amortized? How should this period be determined? Discuss the justification for amortization of intangible assets with indeterminable lives.
3.   Describe the financial statement disclosure requirements relating to Broca's intangible assets and expenses. Do not write the related footnotes.

b. Prepare a schedule showing the intangibles section of Broca's balance sheet at December 31, 1999, and a schedule showing the related expenses that would appear on Broca's 1999 income statement. Show supporting computations.

Problem 5   (15 to 25 minutes)

Mono Tech Co. began operations in 1996 and confined its activities to one project. It purchased equipment to be used exclusively for research and development on the project, and other equipment that is to be used initially for research and development and subsequently for production. In 1997, Mono constructed and paid for a pilot plant that was used until December 1998 to determine the best manufacturing process for the project's product. In December 1998, Mono obtained a patent and received cash from the sale of the pilot plant. In 1999, a factory was constructed and commercial manufacture of the product began.

Required:

a.   1.   According to the FASB conceptual framework, what are the three essential characteristics of an asset?

2.   How do Mono's project expenditures through 1998 meet the FASB conceptual framework's three essential characteristics of an asset? Do **not** discuss why the expenditures may **not** meet the characteristics of an asset.

3.   Why is it difficult to justify the classification of research and development expenditures as assets?

b.   How should Mono report

1.   The effects of equipment expenditures in its income statements and balance sheets from 1996 through 1999?

2.   Pilot plant construction costs and sale proceeds in its 1997 and 1998 statements of cash flows using the direct method?

MULTIPLE-CHOICE ANSWERS

1. a __ __	15. a __ __	29. b __ __	43. b __ __	57. d __ __
2. a __ __	16. d __ __	30. d __ __	44. c __ __	58. a __ __
3. b __ __	17. c __ __	31. c __ __	45. c __ __	59. c __ __
4. a __ __	18. d __ __	32. b __ __	46. a __ __	
5. d __ __	19. c __ __	33. d __ __	47. a __ __	
6. a __ __	20. b __ __	34. b __ __	48. b __ __	
7. b __ __	21. a __ __	35. d __ __	49. d __ __	
8. b __ __	22. b __ __	36. c __ __	50. b __ __	
9. a __ __	23. a __ __	37. b __ __	51. c __ __	
10. c __ __	24. d __ __	38. a __ __	52. d __ __	
11. d __ __	25. b __ __	39. b __ __	53. a __ __	
12. b __ __	26. c __ __	40. b __ __	54. b __ __	
13. d __ __	27. d __ __	41. b __ __	55. c __ __	1st: __/59 = __%
14. b __ __	28. a __ __	42. d __ __	56. a __ __	2nd: __/59 = __%

MULTIPLE-CHOICE ANSWER EXPLANATIONS

A. Acquisition Cost

1.   (a)   The cost of machinery includes all expenditures incurred in acquiring the asset and preparing it for use. Cost includes the purchase price, freight and handling charges, insurance on the machine while in transit, cost of special foundations, and costs of assembling, installation, and testing. All of the costs given in this problem are properly recorded as the cost of the machine. Therefore the cost to be recorded is $155,000 ($125,000 + $20,000 + $10,000).

2.   (a)   Any cost involved in preparing land for its ultimate use (such as a factory site) is considered part of the cost of the land. Before the land can be used as a building site, it must be purchased (involving costs such as purchase price, legal fees, and title insurance) and the old building must be razed (cost of demolition less proceeds from sale of scrap). The total balance in the land account should be $464,000.

Purchase price	$400,000
Legal fees	10,000
Title insurance	12,000
Net cost of demolition ($50,000 – $8,000)	42,000
	$464,000

B. Capitalization of Interest

3.   (b)   The amount of interest cost which should be capitalized during building construction is the **lower** of **avoidable interest** or **actual interest**. Avoidable interest equals the interest computed on the weighted-average amount of accumulated expenditures on the building ($40,000). Since actual interest is $70,000 ($50,000 + $20,000), the amount capitalized should be $40,000.

4.   (a)   The requirement is to calculate the amount of capitalized interest at 12/31/99. The requirements of SFAS 34, para 17, for capitalization of interest are met: (1) expenditures for the asset have been made, (2) activities that are necessary to get the asset ready for its intended use are in progress, and (3) interest cost is being incurred. The amount to be capitalized is the lower of avoidable interest or actual interest. Avoidable interest is the average accumulated expenditures multiplied by the appropriate interest rate

or rates. Since $2,000,000 was spent on the building evenly throughout the year, the average accumulated expenditures were $1,000,000 ($2,000,000 ÷ 2) and the avoidable interest was $120,000 ($1,000,000 x 12%). Since actual interest ($102,000) is less than avoidable interest, the actual interest cost is capitalized.

5.   (d)   SFAS 34, para 9, defines certain assets for which interest costs incurred in their production should be capitalized rather than expensed. Assets which "qualify" for interest capitalization are those constructed or otherwise produced for an enterprise's own use and those intended for sale or lease that are constructed or otherwise produced as **discrete projects**. Para 18 further stipulates that the capitalization period shall end when the asset is substantially complete and ready for its intended use. Based upon these criteria, the interest costs associated with the machinery for Bay's own use should be capitalized during the construction period and expensed after completion. Additionally, all costs associated with the machinery held for sale should be expensed because the machinery does not meet the "discrete project" criterion. Therefore, answer (d) is correct.

C. Nonmonetary Exchanges

6.   (a)   When the investment was acquired, it was recorded at cost--the fair market value of the asset surrendered to acquire it. The July 1 entry was

Inv. in Ace stock	3,000	
Truck		2,500
Gain on disposal		500 ($3,000 – $2,500)

The investment would be reported in the 12/31/99 balance sheet at $3,000. The book value of Ace's stock does not affect the amount recorded on Balt's books.

7.   (b)   The cash price of the new machine represents its fair market value (FMV). The FMV of the old machine can be determined by subtracting the cash portion of the purchase price ($6,000) from the total cost of the new machine: $20,500 – $6,000 = $14,500. Since the book value of the machine ($16,800) exceeds its FMV on the date of the trade-in ($14,500), the difference of $2,300 must be recognized as a loss. Note, however, that if the FMV of the old machine had **exceeded** its book value, the gain would not be recognized. In accordance with APB 29, gains on nonmonetary transactions involving similar productive assets are not recognized when boot is given.

8.   (b) When similar assets are exchanged, boot is received, and a gain results, the exchange is treated as part sale and part exchange. The earnings process is assumed to be complete for the portion relating to the boot received. The gain recognized is computed as follows:

$$\frac{\text{Boot}}{\text{Boot} + \text{FMV of assets received}} \times \text{Total Gain} = \text{Gain Recognized}$$

Total Gain =   (15,000 + 5,000)   –   12,000   = 8,000

Assets received   Book Value of asset
by Amble   given up by Beam

The gain recognized would be calculated as follows:

$$\frac{5,000}{15,000 + 5,000} \times 8,000 = \$2,000 \text{ gain recognized}$$

The asset acquired is recorded at its FMV less the gain not recognized ($15,000 – $6,000 = $9,000). This amount can also be computed as the **book** value of the asset surrendered plus the gain recognized less boot received ($12,000 + $2,000 – $5,000 = $9,000). The journal entry is

Truck (new)	9,000	
Cash	5,000	
Truck (old)		12,000
Gain on sale		2,000

9.   (a) Per APB 29, para 22, if a loss is indicated by the terms of the transaction, the entire loss on the exchange should be recognized. In this case, a loss results because Transit received a similar asset whose book value equaled the fair market value of the asset received and paid cash. Therefore, Transit gave up more than they received, the difference being the loss. Therefore, answer (a) is correct. Answers (c) and (d) are incorrect because there was no gain recognized as a result of the transaction. Answer (b) is incorrect because the entire loss is recognized, not merely a portion of the loss.

10.   (c) Per APB 29, para 22, when the exchange of nonmonetary assets includes an amount of monetary consideration, the Board believes that the receiver of monetary consideration has realized a partial gain on the exchange. To determine the partial gain to be recognized, first compute the total gain which is the difference between the fair market value of the nonmonetary asset given up and its book value. Then multiply the ratio of the **monetary** consideration received to the **total** consideration received (i.e., monetary consideration plus the estimated fair market value of the asset received) times the total gain. The result is the realized gain to be recognized. The Board further believes that the entity paying the monetary consideration should **not** recognize any gain until the earnings process is culminated. Therefore, answer (c) is correct. Note, however, that **all losses** on sales or exchanges are recognized immediately.

11.   (d) Per APB 29, nonmonetary exchanges of dissimilar assets are accounted for on the basis of fair values, and both gains and losses recognized. The gain (or loss) for Vik is calculated as the difference between the fair value and cost of the car. Note that the retail/list price of an asset is not always representative of the FMV of the asset. An asset can often be purchased for less than the retail/list price.

12.   (b) When similar assets are exchanged, boot is received, and a gain results, the exchange is treated as part sale and part exchange. The earnings process is assumed to be complete for the portion relating to the boot received. The gain recognized is computed as follows:

$$\frac{\text{Boot}}{\text{Boot} + \text{FMV of assets received}} \times \text{Total gain} = \text{Gain Recognized}$$

Total Gain   =   (120,000 + 30,000)   –   126,000   =   24,000

Assets received by Zaro   Book value of
asset given up by Zaro

In this case, it would be calculated as follows:

$$\frac{30,000}{(30,000 + 120,000)} \times 24,000 = \$4,800$$

13.   (d) Per APB 29, para 18, a transfer of a nonmonetary asset in a nonreciprocal transfer should be recorded at the fair value of the asset transferred, with a gain or loss recognized on the disposition, whether the transfer is made to a stockholder or to another entity. Therefore, answer (d) is correct.

14.   (b) A gain (loss) must be recognized when a nonmonetary asset is involuntarily converted into monetary assets even if the company reinvests the monetary assets in replacement nonmonetary assets. The gain or loss is the difference between the insurance proceeds received ($3,500) and the carrying value of the asset destroyed. The unadjusted carrying value ($2,500) must be adjusted for the capital expenditure ($700) which has not yet been recorded. When a major component of an asset like an engine is replaced, the preferred treatment is to take the old component off the books (with a loss recognized) and record the new component. When the book value of the component is unknown (as in this case), the cost of the new component ($700) is simply debited to the accumulated depreciation account. This increases the van's carrying value to $3,200 ($2,500 + $700), which means the gain is $300 ($3,500 – $3,200). Note that the $500 invoice should be recorded as repairs expense, and therefore does not affect the van's carrying value.

15.   (a) Per FASB Interpretation 30, para 2, involuntary conversions of nonmonetary assets to monetary assets are monetary transactions for which gain or loss shall be recognized even though an enterprise reinvests or is obligated to reinvest the monetary assets in replacement nonmonetary assets. Accordingly, Lano would record the condemnation and replacement of the forest land as two separate transactions. Lano should recognize a gain on the condemnation and subsequently record the replacement land at the total purchase price. The net effect of these events is to increase the amount of forest land on Lano's balance sheet by the excess of the replacement land's cost over the condemned land's carrying amount, as shown below.

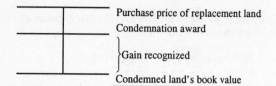

	Purchase price of replacement land
	Condemnation award
	Gain recognized
	Condemned land's book value

Loss		xxx	(Plug)
Acc. Depr.		xxx	
Building			xxx
Building		xxx	
Cash			xxx

D. Purchase of Groups of Fixed Assets

16. (d) The requirement is to determine the amount at which land acquired in a group purchase of fixed assets should be recorded. The total cost ($540,000) of the land and building should be allocated based on their relative fair market value (FMV). Current appraised value is a better indicator of FMV than the seller's original cost. Therefore, the land should be recorded at $216,000.

$$\frac{\text{FMV land}}{\text{Total FMV of assets purchased}} \times \begin{array}{c}\text{Purchase price}\\\text{of group assets}\end{array}$$

$$\frac{200,000}{500,000} \times 540,000 = \$216,000$$

There is no problem in recording the land at more than its appraised value since value is only an estimate of FMV.

E. Capital Versus Revenue Expenditures

17. (c) The requirement is to calculate the amount to be charged to repair and maintenance expense in 1999. Generally, a cost should be capitalized if it improves the asset and expensed if it merely maintains the asset at its current level. Continuing and frequent repairs ($40,000) should be expensed. Similarly, the cost of repainting the plant building ($10,000) and the cost of partially replacing the roof tiles ($14,000) should be expensed. These are ordinary, regularly occurring expenditures which maintain, rather than improve, the plant building. The work on the electrical wiring system ($32,000) is capitalized instead of expensed since it is a major improvement. Therefore, the total amount expensed is $64,000 ($40,000 + $10,000 + $14,000).

18. (d) The cost of the attachment ($84,000) should be capitalized because it is an **addition**. The cost of installing the attachment ($36,000) is also capitalized because this expenditure was required to get the attachment ready for its intended use. The overhaul costs ($26,000 + $14,000 = $40,000) are also capitalized. Even though the overhaul did not increase useful life, it is a capital expenditure because it increased productivity. The total amount capitalized is $160,000 ($84,000 + $36,000 + $40,000).

19. (c) When an entity suffers a casualty loss to an asset, the accounting loss is recorded at the net carrying value of the damaged asset, if known. In this case, the cost and related accumulated depreciation are identifiable. The entity should therefore recognize a loss in the current period equal to the carrying amount of the damaged portion of the building. The refurbishing of the building, which is an economic event separate from the fire damage, should be treated similarly to the purchase of other assets or betterments. The cost of refurbishing the building should therefore be capitalized and depreciated over the shorter of the refurbishment's useful lives or the useful life of the building.

Therefore, answer (c) is correct and answer (b) is incorrect. Answer (a) is incorrect because in order to reduce the accumulated depreciation account, the useful life of the asset must be extended. In this case, there is no mention of this fact. Answer (d) is incorrect because it fails to recognize the casualty loss and properly remove the cost and accumulated depreciation on the damaged portion of the building from the accounting records.

NOTE: If the components of the damaged portion are not identifiable, the following entry would be made:

Loss	xxx	
Cash		xxx

20. (b) Generally, a cost should be capitalized if it improves the efficiency of the asset or extends its useful life and expensed if it merely maintains the asset at its current level. Since an overall reduction in production costs is expected, efficiency must have been improved by the steps taken by Derby. In this problem, it appears that both the building modification and the production line rearrangement contributed to the improved efficiency in the production process. Therefore, both costs should be capitalized and answer (b) is correct.

F. Depreciation

21. (a) Machinery is recorded at its historical cost, which is measured by the cash or **cash equivalent price** of obtaining the machine and preparing it for use. The journal entry to record this acquisition would be

Machinery	110,000	(cash equiv.)
Discount on N.P.	20,000	($130,000 – $110,000)
Notes payable	120,000	(24 x $5,000)
Cash	10,000	

The $20,000 discount represents future interest expense (the cost associated with paying for the asset over 2 years instead of immediately) rather than part of the cost of the machine. Straight-line depreciation for 1999 is computed as follows:

(Cost – Salvage value)	x	1/useful life	=		Depr. expense
($110,000 – $5,000)	x	1/10	=		$10,500

22. (b) The formula for 200% double-declining balance (DDB) depreciation is

$$\left(\begin{array}{c}\text{Beginning-of-year}\\\text{book value}\end{array}\right) \times \left(\begin{array}{c}\text{DDB}\\\text{rate}\end{array}\right) = \text{Depreciation expense}$$

The DDB rate is two times the straight-line rate (in this case, 1/5 x 2 = 2/5 or 40%). Therefore, depreciation for the first 2 years is

1997:	$50,000 x 40% =	$20,000
1998:	($50,000 – $20,000) x 40% =	12,000
		$32,000

In 1999, Turtle switches to the straight-line method. The book value ($50,000 – $32,000 = $18,000) would be depreciated over the remaining 3 years (5 years less 2 gone by). Therefore, 1999 depreciation is $6,000 ($18,000 x 1/3) and

12/31/99 accumulated depreciation is $38,000 ($32,000 + $6,000).

23.   (a)   The requirement is to calculate the amount of depreciation expense to be recorded in 1999. After 3 years (1997-1999), accumulated depreciation is $72,000. Therefore, the method which was used was the sum-of-the-years' digits (SYD) method. Using this method, after 3 years the balance in accumulated depreciation would be 12/15 of the depreciable base (5/15 + 4/15 + 3/15). The depreciable base is the cost ($110,000) less the residual value ($20,000), or $90,000. Thus, using the SYD method, accumulated depreciation at 12/31/98 would be $72,000 ($90,000 x 12/15), which matches the amount given in the problem. 1999 depreciation expense, using the SYD method is $12,000 ($90,000 x 2/15).

24.   (d)   From 1/2/99 to 12/31/98, depreciation was recorded using an 8-year life. Yearly depreciation was $33,000 ($264,000 ÷ 8), and accumulated depreciation at 12/31/98 was $99,000 (3 x $33,000). In 1999, the estimated useful life was changed to 6 years total with a salvage value of $24,000. Therefore, the 12/31/98 book value ($264,000 – $99,000 = $165,000) is depreciated down to the $24,000 salvage value over a remaining useful life of 3 years (6 years total – 3 years already recorded). The 1999 depreciation expense is $47,000 [($165,000 – $24,000) ÷ 3], increasing accumulated depreciation to $146,000 ($99,000 + $47,000).

25.   (b)   The solutions approach is to set up a T-account for **accumulated depreciation** and solve for the unknown.

Accumulated Depreciation		
	370,000	12/31/98
1999 retirements ?	55,000	1999 depr. expense
	400,000	12/31/99

The 12/31/98 and 12/31/99 balances were given in the schedule. The 1999 depreciation expense would be recorded by debiting the expense account and crediting accumulated depreciation. The accumulated depreciation would be debited for the property, plant, and equipment retirements. To balance the T-account, the debit must be $25,000. Alternatively, an equation can be used as shown below.

$$\$370,000 + \$55,000 - X = \$400,000$$
$$425,000\ 0 - X = 400,000$$
$$X = 25,000$$

$$370,000 = 12/31/98\ balance$$
$$55,000 = 1999\ depreciation\ expense$$
$$400,000 = 12/31/99\ balance$$
$$X = retirements$$

26.   (c)   After reviewing the different methods, you might realize that the method with the highest carrying amount would result in a loss or

Gain/loss = Proceeds – Carrying amount

"   = 50% C – [C – 50% (C – S)]

"   = 50% C – [C – 50% (C – 20%C)]

"   = .5C – [1.00C – .5(1.00C – .2C)]

"   = .5C – [.6C]

Carrying amount > Proceeds

∴ Loss

27.   (d)   The formula to compute straight-line depreciation is

$$\frac{Original\ cost\ less\ salvage\ value}{Estimated\ useful\ life}$$

The formula to determine depreciation using the productive output method is

$$\left(\frac{Current\ activity\ (output)}{Total\ expected\ activity}\right) \times \left(\begin{array}{c}Original\ cost\ less\\ salvage\ value\end{array}\right)$$

Note that both of these methods use cost minus salvage value as the depreciable base of the asset. This means that after all depreciation has been recorded using either method, the net asset will be recorded at salvage value, and accumulated depreciation will equal the original cost minus salvage value. Therefore, answer (d) is correct.

28.   (a)   Depreciation is a method of allocating the cost of an asset in a systematic and rational manner. Since the units-of-production method of depreciation is most appropriate when depreciation is a function of activity, answer (a) is correct. Answer (b) is incorrect because this situation warrants the use of a depreciation method based on the passage of time. Answers (c) and (d) are incorrect because both support the use of an accelerated method of depreciation.

29.   (b)   Under the sum-of-the-years' digits (SYD) method, depreciation expense is computed by applying declining fractions to the depreciable cost of the asset. The denominator is the sum of the years in the life of the asset (1 + 2 + 3 + 4 + 5 = 15 in this case). Annual depreciation would be computed as follows:

1996	$\left(\begin{array}{c}\text{original cost}\\ \text{less salvage value}\end{array}\right)$	x	(5/15)
1997	$\left(\begin{array}{c}\text{original cost}\\ \text{less salvage value}\end{array}\right)$	x	(4/15)
1998	$\left(\begin{array}{c}\text{original cost}\\ \text{less salvage value}\end{array}\right)$	x	(3/15)
1999	$\left(\begin{array}{c}\text{original cost}\\ \text{less salvage value}\end{array}\right)$	x	(2/15)
Total	$\left(\begin{array}{c}\text{original cost}\\ \text{less salvage value}\end{array}\right)$	x	(14/15)

Accumulated depreciation at December 31, 1999, would be (original cost less salvage value) multiplied by 14/15, therefore answer (b) is correct.

30.   (d)   Line I represents depreciation expense that stays constant over time (i.e., straight-line). Both sum-of-the-years' digits and double-declining balance are accelerated depreciation methods, and hence the depreciation expense for these two methods does not stay constant over time. Line II represents depreciation expense that decreases at a constant rate (i.e., a linear function) and thus would be the pattern of depreciation for sum-of-the-years' digits. Line III represents depreciation expense that decreases at a decreasing rate (i.e., a nonlinear function) and thus would be the pattern of depreciation for the double-declining balance method.

31. (c) Composite (group) depreciation averages the service life of a number of property units and depreciates the group as if it were a single unit. The term "group" is used when the assets are similar; the term "composite" is used when they are dissimilar. The mechanical application of both of these methods is identical. The depreciation rate is the following ratio:

$$\frac{\text{Sum of annual SL depreciation of individual assets}}{\text{Total asset cost}}$$

Thus, both group and composite depreciation utilize the straight-line depreciation method. Therefore, answer (c) is correct, and answers (a), (b), and (d) are incorrect.

32. (b) The solutions approach is to prepare the journal entry that would be made when an asset is retired under the composite depreciation method.

Cash	(cash proceeds)	
Accum. dep.	(plug)	
Truck		(original cost)

The net decrease in the carrying amount of the assets is the credit to the asset account less the plug to accumulated depreciation. This amount would be equal to the **cash proceeds received**. Therefore, answer (b) is correct and answers (a), (c), and (d) are incorrect.

G. Disposals and Impairment of Value

33. (d) SFAS 121, para 15, requires that when management plans to dispose of long-lived assets and certain identifiable intangibles, the assets shall be reported at the lower of carrying amount or fair value less cost to sell. Therefore, answer (d) is correct.

34. (b) Per SFAS 121, para 18, losses associated with long-lived assets which are to be disposed of are to be reported as a component of income from continuing operations before income taxes for entities preparing income statements. Therefore, answer (b) is correct. Answer (a) is incorrect because losses on long-lived assets to be disposed of are neither unusual nor infrequent occurrences. Answer (c) is incorrect because these losses are not part of selling or general and administrative expenses and they are not disclosed net of tax. Discontinued operations result from disposal of a business segment or a line of business, not the disposal of long-lived assets held for resale; therefore answer (d) is incorrect.

35. (d) In 1998, Taft recognized a loss on the long-lived assets that were to be sold and changed the carrying amount of these assets to fair value less cost to sell. In 1999, the assets have still not been sold. The loss recognized has been more than recovered. Per SFAS 121, subsequent revisions in estimates of fair value less cost to sell shall be reported as adjustments of the carrying amount of an asset to be disposed of. However, the carrying amount may not be increased above the carrying amount prior to impairment. The same amount recognized as a loss in 1998 would be recognized as a recovery (gain) in the 1999 income statement. Therefore, answer (d) is correct.

36. (c) The requirement is to determine when an asset is impaired. An asset is impaired when the sum of the ex-

pected future cash flows is less than the carrying amount of the asset. Per SFAS 121, the expected future cash flows are **not** discounted and do not consider interest charges. Answer (c) refers to one way to measure a loss once it has been determined that an asset has been impaired.

37. (b) Under SFAS 121, when an asset has been determined to be impaired, it is written down to fair value and loss on impairment is recognized. SFAS 121 specifically states that restoration of previously recognized impairment losses is prohibited.

38. (a) The undiscounted expected future cash flows ($175,000) are less than the carrying amount of the equipment ($200,000). Therefore, the equipment is deemed impaired. The impairment loss is calculated in the following way:

Carrying amount of the equipment on December 31, 1999	$200,000
Fair value of the equipment on December 31, 1999	125,000
Impairment loss reported on 1999 income statement	$ 75,000

39. (b) According to SFAS 121, paragraph 11, "after an impairment loss is recognized, the reduced carrying amount of the asset shall be accounted for as its new cost." This new cost (the fair value of the asset at the date of impairment, or $135,000) shall be depreciated over the asset's remaining useful life (27 months). Therefore, the depreciation expense for June is $5,000 ($135,000 ÷ 27 months x 1 month).

40. (b) Per para 11 of SFAS 121, recoveries of impairment losses shall not be recognized. Therefore, answer (b) is correct and answers (a), (c), and (d) are incorrect.

H. Depletion

41. (b) The depletion charge per unit is the **depletion base** (net cost of the resource) divided by the **estimated units of the resource**. Vorst's depletion base is $2,880,000, as computed below.

Cost of mine	$2,640,000
Development cost	360,000
Restoration cost	180,000
Residual value	(300,000)
	$2,880,000

Therefore, the depletion charge is $2.40 per ton ($2,880,000 ÷ 1,200,000 tons). Since 60,000 tons were removed and sold, depletion of $144,000 (60,000 x $2.40) is included in Vorst's 1999 income statement. Note that the amount of depletion included in the income statement depends on the tons **sold**. If more tons were removed than sold, part of the depletion would be included in the cost of ending inventory rather than in the income statement.

J. Intangible Assets (APB 17)

42. (d) Judd Company would record the trademark at its cost of $500,000. The unamortized cost on the seller's books ($380,000) is irrelevant to the buyer. Although the trademark has a remaining useful life of 50 years, intangible assets must be amortized over a maximum period of 40 years per para 29 of APB 17. Therefore, the 1999 amortization expense and 12/31/99 accumulated amortization is $12,500 ($500,000 ÷ 40 years).

43.   (b)   Para 24 of APB 17 states that a company should record as an asset the cost of intangible assets such as goodwill **acquired from other entities**. Para 24 also states that **costs of developing** intangible assets such as goodwill "which are not specifically identifiable, have indeterminate lives, or are inherent in a continuing business and related to an enterprise as a whole" should be expensed when incurred. Therefore, only the $200,000 (and not the additional $80,000) should be capitalized as goodwill. Amortization at 12/31/99 is recorded using the best estimate of useful life at that time (40 years). Therefore, the net amount reported for goodwill at 12/31/99 is $195,000 [$200,000 – ($200,000 x 1/40)].

AUTHOR'S NOTE: This question is confusing because the $80,000 expenditure that must be expensed apparently extended the goodwill's life.

44.   (c)   Goodwill should be allocated to the long-lived assets and identifiable intangible assets being tested for recoverability on a pro rata basis using the relative fair values of the long-lived assets and identifiable intangibles acquired at the acquisition date. In Carver's case, the amount of goodwill that should be allocated is $30,000, not $50,000. The amount of goodwill allocated is the unamortized balance on the date recoverability is being tested. Since Carver was amortizing goodwill over a 5-year period, the unamortized balance of goodwill on December 31, 1999, was $30,000. This amount should be allocated to the long-lived assets and identifiable intangibles using the relative fair values of these assets on January 2, 1998. This allocation is shown below.

Goodwill allocated to long-lived assets

$720,000/$900,000   x $30,000   = $24,000

Goodwill allocated to identifiable intangibles

$180,000/$900,000   x $30,000   = $ 6,000

The amounts allocated to long-lived assets and identifiable intangible assets would be added to the carrying amounts of the assets ($720,000 and $180,000 reduced by depreciation and amoritization respectively) before performing the test for recoverability.

45.   (c)   Before 1999, Lava would record total amortization of $27,000 [($90,000 x 1/10) x 3 years], resulting in a 12/31/98 carrying amount of $63,000 ($90,000 – $27,000). Since the patent became worthless at 12/31/99 due to government prohibition of the product, the entire carrying amount ($63,000) should be charged against income in 1999.

46.   (a)   Because Malden has a weak case on patent A34, the legal fees incurred in its defense should be expensed, rather than capitalized as an asset. This is in accordance with the doctrine of conservatism. As a result of this occurrence, Malden should also consider whether the patent will provide benefit to future periods. Malden has a strong case in regard to patent B19, however, and can expect to receive benefits in the future as a result of its successful defense. Consequently, the legal fees to stop infringement on B19 should be capitalized as an asset and answers (b), (c), and (d) are incorrect.

47.   (a)   Costs incurred in connection with securing a patent, as well as attorney's fees and other unrecovered costs of a successful legal suit to protect the patent, can be capitalized as part of patent costs. Therefore, answer (a) is correct because legal fees and other costs incurred to successfully defend a patent should be amortized along with the acquisition cost over the remaining economic life of the patent. Answer (b) is incorrect because legal fees and other direct costs incurred in registering a patent should be capitalized and amortized on a straight-line basis over its economic life, not 5 years. Answers (c) and (d) are incorrect because research and development costs related to the development of the product, process or idea that is subsequently patented must be expensed as incurred, not capitalized and amortized.

K. Deferred Charges

48.   (b)   Organization costs are those incurred in the formation of a corporation. Since these costs will benefit the company in future years, they are properly recorded as an intangible asset to be amortized over a designated period of time. Income tax regulations require that organization costs be amortized over a period of at least 5 years. Therefore, the maximum allowable deduction for tax purposes is 1/5 of cost. If Kew chooses this basis, 1/5 of the cost is expensed in 1999 while 4/5 is deferred to later years (4/5 x $24,000 = $19,200).

L. Research and Development Costs (SFAS 2)

49.   (d)   Research and development (R&D) costs are defined in para 8 of SFAS 2. Paras 9 and 10 provide detailed lists of examples of activities that would be included in R&D costs and expenses (para 9), and that would be excluded from R&D costs and possibly capitalized (para 10). Among those items listed as being part of R&D costs are design of tools, jigs, molds, and dies involving new technology ($125,000) and modification of the formulation of a process ($160,000), for a total R&D expense of $285,000. Included in the items listed in SFAS 2 as **not** being part of R&D costs are troubleshooting breakdowns during production ($100,000), and adaptation of existing capability for a specific customer ($110,000).

50.   (b)   Per SFAS 2, all R&D costs must be expensed when incurred. However, R&D costs incurred when performing R&D work under contract for other entities are specifically excluded from the requirements of SFAS 2. Generally such costs are deferred and matched with revenue under the completed-contract or percentage-of-completion method. The other costs listed would all be expensed in 1999. Therefore, Ball's 1999 research and development expense is $1,380,000 ($300,000 + $700,000 + $200,000 + $180,000).

51. **(c)** Per SFAS 2, all R&D costs are to be charged to expense when incurred. SFAS 2 specifically includes as R&D costs the cost of designing, constructing, and testing preproduction prototypes, and the cost of R&D equipment (unless it has alternative future uses). Therefore, $340,000 ($60,000 + $200,000 + $80,000) is classified as R&D costs and expensed. The legal costs incurred to obtain a patent ($10,000) are capitalized in the patents account.

52. **(d)** In SFAS 2, the FASB excludes from its definitions of research and development expense the acquisition, development, or improvement of a product or process for use in its **selling or administrative activities**. Both costs given in this problem relate to selling or administrative activities, so the expenditures of $175,000 would not be reported as research and development expense.

53. **(a)** SFAS 2 requires research and development costs to be expensed as incurred except for fixed assets, intangible assets, or materials purchased that have alternative future uses. Tambon purchased equipment to be used for research and development, but the equipment can only be used for that project. Therefore, the cost of the equipment must be expensed in 1999 as it has no alternative future uses, and answer (a) is correct.

M. Computer Software Costs (SFAS 86)

54. **(b)** Costs incurred in creating a computer software product should be charged to research and development expense when incurred until **technological feasibility** has been established for the product. Technological feasibility is established upon completion of a detailed program design or working model. In this case, $23,000 would be recorded as expense ($13,000 for completion of detailed program design and $10,000 for coding and testing to establish technological feasibility). Costs incurred from the point of technological feasibility until the time when product costs are incurred are capitalized as software costs. In this situation, $59,000 is capitalized as software cost ($24,000 + $20,000 + $15,000). Product costs which can be easily associated with the inventory items are reported as inventory (in this case, $25,000 for duplication of computer software and training materials and $9,000 of packaging costs, for a total of $34,000).

55. **(c)** Costs incurred in creating a computer software product should be charged to research and development expense when incurred until **technological feasibility** has been established. Technological feasibility is established upon completion of a detailed program design or working model. In this case, $23,000 would be recorded as expense ($13,000 for completion of detailed program design and $10,000 for coding and testing to establish technological feasibility). Costs incurred from the point of technological feasibility until the time when product costs are incurred are capitalized as software costs. In this situation, $59,000 is capitalized as software cost ($24,000 + $20,000 + $15,000). Product costs which can be easily associated with the inventory items are reported as inventory (in this case, $25,000 for duplication of computer software and training materials and $9,000 of packaging costs, for a total of $34,000).

N. Development Stage Enterprises

56. **(a)** Per SFAS 86, para 8, the annual amortization of capitalized software costs shall be the greater of

1. The ratio of the software's current sales to its expected total sales, or
2. The straight-line method over the economic life of the product.

In this case, the ratio of current to expected total sales is 30% (given). The annual straight-line rate is 20% per year (1 ÷ economic life of 5 years). The 30% amortization should be recorded in 1999, since it is the higher of the two. The unamortized cost on the 12/31/99 balance sheet should, therefore, be 70% (100% – 30% amortization), which is answer (a). Note that para 10 of SFAS 86 requires that the unamortized cost of capitalized software products must be compared to the net realizable value of those assets at each balance sheet date. Any excess of the amortized cost over the net realizable value must be written off. In this case, the net realizable value (90%) was **above** the unamortized cost (70%), so no additional write-off was required.

57. **(d)** Costs incurred in the formation of a corporation such as legal fees, state fees of various sorts, and certain promotional expenditures may be capitalized as **organization costs** and amortized over the period of benefit. Costs associated with initial stock offerings may be treated as a reduction of paid-in capital or, alternatively, capitalized as an organizational cost. Although both methods are accepted by the SEC, the treatment of these costs as a reduction in paid-in capital predominates. Thus, Tanker Oil Co. may capitalize $55,000. The costs of exploration and purchases of mineral rights may be expensed or capitalized as part of the cost of natural resources. The fact that Tanker is a development stage enterprise has no effect on the amount capitalized. SFAS 7 requires development stage companies to capitalize costs in the same manner as companies carrying on normal operations. Thus, answer (d) is correct.

58. **(a)** Per SFAS 7, para 11b, a development stage enterprise shall follow the same revenue and expense recognition principles and issue the same basic financial statements as an established operating enterprise, but shall disclose certain additional information. Therefore, answer (a) is correct. Answers (b), (c), and (d) are incorrect because per SFAS 7, para 10, a development stage company shall use the same generally accepted accounting principles that apply to established operating enterprises to govern the recognition of revenue and to determine whether a cost is to be capitalized or expensed as incurred.

59. **(c)** Per SFAS 7, para 11b, a development stage enterprise shall issue the same basic financial statements as an established operating enterprise, but shall disclose certain additional information. An income statement, in addition to showing amounts of revenues and expenses for each period covered by the income statement, shall include the cumulative amounts from the enterprise's inception. Therefore, answer (c) is correct.

OTHER OBJECTIVE ANSWERS AND ANSWER EXPLANATIONS

Problem 1

Items 1 through 6 represent questions concerning expenditures for goods held for resale and equipment and whether these expenditures should be capitalized or expensed as a period cost. The general concept which determines whether expenditures should be product costs and, therefore, capitalized or expensed as period costs is whether or not these expenditures "attach" themselves to the assets of inventory or equipment. Costs that "attach" themselves to assets are those that are directly connected with bringing the goods or equipment to the place of business of the buyer and converting such goods to a salable (inventory) or unusable (equipment) condition.

1. **(C)** Freight charges are directly connected with bringing the goods to the place of business of the buyer.

2. **(C)** Insurance charges are directly connected with bringing the goods to the place of business of the buyer.

3. **(E)** Only interest costs related to continued assets constructed for internal use or assets produced as discrete products for sale or lease should be capitalized. The informational benefit of capitalization does not justify the cost of the accounting for the interest as a product cost.

4. **(C)** Direct cost of bringing the equipment to the buyer.

5. **(C)** Direct cost of converting the equipment to a usable condition.

6. **(E)** Does not relate to bringing the equipment to the buyer or putting it into a usable condition.

7. **(600,000)** Since the land and building were purchased together, the cost of each must be allocated based on the relative market value. The land and building were purchased together for a total cost of $1,000,000 ($800,000 cash + $200,000 mortgage assumption). For property tax purposes, the building is deemed to be 60% of the value of the land and building. Therefore, the cost of the building should be recorded at $600,000 ($1,000,000 x 60%).

8. **(503,000)** As the lease is classified as a capital lease, Link must record an asset and liability based on the present value of the minimum lease payments. However, the leased assets cannot be recorded at an amount greater than the fair value. To determine the minimum value of the lease payments, Link should discount the future payments using the **lesser** of the lessee's (Link's) incremental borrowing rate (9%) or the lessor's implicit rate if **known** by the lessee. Therefore, since Link does not know the lessor's implicit rate, Link's rate of 9% should be used. The recorded value would be $100,000 x 5.03 = $503,000, which is less than the fair value.

9. **(370,000)** In recording a nonmonetary exchange, the asset received is recorded at the book value of the asset given up plus any boot given when gains and losses are not recognized. Gains and losses are not recognized when the earnings process is not considered complete (when **similar** assets are exchanged), and when the gain or loss cannot be computed. In Link's case, the earnings process is not complete as similar assets are being exchanged. The following fact pattern exists for Link:

	Boot	*FV*	*BV*	*Gain (Loss)*
Land given	50,000	450,000	320,000	130,000
Land received		500,000		

Link will record the land received from Club at the book value of the land given up plus the boot given ($320,000 + 50,000 = $370,000).

An alternative method to calculate the value to record the land at is to subtract the deferred gain from the fair value of the land received ($500,000 – 130,000 = $370,000).

10. **(315,000)** On Club's books the following situation exists:

	Boot	*FV*	*BV*	*Gain (Loss)*
Land given		500,000	350,000	150,000
Land received	50,000	450,000		

An exception to the nonrecognition of gain on similar assets exists when boot is received. The earnings process is considered complete for the portion related to the boot received, but not complete for the portion related to the asset received. A gain is recognized only for the portion related to the boot. The gain is computed as follows:

$$\left(\frac{\text{Boot}}{\text{Boot} + \text{FV of asset received}}\right) \quad \text{x} \quad \text{Total gain} \quad = \quad \text{Gain recognized}$$

$$\left(\frac{50,000}{50,000 + 450,000}\right) \quad \text{x} \quad 150,000 \quad = \quad \$15,000$$

The land received will be recorded at its fair value less the gain deferred.

$450,000 – (150,000 – 15,000) = $315,000.

An alternative method is to record the land received at the book value of the land given less the boot received plus the gain recognized, as follows:

$350,000 - 50,000 + 15,000 = $315,000.

11.   (90,000)   Under the straight-line method of depreciation, the depreciation expense would be calculated as follows:

$$\frac{\text{Cost Salvage value}}{\text{Estimated life}} = \frac{\$864,000 - 144,000}{8} = \$90,000$$

Depreciation expense would be $90,000 for all 8 years, 1996-2003.

12.   (162,000)   The double-declining balance method is calculated by taking two times the straight-line rate times the net book value at the beginning of each year, but not below the salvage value. Furthermore the salvage value is not deducted to arrive at the depreciable base. The calculation would be as follows:

	NBV		*Depreciation expense*
1998	$864,000 x (1/8 x 2)	=	$216,000
1999	($864,000 – 216,000) x (1/8 x 2)	=	$162,000

13.   (140,000)   Under the sum-of-the-years' digits method, the depreciation expense is calculated as follows:

1998	$8 \div \left[\dfrac{8(8+1)}{2}\right]$	x	($864,000 – $144,000)	=	$160,000
1999	$(7 \div 36)$	x	($864,000 – $144,000)	=	$140,000

14.   (120,000)   The units of production method is a type of physical usage depreciation that is based on activity. The formula is as follows:

$$\frac{\text{Current activity/output}}{\text{Total expected activity/output}} \quad x \quad \text{Depreciable base} \quad = \quad \text{Annual depreciation}$$

Depreciation expense for 1997 is calculated as follows:

$$\frac{300,000 \text{ units}}{1,800,000 \text{ units}} \quad x \quad (\$864,000 - \$144,000) \quad = \quad \$120,000$$

ANSWER OUTLINE

Problem 1   Replacement of Components; Accelerated Depreciation; Inventory Method of Depreciation

a.   1.   Old engines' costs **known**

- Remove old engines' costs and accumulated depreciation from account balances
- Record current asset (prepaid repairs and maintenance) at FMV of old engines
- Operating gain/loss = difference between old engines' carrying value and fair value
- Record new engines and related liability at new engines' cost

2.   Old engines' costs **unknown**

- Record current asset (prepaid repairs and maintenance) at FMV of old engines
- Increase snowmobiles account by difference between new engines' costs and old engines' fair value or
- Decrease accumulated depreciation by same amount
- Record liability at new engines' cost

b.   1.   Assumptions underlying use of accelerated depreciation

- Asset productivity greater in earlier years
- Provides a more constant cost over the years
- Avoids risk of obsolescence

2.   Depreciation expense = double the straight-line rate times book value

c.   Balance Sheet

- Report as noncurrent asset
- Record amount equal to physical quantities of items times an appraised amount

Income Statement

- Report depreciation expense
- Depreciation exp. = BI + Purchases – EI

UNOFFICIAL ANSWER

Problem 1   Replacement of Components; Accelerated Depreciation; Inventory Method of Depreciation

a.   1.   When the old engines' costs are known, the snowmobiles account is decreased by the old engines' costs, and accumulated depreciation is decreased by the accumulated depreciation on the old engines. A current asset would be recorded for the fair value of the future repair and maintenance services. The net difference between the old engines' carrying amounts and their fair values is recorded as an operating gain or loss. To record the new engines' acquisition, both the snowmobiles account and accounts payable are increased by the new engines' costs.

2.   If the old engines' costs are unknown, then either the snowmobiles account would be increased or accumulated depreciation would be decreased by the difference

between the new engines' costs and the old engines' fair values.

b.   1.   Assumptions underlying use of an accelerated depreciation method include

- An asset is more productive in the earlier years of its estimated useful life. Therefore, greater depreciation charges in the earlier years would be matched against the greater revenues generated in the earlier years.
- Repair and maintenance costs are often higher in later periods and an accelerated depreciation method results in a more nearly annual constant total cost over the years of use.
- An asset may become obsolete before the end of its originally estimated useful life. The risk associated with estimated long-term cash flows is greater than the risk associated with near-term cash flows. Accelerated depreciation recognizes this condition.

2.   Winter should calculate snowmobile depreciation by applying twice the straight-line rate to their carrying amounts.

c.   Under the inventory (appraisal) method, Winter calculates the ending undepreciated cost on the skis, poles, and boots by multiplying the physical quantities of these items on hand by an appraised amount. This ending undepreciated cost is classified as a noncurrent asset. Depreciation included in continuing operations equals the sum of the beginning balance and purchases for the year less the ending undepreciated cost.

ANSWER OUTLINE

Problem 2   Selection of Deprec. Method, Nonmonetary Exchange, and Composite Deprec. Method

a.   Factors influencing selection of SL method
   Equal amounts of asset's service potential used each period
   If reasons for decline in service potential are unclear, other reasons are
      Ease of recordkeeping
      Use of SL for similar assets
      Use by others in industry

b.   Accounting for the truck exchange
   First, record AD to date of exchange
   Then, if original truck's carrying value > FMV:

Truck (new)	xxx	(Recorded at FMV)
Loss	xxx	(Part of income from continuing operations)
AD	xxx	
Truck (old)		xxx } (Original truck's carrying value)
Cash		xxx

If original truck's carrying value is < FMV:

Truck (new)	xxx	(FMV – unrecognized gain)
AD	xxx	
Truck (old)		xxx } (Original truck's carrying value)
Cash		xxx

Gain not recognized, but decreases carrying value of new truck

c. 1. Benefits derived from using composite method
        Bookkeeping greatly simplified
        Avoids income fluctuations as result of recognizing gains (losses) on dispositions
        Unrecognized losses on early dispositions offset by continuing depreciation on machines used beyond average life

2. Calculation of manufacturing machinery's annual depreciation expense

(a) $\dfrac{\text{Depreciable cost (C – RV) for a single machine}}{\text{Estimated life for that machine}}$

     = Annual S-L depreciation for each machine

(b) $\dfrac{\text{S Annual depreciation for each machine}}{\text{S Individual capitalized cost}}$

     = Annual composite depreciation rate (%)

UNOFFICIAL ANSWER

Problem 2   Selection of Deprec. Method, Nonmonetary Exchange, and Composite Deprec. Method

a.   Portland should have selected the straight-line depreciation method when approximately the same amount of an asset's service potential is used up each period. If the reasons for the decline in service potential are unclear, then the selection of the straight-line method could be influenced by the ease of recordkeeping, its use for similar assets, and its use by others in the industry.

b.   Portland should record depreciation expense to the date of the exchange. If the original truck's carrying amount is greater than its fair value, a loss results. The truck's capitalized cost and accumulated depreciation are eliminated, and the loss on trade-in is reported as part of income from continuing operations. The newly acquired truck is recorded at fair value. If the original truck's carrying amount is less than its fair value at trade-in, then there is an unrecognized gain. The newly acquired truck is recorded at fair value less the unrecognized gain. Cash is decreased by the amount paid.

c. 1.   By associating depreciation with a group of machines instead of each individual machine, Portland's bookkeeping process is greatly simplified. Also, since actual machine lives vary from the average depreciable life, unrecognized net losses on early dispositions are expected to be offset by continuing depreciation on machines usable beyond the average depreciable life. Periodic income does not fluctuate as a result of recognizing gains and losses on manufacturing machine dispositions.

2.   Portland should divide the depreciable cost (capitalized cost less residual value) of each machine by its estimated life to obtain its annual depreciation. The sum of the individual annual depreciation amounts should then be divided by the sum of the individual capitalized costs to obtain the annual composite depreciation rate.

ANSWER OUTLINE

Problem 3   Impairment

a.   Asset impaired if carry. amt. not recoverable

b.   One or more factors indicate possible impairment

- FMV decline
- Δ in asset use or physical Δ.
- Legal factors, Δ business climate, or regular action
- Asset cost > planned
- Operating (xxx) or cash flow (xxx)

If possible impairment indicated, do recoverability test
Σ fut. cash flows < or > carry. amt.
If cash flows
< carry amt., assets impaired
> carry amt,, assets not impaired
If impairment confirmed by recoverability test, measure loss
Fair value – Carry. amt.

c.   Current period
Impairment loss   xx
A/D   xx
Future periods
Recognize additional losses
Recoveries prohibited
Losses reported in income from cont. oper.

d.   Compare NRV to carry. amt.
Report lower amt.
Loss = Carry. amt. – NRV
Asset no longer depreciated
Recoveries in future periods recognized limited to previous losses
Report losses in continuing operations income
Report assets under other assets

UNOFFICIAL ANSWER

Problem 3   Impairment

a.   An operational asset is impaired if some or all of the carrying amount of that asset will not be recovered.

b.   An asset could be impaired if one or more of the following conditions exists:

- Significant decrease in market value
- Change in way asset used or physical change in asset
- Legal factors or change in business climate that might affect asset's fair value or adverse action or assessment by regulator
- Asset cost incurred greater than planned
- Operating or cash flow losses from the asset

If a least one of these conditions exist, a recoverability test shall be performed. Under this test, a loss on operational assets shall be recognized if the expected total net future cash flows are less than the carrying amounts of the assets. Assets should be grouped at lowest level for which there are identifiable cash flows independent of other groupings. Expected net future cash flows are future cash inflows to be generated by the assets less the future cash outflows expected to be necessary to obtain those inflows. Expected future cash flows are not discounted. If the ability to recover the asset is not demonstrated (sum of future cash flows < carrying amount) a loss shall be measured and recorded. The loss is measured as the difference between the fair value of the asset(s) and the carrying amount.

c. A loss is recognized in the current period by a debit to an impairment loss account and a credit to accumulated depreciation. In future periods, if additional impairment is confirmed, an additional loss shall be recognized. However, recoveries of losses recognized in prior periods are not permitted. Impairment losses are reported in income from continuing operations.

d. In situations in which management has made a decision to dispose of an asset, such asset should be recorded at the lower of the asset's carrying amount or net realizable value (NRV). These assets shall no longer be depreciated. In future periods, recoveries are permitted, but are limited to losses previously recognized on these assets. Losses recognized are reported as part of income from continuing operations. The assets to be disposed of shall be reported under other assets on the company's balance sheet.

ANSWER OUTLINE

Problem 4   Intangible Assets

a.   1.   Characteristics of intangible assets

- Lack physical existence
- Value difficult to estimate
- High degree of uncertainty concerning future benefits

Purchased intangibles

- Record at cost

Internally generated intangibles

- Expense currently

2.   Amortized over useful lives
Factors affecting useful life

- Legal life
- Contractual provisions
- Effects of obsolescence, demand, etc.
- Expected actions of competitors
- Other economic factors

Useful life may be indefinite

- Set arbitrarily at 40 years or less
- Justified because value will become zero at an unknown time

3.   Disclose method and period of amortization

b.   1.   Part (b) consists of two requirements: a schedule showing the intangibles section of Broca's 12/31/99 balance sheet, and a schedule showing the related expenses that would appear on Broca's 1999 income statement. The solutions approach for problems in which the requirements are interrelated is to make all the computations for each item at one time. After making the computations, label each computation according to the requirement (BS = balance sheet, IS = income statement) to which it relates.

2.   In a purchase, the net assets acquired are recorded at their FMV. The excess of the cost of the investment ($360,000) over the FMV of the net assets acquired ($172,000) is allocated to goodwill

($360,000 – $172,000 = $188,000). Intangible assets with an indeterminate or unlimited life, such as this goodwill, must be amortized over a period not to exceed 40 years ($188,000 x 1/40 = $4,700 amortization). The goodwill is reported in the 12/31/99 balance at its cost less accumulated amortization ($188,000 – $4,700 = $183,300).

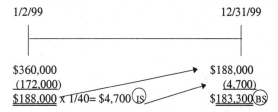

3.   The franchise acquired on 2/1/99 is recorded at its cost of $60,000. Since Broca amortizes all intangibles on a straight-line basis, and takes a full year's amortization in the year of acquisition, 1999 amortization is $12,000 ($60,000 x 1/5), and the franchise is reported at cost less accumulated amortization at 12/31/99 ($60,000 – $12,000 = $48,000). In addition to the amortization expense, there is also an annual fee which must be expensed, equal to 1% of ferry revenues. For 1999, this fee is $200 ($20,000 x 1%).

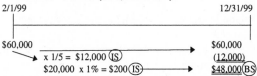

4.   Patents are initially recorded at cost of acquisition, which is purchase price for a purchased patent, or legal and other costs of registration ($51,000) for an internally generated patent. Legal fees incurred in **successfully** defending the patent ($85,000) are also capitalized because such fees help establish the legal right of the holder to any future benefits that will be derived from the patent. Therefore, this patent is capitalized at a total amount of $136,000 ($51,000 + $85,000). Since Broca amortizes all intangibles on a straight-line basis and takes a full 9amortization is $13,600 ($136,000 x1/10). The patent is reported at cost less accumulated amortization at 12/31/99 ($136,000 – $13,600 = $122,400).

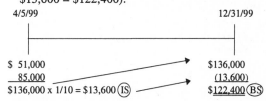

UNOFFICIAL ANSWER

Problem 4   Intangible Assets

a.   1.   The main characteristics of intangible assets are their lack of physical substance, the difficulty of estimating their value, and the high degree of uncertainty regarding their future life. Accounting for intangible assets depends on whether they have been purchased or developed internally.

Intangible assets purchased from others should be recorded at cost. The costs of developing intangible assets with indeterminable lives, such as goodwill, are ordinarily not distinguishable from the current costs of operations and thus are not assignable to specific assets but are expensed immediately.

2. Intangible assets should be amortized over their estimated useful life. Estimated useful life should be determined by consideration of such factors as legal life; provisions for renewal or extensions of contracts; the effects of obsolescence, demand, and competition; and other economic factors.

An apparently unlimited useful life may in fact be indefinite. The justification for amortizing the cost of goodwill or other intangible assets with an indeterminate life over time is that the value almost inevitably becomes zero at some future date. Since the date at which the value becomes zero is indeterminable, the useful life has been set arbitrarily at a period not to exceed 40 years.

3. The financial statements should disclose the method and period of amortization of all intangible assets.

b. *Broca Co.*
INTANGIBLES SECTION OF BALANCE SHEET
December 31, 1999

Goodwill, net of accumulated amortization of $4,700	$183,300	[1]
Franchise, net of accumulated amortization of $12,000	48,000	[2]
Patent, net of accumulated amortization of $13,600	122,400	[3]

[1]	Cash paid	$360,000
	Value of net assets	(172,000)
	Goodwill	188,000
	Amortization over 40 years	(4,700)
	Balance	$183,300
[2]	Franchise	$60,000
	Amortization over 5 years	(12,000)
	Balance	$48,000
[3]	Legal costs ($51,000 + $85,000)	$136,000
	Amortization over 10 years	(13,600)
	Balance	$122,400

EXPENSES RESULTING FROM INTANGIBLES
For the Year Ended December 31, 1999

Amortization:		
	Goodwill	$ 4,700
	Franchise	12,000
	Patent	13,600
		$30,300
Franchise fee		200
		$30,500

ANSWER OUTLINE

Problem 5   R&D Costs

a.   **1.**   Asset characteristics
         Probable future benefit in form of net cash inflows

Obtain benefit and control access to it
         Transaction or event that gives entity right to or control of benefit has already occurred

2.   Intent to produce the product, presuming future net cash inflows
         Patent enables control of benefits
         Consequences of past events (R&D)

3.   Future benefits are uncertain and difficult to measure as R&D expenditures incurred

b.   **1.**   Equipment exclusively for R&D
         Expensed on IS as R&D in period incurred
         Equipment used for R&R and production
            Capitalize as fixed assets less accumulation depr. on BS for 1996 through 1999
            Depreciate asset from 1996 to 1999 as R&D expense in IS
            Depreciation for 1999 should be added to cost of inventory, via overhead, and expensed as CGS in the IS

2.   Cash payments for pilot plant as cash outflow in operating activities in 1997 SCF
         Cash received from sale as cash inflow from operating activities in 1998 SCF

UNOFFICIAL ANSWER

Problem 5   R&D Costs

a.   **1.**   According to the FASB conceptual framework, the three essential characteristics of an asset are

•   It embodies a probable future benefit that involves a capacity to contribute to future net cash inflows.

•   A particular entity can obtain the benefit and control others' access to it.

•   The transaction or other event giving rise to the entity's right to or control of the benefit has already occurred.

2.   Mono's project expenditures through 1996 meet the FASB conceptual framework's three essential characteristics of an asset as follows:

•   Since Mono intends to produce the product, it presumably anticipates future net cash inflows.

•   Mono has obtained a patent that will enable it to control the benefits arising from the product.

•   The control is a consequence of past events.

3.   It is difficult to justify the classification of research and development expenditures as assets because at the time expenditures are made the future benefits are uncertain, and difficult to measure.

b.   **1.**   Expenditures for equipment to be used exclusively for research and development should be reported as research and development expense in the period incurred. Expenditures for equipment to be used both for research and development and for production should be capitalized and reported as fixed assets, less accumulated depreciation, on Mono's balance sheets from 1996 through 1999. An appropriate depreciation method should be used, with depreciation from 1996 through 1999 reported as research and development expense. Depreciation for 1999 should be added to cost of inventory, via factory overhead, and expensed as cost of goods sold.

2. Cash payments for the pilot plant construction should be reported as cash outflows from operating activities on Mono's 1997 statement of cash flows. Cash received from the sale of the pilot plant should be reported as a cash inflow from operating activities on Mono's 1998 statement of cash flows.

MONETARY CURRENT ASSETS AND CURRENT LIABILITIES

Chapter 3A of ARB 43 defines current assets and current liabilities. This study module reviews the accounting for current assets (except inventory which is presented in Module 23 and short-term investments which are presented in Module 29). This module also reviews current liabilities.

A. Cash

Per SFAS 95 (see outline), the definition of cash includes both cash (cash on hand and demand deposits) and cash equivalents (short-term, highly liquid investments). Cash equivalents have to be readily convertible into cash and so near maturity that they carry little risk of changing in value due to interest rate changes. Generally this will include only those investments with original maturities of 3 months or less from the **date of purchase** by the enterprise. Common examples of cash equivalents include Treasury bills, commercial paper, and money market funds. Unrestricted cash and cash equivalents available for general use are presented as the first current asset.

Cash set aside for special uses is usually disclosed separately. The entry to set up a special fund is

Special cash fund	xx	
Cash		xx

Cash restricted as to use (e.g., not transferable out of a foreign country) should be disclosed separately, but not as a current asset if it cannot be used in the next year (this is true of special funds also).

Imprest (petty) cash funds are generally included in the total cash figure, but unreimbursed expense vouchers are excluded.

1. Bank reconciliations

Bank reconciliations are prepared by bank depositors when they receive their monthly bank statements. The reconciliation is made to determine any required adjustments to the cash balance. Two types of reconciling items are possible.

a. Reconciling items not requiring adjustment on the books (type A)
b. Reconciling items requiring adjustment on the books (type B)

There are three type A reconciling items. They do not require adjusting journal entries.

(1) Outstanding checks
(2) Deposits in transit
(3) Bank errors

All other reconciling items (type B) require adjusting journal entries. Examples of type B reconciling items include

(1) Unrecorded returned nonsufficient funds (NSF) checks
(2) Unrecorded bank charges
(3) Errors in the cash account
(4) Unrecorded bank collections of notes receivable

Two types of formats are used in bank reconciliations.

Format 1	*Format 2*
Balance per bank	Balance per bank
+(–) A adjustments	+(–) A adjustments
Correct cash balance	+(–) B adjustments
	Balance per books
Balance per books	+(–) B adjustments
+(–) B adjustments	Correct cash balance
Correct cash balance	

Type A and B adjustments can be either added or subtracted depending upon the type of format and the nature of the item.

Reconciling items must be analyzed to determine whether they are included in (1) the balance per bank, and/or (2) the balance per books. If they are included in one, but not the other, an adjustment is required. For instance, the $1,800 deposit in transit in the following example is included in the balance per books but not in the balance per bank. Thus, it must be added to the balance per bank to reconcile to the correct cash balance. Deposits in transit do not require an adjusting journal entry. Analyze all reconciling items in this manner, but remember, only journalize type B reconciling items.

SAMPLE BANK RECONCILIATION (FORMAT 1)

Per bank statement	$ 4,702
Deposits in transit	1,800
Outstanding checks	(1,200)
Bank error	50
Correct cash balance	$ 5,352
Per books	$ 5,332
Service charges	(5)
Note collected by bank	150
Customer's NSF check	(170)
Deposit of July 10 recorded as $749 instead of $794	45
Correct cash balance	$ 5,352

Note that the balance per bank and balance per books each are reconciled directly to the corrected balance.

a. **Adjusting journal entries**

All of the items in the per books section of a bank reconciliation (type B) require adjusting entries. The entries for the above example appear below.

Miscellaneous expense	5		AR	170	
Cash		5	Cash		170
Cash	150		Cash	45	
Notes receivable		150	AR (or sales)		45

b. **Four-column cash reconciliation**

Unlike the bank reconciliation above, which is as of a specific date, a four-column cash reconciliation, also known as a "proof of cash," reconciles bank and book cash balances over a specified time period. A proof of cash consists of four columns: beginning of the period bank reconciliation, receipts, disbursements, and end-of-the-period bank reconciliation. Thus, the proof of cash cross-foots as well as foots.

SAMPLE PROOF OF CASH (FORMAT 2)

	Bank reconciliation June 30, 1999	Receipts	Disbursements	Bank reconciliation July 31, 1999
Balance per bank statement	$3,402	$25,200	$23,900	$ 4,702
Deposits in transit				
June 30, 1999	1,610	(1,610)		
July 31, 1999		1,800		1,800
Outstanding checks				
June 30, 1999	(450)		(450)	
July 31, 1999			1,200	(1,200)
Service charges			(5)	5
Note collected by bank		(150)		(150)
Customer's NSF check			(170)	170
Deposit of July 10 recorded as $749 instead of $794		(45)		(45)
Bank error			(50)	50
Balance per books	$4,562	$25,195	$24,425	$ 5,332

Note that there are no type B reconciling items in the beginning reconciliation column. This is because the $4,562 has been adjusted when the June bank statement was reconciled. Notice that figures appearing in the center columns have unlike signs if they are adjacent and like signs if they are not adjacent to amounts in the side columns.

The purpose of the proof of cash is to disclose any irregularities, such as unrecorded disbursements and receipts within a month, which would not be detected by a bank reconciliation. For example, if the center two columns each required a negative $1,000 to make the top line reconcile with the bottom line, there may be unrecorded receipts and deposits of $1,000.

B. Receivables

Accounts receivable should be disclosed in the balance sheet at net realizable value (gross amount less estimated uncollectibles) by source (e.g., trade, officer, etc.). Officer, employee, and affiliate company receivables should be separately disclosed (ARB 43, chap 1A). Unearned interest and finance charges should be deducted from gross receivables (APB 6, para 14).

1. Anticipation of sales discounts

Cash discounts are generally recognized as expense when cash payment is received within the discount period. As long as cash discounts to be taken on year-end receivables remain constant from year to year, there is no problem. If, however, discounts on year-end receivables fluctuate, a year-end allowance can be set up or sales can be recorded net of the discounts. The entries to record sales at net are shown below in comparison to the sales recorded gross.

		Sales at net		*Sales at gross*	
a.	Sale	AR	(net)	AR	(gross)
		Sales	(net)	Sales	(gross)
b.	Cash receipt within discount period	Cash	(net)	Sales disc.	(disc.)
		AR	(net)	Cash	(net)
				AR	(gross)
c.	Cash receipt after discount period	Cash	(gross)	Cash	(gross)
		AR	(net)	AR	(gross)
		Disc. not taken	(disc.)		

The rationale for the net method is that sales are recorded at the cash equivalent amount and receivables nearer realizable value. Note that under both the net and gross methods, sales and accounts receivable are recorded net of trade discounts for the same reason. If a sales discount allowance method is used, the entry below is made with the gross method entries. The entry should be reversed.

Sales discounts	(expected disc. on year-end AR)
Allowance for sales disc.	(expected disc. on year-end AR)

Similarly, when using the "net method," an entry should be made to pick up discounts not expected to be taken on year-end receivables. Generally, however, these latter adjustments are not made, because they are assumed to be about the same each period.

2. **Bad debts expense**

There are two approaches to bad debts.

- Direct write-off method
- Allowance method

a. Under the direct write-off method, bad debts are considered expenses in the period in which they are written off. Note that this method is not considered acceptable under GAAP, unless the amounts are immaterial.

Bad debts expense	(uncollectible AR)
AR	(uncollectible AR)

b. The allowance method seeks to estimate the amount of uncollectible receivables, and establishes a contra valuation account (allowance for bad debts) for the amount estimated to be uncollectible. The adjusting entry to set up the allowance is

Bad debts expense	(estimated)
Allowance for bad debts	(estimated)

The entry to write off bad debts is

Allowance for bad debts	(uncollectible AR)
AR	(uncollectible AR)

There are two methods to determine the annual charge to bad debts expense.

   (1) Annual sales
   (2) Year-end AR

For example, charging bad debts expense for 1% of annual sales is based on the theory that bad debts are a function of sales; this method emphasizes the income statement.

Charging bad debts on year-end AR is based on the theory that bad debts are a function of AR collections during the period; this method emphasizes the balance sheet. A bad debts percentage can be applied to total AR or subsets of AR. Often an aging schedule is prepared for this purpose. An AR aging schedule classifies AR by their age (e.g., 30, 60, 90, 120, etc., days overdue).

When bad debts expense is estimated as a function of sales, any balance in the allowance account is ignored in making the adjusting entry. Bad debts expense under this method is simply the total amount computed (i.e., Sales x Percentage). However, when bad debts expense is estimated using outstanding receivables, the expense is the amount needed to adjust the allowance account to the amount computed (i.e., AR x Percentage[s]). Thus, bad debts expense under this method is the amount computed less any credit balance currently in the allowance account (or plus any debit balance).

Net accounts receivable is the balance in accounts receivable less the allowance for bad debts. Also remember that net receivables **do not change** when a specific account is written off since both accounts receivable and the allowance account are reduced by the same amount.

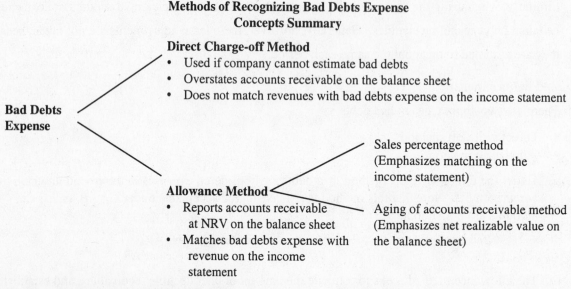

Methods of Recognizing Bad Debts Expense
Concepts Summary

Bad Debts Expense

Direct Charge-off Method
- Used if company cannot estimate bad debts
- Overstates accounts receivable on the balance sheet
- Does not match revenues with bad debts expense on the income statement

Allowance Method
- Reports accounts receivable at NRV on the balance sheet
- Matches bad debts expense with revenue on the income statement

Sales percentage method (Emphasizes matching on the income statement)

Aging of accounts receivable method (Emphasizes net realizable value on the balance sheet)

3. **Pledging, assigning, selling (factoring) AR**

Sometimes businesses cannot wait for the cash flow from the normal collection of AR.

Pledging of receivables. Pledging is an agreement where accounts receivable are used as collateral for loans. Generally, the lender has limited rights to inspect the borrower's records to achieve assurance that the receivables do exist. The customers whose accounts have been pledged are not aware of this event, and their payments are still remitted to the original obligee. The pledged accounts merely serve as security to the lender, giving comfort that sufficient assets exist which will generate cash flows adequate in amount and timing to repay the debt. However, the debt is paid by the borrower whether or not the pledged receivables are collected and whether or not the pattern of such collections matches the payments due on the debt.

The only accounting issue relating to pledging is that of adequate disclosure. The accounts receivable, which remain assets of the borrowing entity, continue to be shown as current assets in its financial statements but must be identified as having been pledged. This identification can be accomplished either parenthetically or by footnote disclosures. Similarly, the related debt should be identified as having been secured by the receivables.

Example of proper disclosure for pledged receivables

Current assets:
Accounts receivable, net of allowance for doubtful accounts of $600,000
   ($3,500,000 of which has been pledged as collateral for bank loans)   8,450,000

Current liabilities:
Bank loans payable (secured by pledged accounts receivable)   2,700,000

Assignment of receivables. The assignment of accounts receivable is a more formalized transfer of the asset to the lending institution. The lender will make an investigation of the specific receivables that are being proposed for assignment and will approve those which are deemed to be worthy as collateral. Customers are not usually aware that their accounts have been assigned and they continue to forward their payments to the original obligee. In some cases, the assignment agreement requires that collection proceeds be immediately delivered to the lender. The borrower is, however, the primary obligor and is required to make timely payment on the debt whether or not the receivables are collected as anticipated. The borrowing is with recourse, and the general credit of the borrower is pledged to the payment of the debt.

Since the lender knows that not all the receivables will be collected on a timely basis by the borrower, only a fraction of the face value of the receivables will be advanced as a loan to the borrower. Typically, this amount ranges from 70 to 90%, depending upon the credit history and collection experience of the borrower.

Assigned accounts receivable remain the assets of the borrower and continue to be presented in its financial statements, with appropriate disclosure of the assignment similar to that illustrated for pledging. Prepaid finance charges would be debited to a prepaid expense account and amortized to expense over the period to which the charges apply.

The journal entries for both the assignor and the assignee follow:

		Assignor	*Assignee*
a.	Cash is advanced for less than total AR assigned	AR assigned AR	Note receivable Finance revenue Cash
		Cash Finance charge Note payable	
b.	Cash is collected and remitted to finance company	Cash AR assigned	
		Note payable Cash	Cash Note receivable
c.	AR are written off	Allowance for doubtful accounts AR assigned	
d.	Financial statement presentation	Current assets: AR assigned Current liabilities: Note payable	Note receivable
e.	Additional cash is collected and note paid	Cash AR assigned	
		Note payable Interest expense Cash	Cash Note receivable Interest revenue
f.	Remainder of AR are transferred back	AR AR assigned	

The assignee discloses either parenthetically or in a footnote the amount of the assigned AR securing the loan.

Factoring of receivables.* This category of financing is the most significant in terms of accounting implications. Factoring traditionally has involved the outright sale of receivables to a financing institution known as a factor. These arrangements involved (1) notification to the customer to forward future payments to the factor and (2) the transfer of receivables **without recourse** which means that the factor assumes the risk of loss from noncollection. Thus, once a factoring arrangement is completed, the entity has no further involvement with the accounts, except for a return of merchandise. In its simplistic form, the receivables are sold and the difference between the cash received and the carrying value is recognized as a gain or loss.

The classical variety of factoring (i.e., without recourse) provides two financial services to the business: it permits the entity to obtain cash earlier and the risk of bad debts is transferred to the factor. The factor is compensated for each of the services. Interest is charged based on the anticipated length of time between the date the factoring is consummated and the expected collection date of the receivables sold. A fee is charged based upon the factor's anticipated bad debt losses.

Example

Thirsty Corp., on July 1, 1999, enters into an agreement with Rich Company to sell a group of its receivables **without recourse**. A total face value of $200,000 of accounts receivable are involved. The factor will charge 20% interest computed on the weighted-average time to maturity of the receivables of 36 days plus a 3% fee.

The entries required are as follows:

Cash	190,055	
Interest expense (or prepaid) (200,000 x .20 x 36/365)	3,945	
Factoring fee (200,000 x .03)	6,000	
Accounts receivable		200,000

The interest expense and factor's fee can be combined into a $9,945 loss on the sale of receivables.

Merchandise returns will normally be the responsibility of the original vendor, who must then make the appropriate settlement with the factor. To protect against the possibility of merchandise returns which diminish the total of receivables to be collected, very often a factoring arrangement will **not** advance the full amount of the factored receivables (less any interest and factoring fee deductions). Rather, the factor will retain a certain fraction of the total proceeds relating to the portion of sales which are anticipated to be returned by customers. This sum is known as the factor's holdback (due from factor). When merchandise is returned to the borrower, an entry is made reducing the receivable from the factor. At the end of the return privilege period, any remaining holdback will become due and payable to the borrower.

Example of accounting for the transfer of receivables without recourse

1. Thirsty Corp., on July 1, 1999, enters into an agreement with Rich Company to sell a group of its receivables **without recourse**. A total face value of $200,000 accounts receivable are involved. The factor will charge 20% interest computed on the weighted-average time to maturity of the receivables of 36 days plus a 3% fee. A 5% holdback will also be retained.
2. Thirsty's customers return for credit $4,800 of merchandise.
3. The customer return privilege period expires and the remaining holdback is paid to the transferor.

The entries required are as follows:

---

* *Taken from Delaney, et. al.,* **GAAP: Interpretation and Application**, *1998 Edition, John Wiley and Sons, Inc., New York, NY, pp. 109-114.*

1. Cash	180,055	
Loss on sale of receivables	9,945*	
Factor's holdback receivable (200,000 x .05)	10,000	
Accounts receivable		200,000

($3,945 interest expense + $6,000 factoring fee)

2. Sales returns and allowances	4,800	
Factor's holdback receivable		4,800

3. Cash	5,200	
Factor's holdback receivable		5,200

Factoring does transfer title. Thus, if there is a **without recourse** provision, the removal of these receivables from the borrower's balance sheet is clearly warranted.

Another variation is known as factoring **with recourse**. Some entities had such a poor history of uncollectible accounts that factors were only willing to purchase their accounts if a substantial fee were collected to compensate for the risk. When the company believed that the receivables were of a better quality, a way to avoid excessive factoring fees was to sell these receivables with recourse. This variation of factoring was really an assignment of receivables with notification to the customers.

In computing the gain or loss to be recognized at the date of the transfer of the receivables, the borrower (transferor) must take into account the anticipated chargebacks from the transferee for bad debts to be incurred. This action requires an estimate by the transferor, based on past experience. Adjustments should also be made at the time of sale for the estimated effects of any prepayments by customers (where the receivables are interest-bearing or where cash discounts are available), and for the effects of any defects in the eligibility of the transferred receivables.

Example of accounting for the transfer of receivables with recourse

1. Thirsty Corp., on July 1, 1999, enters into an agreement with Rich Company to sell a group of its receivables with a face value of $200,000. Rich Company (the factor) will charge 20% interest computed on the weighted-average time to maturity of the receivables of 36 days and a 3% fee. A 5% holdback will also be retained.
2. Generally, 40% of Thirsty's customers take advantage of a 2% cash discount.
3. Assume Thirsty Corp. surrenders control of the receivables, per SFAS 125, Thirsty's future obligation is reasonably estimable, and Rich Co. does not have a unilateral ability to require Thirsty to repurchase the receivables.
4. The factor accepts the receivables **subject to recourse** for nonpayment. This means that the transferor has **continuing involvement**. The recourse obligation has a fair value of $10,000.

According to the requirements of SFAS 125, this situation qualifies as a sale. Under this standard, Thirsty must record a liability for the recourse liability due to its continuing involvement with the receivables transferred. It has accepted the obligation for all credit losses and has, in effect, guaranteed the receivables.

The entries required to record the sale are

Cash	180,055	
Interest expense	3,945	
Factoring fee	6,000	
Factor's holdback receivable (200,000 x .05)	10,000	
Loss on sale of receivables	11,600	
Due to factor (200,000 x .40 x .02)		1,600
Accounts receivable		200,000
Recourse obligation		10,000

Simplified, the entry is

Cash	180,055	
Factor's holdback receivable (200,000 x .05)	10,000	
Loss on sale of receivables (3,945 + 6,000 + 11,600)	21,545	
Accounts receivable		200,000
Recourse obligation (10,000 + 1,600)		11,600

The accounts receivable are removed from the transferor's books because they have been sold. The loss on sale of receivables is the sum of the interest charged by the factor ($3,945), the factor's fee ($6,000), the expected chargeback for cash discounts to be taken ($1,600), and the fair value of the recourse obligation ($10,000).

Because the transaction resulted in a "sale" rather than a borrowing, the "interest" and "fee" elements relate directly to the sale transaction. Note that in a sale, these components are in essence part of a negotiated price for the receivables. All you need to remember is that in sales transactions, amounts that would ordinarily be income statement amounts are netted together to get the total loss.

If, subsequent to the sale of the receivables, the actual experience relative to the recourse terms differs from the provision made at the time of the sale, a change in an accounting estimate results. It is reflected as an additional gain or loss in the subsequent period. These changes are not corrections of errors or retroactive adjustments.

Secured borrowings. If the facts in the example right above apply, but the transfer does not qualify as a sale, because the transferor does not surrender control of the receivables, the borrower's entry will be

Cash	190,055	
Interest expense (or prepaid)	3,945	
Factoring fee	6,000	
Factor borrowing payable		200,000

The accounts receivable remain on the borrower's books. Both the accounts receivable and the factor borrowings payable should be cross-referenced in the balance sheet.

Transfers of financial assets under SFAS 125. The FASB adopted a financial-components approach for SFAS 125. In doing so, the previous approach that viewed a financial asset as an indivisible unit has become obsolete. Financial assets are now to be viewed as a variety of components with a focus on who controls the components and on whether control has changed with a given transaction.

The basic accounting problem in this area involves instances of possible continuing involvement through recourse, repurchase agreements, options generated, servicing, and collateral. The issue is whether the transfer has resulted in a sale or a secured borrowing. A sale results, to the extent that consideration other than beneficial interests has been received, when the transferor gives up control.

Under SFAS 125, transfers of financial assets are disaggregated into separate assets and liabilities. Each entity involved in the transaction then

1. Recognizes only the assets controlled and liabilities incurred, and
2. Derecognizes assets where control has been given up or lost and liabilities where extinguishment has occurred.

Control is deemed to have been surrendered by the transferor only if **all** of the following conditions are met:

1. The **assets** transferred are **beyond the reach of the transferor** and its affiliates, its creditors, bankruptcy trustees or other receivers, except for an affiliate that is a qualifying special-purpose entity.
2. The **transferee can pledge or exchange freely** the assets transferred without unreasonable constraints or conditions imposed on its contractual right **or** the holders of beneficial interests in a qualifying special-purpose entity can pledge or exchange those interests freely without unreasonable constraints or conditions imposed on their right.
3. The **transferor has not kept effective control** of the financial assets transferred through a re-purchase or redemption agreement that entitles and obligates repurchase or redemption before maturity at a determinable price **or** through an agreement (except for a cleanup call) to repur-chase or redeem before maturity assets not readily obtainable elsewhere. To meet this condi-tion, the transferor must have received cash or other collateral sufficient at all time to sub-stantially fund repurchase or redemption.

4. **Discounting notes receivable***

   Notes are simply formal receivables with a written promise to pay and may be negotiable and/or interest bearing. Traditionally, notes receivable have been accounted for independently of accounts receivable. Aside from accruing interest revenue, etc., the common transaction involving notes re-ceivable is discounting them.

   For a discounting of notes receivable, the same criteria for transfer of receivables discussed above apply.

   The following is an example of calculating interest expense (revenue) in discounting a note re-ceivable with recourse (continuing involvement).

   a. **Compute maturity value of the note.** Face value plus (Face value x Contract interest rate for number of days of note).
   b. **Compute discount (i.e., bank interest).** Maturity value x Bank interest or discount rate for days remaining to maturity date.
   c. **Subtract discount from maturity value.** Note that the bank is lending the maturity value (i.e., the amount to be collected at the maturity date).
   d. **Compute interest earned prior to discounting.** Face value x Contract interest rate for num-ber of days prior to discounting.
   e. **Compute loss (gain).** (Face value + Prior interest) minus cash proceeds.

   EXAMPLE: 60 days, 9%, $1,000 note discounted with the bank when 30 days remain to maturity. Bank interest rate is 11%. The note does not meet all three criteria of SFAS 125 and is appropriately treated as a borrowing.

   a. $\frac{60}{360}$ *x 9% x $1,000 + $1,000 = $1,015 maturity value*

   b. $\frac{30}{360}$ *x 11% x $1,015 = $9.30 bank discount (interest charge)*

   c. *$1,015 − $9.30 = $1,005.70 cash proceeds*

   d. $\frac{30}{360}$ *x 9% x $1,000 = $7.50 interest earned*

   e. *($1,000 + $7.50) − $1,005.70 = $1.80 interest expense*

   The journal entry to record the discounting is

Cash	1,005.70	
Interest expense	1.80	
Liability on NR discounted		1,000.00
Interest revenue		7.50

---

* *Other considerations in accounting for notes receivable are covered in Module 26, Section A.9.*

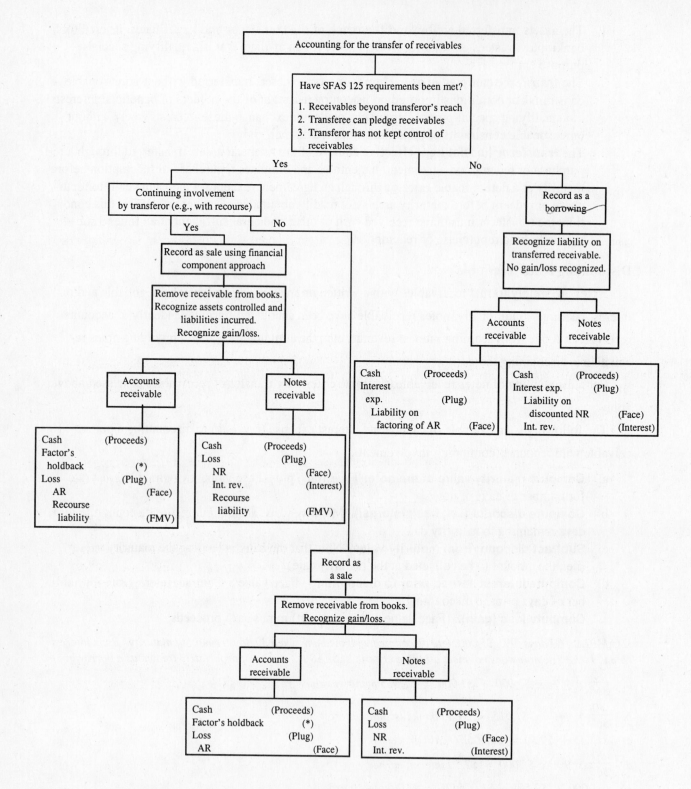

The "factor's holdback" provides a margin of protection against sales returns and allowances and disputed accounts. It may be referred to as "Due from factor" or "Receivable from factor."

"Liability on NR discounted" is a current liability. At the maturity date when the discounted note is honored or dishonored, the following entry is recorded:

Liability on NR discounted	(face)	
NR		(face)

If the note is dishonored, the following entry is also made:

AR	(Maturity value + Penalty)	
Cash		(Maturity value + Penalty)

The AR is from the maker who dishonored the note.

If notes are transferred that meet all SFAS 125 requirements, the transfer is a sale and the credit in the entry above would be to "notes receivable." If continuing involvement is present, a liability would be recorded for that component.

The chart on the previous page summarizes the accounting for transfers of receivables.

 2

C. Current Liabilities

"Obligations whose liquidation is reasonably expected to require the use of existing resources properly classifiable as current assets, or the creation of other current liabilities" (ARB 43, chap 3, para 7).

1. **Examples of current liabilities** (as they fall within the above definition)

    a. Trade accounts and notes payable
    b. Loan obligations--Including current portions of long-term debt. This is not true if the current portion of long-term debt will not require the use of current assets (e.g., be paid from a sinking fund which is not classified as current).
    c. Short-term obligations expected to be refinanced cannot be reclassified as noncurrent liabilities unless there is both an intent and an ability to refinance. See the outline of SFAS 6.
    d. Dividends payable--Cash dividends are a liability when declared. They cannot be rescinded.
    e. Accrued liabilities--Adjusting entries to reflect our use of goods or services before we pay for them. We will pay in future periods even though we have incurred the expense in this period (e.g., interest, payroll, rent expenses).

Expense account	xx	
Liability (usually current) account		xx

    f. Payroll--There are two entries to record payroll. The first records the employee's payment and our deductions on behalf of the employee. The second is to record the employer's taxes.

Payroll expense	xx (gross pay)	
Payroll payable, cash		xx (net pay)
Income taxes payable		xx
FICA taxes payable		xx
Union dues payable		xx
Medical insurance payable		xx
Payroll tax expense	xx	
FICA taxes payable		xx
Federal unemployment tax payable		xx
State unemployment tax payable		xx

    g. Property taxes. See the outline of ARB 43, chap 10A. Generally, there is a monthly accrual for property taxes over the fiscal period of the taxing authority. If taxes are payable at the end of the tax authority's fiscal period, the monthly accrual would be

Property tax expense	xx
Property tax payable	xx

If the taxes were paid at the beginning of the period, the entry to record the prepayment would be followed by monthly entries to expense the prepayment.

Prepaid property taxes	xx		Property tax expense	xx
Cash		xx	Prepaid property taxes	xx

If taxes are due, but not paid at the beginning of the year, the liability should be recorded and the deferred charge expensed over the fiscal year of the taxing body.

Deferred property taxes	xx		Property tax expense	xx
Property tax payable		xx	Deferred property taxes	xx

h. Bonus arrangements

Bonus expense	xx
Bonus payable	xx

Set up equations to describe the terms of the bonus agreement. The general forms of the equations follow:

$$B = P(NI - B - T)$$
$$T = R(NI - B)$$
$$B = Bonus$$
$$P = Bonus \text{ or profit sharing rate } (10\%)$$
$$NI = Net \text{ income } (\$150,000)$$
$$T = Taxes$$
$$R = Tax \text{ rate } (40\%)$$

EXAMPLE: Work through the above equations using the data in parentheses.

$$T = .40(150,000 - B)$$
$$T = 60,000 - .4B$$
$$B = .10(150,000 - B - T)$$
$$B = .10(150,000 - B - 60,000 + .4B)$$
$$B = 15,000 - .1B - 6,000 + .04B$$
$$1.06B = 9,000$$
$$B = \$8,491$$

i. Advances from customers--Record as deferred revenue and recognize as revenue when earned

Cash	xx		Deferred revenue	xx
Deferred revenue		xx	Revenue	xx

2. **Contingencies**

a. **Definitions**--An obligation may be either determinable (fixed) or contingent in accordance with the following definitions.

(1) **Determinable liabilities**--The amount of cash and time of payment are known and reasonably precise. Such liabilities are usually evidenced by written contracts but may also arise from implied agreements or imposed legal statutes. Examples include notes payable and liabilities for various taxes as shown above.

(2) **Contingent liabilities**--Such obligations **may** exist but are dependent on uncertain future events. According to SFAS 5 a contingency is defined as an existing condition, situation, or set of circumstances involving uncertainty as to possible gain or loss to an enterprise that will ultimately be resolved when one or more future events occur or fail to occur.

b. **Recording and disclosing contingencies**--The accounting problems related to contingencies involve the following issues.

(1) When is it appropriate to record and report the effects of a contingency in the financial statements? Should the financial impact of the contingency be reported in the period when the contingency is still unresolved or in the period in which the contingency is resolved?

(2) For contingencies not recorded and reported on the financial statements before they are resolved, what disclosures, if any, are needed in the footnotes to the financial statements?

According to SFAS 5 (see outline), a loss contingency should be accrued if it is **probable** that an asset has been impaired or a liability has been incurred at the balance sheet date **and** the amount of the loss is **reasonably estimable**. When loss contingencies are accrued, a debit should be made to an expense or to a loss account and a credit should be made to either a liability or to a contra asset account. Note that to accrue a loss contingency means that the financial effects of a contingency are reported in the financial statements **before** the contingency is resolved.

When making the decision concerning the accrual of a loss contingency, the term **probable** relates to the likelihood of a future event taking place or failing to take place which would resolve the uncertainty. However, the likelihood of a future event taking place or failing to take place may not always be judged to be probable. The likelihood of the future event taking place or failing to take place may instead be judged to be **reasonably possible** or **remote**. In these last two situations, it is **not** appropriate to accrue the loss contingency as of the balance sheet date, although footnote disclosure may be necessary. Footnote disclosure will be discussed later in this section.

In addition to being probable, the accrual of a loss contingency also requires that the amount of the loss be **reasonably estimable**. In most situations, a single amount can be estimated, and this represents the loss that is accrued. In other situations, the loss may be estimated in terms of a range, for example, the range of loss may be $100,000 to $500,000. In these situations, the amount of loss to accrue is the best estimate within the range. For example, if the best estimate within the range is $200,000, the loss should be accrued in the amount of $200,000. However, if no number in the range is a better estimate of the loss than any other number in the range, the lower number in the range is accrued as the loss. Thus, $100,000 would be accrued if no other number in the range from $100,000 to $500,000 were a better estimate of the loss than any other number in the range.

c. **Examples of loss contingencies**--The accounting problems related to contingencies involve the following issues:

- Collectibility of receivables (Bad debts expense/Allowance for uncollectible accounts),
- Obligations related to product warranties and product defects (Warranty expense/ Warranty liability), and
- Premiums offered to customers (Premium expense/Premium liability)

These contingencies are usually accrued because it is **probable** that some receivables will not be collected, that some of the products sold will be defective and may need warranty work, and that some customers will take advantage of premiums offered by the company. In addition, the **amounts** in each case can usually be **estimated** because of past experience with each of these situations.

To illustrate the accrual of a loss contingency, let's focus on a **product warranty** situation. Here are the facts related to the illustration for ABC Company.

Year	Sales	Actual warranty expenditures	Estimated warranty costs related to dollar sales
1998	$500,000	$15,000	Year of sale 4%
1999	$700,000	$47,000	Year after sale 6%

In 1998, ABC should accrue a loss contingency related to product warranties for $50,000 [$500,000 x (4% + 6%)]. The entry would appear as follows:

Warranty expense	50,000	
Liability for product warranty		50,000

The **actual** warranty expenditures in 1998 would be recorded in the following manner. (Note that the actual expenditures reduce the liability and have no effect on the expense account.)

Liability for product warranty	15,000	
Cash, parts inventory, etc.		15,000

ABC's income statement for 1998 would report an expense for $50,000 related to its product warranty, and its December 31, 1998 balance sheet would report a current liability for product warranty of $35,000 ($50,000 – $15,000). In 1999, ABC should accrue a loss contingency related to product warranties for $70,000 [$700,000 x (4% + 6%)]. The entry would appear as follows:

Warranty expense	70,000	
Liability for product warranty		70,000

The actual warranty expenditures for 1999 would be recorded in the following manner. (Again, note that the actual expenditures only affect the liability account.)

Liability for product warranty	47,000	
Cash, parts inventory, etc.		47,000

ABC's income statement for 1999 should report an expense related to product warranties of $70,000, and its December 31, 1999 balance sheet should report a current liability for product warranty of $58,000 (the 1/1/99 balance of $35,000 + the 1999 expense of $70,000 less the actual warranty expenditures of $47,000 in 1999).

Another example of accrual of a contingent liability involves companies offering **premiums** (e.g., towels, knives, and other prizes) to promote their products. Such companies often have premium liability for outstanding coupons when it is probable that some of the coupons will be redeemed and the amount can be estimated. The expense should be accrued in the period of sale based on the estimated redemption rate.

Premium plan expense	xx	
Premium plan liability		xx

As coupons are actually redeemed by customers, the liability is reduced.

Premium plan liability	xx	
Premiums		xx

Loss contingencies that may be accrued (depending upon whether or not the two conditions of probable and reasonably estimable are satisfied) include the following events.

- Threat of expropriation of assets
- Pending or threatened litigation
- Actual or possible claims and assessments
- Guarantees of indebtedness of others
- Obligations of commercial banks under "Standby letters of credit," and
- Agreements to repurchase receivables (or the related property) that have been sold

Litigation--The one event listed above that appears frequently on the exam involves pending litigation. If the loss from litigation is reasonably estimable, and it is probable as of the balance sheet date that the lawsuit will be lost, the loss should be accrued.

To illustrate this point, assume that XYZ Company is presently involved in litigation involving patent infringement that allegedly occurred during 1998. The financial statements for 1999 are being prepared, and XYZ's legal counsel believes it is probable that XYZ will lose the lawsuit and that the damages will be in the range from $500,000 to $800,000 with the most likely amount being $700,000. Based upon XYZ's legal counsel, it should accrue the loss contingency in the following manner at December 31, 1999.

Loss from litigation	700,000	
Liability from litigation		700,000

The $700,000 loss from litigation should be reported on XYZ's 1999 income statement, and the liability should be reported on the December 31, 1999 balance sheet.

If XYZ settles the litigation in 2000 by paying damages of $600,000, the following journal entry should be made.

Liability from litigation	700,000	
Cash		600,000
Gain from settlement of litigation		100,000

The above entry results in a gain for 2000 because the damages were settled for less than their expected amount. This situation is not unusual because the loss contingency related to the litigation was based upon an estimated amount. Note that it would be incorrect to revise the 1999 financial statements so that the loss contingency reflected the actual damages of $600,000. When the financial statements for 1999 were issued, the best estimate of loss was $700,000. This estimate is not revised subsequent to the issuance of the 1999 financial statements.

Since loss contingencies involving litigation are only accrued if the conditions of probable and reasonably estimable are present, you should be aware of what is reported if either or both of these conditions are not present. For XYZ's case, suppose that its legal counsel believed it was only **reasonably possible** (not probable) as of the balance sheet date, December 31, 1999, that XYZ would lose its lawsuit. In this situation, it would not be appropriate for XYZ to accrue a loss at December 31, 1999. However, because XYZ's legal counsel believes it is reasonably possible to lose the lawsuit, XYZ should disclose this litigation in its footnotes for its 1999 financial statements. The range of loss, noted before as being from $500,000 to $800,000, would also be disclosed in the footnote. In 2000, when the actual damages of $600,000 are known, XYZ would record a loss of this amount and report it on its 2000 income statement.

If XYZ's legal counsel believed that it was **remote** as of December 31, 1999, that the lawsuit would be lost, no accrual or disclosure of the litigation would be necessary.

Loss contingencies that are not accrued or even disclosed in the footnotes include the following events.

- Risk of loss or damage of enterprise property by fire, explosion, or other hazards
- General or unspecified business risks
- Risk of loss from catastrophes assumed by property and casualty insurance companies including reinsurance companies

Losses which result from the above events are recorded and reported in the period when the event occurs that causes the loss. For example, if XYZ's factory is destroyed by fire in 1999, the loss from this event should be recorded and reported in 1999. If the damages from the fire amount to $1,000,000, and XYZ's insurance company reimburses XYZ $800,000, XYZ's loss is $200,000. If XYZ does not insure for fire with an insurance company, XYZ's loss for 1999 would be $1,000,000.

Compensated absences--Knowledge of the conditions that must be present in order to accrue a loss contingency is helpful in the accounting for **compensated absences** (vacation, sick leave pay, etc.). According to SFAS 43 (see outline), an employer shall accrue a liability for employees' compensation for future absences if all of the following conditions are met.

- The employer's obligation relating to employees' rights to receive compensation for future absences is attributable to employees' services already rendered
- The obligation relates to rights that vest or accumulate
- Payment of the compensation is probable
- The amount can be reasonably estimated

To illustrate the accounting for compensated absences, assume MNO Company employees earn 2 weeks of paid vacation for each year of employment. Unused vacation time can be accumulated and carried forward to succeeding years, and will be paid at the salary level in effect when the vacation is taken. As of December 31, 1998, when John Baker's salary was $600 per week, John Baker had earned 18 weeks vacation time and had used 12 weeks of accumulated vacation time. At December 31, 1998, MNO should report a liability for John Baker's accumulated vacation time of $3,600 (6 weeks of accumulated vacation time times $600 per week). The journal entry at December 31, 1998, would appear as follows (assume previous year's entry was reversed).

Salary and wages expense	3,600	
Accrued liability for compensated absences		3,600

Gain contingencies--The discussion relating to contingencies has focused on the accounting for loss contingencies. On the other hand, contingencies exist that may also result in possible **gains**. According to SFAS 5, contingencies that might result in gains usually are not reflected in the accounts since to do so might be to recognize revenue prior to its realization. This means that any gains that result from gain contingencies should be recorded and reported in the period during which the contingency is resolved. For example, the plaintiff in a lawsuit should not record or report the expected damages to be received until the lawsuit has been decided.

D. **Ratios**

1. **Solvency**--Measure short-term viability

   a. **Acid-test (quick) ratio**--Measures ability to pay current liabilities from cash and near-cash items

$$\frac{\text{Cash, Net receivables, Marketable securities}}{\text{Current liabilities}}$$

   b. **Current ratio**--Measures ability to pay current liabilities from cash, near-cash, and cash flow items

$$\frac{\text{Current assets}}{\text{Current liabilities}}$$

2. **Operational efficiency**--Measure utilization of assets

   a. **Receivable turnover**

$$\frac{\text{Net credit sales}}{\text{Average net receivables}}$$

   b. **Number of days' sales in average receivables**--Average length of time receivables are outstanding, which reflects credit and collection policies

$$\frac{365}{\text{Receivable turnover}}$$

   c. **Length of operating cycle**--Measures length of time from purchase of inventory to collection of cash

$$\begin{array}{c}\text{Number of days'} \\ \text{supply in average} \\ \text{inventory}\end{array} + \begin{array}{c}\text{Number of days'} \\ \text{sales in average} \\ \text{receivables}\end{array}$$

MULTIPLE-CHOICE QUESTIONS (1-96)

1. Burr Company had the following account balances at December 31, 1999:

Cash in banks	$2,250,000
Cash on hand	125,000
Cash legally restricted for additions to plant (expected to be disbursed in 2000)	1,600,000

Cash in banks includes $600,000 of compensating balances against short-term borrowing arrangements. The compensating balances are not legally restricted as to withdrawal by Burr. In the current assets section of Burr's December 31, 1999 balance sheet, total cash should be reported at

     a. $1,775,000
     b. $2,250,000
     c. $2,375,000
     d. $3,975,000

2. Ral Corp.'s checkbook balance on December 31, 1999, was $5,000. In addition, Ral held the following items in its safe on that date:

Check payable to Ral Corp., dated January 2, 2000, in payment of a sale made in December 1999, not included in December 31 checkbook balance	$2,000
Check payable to Ral Corp., deposited December 15 and included in December 31 checkbook balance, but returned by bank on December 30 stamped "NSF." The check was redeposited on January 2, 2000, and cleared on January 9	500
Check drawn on Ral Corp.'s account, payable to a vendor, dated and recorded in Ral's books on December 31 but not mailed until January 10, 2000	300

The proper amount to be shown as Cash on Ral's balance sheet at December 31, 1999 is

     a. $4,800
     b. $5,300
     c. $6,500
     d. $6,800

3. At October 31, 1999, Dingo, Inc. had cash accounts at three different banks. One account balance is segregated solely for a November 15, 1999 payment into a bond sinking fund. A second account, used for branch operations, is overdrawn. The third account, used for regular corporate operations, has a positive balance. How should these accounts be reported in Dingo's October 31, 1999 classified balance sheet?

     a.   The segregated account should be reported as a noncurrent asset, the regular account should be reported as a current asset, and the overdraft should be reported as a current liability.
     b.   The segregated and regular accounts should be reported as current assets, and the overdraft should be reported as a current liability.
     c.   The segregated account should be reported as a noncurrent asset, and the regular account should be reported as a current asset net of the overdraft.
     d.   The segregated and regular accounts should be reported as current assets net of the overdraft.

4. In preparing its August 31, 1999 bank reconciliation, Apex Corp. has available the following information:

Balance per bank statement, 8/31/99	$18,050
Deposit in transit, 8/31/99	3,250
Return of customer's check for insufficient funds, 8/31/99	600
Outstanding checks, 8/31/99	2,750
Bank service charges for August	100

At August 31, 1999, Apex's correct cash balance is

     a. $18,550
     b. $17,950
     c. $17,850
     d. $17,550

5. Poe, Inc. had the following bank reconciliation at March 31, 1999:

Balance per bank statement, 3/31/99	$46,500
Add deposit in transit	10,300
	56,800
Less outstanding checks	12,600
Balance per books, 3/31/99	$44,200

Data per bank for the month of April 1999 follow:

Deposits	$58,400
Disbursements	49,700

All reconciling items at March 31, 1999, cleared the bank in April. Outstanding checks at April 30, 1999, totaled $7,000. There were no deposits in transit at April 30, 1999. What is the cash balance per books at April 30, 1999?

     a. $48,200
     b. $52,900
     c. $55,200
     d. $58,500

6. On the December 31, 1999 balance sheet of Mann Co., the current receivables consisted of the following:

Trade accounts receivable	$ 93,000
Allowance for uncollectible accounts	(2,000)
Claim against shipper for goods lost in transit (November 1999)	3,000
Selling price of unsold goods sent by Mann on consignment at 130% of cost (**not** included in Mann's ending inventory)	26,000
Security deposit on lease of warehouse used for storing some inventories	30,000
Total	$150,000

At December 31, 1999, the correct total of Mann's current net receivables was

     a. $ 94,000
     b. $120,000
     c. $124,000
     d. $150,000

7. The following information relates to Jay Co.'s accounts receivable for 1999:

Accounts receivable, 1/1/99	$ 650,000
Credit sales for 1999	2,700,000
Sales returns for 1999	75,000
Accounts written off during 1999	40,000
Collections from customers during 1999	2,150,000

Estimated future sales returns at 12/31/99	50,000
Estimated uncollectible accounts at 12/31/99	110,000

What amount should Jay report for accounts receivable, before allowances for sales returns and uncollectible accounts, at December 31, 1999?

   a. $1,200,000
   b. $1,125,000
   c. $1,085,000
   d. $ 925,000

8. Frame Co. has an 8% note receivable dated June 30, 1997 in the original amount of $150,000. Payments of $50,000 in principal plus accrued interest are due annually on July 1, 1998, 1999, and 2000. In its June 30, 1999 balance sheet, what amount should Frame report as a current asset for interest on the note receivable?

   a. $0
   b. $ 4,000
   c. $ 8,000
   d. $12,000

9. On December 1, 1999, Tigg Mortgage Co. gave Pod Corp. a $200,000, 12% loan. Pod received proceeds of $194,000 after the deduction of a $6,000 nonrefundable loan origination fee. Principal and interest are due in 60 monthly installments of $4,450, beginning January 1, 2000. The repayments yield an effective interest rate of 12% at a present value of $200,000 and 13.4% at a present value of $194,000. What amount of accrued interest receivable should Tigg include in its December 31, 1999 balance sheet?

   a. $4,450
   b. $2,166
   c. $2,000
   d. $0

10. On Merf's April 30, 1999 balance sheet a note receivable was reported as a noncurrent asset and its accrued interest for 8 months was reported as a current asset. Which of the following terms would fit Merf's note receivable?

   a. Both principal and interest amounts are payable on August 31, 1999, and August 31, 2000.
   b. Principal and interest are due December 31, 1999.
   c. Both principal and interest amounts are payable on December 31, 1999, and December 31, 2000.
   d. Principal is due August 31, 2000, and interest is due August 31, 1999, and August 31, 2000.

11. On August 15, 1999, Benet Co. sold goods for which it received a note bearing the market rate of interest on that date. The 4-month note was dated July 15, 1999. Note principal, together with all interest, is due November 15, 1999. When the note was recorded on August 15, which of the following accounts increased?

   a. Unearned discount.
   b. Interest receivable.
   c. Prepaid interest.
   d. Interest revenue.

12. Delta, Inc. sells to wholesalers on terms of 2/15, net 30. Delta has no cash sales but 50% of Delta's customers take advantage of the discount. Delta uses the gross method of recording sales and trade receivables. An analysis of

Delta's trade receivables balances at December 31, 1999, revealed the following:

Age	Amount	Collectible
0 - 15 days	$100,000	100%
16 - 30 days	60,000	95%
31 - 60 days	5,000	90%
Over 60 days	2,500	$500
	$167,500	

In its December 31, 1999 balance sheet, what amount should Delta report for allowance for discounts?

   a. $1,000
   b. $1,620
   c. $1,675
   d. $2,000

13. Fenn Stores, Inc. had sales of $1,000,000 during December, 1999. Experience has shown that merchandise equalling 7% of sales will be returned within 30 days and an additional 3% will be returned within 90 days. Returned merchandise is readily resalable. In addition, merchandise equalling 15% of sales will be exchanged for merchandise of equal or greater value. What amount should Fenn report for net sales in its income statement for the month of December 1999?

   a. $900,000
   b. $850,000
   c. $780,000
   d. $750,000

14. At January 1, 1999, Jamin Co. had a credit balance of $260,000 in its allowance for uncollectible accounts. Based on past experience, 2% of Jamin's credit sales have been uncollectible. During 1999, Jamin wrote off $325,000 of uncollectible accounts. Credit sales for 1999 were $9,000,000. In its December 31, 1999 balance sheet, what amount should Jamin report as allowance for uncollectible accounts?

   a. $115,000
   b. $180,000
   c. $245,000
   d. $440,000

15. The following accounts were abstracted from Roxy Co.'s unadjusted trial balance at December 31, 1999:

	Debit	Credit
Accounts receivable	$1,000,000	
Allowance for uncollectible accounts		8,000
Net credit sales		$3,000,000

Roxy estimates that 3% of the gross accounts receivable will become uncollectible. After adjustment at December 31, 1999, the allowance for uncollectible accounts should have a credit balance of

   a. $90,000
   b. $82,000
   c. $38,000
   d. $30,000

16. Inge Co. determined that the net value of its accounts receivable at December 31, 1999, based on an aging of the receivables, was $325,000. Additional information is as follows:

Allowance for uncollectible accounts--1/1/99	$ 30,000
Uncollectible accounts written off during 1999	18,000
Uncollectible accounts recovered during 1999	2,000
Accounts receivable at 12/31/99	350,000

For 1999, what would be Inge's uncollectible accounts expense?

    a. $ 5,000
    b. $11,000
    c. $15,000
    d. $21,000

17. The following information pertains to Tara Co.'s accounts receivable at December 31, 1999:

Days outstanding	Amount	Estimated % uncollectible
0 - 60	$120,000	1%
61 - 120	90,000	2%
Over 120	100,000	6%
	$310,000	

During 1999, Tara wrote off $7,000 in receivables and recovered $4,000 that had been written off in prior years. Tara's December 31, 1998 allowance for uncollectible accounts was $22,000. Under the aging method, what amount of allowance for uncollectible accounts should Tara report at December 31, 1999?

    a. $ 9,000
    b. $10,000
    c. $13,000
    d. $19,000

18. A method of estimating uncollectible accounts that emphasizes asset valuation rather than income measurement is the allowance method based on

    a. Aging the receivables.
    b. Direct write-off.
    c. Gross sales.
    d. Credit sales less returns and allowances.

19. Which method of recording uncollectible accounts expense is consistent with accrual accounting?

	Allowance	Direct write-off
a.	Yes	Yes
b.	Yes	No
c.	No	Yes
d.	No	No

20. When the allowance method of recognizing uncollectible accounts is used, the entry to record the write-off of a specific account

    a. Decreases both accounts receivable and the allowance for uncollectible accounts.
    b. Decreases accounts receivable and increases the allowance for uncollectible accounts.
    c. Increases the allowance for uncollectible accounts and decreases net income.
    d. Decreases both accounts receivable and net income.

21. A company uses the allowance method to recognize uncollectible accounts expense. What is the effect at the time of the collection of an account previously written off on each of the following accounts?

	Allowance for uncollectible accounts	Uncollectible accounts expense
a.	No effect	Decrease
b.	Increase	Decrease
c.	Increase	No effect
d.	No effect	No effect

22. Which of the following is a method to generate cash from accounts receivables?

	Assignment	Factoring
a.	Yes	No
b.	Yes	Yes
c.	No	Yes
d.	No	No

23. Gar Co. factored its receivables. Control was surrendered in the transaction which was on a without recourse basis with Ross Bank. Gar received cash as a result of this transaction, which is best described as a

    a. Loan from Ross collateralized by Gar's accounts receivable.
    b. Loan from Ross to be repaid by the proceeds from Gar's accounts receivable.
    c. Sale of Gar's accounts receivable to Ross, with the risk of uncollectible accounts retained by Gar.
    d. Sale of Gar's accounts receivable to Ross, with the risk of uncollectible accounts transferred to Ross.

Items 24 through 26 are based on the following:

Taylored Corp. factored $400,000 of accounts receivable to Rich Corp. on July 1, 1999. Control was surrendered by Taylored. Rich accepted the receivables subject to recourse for nonpayment. Rich assessed a fee of 2% and retains a holdback equal to 5% of the accounts receivable. In addition, Rich charged 15% interest computed on a weighted-average time to maturity of the receivables of 41 days. The fair value of the recourse obligation is $8,000.

24. Taylored will receive and record cash of
    a. $385,260
    b. $357,260
    c. $365,260
    d. $377,260

25. Which of the following statements is correct?
    a. Rich should record an asset of $8,000 for the recourse obligation.
    b. Taylored should record a liability and corresponding loss of $8,000 related to the recourse obligation.
    c. Taylored should record a liability of $8,000, but no loss, related to the recourse obligation.
    d. No entry for the recourse obligation should be made by Taylored or Rich until the debtor fails to pay.

26. Assuming all receivables are collected, Taylored's cost of factoring the receivables would be
    a. $ 8,000
    b. $34,740
    c. $42,740
    d. $14,740

27. Which of the following is used to account for probable sales discounts, sales returns, and sales allowances?

	Due from factor	*Recourse liability*
a.	Yes	No
b.	Yes	Yes
c.	No	Yes
d.	No	No

28. All but one of the following are required before a transfer of receivables can be recorded as a sale.
  a. The transferred receivables are beyond the reach of the transferor and its creditors.
  b. The transferor has not kept effective control over the transferred receivables through a repurchase agreement.
  c. The transferor maintains continuing involvement.
  d. The transferee can pledge or sell the transferred receivables.

29. Roth, Inc. received from a customer a 1-year, $500,000 note bearing annual interest of 8%. After holding the note for 6 months, Roth discounted the note at Regional Bank at an effective interest rate of 10%. What amount of cash did Roth receive from the bank?
  a. $540,000
  b. $523,810
  c. $513,000
  d. $495,238

30. Which of the following is not an objective for each entity accounting for transfers of financial assets?
  a. To derecognize assets when control is gained.
  b. To derecognize liabilities when extinguished.
  c. To recognize liabilities when incurred.
  d. To derecognize assets when control is given up.

31. On November 1, 1999, Davis Co. discounted at 10% a 1-year, noninterest bearing, $20,500 note receivable maturing on January 31, 2000. Control was surrendered in this without recourse transfer. What is the amount of the liability for this note that Davis must disclose in its financial statements for the year ended December 31, 1999?
  a. $0
  b. $20,000
  c. $20,333
  d. $20,500

32. After being held for 40 days, a 120-day 12% interest-bearing note receivable was discounted at a bank at 15%. The proceeds received from the bank equal
  a. Maturity value less the discount at 12%.
  b. Maturity value less the discount at 15%.
  c. Face value less the discount at 12%.
  d. Face value less the discount at 15%.

 2

33. Lyle, Inc. is preparing its financial statements for the year ended December 31, 1999. Accounts payable amounted to $360,000 before any necessary year-end adjustment related to the following:

  •   At December 31, 1999, Lyle has a $50,000 debit balance in its accounts payable to Ross, a supplier, resulting

from a $50,000 advance payment for goods to be manufactured to Lyle's specifications.
  •   Checks in the amount of $100,000 were written to vendors and recorded on December 29, 1999. The checks were mailed on January 5, 2000.

What amount should Lyle report as accounts payable in its December 31, 1999 balance sheet?
  a. $510,000
  b. $410,000
  c. $310,000
  d. $210,000

34. Rabb Co. records its purchases at gross amounts but wishes to change to recording purchases net of purchase discounts. Discounts available on purchases recorded from October 1, 1998, to September 30, 1999, totaled $2,000. Of this amount, $200 is still available in the accounts payable balance. The balances in Rabb's accounts as of and for the year ended September 30, 1999, before conversion are

Purchases	$100,000
Purchase discounts taken	800
Accounts payable	30,000

What is Rabb's accounts payable balance as of September 30, 1999, after the conversion?
  a. $29,800
  b. $29,200
  c. $28,800
  d. $28,200

35. On March 1, 1998, Fine Co. borrowed $10,000 and signed a 2-year note bearing interest at 12% per annum compounded annually. Interest is payable in full at maturity on February 28, 2000. What amount should Fine report as a liability for accrued interest at December 31, 1999?
  a. $0
  b. $1,000
  c. $1,200
  d. $2,320

36. On September 1, 1998, Brak Co. borrowed on a $1,350,000 note payable from Federal Bank. The note bears interest at 12% and is payable in 3 equal annual principal payments of $450,000. On this date, the bank's prime rate was 11%. The first annual payment for interest and principal was made on September 1, 1999. At December 31, 1999, what amount should Brak report as accrued interest payable?
  a. $54,000
  b. $49,500
  c. $36,000
  d. $33,000

37. In its 1999 financial statements, Cris Co. reported interest expense of $85,000 in its income statement and cash paid for interest of $68,000 in its cash flow statement. There was no prepaid interest or interest capitalization either at the beginning or end of 1999. Accrued interest at December 31, 1998, was $15,000. What amount should Cris report as accrued interest payable in its December 31, 1999 balance sheet?
  a. $ 2,000
  b. $15,000

c. $17,000
d. $32,000

38. Ames, Inc. has $500,000 of notes payable due June 15, 2000. Ames signed an agreement on December 1, 1999, to borrow up to $500,000 to refinance the notes payable on a long-term basis with no payments due until 1999. The financing agreement stipulated that borrowings may not exceed 80% of the value of the collateral Ames was providing. At the date of issuance of the December 31, 1999 financial statements, the value of the collateral was $600,000 and is not expected to fall below this amount during 2000. In Ames' December 31, 1999 balance sheet, the obligation for these notes payable should be classified as

	Short-term	Long-term
a.	$500,000	$0
b.	$100,000	$400,000
c.	$ 20,000	$480,000
d.	$0	$500,000

39. A company issued a short-term note payable with a stated 12% rate of interest to a bank. The bank charged a .5% loan origination fee and remitted the balance to the company. The effective interest rate paid by the company in this transaction would be
a.   Equal to 12.5%.
b.   More than 12.5%.
c.   Less than 12.5%.
d.   Independent of 12.5%.

40. Cali, Inc. had a $4,000,000 note payable due on March 15, 1999. On January 28, 1999, before the issuance of its 1998 financial statements, Cali issued long-term bonds in the amount of $4,500,000. Proceeds from the bonds were used to repay the note when it came due. How should Cali classify the note in its December 31, 1998 financial statements?
a.   As a current liability, with separate disclosure of the note refinancing.
b.   As a current liability, with no separate disclosure required.
c.   As a noncurrent liability, with separate disclosure of the note refinancing.
d.   As a noncurrent liability, with no separate disclosure required.

41. On December 31, 1999, Largo, Inc. had a $750,000 note payable outstanding, due July 31, 2000. Largo borrowed the money to finance construction of a new plant. Largo planned to refinance the note by issuing long-term bonds. Because Largo temporarily had excess cash, it prepaid $250,000 of the note on January 12, 2000. In February 2000, Largo completed a $1,500,000 bond offering. Largo will use the bond offering proceeds to repay the note payable at its maturity and to pay construction costs during 2000. On March 3, 2000, Largo issued its 1999 financial statements. What amount of the note payable should Largo include in the current liabilities section of its December 31, 1999 balance sheet?
a. $750,000
b. $500,000
c. $250,000

d. $0

42. Rice Co. salaried employees are paid biweekly. Advances made to employees are paid back by payroll deductions. Information relating to salaries follows:

	12/31/98	12/31/99
Employee advances	$24,000	$ 36,000
Accrued salaries payable	40,000	?
Salaries expense during the year		420,000
Salaries paid during the year (gross)		390,000

In Rice's December 31, 1999 balance sheet, accrued salaries payable was
a. $94,000
b. $82,000
c. $70,000
d. $30,000

43. Fay Corp. pays its outside salespersons fixed monthly salaries and commissions on net sales. Sales commissions are computed and paid on a monthly basis (in the month following the month of sale), and the fixed salaries are treated as advances against commissions. However, if the fixed salaries for salespersons exceed their sales commissions earned for a month, such excess is not charged back to them. Pertinent data for the month of March 1999 for the 3 salespersons are as follows:

Salesperson	Fixed salary	Net sales	Commission rate
A	$10,000	$ 200,000	4%
B	14,000	400,000	6%
C	18,000	600,000	6%
Totals	$42,000	$1,200,000	

What amount should Fay accrue for sales commissions payable at March 31, 1999?
a. $70,000
b. $68,000
c. $28,000
d. $26,000

44. Lime Co.'s payroll for the month ended January 31, 1999, is summarized as follows:

Total wages	$10,000
Federal income tax withheld	1,200

All wages paid were subject to FICA. FICA tax rates were 7% each for employee and employer. Lime remits payroll taxes on the 15th of the following month. In its financial statements for the month ended January 31, 1999, what amounts should Lime report as total payroll tax liability and as payroll tax expense?

	Liability	Expense
a.	$1,200	$1,400
b.	$1,900	$1,400
c.	$1,900	$ 700
d.	$2,600	$ 700

45. Under state law, Acme may pay 3% of eligible gross wages or it may reimburse the state directly for actual unemployment claims. Acme believes that actual unemployment claims will be 2% of eligible gross wages and has chosen to reimburse the state. Eligible gross wages are defined as the first $10,000 of gross wages paid to each employee. Acme had 5 employees, each of whom earned $20,000 during 1999. In its December 31, 1999 balance sheet, what amount should Acme report as accrued liability for unemployment claims?

    a. $1,000
    b. $1,500
    c. $2,000
    d. $3,000

46. Pine Corp. is required to contribute, to an employee stock ownership plan (ESOP), 10% of its income after deduction for this contribution but before income tax. Pine's income before charges for the contribution and income tax was $75,000. The income tax rate is 30%. What amount should be accrued as a contribution to the ESOP?

    a. $7,500
    b. $6,818
    c. $5,250
    d. $4,773

47. Able Co. provides an incentive compensation plan under which its president receives a bonus equal to 10% of the corporation's income before income tax but after deduction of the bonus. If the tax rate is 40% and net income after bonus and income tax was $360,000, what was the amount of the bonus?

    a. $36,000
    b. $60,000
    c. $66,000
    d. $90,000

48. Ivy Co. operates a retail store. All items are sold subject to a 6% state sales tax, which Ivy collects and records as sales revenue. Ivy files quarterly sales tax returns when due, by the 20th day following the end of the sales quarter. However, in accordance with state requirements, Ivy remits sales tax collected by the 20th day of the month following any month such collections exceed $500. Ivy takes these payments as credits on the quarterly sales tax return. The sales taxes paid by Ivy are charged against sales revenue.

Following is a monthly summary appearing in Ivy's first quarter 1999 sales revenue account:

	Debit	Credit
January	$ ---	$10,600
February	600	7,420
March	---	8,480
	$600	$26,500

In its March 31, 1999 balance sheet, what amount should Ivy report as sales taxes payable?

    a. $ 600
    b. $ 900
    c. $1,500
    d. $1,590

49. Hudson Hotel collects 15% in city sales taxes on room rentals, in addition to a $2 per room, per night, occupancy tax. Sales taxes for each month are due at the end of the following month, and occupancy taxes are due 15 days after the end of each calendar quarter. On January 3, 2000, Hudson paid its November 1999 sales taxes and its fourth quar-

ter 1999 occupancy taxes. Additional information pertaining to Hudson's operations is

1999	*Room rentals*	*Room nights*
October	$100,000	1,100
November	110,000	1,200
December	150,000	1,800

What amounts should Hudson report as sales taxes payable and occupancy taxes payable in its December 31, 1999 balance sheet?

	Sales taxes	*Occupancy taxes*
a.	$39,000	$6,000
b.	$39,000	$8,200
c.	$54,000	$6,000
d.	$54,000	$8,200

50. On July 1, 1999, Ran County issued realty tax assessments for its fiscal year ended June 30, 2000. On September 1, 1999, Day Co. purchased a warehouse in Ran County. The purchase price was reduced by a credit for accrued realty taxes. Day did not record the entire year's real estate tax obligation, but instead records tax expenses at the end of each month by adjusting prepaid real estate taxes or real estate taxes payable, as appropriate. On November 1, 1999, Day paid the first of two equal installments of $12,000 for realty taxes. What amount of this payment should Day record as a debit to real estate taxes payable?

    a. $ 4,000
    b. $ 8,000
    c. $10,000
    d. $12,000

51. Kemp Co. must determine the December 31, 1999 year-end accruals for advertising and rent expenses. A $500 advertising bill was received January 7, 2000, comprising costs of $375 for advertisements in December 1999 issues, and $125 for advertisements in January 2000 issues of the newspaper.

A store lease, effective December 16, 1998, calls for fixed rent of $1,200 per month, payable 1 month from the effective date and monthly thereafter. In addition, rent equal to 5% of net sales over $300,000 per calendar year is payable on January 31 of the following year. Net sales for 1999 were $550,000.

In its December 31, 1999 balance sheet, Kemp should report accrued liabilities of

    a. $12,875
    b. $13,000
    c. $13,100
    d. $13,475

52. On May 1, 1999, Marno County issued property tax assessments for the fiscal year ended June 30, 2000. The first of two equal installments was due on November 1, 1999. On September 1, 1999, Dyur Co. purchased a 4-year-old factory in Marno subject to an allowance for accrued taxes. Dyur did not record the entire year's property tax obligation, but instead records tax expenses at the end of each month by adjusting prepaid property taxes or property taxes payable, as appropriate. The recording of the November 1, 1999 payment by Dyur should have been allocated between an increase in prepaid property taxes and a decrease in property taxes payable in which of the following percentages?

	Percentage allocated to	
	Increase in pre-paid property taxes	Decrease in property taxes payable
a.	66 2/3%	33 1/3%
b.	0%	100%
c.	50%	50%
d.	33 1/3%	66 2/3%

53. Black Co. requires advance payments with special orders for machinery constructed to customer specifications. These advances are nonrefundable. Information for 1999 is as follows:

Customer advances--balance 12/31/98	$118,000
Advances received with orders in 1999	184,000
Advances applied to orders shipped in 1999	164,000
Advances applicable to orders cancelled in 1999	50,000

In Black's December 31, 1999 balance sheet, what amount should be reported as a current liability for advances from customer?

  a. $0
  b. $ 88,000
  c. $138,000
  d. $148,000

54. Marr Co. sells its products in reusable containers. The customer is charged a deposit for each container delivered and receives a refund for each container returned within 2 years after the year of delivery. Marr accounts for the containers not returned within the time limit as being retired by sale at the deposit amount. Information for 1999 is as follows:

Container deposits at December 31,
  1998, from deliveries in

1997	$150,000	
1998	430,000	$580,000

Deposits for containers
  delivered in 1999   780,000

Deposits for containers returned
  in 1999 from deliveries in

1997	$ 90,000	
1998	250,000	
1999	286,000	626,000

In Marr's December 31, 1999 balance sheet, the liability for deposits on returnable containers should be

  a. $494,000
  b. $584,000
  c. $674,000
  d. $734,000

55. Kent Co., a division of National Realty, Inc., maintains escrow accounts and pays real estate taxes for National's mortgage customers. Escrow funds are kept in interest-bearing accounts. Interest, less a 10% service fee, is credited to the mortgagee's account and used to reduce future escrow payments. Additional information follows:

Escrow accounts liability, 1/1/99	$ 700,000
Escrow payments received during 1999	1,580,000

Real estate taxes paid during 1999	1,720,000
Interest on escrow funds during 1999	50,000

What amount should Kent report as escrow accounts liability in its December 31, 1999 balance sheet?

  a. $510,000
  b. $515,000
  c. $605,000
  d. $610,000

56. Cobb Company sells appliance service contracts agreeing to repair appliances for a 2-year period. Cobb's past experience is that, of the total dollars spent for repairs on service contracts, 40% is incurred evenly during the first contract year and 60% evenly during the second contract year. Receipts from service contract sales for the 2 years ended December 31, 1999, are as follows:

1998	$500,000
1999	600,000

Receipts from contracts are credited to unearned service contract revenue. Assume that all contract sales are made evenly during the year. What amount should Cobb report as unearned service contract revenue at December 31, 1999?

  a. $360,000
  b. $470,000
  c. $480,000
  d. $630,000

57. Toddler Care Co. offers 3 payment plans on its 12-month contracts. Information on the 3 plans and the number of children enrolled in each plan for the September 1, 1999 through August 31, 2000 contract year follows:

Plan	Initial payment per child	Monthly fees per child	Number of children
#1	$500	$ --	15
#2	200	30	12
#3	--	50	9
			36

Toddler received $9,900 of initial payments on September 1, 1999, and $3,240 of monthly fees during the period September 1 through December 31, 1999. In its December 31, 1999 balance sheet, what amount should Toddler report as deferred revenues?

  a. $3,300
  b. $4,380
  c. $6,600
  d. $9,900

58. For $50 a month, Rawl Co. visits its customers' premises and performs insect control services. If customers experience problems between regularly scheduled visits, Rawl makes service calls at no additional charge. Instead of paying monthly, customers may pay an annual fee of $540 in advance. For a customer who pays the annual fee in advance, Rawl should recognize the related revenue

  a. When the cash is collected.
  b. At the end of the fiscal year.
  c. At the end of the contract year after all of the services have been performed.
  d. Evenly over the contract year as the services are performed.

59. A retail store received cash and issued gift certificates that are redeemable in merchandise. The gift certificates lapse 1 year after they are issued. How would the deferred revenue account be affected by each of the following transactions?

	Redemption of certificates	Lapse of certificates
a.	Decrease	No effect
b.	Decrease	Decrease
c.	No effect	No effect
d.	No effect	Decrease

60. On March 31, 1999, Dallas Co. received an advance payment of 60% of the sales price for special-order goods to be manufactured and delivered within 5 months. At the same time, Dallas subcontracted for production of the special-order goods at a price equal to 40% of the main contract price. What liabilities should be reported in Dallas' March 31, 1999 balance sheet?

	Deferred revenues	Payables to subcontractor
a.	None	None
b.	60% of main contract price	40% of main contract price
c.	60% of main contract price	None
d.	None	40% of main contract price

61. In June 1999, Northan Retailers sold refundable merchandise coupons. Northan received $10 for each coupon redeemable from July 1 to December 31, 1999, for merchandise with a retail price of $11. At June 30, 1999, how should Northan report these coupon transactions?

a. Unearned revenues at the merchandise's retail price.
b. Unearned revenues at the cash received amount.
c. Revenues at the merchandise's retail price.
d. Revenues at the cash received amount.

62. Delect Co. provides repair services for the AZ195 TV set. Customers prepay the fee on the standard 1-year service contract. The 1998 and 1999 contracts were identical, and the number of contracts outstanding was substantially the same at the end of each year. However, Delect's December 31, 1999 deferred revenues' balance on unperformed service contracts was significantly less than the balance at December 31, 1998. Which of the following situations might account for this reduction in the deferred revenue balance?

a. Most 1999 contracts were signed later in the calendar year than were the 1998 contracts.
b. Most 1999 contracts were signed earlier in the calendar year than were the 1998 contracts.
c. The 1999 contract contribution margin was greater than the 1998 contract contribution margin.
d. The 1999 contribution margin was less than the 1998 contract contribution margin.

63. Brad Corp. has unconditional purchase obligations associated with product financing arrangements. These obligations are reported as liabilities on Brad's balance

sheet, with the related assets also recognized. In the notes to Brad's financial statements, the aggregate amount of payments for these obligations should be disclosed for each of how many years following the date of the latest balance sheet?

a. 0
b. 1
c. 5
d. 10

64. On January 17, 1999, an explosion occurred at a Sims Co. plant causing extensive property damage to area buildings. Although no claims had yet been asserted against Sims by March 10, 1999, Sims' management and counsel concluded that it is likely that claims will be asserted and that it is reasonably possible Sims will be responsible for damages. Sims' management believed that $1,250,000 would be a reasonable estimate of its liability. Sims' $5,000,000 comprehensive public liability policy has a $250,000 deductible clause. In Sims' December 31, 1998 financial statements, which were issued on March 25, 1999, how should this item be reported?

a. As an accrued liability of $250,000.
b. As a footnote disclosure indicating the possible loss of $250,000.
c. As a footnote disclosure indicating the possible loss of $1,250,000.
d. No footnote disclosure or accrual is necessary.

65. Brite Corp. had the following liabilities at December 31, 1999:

Accounts payable	$55,000
Unsecured notes, 8%, due 7/1/00	400,000
Accrued expenses	35,000
Contingent liability	450,000
Deferred income tax liability	25,000
Senior bonds, 7%, due 3/31/00	1,000,000

The contingent liability is an accrual for possible losses on a $1,000,000 lawsuit filed against Brite. Brite's legal counsel expects the suit to be settled in 1999, and has estimated that Brite will be liable for damages in the range of $450,000 to $750,000.

The deferred income tax liability is not related to an asset for financial reporting and is expected to reverse in 1999.

What amount should Brite report in its December 31, 1999 balance sheet for current liabilities?

a. $ 515,000
b. $ 940,000
c. $1,490,000
d. $1,515,000

66. On February 5, 2000, an employee filed a $2,000,000 lawsuit against Steel Co. for damages suffered when one of Steel's plants exploded on December 29, 1999. Steel's legal counsel expects the company will lose the lawsuit and estimates the loss to be between $500,000 and $1,000,000. The employee has offered to settle the lawsuit out of court for $900,000, but Steel will not agree to the settlement. In its December 31, 1999 balance sheet, what amount should Steel report as liability from lawsuit?

a. $2,000,000
b. $1,000,000
c. $ 900,000
d. $ 500,000

67. On November 5, 1999, a Dunn Corp. truck was in an accident with an auto driven by Bell. Dunn received notice on January 12, 2000, of a lawsuit for $700,000 damages for personal injuries suffered by Bell. Dunn Corp.'s counsel believes it is probable that Bell will be awarded an estimated amount in the range between $200,000 and $450,000, and that $300,000 is a better estimate of potential liability than any other amount. Dunn's accounting year ends on December 31, and the 1999 financial statements were issued on March 2, 2000. What amount of loss should Dunn accrue at December 31, 1999?

a. $0
b. $200,000
c. $300,000
d. $450,000

68. During 1999, Haft Co. became involved in a tax dispute with the IRS. At December 31, 1999, Haft's tax advisor believed that an unfavorable outcome was probable. A reasonable estimate of additional taxes was $200,000 but could be as much as $300,000. After the 1999 financial statements were issued, Haft received and accepted an IRS settlement offer of $275,000. What amount of accrued liability should Haft have reported in its December 31, 1999 balance sheet?

a. $200,000
b. $250,000
c. $275,000
d. $300,000

69. Management can estimate the amount of loss that will occur if a foreign government expropriates some company assets. If expropriation is reasonably possible, a loss contingency should be

a.   Disclosed but **not** accrued as a liability.
b.   Disclosed and accrued as a liability.
c.   Accrued as a liability but **not** disclosed.
d.   Neither accrued as a liability **nor** disclosed.

70. Invern, Inc. has a self-insurance plan. Each year, retained earnings is appropriated for contingencies in an amount equal to insurance premiums saved less recognized losses from lawsuits and other claims. As a result of a 1999 accident, Invern is a defendant in a lawsuit in which it will probably have to pay damages of $190,000. What are the effects of this lawsuit's probable outcome on Invern's 1999 financial statements?

a.   An increase in expenses and **no** effect on liabilities.
b.   An increase in both expenses and liabilities.
c.   No effect on expenses and an increase in liabilities.
d.   No effect on either expenses or liabilities.

71. In 1998, a personal injury lawsuit was brought against Halsey Co. Based on counsel's estimate, Halsey reported a $50,000 liability in its December 31, 1998 balance sheet. In November 1999, Halsey received a favorable judgment, requiring the plaintiff to reimburse Halsey for expenses of $30,000. The plaintiff has appealed the decision, and Halsey's counsel is unable to predict the outcome of the appeal. In its December 31, 1999 balance sheet, Halsey should report what amounts of asset and liability related to these legal actions?

	Asset	*Liability*
a.	$30,000	$50,000
b.	$30,000	$0
c.	$0	$20,000
d.	$0	$0

72. During January 1999, Haze Corp. won a litigation award for $15,000 which was tripled to $45,000 to include punitive damages. The defendant, who is financially stable, has appealed only the $30,000 punitive damages. Haze was awarded $50,000 in an unrelated suit it filed, which is being appealed by the defendant. Counsel is unable to estimate the outcome of these appeals. In its 1999 financial statements, Haze should report what amount of pretax gain?

a. $15,000
b. $45,000
c. $50,000
d. $95,000

73. In May 1996, Caso Co. filed suit against Wayne, Inc. seeking $1,900,000 damages for patent infringement. A court verdict in November 1999 awarded Caso $1,500,000 in damages, but Wayne's appeal is not expected to be decided before 2001. Caso's counsel believes it is probable that Caso will be successful against Wayne for an estimated amount in the range between $800,000 and $1,100,000, with $1,000,000 considered the most likely amount. What amount should Caso record as income from the lawsuit in the year ended December 31, 1999?

a. $0
b. $ 800,000
c. $1,000,000
d. $1,500,000

74. During 1998, Smith Co. filed suit against West, Inc. seeking damages for patent infringement. At December 31, 1998, Smith's legal counsel believed that it was probable that Smith would be successful against West for an estimated amount in the range of $75,000 to $150,000, with all amounts in the range considered equally likely. In March 1999, Smith was awarded $100,000 and received full payment thereof. In its 1998 financial statements, issued in February 1999, how should this award be reported?

a.   As a receivable and revenue of $100,000.
b.   As a receivable and deferred revenue of $100,000.
c.   As a disclosure of a contingent gain of $100,000.
d.   As a disclosure of a contingent gain of an undetermined amount in the range of $75,000 to $150,000.

75. In 1999, a contract dispute between Dollis Co. and Brooks Co. was submitted to binding arbitration. In 1999, each party's attorney indicated privately that the probable award in Dollis' favor could be reasonably estimated. In 2000, the arbitrator decided in favor of Dollis. When should Dollis and Brooks recognize their respective gain and loss?

	Dollis' gain	*Brooks' loss*
a.	1999	1999
b.	1999	2000
c.	2000	1999
d.	2000	2000

76. Eagle Co. has cosigned the mortgage note on the home of its president, guaranteeing the indebtedness in the event that the president should default. Eagle considers the likelihood of default to be remote. How should the guarantee be treated in Eagle's financial statements?

    a.   Disclosed only.
    b.   Accrued only.
    c.   Accrued and disclosed.
    d.   Neither accrued nor disclosed.

77. North Corp. has an employee benefit plan for compensated absences that gives employees 10 paid vacation days and 10 paid sick days. Both vacation and sick days can be carried over indefinitely. Employees can elect to receive payment in lieu of vacation days; however, no payment is given for sick days not taken. At December 31, 1999, North's unadjusted balance of liability for compensated absences was $21,000. North estimated that there were 150 vacation days and 75 sick days available at December 31, 1999. North's employees earn an average of $100 per day. In its December 31, 1999 balance sheet, what amount of liability for compensated absences is North required to report?

    a. $36,000
    b. $22,500
    c. $21,000
    d. $15,000

78. Ross Co. pays all salaried employees on a Monday for the 5-day workweek ended the previous Friday. The last payroll recorded for the year ended December 31, 1999, was for the week ended December 25, 1999. The payroll for the week ended January 1, 2000, included regular weekly salaries of $80,000 and vacation pay of $25,000 for vacation time earned in 1999 not taken by December 31, 1999. Ross had accrued a liability of $20,000 for vacation pay at December 31, 1998. In its December 31, 1999 balance sheet, what amount should Ross report as accrued salary and vacation pay?

    a. $64,000
    b. $68,000
    c. $69,000
    d. $89,000

79. Gavin Co. grants all employees 2 weeks of paid vacation for each full year of employment. Unused vacation time can be accumulated and carried forward to succeeding years and will be paid at the salaries in effect when vacations are taken or when employment is terminated. There was no employee turnover in 1999. Additional information relating to the year ended December 31, 1999, is as follows:

Liability for accumulated vacations at 12/31/98	$35,000
Pre-1999 accrued vacations taken from 1/1/99 to 9/30/99 (the authorized period for vacations)	20,000
Vacations earned for work in 1999 (adjusted to current rates)	30,000

Gavin granted a 10% salary increase to all employees on October 1, 1999, its annual salary increase date. For the year ended December 31, 1999, Gavin should report vacation pay expense of

    a. $45,000
    b. $33,500
    c. $31,500
    d. $30,000

80. At December 31, 1999, Taos Co. estimates that its employees have earned vacation pay of $100,000. Employees will receive their vacation pay in 2000. Should Taos accrue a liability at December 31, 1999, if the rights to this compensation accumulated over time or if the rights are vested?

	Accumulated	*Vested*
a.	Yes	No
b.	No	No
c.	Yes	Yes
d.	No	Yes

81. If the payment of employees' compensation for future absences is probable, the amount can be reasonably estimated, and the obligation relates to rights that accumulate, the compensation should be

    a.   Accrued if attributable to employees' services **not** already rendered.
    b.   Accrued if attributable to employees' services already rendered.
    c.   Accrued if attributable to employees' services whether already rendered or not.
    d.   Recognized when paid.

82. During 1999, Gum Co. introduced a new product carrying a 2-year warranty against defects. The estimated warranty costs related to dollar sales are 2% within 12 months following the sale and 4% in the second 12 months following the sale. Sales and actual warranty expenditures for the years ended December 31, 1999 and 2000, are as follows:

	Sales	*Actual warranty expenditures*
1999	$150,000	$2,250
2000	250,000	7,500
	$400,000	$9,750

What amount should Gum report as estimated warranty liability in its December 31, 2000 balance sheet?

    a. $ 2,500
    b. $ 4,250
    c. $11,250
    d. $14,250

83. Vadis Co. sells appliances that include a 3-year warranty. Service calls under the warranty are performed by an independent mechanic under a contract with Vadis. Based on experience, warranty costs are estimated at $30 for each machine sold. When should Vadis recognize these warranty costs?

    a.   Evenly over the life of the warranty.
    b.   When the service calls are performed.
    c.   When payments are made to the mechanic.
    d.   When the machines are sold.

84. Case Cereal Co. frequently distributes coupons to promote new products. On October 1, 1999, Case mailed 1,000,000 coupons for $.45 off each box of cereal purchased. Case expects 120,000 of these coupons to be redeemed before the December 31, 1999, expiration date. It takes 30 days from the redemption date for Case to receive the coupons from the retailers. Case reimburses the retailers an additional $.05 for each coupon redeemed. As of December 31, 1999, Case had paid retailers $25,000 related to these coupons and had 50,000 coupons on hand that had not been processed for payment. What amount should Case report as a liability for coupons in its December 31, 1999 balance sheet?

    a. $35,000
    b. $29,000
    c. $25,000
    d. $22,500

85. Dunn Trading Stamp Co. records stamp service revenue and provides for the cost of redemptions in the year stamps are sold to licensees. Dunn's past experience indicates that only 80% of the stamps sold to licensees will be redeemed. Dunn's liability for stamp redemptions was $6,000,000 at December 31, 1998. Additional information for 1999 is as follows:

Stamp service revenue from stamps sold to licensees	$4,000,000
Cost of redemptions (stamps sold prior to 1/1/99)	2,750,000

If all the stamps sold in 1999 were presented for redemption in 2000, the redemption cost would be $2,250,000. What amount should Dunn report as a liability for stamp redemptions at December 31, 1999?

    a. $7,250,000
    b. $5,500,000
    c. $5,050,000
    d. $3,250,000

Items 86 and 87 are based on the following:

The following trial balance of Trey Co. at December 31, 1999, has been adjusted except for income tax expense.

	Dr.	Cr.
Cash	$ 550,000	
Accounts receivable, net	1,650,000	
Prepaid taxes	300,000	
Accounts payable		$ 120,000
Common stock		500,000
Additional paid-in capital		680,000
Retained earnings		630,000
Foreign currency translation adjustment	430,000	
Revenues		3,600,000
Expenses	2,600,000	
	$5,530,000	$5,530,000

Additional information

• During 1999, estimated tax payments of $300,000 were charged to prepaid taxes. Trey has not yet recorded income tax expense. There were no differences between financial statement and income tax income, and Trey's tax rate is 30%.

• Included in accounts receivable is $500,000 due from a customer. Special terms granted to this customer require payment in equal semiannual installments of $125,000 every April 1 and October 1.

86. In Trey's December 31, 1999 balance sheet, what amount should be reported as total current assets?

    a. $1,950,000
    b. $2,200,000
    c. $2,250,000
    d. $2,500,000

87. In Trey's December 31, 1999 balance sheet, what amount should be reported as total retained earnings?

    a. $1,029,000
    b. $1,200,000
    c. $1,330,000
    d. $1,630,000

88. The following is Gold Corp.'s June 30, 1999 trial balance:

Cash overdraft		$ 10,000
Accounts receivable, net	$ 35,000	
Inventory	58,000	
Prepaid expenses	12,000	
Land held for resale	100,000	
Property, plant, and equipment, net	95,000	
Accounts payable and accrued expenses		32,000
Common stock		25,000
Additional paid-in capital		150,000
Retained earnings		83,000
	$300,000	$300,000

Additional information

• Checks amounting to $30,000 were written to vendors and recorded on June 29, 1999, resulting in a cash overdraft of $10,000. The checks were mailed on July 9, 1999.

• Land held for resale was sold for cash on July 15, 1999.

• Gold issued its financial statements on July 31, 1999.

In its June 30, 1999 balance sheet, what amount should Gold report as current assets?

    a. $225,000
    b. $205,000
    c. $195,000
    d. $125,000

89. Mill Co.'s trial balance included the following account balances at December 31,1999:

Accounts payable	$15,000
Bonds payable, due 2000	25,000
Discount on bonds payable, due 2000	3,000
Dividends payable 1/31/00	8,000
Notes payable, due 2001	20,000

What amount should be included in the current liability section of Mill's December 31,1999 balance sheet?

    a. $45,000
    b. $51,000

c. $65,000
d. $78,000

Items 90 and 91 are based on the following:

Rey, Inc.
SELECTED FINANCIAL DATA
December 31,

	1999	*1998*
Cash	$ 170,000	$ 90,000
Accounts receivable (net)	450,000	400,000
Merchandise inventory	540,000	420,000
Short-term marketable securities	80,000	40,000
Land and building (net)	1,000,000	1,000,000
Mortgage payable-- current portion	60,000	50,000
Accounts payable and accrued liabilities	240,000	220,000
Short-term notes payable	100,000	140,000

Net credit sales totaled $3,000,000 and $2,000,000 for the years ended December 31, 1999 and 1998, respectively.

90. At December 31, 1999, Rey's quick (acid-test) ratio was

a. 1.50 to 1.
b. 1.75 to 1.
c. 2.06 to 1.
d. 3.10 to 1.

91. For 1999, Rey's accounts receivable turnover was

a. 1.13
b. 1.50
c. 6.67
d. 7.06

92. Which of the following ratios is(are) useful in assessing a company's ability to meet currently maturing or short-term obligations?

	Acid-test ratio	*Debt to equity ratio*
a.	No	No
b.	No	Yes
c.	Yes	Yes
d.	Yes	No

93. At December 30, 1999, Vida Co. had cash of $200,000, a current ratio of 1.5:1 and a quick ratio of .5:1. On December 31, 1999, all cash was used to reduce accounts payable. How did these cash payments affect the ratios?

	Current ratio	*Quick ratio*
a.	Increased	Decreased
b.	Increased	No effect
c.	Decreased	Increased
d.	Decreased	No effect

94. Tod Corp. wrote off $100,000 of obsolete inventory at December 31, 1999. The effect of this write-off was to decrease

a. Both the current and acid-test ratios.
b. Only the current ratio.
c. Only the acid-test ratio.
d. Neither the current nor the acid-test ratios.

95. The following computations were made from Clay Co.'s 1999 books:

Number of days' sales in inventory	61
Number of days' sales in accounts receivable	33

What was the number of days in Clay's 1999 operating cycle?

a. 33
b. 47
c. 61
d. 94

96. On December 31, 1999, Northpark Co. collected a receivable due from a major customer. Which of the following ratios would be increased by this transaction?

a. Inventory turnover ratio.
b. Receivable turnover ratio.
c. Current ratio.
d. Quick ratio.

OTHER OBJECTIVE QUESTIONS

Problem 1   (15 to 25 minutes)

The following items relate to the transfer of accounts and notes receivable.

Required:

a.   Items 1 through 6. For each item, match the transaction with the appropriate journal entry. Entries may be used once, more than once, or not at all.

Transaction		*Journal entry*		
1. A company transfers receivables by surrendering control. Collection is to be made by the purchaser (factor), who assumes risk of loss.	A.	Cash	xxx	
		Interest expense	xxx	
		Liability on discounted NR		xxx
		Interest revenue		xxx
2. A company specifically assigns a portion of its receivables as collateral for a loan. Collections from the assigned receivables will be used to repay the loan and interest.	B.	Cash	xxx	
		Factor's holdback	xxx	
		Interest expense (Discount)	xxx	
		Liability on transferred AR		xxx
3. A company pledges its receivables as collateral to secure a loan and the debtor collects the proceeds.	C.	Cash	xxx	
		Finance charge	xxx	
		AR assigned	xxx	
		Note payable		xxx
		AR		xxx
4. A company sells accounts receivable to a factor in a transaction considered a borrowing.				
5. A company transfers a note receivable by surrendering control over it. The transfer was on a without recourse basis.	D.	Cash	xxx	
		Factor's holdback	xxx	
		Loss on sale of AR	xxx	
		AR		xxx
6. A company pledges its accounts receivable as security for a loan.	E.	Parenthetical or note disclosure only.		
	F.	Cash	xxx	
		Loss on sale of NR	xxx	
		NR		xxx
		Interest revenue		xxx

b.   Items 7 through 11. Determine whether each statement is true or false.

7. The balance in "factor's holdback" (due from factor) is reported as an expense of the period.

8. In a specific assignment of receivables, collections on the assigned accounts are generally remitted to the assignor.

9. Factors are banks or finance companies that purchase receivables for a fee and then collect the remittances directly from the selling company.

10. A transfer of receivables with recourse may be accounted for as a sale, provided the transferee can require the transferor to repurchase the receivables.

11. In a transfer of receivables with recourse accounted for as a borrowing, the difference between the receivables and the total of the factor's holdback plus the proceeds is a financing cost that should be amortized to interest expense over the term of the receivables.

Problem 2 *   (10 to 15 minutes)

Items 1 through 6 are based on the following:

Town, Inc. is preparing its financial statements for the year ended December 31, 1999.

Required:

Items 1 through 6 represent various commitments and contingencies of Town at December 31, 1999, and events subsequent to December 31, 1999, but prior to the issuance of the 1999 financial statements. For each item, select from the following list the reporting requirement and blacken the corresponding oval on the Objective Answer Sheet. A reporting requirement may be selected once, more than once, or not at all.

---

* *This is Part B of 1195, FARE 3. Part A appears in Module 26B, Problem 1.*

	Reporting requirement
D	Disclosure only.
A	Accrual only.
B	Both accrual and disclosure.
N	Neither accrual nor disclosure.

1. On December 1, 1999, Town was awarded damages of $75,000 in a patent infringement suit it brought against a competitor. The defendant did not appeal the verdict, and payment was received in January 2000.

2. A former employee of Town has brought a wrongful-dismissal suit against Town. Town's lawyers believe the suit to be without merit.

3. At December 31, 1999, Town had outstanding purchase orders in the ordinary course of business for purchase of a raw material to be used in its manufacturing process. The market price is currently higher than the purchase price and is not anticipated to change within the next year.

4. A government contract completed during 1999 is subject to renegotiation. Although Town estimates that it is reasonably possible that a refund of approximately $200,000 – $300,000 may be required by the government, it does not wish to publicize this possibility.

5. Town has been notified by a governmental agency that it will be held responsible for the cleanup of toxic materials at a site where Town formerly conducted operations. Town estimates that it is probable that its share of remedial action will be approximately $500,000.

6. On January 5, 2000, Town redeemed its outstanding bonds and issued new bonds with a lower rate of interest. The reacquisition price was in excess of the carrying amount of the bonds.

Problem 3

See the solutions approach example in Chapter 3, Solutions Approach, Problem 2.

PROBLEMS

Problem 1   (15 to 25 minutes)

Magrath Company has an operating cycle of less than 1 year and provides credit terms for all of its customers. On April 1, 1999, the company transferred some of its accounts receivable. Control over the receivables was surrendered by Magrath.

On July 1, 1999, Magrath sold special order merchandise and received a noninterest-bearing note due June 30, 2000. The market rate of interest for this note is determinable.

Magrath uses the allowance method to account for uncollectible accounts. During 1999, some accounts were written off as uncollectible and other accounts previously written off as uncollectible were collected.

Required:

a. How should Magrath account for and report the accounts receivable factored on April 1, 1999? Why is this accounting treatment appropriate?

b. How should Magrath report the effects of the noninterest-bearing note on its income statement for the year ended December 31, 1999, and its December 31, 1999 balance sheet?

c. How should Magrath account for the collection of the accounts previously written off as uncollectible?

d. What are the two basic approaches to estimating uncollectible accounts under the allowance method? What is the rationale for each approach?

Problem 2   (20 to 25 minutes)

Sigma Co. began operations on January 1, 1998. On December 31, 1998, Sigma provided for uncollectible accounts based on 1% of annual credit sales. On January 1, 1999, Sigma changed its method of determining its allowance for uncollectible accounts by applying certain percentages to the accounts receivable aging as follows:

Days past invoice date	Percent deemed to be uncollectible
0 - 30	1
31 - 90	5
91 - 180	20
Over 180	80

In addition, Sigma wrote off all accounts receivable that were over 1 year old. The following additional information relates to the years ended December 31, 1999, and 1998:

	1999	1998
Credit sales	$3,000,000	$2,800,000
Collections	2,915,000	2,400,000

	1999	1998
Accounts written off	27,000	None
Recovery of accounts previously written off	7,000	None

Days past invoice date at 12/31		
0 - 30	300,000	250,000
31 - 90	80,000	90,000

| 91 - 180 | 60,000 | 45,000 |
| Over 180 | 25,000 | 15,000 |

Required:

a. Prepare a schedule showing the calculation of the allowance for uncollectible accounts at December 31, 1999.

b. Prepare a schedule showing the computation of the provision for uncollectible accounts for the year ended December 31, 1999.

Problem 3   (15 to 25 minutes)

Gregor Wholesalers Co. sells industrial equipment for a standard 3-year note receivable. Revenue is recognized at time of sale. Each note is secured by a lien on the equipment and has a face amount equal to the equipment's list price. Each note's stated interest rate is below the customer's market rate at date of sale. All notes are to be collected in 3 equal annual installments beginning 1 year after sale. Some of the notes are subsequently discounted at a bank with recourse that qualify as sales, some are subsequently discounted without recourse, and some are retained by Gregor. At year end, Gregor evaluates all outstanding notes receivable and provides for estimated losses arising from defaults.

Required:

a. What is the appropriate valuation basis for Gregor's notes receivable at the date it sells equipment?

b. How should Gregor account for the discounting, without recourse, of a February 1, 1999 note receivable discounted on May 1, 1999? Why is it appropriate to account for it in this way?

c. At December 31, 1999, how should Gregor measure and account for the impact of estimated losses resulting from notes receivable that it
  1. Retained and did **not** discount?
  2. Discounted at a bank with recourse?

Problem 4   (15 to 25 minutes)

Smith, Inc. is planning to obtain cash by transferring some of its accounts receivable to a factor.

a. With regard to transfers of financial assets, what is the meaning of the financial components approach?

b. Describe the criteria for determining when control has been surrendered in a transfer of receivables.

c. How are transfers of receivables accounted for if one or more of the criteria for determining whether control has been surrendered are not met?

d. Describe the accounting for transfers of receivables in which control is surrendered, but the agreement contains a recourse provision that allows the transferee to recover losses from the transferor and provides for a factor's holdback.

Problem 5   (15 to 25 minutes)

Chester Company has the following contingencies:

• A threat of expropriation exists for one of its manufacturing plants located in a foreign country. Expropriation is deemed to be reasonably possible. Any compensation from the foreign government would be less than the carrying amount of the plant.

• Potential costs exist due to the discovery of a safety hazard related to one of its products. These costs are probable and can be reasonably estimated.

• One of its warehouses located at the base of a mountain could no longer be insured against rockslide losses. No rockslide losses have occurred.

Required:

a. How should Chester report the threat of expropriation of assets? Why?

b. How should Chester report the potential costs due to the safety hazard? Why?

c. How should Chester report the noninsurable rock-slide risk? Why?

Problem 6   (15 to 25 minutes)

Supey Chemical Co. encountered the following two situations in 1999:

• Supey must pay an indeterminate amount for toxic waste cleanup on its land. An adjoining land owner, Gap Toothpaste, sold its property because of possible toxic contamination by Supey of the water supply and resulting potential adverse public reaction towards its product. Gap sued Supey for damages. There is a reasonable possibility that Gap will prevail in the suit.

• At December 31, 1999, Supey had a noncancellable purchase contract for 10,000 pounds of Chemical XZ, for delivery in June 2000. Supey does not hedge its contracts. Supey uses this chemical to make Product 2-Y. In December 1999, the US Food and Drug Administration banned the sale of Product 2-Y in concentrated form. Supey will be allowed to sell Product 2-Y in a diluted form; however, it will take at least 5 years to use the 10,000 pounds of Chemical XZ. Supey believes the sales price of the diluted product will not be sufficient to recover the contract price of Chemical XZ.

Required:

a. **1.** In its 1999 financial statements, how should Supey report the toxic waste cleanup? Why is this reporting appropriate?

   2. In its 1999 financial statements, how should Supey report Gap's claim against it? Why is this reporting appropriate?

b. In its 1999 financial statements, how should Supey report the effects of the contract to purchase Chemical XZ? Why is this reporting appropriate?

Problem 7 *   (15 to 25 minutes)

*Part C of this essay question deals with accruing compensation for future vacations. It can be found in Module 26, Present Value, D. Pensions, Problem 1.

MULTIPLE-CHOICE ANSWERS

1. c	18. a	35. d	52. d	69. a	85. c
2. a	19. b	36. c	53. b	70. b	86. a
3. a	20. a	37. d	54. c	71. d	87. c
4. a	21. c	38. c	55. c	72. a	88. a
5. a	22. b	39. b	56. d	73. a	89. a
6. a	23. d	40. c	57. c	74. d	90. b
7. c	24. c	41. c	58. c	75. c	91. d
8. c	25. b	42. c	59. b	76. a	92. d
9. c	26. d	43. c	60. c	77. d	93. a
10. d	27. a	44. d	61. b	78. d	94. b
11. b	28. c	45. a	62. b	79. c	95. d
12. a	29. c	46. b	63. c	80. c	96. b
13. a	30. a	47. b	64. b	81. b	
14. a	31. a	48. b	65. c	82. d	
15. d	32. b	49. b	66. d	83. d	
16. b	33. a	50. b	67. c	84. a	1st: __/96 = __%
17. a	34. a	50. d	68. a		2nd: __/96 = __%

MULTIPLE-CHOICE ANSWER EXPLANATIONS

A. Cash

1.   **(c)**   Cash on hand ($125,000) and cash in banks ($2,250,000) are both reported as cash in the current asset section of the balance sheet because they are both unrestricted and readily available for use. Cash legally restricted for additions to plant ($1,600,000) is not available to meet current operating needs, and therefore should be excluded from current assets. Instead, it should be shown in the long-term asset section of the balance sheet as an investment. The amount to be reported as cash is $2,375,000 ($2,250,000 + $125,000).

2.   **(a)**   To be classified as cash, the item must be readily available for current needs with no legal restrictions limiting its use. A postdated check is not acceptable for deposit and therefore is not considered cash. Thus, the $2,000 check was correctly excluded from the 12/31 checkbook balance and no adjustment is necessary. An NSF check should not be included in cash until it has been redeposited and has cleared the bank. At 12/31, the NSF check ($500) had not yet been redeposited, so it was incorrectly included in the 12/31 checkbook balance, and an adjustment must be made. The check which was not mailed until 1/10/00 ($300) should not be subtracted from cash until the company gives up physical control of that amount. Therefore, $300 must be added back to the checkbook balance. As a result of these adjustments, the correct cash balance is $4,800 ($5,000 – $500 + $300).

3.   **(a)**   Cash which is segregated and deposited into a bond sinking fund is presented in a classified balance sheet as a noncurrent asset because its use is restricted. Bank overdrafts are presented as current liabilities, unless other accounts at the **same bank** contain sufficient cash to offset the overdraft. The operating account, which has a positive balance, should be presented as a current asset. Therefore, answer (a) is correct, and answers (b), (c), and (d) are incorrect.

A.1. Bank Reconciliations

4.   **(a)**   To determine the correct 8/31/99 cash balance, a partial bank reconciliation should be prepared. The balance per bank statement ($18,050) must be adjusted for any items which the bank has not yet recorded and also for any bank errors (none in this problem).

Balance per bank statement	$18,050
Deposits in transit	3,250
Outstanding checks	(2,750)
Correct balance	$18,550

The deposits in transit and outstanding checks represent transactions which the company has recorded, but the bank has not yet recorded. The insufficient funds check ($600) and bank service charge ($100) are both items which the bank has recorded but the company has not. They would be adjustments to the **book balance**, not the **bank balance**.

5.   **(a)**   The balance per books at 3/31/99 is $44,200. The amount would be increased by cash receipts per books and decreased by cash disbursements per books. Cash receipts per the bank in April were $58,400, but this amount includes the $10,300 in transit at 3/31. Therefore, cash receipts per books in April are $48,100 ($58,400 – $10,300). Cash disbursements per the bank in April were $49,700. This amount includes the 3/31 outstanding checks ($12,600) but does **not** include the 4/30 outstanding checks ($7,000). Therefore, April cash disbursements per books is $44,100 ($49,700 – $12,600 + $7,000). The cash balance per books at 4/30/99 is $48,200 ($44,200 at 3/31/99, plus $48,100 receipts, less $44,100 disbursements). An alternative solutions approach is to first compute the 4/30/99 bank balance ($46,500 + $58,400 – $49,700 = $55,200), and then adjust for outstanding checks ($55,200 – $7,000 = $48,200).

B. Receivables

6.   **(a)**   The 12/31/99 current net receivables would include the trade receivables, net of the allowance account ($93,000 – $2,000) = $91,000). The claim against a shipper for goods lost in transit ($3,000) is also a valid receivable at year end. Therefore, the total current net receivables are $94,000 ($91,000 + $3,000), and answer (a) is correct. The **unsold** goods on consignment do not represent a receivable until sold. Therefore, the $26,000 should be removed from receivables and sales and the cost ($26,000 ÷ 130% = $20,000) should be removed from cost of goods sold and reported as ending inventory. The security deposit ($30,000) should be reported as a **long-term** receivable.

7.   (c)   The solutions approach is to set up a T-account for accounts receivable.

	AR		
1/1/99	650,000		
Credit sales	2,700,000	75,000	Sales returns
		40,000	Write-offs
		2,150,000	Collections
12/31/99	1,085,000		

Credit sales are debited to **AR** and credited to **sales**. Sales returns are debited to **sales returns** and credited to **AR**; write-offs are debited to the **allowance for doubtful accounts** and credited to **AR**; and cash collections are debited to **cash** and credited to **AR**. The estimated future sales returns ($50,000) and estimated uncollectible accounts ($110,000) do not affect the accounts receivable account but are instead recorded in separate allowance accounts. Since the requirement is to determine accounts receivable **before** these allowances, the balance of accounts receivable should include only sales returns and write-offs for 1999. Thus, answer (c) is correct.

8.   (c)   Accrued interest receivable at 6/30/99 is interest revenue which has been earned by 6/30/99, but has not yet been received by that date. Interest was last received on 7/1/98; the accrued interest receivable includes interest revenue earned from 7/1/98 through 6/30/99 (a full year). The original balance of the note receivable was $150,000 but the 7/1/98 principal payment of $50,000 reduced this balance to $100,000. Therefore, the 6/30/99 interest receivable is $8,000 ($100,000 x 8%).

9.   (c)   Per SFAS 91, loan origination fees are recognized over the life of the related loan as an adjustment of yield. These fees are recorded as a discount on the note receivable. Therefore, Tigg's 12/1/99 entry is:

Notes receivable	200,000	
Discount on NR		6,000
Cash		194,000

Using the effective interest method, Tigg's 12/31/99 adjusting entry is:

Int. receivable	2,000	
Discount on NR	166	
Int. revenue		2,166

The interest receivable is:

Face value	x	Stated rate	x	Time		
$200,000	x	12%	x	1/12	=	$2,000

The interest revenue is:

Carrying amount	x	Effective rate	x	Time		
$194,000	x	13.4%	x	1/12	=	$2,166

10.   (d)   A current asset is an asset that can be reasonably expected to be converted into cash, sold or consumed in operations, within a single operating cycle or within a year if more than one cycle is completed each year. A noncurrent asset is an asset that can not be expected to be converted to cash, sold or consumed within a single operating cycle or within 1 year, whichever is longer. Because accrued interest was reported as a current asset on the 1999 balance sheet, it can be assumed interest will be received on August 31, 1999, since current assets are received within 1 year. Also, because the note receivable was reported as a noncurrent asset it can be assumed that the principal will not be collected within the next 12 months. Principal that is not due until August 31, 2000, coincides with reporting the note as a noncurrent asset. Therefore, answer (d) is correct and (a), (b), and (c) are incorrect.

11.   (b)   Upon receipt of the interest-bearing note for the sale of goods, Benet would record the following entry:

Notes receivable	(face value)
Interest receivable	(interest from 7/15 to 8/15)
Sales	(face + interest)

Note that the interest which accrued on the note from July 15 to August 15 represents part of the sales price of the merchandise (rather than interest income) because Benet did not hold the note during this period. On November 15, Benet will record the following entry:

Cash	(Plug)
Note receivable	(face value)
Interest revenue	(interest from 8/15 to 11/15)
Interest receivable	(interest from 7/15 to 8/15)

B.1.   Anticipation of Sales Discounts

12.   (a)   If material, an allowance for discounts must be reported at year end in order to match the discounts with the related sales and to report receivables at their collectible amount. At 12/31/99, $100,000 of the accounts receivable have the potential to be discounted by 2% because they are less than 15 days old (terms 2/10, net 30). Since 50% of the customers are expected to take advantage of the 2% discount, the allowance for discounts should be $1,000 [($100,000 x 50%) x 2%]. None of the other categories require a discount allowance because they are older than the maximum age of 15 days to receive the 2% discount (terms = 2/15, net 30).

13.   (a)   SFAS 48 requires that when revenue is recognized from sales where a right of return exists, sales revenue must be reduced to reflect estimated returns. In this case, sales of $1,000,000 must be reduced by estimated returns of $100,000 [(7% + 3%) x $1,000,000], resulting in net sales of $900,000. The estimated exchanges (15%) will not result in a future reduction of sales.

B.2.   Bad Debts Expense

14.   (a)   To compute the 12/31/99 allowance for uncollectible accounts, the solutions approach is to set up a T-account for the allowance.

Allowance for U.A.

		260,000	1/1/99
		180,000	Expense (2% x 9,000,000)
Write-offs	325,000		
		115,000	12/31/99

The 1/1/99 balance is increased by bad debts expense recorded (2% x credit sales of $9,000,000) and decreased by write-offs of specific uncollectible accounts.

15.   (d) The balance in the allowance for doubtful accounts should reflect the amount of accounts receivable that are estimated to be uncollectible. Since it is estimated that 3% of the gross accounts receivable will become uncollectible, the allowance account should have a 12/31/99 balance of $30,000 (3% x $1,000,000). Note that **bad debt expense** of $38,000 would be recorded for 1999, as indicated below:

Allowance

Bal. before adj.	8,000		
		?	Bad debt expense ($38,000)
		30,000	12/31/98 (3% x $1,000,000)

16.   (b) The solutions approach is to set up a T-account for the allowance for doubtful accounts.

Allowance

		30,000	1/1/99
1999 Write-offs	18,000	2,000	1999 Recoveries
		14,000	12/31/99 Before adj.
		?	Unc. accts. expense
		25,000	12/31/99

In 1999, $18,000 of accounts were written off as uncollectible (debit allowance, credit AR). Also, $2,000 of AR were recovered (debit AR, credit allowance; then, debit cash, credit AR), leaving a balance in the allowance account of $14,000 ($30,000 – $18,000 + $2,000). The desired 12/31/99 balance is $25,000 ($350,000 AR less $325,000 net value per aging schedule). Therefore, to increase the allowance from $14,000 to $25,000, uncollectible accounts expense of $11,000 must be recorded.

17.   (a) When an aging schedule is used to estimate uncollectibles, the total uncollectibles computed is the amount used for the ending balance in the allowance account. As computed below, the 12/31/99 allowance for uncollectible accounts should be $9,000.

$$\$120,000 \times 1\% = \$1,200$$
$$90,000 \times 2\% = 1,800$$
$$100,000 \times 6\% = \underline{6,000}$$
$$\underline{\$9,000}$$

The other information given (12/31/98 allowance, write-offs, and recoveries) would be used to determine the bad debt expense adjustment, not the allowance balance. In this case, apparently due to a change in estimate, the bad debt expense adjustment would actually be a credit (to offset the necessary debit to the allowance account).

Allowance for U.A.

		22,000	12/31/98
Write-offs	7,000	4,000	Recoveries
		19,000	
Adjustment	10,000		
		9,000	12/31/99

18.   (a) The aging of receivables method of estimating uncollectible accounts is based on the theory that bad debts are a function of accounts receivable collections during the period. The aging of receivables method emphasizes reporting accounts receivable at their net realizable value. It is a "balance-sheet" approach, which stresses the collectibility (valuation) of the receivable balance. Once the balance of the allowance account required to reduce net accounts receivable to their realizable value has been computed, bad debts expense is merely the amount needed to adjust the allowance account to the computed balance. Answer (b) is incorrect because under the direct write-off method, bad debts are considered expenses in the period in which they are written off; no consideration is given to the valuation of accounts receivable. Answers (c) and (d) are incorrect because both of these methods are based on the theory that bad debts are a function of sales. Thus, these methods emphasize reporting the bad debts expense amount accurately on the income statement.

19.   (b) A primary objective of accrual accounting is to record the cash consequences of events that change an entity's financial position in the period in which the events occur. This means recognizing revenues when earned rather than when cash is received, and recognizing expenses when incurred rather than when cash is paid. Expenses are incurred when they help the firm earn revenue. Under the allowance method, uncollectible accounts expense is recognized in the same period as the related revenue. The same credit decisions which enabled the entity to earn revenue caused it to incur uncollectible accounts expense. Therefore, under accrual accounting that expense should be recognized in the same period. On the other hand, when the direct write-off method is used, the uncollectible accounts expense is generally recognized after the period in which the revenue is recognized; after the event (credit decision) which changed financial position. Therefore, the direct write-off method is **not** consistent with accrual accounting.

20.   (a) When the allowance method for recognizing uncollectible accounts is used, the entry to write off a specific account is:

Allowance for unc. accts.	xxx	
Accts. receivable		xxx

Answer (a) is correct because this entry decreases both accounts. Answer (b) is wrong because the entry does not increase, or credit, the allowance account. Answer (c) is incorrect because the entry neither increases the allowance account nor affects net income (NI is affected by the recognition of bad debt expense, not by the write-off of a specific account). Answer (d) is wrong, again because the entry does not affect NI.

21.   (c) When an account receivable which was previously written off is collected, two entries must be made.

The first entry reverses the write-off and reestablishes the receivable:

Accounts receivable	xxx	
Allowance for uncollectible accounts		xxx

The second entry records the cash receipt:

Cash	xxx	
Accounts receivable		xxx

The credit to the allowance account in the first entry increases its balance. Uncollectible accounts expense, however, is not affected by this transaction. Therefore, answer (c) is correct.

B.3. Pledging, Assigning, Selling AR

22. (b)   An **assignment** of accounts receivable is a financing arrangement whereby the owner of the receivables (assignor) obtains a loan from the lender (assignee) by pledging the accounts receivable as collateral. A **factoring** of accounts receivable is basically a sale of, or borrowing on, the receivables. "Factors" are intermediaries that buy receivables from companies (for a fee) and then collect payments directly from the customers. Thus, both of these are methods of generating cash from accounts receivable, and answer (b) is correct.

23. (d)   When receivables are factored and control is surrendered the transaction is treated as a **sale**. Therefore, answer (d) is correct. Answers (a) and (b) are incorrect because, under SFAS 125, a transfer in which control is surrendered will not be treated as a borrowing. Answer (c) is incorrect because the risk of uncollectible accounts is **not** retained by the seller in a sale without recourse.

24. (c)   Taylored will receive the value of the receivables ($400,000), reduced by $20,000 for the amount of the holdback ($400,000 x .05), $8,000 withheld as fee income ($400,000 x .02), and $6,740 withheld as interest expense ($400,000 x .15 x 41/365). Answer (c) is therefore correct ($400,000 – $8,000 – $6,740 – $20,000).

25. (b)   Under SFAS 125, a sale of receivables with recourse is recorded using a financial components approach because the seller has a continuing involvement. Under this approach the seller would reduce receivables, recognize assets obtained and liabilities incurred, and record gain or loss. The entry would be

Cash	$365,260	
Factor's holdback	20,000	
Loss	22,740*	
Accounts receivable		$400,000
Liability under recourse provision		8,000

*($6,740 + $8,000 + $8,000)

26. (d)   If all receivables are collected, Taylored would eliminate its recourse liability and the corresponding loss. The costs incurred by Taylored would include a fee of $8,000 ($400,000 x .02) and interest expense of $6,740 ($400,000 x .15 x 41/365) for a total of $14,740.

27. (a)   The seller uses a Due from Factor account to account for probable sales discounts, sales returns, and sales allowances. The Recourse liability account is recorded to indicate probable uncollectible accounts.

28. (c)   Under SFAS 125, a sale occurs if the seller surrenders control of the receivables transferred. Control is deemed to have been surrendered by the seller only if all three conditions listed in (a), (b), and (d) are met. Answer (c) is used to determine whether a recourse liability is recorded as part of the sale, not whether a transaction can be recorded as a sale.

B.4. Discounting Notes Receivable

29. (c)   To compute the proceeds from discounting the note, the maturity value of the note must first be computed [$500,000 + ($500,000 x 8%) = $540,000]. The discount charged by the bank is equal to the **maturity value** times the **discount rate** times the **time until maturity** ($540,000 x 10% x 6/12 = $27,000). The cash received is equal to the **maturity value** less **the discount** ($540,000 – $27,000 = $513,000).

30. (a)   The correct answer is (a). To derecognize assets when control is gained is not an objective in accounting for transfers of financial assets. When control is gained, the assets should be recognized. Answer (b) is incorrect because an objective is to derecognize liabilities when extinguished. A liability no longer exists, and it should be removed from the balance sheet. Answer (c) is incorrect because recognizing liabilities when incurred is an objective. Answer (d) is incorrect because derecognizing assets when control is given up is an objective in accounting for transfers of financial assets.

31. (a)   When a note receivable is discounted **without recourse**, the company discounting the note has no obligation to the bank if the maker of the note fails to pay. Thus, the answer is $0.

32. (b)   The proceeds of a discounted note receivable are equal to the maturity value of the note, using the original interest rate, less the discount, calculated as the maturity value times the bank's discount rate for the number of days to maturity. Therefore, answer (b) is correct. Answer (a) is incorrect because it uses the note's discount rate of 12% instead of the bank's 15%. Answers (c) and (d) are incorrect because they use the face value of the note in calculating the proceeds.

C.1. Examples of Current Liabilities

33. (a)   Before adjustment, the balance in the Accounts Payable account is $360,000. This amount is net of a $50,000 debit balance in Lyle's account payable to Ross resulting from a $50,000 advance payment for goods to be manufactured to Lyle's specifications. The $50,000 should be reclassified as a current asset, **Advance to Suppliers**. The checks recorded on 12/29/99 incorrectly reduced the accounts payable balance by $100,000. The $100,000 reduction should not have been recorded until the checks were mailed on 1/5/00. The 12/31/99 accounts payable must be increased by $100,000. Therefore, the corrected 12/31/99 accounts payable is $510,000.

Unadjusted AP	$360,000
Reclassification of advance	50,000
Error correction	100,000
	$510,000

34.   (a)   When purchases are recorded using the net method, purchases and accounts payable are recorded at an amount net of the cash discounts, and the failure to take advantage of a discount is recorded in a Purchase Discounts Lost account. Therefore, when Rabb changes to the net method, gross accounts payable ($30,000) must be adjusted down to the net amount. Since $200 of discounts are still available in the accounts payable balance, the net accounts payable at 9/30/99 is $29,800 ($30,000 – $200). The journal entry is:

Purchase discounts lost	1,000	
Purchase discounts	800	
Accts. payable	200	
Purchases		2,000

35.   (d)   Accrued interest payable at 12/31/99 is interest expense which has been incurred by 12/31/99, but has not yet been paid by that date. The note was issued on 3/1/98 and interest is payable in full at maturity on 2/28/00. Therefore, there is 1 year and 10 months of unpaid interest at 12/31/99 (3/1/98 to 12/31/99). Interest for the first year is $1,200 ($10,000 x 12%). Since interest is compounded annually, the new principal amount for the second year includes the original principal ($10,000) plus the first year's interest ($1,200). Therefore, accrued interest for the 10 months ended 12/31/99 is $1,120 ($11,200 x 12% x 10/12), and total accrued interest at 12/31/99 is $2,320 ($1,200 + $1,120).

36.   (c)   Accrued interest payable at 12/31/99 is interest expense which has been incurred by 12/31/99, but has not yet been paid by that date. Interest was last paid on 9/1/99; the accrued interest payable includes interest expense incurred from 9/1/99 through 12/31/99 (4 months). The original balance of the note payable was $1,350,000 but the 9/1/99 principal payment of $450,000 reduced this balance to $900,000. Therefore, the interest payable at 12/31/99 is $36,000 ($900,000 x 12% x 4/12). The prime rate (11%) does not affect the computation because it is not the stated rate on this note.

37.   (d)   The solutions approach is to analyze the interest payable T-account for 1999, assuming all interest payments flow through interest payable.

Interest Payable			
		15,000	12/31/98
1999 Int. paid	68,000	85,000	1999 Expense
		?	12/31/99

The beginning interest payable balance ($15,000) is increased by interest expense (debit interest expense, credit interest payable for $85,000) and decreased by interest paid (debit interest payable, credit cash for $68,000), resulting in a 12/31/99 balance of $32,000 ($15,000 + $85,000 –

$68,000). Therefore, answer (d) is the correct interest payable balance at year end.

38.   (c)   All of the notes are due 6/15/00, and normally the entire amount would be classified as current. However, SFAS 6 states that a short-term obligation can be reclassified as long-term if the enterprise intends to refinance the obligation on a long-term basis **and** the intent is supported by the ability to refinance. Ames demonstrated its ability by entering into a financing agreement before the statements are issued. SFAS 6 further states that the amount to be excluded from current liabilities cannot exceed the amount available for refinancing under the agreement. Ames expects to be able to refinance at least $480,000 (80% x $600,000) of the notes. Therefore, that amount can be classified as long-term, while the remaining $20,000 must be classified as short-term.

39.   (b)   The effective rate of interest paid on a note is computed as follows:

$$\frac{\text{Effective}}{\text{interest rate}} = \frac{\text{Interest paid}}{\text{Cash received}}$$

In this case, let's assume the short-term note payable was in the amount of $100,000. The effective interest rate would be 12.56%.

$$\frac{(\$100,000 \times .12) + (\$100,000 \times .005)}{\$100,000 - (\$100,000 \times .005)} = 12.56$$

This is because the loan origination fee increases the interest paid on the note and reduces the net cash received from the note.

40.   (c)   The $4,000,000 note payable is due March 15, 1999, and normally would be classified as a current liability in the December 31, 1998 financial statements. However, SFAS 6 states that a short-term obligation can be reclassified as long-term if the enterprise intends to refinance the obligation on a long-term basis and the intent is supported by the ability to refinance. Cali demonstrated its ability to refinance by actually issuing bonds and refinancing the note prior to the issuance of the December 31, 1998 financial statements. Since the proceeds from the bonds exceeded the amount needed to retire the note, the entire $4,000,000 notes payable would be classified as a noncurrent liability, with separate disclosure of the note refinancing required by SFAS 6 [answer (c)].

41.   (c)   The notes payable ($750,000) are due 7/31/00, and would normally be included in 12/31/99 current liabilities. However, SFAS 6 states that a short-term obligation can be reclassified as long-term if the enterprise intends to refinance the obligation on a long-term basis and the intent is supported by the ability to refinance. Largo demonstrated its ability to refinance by actually issuing $1,500,000 of bonds in February 2000 before the 12/31/99 financial statements were issued on 3/3/00. The bond proceeds will be used to retire the note at maturity. SFAS 6 also states that the amount excluded from current liabilities cannot exceed the amount actually refinanced. Since Largo prepaid $250,000 of the note on 1/12/00 with excess cash, that amount must be included in 12/31/99 current liabilities.

Only the remaining $500,000 can be excluded from current liabilities.

42.   (c)   A key to solving this problem is understanding that the employee advances do **not** affect the accrued salaries payable. When advances are made to employees, they are a cash payment separate from the payroll function. The advances made, therefore, are not reflected in salaries expense ($420,000) or **gross** salaries paid ($390,000). Therefore, the solutions approach is to analyze the salaries payable T-account for 1999 (disregarding the employee advances).

Salaries Payable		
	40,000	12/31/98
1999 sal. paid 390,000	420,000	1998 sal. expense
	?	12/31/99

The beginning salaries payable balance ($40,000) is increased by salaries expense ($420,000) and decreased by salaries paid ($390,000), resulting in a 12/31/99 balance of $70,000.

43.   (c)   No sales commission is due to salesperson A because his commissions earned ($200,000 x 4% = $8,000) are less than his fixed salary ($10,000). Note that the excess of the fixed salary over commissions earned is not charged back against A. Commissions totaling $28,000 are due to salespersons B and C as computed below:

	Commissions earned		Fixed salary paid	Commissions payable
B	(6% x $400,000)	–	$14,000	$10,000
C	(6% x $600,000)	–	$18,000	18,000
				$28,000

44.   (d)   Lime's payroll tax liability includes amounts withheld from payroll checks [$1,200 of federal income taxes withheld and $700 of the **employees'** share of FICA ($10,000 x 7%)] plus the **employer's** share of FICA (an additional $700). Therefore, the total payroll tax liability is $2,600 ($1,200 + $700 + $700). The amount recorded as payroll tax expense consists only of the employer's share of FICA ($700), since no unemployment taxes are mentioned in the problem.

45.   (a)   The contingent unemployment claims liability is both probable and reasonably estimable, so it must be accrued at 12/31/99. Acme's reasonable estimate of its probable liability is 2% of eligible gross wages. Eligible gross wages are the first $10,000 of gross wages paid to each of the 5 employees (5 x $10,000 = $50,000), so the accrued liability should be $1,000 (2% x $50,000). Note that the 3% rate is not used because Acme has chosen the option to reimburse the state directly, and its best estimate of this liability is based on 2%, not 3%.

46.   (b)   To compute the amount of the contribution, the requirements described in the problem must be translated into an equation. The contribution must equal 10% of income **after** deduction of the contribution, but **before** income tax. Therefore, the tax rate (30%) does not enter into the computation. The equation is solved below.

$$C = .10 \times (\$75,000 - C)$$
$$C = \$7,500 - .10C$$
$$1.1C = \$7,500$$
$$C = \$7,500 \div 1.1$$
$$C = \$6,818$$

The amount to be accrued as an expense and liability is $6,818.

47.   (b)   If net income **after** bonus and income tax is $360,000, income before taxes can be computed by dividing **$360,000** by **1 minus the tax rate**.

$$\text{Income before taxes} = \frac{\$360,000}{1 - .40} = \$600,000$$

The bonus is equal to 10% of income **before** income tax but **after** the bonus. The $600,000 computed above **is** income before tax but after all other expenses including the bonus. Therefore, the bonus must be $60,000 (10% x $600,000). Note that this problem is different from other bonus problems because usually the income before taxes and bonus ($660,000 in this case) is given as the starting point, rather than net income.

48.   (b)   To determine the correct amount for sales revenue, Ivy must divide the total of sales and sales taxes by 100% plus the sales tax percentage (6%) as indicated below.

Month	Total		Percentage		Sales revenue
Jan.	$10,600	÷	106%	=	$10,000
Feb.	$7,420	÷	106%	=	7,000
March	$8,480	÷	106%	=	8,000
Total					$25,000

Sales taxes payable would include all sales taxes collected, less any sales taxes already remitted.

January sales taxes ($10,600 – $10,000)	$600
*February sales taxes ($7,420 – $7,000)	420
March sales taxes ($8,480 – $8,000)	480
Total	$1,500
Less taxes remitted	600
Sales taxes payable	$ 900

*Note February sales taxes were not remitted since it did not exceed $500.

49.   (b)   As of 12/31/99 the October sales taxes should have been paid, so there would be no 12/31/99 current liability for those taxes. However, at 12/31/99 sales taxes payable must be reported for the November room rentals as they were not paid until 1/3/00 and the December room rentals [15% x ($110,000 + $150,000) = $39,000]. The fourth quarter occupancy taxes were not paid until 1/3/00, so they would also represent a current liability at 12/31/99 [(1,100 + 1,200 + 1,800) x $2 = $8,200].

50.   (b)   When the warehouse was purchased on 9/1/99, it would be recorded at its total cost before any credit for accrued realty taxes. The offsetting credits would be to **cash** for the net amount paid, and to **real estate taxes payable** for 2 months' taxes ($12,000 x 2/6 = $4,000). At the end of

September and of October, Day would record property tax expense each month as follows:

Real estate tax expense	2,000	
Real estate taxes payable		2,000

Therefore, at October 31, Day has a balance of $8,000 in the payable account ($4,000 + $2,000 + $2,000). On 11/1/99, Day would record the semiannual payment as follows:

Real estate taxes payable	8,000	
Prepaid real estate taxes	4,000	
Cash		12,000

The prepaid real estate taxes would then be expensed $2,000 per month at the end of November and December. Thus, answer (b) is the correct amount debited to the payable.

51.   (d)   An accrued liability is an expense which has been incurred, but has not been paid. Of the $500 advertising bill, $375 had been incurred as an expense as of 12/31/99 and should be reported as an accrued liability at that time. For the store lease, the fixed portion ($1,200 per month) is payable on the 16th of each month for the preceding month. Therefore, on 12/16/99, rent was paid for the period 11/16/99 to 12/15/99. An additional one-half month's rent expense (1/2 x $1200 = $600) has been incurred but not paid as of 12/31/99. The variable portion of the rent [5% x ($550,000 – $300,000), or $12,500] was incurred during 1999, but will not be paid until 1/31/00. It, too, is an accrued liability at 12/31/99. Total 12/31/99 accrued liabilities are $13,475.

Advertising	$ 375
Fixed rent (1/2 x $1200)	600
Variable rent [5% x ($550,000 –	
$300,000)]	12,500
Total	$13,475

52.   (d)   The solutions approach to this problem is to construct a time line documenting the events in the question.

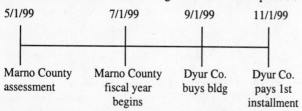

5/1/99	7/1/99	9/1/99	11/1/99
Marno County assessment	Marno County fiscal year begins	Dyur Co. buys bldg	Dyur Co. pays 1st installment

Note that on May 1, 1999, the County has merely determined the amount of property tax owed by each property owner, and no entries would be made by companies subject to property taxes on that date. The fiscal year 2000 taxes are for the period from July 1, 1999, to June 30, 2000. On September 1, 1999, the date on which Dyur purchased the building, 2 months of the fiscal year had passed, and the property tax expense related to those months was borne by the seller. At October 31, 1999, Dyur would have a liability for 4 months of property taxes (even though only the months of September and October would have been expensed by Dyur). On November 1, 1999, 4 months of the fiscal year had passed, and Dyur paid taxes for the first 6 months of the fiscal year. The entry recorded upon the payment would be

Property taxes payable	(4 months)
Prepaid property taxes	(2 months)
Cash	(6 months)

The payment would therefore be allocated as two-sixths (33 1/3%) to an increase in prepaid property taxes and four-sixths (66 2/3%) to a decrease in property taxes payable. Therefore, answer (d) is correct.

53.   (b)   To determine the 12/31/99 balance of the liability for customer advances, the solutions approach is to set up a T-account for the liability.

Customer Advances

		118,000	12/31/98
		184,000	1999 adv. received
1999 adv. applied	164,000		
1999 cancellations	50,000		
		88,000	12/31/99

When advances are received ($184,000), cash is debited and the liability account is credited. When advances are applied to orders shipped ($164,000), the liability account is debited and sales is credited. When an order is cancelled ($50,000), the liability account is debited and a revenue account is credited, since the advance payments are nonrefundable. Thus, the customer advances balance on 12/31/99 is $88,000 [answer (b)].

54.   (c)   The solutions approach is to set up a T-account for the liability.

Liability for Deposits

		580,000	12/31/99 balance
		780,000	1999 deliveries
1999 returns	626,000		
1999 sales	60,000		
		674,000	12/31/99 balance

When customers pay the deposit for a container, cash is debited and the liability is credited. Therefore, at 12/31/98 the liability consists of deposits for containers still held by customers from the last 2 years ($580,000). During 1999, the liability was increased for deposits on containers delivered ($780,000). When containers are returned, the deposits are returned to the customers; in 1999, the liability was debited and cash credited for $626,000. Also, at 12/31/99, some customers still held containers from 1997 ($150,000 – $90,000 = $60,000). The 2-year time limit has expired on these, so the company is no longer obligated to return the deposit. The containers are considered sold to the customers, so the liability account is debited and sales credited for $60,000. This results in a 12/31/99 balance of $674,000.

55.   (c)   To compute the escrow liability, the solutions approach is to use a T-account.

Escrow Liability

		700,000	1/1/99
Taxes paid	1,720,000	1,580,000	Receipts
		45,000	Net interest
		605,000	12/31/99

Escrow payments received ($1,580,000) would increase the liability because these amounts are payable to taxing authorities. Taxes paid ($1,720,000) decrease the liability.

The net interest credited to the escrow accounts [$50,000 − (10% x $50,000) = $45,000] would increase the liability, resulting in a 12/31/99 balance of $605,000.

56.   (d)   All contract sales are made **evenly** during the year. Therefore, the 1998 contracts range from 1 year expired (if sold on 12/31/98) to 2 years expired (if sold on 1/1/98), for an average of 1 1/2 years expired [(2+1)/2]. Similarly, the 1999 contracts range from 0 years expired to 1 year expired, for an average of 1/2 year expired [(0+1)/2]. The average **unearned** portion of the 1998 contracts is 1/2 year (2 years − 1 1/2 years), the last half of the second contract year. The amount of unearned revenue related to 1998 contracts is computed as follows:

$$\$500,000 \times 60\% \times 1/2 = \underline{\$150,000}$$

The average **unearned** portion of the 1999 contracts is 1 1/2 years (2 years − 1/2 year), the last half of the first contract year and all of the second contract year. The amount of unearned revenue related to the 1999 contracts is computed as follows:

1999:	$600,000 x 40% x 1/2	=	$120,000
	$600,000 x 60%	=	360,000
			$480,000

Therefore, the total unearned revenue is $630,000 ($150,000 + $480,000).

57.   (c)   Revenue is earned by Toddler Care Co. as time goes by and care is provided. Therefore, revenue should be recognized on a straight-line basis regardless of the timing of cash receipts. The monthly fees can simply be recognized on a monthly basis, but the initial payment must be deferred and recognized as revenue on a straight-line basis over the 12-month period. The 12/31/99 deferred revenues are $6,600, as computed below.

Plan	Initial fees	1999 revenue (4/12)	12/31/99 def. rev. (8/12)
1	15 x $500 = $7,500	$2,500	$5,000
2	12 x $200 = $2,400	800	1,600
3	$ 0	0	0
	$9,900	$3,300	$6,600

Since the total initial payments received are given ($9,900), a shortcut is to multiply that amount by 8/12 ($9,900 x 8/12 = $6,600).

58.   (d)   Revenue is generally recognized when **realized or realizable** and **earned**. Revenues are considered earned when the entity has substantially accomplished what it must do to be entitled to the benefits represented by the revenues. Therefore, service revenue generally is earned as the work is performed, and it should be recognized evenly over the contract year as the monthly services are performed [answer (d)]. Answer (a) is incorrect because accrual basis accounting is preferable; FASB Concept Statement 6, paras 144-5, explains that cash method provides little information about the results of operations. Answer (b) is incorrect because revenue should be recognized when earned. Answer (c) is incorrect because the completed-contract method should only be used when reasonable estimates of contract costs, revenues, and the extent of progress toward completion cannot be reasonably estimated.

59.   (b)   When a company issues gift certificates for cash, the following journal entry is made:

Cash	(amount of certificate)	
Deferred revenue		(amount of certificate)

When the gift certificates are subsequently redeemed, the following journal entry is made:

Deferred revenue	(amount of certificate)	
Revenue		(amount of certificate)

However, if the gift certificates are not redeemed and lapse, the following journal entry is made:

Deferred revenue	(amount of certificate)	
Gain on lapse of certificates		(amount of certificate)

Please note that although different accounts are credited depending on whether the certificates are redeemed or lapse, the Deferred Revenue account is decreased in both cases.

60.   (c)   Per SFAC 5, paras 83a and b, revenues are generally recognized when they are both **realized** or **realizable** and **earned**. Therefore, Dallas Co. should report a liability for deferred revenues equal to the advance payment of 60% of the main contract price. Per SFAC 6, para 36, one of three essential characteristics of a liability is that the transaction or other event obligating the entity has already happened. Since the subcontractor had not produced the special-order goods as of March 31, Dallas should not record a liability at that time. Therefore, no payable to the subcontractor would be reported for this activity as of March 31, and answer (c) is correct.

61.   (b)   At June 30, 1999, Northan Retailers should report the coupon transactions as unearned revenues because the sale of the coupons is not the culmination of the earnings process (i.e., Northan must allow customers to exchange the coupons for merchandise or refund the cost of the coupons at some later date). Therefore, answers (c) and (d) are incorrect. The unearned revenues should be recorded at the amount of the cash received by debiting cash and crediting an unearned revenue account. Therefore, answer (b) is correct. Answer (a) is incorrect because the retail price of the merchandise for which coupons may be redeemed does not impact the monetary amount of Northan's liability to its customers, and each coupon redeemed will ultimately result in the recognition of sales of $10, the amount of cash previously received.

62.   (b)   The requirement is to determine the situation which might account for the reduction in the deferred revenue balance. When a service contract is purchased by a customer and the fee prepaid, deferred revenue is recognized at the date of payment. Revenue cannot be recorded because revenue has not yet been earned. Revenue is only recorded when services are performed under the contract. The deferred revenue balance is reduced by the **actual** amount of revenue earned when services are performed under the services contract. If more contracts were signed earlier in 1 year than another year, there is a greater period of time in which to perform actual services. As previously stated, when actual services are performed, the deferred revenue balance is decreased. Therefore, the more actual services that are performed, the greater the reduction in the deferred revenue balance. Therefore, (b) is the correct answer. Answer (a) is incorrect because if more 1999 contracts were signed later in 1999 than 1998, the deferred revenue balance in 1999 would be larger than 1998. There would be less time to perform actual services, therefore less actual revenue would be recognized, creating a larger deferred revenue balance at year end. Answers (c) and (d) are incorrect because there is no contribution margin recognized on service contracts.

63.   (c)   Per SFAS 47, para 10, the aggregate amount of payments for unconditional purchase obligations that have been recognized on the purchaser's balance sheet shall be disclosed for each of the **5** years following the date of the latest balance sheet presented.

C.2. Current Liabilities--Contingencies

64.   (b)   Per SFAS 5, a loss contingency should be accrued if it is **probable** that a liability has been incurred at the balance sheet date and the amount of the loss is reasonably estimable. With respect to unfiled claims, the enterprise must consider both the probability that a claim will be filed and the probability of an unfavorable outcome. Although it is probable that claims will be asserted against Sims, it is only **reasonably possible** that the claims will be successful. Therefore, this contingent liability should not be accrued, but should be disclosed. The potential loss to be disclosed is $250,000, since the additional amount above the deductible would be covered by the insurance policy, and therefore is not a loss or liability for Sims.

65.   (c)   ARB 43 states that current liabilities are obligations whose liquidation is reasonably expected to require the use of current assets or the creation of other current liabilities. This means that generally, current liabilities are the liabilities which are due within 1 year of the balance sheet date. Clearly, accounts payable ($55,000) and accrued expenses ($35,000) are current liabilities. Notes payable ($400,000) and bonds payable ($1,000,000) are usually considered to be long-term, but the maturity dates given (7/1/00 and 3/1/00 respectively) indicate they are current liabilities at 12/31/99. The contingent liability ($450,000) and deferred tax liability ($25,000) will not be settled until 2001 and therefore should be classified as long-term at 12/31/99. Thus, the 12/31/99 current liabilities total is $1,490,000 as follows:

Accounts payable	$ 55,000
Accrued expenses	35,000
Unsecured notes 8% - due 7/1/00	400,000
Senior bonds 7% - due 3/31/00	1,000,000
Total current liabilities	$1,490,000

66.   (d)   The lawsuit damages must be accrued as a loss contingency in accordance with SFAS 5 because an unfavorable outcome is **probable** and the amount of the loss is **reasonably estimable**. Per SFAS Interpretation 14, when a range of possible loss exists, the best estimate within the range is accrued. When no amount within the range is a better estimate than any other amount, the dollar amount at the low end of the range is **accrued** (in this case, $500,000) and the dollar amount of the high end of the range is **disclosed**.

67.   (c)   Per SFAS 5, a loss contingency should be accrued if it is **probable** that a liability has been incurred at the balance sheet date and the amount of the loss is **reasonably estimable**. This loss must be accrued because it meets both criteria. Notice that even though the lawsuit was not initiated until 1/12/00, the liability was incurred on 11/5/99 when the accident occurred. FASB Interpretation 14 requires that when some amount within an estimated range is a better estimate than any other amount in the range, that amount is accrued. Therefore, a loss of $300,000 should be accrued. If no amount within the range is a better estimate than any other amount, the amount at the low end of the range is accrued and the amount at the high end is disclosed.

68.   (a)   The additional tax liability must be accrued as a loss contingency in accordance with SFAS 5 because an unfavorable outcome is **probable** and the amount of the loss is **reasonably estimable**. Since $200,000 is the reasonable estimate, that amount should be accrued by debiting Income Tax Expense and crediting Income Tax Payable. The possibility of the liability being as high as $300,000 would be disclosed in the notes. The settlement offer of $275,000 is not accrued at 12/31/99 because prior to financial statement issuance, Haft was unaware of the offer, and $200,000 was the best estimate. In 2000, when the settlement offer was accepted, Haft would record an additional $75,000 of expense and liability.

69.   (a)   Per SFAS 5, a loss contingency is accrued if it is **probable** that a liability has been incurred at the balance sheet date and the amount of the loss is reasonably estimable. If no accrual is made for a loss contingency because one or both of the conditions above are not met, disclosure of the contingency shall be made when it is at least **reasonably possible** that a loss was incurred. Therefore, this loss should be disclosed, but not accrued as a liability. Answers (b) and (c) are incorrect because the contingency is only reasonably possible, thus no accrual is made. Answer (d) is incorrect because a disclosure is required when the contingency is reasonably possible.

70.   (b)   Invern's appropriation of retained earnings for contingencies is merely a reclassification of retained earnings on the balance sheet which tells the readers of the financial statements that such amounts are generally not available to pay dividends. This appropriation has no effect on the income statement. When a loss contingency is probable (as in this instance) **and** reasonably estimable ($190,000 in this instance), SFAS 5, para 8, requires accrual of the loss. Therefore, Invern must accrue both a liability and an expense of $190,000, and answer (b) is correct. Note that Invern will also reclassify $190,000 of appropriated retained earnings into the "general" retained earnings.

71.   (d)   At 12/31/99, Halsey's contingent liability of $50,000 is no longer probable due to the favorable judgment and the inability to predict the outcome of the appeal. Therefore, no liability should be reported in the balance sheet. Para 17 of SFAS 5 states that **gain** contingencies are not reflected in the accounts until realized, so the $30,000 asset is not reported in the 12/31/99 balance sheet, either.

72. **(a)** Para 17 of SFAS 5 states that gain contingencies are not recognized in the income statement until realized. As only $15,000 of the litigation awards has been resolved as of December 31, 1999, Haze should report only $15,000 as a gain in its 1999 financial statements.

73. **(a)** Para 17 of SFAS 5 states that **gain** contingencies are not reflected in the accounts until realized. Since the case is unresolved at 12/31/99, none of this contingent gain should be recorded as income in 1999. Adequate disclosure should be made of the gain contingency, but care should be taken to avoid misleading implications as to the likelihood of realization. Therefore, answer (a) is correct.

74. **(d)** Para 17 of SFAS 5 states that **gain** contingencies are not reflected in the accounts until realized. Since the case was unresolved at 12/31/98, none of this contingent gain can be recorded as a receivable and/or revenue in 1998. Since the contingency is probable, it should be disclosed along with the 12/31/98 estimate of a range of $75,000 to $150,000. Answers (a) and (b) are incorrect because a gain contingency would not be accrued as a receivable. Answer (c) is incorrect because the amount disclosed should be the range because all amounts within the range are considered equally likely.

75. **(c)** Per SFAS 5, para 8, an estimated loss from a loss contingency shall be accrued by a charge to income if **both** of the following conditions are met:

1. Information available indicates that it is **probable** that an asset has been impaired or a liability has been incurred.
2. The amount of the loss can be **reasonably estimated**.

However, per SFAS 5, para 17, gain contingencies are only recognized when a specific event actually occurs, not prior to the event, because to do so would recognize the gain prior to its realization. Therefore, Brooks should recognize the loss in 1999 due to the fact that the event is probable and can be reasonably estimated. Dollis, on the other hand, cannot recognize the gain until 2000, the year they receive the actual award. Therefore, answer (c) is correct and (a), (b), and (d) are incorrect.

76. **(a)** Eagle Co. has a contingent liability where the possibility of loss is **remote**. Loss contingencies are accrued when they are **probable** and **reasonably estimable**. All others are disclosed unless remote. However, per SFAS 5, some contingencies, such as guarantees of others' debts, standby letters of credit by banks, and agreements to repurchase receivables, are disclosed even if remote. Eagle's contingent liability is **not** accrued, because it is not probable. It **is** disclosed for two reasons: it is a guarantee of other's debt, and it is a related-party transaction.

77. **(d)** SFAS 43 states that accrual of a liability for future vacation pay is required if all the conditions below are met.

1. Obligation arises from employee services already performed.
2. Obligation arises from rights that vest or accumulate.

3. Payment is probable.
4. Amount can be reasonably estimated.

The criteria are met for the vacation pay (150 x $100 = $15,000), so North is required to report a $15,000 liability. The same criteria apply to accrual of a liability for future sick pay, **except** that if sick pay benefits accumulate but do not vest, accrual is **permitted** but not **required** because its payment is contingent upon future employee sickness. Therefore, no liability is **required** for these sick pay benefits (75 x $100 = $7500). Note that the unadjusted balance of the liability account ($21,000) does not affect the computation of the required 12/31/99 liability.

78. **(d)** The week ended 1/1/00 included 4 days in 1999 and 1 day in 2000. The pay due for this week won't be paid until the following Monday (1/4/00). Therefore, Ross has a liability for 4 days' accrued salaries at 12/31/99 (4/5 x $80,000 = $64,000). The entire $25,000 of vacation pay is an accrued liability at 12/31/99 because it represents vacation time earned by employees in 1999 but not taken by 12/31/99. Therefore, the total accrued salary and vacation pay is $89,000 ($64,000 + $25,000).

79. **(c)** Per SFAS 43, an employer is required to accrue a liability for employees' rights to receive compensation for future absences, such as vacations, when certain conditions are met. The Statement does **not**, however, specify how such liabilities are to be measured. Since vacation time is paid by Gavin Co. at the salaries in effect when vacations are taken or when employment is terminated, Gavin adjusts its vacation liability and expense to current salary levels. Gavin's 1999 vacation pay expense consists of vacations earned for work in 1999 (adjusted to current rates) of $30,000 plus the amount necessary to adjust its pre-1999 vacation liability for the 10% salary increase. The amount of this adjustment is equal to 10% of the preexisting liability balance at December 31, 1999 [($35,000 −$20,000) x 10% = $1,500]. Therefore, total vacation pay expense for the period is equal to $31,500 ($30,000 + $1,500).

80. **(c)** Per SFAS 43, para 6, an employer shall accrue a liability for employees' future absences if **all** of the following conditions are met: (1) the employer's obligation relates to employees' service already rendered, (2) the employees' rights vest **or** accumulate, (3) payment of the compensation is probable, and (4) the amount can be reasonably estimated. Since all of these conditions are met whether Taos Co.'s employees' rights either accumulate or vest, answer (c) is correct.

81. **(b)** SFAS 43 states that accrual of a liability for employees' compensation for future absences is required if all of the conditions below are met:

1. Obligation arises from employee services already performed.
2. Obligation arises from rights which vest or accumulate.
3. Payment is probable.
4. Amount can be reasonably estimated.

Therefore, answer (b) is correct.

82. (d) The solutions approach is to set up a T-account for warranty liability.

Warranty Liability			
1999 payments	2,250	9,000	1999 exp. (6% x $150,000)
2000 payments	7,500	15,000	2000 exp. (6% x $250,000)
		14,250	12/31/00 liability

Each year warranty expense is estimated at 6% of sales and recorded by debiting the expense account and crediting the liability. As warranty expenditures are made, the liability is debited and cash is credited. Note that the total estimated warranty cost for **both** years (2% + 4% = 6%) is recorded in the year of sale in compliance with the matching principle.

83. (d) The warranty expense of $30 for each machine sold, although it will be incurred over the 3-year warranty period, is directly related to the sales revenue as an integral and inseparable part of the sale and recognized at the time of the sale. The warranty costs make their contribution to revenue in the year of sale by making the product more attractive to the customer. Therefore, in accordance with the matching principle, the warranty costs should be expensed when the machines are sold with a corresponding credit to accrued liability. Thus, answer (d) is correct. Answers (a) and (b) are incorrect; this is sales warranty approach in which the warranty is sold separately from the product. The revenue is recognized on the straight-line basis and they are expensed as incurred. Answer (c) is incorrect because this describes a cash basis method.

84. (a) Case expects 120,000 coupons to be redeemed at a total cost of $.50 per coupon ($.45 + $.05). Therefore, total expected redemptions are $60,000 (120,000 x $.50). By 12/31/99, $25,000 has been paid on coupon redemptions, so a liability of $35,000 must be established ($60,000 – $25,000). Note that this liability would include both payments due for the 50,000 coupons on hand, and payments due on coupons to be received within the first 30 days after the expiration date.

85. (c) Dunn records stamp service revenue and provides for the cost of redemptions in the year stamps are sold. Therefore, Dunn's entries are:

To record sales of stamps
Cash	4,000,000	
Stamp service revenue		4,000,000

To record cost of redemptions
Liability for stamp reds.	2,750,000	
Inventory		2,750,000

To provide for cost of future redemptions
Cost of redemptions	1,800,000	
Liability for stamp reds.		1,800,000
(80% x $2,250,000)		

The 12/31/99 liability balance is $5,050,000 as shown below.

Liability for Stamp Redemptions			
		6,000,000	12/31/98
Redemptions	2,750,000	1,800,000	Provision for reds.
		5,050,000	12/31/99

Miscellaneous

86. (a) Current assets listed in the trial balance are cash ($550,000), accounts receivable ($1,650,000), and prepaid taxes ($300,000). However, part of the AR must be reclassified, and income tax expense has not yet been recorded. Included in AR is $500,000 due from a customer, for which $250,000 is collectible in 2000 (2 x $125,000) and $250,000 is collectible in 2001. The portion collectible in 2001 should be reclassified as a noncurrent asset. Revenues ($3,600,000) less expenses ($2,600,000) result in pretax income of $1,000,000. Since the tax rate is 30%, tax expense is $300,000 (30% x $1,000,000). Therefore, an adjustment is necessary to debit **income tax expense** and credit **prepaid taxes** for $300,000. Total current assets, after reclassification and adjustment, are $1,950,000 [answer (a)] as calculated below.

Cash	$ 550,000
AR ($1,650,000 – $250,000)	1,400,000
Prepaid taxes ($300,000 – $300,000)	-0-
	$1,950,000

87. (c) Before closing entries, retained earnings is $630,000. 1999 net income is revenues ($3,600,000) less expenses ($2,600,000) and income tax expense [30% x ($3,600,000 – $2,600,000) = $300,000]. After adjusting for income tax expense, net income is $700,000 [$3,600,000 – ($2,600,000 + $300,000)]. After closing entries, 12/31/99 retained earnings is $1,330,000 ($630,000 + $700,000). Thus, answer (c) is correct. The foreign currency translation adjustment ($430,000) does not affect retained earnings; it is reported as a separate component of stockholders' equity.

88. (a) Current assets are cash and other assets that are expected to be converted into cash, sold, or consumed either in 1 year, or in the operating cycle, whichever is longer. Generally included in this category are cash, temporary investments, short-term receivables, inventories, and prepaid expenses. In this situation, there are two special items. Cash must be adjusted because checks which were not mailed until July 9 were recorded June 29. To compute the correct June 30 cash balance, this $30,000 of checks must be added back to the cash balance, turning the $10,000 overdraft into a $20,000 positive balance [(– $10,000) + $30,000 = $20,000]. Also, land held for resale ($100,000) must be included in current assets because, like inventory, at June 30 it is expected to be sold for cash within the next year. Therefore, June 30 current assets total $225,000.

Cash	$20,000
AR, net	35,000
Inventory	58,000
Prepaid expenses	12,000
Land held for resale	100,000
	$225,000

89. (a) ARB 43 states that current liabilities are obligations whose liquidation is reasonably expected to require the use of current assets or the creation of other current liabilities. This means that generally, current liabilities are liabilities due within 1 year of the balance sheet date. Clearly, accounts payable ($15,000) and dividends payable ($8,000) are current liabilities. Generally, bonds payable are a long-term liability; however, since these bonds are due in 2000, they must be reported as a current liability at 12/31/99 ($25,000 fair value less $3,000 discount, or $22,000). Therefore, total current liabilities are $45,000 ($15,000 + $8,000 + $22,000). The notes payable ($20,000) are classified as long-term because they are not due until 2001.

D. Ratios

90. (b) The quick (acid-test) ratio is quick assets (cash, temporary investments in marketable equity securities, and net receivables) divided by current liabilities. The quick ratio measures the ability to pay current liabilities from cash and near-cash items. In this case, quick assets total $700,000 ($170,000 + $450,000 + $80,000) and current liabilities total $400,000 ($60,000 + $240,000 + $100,000), resulting in a quick ratio of 1.75 to 1 ($700,000 ÷ $400,000).

91. (d) The formula to compute accounts receivable turnover is:

$$\frac{\text{Net credit sales}}{\text{Average accounts receivable}}$$

The average receivable is the sum of the beginning and ending net accounts receivable divided by 2. The 1999 beginning accounts receivable equals the 1998 ending balance in accounts receivable. Average accounts receivable is $425,000 [($450,000 + $400,000) ÷ 2]. Applying the formula, the 1999 accounts receivable turnover is 7.06 times ($3,000,000 ÷ $425,000).

92. (d) Ratios which are useful in assessing a company's ability to meet currently maturing or short-term obligations are referred to as solvency ratios. The acid-test ratio is classified as a solvency ratio, and it measures the ability to pay current liabilities from cash and near-cash items. The acid-test ratio is:

$$\frac{\text{Cash + Net receivables + Marketable securities}}{\text{Current liabilities}}$$

The debt to equity ratio is a leverage ratio which measures the relative amount of leverage or debt a company has. The debt to equity ratio is:

$$\frac{\text{Total liabilities}}{\text{Common stockholders' equity}}$$

Therefore, answer (d) is correct because the acid-test ratio is useful in assessing a company's ability to meet currently maturing or short-term obligations while the debt to equity ratio is not.

93. (a) The solutions approach is to create a numerical example that conforms to the facts given in the question. Assume the following:

$$\text{Current ratio} = \frac{\$900,000}{\$600,000} = 1.5 \text{ to } 1$$

$$\text{Quick ratio} = \frac{\$300,000}{\$600,000} = .5 \text{ to } 1$$

Payments of accounts payable decrease both cash (a current and quick asset) and accounts payable (a current liability). After payment the following ratios result:

$$\text{Current ratio} = \frac{900 - 200}{600 - 200} = \frac{700}{400} = 1.75 \text{ to } 1$$

$$\text{Quick ratio} = \frac{300 - 200}{600 - 200} = \frac{100}{400} = .25 \text{ to } 1$$

Subtracting equal amounts from the numerator and the denominator of a ratio **greater than one** will **increase** the ratio. Subtracting equal amounts from the numerator and the denominator of a ratio **less than one** will **decrease** the ratio. Therefore, the current ratio will increase while the quick ratio decreases, making answer (a) correct and answers (b), (c), and (d) incorrect.

94. (b) The formula to compute the current ratio is:

$$\text{Current ratio} = \frac{\text{Current assets}}{\text{Current liabilities}}$$

The write-off of inventory would decrease current assets and the current ratio. The formula to compute the acid-test (quick) ratio is:

$$\text{Acid-test ratio} = \frac{\text{Cash + Net receivables + Marketable securities}}{\text{Current liabilities}}$$

The write-off of inventory has no effect on the acid-test ratio. Thus, answer (b) is correct.

95. (d) The number of days in the operating cycle measures the length of time from purchase of inventory to collection of cash. The formula is:

$$\left(\begin{array}{c}\text{Number of days'}\\ \text{sales in}\\ \text{inventories}\end{array}\right) + \left(\begin{array}{c}\text{Number of days'}\\ \text{sales in}\\ \text{accts. receivable}\end{array}\right) = \left(\begin{array}{c}\text{Number of days}\\ \text{in}\\ \text{operating cycle}\end{array}\right)$$

$$61 \text{ days} \quad + \quad 33 \text{ days} \quad = \quad \underline{94 \text{ days}}$$

Note that the number of days' sales in inventories measures the number of days from the purchase of inventory to the sale of inventory, while the number of days' sales in accounts receivable measures the number of days from the sale of inventory to the collection of cash.

96. (b) Collection of a receivable results in an increase in cash and a decrease in the accounts receivable balance. The accounts receivable turnover ratio is computed by dividing net credit sales by the average net accounts receivable balance. Collection of a receivable reduces the average net accounts receivable balance. Thus the receivable turnover ratio increases. Answer (b) is correct. Since this transaction does not affect cost of goods sold or inventory, the inventory turnover ratio is unaffected and answer (a) is incorrect. Answers (c) and (d) are incorrect because neither the current ratio nor the quick ratio is affected by the collection; neither current assets nor quick assets would change as a result of the collection.

OTHER OBJECTIVE ANSWERS AND ANSWER EXPLANATIONS

Problem 1

Part a.

1.   (D)   In this transaction, receivables are factored by surrendering control and without recourse. This constitutes an outright sale of the receivables in that title, risk of loss, and rights to future benefits are all transferred. Therefore, a loss on the transaction is recognized.

2.   (C)   In a specific assignment of receivables, AR assigned are identified by placing them in an AR assigned account. A finance charge is assessed on assignment transactions which are borrowings.

3.   (E)   When AR are pledged, the receivables serve as collateral for a loan but the proceeds are not remitted to the lender. In this case, the amount of AR pledged is reported at the balance sheet date either parenthetically or in the notes.

4.   (B)   In this transaction, considered a borrowing, receivables are considered to be factored with recourse. Thus, the transaction is viewed as a loan collateralized by AR and the amount of the proceeds plus the factor's holdback and interest charged should be reported as a liability.

5.   (F)   A note discounted on which control is surrendered and the terms include without recourse is considered a sales transaction upon which a loss should be recognized. Notes receivable should be credited.

6.   (E)   A general assignment of receivables is another term for pledging AR, and thus should be disclosed parenthetically or in the notes to the financial statements (no journal entry).

Part b.

7.   (F)   "Factor's holdback" accounts for the proceeds retained by the factor to cover estimated sales discounts, sales returns, and sales allowances. When all amounts have been collected by the factor, the balance in factor's margin is returned to the seller. Therefore, this account is a receivable reported as a current asset on the balance sheet.

8.   (T)   A specific assignment of receivables bestows more formal rights upon the assignee (lender) in that the AR do not simply collateralize the loan, but collections on the assigned accounts are actually remitted to the assignor who remits them to the assignee (lender).

9.   (F)   Once a company sells receivables to a factor it normally has no further involvement with the receivables. The factor usually collects the remittances directly from the **customer.**

10.   (F)   Per SFAS 125, transfers of receivables in which the transferee can require the transferor to repurchase the receivables may not be considered a sale.

11.   (T)   The difference between the amount of receivables sold to a factor in a borrowing transaction and the total of the factor's holdback plus the proceeds is recorded in a "Discount on Transferred AR" or interest expense account (see journal entry (B) in part a.). This account represents interest cost and should be recognized over the term of the receivables. If interest expense is debited, an adjusting entry to defer some of the interest as "Discount" would be required if some of the discount pertains to a later period.

Problem 2

1.   (B)   SFAS 5, para 17a, states "contingencies that might result in gains usually are not reflected in the accounts since to do so might be to recognize revenue prior to its realization." Since this gain contingency was resolved before the issuance of the financial statements, it is handled similar to an ordinary transaction which occurred prior to the year end and is accrued in the year of its occurrence.

SFAS 5, para 17b, states "adequate disclosure shall be made of contingencies that might result in gains...."

2.   (N)   To accrue an estimated loss from a loss contingency it is necessary that it is probable that an asset has been impaired or a liability has been incurred and that the amount of loss can be reasonably estimated. Since Town's lawyers believe the suit to be without merit, neither condition has been met.

SFAS 5, para 10, states "disclosure is also required of some loss contingencies that do not meet 'the accrual requirements mentioned above if' there is a **reasonable possibility** that a loss may be incurred." Again, this condition has not been met.

3.   (N)   The conditions described in this question would be considered general or unspecified business risks that do not meet the conditions for accrual or disclosure.

4.   (D)   The words "reasonably possible" require the disclosure of this item. No accrual need be made since the question does not state it is **probable** that an asset has been impaired or a liability incurred and that the amount of loss can be reasonably estimated.

5.   (B)   The word "probable" and the inclusion of the estimated amount of $500,000 mean that this situation meets the criteria of (1) a probable incurrence of a liability and (2) a reasonable estimate of an amount.

6.   (D)   SFAS 5, para 18, quotes para 6 of ARB 50 which "required disclosure of a number of situations including...commitments such as those for an obligation to reduce debts." SFAS 5, para 19, states "situations of the type described...shall continue to be disclosed in financial statements." Since the entire transaction took place in the next accounting period it does not meet the conditions for an accrual in the current period even though it would be disclosed in a footnote.

ANSWER OUTLINE

Problem 1   AR Factored, Noninterest NR, Bad Debts

a. Accounting for AR factored
    Cash (amount received)
    Loss (cash received – AR factored)
        AR   (amount factored)

    Loss reported on IS
    Transfers with control surrendered equivalent to sale

b. Carrying value at 7/1/99 is maturity value discounted
    for 2 years at market interest rate
    Income Statement effects
        Interest revenue for 1999 = Carrying value at 7/1/99
            x Market rate of interest at 7/1/99 x 1/2 year
    Balance Sheet effects
        Noninterest-bearing NR should be reported as non-
            current asset at face value less unamortized discount
            Because it is due more than 1 year from BS date

c. Reinstatement of AR previously WO
    AR   xx
        Allowance for DA   xx

    Collection of AR previously WO
    Cash   xx
        AR   xx

d. **Credit Sales Basis**
    Emphasizes IS
    Attempts to match uncollectible accounts with reve-
        nue earned in same period
    Receivable Account Basis
    Emphasizes BS
    Reports receivables at estimated future collectible
        amounts (net realizable value)

UNOFFICIAL ANSWER

Problem 1   AR Factored, Noninterest NR, Bad Debts

a. To account for the accounts receivable factored on April 1, 1999, Magrath should decrease accounts receivable by the amount of accounts receivable factored, increase cash by the amount received from the factor, and record a loss equal to the difference. The loss should be reported in the income statement. Transfers of accounts receivable with control over the receivables surrendered is equivalent to a sale.

b. The carrying amount of the note at July 1, 1999, is the maturity amount discounted for 2 years at the market interest rate. For the noninterest-bearing note receivable, the interest revenue for 1999 should be determined by multiplying the carrying amount of the note at July 1, 1999, times the market rate of interest at the date of the note times one-half.

    The noninterest-bearing note receivable should be reported in the December 31, 1999 balance sheet, as a noncurrent asset at its face amount less the unamortized discount.

c. Magrath should account for the collection of the accounts previously written off as uncollectible as follows:

    •   Increase both accounts receivable and the allowance for uncollectible accounts.

    •   Increase cash and decrease accounts receivable.

d. One approach estimates uncollectible accounts based on credit sales. This approach focuses on income determination by attempting to match uncollectible accounts expense with the revenues generated.

    The other allowance approach estimates uncollectible accounts based on the balance in or aging of receivables. The approach focuses on asset valuation by attempting to report receivables at realizable value.

ANSWER OUTLINE

Problem 2   Schedule to Calculate Provision and Allowance for Bad Debts

1.   This problem consists of two related parts: part a. requires a calculation of the allowance for uncollectible accounts at 12/31/99 using an aging approach, and part b. requires a computation of the 1999 provision for uncollectible accounts (uncollectible accounts expense). The solutions approach is to quickly review the basics of accounting for uncollectible accounts, visualize the solution format, and begin. Some candidates may benefit from preparation of T-accounts (see item 4 below).

2.   When using the aging approach, the **total** uncollectible accounts (in other words, the required ending balance in the allowance account) is estimated by applying a different percentage to the various age categories. The percentage increases as the age of the receivables increases because the older a receivable is, the less likely is its ultimate collection.

2.1   In this case, Sigma estimates that 1% of its receivables in the 0-30 days age category will prove to be uncollectible. Therefore, of that $300,000 of accounts receivable, it is estimated that $3,000 (1% x $300,000) will be uncollectible. Similar computations are performed for the other age categories, resulting in an estimate that $39,000 of the $465,000 accounts receivable will prove to be uncollectible. This is the required 12/31/99 balance in the allowance account.

3.   When using the aging approach, the first step is to compute the required ending balance in the allowance account (as discussed in items 2 and 2.1 above). The second step is to compute the uncollectible accounts expense necessary to bring the **unadjusted** allowance balance up to the **required** allowance balance.

3.1   The only item affecting the allowance account in 1998 was the recording of uncollectible accounts expense of $28,000 (1% x $2,800,000 credit sales). Therefore, the 1/1/99 balance in this account is $28,000. No adjustment is necessary for the change in the method of estimating this expense (from percent of sales to aging schedule) because any such change is handled prospectively (Author's note: using the aging percents given also results in a $28,000 balance at 1/1/99. Even if the result was different, though, no adjustment is necessary).

3.2   During 1999, this $28,000 credit balance was decreased by write-offs of $27,000 (debit allowance, credit AR) and increased by $7,000 of recoveries (debit AR, credit allowance; and debit cash, credit AR). Therefore, the 12/31/99 balance in the allowance account, **before adjustment**, is $8,000 ($28,000 − $27,000 + $7,000).

3.3   To increase the allowance account from $8,000 (see 3.2 above) to $39,000 (see 2.1 above), a provision for uncollectible accounts (uncollectible accounts expense) of $31,000 must be recorded for 1999.

4.   Some candidates may benefit from the preparation of T-accounts for the allowance account and accounts receivable. These T-accounts are provided below.

T-accounts for 1998

	AR		
Sales	2,800,000	2,400,000	Collections
12/31/98	400,000		

	Allowance		
		28,000	Provision
		28,000	12/31/98

T-accounts for 1999

	AR		
1/1/99	400,000		
Sales	3,000,000		
		2,908,000*	Collections
Recoveries	7,000	27,000	Write-offs
		7,000	Recoveries
12/31/99	465,000		

	Allowance		
		28,000	1/1/99
Write-offs	27,000		
		7,000	Recoveries
		8,000	12/31/99 before adj.
		31,000	Provision
		39,000	12/31/99

* The collections given ($2,915,000) apparently includes the recoveries of $7,000. In the T-accounts above these are shown separately, but total collections are $2,915,000. Note that the ending balance of AR ($465,000) corresponds to the information given in the problem ($300,000 + $80,000 + $60,000 + $25,000 = $465,000)

UNOFFICIAL ANSWER

Problem 2   Schedule to Calculate Provision and Allowance for Bad Debts

a.

Sigma Co.
SCHEDULE OF CALCULATION OF
ALLOWANCE FOR UNCOLLECTIBLE ACCOUNTS
December 31, 1999

0 to 30 days	$300,000	x	1%	$ 3,000
31 to 90 days	80,000	x	5%	4,000
91 to 180 days	60,000	x	20%	12,000
Over 180 days	25,000	x	80%	20,000
Accounts receivable	$465,000			
Allowance for uncollectible accounts				$39,000

b. Computation of 1999 provision:

Balance December 31, 1998	$28,000
Write-offs during 1999	(27,000)
Recoveries during 1999	7,000
Balance before 1999 provision	8,000
Required allowance at December 31, 1999	39,000
1999 provision	$31,000

ANSWER OUTLINE

Problem 3   Notes Receivable: Valuation, Discounting, and Estimating Losses

a.   Note's valuation basis
         Discounted present value of the future principal and interest receivable at customer's market rate of % on sale date

b.   Discounting of note
         Increase CV of note by effective interest revenue earned to 5/1/99
         Discounting shall be treated as sale
         Recognize a gain (loss)
         Since note discounted without recourse, treat as sale

c.   1.   NR not discounted
               Uncollectible notes expense equals adjustment necessary to make balance needed in allowance for uncollectible notes equal estimated uncollectible less FMV of recoverable equipment

     2.   Recognize recourse liability at time of transfer
               Review and adjust this liability at year end
                    Adjustment of prior year amounts are Δs in estimate

UNOFFICIAL ANSWER

Problem 3   Notes Receivable: Valuation, Discounting, and Estimating Losses

a.   The appropriate valuation basis of a note receivable at the date of sale is its discounted present value of the future amounts receivable for principal and interest using the customer's market rate of interest, if known or determinable, at the date of the equipment's sale.

b.   Gregor should increase the carrying amount of the note receivable by the effective interest revenue earned for the period February 1 to May 1, 1999. Gregor should account for the discounting of the note receivable without recourse by increasing cash for the proceeds received, eliminating the carrying amount of the note receivable, and recognizing a loss (gain) for the resulting difference.

This reporting is appropriate since the note's carrying amount is correctly recorded at the date it was discounted and the discounting of a note receivable without recourse is equivalent to a sale of that note. Thus the difference between the cash received and the carrying amount of the note at the date it is discounted is reported as a loss (gain).

c.   1.   For notes receivable not discounted, Gregor should recognize an uncollectible notes expense. The expense equals the adjustment required to bring the balance of the allowance for uncollectible notes receivable equal to the estimated uncollectible amounts less the fair values of recoverable equipment.

2.   When a transfer with recourse qualifies as a sale, a components approach is used. The notes receivable are removed from the books but a liability for recourse provisions is recognized. At year end, the recourse liability must be reviewed and adjusted upward or downward with a corresponding gain (loss) recognized. Any changes relating to prior years is a change of accounting estimate.

ANSWER OUTLINE

Problem 4   Receivable Transfers

a.   Financial components approach
  Accounts for transactions as part asset and part liability using surrender of control criteria

b.   Transferred assets isolated
  Transferee may pledge/exchange assets
  Transferor has no effective control
    No obligatory repurchase agreement
    No entitlement to repurchase based on availability

c.
Cash	xx	
Finance expense	xx	
Liability for loan		xx

d.
Cash	xx	
Factor's holdback	xx	
Loss from transfer	xx	
Receivables		xx
Recourse obligation		xx

UNOFFICIAL ANSWER

Problem 4   Receivable Transfers

a.   The financial components approach as applied to transfers of financial assets provides that the transaction can be separated into the elements comprising it using criteria to ascertain whether control is surrendered. This means that the event can be accounted for by recognizing assets and liabilities in a transfer rather than only as an exchange of assets or an incurrence of a liability.

b.   The criteria for determining when control has been surrendered are

- Transferred assets have been isolated from the transferor or its creditors,
- Transferee has the unconstrained right to pledge or exchange the transferred assets, and
- Transferor does not maintain effective control over the transferred assets through
  - An agreement that obligates the transferor to repurchase or redeem them before their maturity, or
  - An agreement that entitles transferor to repurchase transferred assets that are not obtainable elsewhere

c.   If one or more criteria for determining whether control has been surrendered are not met, the transfer should be recorded as a borrowing by debiting cash and finance expense and crediting a loan liability account.

d.   If control is surrendered in a transfer of receivables, the transaction shall be accounted for by derecognizing the receivables with an entry that debits cash, an asset account entitled "Factor's Holdback," and a loss account. Additionally, the entry would include credits to receivables and a liability account entitled "Recourse Obligation."

ANSWER OUTLINE

Problem 5   Contingencies

a.   Disclose threat of expropriation in notes to FS
  Include estimate of possible loss or range thereof
  Accrual inappropriate because threat only reasonably possible, not probable

b.   Accrue loss and liability from safety hazard and report in FS
  Because both recognition conditions met
    Probable that liability incurred
    Amount of loss can be reasonably estimated
  Additionally, disclose nature of hazard in notes to FS

c.   Do not recognize loss and liability
  Because no asset impaired/liability incurred at BS date
  Disclosure of uninsured risk permitted, but not required

UNOFFICIAL ANSWER

Problem 5   Contingencies

a.   Chester should disclose the threat of expropriation of assets in the notes to the financial statements. Disclosure would include an estimate of the possible loss or an estimate of the range of loss. Accrual of a loss is inappropriate because the threat of expropriation is only reasonably possible.

b. Chester should report the potential costs due to the safety hazard by accruing a loss in the income statement and a liability in the balance sheet. Accrual is required because both of the following conditions are met:

- It is considered probable that a liability has been incurred.
- The amount of the loss can be reasonably estimated.

In addition, Chester should separately disclose in the notes to the financial statements the nature of the safety hazard.

c. Chester should not accrue a loss because an asset has not been impaired nor has a liability been incurred. Disclosure of the uninsured rockslide risk, while permitted, is not required.

ANSWER OUTLINE

Problem 6   Contingencies

a. **1.**   Reporting toxic waste cleanup in 1999 FS
Footnote disclosure of loss
Nature of loss
Indication that an estimate cannot be made
No accrual
Loss not reasonably estimable
Uncertain amount would impair integrity of FS
    2.   Reporting Gap's claim in 1999 FS
Footnote disclosure
Nature of claim
Include estimate of potential loss
No accrual
Only reasonably possible that Supey will lose
the suit

b.   Reporting effects of contract to purchase Chemical XZ
in 1999 FS
Report estimated loss equal to unrecoverable amount
of contract price
Part of income from continuing operations
CL

Reporting appropriate because:
Net loss on purchase commitment should be measured and recognized in period it occurs
Reporting loss recognizes commitment's impact on future cash flows

UNOFFICIAL ANSWER

Problem 6   Contingencies

a. **1.**   Notes to Supey's 1999 financial statements should disclose the nature of the loss on cleanup and indicate that an estimate of the loss, or range of the loss, cannot be made. No accrual should be made because the loss cannot be reasonably estimated and accrual of an uncertain amount would impair the integrity of the financial statements.

2.   Supey should disclose the nature of Gap's claim in the notes to the 1999 financial statements. Disclosure should include an estimate of the potential loss. Supey should not accrue the loss because it is only reasonably possible that it will have to pay for Gap's losses.

b.   An estimated loss on the purchase commitment, equal to the unrecoverable amount of the contract price, should be reported as part of 1999 income from continuing operations and as a current liability at December 31, 1999. The net loss on the purchase commitment should be measured and recognized in the period in which it occurs. Since Supey did not hedge this contract, reporting this loss recognizes the commitment's impact on future cash flows.

PRESENT VALUE

This module begins by reviewing the basic concepts related to time value of money. The module then covers four major topics in which time value of money applications are used extensively: (1) bonds payable and bond investments, (2) debt restructure, (3) pensions, and (4) leases.

A. Fundamentals

The concepts of time value of money are essential for successful completion of the CPA exam. Time value of money concepts are central to capital budgeting, leases, pensions, bonds, and other topics. You must understand the mechanics as well as the concepts. After studying the next few pages, work the multiple-choice questions entitled "Fundamentals." Note that the following abbreviations are used in the text that follows.

> i = interest rate
> n = number of periods or rents

On the CPA exam, you do not have to know the complex formulas that are used to compute time value of money factors (TVMF). The factors will be given to you or enough information will be given to you so that you can easily compute them (See A.8. TVMF Applications). Your main focus of attention should be centered on understanding which TVMF should be used in a given situation.

1. **Future Value (FV) of an Amount** (future value of $1)

The future value of an amount is the amount that will be available at some point in the future if an amount is deposited today and earns compound interest for "n" periods. The most common application is savings deposits. For example, if you deposited $100 today at 10%, you would have $110 [$100 + ($100 x 10%)] at the end of the first year, $121[$100 + ($110 x 10%)] at the end of the second year, etc. The compounding feature allows you to earn interest on interest. In the second year of the example you earn $11 interest: $10 on the original $100 and $1 on the first year's interest of $10.

2. **Present Value (PV) of a Future Amount** (present value of $1)

The present value of a future amount is the amount you would pay now for an amount to be received "n" periods in the future given an interest rate of "i." A common application would be the money you would lend today for a noninterest-bearing note receivable in the future. For example, if you were lending money at 10%, you would lend $100 for a $110 note due in 1 year or for a $121 note due in 2 years.

The present value of $1 is the inverse of the future value of $1. Thus, given a future value of $1 table, you have a present value of $1 by dividing each value into 1.00. Look at the present value of $1 and future value of $1 tables on the next page. The future value of $1 at 10% in 5 years is 1.611. Thus, the present value of $1 in 5 years would be 1.00 ÷ 1.611 which is .621 (check the table). Conversely, the future value of $1 is found by dividing the present value of $1 into 1.00, that is, 1.00 ÷ .621 = 1.611.

3. **Compounding**

When interest is compounded more than once a year, two extra steps are needed. First, **multiply** "n" by the number of times interest is compounded annually. This will give you the total number of interest periods. Second, **divide** "i" by the number of times interest is compounded annually. This will give you the appropriate interest rate for each interest period. For example, if the 10% was compounded semiannually, the amount of $100 at the end of 1 year would be $110.25 [$(1.05)^2$] instead of $110.00. The extra $.25 is 5% of the $5.00 interest earned in the first half of the year.

4. **Future Value of an Ordinary Annuity**

The future value of an ordinary annuity is the amount available "n" periods in the future as a result of the deposit of an amount (A) at the end of every period 1 through "n." Compound interest is earned at the rate of "i" on the deposits. A common application is a bond sinking fund. A deposit is made at the end of the first period and earns compound interest for n-1 periods (not during the first period, because the deposit is made at the end of the first period). The next to the last payment earns one period's interest, that is, n – (n-1) = 1. The last payment earns no interest, because it is deposited at the end of the last (nth) period. Remember that in the FUTURE AMOUNT OF AN ORDINARY ANNUITY TABLE, all of the factors for any "n" row are based on one less interest period than the number of payments.

TIME VALUE OF MONEY FACTOR (TVMF) TABLES

Future Value (Amount) of $1

n	*6%*	*8%*	*10%*	*12%*	*15%*
1	1.060	1.080	1.100	1.120	1.150
2	1.124	1.166	1.210	1.254	1.323
3	1.191	1.260	1.331	1.405	1.521
4	1.262	1.360	1.464	1.574	1.749
5	1.338	1.469	1.611	1.762	2.011

Present Value of $1

n	*6%*	*8%*	*10%*	*12%*	*15%*
1	.943	.926	.909	.893	.870
2	.890	.857	.826	.797	.756
3	.840	.794	.751	.712	.658
4	.792	.735	.683	.636	.572
5	.747	.681	.621	.567	.497

Future Value (Amount) of an Ordinary Annuity of $1

n	*6%*	*8%*	*10%*	*12%*	*15%*
1	1.000	1.000	1.000	1.000	1.000
2	2.060	2.080	2.100	2.120	2.150
3	3.184	3.246	3.310	3.374	3.473
4	4.375	4.506	4.641	4.779	4.993
5	5.637	5.867	6.105	6.353	6.742

Present Value of an Ordinary Annuity of $1

n	*6%*	*8%*	*10%*	*12%*	*15%*
1	.943	.926	.909	.893	.870
2	1.833	1.783	1.736	1.690	1.626
3	2.673	2.577	2.487	2.402	2.283
4	3.465	3.312	3.170	3.037	2.855
5	4.212	3.993	3.791	3.605	3.352

5. **Present Value of an Ordinary Annuity**

The present value of an ordinary annuity is the value today, given a discount rate, of a series of future payments. A common application is the capitalization of lease payments by either lessors or lessees. Payments "1" through "n" are assumed to be made at the end of years "1" through "n," and are discounted back to the present.

> *EXAMPLE:*
>
> *Assume a 5-year lease of equipment requiring payments of $1,000 at the end of each of the 5 years, which is to be capitalized. If the discount rate is 8%, the present value is $3,993 ($1,000 x 3.993).*

6. **Distinguishing a Future Value of an Annuity from a Present Value of an Annuity**

Sometimes confusion arises in distinguishing between the future value (amount) of an annuity and the present value of an annuity. These two may be distinguished by determining whether the total dollar amount in the problem comes at the beginning (e.g., cost of equipment acquired for leasing) or at the end (e.g., the amount needed to retire bonds) of the series of payments as illustrated below.

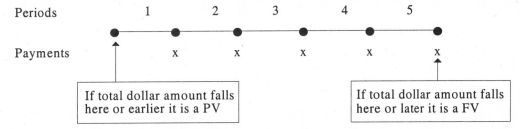

Remember: if the total amount comes at the end of the series of payments, it is a **future value** of annuity situation. If the total amount comes at the beginning of the series of payments, it is a **present value** of annuity situation. The total dollar amount may be given in the problem or you may have to compute it; either way, it makes no difference in determining whether a problem involves a present value or future value situation.

Some students feel the need to "convert" all time value of money problems into either present value or future value problems, depending on which they're most comfortable with. This process involves more work and more chance for errors, because an additional TVMF equation must be solved in the conversion. This is inefficient, and unnecessary if you are able to correctly identify between the two initially. Become proficient at determining present value and future value situations, so that you may efficiently select the correct TVMF from the corresponding table.

7. **Annuities Due**

In some cases, the payments or annuities may not conform to the assumptions inherent in the annuity tables. For example, the payments might be made at the beginning of each of the 5 years instead of at the end of each year. This is an annuity due (annuity in advance) in contrast to an ordinary annuity (annuity in arrears). Both annuity due and ordinary annuity payments are represented by the "x's" in the illustration below.

Periods		1	2	3	4	5	
Annuity			x	x	x	x	x
Annuity Due	x		x	x	x	x	x

If the payments in the 5-period lease example above were made at the beginning of the period, the present value of the first payment which is made today is $1,000 (i.e., the TVMF is 1.00). The remaining 4 payments comprise an ordinary annuity for 4 periods as you can see on the above diagram. Always use time diagrams to analyze application of annuities.

To convert either a future value of an ordinary annuity or the present value of an ordinary annuity factor to an annuity due factor, multiply the ordinary annuity factor times $(1 + i)$. For the above lease example, you would find the present value of an ordinary annuity factor for $n = 5$ which is 3.993. Then multiply 3.993 by 1.08 to arrive at the annuity due factor, 4.312. The present value of the payments would be $4,312 (4.312 x $1,000). Notice that the present value of the annuity due in the above example is $319 greater than the present value of the ordinary annuity because the payments are moved closer to the present.

8. **TVMF Applications**

The basic formula to use is

$$FV \text{ or } PV = TVMF \times Amount$$

If an annuity is involved, the amount is the periodic payment or deposit; if not, it is a single sum. Note that FV or PV is determined by three variables: time, interest rate, and payment. TVMF represents two variables: time and interest rate. The tables usually have the interest rate on the horizontal axis and time on the vertical axis. The above formula may also be stated as

$$Amount = \frac{FV \text{ or } PV}{TVMF}$$

For example, if we need to accumulate $12,210 in 5 years to repay a loan, we could determine the required annual deposit with the above formula. If the savings rate were 10%, we would divide the FV ($12,210) by the TVMF of the future value of annuity, n=5, i=.10 (6.105) and get $2,000. Thus, $2,000 deposited at the end of each of 5 years earning 10% will result in $12,210. This formula may also be used to find future values of an amount, present values of amounts, and annuities in the same manner.

Another variation of the formula is

$$TVMF = \frac{FV \text{ or } PV}{Amount}$$

For example, we may be offered a choice between paying $3,312 in cash or $1,000 a year at the end of each of the next 4 years. We determine the interest rate by dividing the annual payment into the present value of the annuity to obtain the TVMF (3.312) for n=4. We then find the interest rate which has the same or similar TVMF (in this case 8%).

Alternatively, using the above formula, we may know the interest rate but not know the number of payments. Given the TVMF, we can determine "n" by looking in the TVMF table under the known interest rate. Remember the TVMF reflects two variables: time and interest rate.

9. **Notes Receivable and Payable**

Notes should be recorded at their present values (see outline of APB 21). Upon receipt or issuance of a note, record the net value of the note receivable or payable (i.e., note plus or minus premium or discount) at

1. Cash received or paid

    a. Assumes no other rights or privileges

2. Established exchange price (fair market value) or property or services received or provided

    a. If not determinable, determine present value with imputed interest rate

Record interest revenue (on notes receivable) or interest expense (on notes payable) as the effective rate of interest times the net receivable or payable during the period.

a. **Note Exchanged for Cash Only**--When a note is exchanged for cash and no other rights or privileges are exchanged, the present value of the note is equivalent to the cash exchanged. The cash exchanged, however, may not be equal to the face amount of the note (the amount paid at maturity). When the face amount of a note does not equal its present value, the difference is either a discount or a premium. A discount results when the face of the note exceeds its present value, and a premium results when the present value of the note exceeds its face (see Section B.1. in this module for a more detailed discussion of discounts and premiums).

b. **Note Exchanged for Cash and Unstated Rights and Privileges**--In the preceding discussion, notes were issued solely for cash, and no other rights or privileges were exchanged. The accounting treatment differs, however, when a note is issued for cash and unstated rights and/or privileges are also exchanged. The cash exchanged for such a note consists of two elements: (1) the present value of the note, and (2) the present value of the unstated right or privilege. Proper accounting for this situation requires that one of the two present values above be determined. Once this is done, the remaining present value is simply the difference between the face amount of the note and the present value that was determined.

For example, on January 1, 1999, Zilch Company borrowed $200,000 from its major customer, Martha Corporation. The borrowing is evidenced by a note payable due in 3 years. The note is noninterest-bearing. In consideration for the borrowing, Zilch Company agrees to supply Martha Corporation's inventory needs for the loan period at favorable prices. This last feature of the transaction is the unstated right or privilege; that is, the ability of Martha to purchase inventory at less than regular prices.

The present value of the note (assuming it is easier to determine) should be based upon the interest rate Zilch would have to pay in a normal borrowing of $200,000 (i.e., in a transaction that did not include unstated rights or privileges). Assume that Zilch would have to pay interest at 12% in a normal borrowing. The present value of $200,000 discounted for 3 years at 12% is $142,400 ($200,000 x .712). The difference between the face amount of the note, $200,000, and its present value of $142,400 represents the present value of the unstated right or privilege. The amount of this present value is $57,600.

The entries below show how both Zilch and Martha should account for this transaction during 1999.

Zilch				*Martha*		
1/1/99				1/1/99		
Cash	142,400			Note receivable	200,000	
Discount on note payable	57,600			Discount on note re-		
Note payable		200,000		ceivable		57,600
Cash	57,600			Cash		142,400
Deferred revenue		57,600		Advance payments on		
				inventory	57,600	
				Cash		57,600
12/31/99				12/31/99		
Interest expense	17,088*			Discount on note receiv-		
Discount on note pay-				able	17,088	
able		17,088		Interest income		17,088
*$142,400 x .12 = $17,088						
Deferred revenue	xx			Inventory (purchases)	xx	
Sales		xx		Advance payments on		
				inventory		xx

The amounts represented by "xx" in the entries above depend upon the amount of goods acquired by Martha during 1999.

On the December 31, 1999 balance sheets of both Zilch and Martha, the above notes should be disclosed in the noncurrent liability (Zilch) and asset (Martha) sections net of the unamortized discount applicable to each note.

c. **Note Exchanged in a Noncash Transaction**--In addition to notes issued for cash, a note may also be received or issued in a noncash transaction; that is, for goods, property, or services. The problem created in this situation is how to determine the note's present value in the absence of cash. One way to solve this problem is to assume that the stated rate or contractual rate stated on the note represents a fair rate of return to the supplier for the use of the related funds. If the interest rate is presumed to be fair, then the face amount of the note is presumed to equal its present value. Interest revenue (expense) is computed by multiplying the interest rate stated on the face of the note by the face of the note. There is no discount or premium to consider because the face of the note is assumed to be equal to its present value.

The assumption that the interest rate on the face of the note is fair is not always valid. According to APB 21, the assumption is not valid if

(1) The interest rate is not stated (usually, this means the note is noninterest bearing), or

(2) The stated rate is unreasonable (this refers to both unreasonably low and high rates), or

(3) The stated face amount of the note is materially different from the current cash sales price for the same or similar items, or from the market value of the note at the date of the transaction.

When the interest rate is not fair, the face amount of the note does not equal its present value. In the absence of cash, the present value of a note is determined according to the following priorities:

(1) First, determine if the goods, property, or services exchanged have a reliable fair market value. If they do, the fair market value is presumed to be the present value of the note.

(2) If a reliable fair market value does not exist for the goods, property, or services exchanged, then determine if the note has a market value. If it does, the note's market value is equal to the present value of the note.

(3) Finally, if market values do not exist for either the goods, property, or services or for the note, then an interest rate must be **imputed**. This imputed interest rate is then used to determine the present value of the note. The imputed interest rate represents the **debtor's** incremental borrowing rate.

To illustrate the situation where the interest rate on a note is not fair, yet the fair market value of the property exchanged is known, assume the following facts: Doink Co. sold a building on January 1, 1999, which originally cost $7,000,000 and which had a book value of $4,000,000 for a $14,000,000 (face amount) noninterest-bearing note due in 3 years. Since zero interest is not considered to be a fair rate of return, the face amount of Doink's note does not equal its present value. In Doink's case, the face of its note is $14,000,000. The present value of the note is the unknown and must be calculated.

To determine the present value of Doink's $14,000,000 noninterest-bearing note, you should first see if the building it sold had a reliable fair market value at the date it was sold. Assume that Doink's building could have sold on January 1, 1999, for $10,000,000 in a straight cash transaction. Given the information about the building, its fair market value of $10,000,000 on January 1, 1999 represents the note's present value. Since the face of the note is $14,000,000 and its present value is $10,000,000, the $4,000,000 difference represents the discount. Doink should record this transaction in the following manner:

Note receivable	14,000,000	
Accumulated depreciation	3,000,000	
Building		7,000,000
Gain on sale of building		6,000,000
Discount on note receivable		4,000,000

It is important that you note how the gain is calculated in the entry above. The gain is the difference between the present value of the note ($10,000,000) and the book value of the property sold ($4,000,000). The difference between the face amount of the note ($14,000,000) and its present value ($10,000,000) represents the discount of $4,000,000. This discount should be amortized to interest income using the effective interest method. However, before this discount can be amortized, the interest rate must be determined. In situations like this, the interest rate can be determined by reference to present value tables. In Doink's situation, the present value of the note, $10,000,000, divided by its face amount, $14,000,000, results in the number .714. This number represents a factor from the present value of $1 table. Since Doink's note is for 3 periods, the factor .712 in the present value of $1 table is under the 12% interest rate. Thus, Doink's interest rate is approximately 12%.

If the building sold by Doink did not have a reliable fair market value on January 1, 1999, the next step would be to determine if the note had a market value on that date.

Finally, if the building sold by Doink did not possess a reliable fair market value on January 1, 1999, and the note did not have a market value on that date, the present value of Doink's note would have to be determined by **imputation**. This means that Doink would determine the present value of its note by reference to the incremental borrowing rate of the company which acquired its building.

The following diagram represents the forementioned relationships and procedures for determining the present value of a note receivable or payable (monetary assets and liabilities) and the amount of a discount/premium.

10. **Lending Activities**

The basic loan situation involves a borrower receiving the face amount of a loan from a lender, with no related discount or premium. The liability is the face amount, and the effective interest rate is the stated interest rate.

Sometimes the lender incurs various loan origination costs when originating or acquiring a loan. According to SFAS 91, the lender shall defer and recognize these costs over the life of the loan only when the costs relate directly to the loan, and would not have been incurred but for the loan. Otherwise, the costs are considered indirect and are charged to expense as incurred.

Sometimes the lender charges the borrower a nonrefundable loan origination fee. According to SFAS 91, both lender and borrower shall defer and recognize the nonrefundable fee over the life of the loan. The fee is frequently assessed in the form of points, where a point is 1% of the face amount of the loan.

> For example, assume that Bannon Bank grants a 10-year loan to VerSteiner, Inc. in the amount of $100,000 with a stated interest rate of 8%. Payments are due monthly, and are computed to be $1,213. In addition, Bannon Bank incurs $3,000 of direct loan origination costs (attorney's fees, title insurance, wages of employees' direct work on loan origination), and also charges VerSteiner a 5-point nonrefundable loan origination fee.
>
> Bannon Bank, the lender, has a carrying amount of $98,000. This reflects the $100,000 face amount of the loan less the $5,000 nonrefundable fee, plus the $3,000 additional investment Bannon Bank incurs to generate the $145,560 total payments from the borrower, VerSteiner. The effective interest rate is approximately 8.5%.
>
> VerSteiner, the borrower, receives 5% less than the face amount of $100,000, or $95,000, but is still required to pay $1,213 per month under the terms of the loan. VerSteiner's carrying amount is then $100,000 – $5,000 = $95,000, with an effective interest rate of approximately 9.2%.

AUTHOR'S NOTE: Both the rates can be derived with a financial calculator. It is not likely that you would be asked to compute these on the CPA exam because only simple 4-function calculators are provided to candidates. What you are expected to know is the concept of effective interest. You also need to know that the loan origination costs are to be added to the principal, by the lender, and any fee charged to the client is deducted from the principal by both parties in calculating the carrying amount.

**ACCOUNTING FOR MONETARY ASSETS AND LIABILITIES WHICH HAVE
MATURITIES GREATER THAN 1 YEAR FROM THE BALANCE SHEET DATE**

MULTIPLE-CHOICE QUESTIONS (1-21)

1.   On March 15, 1999, Ashe Corp. adopted a plan to accumulate $1,000,000 by September 1, 2003. Ashe plans to make four equal annual deposits to a fund that will earn interest at 10% compounded annually. Ashe made the first deposit on September 1, 1999. Future value and future amount factors are as follows:

Future value of $1 at 10% for 4 periods   1.46
Future amount of ordinary annuity of $1
  at 10% for 4 periods   4.64
Future amount of annuity in advance of
  $1 at 10% for 4 periods   5.11

Ashe should make four annual deposits (rounded) of
  a. $250,000
  b. $215,500
  c. $195,700
  d. $146,000

2.   On July 1, 1999, James Rago signed an agreement to operate as a franchisee of Fast Foods, Inc. for an initial franchise fee of $60,000. Of this amount, $20,000 was paid when the agreement was signed and the balance is payable in four equal annual payments of $10,000 beginning July 1, 2000. The agreement provides that the down payment is not refundable and no future services are required of the franchisor. Rago's credit rating indicates that he can borrow money at 14% for a loan of this type. Information on present and future value factors is as follows:

Present value of $1 at 14% for 4 periods   0.59
Future amount of $1 at 14% for 4 periods   1.69
Present value of an ordinary annuity of $1
  at 14% for 4 periods   2.91

Rago should record the acquisition cost of the franchise on July 1, 1999 at
  a. $43,600
  b. $49,100
  c. $60,000
  d. $67,600

3.   On November 1, 1999, a company purchased a new machine that it does not have to pay for until November 1, 2001. The total payment on November 1, 2001, will include both principal and interest. Assuming interest at a 10% rate, the cost of the machine would be the total payment multiplied by what time value of money concept?
  a.   Present value of annuity of $1.
  b.   Present value of $1.
  c.   Future amount of annuity of $1.
  d.   Future amount of $1.

4.   For which of the following transactions would the use of the present value of an annuity due concept be appropriate in calculating the present value of the asset obtained or liability owed at the date of incurrence?
  a.   A capital lease is entered into with the initial lease payment due 1 month subsequent to the signing of the lease agreement.

  b.   A capital lease is entered into with the initial lease payment due upon the signing of the lease agreement.
  c.   A 10-year 8% bond is issued on January 2 with interest payable semiannually on July 1 and January 1 yielding 7%.
  d.   A 10-year 8% bond is issued on January 2 with interest payable semiannually on July 1 and January 1 yielding 9%.

5.   On December 30, 1999, Chang Co. sold a machine to Door Co. in exchange for a noninterest-bearing note requiring 10 annual payments of $10,000. Door made the first payment on December 30, 1999. The market interest rate for similar notes at date of issuance was 8%. Information on present value factors is as follows:

Period	Present value of $1 at 8%	Present value of ordinary annuity of $1 at 8%
9	0.50	6.25
10	0.46	6.71

In its December 31, 1999 balance sheet, what amount should Chang report as note receivable?
  a. $45,000
  b. $46,000
  c. $62,500
  d. $67,100

Items 6 and 7 are based on the following:

On January 2, 1999, Emme Co. sold equipment with a carrying amount of $480,000 in exchange for a $600,000 noninterest-bearing note due January 2, 2002. There was no established exchange price for the equipment. The prevailing rate of interest for a note of this type at January 2, 1999, was 10%. The present value of $1 at 10% for three periods is 0.75.

6.   In Emme's 1999 income statement, what amount should be reported as interest income?
  a. $ 9,000
  b. $45,000
  c. $50,000
  d. $60,000

7.   In Emme's 1999 income statement, what amount should be reported as gain (loss) on sale of machinery?
  a. $(30,000) loss.
  b. $ 30,000 gain.
  c. $120,000 gain.
  d. $270,000 gain.

8.   On December 31, 1999, Jet Co. received two $10,000 notes receivable from customers in exchange for services rendered. On both notes, interest is calculated on the outstanding principal balance at the annual rate of 3% and payable at maturity. The note from Hart Corp., made under customary trade terms, is due in 9 months and the note from Maxx, Inc. is due in 5 years. The market interest rate for similar notes on December 31, 1999, was 8%. The compound interest factors to convert future values into present values at 8% follow:

Present value of $1 due in 9 months: .944
Present value of $1 due in 5 years: .680

At what amounts should these two notes receivable be reported in Jet's December 31, 1999 balance sheet?

	Hart	Maxx
a.	$ 9,440	$6,800
b.	$ 9,652	$7,820
c.	$10,000	$6,800
d.	$10,000	$7,820

9. Leaf Co. purchased from Oak Co. a $20,000, 8%, 5-year note that required five equal annual year-end payments of $5,009. The note was discounted to yield a 9% rate to Leaf. At the date of purchase, Leaf recorded the note at its present value of $19,485. What should be the total interest revenue earned by Leaf over the life of this note?

    a. $5,045
    b. $5,560
    c. $8,000
    d. $9,000

Items 10 and 11 are based on the following:

House Publishers offered a contest in which the winner would receive $1,000,000, payable over 20 years. On December 31, 1999, House announced the winner of the contest and signed a note payable to the winner for $1,000,000, payable in $50,000 installments every January 2. Also on December 31, 1999, House purchased an annuity for $418,250 to provide the $950,000 prize monies remaining after the first $50,000 installment, which was paid on January 2, 2000.

10. In its December 31, 1999 balance sheet, what amount should House report as note payable--contest winner, net of current portion?

    a. $368,250
    b. $418,250
    c. $900,000
    d. $950,000

11. In its 1999 income statement, what should House report as contest prize expense?

    a. $0
    b. $ 418,250
    c. $ 468,250
    d. $1,000,000

12. On December 31, 1999, Roth Co. issued a $10,000 face value note payable to Wake Co. in exchange for services rendered to Roth. The note, made at usual trade terms, is due in 9 months and bears interest, payable at maturity, at the annual rate of 3%. The market interest rate is 8%. The compound interest factor of $1 due in nine months at 8% is .944. At what amount should the note payable be reported in Roth's December 31, 1999 balance sheet?

    a. $10,300
    b. $10,000
    c. $ 9,652
    d. $ 9,440

13. On January 1, 1999, Parke Company borrowed $360,000 from a major customer evidenced by a

noninterest-bearing note due in 3 years. Parke agreed to supply the customer's inventory needs for the loan period at lower than market price. At the 12% imputed interest rate for this type of loan, the present value of the note is $255,000 at January 1, 1999. What amount of interest expense should be included in Parke's 1999 income statement?

    a. $43,200
    b. $35,000
    c. $30,600
    d. $0

14. Pie Co. uses the installment sales method to recognize revenue. Customers pay the installment notes in 24 equal monthly amounts, which include 12% interest. What is an installment note's receivable balance 6 months after the sale?

    a.   75% of the original sales price.
    b.   Less than 75% of the original sales price.
    c.   The present value of the remaining monthly payments discounted at 12%.
    d.   Less than the present value of the remaining monthly payments discounted at 12%.

15. On July 1, 1999, a company obtained a 2-year 8% note receivable for services rendered. At that time the market rate of interest was 10%. The face amount of the note and the entire amount of the interest are due on June 30, 2001. Interest receivable at December 31, 1999 was

    a.   5% of the face value of the note.
    b.   4% of the face value of the note.
    c.   5% of the July 1, 1999, present value of the amount due June 30, 2001.
    d.   4% of the July 1, 1999, present value of the amount due June 30, 2001.

16. Which of the following is reported as interest expense?

    a.   Pension cost interest.
    b.   Postretirement healthcare benefits interest.
    c.   Imputed interest on noninterest-bearing note.
    d.   Interest incurred to finance construction of machinery for own use.

17. The discount resulting from the determination of a note payable's present value should be reported on the balance sheet as a(n)

    a.   Addition to the face amount of the note.
    b.   Deferred charge separate from the note.
    c.   Deferred credit separate from the note.
    d.   Direct reduction from the face amount of the note.

18. In calculating the carrying amount of a loan, the lender adds to the principal

	Direct loan origination costs incurred by the lender	Loan origination fees charged to the borrower
a.	Yes	Yes
b.	Yes	No
c.	No	Yes
d.	No	No

19. Duff, Inc. borrowed from Martin Bank under a 10-year loan in the amount of $150,000 with a stated interest rate of 6%. Payments are due monthly, and are computed to be

$1,665. Martin Bank incurs $4,000 of direct loan origination costs and $2,000 of indirect loan origination costs. In
addition, Martin Bank charges Duff, Inc. a 4-point nonrefundable loan origination fee.

   Martin Bank, the lender, has a carrying amount of
   a. $144,000
   b. $148,000
   c. $150,000
   d. $152,000

20. Martin Bank grants a 10-year loan to Duff, Inc. in the
amount of $150,000 with a stated interest rate of 6%. Pay-
ments are due monthly, and are computed to be $1,665.
Martin Bank incurs $4,000 of direct loan origination costs
and $2,000 of indirect loan origination costs. In addition,
Martin Bank charges Duff, Inc. a 4-point nonrefundable
loan origination fee.

   Duff, the borrower, has a carrying amount of
   a. $144,000
   b. $148,000
   c. $150,000
   d. $152,000

21. On December 1, 1999, Money Co. gave Home Co. a
$200,000, 11% loan. Money paid proceeds of $194,000
after the deduction of a $6,000 nonrefundable loan origina-
tion fee. Principal and interest are due in 60 monthly installments of $4,310, beginning January 1, 2000. The re-
payments yield an effective interest rate of 11% at a present
value of $200,000 and 12.4% at a present value of
$194,000. What amount of income from this loan should
Money report in its 1999 income statement?
   a. $0
   b. $1,833
   c. $2,005
   d. $7,833

OTHER OBJECTIVE QUESTIONS

Problem 1   (15 to 25 minutes)

Presented below is selected information regarding the sale of a building by Catrina Corporation.

On January 1, 1999, Catrina Corporation sold a building which originally cost $300,000 with accumulated depreciation of $75,000 for a noninterest-bearing note with a face value of $300,000 due January 1, 2003. The FMV of the building is readily determinable and the market rate for a note of this type is 6%.

Required:

a.   Items 1 through 5 represent statements regarding the proper treatment of items in the sale of the building. Determine if the statement is true or false. To record your answer blacken the corresponding oval ⟨ T ⟩ for true and ⟨ F ⟩ for false on the objective answer sheet. These items cannot be graded if you fail to blacken the ovals.

Items to be answered

1.   The gain or loss on the sale of the building would be equal to the face value of the note less the book value of the building.

2.   The difference between the face value of the note and the present value of the note represents the discount or premium on the note.

3.   If the fair market value of the building was not determinable, then 6% would be considered the imputed interest rate.

4.   Even though the note is a noninterest-bearing note, the interest revenue for Catrina Corp. can be computed using the effective interest method.

5.   The amount recorded as the present value of the note should be equal to the fair market value of the building.

b.   Items 6 through 14 require the candidate to select the best answer from the Responses to be selected. For each item blacken the corresponding oval on the objective answer sheet. This item cannot be graded if you fail to blacken the ovals on the answer sheet.

Items to be answered	*Responses to be selected*
6. Annuity due	A. Effective interest rate x Net receivable or payable balance at the beginning of the period
7. Imputed interest rate	B. Periodic interest is computed on principal balance and interest earned to date
8. Market value of note	C. Represents the debtor's incremental borrowing rate
9. Note issued at a discount	D. Series of payments/receipts which occur at beginning of the period
10. Premium on a note	E. The difference between the present value of the note and the cash exchanged when the market rate of interest < rate on note
11. Simple interest method	F. Periodic interest is computed based on the principal balance only
12. Interest revenue/expense	G. Maturity value of note and interest payments discounted to the present value
13. Future value of annuity	H. This will result when face rate of the note < yield rate
14. Face of note equals present value of the note	I. The amount which will be available in the future as a result of consecutive payments/receipts at the end of each period--compounded at a specified interest rate
	J. Series of payments/receipts which are made at the end of the period
	K. No premium or discount exists

PROBLEMS

Problem 1   (15 to 25 minutes)

On September 30, 1998, Industrial Machinery Co. sold a machine and accepted the customer's noninterest-bearing note. Industrial normally makes sales on a cash basis. Since the machine was unique, its sales price was not determinable using Industrial's normal pricing practices.

After receiving the first of two equal annual installments on September 30, 1999, Industrial immediately discounted the note. Industrial had no continuing involvement with the note. On October 9, 2000, Industrial received notice that the note was dishonored, and it paid all amounts due. At all times prior to default, the note was reasonably expected to be paid in full.

Required:

a.   1.   How should Industrial determine the sales price of the machine?

2.   How should Industrial report the effects of the noninterest-bearing note on its income statement for the year ended December 31, 1998? Why is this accounting presentation appropriate?

b.   What are the effects of the discounting of the note receivable with recourse on Industrial's income statement for the year ended December 31, 1999, and its balance sheet at December 31, 1999?

c.   How should Industrial account for the effects of the note being dishonored?

———————————

Problem 2   (45 to 55 minutes)

Kern, Inc. had the following long-term receivable account balances at December 31, 1998:

Note receivable from the sale of an idle building	$750,000
Note receivable from an officer	200,000

Transactions during 1999 and other information relating to Kern's long-term receivables follow:

•   The $750,000 note receivable is dated May 1, 1998, bears interest at 9%, and represents the balance of the consideration Kern received from the sale of its idle building to Able Co. Principal payments of $250,000 plus interest are due annually beginning May 1, 1999. Able made its first principal and interest payment on May 1, 1999. Collection of the remaining note installments is reasonably assured.

•   The $200,000 note receivable is dated December 31, 1996, bears interest at 8%, and is due on December 31, 2001. The note is due from Frank Black, president of Kern, Inc., and is collateralized by 5,000 shares of Kern's common stock. Interest is payable annually on December 31, and all interest payments were made through December 31, 1999. The quoted market price of Kern's common stock was $45 per share on December 31, 1999.

•   On April 1, 1999, Kern sold a patent to Frey Corp. in exchange for a $100,000 noninterest-bearing note due on April 1, 2001. There was no established exchange price for the patent, and the note had no ready market. The prevailing interest rate for this type of note was 10% at April 1, 1999.

The present value of $1 for two periods at 10% is 0.826. The patent had a carrying amount of $40,000 at January 1, 1999, and the amortization for the year ended December 31, 1999, would have been $8,000. Kern is reasonably assured of collecting the note receivable from Frey.

•   On July 1, 1999, Kern sold a parcel of land to Barr Co. for $400,000 under an installment sale contract. Barr made a $120,000 cash down payment on July 1, 1999, and signed a 4-year 10% note for the $280,000 balance. The equal annual payments of principal and interest on the note will be $88,332, payable on July 1 of each year from 2000 through 2003. The fair value of the land at the date of sale was $400,000. The cost of the land to Kern was $300,000. Collection of the remaining note installments is reasonably assured.

Required:

Prepare the following and show supporting computations:

a.   Long-term receivables section of Kern's December 31, 1999 balance sheet.

b.   Schedule showing current portion of long-term receivables and accrued interest receivable to be reported in Kern's December 31, 1999 balance sheet.

c.   Schedule showing interest revenue from long-term receivables and gains recognized on sale of assets to be reported in Kern's 1999 income statement.

MULTIPLE-CHOICE ANSWERS

1. c __ __	6. b __ __	11. c __ __	16. c __ __	20. a __ __
2. b __ __	7. a __ __	12. b __ __	17. d __ __	21. c __ __
3. b __ __	8. d __ __	13. c __ __	18. b __ __	
4. b __ __	9. b __ __	14. c __ __	19. b __ __	1st: __/21 = __%
5. c __ __	10. b __ __	15. b __ __		2nd: __/21 = __%

MULTIPLE-CHOICE ANSWER EXPLANATIONS

A. Fundamentals

1.   (c)   The desired fund balance on September 1, 2003, ($1,000,000) is a **future amount**. The series of four equal annual deposits is an **annuity in advance**, as illustrated in the diagram below.

D   D   D   D $1,000,000

9/1/99   9/1/00   9/1/01   9/1/02   9/1/03

This is an annuity in advance, rather than an ordinary annuity, because the last deposit (9/1/02) is made 1 year prior to the date the future amount is needed. Therefore, these are beginning-of-year payments. The deposit amount is computed by dividing the future amount by the factor for the future amount of an annuity in advance.

$$\$1,000,000 \div 5.11 = \underline{\$195,700}$$

2.   (b)   The requirement is to determine the acquisition cost of a franchise. The cost of this franchise is the down payment of $20,000 plus the present value of the four equal annual payments of $10,000. The annual payments represent an annuity, so the $10,000 annual payment is multiplied by the present value factor of 2.91. Therefore, the franchise cost is $49,100 ($20,000 + $29,100). The journal entry is

Franchise	49,100	
Discount on notes payable	10,900	
Notes payable		40,000
Cash		20,000

3.   (b)   The requirement is to determine what time value of money concept would be used to determine the cost of a machine when a payment (principal plus interest) is to be made in 2 years. Answer (b) is correct because the cost of the machine is to be recorded immediately; therefore, the cost of the present value of a lump-sum payment would be used. Answer (c) is incorrect because a future amount would be used in computing the payment and not the cost of the machine. Also, a lump-sum payment is involved and not an annuity. Answer (d) is incorrect because a future amount would be used in computing the payment and not the cost. Answer (a) is incorrect because a lump-sum payment is involved, not an annuity.

4.   (b)   The requirement is the situation which illustrates an annuity due. An annuity due (annuity in advance) is a series of payments where the first payment is made at the beginning of the first period, in contrast to an ordinary annuity (annuity in arrears), in which the first payment is made at the end of the first period. Answer (b) is correct because the initial lease payment is due immediately (at the beginning of the first period). Answers (a), (c), and (d) all illustrate situations in which the first lease or interest payment occurs

at the end of the first period. Note that in answers (c) and (d), the stated rate and yield rate of the bonds differ; while this would affect the present value of the bonds, it has no effect on the classification as an annuity due or an ordinary annuity.

A.9. Notes Receivable and Payable

5.   (c)   If the FMV of the machine and the FMV of the note are not known, the transaction should be recorded at the PV of the note by imputing interest at the prevailing rate (8%) for similar notes. This series of 10 payments is an **annuity in advance**, because the first payment is due immediately on 12/30/99. However, the problem requires the amount to be reported for the note receivable on **12/31/99**, after the first payment is received. The remaining nine payments are an ordinary annuity, as illustrated in the diagram below.

PV = ?

R1   R2   R8   R9

12/31/99   12/30/00   12/30/01   12/30/07   12/30/08

In a PV computation, one must look at the first rent to see if it is an ordinary annuity or annuity in advance. If the first rent occurs one period after the computation date, it is an ordinary annuity. Therefore, the PV to be reported for the note receivable at 12/31/99 is $62,500 (10,000 x 6.25).

6.   (b)   The $600,000 noninterest-bearing note should be recorded at its present value of $450,000 ($600,000 x .75). The journal entry is

Loss on sale of equip.	30,000	
Note receivable	600,000	
Discount on NR		150,000 } 450,000
Equipment (net)		480,000

At 12/31/99, interest income would be recognized using the effective interest method. Using this method, interest is computing by multiplying the book value of the note ($600,000 – $150,000 = $450,000) by the effective interest rate ($450,000 x 10% = $45,000).

7.   (a)   The $600,000 noninterest-bearing note should be recorded at its present value of $450,000 ($600,000 x .75). The journal entry is

Loss on sale of equip.	30,000	
Note receivable	600,000	
Discount on NR		150,000 } 450,000
Equipment (net)		480,000

The loss is recognized because the fair value of the note received ($450,000) is $30,000 less than the carrying amount of the equipment sold ($480,000).

8. (d) APB 21 states that receivables bearing an unreasonably low stated interest rate should be recorded at their present value. However, APB 21 does **not** apply to receivables arising through the normal course of business which mature in less than 1 year. Therefore, the Hart receivable would be recorded at face value ($10,000), since it matures in 9 months. The Maxx receivable would be recorded at its present value, since it matures in 5 years. The Maxx receivable will result in a lump-sum collection of $11,500 [$10,000 + (10,000 x 3% x 5)], so its present value is $7,820 ($11,500 x .680).

9. (b) The total interest revenue earned over the life of the note equals the excess of the cash received over the cash paid to acquire the note. The cash received over the 5 years is $25,045 (5 receipts of $5,009 each). The cash paid to acquire the $20,000 note was $19,485. Therefore, the total interest revenue is $5,560 ($25,045 – $19,485).

10. (b) The $1,000,000 note is payable $50,000 in 2000 (current portion) and $950,000 after 2000 (long-term portion). Per APB 21, this noninterest-bearing long-term note should be recorded at its present value, which can be measured as the amount required to purchase an annuity sufficient to provide the funds to satisfy the obligation. Therefore, the note payable, net of current portion, should be reported at $418,250.

11. (c) The contest prize expense must be recognized at the present value of the obligation incurred as a result of the contest. The obligation consists of $50,000 payable in 2 days, and $950,000 payable over the next 19 years. The $950,000 long-term portion has a present value of $418,250, as evidenced by the cost of an annuity contract sufficient to satisfy it. Therefore, the total PV of the obligation is $468,250 ($50,000 + $418,250). The journal entry to record the expense is:

Contest prize expense	$468,250	
Discount on NP	$531,750	
Notes payable		$1,000,000

Thus, answer (c) is correct.

12. (b) APB 21 states that all receivables and payables are subject to present value measurement techniques and interest imputation, if necessary, with certain exceptions. One exception is normal course of business receivables and payables maturing in less than 1 year. Therefore this note payable, due in 9 months at usual trade terms, would be reported at face value ($10,000) rather than at present value ($10,225 x .944 = $9,652).

13. (c) The requirement is to determine the amount of interest expense to be recognized in 1999 from a noninterest-bearing note. Parke Company is able to borrow on a noninterest basis because they agree to sell their product at less than the market price. In this type of situation, the note payable is recorded at present value, and the difference between the present value and the cash received is recorded as **unearned sales revenue** (to be recognized when the

product is sold at less than market value). The initial journal entry is

Cash	360,000	
Discount on N.P.	105,000	
Note payable		360,000 / 255,000
Unearned sales revenue		
		105,000

When interest expense is recognized at the end of 1999, the effective interest method must be used. Using this method, interest expense is computed by multiplying the book value of the liability ($360,000 – $105,000 = $255,000) by the effective interest rate (12%), resulting in interest expense of $30,600.

14. (c) The entry made to record an installment sale (ignoring the cost of sale and inventory) is as follows:

Note receivable	(Sale price)
Installment sales	(PV of note @ 12%)
Discount on notes	
Receivable	(Plug)

Although the customer would have paid 25% (6 out of 24 months) of the total payments due under the terms of the installment sale, the **net** carrying value of the note (equal to the principal balance of the note less the unamortized discount) is equal to the present value of the remaining monthly payments discounted at 12%. Therefore, answer (c) is correct and answers (a), (b), and (d) are incorrect. Under the effective interest method, the carrying value of the note will at all times be equal to the present value of the remaining installment payments, regardless of whether the note is recorded gross or net in Pie Co.'s accounts.

15. (b) When a note is issued with a stated rate (8% in this case) below the market rate (10% in this case), the note will be issued at a discount. The entry for the recipient of the note on July 1 would be as follows:

Notes receivable	xxx	
Disc. on notes rec.		xxx
Service revenue		xxx

On December 31, the company must accrue interest on the note. The following entry would be made:

Interest receivable	(6 months at stated rate)
Disc. on notes rec.	(6 months amortization)
Interest revenue	(6 months interest at market rate)

Note that interest receivable is debited for an amount based upon the **stated** (face) rate of the note. This is because the stated rate will determine the amount of cash interest which will be received upon maturity of the note. Since the bond was held for 6 months (7/1/99 to 12/31/99) as of 12/31/99, the amount of the receivable would be determined as follows:

$$\frac{\text{Interest}}{\text{receivable}} = \left(\begin{array}{c}\text{Face value}\\ \text{of note}\end{array}\right) \times \left(\begin{array}{c}\text{Stated}\\ \text{rate}\end{array}\right) \times \left(\begin{array}{c}\text{Period}\\ \text{held}\end{array}\right)$$

$$= \text{Face value} \times 8\% \times (6/12 \text{ months})$$

$$= 4\% \times \text{Face value}$$

Therefore, answer (b) is correct.

16. (c) When a noninterest-bearing note is issued, APB 21 states that interest must be imputed on the note and amortized to interest expense over the life of the note using the effective interest rate. Therefore, answer (c) is correct. Answers (a) and (b) are incorrect because interest on pension cost and postretirement healthcare benefits are included as a component of future benefit obligation. Answer (d) is incorrect because interest incurred to finance construction of machinery for a company's own use may be capitalized and amortized.

17. (d) **Discount on notes payable** is a liability valuation account. It should be reported as a direct reduction from the face amount of the note (contra account). A **premium on notes payable** would be reported as an addition to the face amount of the note [answer (a)]. A discount is not recorded as a separate asset [answer (b)] because it does not provide any future economic benefit. It is not a deferred credit separate from the note [answer (c)] because it is a debit, not a credit, and because it is inseparable from the note. Thus, a discount on notes payable should be reported on the balance sheet as a direct reduction from the face amount of the note.

A.10. Lending Activities

18. (b) In calculating the carrying amount of a loan, loan origination costs are added to the principal by the lender. Any fee charged to the borrower is **deducted** from the principal by both parties (the lender and the borrower) in calculating the carrying amount.

19. (b) The lender's carrying amount of the loan is calculated by adding the direct loan origination costs to the principal and deducting the loan origination fee charged to the borrower. Indirect loan origination costs are charged to expense as incurred, and are not considered when calculating the carrying amount of the loan. Therefore, Martin Bank has a carrying amount of $148,000 [$150,000 principal plus $4,000 direct loan origination costs minus $6,000 ($150,000 x 0.04) nonrefundable loan origination fee]. The $2,000 indirect loan origination costs are expensed in the period incurred.

20. (a) Duff, Inc., the borrower, receives 4% less than the face amount of $150,000. Duff's carrying amount is, therefore, $150,000 – $6,000, or $144,000. Loan origination fees charged to the borrower are deducted from the principal in calculating the carrying amount.

NOTE: Loan origination fees are frequently assessed in the form of points, where a point is 1% of the face amount of the loan.

21. (c) Money Co. made a cash outflow of $194,000 for the $200,000 loan Money gave to Home Co. The book value of the loan is $194,000 on Money's books. Money will receive an effective interest rate of 12.4% on its cash outflow. Income from the loan would be calculated by multiplying the book value, times the effective interest rate, and the number of months of the year (in this case just 1--December). $194,000 x .124 x 1/12 = $2,004.67. The stated rate is 11% and is not used in the calculation. Money Co. will receive equal monthly installments over the 60-month life of the loan. Money Co. will effectively earn 12.4% on its initial cash outflow of $194,000, because Home Co. will repay principal for the total loan amount of $200,000.

OTHER OBJECTIVE ANSWERS AND ANSWER EXPLANATIONS

Problem 1

   1.   (F)   The gain or loss on the sale of the building is calculated by taking the difference between the present value of the note and the book value of the building. When the fair market value (FMV) of the building is readily determinable then the FMV will represent the present value of the note. If the FMV of building was not readily determinable then the PV would be calculated using the market rate. Therefore, this statement is false because the gain or loss would be equal to the **present value of the note** less the book value of the building.

   2.   (T)   The difference between the face value of the note and its present value will be equal to the discount or premium. If the face of the note > present value, then a discount exists and if the face of the note < present value, then a premium exists. Therefore, the statement is true.

   3.   (T)   When the stated interest rate is not fair, and the FMV of the goods being exchanged does not exist, an interest rate must be imputed. The imputed rate would be used to determine the present value of the note. The imputed interest rate represents the rate at which a debtor could obtain financing of a similar nature from a different source, which is known as the incremental borrowing rate. The problem states that the market rate of interest for a note of this type is 6%, thus the debtor's incremental borrowing rate is 6%. Therefore, the statement is true.

   4.   (T)   The difference between the face value of the note and the present value will equal the discount or premium. The discount or premium should be amortized using the effective interest method. The effective interest rate is assumed to be equal to the imputed interest rate. Therefore, the statement is true.

   5.   (T)   The present value of the note will be equal to the fair market value of the building if it is determinable. Therefore, this statement is true because the problem states that the FMV is readily determinable.

   6.   (D)   An annuity due (annuity in advance) represents a series of payments made or received at the beginning of the period.

   7.   (C)   An imputed interest rate is used when the rate on a note is not fair and the market value of the items being exchanged is not readily determinable. An imputed interest rate represents the rate at which the debtor could obtain financing from a different source, this is known as the debtor's incremental borrowing rate.

   8.   (G)   The market value of a note is equal to the maturity value and the interest payments discounted to the present value. The present value represents the amount you would pay now for an amount to be received in the future. Thus, answer G is the correct response, as the present value equals the current market value of the principal and interest amounts.

   9.   (H)   When a note is exchanged for cash and no other rights or privileges exist, the present value of the note will equal the cash received if the stated rate on the note equals the market yield rate. However, if the stated rate is less than the market rate, then the note will be issued at a discount to compensate.

   10.   (E)   A premium on a note occurs when the interest rate on a note is greater than the market yield rate. The market bids up the price of the bond above par until the effective interest rate on the note equals the market yield rate.

   11.   (F)   The simple interest method computes interest based upon the amount of principal only. Interest is computed as Principal x Interest x Time. The compound interest method computes interest on principal and any interest earned and not withdrawn.

   12.   (A)   The interest revenue or expense on a note is computed by taking the effective interest rate times the net receivable or payable balance.

   13.   (I)   An annuity is a periodic payment or receipt made in consecutive intervals over time compounded at a stated interest rate. The future value of an annuity represents the total of the periodic payments and accumulated interest at some point in the future.

   14.   (K)   When a note is exchanged for cash and no other rights or privileges exist, the present value of the note will be equal to the cash exchanged if the stated rate of interest equals the market yield rate. No premium or discount exists if the stated rate on the note equals the market yield rate.

ANSWER OUTLINE

Problem 1   Noninterest-Bearing Note

a. **1.**   Determination of sales price
         Machine's FMV is indeterminable
         Use PV of future cash flows at 9/30/98
            Discount at buyer's 9/30/98 market rate of interest

              PV of payment 1 to be received in 1 year
           + <u>PV of payment 2 to be received in 2 years</u>
              Fair value of note on 9/30/98

          PV = Fair value of note at sale = sales price

  2.   Reporting effects of note on 12/31/98 IS

$$\substack{\text{1998 interest}\\\text{revenue}} = \substack{\text{Carrying Amount}\\\text{(9/30/98)}} \times \substack{\text{Buyer's Market}\\\text{Rate (9/30/98)}} \times \text{3/12 Year}$$

        Presentation appropriate because:
          Interest factor implicit in note
          Interest earned with passage of time
          Rate used should be market rate established by
          original PV

b.   Effects of discounting NR with no continuing
     involvement

   On 12/31/99 IS:
     Gain/loss reported as income from continuing operations

   On 12/31/99 BS:
     Increase in cash
     Decrease in NR

c.   Accounting for dishonored note

  * Increase NR (AR) for all payments caused by dishonor and write down to estimated recoverable amount

UNOFFICIAL ANSWER

Problem 1   Noninterest-Bearing Note

a. **1.**   It was not possible to determine the machine's fair value directly, so the sales price of the machine is reported at the note's September 30, 1998 fair value. The note's September 30, 1998 fair value equals the present value at that date of the two installments discounted at the buyer's September 30, 1998 market rate of interest from their due dates of September 30, 1999, and September 30, 2000.

  2.   Industrial reports 1998 interest revenue determined by multiplying the note's carrying amount at September 30, 1998, times the buyer's market rate of interest at the date of issue, times 3/12. Industrial should recognize that there is an interest factor implicit in the note, and this interest is

earned with the passage of time. Therefore, interest revenue for 1998 should include 3 months' revenue. The rate used should be the market rate established by the original present value, and this is applied to the carrying amount of the note.

b.   To report the discounting of the note receivable with no continuing involvement, Industrial should decrease notes receivable by the carrying amount of the discounted note, increase cash by the amount received, and report the difference as a loss or gain as part of income from continuing operations.

c.   Industrial should decrease cash, and increase its notes (accounts) receivable past due for all payments caused by the note's dishonor. The note (account) receivable should be written down to its estimated recoverable amount (or an allowance for uncollectibles established), and a loss on uncollectible notes should be recorded for the difference.

SOLUTION GUIDE

Problem 2   Notes Receivable

1.   This problem consists of three related requirements. The candidate is required to prepare a long-term receivables section, prepare a schedule showing the current portion of the receivables and accrued interest receivable, and prepare a schedule showing the interest income and gains recognized on the sale of assets. Information pertaining to four notes is given.

1.1   The solutions approach for problems of this type where the requirements are interrelated is to prepare time lines for each note, make all computations for each note at one time, and label each computation according to the requirement to which it relates. For example, if a number or computation relates to requirement **a.**, it can be labeled "a." Using this approach, the candidate will be solving a part of two to three requirements as each note is covered, but not necessarily in the same order as given on the exam. After working through all the information given, the formal required schedules can be prepared.

1.2   The requirement in part **a.** is to prepare the long-term receivables section of the balance sheet dated 12/31/99. The solutions approach is to determine the amount of each note which is due after 12/31/00. In preparing the receivables section, all relevant information must be disclosed, [interest rates, due dates, less current installment (if applicable), etc.].

1.3   Part **b.** is essentially two subrequirements requiring the preparation of a schedule showing the current portion of the long-term receivables (label as b1.) and accrued interest receivable (label as b2.) that would appear in the balance sheet at 12/31/99.

1.4   Part **c.** is also essentially two subrequirements requiring the preparation of a schedule showing interest income from long-term receivables (c1.) and gains recognized on the sale of assets (c2.) that would appear on the income statement for the year ending 12/31/99.

2.   For the note arising from the sale of the building, $250,000 of the $750,000 principal was received on 5/1/99, leaving $500,000 to be received. Of this amount, $250,000 is due on 5/1/00 and represents the current portion. The remaining principal amount of $250,000 is due after 12/31/00 and is classified as long-term (see time line after 2.2).

2.1   Interest has accrued on this note since the last interest payment date (5/1/99) in the amount of $30,000 ($500,000 x 9% x 8/12). See time line after 2.2.

2.2   The interest income on this note is $52,500. This is equal to 9% of the note's balance outstanding from 1/1/99 to the first principal payment on 5/1/99 ($750,000 x 9% x 4/12 = $22,500) plus the interest earned on the remaining balance from the payment date to 12/31/99 ($500,000 x 9% x 8/12 = $30,000).

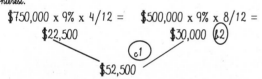

3.   The $200,000 note receivable from the officer is due 12/31/01; therefore, the entire amount is classified as long-term (see time line after 3.3).

3.1   Since the interest is payable annually on 12/31 and all the schedule interest payments have been made, there is no accrued interest from this note at 12/31/99.

3.2   A full year's interest was earned on the officer's note ($200,000 x 8% = $16,000). See the time line after 3.3.

3.3   No gain or loss is recorded on the stock acting as collateral. However, data relating to the collateral should be disclosed.

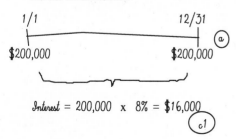

4.   The carrying value of the patent is its 1/1/99 book value of $40,000, less the 1/1/99 to 4/1/99 amortization of $2,000 ($8,000 x 3/12), or $38,000. Subtracting the 4/1/99 carrying value from the present value of the note received for the patent ($82,600) equals the gain on the sale of the patent, $44,600 (see time line after 4.2).

4.1   The $100,000 note arising from the sale of the patent is due 4/1/01 and is therefore considered long-term. Per APB 21, paras 12-14, a noninterest-bearing note should be recorded at its present value using the prevailing rate of interest on similar notes with any difference recorded as a discount or premium. Therefore, at the time this note was received, a discount was recorded for the difference between the face value ($100,000) and present value ($100,000 x .826 = $82,600) of the note, or $17,400, which will be amortized as interest revenue over the life of the note. The effective interest method should be used. The straight-line method is used for intraperiod allocation. Interest was earned for 9 months (4/1 - 12/31) on the carrying value of the note; therefore, the 1999 interest revenue and discount amortization is $6,195 ($82,600 x 10% x 9/12). After this amortization is recorded, the unamortized discount on 12/31/99 is $11,205 ($17,400 – $6,195). The note is presented net of the discount (see time line after 4.2).

4.2   No accrued interest will be recorded in the receivable account pertaining to this note. Even though interest revenue is recorded, the interest is a direct result of amortizing the related discount on the note and is not recorded as a receivable.

5.   The gain on the land sale is the selling price, $400,000 less its cost, $300,000, or $100,000 (see time line after 5.2).

5.1   Since the principal (and interest) on this note will be paid in four equal annual installments, the note must be divided between its current and long-term portions. Subtracting the first year's interest, ($280,000 x 10% = $28,000) from the installment to be received on 7/1/00 equals the current portion ($88,332 – $28,000 = $60,332). The remainder of the note ($280,000 – $60,332 = $219,668) is the long-term receivable (see time line after 5.2).

5.2   Six months' interest was earned and accrued in 1999 on this note ($280,000 x 10% x 6/12 = $14,000).

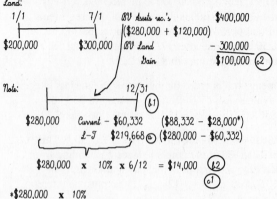

UNOFFICIAL ANSWER

Problem 2   Notes Receivable

a.

Kern, Inc.
LONG-TERM RECEIVABLES SECTION
OF BALANCE SHEET
December 31, 1999

9% note receivable from sale of idle building, due in annual installments of $250,000 to May 1, 2001, less current installment	$250,000	[1]
8% note receivable from officer, due December 31, 2001, collateralized by 5,000 shares of Kern, Inc. common stock with a fair value of $225,000	200,000	
Noninterest-bearing note from sale of patent, net of 10% imputed interest, due April 1, 2001	88,795	[2]
Installment contract receivable, due in annual installments of $88,332 to July 1, 2003, less current installment	219,668	[3]
Total long-term receivables	$758,463	

b.

Kern, Inc.
SELECTED BALANCE SHEET ACCOUNTS
December 31, 1999

Current portion of long-term receivables:		
Note receivable from sale of idle building	$250,000	[1]
Installment contract receivable	60,332	[3]
Total	$310,332	
Accrued interest receivable:		
Note receivable from sale of idle building	$30,000	[4]
Installment contract receivable	14,000	[5]
Total	$44,000	

c.

Kern, Inc.
INTEREST REVENUE FROM LONG-TERM RECEIVABLES
AND GAINS RECOGNIZED ON SALE OF ASSETS
For the Year Ended December 31, 1999

Interest revenue:		
Note receivable from sale of idle building	$52,500	[6]
Note receivable from sale of patent	6,195	[2]
Note receivable from officer	16,000	[7]
Installment contract receivable from sale of land	14,000	[5]
Total interest revenue	$88,695	
Gains recognized on sale of assets:		
Patent	$ 44,600	[8]
Land	100,000	[9]
Total gains recognized	$144,600	

Explanation of Amounts

[1]   Long-term portion of 9% note receivable at 12/31/99

Face amount, 5/1/98	$750,000
Less installment received 5/1/99	250,000
Balance, 12/31/99	500,000
Less installment due 5/1/00	250,000
Long-term portion, 12/31/99	$250,000

[2]   Noninterest-bearing note, net of imputed interest at 12/31/99

Face amount, 4/1/99	$100,000
Less imputed interest [$100,000 – $82,600 ($100,000 x 0.826)]	17,400
Balance, 4/1/99	82,600
Add interest earned to 12/31/99 [$82,600 x 10% x 9/12]	6,195
Balance, 12/31/99	$ 88,795

[3]   Long-term portion of installment contract receivable at 12/31/99

Contract selling price, 7/1/99	$400,000
Less cash down payment	120,000
Balance, 12/31/99	280,000
Less installment due 7/1/00 [$88,332 – $28,000 ($280,000 x 10%)]	60,332
Long-term portion, 12/31/99	$219,668

[4]   Accrued interest--note receivable, sale of idle building at 12/31/99

Interest accrued from 5/1 to 12/31/99 [$500,000 x 9% x 8/12]	$ 30,000

[5]   Accrued interest--installment contract at 12/31/99

Interest accrued from 7/1 to 12/31/99 [$280,000 x 10% x 1/2]	$ 14,000

[6]   Interest revenue--note receivable, sale of idle building, for 1999

Interest earned from 1/1/ to 5/1/99 [$750,000 x 9% x 4/12]	$ 22,500
Interest earned from 5/1 to 12/31/99 [$500,000 x 9% x 8/12]	30,000
Interest revenue	$ 52,500

[7]   Interest revenue--note receivable, officer, for 1999

Interest earned 1/1 to 12/31/99 [$200,000 x 8%]	$ 16,000

[8]   Gain recognized on sale of patent

Stated selling price		$100,000
Less imputed interest		17,400 [2]
Actual selling price		82,600
Less cost of patent (net)		
Carrying value 1/1/99	$40,000	
Less amortization 1/1 to 4/1/99 [$8,000 x 1/4]	2,000	38,000
Gain recognized		$ 44,600

[9]   Gain recognized on sale of land

Selling price	$400,000
Less cost	300,000
Gain recognized	$100,000

B. **Bonds**

1. **Bonds Payable and Bond Investments**

Investment in bonds and bonds payable are discussed together to contrast their treatment.* Bonds generally provide for periodic fixed interest payments at a contract rate of interest. At issuance, or thereafter, the market rate of interest for the particular type of bond may be above, the same, or below the contract rate. If the market rate exceeds the contract rate, the book value will be less than the maturity value. The difference (discount) will make up for the contract rate being below the market rate.

Conversely, when the contract rate exceeds the market rate, the bond will sell for more than maturity value to bring the effective rate to the market rate. This difference (premium) will make up for the contract rate being above the market rate. When the contract rate equals the market rate, the bond will sell for the maturity value.

The market value of a bond is equal to the maturity value and interest payments discounted to the present. You may have to refer to the discussion of time value of money concepts in the previous section before working with the subsequent material. Finally, when solving bond problems, candidates must be careful when determining the number of months to use in the calculation of interest and discount/premium amortization. For example, candidates frequently look at a bond issue with an interest date of September 1 and count 3 months to December 31. This error is easy to make because candidates focus only on the fact that September is the ninth month instead of also noting whether the date is at the beginning or end of the month. Candidates should also be aware that bond issues that mature on a single date are called term bonds, and bond issues that mature in installments are called serial bonds.

2. **Bond Valuation Example**

$10,000 in bonds, semiannual interest at 6% contract rate, maturing in 6 years, and market rate of 5%.

a. Find present value of maturity value. Use present value of $1 factor. Discount $10,000 back 12 periods at 2 1/2% interest (Factor = .7436). (Semiannual compounding is going to be required to discount the semiannual payments so it is also assumed here.)

$$\$10,000 \quad x \quad .7436 \quad = \quad \$7,436$$

b. Find the present value of the annuity of twelve $300 interest payments. Use present value of an ordinary annuity of $1 factor for 12 periods at 2 1/2% interest (Factor = 10.26).

$$\$300 \; x \; 10.26 = \$3,078$$

c. Today's value is $10,514 (7,436 + 3,078)

The $514 premium is to be recognized over the life of the bond issue. It is a reduction of interest expense on the books of the issuer and a reduction of interest revenue on the books of the investor. Amortization is to be the interest, or present value basis. (See outline of APB 21.)

---

* *Coverage in this module focuses on a bond's book or carrying value. Issues concerning FMV, holding gains and losses, and financial statement presentation of bond investments are covered with other marketable debt securities in Module 29, Investments.*

3. **Journal Entries**

The issuer's books will be illustrated at gross (including a premium or discount account) and the investor's books will be illustrated at net (no discount or premium account). The investor may record the bonds either net or gross, but the issuer records at gross. In the past, CPA examination problems and solutions have followed the net method on the books of the investor.

		Issuer			*Investor*		
a.	Issue and						
	Acquisition	Cash	10,514		Bond invest.	10,514	
		Bonds pay.		10,000	Cash		10,514
		Bonds prem.		514			
b.	First int.						
	payment	Interest exp.	300		Cash	300	
		Cash		300	Interest rev.		300
c.	Premium--						
	Amortization	Bond prem.	37.15*		Interest rev.	37.15	
		Interest exp.		37.15	Bond invest.		37.15*

Interest receipt (payment) minus effective interest = 300 – 262.85 = 37.15
Effective interest = net book value times effective rate = 10,514 x .025 = 262.85

Entry a. assumes that the bonds are issued on the interest payment date. If bonds are purchased between interest payment dates, the purchaser will also include accrued interest through the purchase date in the total cash paid for the bonds. The payment of this accrued interest on the purchase date will serve to reduce the subsequent receipt of interest income (which covers a time period longer than the time the purchaser held the bond).

Subsequent interest payments are recorded the same as entry b. shown above. The amount of subsequent amortization (entry c. above) changes. Interest to be recorded under the interest method is always computed by

Effective interest rate x Net book value

This formula is true of all applications of the interest method. The effective rate of interest times net book value is the actual interest revenue or expense for the period. The difference between the actual interest and the amount received or paid is the amortization. The amortization table below shows the effective interest amounts and premium amortizations for the first 4 periods.

Period	*3% cash interest*	*2 1/2% effective interest*	*Decrease in book value*	*Book value of bonds*
0				$10,514.00
1	$300[(a)]	$262.85[(b)]	$37.15[(c)]	10,476.85[(d)]
2	300	261.92	38.08	10,438.77
3	300	260.97	39.03	10,399.74
4	300	259.99	40.01	10,359.73

(a) 3% x $10,000   (c) $300 – $262.85
(b) 2 1/2% x $10,514.00   (d) $10,514.00 – $37.15

Since the interest is paid semiannually, interest (including premium amortization) is recorded every 6 months. The journal entries for periods 2, 3, and 4 are:

	Issuer			*Investor*		
Period 2	Interest expense	261.92		Cash	300.00	
	Bond premium	38.08		Interest rev.		261.92
	Cash		300.00	Bond invest.		38.08

Period 3	Interest expense	260.97		Cash	300.00
	Bond premium	39.03		Interest rev.	260.97
	Cash		300.00	Bond invest.	39.03
Period 4	Interest expense	259.99		Cash	300.00
	Bond premium	40.01		Interest rev.	259.99
	Cash		300.00	Bond invest.	40.01

Notice that the interest (revenue and expense) decreases over time. This is because the net book value (which is also the present value) is decreasing from the maturity value plus premium to the maturity value. Thus, the effective rate is being multiplied by a smaller amount each 6 months.

Also, note that the change in interest each period is the prior period's premium amortization times the effective rate. For example, the interest in period 3 is $.95 less than in period 2, and $38.08 of premium was amortized in period 2. The effective rate of 2.5% (every 6 months) times $38.08 is $.95. Thus, if the interest changes due to the changing level of net book value, the change in interest will be equal to the change in the net book value times the effective rate of interest.

Another complication may arise if the year end does not coincide with the interest dates. In such a case, an adjusting entry must be made. The proportional share of interest payable or receivable should be recognized along with the amortization of discount or premium. The amortization of discount or premium should be straight-line within the amortization period.

EXAMPLE: *Assume that in the above example, both issuer and investor have reporting periods ending 3 months after the issuance of the bonds.*

	Issuer			*Investor*	
Entries on the					
closing date	*Interest expense*	*150*		*Interest receivable*	*150*
	Interest payable	*150*		*Interest revenue*	*150*
	Bond premium	*18.57*		*Interest revenue*	*18.57*
	Interest expense	*18.57*		*Bond investment*	*18.57*

Reverse at beginning of new period and make regular entry at next interest payment date.

If bonds are sold (bought) between interest dates, premium/discount amortization must be computed for the period between sale (purchase) date and last (next) interest date. This is accomplished by straight-lining the 6-month amount which was calculated using the effective interest method.

EXAMPLE: *The investor sold $5,000 of bonds in the above example, 2 months after issuance, for $5,250 plus interest.*

1. *The bond premium which must be amortized to the point of sale ($5,000 for 2 months) is 1/2 x 1/3 x $37.15 or $6.19.*

Interest revenue	*6.19*	
Investment		*6.19*

2. *The sale is recorded. The investment account was $5,257 before amortization of $6.19. The cash received would be $5,250 plus $50 interest (1/2 x 1/3 x $300). The loss is a forced figure.*

Cash	*5,300.00*	
Loss	*.81*	
Interest revenue		*50.00*
Investment		*5,250.81*

3. *Check the interest revenue recorded ($50.00 – $6.19) to the interest earned: $5,257 x 2 1/2% x 1/3 (which equals $43.81).*

Costs incurred in connection with the issuance of bonds (e.g., printing and engraving, accounting and legal fees, and commissions), according to SFAC 6, may be treated two ways. **However**, APB Opinion 21 currently allows the treatment of bond issue costs only in one of these ways.

SFAC 6 (see outline) states that the bond issue costs can be treated as either an expense or a reduction of the related bond liability. Bond issue costs are not considered as assets because they provide no future economic benefit. The argument for treating them as a reduction of the related bond liability is that they reduce bond proceeds thereby increasing the effective interest rate. Thus, they should be accounted for the same as unamortized discounts.

In practice, however, the only acceptable GAAP for bond issue costs is to treat them as deferred charges and amortize them on a straight-line basis over the life of the bond.

4. **Comparison of Effective Interest and Straight-Line Amortization Methods**

Although APB 21 requires use of the effective interest method for determining interest on receivables and payables, the straight-line method may be used if the result obtained is not materially different from that obtained using the effective interest method.

Several recent CPA exam questions have asked candidates to compare the dollar amount of interest revenue (expense) and the interest rate obtained under each method. The table below summarizes the relationships which are obtained under both methods when a note is issued at: (1) a premium or (2) a discount.

	Effective interest				*Straight-line method*		
	(a)	(b)	(c)		(d)	(e)	(f)
	Effective	X Carrying	= Amount of			± Discount	=
Note Is-	Interest	(Book)	Interest In-		Cash	(Premium)	Amount of
sued At:	Rate	Value	come (Expense)		Interest	Amortization	Interest
(1) Discount	Constant	Increasing	Increasing		Constant	Constant	Constant
(2) Premium	Constant	Decreasing	Decreasing		Constant	Constant	Constant

In the above chart, the three columnar headings under each method are written in the form of an equation. Under the effective interest method, the dollar amount of interest revenue (expense), column (c), is derived by multiplying the effective rate (a constant percentage), column (a), by an increasing (decreasing) carrying value, column (b), resulting in an increasing (decreasing) dollar amount of interest, column (c).

Under the straight-line method, the dollar amount of interest revenue (expense), column (f), is the dollar amount of cash interest (nominal or stated rate times the face of the note), column (d) plus (minus) the discount (premium) amortization, column (e). When the constant dollar amount of interest revenue (expense) is related to an increasing (decreasing) carrying value, the result is a decreasing (increasing) interest rate which is, essentially, an "accounting" or "book" interest rate. This rate is the result of using an arbitrary method (straight-line) which ignores the economic facts of the situation. The effective interest method gives recognition to the economic facts by using the rate (effective) which resulted from the bargaining of the parties to the note.

When the note is a bond, this may involve many parties (i.e., the market), and the effective rate is referred to as the "market" or "yield" rate.

5. **Convertible Bonds** (See outlines of APB 14 and SFAS 84)

Bonds are frequently issued with the right to convert the bonds into common stock. When issued, no value is apportioned to the conversion feature. Two approaches are possible to account for bond conversions: valuing the transaction at cost (book value of the bonds), or valuing at market (of the stocks or bonds, whichever is more reliable). At market, assuming market value exceeds book value, the entries would be

Issuer			*Investor*		
Loss on redemption	(plug)		Stock invest	(mkt)	
Bonds payable	(book value)		Invest in bonds		(carrying value)
Bond premium	(book value)		Gain on conver-		
Common stock		(par)	sion		(plug)
Paid-in excess of par		(mkt-par)			

On the issuer's books, the debit (credit) to the loss (gain) account (ordinary) would be for the difference between the market value of the stock (bonds) and the book value of the bonds. The conversion is treated as the culmination of an earnings process; thus the loss (gain) should be recognized. The bonds and the related accounts must be written off, and paid-in excess of par is credited for the excess of the market value of the stock (bonds) over the stock's par value. On the investor's books, the gain (loss) would also be the difference between the market value the stock (bonds) and the book value of the bonds. Remember in both cases that the accrued interest and discount or premium amortization must be recorded prior to the conversion.

Conversion under the cost method would result in debits to bonds payable and bond premium (or a credit to bond discount) equal to the book value of the bonds, and credits to common stock and paid-in excess of par equal to the book value. In practice, conversions are usually recorded at book value. Note that under this method no gain (loss) is recorded, as no gain (loss) should result from an equity transaction.

To induce conversion, firms sometimes change the original conversion privilege or give additional considerations to the bondholders. Per SFAS 84 (see outline), the fair market value of these "sweeteners" should be recognized as an expense (ordinary in nature) upon conversion, determined as the excess of the FMV of all securities and consideration transferred over the FMV of the securities issuable per the original conversion terms.

6. **Debt Issued with Detachable Purchase Warrants**

APB 14 (see outline) requires the proceeds of debt issued with detachable stock purchase warrants to be allocated between the debt and stock warrants based on relative market values. Example: units of one bond and one warrant (to buy 10 shares of stock at $50/share) are issued for $1,030. Thereafter, warrants trade at $40 and the bonds at $960. The relative market value of the warrants is 4% (40/1,000) and the relative market value of the bonds is 96% (960/1,000). Thus, $41.20 (.04 x $1,030) of the issue price is assigned to the warrants.

Cash	1,030.00	
Bond discount	11.20	
Bonds payable		1,000.00
Paid-in capital--stock warrants		41.20

If one warrant was subsequently exercised

Cash	500.00	
Paid-in capital--stock warrants	41.20	
Common stock		(par of 10 shs)
Paid-in excess		(plug)

Alternatively, the example above could have indicated the market value of the stock (e.g., $54) rather than the market values of the bonds and warrants. In such a case, one would value the warrants based on the difference between option price and market price, for example, [$54 (market) – $50 (option)] x 10 shares = $40 value for the warrants.

Notice the effect of requiring allocation of the cash received to the stock warrants. The final effect is to increase interest costs on the bond issue by reducing the premium or increasing the discount.

Note that the allocation to equity shown above is only applicable where the purchase warrants are **detachable**. In contrast, no allocation is made to equity if the bonds are issued with **nondetachable** stock purchase warrants. Detachable warrants are often traded separately from the debt and therefore have a readily determinable market value of their own. The inseparability of nondetachable warrants prevents the determination of a separate market value; therefore, no allocation to equity is permitted by APB 14.

7. **Extinguishment of Debt** (See outline of APB 26)

Debt is considered extinguished whenever the debtor pays the creditor and is relieved of all obligations relating to the debt. Typical examples of this are the calling of a bond by the debtor, requiring the bondholder to sell the bond to the issuing corporation at a certain date and stated price, and the open market repurchase of a debt issue. Refunding of debt (replacement of debt with other debt) is also considered an extinguishment. However, troubled debt restructures (situations where creditors agree to grant relief to debtors) and debt conversions initiated by the debt holders are not. Additionally, when the debtor is legally released from being the primary obligor of the debt either judicially, or by the creditor, and it is probable the debtor will make no further payments on it, the debt is considered extinguished.

All gains (losses) resulting from the extinguishment of debt should be recognized in the period of extinguishment. The gain (loss) is the difference between the bond's reacquisition price and its net book value [face value plus (minus) any unamortized premium (discount) and issue costs]. The rule is not affected by the reissuance of debt before or after the refunding. Furthermore, this rule applies to convertible bonds when reacquired with cash. The gain or loss is **extraordinary** (see SFAS 4 and 64).

Loss or gain	xx	xx
Bonds payable	xx	
Bond premium	xx	
Unamortized issue costs		xx
Bond discount		xx
Cash		xx

MULTIPLE-CHOICE QUESTIONS (1-41)

1.   Hancock Co.'s December 31, 1999 balance sheet contained the following items in the long-term liabilities section:

Unsecured

9.375% registered bonds ($25,000 maturing annually beginning in 2003)	$275,000
11.5% convertible bonds, callable beginning in 2008, due 2019	125,000

Secured

9.875% guaranty security bonds, due 2019	$250,000
10.0% commodity backed bonds ($50,000 maturing annually beginning in 2004)	200,000

What are the total amounts of serial bonds and debenture bonds?

	Serial bonds	*Debenture bonds*
a.	$475,000	$400,000
b.	$475,000	$125,000
c.	$450,000	$400,000
d.	$200,000	$650,000

2.   Blue Corp.'s December 31, 1999 balance sheet contained the following items in the long-term liabilities section:

9 3/4% registered debentures, callable in 2010, due in 2015	$700,000
9 1/2% collateral trust bonds, convertible into common stock beginning in 2008, due in 2018	600,000
10% subordinated debentures ($30,000 maturing annually beginning in 2005)	300,000

What is the total amount of Blue's term bonds?
a. $ 600,000
b. $ 700,000
c. $1,000,000
d. $1,300,000

3.   Bonds payable issued with scheduled maturities at various dates are called

	Serial bonds	*Term bonds*
a.	No	Yes
b.	No	No
c.	Yes	No
d.	Yes	Yes

4.   The following information pertains to Camp Corp.'s issuance of bonds on July 1, 1999:

Face amount	$800,000
Term	10 years
Stated interest rate	6%
Interest payment dates	Annually on July 1
Yield	9%

	At 6%	*At 9%*
Present value of 1 for 10 periods	0.558	0.422
Future value of 1 for 10 periods	1.791	2.367
Present value of ordinary annuity of 1 for 10 periods	7.360	6.418

What should be the issue price for each $1,000 bond?
a. $1,000
b. $ 864
c. $ 807
d. $ 700

5.   The market price of a bond issued at a discount is the present value of its principal amount at the market (effective) rate of interest
a.   Less the present value of all future interest payments at the market (effective) rate of interest.
b.   Less the present value of all future interest payments at the rate of interest stated on the bond.
c.   Plus the present value of all future interest payments at the market (effective) rate of interest.
d.   Plus the present value of all future interest payments at the rate of interest stated on the bond.

6.   On July 1, 1999, Eagle Corp. issued 600 of its 10%, $1,000 bonds at 99 plus accrued interest. The bonds are dated April 1, 1999 and mature on April 1, 2009. Interest is payable semiannually on April 1 and October 1. What amount did Eagle receive from the bond issuance?
a. $579,000
b. $594,000
c. $600,000
d. $609,000

7.   During 1999, Lake Co. issued 3,000 of its 9%, $1,000 face value bonds at 101 1/2. In connection with the sale of these bonds, Lake paid the following expenses:

Promotion costs	$ 20,000
Engraving and printing	25,000
Underwriters' commissions	200,000

What amount should Lake record as bond issue costs to be amortized over the term of the bonds?
a. $0
b. $220,000
c. $225,000
d. $245,000

8.   Dixon Co. incurred costs of $3,300 when it issued, on August 31, 1999, 5-year debenture bonds dated April 1, 1999. What amount of bond issue expense should Dixon report in its income statement for the year ended December 31, 1999?
a. $ 220
b. $ 240
c. $ 495
d. $3,300

9.   On November 1, 1999, Mason Corp. issued $800,000 of its 10-year, 8% term bonds dated October 1, 1999. The bonds were sold to yield 10%, with total proceeds of $700,000 plus accrued interest. Interest is paid every April 1 and October 1. What amount should Mason report for interest payable in its December 31, 1999 balance sheet?
a. $17,500
b. $16,000
c. $11,667
d. $10,667

10. On July 1, 1999, Day Co. received $103,288 for $100,000 face amount, 12% bonds, a price that yields 10%. Interest expense for the 6 months ended December 31, 1999, should be

    a. $6,197
    b. $6,000
    c. $5,164
    d. $5,000

11. On January 2, 1999, West Co. issued 9% bonds in the amount of $500,000, which mature on January 2, 2009. The bonds were issued for $469,500 to yield 10%. Interest is payable annually on December 31. West uses the interest method of amortizing bond discount. In its June 30, 1999 balance sheet, what amount should West report as bonds payable?

    a. $469,500
    b. $470,475
    c. $471,025
    d. $500,000

12. Webb Co. has outstanding a 7%, 10-year $100,000 face-value bond. The bond was originally sold to yield 6% annual interest. Webb uses the effective interest rate method to amortize bond premium. On June 30, 1999, the carrying amount of the outstanding bond was $105,000. What amount of unamortized premium on bond should Webb report in its June 30, 2000 balance sheet?

    a. $1,050
    b. $3,950
    c. $4,300
    d. $4,500

13. A bond issued on June 1, 1999, has interest payment dates of April 1 and October 1. Bond interest expense for the year ended December 31, 1999, is for a period of

    a. 3 months.
    b. 4 months.
    c. 6 months.
    d. 7 months.

14. For the issuer of a 10-year term bond, the amount of amortization using the interest method would increase each year if the bond was sold at a

	Discount	*Premium*
a.	No	No
b.	Yes	Yes
c.	No	Yes
d.	Yes	No

15. On January 2, 1999, Nast Co. issued 8% bonds with a face amount of $1,000,000 that mature on January 2, 2005. The bonds were issued to yield 12%, resulting in a discount of $150,000. Nast incorrectly used the straight-line method instead of the effective interest method to amortize the discount. How is the carrying amount of the bonds affected by the error?

	At December 31, 1999	*At January 2, 2005*
a.	Overstated	Understated
b.	Overstated	No effect
c.	Understated	Overstated
d.	Understated	No effect

16. The following information relates to noncurrent investments that Fall Corp. placed in trust as required by the underwriter of its bonds:

Bond sinking fund balance, 12/31/99	$ 450,000
1998 additional investment	90,000
Dividends on investments	15,000
Interest revenue	30,000
Administration costs	5,000
Carrying amount of bonds payable	1,025,000

What amount should Fall report in its December 31, 2000 balance sheet related to its noncurrent investment for bond sinking fund requirements?

    a. $585,000
    b. $580,000
    c. $575,000
    d. $540,000

17. Witt Corp. has outstanding at December 31, 2000, two long-term borrowings with annual sinking fund requirements and maturities as follows:

	Sinking fund requirements	*Maturities*
2000	$1,000,000	$ --
2001	1,500,000	2,000,000
2002	1,500,000	2,000,000
2003	2,000,000	2,500,000
2004	2,000,000	3,000,000
	$8,000,000	$9,500,000

In the notes to its December 31, 2000 balance sheet, how should Witt report the above data?

    a. No disclosure is required.
    b. Only sinking fund payments totaling $8,000,000 for the next 5 years detailed by year need be disclosed.
    c. Only maturities totaling $9,500,000 for the next 5 years detailed by year need to be disclosed.
    d. The combined aggregate of $17,500,000 of maturities and sinking fund requirements detailed by year should be disclosed.

18. On March 1, 1995, a company established a sinking fund in connection with an issue of bonds due in 2007. At December 31, 1999, the independent trustee held cash in the sinking fund account representing the annual deposits to the fund and the interest earned on those deposits. How should the sinking fund be reported in the company's balance sheet at December 31, 1999?

    a. The cash in the sinking fund should appear as a current asset.
    b. Only the accumulated deposits should appear as a noncurrent asset.
    c. The entire balance in the sinking fund account should appear as a current asset.
    d. The entire balance in the sinking fund account should appear as a noncurrent asset.

19. An issuer of bonds uses a sinking fund for the retirement of the bonds. Cash was transferred to the sinking fund and subsequently used to purchase investments. The sinking fund

    I. Increases by revenue earned on the investments.

II. Is **not** affected by revenue earned on the investments.

III. Decreases when the investments are purchased.

    a. I only.

    b. I and III.

    c. II and III.

    d. III only.

20. On July 2, 1999, Wynn, Inc., purchased as a short-term investment a $1,000,000 face value Kean Co. 8% bond for $910,000 plus accrued interest to yield 10%. The bonds mature on January 1, 2006, pay interest annually on January 1, and are classified as trading securities. On December 31, 1999, the bonds had a market value of $945,000. On February 13, 2000, Wynn sold the bonds for $920,000. In its December 31, 1999 balance sheet, what amount should Wynn report for short-term investments in trading debt securities? (Answer should be in accordance with SFAS 115.)

    a. $910,000

    b. $920,000

    c. $945,000

    d. $950,000

21. On July 1, 1999, East Co. purchased as a long-term investment $500,000 face amount, 8% bonds of Rand Corp. for $461,500 to yield 10% per year. The bonds pay interest semiannually on January 1 and July 1. In its December 31, 1999 balance sheet, East should report interest receivable of

    a. $18,460

    b. $20,000

    c. $23,075

    d. $25,000

22. On October 1, 1998, Park Co. purchased 200 of the $1,000 face value, 10% bonds of Ott, Inc., for $220,000, including accrued interest of $5,000. The bonds, which mature on January 1, 2005, pay interest semiannually on January 1 and July 1. Park used the straight-line method of amortization and appropriately classified the bonds as held-to-maturity. On Park's December 31, 1999 balance sheet, the bonds should be reported at

    a. $215,000

    b. $214,400

    c. $214,200

    d. $212,000

23. On July 1, 1999, York Co. purchased as a held-to-maturity investment $1,000,000 of Park, Inc.'s 8% bonds for $946,000, including accrued interest of $40,000. The bonds were purchased to yield 10% interest. The bonds mature on January 1, 2006, and pay interest annually on January 1. York uses the effective interest method of amortization. In its December 31, 1999 balance sheet, what amount should York report as investment in bonds?

    a. $911,300

    b. $916,600

    c. $953,300

    d. $960,600

24. In 1998, Lee Co. acquired, at a premium, Enfield, Inc. 10-year bonds as a long-term investment. At December 31, 1999, Enfield's bonds were quoted at a small discount. Which of the following situations is the most likely cause of the decline in the bonds' market value?

    a. Enfield issued a stock dividend.

    b. Enfield is expected to call the bonds at a premium, which is less than Lee's carrying amount.

    c. Interest rates have declined since Lee purchased the bonds.

    d. Interest rates have increased since Lee purchased the bonds.

25. An investor purchased a bond as a held-to-maturity investment on January 2. The investor's carrying value at the end of the first year would be highest if the bond was purchased at a

    a. Discount and amortized by the straight-line method.

    b. Discount and amortized by the effective interest method.

    c. Premium and amortized by the straight-line method.

    d. Premium and amortized by the effective interest method.

26. An investor purchased a bond as a long-term investment on January 1. Annual interest was received on December 31. The investor's interest income for the year would be highest if the bond was purchased at

    a. Par.

    b. Face value.

    c. A discount.

    d. A premium.

27. On March 1, 1999, Clark Co. issued bonds at a discount. Clark incorrectly used the straight-line method instead of the effective interest method to amortize the discount. How were the following amounts, as of December 31, 1999, affected by the error?

	Bond carrying amount	Retained earnings
a.	Overstated	Overstated
b.	Understated	Understated
c.	Overstated	Understated
d.	Understated	Overstated

28. Jent Corp. purchased bonds at a discount of $10,000. Subsequently, Jent sold these bonds at a premium of $14,000. During the period that Jent held this investment, amortization of the discount amounted to $2,000. What amount should Jent report as gain on the sale of bonds?

    a. $12,000

    b. $22,000

    c. $24,000

    d. $26,000

29. On July 1, 1999, after recording interest and amortization, York Co. converted $1,000,000 of its 12% convertible bonds into 50,000 shares of $1 par value common stock. On the conversion date the carrying amount of the bonds was $1,300,000, the market value of the bonds was $1,400,000, and York's common stock was publicly trading at $30 per share. Using the book value method, what amount of additional paid-in capital should York record as a result of the conversion?

    a. $ 950,000

b. $1,250,000
c. $1,350,000
d. $1,500,000

30. On March 31, 1999, Ashley, Inc.'s bondholders exchanged their convertible bonds for common stock. The carrying amount of these bonds on Ashley's books was less than the market value but greater than the par value of the common stock issued. If Ashley used the book value method of accounting for the conversion, which of the following statements correctly states an effect of this conversion?

a.   Stockholders' equity is increased.
b.   Additional paid-in capital is decreased.
c.   Retained earnings is increased.
d.   An extraordinary loss is recognized.

Items 31 and 32 are based on the following:

On January 2, 1996, Chard Co. issued 10-year convertible bonds at 105. During 1999, these bonds were converted into common stock having an aggregate par value equal to the total face amount of the bonds. At conversion, the market price of Chard's common stock was 50% above its par value.

31. On January 2, 1996, cash proceeds from the issuance of the convertible bonds should be reported as
a.   Contributed capital for the entire proceeds.
b.   Contributed capital for the portion of the proceeds attributable to the conversion feature and as a liability for the balance.
c.   A liability for the face amount of the bonds and contributed capital for the premium over the face amount.
d.   A liability for the entire proceeds.

32. Depending on whether the book value method or the market value method was used, Chard would recognize gains or losses on conversion when using the

	Book value method	Market value method
a.	Either gain or loss	Gain
b.	Either gain or loss	Loss
c.	Neither gain **nor** loss	Loss
d.	Neither gain **nor** loss	Gain

33. On December 30, 1999, Fort, Inc. issued 1,000 of its 8%, 10-year, $1,000 face value bonds with detachable stock warrants at par. Each bond carried a detachable warrant for one share of Fort's common stock at a specified option price of $25 per share. Immediately after issuance, the market value of the bonds without the warrants was $1,080,000 and the market value of the warrants was $120,000. In its December 31, 1999 balance sheet, what amount should Fort report as bonds payable?
a. $1,000,000
b. $ 975,000
c. $ 900,000
d. $ 880,000

34. On December 31, 1999, Moss Co. issued $1,000,000 of 11% bonds at 109. Each $1,000 bond was issued with 50 detachable stock warrants, each of which entitled the bondholder to purchase one share of $5 par common stock for

$25. Immediately after issuance, the market value of each warrant was $4. On December 31, 1999, what amount should Moss record as discount or premium on issuance of bonds?
a. $ 40,000 premium.
b. $ 90,000 premium.
c. $110,000 discount.
d. $200,000 discount.

35. On March 1, 1999, Evan Corp. issued $500,000 of 10% nonconvertible bonds at 103, due on February 28, 2009. Each $1,000 bond was issued with 30 detachable stock warrants, each of which entitled the holder to purchase, for $50, one share of Evan's $25 par common stock. On March 1, 1999, the market price of each warrant was $4. By what amount should the bond issue proceeds increase stockholders' equity?
a. $0
b. $15,000
c. $45,000
d. $60,000

36. Main Co. issued bonds with detachable common stock warrants. Only the warrants had a known market value. The sum of the fair value of the warrants and the face amount of the bonds exceeds the cash proceeds. This excess is reported as
a.   Discount on bonds payable.
b.   Premium on bonds payable.
c.   Common stock subscribed.
d.   Contributed capital in excess of par--stock warrants.

37. When bonds are issued with stock purchase warrants, a portion of the proceeds should be allocated to paid-in capital for bonds issued with

	Detachable stock purchase warrants	Nondetachable stock purchase warrants
a.	No	Yes
b.	No	No
c.	Yes	No
d.	Yes	Yes

38. On June 30, 1999, King Co. had outstanding 9%, $5,000,000 face value bonds maturing on June 30, 2004. Interest was payable semiannually every June 30 and December 31. On June 30, 1999, after amortization was recorded for the period, the unamortized bond premium and bond issue costs were $30,000 and $50,000, respectively. On that date, King acquired all its outstanding bonds on the open market at 98 and retired them. At June 30, 1999, what amount should King recognize as gain before income taxes on redemption of bonds?
a. $ 20,000
b. $ 80,000
c. $120,000
d. $180,000

39. On January 1, 1994, Fox Corp. issued 1,000 of its 10%, $1,000 bonds for $1,040,000. These bonds were to mature on January 1, 2004 but were callable at 101 any time after December 31, 1997. Interest was payable semiannually on July 1 and January 1. On July 1, 1999, Fox called all of the bonds and retired them. Bond premium was amortized on a straight-line basis. Before income taxes, Fox's gain or loss in 1999 on this early extinguishment of debt was

- a. $30,000 gain.
- b. $12,000 gain.
- c. $10,000 loss.
- d. $ 8,000 gain.

40. On January 1, 1999, Hart, Inc. redeemed its 15-year bonds of $500,000 par value for 102. They were originally issued on January 1, 1987 at 98 with a maturity date of January 1, 2002. The bond issue costs relating to this transaction were $20,000. Hart amortizes discounts, premiums, and bond issue costs using the straight-line method. What amount of extraordinary loss should Hart recognize on the redemption of these bonds?

- a. $16,000
- b. $12,000
- c. $10,000
- d. $0

41. Weald Co. took advantage of market conditions to refund debt. This was the fifth refunding operation carried out by Weald within the last 4 years. The excess of the carrying amount of the old debt over the amount paid to extinguish it should be reported as a(n)

- a.   Deferred credit to be amortized over life of new debt.
- b.   Part of continuing operations.
- c.   Extraordinary gain, net of income taxes.
- d.   Extraordinary loss, net of income taxes.

OTHER OBJECTIVE QUESTIONS

Problem 1*   (10 to 15 minutes)

   Question Number 1 consists of 7 items. Select the **best** answer for each item. Use a No. 2 pencil to blacken the appropriate ovals on the Objective Answer Sheet to indicate your answers. **Answer all items.** Your grade will be based on the total number of correct answers.

Items 1 through 7 are based on the following:

   On January 2, 19997, North Co. issued bonds payable with a face value of $480,000 at a discount. The bonds are due in 10 years and interest is payable semiannually every June 30 and December 31. On June 30, 1999, and on December 31, 1999, North made the semiannual interest payments due, and recorded interest expense and amoritization of bond discount.

Required:

   Items 1 through 7, contained in the partially-completed amortization table below, represent information needed to complete the table. For each item, select from the following lists the correct numerical response and blacken the corresponding oval on the Objective Answer Sheet. A response may be selected once, more than once, or not at all.

	Cash	Interest expense	Amortization	Discount	Carrying amount
1/2/99					(3)
6/30/99	(2)	18,000	3,600	(1)	363,600
12/31/99	$14,400	(6)	(7)		

Annual Interest Rates: Stated   (4)
                         Effective (5)

Rates	
A	3.0%
B	4.5%
C	5.0%
D	6.0%
E	9.0%
F	10.0%

Amounts			
G	$ 3,420	P	$ 21,600
H	$ 3,600	Q	$116,400
I	$ 3,780	R	$120,000
J	$ 3,960	S	$123,600
K	$14,400	T	$360,000
L	$17,820	U	$363,600
M	$18,000	V	$367,200
N	$18,180	W	$467,400
O	$18,360	X	$480,000

Problem 2   (5 to 10 minutes)

   This question consists of 5 items. Select the best answer for each item. Use a No. 2 pencil to blacken the appropriate ovals on the Objective Answer Sheet to indicate your answers. **Answer all items.** Your grade will be based on the total number of correct answers.

Items 1 through 5 are based on the following:

   Hamnoff, Inc.'s $50 par value common stock has always traded above par. During 1999, Hamnoff had several transactions that affected the following balance sheet accounts:

   I.   Bond discount
   II. Bond premium
   III. Bonds payable
   IV. Common stock
   V.   Additional paid-in capital
   VI. Retained earnings

_____

* *This is Part A of 1195, FARE3. Part B appears in Module 25, Problem 2.*

Required:

For **items 1 through 5**, determine whether the transaction increased ⓘ , decreased ⓓ , or had no effect ⓝ on each of the balances in the above accounts, and blacken the corresponding oval on the Objective Answer Sheet.

1. Hamnoff issued bonds payable with a nominal rate of interest that was less than the market rate of interest.

2. Hamnoff issued convertible bonds, which are common stock equivalents, for an amount in excess of the bonds' face amount.

3. Hamnoff issued common stock when the convertible bonds described in item 2 were submitted for conversion. Each $1,000 bond was converted into 20 common shares. The book value method was used for the early conversion.

4. Hamnoff issued bonds, with detachable stock warrants, for an amount equal to the face amount of the bonds. The stock warrants have a determinable value.

5. Hamnoff declared and issued a 2% stock dividend.

Problem 3   (15 to 25 minutes)

The illustrations below represent transactions that occur within the scope of bond investments and bond issuances. Assume that the transactions occur from the date of investment or issuance to the maturity date.

Required:

For each illustration below, select the **best** answer from the answers (A) Increase, (B) Decrease, or (C) Remains constant. An answer may be used once, more than once, or not at all. (On the CPA Exam, candidates would be instructed to blacken in ovals on the Objective Answer Sheet.)

	(A)	*(B)*	*(C)*
			Remains
	Increases	*Decreases*	*constant*
1. Interest expense on a bond issued at a premium from the date of issuance to maturity using the effective interest method.	___	___	___
2. Semiannual receipt of cash by an investor in bonds originally purchased at a premium.	___	___	___
3. Net book value of a bond investment originally issued at a discount using the straight-line method of amortization.	___	___	___
4. The rate applied to the carrying value of bonds payable originally issued at a discount to determine interest expense for a period, using the effective interest method.	___	___	___
5. Interest revenue from bonds purchased at a premium from the purchase date to maturity using the effective interest method.	___	___	___
6. Unamortized discount on bond issuance from issuance date to maturity using the straight-line method.	___	___	___
7. Amortization of a bond premium using the straight-line method.	___	___	___
8. Interest revenue from bonds purchased at a discount using the effective interest method.	___	___	___
9. In practice, the acceptable treatment for the amortization of bond issue costs for bonds issued at a discount.	___	___	___
10. The unamortized premium on bonds payable from issuance date to maturity using the effective interest method.	___	___	___

PROBLEMS

Problem 1   (15 to 25 minutes)

On January 2, 1997, Drew Company issued 9% term bonds dated January 2, 1997 at an effective annual interest rate (yield) of 10%. Drew uses the effective interest method of amortization. On July 1, 1999, the bonds were extinguished early when Drew acquired them in the open market for a price greater than their face amount.

On September 1, 1999, Drew issued for cash 7% nonconvertible bonds dated September 1, 1999, with detachable stock purchase warrants. Immediately after issuance, both the bonds and the warrants had separately determined market values.

Required:

a.   1. Were the 9% term bonds issued at face amount, at a discount, or at a premium? Why?

2. Would the amount of interest expense for the 9% term bonds using the effective interest method of amortization be higher in the first or second year of the life of the bond issue? Why?

b.   1. How should gain or loss on early extinguishment of debt be determined? Does the early extinguishment of the 9% term bonds result in a gain or loss? Why?

2. How should Drew report the early extinguishment of the 9% term bonds on the 1999 income statement?

c. How should Drew account for the issuance of the 7% nonconvertible bonds with detachable stock purchase warrants?

Problem 2   (15 to 25 minutes)

On June 30, 1996, Corval Co. issued 15-year 12% bonds at a premium (effective yield 10%). On November 30, 1999, Corval transferred both cash and property to the bondholders to extinguish the entire debt. The fair value of the transferred property equaled its carrying amount. The fair value of the cash and property transferred exceeded the bonds carrying amount. [Ignore income taxes.]

Required:

a. Explain the purpose of the effective interest method and the effect of applying the method in 1996 on Corval's bond premium.

b. What would have been the effect on 1996 interest expense, net income, and the carrying amount of the bonds if Corval had incorrectly adopted the straight-line interest method instead of the effective interest method?

c. How should Corval calculate and report the effects of the November 30, 1999 transaction in its 1999 income statement? Why is this presentation appropriate?

d. How should Corval report the effects of the November 30, 1999 transaction in its statement of cash flows using the indirect method?*

Problem 3   (10 to 15 minutes)

Columbine Co.'s 10-year convertible bonds, were issued and dated October 1, 1997. Each $1,000 bond is convertible, at the holder's option, into 20 shares of Columbine's $25 par value common stock. The bonds were issued at a premium when the common stock traded at $45 per share. After payment of interest on October 1, 1999, 30% of the bonds were tendered for conversion when the common stock was trading at $57 per share. Columbine used the book value method to account for the conversion.

Required:

a.   1. How would the issue price of Columbine's convertible bonds be determined?

2. How should Columbine account for the issuance of the convertible bonds? Give the rationale for this accounting practice.

3. How should Columbine account for the conversion of the bonds into common stock?

Problem 4

This problem can be found in Module 27. It is problem 2 and requires preparation of the long-term liabilities section of the balance sheet and a schedule of interest expense.

Author's note: Part D of this problem is covered in Module 30.

MULTIPLE-CHOICE ANSWERS

1. a __ __	11. b __ __	21. b __ __	31. d __ __	41. c __ __
2. d __ __	12. c __ __	22. d __ __	32. c __ __	
3. c __ __	13. d __ __	23. a __ __	33. c __ __	
4. c __ __	14. b __ __	24. d __ __	34. c __ __	
5. c __ __	15. b __ __	25. d __ __	35. d __ __	
6. d __ __	16. b __ __	26. c __ __	36. a __ __	
7. d __ __	17. d __ __	27. c __ __	37. c __ __	
8. b __ __	18. d __ __	28. b __ __	38. b __ __	
9. b __ __	19. a __ __	29. b __ __	39. d __ __	1st: __/41 = __%
10. c __ __	20. c __ __	30. a __ __	40. a __ __	2nd: __/41 = __%

MULTIPLE-CHOICE ANSWER EXPLANATIONS

B.1.-4. Bonds

1.   (a)   Serial bonds are bond issues that mature in installments (usually on the same date each year over a period of years). In this case, serial bonds total $475,000 ($275,000 + $200,000). **Debenture** bonds are bonds which are **not** secured by specifically designated collateral, but rather by the general assets of the corporation. The unsecured bonds total $400,000 ($275,000 + $125,000).

2.   (d)   Term bonds are bond issues that mature on a single date, as opposed to **serial bonds**, which mature in installments. In this case, the 9 3/4% bonds and the 9 1/2% bonds are term bonds ($700,000 + $600,000 = $1,300,000), while the 10% bonds are serial bonds ($300,000).

3.   (c)   Serial bonds are bond issues that mature in installments (i.e., on the same date each year over a period of years). Term bonds, on the other hand, are bond issues that mature on a single date. Therefore, answer (c) is correct.

**4.   (c)   The issue price of each bond is equal to the present value (PV) of the maturity value plus the PV of the interest annuity. The PV must be computed using the yield rate (9%). The computation is:

Amount		PV factor		PV
$1,000	x	.422	=	$422
60	x	6.418	=	385
				$807

The annuity interest amount above ($60) is the principal ($1,000) times the stated cash rate (6%).

**5.   (c)   The market price of a bond issued at any amount (par, premium, or discount) is equal to the present value of all of its future cash flows, discounted at the current market (effective) interest rate. The market price of a bond issued at a discount is equal to the present value of both its principal and periodic future cash interest payments at the stated (cash) rate of interest, discounted at the current market (effective) rate. Therefore, answer (c) is correct and answers (a), (b), and (d) are incorrect.

**6.   (d)   To determine the net cash received from the bond issuance, the solutions approach is to prepare the journal entry for the issuance:

Cash	?	
Discount on BP	6,000	
Bonds payable		600,000
Interest expense		15,000

The bonds were issued at 99 ($600,000 x 99% = $594,000), so the discount is $6,000 ($600,000 – $594,000). The accrued interest covers the 3 months from 4/1 to 7/1 ($600,000 x 10% x 3/12 = $15,000). The cash received includes the $594,000 for the bonds and the $15,000 for the accrued interest, for a total of $609,000.

**7.   (d)   SFAS 91 states that engraving and printing costs, legal and accounting fees, commissions, promotion costs, and other similar costs should be recorded as bond issue costs and amortized over the term of the bonds. All the costs given are bond issue costs, so the amount reported as bond issue costs is $245,000 ($20,000 + $25,000 + $200,000).

**8.   (b)   Bond issue costs are treated as deferred charges and amortized on a straight-line basis over the life of the bond. These 5-year bonds were issued 5 months late (4/1/99 to 8/31/99), so they will be outstanding only 55 months (60 – 5). During 1999, the bonds were outstanding for 4 months (8/31/99 to 12/31/99). Therefore, the bond issue costs must be amortized for 4 months out of 55 months total, resulting in bond issue expense of $240 ($3,300 x 4/55).

**9.   (b)   Interest payable reported in the 12/31/99 balance sheet would consist of interest due from the bond date (10/1/99) to the year end (12/31/99); in other words, 3 months' interest. The formula for interest payable is:

$$\left(\begin{array}{c}\text{Face}\\\text{value}\end{array}\right) \times \left(\begin{array}{c}\text{Stated}\\\text{rate}\end{array}\right) \times \left(\begin{array}{c}\text{Time}\\\text{period}\end{array}\right) = \left(\begin{array}{c}\text{Interest}\\\text{payable}\end{array}\right)$$

$$\$800,000 \quad \times \quad 8\% \quad \times \quad 3/12 \quad = \quad \underline{\$16,000}$$

This amount would result from two entries:

Issuance

Cash	705,333		
Discount on BP	100,000		
Bonds payable		800,000	
Int. payable		5,333	(800,000 x 8% x 1/12)

Adjusting entry

Interest expense	11,667		(700,000 x 10% x 2/12)
Int. payable		10,667	(800,000 x 8% x 2/12)
Discount on BP		1,000	

**10.   (c)   A bond premium must be amortized using the interest method or the straight-line method if the results are not materially different. To use the straight-line method, the amount of time the bonds will be outstanding must be known. Since this time period is not given, the interest method must be used. Under the interest method, interest expense is computed as follows:

$$\begin{pmatrix} BV\ of \\ bonds \end{pmatrix} \times \begin{pmatrix} Yield \\ rate \end{pmatrix} \times \begin{pmatrix} Time \\ period \end{pmatrix} = \begin{pmatrix} Interest \\ expense \end{pmatrix}$$

$$\$103,288 \quad \times \quad 10\% \quad \times \quad 6/12 \quad = \quad \$5,164$$

The interest payable at 12/31/99 is $6,000 ($100,000 x 12% x 6/12), so the 12/31/99 journal entry is:

Interest expense	5,164	
Premium on BP	836	
Interest payable		6,000

11. (b) Under the effective interest method, interest expense is computed as follows:

$$\begin{pmatrix} BV\ of \\ bonds \end{pmatrix} \times \begin{pmatrix} Yield \\ rate \end{pmatrix} \times \begin{pmatrix} Time \\ period \end{pmatrix} = \begin{pmatrix} Interest \\ expense \end{pmatrix}$$

$$\$469,500 \quad \times \quad 10\% \quad \times \quad \frac{6}{12} \quad = \quad \underline{\$23,475}$$

The cash interest payable is computed below:

$$\begin{pmatrix} FV\ of \\ bonds \end{pmatrix} \times \begin{pmatrix} Stated \\ rate \end{pmatrix} \times \begin{pmatrix} Time \\ period \end{pmatrix} = \begin{pmatrix} Interest \\ expense \end{pmatrix}$$

$$\$500,000 \quad \times \quad 9\% \quad \times \quad \frac{6}{12} \quad = \quad \underline{\$22,500}$$

The bond discount amortization is the difference between these two amounts computed above ($23,475 – $22,500 = $975). This amortization would increase the carrying amount of the bonds to $470,475 ($469,500 original carrying amount + $975 amortization).

12. (c) Under the effective interest method, interest expense is computed as follows:

$$\begin{pmatrix} CA\ of \\ bonds \end{pmatrix} \times \begin{pmatrix} Yield \\ rate \end{pmatrix} \times \begin{pmatrix} Time \\ period \end{pmatrix} = \begin{pmatrix} Interest \\ expense \end{pmatrix}$$

$$\$105,000 \quad \times \quad 6\% \quad \times \quad 12/12 \quad = \quad \underline{\$6,300}$$

The cash interest payable is computed as follows:

$$\begin{pmatrix} FV\ of \\ bonds \end{pmatrix} \times \begin{pmatrix} Stated \\ rate \end{pmatrix} \times \begin{pmatrix} Time \\ period \end{pmatrix} = \begin{pmatrix} Cash \\ interest \end{pmatrix}$$

$$\$100,000 \quad \times \quad 7\% \quad \times \quad 12/12 \quad = \quad \underline{\$7,000}$$

The bond premium amortization is the difference between these two amounts ($7,000 – $6,300 = $700). Therefore, the unamortized premium at 6/30/97 is $4,300 ($5,000 – $700).

13. (d) Under the accrual basis of accounting, expenses should be recognized when incurred, regardless of when cash is paid. Therefore, expense from the bond issue date (6/1/99) through year end (12/31/99) should be recognized in 1999.

```
      1     2     3     4     5     6     7    ⎫
   |--|--|--|--|--|--|--|--|--|--|--|--|--|--| ⎬  7
  6/1/99  7/1  8/1  9/1  10/1 11/1 12/1 12/31 ⎭ months
```

The 7 months (6/1/99 - 12/31/99) of interest expense would be the net effect of entries prepared on the issuance date, the October 1 interest date, and December 31 (adjusting entry).

14. (b) The requirement is to determine whether the amount of amortization increases each year using the interest method when a bond is sold either at a discount or premium or both. Using the interest method, interest expense for the period is based on the carrying value of the bond multiplied by the effective rate of interest. Cash interest paid for the period equals the face value of the bond multiplied by the stated rate of interest. The difference between these two resulting figures is the amortization of the discount or premium each period. The solutions approach is to prepare a table for a bond issued at a discount and at a premium and examine the direction of the successive amortization amounts. Consider $100,000 of 8% bonds issued on January 1, 1999, due on January 1, 2006, with interest payable each July 1 and January 1. Investors wish to obtain a yield of 10% on the issue. The amortization for the first two periods is as follows:

Date	Credit cash	Debit interest expense	Credit bond discount	Carrying value of bonds
1/1/99				$92,278
7/1/99	$4,000	$4,614	$614	92,892
1/1/00	4,000	4,645	645	93,537

Assume the same facts, except the investors wish to obtain a yield of only 6% on the issue:

Date	Credit cash	Debit interest expense	Credit bond premium	Carrying value of bonds
1/1/99				$108,530
7/1/99	$4,000	$3,256	$744	107,786
1/1/00	4,000	3,234	766	107,020

The above tables show that when bonds are sold at either a discount or a premium, the amount of amortization using the interest method will increase each year.

15. (b) Using the effective interest method, interest expense is computed as the **carrying amount** of the bonds multiplied by the **effective rate** of interest. Cash interest paid equals the **face value** of the bonds multiplied by the **stated rate** of interest. The difference between interest expense and cash interest paid is discount amortization. When bonds are issued at a discount, the carrying amount increases each year, so interest expense increases each year, which causes a larger difference between interest expense and interest paid. Therefore, under the effective interest method, the discount amortization amount increases yearly. Under the straight-line method, discount amortization is constant each period. After 1 year, the incorrect use of the straight-line method would overstate the carrying amount of the bonds since more discount would have been amortized than under the effective interest method. By the time the bonds mature at 1/2/05, the entire discount would have been amortized under both methods, so the carrying amount would be the same for both methods.

16. (b) The 12/31/99 bond sinking fund balance ($450,000) was increased by the additional investment ($90,000), dividends ($15,000), and interest ($30,000). It was decreased by administration costs ($5,000), resulting in a 12/31/00 balance of $580,000 ($450,000 + $90,000 + $15,000 + $30,000 – $5,000).

17. **(d)** SFAS 47 requires disclosure at the balance sheet date of future payments for sinking fund requirements and maturity amounts of long-term debt during each of the next 5 years. Therefore, the combined aggregate of $17,500,000 of maturities and sinking fund requirements detailed by year should be disclosed.

18. **(d)** Companies sometimes place assets in segregated funds for special needs. These funds may become unavailable for normal operations due to debt covenants or other contractual requirements. Funds segregated for long-term needs, such as the bond sinking fund established in this problem, are reported as investments in the noncurrent section of the balance sheet. Therefore, answers (a) and (c) are incorrect. When interest is earned on investments held in a bond sinking fund, the following journal entry would be made:

Bond sinking fund cash   (revenue earned)
    Bond sinking fund revenue   (revenue earned)

The debit to the bond sinking fund increases the balance of the fund. The amount credited to bond sinking fund revenue is reported in the "Other Income (Expense)" section of the income statement. Therefore, answer (d) is correct and answer (b) is incorrect.

19. **(a)** Businesses occasionally accumulate a fund of cash and/or investments for a specific purpose, such as the retirement of bonds in this problem. These funds are referred to as "sinking funds." The sinking fund is increased when periodic additions are made to the fund and when revenue is earned on the investments held in the fund. When cash is used to purchase investments, the components of the fund change (i.e., cash is invested and replaced by bonds or other securities), but the total fund balance is not affected. Therefore, answer (a) is correct, and answers (b), (c), and (d) are incorrect.

20. **(c)** Debt and equity securities that are classified as **trading securities** are reported at fair market value, with unrealized gains and losses included in earnings. Therefore, at 12/31/99 Wynn would recognize an unrealized holding gain of $35,000 ($945,000 – $910,000) on the income statement, and report the securities at their fair market value of $945,000. Therefore, the answer is (c). Answers (a), (b) and (d) are incorrect because in accordance with SFAS 115 securities classified as trading securities are reported at fair market value on the balance sheet.

21. **(b)** Interest **receivable** on an investment in bonds is computed using the basic interest formula:

$$\begin{pmatrix} \text{Face} \\ \text{value} \end{pmatrix} \times \begin{pmatrix} \text{Stated} \\ \text{rate} \end{pmatrix} \times \begin{pmatrix} \text{Time} \\ \text{period} \end{pmatrix} = \begin{pmatrix} \text{Interest} \\ \text{receivable} \end{pmatrix}$$
$$\$500,000 \quad \times \quad 8\% \quad \times \quad 6/12 \quad = \quad \$20,000$$

Note that interest **revenue** is $23,075 ($461,500 x 10% x 6/12) using the interest method.

22. **(d)** The bonds should be recorded at an original cost of $215,000 ($220,000 less accrued interest of $5,000). The premium of $15,000 is amortized using the straight-line method over the period from the 10/1/98 date of purchase to the 1/1/05 maturity date (75 months). By 12/31/99, amorti-

zation has been recorded for 15 months (10/1/98 to 12/31/99), so total amortization is $3,000 ($15,000 x 15/75). Therefore, the bonds should be reported on the 12/31/99 balance sheet at $212,000 ($215,000 – $3,000).

23. **(a)** When using the interest method of amortization, interest revenue is computed as follows:

$$\begin{pmatrix} \text{BV of} \\ \text{bonds} \end{pmatrix} \times \begin{pmatrix} \text{Yield} \\ \text{rate} \end{pmatrix} \times \begin{pmatrix} \text{Time} \\ \text{period} \end{pmatrix} = \begin{pmatrix} \text{Interest} \\ \text{expense} \end{pmatrix}$$
$$\$906,000 \quad \times \quad 10\% \quad \times \quad 6/12 \quad = \quad \$45,300$$

The initial BV is the total amount paid less the accrued interest ($946,000 – $40,000 = $906,000). The amount of interest receivable for the 6 months is computed below:

$$\begin{pmatrix} \text{FV of} \\ \text{bonds} \end{pmatrix} \times \begin{pmatrix} \text{Stated} \\ \text{rate} \end{pmatrix} \times \begin{pmatrix} \text{Time} \\ \text{period} \end{pmatrix} = \begin{pmatrix} \text{Interest} \\ \text{receivable} \end{pmatrix}$$
$$\$1,000,000 \quad \times \quad 8\% \quad \times \quad 6/12 \quad = \quad \$40,000$$

The discount amortized at 12/31/99 is the difference in these two amounts ($45,300 – $40,000 = $5,300). This increases the book value of the investment to $911,300 ($906,000 + $5,300).

24. **(d)** The requirement is to determine the most likely cause of the decline in the bonds' market value. When the bonds were acquired at a premium, they sold above their face value. This meant that the stated rate of the bonds was greater than the market rate of interest on an alternative investment of equal risk. Thus, the investors paid more than the face value to acquire the bonds. However, when bonds are quoted at a discount, the stated rate of the bonds is less than the market rate. Therefore, answer (d) is correct because the market rate of interest has increased since Lee purchased the bonds.

25. **(d)** At any point in time, an investor's carrying value of a bond held as a long-term investment is equal to the par value of the bond, plus the amount of the unamortized premium, or less the amount of the unamortized discount. A bond purchased at a premium, thus, has a higher carrying value at any point in time than if it had been purchased at a discount. This is logical since its initial cost is also higher when purchased at a premium. Therefore, answers (a) and (b) are incorrect.

Having determined that the bond purchased at a premium will result in the highest carrying value, we must now determine which amortization method will result in the higher carrying value at the end of the first year. Under the straight-line method, the periodic amortization is constant; it is computed by dividing the total premium by the number of periods involved. Under the effective interest method, the periodic amortization changes over the term of the bond. A review of amortization tables for bonds issued at a premium will demonstrate that the periodic amortization of the premium is lowest in the first period, but increases over subsequent periods. Therefore, the straight-line method would result in higher amortization of the premium at the end of the first year than under the effective interest method. The higher amortization would result in a smaller unamortized premium and lower, overall carrying value at the end of the first year under the straight-line method than under the effective interest method. Therefore, answer (d) is correct.

26. (c)   The requirement is to determine the purchase price of a bond which will yield the highest interest income for the investor. If the bond's market rate of interest on the date of acquisition is different than the stated rate, the bonds will sell at a premium or discount. If the market rate of interest is higher than the bond's stated rate, the purchase price will be lower than the face value (i.e., discounted). The discount will be recognized over the life of the investment as an addition to interest income. Annual interest income will equal the cash interest received plus the discount amortization for the year. Answers (a) and (b) are incorrect because if the bonds are purchased at par (face value), the interest income will equal the cash interest received. Answer (d) is incorrect because the interest income for a bond purchased at a premium would equal the cash interest received less the premium amortization for the year.

27. (c)   When a company uses the effective interest method to amortize a discount on bonds payable, interest expense (which is based on the carrying value of the bonds) is lower in earlier years when compared to interest expense under the straight-line method. Therefore, the straight-line method results in higher interest expense, lower net income, and **understated** retained earnings. Since more interest expense is recorded under the straight-line method, amortization of the discount on bonds payable will be greater under the straight-line method when compared to the effective-interest method. Therefore, the carrying amount of the bonds under the straight-line method is **overstated**, and answer (c) is correct.

28. (b)   The gain on sale of the bond investment is the excess of the selling price over the carrying amount. The selling price was $14,000 **above** face value. The bonds were purchased at a discount of $10,000, but after amortization of $2,000 the carrying amount at the time of sale was $8,000 **below** face value. Therefore, the selling price exceeded the carrying amount by $22,000 ($14,000 premium + $8,000 remaining discount).

B.5. Convertible Bonds

29. (b)   Using the book value method, the common stock is recorded at the carrying amount of the converted bonds, less any conversion expenses. Since there are no conversion expenses in this case, the common stock is recorded at the $1,300,000 carrying amount of the converted bonds. The par value of the stock issued is $50,000 (50,000 x $1), so additional paid-in capital (APIC) of $1,250,000 ($1,300,000 – $50,000) is recorded. The entry is

Bonds payable	1,000,000	
Premium on B.P.	300,000	
Common stock		50,000
APIC		1,250,000

Note that when the book value method is used, FMV are not considered, and no gain or loss is recognized.

30. (a)   Under the book value method, the common stock will be recorded at the book value of the bonds at the date of conversion. Thus, no gain or loss is recognized on the conversion. The conversion entry credits common stock and APIC, which increases stockholders' equity. Therefore,

answer (a) is correct. The amount of additional paid-in capital is the difference between the book value of the bonds and the par value of the stock. The effect of the conversion would be to increase the APIC, therefore (b) is incorrect. Answer (c) is incorrect because the conversion has no effect on retained earnings. Answer (d) is incorrect because no gain or loss is recognized.

31. (d)   Per APB 14, convertible debt securities which may be converted into common stock at the option of the holder, and whose issue price is not significantly greater than face value, should be reported as debt upon issuance for the entire proceeds of the bonds. This reasoning is based on the inseparability of the debt and the conversion option, and the mutually exclusive options of the holder (i.e., holding either bonds or stock). Therefore, answer (d) is correct. Answers (a), (b), and (c) are all incorrect since contributed capital would be recorded only upon conversion of the bonds to common stock.

32. (c)   When the **book value method** of accounting for the conversion of bonds into common stock is used, the common stock will be recorded at the book value of the bonds at the date of conversion. Thus, no gain or loss is recognized on the conversion. When the **market value method** of accounting for the conversion is used, the following journal entry would be made on the books of the issuer (assuming market value > book value):

Loss on redemption	(plug)
Bonds payable	(book value)
Common stock	(par)
APIC-common stock	(mkt.-par)

The debit to the loss account would be for the difference between the market value of the stock and the book value of the bonds. The market value method assumes a culmination of the earnings process, and a gain or loss on the conversion may be recognized. In this case, the market value of the stock exceeds the book value of the bonds, and a loss is recognized. Therefore, answer (c) is correct.

B.6. Debt Issued with Detachable Purchase Warrants

33. (c)   APB 14 states that the proceeds of bonds issued with **detachable** warrants are allocated between the bonds and the warrants based upon their relative FMV at the time of issuance. In this case, the portion allocated to the bonds is $900,000, calculated as follows:

$$\frac{\$1,080,000}{\$1,080,000 + \$120,000} = 90\%; 90\% \times \$1,000,000 = \underline{\$900,000}$$

Therefore, the bonds payable are reported at $900,000 (face value $1,000,000 less discount $100,000).

34. (c)   Para 13 of APB 14 states that the proceeds from the issuance of debt with **detachable** stock warrants should be allocated between the debt and equity elements. 1,000 bonds ($1,000,000 ÷ $1,000) were issued with 50 detachable stock warrants each, for a total of 50,000 warrants. Paid-in capital from stock warrants is $200,000 (50,000 x $4). Since the bonds and warrants were issued for $1,090,000 ($1,000,000 x 109%), the portion of the proceeds allocated to the bonds is $890,000 ($1,090,000 –

$200,000) and the discount is $110,000 ($1,000,000 – $890,000). Note that if a FMV is given for the **bonds without warrants**, APB 14 states that the proceeds should be allocated between the bonds and warrants based on their relative FMV at the time of issuance.

35.   **(d)**   Para 13 of APB 14 states that the proceeds from the issuance of debt with **detachable** stock warrants should be allocated between the debt and equity elements. 500 bonds ($500,000 ÷ $1,000) were issued with 30 detachable stock warrants each, for a total of 15,000 warrants. Paid-in capital from stock warrants is $60,000 (15,000 x $4). Note that if a FMV was given for the **bonds without warrants**, APB 14 states that the proceeds should be allocated between the bonds and warrants based on their relative FMV at the time of issuance.

36.   **(a)**   The solutions approach is to set up the original journal entry on the books of the issuer. The entry would be made as follows:

Cash	(proceeds)
Discount on bonds payable	(plug)
Bonds payable	(face)
APIC--Stock warrants	(fair value)

Since the APIC--Stock warrants account is already stated at market value, any remaining difference must be allocated to the **bonds**. Bonds payable would be credited only at their face (par) value. Therefore, Discount on bonds payable is debited for the excess of the fair value of the warrants and the face amount of the bonds over cash proceeds, and answer (a) is correct.

37.   **(c)**   Bonds issued with stock purchase warrants are, in substance, composed of two elements: a debt element, and a stockholders' equity element. Per APB 14, para 15, proceeds from bonds issued with **detachable** stock purchase warrants should be allocated between the bonds and the warrants on the basis of their relative fair market values. Detachable warrants trade separately from the debt; thus, a market value is available. The amount allocated to the warrants should be accounted for as paid-in capital. Bonds issued with **nondetachable** stock purchase warrants must be surrendered in order to exercise the warrants. Since this inseparability prevents the determination of individual market values, no allocation is permitted under APB 14.

B.7. Extinguishment of Debt

38.   **(b)**   A gain or loss on redemption of bonds is the difference between the **cash paid** ($5,000,000 x 98% = $4,900,000) and the **net book value of the bonds**. To compute the net book value, premium or discount and bond issue costs must be considered. Book value is $4,980,000 ($5,000,000 face value, less $50,000 bond issue costs, plus $30,000 premium). Therefore the gain or redemption is $80,000 ($4,980,000 book value less $4,900,000 cash paid).

39.   **(d)**   The gain on early extinguishment of debt is the excess of the book value of the bonds at the time of retirement over the cash paid ($1,000,000 x 101% = $1,010,000). On 1/1/94, the original balance in the premium account was $40,000 ($1,040,000 – $1,000,000). At 7/1/99, the pre-

mium had been amortized for 5 1/2 years, or 11 6-month periods (1/1/94 to 7/1/99). Since the bond term was 10 years, or 20 6-month periods, the total premium amortized was $22,000 ($40,000 x 11/20). Therefore, the unamortized premium was $18,000 ($40,000 – $22,000) and the book value of the bonds was $1,018,000 ($1,000,000 + $18,000). A shortcut approach is to take the 1/1/94 book value ($1,040,000) and subtract the amortization ($22,000) to determine the 7/1/99 book value of $1,018,000. The gain is $8,000 ($1,018,000 book value less $1,010,000 cash paid).

40.   **(a)**   The total bond discount and bond issue costs were $30,000 at the time of issuance [(.02 x $500,000) + $20,000]. By 1/1/99, 12 years have passed since the bonds were issued on 1/1/87. Since the bonds have a 15-year life, 12/15 of the discount and issue costs have been amortized, leaving 3/15 unamortized (3/15 x $30,000 = $6,000). When bonds are retired, the bonds and unamortized premium or discount, and/or issue costs must be removed from the books. In this situation, the difference between the net book value of the bonds ($500,000 – $6,000 = $494,000) and the cash paid ($500,000 x 1.02 = $510,000) is recognized as an extraordinary loss ($510,000 – $494,000 = $16,000).

41.   **(c)**   APB 30, para 20, provides general guidance on the reporting of extraordinary items. This guidance requires events and transactions which are both unusual in nature and infrequent in occurrence to be reported as extraordinary items. Paragraph 10 of SFAS 4, however, amends APB 30 to the extent that classification of gains or losses from extinguishment of debt are always reported as an extraordinary item, without regard to the criteria in para 20 of APB 30. When the carrying value of the old debt exceeds the amount paid to extinguish the debt, the following entry would be recorded:

Debt	(carrying value)
Cash	(amount paid)
Extraordinary gain	(difference)

Therefore, answer (c) is correct.

OTHER OBJECTIVE ANSWER EXPLANATIONS

Problem 1

1.   **(Q; $116,400)**   The "discount" column in the problem is the **unamortized** discount. The unamortized discount at any point in time is equal to the difference between the face value of the bonds ($480,000) and the carrying amount of the bonds ($363,600) at that point in time.

2.   **(K; $14,400)**   The cash interest is the product of the stated interest rate x the face value of the bonds. The cash interest is a constant as long as neither the stated interest rate nor the face value of the bonds changes. Since neither one has changed in the problem, the **given** amount of cash interest on 12/31/99 is the same as the missing amount of cash interest on 6/30/99.

3.   **(T; $360,000)**   The carrying amount is equal to the face value minus the unamortized discount. The amortization of the unamortized discount increases the carrying amount. The carrying amount was increased by the amortization of $3,600 at 6/30/99. To obtain the carrying amount at 1/2/99 one reverses the increase of $3,600 which occurred at 6/30/99. Thus:

Carrying amount 6/30/99	$363,600
Reverse increase in carrying amount at 6/30/99	
due to amortization of discount	(3,600)
Carrying amount 1/2/99	$360,000

4.   **(D; 6.0%)**   The stated interest rate is equal to cash interest $14,400 ÷ face value $480,000. $14,000 ÷ $480,000 = .03. Since the table is set up on a semiannual basis and the answer required is on an annual basis, the .03 is doubled to equal 6.0%

5.   **(F; 10.0%)**   Effective interest is equal to interest expense. Interest expense is the product of the effective interest rate x the carrying value at the beginning of the interest period. In this case, interest expense is $18,000; carrying amount at the beginning of the period is $360,000 (from question 3). Thus: $18,000 ÷ $360,000 = .05 for 6 months; .05 x 2 =.10 on an annual basis.

6.   **(N; $18,180)**   As stated in question 5, interest expense is the product of the effective interest rate (.05) x the carrying value at the beginning of the period $363,600. Thus: $363,600 x .05 = $18,180.

7.   **(I; $3,780)**   Amortization is the difference between interest expense $18,180 and cash interest $14,400. Thus: $18,180 – $14,400 = $3,780.

Problem 2

		1	2	3	4	5
I.	Bond discount	I	N	N	I	N
II.	Bond premium	N	I	D	N	N
III.	Bonds payable	I	I	D	I	N
IV.	Common stock	N	N	I	N	I
V.	Additional paid-in capital	N	N	I	I	I
VI.	Retained earnings	N	N	N	N	D

1.   Since the nominal rate of interest was less than the market rate of interest, the bonds sold at a discount. In other words, the investors paid less than the face value to acquire the bonds. The journal entry to record the transaction is:

Cash	xx	
Discount on bonds payable	xx	
Bonds payable		xx

Therefore, the issuance of the bonds would increase both bonds payable and discount on bonds payable.

2.   Per APB 14, convertible debt securities which may be converted into common stock at the option of the holder, and whose issue price is not significantly greater than face value, should be reported as debt upon issuance for the entire proceeds of the bonds. This reasoning is based on the inseparability of the debt and the conversion option, and the mutually exclusive options of the holder (i.e., holding either bonds or stock). The journal entry to record the transaction is:

Cash	xx	
Premium on bonds payable		xx
Bonds payable		xx

Therefore, the issuance of the convertible bonds would increase both bonds payable and premium on bonds payable.

3.   When the book value method of accounting for the conversion of bonds into common stock is used, the common stock will be recorded at the book value of the bonds at the date of conversion. Thus, no gain or loss is recognized on the conversion. The journal entry to record the transaction is:

Bonds payable	xx	
Premium on bonds payable	xx	

Common stock	xx
Additional paid-in capital	xx

Therefore, the conversion of the bonds would decrease bonds payable and premium on bonds payable while increasing common stock and additional paid-in capital.

4.   APB 14, para 13, states that the proceeds of bonds issued with detachable warrants are allocated between the bonds and the warrants based upon their relative fair market values at the time of issuance. In this case, the bonds, with detachable stock warrants, were issued for an amount equal to the face amount of the bonds. Since part of the proceeds are allocated to the stock warrants, the bonds were issued at a discount. The journal entry to record the transaction is:

Cash	xx	
Discount on bonds payable	xx	
Bonds payable		xx
Additional paid-in capital - Stock warrants		xx

Therefore, the issuance of the bonds, with detachable stock warrants, would increase bonds payable, discount on bonds payable, and additional paid-in capital.

5.   The issuance of a "small" stock dividend (less than 20-25%) requires that the market value of the stock be transferred from retained earnings. The journal entry to record the transaction is:

Retained earnings	xx	
Common stock		xx
Additional paid-in capital		xx

Therefore, a 2% stock dividend would decrease retained earnings while increasing both common stock and additional paid-in capital.

Problem 3

1.   **(B)**   Interest expense on a bond issued at a premium which is calculated using the effective interest method would decrease each period. This is due to the reduction in the bond's carrying value, which is multiplied by the effective rate of interest to determine interest expense for the period.

2.   **(C)**   The receipt of cash by an investor in bonds is determined as follows:

$$\begin{matrix} \text{Cash} \\ \text{received} \end{matrix} = \begin{matrix} \text{Principal} \\ \text{(Face value)} \end{matrix} \times \begin{matrix} \text{Rate} \\ \text{(Stated or} \\ \text{coupon rate)} \end{matrix} \times \begin{matrix} \text{Time} \\ \text{(Semiannual} \\ \text{payments)} \end{matrix}$$

All factors in the determination of interest received are constant throughout the bond issuance. Therefore, the cash received would be a constant amount each period.

3.   **(A)**   The net book value of a bond investment originally issued at a discount would increase each period, until at maturity the book value equalled the face value of the bonds. The method of amortization used (straight-line or effective interest) is irrelevant to the problem.

4.   **(C)**   The rate applied to the carrying value of the bonds, whether applied to bonds issued at a discount or premium, is a constant rate known as the effective rate of interest. Thus, interest expense for the period is derived by multiplying the effective rate times the carrying value of the bonds.

5.   **(B)**   Interest revenue (or interest expense--see explanation (1) above) that is determined each period from bonds purchased at a premium decreases over the term of the bond investment. This is due to the decrease of the net book value each period. The net book value is multiplied by the effective rate of interest to determine interest revenue each period.

6.   **(B)**   The unamortized discount on bond issuance, regardless of whether the straight-line or effective interest method is used, would decrease each period as amortization of the discount occurs.

7.   **(C)**   Amortization of a premium or discount using the straight-line method results in a constant amount of amortization each period.

8.   **(A)**   Interest revenue from bonds issued at a discount using the effective interest method would increase each period due to the increase in the net book value of the bond investment. The net book value each period is multiplied by the effective rate to determine the interest revenue for the period.

9.   **(C)**   It is common for bond issue costs to be incurred in connection with the issuance of bonds. Although SFAC 6 states that bond issue costs can be treated as either an expense or a reduction of related bond liability, APB Opinion 21 currently allows the treatment of bond issue costs as deferred charges (assets) to be amortized on a straight-line basis over the life of the bond. This straight-line basis results in a constant amount of amortization each period.

10.   **(B)**   Regardless of the method of amortization, the unamortized premium on bonds payable would always decrease each period as the amortization of the premium occurs.

ANSWER OUTLINE

Problem 1   Issuance of Bonds

a. **1.**   9% bonds issued at discount
Stated rate (9%) < market rate (10%)
Bonds must sell at discount to yield 10%
(Issue price = PV) < face amount

2.   Interest expense higher in second year than in first year
10% effective rate applied to increasing bond carrying value each year
Results in higher interest expense each successive year

b. **1.**   Gain (loss) on early extinguishment is difference between net carrying value of bonds and acquisition price
Net carrying value > acquisition price -- gain results
Net carrying value < acquisition price -- loss results
Early extinguishment of 9% bonds results in loss
Bonds issued at discount
Carrying value at date of extinguishment must be less than face value
Acquisition price exceeds net carrying value

2.   Report loss on early extinguishment in 1999 IS
Extraordinary item, net of tax

c.   Proceeds from issuance increases cash
Allocate proceeds between bonds and warrants on basis of relative FMV
Portion allocated to bonds accounted for as LT debt
Portion allocated to warrants accounted for as APIC

UNOFFICIAL ANSWER

Problem 1   Issuance of Bonds

a. **1.**   The 9% bonds were issued at a discount (less than face amount). Although the bonds provide for payment of interest of 9% of face amount, this rate was less than the prevailing or market rate for bonds of similar quality at the time the bonds were issued. Thus, the issue price of the bonds, which is the present value of the principal and interest payments discounted at 10%, is less than the face amount.

2.   The amount of interest expense would be higher in the second year of the life of the bond issue than in the first year of the life of the bond issue. According to the effective interest method of amortization, the 10% effective interest rate is applied to the bond carrying amount. In a discount situation, the bond carrying amount increases each year, and this results in a greater interest in each successive year.

b. **1.**   Gain or loss on early extinguishment of debt should be determined by comparing the carrying amount of the bonds at the date of extinguishment with the acquisition price. If the carrying amount exceeds the acquisition price, a gain results. If the carrying amount is less than the acquisition price, a loss results.

In this case, a loss results. The term bonds were issued at a discount. Therefore, the carrying amount of the

bonds at the date of extinguishment must be less than the face amount, which is less than the acquisition price.

2.   Drew should report the loss from early extinguishment of debt in its 1999 income statement as an extraordinary item, net of income taxes.

c.   The proceeds from the issuance of the 7% nonconvertible bonds with detachable stock purchase warrants should be recorded as an increase in cash. These proceeds should be allocated between the bonds and the warrants on the basis of their relative market values. The portion of the proceeds allocable to the bonds should be accounted for as long-term debt, while the portion allocable to the warrants should be accounted for as paid-in capital.

ANSWER OUTLINE

Problem 2   Effective Interest Method; Effect of Using SL versus Effective Interest Method; Extinguishment of Debt in IS and SCF

a.   Effective interest method
Periodic interest expense = constant percentage of BV of bonds
In 1996, premium decrease less than if straight-line method used

b.   For 1996,

Interest expense	--	understated
Net income	--	overstated
BV of bonds	--	understated

c.   Report as XO loss after income from continuing operations
Loss = excess of FMV of cash and property transferred over BV of bonds
Early extinguishment of debt is XO item

d.   Operating activities
Add gross extraordinary loss to NI
Financing activities
Show extinguishment as cash outflow

Significant noncash transactions
Show noncash elements of transaction at bottom of SCF/notes to FS

UNOFFICIAL ANSWER

Problem 2   Effective Interest Method; Effect of Using SL versus Effective Interest Method; Extinguishment of Debt in IS and SCF

a.   The purpose of the effective interest method is to provide periodic interest expense based on a constant rate over the life of the bonds. The impact of applying the effective interest method on Corval's bond premium is to decrease the premium by a lesser amount in 1996 compared to using the straight-line method of amortization.

b.   Under the straight-line interest method, the premium is amortized at a constant periodic amount, and in 1996 the premium amortization would have been greater than amortization under the effective interest method. Consequently, for 1996, interest expense would have been understated, net income would have been overstated, and the carrying amount of the bonds would have been understated.

c.   The November 30, 1999, transaction is reported as an extraordinary loss after income from continuing operations. This loss equals the excess of the fair value of the cash and property transferred over the bonds' carrying amount on November 30, 1999. This presentation is appropriate because this is an early extinguishment of debt.

d.   The gross amount of the extraordinary loss is added to net income under cash flows from operating activities. The cash payment is reported as a cash outflow from financing activities.

Corval should disclose details of the noncash elements of the transaction either on the same page as the statement of cash flows or in the notes to the financial statements.

ANSWER OUTLINE

Problem 3   Convertible Debt and EPS

a.   **1.**   Issue price = Expected future cash flows discounted at market rate + Value of conversion option

   2.   Accounting for issuance

   Cash   (issue price)
       Bonds payable   (face amount)
       Premium   (plug)

   Convertible debt accounted for as debt
   Conversion option not recognized

   3.   Accounting for conversion

   Bonds payable   (30% of balance)
   Premium   (30% of balance)
       Common stock   ($25/share issued)
       Additional PIC   (plug)

UNOFFICIAL ANSWER

Problem 3   Convertible Debt and EPS

a.   **1.**   The bond issue price would be determined by the expected future cash flows of principal and interest, discounted at the market rate of interest, plus the value of the conversion option at the date of issuance.

2.   Columbine should account for the issuance of the convertible bonds by increasing cash for the issue price, increasing bonds payable by the face amount, and increasing premium on bonds payable for the balance. The convertible debt is accounted for solely as debt. The conversion option is not recognized primarily because it is inseparable from the debt, and secondarily because of the practical difficulty of assigning it a value.

3.   Columbine should account for the conversion of the bonds into common stock by decreasing both bonds payable and unamortized bond premium by 30%, increasing common stock by $25 for each share issued, and increasing additional paid-in capital by the difference between the three previous amounts.

C. Debt Restructure

SFAS 15 (see outline) prescribes accounting for debtors in situations where creditors are compelled to grant relief (i.e., restructure debt) to debtors. Two types of restructure are described. The first is a settlement of the debt at less than the carrying amount and the second is a continuation of the debt with a modification of terms.

SFAS 114 (see outline), as amended by SFAS 118, addresses the accounting by creditors for impairment of certain loans. Impaired loans include all loans that are restructured in a troubled debt restructuring involving a modification of terms.

1. Settlement of Debt

a. **Debtors**--If the debt is settled by the exchange of assets, an extraordinary gain is recognized for the difference between the carrying amount of the debt and the consideration given to extinguish the debt. If a noncash asset is given, a separate, ordinary gain or loss is recorded to revalue the noncash asset to FMV as the basis of the noncash asset given. Thus, a two-step process is used: (1) revalue the noncash asset to FMV and (2) determine the restructuring gain. If stock is issued to settle the liability, record the stock at FMV.

b. **Creditors**

    (1) Assets received in full settlement are recorded at FMV

        (a) Excess of receivable over asset FMV is an ordinary loss

        (b) Subsequently account for the assets as if purchased for cash

        ***Example 1: Settlement of Debt**--Debtor company transfers land in full settlement of its loan payable.*

Loan payable (5 years remaining)	$90,000
Accrued interest payable on loan	10,000
Land:	
Book value	70,000
Fair value	80,000

	Debtor				*Creditor*		
1.	Land	10,000		1.	Land	80,000	
	Gain on trans-				Loss on settlement	20,000	
	fer of assets		10,000		Loan receivable		90,000
2.	Loan payable	90,000			Interest receivable		10,000*
	Interest payable	10,000					
	Land		80,000				
	Extraordinary						
	gain on settle-						
	ment of debt		20,000				

*If the creditor was a bank or other finance company, this amount would be included as part of Loan receivable.

2. Impairment

If the creditor determines that, based on current information and events, it is probable that they will be unable to collect all amounts due on an outstanding note receivable, then the note is considered to be impaired. The criteria for determining uncollectibility of a note should be based on the creditor's normal review procedures. When a note receivable is considered to be impaired, a loss should be recorded at the time the impairment is discovered. The loss will be based upon the difference between the current carrying value of the note and the present value of the expected future cash flows from the impaired note, discounted at the loan's contractual rate.

EXAMPLE:

On January 1, 1997 Spot Corporation issued a $100,000, 3-year noninterest-bearing note to yield 10%, to Grover Corporation. On December 31, 1997, Spot Co. management determines that it is probable that Grover Co. will be unable to repay the entire note. It appears as though only $75,000 will be repaid. Using the effective interest method the impairment is calculated as follows:

Date	10% interest	Carrying value	
1/1/97	--	$ 75,132	(present value of 100,000 at 10% for 3 periods, 100,000 x .75132)
12/31/97	7,513	82,645	(75,132 + 7,513)
12/31/98	8,265	90,910	(82,645 + 8,265)
12/31/99	9,090	100,000	(90,910 + 9,090)

Carrying value at 12/31/97	$82,645
Present value of future receipts	
(75,000, 10%, 2 periods = 75,000 x .82645)	61,984
Impairment at 12/31/97	$20,661

The loss due to the impairment of the Grover Co. note will be recorded on the creditor's books as follows:

Bad debt expense	20,661	
Allowance for doubtful accounts		20,661

The debtor, Grover Co., should not record anything as it still has a legal obligation to repay the entire $100,000. The future interest revenue recorded by Spot Co. will be based upon the new carrying value of $61,984. If there is a significant change in the expected future cash flows, then the impairment should be recalculated and the allowance adjusted accordingly.

3. **Modification of Terms**

   a. **Debtors**

   If the debt is continued with a modification of terms, it is necessary to compare the total future cash flows of the restructured debt (both principal and stated interest) with the prerestructured carrying value. If the total amount of future cash flows is greater than the carrying value, no adjustment is made to the carrying value of the debt; however, a new effective interest rate must be computed. This rate makes the present value of the total future cash flows equal to the present carrying value of debt (principal and accrued interest). If the total future cash flows of the restructured debt are less than the present carrying value, the current debt should be reduced to the amount of the future cash flows and an extraordinary gain should be recognized. No interest expense would be recognized in subsequent periods because the loan was written down below its carrying value. All payments including those designated as interest would be applied to the principal amount.

   If the restructuring consists of part settlement and part modification of payments, first account for the part settlement per the above, and then account for the modification of payments per the above.

   b. **Creditors**

   Under SFAS 114 a creditor measures impairment based on the present value of expected future cash flows discounted at the loan's effective interest rate. The effective interest rate for a loan restructured in a troubled debt restructuring is based on the original contractual rate, not the rate specified in the restructuring agreement. As a practical expedient, a creditor may measure impairment based on a loan's observable market price, or the fair value of the collateral if the loan is collateral dependent. A loan is collateral dependent if the repayment of the loan is expected to be provided solely by the underlying collateral.

   If the measure of the impaired loan is less than the recorded investment in the loan (including accrued interest, net deferred loan fees or costs, and unamortized premium or discount), a creditor shall recognize an impairment by creating a valuation allowance with a corresponding charge to bad debt expense or by adjusting an existing valuation allowance for the impaired loan with a corresponding charge or credit to bad debt expense.

The present value of an impaired loan's expected future cash flows will change from one reporting period to the next because of the passage of time and also may change because of revised estimates in the amount or timing of those cash flows. No guidance is provided on how the creditor should recognize the change in the present value.

The following example of the treatment of modification of terms for creditors demonstrates the accounting for the **debtor** under SFAS 15 and for the **creditor** under SFAS 114.

Example 2: Modification of Terms--Gain/Loss Recognized--Assume the interest rate on above loan is 5% and the following modification of terms is made:

1. Interest rate is reduced to 4%.
2. The accrued interest is forgiven.
3. The principal at date of restructure is reduced to $80,000.

Debtor

Future cash flows (after restructuring):

Principal	$80,000
Interest (5 years x $80,000 x 4%; 3,200 per year)	+ 16,000
Total cash to be received	$96,000
Amount prior to restructure	
($90,000 principal + $10,000 accrued interest)	– 100,000
Extraordinary gain to be recognized	$ 4,000

Analysis of Debtor's Loan Payable Account

Gain	4,000			
	3,200*		90,000	Loan payable before modification of terms
4% modified interest payments in years 1-5	3,200			
	3,200			
	3,200		10,000	Additional amount payable from accrued interest
	3,200			
				Bal. before principal pay 80,000

Creditor

Present value of future cash flows (after restructuring)
discounted at the original effective interest rate of 5%
for the 5 years remaining:

Principal ($80,000 x .78353)**	$ 62,682
Interest ($80,000 x 4% x 4.32948)***	13,854
Present value of future cash flows	$ 76,536
Recorded investment in loan by creditor	$100,000
Present value of future cash flows after restructuring	76,536
Impairment loan loss to be recognized by creditor	$ 23,464

 ** PV of 1 for 5 periods at 5%.
*** PV of ordinary annuity for 5 periods at 5%.

Debtor (SFAS 15)			*Creditor (SFAS 114)*		
Beginning of Year 1			*Beginning of Year 1*		
Interest payable	10,000		Bad debt expense	23,464	
Loan payable	4,000		Loan receivable		10,000
Loan payable		10,000	Accrued interest re-		
Extraordinary gain			ceivable		10,000
on restructure of			Valuation allowance		
debt		4,000	for impaired loans		3,464

---

* *Note that the $3,200 is recorded as a reduction of principal, not as interest expense.*

End of Year 1			*End of Year 1*		
Loan payable	3,200		Cash	3,200	
Cash		3,200	Valuation allowance for		
			impaired loans	627	
			Interest revenue/bad		
			debts expense		3,827*

* [($80,000 – $3,464)] x 5% = $3,827

End of Year 2			*End of Year 2*		
Loan payable	3,200		Cash	3,200	
Cash		3,200	Valuation allowance for		
			impaired loans	658	
			Interest revenue/bad		
			debts expense		3,858*

* [$80,000 – ($3,464 – $627)] x 5% = $3,858

End of Year 3			*End of Year 3*		
Loan payable	3,200		Cash	3,200	
Cash		3,200	Valuation allowance for		
			impaired loans	691	
			Interest revenue/bad		
			debts expense		3,891*

* [$80,000 – ($3,464 – $627 – $658)] x 5% = $3,891

End of Year 4			*End of Year 4*		
Loan payable	3,200		Cash	3,200	
Cash		3,200	Valuation allowance for		
			impaired loans	726	
			Interest revenue/bad		
			debts expense		3,926*

* [$80,000 – ($3,464 – $627 – $658 – $691)] x 5% = $3,926

End of Year 5			*End of Year 5*		
Loan payable	3,200		Cash	3,200	
Cash		3,200	Valuation allowance for		
			impaired loans	762	
			Interest revenue/bad		
			debts expense		3,962*

* [$80,000 – ($3,464 – $627 – $658 – $691 – $726)] x 5% = $3,962

Loan payable	80,000		Cash	80,000	
Cash		80,000	Loan receivable		80,000

AUTHOR'S NOTE: This example does not include any future changes in the amount and timing of future cash flows, due to the complexity of the accounting.

Example 3: Modification of Terms--No Gain Recognized By Debtor--Assume the $90,000 principal is reduced to $85,000. The interest rate of 5% is reduced to 4%.

Future cash flows (after restructuring):	
Principal	$ 85,000
Interest (5 years x $85,000 x 4%)	17,000
Total cash to be received	$102,000
Amount prior to restructure:	
($90,000 principal + $10,000 accrued interest)	– 100,000
Interest expense/revenue to be recognized over 5 years	$ 2,000

In Example 3, a new effective interest rate must be computed so that the PV of future payments = $100,000. A trial and error approach would be used. For the exam, you need to be prepared to describe this process and the related entries, but you will not have to make such a computation.

End of Year 1-5

	Debtor		
Loan payable		xxxx	
Interest expense		xxx	
Cash			3,400

End of Year 5

Loan payable	85,000	
Cash		85,000

NOTE: x's equal different amounts each year based on effective interest rate computed.

By Creditor--The creditor would account for the modification in the same way as in the previous example that shows the SFAS 114 approach. That is, the original effective rate would be used to measure the loss.

To summarize the two basic situations

1. **Settlement of Debt**: The debtor transfers assets or grants an equity interest to the creditor in full satisfaction of the claim. Both debtor and creditor account for the fair values of assets transferred and equity interest granted. A gain or loss is recognized on the asset transferred. The debtor recognizes a gain and the creditor recognizes a loss for the difference between the recorded value of the debt and the fair values accounted for.

2. **Restructuring of the Debt**: Under SFAS 15, the terms of the debt are modified in order to reduce or defer cash payments that the debtor is obligated to make to the creditor, but the debt itself is continued. The debtor accounts for the modification of terms as a reduction in interest expense from the date of restructuring until maturity. Gains and losses will generally not be recognized unless the total future cash payments specified by the new terms are less than the recorded amount of the debt. Then the debtor would recognize a gain for the difference. The debtor's gain is considered extraordinary. Under SFAS 114, the creditor accounts for a restructuring using the original effective rate to measure losses.

Refer to the outlines of SFAS 15 and SFAS 114 for the disclosure requirements.

MULTIPLE-CHOICE QUESTIONS (1-6)

Items 1 and 2 are based on the following:

The following information pertains to the transfer of real estate pursuant to a troubled debt restructuring by Knob Co. to Mene Corp. in full liquidation of Knob's liability to Mene:

Carrying amount of liability liquidated	$150,000
Carrying amount of real estate transferred	100,000
Fair value of real estate transferred	90,000

1. What amount should Knob report as a pretax extraordinary gain (loss) on restructuring of payables?

    a.   ($10,000)
    b. $0
    c. $50,000
    d. $60,000

2. What amount should Knob report as ordinary gain (loss) on transfer of real estate?

    a.   ($10,000)
    b. $0
    c. $50,000
    d. $60,000

3. On October 15, 1999, Kam Corp. informed Finn Co. that Kam would be unable to repay its $100,000 note due on October 31 to Finn. Finn agreed to accept title to Kam's computer equipment in full settlement of the note. The equipment's carrying value was $80,000 and its fair value was $75,000. Kam's tax rate is 30%. What amounts should Kam report as ordinary gain (loss) and extraordinary gain for the year ended September 30, 2000?

	Ordinary gain (loss)	*Extraordinary gain*
a.	$(5,000)	$17,500
b.	$0	$20,000
c.	$0	$14,000
d.	$20,000	$0

4. Colt, Inc. is indebted to Kent under an $800,000, 10%, 4-year note dated December 31, 1996. Annual interest of $80,000 was paid on December 31, 1997 and 1998. During 1999 Colt experienced financial difficulties and is likely to default unless concessions are made. On December 31, 1999, Kent agreed to restructure the debt as follows:

    •   Interest of $80,000 for 1999, due December 31, 1999, was made payable December 31, 2000.
    •   Interest for 2000 was waived.
    •   The principal amount was reduced to $700,000.

Assuming an income tax rate of 40%, how much should Colt report as extraordinary gain in its income statement for the year ended December 31, 1999?

    a. $0
    b. $ 60,000
    c. $100,000
    d. $108,000

5. Grey Company holds an overdue note receivable of $800,000 plus recorded accrued interest of $64,000. The effective interest rate is 8%. As the result of a court im-

posed settlement on December 31, 1999, Grey agreed to the following restructuring arrangement:

    •   Reduced the principal obligation to $600,000.
    •   Forgave the $64,000 accrued interest.
    •   Extended the maturity date to December 31, 2001.
    •   Annual interest of $40,000 is to be paid to Grey on December 31, 2000 and 2001.

The present value of the interest and principal payments to be received by Grey Company discounted for 2 years at 8% is $585,734. On December 31, 1999, Grey would recognize a valuation allowance for impaired loans of

    a. $ 14,266
    b. $184,000
    c. $278,266
    d. $0

6. On December 31, 1997, Marsh Company entered into a debt restructuring agreement with Saxe Company, which was experiencing financial difficulties. Marsh restructured a $100,000 note receivable as follows:

    •   Reduced the principal obligation to $70,000.
    •   Forgave $12,000 of accrued interest.
    •   Extended the maturity date from December 31, 1997 to December 31, 1999.
    •   Reduced the interest rate from 12% to 8%. Interest was payable annually on December 31, 1998 and 1999.

Present value factors:

Single sum, 2 years @ 8%	.85734
Single sum, 2 years @ 12%	.79719
Ordinary annuity, 2 years @ 8%	1.78326
Ordinary annuity, 2 years @ 12%	1.69005

In accordance with the agreement, Saxe made payments to Marsh on December 31, 1998 and 1999. How much interest income should Marsh report for the year ended December 31, 1999?

    a. $0
    b. $ 5,600
    c. $ 8,100
    d. $11,200

| 1. d __ __ | 3. a __ __ | 5. a __ __ | 6. c __ __ | 1st: __/6 = __% |
| 2. a __ __ | 4. b __ __ | | | 2nd: __/6 = __% |

MULTIPLE-CHOICE ANSWER EXPLANATIONS

C. Debt Restructure

1.   (d)   In this restructure, the debt is retired by the transfer of real estate to the creditor. Per SFAS 15, an ordinary operating gain or loss is recognized on the transfer of real estate, and an extraordinary gain or loss is recognized on the restructuring. The ordinary loss is the excess of the real estate's carrying amount over its FMV ($100,000 – $90,000 = $10,000). The extraordinary gain is the excess of the carrying amount of the liability over the FMV of the real estate transferred, net of the related tax effect. The pretax extraordinary gain is $60,000 ($150,000 – $90,000). The journal entry is:

Liability	150,000	
Loss on transfer	10,000	
Real estate		100,000
X/O gain		60,000

2.   (a)   In this restructure, the debt is retired by the transfer of real estate to the creditor. Per SFAS 15, an ordinary operating gain or loss is recognized on the transfer of real estate, and an extraordinary gain or loss is recognized on the restructuring. The ordinary loss is the excess of the real estate's carrying amount over its FMV ($100,000 – $90,000 = $10,000). The extraordinary gain is the excess of the carrying amount of the liability over the FMV of the real estate transferred, net of the related tax effect. The pretax extraordinary gain is $60,000 ($150,000 – $90,000). The journal entry is:

Liability	150,000	
Loss on transfer	10,000	
Real estate		100,000
X/O gain		60,000

3.   (a)   In this restructure, the debt is retired by the transfer of equipment to the creditor. Per SFAS 15, an ordinary operating gain or loss is recognized on the transfer of the equipment, and an extraordinary gain or loss is recognized on the retirement of the debt. The ordinary loss is the excess of the equipment's carrying amount over its fair value ($80,000 – $75,000 = $5,000). The extraordinary gain is the excess of the carrying amount of the debt over the fair value of the equipment transferred, net of the related tax effect [$100,000 – $75,000 = $25,000; $25,000 – (30% x $25,000) = $17,500].

4.   (b)   The requirement is to determine the amount of extraordinary gain to be recognized from a troubled debt restructure. According to SFAS 15, if the debt is continued with a modification of terms, an extraordinary gain is recognized by the debtor if the future cash payments on the debt are less than the carrying value of the debt. For troubled debt restructures, carrying value is defined as the principal amount ($800,000) plus accrued interest ($80,000), or $880,000. The future payments total $780,000 ($700,000 reduced principal and $80,000 interest). The $100,000 difference ($880,000 – $780,000) is recognized as an extraor-

dinary gain, net of the related tax effect [$100,000 – (40% x $100,000) = $60,000]. The following entry would be made:

Notes payable	800,000	
Interest payable	80,000	
Notes payable (restructured amt)		780,000
Extraordinary gain		100,000

5.   (a)   Under SFAS 114, if the present value of future cash flows is less than the carrying amount of the loan (Principal + Accrued interest) then bad debt expense should be recorded for the total impairment, the accrued interest account should be written off, and the principal balance in the loan receivable account should be reduced to reflect any amounts forgiven. Any remaining balance should be recorded in an allowance account, as follows:

Present value of interest and principal payments to be received by Grey Company (as stated in the problem)	585,734
Recorded investment by Grey Company (800,000 principal + 64,000 interest)	864,000
Less present value of future cash flows	(585,734)
	278,266

Bad debt expense	278,266	
Loan receivable		200,000
Accrued interest receivable		64,000
Valuation allowance for impaired loans		14,266

Thus, under SFAS 114, the valuation allowance Grey must recognize is $14,266. Therefore, the correct answer is (a).

6.   (c)   The requirement is to determine the amount of interest revenue to be recorded by Marsh, after a modification of terms type of troubled debt restructure on December 31, 1997.

Under SFAS 114, when a modification of terms results in the present value of future cash flows being less than the carrying amount, then the interest revenue is calculated by using the effective interest method. In this problem the expected future cash flows is determined by discounting the principal and interest at the original effective rate of 12%.

70,000	x	.79719	=	55,803
5,600	x	1.69005	=	9,464
Present value of future cash flows				65,267

The interest revenue to be recognized can then be determined using the effective interest method.

PV at 12/31/97		$65,267
Interest income at 12/31/98		
($65,267 x 12%)	$7,832	
Interest receivable at 12/31/98		
(70,000 x 8%)	5,600	
Increase in carrying value of loan		2,232
PV at 12/31/98		67,499
Interest revenue at 12/31/99		
(67,499 x 12%)	$8,100	

Thus, answer (c) $8,100, is the correct answer under SFAS 114.

D. Pensions

Accounting for pensions involves the use of special terminology. Mastery of this terminology is essential both to an understanding of problem requirements and to the ability to respond correctly to theory questions. Review the definitions at the beginning of the outline of SFAS 87 before proceeding with this section of the module. When you are finished with this section, review the remaining portion of the outline of SFAS 87. Additionally, you should look over the contents of SFAS 88 and SFAS 132; SFAS 88 has been tested lightly. SFAS 132 deals solely with employer disclosures about pensions and other postretirement benefits. It amends Statements 87, 88, and 106. SFAS 106, which deals with postemployment benefits other than pensions, is modeled very closely after SFAS 87. Therefore, your knowledge of pensions from SFAS 87 and SFAS 132 should enable you to answer questions on SFAS 106.

In this section the key points covered are as follows:

1. The differences between a defined contribution pension plan and a defined benefit pension plan and the resulting accounting and reporting differences between these two types of plans.
2. The bookkeeping entries made to record an employer's pension expense and the funding of pension cost.
3. The difference between the accumulated benefits actuarial approach and the benefits-years-of-service approach.
4. The calculation and reporting of the additional minimum liability for employers who sponsor defined benefit pension plans.
5. The five elements which, if they all exist, an employer sponsoring a defined benefit pension plan must evaluate for inclusion in its pension expense each year. These factors are: (1) service cost, (2) interest cost, (3) actual return on plan assets, (4) amortization of unrecognized prior service cost, and (5) gain or loss.
6. The required disclosures in the financial statements of employers who sponsor pension plans.

1. Employer Sponsor's Versus Plan's Accounting and Reporting

In order to understand the accounting and reporting requirements for pension plans, you must keep in mind that there are two accounting entities involved: (1) the employer sponsor of the plan, and (2) the pension plan which is usually under the control of a pension trustee.

The employer sponsor reports Pension Expense in its income statement. In its balance sheet it usually reports a pension liability labeled Accrued/Prepaid Pension Cost (the sum of two accounts, Accrued/Prepaid Pension Cost and Additional Pension Liability, if required) and an Intangible Asset--Deferred Pension Cost (if required). As discussed later, a third balance sheet account, Net Loss Not Recognized As Pension Expense, is possible. In order to fund the plan, the employer sponsor contributes money to the plan.

A separate accounting entity, the pension plan, maintains the following accounts: Projected Benefit Obligation, Accumulated Benefit Obligation (for reporting purposes only), Vested Benefits (for reporting purposes only), and Plan Assets. The pension plan pays benefits to the retired employees.

The diagram below shows the relationship of the entities involved in a pension plan, the accounts usually used by each, and the flow of cash.

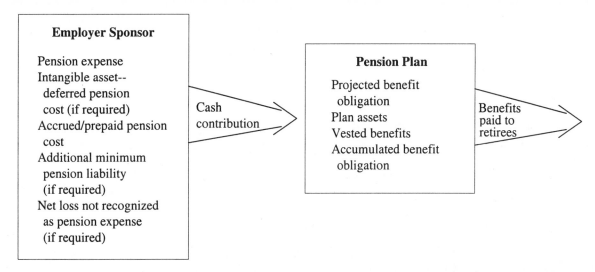

In addition to the accounts shown in the diagram above, the employer sponsor must also maintain, on a memo basis, accounts for Unrecognized Past Service Cost and Unrecognized Gains and Losses.

You should note as you read the sections below that the projected benefit obligations of the pension plan, the interest on these obligations, the pension plan assets available to meet these obligations, and returns (income) on these plan assets are all economic variables which impact the employer sponsor's yearly calculations of pension expense and its year-end pension liability (or prepaid pension cost).

In the following presentation, key concepts are **boldfaced** to call attention to those terms and phrases that must be clearly understood.

2.   **An Overview of Employer's Accounting for Pension Plans**

Under a **defined contribution plan** the employer agrees to make a defined contribution to a pension plan as determined by the provisions of the plan. Consequently, plan participants will receive at retirement whatever benefits (i.e., payments) the contributions can provide. Accounting for a defined contribution plan is relatively straightforward. Each year the employer records an expense and a related liability for the agreed upon contribution. Payments are charged against the liability with an offsetting reduction in cash. Additional disclosure requirements include a description of the plan including: employee groups covered, the basis for determining contributions, and the nature and effects of events affecting comparability.

Under a **defined benefit plan** the employer agrees to provide a benefit at retirement that is defined or fixed by a formula. Because the benefits are defined, the employer accepts the risk associated with changes in the variables that determine the amounts needed to meet the obligation to plan participants. These amounts require the use of estimates that may become very complex. However, these estimates are made by actuaries hired by the management of the employer sponsor. They are not made by the sponsoring company's accountants. The remainder of our pension coverage is devoted to a discussion of the issues that arise under this type of plan.

The **accrual accounting objective** for pension costs recognized the compensation cost of an employee's pension benefits including prior service costs over that employee's service period. Under accrual accounting, pension expense should not be determined on the basis of the employer's cash payout (funding) practices. The **funding of the pension obligation** refers to the amount that the employer contributes to an independent trustee for the pension plan (plans where the fund is under the control of the employer are considered unfunded). Many factors including tax considerations, working capital management, and contractual agreements influence funding decisions. Thus, the amount selected for funding should not govern the determination of the amount to be reported as pension expense under accrual accounting; these events should be distinguished. Although both events can be recorded with one entry, we use two entries to better illustrate this distinction.

Pension expense	xxxx	
Accrued/prepaid pension cost		xxxx

This adjusting entry is to record the accrued expense. The optional use of the Accrued/Prepaid Pension Cost account simplifies the accounting. If the account has a net debit balance, it is a prepaid asset account. If the account has a net credit balnce, it is a liability.

Accrued/prepaid pension cost	xxxx	
cash		xxxx

This entry is to record the funding of the pension obligation at the time cash is transferred to the plan's trustee.

The determination of the amounts to be used in the above entries requires the professional expertise of actuaries who assess the benefits to be provided under the pension formula and the characteristics of the employees covered under the plan (e.g., average age). With these factors as given, the actuaries must estimate the values of the variables that will influence the actual amounts to be paid at retirement by making **actuarial assumptions** about factors such as longevity, early retirements, turnover rate, and the rates of return to be earned on invested funds.

Of the many methods employed by actuaries to estimate pension related amounts, the methods of particular importance in accounting for pensions are the accumulated benefits approach and the benefits-years-of-service approach. The **accumulated benefits approach** (also referred to as the unit credit approach) provides estimates of period expenses and end of period pension obligations based on service to date, actuarial assumptions, and **current** salary levels. The **benefits-years-of-service approach** (also referred to as the projected unit credit approach) provides these same estimates based on service to date, actuarial assumptions, and **projected** salary levels. The actual pension payouts to retirees will be based upon projected salary levels rather than current salary levels. The actuarial present value of the obligation determined under the accumulated benefits method is referred to as the **accumulated benefit obligation**. The actuarial present value of the obligation determined under the benefits-years-of-service method is referred to as the **projected benefit obligation**. If the defined benefit formula is not dependent on the amount of a future salary (say a retiree receives a fixed amount for each month worked), there would be no difference between the two approaches. If the defined benefit formula is pay-related and salaries are assumed to increase over time, the projected benefit obligation will be a greater amount than the accumulated benefit obligation.

Many of the provisions of SFAS 87 employ the use of amortization procedures that will significantly reduce, over time, the amount of the unrecognized pension liability associated with defined benefit plans. While the FASB conceptually supported immediate recognition of the projected benefit obligation as a balance sheet liability, this position was not adopted because it represented too significant a departure from past practices. The FASB did, however, require a minimum pension liability. This minimum liability requirement is independent of other reporting requirements for defined benefit plans. The minimum liability must be recognized to the extent that the accumulated benefit obligation at year end exceeds the fair value of the plan assets at year end. However, it should be noted that an asset may not be recorded by the employer when the fair value of plan assets exceeds the amount of the accumulated benefit obligation.

The accounting for the **minimum liability** is complex because the ML is a combination of two accounts: the Additional Pension Liability and the Accrued/Prepaid Pension Cost. Assume that the excess of the ABO over the fair value of the plan assets (i.e., ML) is $5,000. That amount is the **final** liability balance that must appear in the balance sheet. If a credit balance (assume $1,000) already exists in the Accrued/Prepaid Pension Cost Account, only an additional $4,000 credit is required to make the combination of the two credit accounts equal to $5,000. The adjusting journal entry is

Intangible asset--deferred pension cost	$4,000	
Additional pension liability		$4,000

Assume that instead of a credit of $1,000 in the Accrued/Prepaid account there is a debit of $1,000 in the account. Since the **final** liability must be a $5,000 credit, and that liability is a combination of a debit of $1,000 in the Accrued/Prepaid account, and a credit amount in the Additional Liability account which must equal a credit balance of $5,000, the adjusting entry will be

Intangible asset--deferred pension cost	$6,000	
Additional pension liability		$6,000

The $6,000 Additional Pension Liability credit will be combined with the $1,000 Accrued/Prepaid Pension Cost debit to result in a final liability credit in the balance sheet which will be labeled Accrued Pension Liability $5,000. The account title Minimum Liability is not used in the balance sheet.

The Intangible Asset--Deferred Pension Cost Account that results from the adjusting entry for the minimum liability cannot exceed the unrecognized prior service cost. If any excess does exist, the debits in the adjusting entry will be: (1) a debit to the intangible asset equal to the unrecognized prior service cost and (2) a second debit for the excess to an "other comprehensive income" account that is closed to "accumulated other comprehensive income." In the example immediately above where the ML is $5,000 assume that the unrecognized prior service cost is $2,000. The adjusting entry would be

Intangible asset--deferred pension cost	$2,000	(equal to unrecognized service cost)
Minimum pension liability adjustment		
(Other comprehensive income)	4,000	
Additional pension liability		$6,000

The minimum pension liability adjustment is closed along with other comprehensive income accounts to "accumulated other comprehensive income account" which is a component of stockholders' equity. It is important to note that the debit balance accounts in the above entry are not amortized.

Instead, at each statement date the amount of the Additional Liability account and the offsetting debit account (or accounts) are adjusted upward or downward to reflect the relationship between the excess of the accumulated benefit obligation over the fair value of plan assets at that date.

This completes the overview of the accounting required by employers for pension plans. In the next section, the determination of Pension Cost is thoroughly reviewed. The general term "**Pension Cost**" is preferred over pension expense because pension cost is included in overhead in the determination of product costs and therefore may be part of inventory in the balance sheet. When permissible the term "Pension Expense" is used instead because it is simpler and clearer. The disclosure of the elements included in pension expense is one of the most significant disclosures required by SFAS 132 and should be carefully studied. A comprehensive illustration is presented in Section 5 below. This illustration integrates the concepts and calculations that have been introduced in the preceding discussions. Section 4 below is concerned with the additional disclosure requirements that apply.

3. **Determination of Pension Expense**

Pension Expense is a net amount calculated by adding together five factors. These factors are: (1) service cost, (2) interest on the projected benefit obligation, (3) actual return on plan assets, (4) amortization of unrecognized prior service cost, and (5) the effect of gains and losses. Each of these components is discussed below.

a. **Service Cost--increases pension expense**

Service cost is defined as the actuarial present value of benefits attributed by the pension benefit formula to employee service during the current period. SFAS 87 requires that future salary levels be taken into consideration in this calculation (i.e., the benefits-years-of-service approach).

b. **Interest on Projected Benefit Obligation--increases expense**

The **interest on the projected benefit obligation** is defined as the increase in the amount of the projected benefit obligation due to the passage of time. Since the pension plan's obligation at the beginning of the year is stated in terms of present value, a provision for interest is required. By the end of the period, the plan's obligation will increase by the amount of interest that would accrue based on the discount (settlement) rate selected. The discount rate selected should be determined by reference to market conditions using such rates as the return on high quality investments or the implicit rate of return in retirement annuities as a basis for comparison. Also, the rate selected must be **explicit** and an unreasonable rate cannot be justified by an argument that the unreasonable rate is **implicitly** valid because of other offsetting actuarial assumptions. The selected discount rate is referred to as the **settlement rate** because it is the rate at which the plan's obligation could be settled.

EXAMPLE: Compute the "interest" component of net pension expense for 1999, if the projected benefit obligation was $4,800,000 on January 1, 1999, and the settlement rate is 9%. Answer: Net pension expense for 1999 is increased by $432,000 (9% x $4,800,000) to provide for interest on the projected benefit obligation.

c. **Actual Return on Plan Assets--decreases or possibly increases pension expense**

The **actual return on plan assets** is defined as the difference in the fair value of plan assets at the beginning and the end of the period adjusted for contributions made to the plan and benefit payments made by the plan during the period. The formula for determining the actual return is as follows:

Actual return = (End. bal. of plan assets at fair value – Beg. bal. of plan assets at fair value) + Benefits – Contributions

The **fair value or market value** of plan assets is defined as the price expected in a sales transaction between a willing buyer and seller. **Plan assets** typically include marketable securities and other investments such as real estate that are held in trust for the plan participants. Assets that are under the control of the employer are not considered to be plan assets. In calculating the return on plan assets, considerable leeway has been allowed in measuring the fair value of plan assets.

EXAMPLE: Compute the "actual return on plan assets" component of net pension expense, if the fair value of plan assets was $3,100,000 at the beginning of the year and $3,820,000 at year end. The employer sponsor contributed $450,000 to the plan and the plan paid benefits of $200,000 during the year. Answer: Net pension expense is decreased by $470,000 [($3,820,000 – $3,100,000) – $450,000 + $200,000] due to the actual return earned on the fair value of plan assets.

Although the **actual** return on plan assets is measured and disclosed as one of the components of net pension expense, net pension expense will include only an amount equal to the **expected** return on plan assets. This methodology is followed because the difference between the actual return on plan assets and the expected return on plan assets is a cancelling adjustment that is included in the gain or loss calculation to be discussed below.

d. **Prior Service Cost--increases or possibly decreases pension expense**

Prior service costs are retroactive adjustments that are granted to recognize services rendered in previous periods. These costs are caused by either an amendment to an existing plan or the initiation of a new plan where a **retroactive allowance** is made for past services rendered. If, as a result of an amendment to an existing plan, the benefits are increased, then the amount of the plan's projected benefit obligation will increase. The amount of the prior service costs is measured by the increase in the projected benefit obligation caused by the amendment or the initiation of the plan.

While the prior service costs are related to the past, it is assumed that the initiation or amendment of the plan was made with the intent of benefiting the employer's future operations rather than its past operations. Because of this assumption, prior service costs should be amortized over the present and future periods affected. Two methods approved for use in determining the assignment of prior service costs are (1) the expected future years of service method, and (2) the straight-line basis over the average remaining service period of active employees method.

Under the **expected future years of service** method, the total number of employee service years is calculated by grouping employees according to the time remaining to their retirement, based on actuarial assumptions, and multiplying the number in each group by the number of periods remaining to retirement. For example, 8 employees expected to work 10 years until retirement would contribute 80 expected future years of service to the total. To calculate the amortization of prior service costs for a given year, the number of employee service years applicable to that period is used as the numerator of the fraction and the denominator is the total employee service years based on all the identified groups. This method produces a declining pattern similar to the amortization applicable to premiums or discounts on serial bonds and the sum-of-the-years' digits method of depreciation.

The **straight-line basis over the average remaining service period** of active employees is a simpler method. The projected average remaining service period for the affected participants is estimated by the use of a weighted-average method. For example, 10 employees with 10 years remaining to retirement, and 15 employees with 20 years remaining to retirement would have a weighted-average service life of 16 years computed as follows: (10 x 10 + 15 x 20)/25. In this example, the prior service costs would be amortized and included in pension expense over 16 years. Note by including these prior service costs in pension expense, these costs will also be included in the employer's Accrued/Prepaid Pension Cost account over the 16 years. Thus, the employer will gradually record on its balance sheet the unrecognized liability associated with these prior service costs.

EXAMPLE: Compute the "amortization of prior service cost" component of net pension expense for the first 3 years after an amendment, based on the following facts. The prior service cost associated with the amendment is determined by the actuaries to be $650,000 (the difference between the projected benefit

*obligation before and after the amendment). The employer has 200 employees at the time of the amend-
ment. It is expected that workers will retire or terminate at the rate of 4% per year, and the employer will
use the "expected future years of service" method of amortization. Answer: Since the workers will leave at
the rate of 8 per year, the denominator of the amortization fraction is computed by summing 200 + 192 +
184 + ... + 8. This series can be written as 8(25 + 24 + 23 + ... + 1) or 8n(n+1) /2 = 8(25) (26) /2 = 2,600.
The calculations for the first 3 years and the unamortized balance at year-end are presented in the table
below.*

Year	Amortization fraction	Annual amortization	Unamortized balances
0			$650,000
1	200/2,600	$50,000	600,000
2	192/2,600	48,000	552,000
3	184/2,600	46,000	506,000

e. Gain or Loss--increases or decreases pension expense

Net gain or loss is defined as the change in the amount of the projected benefit obligation as
well as the change in the value of plan assets (realized and unrealized), resulting from experience
being different from that assumed, or from a change in an actuarial assumption. For this calculation, plan assets are valued at the market-related value. The **market-related value of plan assets**
can be either fair market value or any calculated value that recognizes changes in fair value in a
rational and systematic manner over not more than 5 years. For example, the market-related value
for a plan's common stocks might be calculated based on a 5-year moving average of the year-end
market prices for these shares. The net effect of permitting several methods of calculating
market-related value is to introduce adjustments that will minimize and "smooth" volatility arising from the use of estimates and dampen the effects of volatile swings in market value.

The gain or loss component included in net pension expense consists of two items: (1) the
current period difference between the actual and expected return [(Expected rate of return on plan
assets) x (Market-related value of plan assets at the beginning of the period)] on plan assets, and
(2) amortization of the unrecognized net gain or loss from **previous** periods. The current period
difference is reported as a component of the current period net pension expense and the unrecognized net gain or loss is subject to amortization. In the unusual case when a gain or loss arises
from an event such as the discontinuation of a business segment, the gain or loss should be recognized immediately and associated with the event that was the cause (e.g., discontinued segment)
rather than the pension plan.

When the amortization of the cumulative unrecognized net gain or loss from previous periods
is required, the procedure is comparable to the amortization of prior service cost and, in general, it
requires the use of a systematic method applied on a consistent basis that is dependent on the average remaining service period for active employees. Unlike past service cost, however, the
amount to be amortized is not necessarily the calculated amount of the cumulative unrecognized
net gain or loss. Instead, the minimum amount subject to amortization is determined by the use of
a method sometimes referred to as the "corridor" approach. The minimum amount of the cumulative unrecognized gain or loss required to be amortized is determined by computing, at the beginning of the fiscal year, the excess of the cumulative unrecognized gain or loss over 10% of the
greater of the projected benefit obligation or the market-related asset value. If the cumulative unrecognized gain or loss is equal to or less than the 10% calculated value, no amount need be amortized.

*EXAMPLE: Compute the "gain or loss" component of net pension expense and the other elements of pen-
sion expense based on the following facts:*

*At the beginning of the year the cumulative unrecognized net loss was $500,000, the fair value and
market-related value of plan assets was $3,100,000, and the projected benefit obligation was $4,800,000.
The expected return on assets for the year was 9% and the settlement rate was 11%. The fair value of plan
assets at the end of the year was $3,400,000. There were no contributions to the plan during the year. The
plan made no benefit payments during the year. Service costs for the year were $400,000. At the beginning*

of the year the average remaining service period of active employees was 10 years. There are no other factors to be considered in computing pension expense for the year.

Answer: The elements of net pension expense are calculated as follows:

Service cost	$400,000	
Interest (.11 x $4,800,000)	528,000	
Actual return on plan assets	(300,000)	(1)
Amortization of unrecognized net loss	2,000	(2)
Asset gain deferred	21,000	(3)
Net pension expense	$651,000	

NOTE: The above components of pension expense are required to be disclosed in the employer sponsor's financial statements. This would be done in the footnotes to those statements.

(1) $3,400,000 less $3,100,000 less contributions to the plan of $0 plus benefit payments of the plan of $0.

(2) Amortization of unrecognized net loss is calculated as follows:

"Corridor" 10% x $4,800,000	$480,000
Cumulative unrecognized net loss at the beginning of the year	500,000
Excess to be amortized	$ 20,000

Amortization of unrecognized loss is: $20,000/10 years = $2,000.

(3) The asset gain deferred of $21,000 is calculated as follows: Actual return on plan assets of $300,000 less expected return on plan assets of $279,000. The expected return on plan assets is determined by multiplying the expected return on plan assets of 9% times the market-related value of plan assets at the beginning of the year of $3,100,000. Note that in the above computation of pension expense actual return on assets of $300,000 is included as required by SFAS 87. However, the expected return on plan assets of $279,000 ($300,000 – $21,000) is the amount that is actually included in pension expense for the year.

4. Disclosures

Under SFAS 87 and SFAS 132, disclosure in the statement of financial position follows the practice of **offsetting** the financial effects of plan assets and obligations where the plan's assets can be used directly to satisfy its obligations. This practice and the practice of **netting** the components of pension expense in the income statement, and the complexities inherent in pension accounting, put added emphasis on the use of notes to the financial statements to provide disclosure. The required disclosures are as follows:

a. A reconciliation schedule of the benefit obligation showing the components separately
b. A reconciliation schedule of the fair value of plan assets with the components shown separately
c. The funded status of the plan(s) and the amounts recognized and not recognized in the statement of financial position (balance sheet)
d. The net periodic benefit cost recognized with the components shown separately
e. The amount of change in the additional minimum pension liability recognized within other comprehensive income
f. The rates and assumptions used for the assumed discount rate, rate of compensation increase, and expected long-term rate of return on plan assets
g. The assumed health care cost trend rate, a description of the pattern of change, and what effect a 1-percentage-point increase or decrease would have on the aggregated service and interest cost components
h. An explanation of any significant changes in the plan assets or the benefit obligation

If an employer sponsors more than one pension plan, the plans may be shown aggregated or disaggregated.

5. **Comprehensive Illustration**

Schaefer Company has sponsored a noncontributory (i.e., employees make no contributions) defined benefit plan for its 100 employees for several years. Within this group of 100 employees, it is
expected that workers will retire or terminate at the rate of 5 per year for the next 20 years starting
January 1, 1999. Prior to 1998, cumulative pension expense recognized in compliance with SFAS 87
exceeded cumulative contributions by $150,000 resulting in a $150,000 balance sheet liability. As of
January 1, 1999, the company has agreed to an amendment to its plan that includes a retroactive provision to recognize prior service. To illustrate how the provisions of SFAS 87 should be applied, assumptions about the facts relevant to the pension plan for the years 1998 and 1999 are presented in
the tables that follow:

	1/1/1998	1/1/1999	12/31/1999
Plan assets (at fair value = market-related value)	$400,000	$455,000	$760,500
Accumulated benefit obligation (ABO; 60% vested)	460,000	640,000*	710,000*
Projected benefit obligation	550,000	821,500*	1,033,650*
Unrecognized cumulative gain (loss)--due to unexpected decrease in asset value	-0-	(106,000)	?
Prior service cost amendment	-0-	105,000	?
Accrued pension cost (liability)	(150,000)	?	?

Includes effects of amendment

	12/31/1998	12/31/1999
Service cost	$117,000	$130,000
Employer's funding contribution	125,000	260,000
Plan assets (at fair value = market-related value)	455,000	760,500
Accumulated benefit obligation (60% vested)	620,000	710,000
Benefits paid by the plan	-0-	-0-
Unrecognized cumulative gain (loss)--due to unexpected decrease in asset value	(106,000)	(103,729)
Rate of return on assets	9%	10%
Settlement rate	9%	10%

Schedule of Changes in Plan Assets

	1998	1999
Plan assets at 12/31	$455,000	$760,500
Plan assets at 1/1	400,000	455,000
Increase in plan assets	55,000	305,500
Add:		
Benefits paid	-0-	-0-
Less:		
Funding contributions for the year	(125,000)	(260,000)
Actual return or (loss) on plan assets	(70,000)	45,500
Expected return on plan assets		
1998: 9% x $400,000	36,000	
1999: 10% x $455,000		45,500
Unrecognized gain (loss)	$(106,000)	$ -0-

Required:

A. Prepare a supporting schedule to determine the amounts to be reported as pension expense for 1998 and 1999. The company has decided to use the "expected future years of service" method to amortize the effects of the amendment made in 1999.

B. Prepare the journal entries required for 1998 and 1999 with respect to the pension plan including any entry necessary to comply with the **minimum liability** requirement.

C. Prepare pension worksheets for 1998 and 1999. Note these worksheets summarize Schaefer's general journal entries and changes in its pension-related accounts. These worksheets also summarize the changes in the pension plan's accounts, unrecognized prior service cost, and unrecognized gain or loss. Study these worksheets as they are an excellent tool for pulling together the elements of this comprehensive illustration.[*]

D. Indicate the pension-related amounts that should appear in the company's financial statements prepared at the end of 1998 and 1999.

E. Prepare disclosures of the funded status of the plan to the liability shown in the company's balance sheet at 1/1/1998, 12/31/1998, and 12/31/1999.

Solution
Part A

REQUIRED FOOTNOTE DISCLOSURE
Pension Expense

	12/31/98	*12/31/99*
Components of net periodic benefit cost		
Service cost	$117,000	$130,000
Interest cost	49,500	82,150
Expected return on plan assets	(36,000)	(45,500)
Amortization of prior service cost	-0-	10,000
Loss amortization	-0-	2,271
Recognized actuarial loss	-0-	-0-
Net periodic benefit cost	$130,500	$178,921

(NOTE: This is one of the required disclosures by SFAS 87 and 132 as discussed above.)

Calculations

1. **Service cost** is given.

2. **Interest:** 9% x $550,000 (1998), and 10% x $821,500 (1999).

3. **Actual return:** ($70,000) for 1998 and $45,500 (same as expected) for 1999. Note that in 1998, the $70,000 actual loss on plan assets less the $106,000 unrecognized loss equals the expected return ($36,000).

4. **Prior service:** Compute the denominator of the fraction for amortization by calculating the sum of the estimated remaining service years by adding $100 + 95 + 90 + ... + 10 + 5$. This series can be written as $5(20 + 19 + 18 + ... + 2 + 1)$ or $5n(n+1)/2 = 5(20)(21)/2 = 1,050$. For 1999 the amount is $(100/1,050)$ x $105,000 = $10,000.

---

[*] *From Paul B. W. Miller, "The New Pension Accounting (Part 2)," **Journal of Accountancy** (February 1987), pp. 86-94.*

5. **Loss:** The $106,000 unrecognized loss that arose in 1998 is not amortized until 1999, because no unrecognized net gain or loss existed at the **beginning** of the year. The amortization of the unrecognized net gain or loss should be included as a component of pension expense only if the unrecognized net gain or loss existed as of the **beginning** of the year and the unrecognized gain or loss exceeded the corridor. At 1/1/1999 10% of the greater of the projected benefit obligation ($821,500) or the market-related asset value ($455,000) is equal to $82,150. The **minimum loss** to be amortized is $106,000 − $82,150 or $23,850. The average employee service remaining as of 1/1/1999 assuming a constant work force of 100 and an attrition rate of 5 workers per year is (100 + 95 + 90 + ... + 10 + 5)/100 or 1,050/100 = 10.5 years. The amount of the loss recognized in 1999 is $23,850/10.5 = $2,271. Since actual and expected returns are equal in 1999, no further adjustment is required.

Part B

Journal Entries

	1998	1999
Pension expense	130,500	178,921
Accrued/prepaid pension cost	130,500	178,921
(to record pension expense)		
Accrued/prepaid pension cost	125,000	260,000
Cash	125,000	260,000
(to record funding)		

The amount of the **minimum liability** is the excess, if any, at the balance sheet date of the accumulated benefit obligation over the fair value of plan assets. An adjustment is required to the extent that the liability has not already been reflected. (Note that this adjustment does not impact the determination of pension expense.)

	1998	1999
Intangible asset--deferred pension cost	9,500	
Additional minimum liability	9,500	
[to adjust as of 12/31/1998 for the minimum liability		
by increasing the liability from $155,500 (credit balance		
in the "Accrued/Prepaid Pension Cost" account below)		
to $165,000 ($620,000 ABO - $455,000 FMV of plan assets)]		
Additional minimum liability		9,500
Intangible asset--deferred pension cost		9,500
[to adjust as of 12/31/1999 the balance in additional liability		
account; no balance is required because the FMV of		
plan assets ($760,500) exceeds the ABO ($710,000)]		

Pension Expense			
1998	130,500		
---	---	---	---
1999	178,921		

Accrued/Prepaid Pension Cost			
1998 Funding	125,000	1/1/1998 balance	150,000
		1998 accrual	130,500
1999 Funding	260,000	12/31/1998 balance	155,500
		1999 accrual	178,921
		12/31/1999 balance	74,421

Intangible Asset--Def. Pension Cost			
1998	9,500	1999	9,500

Additional Minimum Liability			
1999	9,500	1998	9,500

Part C

SCHAEFER COMPANY
Pension Work Sheet--1998

	Debit (credit)					Debit (credit)			
	General journal entries					Memo entries			
Items	*Pension expense*	*Cash*	*Prepaid/ accrued cost*	*Add'l liability*	*Intangible asset*	*Projected benefit obligation*	*Plan assets*	*Unrecog- nized prior ser- vice cost*	*Unrecog- nized net gain or loss*
Bal. 1/1/1998			(150,000)			(550,000)	400,000		
Service cost	117,000					(117,000)			
Interest cost	49,500					(49,500)			
Actual loss	70,000						(70,000)		
Deferred gain	(106,000)								106,000
Contribution		(125,000)					125,000		
Min. lia. adj.				(9,500)	9,500				
Journal entry for 1998	130,500	(125,000)	(5,500)						
Bal. 12/31/1998			(155,500)	(9,500)	9,500	(716,500)	455,000		106,000

SCHAEFER COMPANY
Pension Work Sheet--1999

	Debit (credit)					Debit (credit)			
	General journal entries					Memo entries			
Items	*Pension expense*	*Cash*	*Prepaid/ accrued cost*	*Add'l liability*	*Intangible asset*	*Projected benefit obligation*	*Plan assets*	*Unrecog- nized prior ser- vice cost*	*Unrecog- nized net gain or loss*
Bal. 1/1/1999			(155,500)	(9,500)	9,500	(716,500)	455,000		106,000
Prior service cost amendment						(105,000)		105,000	
Service cost	130,000					(130,000)			
Interest cost	82,150					(82,150)			
Actual return	(45,500)						45,500		
Prior service cost amort.	10,000							(10,000)	
Gain amort.	2,271								(2,271)
Contribution		(260,000)					260,000		
Min. lia. adj.				9,500	(9,500)				
Journal entry for 1999	178,921	(260,000)	81,079						
Bal. 12/31/1999			(74,421)	-0-	-0-	(1,033,650)	760,500	95,000	103,729

Part D

Financial Statements

	12/31/1998	12/31/1999
Assets		
Intangible asset--deferred Pension cost	$ 9,500	$ --
Liabilities		
Accrued pension cost**	165,000*	74,421
Income statement		
Pension expense	130,500	178,921

*Accrued liability ($155,500) plus adjustment for minimum liability ($9,500)

Although not specifically addressed by SFAS 87, we believe these amounts **should be classified as noncurrent, unless evidence indicates otherwise, in accordance with ARB 43, Chapter 3A (current assets and liabilities).

Part E

Required Footnote Disclosure

	12/31/1998	*12/31/1999*
Change in benefit obligation		
Benefit obligation at beginning of year	$550,000	$ 716,500*
Service cost	117,000	130,000
Interest cost	49,500	82,150
Amendment (prior service cost)	-0-	105,000
Actuarial loss (gain)	-0-	-0-
Benefits paid	-0-	-0-
Benefit obligation at end of year	$716,500	$1,033,650

*Before effect of plan amendment.

Change in plan assets		
Fair value of plan assets at beginning of year	$ 400,000	$ 455,000
Actual return (loss) on plan assets	(70,000)	45,500
Employer contribution	125,000	260,000
Benefits paid	-0-	-0-
Fair value of plan assets at end of year	$ 455,000	$ 760,500
Funded status	$(261,500)	$ (273,150)
Unrecognized loss on assets	106,000	103,729
Unrecognized prior service cost	-0-	95,000
Net amount recognized	$(155,500)	$ (74,421)

Amounts recognized in the statement of		
financial position (balance sheet) consist of		
Accrued benefit liability	$(165,000)*	$ (74,421)
Intangible asset	9,500	-0-
Accumulated other comprehensive income	-0-	-0-
Net amount recognized	$(155,500)	$ (74,421)

*Accrued pension cost plus adjustment for minimum liability ($9,500).

6. Postretirement Benefits Other Than Pensions (OPEB)

SFAS 106 (refer to outline) establishes the standard for employers' accounting for other (than pension) postretirement benefits (OPEB). This standard requires a single method for measuring and recognizing an employer's accumulated postretirement benefit obligation (APBO). It applies to all forms of postretirement benefits, although the most material benefit is usually postretirement health care. It uses the fundamental framework established by SFAS 87 and SFAS 88. To the extent that the promised benefits are similar, the accounting provisions are similar. Only when there is a compelling reason is the accounting different. SFAS 132 states the required disclosures for employers' with post-retirement benefits and pensions.

There are, however, some fundamental differences between defined benefit pension plans and postretirement benefits other than pensions. The following list presents these differences.

Differences Between Pensions and Postretirement Health Care Benefits*

Item	Pensions	Health care benefits
Funding	Generally funded.	Generally *NOT* funded.
Benefit	Well-defined and level dollar amount.	Generally uncapped and great variability.
Beneficiary	Retiree (maybe some benefit to surviving spouse).	Retiree, spouse, and other dependents.
Benefit payable	Monthly.	As needed and used.
Predictability	Variables are reasonably predictable.	Utilization difficult to predict. Level of cost varies geographically and fluctuates over time.

*D. Gerald Searfoss and Naomi Erickson, "The Big Unfunded Liability: Postretirement Health Care Benefits," **Journal of Accountancy**, November 1988, pp. 28-39.*

SFAS 106 requires accrual accounting and adopts the three primary characteristics of pension accounting: (1) delayed recognition (changes are not recognized immediately, but are subsequently recognized in a gradual and systematic way), (2) reporting net cost (aggregates of various items are reported as one net amount), and (3) offsetting assets and liabilities (assets and liabilities are sometimes shown net).

SFAS 106 distinguishes between the **substantive** plan and **written** plan. Although generally the same, the substantive plan (the one understood as evidenced by past practice or by communication of intended changes) is the basis for the accounting if it differs from the written plan.

OPEBs are considered to be deferred compensation earned in an exchange transaction during the time periods that the employee provides services. The expected cost generally should be attributed in equal amounts (unless the plan attributes a disproportionate share of benefits to early years) over the periods from the employee's hiring date (unless credit for the service is only granted from a later date) to the date that the employee attains full eligibility for all benefits expected to be received. This accrual should be followed even if the employee provides service beyond the date of full eligibility.

The transition obligation, under SFAS 106, is the unrecognized and unfunded APBO (accumulated postretirement benefit obligation) for all of the participants in the plan. This obligation can either (1) be recognized immediately as the effect of an accounting change, subject to certain limitations, or (2) be recognized on a delayed basis over future service periods with disclosure of the unrecognized amount. The delayed recognition has to result in, at least, as rapid a recognition as would have been recognized on a pay-as-you-go basis.

> EXAMPLE: A sample illustration of the basic accounting for OPEB as established by SFAS 106 follows: Firstime Accrual Co. plans to adopt accrual accounting for OPEB as of January 1, 1999. All employees were hired at age 30 and are fully eligible for benefits at age 60. There are no plan assets. This first calculation determines the unrecognized transition obligation (UTO).

Firstime Accrual
December 31, 1998

Employee	Age	Years of service	Total years when fully eligible	Expected retirement age	Remaining service to retirement	EPBO	APBO
A	35	5	30	60	25	$ 14,000	$ 2,333
B	40	10	30	60	20	22,000	7,333
C	45	15	30	60	15	30,000	15,000
D	50	20	30	60	10	38,000	25,333
E	55	25	30	65	10	46,000	38,333
F	60	30	30	65	5	54,000	54,000
G	65	RET	--		--	46,000	46,000
H	70	RET	--		--	38,000	38,000
					85	$288,000	$226,332

Calculations

1. EPBO (expected postretirement benefit obligation) is usually determined by an actuary, although it can be calculated if complete data is available.
2. APBO is calculated using the EPBO. Specifically, it is EPBO x (Years of service/total years when fully eligible)
3. The unrecognized transition obligation (UTO) is the APBO at 12/31/98 since there are no plan assets to be deducted. The $226,332 can be amortized over the average remaining service to retirement of 14.17 (85/6) years or an optional period of 20 years, if longer. Firstime Accrual selected the 20-year period of amortization.
4. Note that Employee F has attained full eligibility for benefits and yet plans to continue working.
5. Note that the above 1998 table is used in the calculation of the 1999 components of OPEB cost that follows.

After the establishment of UTO, the next step is to determine the benefit cost for the year ended December 31, 1999. This calculation follows the framework established by SFAS 87. The discount rate is assumed to be 10%.

Firstime Accrual
OPEB COST
December 31, 1999

1.	Service Cost	$ 5,000
2.	Interest Cost	22,633
3.	Actual Return on Plan Assets	--
4.	Gain or Loss	--
5.	Amortization of Unrecognized Prior Service Cost	--
6.	Amortization of UTO	11,317
	Total OPEB Cost	$38,950

Calculations

1. Service cost calculation uses only employees not yet fully eligible for benefits.

Employee	1/1/99 EPBO	Total years when fully eligible	Service cost
A	$14,000	30	$ 467
B	22,000	30	733
C	30,000	30	1,000
D	38,000	30	1,267
E	46,000	30	1,533
Total service cost			$5,000

2. Interest cost is the 1/1/99 APBO of $226,332 x 10% = $22,633.
3. There are no plan assets so there is no return.

4. *There is no gain (loss) since there are no changes yet.*
5. *There is no unrecognized prior service cost initially.*
6. *Amortization of UTO is the 1/1/99 UTO of $226,332/20 year optional election = $11,317.*

Assume that Firstime Accrual makes a year-end cash benefit payment of $20,000. Firstime Accrual's year-end entry to record other postretirement benefit cost for 1999 would be as follows:

Postretirement benefit cost	*38,950*	
Cash		*20,000*
Accrued postretirement benefit cost		*18,950*

Disclosures

Required disclosures for a postretirement benefit plan are stated in SFAS 106 and SFAS 132. The requirements are the same as the requirements for pensions, which have already been covered in this module.

7. **Postemployment Benefits**

(See the outline of SFAS 112)

MULTIPLE-CHOICE QUESTIONS (1-30)

1. The following information pertains to Lee Corp.'s defined benefit pension plan for 1999:

Service cost	$160,000
Actual and expected gain on plan assets	35,000
Unexpected loss on plan assets related to a 1999 disposal of a subsidiary	40,000
Amortization of unrecognized prior service cost	5,000
Annual interest on pension obligation	50,000

What amount should Lee report as pension expense in its 1999 income statement?
   a. $250,000
  -b. $220,000
   c. $210,000
   d. $180,000

2. Jordon Corporation obtains the following information from its actuary. All amounts given are **as of** 1/1/99 (beginning of the year).

	1/1/99
Projected benefit obligation	$1,530,000
Market-related asset value	1,650,000
Unrecognized net loss	235,000
Average remaining service period	5.5 years

What amount of unrecognized net loss should be recognized as part of pension expense in 1999?
   a. $70,000
   b. $42,727
   c. $14,909
   d. $12,727

3. Bulls Corporation amends its pension plan on 1/1/99. The following information is available:

	1/1/99 before amendment	1/1/99 after amendment
Accumulated benefit obligation	$ 950,000	$1,425,000
Projected benefit obligation	1,300,000	1,900,000

The total amount of unrecognized prior service cost to be amortized over future periods as a result of this amendment is
   a. $950,000
   b. $600,000
   c. $475,000
   d. $125,000

4. On January 2, 1999, Loch Co. established a noncontributory defined benefit plan covering all employees and contributed $1,000,000 to the plan. At December 31, 1999, Loch determined that the 1999 service and interest costs on the plan were $620,000. The expected and the actual rate of return on plan assets for 1999 was 10%. There are no other components of Loch's pension expense. What amount

should Loch report in its December 31, 1999 balance sheet as prepaid pension cost?
   a. $280,000
   b. $380,000
   c. $480,000
   d. $620,000

5. Webb Co. implemented a defined benefit pension plan for its employees on January 1, 1997. During 1997 and 1998, Webb's contributions fully funded the plan. The following data are provided for 2000 and 1999:

	2000 Estimated	1999 Actual
Projected benefit obligation, December 31	$750,000	$700,000
Accumulated benefit obligation, December 31	520,000	500,000
Plan assets at fair value, December 31	675,000	600,000
Projected benefit obligation in excess of plan assets	75,000	100,000
Pension expense	90,000	75,000
Employer's contribution	?	50,000

What amount should Webb contribute in order to report an accrued pension liability of $15,000 in its December 31, 2000 balance sheet?
   a. $ 50,000
   b. $ 60,000
   c. $ 75,000
   d. $100,000

6. Visor Co. maintains a defined benefit pension plan for its employees. The service cost component of Visor's net periodic pension cost is measured using the
   a. Unfunded accumulated benefit obligation.
   b. Unfunded vested benefit obligation.
   c. Projected benefit obligation.
   d. Expected return on plan assets.

7. Which of the following components should be included in the calculation of net pension cost recognized for a period by an employer sponsoring a defined benefit pension plan?

	Actual return on plan assets, if any	Amortization of unrecognized prior service cost, if any
a.	No	Yes
b.	No	No
c.	Yes	No
d.	Yes	Yes

8. Interest cost included in the net pension cost recognized by an employer sponsoring a defined benefit pension plan represents the
   a. Amortization of the discount on unrecognized prior service costs.
   b. Increase in the fair value of plan assets due to the passage of time.
   c. Increase in the projected benefit obligation due to the passage of time.
   d. Shortage between the expected and actual returns on plan assets.

9. On July 31, 1999, Tern Co. amended its single employee defined benefit pension plan by granting increased benefits for services provided prior to 1999. This prior service cost will be reflected in the financial statement(s) for
   a.   Years before 1999 only.
   b.   Year 1999 only.
   c.   Year 1999, and years before and following 1999.
   d.   Year 1999, and following years only.

10. Effective January 1, 1999, Flood Co. established a defined benefit pension plan with no retroactive benefits. The first of the required equal annual contributions was paid on December 31, 1999. A 10% discount rate was used to calculate service cost and a 10% rate of return was assumed for plan assets. All information on covered employees for 1999 and 2000 is the same. How should the service cost for 2000 compare with 1999, and should the 1999 balance sheet report an accrued or a prepaid pension cost?

	Service cost for 2000 compared to 1999	Pension cost reported on the 1999 balance sheet
a.	Equal to	Accrued
b.	Equal to	Prepaid
c.	Greater than	Accrued
d.	Greater than	Prepaid

11. A company that maintains a defined benefit pension plan for its employees reports an unfunded accrued pension cost. This cost represents the amount that the
   a.   Cumulative net pension cost accrued exceeds contributions to the plan.
   b.   Cumulative net pension cost accrued exceeds the vested benefit obligation.
   c.   Vested benefit obligation exceeds plan assets.
   d.   Vested benefit obligation exceeds contributions to the plan.

12. The following information pertains to Seda Co.'s pension plan:

Actuarial estimate of projected benefit obligation at 1/1/99	$72,000
Assumed discount rate	10%
Service costs for 1999	18,000
Pension benefits paid during 1999	15,000

If **no** change in actuarial estimates occurred during 1999, Seda's projected benefit obligation at December 31, 1999 was
   a. $64,200
   b. $75,000
   c. $79,200
   d. $82,200

13. Which of the following terms includes assumptions concerning projected changes in future compensation when the pension benefit formula is based on future compensation levels (e.g., pay-related and final pay plans)?

	Service cost component	Projected benefit obligation	Accumulated benefit obligation
a.	Yes	Yes	Yes
b.	Yes	Yes	No
c.	No	Yes	No
d.	Yes	No	Yes

14. For a defined benefit pension plan, the discount rate used to calculate the projected benefit obligation is determined by the

	Expected return on plan assets	Actual return on plan assets
a.	Yes	Yes
b.	No	No
c.	Yes	No
d.	No	Yes

15. At December 31, 1999, the following information was provided by the Kerr Corp. pension plan administrator:

Fair value of plan assets	$3,450,000
Accumulated benefit obligation	4,300,000
Projected benefit obligation	5,700,000

What is the amount of the pension liability that should be shown on Kerr's December 31, 1999 balance sheet?
   a. $5,700,000
   b. $2,250,000
   c. $1,400,000
   d. $ 850,000

16. Nome Co. sponsors a defined benefit plan covering all employees. Benefits are based on years of service and compensation levels at the time of retirement. Nome determined that, as of September 30, 1999, its accumulated benefit obligation was $380,000, and its plan assets had a $290,000 fair value. Nome's September 30, 1999 trial balance showed prepaid pension cost of $20,000. In its September 30, 1999 balance sheet, what amount should Nome report as additional pension liability?
   a. $110,000
   b. $360,000
   c. $380,000
   d. $400,000

17. Payne, Inc. implemented a defined-benefit pension plan for its employees on January 2, 1999. The following data are provided for 1999, as of December 31, 1999:

Accumulated benefit obligation	$103,000
Plan assets at fair value	78,000
Net periodic pension cost	90,000
Employer's contribution	70,000

What amount should Payne record as additional minimum pension liability at December 31, 1999?
   a. $0
   b. $ 5,000
   c. $20,000
   d. $45,000

Items 18 and 19 are based on the following:

The following data pertains to Hall Co.'s defined-benefit pension plan at December 31, 1999:

Unfunded accumulated benefit obligation	$25,000
Unrecognized prior service cost	12,000
Net periodic pension cost	8,000

Hall made no contributions to the pension plan during 1999.

18. At December 31, 1999, what amount should Hall record as additional pension liability?

a. $ 5,000
b. $13,000
c. $17,000
d. $25,000

19. In its December 31, 1999, statement of stockholders' equity, what amount should Hall report as excess of additional pension liability over unrecognized prior service cost?

a. $ 5,000
b. $13,000
c. $17,000
d. $25,000

20. An employer sponsoring a defined benefit pension plan is subject to the minimum pension liability recognition requirement. An additional liability must be recorded equal to the unfunded

a. Accumulated benefit obligation plus the previously recognized accrued pension cost.
b. Accumulated benefit obligation less the previously recognized accrued pension cost.
c. Projected benefit obligation plus the previously recognized accrued pension cost.
d. Projected benefit obligation less the previously recognized accrued pension cost.

21. In which of the following pension instances would the account adjustment for minimum pension liability be reported on the balance sheet for a particular year?

a. When the additional pension liability required to be recognized exceeds the unrecognized prior service cost.
b. When the unrecognized prior service cost exceeds the additional pension liability required to be recognized.
c. Only when an employer sponsors two or more separate defined benefit pension plans.
d. Only when there is an amendment to a defined benefit pension plan.

22. On September 1, 1999, Howe Corp. offered special termination benefits to employees who had reached the early retirement age specified in the company's pension plan. The termination benefits consisted of lump-sum and periodic future payments. Additionally, the employees accepting the company offer receive the usual early retirement pension benefits. The offer expired on November 30, 1999. Actual or reasonably estimated amounts at December 31, 1999 relating to the employees accepting the offer are as follows:

- Lump-sum payments totaling $475,000 were made on January 1, 2000.
- Periodic payments of $60,000 annually for 3 years will begin January 1, 2001. The present value at December 31, 1999 of these payments was $155,000.
- Reduction of accrued pension costs at December 31, 1999 for the terminating employees was $45,000.

In its December 31, 1999 balance sheet, Howe should report a total liability for special termination benefits of

a. $475,000
b. $585,000
c. $630,000
d. $655,000

23. A company with a defined benefit pension plan must disclose in the notes to its financial statements a reconciliation of

a. The vested and nonvested benefit obligation of its pension plan with the accumulated benefit obligation.
b. The accrued or prepaid pension cost reported in its balance sheet with the pension expense reported in its income statement.
c. The accumulated benefit obligation of its pension plan with its projected benefit obligation.
d. The funded status of its pension plan with the accrued or prepaid pension cost reported in its balance sheet.

24. Which of the following defined benefit pension plan disclosures should be made in a company's financial statements?

I. The amount of net periodic pension cost for the period.
II. The fair value of plan assets.

a. I and II.
b. I only.
c. II only.
d. None of the above.

 6

25. The following information pertains to Foster Co.'s defined benefit postretirement plan for the year 1999.

Service cost	$120,000
Benefit payment	55,000
Interest on the accumulated postretirement benefit obligation	20,000
Unrecognized transition obligation (to be amortized over 20 years)	200,000

Foster Co.'s 1999 net periodic postretirement benefit cost was

a. $205,000
b. $150,000
c. $ 95,000
d. $285,000

26. Kemp Company provides a defined benefit postretirement plan for its employees. Kemp adopted the plan on January 1, 1999, in accordance with the provisions of SFAS Statement No. 106, *Employer's Accounting for Postretirement Benefits Other Than Pensions.* Data relating to the pension plan for 1999 are as follows:

Service cost for 1999	28,000
Interest on the accumulated postretirement benefit obligation	5,000
Amortization of the unrecognized transition obligation	8,000

At the end of 1999, Kemp makes a benefit payment of $10,000 to employees. In its December 31, 1999 balance sheet, Kemp should record accrued postretirement benefit cost of

a. $35,000
b. $31,000
c. $51,000
d. $15,000

27. Bounty Co. provides postretirement health care benefits to employees who have completed at least 10 years service and are aged 55 years or older when retiring. Employees retiring from Bounty have a median age of 62, and no one has worked beyond age 65. Fletcher is hired at 48 years old. The attribution period for accruing Bounty's expected postretirement health care benefit obligation to Fletcher is during the period when Fletcher is aged

- a. 48 to 65.
- b. 48 to 58.
- c. 55 to 65.
- d. 55 to 62.

28. An employer's obligation for postretirement health benefits that are expected to be provided to or for an employee must be fully accrued by the date the

- a. Employee is fully eligible for benefits.
- b. Employee retires.
- c. Benefits are utilized.
- d. Benefits are paid.

29. Which of the following are correct regarding a transition obligation resulting from the adoption of a defined benefit postretirement plan?

I. A transition obligation may be recognized immediately.
II. The transition obligation represents the difference between the accumulated postretirement benefit obligation and the fair value of plan assets at the beginning of the year the plan is adopted.
III. A transition obligation may be amortized on a straight-line basis over a maximum period of 20 years.

- a. I and II.
- b. II only.
- c. I, II, and III.
- d. II and III.

30. Which of the following information should be disclosed by a company providing health care benefits to its retirees?

I. The assumed health care cost trend rate used to measure the expected cost of benefits covered by the plan.
II. The accumulated postretirement benefit obligation.

- a. I and II.
- b. I only.
- c. II only.
- d. Neither I **nor** II.

OTHER OBJECTIVE QUESTIONS

Problem 1   (20 to 25 minutes)

This problem consists of 10 items. Select the **best** answer for each item. Use a No. 2 pencil to blacken the appropriate ovals on the Objective Answer Sheet to indicate your answers. **Answer all items**. Your grade will be based on the total number of correct answers.

The following information pertains to Sparta Co.'s defined benefit pension plan.

Discount rate	8%
Expected rate of return	10%
Average service life	12 years

At January 1, 1999:

Projected benefit obligation	$600,000
Fair value of pension plan assets	720,000
Unrecognized prior service cost	240,000
Unamortized prior pension gain	96,000

At December 31, 1999:

Projected benefit obligation	910,000
Fair value of pension plan assets	825,000

Service cost for 1999 was $90,000. There were no contributions made or benefits paid during the year. Sparta's unfunded accrued pension liability was $8,000 at January 1, 1999. Sparta uses the straight-line method of amortization over the maximum period permitted.

Required:

a.   For items 1 through 5, calculate the amounts to be recognized as components of Sparta's unfunded accrued pension liability at December 31, 1999. To record your entry, write the number in the boxes on the Objective Answer Sheet and blacken the corresponding oval below each box. These items cannot be graded if you fail to blacken the ovals.

Amounts to be calculated

1. Interest cost.

2. Expected return on plan assets.

3. Actual return on plan assets.

4. Amortization of prior service costs.

5. Minimum amortization of unrecognized pension gain.

b.   For items 6 through 10, determine whether the component increases (I) or decreases (D) Sparta's unfunded accrued pension liability and blacken the corresponding oval on the Objective Answer Sheet.

Items to be answered

6. Service cost.

7. Deferral of gain on plan assets.

8. Actual return on plan assets.

9. Amortization of prior service costs.

10. Amortization of unrecognized pension gain.

PROBLEMS

Problem 1   (15 to 25 minutes)

Essex Company has a single-employer defined benefit pension plan, and a compensation plan for future vacations for its employees.

Required:

a. Define the interest cost component of net pension cost for a period. How should Essex determine its interest cost component of net pension cost for a period?

b. Define prior service cost. How should Essex account for prior service cost? Why?

c. What conditions must be met for Essex to accrue compensation for future vacations? What is the theoretical rationale for accruing compensation for future vacations?

AUTHOR'S NOTE: Part C of this question is covered in Module 25.

Problem 2   (15 to 25 minutes)

At December 31, 1999, as a result of its single employer defined benefit pension plan, Bighorn Co. had an unrecognized net loss and an unfunded accrued pension cost. Bighorn's pension plan and its actuarial assumptions have not changed since it began operations in 1995. Bighorn has made annual contributions to the plan.

Required:

a. Identify the components of net pension cost that should be recognized in Bighorn's 1999 financial statements.

b. What circumstances caused Bighorn's
1. Unrecognized net loss?
2. Unfunded accrued pension cost?

c. How should Bighorn compute its minimum pension liability and any additional pension liability?

Problem 3   (30 to 40 minutes)

Deck Co. has just hired a new president, Palmer, and is reviewing its employee benefit plans with the new employee. For current employees, Deck offers a compensation plan for future vacations. Deck also provides postemployment benefits to former or inactive employees.

On the date of Palmer's hire, Palmer entered into a deferred compensation contract with Deck. Palmer is expected to retire in 10 years. The contract calls for a payment of $150,000 upon termination of employment following a minimum 3-year service period. The contract also provides that interest of 10%, compounded annually, be credited on the amount due each year after the third year.

Required:

a. Give an example of postemployment benefits. State the conditions under which Deck is required to accrue liabilities for compensated absences and postemployment benefits. State Deck's disclosure requirements if these conditions, in full or in part, are not met.

b. Describe the general accrual period for amounts to be paid under a deferred compensation contract. State the theoretical rationale for requiring accrual of these liabilities and related expenses.

c. Prepare a schedule of the expense and accrued liability related to Palmer's deferred compensation agreement to be reported in Deck's financial statements for the first 4 years of the contract.

Problem 4

Requirement b. covers postretirement benefits other than pensions. Return to Module 22A and complete that requirement.

MULTIPLE-CHOICE ANSWERS

1. d __ __	8. c __ __	15. d __ __	22. c __ __	29. c __ __
2. d __ __	9. d __ __	16. a __ __	23. d __ __	30. a __ __
3. b __ __	10. d __ __	17. b __ __	24. a __ __	
4. c __ __	11. a __ __	18. c __ __	25. b __ __	
5. d __ __	12. d __ __	19. a __ __	26. b __ __	
6. c __ __	13. b __ __	20. b __ __	27. b __ __	1st: __/30 = __%
7. d __ __	14. b __ __	21. a __ __	28. a __ __	2nd: __/30 = __%

MULTIPLE-CHOICE ANSWER EXPLANATIONS

D.1.-5. Pensions

1. **(d)** Per SFAS 87, para 20, the six elements which an employer sponsoring a defined benefit pension plan must include in its net pension cost are service cost, interest cost, actual return on plan assets, amortization of unrecognized prior service cost, deferral of unexpected gain or loss, and amortization of the unrecognized net obligation or unrecognized net asset existing at the date of initial application of SFAS 87. Lee Corp's pension expense is calculated as follows:

Service cost	$160,000
Gain (actual and expected) on plan assets	(35,000)
Amortization	5,000
Interest	50,000
	180,000

Note that per SFAS 87, gains and losses that arise from a single occurrence which is not directly related to the operation of the plan should be reported as part of that occurrence and not as part of the plan's activity. Therefore, the $40,000 unexpected loss on plan assets related to a 1999 disposal of a subsidiary should be reported as part of the "loss on disposal" and not as part of the 1999 pension cost.

2. **(d)** The requirement is to determine the amount of unrecognized net loss to be recognized as a part of pension expense in 1999. Per SFAS 87, the **corridor approach** is to be used to determine gain or loss amortization. Under this approach, only the unrecognized net gain or loss in excess of 10% of the **greater** of the projected benefit obligation (PBO) or the market-related asset value (M-RAV) is amortized. In this case, the M-RAV ($1,650,000) is larger than the PBO ($1,530,000). The corridor is $165,000 (10% x $1,650,000). The unrecognized net loss ($235,000) exceeds the corridor by $70,000 ($235,000 – $165,000). This excess is amortized over the average remaining service period of active employees expected to participate in the plan ($70,000 ÷ 5.5 = $12,727).

3. **(b)** The requirement is to calculate the total amount of unrecognized prior service cost to be amortized over future periods as a result of a pension plan amendment. Prior service cost is the present value of retroactive benefits given to employees for years of service provided before the date of an amendment to the plan. Per SFAS 87, the cost of these retroactive benefits is measured by the increase in the projected benefit obligation at the date of amendment ($1,900,000 – $1,300,000 = $600,000). This amount will be recognized as expense (amortized) during the service periods of those employees who are expected to receive benefits under the plan.

4. **(c)** Prepaid pension cost is the cumulative excess of the amount funded over the amount recorded as pension expense. In 1999, pension expense is $520,000.

Service cost and interest on PBO	$620,000
Actual return on plan assets	
($1,000,000 x 10%)	(100,000)
Pension expense	$520,000

Since 1999 funding was $1,000,000, 12/31/99 prepaid pension cost is $480,000 ($1,000,000 – $520,000).

5. **(d)** The solutions approach is to set up a T-account for prepaid/accrued pension cost

Prepaid/Accrued Pension Cost			
		0	1/1/99 bal.
1999 cont.	50,000	75,000	1999 expense
2000 cont.	?	90,000	2000 expense
		15,000	Desired 12/31/00 bal.

The 1/1/99 balance is $0 because prior to 1999, Webb's contributions fully funded the plan. The missing amount can be solved as $100,000. Note that minimum liability considerations do not affect the accrued pension liability because in both years the fair value of plan assets exceeds the accumulated benefit obligation.

6. **(c)** The requirement is to determine how the service cost component of the net periodic pension cost is measured in a defined benefit pension plan. Per SFAS 87 the service cost component recognized shall be determined as *the actuarial present value of benefits attributed by the pension benefit formula to employee service during the period* which is known as the **projected benefit obligation.** Therefore answer (c) is correct. Answers (a), (b), and (d) are incorrect because they are not related to the measurement of service cost.

7. **(d)** Per SFAS 87, para 20, among the components which should be included in the net pension cost recognized for a period by an employer sponsoring a defined benefit pension plan are **both** actual return on plan assets, if any, and amortization of unrecognized prior service cost, if any. Therefore, answer (d) is correct, and answers (a), (b), and (c) are incorrect.

8. **(c)** Net pension cost (expense) is comprised of six elements. One of these elements is interest on the projected benefit obligation, which is defined as the increase in the amount of the projected benefit obligation due to the passage of time. Therefore, answer (c) is correct. Candidates must be careful so as not to confuse "interest cost" with the "actual return" component of net pension cost which is the earnings on the plan assets. If the latter component is positive, it reduces the net pension cost for the period.

9. (d) Per SFAS 87, para 24, "because plan amendments are granted with the expectation that the employer will realize economic benefits in future periods, this Statement...provides for recognition during the future periods of those employees." Therefore, the prior service cost will be reflected in the financial statements for 1999 and future years only.

10. (d) This question addresses the behavior of the components of pension expense over a period of time. The glossary in Appendix D of SFAS 87 defines service cost as the actuarial present value of benefits attributed by the pension benefit formula to services rendered by employees during that period. This problem states that "all information on covered employees for 1999 and 2000 is the same," which indicates that there has been no change in Flood's work force during this 2-year period. The only difference in the service cost for these 2 years would, therefore, be attributable to differences in the discounting of the benefits. Each year a group of employees works, the group becomes 1 year closer to retirement age and to collecting their retirement benefits. The present value of the benefits earned by employees each year grows as their retirement date grows nearer, because the benefits are discounted over a shorter period of time. If, for instance, the "average" retirement date for Flood's employees is January 1, 2010, the present value of the benefits for 2000's service will be greater than the present value of 1999's service, because it is discounted 11 years for 1999 versus 10 years for 2000. (This is because every additional year of discounting reduces the present value of the benefits.) Therefore, the service cost for 2000 will be greater than for 1999. The problem also states that Flood intends to fund the plan in equal annual installments, and that the discount rate which was used to calculate the service cost is equal to the assumed rate of return on plan assets. Under these circumstances, to fully fund the pension obligation in equal payments, Flood will contribute an amount which exceeds the pension cost in the first years of the plan and which is less than the pension cost in later years. The glossary of SFAS 87 defines prepaid pension cost as the cumulative employer contributions in excess of accrued pension cost. Since 1999's funding would exceed its pension cost, Flood would report a prepaid pension cost on its 1999 balance sheet. The journal entry to record the funding would be:

Pension expense	xxx	
Prepaid pension cost	xx	
Cash		xxx

Therefore, answer (d) is correct.

11. (a) The requirement is to determine what the "unfunded accrued pension cost" represents. Per SFAS 87, para 35, the unfunded accrued pension cost is a liability recognized when the net periodic pension cost exceeds the amount the employer has contributed to the plan. Therefore, answer (a) is correct. Answers (b), (c), and (d) are incorrect

because the vested benefit obligation is not used to calculate the unfunded accrued pension cost.

12. (d) The projected benefit obligation is the actuarial present value of the pension obligation at the end of the period. Since there were no changes in actuarial estimates during the year, the end of period projected benefit obligation is computed as follows:

Projected benefit obligation, 1/1/99	$72,000
Service cost	18,000
Interest on projected benefit obligation	
(10% x $72,000)	7,200
Benefit payments	(15,000)
Pension benefit obligation, 12/31/99	$82,200

Service cost and interest on the projected benefit obligation increase the projected benefit obligation; benefit payments decrease the projected benefit obligation.

13. (b) The requirement is to determine which of the listed pension terms includes assumptions concerning projected changes in future compensation levels if the pension benefit formula is based on future compensation levels. Answer (b) is correct because per SFAS 87, paras 46 and 47, the service cost component and the projected benefit obligation reflect projected future compensation levels while the accumulated benefit obligation is measured based on employees' history of service and compensation without an estimate of projected future compensation levels. Therefore, answers (a), (c), and (d) are incorrect.

14. (b) Per SFAS 87, the assumed discount rate should reflect the rates at which pension benefits could be effectively settled. This rate is sometimes referred to as the "settlement rate." To determine the settlement rate, it is appropriate to look at rates implicit in current prices of annuity contracts that could be used to settle the obligation under the defined benefit plan. The expected return on plan assets is **not** used to calculate the projected benefit obligation. The actual return on plan assets is also **not** used to calculate the projected benefit obligation. Therefore, answer (b) is correct.

15. (d) SFAS 87 requires that a minimum pension liability be reported for the excess of the accumulated benefit obligation over the fair value of the plan assets ($4,300,000 − $3,450,000 = **$850,000**). Note that this is the amount to be **reported in the balance sheet**. The amount of **additional liability to be recorded** would be this amount plus prepaid pension cost or less accrued pension cost.

16. (a) SFAS 87 requires the recognition of a **minimum liability** if the accumulated benefit obligation (ABO) exceeds the FV of the plan assets. In this case, the excess of the ABO over the FV of plan assets is $90,000 ($380,000 − $290,000). The **additional liability** to be recorded is the minimum liability **less accrued pension cost**, or plus **prepaid pension cost**. Therefore, the additional liability is $110,000 ($90,000 + $20,000).

17. (b) SFAS 87 requires the reporting of a **minimum liability** if the accumulated benefit obligation (ABO) exceeds the FV of the plan assets. In this case, the excess of the ABO over the FV of plan assets is $25,000 ($103,000 – $78,000). The **additional liability** to be recorded is equal to the minimum liability **less accrued pension cost**, or **plus prepaid pension cost**. At the end of the first year, accrued pension cost is $20,000 ($90,000 pension expense less $70,000 cash contribution). Therefore, the additional liability is $5,000 ($25,000 – $20,000).

18. (c) SFAS 87 requires that a **minimum pension liability** be reported for the excess of the accumulated benefit obligation (ABO) over the fair value of the plan assets. This excess is also called the unfunded ABO ($25,000). The **additional liability** to be recorded is the minimum liability less **accrued pension cost** or plus **prepaid pension cost**. Since Hall made no contributions to the pension plan during 1999, accrued pension cost equals net periodic pension cost of $8,000. Therefore, the additional pension liability to be recorded is $17,000 ($25,000 – $8,000).

19. (a) SFAS 87 requires that a **minimum pension liability** be reported for the excess of the accumulated benefit obligation (ABO) over the fair value of the plan assets. This excess is also called the unfunded ABO ($25,000). The **additional liability** to be recorded is the minimum liability less **accrued pension cost** or plus **prepaid pension cost**. Since Hall made no contributions to the pension plan during 1999, accrued pension cost equals net periodic pension cost of $8,000. Therefore, the additional liability to be recorded is $17,000 ($25,000 – $8,000). Generally, the credit to **additional liability** is offset by a debit to an **intangible asset** account. However, when the additional liability exceeds the unrecognized prior service cost, the excess is reported as a component of **other comprehensive income** entitled "adjustment for minimum pension liability" and as accumulated other comprehensive income which is reported in one of three places, including the statement of changes in stockholder's equity, rather than as an intangible asset. For Hall, the excess reported in the equity account is $5,000 ($17,000 additional liability less $12,000 unrecognized prior service cost).

20. (b) Per SFAS 87, para 36, the recognition of an additional minimum liability is required if an unfunded accumulated benefit obligation (excess of accumulated benefit obligation over fair value of plan assets) exists and (1) an asset has been recognized as prepaid pension cost, (2) the liability already recognized as unfunded accrued pension cost is less than the unfunded accumulated benefit obligation, or (3) no accrued or prepaid pension cost has been recognized. Answer (b) is correct and answer (a) is incorrect because the additional liability which must be recorded is the amount necessary to make the **total** liability equal to the unfunded accumulated benefit obligation (i.e., the accumulated benefit obligation **less** the fair market value of plan assets). Answers (c) and (d) are incorrect because the **projected** benefit obligation is not involved in the calculation of the minimum liability.

21. (a) The requirement is to determine when the **accumulated other comprehensive income** account, adjustment for minimum pension liability, should be reported on the balance sheet for a particular year. Per SFAS 87, para 37, when the additional liability required to be recognized exceeds the unrecognized prior service cost, the excess should be reported as a separate component (that is, a reduction) of **other comprehensive income and accumulated other comprehensive income**, net of any tax benefits. Therefore, answer (a) is correct and answer (b) is incorrect. Answer (c) is incorrect because an employer that sponsors only one defined benefit pension plan may be required to report the equity account as well as an employer with two or more defined benefit pension plans. Answer (d) is incorrect because an amendment to an existing plan does not always cause the difference between the fair value of the plan assets and the accumulated benefit obligation.

22. (c) Per SFAS 88, when special termination benefits are offered to employees, a loss and liability must be recognized when the employee accepts the offer and the amount can be reasonably estimated. The amount to be recognized shall include any lump-sum payments ($475,000) and the present value of any expected future payments ($155,000). Therefore, the total liability for special termination benefits is $630,000 ($475,000 + $155,000). Note that the reduction of accrued pension costs ($45,000) would reduce the amount of the loss, but would **not** affect the liability. Instead it would be recorded as a reduction of accrued pension costs. The journal entry would be:

Loss from termination benefits	585,000	
Accrued pension costs	45,000	
Liability from termination benefits		630,000

23. (d) SFAS 132 requires disclosure of a schedule reconciling the funded status of the pension plan (PBO less FV of plan assets) with the accrued or prepaid pension cost reported in the balance sheet [answer (d)]. The reconciliations described in answers (a), (b), and (c) are not required by SFAS 132.

24. (a) Per SFAS 132, an employer sponsoring a defined benefit pension plan must disclose a great deal of information related to the plan. These disclosures include the amount of net periodic pension cost for the period and the fair value of plan assets. Therefore, answer (a) is correct, and answers (b), (c), and (d) are incorrect.

D.6. Postretirement Benefits Other Than Pensions (OPEB)

25. (b) Net periodic postretirement benefit cost is a net amount calculated by adding or subtracting six components. Three components present in this problem are combined as follows:

Service cost	$120,000
Interest on the accumulated postretirement benefit obligation	20,000
Amortization of transition obligation ($200,000 ÷ 20 years)	10,000
Postretirement benefit cost	$150,000

Service cost and interest on the accumulated postretirement benefit obligation always increase postretirement benefit cost. Foster Co. has elected to amortize the unrecognized transition obligation over a 20-year period. Amortization of the $200,000 obligation on the straight-line basis increases postretirement benefit cost by $10,000 per year. Thus, answer (b) is correct. The benefit payment represents a cash payment made for benefits by the employer; however, this is not a component of net periodic postretirement benefit cost.

26. (b) To determine the accrued postretirement benefit cost, the net periodic postretirement benefit cost must first be calculated as follows:

Service cost	$28,000
Interest on the accumulated postre-	
tirement benefit obligation	5,000
Amortization of the unrecognized	
transition obligation	8,000
Net periodic postretirement benefit	
cost	$41,000

An adjusting entry is required at year end to record net periodic postretirement benefit cost and the cash benefit payments made to employees. An accrued postretirement benefit cost will be recorded if the net postretirement benefit cost exceeds the cash payments to employees. The journal entry would be:

Postretirement benefit cost	41,000	
Cash		10,000
Accrued postretirement benefit cost		31,000

Therefore, answer (b) is correct. The balance in the accrued postretirement benefit cost account would be $31,000.

27. (b) The requirement is to determine the attribution period for accruing the expected postretirement health care benefit obligation. In accordance with SFAS 106, para 44, the beginning of the attribution period is generally the date of hire, and the end shall be the date of full eligibility. Therefore, answer (b) is correct. Answers (a), (c), and (d) are incorrect because Fletcher's age at the date of hire is 48 and the period of eligibility is 10 years. Thus, the attribution period is 48 to 58.

28. (a) SFAS 106 requires an employer's obligation for postretirement benefits expected to be provided to an employee be fully accrued by the full eligibility date of the employee, even if the employee is to render additional service beyond that date. Answers (b), (c),and (d) all indicate points in time after full eligibility.

29. (c) Per SFAS 106, para 110, a transition obligation is measured as the difference between the accumulated postretirement benefit obligation and the fair value of plan assets at the beginning of the fiscal year for which SFAS 106 is adopted. A transition obligation may be recognized immediately in net income of the period of the change, or recognized on a delayed basis as a component of net periodic postretirement benefit cost. If delayed recognition is elected, SFAS 106, para 112, states that in general the transition obligation should be amortized on a straight-line basis over the average remaining service period of plan participants. If the average remaining service period is less than 20 years, the employer may elect to use a 20-year amortization period. Therefore, answer (c) is correct.

30. (a) SFAS 106, para 74c, requires that the employer disclose the amount of the accumulated postretirement benefit obligation. Paragraph 74d requires that the employer also disclose the assumed health care cost trend rate used to measure the expected cost of benefits covered by the plan. Therefore, answer (a) is correct, and answers (b), (c), and (d) are incorrect.

OTHER OBJECTIVE ANSWER EXPLANATIONS

Problem 1

1.   **($48,000)**   The solutions approach is to set up the formula for calculating interest cost:

Beginning balance of projected benefit obligation (1/1/99)	x	Discount rate	=	Interest cost
$600,000	x	.08	=	$48,000

2.   **($72,000)**   The solutions approach is to set up the formula for calculating the expected return on plan assets:

Beginning balance of fair value of the plan assets (1/1/99)	x	Expected rate of return on plan assets	=	Expected return on plan assets
$720,000	x	10%	=	$72,000

3.   **($105,000)**   The solutions approach is to set up a T-account for the fair value of pension plan assets:

(Pension plan account, but not on Sparta's books)

	Fair Value of Pension Plan Assets	
1/1/99	$720,000	
Contributions during the year	$0	$0 Pension benefits paid during 1999
Actual return on plan assets	?	
12/31/99	$825,000	

Actual return on plan assets = $825,000 – $720,000 + $0 – $0 = $105,000

The problem states that there were no contributions made or benefits paid, thus the actual return on plan assets is the only change not accounted for.

4.   **($20,000)**   The solutions approach is to set up the formula for amortization of prior service cost:

Unrecognized prior service cost (1/1/99)   ÷   Average service life of employees   =   Amortization of prior service costs

$$\frac{\$240,000}{12} = \$20,000$$

5.   **($2,000)**   The solutions approach is to set up the steps needed to calculate the minimum amortization of unrecognized pension gain:

       (1)   Determine the greater of the:

            Projected benefit obligation ($600,000), or
            Fair value of the plan assets ($720,000)

       (2)   Multiply the larger amount in #1 by 10%:

            $720,000 x 10% = $72,000

       (3)   Calculate the difference between the value in #2 and the unamortized prior pension gain:

            $96,000 – $72,000 = $24,000

       (4)   Amortize the value in #3 by dividing it by the average service life of employees:

$$\frac{\$24,000}{12} \quad = \quad \$2,000$$

          Minimum amortization   = $2,000

     When the amortization of the cumulative unrecognized net gain or loss from previous periods is required, the procedure is comparable to the amortization of prior service cost and, in general, it requires the use of the average remaining service period for active employees. Unlike prior service cost, however, the amount to be amortized is not necessarily the calculated amount of the cumulative unrecognized net gain or loss. Instead, the minimum amount subject to amortization, is determined by the use of a method sometimes referred to as the "corridor" approach. The minimum amount of the cumulative unrecognized gain or loss required to be amortized is determined by computing, at the beginning of the fiscal year, the excess of the cumulative unrecognized gain or loss over 10% of the greater of the projected benefit obligation or the market-related asset value. If the cumulative unrecognized gain or loss is equal to or less than the 10% calculated value, no amount need be amortized.

6.   **(I)**   Service cost increases the unfunded accrued pension liability. Service cost is defined as the actuarial present value of benefits attributed by the pension benefit formula to employee services performed during the current period. In other words, this represents the obligation a company is responsible to pay, for work employees perform during the current year, which increases a company's pension liability.

7.   **(I)**   The deferral of a gain on pension plan assets will increase the unfunded pension liability. A gain consists of two components: (1) the current period difference between the expected return on plan assets and the actual return on plan assets **and** (2) the unrecognized net gain from **previous periods**. When the expected return is less than the actual return, a gain arises. However, the pension cost for the year will report the expected return on plan assets, not the actual return on plan assets. This is done to record a more consistent, smooth yearly return, rather than one which is erratic, based on actual results. Therefore, if the expected return is less than the actual return, the actual return which originally decreased pension cost, will be offset by an increase in pension cost for the difference between the actual and expected return. A numerical example will help to clarify this point:

Actual return	=	$60,000
Expected return	=	25,000
Difference		$35,000 gain

The $35,000 gain cannot be recognized, because only the expected return is recorded as a decrease in pension cost. Therefore, because $60,000 was recorded, and only $25,000 should be used to decrease pension cost, the $35,000 gain will be subtracted from pension cost, **increasing** pension liability by $35,000.

8.   **(D)**   The actual return on plan assets will decrease the unfunded accrued pension liability. The actual return represents the return on the assets that are invested, to generate income, for paying pension benefits. This return will then decrease the amount of funds a company must contribute, to accumulate funds to pay pension benefits to their employees, thereby decreasing pension liability. Recall, from the discussion in (7), there will be an adjustment in the calculation of pension cost for the difference between the actual return and the expected return on plan assets.

9.   **(I)**   The amortization of prior service costs will increase the unfunded accrued pension liability. Prior service costs represent additional benefits, which are granted to employees, for services performed in previous periods. These benefits are then amortized over the average service life of the employees, from the time period the benefits were granted. The benefits increase the pension liability on Sparta's books as they are amortized because they represent the additional benefits that must be paid to employees.

10.   **(D)**   The amortization of unrecognized pension gain decreases the unfunded accrued pension liability. Please refer to question (7) for an explanation of how a pension gain arises. Also, refer to question (5) for an explanation of how gain amortization is calculated. The amortization decreases the pension liability because it is a deduction in the pension cost calculation. Therefore, the pension liability decreases.

ANSWER OUTLINE

Problem 1   Pension Terms and Accrual of Vacation Pay

a.   Interest cost component = Increase in PBO caused by passage of time
Calculation
    Assumed discount rate x Beginning PBO

b.   PSC = increased benefits based on services rendered in prior periods
    Granted at adoption or amendment date
Accounting
    Include amortization of PSC in net pension cost during future service periods of employees active at date of adoption/amendment
    Because PSC incurred in anticipation of future economic benefits to employer

c.   Conditions necessary for accrual of future vacation compensation
    Obligation stems from services already performed
    Obligation relates to vested/accumulated rights
    Payment is probable
    Amount can reasonably be estimated
    Rationale for accrual
    Matches costs and revenues
    Recognizes measurable liability

UNOFFICIAL ANSWER

Problem 1   Pension Terms and Accrual of Vacation Pay

a.   The interest cost component of the net pension cost for a period is the increase in the projected benefit obligation due to the passage of time. Essex would determine its interest cost component by applying an assumed discount rate to the beginning projected benefit obligation.

b.   Prior service cost is the cost of retroactive benefits (increased benefits based on services rendered in prior periods) granted at the date of adoption or amendment of a pension plan. Prior service cost should be included in net pension cost during the future service periods of those employees active at the date of the pension plan adoption or amendment, as appropriate, who are expected to receive benefits under the pension plan. Prior service cost is incurred with the expectation that the employer will realize economic benefits in future periods.

c.   Essex must accrue compensation for future vacations if all of the following conditions are met:

• Essex's obligation relating to employees' rights to receive compensation for future vacations is attributable to employees' services already rendered.
• The obligation relates to rights that vest or accumulate.
• Payment of the vacation benefits is probable.
• The amount can be reasonably estimated.

The theoretical rationale is that accruing compensation matches the cost of vacation benefits to the period in which services are rendered, and results in recognition of a measurable liability.

ANSWER OUTLINE

Problem 2   Pension Cost Components: Causes of Unrecognized Net Loss and Accrual Pension Cost; Minimum Liability

a.   Components of net pension cost

• Service cost
• Interest cost
• Actual return on plan assets
• Gain or loss
    (Actual – Expected return) + Amortization of unrecognized gain/loss

b.   **1.**   Unrecognized net loss
    Actuarial assumptions ≠ experience for PBO and returns on plan assets
    2.   Unfunded accrued pension cost
    Cumulative net pension expense > cash contributed to fund

c.   Minimum pension liability = ABO – FV of plan assets
    Additional pension liability = minimum liability – unfunded accrued pension cost

UNOFFICIAL ANSWER

Problem 2   Pension Cost Components: Causes of Unrecognized Net Loss and Accrual Pension Cost; Minimum Liability

a.   The components of Bighorn's 1999 net pension cost calculation are:

• Service cost.
• Interest cost.
• Actual return on plan assets.
• Gain or loss consisting of:

    • The difference between the actual and expected return on plan assets.
    • Any amortization of the unrecognized gain or loss from previous periods.

b.   **1.**   Bighorn's unrecognized net loss results from differences between actuarial assumptions and experiences for both its projected benefit obligation and returns on plan assets.
    2.   Bighorn's unfunded accrued pension cost occurs because cumulative net pension expense exceeds cash contributed to the pension fund.

c.   Bighorn's minimum pension liability equals the excess of the accumulated benefit obligation over the fair value of plan assets. Bighorn's additional pension liability would equal any excess of this minimum pension liability over the unfunded accrued pension cost.

ANSWER OUTLINE

Problem 3   Postemployment Benefits; Deferred Compensation Contracts

a.   Example of postemployment benefits:
    Health care benefits
    Conditions which require accrued liabilities:

Obligation is attributable to employees' services already rendered,

Employee's rights accumulate or vest,

Payment is probable, and

Amount of benefits can be reasonably estimated

Disclosure requirements

Mention that obligation amount is **not** reasonably estimable

b. General accrual period

Active employment period through full eligibility date

Beginning with contract date

Theoretical rationale

Matching

Cost of benefits matched to period services rendered

Recognize measurable liability

c. Record deferred compensation expense and increase accrued liability first 3 years (1999-2001)

Record interest in year 4 (2001)

UNOFFICIAL ANSWER

Problem 3   Postemployment Benefits; Deferred Compensation Contracts

a.   An example of postemployment benefits offered by employers is continuation of health care benefits. Deck is required to accrue liabilities for compensated absences and postemployment benefits if all of the following conditions are met:

• The obligation is attributable to employees' services already rendered,

• The employees' rights accumulate or vest,

• Payment is probable, and

• The amount of the benefits can be reasonably estimated

If an obligation cannot be accrued solely because the amount cannot be reasonably estimated, the financial statements should disclose that fact.

b.   Estimated amounts to be paid under a deferred compensation contract should be accrued over the period of an employee's active employment from the time the contract is signed to the employee's full eligibility date. The theoretical rationale for accrual of these obligations to be paid in the future is that accrual matches the cost of the benefits to the period in which services are rendered, and results in recognition of a measurable liability.

c.

Deck Co.

SCHEDULE OF DEFERRED COMPENSATION AMOUNTS

For the Years 1999 through 2000

For the year ended	*Accrued liability*	*Deferred compensation expense*
12/31/99	$ 50,000	$50,000 [a]
12/31/00	$100,000	$50,000
12/31/01	$150,000	$50,000
12/31/00	$165,000	$15,000 [b]

[a] $150,000 ÷ 3 (straight-line method)

[b] $150,000 x 10%

E. Leases

A lease is a contract between two parties--a lessor and a lessee. A lease contract gives a lessee rights to use the lessor's property for a specified period of time in return for periodic cash payments (rent) to the lessor.

A major goal in accounting for leases is to recognize the economic substance of the lease agreement over its mere legal form. For example, many lease agreements are similar to the purchase of an asset financed by the issuance of debt. The economic substance of a lease agreement generally takes one of two forms:

1.   Periodic payments of rent by the lessee for the **use** of the lessor's property
2.   Periodic payments similar to an installment purchase by the lessee for the rights to **acquire** the lessor's property in the future (i.e., acquisition of property by financing)

In (1), the risks and rewards of owning the asset remain with the lessor. Accordingly, the asset is **not** treated as sold by the lessor to the lessee, and remains on the lessor's books. This form of leasing arrangement is called an **operating lease**. By contrast, in (2), a lease agreement may transfer many of the risks and rewards of ownership to the lessee. This form of lease is treated as a sale by the lessor and as a purchase by the lessee. This concept is clearly stated in SFAS 13 as follows:

> "A lease that transfers substantially all of the benefits and risks incident to ownership of property should be accounted for as the acquisition of an asset and the incurrence of an obligation by the lessee and as a sale or financing by the lessor."

When the risks and rewards of ownership are deemed to have been passed from the lessor to the lessee, the lessor will account for the lease as either a **direct financing** or as a **sales-type lease**, and the lessee will account for the lease as a **capital lease**.

To determine whether the risks and rewards of ownership have been transferred to the lessee, **at least one** of the following four criteria must be met:

1.   The lease **transfers title** to the lessee
2.   The lease contains a **bargain purchase** option
3.   The lease **term is 75% or more** of useful life and the lease is not first executed within the last 25% of the original useful life
4.   The **present value** of minimum lease payments **is 90% or more** of the net of the **fair market value** of the asset reduced by the investment tax credit (when in effect) retained by the lessor and the lease is not executed in the last 25% of the original useful life

These four criteria apply to both the lessor and to the lessee. The lessor, however, must meet two additional criteria:

1.   **Collectibility** of minimum lease payments is predictable, and
2.   There are **no important uncertainties** concerning costs yet to be incurred by the lessor under the lease.

Both of the above must be satisfied by the lessor in order for the lessor to treat the lease in substance as an installment sale.

The classification of leases can be summarized as follows:

| Risks and rewards remain with lessor (no sale and purchase of asset) | *Lessor* Operating ···························· | *Lessee* Operating |
| Risks and rewards transfer to lessee (sale and purchase of asset) | Direct financing ···················· Sales-type ············· | Capital |

1. **Study Program for Leases**

   a. Begin by reviewing the terms peculiar to leases that appear at the beginning of the outline of SFAS 13 in the pronouncement outlines that begin after Module 33.

   b. Review the material in this module so that you will be familiar with the major concepts and applications in the leasing area.

   c. After you have developed a solid base of understanding, you should review the outline of SFAS 13.

   d. The discussion of accounting for leases is structured to follow the lease classification matrix listed above.

   (1) **Operating Lease--Lessor/Lessee**

   An operating lease is any lease not meeting the criteria for a direct financing or sales-type lease in the case of a lessor, or for a capital lease in the case of a lessee. Under an operating lease, leased assets continue to be carried on the lessor's balance sheet and are depreciated in the normal manner. These assets, however, are not shown on the lessee's balance sheet since the lessee cannot expect to derive any future economic benefit from the assets beyond the lease term. Several issues are frequently encountered when dealing with operating leases. These issues are discussed in the remainder of this section.

   (a) **Free rent/uneven payments**

   Some lease agreements might call for uneven payments or scheduled rent increases over the lease term. Other agreements might include, as an incentive to the lessee, several months of "free rent" during which the lessee may use the asset without owing rent to the lessor. In these cases, rental revenue (expense) is still recognized by the lessor (lessee) on a straight-line basis and is prorated over the full term of the lease during which the lessee has possession of the asset. This is due to the matching principle; if physical usage is relatively the same over the lease term, then an equal amount of benefit is being obtained by both parties to the lease.

   NOTE: Another method to allocate rental revenue (expense) may be used if it better represents the actual physical use of the leased asset.

   When the pattern of actual cash received (paid) as rent is other than straight-line, it will be necessary for both parties to record accruals, or deferrals, depending upon the payment schedule.

	Accruals	(or)	*Deferrals*
Lessor --	Rent receivable		Unearned rent
Lessee --	Rent payable		Prepaid rent

Numerical Example 1:

Lease Information

   1) A 10 year lease is initiated on 1/1/99

   2) Payments are $100,000 per year payable January 1 (except for the first year)

   3) Payment for the first year is $50,000, due on 7/1/99

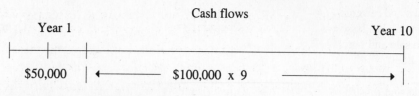

Cash flows

Recognition of revenue/expense:

Actual cash received/paid =
(9 years   x $100,000) + $50,000 = $950,000 total

Revenue and expense per year =
$950,000   ÷   10 years   = $95,000 per year

Journal entries for the lessor				*Journal entries for the lessee*		
Year 1				**Year 1**		
Cash	50,000			Rent expense	50,000	
Rent revenue		50,000		Cash		50,000
Rent receivable	45,000			Rent expense	45,000	
Rent revenue		45,000		Rent payable		45,000
Years 2-10				**Years 2-10**		
Cash	100,000			Rent expense	95,000	
Rent revenue		95,000		Rent payable	5,000 (b)	
Rent receivable		5,000 (a)		Cash		100,000

	Rent Receivable		(a)		(b)	Rent Payable	
yr. 1	45,000	5,000	yr. 2	yr. 2	5,000	45,000	yr. 1
		•			•		
		•			•		
		•	yr. 10	yr. 10	•		

(b)   **Initial direct costs**

    The lessor may incur costs in setting up the lease agreement. Such costs might include finder's fees, appraisal fees, document processing fees, negotiation fees, and any costs in closing the transaction. These costs, called initial direct costs, are carried as an asset on the lessor's balance sheet. Initial direct costs are amortized on a straight-line basis to expense over the lease term by the lessor, and are shown net of accumulated amortization on the lessor's balance sheet.

(c)   **Lease bonus (fee)**

    At the inception of the lease, the lessee may pay a nonrefundable lease bonus (fee) to the lessor in order to obtain more favorable leasing terms (e.g., a lease term of 3 years instead of 5 years). The lease bonus (fee) would be treated as unearned rent by the lessor and would be amortized to rental revenue on a straight-line basis over the lease term. The lessee would treat the lease bonus (fee) as prepaid rent and would recognize it as rental expense over the lease term on a straight-line basis.

(d)   **Security deposits**

    Some lease agreements may require that the lessee pay the lessor a security deposit at the inception of the lease. Security deposits may be either refundable or nonrefundable. A **refundable** security deposit is treated as a liability by the lessor and as a receivable by the lessee until the deposit is returned to the lessee. A **nonrefundable** security deposit is recorded as unearned revenue by the lessor and as prepaid rent by the lessee until the deposit is considered earned by the lessor (usually at the end of the lease term).

(e)   **Leasehold improvements**

Frequently, the lessee will make improvements to leased property by constructing new buildings or improving existing structures. The lessee has the right to use these leasehold improvements over the term of the lease; however, these improvements will revert to the lessor at the expiration of the lease. Leasehold improvements are capitalized to "Leasehold Improvements" (a property, plant and equipment account) by the lessee and are amortized over the **shorter** of (1) the remaining lease term, **or** (2) the useful life of the improvement. Improvements made in lieu of rent should be expensed in the period incurred. If the lease contains an option to renew and the likelihood of renewal is uncertain, the leasehold improvement should be written off over the life of the initial lease term or useful life of the improvement, whichever is shorter.

*NOTE: Moveable equipment or office furniture that is not attached to the leased property is **not** considered a leasehold improvement.*

The summary below lists the elements commonly encountered in operating leases:

Operating Lease FS Elements

	Lessor	*Lessee*
Balance sheet:	• Leased asset (net of accumulated depreciation)	• Prepaid rent (including lease bonus/fee and nonrefundable security deposit)
	• Rent receivable	
	• Initial direct costs (net of accumulated amortization)	• Leasehold improvements (net of accumulated amortization)
	• Unearned rent (including lease bonus/fee and nonrefundable security deposit)	• Deposit receivable
	• Deposit liability	
Income statement:	• Rent revenue (including amortization of lease bonus/fee and nonrefundable security deposit)	• Rent expense (including amortization of lease bonus/fee and nonrefundable security deposit)
	• Depreciation expense	• Amortization of leasehold improvements
	• Amortization of initial direct costs	
	• Other maintenance expenses	

Knowledge of these elements is helpful in answering questions that require a determination of lessor's net income or lessee's total expense in connection with an operating lease.

(2) **Direct Financing Lease--Lessor**

Although most discussions, including SFAS 13, begin with the lessee's accounting for a capital lease, we have chosen to present the lessor's accounting first because the lessor is the party that determines the fixed cash schedule of lease payments that are to be made by the lessee.

A direct financing lease arises when a consumer needs equipment but does not want to purchase the equipment outright, and/or is unable to obtain conventional financing. In this situation, the consumer will turn to a leasing company (e.g., a bank) which will purchase the desired asset from a manufacturer (or dealer) and lease it to the consumer. Direct financing leases apply to leasing companies, as opposed to manufacturers or dealers, because leasing companies purchase the assets solely for leasing, not for resale. Leasing companies are usually involved in financing activities (e.g., banking and insurance), not in the sale of property of the type being leased. The following situation shows when a direct financing lease would arise:

ABC Company needs new equipment to expand its manufacturing operations but does not have enough capital to purchase the equipment at present. ABC Company employs Universal Leasing Company to purchase the equipment. ABC will lease the asset from Universal. Universal records a direct financing lease.

The relationships in a direct financing lease arrangement are illustrated below.

*Title would stay with the lessor unless criterion (1) or (2) above is met in which case title would pass to the lessee.

As mentioned, a lease is considered to be a direct financing lease by the **lessor** if at least one of the four criteria applicable to both lessors and lessees is met, and **both** of the additional criteria applicable to lessors is met.

Direct financing leases result in only interest revenue for the lessor. In essence, no product has been sold by the lessor, so no gain/loss, sales, or cost of sales is recognized from the lease transaction. Thus the FMV (selling price) of the leased asset equals its cost to the lessor.

The lessor's entry to record the acquisition of title to the asset to be leased is as follows:

Asset to be leased	(cost of asset = FMV)
Cash	(cash paid)

At the inception of the lease, the lessor makes the following entry:

Lease receivable	xx	
Asset to be leased		xx
Unearned interest revenue		xx

In effect, the asset is removed from the lessor's books; it will be transferred to the lessee's books if one of the four criteria applicable to lessees is met. It is possible that the lessee's analysis might result in an operating lease.

In order to calculate the amounts in the entry above, you must first become familiar with several important terms.

(a) **Minimum lease payments (MLP)**

MLP are the payments that the lessor/lessee is or can be required to make in connection with the leased property:

1. Rent payments (excluding executory costs and contingent rentals)
2. Bargain purchase option (if any)
3. Guaranteed residual value (if any)
4. Penalty for failure to renew (if any)

Executory costs (e.g., property taxes, insurance, etc.) and contingent rentals are treated as revenues in the period earned.

(b) **Bargain purchase option (BPO)**

This option allows the lessee to purchase leased property for an amount substantially lower than the expected FMV at the exercise date of the option.

(c)   **Residual value**

Residual value can be unguaranteed or guaranteed. Some lease contracts require lessees to guarantee residual value to lessors. The lessee can either buy the leased asset at the end of the lease term for the guaranteed residual value or allow the lessor to sell the leased asset (with the lessee paying any deficiency or receiving any excess over the guaranteed residual value).

Guaranteed residual value is considered part of the "minimum lease payment" and is reflected in the lessor's lease receivable account and the lessee's lease payable account. At the end of the lease term, the receivable and payable on the respective lessor's and lessee's books should be equal to the guaranteed residual value. Both lessor and lessee consider the guaranteed residual value a final lease payment. The lessee should amortize (depreciate) the asset down to the guaranteed residual value.

Unguaranteed residual value is the estimated residual value of the leased asset at the end of the lease (if a guaranteed residual value exists, the unguaranteed residual value is the excess of estimated value over the guaranteed residual value). The present value of the unguaranteed residual value should be included in the lessor's net investment in the lease unless the lease transfers title to the leased asset or there is a bargain purchase option.

At the end of the lease, the lessor's receivable account should be equal to the unguaranteed residual value. The lessor must review the estimated residual value annually and recognize any decreases as a loss. No upward adjustments of the residual value are permitted.

Now you are ready to calculate the amounts for the lessor's entry using the following formulas:

Lease receivable*
(= gross investment)   =   Total MLP**   +   URV (if any)

Asset to be leased
(= net investment)   =   PV of gross investment
(= FMV or cost of asset)

Unearned interest revenue   =   Gross investment   −   FMV (or cost) of asset

> * *The title* **Gross investment** *is used when there is an unguaranteed residual value because the lower probability of collection of the residual value makes the use of the term* **Receivable** *undesirable.*
> ** *Include guaranteed residual value.*

Alternative methods of recording the lease transaction are shown below.

Lease receivable (gross)	xx			Lease receivable (net)	xx
Asset to be leased		xx	-or-	Asset to be leased		xx
Unearned interest revenue		xx			

We will follow the gross method in our examples for the lessor because it is consistent with SFAS 13 and the questions on the CPA exam.

SFAS 13 specifies additional guidelines when accounting for the lessor:

- The lease receivable should be separated into current and noncurrent components on the lessor's balance sheet.
- Unearned interest revenue must be amortized to produce a constant periodic rate of return on the net investment using the interest method.
- No residual value is assumed to accrue to the value of the lessor if the lease transfers ownership or contains a BPO.

- At the termination of the lease, the balance in the receivable should equal the guaranteed or unguaranteed residual value, assuming title is not transferred and there is no bargain purchase option.

Numerical Example 2:

Lease Information

1) A 3-year lease is initiated on 1/1/99 for equipment costing $131,858 with an expected useful life of 5 years. The FMV of the equipment on 1/1/99 is $131,858.
2) Three annual payments are due to the lessor beginning 12/31/99. The property reverts back to the lessor upon termination of the lease.
3) The guaranteed residual value at the end of year 3 is $10,000.
4) The lessor is to receive a 10% return (implicit rate).
5) Collectivity of minimum lease payments is predictable, and there are no important uncertainties concerning costs yet to be incurred by the lessor under the lease.
6) The cost (FMV) of the asset incurred by the lessor to acquire the asset for leasing is to be recovered through two components: annual rent payments and guaranteed residual value using a discount (implicit) rate of 10%.
7) The annual rent payment to the lessor is computed as follows:

   a) Find PV of guaranteed residual value

   $$\underset{\text{GRV}}{\$\,10,000} \quad \times \quad .7513 \quad = \quad \$\,7,513$$

   b) Find PV of annual rent payments

   $$\underset{\text{FMV of asset}}{\$131,858} \quad - \quad \$7,513 \quad = \quad \$124,345$$

   c) Find annual rent payment

   $$\$124,345 \quad \div \quad \text{PVA}_{n=3;\,i=10\%}$$

   $$\$124,345 \quad \div \quad 2.4869 \quad = \quad \$50,000$$

Lease Classification

This lease is a direct financing lease because criterion 4 (the 90% test) is satisfied.

$$\$124,345 + \$7,513 \ge (.9)(\$131,858)$$

(Since the residual value is guaranteed, the PV of the MLP is 100% of the FMV). The two additional criteria for the lessor are satisfied, and FMV equals cost. If the residual value had been unguaranteed, the 90% test would still have been met because $\$124,345 \ge (.9)\,(\$131,858)$.

Accounting for Lease

1) The lease should be recorded at the beginning of year 1 by the lessor.
2) The lease receivable is calculated as follows:

(Annual rent payment	x	Lease term)	+	GRV	
$50,000		3 yrs.		$10,000	= $160,000

3) Unearned interest revenue is calculated as follows:

Lease receivable	–	FMV of asset	
$160,000		$131,858	= $ 28,142

4) Unearned interest is amortized during the lease term using the following amortization schedule:

AMORTIZATION SCHEDULE

Carrying value at beg. of yr. 1 (= PV of gross investment)		$131,858
Interest revenue (10%)	$ 13,186	
Rent payment	(50,000)	(36,814)
Carrying value at beg. of yr. 2		95,044
Interest revenue	9,504	
Rent payment	(50,000)	(40,496)
Carrying value at beg. of yr. 3		54,548
Interest revenue	5,452	
Rent payment	(50,000)	(44,548)
Carrying value at end of yr. 3 (= residual value)		10,000

Lease receivable on balance sheet:

End of Year 1	–	current portion	= $40,496	principal reduction in year 2
		noncurrent portion	= $54,548	principal reductions after year 2
End of Year 2	–	current portion	= $54,548	principal reduction in the follow-ing year (includes residual value)

NOTE: As the lease expires, interest revenue decreases and the reduction of principal increases.

5)   The journal entries for the lessor are shown below.

JOURNAL ENTRIES FOR THE LESSOR

Initial entries (Beg. of Yr. 1)

Equipment for leasing	131,858	
Cash		131,858
Lease receivable	160,000	
Equipment for leasing		131,858
Unearned interest		28,142

End of Year 1

Cash	50,000	
Lease receivable		50,000
Unearned interest	13,186	
Interest revenue		13,186

End of Year 2

Cash	50,000	
Lease receivable		50,000
Unearned interest	9,504	
Interest revenue		9,504

End of Year 3

Cash	50,000	
Lease receivable		50,000
Unearned interest	5,452	
Interest revenue		5,452

6)   Assume that when the asset is returned at the end of year 3 the asset has a FMV of only $4,000. The lessee will need to make a payment of $6,000 ($10,000 – $4,000) because the residual value was guaranteed. The lessor would make the following entry:

Cash	6,000	
Residual value of equipment	4,000	
Lease receivable		10,000

(3) Sales-Type Lease--Lessor

A sales-type lease arises when a manufacturer or dealer leases an asset which otherwise might be sold outright for a profit. These manufacturers (dealers) use leasing as a way to market their own products (e.g., a car dealership). The leasing, or financing arrangement, is a means for the manufacturer to sell its products and realize a profit from sales. (By contrast, direct financing leases serve purely as financing arrangements.) The following situation shows when a sales-type lease would arise:

ABC Company needs equipment to expand its manufacturing operations. ABC Company enters into a lease agreement with XYZ Manufacturing, Inc. for the equipment. XYZ Manufacturing Inc. records a sales-type lease.

The relationships in a sales-type lease arrangement are illustrated below.

* *Title stays with lessor and property will be returned to lessor at the end of the lease term unless criterion (1) or (2) above is met.*

Sales-type leases, unlike direct financing leases, result in **both** (1) gross profit (loss) in the period of sales, **and** (2) interest revenue to be earned over the lease term using the effective interest method. The diagram below compares and contrasts direct financing leases with sales-type leases.

Direct Financing Lease (Lessor)

Gross investment
= *total amount lessor receives*
= *MLPs + URV*
= *Lease Receivable*

FMV
= *cost of asset*
= *PV of gross investment*
= *Asset*

0

Unearned interest revenue
•*Recognize as revenue using the (effective) interest method*

Sales-Type Lease (Lessor)

Gross investment
= *total amount lessor receives*
= *MLPs + URV*
= *Lease Receivable*

FMV
= *sales price*
= *PV of MLPs*
= *Sales*

Cost
= *Cost of Goods Sold*

0

Unearned interest revenue
•*Recognize as revenue using the (effective) interest method*

Gross (dealer's) profit
•*Recognize immediately*
•*Sales less CGS on income statement*

A lease is considered to be a sales-type lease from the viewpoint of the lessor if the criteria mentioned earlier for direct financing leases are satisfied. However, in the case of a sales-type lease, the FMV of the asset, which is the sales price in the ordinary course of the lessor's business is **greater than** the cost or carrying value of the leased asset. Because of this difference, a sales-type lease is more complex than a direct financing lease. The journal entries to record a sales-type are

Lease receivable (Gross)	xx	
Sales		xx
Unearned interest		xx
CGS	xx	
Inventory		xx

Note the similarity of these entries to those made for a sale on account. The differences are "lease receivable" instead of "accounts receivable" and the "unearned interest" for the excess of the receivables over the sales price (present value of future payments).

SFAS 13 specifies additional guidelines unique to sales-type leases:

- The lessor bases the lease payment schedule on the amount the lessee would have paid to purchase the asset outright (i.e., the sales price). Therefore, sales are equal to the present value of the minimum lease payments.
- The cost of goods sold to be charged against income is equal to the historic cost or carrying value of the leased asset (most likely inventory) **less** the present value of any unguaranteed residual value.
- The difference between the selling price and cost of goods sold is the gross profit (loss) recognized by the lessor at the inception of the lease.
- When accounting for sales-type leases, guaranteed residual value is considered part of sales revenue because the lessor knows the entire asset has been sold. Unguaranteed residual value, however, is excluded from both sales and cost of sales at its present value because there is less certainty that unguaranteed residual value will be realized.

Numerical Example 3:

Lease Information

Assume same information as in previous example except

1) The cost of the equipment is $100,000 (either manufactured cost or purchase price paid by dealer).
2) The normal selling price of the equipment is $131,858 which is greater than the $100,000 cost.
3) The residual value is **unguaranteed.**
4) The lease payments are $50,000, the same as computed in the previous example, because the lessor treats an **un**guaranteed residual value in the same way as a guaranteed residual value. However, as mentioned below, the present value of the unguaranteed residual value is not included in the 90% test.

Lease Classification

This is a sales-type lease since the 90% test is satisfied; 90% of the $131,858 FMV = $118,672, which is less than $124,345, the present value of the minimum lease payments (see Numerical Example 2); the present value of the residual value is excluded because it is unguaranteed. Additionally, the cost of the asset is less than its fair market value (also the present value of the minimum lease payments plus the unguaranteed residual value). Assume the two additional criteria for the lessor have been satisfied.

Accounting for Lease

1) The gross investment is: $160,000 [3 payments of $50,000 (same as Numerical Example 2) plus a $10,000 unguaranteed residual value]
   The PV of gross investment is: $131,858 [($50,000 x 2.4869) + ($10,000 x .7513)]

The unearned interest revenue is: $28,142 ($160,000 − $131,858)
Sales are: $124,345 [$131,858 − ($10,000 x .7513)*]
CGS is: $92,487 [$100,000 − ($10,000 x .7513)*]

Note that there is no effect on gross profit of not including the present value of the unguaranteed residual value in either sales or cost of goods sold. If the residual value were guaranteed, this adjustment would not be made.

2) The entry to record the lease is

Lease receivable**	160,000	
Cost of goods sold	92,487	
Sales		124,345
Inventory***		100,000
Unearned interest		28,142

**** On the balance sheet this amount is termed gross investment since it includes an unguaranteed residual value.*
***** Either acquisition cost to dealer or manufacturer's cost of production.*

Interest revenue will be recognized at 10% of the outstanding net investment (lease receivable less unearned interest) each period (i.e., interest revenue in year 1 is $131,858 x 10% = $13,186).

At the end of year 1, the following entry(ies) would be made:

Cash	50,000	
Lease receivable		50,000
Unearned interest revenue	13,186	
Interest revenue		13,186

At termination, the lease receivable will have a balance of $10,000 which is the unguaranteed residual value. Note that the same amortization schedule that appears in Numerical Example 2 above is applicable to this one. The fact that the residual value is unguaranteed in this example does not affect the amortization schedule because the lessor is projecting that it will get back an asset worth $10,000. If the asset is returned to the lessor and its fair market value is only $4,000, the following entry is made on the lessor's books:

Loss	6,000	
Residual value of equipment	4,000	
Lease receivable		10,000

Now that we have completed our discussion of lessor's direct financing and sales-type leases, it should be helpful to review the financial statement elements for the lessor, and to preview elements that appear on the lessee's financial statements. These balance sheet elements are shown below.

Lessor

	Direct financing lease	Sales-type lease
Balance sheet:	Lease receivable (current and noncurrent)	Lease receivable (current and noncurrent)
	Initial direct costs (added to net investment causing a new implicit rate of interest)	
	Unearned interest revenue	Unearned interest revenue
Income statement:	Interest revenue	Interest revenue
	Amortization of initial direct costs	Initial direct costs (expensed immediately)
		Dealer's profit

Lessee

Capital lease

Balance *sheet:*	Leased asset (net of accumulated depreciation) Lease obligation (current and noncurrent)
Income *statement:*	Depreciation expense Interest expense Other maintenance expense

(4) **Capital Leases--Lessee**

When a lessor records a direct financing or sales-type lease, the lessee, in turn, must record a capital lease. Capital leases reflect the transfer of risks and benefits associated with the asset to the lessee. A lease is considered to be a capital lease to the lessee if **any one** of the four criteria of SFAS 13 is satisfied.

1.   Transfer of title
2.   Bargain purchase
3.   75% of useful life
4.   90% of net FMV

Lease agreements not meeting at least one of the criteria for capital leases are treated as operating leases on the lessee's books. If the lease is classified as a capital lease, the lessee must record an asset and a liability based on the present value of the minimum lease payments as follows:

Leased asset	(PV of MLP)	
Lease obligation		(PV of MLP)

Note that the above entry reflects recording the transaction "net" (i.e., at present value). If the lease was recorded gross, the lease obligation would be credited for the total amount of the MLP and there would be a debit to "Discount on lease obligation."

Leased asset	(PV of MLP)	
Discount on lease obligation	(PLUG)	
Lease obligation		(gross MLP)

The gross method is similar to the accounting for deferred payment contracts.

To determine the present value of the MLP, the lessee discounts the future payments using the **lesser** of:

1.   The lessee's incremental borrowing rate, **or**
2.   The lessor's implicit rate if known by the lessee

NOTE: Using a lower interest rate increases the present value.

Leased assets, however, should **not** be recorded at an amount greater than the FMV of the asset. If the FMV is less than the PV of the MLP, the lease should be recorded at the FMV and a new implicit interest rate calculated to reflect a constant periodic rate applied to the remaining balance of the obligation.

During the term of the lease, the lessee must use the (effective) interest method to allocate cash paid between interest expense and reduction of the lease obligation. This method is the same as the one used by the lessor as previously described.

Lessees must amortize leased assets recorded on the books under a capital lease. The amortization (depreciation) method used should be consistent with the lessee's normal depreciation policy. The term over which the asset is amortized may differ depending upon which criteria qualified the lease as a capital lease.

1.   If the lease transfers ownership or contains a BPO (criteria 1 or 2), the asset will be amortized over its estimated useful life (since the asset actually becomes the prop-

erty of the lessee at the end of the lease term and will be used for the remainder of its useful life).

2. If the 75% of useful life or the 90% test (criteria 3 or 4) is met, the leased asset is amortized over the lease term only (since the property will revert to the lessor at the end of the lease term and will be used for the remainder of its useful life).

The lease term does not extend beyond the date of a bargain purchase option. Lease terms, however, may include the following:

1. Bargain renewal periods
2. Periods when the lessor has the option to renew or extend
3. Periods during which the lessee guarantees the debt of the lessor
4. Periods in which a material penalty exists for failure to renew

When the lease terminates, the balance in the obligation account should equal the bargain purchase option price or the expected residual value (guaranteed residual value, or salvage value if lower).

Leased assets and obligations should be disclosed as such in the balance sheet. The lease obligation should be separated into both current and noncurrent components.

Numerical Example 4:

Lease Information

1) A 3-year lease is initiated on 1/1/99 for equipment with an expected useful life of 5 years. The equipment reverts back to the lessor upon expiration of the lease agreement.
2) Three payments are due to the lessor in the amount of $50,000 per year beginning 12/31/99. An additional sum of $1,000 is to be paid annually by the lessee for insurance.
3) Lessee guarantees a $10,000 residual value on 12/31/01 to the lessor.
4) The leased asset is expected to have only a $7,000 salvage value on 12/31/01 despite the $10,000 residual value guarantee; therefore, the asset should be depreciated down to the $7,000 expected residual value.
5) The lessee's incremental borrowing rate is 10% (same as lessor's implicit rate).
6) The present value of the lease obligation is

PV of guaranteed residual value	=	$10,000	x	.7513	=	$	7,513
PV of annual payments	=	$50,000	x	2.4869	=		124,345
							$131,858

Note that since the lessee's incremental borrowing rate is 10% and the residual value is guaranteed, the present value of $131,858 is the same amount used by the lessor in the direct financing lease example (Numerical Example 2) to determine the payments to be made by the lessee. If an incremental borrowing rate different than the lessor's is used and/or the lease contains an unguaranteed residual value, the present value computed by the lessee will differ from the lessor's present value (FMV). These differences account for the fact that many leases are not capitalized by lessees because they don't meet the 90% test.

Lease Classification

The 90% test is met because the present value of the minimum lease payments ($131,858) is 100% of the FMV of the leased asset.

Accounting for Lease

1) Note that executory costs (e.g., insurance, property taxes, etc.) are not included in the present value calculations
2) The entry to recognize the lease is

1/1/99	Leased equipment	131,858	
	Lease obligation		131,858

3) The entries to record the payments and depreciation are

	12/31/99		12/31/00		12/31/01	
Insurance expense	1,000		1,000		1,000	
Lease obligation*	36,814		40,496		44,548	
Interest expense*	13,186		9,504		5,452	
Cash		51,000		51,000		51,000
Depreciation expense**	41,619		41,619		41,620	
Accumulated depreciation		41,619		41,619		41,620***

* *Refer to the amortization table in the direct financing lease discussion (Numeric Example 2). Note that classification of the lease obligation into current and noncurrent on the lessee's books would parallel classification of the lease receivable on the lessor's books.*

** *[($131,858 – 7,000) ÷ 3 years]*

*** *Rounding error of $1*

4) The 12/31/01 entry to record the guaranteed residual value payment (assuming salvage value = estimated residual value = $7,000) and to clear the lease related accounts from the lessee's books is

Lease obligation	10,000	
Accumulated depreciation	124,858	
Cash		3,000
Leased equipment		131,858

If the actual residual value were only $5,000, the credit to "cash" would be $5,000 and a $2,000 loss would be recognized by the lessee.

Remember that leased assets are amortized over the lease term unless title transfers or a bargain purchase option exists--then over the useful life of the leased asset. At the end of the lease, the balance of the lease obligation should equal the guaranteed residual value or the bargain purchase option price. To illustrate, consider the example below.

Numerical Example 5:

Lease Information
1) A 3-year lease is initiated on 1/1/99 for equipment with an expected useful life of 5 years.
2) Three annual $50,000 payments are due the lessor beginning 1/1/99.
3) The lessee can exercise a bargain purchase option on 12/31/01 for $10,000. The expected residual value at 12/31/03 is $1,000.
4) The lessee's incremental borrowing rate is 10% (lessor's implicit rate is unknown).

Lease Classification
Although the lease term is for only 60% of the asset's useful life, the lessee would account for this as a capital lease because it contains a bargain purchase option.

Accounting for Lease
1) The present value of the lease obligation is

PV of bargain purchase option	=	$10,000	x	.7513	=	$ 7,513
PV of annual payments	=	$50,000	x	2.7355	=	136,775
						$144,288

2) The following amortization table summarizes the liability amortization:

AMORTIZATION TABLE

Carrying value at beg. of yr. 1		$144,288
Lease payment	$(50,000)	(50,000)
Carrying value at beg. of yr. 1 after first payment		94,288
Interest expense	9,429	
Lease payment	(50,000)	(40,571)
Carrying value at beg. of year 2 after second payment		53,717
Interest expense	5,372	
Lease payment	(50,000)	(44,628)
Carrying value at beg. of yr. 3 after third payment		9,089
Interest expense	911*	911
Bargain purchase option		10,000
Option payment	(10,000)	(10,000)
		-0-

* Rounding error of $2

NOTE: *This table reflects the fact that the lease is an annuity due with cash payments on 1/1 and interest expense accruals on 12/31; thus, the first payment does not include any interest expense.*

3) The entry to record the lease is

1/1/99	Leased equipment	144,288	
	Lease obligation		144,288

4) The entries to record the payments, interest expense, depreciation (amortization) expense, and the exercise of the bargain purchase are

		1999		2000		2001	
1/1	Lease obligation	50,000		40,571		44,628	
	Accrued interest payable or interest expense*			9,429		5,372	
	Cash		50,000		50,000		50,000
12/31	Interest expense	9,429		5,372		911	
	Accrued int. payable		9,429		5,372		
	Lease obligation						911
12/31	Depreciation expense**	28,658		28,658		28,658	
	Accumulated depreciation		28,658		28,658		28,658
12/31	Lease obligation					10,000	
	Cash						10,000

*If 12/31 accruals are reversed
**(143,288 ÷ 5 years)

2. Other Considerations

To supplement the review of lease accounting presented above, the following topics have been selected for further discussion:

 a. Initial direct costs
 b. Sale-leaseback
 c. Disclosure requirements

a. Initial direct costs

Initial direct costs are the lessor's costs directly associated with negotiation and consummation of leases. These costs include commissions, legal fees, credit investigations, document preparation, etc. In operating leases, initial direct costs are capitalized and subsequently amortized to expense in proportion to the recognition of rental revenue (which is usually straight-line).

Initial direct costs of direct financing and sales-type leases are accounted for differently: (1) In sales-type leases, charge initial direct costs to operations in the year the sale is recorded; (2) In direct financing leases add the initial direct costs to the net investment in the lease. Compute a new effective interest rate that equates the minimum lease payments and any unguaranteed residual value with the combined outlay for the leased asset and initial direct costs. Finally, the unearned lease (interest) revenue and the initial direct costs are to be amortized to income over the lease term so that a constant periodic rate is earned on the net investment.

b. **Sale-leaseback**

Sale-leaseback describes a transaction where the owner of property (seller-lessee) sells the property, and then immediately leases all or part of it back from the new owner (buyer-lessor). The important consideration in this type of transaction is the recognition of two separate and distinct economic transactions. It is important, however, to note that there is not a physical transfer of property. First, there is a sale of property, and second, there is a lease agreement for the same property in which the seller is the lessee and the buyer is the lessor. This is illustrated below.

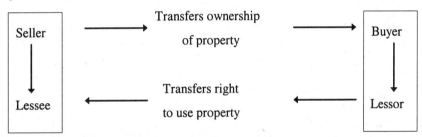

Note that sale-leaseback transactions only affect accounting for the seller-lessee. Buyer-lessor accounting is unaffected.

The accounting treatment from the seller-lessee's point of view will depend upon the degree of rights to use the property retained by the seller-lessee. The degree of rights may be categorized in one of three ways:

1. Substantially all
2. Minor
3. More than minor but less than substantially all

A seller-lessee retains **substantially all** the rights to use the property if the PV of the rental payments is 90% or more of the fair value of the asset sold. This test is based on the criteria used earlier to classify leases. Since the seller-lessee retains use of the asset, this type of sale-leaseback is considered, in substance, a form of financing to the seller-lessee rather than a sale. In this case, any gain on the sale is deferred by the seller-lessee.

Cash	(selling price)
Asset	(carrying value)
Deferred gain	(excess)

The asset would be reported on the seller-lessee's balance sheet as follows:

Leased asset	xx
Less: Deferred gain	(xx)
	xx

The net value of the leased asset is the same amount the asset would be if it had not been sold.

If the lease is classified as a capital lease, the deferred gain is amortized over the life of the asset at the same rate as the asset is being depreciated. As deferred gain is amortized, it is charged to depreciation expense.

Deferred gain	xx	
Depreciation expense		xx

Alternatively, the gain may be recognized as income over the term of the lease.

Although most leases in the "substantially all" category are capital leases, a sale-leaseback occurring in the last 25% of an asset's economic life would be classified as an operating lease.

If the lease is classified as an operating lease, any deferred gain is amortized over the lease term in proportion to the related gross rental charges to expense over the lease term. Amortization in this case is charged to rent expense by the seller-lessee.

Deferred gain	xx	
Rent expense		xx

The seller-lessee retains only a **minor** portion of rights to use the property when the PV of the rental payments is 10% or less of the fair value of the asset sold. Since the seller-lessee has given up the right to use the asset, the leaseback is considered in substance a sale. Any gain on the sale is recognized in full since the earnings process is considered complete.

Cash	(selling price)
Asset	(carrying value)
Gain	(excess)

When only a minor portion of use is retained, the seller-lessee accounts for the lease as an operating lease.

The seller-lessee retains **more than a minor portion but less than substantially all** the rights to use the property when the PV of the rental payments is more than 10% but less than 90% of the fair value of the asset sold. In this situation, gain is recognized only to the extent that it exceeds the PV of the rental payments.

Cash	(selling price)
Asset	(carrying value)
Deferred gain	(PV of rental payments)
Gain	(excess)

Recognized gain for capital and operating leases is derived as follows:

1. If the leaseback is classified as an operating lease, recognized gain is the portion of gain that exceeds the PV of the MLP over the lease term. The seller-lessee should use its incremental borrowing rate to compute the PV of the MLP. If the implicit rate of interest in the lease is known and lower, it should be used instead.
2. If the leaseback is classified as a capital lease, recognized gain is the amount of gain that exceeds the recorded amount of the leased asset.

In all cases, the seller-lessee should immediately recognize a loss when the fair value of the property at the time of the leaseback is less than its undepreciated cost (book value). In the example below, the sales price is less than the book value of the property. However, there is no economic loss because the FMV which equals the PV is greater than the book value.

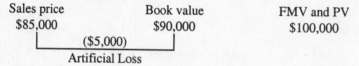

Sales price	Book value	FMV and PV
$85,000	$90,000	$100,000

The artificial loss must be deferred and amortized as an addition to depreciation.

In the chart below, when the leased asset is land only, any amortization should be on a straight-line basis over the lease term, regardless of whether the lease is classified as a capital or operating lease.

The buyer-lessor should account for the transaction as a purchase and a direct financing lease if the agreement meets the criteria of **either** a direct financing lease **or** a sales-type lease. Otherwise, the agreement should be accounted for as a purchase and an operating lease.

To illustrate a sale-leaseback transaction, consider the example below.

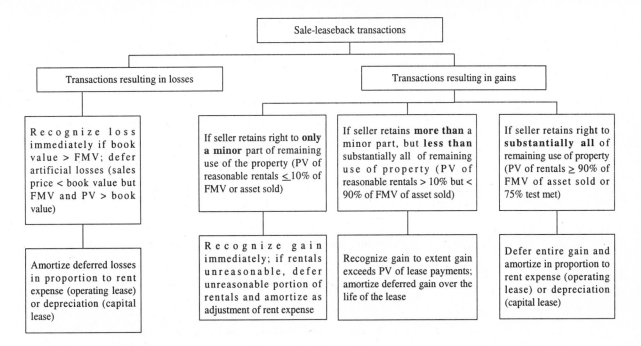

Numerical Example 6:

Lease Information

1) Lessee Corporation sells equipment that has a book value of $80,000 and a fair value of $100,000 to Lessor Corporation, and then immediately leases it back.

2) The sale date is January 1, 1999, and the equipment has a fair value of $100,000 on that date and an estimated useful life of 15 years.

3) The lease term is 15 years, noncancelable, and requires equal rental payments of $13,109 at the beginning of each year.

4) Lessee Corp. has the option to renew the lease annually at the same rental payments upon expiration of the original lease.

5) Lessee Corp. has the obligation to pay all executory costs.

6) The annual rental payments provide the lessor with a 12% return on investment.

7) The incremental borrowing rate of Lessee Corp. is 12%.

8) Lessee Corp. depreciates similar equipment on a straight-line basis.

Lease Classification

Lessee Corp. should classify the agreement as a capital lease since the lease term exceeds 75% of the estimated economic life of the equipment, and because the present value of the lease payments is greater than 90% of the fair value of the equipment. Assuming that collectibility of the lease payments is reasonably predictable and that no important uncertainties exist concerning the amount of unreimbursable costs yet to be incurred by the lessor, Lessor Corp. should classify the transaction as a direct financing lease because the present value of the minimum lease payments is equal to the fair market value of $100,000.

Accounting for Lease

Lessee Corp. and Lessor Corp. would normally make the following journal entries during the first year:

Upon Sale of Equipment on January 1, 1999

	Lessee Corp.			Lessor Corp.	
Cash	100,000		Equipment	100,000	
Equipment		80,000	Cash		100,000
Unearned profit on			Lease receivable	196,635*	
sale-leaseback		20,000	Equipment		100,000
Leased equipment	100,000		Unearned interest		96,635
Lease obligations		100,000			

*($13,109 x 15)

To Record First Payment on January 1, 1999

	Lessee Corp.			Lessor Corp.	
Lease obligations	13,109		Cash	13,109	
Cash		13,109	Lease receivable		13,109

To Record Incurrence and Payment of Executory Costs

	Lessee Corp.		Lessor Corp.
Insurance, taxes, etc.	xxx		(No entry)
Cash (accounts			
payable)		xxx	

To Record Depreciation Expense on the Equipment, December 31, 1999

	Lessee Corp.		Lessor Corp.
Depreciation expense	6,667		(No entry)
Accum. depr. --			
capital leases			
($100,000 ÷ 15)		6,667	

To Amortize Profit on Sale-Leaseback by Lessee Corp., December 31, 1999

	Lessee Corp.		Lessor Corp.
Unearned profit on			(No entry)
sale-leaseback	1,333		
Depr. expense			
($20,000 ÷ 15)		1,333	

To Record Interest for 1999, December 31, 1999

	Lessee Corp.			Lessor Corp.	
Interest expense	10,427		Unearned interest		
Accrued interest			income	10,427	
payable		10,427	Interest income		10,427

(Carrying value $86,891 x .12 = $10,427)

c. **Disclosure requirements**

    The disclosures required of the lessor and lessee are very comprehensive and detailed. In essence, all terms of the leasing arrangement are required (i.e., contingent rentals, subleases, residual values, unearned interest revenue, etc.). For the details see the outline of SFAS 13 (D.5.). There are, however, a couple of generic disclosure requirements. First, a **general description** of the leasing arrangement is required. Second, the minimum future payments to be received (paid) by the lessor (lessee) for each of the **5 succeeding fiscal years** should also be disclosed.

SUMMARY OF KEY PROBLEM SOLUTION POINTS

- *Lessor--direct financing and sales-type leases*

  - Periodic lease payments (PLP) $\quad=\quad$ $\dfrac{\text{FMV of leased property} - \text{PV of RV*/BPO}}{\begin{bmatrix}\text{PV of an annuity factor** using} \\ \text{the lessor's implicit rate}\end{bmatrix}}$

    *guaranteed/unguaranteed

    **annuity due or ordinary

- Lease payments receivable/   = $\begin{bmatrix} \text{Periodic lease} & \times & \text{Number} \\ \text{payments} & & \text{of rents} \end{bmatrix}$ +   Residual value/
  Gross investment   Bar. Pur. Opt.

- Unearned interest revenue   =   Gross investment   –   PV of PLP,
                                                                            PV of G/UC RV,
                                                                            PV of BPO

- Net investment   =   Gross investment   –   Unearned interest
                                                                                                revenue

- Gross profit   =   Selling price*   –   Cost of leased asset sold
  (only for sales-
  type leases)   *   *(FMV/PV of PLP + G/UGRV + BPO)*

- Interest revenue   = $\begin{bmatrix} \text{Carrying value} \\ \text{of lease} \\ \text{receivable*} \end{bmatrix}$ x   Implicit % x Time

           * *(Gross investment – Unearned interest)*

Periodic Journal Entries:

Unearned interest revenue	xxx	
Interest revenue		xxx
Cash	xxx	
Lease payments receivable		xxx

- **Lessee--Capital Lease**

  - Determine capital lease liability   = $\begin{pmatrix} \text{Periodic} \\ \text{lease} \\ \text{payment (PLP)} \end{pmatrix} \times \begin{pmatrix} \text{Present} \\ \text{value} \\ \text{factor*} \end{pmatrix} + \begin{bmatrix} \text{G/UGRV} & & \text{PV} \\ \text{OR} & \times & \text{of} \\ \text{BPO} & & \text{1.00} \\ & & \text{factor} \end{bmatrix}$

       * *Annuity Due or Ordinary Annuity*

    - Use lessee's incremental borrowing %, unless lessor's implicit % is lower and lessee knows it

    - PLP is exclusive of executory costs

  - Leased asset   =   Capital lease liability at inception of lease as com-puted above--PV x MLP [Exception: where FMV of leased asset < PV of MLP (PLP + Guar. RV or BPO), then leased asset and capital lease liability are recorded at the FMV of leased asset.]

  - Depreciation (amortization) of leased asset
    - Over useful life, regardless of lease term, if either cri-terion (1) or (2) is met: title transfer or bargain pur-chase option.
    - Over lease term if criterion (3) or (4) is met: $\geq 75\%$ test or $\geq 90\%$ test

- Lease liability   =   (1) Carrying value at inception of lease $xxx

                                   (2) Less first payment (usually the first payment is all principal because the lease liability is the PV of an annuity due)   (xx)

                                   (3) Carrying value (CV) $xxx

- CV x % = Interest expense   (4) Less principal part of 2**nd** payment [PLP – (CV x interest %)]   (xxx)

                                   (5) Carrying value $xxx

                                                           etc.

MULTIPLE-CHOICE QUESTIONS (1-52)

 7

1. Rapp Co. leased a new machine to Lake Co. on January 1, 1999. The lease expires on January 1, 2004. The annual rental is $90,000. Additionally, on January 1, 1999, Lake paid $50,000 to Rapp as a lease bonus and $25,000 as a security deposit to be refunded upon expiration of the lease. In Rapp's 1999 income statement, the amount of rental revenue should be

    a. $140,000
    b. $125,000
    c. $100,000
    d. $ 90,000

2. Wall Co. leased office premises to Fox, Inc. for a 5-year term beginning January 2, 1999. Under the terms of the operating lease, rent for the first year is $8,000 and rent for years 2 through 5 is $12,500 per annum. However, as an inducement to enter the lease, Wall granted Fox the first 6 months of the lease rent-free. In its December 31, 1999 income statement, what amount should Wall report as rental income?

    a. $12,000
    b. $11,600
    c. $10,800
    d. $ 8,000

3. On January 1, 1999, Wren Co. leased a building to Brill under an operating lease for 10 years at $50,000 per year, payable the first day of each lease year. Wren paid $15,000 to a real estate broker as a finder's fee. The building is depreciated $12,000 per year. For 1999, Wren incurred insurance and property tax expense totaling $9,000. Wren's net rental income for 1999 should be

    a. $27,500
    b. $29,000
    c. $35,000
    d. $36,500

4. On July 1, 1997, Gee, Inc. leased a delivery truck from Marr Corp. under a 3-year operating lease. Total rent for the term of the lease will be $36,000, payable as follows:

12 months at $ 500 = $ 6,000
12 months at $ 750 =   9,000
12 months at $1,750 = 21,000

All payments were made when due. In Marr's June 30, 1999 balance sheet, the accrued rent receivable should be reported as

    a. $0
    b. $ 9,000
    c. $12,000
    d. $21,000

5. On January 1, 1999, Glen Co. leased a building to Dix Corp. for a 10-year term at an annual rental of $50,000. At inception of the lease, Glen received $200,000 covering the first 2 years' rent of $100,000 and a security deposit of $100,000. This deposit will not be returned to Dix upon expiration of the lease but will be applied to payment of rent for the last 2 years of the lease. What portion of the $200,000 should be shown as a current and long-term liabil-

ity, respectively, in Glen's December 31, 1999 balance sheet?

	Current liability	Long-term liability
a.	$0	$200,000
b.	$ 50,000	$100,000
c.	$100,000	$100,000
d.	$100,000	$ 50,000

6. As an inducement to enter a lease, Graf Co., a lessor, granted Zep, Inc., a lessee, 12 months of free rent under a 5-year operating lease. The lease was effective on January 1, 1999, and provides for monthly rental payments to begin January 1, 2000. Zep made the first rental payment on December 30, 1999. In its 1999 income statement, Graf should report rental revenue in an amount equal to

    a. Zero.
    b. Cash received during 1999.
    c. One-fourth of the total cash to be received over the life of the lease.
    d. One-fifth of the total cash to be received over the life of the lease.

7. Quo Co. rented a building to Hava Fast Food. Each month Quo receives a fixed rental amount plus a variable rental amount based on Hava's sales for that month. As sales increase so does the variable rental amount, but at a reduced rate. Which of the following curves reflects the monthly rentals under the agreement?

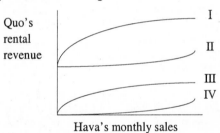

    a. I
    b. II
    c. III
    d. IV

8. As an inducement to enter a lease, Arts, Inc., a lessor, grants Hompson Corp., a lessee, 9 months of free rent under a 5-year operating lease. The lease is effective on July 1, 1999 and provides for monthly rental of $1,000 to begin April 1, 2000. In Hompson's income statement for the year ended June 30, 2000, rent expense should be reported as

    a. $10,200
    b. $ 9,000
    c. $ 3,000
    d. $ 2,550

9. On January 1, 1999, Park Co. signed a 10-year operating lease for office space at $96,000 per year. The lease included a provision for additional rent of 5% of annual company sales in excess of $500,000. Park's sales for the year ended December 31, 1999 were $600,000. Upon execution of the lease, Park paid $24,000 as a bonus for the lease. Park's rent expense for the year ended December 31, 1999 is

    a. $ 98,400
    b. $101,000

c. $103,400
d. $125,000

10. On July 1, 1999, South Co. entered into a 10-year oper-ating lease for a warehouse facility. The annual minimum lease payments are $100,000. In addition to the base rent, South pays a monthly allocation of the building's operating expenses, which amounted to $20,000 for the year ended June 30, 2000. In the notes to South's June 30, 2000 finan-cial statements, what amounts of subsequent years' lease payments should be disclosed?
a. $100,000 per annum for each of the next 5 years and $500,000 in the aggregate.
b. $120,000 per annum for each of the next 5 years and $600,000 in the aggregate.
c. $100,000 per annum for each of the next 5 years and $900,000 in the aggregate.
d. $120,000 per annum for each of the next 5 years and $1,080,000 in the aggregate.

11. On January 1, 1999, Mollat Co. signed a 7-year lease for equipment having a 10-year economic life. The present value of the monthly lease payments equaled 80% of the equipment's fair value. The lease agreement provides for neither a transfer of title to Mollat nor a bargain purchase option. In its 1999 income statement Mollat should report
a.   Rent expense equal to the 1999 lease payments.
b.   Rent expense equal to the 1999 lease payments less interest expense.
c.   Lease amortization equal to one-tenth of the equipment's fair value.
d.   Lease amortization equal to one-seventh of 80% of the equipment's fair value.

12. A 20-year property lease, classified as an operating lease, provides for a 10% increase in annual payments every 5 years. In the sixth year compared to the fifth year, the lease will cause the following expenses to increase

	Rent	Interest
a.	No	Yes
b.	Yes	No
c.	Yes	Yes
d.	No	No

13. On December 1, 1999, Clark Co. leased office space for 5 years at a monthly rental of $60,000. On the same date, Clark paid the lessor the following amounts:

First month's rent	$ 60,000
Last month's rent	60,000
Security deposit (refundable at lease expiration)	80,000
Installation of new walls and offices	360,000

What should be Clark's 1999 expense relating to utilization of the office space?
a. $ 60,000
b. $ 66,000
c. $120,000
d. $140,000

14. Star Co. leases a building for its product showroom. The 10-year nonrenewable lease will expire on Decem-ber 31, 2004. In January 1999, Star redecorated its show-room and made leasehold improvements of $48,000. The estimated useful life of the improvements is 8 years. Star uses the straight-line method of amortization. What amount of leasehold improvements, net of amortization, should Star report in its June 30, 1999 balance sheet?
a. $45,600
b. $45,000
c. $44,000
d. $43,200

15. On January 2, 1999, Ral Co. leased land and building from an unrelated lessor for a 10-year term. The lease has a renewal option for an additional 10 years, but Ral has not reached a decision with regard to the renewal option. In early January of 1999, Ral completed the following im-provements to the property:

Description	Estimated life	Cost
Sales office	10 years	$47,000
Warehouse	25 years	75,000
Parking lot	15 years	18,000

Amortization of leasehold improvements for 2000 should be
a. $ 7,000
b. $ 8,900
c. $12,200
d. $14,000

16. On January 1, 1997, Nobb Corp. signed a 12-year lease for warehouse space. Nobb has an option to renew the lease for an additional 8-year period on or before January 1, 2001. During January 1999, Nobb made substantial improvements to the warehouse. The cost of these improvements was $540,000, with an estimated useful life of 15 years. At De-cember 31, 1999, Nobb intended to exercise the renewal option. Nobb has taken a full year's amortization on this leasehold. In Nobb's December 31, 1999 balance sheet, the carrying amount of this leasehold improvement should be
a. $486,000
b. $504,000
c. $510,000
d. $513,000

17. During January 1999, Vail Co. made long-term im-provements to a recently leased building. The lease agree-ment provides for neither a transfer of title to Vail nor a bargain purchase option. The present value of the minimum lease payments equals 85% of the building's market value, and the lease term equals 70% of the building's economic life. Should assets be recognized for the building and the leasehold improvements?

	Building	Leasehold improvements
a.	Yes	Yes
b.	No	Yes
c.	Yes	No
d.	No	No

18. A lessee incurred costs to construct office space in a leased warehouse. The estimated useful life of the office is 10 years. The remaining term of the nonrenewable lease is 15 years. The costs should be
a.   Capitalized as leasehold improvements and depre-ciated over 15 years.
b.   Capitalized as leasehold improvements and depre-ciated over 10 years.

c.   Capitalized as leasehold improvements and expensed in the year in which the lease expires.

d.   Expensed as incurred.

19. Glade Co. leases computer equipment to customers under direct-financing leases. The equipment has no residual value at the end of the lease and the leases do not contain bargain purchase options. Glade wishes to earn 8% interest on a 5-year lease of equipment with a fair value of $323,400. The present value of an annuity due of $1 at 8% for 5 years is 4.312. What is the total amount of interest revenue that Glade will earn over the life of the lease?

a. $ 51,600
b. $ 75,000
c. $129,360
d. $139,450

20. On January 1, 1997, JCK Co. signed a contract for an 8-year lease of its equipment with a 10-year life. The present value of the 16 equal semiannual payments in advance equaled 85% of the equipment's fair value. The contract had no provision for JCK, the lessor, to give up legal ownership of the equipment. Should JCK recognize rent or interest revenue in 1999, and should the revenue recognized in 1999 be the same or smaller than the revenue recognized in 1998?

	1999 revenues recognized	1999 amount recognized compared to 1998
a.	Rent	The same
b.	Rent	Smaller
c.	Interest	The same
d.	Interest	Smaller

21. Peg Co. leased equipment from Howe Corp. on July 1, 1999 for an 8-year period expiring June 30, 2007. Equal payments under the lease are $600,000 and are due on July 1 of each year. The first payment was made on July 1, 1999. The rate of interest contemplated by Peg and Howe is 10%. The cash selling price of the equipment is $3,520,000, and the cost of the equipment on Howe's accounting records is $2,800,000. The lease is appropriately recorded as a sales-type lease. What is the amount of profit on the sale and interest revenue that Howe should record for the year ended December 31, 1999?

	Profit on sale	Interest revenue
a.	$720,000	$176,000
b.	$720,000	$146,000
c.	$ 45,000	$176,000
d.	$ 45,000	$146,000

22. Howe Co. leased equipment to Kew Corp. on January 2, 1999, for an 8-year period expiring December 31, 2006. Equal payments under the lease are $600,000 and are due on January 2 of each year. The first payment was made on January 2, 1999. The list selling price of the equipment is $3,520,000 and its carrying cost on Howe's books is $2,800,000. The lease is appropriately accounted for as a sales-type lease. The present value of the lease payments is $3,300,000. What amount of profit on the sale should Howe report for the year ended December 31, 1999?

a. $720,000
b. $500,000

c. $ 90,000
d. $0

23. The excess of the fair value of leased property at the inception of the lease over its cost or carrying amount should be classified by the lessor as

a.   Unearned income from a sales-type lease.
b.   Unearned income from a direct-financing lease.
c.   Manufacturer's or dealer's profit from a sales-type lease.
d.   Manufacturer's or dealer's profit from a direct-financing lease.

24. In a lease that is recorded as a sales-type lease by the lessor, interest revenue

a.   Should be recognized in full as revenue at the lease's inception.
b.   Should be recognized over the period of the lease using the straight-line method.
c.   Should be recognized over the period of the lease using the interest method.
d.   Does **not** arise.

25. Lease M does not contain a bargain purchase option, but the lease term is equal to 90% of the estimated economic life of the leased property. Lease P does not transfer ownership of the property to the lessee at the end of the lease term, but the lease term is equal to 75% of the estimated economic life of the leased property. How should the lessee classify these leases?

	Lease M	Lease P
a.	Capital lease	Operating lease
b.	Capital lease	Capital lease
c.	Operating lease	Capital lease
d.	Operating lease	Operating lease

26. On December 31, 1999, Day Co. leased a new machine from Parr with the following pertinent information:

Lease term	6 years
Annual rental payable at beginning of each year	$50,000
Useful life of machine	8 years
Day's incremental borrowing rate	15%
Implicit interest rate in lease (known by Day)	12%
Present value of annuity of 1 in advance for 6 periods at	
12%	4.61
15%	4.35

The lease is not renewable, and the machine reverts to Parr at the termination of the lease. The cost of the machine on Parr's accounting records is $375,500. At the beginning of the lease term, Day should record a lease liability of

a. $375,500
b. $230,500
c. $217,500
d. $0

27. On January 1, 1999, Day Corp. entered into a 10-year lease agreement with Ward, Inc. for industrial equipment. Annual lease payments of $10,000 are payable at the end of each year. Day knows that the lessor expects a 10% return on the lease. Day has a 12% incremental borrowing rate. The equipment is expected to have an estimated useful life of 10 years. In addition, a third party has guaranteed to pay Ward a residual value of $5,000 at the end of the lease.

The present value of an ordinary annuity of $1 at
    12% for 10 years is 5.6502
    10% for 10 years is 6.1446

The present value of $1 at
    12% for 10 years is .3220
    10% for 10 years is .3855

In Day's October 31, 1999 balance sheet, the principal amount of the lease obligation was
    a. $63,374
    b. $61,446
    c. $58,112
    d. $56,502

28. Robbins, Inc. leased a machine from Ready Leasing Co. The lease qualifies as a capital lease and requires 10 annual payments of $10,000 beginning immediately. The lease specifies an interest rate of 12% and a purchase option of $10,000 at the end of the tenth year, even though the machine's estimated value on that date is $20,000. Robbins' incremental borrowing rate is 14%.

The present value of an annuity due of 1 at:
    12% for 10 years is 6.328
    14% for 10 years is 5.946

The present value of 1 at:
    12% for 10 years is .322
    14% for 10 years is .270

What amount should Robbins record as lease liability at the beginning of the lease term?
    a. $62,160
    b. $64,860
    c. $66,500
    d. $69,720

29. Neal Corp. entered into a 9-year capital lease on a warehouse on December 31, 1999. Lease payments of $52,000, which includes real estate taxes of $2,000, are due annually, beginning on December 31, 2000, and every December 31 thereafter. Neal does not know the interest rate implicit in the lease; Neal's incremental borrowing rate is 9%. The rounded present value of an ordinary annuity for nine years at 9% is 5.6. What amount should Neal report as capitalized lease liability at December 31, 1999?
    a. $280,000
    b. $291,200
    c. $450,000
    d. $468,000

30. East Company leased a new machine from North Company on May 1, 1999, under a lease with the following information:

Lease term	10 years
Annual rental payable atbeginning of each lease year	$40,000
Useful life of machine	12 years
Implicit interest rate	14%

Present value of an annuity of 1 in advance
    for 10 periods at 14%   5.95
Present value of 1 for 10 periods at 14%   0.27

East has the option to purchase the machine on May 1, 2009 by paying $50,000, which approximates the expected fair value of the machine on the option exercise date. On May 1, 1999, East should record a capitalized lease asset of
    a. $251,500
    b. $238,000
    c. $224,500
    d. $198,000

31. On January 1, 1999, Babson, Inc. leased two automobiles for executive use. The lease requires Babson to make 5 annual payments of $13,000 beginning January 1, 1999. At the end of the lease term, December 31, 2003, Babson guarantees the residual value of the automobiles will total $10,000. The lease qualifies as a capital lease. The interest rate implicit in the lease is 9%. Present value factors for the 9% rate implicit in the lease are as follows:

For an annuity due with 5 payments	4.240
For an ordinary annuity with 5 payments	3.890
Present value of $1 for 5 periods	0.650

Babson's recorded capital lease liability immediately after the first required payment should be
    a. $48,620
    b. $44,070
    c. $35,620
    d. $31,070

32. On December 30, 1999, Rafferty Corp. leased equipment under a capital lease. Annual lease payments of $20,000 are due December 31 for 10 years. The equipment's useful life is 10 years, and the interest rate implicit in the lease is 10%. The capital lease obligation was recorded on December 30, 1999, at $135,000, and the first lease payment was made on that date. What amount should Rafferty include in current liabilities for this capital lease in its December 31, 1999 balance sheet?
    a. $ 6,500
    b. $ 8,500
    c. $11,500
    d. $20,000

33. Oak Co. leased equipment for its entire 9-year useful life, agreeing to pay $50,000 at the start of the lease term on December 31, 1998, and $50,000 annually on each December 31 for the next 8 years. The present value on December 31, 1998, of the 9 lease payments over the lease term, using the rate implicit in the lease which Oak knows to be 10%, was $316,500. The December 31, 1998 present value of the lease payments using Oak's incremental borrowing rate of 12% was $298,500. Oak made a timely second lease payment. What amount should Oak report as capital lease liability in its December 31, 1999 balance sheet?
    a. $350,000
    b. $243,150
    c. $228,320
    d. $0

34. On December 31, 1998, Roe Co. leased a machine from Colt for a 5-year period. Equal annual payments under the lease are $105,000 (including $5,000 annual executory costs) and are due on December 31 of each year. The first payment was made on December 31, 1998, and the second payment was made on December 31, 1999. The 5 lease payments are discounted at 10% over the lease term. The present value of minimum lease payments at the inception of the lease and before the first annual payment was $417,000. The lease is appropriately accounted for as a capital lease by Roe. In its December 31, 1999 balance sheet, Roe should report a lease liability of

- a. $317,000
- b. $315,000
- c. $285,300
- d. $248,700

35. In the long-term liabilities section of its balance sheet at December 31, 1998, Mene Co. reported a capital lease obligation of $75,000, net of current portion of $1,364. Payments of $9,000 were made on both January 2, 1999, and January 2, 2000. Mene's incremental borrowing rate on the date of the lease was 11% and the lessor's implicit rate, which was known to Mene, was 10%. In its December 31, 1999 balance sheet, what amount should Mene report as capital lease obligation, net of current portion?

- a. $66,000
- b. $73,500
- c. $73,636
- d. $74,250

36. For a capital lease, the amount recorded initially by the lessee as a liability should normally

- a. Exceed the total of the minimum lease payments.
- b. Exceed the present value of the minimum lease payments at the beginning of the lease.
- c. Equal the total of the minimum lease payments.
- d. Equal the present value of the minimum lease payments at the beginning of the lease.

37. At the inception of a capital lease, the guaranteed residual value should be

- a. Included as part of minimum lease payments at present value.
- b. Included as part of minimum lease payments at future value.
- c. Included as part of minimum lease payments only to the extent that guaranteed residual value is expected to exceed estimated residual value.
- d. Excluded from minimum lease payments.

38. A 6-year capital lease entered into on December 31, 1999, specified equal minimum annual lease payments due on December 31 of each year. The first minimum annual lease payment, paid on December 31, 1999, consists of which of the following?

	Interest expense	Lease liability
a.	Yes	Yes
b.	Yes	No
c.	No	Yes
d.	No	No

39. A 6-year capital lease expiring on December 31 specifies equal minimum annual lease payments. Part of this payment represents interest and part represents a reduction

in the net lease liability. The portion of the minimum lease payment in the fifth year applicable to the reduction of the net lease liability should be

- a. Less than in the fourth year.
- b. More than in the fourth year.
- c. The same as in the sixth year.
- d. More than in the sixth year.

40. A lessee had a 10-year capital lease requiring equal annual payments. The reduction of the lease liability in year 2 should equal

- a. The current liability shown for the lease at the end of year 1.
- b. The current liability shown for the lease at the end of year 2.
- c. The reduction of the lease obligation in year 1.
- d. One-tenth of the original lease liability.

41. On January 2, 1999, Cole Co. signed an 8-year noncancelable lease for a new machine, requiring $15,000 annual payments at the beginning of each year. The machine has a useful life of 12 years, with no salvage value. Title passes to Cole at the lease expiration date. Cole uses straight-line depreciation for all of its plant assets. Aggregate lease payments have a present value on January 2, 1999, of $108,000 based on an appropriate rate of interest. For 1999, Cole should record depreciation (amortization) expense for the leased machine at

- a. $0
- b. $ 9,000
- c. $13,500
- d. $15,000

42. On January 2, 1999, Nori Mining Co. (lessee) entered into a 5-year lease for drilling equipment. Nori accounted for the acquisition as a capital lease for $240,000, which includes a $10,000 bargain purchase option. At the end of the lease, Nori expects to exercise the bargain purchase option. Nori estimates that the equipment's fair value will be $20,000 at the end of its 8-year life. Nori regularly uses straight-line depreciation on similar equipment. For the year ended December 31, 1999, what amount should Nori recognize as depreciation expense on the leased asset?

- a. $48,000
- b. $46,000
- c. $30,000
- d. $27,500

43. The lessee should amortize the capitalizable cost of the leased asset in a manner consistent with the lessee's normal depreciation policy for owned assets for leases that

	Contain a bargain purchase option	Transfer ownership of the property to the lessee by the end of the lease term
a.	No	No
b.	No	Yes
c.	Yes	Yes
d.	Yes	No

44. On January 1, 1999, Harrow Co. as lessee signed a 5-year noncancelable equipment lease with annual payments of $100,000 beginning December 31, 1999. Harrow treated this transaction as a capital lease. The five lease payments have a present value of $379,000 at January 1, 1999, based on interest of 10%. What amount should Harrow report as interest expense for the year ended December 31, 1999?

    a. $37,900
    b. $27,900
    c. $24,200
    d. $0

45. On January 1, 1998, West Co. entered into a 10-year lease for a manufacturing plant. The annual minimum lease payments are $100,000. In the notes to the December 31, 1999 financial statements, what amounts of subsequent years' lease payments should be disclosed?

	Amount for appropriate required period	Aggregate amount for the period thereafter
a.	$100,000	$0
b.	$300,000	$500,000
c.	$500,000	$300,000
d.	$500,000	$0

46. On December 31, 1999, Lane, Inc. sold equipment to Noll, and simultaneously leased it back for 12 years. Pertinent information at this date is as follows:

Sales price	$480,000
Carrying amount	360,000
Estimated remaining economic life	15 years

At December 31, 1999, how much should Lane report as deferred gain from the sale of the equipment?

    a. $0
    b. $110,000
    c. $112,000
    d. $120,000

47. The following information pertains to a sale and leaseback of equipment by Mega Co. on December 31, 1999:

Sales price	$400,000
Carrying amount	$300,000
Monthly lease payment	$3,250
Present value of lease payments	$36,900
Estimated remaining life	25 years
Lease term	1 year
Implicit rate	12%

What amount of deferred gain on the sale should Mega report at December 31, 1999?

    a. $0
    b. $ 36,900
    c. $ 63,100
    d. $100,000

48. On December 31, 1999, Parke Corp. sold Edlow Corp. an airplane with an estimated remaining useful life of 10 years. At the same time, Parke leased back the airplane for 3 years. Additional information is as follows:

Sales price	$600,000
Carrying amount of airplane at date of sale	$100,000
Monthly rental under lease	$ 6,330

Interest rate implicit in the lease as computed by Edlow and known by Parke (this rate is lower than the lessee's incremental borrowing rate)   12%

Present value of operating lease rentals ($6,330 for 36 months @ 12%) $190,581

The leaseback is considered an operating lease. In Parke's December 31, 1999 balance sheet, what amount should be included as deferred revenue on this transaction?

    a. $0
    b. $190,581
    c. $309,419
    d. $500,000

49. On June 30, 1999, Lang Co. sold equipment with an estimated useful life of 11 years and immediately leased it back for 10 years. The equipment's carrying amount was $450,000; the sale price was $430,000; and the present value of the lease payments, which is equal to the fair value of the equipment, was $465,000. In its June 30, 1999 balance sheet, what amount should Lang report as deferred loss?

    a. $35,000
    b. $20,000
    c. $15,000
    d. $0

50. On January 1, 1999, Hooks Oil Co. sold equipment with a carrying amount of $100,000, and a remaining useful life of 10 years, to Maco Drilling for $150,000. Hooks immediately leased the equipment back under a 10-year capital lease with a present value of $150,000 and will depreciate the equipment using the straight-line method. Hooks made the first annual lease payment of $24,412 in December 1999. In Hooks' December 31, 1999 balance sheet, the unearned gain on equipment sale should be

    a. $50,000
    b. $45,000
    c. $25,588
    d. $0

51. In a sale-leaseback transaction, the seller-lessee has retained the property. The gain on the sale should be recognized at the time of the sale-leaseback when the lease is classified as a(n)

	Capital lease	Operating lease
a.	Yes	Yes
b.	No	No
c.	No	Yes
d.	Yes	No

52. Able sold its headquarters building at a gain, and simultaneously leased back the building. The lease was reported as a capital lease. At the time of sale, the gain should be reported as

    a.   Operating income.
    b.   An extraordinary item, net of income tax.
    c.   A separate component of stockholders' equity.
    d.   An asset valuation allowance.

PROBLEMS

Problem 1 (15 to 20 minutes)

On January 2, 1999, Elsee Co. leased equipment from Grant, Inc. Lease payments are $100,000, payable annually every December 31 for 20 years. Title to the equipment passes to Elsee at the end of the lease term. The lease is noncancelable.

Additional facts

- The equipment has a $750,000 carrying amount on Grant's books. Its estimated economic life was 25 years on January 2, 1999.
- The rate implicit in the lease, which is known to Elsee, is 10%. Elsee's incremental borrowing rate is 12%.
- Elsee uses the straight-line method of depreciation.

The rounded present value factors of an ordinary annuity for 20 years are as follows:

12%	7.5
10%	8.5

Required:

Prepare the necessary journal entries, without explanations, to be recorded by Elsee for:

1. Entering into the lease on January 2, 1999.
2. Making the lease payment on December 31, 1999.
3. Expenses related to the lease for the year ended December 31, 1999.

Show supporting calculations for all entries.

Problem 2 (15 to 25 minutes)

On December 31, 1999, Jen, Inc. sold a building for its fair value and leased it back. The building was sold for more than its carrying amount and a gain was recorded. Lease payments are due at the end of each month. Jen accounted for the transaction as a capital lease. The lease's interest rate was equal to Jen's incremental borrowing rate.

Required:

a. How should Jen account for the sale portion of the sale-leaseback transaction at December 31, 1999? Why is this an appropriate method of accounting for this portion of the contract?

b. How should Jen report the leaseback portion of the sale-leaseback transaction on its December 31, 2000 balance sheet? How are these reported amounts determined?

MULTIPLE-CHOICE ANSWERS

1. c __ __	13. b __ __	25. b __ __	37. a __ __	49. b __ __
2. c __ __	14. c __ __	26. b __ __	38. c __ __	50. b __ __
3. a __ __	15. d __ __	27. b __ __	39. b __ __	51. b __ __
4. b __ __	16. b __ __	28. c __ __	40. a __ __	52. d __ __
5. b __ __	17. b __ __	29. a __ __	41. b __ __	
6. d __ __	18. b __ __	30. b __ __	42. d __ __	
7. a __ __	19. a __ __	31. a __ __	43. c __ __	
8. a __ __	20. d __ __	32. b __ __	44. a __ __	
9. c __ __	21. b __ __	33. b __ __	45. c __ __	
10. c __ __	22. b __ __	34. d __ __	46. d __ __	
11. a __ __	23. c __ __	35. b __ __	47. a __ __	1st: __/52 = __%
12. d __ __	24. c __ __	36. d __ __	48. b __ __	2nd: __/52 = __%

MULTIPLE-CHOICE ANSWER EXPLANATIONS

E.1.d.(1)   Operating Leases: Lessor/Lessee

1. (c)   SFAS 13 specifies that, in an operating lease, the lessor should recognize rental revenue on a straight-line basis. This means that the lease bonus ($50,000) should be recorded as unearned revenue on 1/1/99, and recognized as rental revenue over the 5-year lease term. Therefore, 1999 rental revenue should be $100,000 [$90,000 + ($50,000 ÷ 5)]. The security deposit ($25,000) does not affect rental revenue. Since it is to be refunded to the lessee upon expiration of the lease, it is recorded as a deposit, a long-term liability when received.

2. (c)   SFAS 13 states that rental revenue on operating leases should be recognized on a straight-line basis unless another method more reasonably reflects the pattern of use given by the lessor. When the pattern of cash flows under the lease agreement is other than straight-line, this will result in the recording of rent receivable or unearned rent. Wall's total rent revenue [(1/2 x $8,000) + (4 x $12,500) = $54,000] should be recognized on a straight-line basis over the 5-year lease term ($54,000 x 1/5 = $10,800). Since cash collected in 1999 is only $4,000 (one-half of $8,000, since the first 6 months are rent-free), Wall would accrue rent receivable and rental revenue of $6,800 ($10,800 – $4,000) at year end to bring the rental revenue up to $10,800.

3. (a)   Net rental income on an operating lease is equal to rental revenue less related expenses, as computed below:

Rental revenue	$50,000
Depreciation expense	(12,000)
Executory costs	(9,000)
Finder's fee ($15,000 ÷ 10)	(1,500)
Net rental income	$27,500

The finder's fee ($15,000) is capitalized as a deferred charge at the inception of the lease and amortized over 10 years to match the expense to the revenues it enabled the lessor to earn.

4. (b)   SFAS 13 states that for an operating lease, rental revenue should be recognized on a straight-line basis unless another method more reasonably reflects the pattern of use given by the lessor. When the pattern of cash flows under the lease agreement is other than straight-line, this will result in the recording of rent receivable or unearned rent. Gee's total rent revenue ($36,000) should be recognized on a

straight-line basis over the 36-month lease, resulting in monthly entries debiting **rent receivable** and crediting **rent revenue** for $1,000. Cash collections will result in entries debiting **cash** and crediting **rent receivable** for $500 per month for the first 12 months and $750 per month for the second 12 months. Therefore, rent receivable at 6/30/99 is $9,000, as indicated by the T-account below.

	Rent Receivable		
Accruals (24 x $1,000)	24,000	6,000	Collections (12 x $500)
		9,000	Collections (12 x $750)
6/30/99 Balance	9,000		

5. (b)   At 1/1/99, Glen would record as a current liability unearned rent of $50,000, and as a long-term liability unearned rent of $150,000. During 1999, the current portion of unearned rent was earned and would be recognized as revenue. At 12/31/99, the portion of the long-term liability representing the second year's rent ($50,000) would be reclassified as current, leaving as a long-term liability the $100,000 representing the last 2 years' rent.

6. (d)   SFAS 13 states that rental revenue on operating leases should be recognized on a straight-line basis unless another method more reasonably reflects the pattern of use given by the lessor. When the pattern of cash flows under the lease agreement is other than straight-line, this will result in the recording of rent receivable or unearned rent. Therefore, even though Graf received only one monthly payment in 1999 (1/48 of the total rent to received over the life of the lease), they would accrue as rent receivable and rent revenue an amount sufficient to increase the rent revenue account to a balance equal to one-fifth of the total cash to be received over the 5-year life of the lease.

7. (a)   The graph presented in the problem can be interpreted as follows:

Line AB is considered to be fixed rental costs per month. Therefore, answers (c) and (d) are incorrect because lines III and IV do not include the fixed portion of the rental payment, in its graphical representation. The problem states that as the variable rental amount increases, it does so at a decreasing rate. Answer (b) is incorrect because line II is increasing, but at an increasing rate, not a decreasing rate, as line I represents. Therefore, answer (a) is the correct answer because line I is increasing, at a decreasing rate.

8. **(a)** SFAS 13 states that rent on operating leases should be expensed on a straight-line basis unless another method is better suited to the particular benefits and costs associated with the lease. In this lease, the lessee must pay rent of $1,000 monthly for 5 years excluding the first 9 months, or 51 months (60 – 9). Therefore, total rent expense for the 5 years is $51,000 (51 x $1,000). Recognizing rent expense on a straight-line basis, rent expense for the first year is $10,200 ($51,000 ÷ 5 years).

9. **(c)** SFAS 13 specifies that, in an operating lease, the lessee should recognize rent expense on a straight-line basis unless another method is better suited to the particular lease. Therefore, the lease bonus should be recognized as rent expense on a straight-line basis over the 10-year lease term ($24,000 ÷ 10 = $2,400). However, the contingent rentals, which are based on company sales, shall be expensed in the period to which they relate. Therefore, in 1999, contingent rentals of $5,000 [5% x ($600,000 – $500,000)] should be included in rent expense. Total rent expense is $103,400, as computed below:

Base rental	$ 96,000
Lease bonus ($24,000 ÷ 10)	2,400
Cont. rental [5% x ($600,000 – $500,000)]	5,000
	$103,400

10. **(c)** For operating leases having noncancellable remaining lease terms of more than one year, the lessee must disclose future minimum lease payments in the aggregate and for each of the 5 succeeding fiscal years. Since the annual **minimum** lease payments are $100,000, South must disclose subsequent years' lease payments of $100,000 per annum for each of the next 5 years and $900,000 (9 remaining payments x $100,000) in the aggregate.

11. **(a)** To qualify for treatment as a capital lease, a lease must meet one or more of the following criteria:

1) Transfers ownership to lessee.
2) Contains bargain purchase option.
3) Lease term is ≥ 75% of the economic life of the leased asset.
4) Present value of minimum lease payments is ≥ 90% of the FMV of the leased asset.

Since the lease signed by Mollat Company does not meet any of these criteria, it must be classified as an operating lease. For operating leases, the lessee's lease payments are recorded as debits to rent expense. Thus, answer (a) is correct because Mollat would report rent expense equal to the 1999 lease payments in its 1999 income statement.

12. **(d)** When a leasing agreement is accounted for as an operating lease, the lessor and the lessee recognize rental revenue and rental expense respectively on a straight-line basis unless another systematic and rational basis more clearly reflects the time pattern in which use benefit is given (received) by the respective parties. Per FASB Technical Bulletin 85-3, para 1, the straight-lining of uneven lease payments includes scheduled rent increases. Even though the amount of the annual lease payment increases in year 6, rental expense would not change. Interest is not an element of revenue (expense) in operating leases. Therefore, the correct answer is (d).

E.1.d.(1)(e) Leasehold Improvements

13. **(b)** The first month's rent ($60,000) should be expensed in 1999. The prepayment of the last month's rent (also $60,000) should be deferred and recognized as an expense in November 2004. The security deposit ($80,000) should be recorded as a long-term receivable, since Clark can expect to receive the deposit back at lease end. The installation of new walls and offices ($360,000) is recorded as a leasehold improvement at 12/1/99. At 12/31/99, amortization must be recorded for one month ($360,000 x 1/60 = $6,000). Therefore, 1998 expense is $66,000 ($60,000 + $6,000). The journal entries are:

Rent expense	60,000	
Prepaid rent	60,000	
Sec. deposit receivable	80,000	
Leasehold improvements	360,000	
Cash		560,000
Amortization expense	6,000	
Leasehold improvements		6,000

14. **(c)** Leasehold improvements are capitalized and amortized over the shorter of the remaining life of the lease (6 years from 1/1/99 to 12/31/04) or the useful life of the improvements (8 years). Therefore, the $48,000 cost is amortized over 6 years, resulting in annual amortization of $8,000 ($48,000 ÷ 6). For the period 1/1/99 to 6/30/99, amortization is $4,000 ($8,000 x 6/12), so the 6/30/99 net amount for leasehold improvements is $44,000 ($48,000 – $4,000).

15. **(d)** Leasehold improvements are properly capitalized and amortized over the shorter of the remaining life of the lease or the useful life of the improvement. If the lease contains an option to renew and the likelihood of renewal is uncertain (as it is in this case), then the remaining life of the lease is based on the initial lease term. In this case, the remaining life of the lease is therefore 10 years. Since the estimated lives of all improvements in this case are greater than or equal to 10 years, the appropriate amortization period is 10 years. The 2000 amortization is thus computed as the total cost of $140,000 ($47,000 + $75,000 + $18,000 = $140,000), divided by 10 years, or $14,000. There is no salvage value for leasehold improvements, because the assets revert to the lessor at the end of the lease term. Note that if the renewal of the lease for an additional 10 years were considered a certainty, the amortization periods would be as follows: 10 years for the sales office (estimated life); 20 years for the warehouse (lease term); and 15 years for the parking lot (estimated life).

16.   (b)   The cost of the leasehold improvements ($540,000) should be amortized over the remaining life of the lease, or over the useful life of the improvements, whichever is **shorter**. The remaining life of the lease should include periods covered by a renewal option **if** it is probable that the option will be exercised. In this case, the remaining life of the lease is 18 years (12 years of original lease + 8 years in option period – 2 years gone by), and the useful life of the improvements is 15 years. Therefore, amortization is based on a 15-year life ($540,000 ÷ 15 = $36,000). The 12/31/99 carrying amount is $504,000 ($540,000 – $36,000).

17.   (b)   Per SFAS 13, para 7, a lease should be classified as a capital lease by the lessee if the lease terms meet any one of the following four criteria: (1) the lease transfers ownership of the property to the lessee by the end of the lease term, (2) the lease contains a bargain purchase option, (3) the lease term is greater than or equal to 75% of the economic life of the leased property, or (4) the present value of the minimum lease payments is greater than or equal to 90% of the fair market value of the leased property. In this question, the terms of Vail's lease do not meet any of the four criteria for treatment as a capital lease, so the lease should be accounted for as an operating lease. Vail should therefore **not** recognize the building as an asset. In an operating lease, the lessee should capitalize the cost of the leasehold improvements, recognizing them as assets, and amortize their cost over the shorter of their useful lives or the term of the lease. Therefore, answer (b) is correct.

18.   (b)   Leasehold improvements are properly capitalized and amortized over the remaining life of the lease, or the useful life of the improvements, whichever is shorter. Since the useful life of the office is only 10 years and the remaining term of the lease is 15 years, the cost should be depreciated over the 10-year period. Therefore, answer (b) is correct, and answers (a), (c), and (d) are incorrect.

E.1.d.(2)   Direct Financing Leases: Lessor

19.   (a)   The annual lease payment is $75,000 ($323,400 ÷ 4.312). After 5 years, total lease payments will be $375,000 (5 x $75,000). The total interest revenue over the life of the lease is the excess of total lease payments over the fair value of the leased asset ($375,000 – $323,400 = $51,600).

20.   (d)   This lease qualifies as a direct financing lease; therefore interest revenue will be recognized rather than rent revenue. Had the lease qualified as an operating lease, rent revenue would have been recognized. The lessor's criteria for direct financing classification is as follows:

(1) The lease transfers ownership to the lessee, at the end of the lease

(2) The lease contains a bargain purchase option

(3) The lease term is ≥ 75% of an asset's economic life

(4) The present value of the minimum lease payments is ≥ 90% of the fair market value of the leased asset.

Note that the question is silent concerning the two additional criteria that apply to lessors: (1) collectibility of minimum lease payments is predictable, and (2) no important uncertainties exist concerning costs yet to be incurred by the lessee. Recall that if one of the 4 criteria are met, the lease is treated as a capital lease. In this case, since the lease term is for 80% of the asset's economic life, test (3) is met, and the lease is properly treated as a capital lease. In addition, the amount of interest revenue will be smaller in 1999 than the revenue in 1998. This result occurs because the present value of the minimum lease payments or carrying value of the obligation decreases each year as lease payments are received. As this occurs, the amount of interest revenue on the outstanding amount of the investment will decrease as well. Over the course of time, the investment reduction portion of each level payment increases and the amount of interest declines. Therefore, answer (d) is correct and answers (a), (b), and (c) are incorrect.

E.1.d.(3)   Sales-Type Leases: Lessor

21.   (b)   This is a sales-type lease, so at the inception of the lease, the lessor would recognize sales of $3,520,000 and cost of goods sold of $2,800,000, resulting in a **profit on sale of $720,000**. In addition, interest revenue is recognized for the period July 1, 1999, to December 31, 1999. The initial net lease payments receivable on 7/1/99 is $3,520,000. The first rental payment received on 7/1/99 consists entirely of principal, reducing the net receivable to $2,920,000 ($3,520,000 – $600,000). Therefore, 1999 **interest revenue for the 6 months from 7/1/99 to 12/31/99 is $146,000** ($2,920,000 x 10% x 6/12).

22.   (b)   This is a sales-type lease, so at the inception of the lease, the lessor would recognize sales of $3,300,000 (the PV of the lease payments), and cost of goods sold of $2,800,000, resulting in profit on the sale of $500,000 ($3,300,000 – $2,800,000). Note that the list selling price of an asset ($3,520,000 in this case) is not always representative of its FMV. An asset can often be purchased for less than its list price.

23.   (c)   Per SFAS 13, para 17, the excess of the fair value of leased property at the inception of the lease over the lessor's cost is defined as the manufacturer's or dealer's profit. Answer (a) is incorrect because the unearned income from a sales-type lease is defined as the difference between the gross investment in the lease and the sum of the present values of the components of the gross investment. Answer (b) is incorrect because the unearned income from a direct-financing lease is defined as the excess of the gross investment over the cost (also the PV of lease payments) of the leased property. Answer (d) is incorrect because a sales-type lease involves a manufacturer's or dealer's profit while a direct financing lease does not.

24.   (c)   Per SFAS 13, para 17b, revenue is to be recognized for a sales-type lease over the lease term so as to produce a **constant rate** of return on the net investment in the lease. This requires the use of the **interest method**. Therefore, answer (c) is correct and answer (b) is incorrect. Answer (d) is incorrect because, per SFAS 13, interest revenue **does** arise in a sales-type lease. Answer (a) is incorrect because the interest is to be earned over the life of the lease, not in full at the lease's inception.

E.1.d.(4)   Capital Leases: Lessee

25.   (b)   Para 7 of SFAS 13 provides criteria for classifying leases as either "capital" or "operating." If **any** of the criteria for classification as a capital lease are met, the lease is classified as such. One of the capital lease criterion is that the lease term is equal to 75% or more of the estimated economic life of the leased property. Thus, both leases M and P should be classified as capital leases, and answer (b) is correct.

26.   (b)   This is a capital lease for the lessee because the lease term is 75% of the useful life of the machine [6 years = (75% x 8 years)]. For a capital lease, the lessee records as a **leased asset** and a **lease obligation** the lower of the PV of the minimum lease payments or the FV of the leased asset (not given in this problem). The PV of the minimum lease payments is computed using the lower of the lessee's incremental borrowing rate (15%) or the implicit rate used by the lessor if known by the lessee (12%). Since the implicit rate is lower, and known by the lessee, it is used to compute the PV ($50,000 x 4.61 = $230,500). The cost of the asset on the lessor's books ($375,500) is irrelevant.

27.   (b)   This is a capital lease since the lease term (10 years) is the same as the useful life of the leased asset. In a capital lease, the lessee records an asset and a liability based on the PV of the minimum lease payments. The minimum lease payments includes rentals and a guaranteed residual value, **if guaranteed by the lessee**. In this case the minimum lease payments include only the rentals, since the residual value is guaranteed by a third party. The minimum lease payments are discounted using the **lower** of the lessee's incremental borrowing rate or the implicit rate used by the lessor, if known. In this case, the lessee knows the implicit rate is 10%, which is lower than the incremental borrowing rate of 12%. Thus, the present value or principal amount of the lease obligation is $61,446 ($10,000 x 6.1446) through the first year. Although accrued interest would be recognized at 10/31/99, the principal amount does not change until 1/1/00.

28.   (c)   The lessee records a capital lease at the present value of the minimum lease payments. The minimum lease payments includes rental payments and bargain purchase options (among other items). The $10,000 purchase option is a **bargain** purchase option because it allows the lessor to purchase the leased asset at an amount **less** than its expected fair value. In accordance with SFAS 13, the lessee computes the present value using its incremental borrowing rate (14%), unless the lessor's implicit rate (12%) is lower and is known by the lessee. This question indicates that the implicit rate is stated in the lease; therefore it would be known to the lessee. At the beginning of the lease term, Robbins should record a leased asset and lease liability at $66,500.

PV of rentals	($10,000 x 6.328)	=	$63,280
PV of BPO	($10,000 x .322)	=	3,220
	PV at 12%		$66,500

29.   (a)   The annual executory costs (real estate taxes of $2,000) are **not** an expense or liability until incurred; therefore they are excluded from the minimum lease payments and are **not** reflected in the initial lease liability. The 12/31/99 capital lease liability is recorded at the PV of the minimum lease payments [5.6 x ($52,000 – $2,000) = $280,000].

30.   (b)   The requirement is to determine the amount to be recorded as a capitalized leased asset. This is a capital lease for the lessee because the lease term exceeds 75% of the economic life of the leased asset (10/12 > 75%). In a capital lease, the lessee records as an asset and liability the present value (PV) of the minimum lease payments (unless the PV exceeds the asset's FMV, in which case the FMV is recorded). The minimum lease payments include rentals, and a lessee-guaranteed residual value or a bargain purchase option. Only rentals apply in this case. Note that the $50,000 purchase option is not a **bargain** purchase option which the lessee would be compelled to exercise. A bargain purchase option is an option to purchase the leased asset at an amount **less** than its expected fair value. Therefore, the present value of the minimum lease payments is $238,000 ($40,000 x 5.95).

31.   (a)   The initial lease liability at 1/1/99, before the 1/1/99 payment, is the present value of the 5 rental payments (an **annuity due** since the first payment is made on 1/1/99) plus the present value of the guaranteed residual value. The computation is below.

PV of rentals ($13,000 x 4.240)	$55,120
PV of residual ($10,000 x 0.650)	6,500
Initial liability	$61,620

The 1/1/99 payment consists entirely of principal, bringing the 1/1/99 liability down to $48,620 ($61,620 – $13,000).

32.   (b)   The initial lease obligation at 12/30/99 was $135,000. The first lease payment was made the same day, and therefore consisted entirely of principal reduction. After the payment, the lease obligation was $115,000 ($135,000 – $20,000). This balance will be reported as current (for the portion to be paid in 2000) and long-term (for the portion to be paid beyond 2000). The next lease payment of $20,000 will be paid 12/31/00, and will consist of both interest ($115,000 x 10% = $11,500) and principal reduction ($20,000 – $11,500 = $8,500). Thus, the portion of the $115,000 lease obligation to be paid in the next year (and therefore reported as a current liability) is $8,500. Note that the interest to be paid next year ($11,500) is not a liability at 12/31/99 because it has not yet been incurred.

33.   (b)   This is a capital lease for the lessee because the lease term (9 years) exceeds 75% of the useful life of the machine (also 9 years). For a capital lease, the lessee records as a **leased asset** and a **lease obligation** at the lower of the PV of the minimum lease payments or the FV of the leased asset (not given in this problem). The PV of the minimum lease payments is computed using the lower of the lessee's incremental borrowing rate (12%) or the implicit rate used by the lessor if known by the lessee (10%). Since the implicit rate is lower, and known by the lessee, it is used to compute the PV ($316,500). The initial lease payment

($50,000) is entirely principal because it was made at the inception of the lease. Therefore, after the 12/31/98 payment, the lease liability is $266,500 ($316,500 – $50,000). The 12/31/99 payment consists of interest incurred during 1999 ($266,500 x 10% = $26,650) and principal reduction ($50,000 – $26,650 = $23,350). Therefore, the 12/31/99 capital lease liability is $243,150 ($266,500 – $23,350).

34. (d) The initial lease liability at 12/31/98 is $417,000 (the PV of the minimum lease payments). The annual executory costs ($5,000) are **not** an expense or liability until incurred; therefore, they are excluded from the minimum lease payments and are **not** reflected in the initial lease liability. The 12/31/98 payment of $105,000 includes $5,000 of executory costs; the remainder ($100,000) is entirely principal since the payment was made at the inception of the lease. Therefore, after the 12/31/98 payment, the lease liability is $317,000 ($417,000 – $100,000). The 12/31/99 payment consists of executory costs ($5,000), interest incurred during 1999 ($317,000 x 10% = $31,700), and reduction of principal ($105,000 – $5,000 – $31,700 = $68,300). Therefore, the 12/31/99 balance sheet should include a lease liability of $248,700 ($317,000 – $68,300).

35. (b) On 1/2/99, Mene made a lease payment of $9,000, which included payment of the current portion of the lease obligation ($1,364) and interest ($9,000 – $1,364 = $7,636). After this payment, the total lease obligation was $75,000. The 1/2/00 payment would include interest of $7,500 ($75,000 x 10%), and principal of $1,500 ($9,000 – $7,500). This $1,500 amount would represent the current portion of the lease obligation at 12/31/99, so the long-term lease obligation net of the current portion at 12/31/99 is $73,500 ($75,000 – $1,500).

36. (d) SFAS 13 specifies that if a lease is classified as a capital lease, the lessee must record an asset and a liability, each for an amount equal to the present value of the minimum lease payments at the beginning of the lease. Therefore, answer (d) is correct.

37. (a) At the inception of a capital lease, the lessee must record an asset and a liability based on the PV of the minimum lease payments. The minimum lease payments are the payments that lessee is required to make in connection with the leased property, including rent payments, bargain purchase option, and guaranteed residual value. Thus, answer (a) is correct. Answer (b) is incorrect because minimum lease payments (MLP) are recorded at present value. Answers (c) and (d) are incorrect because the whole guaranteed residual value is included in MLP.

38. (c) In a capital lease where the first annual lease payment is made immediately upon signing the lease (annuity due), the first payment consists solely of lease liability reduction, since no time has transpired during which interest expense could be incurred. Subsequent payments include both interest expense and reduction of the liability.

39. (b) Per SFAS 13, para 12, each minimum lease payment shall be allocated between a reduction of the obligation and interest expense so as to produce a constant periodic rate of interest on the remaining balance of the obliga-

tion. Since the interest will be computed based upon a **declining** obligation balance, the interest component of each payment will also be declining. The result will be a relatively larger portion of the minimum lease payment allocated to the reduction of the lease obligation in the latter portion of the lease term. Therefore, answer (b) is correct and answers (a), (c), and (d) are incorrect.

40. (a) When a leasing agreement is accounted for as capital lease, the lessee recognizes a liability on its books equal to the present value of the minimum lease payments. The liability should be divided between current and noncurrent based upon when each lease payment is due. At the end of year 1, the current lease liability should equal the principal portion of the lease payment due in year 2. Therefore, when the lease payment is made in year 2, the reduction of the lease liability will equal the current liability shown at the end of year 1.

41. (b) This is a capital lease since title passes to Cole, the lessee, at the end of the lease. At the inception of the lease on 1/2/99, the lessee records the PV of the lease payments ($108,000) as an asset and a liability. The asset is depreciated on a straight-line basis over its useful life of 12 years, resulting in a yearly depreciation charge of $9,000 ($108,000 ÷ 12). The asset is depreciated over its useful life rather than over the lease term (8 years) because title transfers to the lessee, allowing the lessee to use the asset for 12 years.

42. (d) A leased asset acquired in a capital lease should be depreciated over the period of time the lessee expects to use the asset (either the lease term or the useful life, depending on the situation). In this case, Nori expects to use the leased asset for its entire 8-year useful life, due to the expected exercise of the bargain purchase option at the end of the 5-year lease term. Therefore, Nori's 1999 depreciation expense is $27,500

$$\frac{(\$240,000 \text{ cost}) - (\$20,000 \text{ salvage})}{8 \text{ years}} = \underline{\$27,500}$$

43. (c) The requirement is to determine whether a lessee should amortize the capitalizable cost of a leased asset in a manner consistent with the lessee's normal depreciation policy for owned assets for leases that contained a bargain purchase option and/or transferred ownership at the end of the lease term. Transfer of ownership of the property to the lessee by the end of the lease term and a lease that contains a bargain purchase option are properly classified as capital leases [SFAS 13, paras 7(a) and 7(b)]. Per SFAS 13, para 11(a), if the lease meets either of the above criteria, the asset shall be amortized in a manner consistent with the lessee's normal depreciation policy for owned assets. Therefore, answers (a), (b), and (d) are incorrect.

44. (a) At the inception of the lease on 1/1/99, the capitalized liability is $379,000 (the present value of the lease payments). Since the first payment is not due until the **end** of the first year, 1999 interest expense is based on the full initial liability ($379,000 x 10% = $37,900).

45. (c) SFAS 13, as amended and interpreted, requires the disclosure of future minimum lease payments (MLP) for each of the next 5 years and the aggregate amount of MLP due after 5 years. At 12/31/99, eight annual payments of $100,000 each have not yet been paid. Therefore, future MLP are $800,000 (8 x $100,000). The amount for the appropriate required period (5 years) is $500,000, while the aggregate amount for the period thereafter is $300,000 ($800,000 – $500,000).

E.2.b.   Sale-Leaseback

46.   (d)   According to SFAS 13, sale-leaseback arrangements are treated as though two transactions were a single financing transaction, if the lease qualifies as a capital lease. Any gain or loss on the sale is deferred and amortized over the lease term (if possession reverts to the lessor) or the economic life (if ownership transfers to the lessee). In this case, the lease qualifies as a capital lease because the lease term (12 years) is 80% of the remaining economic life of the leased property (15 years). Therefore, at 12/31/99, all of gain ($480,000 – $360,000 = $120,000) would be deferred and amortized over 12 years. Since the sale took place on 12/31/99, there is no amortization for 1999.

47.   (a)   SFAS 13, para 33, generally treats a sale-leaseback as a single financing transaction in which any profit on the sale is deferred and amortized by the seller. However, SFAS 28 amends this general rule when either **only a minor part** of the remaining use of the leased asset is retained (case 1) or when **more than a minor part but less than substantially all** of the remaining use of the leased asset is retained (case 2). Case 1 occurs when the PV of the lease payments is 10% or less of the FMV of the sale-leaseback property. Case 2 occurs when the leaseback is more than minor but does **not** meet the criteria of a capital lease. This problem is an example of case 1, because the PV of the lease payments ($36,900) is less than 10% of the FMV of the asset (10% x $400,000 = $40,000). SFAS 28 specifies that under these circumstances, the full gain ($400,000 – $300,000 = $100,000) is recognized, and **none is deferred**.

48.   (b)   SFAS 13, para 33, generally treats a sale-leaseback as a single financing transaction in which any profit on the sale is deferred and amortized by the seller. However, SFAS 28 amends this general rule when either **only a minor part** of the remaining use of the leased asset is retained (case 1), or when **more than a minor part but less than substantially all** of the remaining use of the leased asset is retained (case 2). Case 1 occurs when the PV of the lease payments is 10% or less of the FMV of the sale-leaseback property. Case 2 occurs when the leaseback is more than minor but does **not** meet the criteria of a capital lease. This is an example of case 2 because while the PV of the lease payments ($190,581) is more than 10% of the FMV of the asset ($600,000), the lease falls into the operating lease category. SFAS 28 specifies that under these circumstances the gain on sale ($600,000 – $100,000 = $500,000) is recognized to the extent that it exceeds the PV of the lease payments ($190,581). The gain reported would be $309,419 ($500,000 – $190,581). The portion of the gain represented by the $190,581 PV of the lease payments

is deferred and amortized on a straight-line basis over the life of the lease.

49.   (b)   On a sale-leaseback, generally **losses** are recognized immediately. However, there can be two types of losses in sale-leasebacks. The type which is **recognized immediately** is a **real economic loss**, where the carrying amount of the asset is higher than its FMV. The type which is **deferred** is an **artificial loss** where the sale price ($430,000) is below the carrying amount ($450,000), but the FMV ($465,000) is above the carrying amount ($450,000). The loss in this problem ($450,000 – $430,000 = $20,000) is an artificial loss which must be deferred.

50.   (b)   According to SFAS 13, sale-leaseback transactions are treated as though two transactions were a single financing transaction, if the lease qualifies as a capital lease. Any gain on the sale is deferred and amortized over the lease term (if possession reverts to the lessor) or the economic life (if ownership transfers to the lessee); both are 10 years in this case. Since this is a capital lease, the entire gain ($150,000 – $100,000 = $50,000) is deferred at 1/1/99. At 12/31/99, an adjusting entry must be prepared to amortize 1/10 of the unearned gain (1/10 x $50,000 = $5,000), because the lease covers 10 years. Therefore, the unearned gain at 12/31/99 is $45,000 ($50,000 – $5,000).

51.   (b)   Per SFAS 28, any profit related to a sale-leaseback transaction in which the seller-lessee retains the property leased (i.e., the seller-lessee retains substantially all of the benefits and risks of the ownership of the property sold), shall be deferred and amortized in proportion to the amortization of the leased asset, if a capital lease. If it is an operating lease, the profit will be deferred in proportion to the related gross rental charged to expense over the lease term. It is important to note that **losses**, however, are recognized immediately for either a capital or operating lease. Since the gain on the sale should be deferred in either case, no gain is recognized at the time of the sale, and answer (b) is correct.

AUTHOR'S NOTE: An example of an operating lease in which substantially all of the remaining use of the leased asset is retained by the lessee occurs when the lease term begins within the last 25% of the asset's original useful life.

52.   (d)   In a sale-leaseback transaction, if the leaseback is recorded as a capital lease and the lessee has retained **substantially all** of the rights to use the property, then any gain on the sale must be deferred and amortized over the life of the property in proportion to the amortization of the leased asset. This deferred gain acts as an asset valuation allowance resulting in the net amount shown for the leased asset being equal to the same carrying value as if the sale and leaseback transaction had not occurred. Therefore, answer (d) is correct. Answers (a) and (b) are incorrect since the gain should not be recognized. Answer (c) is incorrect since the deferred gain acts as an asset valuation allowance, and should not be reported as a component of stockholders' equity.

SOLUTION GUIDE

Problem 1   Capital Lease Entries

1. This problem requires preparation of the lessee's journal entries for the first year of a lease. The lease is a capital lease because title passes to the lessee at the end of the lease and the lease term (20 years) is greater than 75% of the useful life (25 years).

2. In a capital lease, the lessee records a **leased asset** and a **lease obligation** at the present value of the minimum lease payments. The lessee's incremental borrowing rate (12%) should be used to determine the present value unless the lessor's implicit rate is lower and is known by the lessee. The lessor's 10% rate is lower and is known by the lessee, so it is used to compute the PV of $850,000 ($100,000 x 8.5).

3. The first lease payment on 12/31/99 consists of interest expense incurred during 1999 ($850,000 x 10% = $85,000) and reduction of lease obligation ($100,000 payment – $85,000 interest = $15,000). The $100,000 credit to cash is offset by debits to interest expense ($85,000) and lease obligation ($15,000)

4. The only other expense related to this lease is depreciation of the leased asset. Leased assets are depreciated over the lease term (20 years) unless the lease transfers ownership (as this one does) or contains a bargain purchase option. If either of these is present, then the asset is depreciated over the estimated useful life of the asset (25 years). Depreciation expense is cost ($850,000) divided by useful life ($850,000 ÷ 25 years = $34,000). If a salvage value had been given, it would be subtracted from cost before dividing by useful life.

UNOFFICIAL ANSWER

Problem 1   Capital Lease Entries

	Debits	_Credits_
1. January 2, 1999--to record lease:		
Equipment	850,000	
Capital lease liability		850,000
2. December 31, 1999--to record payment:		
Capital lease liability	100,000	
Cash		100,000
3. December 31, 1999--to record depreciation:		
Depreciation expense	34,000	
Accumulated depreciation		34,000
Interest expense	85,000	
Capital lease liability		85,000

ANSWER OUTLINE

Problem 2   Sale-Leaseback Accounting and Reporting

a. Accounting for sale-leaseback, 12/31/99

Cash	xx	
PP&E		xx
Deferred gain		xx

Appropriate because Jen retains substantial ownership rights and obligations
   Earning process not complete
   Financing transaction, not a sale
   Gain should be deferred

b. BS reporting 12/31/00
   Leased property at discounted PV 12/31/99 less acc. depr. and unamortized deferred gain on sale
      Discounted PV at 12/31/99 represents future lease payments, discounted at Jen's interest rate
   Lease obligation equals the 12/31/99 PV less principal repaid in 2000
      2001 principal reduction reported as CL
      Balance due reported as NCL

UNOFFICIAL ANSWER

Problem 2   Sale-Leaseback Accounting and Reporting

a.   Jen should account for the sale portion of the sale-leaseback transaction by increasing cash for the sale price, decreasing property, plant, and equipment for the building's carrying amount, and recording a deferred gain for the excess of the sale price over the building's carrying amount.

This accounting is appropriate because Jen still retains substantial ownership rights and obligations pertaining to the building. Since no earning process occurred, this sale-leaseback is not in substance a sale but a financing transaction. Therefore, the gain should be deferred.

b.   The leased building is included on Jen's December 31, 2000 balance sheet as leased property at its discounted present value on December 31, 1999, less accumulated depreciation, and less unamortized deferred gain on the sale. Its discounted present value at December 31, 1999, represents the future lease payments, discounted at Jen's interest rate.

The lease obligation on Jen's December 31, 2000 balance sheet equals the building's December 31, 1999 present value less principal repaid in 2000. An amount equal to the principal to be repaid in 2001 should be reported as a current liability. The balance of the obligation should be reported as a noncurrent liability.

DEFERRED TAXES

SFAS 109, "*Accounting for Income Taxes*," requires an asset and liability (balance sheet) approach to recognizing and measuring deferred taxes. To understand the basic concepts of deferred taxes, study this module and the outlines of SFAS 109 and APB 23.

A. Overview of Deferred Tax Theory

There are numerous differences between the recognition and measurement of pretax financial (book) income and asset/liability valuation under GAAP and the recognition and measurement of taxable income and asset/liability valuation under the Internal Revenue Code. Because of these differences between the two bodies of promulgated rules, pretax financial (book) income usually differs from taxable income. The amount of Income Tax Expense and the amount of Income Taxes Payable are, therefore, often different amounts.

According to SFAS 109, financial income tax expense (the **current and deferred** tax consequences of **all** events that have been recognized in the financial statements) is charged to Income Tax Expense. Income Tax Expense equals the taxes actually owed (a current tax liability) for the current period plus or minus the change during the current period in amounts payable in the future and in future tax benefits. By using this procedure, any possible income statement or balance sheet distortion that may result from differences in the timing of revenue recognition or expense deductibility and asset or liability valuation between GAAP and the Internal Revenue Code is avoided. The Income Tax Expense reported in the entity's income statement reflects the amount of taxes related to transactions recognized in the financial statements prepared under GAAP for the specific period. The deferred tax asset or liability (the difference between Income Tax Expense and Income Tax Payable) reported in the entity's balance sheet clearly reflects the amount of taxes that the entity has prepaid (an asset) or will have to pay in the future (a liability) because of temporary differences that result from differences in timing of revenue recognition or expense deductibility between GAAP and the Internal Revenue Code.

B. Permanent and Temporary Differences Defined

Differences between pretax financial (book) income and taxable income can be divided into two types: temporary differences or permanent differences. SFAS 109 does **not** use the term permanent differences. However, to ease our explanation and your comprehension, the term "permanent difference" will be used in this module, as it is in several intermediate accounting textbooks.

1. Temporary Differences

SFAS 109 defines a temporary difference as "a difference between the tax basis of an asset or liability and its reported amount in the financial statements that will result in taxable or deductible amounts in future years when the reported amount of the asset or liability is recovered or settled, respectively." This definition of a temporary difference is based on the assumption that assets and liabilities reported on an entity's balance sheet will eventually be recovered or settled at their net reported (book) value. This recovery or settling process will create income statement items (revenues/gains or expenses/losses) as the life of the asset or liability progresses. If the reported financial (book) value of the balance sheet item differs from its tax basis, the correct period for recognition of the related income statement item will differ between the entity's financial statements and the entity's tax return. Thus, from an income statement perspective, a temporary difference occurs when a revenue or expense item: (1) is included in both financial accounting income and taxable income, **and**, (2) is recognized in one period for financial accounting purposes and in another period for income tax purposes because of differences between the promulgated rules of GAAP and the Internal Revenue Code. If such a timing (temporary) difference exists, an amount will be recorded and reported as either a deferred tax liability or a deferred tax asset depending upon the relationship between the reported net financial (book) value and the tax basis of the related asset or liability. When the temporary difference reverses, the recorded deferred tax amount is removed from the balance sheet; the amount removed results in an increase or decrease in income tax expense. Some examples of temporary differences are presented below.

a. **Estimated Warranty Liability:** Expense recognized in the financial statements when the liability is incurred. Deduction recognized for tax purposes when the work is actually performed.

b. **Unearned Rent (Royalty) Revenue:** Recognized in the financial statements as a liability when the rent (royalty) is received and as revenue when earned. Recognized as revenue for tax purposes when the cash is received. (Note that the Internal Revenue Code refers to revenue received in advance as "prepaid income," not "unearned revenue.")

c. **Plant Assets and Accumulated Depreciation:** Changes in these assets and the related contra asset are recognized in the financial statements according to depreciation methods acceptable to GAAP. Changes in these assets and the related contra asset are usually recognized for tax purposes according to accelerated methods acceptable to the IRS such as ACRS and MACRS. Note that recovery of these assets occurs as the asset is used in the entity's operations to generate revenue. In essence, a portion of the investment in the asset is being recovered as the product or service is sold.

d. **Donated Asset:** According to GAAP, initial valuation in the financial statements of a donated asset is based upon fair market value, and revenue is recognized for the same amount. Depreciation on the asset is computed according to the entity's normal policies. Upon sale of the asset, a gain is recognized for the difference between cash received and net book value. According to the Internal Revenue Code, a donated asset has the same basis for the donee as it did in the donor's hands. Thus, no tax deductions for depreciation are allowed for the asset if the tax basis is zero. When the asset is sold, the entire amount received is a taxable gain.

e. **Involuntary Conversion of Assets:** According to GAAP (FASB Interpretation 30), a gain (loss) must be recognized when a nonmonetary asset is involuntarily converted into a monetary asset, even though the entity reinvests the monetary assets in replacement nonmonetary assets. The replacement asset is valued at its cost or fair market value on date of acquisition. According to the Internal Revenue Code, no gain is recognized on an involuntary conversion if the amount reinvested in replacement property equals or exceeds the amount realized from the converted property. The tax basis of the replacement asset is valued at its cost less the deferred gain.

f. **Goodwill:** Under GAAP, goodwill must be amortized over a period not to exceed 40 years. The Internal Revenue Code however, mandates an amortization period of 15 years.

2. **Permanent Differences**

A permanent difference occurs when a revenue or expense item is only included in pretax financial (book) income or in taxable income but will never be included in both. For example, interest income on municipal bonds is included in pretax financial (book) income but is never included in taxable income because it is tax exempt by law. No deferred taxes need to be recognized because no future tax consequences are created. The tax exempt income (or deduction not allowed for taxes) is simply subtracted from (or added to) book income in the book to tax reconciliation. Thus, a permanent difference affects only the current reconciliation of book income to taxable income, and has no effect on the computation of deferred taxes. Some common permanent differences are

a. **State and municipal bond interest income:** included in book income but not included in taxable income.
b. **Life insurance premium expense when the corporation is the beneficiary:** deducted for book income but not for taxable income; proceeds received on such policies result in a book gain but are not taxable.
c. **Federal income tax expense:** deducted for book income but not for taxable income.
d. **Payment of penalty or fine:** deducted for book income but not for taxable income.
e. **Dividend received deduction (DRD):** deducted for taxable income but not for book income.

The example below shows how permanent and temporary differences are used in calculating taxable income, given a corporation's pretax financial (book) income.

> EXAMPLE 1: *A corporation has pretax financial accounting (book) income of $146,000 in 1999. Additional information is as follows:*
>
> 1. *Municipal bond interest income is $35,000.*
> 2. *Life insurance premium expense, where the corporation is the beneficiary, per books is $4,000.*
> 3. *Accelerated depreciation is used for tax purposes, while straight-line is used for books. Tax depreciation is $10,000; book depreciation is $5,000.*
> 4. *Estimated warranty expense of $500 is accrued for book purposes.*
>
> *Taxable income can be determined as follows:*
>
> | | |
> |---|---:|
> | Financial (book) income before income taxes | $146,000 |
> | Permanent differences | |
> | Life insurance premium | 4,000 |
> | Municipal bond interest | (35,000) |
> | Temporary differences | |
> | Amount added to book accum. deprec. and deprec. exp. < amount added to tax accum. depr. and deducted on the tax return | (5,000) |
> | Amount recognized for book estimated warranty liability and warranty exp. not recognized on the tax return | 500 |
> | Taxable income | $110,500 |
>
> *The above schedule is known as the reconciliation of book income to taxable income. It is similar to the Schedule M-1 of the US Corporate Income Tax Return (Form 1120) except it starts with pretax financial accounting income instead of net income as Schedule M-1 does. Note that the permanent differences only impact the current year (1999 in this case) whereas the temporary differences will have future tax consequences.*

C. Deferred Tax Assets and Liabilities

SFAS 109 defines a deferred tax asset as the deferred tax consequences attributable to deductible temporary differences and carryforwards. SFAS 109 requires that the deferred tax asset be reduced by a valuation allowance if a portion or all of the deferred tax asset will not be realized in the future. A deferred tax liability is defined as an amount that is recognized for the deferred tax consequence of temporary differences that will result in taxable amounts in future years. SFAS 109, like its predecessor pronouncements, does **not** permit discounting of these deferred tax assets and liabilities.

1. **Identification & Measurement of Deferred Tax Items**

    The candidate's ability to work an income tax accounting problem depends upon his/her ability to correctly identify permanent and temporary differences. In order to recognize the tax consequences of a temporary difference, it must be the result of event(s) that have already been recognized in the entity's financial statements for the current or previous years. With regard to a fixed asset, this means that the fixed asset has been acquired before the end of the year for which income taxes are being determined. Thus, planned asset acquisitions for future years cannot result in temporary differences and thereby affect the determination of deferred income taxes.

    A **temporary difference** between pretax financial (book) income and taxable income occurs when the tax basis of an asset (or liability) differs from its reported financial statement amount. As shown in *Example 1*, a temporary difference resulting from timing of GAAP recognition vs. timing of recognition for tax purposes can create the need for additions to or subtractions from book income in order to arrive at taxable income. These **additions (taxable amounts)** or **subtractions (deductible amounts)** can occur in the year an asset is acquired or a liability is incurred as well as in future years as the asset is recovered or the liability is settled. The table below presents the various possible relationships between financial statement (book) and tax recognition of revenue and expense and assets and liabilities as well as the nature of the resulting future tax consequences.

Acctg. income >or< taxable income*	B/S relationships	Temp. differ.** Cur.	Temp. differ.** Fut.	Type of BS tax deferral	Current deferred tax expense effect	Future deferred tax expense effect
	Assets					
>	(1) on books > tax return	D	T	Liability	(+)	(−)
<	(2) on books < tax return	T	D	Asset	(−)	(+)
	Liabilities					
<	(3) on books > tax return	T	D	Asset	(−)	(+)
	(4) on books < tax return	D	T	Liability	(+)	(−)

    Relationship in the year the temporary difference originates.
    ***Deductible (D) /Taxable (T)*

    For example, a type 1 temporary difference (such as the difference between the financial statement amount and the **zero** tax basis of an asset obtained by a donation) creates a deferred tax liability. If the donated asset is sold for more than its tax basis, recognition of the difference between the asset's financial statement amount and its tax return basis results in a gain for taxable income and either a smaller gain or a loss for book income depending on the amount of book depreciation taken on the asset since it was received by the enterprise. The amount of cash that will be needed to pay the taxes due will be increased because the entire amount of cash received for the donated asset will be reported as gain (taxable amount) on the tax return. A liability is defined in Statement of Financial Accounting Concepts 6 as "probable future sacrifices of economic benefits arising from present obligations of a particular entity to transfer assets...as a result of past transactions or events." The increase in cash paid out for taxes (a sacrifice of economic benefits) will result when the donated asset (from a past transaction or event) is disposed of; therefore, the future tax impact of the current period difference between financial statement value and tax basis represents a deferred liability. When the liability is recognized, deferred income tax expense is also recognized.

In contrast, a contingent liability recognized in the current period financial statements represents a type 3 temporary difference because a contingent liability has a zero basis for tax accounting. The amount of expense stemming from this contingent liability must be added back to financial (book) income to arrive at taxable income. Therefore, a deferred tax asset is created. When the probable and measurable future event does actually occur, the contingent liability will then represent a loss (deductible amount) on the tax return. Because the tax loss recognized will reduce taxable income and income taxes payable, the amount of cash that will be needed to pay the taxes due will be decreased. Remember, an asset is defined in Statement of Financial Accounting Concepts 6 as a "probable future economic benefit obtained or controlled by a particular entity as a result of past transactions or events." The reduction of current tax expense and the resulting future decrease in cash paid out for taxes (an economic benefit) will result from the contingent liability (a past transaction or event). Therefore, the future tax impact of the current period difference between the financial statement value and tax basis represents a deferred tax asset in the year the contingency is recognized. Note that the deferred tax expense recorded in this situation is a credit because it represents a current period benefit.

2. **Scheduling and Recording Deferred Tax Amounts**

An entity's total income statement provision for income taxes is the sum of that entity's current and deferred tax amounts. The current tax expense or benefit is defined by SFAS 109 as "the amount of income taxes paid or payable (or refundable) for a year as determined by applying the provisions of the tax law to the taxable income or excess of deductions over revenues for that year." The deferred tax expense or benefit is defined as "the change during the year in an enterprise's deferred tax liabilities or assets." Thus, SFAS 109 requires that current and deferred tax amounts be computed independently.

The deferred tax amount (the future tax consequences of temporary differences) should be recorded in the current financial statements at the amounts that will be paid or recovered based upon tax laws and rates that are already in place and due to be in effect at the date of payment or recovery. These are known as **enacted** tax laws and **enacted** tax rates. In order to comply with SFAS 109, an entity must, therefore, determine when the identified and measured temporary differences will become taxable or deductible. Future **taxable amounts** cause taxable income to be greater than financial (book) income in future periods. They are a result of existing temporary differences and are reported as deferred tax liabilities in the current year. Future **deductible amounts** cause taxable income to be less than financial (book) income in future periods. They are a result of existing temporary differences and are reported as a deferred tax asset in the current year. For illustrative purposes, the following examples show the scheduling of future temporary differences. However, in practice and on the CPA exam, extensive scheduling is generally not necessary unless (1) there is a change in future enacted tax rates or (2) the problem requires the use of a valuation allowance account.

According to SFAS 109, deferred tax liabilities and assets are determined separately for each tax-paying component (an individual entity or group of entities that is consolidated for tax purposes) in each tax jurisdiction. That determination includes the following procedures:

1. Identify the types and amounts of existing temporary differences
2. Identify the nature and amount of each type of operating loss and tax credit carryforward and the remaining length of the carryforward period
3. Measure the total deferred tax liability for taxable temporary differences using the applicable tax rate
4. Measure the total deferred tax asset for deductible temporary differences and operating loss carryforwards using the applicable tax rate
5. Measure deferred tax assets for each type of tax credit carryforward
6. Reduce deferred tax assets by a valuation allowance if, based on the weight of available evidence, it is *more likely than not* (a likelihood of more than 50%) that some portion or all of the deferred tax assets will not be realized. The valuation allowance should be sufficient to reduce the deferred tax asset to the amount that is more likely than not to be realized.
7. Deferred tax assets and liabilities are **not** discounted to reflect their present value.

*EXAMPLE 2: This example shows the **deferred tax accounting in 1999, 2000, and 2001** for the temporary differences included in EXAMPLE 1 earlier in this module. Additional details are*

a. *On 1/1/97 the enterprise acquired a depreciable asset for $30,000 that had an estimated life of 6 years and is depreciated on a straight-line basis for book purposes. For tax purposes, the asset is depreciated using the straight-line election under MACRS and qualifies as a 3-year asset.*
b. *The enterprise deducted warranty expense of $500 for book purposes in 1999 that is expected to be deductible for tax purposes in 2000.*
c. *Taxable income was $110,500 in 1999, $112,000 in 2000, and $113,500 in 2001.*
d. *The applicable tax rate is 40% for all years affected.*

*The deferred component of income tax expense for 1999 is computed as follows. First, a schedule of the **temporary depreciation differences** for all affected years is prepared:*

	1994	1998	1999	2000	2001	2002
Book depreciation	$ 5,000	$ 5,000	$ 5,000	$5,000	$5,000	$5,000
Tax depreciation	5,000*	10,000	10,000	5,000*	-	-
Temporary difference:						
No difference	$ 0			$ 0		
Book deprec. < Tax deprec.		($5,000)	($5,000)			
Book deprec. > Tax deprec.					$5,000	$5,000

*Due to MACRS half-year convention

*Then, a schedule of **future taxable (deductible) amounts** is prepared.*

	2000 Taxable (deductible)	2001 Taxable (deductible)	2002 Taxable (deductible)	Tax rate	Deferred tax liability (asset)
Scheduled taxable (deductible) amounts:					
Depreciation differences: taxable amounts		$5,000	$5,000	40%	$4,000 Noncurrent
Warranty differences: deductible amounts	$(500)			40%	$(200) Current

The above schedule shows that the future tax benefit (deductible amount) in 2000 of the $500 temporary difference resulting from the Warranty Expense Liability must be recognized automatically as a deferred tax as-

set in 1999. The deferred tax asset of $200 ($500 x 40%) should be reported as a current asset at 12/31/99 because the classification of the temporary difference is based on the related asset or liability, in this case a warranty liability that is expected to be satisfied in the next year. The amount of future taxes payable (deferred tax liability) associated with the total temporary difference of $10,000 resulting from excess depreciation [$5,000 (2001) + $5,000 (2002)] is $4,000 [($5,000 + 5,000) x 40%]. The $4,000 amount is reported as a noncurrent deferred tax liability at 12/31/99, because classification as current or noncurrent is based on the classification of the related asset or liability, in this case a depreciable asset that is noncurrent.

Once the deferred tax asset and deferred tax liability have been measured at year end, a journal entry is necessary to adjust the deferred tax account balances to the current year-end amount. As stated earlier, income tax expense for the year will consist of the taxes currently payable (based on taxable income) plus or minus any change in the deferred tax accounts.

EQUATION FOR DETERMINING INCOME TAX EXPENSE

$$\begin{matrix} Income\ tax \\ expense\ for \\ financial\ reporting \end{matrix} = \begin{matrix} Income\ tax \\ payable \\ from\ the\ tax \\ return \end{matrix} \pm \begin{matrix} Change\ in \\ deferred \\ taxes\ (net)* \end{matrix}$$

*Ending balance of deferred tax liability/asset (net) less beginning balance of deferred tax liability/asset (net)

NOTES:
1. Income Tax Expense is the sum of the two numbers on the right side of the equation. Each of these two numbers is determined directly using independent calculations. It is not possible to derive Income Tax Expense from pretax financial accounting income adjusted for permanent differences, unless the tax rate is constant for all years affected.
2. The $\pm$ refers to whether the change is a credit or additional liability (+) or a debit or additional asset (–).
3. Income Tax Payable is the amount of taxes calculated on the corporate tax return. It is the amount legally owed the government (after credits).
4. One deferred tax (net) balance sheet account may be used in practice. If separate asset and liability accounts are used, the changes in each account would all be netted to determine the deferred tax component of income tax expense.

To illustrate, we will use the deferred tax liability computed in Example 2 above and the taxable income derived in Example 1. Note that prior to adjustment, the deferred tax asset account had a zero balance and the deferred tax liability account had a balance of $2,000 ($5,000 x 40%) that was recognized as a result of the accumulated depreciation temporary difference that originated in 1995. (Refer to the schedule following the additional information given in Example 2 showing depreciation and the pattern of temporary differences and to the T-account under (c) below.) To focus on the two components of income tax expense, two entries rather than the typical combined entry will be used:

Income tax expense--current	44,200	
Income tax payable (a)		44,200

(a) $110,500 taxable income (from Example 1) x 40% = $44,200

Income tax expense--deferred (d)	1,800	
Deferred tax asset--current (b)	200	
Deferred tax liability--noncurrent (c)		2,000

(b) $500 x 40% = $200 needed Ending balance; $200 Ending balance – $0 Beginning balance = $200 increase needed in the account

	Deferred Tax Asset	
Beg. bal.	0	
(b) Increase	200	
End. bal.	200	

(c) $10,000 x 40% = $4,000 needed Ending balance; $4,000 Ending balance – $2,000 Beginning balance = $2,000 increase needed in the account

Deferred Tax Liability

2,000	Beg. bal.
2,000	Increase (c)
4,000	End. bal.

(d) $2,000 increase in noncurrent deferred tax liability account – $200 increase in current deferred tax asset account = $1,800

The bottom of the income statement for 1999 would appear as follows:

Income before income tax		$146,000
Income tax expense		
Current	$44,200	
Deferred	1,800	46,000
Net income		$100,000

To determine the deferred component of income tax expense for **2000**, a schedule of future taxable (deductible) amounts is prepared.

	2000 Taxable (deductible)	2001 Taxable (deductible)	2002 Taxable (deductible)	Tax rate	Deferred tax liability (asset)
Scheduled taxable (deductible) amounts:					
Depreciation differences:					
taxable amounts	-0-	$5,000	$5,000	40%	$4,000 Noncurrent

The temporary depreciation difference of $10,000 results in future taxes payable (a deferred tax liability) of $4,000 [($5,000 + 5,000) x 40%]. Note that the amount of the deferred tax liability in this example does not change from 1999 to 2000. The $4,000 amount would be reported as a noncurrent deferred tax liability at 12/31/00, based upon the noncurrent classification of the related depreciable asset. The $500 warranty expense deducted in 1999 for book purposes is deducted in 2000 for tax purposes. Therefore, the deferred tax asset related to warranty expense is realized in 2000 and the temporary difference related to warranty expense no longer exists.

Once the deferred tax amounts have been measured at year end, a journal entry is required to adjust the deferred tax account balances to the current year-end amount. Income tax expense for the year consists of the taxes currently payable plus or minus any change in the deferred tax accounts. The following journal entries are needed to record income tax expense for 2000:

Income tax expense--current	44,800	
Income tax payable (a)		44,800

(a) $112,000 taxable income x 40% = $44,800

Income tax expense--deferred (c)	200	
Deferred tax asset--current (b)		200

(b) The credit to the deferred tax asset is the adjustment necessary to reduce the existing balance to the desired ending balance.

Deferred Tax Asset

Beg. bal.	200		
		200	Decrease (b)
End. bal.	0		

(c) Income tax expense--deferred results from the decrease in the deferred tax asset. There is no adjustment to the deferred tax liability account.

Deferred Tax Liability

4,000	Beg. bal.
0	
4,000	End. bal.

To determine the deferred component of income tax expense for **2001** *the following journal entries are required:*

Income tax expense--current	45,400	
Income tax payable (a)		45,400

   (a) *$113,500 taxable income x 40% = $45,400*

Deferred tax liability--noncurrent (b)	2,000	
Income tax expense--deferred (c)		2,000

   (b) *The debit to the deferred tax liability is the adjustment necessary to reduce the existing balance to the desired ending balance.*

Deferred Tax Liability

		4,000	Beg. bal.
2,000			Decrease (b)
		2,000	End. bal.

   (c) *Income tax expense--deferred results from the decrease in the deferred tax liability. The deferred tax asset account was closed in 2000 because all temporary differences have reversed.*

The income tax liability per the tax return in 2001 is higher than total tax expense reported on the income statement since depreciation is not deducted for tax purposes anymore. In effect, the income tax liability in 2001 includes a portion of the tax deferred from 1999-2000 that was recorded as a liability; therefore, the deferred tax liability is reduced in 2001. There is a corresponding decrease in income tax expense--deferred that will reconcile the income tax liability per the tax return to income tax expense on the books.

Income tax expense--current	45,400
Income tax expense--deferred	(2,000)
Income tax expense per income	
statement	43,400

Changing tax rates. The previous examples assumed a constant enacted tax rate of 40%. Under the liability method upon which SFAS 109 is predicated, future taxable or deductible amounts must be measured using enacted tax rates expected to be in effect in the periods such amounts will impact taxable income. Similarly, a deferred tax asset is measured using the applicable enacted tax rate and provisions of the enacted tax law. However, when tax rates change, adjustments to reflect such changes are automatically included in the journal entry amount to increase or decrease the deferred tax accounts to the balances needed to properly reflect balance sheet amounts and to recognize the deferred component of income tax expense. The rate change effect would be included because the amount of the journal entry is determined by comparing the needed balance in deferred taxes at the end of the period which would be based on the newly enacted rates with the balance at the beginning of the period and taking the difference.

EXAMPLE 3: *Assume that in June 2001 a new income tax law is passed which lowers the corporate tax rate to 35% effective January 1, 2002. The entry debiting income tax expense--current and crediting income tax payable for 2001 is identical to that above.*

   However, the debit to the deferred tax liability account is the adjustment necessary to reduce the existing balance to the desired ending balance **under the new tax rate.**

Deferred tax liability--noncurrent	2,250	
Income tax expense--deferred		2,250

Deferred Tax Liability

		4,000	Beg. bal.
2,250			Decrease
		1,750	End. bal.

The $1,750 is the necessary balance for the 2002 reversal of the remaining $5,000 at 35%.

EXAMPLE 4: Dart Corporation has the following temporary differences from its first year of operations:

		Treatment in the book to tax reconciliation
1. **Long-term contracts:**		
Year 1 (Current year):	Book contract income > tax contract income	$300 subtraction
Year 2:	Book contract income < tax contract income	$300 addition
2. **Accumulated depreciation:**		
Year 1 (Current year):	Book deprec. < tax deprec.	$1,000 subtraction
Year 2:	Book deprec. < tax deprec.	$500 subtraction
Year 3:	Book deprec. > tax deprec.	$600 addition
Year 4:	Book deprec. > tax deprec.	$400 addition
Year 7:		$500 addition
3. **Estimated expense liability:**		
Year 1 (Current year):	Book est. exp./loss > tax deduction	$200 addition
Year 7:	Book exp./loss < tax deduction	$200 subtraction
4. **Rent revenue:**		
Year 1 (Current year):	Book rev. < tax rev.	$500 addition
Year 4:	Book rev. > tax rev.	$200 subtraction
Year 7:	Book rev. > tax rev.	$300 subtraction
5. **Tax rates:** Current year:	40%	
Years 2-4:	35%	
Years 5-7:	30%	

*The schedule below combines (1) the pretax accounting income to taxable income reconciliation and (2) the future taxable (deductible) amounts schedule. Remember that **taxable amounts** are added to financial (book) income in the book to tax reconciliation schedule in the future years in which they increase taxable income. **Deductible amounts** are subtracted from financial (book) income in the book to tax reconciliation schedule in the future years in which they decrease taxable income. Taxable income and deferred tax liability (asset) balances for Year 1 (the current year) would be determined as follows:*

	Current year	Future years				
	Year 1	Year 2 taxable (deductible)	Year 3 taxable (deductible)	Year 4 taxable (deductible)	Year 7 taxable (deductible)	Deferred tax liability (asset)
Tax rate	40%	35%	35%	35%	30%	
Pretax accounting income	$1,600					
Temporary differences:						
LT contracts	(300)	300				$105 Current
Accumulated deprec.	(1,000)	(500)	600	400	500	$325 Noncurrent
Estimated expense liability	200				(200)	$ (60) Noncurrent
Rent revenue	500			(200)	(300)	$(160) Noncurrent
Taxable income	$1,000					
Income tax payable	$ 400 ($1,000 x 40%)					

Income tax expense would be computed as follows:

$$\text{Income tax expense} = \text{Income taxes payable} \pm \text{Change in deferred taxes (net)}$$

Under SFAS 109, deferred tax assets and liabilities are classified as current or long-term based on the related asset or liability, rather than on the expected timing of the future deductible or taxable amounts. However, if a deferred tax asset or liability is not related to an asset or liability for financial reporting purposes, it is classified based upon its expected reversal date. Presented below is a solution for Example 4.

Temporary difference	Deferred tax asset or liability	Related account	Classification*
LT Contracts	$300 x 35% = $105 liability	Const-in-Progress	Current
Depreciation	[(500) + 600 + 400] x 35% + $500 x 30% = $325 liability	Accumulated depr.	Noncurrent
Est. expense	$200 x 30% = $60 asset	Estimated liability	Noncurrent
Rent Revenue	$200 x 35% + $300 x 30% = $160 asset	Unearned rent	Noncurrent

Balance sheet disclosure is explained for this example in Section F.3.

The journal entries required are as follows:

Income tax expense--current	400	
Income tax payable		400 (a)

(a) $1,000 taxable income x 40% = $400

Income tax expense--deferred (e)	210	
Deferred tax asset--noncurrent (b)	220	
Deferred tax liability--current (c)		105
Deferred tax liability--noncurrent (d)		325

(b) $200 x 30% + $200 x 35% + $300 x 30%= $220 needed Ending balance; $220 Ending balance – $0 Beginning balance = $220 increase needed in the account.

Deferred Tax Asset--Noncurrent			
Beg. bal.	-0-		
(b) Increase	220		
End. bal.	220		

(c) $300 x 35% = $105 Ending balance; $105 Ending balance – $0 Beginning balance = $105 increase needed in the account

Deferred Tax Liability--Current			
		-0-	Beg. bal.
		105	Increase (c)
		105	End. bal.

(d) $1,000 x 35% + ($500) x 35% + $500 x 30% = $325 Ending balance; $325 Ending balance – zero Beginning balance = $325 increase needed in the account.

Deferred Tax Liability--Noncurrent			
		-0-	Beg. bal.
		325	Increase (d)
		325	End. bal.

(e) $105 increase in current deferred tax liability amount + $325 increase in noncurrent deferred tax liability account – $220 increase in noncurrent deferred tax asset account = $210.

Note that since this is the firm's first year of operations, there are no beginning balances in the deferred tax accounts. If there were any permanent differences, such differences would affect only the current year as they did in Example 1. In addition, the need for a valuation allowance to reduce the deferred tax asset to its net realizable value would need to be considered.

Deferred tax asset valuation allowance. SFAS 109 does require that a deferred tax asset be reduced by a valuation allowance if, based on the weight of available evidence, it is more likely than not (a likelihood of more than 50%) that some portion or all of the deferred tax asset will not be realized. All available evidence, both positive and negative, should be considered to determine whether a valuation allowance is needed. The need for a valuation allowance ultimately depends on the existence of sufficient taxable income (necessary to receive the benefit of a future deductible amount) within the carryback/carryforward period, as described in Section E of this module. SFAS 109 provides the following list of possible sources of taxable income; if any one of these sources is sufficient to support a conclusion that a valuation allowance is not necessary, other sources need not be considered.

1. Possible Sources of Taxable Income

    a. Future reversals of existing taxable temporary differences
    b. Future taxable income exclusive of reversing temporary differences and carryforwards
    c. Taxable income in prior carryback year(s) if carryback is permitted under the tax law
    d. **Tax-planning strategies** that would, if necessary, be implemented to

        (1) Accelerate taxable amounts to utilize expiring carryforwards
        (2) Change the character of taxable or deductible amounts from ordinary income or loss to capital gain or loss
        (3) Switch from tax-exempt to taxable investments.

SFAS 109 also provides some examples of evidence to be considered when evaluating the need for a valuation allowance. These are summarized in the table below.

1. Negative Evidence--Indicates Need for a Valuation Allowance

    a. Cumulative losses in recent years
    b. A history of operating loss or tax credit carryforwards expiring unused
    c. Losses expected in early future years (by a presently profitable entity)
    d. Unsettled circumstances that, if unfavorably resolved, would adversely affect future operations and profit levels on a continuing basis in future years
    e. A carryback/carryforward period that is so brief that it would limit realization of tax benefits if (1) a significant deductible temporary difference is expected to reverse in a single year or (2) the enterprise operates in a traditionally cyclical business.

2. Positive Evidence--Can Offset the Impact of Negative Evidence

    a. Existing contracts or firm sales backlog that will produce more than enough taxable income to realize the deferred tax asset based on existing sales prices and cost structures
    b. An excess of appreciated asset value over the tax basis of the entity's net assets in an amount sufficient to realize the deferred tax asset
    c. A strong earnings history exclusive of the loss that created the future deductible amount (tax loss carryforward or deductible temporary difference) coupled with evidence indicating that the loss (for example, an unusual, infrequent, or extraordinary item) is an aberration rather than a continuing condition.

For an example of the recording of a valuation allowance, assume Jeremiah Corporation has determined it has a noncurrent deferred tax asset of $800,000. Note that in the current and prior periods when this asset was recognized, income tax expense was reduced. Based on the weight of available evidence, Jeremiah feels it is more likely than not that $300,000 of this deferred tax asset will not be realized. Jeremiah would prepare the following journal entry:

Income tax expense	300,000	
Allowance to reduce deferred tax asset to expected realizable value		300,000

The balance sheet presentation is

Other Assets (Noncurrent)	
Deferred tax asset	$800,000
Less Allowance to reduce deferred tax asset to expected realizable value	(300,000)
	$ 500,000

At each year end, the balance on the allowance account is adjusted upward or downward based on the evidence available at that time, resulting in an increase or decrease of income tax expense. For example, if $600,000 was deemed to be the net realizable value at the end of the next year, the following entry would be made:

Allowance to reduce deferred tax asset to ex- pected realizable value	100,000	
Deferred income tax expense		100,000

D. Deferred Tax Related to Business Investments

One additional issue concerns temporary differences from income on long-term investments that are accounted for using the equity method. For these investments a corporation may assume that the temporary difference (the undistributed income since date of acquisition) will ultimately become taxable in the form of a dividend or in the form of a capital gain. Obviously, the tax expense and deferred tax liability recorded when the difference originates will be a function of whichever of these assumptions is made.

To illustrate the application of the requirements of SFAS 109 and APB 23 assume the Parent Company owns 70% of the outstanding common stock of the Subsidiary Company and 30% of the outstanding common stock of Investee Company. Additional data for Subsidiary and Investee Companies for the year 1999 are as follows:

	Investee Co	*Subsidiary Co*
Net income	$50,000	$100,000
Dividends paid	20,000	60,000

1. Income Tax Effects From Investee Co.

The pretax accounting income of Parent Company will include equity in investee income equal to $15,000 ($50,000 x 30%). Parent's taxable income, however, will include dividend income of $6,000 ($20,000 x 30%), and a dividends received deduction of 80% of the $6,000, or $4,800, will also be allowed for the dividends received. This 80% dividends received deduction is a permanent difference between pretax accounting and taxable income and is allowed for dividends received from domestic corporations in which the ownership percentage is less than 80% and equal to or greater than 20%. The originating temporary difference results from Parent's equity ($9,000) in Investee's undistributed income of $30,000 ($50,000 – $20,000). The amount by which the deferred tax liability account would increase in 1999 depends upon the expectations of Parent Co. as to the manner in which the $9,000 of undistributed income will be received. If the expectation of receipt is via dividends, then the temporary difference is 20% of $9,000 because 80% of the expected dividend will be excluded from taxable income when received. This temporary difference in 1999 of $1,800, multiplied by the tax rate, will give the amount of the increase in the deferred tax liability. If the expectation of receipt, however, is through future sale of the investment, then the temporary difference is $9,000, and the change in the deferred tax liability is the capital gains rate (currently the same as ordinary rate) times the $9,000.

The entries below illustrate these alternatives. A tax rate of 34% is used for both ordinary income and capital gains. Note that the amounts in the entries below relate only to Investee Company's incremental impact upon Parent Company's tax accounts.

	Expectations for undistributed income	
	Dividends	Capital gains
Income tax expense	1,020	3,468
Deferred taxes (net)	612[b]	3,060[c]
Income taxes payable	408[a]	408[a]

[a]Computation of income taxes payable

Dividend income--30% ($20,000)	$6,000
Less: 80% dividends received deduction	(4,800)
Amount included in Parent's taxable income	$1,200
Tax liability--34% ($1,200)	$ 408

[b]Computation of deferred tax liability (dividend assumption)

Temporary difference

Parent's share of undistributed income-- 30% ($30,000)	$ 9,000
Less: 80% dividends received deduction	(7,200)
Originating temporary difference	$1,800
Deferred tax liability--34% ($1,800)	$ 612

[c]Computation of deferred tax liability (capital gain assumption)

Temporary difference--Parent's share of undistributed income--

30% ($30,000)	$9,000
Deferred tax liability--34% ($9,000)	$3,060

2. **Income Tax Effects From Subsidiary Co.**

The pretax accounting income of Parent will also include equity in subsidiary income of $70,000 (70% of $100,000). Note also that this $70,000 will be included in pretax consolidated income if Parent and Subsidiary consolidate. For tax purposes, Parent and Subsidiary cannot file a consolidated tax return because the minimum level of control (80%) is not present. Consequently, the taxable income of Parent will include dividend income of $42,000 (70% of $60,000) and there will be an 80% dividends received deduction of $33,600. The temporary difference results from Parent's equity ($28,000) in Subsidiary's undistributed earnings of $40,000 ($100,000 – $60,000). Remember that the undistributed income of Subsidiary has been recognized for book purposes, but only distributed income (dividends) has been included in taxable income. The amount of the deferred tax liability in 1997 depends upon the expectations of Parent Company as to the manner in which this $28,000 of undistributed income will be received in the future. The same expectations can exist as previously discussed for Parent's equity in Investee's undistributed earnings (i.e., through future dividend distributions or capital gains). Determination of the amounts and the accounts affected for these 2 assumptions would be similar. The diagram below illustrates the accounting and income tax treatment of the undistributed investee/subsidiary earnings by corporate investors under different levels of ownership.

SUMMARY OF TEMPORARY DIFFERENCES OF INVESTEES AND SUBSIDIARIES

Level of Ownership Interest

Recognition of Temporary Differences

> * *Both pretax financial accounting and taxable income would include only dividends declared by the investee. If evidence indicates that significant influence exists at an ownership level less than 20%, a temporary difference would be recognized.*

E. **Loss Carryforwards and Carrybacks**

Operating losses of a particular period can be carried back to the two immediate past periods' income resulting in a refund. Losses still remaining after carrybacks may also be carried forward for 20 years to offset income if income arises in any of those 20 years. Companies may at the time of the loss elect to use only the carryforward provision.

Loss carrybacks occur when losses in the current period are carried back to periods in which there was income. Loss carrybacks result in tax refunds in the loss period and thus should be recognized in the year of the loss. The entry to record the benefit is

Tax refund receivable	(based on tax credit due to loss)	
Tax loss benefit (income tax expense)		(same)

The tax loss benefit account would be closed to revenue and expense summary in the year of the loss.

Tax loss carryforwards are recognized in the year the loss occurs. Under SFAS 109, the benefit of a loss carryforward is **always** recognized as a deferred tax asset which may be reduced by a valuation allowance if necessary. For example, assume Caleb Corporation has a loss carryforward of $300,000 which could result in future tax savings of $120,000 (40% x $300,000). Caleb feels that based on the weight of available evidence it is more likely than not that $50,000 of these savings will not be realized. Caleb's entries to record the benefit and the valuation allowance are

Deferred tax asset	120,000	
Tax loss benefit (income tax expense)		120,000
Tax loss benefit (income tax expense)	50,000	
Allowance to reduce deferred tax asset to expected realizable value		50,000

Income statement presentation

The income statement for the year in which both a loss carryback and carryforward are realized would appear as follows:

Loss before income taxes		($xx)
Less:		
Benefit from operating loss carryback	xx	
Benefit from operating loss carryforward	<u>xx</u>	<u>xx</u>
Net loss		($<u>xx</u>)

F. **Financial Statement Presentation of Income Tax**

1. Income Statement

    Continuing Operations. For each year presented, the significant components of income tax expense arising from continuing operations shall be disclosed on the face of the income statement or in the notes. These components would include

    a. Current tax expense or benefit
    b. Deferred tax expense or benefit (exclusive of the effects of other components listed below)
    c. The benefits of operating loss carryforwards
    d. Adjustments of a deferred tax liability or asset for enacted changes in tax laws or rates or a change in the tax status of the enterprise
    e. Adjustments of the beginning-of-the-year balance of a valuation allowance because of a change in circumstances that causes a change in judgment about the realizability of the related deferred tax asset in future years.

    Other Components of Net Income. Income tax expense must be allocated within an accounting period between continuing operations and other components of net income (i.e., discontinued operations, extraordinary items, etc.). The amount of income tax expense allocated to continuing operations is equal to the tax on pretax income or loss from continuing operations. However, if net income includes "special items" such as discontinued operations, extraordinary items, and accounting changes, the amount of income tax expense allocated to continuing operations must consider these items. The amount allocated to an item other than continuing operations (e.g., discontinued operations, extraordinary items, and accounting changes) is equal to the incremental effect on income taxes resulting from that item.

    > EXAMPLE: *Alco Co. has income from continuing operations of $2,000,000, an extraordinary gain of $450,000, and no permanent or temporary differences. The current tax rate is 34%. Total income tax expense is $833,000 ($2,450,000 x 34%). This amount will first be allocated to income from continuing operations, and the remainder (incremental tax consequences attributable to the remaining components of net income) will be allocated to the extraordinary gain.*

Total income tax expense	*$833,000*
Tax consequences associated	
* with income from continuing operations ($2,000,000 x 34%)*	*<u>680,000</u>*
Remainder to extraordinary gain	*$<u>153,000</u>*
The bottom of the income statement would appear as follows:	
Income from continuing operations	*$2,000,000*
Income tax expense	*<u>680,000</u>*
Income before extraordinary item	*$1,320,000*
Extraordinary gain (net of $153,000 tax)	*<u>297,000</u>*
Net income	*$<u>1,617,000</u>*

EXAMPLE: Benjamin Corporation's ordinary loss from continuing operations is $1,000. Benjamin also has an extraordinary gain of $1,800 that is a capital gain for tax purposes. The tax rate is 40% on ordinary income and 30% on capital gains. Income taxes currently payable are $240 [($1,800 – $1,000) x 30%]. Since the effect of the $1,000 loss was to offset a capital gain, the benefit allocated to continuing operations is $300 (30% x $1,000) rather than $400 (40% x $1,000). The incremental tax expense allocated to the extraordinary gain is $540 (difference between the $300 tax benefit and the $240 total tax expense).

2. Retained Earnings

    Any income tax effects associated with adjustments of the opening balance of retained earnings for a **special type** change in accounting principle or correction of an error are to be charged or credited directly to retained earnings. The income tax effects of other stockholders' equity items (e.g., cumulative translation adjustment) are charged or credited to stockholders' equity.

3. Balance Sheet

    The classification of deferred tax liabilities and assets is a two-stage process. First, all deferred tax liabilities and assets are classified as current or noncurrent. Deferred tax liabilities and assets are classified as current or long-term based on the related asset or liability. A deferred tax liability or asset is related to an asset or liability if reduction of the asset or liability will cause the temporary difference to reverse. If the deferred tax liability or asset is **not** related to any asset or liability for financial reporting purposes (such as a deferred tax asset caused by a loss carryforward), it is classified based on the timing of its expected reversal or utilization date. Once classification has been determined, all current amounts are netted to get a net current asset or liability and the noncurrent amounts are likewise netted to obtain a net noncurrent amount.

    This process is illustrated in Example 4 that appeared earlier in this module. In Example 4, the only current deferred tax asset/liability is the $105 current liability. Thus the net current amount is a $105 liability. The other amounts are netted to find the net noncurrent amount. In this case the net noncurrent amount is a $105 liability ($325 – 220).

    If an allowance account has been recognized for a deferred tax asset, it would be deducted from the related deferred tax asset before the netting process described above is done. If the allowance account balance relates to a deferred tax asset that is classified partially as current and partially as noncurrent, the allowance balance should be allocated between them in the ratio of each asset balance to the total asset balance.

    Note that if a tax refund receivable results from a loss carryback in the current period, this element would not be included in the netting process; only deferred tax assets and liabilities are netted.

G. **Treatment of Selected Temporary Differences**

    On the following page we have summarized the treatment of selected temporary differences from the period of origination to the period of reversal.

TREATMENT OF SELECTED TEMPORARY DIFFERENCES

	Book value	Less	Tax basis	=	Previous and current reconciliations of book income to tax income	Future years(s) reconciliation of book income to tax income	Deferred consequence*
a. Estimated liability under warranties	56,000	Less	-0-	=	56,000 addition(s)	56,000 subtraction(s)	Asset (3)
b. Unearned rent (royalty) revenue received (liability)	40,000	Less	-0-	=	40,000 addition(s)	40,000 subtraction(s)	Asset (3)
c. Long term contracts:							
Construction in process (asset)	1,125,000	Less	1,000,000	=	125,000 subtraction	125,000 addition	Liability (1)
d. Plant assets and accumulated depreciation:							
Equipment (asset)	50,000		50,000				
Accumulated depreciation (contra asset)	10,000	Less	18,500				
End of period basis	40,000		31,500	=	8,500 subtraction(s)	8,500 addition(s)	Liability (1)
e. Donated assets:							
Year of acquisition:							
Machinery (asset)	90,000	Less	-0-	=	Not included because donat. recorded in S/E	See deprec. below	Liability (1)
Depreciation:							
Machinery (asset)	90,000		-0-				
Accumulated depreciation (contra asset)	18,000	Less	-0-				
End of period basis	72,000		-0-	=	18,000 addition(s)	18,000 addition(s)	Reduction of liability
Sale of asset:							
Cash received	80,000		80,000				
Basis of asset	72,000	Less	-0-				
Gain (revenue)	8,000		80,000	=		72,000 addition	Reduction of liability
f. Replacement asset for involuntarily converted asset:							
Year of acquisition:							
Building (asset)	280,000		280,000				
Deferred gain from involuntary conversion	-0-**	Less	(110,000)				
Initial basis of asset	280,000		170,000	=	110,000 subtraction		Liability (1)
Depreciation:							
Building (asset)	280,000		170,000				
Accumulated depreciation (contra asset)	(14,000)	Less	(28,900)				
End of period basis	266,000		141,100	=	14,900 subtraction		Liability (1)
Sale of replacement asset:							
Cash received	270,000		270,000				
Basis of asset	(266,000)	Less	(141,100)				
Gain (revenue)	4,000		128,900	=		124,900 addition	Reduction of liability

* The numbers in parenthesis refer to the relationships presented on p. 730.

** The $110,000 gain was recognized in the financial statements in the period the involuntary conversion occurred.

MULTIPLE-CHOICE QUESTIONS (1-40)

1. Justification for the method of determining periodic deferred tax expense is based on the concept of

a. Matching of periodic expense to periodic revenue.
b. Objectivity in the calculation of periodic expense.
c. Recognition of assets and liabilities.
d. Consistency of tax expense measurements with actual tax planning strategies.

2. Among the items reported on Cord, Inc.'s income statement for the year ended December 31, 1999, were the following:

Payment of penalty	$ 5,000
Insurance premium on life of an officer with Cord as owner and beneficiary	10,000

Temporary differences amount to

a. $0
b. $ 5,000
c. $10,000
d. $15,000

3. Caleb Corporation has three financial statement elements for which the December 31, 1999, book value is different than the December 31, 1999, tax basis:

	Book value	Tax basis	Difference
Equipment	$200,000	$120,000	$80,000
Prepaid officers insurance policy	75,000	0	75,000
Warranty liability	50,000	0	50,000

As a result of these differences, future taxable amounts are

a. $ 50,000
b. $ 80,000
c. $155,000
d. $205,000

4. Temporary differences arise when revenues are taxable

	After they are recognized in financial income	Before they are recognized in financial income
a.	Yes	Yes
b.	Yes	No
c.	No	No
d.	No	Yes

5. Which of the following differences would result in future taxable amounts?

a. Expenses or losses that are deductible after they are recognized in financial income.
b. Revenues or gains that are taxable before they are recognized in financial income.
c. Expenses or losses that are deductible before they are recognized in financial income.
d. Revenues or gains that are recognized in financial income but are never included in taxable income.

6. Dunn Co.'s 1999 income statement reported $90,000 income before provision for income taxes. To compute the provision for federal income taxes, the following 1999 data are provided:

Rent received in advance	$16,000
Income from exempt municipal bonds	20,000
Depreciation deducted for income tax purposes in excess of depreciation reported for financial statements purposes	10,000
Enacted corporate income tax rate	30%

If the alternative minimum tax provisions are ignored, what amount of current federal income tax liability should be reported in Dunn's December 31, 1999 balance sheet?

a. $18,000
b. $22,800
c. $25,800
d. $28,800

7. Pine Corp.'s books showed pretax income of $800,000 for the year ended December 31, 1999. In the computation of federal income taxes, the following data were considered:

Gain on an involuntary conversion (Pine has elected to replace the property within the statutory period using total proceeds.)	$350,000
Depreciation deducted for tax purposes in excess of depreciation deducted for book purposes	50,000
Federal estimated tax payments, 1999	70,000
Enacted federal tax rates, 1999	30%

What amount should Pine report as its current federal income tax liability on its December 31, 1999 balance sheet?

a. $ 50,000
b. $ 65,000
c. $120,000
d. $135,000

8. For the year ended December 31, 1999, Tyre Co. reported pretax financial statement income of $750,000. Its taxable income was $650,000. The difference is due to accelerated depreciation for income tax purposes. Tyre's effective income tax rate is 30%, and Tyre made estimated tax payments during 1999 of $90,000. What amount should Tyre report as current income tax expense for 1999?

a. $105,000
b. $135,000
c. $195,000
d. $225,000

9. Tower Corp. began operations on January 1, 1998. For financial reporting, Tower recognizes revenues from all sales under the accrual method. However, in its income tax returns, Tower reports qualifying sales under the installment method. Tower's gross profit on these installment sales under each method was as follows:

Year	Accrual method	Installment method
1998	$1,600,000	$ 600,000
1999	2,600,000	1,400,000

The income tax rate is 30% for 1998 and future years. There are no other temporary or permanent differences. In its December 31, 1999 balance sheet, what amount should Tower report as a liability for deferred income taxes?

    a. $840,000
    b. $660,000
    c. $600,000
    d. $360,000

10. On June 30, 1999, Ank Corp. prepaid a $19,000 premium on an annual insurance policy. The premium payment was a tax deductible expense in Ank's 1996 cash basis tax return. The accrual basis income statement will report a $9,500 insurance expense in 1999 and 2000.

Ank's income tax rate is 30% in 1999 and 25% thereafter. In Ank's December 31, 1999 balance sheet, what amount related to the insurance should be reported as a deferred income tax liability?

    a. $5,700
    b. $4,750
    c. $2,850
    d. $2,375

11. Mill, which began operations on January 1, 1997, recognizes income from long-term construction contracts under the percentage-of-completion method in its financial statements and under the completed-contract method for income tax reporting. Income under each method follows:

Year	Completed contract	Percentage-of-completion
1997	$ --	$300,000
1998	400,000	600,000
1999	700,000	850,000

The income tax rate was 30% for 1997 through 1999. For years after 1999, the enacted tax rate is 25%. There are no other temporary differences. Mill should report in its December 31, 1999 balance sheet a deferred income tax liability of

    a. $ 87,500
    b. $105,000
    c. $162,500
    d. $195,000

Items 12 and 13 are based on the following:

Zeff Co. prepared the following reconciliation of its pretax financial statement income to taxable income for the year ended December 31, 1999, its first year of operations:

Pretax financial income	$160,000
Nontaxable interest received on municipal securities	(5,000)
Long-term loss accrual in excess of deductible amount	10,000
Depreciation in excess of financial statement amount	(25,000)
Taxable income	$140,000

Zeff's tax rate for 1999 is 40%.

12. In its 1999 income statement, what amount should Zeff report as income tax expense--current portion?

    a. $52,000
    b. $56,000

    c. $62,000
    d. $64,000

13. In its December 31, 1999 balance sheet, what should Zeff report as deferred income tax liability?

    a. $2,000
    b. $4,000
    c. $6,000
    d. $8,000

14. West Corp. leased a building and received the $36,000 annual rental payment on June 15, 1999. The beginning of the lease was July 1, 1999. Rental income is taxable when received. West's tax rates are 30% for 1999 and 40% thereafter. West had no other permanent or temporary differences. West determined that no valuation allowance was needed. What amount of deferred tax asset should West report in its December 31, 1999 balance sheet?

    a. $ 5,400
    b. $ 7,200
    c. $10,800
    d. $14,400

15. Black Co., organized on January 2, 1999, had pretax accounting income of $500,000 and taxable income of $800,000 for the year ended December 31, 1999. The only temporary difference is accrued product warranty costs which are expected to be paid as follows:

2000	$100,000
2001	50,000
2002	50,000
2003	100,000

Black has never had any net operating losses (book or tax) and does not expect any in the future. There were no temporary differences in prior years. The enacted income tax rates are 35% for 1996, 30% for 2000 through 2001, and 25% for 2000. In Black's December 31, 1999 balance sheet, the deferred income tax asset should be

    a. $ 60,000
    b. $ 70,000
    c. $ 85,000
    d. $105,000

16. A temporary difference which would result in a deferred tax liability is

    a.   Interest revenue on municipal bonds.
    b.   Accrual of warranty expense.
    c.   Excess of tax depreciation over financial accounting depreciation.
    d.   Subscriptions received in advance.

17. Orleans Co., a cash basis taxpayer, prepares accrual basis financial statements. In its 1999 balance sheet, Orleans' deferred income tax liabilities increased compared to 1998. Which of the following changes would cause this increase in deferred income tax liabilities?

    I.   An increase in prepaid insurance.
    II.   An increase in rent receivable.
    III.   An increase in warranty obligations.

    a.   I only.

b. I and II.
c. II and III.
d. III only.

18. At the end of year 1, Cody Co. reported a profit on a partially completed construction contract by applying the percentage-of-completion method. By the end of year 2, the total estimated profit on the contract at completion in year 3 had been drastically reduced from the amount estimated at the end of year 1. Consequently, in year 2, a loss equal to one-half of the year 1 profit was recognized. Cody used the completed-contract method for income tax purposes and had no other contracts. The year 2 balance sheet should include a deferred tax

	Asset	Liability
a.	Yes	Yes
b.	No	Yes
c.	Yes	No
d.	No	No

19. A deferred tax liability is computed using
a. The current tax laws, regardless of expected or enacted future tax laws.
b. Expected future tax laws, regardless of whether those expected laws have been enacted.
c. Current tax laws, unless enacted future tax laws are different.
d. Either current or expected future tax laws, regardless of whether those expected laws have been enacted.

20. For the year ended December 31, 1999, Grim Co.'s pretax financial statement income was $200,000 and its taxable income was $150,000. The difference is due to the following:

Interest on municipal bonds	$70,000
Premium expense on keyman life insurance	(20,000)
Total	$50,000

Grim's enacted income tax rate is 30%. In its 1999 income statement, what amount should Grim report as current provision for income tax expense?
a. $45,000
b. $51,000
c. $60,000
d. $66,000

Items 21 and 22 are based on the following:

Venus Corp.'s worksheet for calculating current and deferred income taxes for 1999 follows:

	1999	*2000*	*2001*
Pretax income	$1,400		
Temporary differences:			
Depreciation	(800)	($1,200)	$2,000
Warranty costs	400	(100)	(300)
Taxable income	$1,000		
Enacted rate	30%	30%	25%
Deferred tax accounts			

	Asset	Liability
Current	$ (30)[a]	
Noncurrent (before netting)	$ (75)[b]	$ 140[c]

[a] [($100) x 30%]
[b] [($300) x 25%]
[c] [($1,200) x 30%] + [$2,000 x 25%]

Venus had no prior deferred tax balances. In its 1999 income statement, what amount should Venus report as

21. Current income tax expense?
a. $420
b. $350
c. $300
d. $0

22. Deferred income tax expense?
a. $350
b. $300
c. $120
d. $ 35

23. Shear, Inc. began operations in 1999. Included in Shear's 1999 financial statements were bad debt expenses of $1,400 and profit from an installment sale of $2,600. For tax purposes, the bad debts will be deducted and the profit from the installment sale will be recognized in 2000. The enacted tax rates are 30% in 1999 and 25% in 2000. In its 1999 income statement, what amount should Shear report as deferred income tax expense?
a. $300
b. $360
c. $650
d. $780

24. Quinn Co. reported a net deferred tax asset of $9,000 in its December 31, 1998 balance sheet. For 1999, Quinn reported pretax financial statement income of $300,000. Temporary differences of $100,000 resulted in taxable income of $200,000 for 1999. At December 31, 1999, Quinn had cumulative taxable differences of $70,000. Quinn's effective income tax rate is 30%. In its December 31, 1999, income statement, what should Quinn report as deferred income tax expense?
a. $12,000
b. $21,000
c. $30,000
d. $60,000

25. Rein Inc. reported deferred tax assets and deferred tax liabilities at the end of 1998 and at the end of 1999. For the year ended 1999, Rein should report deferred income tax expense or benefit equal to the
a. Decrease in the deferred tax assets.
b. Increase in the deferred tax liabilities.
c. Amount of the current tax liability plus the sum of the net changes in deferred tax assets and deferred tax liabilities.
d. Sum of the net changes in deferred tax assets and deferred tax liabilities.

26. On its December 31, 1999 balance sheet, Shin Co. had income taxes payable of $13,000 and a current deferred tax asset of $20,000 before determining the need for a valuation account. Shin had reported a current deferred tax asset of $15,000 at December 31, 1998. No estimated tax payments were made during 1999. At December 31, 1999, Shin determined that it was more likely than not that 10% of the deferred tax asset would not be realized. In its 1999 income statement, what amount should Shin report as total income tax expense?

    a. $ 8,000
    b. $ 8,500
    c. $10,000
    d. $13,000

27. Bart, Inc., a newly organized corporation, uses the equity method of accounting for its 30% investment in Rex Co.'s common stock. During 1999, Rex paid dividends of $300,000 and reported earnings of $900,000. In addition:

- The dividends received from Rex are eligible for the 80% dividends received deductions.
- All the undistributed earnings of Rex will be distributed in future years.
- There are no other temporary differences.
- Bart's 1999 income tax rate is 30%.
- The enacted income tax rate after 1999 is 25%.

In Bart's December 31, 1999 balance sheet, the deferred income tax liability should be

    a. $10,800
    b. $ 9,000
    c. $ 5,400
    d. $ 4,500

28. Leer Corp.'s pretax income in 1999 was $100,000. The temporary differences between amounts reported in the financial statements and the tax return are as follows:

- Depreciation in the financial statements was $8,000 more than tax depreciation.
- The equity method of accounting resulted in financial statement income of $35,000. A $25,000 dividend was received during the year, which is eligible for the 80% dividends received deduction.

Leer's effective income tax rate was 30% in 1999. In its 1999 income statement, Leer should report a current provision for income taxes of

    a. $26,400
    b. $23,400
    c. $21,900
    d. $18,600

29. Dix, Inc., a calendar-year corporation, reported the following operating income (loss) before income tax for its first 3 years of operations:

1997	$100,000
1998	(200,000)
1999	400,000

There are no permanent or temporary differences between operating income (loss) for financial and income tax reporting purposes. When filing its 1998 tax return, Dix did not elect to forego the carryback of its loss for 1998. Assume a 40% tax rate for all years. What amount should Dix report as its income tax liability at December 31, 1999?

    a. $160,000
    b. $120,000
    c. $ 80,000
    u. $ 60,000

30. Town, a calendar-year corporation incorporated in January 1997, experienced a $600,000 net operating loss (NOL) in 1998 due to a prolonged strike. Town never had a strike in the past that significantly affected its income and does not expect such a strike in the future. Additionally, there is no other negative evidence concerning future operating income. For the years 1997-1999, Town reported a taxable income in each year, and a total of $450,000 for the 3 years. Assume that: (1) there is no difference between pretax accounting income and taxable income for all years, (2) the income tax rate is 40% for all years, (3) the NOL will be carried back to the profit years 1997-1999 to the extent of $450,000, and $150,000 will be carried forward to future periods. In its 1999 income statement, what amount should Town report as the reduction of loss due to NOL carryback and carryforward?

    a. $240,000
    b. $180,000
    c. $270,000
    d. $360,000

31. Bishop Corporation began operations in 1997 and had operating losses of $200,000 in 1997 and $150,000 in 1998. For the year ended December 31, 1999, Bishop had pretax book income of $300,000. For the 3-year period 1997 to 1999, assume an income tax rate of 40% and no permanent or temporary differences between book and taxable income. Because Bishop began operations in 1997, the entire amount of deferred tax assets recognized in 1997 and 1998 were offset with amounts added to the allowance account. In Bishop's 1999 income statement, how much should be reported as current income tax expense?

    a. $0
    b. $ 40,000
    c. $ 60,000
    d. $120,000

32. Mobe Co. reported the following operating income (loss) for its first 3 years of operations:

1997	$ 300,000
1998	(700,000)
1999	1,200,000

For each year, there were no deferred income taxes, and Mobe's effective income tax rate was 30%. In its 1998 income tax return, Mobe elected to carry back the maximum amount of loss possible. Additionally, there was more negative evidence than positive evidence concerning profitability for Mobe in 1999. In its 1999 income statement, what amount should Mobe report as total income tax expense?

- a. $120,000
- b. $150,000
- c. $240,000
- d. $360,000

33. In 1996, Rand, Inc. reported for financial statement purposes the following items, which were not included in taxable income:

Installment gain to be collected equally in 2000 through 2002	$1,500,000
Estimated future warranty costs to be paid equally in 2000 through 2002	2,100,000

There were no temporary differences in prior years. Rand's enacted tax rates are 30% for 1999 and 25% for 2000 through 2002.

In Rand's December 31, 1999 balance sheet, what amounts of the deferred tax asset should be classified as current and noncurrent?

	Current	*Noncurrent*
a.	$60,000	$100,000
b.	$60,000	$120,000
c.	$50,000	$100,000
d.	$50,000	$120,000

34. Thorn Co. applies Statement of Financial Accounting Standards 109, *Accounting for Income Taxes*. At the end of 1999, the tax effects of temporary differences were as follows:

	Deferred tax assets (liabilities)	*Related asset classification*
Accelerated tax depreciation	($75,000)	Noncurrent asset
Additional costs in inventory for tax purposes	25,000	Current asset
	($50,000)	

A valuation allowance was not considered necessary. Thorn anticipates that $10,000 of the deferred tax liability will reverse in 2000. In Thorn's December 31, 1999 balance sheet, what amount should Thorn report as noncurrent deferred tax liability?

- a. $40,000
- b. $50,000
- c. $65,000
- d. $75,000

35. Because Jab Co. uses different methods to depreciate equipment for financial statement and income tax purposes, Jab has temporary differences that will reverse during the next year and add to taxable income. Deferred income taxes that are based on these temporary differences should be classified in Jab's balance sheet as a

- a. Contra account to current assets.
- b. Contra account to noncurrent assets.
- c. Current liability.
- d. Noncurrent liability.

36. At the most recent year end, a company had a deferred income tax liability arising from accelerated depreciation that exceeded a deferred income tax asset relating to rent received in advance which is expected to reverse in the next year. Which of the following should be reported in the company's most recent year-end balance sheet?

- a. The excess of the deferred income tax liability over the deferred income tax asset as a noncurrent liability.
- b. The excess of the deferred income tax liability over the deferred income tax asset as a current liability.
- c. The deferred income tax liability as a noncurrent liability.
- d. The deferred income tax liability as a current liability.

37. On December 31, 1999, Oak Co. recognized a receivable for taxes paid in prior years and refundable through the carryback of all of its 1999 operating loss. Also, Oak had a 1999 deferred tax liability derived from the temporary difference between tax and financial statement depreciation, which reverses over the period 2000-2004. The amount of this tax liability is less than the amount of the tax asset. Which of the following 1999 balance sheet sections should report tax-related items?

- I. Current assets.
- II. Current liabilities.
- III. Noncurrent liabilities.

- a. I only.
- b. I and III.
- c. I, II, and III.
- d. II and III.

38. The amount of income tax applicable to transactions that are not reported in the continuing operations section of the income statement is computed

- a. By multiplying the item by the effective income tax rate.
- b. As the difference between the tax computed based on taxable income without including the item and the tax computed based on taxable income including the item.
- c. As the difference between the tax computed on the item based on the amount used for financial reporting and the amount used in computing taxable income.
- d. By multiplying the item by the difference between the effective income tax rate and the statutory income tax rate.

39. No net deferred tax asset (i.e., deferred tax asset net of related valuation allowance) was recognized in the 1998 financial statements by the Chaise Company when a loss from discontinued segments was carried forward for tax purposes because it was more likely than not that none of this deferred tax asset would be realized. Chaise had no temporary differences. The tax benefit of the loss carried forward reduced current taxes payable on 1999 continuing operations. The 1999 income statement would include the tax benefit from the loss brought forward in

    a.   Income from continuing operations.
    b.   Gain or loss from discontinued segments.
    c.   Extraordinary gains.
    d.   Cumulative effect of accounting changes.

40. Which of the following statements is correct regarding the provision for income taxes in the financial statements of a sole proprietorship?

    a.   The provision for income taxes should be based on business income using individual tax rates.
    b.   The provision for income taxes should be based on business income using corporate tax rates.
    c.   The provision for income taxes should be based on the proprietor's total taxable income, allocated to the proprietorship at the percentage that business income bears to the proprietor's total income.
    d.   No provision for income taxes is required.

OTHER OBJECTIVE QUESTIONS

Problem 1   (15 to 25 minutes)

This question consists of 2 parts. Each part consists of 4 items. Select the **best** answer for each item. Use a No. 2 pencil to blacken the appropriate ovals on the Objective Answer Sheet to indicate your answers. **Answer all items**. Your grade will be based on the total number of correct answers.

Required:

a.   **Items 1 through 4**, describe circumstances resulting in differences between financial statement income and taxable income. For each numbered item, determine whether the difference is:

List
Ⓐ   A temporary difference resulting in a deferred tax asset.
Ⓑ   A temporary difference resulting in a deferred tax liability.
Ⓒ   A permanent difference.

Blacken the corresponding oval in the Objective Answer Sheet. An answer may be selected once, more than once, or not at all.

1.   For plant assets, the depreciation expense deducted for tax purposes is in excess of the depreciation expense used for financial reporting purposes.

2.   A landlord collects some rents in advance. Rents received are taxable in the period in which they are received.

3.   Interest is received on an investment in tax-exempt municipal obligations.

4.   Costs of guarantees and warranties are estimated and accrued for financial reporting purposes.

b.   The following partially completed worksheet contain Lane Co.'s reconciliation between financial statement income and taxable income for the 3 years ended April 30,2000, and additional information.

Lane Co.
INCOME TAX WORKSHEET
For the Three Years Ended April 30, 2000

	April 30, 1998	*April 30, 1999*	*April 30, 2000*
Pretax financial income	$900,000	$1,000,000	$1,200,000
Permanent differences	100,000	100,000	100,000
Temporary differences	200,000	100,000	150,000
Taxable income	$600,000	$ 800,000	$ 950,000
Cumulative temporary differences (future taxable amounts)	$200,000	$ (6)	$ 450,000
Tax rate	20%	25%	30%
Deferred tax liability	$ 40,000	$ 75,000	$ (8)
Deferred tax expense	$ --	$ (7)	$ --
Current tax expense	$ (5)	$ --	$ --

The tax rate changes were enacted at the beginning of each tax year and were not known to Lane at the end of the prior year.

Required:

Items 5 through 8 represent amounts omitted from the worksheet. For each item, determine the amount omitted from the worksheet. Select the amount from the following list and blacken the corresponding oval on the Objective Answer Sheet. An answer may be used once, more than once, or not at all.

5. Current tax expense for the year ended April 30, 1998.

6. Cumulative temporary differences at April 30, 1999.

7. Deferred tax expense for the year ended April 30, 1999.

8. Deferred tax liability at April 30, 2000.

Amount			
A	$ 25,000	H	$135,000
B	$ 35,000	I	$140,000
C	$ 45,000	J	$160,000
D	$ 75,000	K	$180,000
E	$100,000	L	$200,000
F	$112,500	M	$300,000
G	$120,000	N	$400,000

PROBLEMS

Problem 1   (15 to 25 minutes)

Chris Green, CPA, is auditing Rayne Co.'s 1999 financial statements. The controller, Dunn, has provided Green with the following information relating to income taxes:

• Dunn has prepared a schedule of all differences between financial statement and income tax return income. Dunn believes that as a result of pending legislation, the enacted tax rate at December 31, 1999, will be increased for 2000. Dunn is uncertain which differences to include and which rates to apply in computing deferred taxes under SFAS 109. Dunn has requested an overview of SFAS 109 from Green.

Required:

Part a. of this problem required a schedule of interest expense; we did not add it to this volume because it was similar to many other questions and problems.

b. Prepare a brief memo to Dunn from Green:

• Identifying the objectives of accounting for income taxes,
• Defining temporary differences,
• Explaining how to measure deferred tax assets and liabilities, and
• Explaining how to measure deferred income tax expense or benefit.

Problem 2   (40 to 50 minutes)

The following is the long-term liabilities section of Tempo Co.'s December 31, 1998 balance sheet:

Long-term liabilities:

Note payable--bank; 15 principal payments of $5,000, plus 10% interest due annually on September 30	$75,000	
Less current portion	5,000	$ 70,000
Capital lease obligation--16 payments of $9,000 due annually on January 1	$76,600	
Less current portion	1,340	75,260
Deferred income tax liability		4,500
Total long-term liabilities		$149,760

• Tempo's incremental borrowing rate on the date of the lease was 11% and the lessor's implicit rate, which was known by Tempo, was 10%.
• The only difference between Tempo's taxable income and pretax accounting income is depreciation on a machine acquired on January 1, 1998, for $250,000. The machine's estimated useful life is 5 years, with no salvage value. Depreciation is computed using the straight-line method for financial reporting purposes and the MACRS method for tax purposes. Depreciation expense for tax and financial reporting purposes for 1999 through 2002 is as follows:

Year	Tax depreciation	Financial depreciation	Tax depreciation (over) under financial depreciation
1999	$80,000	$50,000	$(30,000)
2000	40,000	50,000	10,000
2001	35,000	50,000	15,000
2002	30,000	50,000	20,000

The enacted federal income tax rates are 30% for 1998 and 1999. A 35% tax rate for 2000 through 2002 was enacted during 1996.

• For the year ended December 31, 1999, Tempo's income before income taxes was $430,000.
• On July 1, 1996, Tempo received proceeds of $459,725 from a $500,000 bond issuance. The bonds mature in 30 years and interest of 11% is payable each January 1 and July 1. The bonds were issued at a price to yield the investors 12%. Tempo uses the effective interest method to amortize the bond discount.

Required:

a. Prepare a schedule showing Tempo's income before income taxes, current income tax expense, deferred income tax expense, and net income. Show supporting calculations for current and deferred income tax amounts.

b. Prepare a schedule showing the calculation of Tempo's interest expense for the year ended December 31, 1999.

c. Prepare the long-term liabilities section of Tempo's December 31, 1999 balance sheet. Show supporting calculations.

Problem 3   (45 to 55 minutes)

[See Problem 2 in Module 22 D. (Requirement b.)]

Problem 4   (45 to 55 minutes)

[See Problem 3 in Module 22 D.]

Problem 5   (40 to 50 minutes)

[See Problem 4 in Module 22 D.]

Problem 6   (15 to 25 minutes)

[See Problem 5 in Module 23 (Requirement d.)]

Problem 7   (40 to 50 minutes)

[See Problem 6 in Module 23 (Requirement c.)]

MULTIPLE-CHOICE ANSWERS

1. c __ __	10. d __ __	19. c __ __	28. b __ __	37. b __ __
2. a __ __	11. c __ __	20. a __ __	29. b __ __	38. b __ __
3. b __ __	12. b __ __	21. c __ __	30. a __ __	39. a __ __
4. a __ __	13. c __ __	22. d __ __	31. a __ __	40. d __ __
5. c __ __	14. b __ __	23. a __ __	32. c __ __	
6. b __ __	15. c __ __	24. c __ __	33. c __ __	
7. a __ __	16. c __ __	25. d __ __	34. d __ __	
8. c __ __	17. b __ __	26. c __ __	35. d __ __	1st: __/40 = __%
9. b __ __	18. b __ __	27. b __ __	36. c __ __	2nd: __/40 = __%

MULTIPLE-CHOICE ANSWER EXPLANATIONS

A. Overview of Deferred Tax Theory

1.   (c)   SFAS 109, para 6, states that the objective of accounting for income taxes is to recognize the amount of current and deferred taxes payable or refundable at the date of the financial statements. The standard further states that this objective is implemented through recognition of deferred tax liabilities or assets. Deferred tax expense results from changes in deferred tax assets and liabilities. Therefore, answer (c) is correct.

B. Permanent and Temporary Differences Defined

2.   (a)   **Temporary** differences are differences between taxable income and accounting income which originate in one period and reverse in one or more subsequent periods. The payment of a penalty ($5,000) and insurance premiums where the corporation is the beneficiary ($10,000) are **not** temporary differences because they never reverse. These are examples of **permanent** differences, which are items that either enter into accounting income but never into taxable income (such as these two items), or enter into taxable income but never into accounting income.

3.   (b)   The officer insurance policy difference ($75,000) is a permanent difference which does not result in future taxable or deductible amounts. The warranty difference ($50,000) is a temporary difference, but it results in future **deductible** amounts in future years when tax warranty expense exceeds book warranty expense. However, the equipment difference ($80,000) is a temporary difference which results in future taxable amounts in future years when tax depreciation is less than book depreciation.

4.   (a)   SFAS 109, para 11, cites examples of temporary differences. Among these examples are revenues which are taxable both before and after they are recognized in financial income. Therefore, answer (a) is correct. Note that emphasis is placed on the difference between book and tax, not the chronological order of the reporting.

5.   (c)   Expenses or losses that are deductible before they are recognized in financial income would result in future taxable amounts. For example, the cost of an asset may have been deducted for tax purposes faster than it was depreciated for financial reporting. In future years, tax depreciation will be less than financial accounting depreciation, meaning future taxable income will exceed future financial

accounting income. Answers (a) and (b) are temporary differences which would result in future deductible amounts. Answer (d) is a permanent difference which does not result in either future taxable or future deductible amounts.

C. Deferred Tax Assets and Liabilities

6.   (b)   To determine the current federal tax liability, **book** income ($90,000) must be adjusted for any temporary or permanent differences to determine **taxable** income.

Book income	$90,000
Rent received in advance	16,000
Municipal interest	(20,000)
Excess tax depreciation	(10,000)
Taxable income	$76,000

Rent received in advance (temporary difference) is added to book income because rent is taxable when received, but is not recognized as book revenue until earned. Municipal interest (permanent difference) is subtracted from book income because it is excluded from taxable income. The excess tax depreciation (temporary difference) is subtracted because this excess amount is an additional tax deduction beyond accounting depreciation. The current tax liability is computed by multiplying taxable income by the tax rate ($76,000 x 30% = $22,800).

7.   (a)   The **current** federal income tax liability is based on **taxable** income, which is computed in the "book to tax reconciliation" below.

Accounting income	$ 800,000
Nontaxable gain	(350,000)
Excess tax depreciation	(50,000)
Taxable income	$ 400,000

The gain on involuntary conversion was included in accounting income but is deferred for tax purposes. Depreciation deducted for tax purposes in excess of book depreciation also causes taxable income to be less than accounting income. Taxes payable before considering estimated tax payments is $120,000 ($400,000 x 30%). Since tax payments of $70,000 have already been made, the 12/31/99 current federal income tax liability is $50,000 ($120,000 – $70,000).

8.   (c)   SFAS 109 states that income tax expense must be reported in two components: the amount currently payable (current portion) and the tax effects of temporary differences (deferred portion). The current portion is computed by multiplying taxable income by the current enacted tax rate ($650,000 x 30% = $195,000). The deferred portion is $30,000 ($100,000 temporary difference x 30%). The estimated tax payments ($90,000) do not affect the amount of tax expense, although the payments would decrease taxes payable.

9.   (b)   Over the 2 years, accounting income on the accrual basis is $4,200,000 ($1,600,000 + $2,600,000) and taxable income using the installment method is $2,000,000 ($600,000 + $1,400,000). This results in future taxable amounts at 12/31/96 of $2,200,000 ($4,200,000 – $2,000,000). Therefore, at 12/31/96, Tower should report a deferred tax liability of $660,000 ($2,200,000 x 30%).

10.   (d)   For accounting purposes, prepaid insurance is $9,500 at 12/31/96. For tax purposes, there was no prepaid insurance at 12/31/96, since the entire amount was expensed on the 1996 tax return. Therefore, the temporary difference is $9,500. This temporary difference will result in a future taxable amount in 1997, when the tax rate is 25%. Therefore, at 12/31/96, a deferred tax liability of $2,375 (25% x $9,500) must be reported.

11.   (c)   Mill's total accounting income using percentage-of-completion ($300,000 + $600,000 + $850,000 = $1,750,000) will eventually be subject to federal income taxes. However, by 12/31/99, only $1,100,000 of income ($400,000 + $700,000) has been reported as taxable income using the completed-contract method. The amount of accounting income which has not yet been taxed ($1,750,000 – $1,100,000 = $650,000 temporary difference) will be taxed eventually when the related contracts are completed. The resulting future taxable amounts will all be taxed after 1999 when the enacted tax rate is 25%. Therefore, the 12/31/99 deferred tax liability is $162,500 ($650,000 x 25%). To record the liability, the following entry would be made:

Income tax expense--deferred	162,500	
Deferred tax liability		162,500

12.   (b)   SFAS 109 states that income tax expense must be reported in two components: the amount currently payable (current portion) and the tax effects of temporary differences (deferred portion). The amount currently payable, or current income tax expense, is computed by multiplying taxable income by the current enacted tax rate ($140,000 x 40% = $56,000).

13.   (c)   The deferred tax liability reported at 12/31/99 results from future taxable (and possibly deductible) amounts which exist as a result of past transactions, multiplied by the appropriate tax rate. The nontaxable interest received on municipal securities ($5,000) is a **permanent** difference which does **not** result in future taxable or deductible amounts. SFAS 109 requires the netting of current deferred tax assets and liabilities, and noncurrent deferred tax assets and liabilities. The future deductible amount ($10,000) resulting from a loss accrual results in a **long-term** deferred tax asset of $4,000 ($10,000 x 40%) because

it is related to a **long-term** loss accrual. The future taxable amount ($25,000) caused by depreciation results in a **long-term** deferred tax liability of $10,000 ($25,000 x 40%) because it is related to a **long-term** asset (property, plant, and equipment). Since these are both long-term, they are netted and a long-term deferred tax liability of $6,000 is reported in the balance sheet ($10,000 liability less $4,000 asset).

14.   (b)   At 12/31/99, unearned rent for financial accounting purposes is $18,000 ($36,000 x 6/12). The tax basis of unearned rent at 12/31/99 is $0 because rental income is taxable when received. This temporary difference ($18,000 – $0 = $18,000) results in future deductible amounts because 2000 taxable rental income ($0) will be less than 2000 financial rental income ($18,000). The deferred tax asset to be recorded is measured using the future enacted tax rate of 40% in accordance with SFAS 109. The deferred tax asset is $7,200 ($18,000 x 40%).

15.   (c)   Under SFAS 109, a deferred tax asset is recognized for all deductible temporary differences. The computation of the deferred tax asset for Black Co. arising from the accrued product warranty costs of $300,000 is shown below.

	2000	2001	2002	2003	Total
Future deductible amounts	100,000	50,000	50,000	100,000	300,000
Tax rate	30%	30%	30%	25%	
Deferred tax asset	30,000	15,000	15,000	25,000	85,000

Thus, the total deferred tax asset at the end of 1999 is $85,000.

16.   (c)   An excess of tax depreciation over financial accounting depreciation results in future taxable amounts and, therefore, a deferred tax liability. Answer (a) is an example of a permanent difference which does not result in future taxable or deductible amounts. Answers (b) and (d) are examples of temporary differences which result in future deductible amounts and a possible deferred tax asset.

17.   (b)   The increase in prepaid insurance in 1999 creates a deductible amount for income tax reporting purposes for the insurance paid; however, for financial reporting purposes the expense is not recognized until years subsequent to 1999. As a result, net taxable income for future years is increased, thus, the deferred income tax liability increases. The increase in rent receivable in 1999 also increases the deferred tax liability. For income tax purposes, rents are not included in income until received (i.e. years subsequent to 1999). However, the amount of the receivable is earned and recognized in the income statement in 1999. The increase in warranty obligations results in warranty expense for 1999 and will provide future deductible amounts, because under the IRC, a deduction for warranty cost is not permitted until such cost is incurred. Future deductible amounts lead to deferred tax assets.

18.   (b)   Per SFAS 109, a deferred tax liability is recognized for temporary differences that will result in **net** taxable amounts (taxable income exceeds book income) in future years. Although Cody Co. has recognized a loss (per books) in year 2 of the construction contract, the contract is still profitable over the 3 years. Therefore, in year 3 when the contract is completed, Cody will recognize the total profit on its tax return, and only a portion of the profit will be recorded in its income statement. Thus, the contract will result in a taxable amount in year 3, and a deferred tax liability exists. Note that this liability was recorded at the end of year 1 and reduced by one-half at the end of year 2 due to the change in estimated profit. Answer (b) is, therefore, the correct answer. Answers (a) and (c) are incorrect because no deferred tax asset is created. Answer (d) is incorrect because Cody will include a deferred tax liability on its balance sheet.

19. (c) Per SFAS 109, a deferred tax liability is recognized for the amount of taxes payable in **future** years as a result of the deferred tax consequences (as measured by the provisions of **enacted** tax laws) of events recognized in the financial statements in the current or preceding years.

20. (a) SFAS 109 states that income tax provision (expense) must be reported in two components: the amount currently payable (current portion) and the tax effects of temporary differences (deferred portion). The current portion is computed by multiplying taxable income by the current enacted tax rate ($150,000 x 30% = $45,000). Note that in this case, the deferred portion is $0, because both differences are permanent differences, which do not result in a deferred tax liability. Therefore, the current provision for income taxes should be reported at $45,000. It is important to note that if temporary differences did exist the tax effects would have been included in the tax expense for the current period.

21. (c) SFAS 109 states that income tax expense must be reported in two components: the amount currently payable (current portion) and the tax effects of temporary differences (deferred portion). The amount currently payable, or current income tax expense, is computed by multiplying taxable income by the current enacted tax rate ($1,000 x 30% = $300).

22. (d) SFAS 109 states that income tax expense must be reported on the IS in two components: the amount currently payable (current portion) and the tax effects of temporary differences (deferred portion). The worksheet indicates two temporary differences: depreciation and warranty costs. The scheduling contained in the worksheet shows that these two temporary differences will result in a deferred tax asset of $105 (30 + 75) and deferred tax liability of $140. The liability has the effect of increasing 1999 tax expense while the asset has the effect of decreasing 1999 tax expense. The net effect is deferred income tax expense of $35 for 1999 [$140 − (30 + 75)].

Not required:

The balance sheet presentation would show a current deferred tax asset of $30 and a noncurrent deferred tax liability of $65 ($140 − 75).

23. (a) The deferred portion of income tax expense can be computed by determining the tax effect of the two temporary differences. The installment sale profit results in a future taxable amount in 2000 of $2,600, and the bad debt expense results in a future deductible amount of $1,400. The deferred tax consequences of these temporary differences will be measured by Shear in 1999 using the enacted tax rate expected to apply to taxable income in the year the deferred amounts are expected to be settled. The following journal entry is necessary to record the deferred tax liability related to the installment sale:

Deferred tax expense	650	
Deferred tax liability		650
[$2,600 x .25]		

To record the deferred tax asset related to the bad debt expense, the following journal entry is required:

Deferred tax asset	350	
Deferred tax expense		350
[$1,400 x .25]		

The amount of deferred tax expense to be reported by Shear in its 1999 income statement is $300 ($650 − 350); therefore, answer (a) is correct. Note that one journal entry could have been used. Using two entries more clearly shows the opposite effect of an asset versus a liability on deferred tax expense.

24. (c) SFAS 109 states that income tax expense must be reported in two components: the amount currently payable (current portion) and the tax effects of temporary differences (deferred portion). The current portion is computed by multiplying taxable income by the current enacted tax rate ($200,000 x 30% = $60,000). The deferred portion is $30,000 ($100,000 temporary difference x 30%). An alternative computation for the deferred portion is shown below.

DT asset at 12/31/99	$ 0	
DT asset at 12/31/98	9,000	
Decrease in DT asset		$9,000
DT liability at 12/31/99 (70,000 x 30%)	$21,000	
DT liability at 12/31/98	0	
Increase in DT liability		21,000
Deferred portion of tax expense		$30,000

25. (d) SFAS 109 defines the deferred income tax expense or benefit as the net change during the year in an enterprise's deferred tax liabilities or assets. Therefore, answer (d) is correct. Answers (a) and (b) are incorrect because the deferred income tax expense or benefit must consider the net effect of changes (both increases and decreases) in both deferred tax assets and deferred tax liabilities. The decrease in deferred tax assets alone or the increase in deferred tax liabilities alone will not be equal to the deferred income tax expense. Answer (c) is incorrect because the amount of income tax liability (current portion which comes off the tax return) plus the sum of the net changes in deferred tax assets and deferred tax liabilities is the total amount of income tax expense or benefit for the year. The question asks only for the deferred portion.

26.   (c) From 12/31/98 to 12/31/99, the deferred tax asset increased by $5,000 (from $15,000 to $20,000). Income taxes payable at 12/31/99 are $13,000. Based on this information, the following journal entries can be recreated.

Income tax expense--current	13,000	
Income tax payable		13,000
Deferred tax asset	5,000	
Income tax expense--deferred		5,000

An additional entry would be prepared by Shin to record an allowance to reduce the deferred tax asset to its realizable value (10% x $20,000 = $2,000).

Income tax expense--deferred	2,000	
Allowance to reduce deferred		
tax asset to realizable value		2,000

Based on these three entries, total 1999 income tax expense is $10,000 ($13,000 − $5,000 + $2,000).

D. Deferred Tax Related to Business Investments

27.   (b) The deferred income tax liability is the result of the undistributed earnings of an equity investee, which are expected to be distributed as dividends in future periods. For accounting purposes, investment revenue is $270,000 ($900,000 x 30%). For tax purposes, dividend revenue is $90,000 ($300,000 x 30%), which will be partially offset by the 80% dividends received deduction. Because of this 80% deduction, the difference ($270,000 − $90,000 = $180,000) is partially a permanent difference (80% x $180,000 = $144,000 which will never be subject to taxes) and partially a temporary difference (20% x $180,000 = $36,000 which will be taxable in future years). This future taxable amount of $36,000 will become taxable after 1999, when the expected tax rate is 25%. Therefore, the deferred tax liability is $9,000 (25% x $36,000). The entry to record the liability is as follows:

Income tax expense--deferred	9,000	
Deferred tax liability		9,000

28.   (b) The **current** provision for income taxes is computed by multiplying taxable income on the Form 1120 by the current tax rate. Since taxable income is not given, pretax book income must be adjusted to compute taxable income.

Pretax book income	$100,000
Excess book depreciation	8,000
Excess book investment revenue	
[$35,000 − (20% x $25,000)]	(30,000)
Taxable income	$78,000

Excess book depreciation is added because it causes book income to be lower than taxable income. For book purposes, investment revenue of $35,000 was recognized using the equity method; for tax purposes, net dividend revenue of $5,000 was recognized [$25,000 − (80% x $25,000)]. The excess book revenue ($35,000 − $5,000 = $30,000) is deducted to compute taxable income. Therefore, the **current** provision for income taxes is $23,400 ($78,000 x 30%).

E. Loss Carryforwards and Carrybacks

29.   (b) Dix did **not** elect to forego the loss carryback, so $100,000 of the $200,000 loss will be carried back to offset 1997 income, resulting in a tax refund of $40,000 (40% x $100,000). The remaining $100,000 of the 1998 loss will be carried forward to offset part of 1999 income. Thus, the income tax **liability** at 12/31/96 will be $120,000 [40% x ($400,000 − $100,000)].

30.   (a) The requirement is to determine the amount to be reported in 1999 as the reduction of loss due to NOL carryback and carryforward [i.e., benefit (negative tax expense) on the face of the IS]. Per SFAS 109, para 16, a deferred tax liability or asset is recognized for all temporary differences, operating losses, and tax credit carryforwards.

Income Tax Return Analysis

	1996/1997/1998	*1999*
Inc (loss)	450,000	($600,000)
Carryback	(450,000)	450,000
Unused NOL		$150,000

Town can thus recognize tax benefits from both the NOL carryback and carryforward. Town may carryback $450,000 of the NOL which will provide a tax benefit of $180,000 ($450,000 x .40). The journal entry to recognize the loss carryback would be as follows:

Tax refund receivable	180,000	
Benefit due to loss carryback		180,000

The additional $150,000 NOL can be carried forward to future periods to provide a benefit of $60,000 ($150,000 x .40). The following journal entry reflects the loss carryforward:

Deferred tax asset	60,000	
Benefit due to loss carryforward		60,000

Therefore, the reduction of the loss due to NOL carryback and carryforward is $240,000 and the correct response is (a). Note that an allowance for nonrealization of the deferred tax asset is not necessary because the information given about the strike indicates that it is not more likely than not that part of the deferred tax asset may not be recognized.

The carryback and carryforward would be shown in the income statement as follows:

Loss before income taxes		
		($600,000)
Less:		
Benefit from operating		
loss carryback	$180,000	
Benefit from operating		
loss carryforward	60,000	240,000
Net loss		($360,000)

31.   (a) The requirement is to determine the amount of 1999 current income tax expense (or income taxes payable from tax return) to be reported in the income statement. For tax purposes, loss carryforwards should not be recognized until they are actually realized.

Income Tax Return Analysis

	1997	*1998*	*1999*
Income or loss	($200,000)	($150,000)	$300,000
Carryforward	200,000	100,000	(300,000)
Unused Carryforward	-0-	$ 50,000	-0-

Bishop would recognize, in the income statement, income tax expense of $0 as the loss carryforward fully offsets the 1999 income.

Not required:

The deferred tax component for 1999 would be as follows.

Balance in the deferred tax asset and allowance accounts at 1/1/99:

	Deferred Tax Asset		Allow for Reduction, etc.	
12/31/97	80,000		80,000	12/31/97
12/31/98	60,000		60,000	12/31/98
12/31/98 balance	140,000		140,000	12/31/98 balance

The deferred tax entry for 1999 would be:

Allow for reduction, etc.	140,000	
Deferred tax asset		120,000
Income tax expense--deferred		20,000

The bottom of the income statement would be:

Income before taxes		$300,000
Income tax expense or benefit		
Current		0
Deferred **benefit**		20,000
Net income		$320,000

32.   (c)   Per para 16 of SFAS 109, a deferred tax liability or asset is recognized for all temporary differences and operating loss carryforwards. In 1998, Mobe would prepare the following entries:

Tax refund receivable ($300,000 x 30%)	90,000	
Deferred tax asset ($400,000 x 30%)	120,000	
Tax loss benefit (income tax expense)		210,000
Tax loss benefit (income tax expense)	120,000	
Allowance to reduce deferred tax asset to realizable value		120,000

The tax refund receivable results from carrying $300,000 of the 1998 loss **back** to offset 1994 taxable income. The deferred tax asset results from the potential **carryforward** of the remaining $400,000 loss ($700,000 – $300,000). However, the inconsistent performance of the company (profitable operations in the first year, loss in the second year) coupled with the lack of positive evidence concerning future operations indicate that at the end of 1998 it is more likely than not that none of the deferred tax asset will be realized. Therefore, Mobe must establish a valuation allowance to reduce this asset to its expected realizable value. In 1999, the entries are:

Income tax expense ($1,200,000 x 30%)	360,000	
Deferred tax asset		120,000
Income taxes payable [($1,200,000 – $400,000) x 30%]		240,000
Allowance to reduce deferred tax asset to realizable value	120,000	
Benefit due to loss carryforward (income tax expense)		120,000

Income taxes payable is 1999 income less the $400,000 loss carryforward, times 30%. Total income tax expense for 1999 is $240,000 ($360,000 – $120,000). Note that if the facts had indicated positive evidence following 1998 for 1999 operations, the allowance account would not have been recognized and 1999 expense would have been $360,000.

F.   Financial Statement Presentation of Income Tax

33.   (c)   The warranty temporary difference results in future deductible amounts of $700,000 per year in 2000 through 2002 ($2,100,000 ÷ 3). The installment temporary difference results in future taxable amounts of $500,000 per year in 2000 through 2002 ($1,500,000 ÷ 3). The portions of the resulting deferred tax asset and deferred tax liability that will be netted to find the amount of the current asset/current liability to be presented on the BS are shown below.

Deferred tax asset: $(700,000) x 25% =	$(175,000)
Deferred tax liability: $500,000 x 25% =	125,000
Current deferred tax asset (CDTA) shown on BS	$(50,000)

The noncurrent deferred tax asset is $100,000 [25% x ($2,100,000 – $1,500,000)] – $50,000 CDTA.

34.   (d)   Per SFAS 109, deferred tax liabilities and assets are classified as current or noncurrent based on the classification of the related asset or liability for financial reporting. The deferred tax liability resulting from accelerated tax depreciation should be considered noncurrent because the related asset is classified as noncurrent. The deferred tax asset resulting from additional costs in inventory for tax purposes is classified as current because the related asset is classified as current. Therefore, Thorn would report a **noncurrent deferred tax liability** of **$75,000**.

35.   (d)   Deferred tax liabilities and assets are classified as current or noncurrent based on the related asset or liability. A deferred tax liability or asset is considered to be related to an asset or liability if reduction of the asset or liability will cause the temporary difference to reverse. If the deferred tax liability or asset is **not** related to any asset or liability, then it is classified based on the timing of its expected reversal or utilization date. This deferred tax liability is related to equipment, which is noncurrent, so the deferred tax liability should also be classified as a noncurrent liability. Answers (a) and (b) are incorrect because deferred taxes are always classified as assets or liabilities, rather than as contra accounts. Answer (c) is incorrect because the deferred tax liability related to equipment is a noncurrent liability.

36. **(c)** Deferred tax assets and liabilities are classified as current or noncurrent based on the classification of the related asset or liability for financial reporting. Therefore, a deferred tax liability relating to depreciation of a fixed asset would be noncurrent in nature. The deferred tax asset relating to rent received in advance that is expected to reverse in the following year would be classified as current. No netting of net current amounts and net noncurrent amounts can occur; thus, answer (c) is the correct answer.

37. **(b)** Per SFAS 109, para 41, a **deferred** tax liability or asset should be classified in two categories (the current amount and the noncurrent amount) on the balance sheet based on the classification of the related asset or liability for financial reporting. The receivable for taxes paid in prior years and refundable through the carryback of the 1999 operating loss is **not** considered a **deferred** tax asset. A current asset should be reported on the balance sheet for the amount of the refund due to Oak Co. Note that if there was a current deferred tax liability it would not be netted with the refund receivable. However, a current deferred tax asset would be so netted. A noncurrent deferred tax liability should be reported on the balance sheet for temporary differences related to depreciation of fixed assets.

38. **(b)** Per SFAS 109, income tax expense must be associated with (i.e., allocated among) income from continuing operations, discontinued operations, extraordinary items, cumulative effect of an accounting change, and prior period adjustments. The tax effect to be associated with any of the special items (other than income from continuing operations) is computed by determining the income tax on overall taxable income and comparing it with the income tax on continuing operations. If more than one special item exists, the difference between tax on ordinary operations and tax on overall taxable income must be allocated proportionately among the special items.

39. **(a)** Per SFAS 109, para 37, the tax benefit of an operating loss carryforward or carryback shall be reported in the same manner as the **source of income (loss) in the current year**. Thus, in 1999, the tax benefit shall be reported under income from continuing operations.

40. **(d)** Sole proprietorships do not pay any income taxes as the tax items related to a sole proprietorship flow through to the owner's tax return. Because the sole proprietorship is not a taxable entity, no provision for income taxes would be included in the financial statements of the sole proprietorship. Thus, answer response (d) is the correct response. Although answer response (a) illustrates the correct formula for calculating the taxes payable related to a sole proprietorship's operations, it is an incorrect response because the tax provision would not be shown on the sole proprietorship's financial statements since it flows through to the owner and is a liability of the owner. Answer response (b) is incorrect because the income tax expense would be calculated using the owner's tax rates, as it is the owner's personal liability, not the entity's. Answer response (c) is incorrect because the proprietorship would have **no** provision for income taxes on its books. The entire income tax liability is the personal responsibility of the owner.

OTHER OBJECTIVE ANSWERS AND ANSWER EXPLANATIONS

Problem 1

1.   **(B)**   In cases in which tax depreciation is greater than accounting (book) depreciation, taxable income will be less than accounting income and a deferred tax liability results. The reason is that in future years tax depreciation will be less than book depreciation and taxable income will be greater than book income. This will result in future cash flows for the income tax liability shown on the Form 1120 exceeding those that would occur based on pretax accounting income. Thus a deferred tax liability will result. The entry is

Deferred income tax expense	xx	
Deferred tax liability		xx

In the reversal year, the entry would be

Deferred tax liability	xx	
Deferred tax expense		xx

2.   **(A)**   Taxable income will exceed pretax accounting (book) income in the year in which the rents are received. In effect, income taxes on the portion of the rent that is unearned for financial reporting under GAAP must be prepaid under the Internal Revenue Code. Thus, a deferred tax asset would result because in future years when the rent received in advance is earned, no taxes will be payable on the amount earned, because the taxes were paid in the year rent was received. The entry is

Deferred tax asset	xx	
Deferred tax expense		xx

3.   **(C)**   Interest earned on a tax-exempt municipal obligation is a permanent difference. The interest is deducted in the year received from pretax accounting income to arrive at taxable income. However, it will never be reported as income on the firm's Form 1120. Therefore, such a difference does not result in deferred income taxes.

4.   **(A)**   Costs of guarantees and warranties are not deductible under the Internal Revenue Code until incurred. Under SFAS 5, however, they are estimated and recorded as an expense (loss) and a liability in the period of sale. In effect, income taxes are prepaid because in later years a benefit is received when these costs are incurred and deducted on the tax return. The entry in the origination year is

Deferred tax asset	xx	
Deferred tax expense		xx

The entry when the warranty costs are deducted is

Deferred tax expense	xx	
Deferred tax asset		xx

5.   **(G)**   Current tax expense for FY 1998 is equal to taxable income (Form 1120) of $600,000 times 20% or $120,000.

6.   **(M)**   The $100,000 temporary difference for FY 1999 is deducted from pretax financial income to arrive at taxable income. Therefore, cumulative temporary differences or future taxable amounts are increased. Thus, $300,000 ($200,000 + $100,000) will be added to pretax financial income in future reversal years.

7.   **(B)**   Deferred tax expense is equal to the increased rate on future taxable amounts outstanding at the beginning of FY 1999 plus the amount related to the $100,000 of temporary differences that originated in FY 1999. Thus, deferred tax expense is equal to $35,000 [$200,000 x (.25 − .20) + $100,000 x .25]. The entry is

Deferred tax expense	35,000	
Deferred tax liability		35,000

8.   **(H)**   In FY 1999 cumulative temporary differences (future taxable amounts) increased by $150,000. The deferred tax liability account for 3 years is shown below.

Deferred Tax Liability

	1998
40,000	(200,000 x .20)
	1999
10,000	[200,000 x (.25 − .20)]
25,000	(100,000 x .25)
	2000
15,000	[300,000 x (.30 − .25)]
45,000	(150,000 x .30)
	Bal. 135,000

The $135,000 is equal to the cumulative temporary differences of $450,000 x.30.

ANSWER OUTLINE

Problem 1   Deferred Tax Memo

Memorandum Format (To:, From:, Subject:)
Objective of accounting for income taxes is to recognize:
    taxes payable/refundable
    deferred tax assets/liabilities
Temporary Differences
    Differences between tax basis and GAAP basis
    Result in future taxable/deductible amounts
Measurement of deferred tax asset/liability
    Based on enacted tax laws
    Allowance for unrealizable assets
Deferred income tax expense
    Equal to Δ during year in deferred tax liabilities and assets

UNOFFICIAL ANSWER

Problem 1   Deferred Tax Memo

To: Dunn
From: Green
Re: Accounting for income taxes

Below is a brief overview of accounting for income taxes in accordance with SFAS 109.

The objectives of accounting for income taxes are to recognize (a) the amount of taxes payable or refundable for the current year, and (b) deferred tax liabilities and assets for the estimated future tax consequences of temporary differences and carryforwards. Temporary differences are differences between the tax basis of assets or liabilities and their reported amounts in the financial statements that will result in taxable or deductible amounts in future years.

Deferred tax assets and liabilities are measured based on the provisions of enacted tax law; the effects of future changes in the tax laws or rates are not anticipated. The measurement of deferred tax assets is reduced, if necessary, by a valuation allowance to reflect the net asset amount that is more likely than not to be realized. Deferred income tax expense or benefit is measured as the change during the year in an enterprise's deferred tax liabilities and assets.

SOLUTION GUIDE

Problem 2   Schedule for Income Taxes; Schedule of Interest Expense Calculations; LT Liabilities Section of BS

1. This problem consists of three related requirements concerning income taxes (part a), interest expense (part b), and long-term liabilities (part c). The solutions approach for problems in which the requirements are interrelated is to make all the computations for each item at one time. After making the computations, label each computation according to the requirement (a, b, or c) to which it relates. Formulas, time lines, journal entries, etc. can be used to analyze each item.

2. The **current** portion of **1999** income tax expense is computed as follows:

Income before taxes – Excess tax depreciation = Taxable income
    $430,000^{(a)}$ – $30,000   = $400,000

Taxable income   x   Current tax rate   =   Current tax expense
   $400,000   x   30%   = $120,000^{(a)}$

The journal entry for the current portion of income taxes would be

Income tax expense--current	120,000	
Income taxes payable		120,000

2.1 The only temporary difference is the depreciation difference. It caused the $4,500 long-term deferred tax liability that appears on the 12/31/98 balance sheet. The excess tax depreciation in 1998 was $15,000 [$250,000 cost – ($80,000 + 40,000 + 35,000 + 30,000) tax depreciation – $50,000 financial (book) depreciation]. The deferred tax liability is equal to $4,500 ($15,000 x 30%).

The schedule below shows the deductible and taxable amounts for 1998 and 1999.

Schedule of (Deductible) and Taxable Amounts

	Originating Years			Future Years	
Years Ended	1998	1999	2000	2001	2002
1998	$(15,000)*		$10,000	$ 5,000	
1999		$(30,000)*		10,000	20,000
Total fut. tax. amts.			$10,000	$15,000	$20,000

Deductions in reconciling book income to taxable income.

The **deferred** portion of 1999 income tax expense is based on the **change** in the deferred tax liability. At 12/31/99, the deferred tax liability is $15,750 [($10,000 + 15,000 + 20,000) x 35%]. At 12/31/98, the deferred liability tax was $4,500. Therefore, the deferred portion of income tax expense is $11,250 ^{(a)} ($15,750 – $4,500). Total income tax expense is $131,250 ($120,000 + $11,250).

Income Tax Expense--Deferred	Deferred Tax Liability
1999	4,500 12/31/98
Adjust. 11,250	11,250 Adjust
	15,750 Bal 12/31/99

Income tax expense--deferred	11,250	
Deferred tax liability		11,250

Note that the 1999 deferred tax expense consists of two components as follows:

Rate increase on
beginning balance   (35% – 30%) x $15,000 = $750

1999 originating
difference   35% x 30,000 = $\underline{10,500}$
                                       $\underline{\$11,250}$

Note that the entire deferred tax liability is noncurrent in accordance with SFAS 109 because the depreciation temporary difference relates to fixed assets which are classified as noncurrent.

2.2 1999 net income is $299,500 ^{(a)} ($430,000 income before income taxes – $130,500 income tax expense).

3. The note payable principal is paid in equal installments of $5,000 each September 30. Therefore, the total note payable balance was $75,000 from 1/1/99 to 9/30/99. After the 9/30 payment, the balance is $70,000 the rest of the year. At 12/31/99, $5,000 of the remaining

$70,000 is current (due 9/30/00), and the other $65,000 is long-term.

3.1 Interest expense on the note payable must be computed in two parts: on the $75,000 balance outstanding from 1/1/99 to 9/30/99, and on the $70,000 balance outstanding from 10/1/99 to 12/31/99. As shown below, total interest expense is $7,375. The interest payable at 12/31/99 ($1,750) is a current liability.

4. A lessee records a capital lease based on the **lesser** of the lessee's incremental borrowing rate (11%) or the lessor's implicit rate if known by the lessee (10%). Therefore, 10% is the appropriate rate for the lease in this problem.

4.1 The interest payable at 12/31/98 (not given) was $7,660 ($76,600 x 10%), so Tempo's 1/1/99 journal entry to record the lease payment was:

Lease obligation	1,340	
Interest payable	7,660	
Cash		9,000

Therefore, during 1999, the lease obligation was $75,260, resulting in 1999 interest expense of $7,526 ($75,260 x 10%).

4.2 The 12/31/99 lease obligation of $75,260 includes a current portion of $1,474 ($9,000 payment due 1/1/00 less $7,526 interest payable.)

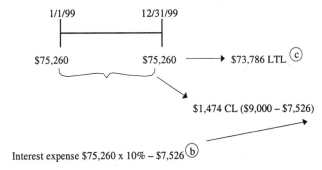

Interest expense $75,260 x 10% – $7,526 (b)

5. On 7/1/99, Tempo issued $500,000 face amount of 11% bonds for $459,725, to yield 12%. Under the effective interest method, interest expense is:

Book value	x	Effective rate	x	Time	=	Interest expense
$459,725	x	12%	x	6/12	=	$27,584

Interest payable is:

Face amount	x	Stated rate	x	Time	=	Interest payable
$500,000	x	11%	x	6/12	=	$27,500

Therefore, Tempo's 12/31/99 adjusting entry is

Interest expense	27,584	
Interest payable		27,500
Discount on BP		84

This entry decreases the discount account, which increases the book value of the bond liability. The interest payable ($27,500) is a current liability.

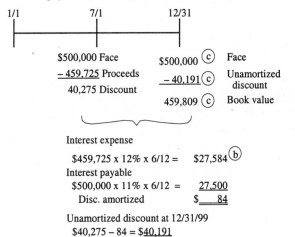

UNOFFICIAL ANSWER

Problem 2   Schedule for Income Taxes; Schedule of Interest Expense Calculation; LT Liabilities Section of BS

a.   *Tempo Co.*
INCOME TAX EXPENSE AND NET INCOME
For the Year Ended December 31, 1999

Income before income taxes		$430,000
Income tax expense:		
Current [30% x (430,000 – 30,000)]	$120,000	
Deferred [see computation below]	11,250	131,250
Net income		$298,750

Computation

Deferred income tax expense

Temporary difference--depreciation

2000	$10,000	
2001	15,000	
2002	20,000	$45,000
Effective tax rate for years 2000 through 2002		35%
Deferred tax liability, 12/31/99		15,750
Less:		
12/31/98 deferred tax liability		4,500
1999 deferred income tax expense		$11,250

b.

Tempo Co.
CALCULATION OF INTEREST EXPENSE
For the Year Ended December 31, 1999

Note payable--bank

1/1/99 to 9/30/99	- $75,000 x 10% x 9/12	$ 5,625	
10/1/99 to 12/31/99	- $70,000 x 10% x 3/12	1,750	$ 7,375

Capital lease obligation

1/1/99 to 12/31/99	- $75,260 x 10%	7,526

Bonds payable

7/1/99 to 12/31/99	- $459,725 x 12% x 6/12	27,584
		$42,485

c.

Tempo Co.
LONG-TERM LIABILITIES SECTION OF BALANCE SHEET
December 31, 1999

Long-term liabilities:

Note payable--bank; 14 principal payments of $5,000 plus 10% interest due annually on September 30	$70,000	
Less current portion	5,000	$ 65,000
Capital lease obligation--15 payments of $9,000 due annually on January 1	75,260	
Less current portion	1,474	73,786
11% bonds payable due June 30, 2026, less unamortized discount of $40,191		459,809
Deferred income tax liability		15,750
Total long-term liabilities		$614,345

STOCKHOLDERS' EQUITY

Stockholders' equity is the residual of assets minus liabilities (i.e., net assets). Due to the number of fraudulent manipulations involving stocks, many states have legislated accounting for stockholders' equity transactions and they are controlled to some degree (e.g., conditions under which dividends may be paid).

Common stockholders' equity consists of two major categories: contributed capital and retained earnings. Retained earnings are either appropriated or unappropriated. Paid-in consists of paid-in excess and legal capital. Legal capital is the par or stated value of stock. An outline of stockholders' equity follows:

- Contributed capital

    - Paid-in (e.g., common and preferred stock)
        - Legal--par, stated, no par
        - Paid-in capital in excess of par or stated value
        - Paid-in capital from other transactions
            - Treasury stock
            - Retirement of stock
            - Stock dividends recorded at market
            - Stock warrants detachable from bonds
            - Lapse of stock purchase warrants
            - Conversion of convertible bonds
            - Any other gain on the company's own stock transactions

- Retained earnings

    - Appropriated
    - Unappropriated

- Accumulated other comprehensive income
- Contra stockholders' equity item (deducted after contributed capital, retained earnings, and accumulated other comprehensive income above are totaled)

    - Treasury stock (cost method)

When significant changes occur in stockholders' equity accounts, enterprises are required to disclose them. (See outline of SFAS 129.) Most companies satisfy this requirement by issuing a statement of changes in stockholders' equity (illustrated below). These statements show changes in the number of shares (not included due to space limits) as well as dollars between balance sheet dates. The statement of changes in stockholders' equity may also be used to report comprehensive income per SFAS 130 (see the second column in the following statement). This is the FASB's least preferable means of disclosing it. See Module 22D, page 153.

Northern Corporation
Statement of Changes in Stockholders' Equity
For the Year Ended December 31, 1999

	Common stock	Comprehensive income	Retained earnings	Accumulated other comprehensive income	Total
Balances, January 1, 1999	$1,500,000		$213,675	$ (3,450)	$1,710,225
Comprehensive income					
Net income		$63,250	63,250		
Other comprehensive income:					
Foreign currency translation adjustments, net of tax		8,000			
Unrealized gains on securities:					
Unrealized holding gains arising during period, net of tax		13,000			
Less: reclassification adjustment, net of tax, for gain included in net income		(1,500)			
Minimum pension liability adjustment, net of tax		(2,500)			
Other comprehensive income		17,000		17,000	
Comprehensive income		$80,250			80,250
Proceeds from issuance of shares	200,000				200,000
Dividends paid	--		(24,825)		(24,825)
Balances, December 31, 1999	$1,700,000		$252,100	$13,550	$1,965,650

A. Common Stock

The entry to record the issuance of common stock is

Cash	(amount received)
Common stock	(par or stated value)
Paid-in capital in excess of par	(forced)

If stock is sold for less than par, a discount account is debited.

Very little stock is issued at a discount because of the resulting potential liability to the original purchaser for the difference between the issue price (when less than par) and par which in many states is legal capital. This liability has been avoided by the use of stated value and no par stock, but is mainly avoided by establishing par values below market.

Control accounts are occasionally used to control unissued stock. At authorization

Unissued common stock	(total par or stated value)
Common stock authorized	(same)

At issuance

Cash	(cash received)
Unissued common stock	(par or stated value)
Paid-in capital in excess of par	(forced)

The credit balance in the authorized account is the total available for issuance. The debit balance in the unissued account is the amount not issued. Thus, authorized (cr) – unissued (dr) = issued (cr). The unissued account is an offset account to the authorized account.

No-par stock is occasionally issued (i.e., no par or stated value exists). All of the proceeds from issuance of no-par stock are credited to "common stock."

Legal expenses	(FMV)	
Assets	(FMV)	
Common stock		(par)
Paid-in capital in excess of par		(forced)

Costs of registering and issuing common stock are generally netted against the proceeds (i.e., reduce "paid-in capital in excess of par"). An alternative method is to consider stock issue costs an organizational cost.

B. Preferred Stock

As implied, preferred stock has preferential rights: most commonly the right to receive dividends prior to common stockholders. Generally the dividend payout is specified (e.g., 7% of par). Additional possible features are

1. Participating--share with common stockholders in dividend distributions after both preferred and common stockholders receive a specified level of dividend payment

   a. Participation with common stockholders in dividends is usually specified in terms of a percentage of legal capital. For example, 7% preferred receive 7% of their par value in dividends before common stockholders receive dividends. Fully participating preferred would receive the same percentage dividend as common stockholders if the common stockholders received over a 7% (of par value) dividend.

2. Cumulative--dividends not paid in any year (dividends in arrears) must be made up before distributions can be made to common stockholders

   a. However, dividends in arrears are not a liability until declared. They should be disclosed parenthetically or in the footnotes.

3. Convertible--preferred stockholders have an option of exchanging their stock for common stock at a specified ratio

   a. Conversion is usually accounted for at book value

Preferred stock	(par converted)	
Preferred paid-in accounts	(related balances)	
Common stock		(par)
Paid-in capital in excess of par		(forced)

   b. If market value is used, common stock and paid-in excess are credited for the market value, usually resulting in a large debit to retained earnings. (Plug figure in the journal entry.)

4. Callable--the corporation has the option to repurchase the preferred stock at a specified price

   a. If called, no gain or loss is recognized. Gains are taken to a paid-in capital account; losses are charged to retained earnings

Preferred stock	(par)
Preferred paid-in accounts	(related balances)
Retained earnings	(if dr. needed)
Cash	(amount paid)
Paid-in capital from preferred	
retirement	(if cr. needed)

Any of the above features present in a preferred stock issuance should be disclosed parenthetically in the balance sheet next to the account title.

C. Stock Subscriptions

Stock (common/preferred) can be subscribed by investors. A receivable is established and "stock subscribed" credited. When the total subscription price is received, the stock (common/preferred) is issued.

At subscription

Cash	(any cash received)
Subscription receivable	(balance)
Common stock subscribed	(par)
Paid-in capital in excess of par	(subscription price > par)

Cash receipt and issuance

Cash	(balance)
Subscriptions receivable	(balance)
Common stock subscribed	(par)
Common stock*	(par)

Unissued common stock, if unissued and authorized accounts are being used.

Upon default of subscription agreements, depending on the agreement, the amount paid to date may be

1. Returned to subscriber

2. Kept by company

3. Held to cover any losses on resale and balance returned

If returned

Common stock subscribed	(par)
Paid-in capital in excess of par	(subscription price > par)
Cash	(any cash received)
Subscriptions receivable	(balance)

If kept by the company, no cash would be paid and "paid-in from subscription default" credited instead of cash.

If held to cover any losses on resale, a "refundable subscription deposit" liability would be credited instead of cash. If the stock were resold at less than the original subscription price, the difference would be debited to "refundable subscription deposit."

Cash	(payment)
Refundable subscription deposit	(forced)
Stock	(par)
Paid-in capital in excess of par	(amount from original sale)

The balance in the refundable subscription account would be paid (possibly in an equivalent number of shares) to the original subscriber.

D. Treasury Stock Transactions

A firm's own stock repurchased on the open market is known as treasury stock. Treasury stock is **not** an asset, as a firm may not own shares of itself. Instead it is treated as a reduction of stockholders' equity. There are two methods of accounting for treasury stock: cost and par value.

1. Cost Method

Under the **cost method**, treasury stock is debited for the cost of treasury stock. Any gain (loss) is recognized at the point of resale. However, such gains (losses) are not included in the determination of periodic income. Gains are credited to "paid-in capital from treasury stock transactions." Losses should be charged first to "paid-in capital from treasury stock (TS) transactions" or "paid-in capital from stock retirement" to the extent that either of these exists for that class of stock. The remainder of any loss is to be charged to retained earnings. In essence a one-transaction viewpoint is used, as the firm is treated as a middle "person" for the transfer of stock between two shareholders.

2. Par Value Method

Under the **par value** method, all capital balances associated with the treasury shares are removed upon acquisition. Any excess of treasury stock cost over par value is accounted for by charging "paid-in capital from common stock" for the amount in excess of par received when the shares were originally issued. Any excess of the cost of acquiring the treasury stock over the original issue cost is charged to retained earnings. If treasury stock is acquired at a cost equal to or less than the original issue cost, "paid-in capital from common stock" is charged (debited) for the original amount in excess of par and "paid-in capital from treasury stock" is credited for the difference between the original issue price and the cost to acquire the treasury stock. When the treasury stock is resold, it is treated as a typical issuance, with the excess of selling price over par credited to "paid-in capital from common stock." Note that the par value method takes on a two-transaction viewpoint. The purchase is treated as a "retirement" of the shares, while the subsequent sale of the shares is treated as a "new" issue.

EXAMPLE: 100 shares ($50 par) are originally sold at $60, reacquired at $70, and subsequently resold at $75.

Cost method			Par value method		
Treasury stock	7,000		Treasury stock	5,000	
Cash		7,000	Paid-in capital--common		
			stock	1,000	
			Retained earnings	1,000	
			Cash		7,000
Cash	7,500		Cash	7,500	
Treasury stock		7,000	Treasury stock		5,000
Paid-in capital--			Paid-in capital--		
treasury stock		500	common stock		2,500

If the shares had been resold at $65

<u>Cost method</u>				<u>Par value method</u>		
Cash	6,500			Cash	6,500	
Retained earnings*	500			Treasury stock		5,000
Treasury stock		7,000		Paid-in capital--		
				common stock		1,500

"Paid-in capital--treasury stock" or "paid-in capital--retired stock" of that issue would be debited first to the extent it exists.

Note that total stockholders' equity is not affected by the method selected; only the allocation among the equity accounts is different.

E. Retirement of Stock

Formal retirement or constructive retirement (purchase with no intent of reissue) of stock is handled very similarly to treasury stock. When formally retired

Common stock	xx	
Paid-in capital in excess of par*	xx	
Retained earnings*	xx	
Treasury stock*		xx

*Assuming a loss on the retirement of treasury stock

1. "Paid-in capital from treasury stock transactions" may be debited to the extent it exists

2. A pro rata portion of all paid-in capital existing for that issue (e.g., if 2% of an issue is retired, up to 2% of all existing paid-in capital for that issue may be debited)

Alternatively, the entire or any portion of the loss may be debited to retained earnings. Any gains are credited to a "paid-in capital from retirement" account.

F. Dividends

1. At the date of declaration, an entry is made to record the dividend liability.

Retained earnings (dividends)	xx	
Dividends payable		xx

2. No entry is made at the date of record. Those owning stock at the date of record will be paid the previously declared dividends.

   a. The stockholder records consist of

      (1) General ledger account
      (2) Subsidiary ledger

         (a) Contains names and addresses of stockholders

      (3) Stock certificate book

   b. Outside services: usually banks

      (1) Transfer agent issues new certificates, canceling old, and maintains stockholder ledger
      (2) Registrar validates new certificates and controls against overissuance
      (3) Functions are now becoming combined

3. At the payment date, the liability is paid.

Dividends payable	xx	
Cash		xx

4. Property dividends are accounted for as cash dividends. They are recorded at FMV of the asset transferred with a gain (loss) recognized on the difference between the asset's BV and FMV at disposition (see APB 29).

5. Liquidation dividends (dividends based on other than earnings) are a return of capital to stockholders and should be so disclosed. Paid-in capital is usually debited rather than retained earnings. Common stock cannot be debited because it is the legal capital which can only be eliminated upon corporate dissolution.

6. Scrip dividends are issuance of promises to pay dividends in the future (and may bear interest) instead of cash.

Retained earnings	xx	
Scrip dividends payable		xx

  Scrip dividends are a liability which is extinguished by payment.

Scrip dividends payable	xx	
Interest expense (maybe)	xx	
Cash		xx

7. Unlike cash and property dividends, stock dividends are not a liability when declared. They can be rescinded as nothing is actually being distributed to stockholders except more stock certificates. Current assets are not used to "pay" the dividend.

  a. After stock dividends, shareholders continue to own the same proportion of the corporation.
  b. At declaration

Retained earnings	(FMV of shares)	
Stock dividend distributable		(par)
Paid-in capital in excess of par		(plug)

  c. At issuance

Stock dividend distributable	xx	
Common stock		xx

  d. Charge retained earnings for FMV of stock dividend if less than 20%-25% increase in stock outstanding; charge RE for **par value** of stock dividend if greater than 20-25% increase in stock outstanding.

   (1) Not required if closely held company

G. **Stock Splits**

  Stock splits change the number of shares outstanding and the par value per share. Par value is reduced in proportion to the increase in the number of shares. The total par value outstanding does not change and no charge is made to retained earnings. If legal requirements preclude changing the par or stated value, charge retained earnings only for the par or stated value issued.

STOCK DIVIDENDS AND SPLITS: SUMMARY OF EFFECTS

	Total S.E.	Par value per share	Total par outstanding	RE	Legal capital	Additional paid-in capital	No. of shares outstanding
Stock dividend < 20-25% of shares outstanding	N/C	N/C	+	Decrease by market value of shares issued	+	+	+
Stock split effected in form of dividend > 20 – 25% of shares outstanding	N/C	N/C	+	Decrease by par value of shares issued	+	N/C	+
Stock split	N/C	Decrease proportionately	N/C	N/C	N/C	N/C	+

N/C = No Change
+ = Increase
Prepared by Professor John R. Simon, Northern Illinois University

H. Appropriations of Retained Earnings (Reserves)

An entry to appropriate retained earnings restricts the amount of retained earnings that is available for dividends.

    RE (or Unappropriated RE)
       Reserve for RE (or Appropriated RE)

It is important to note, however, that the restriction of retained earnings does not necessarily provide cash for any intended purpose. The purpose is to show that **assets** in the amount of the appropriation are not available for dividends. SFAS 5 requires that when a reserve is no longer needed it must be returned directly to unappropriated retained earnings by reversing the entry that created it.

I. Compensation Cost

1. Stock Options

Study ARB 43, chap 13B, and APB 25 before studying this section. SFAS 123 is introduced at the end of this section. The outline of this standard should be studied at that point.

Compensation is generally measured by the dollar value difference between the option price and the market price if the option price is below the market price.

For financial reporting purposes, compensation is measured on the measurement date--that date on which both the number of shares the individual employee is entitled to and the option or purchase price are known. The measurement date is usually, though not always, the grant date.

Many options are granted at a price equal to or greater than the market price when the option is granted for a fixed number of shares. Thus, there is no compensation expense and no journal entry involving compensation expense is recorded. Disclosure, however, as to the options outstanding, is required. When the employee acquires stock under these circumstances, the corporation debits cash for the option price, and credits common stock for par and paid-in capital for the excess.

If the measurement date is the grant date and deferred compensation is recorded, it is amortized over the periods in which the employee provides the services for which the option contract is the reward. For example, an option is granted to a corporate officer to purchase 100 shares of $1 par common at $52 when the market price is $58. The entry to record the granting of the option is

Deferred compensation expense	600	(a contra paid-in capital account)
Stock options outstanding	600	(a paid-in capital account)

Deferred compensation is subtracted from stock options outstanding in the paid-in capital section of owners' equity to indicate the net contributed services on any date--that is, on the grant date nothing has yet been contributed by the option holder, and this would be measured by ($600 – $600 = 0). As the employee provides services to earn the option, an entry is made assigning compensation expense to periods (assume a 5-year period).

Compensation expense	120
Deferred compensation exp.	120

When the option is exercised, cash is received and stock is issued as reflected in the following entry (assume exercise after the 5-year period):

Cash	5,200	(option price)
Stock options outstanding	600	
Common stock	100	(par)
Additional paid-in capital	5,700	(plug)

If the options are forfeited due to the employee(s) failing to fulfill an obligation (e.g., staying with the company) compensation expense is credited in the year of forfeiture. The amount credited reflects the total compensation expense previously charged to the income statement for the employee(s) who forfeited the options. In the example, assume the officer leaves the company in year 3, 2 years before the options can be exercised. The following entry is made in year 3:

Stock options outstanding	600
Deferred compensation expense	360
Compensation expense	240

In the example above, the grant date and the measurement date coincide. If the measurement date follows the grant date, it is necessary to assume compensation expense based on the market values of the common stock that exist at the end of each period until the measurement date is reached. For example, assume that on 1/1/97, a company grants an option to purchase 100 shares of common stock at 90% of the market price at 12/31/99 and that the compensation period is 4 years. Note that at 1/1/97, the number of shares is determinable, but the option price is unknown. The market values and option prices of the common shares are as follows:

12/31/97	$10 x 90% = $ 9.00
12/31/98	13 x 90% = 11.70
12/31/99	15 x 90% = 13.50

The following entries for compensation expense are recorded:

	_1997_	_1998_	_1999_	_2000_
Compensation expense	25	40*	47.50*	37.50
Stock options outstanding	25	40	47.50	37.50

* *Results from change in accounting estimate*

1997: [($10 – 9.00) x 100 shares x 1/4)] = $25
1998: [($13 – 11.70) x 100 shares x 2/4)] – expense recognized to date = $40
1999: [($15 – 13.50) x 100 shares x 3/4)] – expense recognized to date = $47.50
2000: [($15 – 13.50) x 100 shares x 4/4)] – expense recognized to date = $37.50

Note that the market value of the stock at the end of 1997 and 1998 is used as an estimate of the market price of the stock at 12/31/99. Also, in accordance with FASB Interpretation 28, changes in the market value of the stock between the date of grant and the measurement date are adjustments to compensation expense **in the period the market value of the stock changes**. The effects of such changes are not spread over future periods.

A time line depicting the actual and estimated compensation expense would appear as follows:

1997	1998	1999	2000
$25	$40	$47.50	$37.50
estimated	estimated	actual	actual

Market price is known for both years

2. **Stock Appreciation Rights**

Study the summary of FASB Interpretation 28, which follows the outline of APB 25, in conjunction with the study of this section.

Stock appreciation rights (SAR) allow employees to receive stock or cash equal in amount to the difference between the market value and some predetermined amount per share for a certain number of shares. SAR allow employees to receive share appreciation without having to make a cash outlay as is common in stock option plans.

For financial reporting purposes, compensation expense is the excess of market value over a predetermined amount. Compensation expense is recorded in each period prior to exercise based on the excess of market value at the end of each period over a predetermined amount. Compensation expense is adjusted up or down as the market value of the stock changes before the measurement date (which is the exercise date). Therefore, compensation expense could be credited if the stock's market value drops from one period to the next.

For example, assume a company grants 100 SAR, payable in cash, to an employee on 1/1/98. The predetermined amount for the SAR plan is $50 per right, and the market value of the stock is $55 on 12/31/98, $53 on 12/31/99, and $61 on 12/31/00. Compensation expense recorded in each year would be

Total expense – Exp. previously accrued = Current expense

1998	100 ($55 – $50) =	$ 500	–	$ 0	=	$500
1999	100 ($53 – $50) =	$ 300	–	$500	=	($200)
2000	100 ($61 – $50) =	$1,100	–	$300	=	$800

The total expense recognized over the 3-year period is $1,100 [100($61 – $50)]. Journal entries would be

1998 and 2000		*1999*	
Compensation expense	$500/$800	Liability under SAR plan	$200
Liability under SAR plan	$500/$800	Compensation expense	$200

If the SAR were to be redeemed in common stock, Stock Rights Outstanding (a paid-in capital account) would replace the liability account in the above entries.

The above example assumes no service or vesting period, which is the period of time until the SAR become exercisable. If the above plan had a 2-year service period, 50% of the total expense would be recognized at the end of the first year, and 100% at the end of the second year and thereafter until exercised. The compensation would be accrued as follows:

1998	($ 500) (50%)	=	$ 250 – $ 0	=	$250
1997	($ 300) (100%)	=	$ 300 – $250	=	$ 50
2000	($1,100) (100%)	=	$1,100 – $300	=	$800

J.   Stock Compensation Under SFAS 123

Under this standard, the FASB encourages that compensation cost be measured at the grant date at **fair value** for stock purchase plans, stock options, restricted stock, and SAR issued to employees. Those plans requiring cash settlement shall measure the appropriate expense at the date of each reporting period.

The fair value of the compensation shall be calculated utilizing an options pricing model (such as the Black-Scholes model) which considers the following variables:

1. Current price of the underlying stock
2. Exercise price of the option
3. Expected life of the option
4. Expected volatility of the underlying stock
5. Expected dividends on the stock
6. Risk-free interest rate during the expected option term

The resulting fair value shall be applied to the number of options expected to vest (based on the grant date estimate) or the total number of options issued; nonpublic companies may use a simplified approach known as the minimum value method. This method considers all of the above variables except volatility. Previously recognized compensation expense shall only be revised for actual forfeitures before vesting or if certain performance conditions are not met.

SFAS 123 is also required for companies issuing stock options or other equity instruments to nonemployees in exchange for goods or services. Such transactions are recorded at the fair value of the goods or services received or the equity instrument issued, whichever is more reliably determinable.

Comparison of SFAS 123 and APB 25.

	APB 25 (Intrinsic value)	SFAS 123 (Fair value)
When to measure compensation expense	Date at which number of shares and exercise price are known, generally grant; each reporting period for plans requiring cash settlement	Date of grant for both fixed and variable stock-based plans; each reporting period for plans requiring cash settlement
How to measure compensation expense	Measure the intrinsic value of options difference between market price and exercise price at measurement date	Measure the fair value of options using option-pricing model (e.g., Black-Scholes or Binomial model); nonpublic entities may use the minimum value method
How to allocate compensation expense	Recognize on a straight-line basis over the vesting period	Recognize on a straight-line basis over the vesting period

To illustrate the recognition and measurement of stock compensation expense, suppose ABC Corporation (a nonpublic company) establishes an employee stock option plan on January 1, 1998. The plan allows its employees to acquire 10,000 shares of its $1 par value common stock at $52 per share, when the market price is also $52. The options may not be exercised until 5 years from the grant date. The risk-free interest rate is 8%, and the stock is expected to pay dividends of $2 annually. The schedule below shows the calculation of deferred compensation expense under SFAS 123 and APB 25.

Accounting for Stock Based Compensation Under the
Minimum Value Method Under SFAS 123

Current market value per share	$52.00
Less: Present value exercise price	
($52 x .681)	$35.39
Present value expected div.	
($2 x 3.993)	$ 7.99
Equals	$ 8.62
Times # of options	10,000
Deferred comp. expense	$86,200

Journal Entry in Year 1:

Deferred comp. expense	86,200	
Stock options outstanding		86,200

Over each of the next 5 years:

Compensation expense	17,240	
Deferred comp. expense		17,240

Accounting for Stock Based Compensation Under the
Method Allowed Under APB 25

Current market value per share	$52.00
Less: Exercise price per share	$52.00
Equals	$ 0.00
Times # of options	10,000
Deferred comp. expense	$ 0

Journal Entries:

No journal entries required because under the provisions of APB 25 in this circumstance no deferred compensation expense is recognized, when the exercise price equals the market price.

Accounting treatment per APB 25 is still acceptable for those organizations opting not to adopt the recommendations of SFAS 123. Such companies, however, are required to include pro forma net income and earnings per share under the new method. All organizations with stock-based compensation plans are required to make detailed disclosures about plan terms, exercise prices, and the assumptions made in measuring the fair value of stock-based grants (read the outline of SFAS 123).

K. Basic Earnings Per Share

In reviewing earnings per share, we recommend that candidates work through this section before reading the outline of SFAS 128.

A corporation is said to have a simple capital structure if it has only common stock outstanding (no potential common shares). In this calculation, all antidilutive securities (those that would **individually** increase EPS based upon outstanding common shares) are disregarded.

In the simple capital structure situation, the calculation of EPS can be stated as follows:

$$\text{Basic earnings per common share} = \frac{\text{Net income} - \text{Applicable preferred dividends}}{\text{Weighted-average number of common shares outstanding}}$$

The following example will illustrate the application of this formula:

Numerator information

a.	Net income	$100,000	
b.	Extraordinary loss (net of tax)	30,000	

c. 6% preferred stock, $100 par, 1,000 shares issued and outstanding ($100,000 x .06)   6,000

Denominator information

a. Common shares outstanding
   1/1/95   100,000

b. Shares issued for cash 4/1   20,000

c. Shares issued in 10% stock
   dividend declared in July   12,000

d. Shares of treasury stock
   purchased 10/1   10,000

When a corporation reports discontinued operations, an extraordinary item, and/or a cumulative effect of an accounting principles change, earnings per share information is required for the following income elements:

1. Income from continuing operations

2. The cumulative effect of the change in principle (net of tax)

3. Net income

4. Discontinued operations

5. Extraordinary items

Reporting EPS on these five income elements is required regardless of whether the capital structure is simple or complex; however, the entity may choose whether to report items 2, 4, and 5 on the face of the statement or in the notes. In the example, earnings per share information is required for the first, third, and fifth income elements. Nonpublic companies do not have to report EPS.

When calculating the amount of the numerator, the claims of senior securities (i.e., preferred stock) should be deducted to arrive at the earnings attributable to common shareholders. In the example, the preferred stock is cumulative. Thus, regardless of whether or not the board of directors declares a preferred dividend, holders of the preferred stock have a claim of $6,000 (1,000 shares x $6 per share) against 1997 earnings. Therefore, $6,000 is deducted from the numerator to arrive at the net income attributable to common shareholders. Note that this $6,000 would have been deducted for noncumulative preferred only if a dividend of this amount had been declared.

To summarize, at this point, the EPS calculations look as follows:

Earnings per common share:

$$\text{On income from continuing operations} = \frac{\$130,000 - 6,000}{\text{Common shares outstanding}}$$

$$\text{On net income} = \frac{\$100,000 - 6,000}{\text{Common shares outstanding}}$$

The numerator of the EPS calculation covers a particular time period such as a month, a quarter, or a year. It is, therefore, consistent to calculate the average number of common shares which were outstanding during this same time period. The calculation below in Table I illustrates the determination of weighted-average common shares outstanding. Note that for stock dividends the number of shares is adjusted retroactively for the shares which were outstanding prior to the stock dividend. Since the stock dividend was issued **after** the issuance of additional shares for cash on 4/1, the shareholders of those additional shares and the shareholders of the shares outstanding at the beginning of the year will receive the stock dividend. However, if the stock dividend had been issued **before** the issuance of additional shares of stock for cash on 4/1, only the shareholders who own the shares outstanding at the beginning of the period would have received the stock dividend. Stock splits are handled in an identical fashion.

TABLE I

Dates	Number common shares outstanding	Months outstanding	Fraction of year	Shares x Fraction of year
1/1 to 4/1	100,000 + 10% (100,000) = 110,000	3	1/4	27,500
4/1 to 10/1	110,000 + 20,000 + 10% (20,000) = 132,000	6	1/2	66,000
10/1 to 12/31	132,000 – 10,000 = 122,000	3	1/4	30,500
Weighted-average of common shares outstanding				124,000

In the weighted-average computation, an additional problem is created if common shares are issued in a business combination during the year. If the combination is accounted for as a purchase, the common shares are weighted from the date of issuance. If the pooling method is used the shares are considered to be outstanding for the entire year, regardless of the date the pooling was consummated. Other complications in the weighted-average calculation are posed by actual conversions of debt and preferred stock to common during the year and by exercise of warrants and options. These situations are introduced in the example presented with diluted earnings per share in the next section.

To complete the basic EPS example, the weighted-average number of common shares determined in Table I is divided into the income elements previously computed to arrive at the following:

Earnings per common share:

On income from continuing operations
$$\frac{\$130,000 - 6,000}{124,000 \text{ common shares}} = \$1.00$$

On net income
$$\frac{\$100,000 - 6,000}{124,000 \text{ common shares}} = \$ .76$$

These EPS numbers should be presented on the face of the income statement. Reporting a $.24 loss per share due to the extraordinary item can be presented on the face of the income statement or in the notes.

L. **Diluted Earnings Per Share**

Diluted EPS measures the performance of the entity over the reporting period (same as basic EPS) while also taking into account the effect of all dilutive potential common shares that were outstanding during the period. The only difference in the computation of diluted and basic EPS is that the denominator of the diluted EPS computation is increased to include the number of additional common shares that would have been outstanding if the dilutive potential common shares had been issued. In addition, the numerator is adjusted to add back any convertible preferred dividends, the after-tax amount of interest recognized in the period associated with any convertible debt, and any other changes in income (loss) that would result from the assumed conversion of the potential common shares. Diluted EPS should be based on the security holder's most advantageous conversion rate or exercise price. Similar to basic EPS, all antidilutive securities are disregarded.

The following two independent examples will illustrate the procedures necessary to calculate basic and diluted EPS. For both examples, assume net income is $50,000, and the weighted-average of common shares outstanding is 10,000.

In the first example, assume the following additional information with respect to the capital structure:

1. 4% nonconvertible, cumulative preferred stock, par $100, 1,000 shares issued and outstanding the entire year
2. Options and warrants to purchase 1,000 shares of common stock at $8 per share. The average market price of common stock during the year was $10 and the closing market price was $12 per share. The options and warrants were outstanding all year.

Diluted EPS must be computed because of the presence of the options and warrants. The preferred stock is not convertible; therefore, it is not a potentially dilutive security.

The first step in the solution of this problem is the determination of the basic EPS. This calculation appears as follows:

$$\frac{\text{Net income} - \text{Preferred dividends}}{\text{Weighted-average of common shares outstanding}} = \frac{\$50,000 - 4,000}{10,000 \text{ shares}} = \$4.60$$

Note that preferred dividends are deducted to arrive at net income applicable to common stock. When preferred stock is cumulative, this deduction is made whether or not dividends have been declared.

The calculation of diluted EPS is based upon outstanding common stock and all dilutive common shares that were outstanding during the period. In the example, the options and warrants are the only potentially dilutive security. Options and warrants are considered to be common stock equivalents at all times. Consequently, the only question that must be resolved is whether or not the options and warrants are dilutive. This question is resolved by comparing the average market price per common share of $10 with the exercise price of $8. If the average market price is > the exercise price, the effect of assuming the exercise of options and warrants is dilutive. However, if the average market price is ≤ the exercise price, the effect of assuming the exercise of options and warrants would be antidilutive (i.e., EPS would stay the same or increase). In the example, the options and warrants are dilutive ($10 > $8).

The method used to determine the dilutive effects of options and warrants is called the **treasury stock method**.

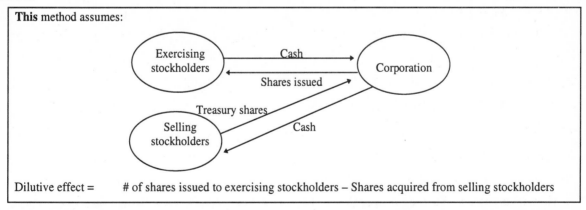

This method assumes:

Dilutive effect =   # of shares issued to exercising stockholders – Shares acquired from selling stockholders

In the example above, all of the options and warrants are assumed to be exercised at the beginning of the year (the options and warrants were outstanding the entire year) and the cash received is used to reacquire shares (treasury stock) at the average market price. The computation below illustrates the "treasury stock" method.

Proceeds from assumed exercise of options and warrants (1,000 shares x $8)	$8,000
Number of shares issued	1,000
Number of shares reacquired ($8,000 ÷ $10)	800
Number of shares assumed issued and not reacquired	200*

An alternative approach that can be used to calculate this number for diluted EPS is demonstrated below.

$$\frac{Ave.\ mar.\ price - Exer.\ price}{Average\ market\ price} \quad x \quad \begin{array}{c} Number\ of \\ Shares\ under \\ options/warrants \end{array} \quad = \quad Shares\ not\ reacquired$$

$$\frac{\$10-8}{\$10} \quad x \quad 1,000\ shares \quad = \quad 200\ shares$$

Diluted EPS can now be calculated, as follows, including the effects of applying the "treasury stock" method.

$$\frac{Net\ income - Preferred\ dividends}{\begin{array}{c}Weighted\text{-}average\ of\ common\ shares\\outstanding + Number\ of\ shares\ not\\acquired\ with\ proceeds\ from\\options\ and\ warrants\end{array}} \quad = \quad \frac{\$50,000 - 4,000}{10,000 + 200\ shares} \quad = \quad \$4.51$$

Note the incremental effects of the treasury stock method; there was no effect on the numerator of the EPS calculation while there were 200 shares added to the denominator. Note also that the options and warrants are dilutive. EPS is reduced from $4.60 to $4.51.

Table II summarizes the calculations made for the first example involving diluted EPS.

TABLE II

	Basic EPS		Diluted EPS	
Items	*Numerator*	*Denominator*	*Numerator*	*Denominator*
Net income	$50,000		$50,000	
Preferred div.	(4,000)		(4,000)	
Common shares outstanding		10,000 shs.		10,000 shs.
Options and warrants				200
Totals	$46,000 ÷	10,000 shs.	$46,000 ÷	10,200 shs.
EPS		$4.60		$4.51

For the second example, assume the following additional information about the capital structure (net income of $50,000 and common shares of 10,000 as in previous example).

1. 8% convertible debt, 200 bonds each convertible into 40 common shares. The bonds were outstanding the entire year. The average Aa corporate bond yield was 10% at the date the bonds were issued. The income tax rate is 40%. The bonds were issued at par ($1,000 per bond). No bonds were converted during the year.

2. 4% convertible, cumulative preferred stock, par $100, 1,000 shares issued and outstanding. Each preferred share is convertible into 2 common shares. The preferred stock was outstanding the entire year, and the average Aa corporate bond yield at the date the preferred stock was issued was 10%. The preferred stock was issued at par. No preferred stock was converted during the year.

The capital structure is complex in this example because of the presence of the two convertible securities. The first step in the solution of this example is the calculation of basic EPS based upon weighted-average of common shares outstanding. This EPS is the same as it was for the first example (i.e., $4.60). The next step is the computation of diluted EPS. The diluted EPS computation will include the convertible preferred stock if it is dilutive.

To determine the dilutive effect of the preferred stock, an assumption (called the **if converted method**) is made that all of the preferred stock is converted at the earliest date that it could have occurred during the year. In this example, the date would be January 1. The effects of this assumption are twofold. One, if the preferred stock is converted, there will be no preferred dividend of $4,000 for the year; and, two, there will be an additional 2,000 shares of common stock outstanding during the year (the conversion rate is 2 common for 1 preferred). EPS is computed, as follows, reflecting these two assumptions.

$$\frac{\text{Net income}}{\substack{\text{Weighted-average of common shares} \\ \text{outstanding + Shares issued upon} \\ \text{conversion of preferred stock}}} = \frac{\$50,000}{10,000 + 2,000 \text{ shares}} = \$4.17$$

The convertible preferred stock is dilutive because it reduced EPS from $4.60 to $4.17.

In the example, the convertible bonds are assumed to have been converted at the beginning of the year. The effects of this assumption are twofold. One, if the bonds are converted, there will be no interest expense of $16,000 (8% x $200,000 face value); and, two, there will be an additional 8,000 shares (200 bonds x 40 shares) of common stock outstanding during the year. One note of caution, however, must be mentioned; namely, the effect of not having $16,000 of interest expense will increase income, but it will also increase tax expense. Consequently, the net effect of not having interest expense is $9,600 [$16,000 – (40% x $16,000)]. Diluted EPS is computed, as follows, reflecting the dilutive preferred stock and the effects noted above for the convertible bonds.

$$\frac{\text{Net income + Interest expense (net of tax)}}{\substack{\text{Weighted-average of common shares} \\ \text{outstanding + Shares issued upon} \\ \text{conversion of preferred and} \\ \text{conversion of bonds}}} = \frac{\$50,000 + 9,600}{10,000 + 2,000 + 8,000 \text{ shares}} = \$2.98$$

The convertible debt is dilutive. Both the convertible bonds and preferred stock reduced EPS from $4.60 to $2.98. Table III summarizes the computations made for the second example.

The income statement disclosures for EPS, as a result of the second example, would be as follows:

Earnings per common share (see Note X)	$4.60
Earnings per common share assuming dilution	2.98

Note X would state the assumptions made in determining both basic and diluted EPS numbers.

TABLE III

Items	Basic EPS Numerator	Basic EPS Denominator	Diluted EPS Numerator	Diluted EPS Denominator
Net income	$50,000		$50,000	
Preferred div.	(4,000)			
Common shares outstanding		10,000 shs.		10,000 shs.
Conversion of preferred				2,000
Conversion of bonds			9,600	8,000
Totals	$46,000 ÷	10,000 shs.	$59,600 ÷	20,000 shs.
EPS	$4.60		$2.98	

In the two examples, all of the potentially dilutive securities were outstanding the entire year and no conversions or exercises were made during the year. If a potentially dilutive security was not outstanding the entire year, then the numerator and denominator effects would have to be "time-weighted." For instance, suppose the convertible bonds in the second example were issued during the current year on July 1. If all other facts remain unchanged, diluted EPS would be computed as follows:

$$\frac{\text{Net income + Interest expense (net of tax)}}{\substack{\text{Weighted-average of common shares} \\ \text{outstanding + Shares issued upon} \\ \text{conversion of preferred and} \\ \text{conversion of bonds}}} = \frac{\$50,000 + 1/2\,(9,600)}{10,000 + 2,000 + 1/2\,(8,000)} = \$3.43$$

The convertible debt is dilutive whether or not it is outstanding the entire year or for part of a year.

If actual conversions or exercises take place during a period, the common shares issued will be outstanding from their date of issuance and, therefore, will be in the weighted-average of common shares outstanding. These shares are then weighted from their respective times of issuance. For example, assume that all the bonds in the second example are converted on July 1 into 8,000 common shares. Several important effects should be noted, as follows:

(1)   The weighted-average of common shares outstanding will be increased by (8,000)(.5) or 4,000. Income will increase $4,800 net of tax, because the bonds are no longer outstanding.

(2)   The "if converted" method is applied to the period January 1 to July 1 because it was during this period that the bonds were potentially dilutive. The interest expense, net of tax, of $4,800 is added to the income, and 4,000 shares (.5 of 8,000) are added to the denominator.

(3)   Interestingly, the net effect of items 1 and 2 is the same for the period whether these dilutive bonds were outstanding the entire period or converted during the period.

It should also be noted that when convertible debt is issued for a premium or discount, the interest expense net of taxes must be computed after giving effect to premium/discount amortization.

The benchmark used to determine if including individual securities decreases income is income from continuing operations unless an enterprise has no discontinued operations. In that case income before extraordinary items or cumulative effect would be the benchmark number.

Contingent issuances of common stock. Also mentioned are **contingent issuances** of common stock (e.g., stock subscriptions). If shares are to be issued in the future with no restrictions on issuance other than the passage of time, they are to be considered issued and treated as outstanding in the computation of dilutive EPS (SFAS 128, para 91). Other issuances that are dependent upon certain conditions being met are to be evaluated in a different respect. SFAS 128 uses as examples the maintenance of current earnings levels and the attainment of specified earnings increases. If the contingency is to merely maintain the earnings levels currently being attained, then the shares are considered outstanding for the entire period and considered in the computation of dilutive EPS if the effect is dilutive. If the requirement is to increase earnings over a period of time, the diluted EPS computation shall include those shares that would be issued based on the assumption that current amount of earnings will remain unchanged, if the effect is dilutive.

Return to Module 22C and review the EPS disclosures there. Also read the outline for SFAS 128.

M. Corporate Bankruptcy

The going concern assumption is one of the basic principles underlying the primary financial statements (balance sheet, income statement and statement of cash flows). However, this assumption of continued existence is threatened in corporations that are in severe financial trouble. A range of alternative actions is available to a company before it enters bankruptcy, such as seeking extensions on due dates of debt, restructuring its debt, or allowing a court-appointed trustee to manage the corporation. These pre-bankruptcy options are presented in the following modules:

> Creditor's agreements--Module 11, Bankruptcy
> Troubled debt restructurings--Module 26, Present Value, Section C

Bankruptcy is the final legal act for a company. In bankruptcy, the accounting and financial reporting must present the information necessary for the liquidation of the business. The **Statement of Affairs** is prepared to present the current market values of the assets and the status of the various categories of the equity interests of the corporation.

The accountant must provide a prioritization of the creditors' claims against the net assets of the corporation. The legal rights of each creditor are determined by the terms of the credit agreement it has with the company and by the National Bankruptcy Act.

The **Statement of Affairs** classifies assets in the following order of priority (highest to lowest):

(1) Assets pledged with fully secured creditors--assets having a fair valuation equal to or greater than the debts for which they serve as collateral
(2) Assets pledged with partially secured creditors--assets having a fair valuation less than their associated debts
(3) Free assets--uncommitted assets available for remaining equity interests

The equity interests are classified in the following order (highest to lowest):

(1) Preferred claims--these claims have priority as specified in the Bankruptcy Act
(2) Fully secured creditors--these are claims which should be fully covered with the realizations from the assets pledged to the claims

(3) Partially secured creditors--these are claims which may not be fully covered by the realizations of the pledged assets for these claims; the amount of the uncovered claims goes to the unsecured creditors category

(4) Unsecured creditors--these are claims that have no priority and do not have any collateral claims to any specific assets

(5) Stockholders' equity--this represents any residual claim

The historical cost valuation principles used in a balance sheet assume a going concern assumption. As a business enters bankruptcy, the liquidation values of the assets become the most relevant measures. In addition, anticipated costs of liquidation should be recognized. The Statement of Affairs begins with the present book values of the company's assets in order to articulate with the balance sheet. After relating the projected proceeds from the liquidation of the assets to the various equity interests, the statement concludes with the estimated dollar amount of unsecured claims that cannot be paid (estimated deficiency).

EXAMPLE: The Vann Corporation's balance sheet for December 31, 1999, is shown below. The corporation is entering bankruptcy and expects to incur $8,000 of costs for the liquidation process. The estimated current values of the assets are determined and the various equity claims are prioritized. The Statement of Affairs for Vann Corporation is presented on the following page.

The Vann Corporation
BALANCE SHEET
December 31, 1999

Assets

Cash	$ 1,500
Marketable securities	10,000
Accounts receivable (net)	18,000
Merchandise inventory	41,000
Prepaid expenses	2,000
Land	6,000
Building (net of depreciation)	65,000
Machinery (net of depreciation)	21,000
Goodwill	10,000
	$174,500

Equities

Accounts payable	$ 30,000
Notes payable	37,000
Accrued wages	6,500
Mortgages payable	45,000
Capital stock ($10 par)	100,000
Retained earnings (deficit)	(44,000)
	$174,500

N. Reorganizations

Chapter 11 of the Bankruptcy Reform Act of 1978 allows legal protection from creditors to provide time for a bankrupt corporation to return its operations to a profitable level. SOP 90-7 provides guidance for financial reporting during Chapter 11 reorganizations. The SOP requires the balance sheet, income statement, and statement of cash flows to distinguish events and transactions related with the reorganization from those related to ongoing operations. Liabilities should be reported at expected amounts per the plan on the balance sheet. Liabilities should be classified as unsecured or secured liabilities before reorganization and liabilities incurred after the filing date for Chapter 11. Transactions directly related to the reorganization should be reported separately on the income statement in the period incurred, and disclo-

The Vann Corporation
STATEMENT OF AFFAIRS
December 31, 1999

ASSETS

Book values		Estimated current values	Amount available to unsecured claims
	(1) Assets Pledged with Fully Secured Creditors:		
$ 6,000	Land	$12,000	
65,000	Building	41,000	
		$53,000	
	Less Mortgages Payable	45,000	$ 8,000
	(2) Assets Pledged with Partially Secured Creditors:		
10,000	Marketable Securities	$12,000	
	Notes Payable	37,000	
	(3) Free Assets		
1,500	Cash	1,500	
18,000	Accounts Receivable (net)	14,000	
41,000	Merchandise Inventory	22,500	
2,000	Prepaid Expenses	0	
21,000	Machinery	13,200	
10,000	Goodwill	0	51,200
	Estimated amount available		59,200
	Less: creditors with priority		(14,500)
	Net Estimated amount available to unsecured creditors (81 cents on the dollar)		44,700
	Estimated deficiency to unsecured creditors		10,300
			$55,000
$174,500			

EQUITIES

Book values		Amount unsecured
	(1) Creditors with Priority	
$ 0	Estimated Liquidation Expenses (accounting, legal and other costs of liquidation process)	$ 8,000
6,500	Accrued Wages	6,500
		$14,500
	(2) Fully Secured Creditors	
45,000	Mortgages Payable	45,000
	(3) Partially Secured Creditors	
37,000	Notes Payable	37,000
	Less Marketable Securities	12,000
		25,000
	(4) Unsecured Creditors	
30,000	Accounts Payable	30,000
	(5) Stockholders' Equity	
100,000	Capital Stock	
(44,000)	Retained Earnings (deficit)	
$174,500		$55,000

sure should be made of any anticipated changes in common stock or common stock equivalents. Cash flows related to the reorganization should be reported separately from those related to regular operations. At confirmation of the plan of reorganization, an entity may be considered a new entity for reporting purposes if the reorganization value of assets before confirmation is less than liabilities incurred after petition for Chapter 11 and voting shareholders before confirmation receive less than 50% of the voting shares of the emerging entity. If the entity does not qualify as a new entity, the reorganization should be accounted for as troubled debt restructuring which is discussed in Module 26C.

O. **Quasi Reorganization (ARB 43, Chapter 7A)**

The purpose of a quasi reorganization is to allow companies to avoid formal bankruptcy proceedings through an informal proceeding. The procedure is applicable for a situation where a going concern exists except for overvalued assets and a possible deficit. The overvalued assets result in high depreciation charges and losses or lower net income. The deficit precludes payment of dividends.

The procedure is applicable during a period of declining price levels (normally associated with decreased economic activity), such as the 1930s.

The procedures involve

(1) Proper authorization including that from stockholders and creditors where required
(2) Revaluation of assets to current values
(3) Elimination of any deficit by charging paid-in capital

   (a) First capital surplus
   (b) Second capital stock

To write down assets: here the adjustments are taken directly to retained earnings. An alternative is to use an intermediary account such as "adjustment account" which would later be closed to retained earnings.

Retained earnings	(writedown)
Assets	(writedown)

To eliminate the deficit

Paid-in capital	(deficit)
Retained earnings	(deficit)

In many cases, paid-in capital in excess of par value will be insufficient, and the par or stated value of the capital stock must be reduced to eliminate the deficit.

Existing paid-in capital	(amount on the books)
Capital stock	(total reduction in par)
Retained earnings	(deficit)
Paid-in capital from	
quasi reorganization	(forced figure)

The paid-in capital arises from reducing the par or stated value from, for example, $100 to $50 rather than to $59.415. The $59.415 would come from dividing the shares outstanding into the retained earnings deficit.

ARB 46 requires retained earnings to be dated for 10 years (less than 10 years justified under exceptional circumstances) after a quasi reorganization takes place. Disclosure similar to "since quasi reorganization of June 30, 1989," would be appropriate.

P. **Stock Rights**

Generally, before additional stock is offered to the public, stock rights are issued to existing shareholders to prevent involuntary dilution of their voting rights (e.g., the preemptive privilege). The stock rights, evidenced by warrants, indicate the number and price at which the shares may be purchased. At issuance, the issuer makes only a memorandum entry. Upon exercise, the following entry is made:

Cash	(proceeds)	
Common stock		(par)
Paid-in capital		(plug)

Information relating to stock rights outstanding must be disclosed. Detachable stock rights issued with preferred stock are treated like those on bonds (see Module 26, Section B.6.). Treatment of stock rights by recipients is discussed in Module 29, Section F.

Q. **Employee Stock Ownership Plan (ESOP)**

An employee stock ownership plan (ESOP) is a qualified stock bonus plan designed to invest primarily in qualifying employer securities, including stock and other marketable obligations. In some instances, the ESOP will borrow funds from a bank or other lender in order to acquire shares of the employer's stock. If such an obligation of the ESOP is guaranteed by the employer (assumption by the employer of the ESOP's debt), it should be recorded as a liability in the employer's financial statements. The offsetting debit to the liability should be accounted for as a reduction of shareholders' equity. Shareholders' equity will increase symmetrically with the reduction of the liability as the ESOP makes payments on the debt. Assets held by an ESOP should not be included in the employer's financial statements, because such assets are owned by the employees, not the employer. Additionally, the employer should charge to compensation expense the amount the employer contributed or committed to be contributed to an ESOP with respect to a given year. This is done regardless of whether or not the ESOP has borrowed funds.

R. **Ratios**

The following ratios use stockholders' equity components in their calculations:

1. **Dividend payout**--measures percentage of earnings distributed as dividends

$$\frac{\text{Dividends per share}}{\text{Earnings per share}}$$

2. **Book value of common stock** (at a point in time)--not a meaningful measure because assets are carried at historical costs

$$\frac{\text{Common stockholders' equity}}{\text{Shares outstanding}}$$

3. **Rate of return on common stockholders' equity**--measures the return earned on the stockholders' investment in the firm

$$\frac{\text{Net income available to common stockholders}}{\text{Common stockholders' equity}}$$

4. **Debt to equity**--shows creditors the corporation's ability to sustain losses

$$\frac{\text{Debt}}{\text{Stockholders' equity}}$$

MULTIPLE-CHOICE QUESTIONS (1-89)

1. East Co. issued 1,000 shares of its $5 par common stock to Howe as compensation for 1,000 hours of legal services performed. Howe usually bills $160 per hour for legal services. On the date of issuance, the stock was trading on a public exchange at $140 per share. By what amount should the additional paid-in capital account increase as a result of this transaction?
   a. $135,000
   b. $140,000
   c. $155,000
   d. $160,000

2. On July 1, 1999, Cove Corp., a closely-held corporation, issued 6% bonds with a maturity value of $60,000, together with 1,000 shares of its $5 par value common stock, for a combined cash amount of $110,000. The market value of Cove's stock cannot be ascertained. If the bonds were issued separately, they would have sold for $40,000 on an 8% yield to maturity basis. What amount should Cove report for additional paid-in capital on the issuance of the stock?
   a. $75,000
   b. $65,000
   c. $55,000
   d. $45,000

3. Beck Corp. issued 200,000 shares of common stock when it began operations in 1997 and issued an additional 100,000 shares in 1998. Beck also issued preferred stock convertible to 100,000 shares of common stock. In 1997, Beck purchased 75,000 shares of its common stock and held it in Treasury. At December 31, 1999, how many shares of Beck's common stock were outstanding?
   a. 400,000
   b. 325,000
   c. 300,000
   d. 225,000

4. A corporation was organized in January 1999 with authorized capital of $10 par value common stock. On February 1, 1999, shares were issued at par for cash. On March 1, 1999, the corporation's attorney accepted 5,000 shares of the common stock in settlement for legal services with a fair value of $60,000. Additional paid-in capital would increase on

	February 1, 1999	March 1, 1999
a.	Yes	No
b.	Yes	Yes
c.	No	No
d.	No	Yes

5. On April 1, 1999, Hyde Corp., a newly formed company, had the following stock issued and outstanding:

   • Common stock, no par, $1 stated value, 20,000 shares originally issued for $30 per share.
   • Preferred stock, $10 par value, 6,000 shares originally issued for $50 per share.

Hyde's April 1, 1999 statement of stockholders' equity should report

	Common stock	Preferred stock	Additional paid-in capital
a.	$ 20,000	$ 60,000	$820,000
b.	$ 20,000	$300,000	$580,000
c.	$600,000	$300,000	$0
d.	$600,000	$ 60,000	$240,000

6. On March 1, 1999, Rya Corp. issued 1,000 shares of its $20 par value common stock and 2,000 shares of its $20 par value convertible preferred stock for a total of $80,000. At this date, Rya's common stock was selling for $36 per share, and the convertible preferred stock was selling for $27 per share. What amount of the proceeds should be allocated to Rya's convertible preferred stock?
   a. $60,000
   b. $54,000
   c. $48,000
   d. $44,000

7. During 1998, Brad Co. issued 5,000 shares of $100 par convertible preferred stock for $110 per share. One share of preferred stock can be converted into three shares of Brad's $25 par common stock at the option of the preferred shareholder. On December 31, 1999, when the market value of the common stock was $40 per share, all of the preferred stock was converted. What amount should Brad credit to Common Stock and to Additional Paid-in Capital--Common Stock as a result of the conversion?

	Common stock	Additional paid-in capital
a.	$375,000	$175,000
b.	$375,000	$225,000
c.	$500,000	$ 50,000
d.	$600,000	$0

8. Quoit, Inc. issued preferred stock with detachable common stock warrants. The issue price exceeded the sum of the warrants' fair value and the preferred stocks' par value. The preferred stocks' fair value was not determinable. What amount should be assigned to the warrants outstanding?
   a. Total proceeds.
   b. Excess of proceeds over the par value of the preferred stock.
   c. The proportion of the proceeds that the warrants' fair value bears to the preferred stocks' par value.
   d. The fair value of the warrants.

9. Blue Co. issued preferred stock with detachable common stock warrants at a price which exceeded both the par value and the market value of the preferred stock. At the time the warrants are exercised, Blue's total stockholders' equity is increased by the

	Cash received upon exercise of the warrants	Carrying amount of warrants
a.	Yes	No
b.	Yes	Yes
c.	No	No
d.	No	Yes

10. When collectibility is reasonably assured, the excess of the subscription price over the stated value of the no par common stock subscribed should be recorded as

   a.   No par common stock.

   b.   Additional paid-in capital when the subscription is recorded.

   c.   Additional paid-in capital when the subscription is collected.

   d.   Additional paid-in capital when the common stock is issued.

11. On December 1, 1999, shares of authorized common stock were issued on a subscription basis at a price in excess of par value. A total of 20% of the subscription price of each share was collected as a down payment on December 1, 1999, with the remaining 80% of the subscription price of each share due in 2000. Collectibility was reasonably assured. At December 31, 1999, the stockholders' equity section of the balance sheet would report additional paid-in capital for the excess of the subscription price over the par value of the shares of common stock subscribed and

   a.   Common stock issued for 20% of the par value of the shares of common stock subscribed.

   b.   Common stock issued for the par value of the shares of common stock subscribed.

   c.   Common stock subscribed for 80% of the par value of the shares of common stock subscribed.

   d.   Common stock subscribed for the par value of the shares of common stock subscribed.

12. In 1998, Seda Corp. acquired 6,000 shares of its $1 par value common stock at $36 per share. During 1999, Seda issued 3,000 of these shares at $50 per share. Seda uses the cost method to account for its treasury stock transactions. What accounts and amounts should Seda credit in 1999 to record the issuance of the 3,000 shares?

	Treasury stock	Additional paid-in capital	Retained earnings	Common stock
a.		$102,000	$42,000	$6,000
b.		$144,000		$6,000
c.	$108,000	$ 42,000		
d.	$108,000		$42,000	

13. At December 31, 1998, Rama Corp. had 20,000 shares of $1 par value treasury stock that had been acquired in 1998 at $12 per share. In May 1999, Rama issued 15,000 of these treasury shares at $10 per share. The cost method is used to record treasury stock transactions. Rama is located in a state where laws relating to acquisition of treasury stock restrict the availability of retained earnings for declaration of dividends. At December 31, 1999, what amount should Rama show in notes to financial statements as a restriction of retained earnings as a result of its treasury stock transactions?

   a. $ 5,000

   b. $10,000

   c. $60,000

   d. $90,000

14. United, Inc.'s unadjusted current assets section and stockholders' equity section of its December 31, 1999 balance sheet are as follows:

Current assets

Cash	$ 60,000
Investments in marketable equity securities (including $300,000 of United, Inc. common stock)	400,000
Trade accounts receivable	340,000
Inventories	148,000
Total	$ 948,000

Stockholders' equity

Common stock	$2,224,000
Retained earnings (deficit)	(224,000)
Total	$2,000,000

The investments and inventories are reported at their costs, which approximate market values.

In its 1999 statement of stockholders' equity, United's total amount of equity at December 31, 1999, is

   a. $2,224,000

   b. $2,000,000

   c. $1,924,000

   d. $1,700,000

15. Cyan Corp. issued 20,000 shares of $5 par common stock at $10 per share. On December 31, 1998, Cyan's retained earnings were $300,000. In March 1999, Cyan reacquired 5,000 shares of its common stock at $20 per share. In June 1999, Cyan sold 1,000 of these shares to its corporate officers for $25 per share. Cyan uses the cost method to record treasury stock. Net income for the year ended December 31, 1999, was $60,000. At December 31, 1999, what amount should Cyan report as retained earnings?

   a. $360,000

   b. $365,000

   c. $375,000

   d. $380,000

16. Victor Corporation was organized on January 2, 1999 with 100,000 authorized shares of $10 par value common stock. During 1999 Victor had the following capital transactions:

January 5--issued 75,000 shares at $14 per share.
December 27--purchased 5,000 shares at $11 per share.

Victor used the par value method to record the purchase of the treasury shares. What would be the balance in the paid-in capital from treasury stock account at December 31, 1999?

   a. $0

   b. $ 5,000

   c. $15,000

   d. $20,000

17. On incorporation, Dee Inc. issued common stock at a price in excess of its par value. No other stock transactions occurred except treasury stock was acquired for an amount exceeding this issue price. If Dee uses the par value method of accounting for treasury stock appropriate for retired stock, what is the effect of the acquisition on the following?

	Net common stock	Additional paid-in capital	Retained earnings
a.	No effect	Decrease	No effect
b.	Decrease	Decrease	Decrease
c.	Decrease	No effect	Decrease
d.	No effect	Decrease	Decrease

18. Posy Corp. acquired treasury shares at an amount greater than their par value, but less than their original issue price. Compared to the cost method of accounting for treasury stock, does the par value method report a greater amount for additional paid-in capital and a greater amount for retained earnings?

	Additional paid-in capital	Retained earnings
a.	Yes	Yes
b.	Yes	No
c.	No	No
d.	No	Yes

19. In 1996, Rona Corp. issued 5,000 shares of $10 par value common stock for $100 per share. In 1999, Rona reacquired 2,000 of its shares at $150 per share from the estate of one of its deceased officers and immediately canceled these 2,000 shares. Rona uses the cost method in accounting for its treasury stock transactions. In connection with the retirement of these 2,000 shares, Rona should debit

	Additional paid-in capital	Retained earnings
a.	$ 20,000	$280,000
b.	$100,000	$180,000
c.	$180,000	$100,000
d.	$280,000	$0

20. The following accounts were among those reported on Luna Corp.'s balance sheet at December 31, 1998:

Marketable securities (market value $140,000)	$ 80,000
Preferred stock, $20 par value, 20,000 shares issued and outstanding	400,000
Additional paid-in capital on preferred stock	30,000
Retained earnings	900,000

On January 20, 1999, Luna exchanged all of the marketable securities for 5,000 shares of Luna's preferred stock. Market values at the date of the exchange were $150,000 for the marketable securities and $30 per share for the preferred stock. The 5,000 shares of preferred stock were retired immediately after the exchange. Which of the following journal entries should Luna record in connection with this transaction?

		Debit	Credit
a.	Preferred stock	100,000	
	Additional paid-in capital on preferred stock	7,500	
	Retained earnings	42,500	
	Marketable securities		80,000
	Gain on exchange of securities		70,000

		Debit	Credit
b.	Preferred stock	100,000	
	Additional paid-in capital on preferred stock	30,000	
	Marketable securities		80,000
	Additional paid-in capital from retirement of preferred stock		50,000
c.	Preferred stock	150,000	
	Marketable securities		80,000
	Additional paid-in capital on preferred stock		70,000
d.	Preferred stock	150,000	
	Marketable securities		80,000
	Gain on exchange of securities		70,000

21. On December 31, 1999, Pack Corp.'s board of directors canceled 50,000 shares of $2.50 par value common stock held in treasury at an average cost of $13 per share. Before recording the cancellation of the treasury stock, Pack had the following balances in its stockholders' equity accounts:

Common stock	$540,000
Additional paid-in capital	750,000
Retained earnings	900,000
Treasury stock, at cost	650,000

In its balance sheet at December 31, 1999, Pack should report common stock outstanding of
a. $0
b. $250,000
c. $415,000
d. $540,000

22. In 1997, Fogg, Inc. issued $10 par value common stock for $25 per share. No other common stock transactions occurred until March 31, 1999, when Fogg acquired some of the issued shares for $20 per share and retired them. Which of the following statements correctly states an effect of this acquisition and retirement?
a. 1999 net income is decreased.
b. 1999 net income is increased.
c. Additional paid-in capital is decreased.
d. Retained earnings is increased.

23. Arp Corp.'s outstanding capital stock at December 15, 1999, consisted of the following:

• 30,000 shares of 5% cumulative preferred stock, par value $10 per share, fully participating as to dividends. No dividends were in arrears.
• 200,000 shares of common stock, par value $1 per share.

On December 15, 1999, Arp declared dividends of $100,000. What was the amount of dividends payable to Arp's common stockholders?
a. $10,000
b. $34,000
c. $40,000
d. $47,500

24. At December 31, 1998 and 1999, Apex Co. had 3,000 shares of $100 par, 5% cumulative preferred stock outstanding. No dividends were in arrears as of December 31, 1997. Apex did not declare a dividend during 1997. During 1999, Apex paid a cash dividend of $10,000 on its preferred stock. Apex should report dividends in arrears in its 1999 financial statements as a(n)

    a. Accrued liability of $15,000.
    b. Disclosure of $15,000.
    c. Accrued liability of $20,000.
    d. Disclosure of $20,000.

25. East Corp., a calendar-year company, had sufficient retained earnings in 1999 as a basis for dividends, but was temporarily short of cash. East declared a dividend of $100,000 on April 1, 1999, and issued promissory notes to its stockholders in lieu of cash. The notes, which were dated April 1, 1999, had a maturity date of March 31, 2000, and a 10% interest rate. How should East account for the scrip dividend and related interest?

    a. Debit retained earnings for $110,000 on April 1, 1999.
    b. Debit retained earnings for $110,000 on March 31, 2000.
    c. Debit retained earnings for $100,000 on April 1, 1999, and debit interest expense for $10,000 on March 31, 2000.
    d. Debit retained earnings for $100,000 on April 1, 1999, and debit interest expense for $7,500 on December 31, 1999.

26. On January 2, 1999, Lake Mining Co.'s board of directors declared a cash dividend of $400,000 to stockholders of record on January 18, 1999, payable on February 10, 1999. The dividend is permissible under law in Lake's state of incorporation. Selected data from Lake's December 31, 1998 balance sheet are as follows:

Accumulated depletion	$100,000
Capital stock	500,000
Additional paid-in capital	150,000
Retained earnings	300,000

The $400,000 dividend includes a liquidating dividend of

    a. $0
    b. $100,000
    c. $150,000
    d. $300,000

27. On June 27, 1999, Brite Co. distributed to its common stockholders 100,000 outstanding common shares of its investment in Quik, Inc., an unrelated party. The carrying amount on Brite's books of Quik's $1 par common stock was $2 per share. Immediately after the distribution, the market price of Quik's stock was $2.50 per share. In its income statement for the year ended June 30, 1999, what amount should Brite report as gain before income taxes on disposal of the stock?

    a. $250,000
    b. $200,000
    c. $ 50,000
    d. $0

28. On December 1, 1999, Nilo Corp. declared a property dividend of marketable securities to be distributed on December 31, 1999, to stockholders of record on December 15, 1999. On December 1, 1999, the marketable securities had a carrying amount of $60,000 and a fair value of $78,000. What is the effect of this property dividend on Nilo's 1999 retained earnings, after all nominal accounts are closed?

    a. $0.
    b. $18,000 increase.
    c. $60,000 decrease.
    d. $78,000 decrease.

29. Long Co. had 100,000 shares of common stock issued and outstanding at January 1, 1999. During 1999, Long took the following actions:

March 15	--	Declared a 2-for-1 stock split, when the fair value of the stock was $80 per share.
December 15	--	Declared a $.50 per share cash dividend.

In Long's statement of stockholders' equity for 1999, what amount should Long report as dividends?

    a. $ 50,000
    b. $100,000
    c. $850,000
    d. $950,000

30. A company declared a cash dividend on its common stock on December 15, 1999, payable on January 12, 2000. How would this dividend affect stockholders' equity on the following dates?

	December 15, 1999	December 31, 1999	January 12, 2000
a.	Decrease	No effect	Decrease
b.	Decrease	No effect	No effect
c.	No effect	Decrease	No effect
d.	No effect	No effect	Decrease

31. Ole Corp. declared and paid a liquidating dividend of $100,000. This distribution resulted in a decrease in Ole's

	Paid-in capital	Retained earnings
a.	No	No
b.	Yes	Yes
c.	No	Yes
d.	Yes	No

32. Instead of the usual cash dividend, Evie Corp. declared and distributed a property dividend from its overstocked merchandise. The excess of the merchandise's carrying amount over its market value should be

    a. Ignored.
    b. Reported as a separately disclosed reduction of retained earnings.
    c. Reported as an extraordinary loss, net of income taxes.
    d. Reported as a reduction in income before extraordinary items.

33. The following stock dividends were declared and distributed by Sol Corp.:

Percentage of common shares outstanding at declaration date	Fair value	Par value
10	$15,000	$10,000
28	40,000	30,800

What aggregate amount should be debited to retained earnings for these stock dividends?

a. $40,800
b. $45,800
c. $50,000
d. $55,000

34. Ray Corp. declared a 5% stock dividend on its 10,000 issued and outstanding shares of $2 par value common stock, which had a fair value of $5 per share before the stock dividend was declared. This stock dividend was distributed 60 days after the declaration date. By what amount did Ray's current liabilities increase as a result of the stock dividend declaration?

a. $0
b. $ 500
c. $1,000
d. $2,500

35. How would total stockholders' equity be affected by the declaration of each of the following?

	Stock dividend	Stock split
a.	No effect	Increase
b.	Decrease	Decrease
c.	Decrease	No effect
d.	No effect	No effect

36. On July 1, 1999, Bart Corporation has 200,000 shares of $10 par common stock outstanding and the market price of the stock is $12 per share. On the same date, Bart declared a 1-for-2 reverse stock split. The par of the stock was increased from $10 to $20 and one new $20 par share was issued for each two $10 par shares outstanding. Immediately before the 1-for-2 reverse stock split, Bart's additional paid-in capital was $450,000. What should be the balance in Bart's additional paid-in capital account immediately after the reverse stock split is effected?

a. $0
b. $450,000
c. $650,000
d. $850,000

37. How would a stock split in which the par value per share decreases in proportion to the number of additional shares issued affect each of the following?

	Additional paid-in capital	Retained earnings
a.	Increase	No effect
b.	No effect	No effect
c.	No effect	Decrease
d.	Increase	Decrease

38. At December 31, 1998, Eagle Corp. reported $1,750,000 of appropriated retained earnings for the construction of a new office building, which was completed in 1999 at a total cost of $1,500,000. In 1999, Eagle appropriated $1,200,000 of retained earnings for the construction of a new plant. Also, $2,000,000 of cash was restricted for the retirement of bonds due in 2000. In its 1999 balance sheet, Eagle should report what amount of appropriated retained earnings?

a. $1,200,000
b. $1,450,000
c. $2,950,000
d. $3,200,000

39. The following information pertains to Meg Corp.:

• Dividends on its 1,000 shares of 6%, $10 par value cumulative preferred stock have not been declared or paid for 3 years.
• Treasury stock that cost $15,000 was reissued for $8,000.

What amount of retained earnings should be appropriated as a result of these items?

a. $0
b. $1,800
c. $7,000
d. $8,800

40. A retained earnings appropriation can be used to

a. Absorb a fire loss when a company is self-insured.
b. Provide for a contingent loss that is probable and reasonably estimable.
c. Smooth periodic income.
d. Restrict earnings available for dividends.

41. On January 1, 1998, Doro Corp. granted an employee an option to purchase 3,000 shares of Doro's $5 par value common stock at $20 per share. The option became exercisable on December 31, 1999, after the employee completed 2 years of service. The option was exercised on January 10, 2000. The market prices of Doro's stock were as follows:

January 1, 1998	$30
December 31, 1999	50
January 10, 2000	45

For 1999, Doro should recognize compensation expense under APB 25 of

a. $45,000
b. $37,500
c. $15,000
d. $0

42. In connection with a stock option plan for the benefit of key employees, Ward Corp. intends to distribute treasury shares when the options are exercised. These shares were bought in 1998 at $42 per share. On January 1, 1999, Ward granted stock options for 10,000 shares at $38 per share as additional compensation for services to be rendered over the next 3 years. The options are exercisable during a 4-year period beginning January 1, 2001, by grantees still employed by Ward. Market price of Ward's stock was $47 per share at the grant date. No stock options were terminated during 1999. In Ward's December 31, 1999 income statement, what amount should be reported as compensation expense pertaining to the options under APB 25?

    a. $90,000
    b. $40,000
    c. $30,000
    d. $0

43. On January 2, 1999, Kine Co. granted Morgan, its president, compensatory stock options to buy 1,000 shares of Kine's $10 par common stock. The options call for a price of $20 per share and are exercisable for 3 years following the grant date. Morgan exercised the options on December 31, 1999. The market price of the stock was $50 on January 2, 1999, and $70 on December 31, 1999. By what net amount should stockholders' equity increase as a result of the grant and exercise of the options under APB 25?

    a. $20,000
    b. $30,000
    c. $50,000
    d. $70,000

44. On January 2, 1999, Morey Corp. granted Dean, its president, 20,000 stock appreciation rights for past services. Those rights are exercisable immediately and expire on January 1, 2002. On exercise, Dean is entitled to receive cash for the excess of the stock's market price on the exercise date over the market price on the grant date. Dean did not exercise any of the rights during 1999. The market price of Morey's stock was $30 on January 2, 1999 and $45 on December 31, 1999. As a result of the stock appreciation rights, Morey should recognize compensation expense for 1999 of

    a. $0
    b. $100,000
    c. $300,000
    d. $600,000

45. Wall Corp.'s employee stock purchase plan specifies the following:

• For every $1 withheld from employees' wages for the purchase of Wall's common stock, Wall contributes $2.

• The stock is purchased from Wall's treasury stock at market price on the date of purchase.

The following information pertains to the plan's 1999 transactions:

• Employee withholdings for the year	$ 350,000
• Market value of 150,000 shares issued	1,050,000
• Carrying amount of treasury stock issued (cost)	900,000

Before payroll taxes, what amount should Wall recognize as expense in 1999 under either APB 25 or SFAS 123 for the stock purchase plan?

    a. $1,050,000
    b. $ 900,000
    c. $ 700,000
    d. $ 550,000

46. In accounting for stock based compensation under SFAS 123, what interest rate is used to discount both the exercise price of the option and the future dividend stream?

    a. The firm's known incremental borrowing rate.
    b. The current market rate that firms in that particular industry use to discount cash flows.
    c. The risk-free interest rate.
    d. Any rate that firms can justify as being reasonable.

47. In accounting for employee stock-based compensation, if the market price is equal to the option price at the date of grant, would any deferred stock compensation expense be measured?

	Under APB 25	*Under SFAS 123*
a.	Yes	No
b.	No	No
c.	No	Yes
d.	Yes	Yes

48. In what circumstances is compensation expense immediately recognized, under SFAS 123?

    a. In all circumstances.
    b. In circumstances when the options are exercisable within 2 years for services rendered over the next 2 years.
    c. In circumstances when options are granted for prior service, and the options are immediately exercisable.
    d. In no circumstances is compensation expense immediately recognized.

49. What is required of companies that continue to use APB 25 for Accounting for stock-based compensation rather than adopting SFAS 123?

    a. Letters of explanation to shareholders.
    b. Footnote disclosures of the effects of adoption.
    c. Approval of stock-compensated employees.
    d. A hearing before the FASB.

50. Which of the following disclosures required by SFAS 123 must be made by companies that continue to employ APB 25?

   I. The weighted-average grant date fair value of options granted during the year.
  II. A description of the method and significant assumptions used to estimate fair values.
 III. The vesting requirements of the plan.

    a. III only.
    b. I and III only.
    c. I, II, and III.
    d. None of these.

51. Shafer Corporation (a nonpublic company) establishes an employee stock option plan on January 1, 1999. The plan allows its employees to acquire $20,000 of its $5 par value common stock at $75 per share, when the market price is also $75. The options may not be exercised until 5 years from the grant date. The risk-free interest rate is 6%, and the stock is expected to pay dividends of $3 annually. What is the amount of deferred compensation expense that should be recorded in year 1 under SFAS 123?

Present value of 1 at 6% for 5 years:	.747
Future vale of 1 at 6% for 5 years:	1.338
Present value of annuity at 6% for 5 years:	4.212
Future value of annuity at 6% for 5 years:	5.637

   a. $ 52,080
   b. $126,780
   c. $379,500
   d. $633,780

52. Normally, dividends are not paid on shares which have not been issued. However, an entity can choose to pay dividend equivalents on options. Under the provisions of SFAS 123, how are these dividend equivalents accounted for on options which vest, and how are they accounted for on options which do not vest?

	Vest	*Not Vest*
a.	Compensation expense	Compensation expense
b.	Compensation expense	Charge against retained earnings
c.	Charge against retained earnings	Compensation expense
d.	Charge against retained earnings	Charge against retained earnings

53. At December 31, 1999 and 1998, Gow Corp. had 100,000 shares of common stock and 10,000 shares of 5%, $100 par value cumulative preferred stock outstanding. No dividends were declared on either the preferred or common stock in 1999 or 1998. Net income for 1999 was $1,000,000. For 1999, basic earnings per share amounted to

   a. $10.00
   b. $ 9.50
   c. $ 9.00
   d. $ 5.00

54. Ute Co. had the following capital structure during 1998 and 1999:

Preferred stock, $10 par, 4% cumulative, 25,000 shares issued and outstanding	$ 250,000
Common stock, $5 par, 200,000 shares issued and outstanding	1,000,000

Ute reported net income of $500,000 for the year ended December 31, 1999. Ute paid no preferred dividends during 1998 and paid $16,000 in preferred dividends during 1999. In its December 31, 1999 income statement, what amount should Ute report as basic earnings per share?

   a. $2.42
   b. $2.45
   c. $2.48
   d. $2.50

55. The following information pertains to Jet Corp.'s outstanding stock for 1999:

Common stock, $5 par value

Shares outstanding, 1/1/99	20,000
2-for-1 stock split, 4/1/99	20,000
Shares issued, 7/1/99	10,000

Preferred stock, $10 par value, 5% cumulative

Shares outstanding, 1/1/99	4,000

What are the number of shares Jet should use to calculate 1999 basic earnings per share?

   a. 40,000
   b. 45,000
   c. 50,000
   d. 54,000

56. Timp, Inc. had the following common stock balances and transactions during 1999:

1/1/99	Common stock outstanding	30,000
2/1/99	Issued a 10% common stock dividend	3,000
3/1/99	Issued common stock in a pooling of interests	9,000
7/1/99	Issued common stock for cash	8,000
12/31/99	Common stock outstanding	50,000

What were Timp's 1999 weighted-average shares outstanding?

   a. 40,000
   b. 44,250
   c. 44,500
   d. 46,000

57. Strauch Co. has one class of common stock outstanding and no other securities that are potentially convertible into common stock. During 1998, 100,000 shares of common stock were outstanding. In 1999, two distributions of additional common shares occurred: On April 1, 20,000 shares of treasury stock were sold, and on July 1, a 2-for-1 stock split was issued. Net income was $410,000 in 1999 and $350,000 in 1998. What amounts should Strauch report as basic earnings per share in its 1999 and 1998 comparative income statements?

	1999	*1998*
a.	$1.78	$3.50
b.	$1.78	$1.75
c.	$2.34	$1.75
d.	$2.34	$3.50

58. Earnings per share data must be reported on the income statement for

	Cumulative effect of a change in accounting principle	*Extraordinary items*
a.	Yes	No
b.	No	No
c.	No	Yes
d.	Yes	Yes

59. On January 31, 2000, Pack, Inc. split its common stock 2 for 1, and Young, Inc. issued a 5% stock dividend. Both companies issued their December 31, 1999 financial statements on March 1, 2000. Should Pack's 1999, basic earnings per share (BEPS) take into consideration the stock split, and should Young's 1999 BEPS take into consideration the stock dividend?

	Pack's 1999 BEPS	*Young's 1999 BEPS*
a.	Yes	No
b.	No	No
c.	Yes	Yes
d.	No	Yes

60. Mann, Inc. had 300,000 shares of common stock issued and outstanding at December 31, 1998. On July 1, 1999, an additional 50,000 shares of common stock were issued for cash. Mann also had unexercised stock options to purchase 40,000 shares of common stock at $15 per share outstanding at the beginning and end of 1999. The average market price of Mann's common stock was $20 during 1999. What is the number of shares that should be used in computing diluted earnings per share for the year ended December 31, 1999?

- a.   325,000
- b.   335,000
- c.   360,000
- d.   365,000

61. Peters Corp.'s capital structure was as follows:

| | December 31 | |
	1998	1999
Outstanding shares of stock:		
Common	110,000	110,000
Convertible preferred	10,000	10,000

During 1999, Peters paid dividends of $3.00 per share on its preferred stock. The preferred shares are convertible into 20,000 shares of common stock and are considered common stock equivalents. Net income for 1999 was $850,000. Assume that the income tax rate is 30%. The diluted earnings per share for 1999 is

- a. $6.31
- b. $6.54
- c. $7.08
- d. $7.45

62. Cox Corporation had 1,200,000 shares of common stock outstanding on January 1 and December 31, 1999. In connection with the acquisition of a subsidiary company in June 1998, Cox is required to issue 50,000 additional shares of its common stock on July 1, 2000, to the former owners of the subsidiary. Cox paid $200,000 in preferred stock dividends in 1999, and reported net income of $3,400,000 for the year. Cox's diluted earnings per share for 1999 should be

- a. $2.83
- b. $2.72
- c. $2.67
- d. $2.56

63. On June 30, 1998, Lomond, Inc. issued twenty, $10,000, 7% bonds at par. Each bond was convertible into 200 shares of common stock. On January 1, 1999, 10,000 shares of common stock were outstanding. The bondholders converted all the bonds on July 1, 1999. On the bonds' issuance date, the average Aa corporate bond yield was 12%. During 1999, the average Aa corporate bond yield was 9%. The following amounts were reported in Lomond's income statement for the year ended December 31, 1999:

Revenues	$977,000
Operating expenses	920,000
Interest on bonds	7,000
Income before income tax	50,000
Income tax at 30%	15,000
Net income	$ 35,000

What is Lomond's 1999 diluted earnings per share?

- a. $2.50
- b. $2.85
- c. $2.92
- d. $3.50

64. West Co. had earnings per share of $15.00 for 1999 before considering the effects of any convertible securities. No conversion or exercise of convertible securities occurred during 1999. However, possible conversion of convertible bonds, not considered common stock equivalents, would have reduced earnings per share by $0.75. The effect of possible exercise of common stock options would have increased earnings per share by $0.10. What amount should West report as diluted earnings per share for 1999?

- a. $14.25
- b. $14.35
- c. $15.00
- d. $15.10

65. In determining diluted earnings per share, dividends on nonconvertible cumulative preferred stock should be

- a.   Disregarded.
- b.   Added back to net income whether declared or not.
- c.   Deducted from net income only if declared.
- d.   Deducted from net income whether declared or not.

66. The if-converted method of computing earnings per share data assumes conversion of convertible securities as of the

- a.   Beginning of the earliest period reported (or at time of issuance, if later).
- b.   Beginning of the earliest period reported (regardless of time of issuance).
- c.   Middle of the earliest period reported (regardless of time of issuance).
- d.   Ending of the earliest period reported (regardless of time of issuance).

67. In determining earnings per share, interest expense, net of applicable income taxes, on convertible debt that is dilutive should be

- a.   Added back to weighted-average common shares outstanding for diluted earnings per share.
- b.   Added back to net income for diluted earnings per share.
- c.   Deducted from net income for diluted earnings per share.
- d.   Deducted from weighted-average common shares outstanding for diluted earnings per share.

68. For contingent issue agreements requiring passage of time or earnings threshold that is met, before issuing stock, these should be

	Included in basic earnings per share	Included in computing diluted earnings per share
a.	No	No
b.	No	Yes
c.	Yes	No
d.	Yes	Yes

69. Kent, Co. filed a voluntary bankruptcy petition on August 15, 1999, and the statement of affairs reflects the following amounts:

	Book value	Estimated current value
Assets		
Assets pledged with fully secured creditors	$ 300,000	$370,000
Assets pledged with partially secured creditors	180,000	120,000
Free assets	420,000	320,000
	$ 900,000	$810,000
Liabilities		
Liabilities with priority	$ 70,000	
Fully secured creditors	260,000	
Partially secured creditors	200,000	
Unsecured creditors	540,000	
	$1,070,000	

Assume that the assets are converted to cash at the estimated current values and the business is liquidated. What amount of cash will be available to pay unsecured nonpriority claims?

- a. $240,000
- b. $280,000
- c. $320,000
- d. $360,000

70. Seco Corp. was forced into bankruptcy and is in the process of liquidating assets and paying claims. Unsecured claims will be paid at the rate of 40 cents on the dollar. Hale holds a $30,000 noninterest-bearing note receivable from Seco collateralized by an asset with a book value of $35,000 and a liquidation value of $5,000. The amount to be realized by Hale on this note is

- a. $ 5,000
- b. $12,000
- c. $15,000
- d. $17,000

71. Kamy Corp. is in liquidation under Chapter 7 of the Federal Bankruptcy Code. The bankruptcy trustee has established a new set of books for the bankruptcy estate. After assuming custody of the estate, the trustee discovered an unrecorded invoice of $1,000 for machinery repairs performed before the bankruptcy filing. In addition, a truck with a carrying amount of $20,000 was sold for $12,000 cash. This truck was bought and paid for in the year before the bankruptcy. What amount should be debited to estate equity as a result of these transactions?

- a. $0
- b. $1,000
- c. $8,000
- d. $9,000

72. On December 30, 1999, Hale Corp. paid $400,000 cash and issued 80,000 shares of its $1 par value common stock to its unsecured creditors on a pro rata basis pursuant to a reorganization plan under Chapter 11 of the bankruptcy statutes. Hale owed these unsecured creditors a total of $1,200,000. Hale's common stock was trading at $1.25 per share on December 30, 1999. As a result of this transaction, Hale's total stockholders' equity had a net increase of

- a. $1,200,000
- b. $ 800,000
- c. $ 100,000
- d. $ 80,000

73. The primary purpose of a quasi reorganization is to give a corporation the opportunity to

- a. Obtain relief from its creditors.
- b. Revalue understated assets to their fair values.
- c. Eliminate a deficit in retained earnings.
- d. Distribute the stock of a newly-created subsidiary to its stockholders in exchange for part of their stock in the corporation.

74. When a company goes through a quasi reorganization, its balance sheet carrying amounts are stated at

- a. Original cost.
- b. Original book value.
- c. Replacement value.
- d. Fair value.

75. The stockholders' equity section of Brown Co.'s December 31, 1999, balance sheet consisted of the following:

Common stock, $30 par, 10,000 shares authorized and outstanding	$300,000
Additional paid-in capital	150,000
Retained earnings (deficit)	(210,000)

On January 2, 2000, Brown put into effect a stockholder-approved quasi reorganization by reducing the par value of the stock to $5 and eliminating the deficit against additional paid-in capital. Immediately after the quasi reorganization, what amount should Brown report as additional paid-in capital?

- a. $ (60,000)
- b. $150,000
- c. $190,000
- d. $400,000

76. On July 1, 1999, Vail Corp. issued rights to stockholders to subscribe to additional shares of its common stock. One right was issued for each share owned. A stockholder could purchase one additional share for 10 rights plus $15 cash. The rights expired on September 30, 1999. On July 1, 1999, the market price of a share with the right attached was $40, while the market price of one right alone was $2. Vail's stockholders' equity on June 30, 1999, comprised the following:

Common stock, $25 par value, 4,000 shares issued and outstanding	$100,000
Additional paid-in capital	60,000
Retained earnings	80,000

By what amount should Vail's retained earnings decrease as a result of issuance of the stock rights on July 1, 1999?

a. $0
b. $ 5,000
c. $ 8,000
d. $10,000

77. In September 1996, West Corp. made a dividend distribution of one right for each of its 120,000 shares of outstanding common stock. Each right was exercisable for the purchase of 1/100 of a share of West's $50 variable rate preferred stock at an exercise price of $80 per share. On March 20, 1999, none of the rights had been exercised, and West redeemed them by paying each stockholder $0.10 per right. As a result of this redemption, West's stockholders' equity was reduced by

a. $ 120
b. $ 2,400
c. $12,000
d. $36,000

78. On November 2, 1998, Finsbury, Inc. issued warrants to its stockholders giving them the right to purchase additional $20 par value common shares at a price of $30. The stockholders exercised all warrants on March 1, 1999. The shares had market prices of $33, $35, and $40 on November 2, 1998; December 31, 1998; and March 1, 1999, respectively. What were the effects of the warrants on Finsbury's additional paid-in capital and net income?

	Additional paid-in capital	*Net income*
a.	Increased in 1999	No effect
b.	Increased in 1998	No effect
c.	Increased in 1999	Decreased in 1998 and 1999
d.	Increased in 1998	Decreased in 1998 and 1999

79. A company issued rights to its existing shareholders to purchase, for $30 per share, unissued shares of $15 par value common stock. Additional paid-in capital will be credited when the

	Rights are issued	*Rights lapse*
a.	Yes	No
b.	No	No
c.	No	Yes
d.	Yes	Yes

Items 80 and 81 are based on the following:

On January 1, 1999, Fay Corporation established an employee stock ownership plan (ESOP). Selected transactions relating to the ESOP during 1999 were as follows:

• On April 1, 1999, Fay contributed $30,000 cash and 3,000 shares of its $10 par common stock to the ESOP. On this date the market price of the stock was $18 a share.

• On October 1, 1999, the ESOP borrowed $100,000 from Union National Bank and acquired 5,000 shares of Fay's common stock in the open market at $17 a share. The note is for 1 year, bears interest at 10%, and is guaranteed by Fay.

• On December 15, 1999, the ESOP distributed 6,000 shares of Fay common stock to employees of Fay in accordance with the plan formula.

80. In its 1999 income statement, how much should Fay report as compensation expense relating to the ESOP?

a. $184,000
b. $120,000
c. $ 84,000
d. $ 60,000

81. In Fay's December 31, 1999 balance sheet, how much should be reported as a reduction of shareholders' equity and as an endorsed note payable in respect of the ESOP?

	Reduction of shareholders' equity	*Endorsed note payable*
a.	$0	$0
b.	$0	$100,000
c.	$100,000	$0
d.	$100,000	$100,000

82. Zinc Co.'s adjusted trial balance at December 31, 1999, includes the following account balances:

Common stock, $3 par	$600,000
Additional paid-in capital	800,000
Treasury stock, at cost	50,000
Net unrealized loss on available-for-sale MES	20,000
Retained earnings: appropriated for uninsured earthquake losses	150,000
Retained earnings: unappropriated	200,000

What amount should Zinc report as total stockholders' equity in its December 31, 1999 balance sheet?

a. $1,680,000
b. $1,720,000
c. $1,780,000
d. $1,820,000

83. Rudd Corp. had 700,000 shares of common stock authorized and 300,000 shares outstanding at December 31, 1998. The following events occurred during 1999:

January 31	Declared 10% stock dividend
June 30	Purchased 100,000 shares
August 1	Reissued 50,000 shares
November 30	Declared 2-for-1 stock split

At December 31, 1999, how many shares of common stock did Rudd have outstanding?

a. 560,000
b. 600,000
c. 630,000
d. 660,000

84. Nest Co. issued 100,000 shares of common stock. Of these, 5,000 were held as treasury stock at December 31, 1998. During 1999, transactions involving Nest's common stock were as follows:

May 3   --1,000 shares of treasury stock were sold.

August 6   --10,000 shares of previously unissued
           stock were sold.

November 18   --A 2-for-1 stock split took effect.

Laws in Nest's state of incorporation protect treasury stock from dilution. At December 31, 1999, how many shares of Nest's common stock were issued and outstanding?

	Shares	
	Issued	*Outstanding*
a.	220,000	212,000
b.	220,000	216,000
c.	222,000	214,000
d.	222,000	218,000

85. The following information pertains to Ali Corp. as of and for the year ended December 31, 1999:

Liabilities	$ 60,000
Stockholders' equity	$500,000
Shares of common stock issued and outstanding	10,000
Net income	$ 30,000

During 1999, Ali's officers exercised stock options for 1,000 shares of stock at an option price of $8 per share. What was the effect of exercising the stock options?

a. Debt to equity ratio decreased to 12%.
b. Earnings per share increased by $0.33.
c. Asset turnover increased to 5.4%.
d. No ratios were affected.

86. Selected information for Irvington Company is as follows:

	December 31	
	1998	*1999*
Preferred stock, 8%, par $100, nonconvertible, noncumulative	$125,000	$125,000
Common stock	300,000	400,000
Retained earnings	75,000	185,000
Dividends paid on preferred stock for year ended	10,000	10,000
Net income for year ended	60,000	120,000

Irvington's return on common stockholders' equity, rounded to the nearest percentage point, for 1999 is

a. 17%
b. 19%
c. 23%
d. 25%

87. Hoyt Corp.'s current balance sheet reports the following stockholders' equity:

5% cumulative preferred stock, par value $100 per share; 2,500 shares issued and outstanding	$250,000
Common stock, par value $3.50 per share; 100,000 shares issued and outstanding	350,000
Additional paid-in capital in excess of par value of common stock	125,000
Retained earnings	300,000

Dividends in arrears on the preferred stock amount to $25,000. If Hoyt were to be liquidated, the preferred stockholders would receive par value plus a premium of $50,000. The book value per share of common stock is

a. $7.75
b. $7.50
c. $7.25
d. $7.00

88. Grid Corp. acquired some of its own common shares at a price greater than both their par value and original issue price but less than their book value. Grid uses the cost method of accounting for treasury stock. What is the impact of this acquisition on total stockholders' equity and the book value per common share?

	Total stockholders' equity	Book value per share
a.	Increase	Increase
b.	Increase	Decrease
c.	Decrease	Increase
d.	Decrease	Decrease

89. How are dividends per share for common stock used in the calculation of the following?

	Dividend per share payout ratio	Earnings per share
a.	Numerator	Numerator
b.	Numerator	Not used
c.	Denominator	Not used
d.	Denominator	Denominator

OTHER OBJECTIVE QUESTIONS

Problem 1   (10 to 15 minutes)

Required:

Items 1 through 10 require the candidate to select the best response from the responses to be selected. On the CPA Exam candidates would be required to blacken the corresponding oval on the objective answer sheet. These items cannot be graded if you fail to blacken the ovals.

Items to be answered	*Responses to be selected*
1. Par value method	A. Contains no potentially dilutive securities
2. Appropriations of retained earnings	B. A form of compensation which allows employees to receive stock or cash for the difference between the stated value and the market value
3. Stock split	C. Legal or contractual restrictions on the number of shares an employee may own
4. Simple capital structure	
5. If converted method	D. Issuance of additional shares in order to reduce the market value
6. Scrip dividend	E. Purchase by the corporation of its own stock
7. Stock appreciation rights	F. The value of treasury shares are recorded at cost of acquisition
8. Stock option	G. A dividend paid which is considered a return of the shareholders' investment
9. Liquidating dividend	H. Actions by the board of directors to disclose amounts not available for dividends
10. Treasury stock	I. The balance of the treasury stock account reflects the par value
	J. A form of compensation which allows employees to purchase shares at a specified price
	K. A dividend issued in the form of a note payable
	L. A stock transaction resulting in a reduced number of shares outstanding and a higher market value
	M. Assumes convertible securities were converted at the beginning of the period

---

Problem 2   (15 to 25 minutes)

This problem consists of 10 items. Select the **best** answer for each item. Use a No. 2 pencil to blacken the appropriate ovals on the Objective Answer Sheet to indicate your answers. **Answer all items.** Your grade will be based on the total number of correct answers.

Min Co. is a publicly held company whose shares are traded in the over-the-counter market. The stockholders' equity accounts at December 31, 1998, had the following balances:

Preferred stock, $100 par value, 6% cumulative;	
5,000 shares authorized; 2,000 issued and outstanding	$200,000
Common stock, $1 par value, 150,000 shares authorized;	
100,000 issued and outstanding	100,000
Additional paid-in capital	800,000
Retained earnings	1,586,000
Total stockholders' equity	$2,686,000

Transactions during 1999 and other information relating to the stockholders' equity accounts were as follows:

• February 1, 1999--Issued 13,000 shares of common stock to Ram Co. in exchange for land. On the date issued, the stock had a market price of $11 per share. The land had a carrying value on Ram's books of $135,000, and an assessed value for property taxes of $90,000.

• March 1, 1999--Purchased 5,000 shares of its own common stock to be held as treasury stock for $14 per share. Min uses the cost method to account for treasury stock. Transactions in treasury stock are legal in Min's state of incorporation.

• May 10, 1999--Declared a property dividend of marketable securities held by Min to common shareholders. The securities had a carrying value of $600,000; fair value on relevant dates were

Date of declaration (May 10, 1999)	$720,000
Date of record (May 25, 1999)	758,000
Date of distribution (June 1, 1999)	736,000

- October 1, 1999--Reissued 2,000 shares of treasury stock for $16 per share.

- November 4, 1999--Declared a cash dividend of $1.50 per share to all common shareholders of record November 15, 1999. The dividend was paid on November 25, 1999.

- December 20, 1999--Declared the required annual cash dividend on preferred stock for 1999. The dividend was paid on January 5, 2000.

- January 16, 2000--Before closing the accounting records for 1999, Min became aware that no amortization had been recorded for 1998 for a patent purchased on July 1, 1998. The patent was properly capitalized at $320,000 and had an estimated useful life of 8 years when purchased. Min's income tax rate is 30%. The appropriate correcting entry was recorded on the same day.

- Adjusted net income for 1999 was $838,000.

Required:

Items 1 through 8 represent amounts to be reported in Min's financial statements. **Items 9 and 10** represent other financial information. For all items, calculate the amounts requested. To record your answer, blacken the ovals on the Objective Answer Sheet. If zeros precede your numerical answer, blacken the zeros in the ovals preceding your answer. **You cannot receive credit for your answers if you fail to blacken an oval in each column.** You may write the numbers in the boxes provided to facilitate blackening the ovals; however, the numbers written in the boxes will **not** be graded.

Items 1 through 4 represent amounts to be reported on Min's 1999 statement of retained earnings.

1. Prior period adjustment.

2. Preferred dividends.

3. Common dividends--cash.

4. Common dividends--property.

Items 5 through 8 represent amounts to be reported on Min's statement of stockholders' equity at December 31, 1999.

5. Number of common shares issued at December 31, 1999.

6. Amount of common stock issued.

7. Additional paid-in capital, including treasury stock transactions.

8. Treasury stock.

Items 9 and 10 represent other financial information for 1998 and 1999.

9. Book value per share at December 31, 1998, before prior period adjustment.

10. Numerator used in calculation of 1999 earnings per share for the year.

PROBLEMS

Problem 1   (15 to 25 minutes)

On November 5, 1998, Gunpowder Corp.'s board of directors approved a stock option plan for key executives. On January 2, 1999, a specific number of stock options were granted. These options were exercisable between January 2, 2001, and December 31, 2003, at 90% of the quoted market price on January 2, 1999. The service period is for 1999 and 2000. Some options were forfeited when an executive resigned in 2000. All other options were exercised during 2001.

Required:

a. Under the intrinsic method (APB 25), when is Gunpowder's stock option measurement date? Why?

b. Using the intrinsic method how should Gunpowder determine the compensation expense, if any, for the stock option plan in 1999?

c. Assuming Gunpowder used the fair value based method (SFAS 123) what factors would be used in the option-pricing model to arrive at the value of an option on January 2, 1998?

d. If Gunpowder used the intrinsic value based method, what pro forma disclosures would be required in the notes to the company's financial statements for 1998?

Problem 2   (15 to 25 minutes)

Columbine Co.'s 10-year convertible bonds were issued and dated October 1, 1999. Each $1,000 bond is convertible, at the holder's option, into 20 shares of Columbine's common stock. Columbine, a public company, had a net loss for the year. There was no change in the number of shares outstanding during the year.

Required:

a. Describe and distinguish between basic and diluted earnings per share. Include in your discussion the meaning of dilutive securities.

b. Determine whether to include the convertible bonds in computing 1999 diluted earnings per share.

Problem 3   (45 to 55 minutes)

Trask Corp., a public company whose shares are traded in the over-the-counter market, had the following stockholders' equity account balances at December 31, 1998:

Common stock	$ 7,875,000
Additional paid-in capital	15,750,000
Retained earnings	16,445,000
Treasury common stock	750,000

Transactions during 1999, and other information relating to the stockholders' equity accounts, were as follows:

• Trask had 4,000,000 authorized shares of $5 par value common stock; 1,575,000 shares were issued, of which 75,000 were held in treasury.

• On January 21, 1999, Trask issued 50,000 shares of $100 par value, 6% cumulative preferred stock in exchange for all of Rover Co.'s assets and liabilities. On that date, the net carrying amount of Rover's assets and liabilities was $5,000,000. The carrying amounts of Rover's assets and liabilities equaled their fair values. On January 22, 1999, Rover distributed the Trask shares to its stockholders in complete liquidation and dissolution of Rover. Trask had 150,000 authorized shares of preferred stock.

• On February 17, 1999, Trask formally retired 25,000 of its 75,000 treasury common stock shares. The shares were originally issued at $15 per share and had been acquired on September 25, 1996, for $10 per share. Trask uses the cost method to account for treasury stock.

• Trask owned 15,000 shares of Harbor, Inc. common stock purchased in 1994 for $600,000. The Harbor stock was included in Trask's short-term marketable securities portfolio. On March 5, 1999, Trask declared a property dividend of one share of Harbor common stock for every 100 shares of Trask common stock held by a stockholder of record on April 16, 1999. The market price of Harbor stock on March 5, 1999, was $60 per share. The property dividend was distributed on April 29, 1999.

• On October 27, 1999, Trask declared a 2-for-1 stock split on its common stock and reduced the per share par value accordingly. Trask stockholders of record on August 2, 1999, received one additional share of Trask common stock for each share of Trask common stock held. The laws in Trask's state of incorporation protect treasury stock from dilution.

• On December 12, 1999, Trask declared the yearly cash dividend on preferred stock, payable on January 11, 2000, to stockholders of record on December 31, 1999.

• On January 16, 2000, before the accounting records were closed for 1999, Trask became aware that depreciation expense was understated by $350,000 for the year ended December 31, 1998. The after-tax effect on 1998 net income was $245,000. The appropriate correcting entry was recorded on the same day.

• Net income for 1999 was $2,400,000.

Required:

a. Prepare Trask's statement of retained earnings for the year ended December 31, 1999. Assume that Trask prepares only single-period financial statements for 1999.

b. Prepare the stockholders' equity section of Trask's balance sheet at December 31, 1999.

c. Compute the book value per share of common stock at December 31, 1999.

Show all supporting calculations in good form.

1. a __ __	20. a __ __	39. a __ __	58. b __ __	76. a __ __
2. b __ __	21. c __ __	40. d __ __	59. c __ __	77. c __ __
3. d __ __	22. c __ __	41. c __ __	60. b __ __	78. a __ __
4. d __ __	23. c __ __	42. c __ __	61. b __ __	79. b __ __
5. a __ __	24. d __ __	43. a __ __	62. d __ __	80. c __ __
6. c __ __	25. d __ __	44. c __ __	63. b __ __	81. d __ __
7. a __ __	26. b __ __	45. c __ __	64. a __ __	82. a __ __
8. d __ __	27. c __ __	46. c __ __	65. d __ __	83. a __ __
9. a __ __	28. c __ __	47. c __ __	66. a __ __	84. a __ __
10. b __ __	29. b __ __	48. c __ __	67. b __ __	85. a __ __
11. d __ __	30. b __ __	49. b __ __	68. b __ __	86. c __ __
12. c __ __	31. d __ __	50. c __ __	69. d __ __	87. d __ __
13. c __ __	32. d __ __	51. b __ __	70. c __ __	88. c __ __
14. d __ __	33. b __ __	52. c __ __	71. d __ __	89. b __ __
15. a __ __	34. a __ __	53. b __ __	72. b __ __	
16. c __ __	35. d __ __	54. b __ __	73. c __ __	
17. b __ __	36. b __ __	55. b __ __	74. d __ __	
18. c __ __	37. b __ __	56. d __ __	75. c __ __	1st: __/89 = __%
19. c __ __	38. a __ __	57. b __ __		2nd: __/89 = __%

MULTIPLE-CHOICE ANSWER EXPLANATIONS

A. Common Stock

1. (a) When stock is issued for services, the transaction should be recorded at either the FMV of the stock issued or the FMV of the services received, whichever is more clearly determinable. The FMV of stock traded on a public exchange is a more objective, reliable measure than a normal billing rate for legal services, which is likely to be negotiable. If the transaction is valued at $140 per share, legal expense would be debited for $140,000 (1,000 x $140), common stock would be credited for the par value of $5,000 (1,000 x $5), and additional paid-in capital would be credited for the difference ($140,000 − $5,000 = $135,000).

2. (b) When stock is issued in combination with other securities (lump sum sales), the proceeds can be allocated by the **proportional method** or by the **incremental method**. If the FMV of each class of securities is determinable, the proceeds should be allocated to each class of securities based on their relative FMV. In the instances where the FMV of all classes of securities is not determinable, the incremental method should be used. The market value of the securities is used as a basis for those classes that are known, and the remainder of the lump sum is allocated to the class for which the market value is not known. In this problem, the FMV of the stock is unknown. As such, the incremental method must be used as follows:

Lump sum receipt	$110,000
FMV of bonds	40,000
Balance allocated to common stock	$ 70,000

As the par value of the common stock is $5,000 (1,000 shares x $5), $65,000 ($70,000 − $5,000) should be reported as additional paid-in capital on the issuance of the stock.

3. (d) The number of common shares outstanding is equal to the issued shares less treasury shares. Beck Corp. had 300,000 shares outstanding at 1/1/97. The purchase of treasury shares in 1999 reduced the number of shares outstanding to 225,000 (300,000 − 75,000). The preferred stock convertible into 100,000 shares of common stock is recorded as preferred stock until it is **converted** by the stockholder.

4. (d) On February 1, 1999, when shares were issued at par for cash, the following journal entry would have been made:

Cash	(cash received)	
Common stock		(par)

On March 1, 1999, however, the issuance of 5,000 shares in settlement for legal services rendered would have been recorded as follows:

Legal fees	60,000	
Common stock ($10 x 5,000 shares)		50,000
Addl. paid-in capital		10,000

Per APB 29, para 18, stock issued for services (i.e., in a nonmonetary transaction) should be recorded at the fair market value of those services (in this case $60,000). Therefore, answer (d) is correct.

B. Preferred Stock

5. (a) When the common stock was issued, it was recorded at stated value with the excess recorded as additional paid-in capital.

Cash	600,000	
Common stock		20,000
Addl. paid-in capital		580,000

The preferred stock was recorded at par value with the excess credited to additional paid-in capital.

Cash	300,000	
Preferred stock		60,000
Addl. paid-in capital		240,000

Therefore, at 4/1/99, the balances are common stock ($20,000), preferred stock ($60,000), and additional paid-in capital ($580,000 + $240,000 = $820,000).

6. (c) In a lump sum issuance of common and preferred stock, the proceeds ($80,000) are generally allocated based on the relative fair market values of the securities issued. The FMV of the convertible preferred stock is $54,000 ($27 x 2,000) and the FMV of the common stock is $36,000 ($36 x 1,000). The proceeds are allocated as follows:

Convertible $\frac{\$54,000}{\$90,000}$ x $80,000 = $48,000
preferred

Common $\frac{\$36,000}{\$90,000}$ x $80,000 = $32,000

7. (a) All 5,000 shares of convertible preferred stock were converted to common stock at a rate of 3 shares of common for every share of preferred. Therefore, 15,000 shares of common stock were issued (5,000 x 3). The common stock account is credited for the par value of these shares (15,000 x $25 = $375,000). APIC – CS ($550,000 – $375,000 = $175,000) is credited for the difference between the carrying amount of the preferred stock (5,000 x $110 = $550,000) and the par value of the common stock. The journal entry is

Preferred stock	500,000	
APIC-PS	50,000	
Common stock		375,000
APIC-CS		175,000

Note that the $40 market value of the common stock is ignored. The book value method must be used for conversion of preferred stock, so no gains or losses can be recognized.

8. (d) Per APB 14, para 15, when an issuance of debt, or in this case preferred stock, contains detachable common stock warrants the total proceeds from the sale should be allocated to both the preferred stock and the detachable stock warrants. This treatment arises due to the separability of the stock and the detachable warrants. The allocation of the proceeds is based on the relative fair values of both the stock and the warrants at the time of the issuance. However, in instances where only one of the fair values is known, the known fair value will be used to allocate proceeds to the security in which the fair value is determinable. The remainder is then allocated to the security for which the fair value is unknown. Therefore, because only the fair value of the warrants is known, answer (d) is correct. Answers (a) and (b) are incorrect because fair market value is used to allocate proceeds to the warrants, not the total proceeds or excess proceeds over par value. Answer (c) is incorrect because proceeds are allocated in proportion to both fair values, if determinable, not the fair market value and par value.

9. (a) When the preferred stock and detachable warrants are issued, the following journal entry is made:

Cash	(cash received)
Preferred stock	(par value)
APIC--preferred stock	(FMV of preferred stock – par value)
APIC--stock warrants	(plug)

When the stock warrants are exercised, the following journal entry is made:

Cash	(cash received)
APIC--stock warrants	(original amount credited)
Common stock	(par value)
APIC--common stock	(plug)

Therefore, stockholders' equity is increased by the cash received upon the exercise of the common stock warrants. The carrying amount of the warrants increased total stockholders' equity when the preferred stock was issued, not when the warrants were issued.

C. Stock Subscriptions

10. (b) When no par common stock is sold on a subscription basis at a price above the stock's stated value, the stock is not issued until the full subscription price is received. The journal entry on the subscription contract date would be

Cash	(amount received--if any)
Subscription receivable	(balance due)
Common stock subscribed	(stated value)
Additional paid-in capital	(plug)

Therefore answer (b) is correct and answer (a) is incorrect. The journal entry on the date the balance of the subscription is collected and the common stock issued would be

Cash	(balance due)
Common stock subscribed	(stated value)
Common stock	(stated value)
Subscription receivable	(balance due)

Since additional paid-in capital increases on the date that the stock is subscribed, not paid for or issued, answers (c) and (d) are incorrect.

11. (d) When stock is sold on a subscription basis, the full price of the stock is not received initially, and the stock is not issued until the full subscription price is received. On the subscription contract date of December 1, 1999, the journal entry would be

Cash	(amount received)
Subscriptions receivable	(balance due)
Common stock subscribed	(par)
Additional paid-in capital	(plug)

Thus, answer (d) is correct, and answers (a), (b), and (c) are incorrect.

D. Treasury Stock Transactions

12. (c) Under the cost method, the treasury stock account is debited for the cost of the shares acquired. If the treasury shares are reissued at a price in excess of the acquisition cost, the excess is credited to an account titled Paid-in Capital from Treasury Stock. This question refers to it as Additional Paid-in Capital because typically companies do not segregate the two accounts on the balance sheet for reporting purposes. If the treasury shares are reissued at less than the acquisition cost, the deficiency is treated first as a reduction to any paid-in capital related to previous reissuances or retirements of treasury stock of the same class. If the balance in Paid-in Capital from Treasury Stock is not sufficient to absorb the deficiency, the remainder is recorded as a reduction of retained earnings. As the shares in this question were reissued at a price in excess of the acquisition price, the following journal entry would be made at the time of reissue:

Cash (3,000 x $50)	150,000	
Treasury Stock (3,000 x $36)		108,000
Additional Paid-in Capital ($150,000 – $108,000)		42,000

Thus, the correct answer is (c).

13. (c) The entry that Rama made on acquisition of treasury stock was as follows using the **cost method**:

Treasury stock (20,000 x $12)	240,000	
Cash		240,000

When some of the shares are later reissued, the entry is

Cash (15,000 x $10)	150,000	
Retained earnings	30,000	
Treasury stock (15,000 x $12)		180,000

It is assumed there was no balance in APIC--Treasury stock prior to this entry. If the problem had stated there was a credit balance, APIC--Treasury stock would be debited before retained earnings to the extent a credit balance existed in APIC--Treasury stock. SFAS 5 requires disclosure when retained earnings are legally restricted. In this case, the net treasury stock account balance is $60,000 ($240,000 – $180,000), and this is the amount of retained earnings that must be disclosed as legally restricted.

14. (d) The unadjusted stockholders' equity section shows a total of $2,000,000. However, analysis of the current asset section reveals that United has incorrectly classified $300,000 of treasury stock as a current asset. Although this account has a debit balance, it is **not an asset**. Treasury stock should be reported as a reduction of stockholders' equity. Therefore, total equity at 12/31/99 should be $1,700,000 ($2,000,000 – $300,000).

15. (a) Under the cost method, when treasury stock is acquired, **treasury stock** is debited and **cash** is credited for the cost.

Treasury stock	100,000	
Cash		100,000

When the treasury stock is resold at an amount above cost, **cash** is debited for the proceeds, **treasury stock** is credited at cost, and the difference is credited to **additional paid-in capital--treasury stock**.

Cash	25,000	
Treasury stock		20,000
APIC-TS		5,000

Neither of these two transactions affect **retained earnings**. Therefore, 12/31/99 retained earnings consists of the 12/31/98 balance ($300,000) plus 1999 net income ($60,000), or $360,000.

16. (c) The requirement is to determine the balance in the paid-in capital from treasury stock account at 12/31/99. Using the par value method, treasury stock is debited for par value (5,000 x $10, or $50,000) when purchased. Any excess over par from the original issuance (5,000 x $4, or $20,000) is removed from the appropriate paid-in capital account. In effect, the total original issuance price (5,000 x $14, or $70,000) is charged to the two accounts. Any difference between the original issue price ($70,000) and the cost of the treasury stock (5,000 x $11, or $55,000) is credited to paid-in capital from treasury stock, as illustrated below.

Treasury stock	50,000	(5,000 x $10)
APIC	20,000	(5,000 x $ 4)
Cash	55,000	(5,000 x $11)
PIC-Treasury stock	15,000	($70,000 – $55,000)

17. (b) When Dee Inc. issued common stock at a price in excess of its par value, the following journal entry was made:

Cash	(Cash received)
Common stock	(Par)
Additional paid-in capital	(Excess of cash received over par)

When Dee Inc. acquires treasury stock using the par method for an amount exceeding the issue price the following journal entry is made:

Treasury stock	(Par)
Additional paid-in capital	(Excess of original issue price over par)
Retained earnings	(Excess of acquisition price over issue price)
Cash	(Cash paid)

Net common stock decreases by the par value of treasury stock acquired. Therefore, answers (a) and (d) are incorrect. Additional paid-in capital decreases by the excess of the original issue price over the par value. Therefore, answer (c) is incorrect. Retained earnings decreases by the excess of the acquisition price over the original issue price. Therefore, answer (b) is correct.

18. (c) Answer (c) is correct because, in this case, the par value method does not report a greater amount for additional paid-in capital or retained earnings than the cost method. The entries for an acquisition of treasury shares at greater than par but less than the original issue price are as follows:

Cost method		_Par value method_	
Treasury stock	xxx	Treasury stock	xxx
Cash	xxx	Pd.-in Cap. in	
		excess of par	xxx
		Cash	xxx
		Pd.-in cap.	
		from trea-	
		sury stock	xxx

Since under the par value method the original paid-in capital in excess of par must be removed from the accounts upon reacquisition, the par value method actually reports a decrease in additional paid-in capital. On the other hand, under the cost method no change in additional paid-in capital is recorded. There is no change in retained earnings under either method.

E. Retirement of Stock

19. (c)   When accounting for the retirement of stock, common stock and additional paid-in-capital are removed from the books based on the original issuance of the stock. Cash is credited for the cost of the shares. Any difference is debited to **retained earnings** or credited to **paid-in capital from retirement**. The entry in this case is

Common stock	20,000 (2,000 x $10)
APIC	180,000 (2,000 x $90)
Retained earnings	100,000 (2,000 x $50)
Cash	300,000

Therefore, APIC should be debited for $180,000 and retained earnings should be debited for $100,000.

20. (a)   In this problem, Luna Corp. is exchanging its marketable equity securities (MES) for its preferred stock (i.e., they are retiring some of their preferred stock by exchanging MES). Upon disposition of the MES, a gain of $70,000, which is the difference between the carrying amount ($80,000) and the FMV ($150,000), must be recognized. Upon retirement of the stock, the preferred stock is debited for the $100,000 par amount (5,000 shares x $20 par). The additional paid-in capital (APIC) is debited for $7,500, which is 1/4 of the original APIC (i.e., 5,000 of the 20,000 shares were retired). The remainder of the FMV of the preferred stock ($42,500 = $150,000 − $100,000 − $7,500) is debited to retained earnings.

21. (c)   When accounting for the retirement of treasury stock that was initially recorded using the cost method, common stock and additional paid-in capital are removed from the books based on the original issuance of the stock. Treasury stock is credited for the cost of the shares acquired. Any difference is debited to retained earnings or credited to paid-in capital from retirement. In this problem, common stock should be debited for $125,000 (50,000 shares x $2.50), and the common stock outstanding at December 31, 1998, is $415,000 ($540,000 − $125,000).

22. (c)   The requirement is to determine which of the statements correctly identifies an effect of the acquisition and retirement of common stock. The entry to record the retirement of common stock appears as follows:

Common stock (par)	xxx	
Additional paid-in capital	xxx	
Retained earnings	xxx	
Cash		xxx

Additional paid-in capital is debited to the extent it exists. In this case, based on the original issuance, the additional paid-in capital (APIC) balance was $15 per share on the shares retired. When stock is repurchased, if the APIC balance is depleted to zero, retained earnings must also be debited. In this case, retained earnings would not be needed, however. Common stock would be debited for $10 per share and additional paid-in capital would be debited for $10 a share. Excess APIC remains, so retained earnings are not needed to retire the stock. Therefore, answer (c) is correct because when common stock is repurchased and retired, additional paid-in capital decreases. Answers (a) and (b) are incorrect because when common stock is retired, net income is never affected, only stockholders' equity balances are affected. Answer (d) is incorrect because if retained earnings are needed to retire stock, the account decreases, not increases.

F. Dividends

23. (c)   When preferred stock is participating, there may be different agreements as to how the participation feature is to be executed. However, in the absence of any specific agreement, the following procedure should be used:

After the preferred stock is allocated its current year dividend, the common stock will receive a "like" percentage of par value outstanding. If there are remaining declared dividends, this amount should be shared by both the preferred and common stock in proportion to the par value dollars outstanding of each stock as follows:

Current year's dividend:

Preferred, 5% of $300,000		
(30,000 shares x $10 Par)	$15,000	
Common, 5% of $200,000		
(200,000 shares x $1 Par)	10,000	$25,000

Amount available for participation ($100,000 − $25,000)	$ 75,000
Par value of stock that is to participate ($300,000 + $200,000)	$500,000

Proportional share of participating dividend:

Preferred	$\dfrac{300,000}{500,000}$	x	75,000	=	$ 45,000
Common	$\dfrac{200,000}{500,000}$	x	75,000	=	$ 30,000

Thus, the dividends payable to common shareholders is $40,000 ($10,000 + $30,000).

24. (d)   For **cumulative** preferred stock, dividends not paid in **any** year will accumulate and must be paid in a later year before any dividends can be paid to common stockholders. The unpaid prior year dividends are called "dividends in arrears." The balance of dividends in arrears should be disclosed in the financial statements rather than accrued, as they are not considered a liability until they are declared. Dividends in arrears at 12/31/99 total $20,000, as computed below.

1998	$300,000 x 5%	=	$15,000
1999	($300,000 x 5%)	=	15,000
Total cumulative preferred dividends			$30,000
Less 1999 dividend payment			(10,000)
Balance of dividends in arrears			$20,000

Answer (c) is incorrect because dividends in arrears are not considered to be a liability until they are declared. They should be disclosed parenthetically or in the notes to the financial statements. Answer (b) is incorrect because the total dividends amount needs to reflect both the 1998 and 1999 unpaid dividends since it is cumulative preferred stock. Answer (a) is incorrect because the dividends in arrears would not be considered a liability until they are declared and the $15,000 amount is the incorrect balance as discussed above.

25. (d) The interest is not an expense or liability until incurred, thus, none of it is recorded on April 1. The April 1 entry would be

Retained earnings	100,000	
Scrip dividends payable		100,000

By December 31 (the year end for this calendar-year company), 9 months' interest had been incurred, which would not be paid until the maturity date of 3/31/00. The $7,500 of interest expense ($100,000 x 10% x 9/12) must be accrued at 12/31/99 with the following entry:

Interest expense	7,500	
Interest payable		7,500

Thus, answer (d) is the correct response as retained earnings is debited for $100,000 on April 1, 1999, and interest expense is debited for $7,500 on December 31, 1999. Answers (a) and (b) are incorrect because the interest expense should not be recorded as a debit to retained earnings; in addition the dates of recording the journal entries are incorrect. Answer (c) is incorrect because interest expense needs to be accrued at December 31, 1999.

26. (b) Dividends that are based on funds other than retained earnings are considered to be liquidating dividends. The cash dividend declared of $400,000 is first assumed to be a return **on** capital for the distribution of the retained earnings balance of $300,000. The excess $400,000 dividend – $300,000 RE = $100,000 is considered to be a return **of** capital or a liquidating dividend rather than a return **on** capital. Note that the amount of liquidating dividend also equals the balance in accumulated depletion. Companies in the extractive industries may pay dividends equal to the accumulated income **and** depletion.

27. (c) Per APB 29, a transfer of a nonmonetary asset to a stockholder or to another entity in a nonreciprocal transfer should be recorded at the fair value of the asset transferred, and a gain or loss should be recognized on the disposition of the asset. The fair value of the nonmonetary asset distributed is measured by the amount that would be realized in an outright sale at or near the time of distribution. In this case, a gain should be recognized for the difference between the fair value of $2.50 per share and the carrying amount of $2 per share, or a total gain of $50,000 [100,000 x ($2.50 – $2.00)].

28. (c) Per APB 29, para 18, a transfer of a nonmonetary asset to a stockholder or to another entity in a nonreciprocal transfer should be recorded at the fair market value of the asset transferred, and a gain or loss should be recognized on the disposition of the asset. At the date of declaration, Nilo records

Marketable securities	18,000	
Gain on disposition of securities		18,000
Retained earnings (dividends)	78,000	
Property dividends payable		78,000

At the date of distribution, Nilo records

Property dividends payable	78,000	
Marketable securities		78,000

After all nominal accounts are closed, the effect on retained earnings from the above entries would be $60,000 ($78,000 debit to retained earnings less $18,000 credit to retained earnings when the "gain on disposition" account is closed out). Therefore, answer (c) is correct.

29. (b) A stock split is **not** a dividend. Stock splits change the number of shares outstanding and the par value per share. Par value per share is reduced in proportion to the increase in the number of shares. Therefore, the total par value outstanding does not change, and no journal entry is required. The only dividend to be reported in Long's 1999 statement of stockholders' equity is the 12/15 cash dividend. The stock split increased the number of shares outstanding to 200,000 (100,000 x 2), so the amount of the cash dividend is $100,000 (200,000 x $.50).

30. (b) The requirement is to determine the effect of a cash dividend on stockholders' equity at the three dates listed. On the date of declaration, December 15, 1999, the following entry should be made:

Retained earnings	xxx	
Dividends payable		xxx

Thus, at December 15, 1999, stockholders' equity is reduced due to the debit to retained earnings, and consequently answers (c) and (d) are incorrect. On December 31, 1999, there is no effect on stockholders' equity because an entry would not be recorded. On January 12, 2000, the following entry would be made:

Dividends payable	xxx	
Cash		xxx

The net effect of this entry is to decrease assets and liabilities by an equal amount. Thus, stockholders' equity (or net assets) would be unaffected. Therefore, answer (b) is correct and answer (a) is incorrect.

31. (d) Any dividend not based on earnings must be a reduction of corporate paid-in capital and, to that extent, it is a liquidating dividend. The following journal entries would be made for this situation:

At date of declaration:

| Additional paid-in capital | 100,000 | |
| Dividends payable | | 100,000 |

At date of payment:

| Dividends payable | 100,000 | |
| Cash | | 100,000 |

Thus, a liquidating dividend would decrease Ole's paid-in capital, not its retained earnings.

32. (d) A property dividend is a nonreciprocal transfer of nonmonetary assets between an enterprise and its owners. APB 29 requires that "nonreciprocal transfers of nonmonetary assets to a stockholder or another entity shall be recorded at the fair value of the asset transferred. Additionally, a gain or loss shall be recognized on the disposition of the asset." Accordingly, Evie Corp. should record the following journal entries to reflect the property dividend:

At the date of declaration:

Loss on decline in inventory value		
(carrying amount – market value)	xxx	
Merchandise inventory		xxx
Retained earnings		
(market value)	xxx	
Property dividends payable		xxx

At the date of distribution:

| Property dividends payable | xxx | |
| Merchandise inventory | | xxx |

The loss recorded in the above journal entry does not qualify as unusual and infrequent, thus it is not an extraordinary item and answer (c) is incorrect. The loss should be reported as a reduction in income before extraordinary items. Therefore, answer (d) is correct.

33. (b) The requirement is to determine the amount to be debited to retained earnings for these stock dividends. Per ARB 43, chap 7B, paras 10-16, the issuance of a stock dividend less than **20-25%** (a "small" stock dividend) requires that the **market value** of the stock be transferred from retained earnings, and a dividend greater than **20-25%** (a "large" stock dividend) requires the **par value** of the stock to be transferred from retained earnings. Thus, a 10% stock dividend is considered to be "small" and should be transferred from retained earnings at the FMV of $15,000. A 28% stock dividend is considered to be "large" and should be transferred at the par value of $30,800. The aggregate amount to be transferred from retained earnings is $45,800.

34. (a) When the stock dividend is less than 20-25% of the common shares outstanding at the time of the declaration, generally accepted accounting principles require that the FMV of the stock issued be transferred from retained earnings. At the date of declaration, the following entry would be made:

Retained earnings (Stock dividends declared)		
(.05 x 10,000 shares x $5)	2,500	
Common stock dividend distributable		
(.05 x 10,000 x $2)		1,000
Additional paid-in capital (plug)		1,500

Note from the entry above that no asset or liability has been affected. The entry merely reflects a reclassification within the equity accounts. When a balance sheet is prepared between the dates of declaration and distribution, the common stock dividend distributable should be shown in the stockholders' equity section as an addition to capital stock.

G. Stock Splits

35. (d) ARB 43, chap 7, defines a stock dividend as an issuance by a corporation of its own common shares to its common shareholders without consideration...to give the recipient shareholders evidence of a part of their respective interests in accumulated corporate earnings without distribution of cash or other property. A stock split is defined as an issuance by a corporation of common shares to its common shareholders without consideration...prompted mainly by a desire to increase the number of outstanding shares for the purpose of effecting a reduction in their unit market price and, thereby, of obtaining wider distribution and improved marketability of the shares. Thus, neither of these transactions results in a transfer of assets among the shareholders and the corporation. While the allocation of stockholders' equity among the various accounts (retained earnings, common stock, and additional paid-in capital) will change, the **total** stockholders' equity is **not** affected. Therefore, answer (d) is correct, and answers (a), (b), and (c) are incorrect.

36. (b) The requirement is to determine the balance of additional paid-in capital immediately after a reverse stock split. Stock splits change the number of shares outstanding and the par value per share, but the total par value outstanding does not change. Stock splits do not affect any account balances, including additional paid-in capital. Therefore, the balance of additional paid-in capital remains at $450,000.

37. (b) A stock split does not affect either the balance of the additional paid-in capital or the retained earnings accounts. The number of shares outstanding and the par value per share merely change in proportion to each other. When this occurs, only a memorandum entry is made. Therefore, answer (b) is correct, and answers (a), (c), and (d) are incorrect.

H. Appropriations of Retained Earnings (Reserves)

38. (a) The requirement is to determine the amount of appropriated retained earnings Eagle should report in its 1999 balance sheet. The entry to record the appropriation of retained earnings in 1999 for the construction of a new plant is as follows:

RE (or Unappropriated RE) $1,200,000
     RE Appropriated for plant expansion $1,200,000

The cash restricted for the retirement of bonds due in 1999 should **not** be reported as an appropriation of retained earnings because the facts in the question do not indicate that appropriation was made by management. SFAS 5 requires that when an appropriation is no longer needed, it must be returned directly to unappropriated retained earnings by reversing the entry that created it. Therefore, when the office building was completed in 1999, the following entry was made:

RE Appropriated for plant expansion $1,750,000
     RE (or Unappropriated RE) $1,750,000

The total cost to complete the building has no effect on appropriated retained earnings. Thus, answer (a) is correct.

39. **(a)** Retained earnings are typically appropriated due to legal requirements, contractual requirements, or through the discretion of the board of directors. Dividends in arrears are not considered a liability to the company, and retained earnings would not be appropriated for this amount. In many cases, retained earnings must be appropriated for an amount equal to the cost of treasury stock acquired. However, this appropriation would be removed upon reissuance of the treasury stock. Therefore, answer (a) is correct.

40. **(d)** SFAS 5, para 15, states that appropriations of retained earnings are not prohibited provided that the appropriation is clearly identified as such in the stockholders' equity section of the balance sheet. Costs or losses cannot be charged to an appropriation of retained earnings. Accordingly, answer (a) is incorrect. Answer (b) is also incorrect because a contingent loss that is probable and reasonably estimable should be accrued as a loss and liability under the guidance of SFAS 5, para 8. Answer (c) is an inappropriate restriction of retained earnings. Therefore, answer (d) is correct.

I.1. Stock Options

41. **(c)** Under APB 25, employee compensation expense as the result of a stock option plan is calculated as the difference between the option price and the market price **at the date of grant** times the number of option shares.

$$\text{Option shares} \times \left(\text{Market price} - \text{Option price}\right) = \text{Total compensation expense}$$

$$3,000 \times (\$30 - \$20) = \$30,000$$

The total compensation expense must be recognized over the period for which the option plan represents compensation. If not otherwise specified, the required service period (2 years) is assumed to be the period benefited. Therefore, 1999 compensation expense is $15,000 ($30,000 ÷ 2). Note that compensation expense is not affected by changes in the market value of the stock after the measurement date.

42. **(c)** Under APB 25, total compensation expense as a result of a stock option plan is calculated as the difference between the option price and the market price at the date of grant times the number of option shares.

$$\text{Option shares} \times \left(\text{Market price} - \text{Option price}\right) = \text{Total compensation expense}$$

$$10,000 \times (\$47 - \$38) = \$90,000$$

The total compensation expense must be recognized over the period for which the option plan represents compensation. Therefore, 1999 compensation expense is $30,000 ($90,000 ÷ 3 years). Note that APB 25 states that the cost of treasury stock distributed in an option plan does not determine compensation expense.

43. **(a)** The net increase in stockholders' equity (SE) as a result of the grant and exercise of the options is equal to the increase in cash (1,000 shares x $20 option price = $20,000). The journal entry to record the options has no effect on SE because a SE account will be credited while a contra SE account will be debited as follows:

Deferred compensation   30,000
     Paid-in capital stock options   30,000
     [1,000 shares x ($50 market price
     – $20 options price)]

The entry to recognize compensation expense has no effect on SE because the debit decreases SE while the credit increases SE by reducing the contra account as follows:

Compensation expense   30,000
     Deferred compensation   30,000

The only entry which does affect SE is the entry for the exercise of the options, which decreases SE by $30,000 while increasing it by $50,000 (a net increase of $20,000).

Cash (1,000 x $20)   20,000
Paid-in capital stock options
  (1,000 x $30)   30,000
     Common stock (1,000 x $10)   10,000
     Paid-in capital in X of PV (plug)   40,000

Thus, the net increase in stockholders' equity is $20,000.

Note that the concept tested in this question would apply in the same way under SFAS 123. Therefore, although compensation expense would differ under the new standard, the answer would be the same.

I.2. Stock Appreciation Rights

44. **(c)** The 20,000 stock appreciation rights (SAR) each entitle the holder to receive cash equal to the excess of the market price of the stock on the exercise date over the market price on the grant date ($30). Since these SAR are payment for past services and are exercisable immediately, there is no required service period. Therefore, the expense computed at 12/31/99 does **not** have to be allocated to more than one period. At 12/31/99, compensation expense is measured based on the excess of the 12/31/99 market price ($45) over the predetermined price ($30), resulting in compensation expense of $300,000 [20,000 ($45 – $30)]. Note that **if** Dean was **required** to work 3 years **before** the SAR could be exercised, the expense would be allocated over the 3 years of required service ($300,000 x 1/3 = $100,000).

J. Stock Compensation Under SFAS 123

45. (c)   Per APB 25 or SFAS 123, when accounting for stock compensation plans, total compensation expense is computed as the excess of the market price of the stock over the amount contributed by employees. In this case, the market value of the 150,000 shares issued in 1999 is $1,050,000, and the employees' contributions for these shares is $350,000. Therefore, Wall should recognize $700,000 ($1,050,000 – $350,000) as expense in 1999 for the stock compensation plan.

46. (c)   According to SFAS 123, *Accounting for Stock Option Employee Compensation Plans*, the rate of interest used to discount both the exercise price and dividends is the risk-free interest rate. Answers (a), (b), and (d) are all incorrect because they indicate a different rate than the risk-free rate.

47. (c)   Using the Black-Scholes method it is more than likely that deferred compensation expense would be measured even if the market value and the option price are equal. Deferred compensation is not measured under APB 25 if the market price is equal to the option price. Therefore, answers (a), (b), and (d) are incorrect.

48. (c)   If the stock options are for past services, as indicated when the options are immediately exercisable by the holders, compensation cost must be fully expensed at the grant date. Answer (a) is incorrect because usually deferred compensation expense is recognized. Answer (b) is incorrect because deferred compensation expense is recognized when service has not yet been provided. Answer (d) is incorrect because when options are provided for prior service compensation expense must immediately be recognized.

49. (b)   SFAS 123 requires that footnote disclosures be presented in the financial statements of entities that do not adopt SFAS 123, which effectively will show what the effect of adoption would have been. This includes pro forma net income and earnings per share reflecting the difference in compensation cost and the related tax effect of using SFAS 123 as opposed to APB 25.

50. (c)   SFAS 123 significantly expanded the disclosures which are required by entities having stock compensation arrangements, and this expansion applies as well, for the most part, to those companies that continue to employ APB 25 for financial statement purposes. Thus, all three items listed are required to be disclosed, and answer (c) is correct.

51. (b)   Accounting for stock-based compensation under the minimum value method under SFAS 123 is as follows:

Current market value per share	$75.00
Less: Present value of exercise price	
($75 x .747)	56.025
Present value of expected	
dividends ($3 x 4.212)	12.636
Equals	6.339
Times # of options	x 20,000
Deferred compensation expense	$126,780

Thus, answer (b) is correct.

52. (c)   Under the provisions of SFAS 123, dividends or dividend equivalents on options which vest are to be accounted for as other dividends--that is, charged against retained earnings--but those paid on options which do not vest are deemed to be compensation expense. The reporting entity can either estimate what fraction of options will vest and allocate such dividend equivalents between retained earnings and compensation expense accordingly, or it can charge the entire amount to retained earnings and account for forfeitures as they occur, by reversing the charge from retained earnings to compensation cost. Thus, answer (c) is correct.

K. Basic Earnings Per Share

53. (b)   The formula for basic earnings per share (BEPS) is

$$\frac{\underset{\text{net income}}{\$1,000,000} - \underset{\text{preferred dividends}}{\$50,000}}{100,000 \text{ common shares outstanding}} = \underline{\$9.50}$$

In calculating the numerator the claims of preferred shareholders against 1999 earnings should be deducted to arrive at the 1999 earnings attributable to common shareholders. This amount is 50,000 (5% x $100 x 10,000 shares). The $50,000 preferred dividends in arrears is not deducted to compute the numerator in determining 1999 BEPS. This is because the $50,000 dividends in arrears is a claim of preferred shareholders against 1998 earnings and would reduce 1998 BEPS.

54. (b)   The formula for basic earnings per share (BEPS) is

$$\frac{\underset{\text{net income}}{\$500,000} - \underset{\text{preferred dividends}}{10,000}}{200,000 \text{ common shares outstanding}} = \underline{\$2.45}$$

In calculating the numerator, the claims of preferred shareholders against 1999 earnings should be deducted to arrive at the 1999 earnings attributable to common shareholders. This amount is $10,000 ($250,000 x 4%). During 1998, the BEPS numerator would have been reduced by $10,000 even though no preferred dividends were declared, because the cumulative feature means that $10,000 of 1998 earnings are reserved for, and will ultimately be paid to, preferred stockholders. In 1999, the 1998 dividends in arrears are paid, as well as $6,000 of the $10,000 1999 preferred dividend. Even though only $6,000 is paid, the entire $10,000 is subtracted for reasons explained above.

55. (b)   Para 54 of SFAS 128 states that for EPS purposes, shares of stock issued as a result of stock dividends or splits should be considered outstanding for the entire period in which they were issued. Therefore, both the original 20,000 shares and the additional 20,000 issued in the 4/1 stock split are treated as outstanding for the entire year (20,000 x 2 = 40,000). The 7/1 issuance of 10,000 shares results in a weighted-average of 5,000 shares (10,000 x 6/12) because the shares were outstanding for only 6 months during the year. Therefore, Jet should use 45,000 shares (40,000 + 5,000) to calculate EPS.

56. (d) The computation of weighted-average shares outstanding is

Date	# of shares		Fraction		W-A
1/1	30,000	x	12/12	=	30,000
2/1	3,000	x	12/12	=	3,000
3/1	9,000	x	12/12	=	9,000
7/1	8,000	x	6/12	=	4,000
					46,000

The 3,000 shares issued as a result of a stock dividend are weighted at 12/12 instead of 11/12 because for EPS purposes stock dividends are treated as if they occurred at the beginning of the year. Similarly, the shares issued in a pooling of interests are treated as if outstanding the entire year for BEPS purposes (weighted at 12/12 instead of 10/12).

57. (b) The formula for computing BEPS for a simple capital structure is

$$\frac{\text{Net income} - \text{Applicable pref. stock dividends}}{\text{Weighted-average \# of common shares outstanding}}$$

Net income is $410,000 and $350,000 in 1999 and 1998, respectively, and there are no preferred dividends. The weighted-average number of common shares outstanding must be computed for 1999. Stock dividends and stock splits are handled retroactively for comparability. The 1999 computation is

Dates	Number of shares	Fraction	WA
1/1 to 3/31	100,000 x 2 = 200,000	3/12	50,000
4/1 to 6/30	(100,000 + 20,000) x 2 = 240,000	3/12	60,000
7/1 to 12/31	120,000 x 2 = 240,000	6/12	120,000
			230,000

The 1998 weighted-average of 100,000 is retroactively restated to 200,000 for comparability. Therefore, the BEPS amounts are

1999

$$\frac{\$410,000}{230,000} = \underline{\$1.78}$$

1998

$$\frac{\$350,000}{200,000} = \underline{\$1.75}$$

58. (b) Per SFAS 128, paras 36 and 37, earnings per share must be shown on the face of the income statement for income from continuing operations and net income. Discontinued operations, extraordinary items, and cumulative effect of change in accounting principle may be shown on the income statement or in the notes. Because they are not required to be shown the face of the income statement, answer (b) is correct.

59. (c) Per para 54 of SFAS 128, if the number of common shares outstanding increases as a result of a stock dividend or stock split or decreases as a result of a reverse split, the computations of EPS should give retroactive recognition for all periods presented. If these events take place after the close of the period but before completion of the financial report, the per share computations should be based on the new number of shares. Therefore, answer (c) is correct. Note that when per share computations reflect such

changes in the number of shares after the close of the period, this fact should be disclosed.

L. Diluted Earnings Per Share

60. (b) The requirement is to determine the number of shares that should be used in computing 1999 diluted earnings per share. The first step is to compute the weighted-average number of common shares outstanding. 300,000 shares were outstanding the entire year, and 50,000 more shares were outstanding for 6 months, resulting in a weighted-average of 325,000 [300,000 + (50,000 x 6/12)]. Second, the stock options increase the number of shares used in the computation **only** if they are dilutive. The stock options are dilutive because the exercise price is less than the market value. Thus, the denominator effect of the options must be computed. This is done using the **treasury stock method,** as illustrated below.

Assumed proceeds	
(40,000 x $15)	$600,000
Shares issued	40,000
Shares reacquired	
($600,000 ÷ $20)	(30,000)
Shares issued,	
not reacquired	10,000

Therefore, the number of shares used for computing diluted earnings per share is 335,000 (325,000 + 10,000).

61. (b) Diluted earnings per share is based on common stock and all dilutive potential common shares. To determine if a security is dilutive, EPS, including the effect of the dilutive security, must be compared to the basic EPS. In this case, basic EPS is 7.45.

$$\frac{850,000 \ (\text{N.I.}) - 30,000 \ (\text{pref. div.})}{110,000 \ \text{shares}} = \underline{7.45}$$

The effect of the convertible preferred stock is to increase the numerator by $30,000 ($3.00 dividend per share x 10,000 shares) for the amount of the preferred dividends that would not be paid (assuming conversion) and increase the denominator by 20,000 shares. This security is dilutive because it decreases the EPS from 7.45 to 6.54.

$$\frac{850,000 - 30,000 + 30,000}{110,000 + 20,000} = \underline{6.54}$$

If the EPS increases due to the inclusion of a security, that security is antidilutive and should not be included.

62. (d) The requirement is to compute the diluted earnings per share for 1999. Therefore, **all** potential common shares that **reduce** current EPS must be included in the computation. The formula for diluted EPS is

$$\frac{\text{Net income available to common shareholders}}{\text{Weighted-average common shares outstanding}}$$

The net income available to common shareholders is $3,200,000. This is the net income of $3,400,000 less the preferred stock dividend of $200,000. The weighted-average common shares outstanding is 1,250,000. This is computed as the actual common shares outstanding for the full year of 1,200,000 plus the contingent common shares of

50,000 which were outstanding for the full year because the contingency was incurred in 1998. Thus,

$$\text{Diluted EPS} = \frac{\$3,200,000}{1,250,000} = \underline{\$2.56}$$

63. (b) The effect of convertible bonds is included in diluted EPS under the if converted method, if they are dilutive. The bonds are dilutive as shown below.

$$\text{Basic EPS} = \frac{\$35,000}{(1/2)10,000 + (1/2)14,000} = \$2.92$$

$$\frac{\text{Incremental}}{\text{per share effect}} = \frac{(7\% \times \$10,000) - 30\% (7\% \times \$10,000)}{200 \text{ Shares per bond}} = \frac{\$490}{200} = \$2.45$$

Since $2.45 < $2.92, the bonds are dilutive. Under the if converted method, the assumption is made that the bonds were converted at the beginning of the current year (1/1) or later in the current year if the bonds were issued during the current year. In this case, conversion is assumed for the first 6 months of 1999 only because the bonds were actually converted on July 1. Under their assumed conversion, the numerator would increase because bond interest expense would not have been incurred for the first 6 months of the year [1/2 ($14,000 – 30% x $14,000) = $4,900]. The denominator would increase because the 4,000 shares (20 x 200) would have been outstanding for the first 6 months of the year (4,000 x 6/12 = 2,000). Therefore, diluted EPS is $2.85.

$$\frac{\$35,000 + \$4,900}{12,000 + 2,000} = \frac{\$39,900}{14,000} = \underline{\$2.85}$$

64. (a) Diluted EPS takes into account the effect of all dilutive potential common shares that were outstanding during the period. Thus, the possible conversion of convertible bonds would be included because they are dilutive (i.e., EPS would be reduced), but the possible exercise of common stock options would not be included because they are antidilutive (i.e., EPS would be increased). Diluted EPS = $15.00 -$.75 = $14.25. Therefore, answer (a) is correct.

65. (d) The requirement is to determine the treatment of nonconvertible cumulative preferred dividends in determining diluted EPS. Per SFAS 128, para 9, dividends on nonconvertible cumulative preferred shares should be deducted from net income whether an actual liability exists or not. This is because cumulative preferred stock owners must receive any dividends in arrears before future dividend distributions can be made to common stockholders. Answer (a) is incorrect because cumulative preferred stock dividends are not disregarded in computing EPS. Answer (b) is incorrect because cumulative preferred dividends are deducted, not added, to net income in EPS calculations. Answer (c) is incorrect because it describes the treatment of dividends for noncumulative preferred stock.

66. (a) Per SFAS 128, para 26, the if converted method of computing earnings per share assumes that convertible securities are converted at the beginning of the earliest period reported or, if later, at the time of issuance. Therefore, answer (a) is correct and answers (b), (c), and (d) are incorrect.

67. (b) Per SFAS 128, if convertible securities are deemed to be dilutive, then interest expense should be added back to net income when computing diluted earnings per share.

68. (b) Per SFAS 128, the effect of contingent issue agreements are not included in basic earnings per share. They are included in diluted earnings per share if the contingency is met.

M. Corporate Bankruptcy

69. (d) The total cash available to pay **all** unsecured claims, including priority claims, is the cash obtained from free assets ($320,000) and any excess cash available from assets pledged with fully secured creditors after they are used to satisfy those claims ($370,000 – $260,000 = $110,000). Therefore, total cash available is $430,000 ($320,000 + $110,000). After paying priority claims, $360,000 will remain to pay all unsecured nonpriority claims ($430,000 – $70,000).

70. (c) Bankruptcy law requires that the claims of secured creditors be satisfied before any unsecured claims are paid. Hale is a secured creditor in the amount of $5,000 (the liquidation value of the collateral). The remainder of Hale's claim ($30,000 – $5,000 = $25,000) is an unsecured claim, because it is not secured by any collateral. Therefore, Hale, will receive a total of $15,000 on this note: $5,000 received in full as a secured creditor, and $10,000 received as an unsecured creditor ($25,000 x $.40).

71. (d) A bankruptcy trustee may establish a new set of accounting records to maintain accountability for the bankruptcy estate. Once the trustee assumes custody of the estate, the trustee will enter any unrecorded assets or liabilities in the estate equity account. Any gains or losses and liquidation expenses incurred will also be recorded. In the Kamy Corp. bankruptcy, both the $8,000 loss on sale of the truck ($20,000 carrying value – $12,000 cash selling price) and the $1,000 unrecorded liability would be debited to the estate equity account as follows:

Estate equity	1,000	
Accounts payable		1,000
Cash	12,000	
Estate equity	8,000	
Truck		20,000

Therefore, answer (d) is correct.

N. Reorganizations

72. (b) The requirement is to determine the net increase in total stockholders' equity as a result of the payments to unsecured creditors pursuant to a reorganization plan under Chapter 11. The net increase in stockholders' equity can be determined as follows:

Fair value of liabilities owed to	
unsecured creditors	$1,200,000
Cash paid	(400,000)
Common stock issued (80,000 x $1.25)	(100,000)
Gain on settlement of debt	$ 700,000

The gain on the settlement of debt would be included in the income statement and closed to retained earnings. The net increase in stockholders' equity would equal $800,000 ($700,000 gain + $100,000 FMV of stock issued).

O. Quasi Reorganization

73. (c) Although assets are often revalued to fair value during a quasi reorganization [answer (b)], the **primary** purpose of a quasi reorganization is to eliminate a deficit in retained earnings [answer (c)], so that dividends may be paid without waiting years to eliminate the deficit through future earnings. A quasi reorganization does not directly allow a corporation to obtain relief from creditors [answer (a)] or result in a distribution of stock [answer (d)].

74. (d) Per ARB 43, chap 7A, paras 1-3, in certain instances an entity may elect to restate its assets, capital stock, and surplus through a readjustment (or "quasi reorganization") and thus avail itself of permission to relieve its future income account or earned surplus account of charges which would otherwise be made there against. In such instances, the entity should present a **fair (value)** balance sheet as of the date of the reorganization. Therefore, answer (d) is correct.

75. (c) A quasi reorganization generally involves (1) revaluing assets, (2) reducing par, and (3) writing the deficit off against additional paid-in capital. In this case, no mention is made of the first step, revaluing assets. The second step, reducing par, results in a decrease to **common stock** and an increase to **additional paid-in capital** of $250,000 [10,000 x ($30 – $5)]. The third step, writing off the deficit, increases **retained earnings** by $210,000 (creating a $0 balance) and decrease **additional paid-in capital** by the same amount. Immediately after the quasi reorganization, Brown should report additional paid-in capital of $190,000 ($150,000 + $250,000 – $210,000).

P. Stock Rights

76. (a) When a corporation issues rights to its stockholders, it only makes a memorandum entry. If rights are later exercised, the corporation would make the following entry:

Cash	xxx	
Common stock		xxx
Additional paid-in capital		xxx

Therefore, answer (a) is correct.

77. (c) The only time a journal entry is recorded for the issuance and exercise of stock rights is on the date of exercise. At the date of issuance, only a memorandum entry is recorded. The redemption of the rights issued to the shareholders should be treated like a dividend. Accordingly, retained earnings will be decreased by the amount paid to the shareholders (120,000 x $0.10 = $12,000).

78. (a) The requirement is to determine the effects of the stock warrants on the additional paid-in capital account and on net income. When a corporation issues stock warrants to its stockholders it only makes a memorandum entry.

Then, when the warrants are exercised, the following entry is made:

Cash	xx	
Common stock		xx
Additional paid-in capital		xx

Net income is not affected by the exercise of stock warrants because the transaction represents a process of raising capital and is not related to the earnings process. Therefore, answer (a) is correct. Answer (b) is incorrect because the additional paid-in capital is not affected until the exercise date in 1999. Answers (c) and (d) are incorrect because there is no effect on net income from the issuance and exercise of stock warrants.

79. (b) Note that the only time an entry related to the issuance and exercise of stock rights, which affects the equity accounts of a corporation, is recorded is on the date of exercise. At the date of issuance, only a memorandum entry is recorded, and on the date of the rights lapsing, no entry is recorded which would affect the company's equity accounts. Thus, the correct answer is (b): the additional paid-in capital account would not be credited at the time the rights are issued or at the date on which the rights lapse.

Q. Employee Stock Ownership Plan (ESOP)

80. (c) Per AICPA Statement of Position 76-3, para 9, the amount contributed or committed to be contributed to an employee stock ownership plan (ESOP) in a given year should be the measure of the amount to be charged to expense by the employer. Therefore, Fay should record 1998 compensation expense of $84,000 [contribution of $30,000 cash and common stock with a FMV of $54,000 (3,000 x $18)].

81. (d) Per AICPA Statement of Position 76-3, para 5, an obligation of an Employee Stock Ownership Plan (ESOP) should be recorded as a liability in the financial statements of the employer when the obligation is covered by either a guarantee of the employer or a commitment by the employer to make future contributions to the ESOP sufficient to meet the debt service requirements. Therefore, the note payable of $100,000 (which is guaranteed by Fay) should be reported in Fay's 12/31/99 balance sheet. The Statement of Position also states that the offsetting debit to the employer's liability should be reported as a reduction of stockholders' equity (para 7). Therefore, Fay should also report $100,000 as a reduction of stockholders' equity.

Stockholders' Equity: Comprehensive

82. (a) All of the accounts given are stockholders' equity accounts. Total stockholders' equity is computed below.

Paid-in capital		
Common stock		$600,000
Addl. paid-in capital		800,000
		1,400,000
Retained earnings		
Appropriated	$150,000	
Unappropriated	200,000	350,000
		1,750,000
Less: Treasury stock	50,000	
Unrealized loss on		
available-for-sale MES	20,000	(70,000)
		$1,680,000

Both **treasury stock** and **net unrealized loss on available-for-sale marketable equity securities** are contra stockholders' equity accounts.

83. (a) The number of shares outstanding is equal to the issued shares less treasury shares. The table below shows the effects of each of the stock transactions on the common shares outstanding.

	Outstanding shares
1/1/99	300,000
1/31/99 declaration of 10% stock dividend	30,000
6/30/99 purchase of TS	(100,000)
8/1/99 sale of TS	50,000
Subtotal	280,000
11/30/99 stock split	x 2
12/31/99	560,000

84. (a) Shares issued and outstanding are computed below.

	Issued	*Outstanding*
12/31/98	100,000	95,000
5/3/99		1,000
8/6/99	10,000	10,000
	110,000	106,000
11/18/99	110,000	106,000
12/31/99	220,000	212,000

At 12/31/98, shares issued were 100,000 and outstanding 95,000 (100,000 issued less 5,000 treasury). The reissuance of treasury stock does not increase shares issued, but does increase shares outstanding by 1,000 to 96,000 (100,000 issued less 4,000 treasury). The issuance of previously unissued stock on 8/6/99 increases both issued and outstanding shares by 10,000, bringing the totals to 110,000 issued and 106,000 outstanding prior to the stock split. Since treasury stock is protected from dilution, shares issued, treasury shares, and outstanding shares are all doubled by the stock split.

R. Ratios

85. (a) The requirement is to determine the effect on Ali Corp. of exercising the stock options. First, the debt to equity ratio is calculated as follows:

$$\text{Debt to equity} = \frac{\text{Total liabilities}}{\text{Common stockholders' equity}}$$

The figures given in the problem reflect the account balances **after** the exercise of the stock options. Thus, Ali's debt to equity ratio after the exercise is

$$\frac{\$60,000}{\$500,000} = 12\%$$

When the options were exercised, total stockholders' equity would have increased by the amount of the option price as follows:

Common stock	↑	by par value x 1,000 shares
Paid-in capital	↑	by (option price-par) x 1,000 shares

Note that the information given is incomplete as to whether compensation was recorded under the stock option plan. However, even if compensation were recorded, the entries are made only to accounts that impact stockholders' equity, and the net effect is no change. Thus, the only change is an increase resulting from the exercise of the options. Since common stockholders' equity increased, the denominator of the debt to equity ratio also increased. As the denominator becomes larger and the numerator remains constant, the quotient becomes smaller. Therefore, the debt to equity ratio must have **decreased** to its current level of 12%, and answer (a) is correct. Answer (b) is incorrect because earnings per share decreased by $.15. Answer (c) is incorrect because not enough information is given to calculate the asset turnover. Answer (d) is incorrect because the debt to equity ratio, rate of return on common stock, earnings per share, price earnings ratio, and book value per share were all affected by exercising the stock options.

86. (c) The requirement is to determine Irvington's return on common stockholders' equity for 1999, which is computed by dividing net income available to common stockholders (net income less preferred dividends) by average common stockholders' equity

$$\frac{\$120,000 - \$10,000}{(\$375,000 + \$585,000)/2} = 23\%$$

87. (d) The requirement is to determine the book value per common share. The book value per common share is the amount each share would receive if the company were liquidated. The book value per common share is calculated as follows:

	Preferred	*Common*
Preferred stock, 5%	$250,000	
Common stock		$350,000
APIC in excess of par value of common stock		125,000
Retained earnings:		
Dividends in arrears	25,000	
Liquidation premium	50,000	
Remainder to common (Plug)		225,000
Totals	$325,000	$700,000
Shares outstanding		100,000
Book value per share		7.00

Note that when calculating the remainder to common, total stockholders' equity before the liquidation must be equal to the amount after the assumed liquidation.

88. **(c)** Under the cost method, treasury stock is debited for the cost of the treasury stock, thus decreasing total stockholders' equity. However, the book value per share will increase due to the acquisition of the treasury stock. Book value per share is calculated by dividing common stockholders' equity by the shares outstanding. An example will help illustrate

Stockholders' equity	
Common stock (30,000 shares),	
$5 par	$150,000
Additional paid-in capital	550,000
Retained earnings	250,000
	$950,000

$$\text{Book value per share} = \frac{\$950,000}{30,000} = \$31.67$$

Per the facts in the question, treasury stock was acquired at more than par and original issue price, but less than book value per share. Therefore, the acquisition price must be greater than $23.33 per share (700,000 ÷ 30,000) and less than $31.67 per share.

Let's say 1,000 shares of treasury stock were acquired at $27.00 per share.

$$\text{Book value per share} = \frac{\$950,000 - (1,000 \times \$27)}{30,000 - 1,000}$$

$$= \frac{923,000}{29,000}$$

$$= \$31.83$$

The book value per share increased after the acquisition of the treasury stock. Therefore, answer (c) is correct.

89. **(b)** Answer (b) is correct because dividends per share is used in the numerator of the dividend payout ratio as shown below.

$$\frac{\text{Dividend}}{\text{payout ratio}} = \frac{\text{Dividends per share}}{\text{Earnings per share}}$$

However, dividends per share are not used in the calculation of earnings per share

$$\frac{\text{Earnings}}{\text{per share}} = \frac{\text{Net income} - \text{Preferred dividends}}{\text{Weighted-average number of shares outstanding}}$$

Therefore, answers (a), (c), and (d) are incorrect.

OTHER OBJECTIVE ANSWERS AND ANSWER EXPLANATIONS

Problem 1

1.   **(I)**   In accordance with the par value method, treasury shares are recorded at par value by debiting treasury stock when acquired. Any additional paid-in capital from the original issue of the acquired shares is also debited, cash is credited, and either additional paid-in capital--treasury stock is credited or retained earnings is debited for the difference between cash and the other two debits previously mentioned.

2.   **(H)**   Appropriations of retained earnings are actions by the board of directors to disclose amounts not available for dividends.

3.   **(D)**   A stock split changes the number of shares outstanding and the par value per share. The purpose of a stock split is to reduce the market price per share.

4.   **(A)**   A simple capital structure for a corporation exists if there are no potentially dilutive securities.

5.   **(M)**   The if converted method for convertible securities assumes that the securities were converted at the later of the beginning of the period or the date of issue. The method thus increases the weighted-average number of shares in the denominator of the EPS equation. Since the method assumes conversion at the beginning of the period, no preferred dividends or interest would be considered to have been paid.

6.   **(K)**   A scrip dividend is a dividend issued by the corporation in the form of a note payable.

7.   **(B)**   A stock appreciation right allows an employee to receive the excess of the market value of the stock over a preestablished value in the form of cash, shares of stock, or both on the exercise date.

8.   **(J)**   A stock option is a form of compensation given to employees which allows them to purchase shares of stock at a specified price.

9.   **(G)**   A dividend paid to shareholders in excess of the retained earnings balance which is considered to be a return of capital and a liquidating dividend.

10.   **(E)**   When a corporation purchases its own stock in the market, the stock is termed treasury stock. Treasury stock is not an asset as a corporation cannot invest in itself. Treasury stock is recorded in a contra equity account.

Problem 2

This problem is a collection of miscellaneous stockholders' equity problems. The candidate should start the problem by scanning the Required information to determine the amounts to be calculated. While scanning, the candidate should recognize that some of the required items are related, such as 2 (preferred dividends) and 10 (numerator used in calculating EPS) and 5 (number of common shares issued) and 6 (amount of common stock issued); 7 (additional paid-in capital) and 8 (treasury stock). These relationships require that the candidate label each answer, so that it will be possible to quickly find that answer when it is used in a subsequent problem.

Unlike many previous exam problems, the order of the information concerning the transactions does not coincide with the order of the required answers. This arrangement makes it necessary to read the required amount and then hunt for the transaction information needed to calculate that required amount.

1. ($14,000)   Prior period adjustment is the term generally applied to corrections of errors of prior periods. In this problem no amortization had been recorded in a prior year--an error. Since this is not a self-correcting error, it still existed in 2000. The calculation is cost ($320,000) ÷ useful life (8 years) for 1/2 year (purchased July 1). Prior period adjustments are disclosed net of tax (30%). $320,000/8 x 1/2 x (1 – .3) = $14,000.

2. ($12,000)   Preferred dividends are 6% and cumulative. They were declared during 1999 and paid in 2000. The declaration is sufficient to record and recognize the dividends legally; they do not have to be paid in the current year to be recognized during that time period. These dividends will be used in the numerator in question 10 when calculating the 1999 EPS. Since these dividends are cumulative, they would be used in the calculation of EPS even if they had not been declared. The amount of preferred dividends is derived by multiplying the par value of the stock by its rate. 6% x $200,000 par = $12,000 dividends.

3. ($165,000)   Common dividends--cash are calculated by the formula: Common shares outstanding x Dividend per share. In this problem the number of shares outstanding is affected by the beginning shares (100,000), shares issued (13,000), and treasury shares purchased and sold (5,000 purchased, 2,000 sold) prior to the dividend date of November 4. 100,000 + 13,000 – 5,000 + 2,000 = 110,000 shares outstanding x dividend rate $1.50 = $165,000.

4. ($720,000)   Common dividends--property differ from cash dividends because the property may be carried in the accounts at an amount which does not equal its fair value (cash is always at its fair value). Management intends to distribute the property at its fair value, therefore it is necessary to bring the property to fair value on the date management is legally forced to distribute it (the declaration date). Value fluctuations beyond that date are irrelevant.

5. **(113,000)**   The number of shares issued differs from the number of shares outstanding which was used in question 3. Shares issued include those outstanding as well as those held in the treasury. Shares outstanding from question 3, 110,000 plus 3,000 treasury shares = 113,000 shares.

6. **($113,000)**   Amount of common stock issued--This question takes the answer from question 5 (113,000 shares) and multiplies that figure by the par value of each share, $1.

7. **($934,000)**   The additional paid-in capital, including treasury stock transactions, is derived by adding the beginning balance ($800,000) to the excess ($10) of issue price ($11) over par value ($1) for the shares issued (13,000) to acquire land on February 1, 1999. In addition, the sale of the treasury stock (2,000 shares) at an amount ($16) greater than cost ($14) gives rise to a nonoperating gain that cannot be included in net income since it was both not related to operations and is a transaction in the company's own stock. $800,000 + (13,000 x $10) + (2,000 x 16-14) = $934,000.

8. **($42,000)**   Treasury stock--Since the Min Co. follows the cost method of accounting for treasury stock, this answer is derived by multiplying the shares of treasury stock (3,000) by their cost ($14). 3,000 x $14 = $42,000.

9. **($24.86)**   Book value per share is a concept that relates common stockholders' equity to shares of common stock. The "per share" referred to is always the **common** shares unless the problem states some other type of shares. In this case it is to be calculated before the prior period adjustment. It is necessary to subtract preferred stock's total liquidating value ($100 x 2,000 sh = $200,000) from total stockholders' equity ($2,686,000) to obtain common stockholders' equity. In this problem no liquidating value is given, so par value is used. The resulting amount ($2,686,000 – $200,000 = $2,486,000) is divided by the common shares outstanding (100,000) to obtain book value per share ($24.86). ($2,686,000 – $200,000) ÷ 100,000 = $24.86.

10. **($826,000)**   The formula for calculating earnings per share is (NI – preferred dividends) ÷ Wtd.-Avg. Shares outstanding. The numerator is income available to common stockholders. The problem states that adjusted net income for 1999 was $838,000. The word "adjusted" tells the candidate that net income includes all information concerning transactions in the problem and need not be changed in any way. Preferred dividends ($12,000) were calculated in question 2. $838,000 – $12,000 = $826,000.

ANSWER OUTLINE

Problem 1   Stock Options

a.   1/2/99 is measurement date
      Date employer knows both:
          # of shares and option or exercise price

b.   Expense = (FMV of Gunpowder stock on 1/2/99 –
      option price) x # of options x 1/2 year

c.   See Unofficial Answer

d.   Required pro forma disclosures
      Pro forma net income
      Pro forma EPS
      Amounts if fair value method used on IS

UNOFFICIAL ANSWER

Problem 1   Stock Options

a.   Gunpowder's stock option measurement date is January 2, 1999. The stock option measurement date is the first date on which the employer knows both

      • The number of shares that an individual is entitled to receive, and
      • The option or purchase price.

b.   The compensation expense for 1999 equals the market price of Gunpowder's stock on January 2, 1999, less the option price times the number of options outstanding times one-half.

c.   For companies whose stock is publicly traded, there are six factors that are used in option-pricing models to estimate the fair value of stock options on the grant date. These factors are

      • The exercise price of the options
      • The current price of the underlying stock
      • The expected volatility of the underlying stock
      • The expected life of the option
      • The expected dividends on the underlying stock
      • The risk-free interest rate of the expected term of the option

d.   If Gunpowder used the intrinsic value based method for its stock options, the company would be required to report pro forma net income and pro forma earnings per share in the notes to its 1998 financial statements. The pro forma amounts would disclose what net income and earnings per share would have been for 1998 if the company used the fair value based method for compensation expense on its income statement.

ANSWER OUTLINE

Problem 2   EPS

a.   Basic EPS $= \dfrac{\text{NI} - \text{Pfd. div.}}{\text{W/A out. shs.}}$

      Pfd. div. deducted if declared or if stk. is cumulative

      Diluted EPS $= \dfrac{\text{NI} - \text{Pfd. div.} + \text{Dilutive security adjust.}}{\text{WA out. shs} + \text{Dilutive security shs.}}$

      Dilutive securities include options & warrants and convert. bonds & pfd. stk.

Dilutive securities decrease EPS
Antidilutive securities increase EPS

b.   Effect of assuming bond conversion is antidilutive
      Addition of interest, net of tax, would decrease loss
        to stockholders in numerator
      Dividing by number of shares including those from
        conversion would result in lower net loss per share
      Only basic net loss per share would be reported

UNOFFICIAL ANSWER

Problem 2   EPS

a.   Basic earnings per share is based on income available for common stockholders divided by the weighted-average number of outstanding shares. Income available to common stockholders is net income less preferred dividends declared. Preferred dividends on cumulative preferred stock are deducted whether declared or not.

      Diluted earnings per share is basic earnings per share adjusted for the effects of dilutive securities. Dilutive securities include options and warrants and convertible bonds and preferred stock. The adjustments include positive numerator adjustments for bond interest, net of tax, and preferred dividends. The positive denominator adjustments are for dilutive shares that would be issued upon conversion of convertible securities and from applying the treasury stock method for dilutive options and warrants.

b.   Columbine's convertible bonds are antidilutive in the diluted EPS calculation because the addition of interest avoided (net of tax) to the numerator and the shares from conversion to the denominator would result in a lower net loss per share than basic net loss per share. Columbine would report only basic net loss per share.

SOLUTION GUIDE

Problem 3   Retained Earnings Statement and Stockholders' Equity Section of Balance Sheet

1.   This problem consists of three related requirements. The candidate must prepare a statement of retained earnings; prepare the stockholders' equity section; and compute the book value per share of common stock. Only single period (1999) financial statements are presented.

2.   The solutions approach for problems of this type, in which the requirements are interrelated, is to make computations for each piece of information and label each computation according to the requirement [(a), (b), or (c)] to which it relates.

2.1   The information on common shares authorized, issued and treasury, and on par value per share will be used to help determine balance sheet disclosures in part (b).

2.2   Preferred stock was issued on 1/21/99. 50,000 shares with a par value per share of $100 were issued, for a total par of $5,000,000 (b). The same $5,000,000 will be subtracted from total stockholders' equity in

(c) to compute the common stockholders' equity. There is no additional paid-in capital since the stock was issued for net assets which had a fair value of $5,000,000. Rover's distribution of the Trask shares to its stockholders has no effect on Trask's books.

2.3 The journal entry to record the retirement of treasury stock is

Common stock	125,000	
Paid-in capital in		
excess of par	250,000	
Treasury stock		250,000
Paid-in capital		
from TS trans.		125,000

Common stock is debited for par (25,000 x $5). Paid-in capital in excess of par from the original issuance [25,000 x ($15 – $5)] is removed from the books, as is the treasury stock (25,000 x $10). The difference of $125,000 is credited to paid in capital from TS transactions. This entry affects the stockholders' equity section (b), reducing common stock by $125,000, additional paid-in capital by a **net** amount of $125,000 ($250,000 – $125,000), and treasury stock by $250,000.

2.4 Property dividends are recorded at the FMV of the asset transferred with a gain (loss) recognized on the difference between the assets' BV and FMV. In this property dividend one share of Harbor is distributed for every 100 outstanding shares. After the 2/17/99 transaction, issued shares total 1,550,000 (1,575,000 – 25,000) and treasury shares total 50,000 (75,000 – 25,000), so outstanding shares amount to 1,500,000 (1,550,000 – 50,000). Therefore, all 15,000 shares of Harbor are distributed (1,500,000 ÷ 100 = 15,000). The dividend results in a decrease to retained earnings of $900,000 [15,000 x $60] (a).

2.5 The 2-for-1 stock split doubles the number of shares authorized, issued, held in treasury, and outstanding, while halving the par value ($5 ÷ 2 = $2.50) (b). No entry is required since the **total** par value outstanding is unaffected. The effect on the number of shares is summarized below.

	1/1/99	Retirement	2/17/99	Issuance	6/1/99	Split	10/27/99	
Auth.	4,000,000		4,000,000		4,000,000	x 2 =	8,000,000	(b)
Iss.	1,575,000	- 25,000 =	1,550,000	+ 150,000 =	1,700,000	x 2 =	3,400,000	(b)
T.S.	75,000	- 25,000 =	50,000		50,000	x 2 =	100,000	(b)
Outs.	1,500,000		1,500,000	+ 150,000 =	1,650,000	x 2 =	3,300,000	(b)

2.6 On 12/12/99, Trask declared the cash dividend on preferred stock, which will be a subtraction in the RE statement. The amount is the preferred dividend rate (6%) times the total par value of preferred stock outstanding ($5,000,000), or $300,000 (a).

2.7 The correction of 1998 depreciation expense is a prior period adjustment to retained earnings. The RE statement should start with the 1/1/99 balance as previously reported, to enable users to correlate this amount with prior years. Then the prior period adjustment is added or subtracted to result in the ad-

justed 1/1/99 balance. In this case, the net of tax adjustment ($245,000) is deducted because the prior period (1998) income was overstated.

2.8 The net income of $2,400,000 (a) is an addition in the RE statement.

3. The retained earnings statement [requirement (a)] contains the beginning balance, prior period adjustment, adjusted beginning balance, net income, property dividends, and cash dividends.

4. Stockholders' equity consists of preferred stock, common stock, additional paid-in capital, retained earnings, and treasury stock. Preferred stock is $5,000,000 from the 1/21/99 issuance; common stock, APIC, and treasury stock are computed by taking the 12/31/98 balances and adding or subtracting the appropriate transactions. The retained earnings amount is obtained from the RE statement.

5. The third requirement of the problem is the computation of book value per share at 12/31/99. It is computed by dividing **common** stockholders' equity by the **common** shares outstanding.

5.1 Common stockholders' equity is total stockholders' equity [$47,075,000 from requirement (b)] less the liquidation value of preferred stock [in this case, par value ($5,000,000)] and any dividends in arrears (none, in this case).

5.2 Common shares **outstanding** at year end was 3,300,000 shares (see 2.6 above).

5.3 The book value per share is $12.75 ($42,075,000 ÷ 3,300,000).

UNOFFICIAL ANSWER

Problem 3   Retained Earnings Statement and Stockholders' Equity Section of Balance Sheet

a.

Trask Corp.
STATEMENT OF RETAINED EARNINGS
For the Year Ended December 31, 1999

Balance, December 31, 1998		
As originally reported		$16,445,000
Less prior period adjustment from error understating depreciation	$350,000	
Less income tax effect	105,000	245,000
As restated		16,200,000
Net income		2,400,000
Deduct dividends		18,600,000
Cash dividend on preferred stock	300,000 [1]	
Dividend in kind on common stock	900,000 [2]	1,200,000
Balance, December 31, 1999		$17,400,000

b.

Trask Corp.
STOCKHOLDERS' EQUITY SECTION OF BALANCE SHEET
December 31, 1999

Preferred stock, $100 par value, 6% cumulative; 150,000 shares authorized;	
50,000 shares issued and outstanding	$ 5,000,000
Common stock, $2.50 par value; 4,000,000 shares authorized; 3,100,000	
shares issued	7,750,000 [3]
Additional paid-in capital	15,625,000 [4]
Retained earnings	17,400,000
	45,775,000
Less common stock in treasury, 100,000 shares at cost	500,000
Total stockholders' equity	$45,275,000

c.

Trask Corp.
COMPUTATION OF BOOK VALUE
PER SHARE OF COMMON STOCK
December 31, 1999

Total stockholders' equity	$45,275,000
Deduct allocation to preferred stock	5,000,000
Allocation to common stock	$40,275,000
Divided by number of common shares outstanding [3,400,000 – 100,000]	÷ 3,300,000
Book value per share of common stock	$12.20

Explanation of Amounts

[1]	Preferred stock dividend		
		Par value of outstanding preferred shares	$ 5,000,000
		Multiplied by dividend rate	x .06
		Dividends paid on preferred stock	$ 300,000
[2]	Dividend in kind on common stock		
		Fair market value of Harbor stock distributed [15,000 shares @ $60]	$ 900,000
[3]	Number of common shares issued and outstanding		
		Number of common shares issued, 12/31/98	1,575,000
		Less: common shares retired	(25,000)
		Number of common shares before stock split	1,550,000
		Two-for-one stock split, 10/27/99	x 2
		Number of common shares after stock split	3,100,000
		Less: common shares held in treasury	(100,000)
		Total number of common shares outstanding	3,000,000
		Amount of common shares issued, 12/31/98	$ 7,875,000
		Less: common shares retired at par value	(125,000)
		Number of common shares issued, 6/1/99	750,000
		Total amount of common shares issued	$ 8,500,000
[4]	Amount of additional paid-in capital		
		Amount at 12/31/98 (1,575,000 @ $10)	$15,750,000
		Less: treasury stock retired [25,000 shares @ $5 ($10 cost – $5 value)]	(125,000)
		Total amount of additional paid-in capital	$15,625,000

INVESTMENTS

A. **Concepts of Accounting and Investment Percentage**

1. **Debt securities** are covered by SFAS 115 (see outline), *Accounting for Certain Investments in Debt and Equity Securities*, which defines debt securities as "any security representing a creditor relationship with an enterprise." This includes corporate debt, convertible bonds, US Treasury and municipal securities, redeemable preferred stock, commercial paper, and other secured debt instruments. Excluded are unsecured trade receivables and consumer loans and notes receivable because they are not normally traded on organized exchanges and because of cost/benefit considerations. SFAS 115 requires that investments in debt securities be classified into three categories: trading securities, available-for-sale securities, and held-to-maturity securities. Debt securities are discussed in Section B of this module and also in Module 26, Section B.

2. **Equity securities** include ownership interests (common, preferred, and other capital stock), rights to acquire ownership interests (rights, warrants, call options), and rights to dispose of ownership interests (put options). The accounting rules for investments in the common stock of another corporation are generally based on the percentage of the voting stock obtained.

   a. Investments of less than 20% of the outstanding stock
      SFAS 115 requires that "small" investments in marketable equity securities be classified into two categories: trading securities and available-for-sale securities. Discussion of these smaller investments is presented in Section B.

   b. Investments between 20% and 50% of the outstanding stock
      At 20% or more ownership, the investor is presumed to be able to significantly influence the operating or financial decisions of the investee. Most investments in this range will result in significant influence; however, the 20% level is just a guide. FASB Interpretation 35 presents several examples in which an investor owning between 20% and 50% may not be able to exercise influence over the investee. An example of this situation is when the majority ownership is concentrated among a small group of investors who ignore the views of the minority investor. Additional examples are included in the summary of Interpretation 35, page 748. The equity method of accounting is used for investments resulting in significant influence. Investments where significant influence does exist are discussed in Section C.

   c. Investments of more than 50% of the outstanding stock
      At more than 50% ownership, the investor has control because of its majority ownership of the voting stock. Most of these investments will require the preparation of consolidated financial statements. Consolidations are discussed in Module 31.

3. Securities are originally recorded at cost, including any broker's fees, taxes, etc.; this amount is the best estimate of fair value at acquisition. Cost equals the cash paid or, in noncash transactions, the fair value of either the securities received or the resources sacrificed, whichever is more clearly determinable. The fair value of debt securities equals the present value of their future cash inflows. The present value is calculated using the current market rate of interest for similar instruments with similar risk. Any accrued interest is accounted for separately. The fair value of equity securities to be marked to market must be readily determinable from quotes obtainable from a securities exchange registered with the SEC or from the over-the-counter market. Investments which are considered to be

nontradeable or investments which do not have determinable market values should be carried at cost and adjusted only for permanent declines in value.

The exhibit below illustrates the major concepts of accounting for investments in equity securities.

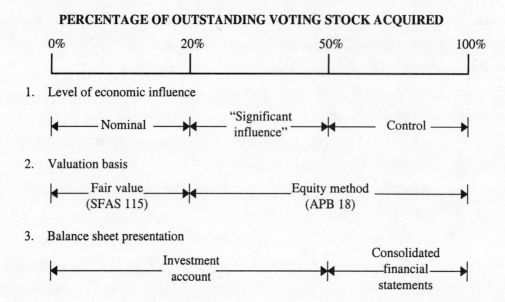

PERCENTAGE OF OUTSTANDING VOTING STOCK ACQUIRED

Several exceptions to these general concepts exist. These exceptions are noted in the following discussions.

B. **Investments in Which Significant Influence Does *Not* Exist**

Investments which do not confer significant influence over the operating or financial decisions of the investee consist of all debt securities and generally all small (less than 20%) investments in equity securities. SFAS 115 dictates that such investments be segregated into held-to-maturity securities (debt securities only), trading securities, and available-for-sale securities; the appropriateness of the classification should be reviewed at each reporting date.

1. **Held-to-Maturity Securities**

This category includes only debt securities and requires the positive intent and ability to hold the securities to maturity (not simply an absence of intent to sell). Held-to-maturity securities are carried at amortized cost (acquisition cost adjusted for amortization of premium or discount) using effective interest method; thus, unrealized holding gains and losses are not reported. However, realized gains and losses are included in earnings, as are interest income and premium and discount amortization. These securities are classified on the balance sheet as current or noncurrent on an individual basis, and on the statement of cash flows as investing activities.

In rare instances, the investor company's intent to hold a security to maturity may change without casting doubt on its intent to hold other debt securities to maturity. The circumstances must be nonrecurring and unforeseeable, such as the continuing deterioration of the issuer's credit. Premature sale of held-to-maturity securities may be considered as maturities if either of the following conditions are met:

a. The sale occurs so close to the maturity date that interest rate risk is virtually eliminated, or

b. The sale occurs after at least 85% of the principal has been collected.

Investments in held-to-maturity securities are accounted for under the cost method, which requires that they be carried at amortized cost (acquisition cost adjusted for amortization of premium or discount). Coverage of accounting for these appears under bond investments in Module 26B.

2. **Trading Securities**

Debt and equity securities purchased and held principally for the purpose of generating gains on current resale are classified as trading securities. Trading securities are accounted for according to the cost adjusted for fair value (mark-to-market) method, under which the carrying amount is adjusted at financial statement dates for subsequent changes in fair value (i.e., they are carried at market value). Trading securities are generally held by brokers, bankers, and other financial institutions which engage in active buying and selling activities. Both unrealized and realized gains and losses are included in income. However, to the extent that realized gains/losses have been previously reported as unrealized, only changes in the current period shall be reported as realized in the period of sale. Other components of earnings include dividend and interest revenue. Dividends on equity securities are recognized as income when received. However, if dividends received exceed cumulative earnings since acquisition, the excess is accounted for as a liquidating dividend. Trading securities appear on the balance sheet as current assets and on the statement of cash flows as operating activities.

Debt securities reported at fair value require special accounting treatment. The securities are to be carried at market value while interest and amortization are to be calculated using the effective interest method. Therefore, any unrealized gain or loss is actually the difference between fair value and amortized cost, that is, the adjustment equals the change in fair value during the period, plus premium amortization (decrease in book value) or minus discount amortization (increase in book value). Both the interest revenue and the unrealized holding gain/loss are included in current earnings. An example of accounting for trading debt securities is presented in the comprehensive example at the end of Section B.

3. **Available-for-Sale Securities**

Available-for-sale securities include debt and equity securities not categorized as either held-to-maturity securities or trading securities. For example, a company such as a manufacturing firm may purchase securities to make use of idle cash. These securities are not actively traded, nor will they necessarily be held to maturity. Included in earnings are realized gains and losses (which include previously unrealized holding gains and losses) and dividend and interest income. Available-for-sale securities are accounted for according to the cost adjusted for fair value (mark-to-market) method, under which the carrying amount is adjusted at financial statement dates for subsequent changes in fair value (i.e., they are carried at market value).

Unrealized gains and losses on available-for-sale debt and equity securities are calculated in the same manner as those on trading securities. These gains and losses, however, are not recognized in income of the period. Instead, the changes in fair value during a period (unrealized gains/losses) are reported as other comprehensive income (see Module 22D), and the accumulated unrealized gain/loss on marketable securities account is presented as accumulated other comprehensive income in stockholders' equity. The fair value of a debt security minus its amortized cost represents the correct unrealized gain or loss for this security in its balance of this stockholders' equity account at year end. The adjusting entry for this account at the end of the period will equal the difference between the account's balance before adjustment and the cumulative unrealized gain or loss on the debt and equity securities at the end of the period.

Available-for-sale securities are classified on the balance sheet as current or noncurrent on an individual basis based on management's intent concerning the holding period and appear on the statement of cash flows as investing activities. The following chart summarizes the three categories of marketable securities and the accounting treatment of each.

ACCOUNTING AND REPORTING OF MARKETABLE DEBT AND EQUITY SECURITIES

Category	Definition	How the security is reported on the balance sheet	How unrealized holding gains and losses are reported on the income statement*	How realized gains and losses are reported on the income statement
Trading (trading securities)	**Debt and equity** securities bought and held principally for the purpose of selling them in the near term	Reported at fair market value, and grouped with current assets on the balance sheet	Unrealized gains and losses are included in earnings in the period they occur	Realized gains and losses not already recognized as unrealized components are recognized
Available-for-sale	**Debt and equity** securities not classified as trading or held-to-maturity	Reported at fair market value and may be classified as current or noncurrent	Unrealized gains and losses for a period are excluded from earnings and reported as other comprehensive income (If decline is "other than temporary" then recognized in earnings)	Realized gains and losses are recognized (which include unrealized holding gains and losses recognized previously as unrealized)
Held-to-maturity	**Debt** securities that the organization has the positive intent and ability to hold to the maturity date	Reported at amortized cost and may be classified as current or noncurrent	Unrealized gains and losses are excluded from earnings (unless decline is "other than temporary")	Realized gains and losses are recognized in accordance with amortized cost method

Or on the statement where items of other comprehensive income are reported.

COMPREHENSIVE EXAMPLE. *On 1/01/99, when interest rates were 12%, STC Corporation purchased the following securities:*

Security description	Acquisition cost
• Shaner Enterprise 10-year, 10%, $1,000 face value bonds (STC Corp. intends to hold the bond until it matures)	$ 887
• Harmony Corporation 5-year, 14%, $5,000 face value bond (STC Corp. expects that interest rates will fall and the bond will be sold at a profit)	$5,360
• 100 shares Keswick Corporation common stock (STC anticipates that the price of the stock will rise 10%, at which time the stock will be sold)	$2,200
• 150 shares Rusell Inc. common stock (STC has no immediate plans to sell this stock)	$5,600

The Shaner bond must be classified as held-to-maturity and carried at amortized cost since management has the ability and intent to hold the investment to the maturity date. The Harmony and Keswick securities are classified as trading securities because STC intends to hold these investments for only a short period of time expressly to realize a quick profit. The Rusell, Inc. stock is classified as available-for-sale because STC has not expressed an intent to hold the stock for current resale. The Harmony, Keswick, and Rusell investments are all carried at fair market value.

At the end of 1999, the fair values of the Keswick and Rusell stock are $2,700 and $5,190, respectively. Interest rates have fallen to 10%, boosting the value of the Harmony bond to $5,634. Interest income, premium amortization, and unrealized gain on this bond are calculated as

Date	14% Cash interest	12% Effective interest	Premium amortization	Carrying value	Fair value	Unrealized gain (loss)
1/01/99				$5,360	$5,360	
12/31/99	$700	$643	$57	5,303	5,634	$331

Note that the unrealized gain ($331) equals the increase in fair value ($274) plus the premium amortization ($57).

Interest income and discount amortization must also be recorded for the Shaner bond. Both the Harmony and Shaner bonds were purchased to yield 12%. The entries required at 12/31/99 are

Interest receivable	700	
Investment in Harmony securities--held-for-trading		57
Interest income		643
Investment in Harmony securities--held-for-trading	331	
Unrealized gain on holding debt securities		
(income statement)		331
Investment in Keswick securities--held-for-trading	500	
Unrealized gain on holding equity securities		
(income statement)		
($2,700 FMV – $2,200 CV)		500
Unrealized loss on Rusell securities--available-for-sale	410	
(other comprehensive income account)		
Investment in Rusell securities--available-for-sale		
($5,600 CV – $5,190 FMV)		410
Interest receivable	100	
Investment in Shaner bond--held-to-maturity	6	
Interest income ($887 x 12%)		106

The unrealized holding gain on trading securities is a nominal account which is closed to income at 12/31/99. The unrealized loss on available-for-sale securities is closed out to the "accumulated other comprehensive income" account at year end, which is presented in the stockholders' equity section of the 12/31/99 balance sheet. **It is important to note that the increases and decreases in market value recorded above may alternatively be recorded in a separate fair value adjustment account (contra asset account).** If a fair value adjustment account is used to carry the holding gains and losses, then the fair value adjustment account and the investment account would be netted for presentation purposes. The carrying amount of the Shaner bond at 12/31/99 is $893 ($887 + $6).

Assume that in January 2000, new information comes to the attention of STC Corporation management regarding the viability of Rusell Corporation. Based upon this new information it is determined that the decline in Rusell Corporation stock is probably other than temporary. In this situation the decline in value of the available-for-sale securities must be reflected in earnings of the current period. The following entry to record the other than temporary decline would be made:

Loss on holding Rusell equity securities	410	
Unrealized loss on Rusell securities--available-		
for-sale (other comprehensive income account)		410

Any subsequent recoveries of the Rusell securities will be excluded from earnings and recorded as accumulated other comprehensive income in stockholders' equity, just as before, so that the securities will be carried at market value. However, any future declines which are also considered to be other than temporary would be recorded the same as the above entry.

Now assume that in July 2000, 75 shares of Rusell stock were sold for $30 per share. The entry to record the sale is

Cash ($30 x 75)	2,250	
Loss on sale of securities	345	
Investment in Rusell Inc.		
($34.60* x 75 shares)		2,595

* Carrying value = $5,190 ($5,600 – 410) market value on books ÷ 150 shares = $34.60.

The loss on securities equals the current carrying value of the securities on the date of the sale less the sales price. Since the Rusell securities are classified as available-for-sale, any unrealized holding gains or losses which had accumulated in the stockholders' equity account would be netted with this loss for inclusion in income. However, since the previous unrealized holding loss was other than temporary, it has already been accounted for in earnings and should **not** be reversed. No other holding gains or losses had accumulated since that time.

In September 2000, Keswick Corp. declared a 10% stock dividend. Stock dividends should not be reflected in income. The stock's current carrying value of $2,700 should be allocated to the additional shares received from the dividend. Since STC holds 100 shares, the dividend will be 10 shares, resulting in a total of 110 shares. After the dividend, the 110 shares will each have a carrying value of $24.55 ($2,700 ÷ 110) which will be adjusted to market at the end of the reporting period.

STC Corporation periodically reviews its intent to hold or actively trade its securities. At 12/31/00, when interest rates are 8%, STC decides that it will hold the Harmony bond indefinitely. Since this bond was originally classified as trading, it must be transferred to available-for-sale. Market value on this date is $5,773. The entries to record interest income and to transfer the bond are

Interest receivable	700	
Investment in Harmony securities--held-for-trading		64
Interest income		636
Investment in Harmony securities--held-for-trading	203	
Unrealized gain on holding debt securities		203
Investment in Harmony securities--available-for-sale	5,773	
Investment in Harmony securities--held-for-trading		5,773

The holding gain of $203 ($5,773 FMV 12/00 – $5,634 FMV 12/99 plus premium amortization of $64) is recognized in current earnings, and the value recorded in the available-for-sale portfolio reflects the market value of $5,773 at the transfer date. Note that from this point forward any holding gains or losses should be recognized as other comprehensive income and included in accumulated other comprehensive income in stockholders' equity in accordance with the available-for-sale classification.

Also on 12/31/00, STC sold its held-for-trading Keswick stock for $32 per share. This transaction was recorded as follows:

Cash ($32 x 110 shares)	3,520	
Investment in Keswick securities		
--held-for-trading		2,700
Gain on sale of securities		820

On 12/31/00, STC also recorded the appropriate entries for amortization of the Shaner bond ($7 discount amortization and $107 interest income) and to adjust the Rusell stock to its current fair value of $29 per share.

Finally, on 12/31/00 STC discovered that Shaner Enterprise is experiencing financial difficulty due to mismanagement, and the full amount of the bond will not be collected. This impairment would be considered other than temporary, so the investment in Shaner Enterprise bonds must be reduced to its current fair value of $500. The realized loss of $400 ($900 12/31/00 current carrying value – $500 FMV) is reported in earnings, and no write-up will be allowed if a recovery is made at a later date.

To summarize STC Corporation's marketable securities transactions for 1999 and 2000, T-accounts for each security are shown below, followed by earnings information relating to the investments.

Harmony Bond--Held-for-Trading			Harmony Bond--Available-for-Sale	
1/01/99 Acquisition $5,360			12/31/00 Transfer $5,773	
	$ 57 12/31/99 Amort.			
12/31/99 Adj. to FMV 331				
	64 12/31/00 Amort.			
12/31/00 Adj. to FMV 203				
	5,773 12/31/00 Transfer			
Bal. 12/31/00 $0			Bal. 12/31/00 $5,773	

Shaner Bond--Held-to-Maturity

Debit		Credit
1/01/99 Acquisition	$887	
12/31/99 Amort.	6	
12/31/00 Amort.	7	
		$400 12/31/00 Write-down
Bal. 12/31/00	$500	

Keswick Stock--Held-for-Trading

Debit		Credit
1/01/997 Acquisition (100 shares)	$2,200	
12/31/99 Adj. to FMV	500	
(9/00 Stock div.--10 shares)		
		$2,700 12/31/00 Sale
Bal. 12/31/00	$0	

Rusell Stock--Available-for-Sale

Debit		Credit
1/01/99 Acquisition (150 shares)	$5,600	
		$ 410 12/31/99 Adj. to FMV
		2,597 7/00 Sale (75 shares)
		420 12/31/00 Adj. to FMV
Bal. 12/31/00	$2,175	

Year	Transaction	Income/Gain	Loss	Net
1999	Harmony adj. to FMV	$331		
	Keswick adj. to FMV	500		
	Interest on Shaner bond	106		
	Interest on Harmony bond	643		
				$ 1,580
2000	Write-down of Rusell stock		$410	
	Write-down of Shaner bond		408	
	Loss on Rusell securities		345	$(1,163)
	Gain on Keswick securities	$820		
	Harmony adj. to FMV	203		
	Interest on Shaner bond	107		
	Interest on Harmony bond	636		1,766
				$ 603

4. Transfers Between Categories

SFAS 115 requires that the classification of securities be reviewed at each balance sheet date. Although a reclassification should be rare, a company may deem it necessary to transfer a security from one category to another. Such transfers are accounted for at fair value, taking into consideration any unrealized holding gains or losses. For example, when a security is transferred **from** trading securities, any recognized unrealized gain or loss as of the date of transfer should not be reversed. On the other hand, in a transfer **to** trading securities, unrealized holding gains and losses are recognized immediately. Held-to-maturity securities reclassified as available-for-sale securities must be restated to fair value; any unrealized holding gain or loss that results is reported as accumulated other comprehensive income in stockholders' equity. However, transfers **from** held-to-maturity should be rare. Unrealized holding gain or loss on securities transferred **to** held-to-maturity from available-for-sale is also reported as accumulated other comprehensive income in stockholders' equity, but this gain or loss is then amortized over the remaining life of the security as an adjustment to yield. The treatment of securities transfers is summarized in the chart below.

Securities Transferred to:

Securities Transferred from:		Held-to-maturity	Available-for-sale	Trading
	Held-to-maturity		Report unrealized G/L as accumulated other comprehensive income in SE	Recognize unrealized G/L immediately
	Available-for-sale	Report unrealized G/L as accumulated other comprehensive income in SE & amortize the gain or loss over remaining life of security		Recognize unrealized G/L immediately
	Trading	Do not reverse unrealized G/L previously recognized in income	Do not reverse unrealized G/L previously recognized in income	

5. **Income Statement Presentation**

Since held-to-maturity and available-for-sale securities are held for some length of time, these securities may become impaired at some point. If the decline in value is other than temporary, then the impaired security must be written down to fair value and the realized loss included in earnings. Any subsequent recovery would not be recognized in earnings unless realized through sale of the security. An other than temporary impairment cannot occur in the context of trading securities because holding gains and losses are recognized in current earnings without limitation.

SFAS 115 does not change the method of recognition of cash dividends or interest income on debt and equity securities. Thus, cash dividends or interest income should be included in the current period's income. The method of recognition for stock dividends is also not affected by SFAS 115; stock dividends should not be reflected in income. Additional shares received from a stock dividend should be added to the original shares and the per share value should be calculated upon the original shares' carrying value. At the end of the period the carrying value of the stock is adjusted to the fair value, and any unrealized holding gain or loss is recorded.

Additionally, SFAS 115 requires that realized and **unrealized** gains and losses on trading securities be included in the current period's earnings. Only realized gains and losses on sales of available-for-sale and held-to-maturity securities should be included in earnings. Unrealized gains (losses) on available-for-sale securities are reported as other comprehensive income in one of three ways (see Module 22D). Finally, amortization of any unrealized holding gain or loss on securities transferred to held-to-maturity from available-for-sale is included in income.

 2

C. **Investments Where Significant Influence *Does* Exist**

APB 18 requires the use of the **equity method** when accounting for investments which give the investor the ability to exercise significant influence over the operating and financial policies of the investee.

APB 18 assumes that ownership of 20% or more of the outstanding stock will result in that ability. Exceptions to the use of the equity method (i.e., the cost adjusted for fair value method) are related to an assessment of the investor's level of influence over the investee. The cost adjusted for fair value method should be used if an investment of more than 20% is judged to be temporary, if the investment is in a company operating in a foreign country which has severe restrictions on the operations of companies and on the transfer of monies to outside the country, and for other investments of more than 20% that do not result in significant influence.

The cost adjusted for fair value and equity methods differ in the treatment of the investment account and in the recognition of earnings from the investment. The cost adjusted for fair value method first records the cost of the investment in the investment account. Income is recognized for dividends distributed from income of the investee earned since the date the investor acquired the stock. Any dividends distributed by the investee which exceed earnings since the acquisition date are classified as return of capital and recorded as a reduction of the investment account. Interest income and amortization are calculated as if the effective interest method had been used. Both debt and equity securities must be adjusted for subsequent changes in market value, but the gain or loss on equity securities equals the current fair value minus the previous period's fair value on the books, while a gain or loss on debt securities equals the current fair value minus the previous period's fair value plus or minus amortization.

The equity method also begins with recording the cost of the investment in the investment account but the two methods differ from this point on. A basic concept of the equity method is the reciprocal relationship formed between the investment account on the investor's books and the book values of the net assets on the investee's books. As changes in the investee's net assets occur (e.g., earnings, dividends, etc.), the investor will recognize in the investment account the percentage of ownership share of those changes.

Another aspect of the equity method is the computation and eventual amortization of the difference between the cost of the investment and the book value of the acquired asset share at the investment date. The abundance of advanced accounting texts currently in print use an assortment of terms to describe the characteristics of this concept. For purposes of uniformity, the following boldfaced terms shall be used throughout this module.

Differential: The difference between the cost of the investment and the underlying book value of the net assets of the investee. This difference can be either positive or negative, as follows:

1. **Excess of Cost Over Book Value**, which is generally attributable to
   a. **Excess of fair value over book value**, when the fair values of the investee's assets are greater than their book values, and
   b. **Goodwill**, when the investee has high earnings potential for which the investor has paid more than the fair values of the other net assets

2. **Excess of Book Value Over Cost**, which is generally attributable to
   a. **Excess of book value over fair value**, when the book values of the net assets of the investee are greater than their fair values, and
   b. **Excess of fair value over cost**, when the cost of the investment is less than even the fair values of the investee's net assets. Some authors term this "negative goodwill."

The differential will be amortized to the investment account. Thus, similar to the amortization of bond investment premium or discount, the original investment in stock will approach the underlying book values of the investee's net assets held at the investment date.

EXAMPLE: A Company purchased 20 shares of B Company's 100 shares of common stock outstanding for $25,000. The book value of B's total net worth (i.e., stockholders' equity) at the date of the investment was $120,000. Any excess of cost over book value is due to goodwill to be amortized over 40 years.

Investment cost		*$25,000*
Book value of B Company	*$120,000*	
Percentage owned	*20%*	
Investor's share		*24,000*
Excess of cost over book value (due to goodwill)		*$ 1,000*

Amortization over 40 years
$1,000 ÷ 40 years = $25

An illustration of accounting just for the amortization is shown below. Other adjustments to the investment account which are normally required are discussed later in this module.

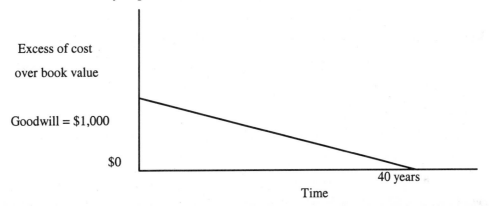

Under the equity method, the Income from Investment account is a parallel income statement account to the Investment in Stock balance sheet account. These two accounts should include all the income recognition and amortization resulting from the investment. Note that under the equity method, dividends received from the investee are a reduction in the balance sheet account and are **not** part of the Income From Investment account.

Alternative levels of recording the results of intercompany transactions and amortization in both the investment and investment income accounts are used in accounting practice. The alternatives are presented below.

1. ***Cost adjusted for fair value method*--**No intercompany transactions or amortization are recognized in either the investment account or investment income account under this method.
2. ***"Partial" equity*--**Includes recognition of percentage share of income or loss, dividends, and any changes in the investment percentage. This method is often used for investments that will be consolidated. Thus, amortization and other adjustments are made on the work sheets, not in the investment account.
3. ***"Full" equity*--**In addition to the factors above, this level includes the amortization of the differential between the investment cost and book value of the investment. This level also recognizes the effects of any intercompany transactions (e.g., inventory, fixed assets, and bonds) between the investor and investee corporations. APB 18 requires that all unconsolidated investments be reported in the financial statements using the "full" equity method.

*EXTENDED EXAMPLE: Assume the same facts for A Company and B Company as stated above. In addition, B Company earned $10,000 income for the year and paid $6,000 in dividends. There were no intercompany transactions. If A Company does **not** have significant influence over B Company, the investment would be accounted for by the cost adjusted for fair value method. If A Company can significantly influence B Company, the equity method is used to account for and report the investment. The appropriate entries are*

	Cost adjusted for fair value method		*Equity method*	
1.	To record purchase of 20% interest			
	Investment in stock of B 25,000		Investment in stock of B 25,000	
	Cash 25,000		Cash 25,000	
2.	To record percentage share of investee's reported income			
	No entry		Investment in stock of B 2,000	
			Income from investment 2,000	
			(20% x $10,000)	
3.	To record percentage share of dividend received as distribution of income			
	Cash 1,200		Cash 1,200	
	Dividend income from		Investment in stock of B 1,200	
	investment 1,200			
	(20% x $6,000)			
4.	To record amortization of goodwill in accordance with APB 18 using maximum period allowed by APB 17			
	No entry		Income from investment 25	
			Investment in stock of B 25	

The differences in the account balances under the equity method vs. the cost adjusted for fair value method reflect the different income recognition processes and underlying asset valuation concepts of the two methods. The investment account balance under the cost adjusted for fair value method remains at the investment cost of $25,000 (although subsequent changes in fair value would require that the investment account be adjusted to market value), while under the equity method, the investment balance increases to $25,775. The $775 difference is the investor's share of the increase in the investee's undistributed earnings less the investor's amortization of the differential (excess of cost over the book value of the investment).

The amount of the investment income to be recognized by the investor also depends upon the length of time during the year the investment is owned. For example, assume that A Company acquired the 20% interest on July 1, 1999, and B Company earned $10,000 of income ratably over the period from January 1 to December 31, 1999. The entry to record A Company's percentage share of B Company's income for the period of July 1 to December 31, 1999, would be

Cost adjusted for fair value method	*Equity method*	
No entry	Investment in stock of B 1,000	
	Income from investment 1,000	
	(20% x $10,000 x 6/12)	

The receipt of the $1,200 dividends after the acquisition date would require additional analysis since the $1,200 dividend received is greater than the investor's share of the investee's income ($1,000) since acquisition. The difference of $200 ($1,200 – $1,000) is a return of capital under the cost adjusted for fair value method, and is recorded as follows:

Cost adjusted for fair value method			_Equity method_		
Cash	1,200		Cash		1,200
Dividend income			Investment in stock		
from investment		1,000	of B		1,200
Investment in stock					
of B		200			

The amortization of goodwill will also be prorated to the time period the investment was held. The entry to record the partial year's amortization since the date of acquisition is:

Cost adjusted for fair value method	_Equity method_	
	Income from investment	12.50
No entry	Investment in stock of B	12.50
	($1,000 ÷ 40 years = $25.00)	
	($25 x 6/12 = $12.50)	

When an investor changes from the cost adjusted for fair value to the equity method, the investment account must be adjusted retroactively and prior years' income and retained earnings must be retroactively restated. A change to the equity method would be made if an investor made additional purchases of stock and, for the first time, is able to exercise significant influence over the operating and financial decisions of the investee. Remember that APB 18 states that investments of 20% or more of the investee's outstanding stock carry the "presumption" that the investor has the ability to exercise significant influence. Therefore, in most cases, when an investment of less than 20% increases to more than 20%, the investor will retroactively change from the cost adjusted for fair value method to the equity method.

The retroactive change to the equity method requires a prior period adjustment for the difference in the investment account and retained earnings account between the amounts that were recognized in prior periods under the cost adjusted for fair value method and the amounts that would have been recognized if the equity method had been used. In the full-year investment example on page 544 where A Company had a $25,000 balance in its Investment in B account under the cost adjusted for fair value method and $25,775 under the equity method, if A changed from the cost to the equity method because of its increased influence over B, the change entry would be

Investment in B Company	775	
Retained earnings		775
($775 = $2,000 – $1,200 – $25)		

In addition, any balance in the Unrealized holding gain or loss account must be reversed. Assume that the fair value of the B Company stock had increased from $25,000 to $27,000 as of the end of the year of acquisition. The investment account would have been debited for $2,000 and the Unrealized gain on MES account credited for $2,000 to bring the carrying value of the stock up to its market value. Upon retroactive change to the equity method, the following reversing entry would be made:

Unrealized gain on MES	2,000	
Investment in stock of B		2,000

If the change is made at any time point other than the beginning of the fiscal period, the change entry would also include an adjustment to the period's Income from investment account to record the difference between the cost adjusted for fair value and equity methods handling of the investor's share of the investee's income for the current period.

When an investor discontinues using the equity method because of an inability to influence the investee's financial and operating policies, no retroactive restatement is allowed. An example of this would be a disposal of stock resulting in a decrease in the percentage of stock owned from more than 20% to less than 20%. The earnings or losses that relate to the shares retained by the investor that were previously recognized by the investor should remain as a part of the carrying amount. However, if dividends received by the investor in subsequent periods exceed the investor's share of the investee's earnings for such periods, the excess should be accounted for as a return of capital and recorded as a reduction in the investment carrying amount.

A T-account is used to exhibit the major changes in the Investment in stock account under the equity method.

Investment in Stock	
Original cost of investment	Percentage share of investee's losses since acquisition
Percentage share of investee's income since acquisition	Percentage share of dividends received
Amortization of excess of book value over cost	Amortization of excess of cost over book value
Increase above "significant influence" ownership--retroactive adjustment for change to equity	Disposal or sales of investment in stock

In addition to the above, several adjustments may be added if the "full equity" method is used. This method eliminates the effects of intercompany profits from transactions such as sales of inventory between the investor and investee corporations. This method is rarely required on the exam but candidates should briefly review these additions in association with the discussion of the elimination entries required for consolidated working papers presented later in this module.

Investment in Stock (continued)	
Realized portion of intercompany profit from last period confirmed this period	Elimination of unrealized portion of intercompany profit transactions from current period

D. **Equity Method and Deferred Income Taxes**

Recognition of deferred taxes may be required when the equity method is used. The difference between the income recognized using the equity method and the dividends received from the investee represents a temporary difference for which interperiod allocation is necessary. Note that companies are allowed to exclude 80% of the dividend income from domestic investees. If an investor owns 80% or more of the investee's stock, the dividend exclusion is increased to 100% (i.e., no taxes are due on investee dividend distributions). The dividend exclusion (dividends received deduction) is a permanent difference.

A discussion of deferred income taxes arising from equity method investments and several examples are provided in Module 27, Deferred Taxes.

E. **Stock Dividends and Splits**

Stock dividends and stock splits are not recorded as income. The recipient continues to own the same proportion of the investee as before the stock split or dividend. The investor should make a memo entry to record the receipt of the additional shares and recompute the per share cost of the stock.

F. Stock Rights

Investors in common stock occasionally receive stock rights to purchase additional common stock below the existing market price. The investee company has probably issued the stock rights to satisfy the investor's preemptive right to maintain an existing level of ownership of the investee. It is possible to waive these preemptive rights in some jurisdictions.

Rights are issued below the existing market price to encourage the exercise of the rights (i.e., the investor's use thereof resulting in acquisitions of additional shares of stock). The rights represent a possible dilution of investor ownership and should be recorded by allocating the cost of the stock between the market value of the rights and the market value of the stock. This is accomplished by multiplying the following ratio by the cost basis of the stock:

$$\frac{\text{Market value of right}}{\text{Market value of right} + \text{Market value of stock}}$$

The following entry is made to record the receipt of the rights:

Investment in stock rights	xx	
Investment in common stock		xx

The rights can be sold or exercised. The entry for exercise is

Investment in common stock	xx	
Investment in stock rights		xx
Cash		xx

If the stock rights lapse

Loss on expiration of stock rights	xx	
Investment in stock rights		xx

EXAMPLE: *A Company acquired 1,000 shares of common stock in B Company for $12,000. A Company subsequently received two stock rights for every share owned in B Company. Four rights and $12 are required to purchase one new share of common stock. At the date of issuance the market value of the stock rights and the common stock is $5 and $20, respectively. The entry to record the receipt of the rights is as follows:*

Investment in stock rights	4,000	
Investment in common stock		4,000

The $4,000 above was computed as follows:

Total market value of rights	2,000 rights x $5 =	$10,000
Total market value of shares	1,000 shares x $20 =	$20,000
Combined market value		$30,000

Cost allocated to stock rights $\dfrac{\$10,000}{\$30,000}$ x $12,000 = $ 4,000

Cost allocated to common stock $\dfrac{\$20,000}{\$30,000}$ x $12,000 = $ 8,000

Note that $2 ($4,000 ÷ 2,000 rights) of cost is assigned to each stock right and $8 ($8,000 ÷ 1,000 shares) of cost to each share of stock.

If A uses 800 rights to purchase 200 additional shares of stock, the following entry would be made to record the transaction.

Investment in common stock	4,000	
Investment in stock rights		1,600*
Cash		2,400**

* *(800 rights x $2/right)*
** *(200 shares x $12/share)*

If 1,000 stock rights are sold outright for $5 per right, the following entry would be made to record the transaction.

Cash	5,000*	
Investment in stock rights		2,000**
Gain on sale of investments		3,000

* *(1,000 rights x $5/right)*
** *(1,000 rights x $2/right)*

If the 200 remaining stock rights are permitted to expire, the following entry would be made:

Loss on expiration of stock rights	400*	
Investment in stock rights		400*

* *(200 rights x $2/right)*

The journal entries above can be summarized as follows:

	Investment in Common Stock				Investment in Stock Rights	
Purchase, 1,000 shares @ $12	$12,000	$ 4,000	← Cost allocated → to stock rights	$ 4,000		
					$ 1,600	Exercise of 800 rights
Purchase, 200 shares by exercise of rights	$ 4,000				$ 2,000	Sale of 1,000 rights
					$ 400	Expiration of 200 rights
	$12,000			-0-		

G. Cash Surrender Value of Life Insurance

The cash surrender value of life insurance policies represents a noncurrent investment when the company is the beneficiary (rather than insured employees). The entry to record insurance premiums that increase cash surrender value is

Insurance expense	(plug)	
Cash surrender value	(increase in CSV)	
Cash		(total premium)

Cash surrender value remains a noncurrent asset unless the company plans to cash in the policy within the next period.

During the first few years of a policy, no cash surrender value may attach to the policy. During this period, the entire insurance premium would be expense. In addition, any dividends received from the life insurance policy are **not** recorded as revenue but instead are offset against insurance expense.

MULTIPLE-CHOICE QUESTIONS (1-49)

1. On April 1, 1999, Saxe, Inc. purchased $200,000 face value, 9% US Treasury Notes for $198,500, including accrued interest of $4,500. The notes mature July 1, 2000, and pay interest semiannually on January 1 and July 1. Saxe uses the straight-line method of amortization and intends to hold the notes to maturity. In its October 31, 1999 balance sheet, the carrying amount of this investment should be

a. $194,000
b. $196,800
c. $197,200
d. $199,000

2. Kale Co. purchased bonds at a discount on the open market as an investment and intends to hold these bonds to maturity. Kale should account for these bonds at

a. Cost.
b. Amortized cost.
c. Fair value.
d. Lower of cost or market.

3. For a marketable debt securities portfolio classified as held-to-maturity, which of the following amounts should be included in the period's net income?

I. Unrealized temporary losses during the period.
II. Realized gains during the period.
III. Changes in the valuation allowance during the period.

a. III only.
b. II only.
c. I and II.
d. I, II, and III.

Items 4 and 5 are based on the following:

The following data pertains to Tyne Co.'s investments in marketable equity securities:

		Market value	
	Cost	12/31/99	12/31/98
Trading	$150,000	$155,000	$100,000
Available-for-sale	150,000	130,000	120,000

4. What amount should Tyne report as unrealized holding gain in its 1999 income statement?

a. $50,000
b. $55,000
c. $60,000
d. $65,000

5. What amount should Tyne report as net unrealized loss on marketable equity securities at December 31, 1999, in accumulated other comprehensive income in stockholders' equity?

a. $0
b. $10,000
c. $15,000
d. $20,000

6. Reed Insurance Co. began operations on January 1, 1999. The following information pertains to Reed's December 31, 1999 portfolio of marketable equity securities:

	Trading securities	Available-for-sale securities
Aggregate cost	$360,000	$550,000
Aggregate market value	320,000	450,000
Aggregate lower of cost or market value applied to each security in the portfolio	304,000	420,000

If the market declines are judged to be temporary, what amounts should Reed report as a loss on these securities in its December 31, 1997 income statement?

	Trading securities	Available-for-sale securities
a.	$40,000	$0
b.	$0	$100,000
c.	$40,000	$100,000
d.	$56,000	$130,000

7. Information regarding Stone Co.'s portfolio of available-for-sale securities is as follows:

Aggregate cost as of 12/31/99	$170,000
Unrealized gains as of 12/31/99	4,000
Unrealized losses as of 12/31/99	26,000
Net realized gains during 1999	30,000

At December 31, 1998, Stone reported an unrealized loss of $1,500 in other comprehensive income to reduce these securities to market. Under the accumulated other comprehensive income in stockholders' equity section of its December 31, 1999 balance sheet, what amount should Stone report?

a. $26,000
b. $22,000
c. $20,500
d. $0

8. Data regarding Ball Corp.'s available-for-sale securities follow:

	Cost	Market value
December 31, 1998	$150,000	$130,000
December 31, 1999	150,000	160,000

Differences between cost and market values are considered temporary. Ball's 1999 other comprehensive income would be

a. $30,000
b. $20,000
c. $10,000
d. $0

9. During 1999, Rex Company purchased marketable equity securities as a short-term investment. These securities are classified as available-for-sale. The cost and market value at December 31, 1999, were as follows:

Security	Cost	Market value
A -- 100 shares	$ 2,800	$ 3,400
B -- 1,000 shares	17,000	15,300
C -- 2,000 shares	31,500	29,500
	$51,300	$48,200

Rex sold 1,000 shares of Company B stock on January 31, 2000, for $15 per share, incurring $1,500 in brokerage commission and taxes. On the sale, Rex should report a realized loss of

- a. $ 300
- b. $1,800
- c. $2,000
- d. $3,500

10. Cap Corp. reported accrued investment interest receivable of $38,000 and $46,500 at January 1 and December 31, 1999, respectively. During 1999, cash collections from the investments included the following:

| Capital gains distributions | $145,000 |
| Interest | 152,000 |

What amount should Cap report as interest revenue from investments for 1999?

- a. $160,500
- b. $153,500
- c. $152,000
- d. $143,500

11. Nola has a portfolio of marketable equity securities which it does not intend to sell in the near term. How should Nola classify these securities, and how should it report unrealized gains and losses from these securities?

	Classify as	*Report as a*
a.	Trading securities	Component of income from continuing operations
b.	Available-for-sale securities	Separate component of other comprehensive income
c.	Trading securities	Separate component of other comprehensive income
d.	Available-for-sale securities	Component of income from continuing operations

12. On December 29, 1999, BJ Co. sold a marketable equity security that had been purchased on January 4, 1998. BJ owned no other marketable equity security. An unrealized loss was reported in 1996 as other comprehensive income. A realized gain was reported in the 1999 income statement. Was the marketable equity security classified as available-for-sale and did its 1998 market price decline exceed its 1999 market price recovery?

	Available-for-sale	*1998 market price decline exceeded 1999 market price recovery*
a.	Yes	Yes
b.	Yes	No
c.	No	Yes
d.	No	No

13. On January 10, 1999, Box, Inc. purchased marketable equity securities of Knox, Inc. and Scot, Inc., neither of which Box could significantly influence. Box classified both securities as available-for-sale. At December 31, 1999, the cost of each investment was greater than its fair market value. The loss on the Knox investment was considered other-than-temporary and that on Scot was considered tem-

porary. How should Box report the effects of these investing activities in its 1999 income statement?

- I. Excess of cost of Knox stock over its market value.
- II. Excess of cost of Scot stock over its market value.

- a. An unrealized loss equal to I plus II.
- b. An unrealized loss equal to I only.
- c. A realized loss equal to I only.
- d. No income statement effect.

14. On both December 31, 1998, and December 31, 1999, Kopp Co.'s only marketable equity security had the same market value, which was below cost. Kopp considered the decline in value to be temporary in 1998 but other than temporary in 1999. At the end of both years the security was classified as a noncurrent asset. Kopp considers the investment to be available-for-sale. What should be the effects of the determination that the decline was other than temporary on Kopp's 1999 net noncurrent assets and net income?

- a. No effect on both net noncurrent assets and net income.
- b. No effect on net noncurrent assets and decrease in net income.
- c. Decrease in net noncurrent assets and **no** effect on net income.
- d. Decrease in both net noncurrent assets and net income.

15. For the last 10 years, Woody Co. has owned cumulative preferred stock issued by Hadley, Inc. During 1999, Hadley declared and paid both the 1999 dividend and the 1998 dividend in arrears. How should Woody report the 1998 dividend in arrears that was received in 1999?

- a. As a reduction in cumulative preferred dividends receivable.
- b. As a retroactive change of the prior period financial statements.
- c. Include, net of income taxes, after 1999 income from continuing operations.
- d. Include in 1999 income from continuing operations.

Items 16 and 17 are based on the following:

Deed Co. owns 2% of Beck Cosmetic Retailers. A property dividend by Beck consisted of merchandise with a fair value lower than the listed retail price. Deed in turn gave the merchandise to its employees as a holiday bonus.

16. How should Deed report the receipt and distribution of the merchandise in its income statement?

- a. At fair value for both dividend revenue and employee compensation expense.
- b. At listed retail price for both dividend revenue and employee compensation expense.
- c. At fair value for dividend revenue and listed retail price for employee compensation expense.
- d. By disclosure only.

17. How should Deed report the receipt and distribution of the merchandise in its statement of cash flows?

- a. As both an inflow and outflow for operating activities.

b.   As both an inflow and outflow for investing activities.

c.   As an inflow for investing activities and outflow for operating activities.

d.   As a noncash activity.

18. Pal Corp.'s 1999 dividend revenue included only part of the dividends received from its Ima Corp. investment. Pal Corp. has an investment in Ima Corp. which it intends to hold indefinitely. The balance of the dividend reduced Pal's carrying amount for its Ima investment. This reflects the fact that Pal accounts for its Ima investment

a.   As an available-for-sale investment, and only a portion of Ima's 1999 dividends represent earnings after Pal's acquisition.

b.   As an available-for-sale investment and its carrying amount exceeded the proportionate share of Ima's market value.

c.   As an equity investment, and Ima incurred a loss in 1999.

d.   As an equity investment, and its carrying amount exceeded the proportionate share of Ima's market value.

19. In its financial statements, Pare, Inc. uses the cost method of accounting for its 15% ownership of Sabe Co. At December 31, 1999, Pare has a receivable from Sabe. How should the receivable be reported in Pare's December 31, 1999 balance sheet?

a.   The total receivable should be reported separately.

b.   The total receivable should be included as part of the investment in Sabe, without separate disclosure.

c.   85% of the receivable should be reported separately, with the balance offset against Sabe's payable to Pare.

d.   The total receivable should be offset against Sabe's payable to Pare, without separate disclosure.

Items 20 and 21 are based on the following:

Sun Corp. had investments in marketable debt securities costing $650,000 which were classified as available-for-sale. On June 30, 1999, Sun decided to hold the investments to maturity and accordingly reclassified them from the held-to-maturity category on that date. The investments' market value was $575,000 at December 31, 1998, $530,000 at June 30, 1999, and $490,000 at December 31, 1999.

20. What amount of loss from investments should Sun report in its 1999 income statement?

a. $ 45,000
b. $ 85,000
c. $120,000
d. $0

21. What amount should Sun report as net unrealized loss on marketable debt securities in its 1999 statement of stockholders' equity?

a. $ 40,000
b. $ 45,000
c. $160,000
d. $120,000

22. A marketable debt security is transferred from available-for-sale to held-to-maturity securities. At the transfer date, the security's carrying amount exceeds its market value. What amount is used at the transfer date to record the security in the held-to-maturity portfolio?

a.   Market value, regardless of whether the decline in market value below cost is considered permanent or temporary.

b.   Market value, only if the decline in market value below cost is considered permanent.

c.   Cost, if the decline in market value below cost is considered temporary.

d.   Cost, regardless of whether the decline in market value below cost is considered permanent or temporary.

Items 23 through 25 are based on the following:

Grant, Inc. acquired 30% of South Co.'s voting stock for $200,000 on January 2, 1998. Grant's 30% interest in South gave Grant the ability to exercise significant influence over South's operating and financial policies. During 1998, South earned $80,000 and paid dividends of $50,000. South reported earnings of $100,000 for the 6 months ended June 30, 1999, and $200,000 for the year ended December 31, 1999. On July 1, 1999, Grant sold half of its stock in South for $150,000 cash. South paid dividends of $60,000 on October 1, 1999.

23. Before income taxes, what amount should Grant include in its 1998 income statement as a result of the investment?

a. $15,000
b. $24,000
c. $50,000
d. $80,000

24. In Grant's December 31, 1998 balance sheet, what should be the carrying amount of this investment?

a. $200,000
b. $209,000
c. $224,000
d. $230,000

25. In its 1999 income statement, what amount should Grant report as gain from the sale of half of its investment?

a. $24,500
b. $30,500
c. $35,000
d. $45,500

26. Moss Corp. owns 20% of Dubro Corp.'s preferred stock and 80% of its common stock. Dubro's stock outstanding at December 31, 1999, is as follows:

10% cumulative preferred stock	$100,000
Common stock	700,000

Dubro reported net income of $60,000 for the year ended December 31, 1999. What amount should Moss record as equity in earnings of Dubro for the year ended December 31, 1999?

a. $42,000
b. $48,000

c. $48,400
d. $50,000

27. Sage, Inc. bought 40% of Adams Corp.'s outstanding common stock on January 2, 1999, for $400,000. The carrying amount of Adams' net assets at the purchase date totaled $900,000. Fair values and carrying amounts were the same for all items except for plant and inventory, for which fair values exceeded their carrying amounts by $90,000 and $10,000, respectively. The plant has an 18-year life. All inventory was sold during 1999. Goodwill, if any, is to be amortized over 40 years. During 1999, Adams reported net income of $120,000 and paid a $20,000 cash dividend. What amount should Sage report in its income statement from its investment in Adams for the year ended December 31, 1999?

a. $48,000
b. $42,000
c. $36,000
d. $32,000

28. Pear Co.'s income statement for the year ended December 31, 1999, as prepared by Pear's controller, reported income before taxes of $125,000. The auditor questioned the following amounts that had been included in income before taxes:

Unrealized gain on available-for-sale investment	$40,000
Equity in earnings of Cinn Co.	20,000
Dividends received from Cinn	8,000
Adjustments to profits of prior years for arithmetical errors in depreciation	(35,000)

Pear owns 40% of Cinn's common stock. Pear's December 31, 1999 income statement should report income before taxes of

a. $ 85,000
b. $117,000
c. $112,000
d. $152,000

29. On January 2, 1999, Saxe Company purchased 20% of Lex Corporation's common stock for $150,000. Saxe Corporation intends to hold the stock indefinitely. This investment did not give Saxe the ability to exercise significant influence over Lex. During 1999 Lex reported net income of $175,000 and paid cash dividends of $100,000 on its common stock. There was no change in the market value of the common stock during the year. The balance in Saxe's investment in Lex Corporation account at December 31, 1999 should be

a. $130,000
b. $150,000
c. $165,000
d. $185,000

30. On January 2, 1999, Well Co. purchased 10% of Rea, Inc.'s outstanding common shares for $400,000. Well is the largest single shareholder in Rea, and Well's officers are a majority on Rea's board of directors. Rea reported net income of $500,000 for 1999, and paid dividends of $150,000. In its December 31, 1999 balance sheet, what amount should Well report as investment in Rea?

a. $450,000
b. $435,000
c. $400,000
d. $385,000

31. On January 2, 1999, Kean Co. purchased a 30% interest in Pod Co. for $250,000. On this date, Pod's stockholders' equity was $500,000. The carrying amounts of Pod's identifiable net assets approximated their fair values, except for land whose fair value exceeded its carrying amount by $200,000. Pod reported net income of $100,000 for 1999, and paid no dividends. Kean accounts for this investment using the equity method and amortizes goodwill over 10 years. In its December 31, 1999 balance sheet, what amount should Kean report as investment in subsidiary?

a. $210,000
b. $220,000
c. $270,000
d. $276,000

32. On January 1, 1999, Mega Corp. acquired 10% of the outstanding voting stock of Penny, Inc. On January 2, 2000, Mega gained the ability to exercise significant influence over financial and operating control of Penny by acquiring an additional 20% of Penny's outstanding stock. The two purchases were made at prices proportionate to the value assigned to Penny's net assets, which equaled their carrying amounts. For the years ended December 31, 1999 and 2000, Penny reported the following:

	1999	2000
Dividends paid	$200,000	$300,000
Net income	600,000	650,000

In 2000, what amounts should Mega report as current year investment income and as an adjustment, before income taxes, to 1999 investment income?

	2000 investment income	Adjustment to 1999 investment income
a.	$195,000	$160,000
b.	$195,000	$100,000
c.	$195,000	$ 40,000
d.	$105,000	$ 40,000

33. Pare, Inc. purchased 10% of Tot Co.'s 100,000 outstanding shares of common stock on January 2, 1999, for $50,000. On December 31, 1999, Pare purchased an additional 20,000 shares of Tot for $150,000. There was no goodwill as a result of either acquisition, and Tot had not issued any additional stock during 1999. Tot reported earnings of $300,000 for 1999. What amount should Pare report in its December 31, 1999 balance sheet as investment in Tot?

a. $170,000
b. $200,000
c. $230,000
d. $290,000

34. When the equity method is used to account for investments in common stock, which of the following affects the investor's reported investment income?

	Goodwill amortization related to purchase	Cash dividends from investee
a.	Yes	Yes
b.	No	Yes
c.	No	No
d.	Yes	No

35. Park Co. uses the equity method to account for its January 1, 1999 purchase of Tun Inc.'s common stock. On January 1, 1999, the fair values of Tun's FIFO inventory and land exceeded their carrying amounts. How do these excesses of fair values over carrying amounts affect Park's reported equity in Tun's 1999 earnings?

	Inventory excess	Land excess
a.	Decrease	Decrease
b.	Decrease	No effect
c.	Increase	Increase
d.	Increase	No effect

36. An investor in common stock received dividends in excess of the investor's share of investee's earnings subsequent to the date of the investment. How will the investor's investment account be affected by those dividends for each of the following investments?

	Available-for-sale securities	Equity method investment
a.	No effect	No effect
b.	Decrease	No effect
c.	No effect	Decrease
d.	Decrease	Decrease

37. Peel Co. received a cash dividend from a common stock investment. Should Peel report an increase in the investment account if it has classified the stock as available-for-sale or uses the equity method of accounting?

	Available-for-sale	Equity
a.	No	No
b.	Yes	Yes
c.	Yes	No
d.	No	Yes

38. On January 1, 1999, Point, Inc. purchased 10% of Iona Co.'s common stock. Point purchased additional shares bringing its ownership up to 40% of Iona's common stock outstanding on August 1, 1999. During October 1999, Iona declared and paid a cash dividend on all of its outstanding common stock. How much income from the Iona investment should Point's 1999 income statement report?

- a. 10% of Iona's income for January 1 to July 31, 1999, plus 40% of Iona's income for August 1 to December 31, 1999.
- b. 40% of Iona's income for August 1 to December 31, 1999 only.
- c. 40% of Iona's 1999 income.
- d. Amount equal to dividends received from Iona.

39. In its financial statements, Pulham Corp. uses the equity method of accounting for its 30% ownership of Angles Corp. At December 31, 1999, Pulham has a receivable from Angles. How should the receivable be reported in Pulham's 1999 financial statements?

- a. None of the receivable should be reported, but the entire receivable should be offset against Angles' payable to Pulham.
- b. 70% of the receivable should be separately reported, with the balance offset against 30% of Angles' payable to Pulham.
- c. The total receivable should be disclosed separately.
- d. The total receivable should be included as part of the investment in Angles, without separate disclosure.

 3

40. Wood Co. owns 2,000 shares of Arlo, Inc.'s 20,000 shares of $100 par, 6% cumulative, nonparticipating preferred stock and 1,000 shares (2%) of Arlo's common stock. During 1999, Arlo declared and paid dividends of $240,000 on preferred stock. No dividends had been declared or paid during 1998. In addition, Wood received a 5% common stock dividend from Arlo when the quoted market price of Arlo's common stock was $10 per share. What amount should Wood report as dividend income in its 1999 income statement?

- a. $12,000
- b. $12,500
- c. $24,000
- d. $24,500

41. Stock dividends on common stock should be recorded at their fair market value by the investor when the related investment is accounted for under which of the following methods?

	Cost	Equity
a.	Yes	Yes
b.	Yes	No
c.	No	Yes
d.	No	No

42. On March 4, 1999, Evan Co. purchased 1,000 shares of LVC common stock at $80 per share. On September 26, 1999, Evan received 1,000 stock rights to purchase an additional 1,000 shares at $90 per share. The stock rights had an expiration date of February 1, 2000. On September 30, 1999, LVC's common stock had a market value, ex-rights, of $95 per share and the stock rights had a market value of $5 each. What amount should Evan report on its September 30, 1999 balance sheet as the cost of its investment in stock rights?

- a. $ 4,000
- b. $ 5,000
- c. $10,000
- d. $15,000

43. On January 3, 1997, Falk Co. purchased 500 shares of Milo Corp. common stock for $36,000. On December 2, 1999, Falk received 500 stock rights from Milo. Each right entitles the holder to acquire one share of stock for $85. The market price of Milo's stock was $100 a share immediately before the rights were issued, and $90 a share immediately after the rights were issued. Falk sold its rights on December 3, 1999, for $10 a right. Falk's gain from the sale of the rights is

a. $0
b. $1,000
c. $1,400
d. $5,000

44. In 1994, Chain, Inc. purchased a $1,000,000 life insurance policy on its president, of which Chain is the beneficiary. Information regarding the policy for the year ended December 31, 1999, follows:

Cash surrender value, 1/1/99	$ 87,000
Cash surrender value, 12/31/99	108,000
Annual advance premium paid 1/1/99	40,000

During 1999, dividends of $6,000 were applied to increase the cash surrender value of the policy. What amount should Chain report as life insurance expense for 1999?
a. $40,000
b. $25,000
c. $19,000
d. $13,000

45. An increase in the cash surrender value of a life insurance policy owned by a company would be recorded by
a. Decreasing annual insurance expense.
b. Increasing investment income.
c. Recording a memorandum entry only.
d. Decreasing a deferred charge.

46. Upon the death of an officer, Jung Co. received the proceeds of a life insurance policy held by Jung on the officer. The proceeds were not taxable. The policy's cash surrender value had been recorded on Jung's books at the time of payment. What amount of revenue should Jung report in its statements?
a. Proceeds received.
b. Proceeds received less cash surrender value.
c. Proceeds received plus cash surrender value.
d. None.

Items 47 through 49 are based on the following data:

Lake Corporation's accounting records showed the following investments at January 1, 1999:

Common stock:	
Kar Corp. (1,000 shares)	$ 10,000
Aub Corp. (5,000 shares)	100,000
Real estate:	
Parking lot (leased to Day Co.)	300,000
Other:	
Trademark (at cost, less accumulated amortization)	25,000
Total investments	$435,000

Lake owns 1% of Kar and 30% of Aub. Lake's directors constitute a majority of Aub's directors. The Day lease, which commenced on January 1, 1997, is for 10 years, at an annual rental of $48,000. In addition, on January 1, 1997, Day paid a nonrefundable deposit of $50,000, as well as a security deposit of $8,000 to be refunded upon expiration of the lease. The trademark was licensed to Barr Co. for royalties of 10% of sales of the trademarked items. Royalties are payable semiannually on March 1 (for sales in July through December of the prior year), and on September 1 (for sales in January through June of the same year).

During the year ended December 31, 1999, Lake received cash dividends of $1,000 from Kar, and $15,000 from Aub, whose 1999 net incomes were $75,000 and $150,000, respectively. Lake also received $48,000 rent from Day in 1999 and the following royalties from Barr:

	March 1	*September 1*
1998	$3,000	$5,000
1999	4,000	7,000

Barr estimated that sales of the trademarked items would total $20,000 for the last half of 1999.

47. In Lake's 1999 income statement, how much should be reported for dividend revenue?
a. $16,000
b. $ 2,400
c. $ 1,000
d. $ 150

48. In Lake's 1999 income statement, how much should be reported for royalty revenue?
a. $14,000
b. $13,000
c. $11,000
d. $ 9,000

49. In Lake's 1999 income statement, how much should be reported for rental revenue?
a. $43,000
b. $48,000
c. $53,000
d. $53,800

OTHER OBJECTIVE QUESTIONS

Problem 1 (10 to 15 minutes)

The following questions relate to investments in debt securities and in equity securities which do not involve significant influence.

Part a.

Required:

Items 1 through 7. For each item, match the accounting treatment with the appropriate concept. Concepts may be used once, more than once, or not at all.

<table>
<tr><td colspan="2">Accounting treatment</td><td colspan="2">Concept</td></tr>
<tr><td>1.</td><td>Cash flows from purchases and sales of these securities are reported as an operating activity on the statement of cash flows.</td><td>A.</td><td>Available-for-sale-securities</td></tr>
<tr><td></td><td></td><td>B.</td><td>Valuation allowance</td></tr>
<tr><td></td><td></td><td>C.</td><td>Transfer from trading to available-for-sale</td></tr>
<tr><td>2.</td><td>Include unrealized holding gains/losses in earnings of current period.</td><td>D.</td><td>Held-to-maturity securities</td></tr>
<tr><td></td><td></td><td>E.</td><td>Permanent impairment</td></tr>
<tr><td></td><td></td><td>F.</td><td>Other-than-temporary securities</td></tr>
<tr><td>3.</td><td>Amortize unrealized holding gain/loss over life of security.</td><td>G.</td><td>Amortization of differential</td></tr>
<tr><td></td><td></td><td>H.</td><td>Trading securities</td></tr>
<tr><td>4.</td><td>Report at amortized cost.</td><td>I.</td><td>Transfer from available-for-sale to held-to-maturity</td></tr>
<tr><td>5.</td><td>Report unrealized holding gains/losses as other comprehensive income and close to accumulated other comprehensive income, a separate component of stockholders' equity.</td><td></td><td></td></tr>
<tr><td>6.</td><td>Classify as a current asset.</td><td></td><td></td></tr>
<tr><td>7.</td><td>Subsequent recovery not recognized unless realized.</td><td></td><td></td></tr>
</table>

Part b.

Required:

Items 8 through 10. Determine whether each statement is true or false.

8. Held-to-maturity securities are classified as current or noncurrent on an individual basis.

9. For trading securities, some realized gains/losses are excluded from earnings.

10. A premature sale of held-to-maturity securities may be considered maturity if at least 80% of the principal has already been collected.

Problem 2 (15 to 25 minutes)

This question consists of 10 items. Select the **best** answer for each item. Use a No. 2 pencil to blacken the appropriate ovals on the Objective Answer Sheet to indicate your answers. **Answer all items.** Your grade will be based on the total number of correct answers.

Items 1 through 4 are based on the following:

Camp Co. purchased various securities during 1999 to be classified as held-to-maturity securities, trading securities, or available-for-sale securities.

Required:

Items 1 through 4 describe various securities purchased by Camp. For each item, select from the following list the appropriate category for each security and blacken the corresponding oval on the Objective Answer Sheet. A category may be used once, more than once, or not at all.

Categories	
(H)	Held-to-maturity.
(T)	Trading.
(A)	Available-for-sale.

1.   Debt securities bought and held for the purpose of selling in the near term.

2.   US Treasury bonds that Camp has both the positive intent and the ability to hold to maturity.

3. $3 million debt security bought and held for the purpose of selling in 3 years to finance payment of Camp's $2 million long-term note payable when it matures.

4.   Convertible preferred stock that Camp does not intend to sell in the near term.

Items 5 through 10 are based on the following:

The following information pertains to Dayle, Inc.'s portfolio of marketable investments for the year ended December 31, 1999:

	Cost	Fair value 12/31/98	1999 activity Purchases	Sales	Fair value 12/31/99
Held-to-maturity securities					
Security ABC			$100,000		$95,000
Trading securities					
Security DEF	$150,000	$160,000			155,000
Available-for-sale securities					
Security GHI	190,000	165,000		$175,000	
Security JKL	170,000	175,000			160,000

Security ABC was purchased at par. All declines in fair value are considered to be temporary.

Required:

Items 5 through 10 describe amounts to be reported in Dayle's 1999 financial statements. For each item, select from the following list the correct numerical response and blacken the corresponding oval on the Objective Answer Sheet. An amount may be selected once, more than once, or not at all. Ignore income tax considerations.

5.   Carrying amount of security ABC at December 31, 1999.

6.   Carrying amount of security DEF at December 31, 1999.

7.   Carrying amount of security JKL at December 31, 1999.

Items 8 through 10 require a second response. For each item, indicate whether a gain ⓖ or a loss ⓛ is to be reported and blacken the corresponding oval on the Objective Answer Sheet.

8.   Recognized gain or loss on sale of security GHI.

9.   Unrealized gain or loss to be reported in 1999 net income.

10. Unrealized gain or loss to be reported at December 31, 1999, as a separate component of stockholders' equity entitled "accumulated other comprehensive income."

Answer List							
Ⓐ	$0	Ⓓ	$ 15,000	Ⓖ	$100,000	Ⓙ	$160,000
Ⓑ	$ 5,000	Ⓔ	$ 25,000	Ⓗ	$150,000	Ⓚ	$170,000
Ⓒ	$ 10,000	Ⓕ	$ 95,000	Ⓘ	$155,000		

PROBLEMS

Problem 1   (15 to 25 minutes)

Vane Insurance Company has two portfolios of marketable equity securities. One is classified as available-for-sale and the other is classified as trading securities. Vane does not have the ability to exercise significant influence over any of the companies in either portfolio. Some securities from each portfolio were sold during the year. One of the securities in the trading securities portfolio was reclassified to the available-for-sale securities portfolio when its market value was less than cost. At the beginning and end of the year, the aggregate cost of each portfolio exceeded its aggregate market value by different amounts.

Required:

a. How should Vane measure and report the income statement effects of the securities sold during the year from each portfolio?

b. How should Vane account for the security which was reclassified from the trading securities portfolio to the available-for-sale securities portfolio?

c. How should Vane report the effects of investments in each portfolio in its balance sheet as of the end of the year and its income statement for the year? Why? **Do not discuss the securities sold.**

Problem 2   (30 to 40 minutes)

On January 2, 1999, Bing Co. purchased 39,000 shares of Latt Co.'s 200,000 shares of outstanding common stock for $585,000. On that date, the carrying amount of the acquired shares on Latt's books was $405,000. Bing attributed the excess of cost over carrying amount to goodwill. Bing's policy is to amortize intangibles over 10 years.

During 1999, Bing's president gained a seat on Latt's board of directors. Latt reported earnings of $400,000 for the year ended December 31, 1999, and declared the paid dividends of $100,000 during 1999. On December 31, 1999, Latt's common stock was trading over-the-counter at $15 per share.

Required:

a. What criteria should Bing consider in determining whether to account for its investment in Latt under the equity method? Is the equity method consistent with accrual accounting? Explain.

b. Assuming Bing accounts for the investment using the equity method, prepare a schedule of the amounts related to this investment to be reported on Bing's income statement for the year ended 1999 and the amount in the investment in Latt account in the balance sheet at December 31, 1999. Show all computations. **Disregard income taxes.**

Problem 3   (40 to 50 minutes)

At December 31, 1998, Poe Corp. properly reported as available-for-sale securities the following marketable equity securities:

	Cost	Fair value
Axe Corp., 1,000 shares, $2.40 convertible preferred stock	$ 40,000	$42,000
Purl, Inc., 6,000 shares of common stock	60,000	66,000
Day Co., 2,000 shares of common stock	55,000	40,000
Total available-for-sale securities	$155,000	$148,000

On January 2, 1999, Poe purchased 100,000 shares of Scott Corp. common stock for $1,700,000, representing 30% of Scott's outstanding common stock and an underlying equity of $1,400,000 in Scott's net assets on January 2. Poe, which had no other financial transactions with Scott during 1999, amortizes goodwill over a 40-year period. As a result of Poe's 30% ownership of Scott, Poe has the ability to exercise significant influence over Scott's financial and operating policies.

During 1999, Poe disposed of the following securities:

• January 18--sold 2,500 shares of Purl for $13 per share.

• June 1--sold 500 shares of Day, after a 10% stock dividend was received, for $21 per share.

• October 1--converted 500 shares of Axe's preferred stock into 1,500 shares of Axe's common stock, when the market price was $60 per share for the preferred stock and $21 per share for the common stock.

The following 1999 dividend information pertains to stock owned by Poe:

• February 14--Day issued a 10% stock dividend, when the market price of Day's common stock was $22 per share.

• April 5 and October 5--Axe paid dividends of $1.20 per share on its $2.40 preferred stock, to stockholders of record on March 9 and September 9, respectively. Axe did not pay dividends on its common stock during 1997.

• June 30--Purl paid a $1.00 per share dividend on its common stock.

• March 1, June 1, September 1, and December 1 --Scott paid quarterly dividends of $0.50 per share on each of these dates. Scott's net income for the year ended December 31, 1999 was $1,200,000.

At December 31, 1999, Poe's management intended to hold Scott's stock on a long-term basis with the remaining investments considered temporary. Market prices per share of the marketable equity securities were as follows:

	At December 31,	
	1999	1998
Axe Corp.--preferred	$56	$42
Axe Corp.--common	20	18
Purl, Inc.--common	11	11
Day Co.--common	22	20
Scott Corp.--common	16	18

All of the foregoing stocks are listed on major stock exchanges. Declines in market value from cost would not be considered permanent.

Required:

a.   Prepare a schedule of Poe's available-for-sale securities at December 31, 1999, including any information necessary to determine unrealized gains and losses for the current year.

b.   Prepare a schedule to show the carrying amount of Poe's long-term securities accounted for by the equity method at December 31, 1999.

c.   Prepare a schedule showing all revenue, gains, and realized losses relating to Poe's investments for the year ended December 31, 1999.

MULTIPLE-CHOICE ANSWERS

1. b __ __	12. b __ __	23. b __ __	34. d __ __	45. a __ __
2. b __ __	13. c __ __	24. b __ __	35. b __ __	46. b __ __
3. b __ __	14. b __ __	25. b __ __	36. d __ __	47. c __ __
4. b __ __	15. d __ __	26. a __ __	37. a __ __	48. d __ __
5. d __ __	16. a __ __	27. b __ __	38. a __ __	49. c __ __
6. a __ __	17. d __ __	28. c __ __	39. c __ __	
7. b __ __	18. a __ __	29. b __ __	40. c __ __	
8. a __ __	19. a __ __	30. b __ __	41. d __ __	
9. d __ __	20. d __ __	31. d __ __	42. a __ __	
10. a __ __	21. d __ __	32. c __ __	43. c __ __	1st: __/49 = __%
11. b __ __	22. a __ __	33. c __ __	44. c __ __	2nd: __/49 = __%

MULTIPLE-CHOICE ANSWER EXPLANATIONS

B.1. No Significant Influence: Held-to-Maturity

1.   (b)   Per SFAS 115, held-to-maturity securities are to be carried at amortized cost. Therefore, the investment is recorded on 4/1/99 at its cost of $194,000 ($198,500 less accrued interest of $4,500). The carrying amount is calculated as cost plus amortized discount, which at 10/31/99 is $196,800 [$194,000 + ($6,000 x 7/15)]. Therefore, answer (b) is correct.

2.   (b)   Per SFAS 115, **held-to-maturity** securities, which include only debt securities, are reported on the balance sheet at **amortized cost** without adjustment to fair value. If the investment in bonds had been classified as trading or available-for-sale, answer (c) would be correct. **Trading** securities are reported at **fair value** with holding gains or losses flowing through the income statements. **Available-for-sale** securities are reported at **fair value** with holding gains or losses reported as a component of other comprehensive income. Cost [answer (a)] and lower of cost or market [answer (d)]are not used as reporting bases for bond investments.

3.   (b)   Per SFAS 115, held-to-maturity securities are carried at cost, so unrealized holding gains and losses are not reported. However, realized gains and losses on held-to-maturity securities should always be included in the income statement of the appropriate period. No valuation allowance exists for any marketable debt or equity securities. Therefore, answer (b) is correct because realized gains for the period are the only item listed that is included in that period's net income.

B.2. No Significant Influence: Trading

4.   (b)   Debt and equity securities that are classified as **trading securities** are reported at fair value with unrealized gains and losses included in earnings. During 1999, Tyne had an unrealized holding gain of $55,000 ($155,000 – $100,000) on its trading securities. The unrealized holding gain on **available-for-sale** securities ($130,000 – $120,000 = $10,000) is excluded from earnings and reported as other comprehensive income.

5.   (d)   The requirement is to determine the accumulated other comprehensive income to be reported in the Decem

ber 31, 1999 statement of stockholders' equity. Unrealized gains and losses on **trading securities** are included in earnings. Unrealized gains and losses on **available-for-sale** securities are excluded from earnings and reported as accumulated other comprehensive income in a separate component of shareholders' equity. This amount is the net unrealized loss on available-for-sale securities at 12/31/99 is $20,000 ($150,000 – $130,000).

6.   (a)   SFAS 115, para 13, states that unrealized holding gains and losses for trading securities are to be reported in earnings. On the other hand, this para also states that unrealized gains or losses on available-for-sale securities should be excluded from earnings and reported as other comprehensive income. Therefore, only the $40,000 ($360,000 – $320,000) unrealized loss on trading securities is included in income and answer (a) is correct.

B.3. No Significant Influence: Available-For-Sale

7.   (b)   Available-for-sale securities are reported at market value on the balance sheet. At 12/31/99, Stone has incurred gross unrealized gains of $4,000 and gross unrealized losses of $26,000 on its available-for-sale securities. Therefore, at 12/31/99, the net unrealized loss is $22,000 ($26,000 – $4,000). Stone would have to increase the balance in accumulated other comprehensive income from $1,500 to $22,000 at 12/31/99.

8.   (a)   SFAS 115, para 13, as amended by SFAS 130, dictates that unrealized holding gains and losses on available-for-sale securities be reported as other comprehensive income. At 12/31/98, available-for-sale securities would have been reported in the balance sheet at their fair value of $130,000, with a corresponding unrealized loss of $20,000. At 12/31/99, the fair value of these securities is $160,000. Therefore, an unrealized gain of $30,000 ($160,000 – $130,000) would result in other comprehensive income of $30,000 as **accumulated** other comprehensive income and answer (a) is correct.

9.   (d)   In accordance with SFAS 115, the securities purchased by Rex are classified as available-for-sale securities and accounted for at fair value. At 12/31/99, the fair value of security B was $15,300; an unrealized loss of $1,700 resulted in other comprehensive income in that amount. At 1/31/00, the stock was sold when its fair value was $15,000 and the following entry would have been made:

Cash (net)	$13,500	
Loss on sale of stock	3,500	
Investment in Security B		$15,300
Unrealized loss on Sec. B		1,700

The unrealized loss of $1,700 on Security B is a credit. It would be netted with unrealized gains and/or losses recognized in 2000. The effect is to offset the $1,700 loss recognized in 1999 that was closed to other comprehensive income, net retained earnings thus avoiding double counting. Therefore, answer (d) is correct.

10. (a) The capital gains distribution ($145,000) would not be reported as interest revenue. The solutions approach is to set up a T-account for interest receivable.

Interest Receivable

Beg. bal.	38,000		
Int. rev.	?	152,000	Int. collected
End. bal.	46,500		

Beginning and ending balances are given in the question. Interest receivable would be credited for cash collections to reduce the receivable.

Cash	$152,000	
Interest receivable		$152,000

Interest receivable would be debited for interest revenue.

Interest receivable	xxx	
Interest revenue		xxx

Solve for interest revenue ($46,500 + $152,000 − $38,000 = $160,500).

11. (b) In accordance with SFAS 115, marketable equity securities (MES) are classified as either trading (held for current resale) or available-for-sale (if not categorized as trading). Since Nola does not intend to sell these securities in the near term, they should be classified as available-for-sale. SFAS 115 requires MES to be carried at market value. The unrealized gains or losses of available-for-sale MES are reported as a separate component of other comprehensive income. It is important to note that unrealized gains or losses on **trading** securities would be reported as a component of income from continuing operations on the income statement. Thus, answer (b) is correct because the securities would be classified as available-for-sale and unrealized gains and losses from these securities would be reported as other comprehensive income.

12. (b) Per SFAS 115, unrealized losses on available-for-sale securities are reported as a separate component of other comprehensive income, while unrealized gains and losses on trading securities are recognized in income and unrealized gains and losses on held-to-maturity securities are ignored. Thus, this security is classified as available-for-sale. A realized gain will be reported only if the security was sold for a price in excess of its cost. Therefore, the 1998 price decline was **less than** the 1999 price recovery. For example, assume that the investment was purchased for $1,000 on 1/04/98. At 12/31/98, its market value was $800, and on 12/29/99 its market value was $1,200. The following entries would have been made:

1/04/98 Investment	$1,000	
Cash		$1,000
12/31/98 Unrealized loss	$200	
Investment		$200
12/29/99 Cash	$1,200	
Investment		$800
Unrealized loss		200
Gain on sale of securities		**200**

13. (c) The requirement is to determine how the losses on the securities classified as available-for-sale should be reported. In accordance with SFAS 115, a decline in market value of a security, which is considered to be **other-than-temporary**, should be reported on the income statement in the current period. A decline in market value, which is considered to be **temporary**, would be recorded as an unrealized loss, and recognized as other comprehensive income. Therefore, answer (c) is correct as the loss on the Knox stock is considered to be other-than-temporary and it would be reported on the income statement. Answer (a) is incorrect because the unrealized loss on the Scot stock would be reported as other comprehensive income. Answer (b) is incorrect because the loss on the Knox stock is considered to be a realized loss as it is other-than-temporary. Answer (d) is incorrect because the other-than-temporary decline in Knox stock results in a realized loss which is reported on the income statement.

14. (b) Per SFAS 115, the carrying amount of a marketable equity security classified as available-for-sale shall be the fair market value and the unrealized holding gain or loss should be reported as other comprehensive income. In 1998 when the value declined, the portfolio was reported at market with an unrealized holding loss recorded as other comprehensive income. In 1999, the decline is considered to be other than temporary. Thus, the security must be written down to market and a realized loss recognized. However, since there is no actual change in value, in 1999 the security will be reported at the same amount (cost − write-down of asset) as in 1998. Therefore, there is no effect on **net** noncurrent assets in 1999. However, net income will be affected because a realized loss is recorded on the income statement. Note that the unrealized loss account charged to other comprehensive income in 1998 would be credited and the realized loss account would be debited for the same amount. The allowance accounts will be closed against each other because the new basis after the write-down will equal the lower FMV amount. Therefore, answer (b) is correct. Answer (a) is incorrect because net income is affected. Note that if the decline was merely temporary, there would be no net income effect because temporary declines in value of noncurrent portfolios are reported as other comprehensive income, rather than net income. Answer (c) is incorrect because there is no net decrease in noncurrent assets, but there is a net income effect. Answer (d) is incorrect because only net income decreases.

15. (d) Dividends in arrears are not a receivable to the cumulative preferred stockholder until the issuing corporation's board of directors formally declares the dividend. In this case, Hadley, Inc. did not declare the 1998 dividends in arrears until 1999. At the 1999 dividend declaration date,

Woody Co. records dividends receivable and dividend income. Dividend income is included in income from continuing operations; thus, answer (d) is correct.

16. **(a)** Per APB 29, para 18, a nonmonetary asset (the merchandise in this case) received in a nonreciprocal transfer should be recorded at the fair value of the asset received. Additionally, the transfer of a nonmonetary asset to a stockholder or other entity (Deed's employees in this case) should be recorded at the fair value of the asset received. Therefore, answer (a) is correct and answers (b), (c), and (d) are incorrect.

17. **(d)** Per SFAS 95, para 74, noncash transactions should be excluded from the statement of cash flows to better achieve the statement's objectives. However, SFAS 95 requires that information about noncash investing and financing transactions be reported in related disclosures. Thus, answer (d) is correct.

18. **(a)** Per SFAS 115, an investor carries an investment in the stock of an investee at market, and recognizes as income dividends received that are distributed from the net accumulated earnings of the investee **since the date of acquisition** by the investor. Dividends received in excess of earnings subsequent to the date of investment are considered to be return of investment or a liquidating dividend and are recorded as reductions of the cost of the investment. Therefore, Pal Corp.'s accounting treatment of the dividend it received from Ima Corp. indicates that Pal is accounting for the securities under SFAS 115 as an available-for-sale investment in Ima, and answer (a) is correct. Answer (b) is incorrect because Ima's market value does not impact Pal's treatment of dividends received. Answers (c) and (d) are incorrect because all dividends received are treated as reductions in an investee's carrying value under the equity method.

19. **(a)** Intercompany receivables and payables are not eliminated unless consolidated financial statements are prepared. Since Pare only has a 15% interest in Sabe, consolidated financial statements would not be prepared. Thus, on the 12/31/99 balance sheet, Pare should separately report the total amount of the receivable [answer (a)]. Answer (b) is incorrect because the receivable should be reported separately. Answers (c) and (d) are incorrect because none of the receivable should be eliminated.

B.4. No Significant Influence: Transfers

20. **(d)** The requirement is to determine the amount of loss on investments to be reported in Sun's 1999 income statement. SFAS 115 requires this transfer to be accounted for at fair market value and any holding gains or losses on securities which are transferred to held-to-maturity from available-for-sale be reported as accumulated other comprehensive income. This amount is then amortized over the remaining life of the security as an adjustment to yield. Since cost is greater than market value by $75,000 at 12/31/98 ($650,000 cost – $575,000 fair market value), the following entry would be recorded:

| Unrealized loss | $75,000 | |
| Marketable debt securities | | $75,000 |

Then on June 30, 1999, when Sun decides to hold the investments to maturity, an additional $45,000 will be recorded in the valuation account ($575,000 value on books – $530,000 FMV) to reflect the change in FMV. The following entry would be recorded:

| Unrealized loss | $45,000 | |
| Marketable debt securities | | $45,000 |

Each year the unrealized loss would be reported as other comprehensive income which would be closed to "accumulated other comprehensive income."

21. **(d)** Per SFAS 115, when a security is transferred to held-to-maturity from available-for-sale the unrealized holding gain or loss continues to be is reported as a separate component of stockholders' equity. Held-to-maturity securities are carried at amortized cost, and any unrealized holding gains or losses are not reported. Thus, the balance in the "accumulated other comprehensive income" in stockholders' equity on the 1999 statement of stockholders' equity would be $120,000 ($75,000 amount reported at 12/31/98 plus the $45,000 amount reported at June 30, 1999). The $120,000 will be amortized over the remaining life of the security as an adjustment to yield. The additional decline in value from 6/30/99 to 12/31/99 would not be reported, as held-to-maturity securities do not report unrealized losses.

22. **(a)** SFAS 115, para 15, states that "the transfer of a security between categories of investments shall be accounted for at fair value." If fair value is less than the security's carrying amount at the date of transfer, it is irrelevant whether the decline is temporary or permanent. Therefore, answer (a) is correct.

C. Investment Where Significant Influence Does Exist

23. **(b)** This investment should be accounted for using the equity method since Grant owns a 30% interest and can exercise significant influence over South. Grant's share of South's 1998 earnings (30% x $80,000 = $24,000) would be recognized as investment revenue under the equity method. If there was any excess of cost over book value resulting from the purchase of the investment, it would be amortized, reducing investment revenue. However, not enough information was given to determine if there was an excess. The dividends received by Grant (30% x $50,000 = $15,000) do not affect investment revenue using the equity method; they are recorded as a reduction of the investment account.

24. **(b)** The equity method is used because Grant owns a 30% interest and can exercise significant influence. Under this method, the investment account is increased by Grant's equity in South's earnings (30% x $80,000 = $24,000) and is decreased by Grant's dividends received from South (30% x $50,000 = $15,000) and amortization of excess of cost over book value (none in this case). This results in a 12/31/98 carrying amount for the investment of $209,000, as indicated in the T-account below.

	Investment in South		
1/2/98	$200,000		
Equity in earnings	24,000	15,000	Dividends
12/31/98	$209,000		

25. (b) The equity method is used because Grant owns a 30% interest and can exercise significant influence. Under this method, the investment account is increased by Grant's equity in South's earnings (30% x $80,000 = $24,000 in 1998; 30% x $100,000 = $30,000 for first 6 months of 1999) and is decreased by Grant's dividends received from South (30% x $50,000 = $15,000 in 1998; none in first 6 months of 1999) and amortization of excess of cost over book value (none in this case). This results in a 7/1/99 carrying amount of $239,000, as indicated in the T-account below.

	Investment in South		
1/2/98	$200,000		
Equity in earnings	24,000	15,000	Dividends
Equity in earnings	30,000		
7/1/99	$239,000		

The gain on sale is the excess of the proceeds ($150,000) over the carrying amount of the shares sold (1/2 x $239,000 = $119,500), or $30,500 ($150,000 – $119,500).

26. (a) An investor's share of the income of a company in which it holds a 20% or greater investment is referred to as the investor's equity in earnings of the investee. Per APB 18, the investor's share of the investee's earnings should be computed after deducting the investee's cumulative preferred dividends (whether declared or not). In this case, the income available to common stockholders is $50,000 [$60,000 income – (10% x $100,000 total pref. div.)], so Moss Corp.'s equity in earnings is $40,000 (80% ownership x $50,000). Since $40,000 is not one of the answer choices, apparently the candidate is expected to include the preferred dividend revenue of $2,000 [20% ownership x ($100,000 x 10% total pref. div.)] on the income statement in the equity in earnings line item. Although preferred dividends are usually classified separately, answer (a) is the best answer given. The answer, therefore, is $42,000.

Equity in earnings	$40,000
Dividend revenue	2,000
	$42,000

27. (b) Sage paid $400,000 for its 40% investment in Adams when Adams' net assets had a carrying amount of $900,000. Therefore, the book value Sage purchased is $360,000 (40% x $900,000), resulting in an excess of cost over book value of $40,000 ($400,000 – $360,000). This excess must be attributed to specific assets of Adams; any amount not attributed to specific assets is attributed to goodwill. In this case, the excess is attributed to plant assets (40% x $90,000 = $36,000) and inventory (40% x $10,000 = $4,000). The portion attributed to plant assets is amortized over 18 years, while the portion attributed to inventory is expensed immediately (since all inventory was sold during 1997). Therefore, Sage's investment income is $42,000, as computed below.

Share of income (40% x $120,000)	$48,000
Excess amortization	
[($36,000/18) + $4,000]	(6,000)
	$42,000

28. (c) The unrealized gain on the available-for-sale securities is improperly included in Pear's $125,000 income before taxes. Per SFAS 115, unrealized holding gains and losses on available-for-sale securities are reported as a separate component of stockholders' equity. The equity in Cinn's earnings is properly included in Pear Co.'s pretax income. However, the dividends from Cinn are also improperly included in income because under the equity method, dividends received are a reduction of the investment account rather than dividend revenue. The adjustments to profits of prior years for arithmetic errors in depreciation ($35,000) should be recorded as a retroactive adjustment to beginning retained earnings and should **not** have been deducted when computing 1999 income before taxes. Therefore, 1999 income before taxes should be $112,000 as computed below.

Tentative income	$125,000
Unrealized holding gain	(40,000)
Dividends received	(8,000)
Prior period adjustment	35,000
Correct income	$112,000

29. (b) The equity method is to be used when the investor owns 20% or more of the investee's voting stock, unless there is evidence that the investor does **not** have the ability to exercise significant influence over the investee. Since this is the case, Saxe must carry the stock at market in the available-for-sale category. Under this method, dividends received are to be recognized as income to the investor, and the investment account is unaffected. Also, under this method, the investor's share of the investee's net income is not recognized. Any changes in the market value of the stock would be reflected in the book value of the stock with a corresponding amount in a separate account in stockholders' equity. As there has been no change in the market value, the investment account would still have a balance of $150,000 at 12/31/99. Note that the dividends received by Saxe were distributed from Lex's net accumulated earnings since the date of acquisition by Saxe. However, if dividends received had been in excess of earnings subsequent to the investment date, they are considered a return of capital and would be recorded as a reduction in the investment account.

30. (b) Ownership of less than 20% leads to the presumption of **no substantial influence** unless evidence to the contrary exists. Well's position as Rea's largest single shareholder and the presence of Well's officers as a **majority** of Rea's board of directors constitute evidence that Well **does have significant influence** despite less than 20% ownership. Therefore, the equity method is used. The investment account had a beginning balance of $400,000 (purchase price). This amount is increased by Well's equity in Rea's earnings (10% ownership x $500,000 income = $50,000) and decreased by Well's dividends received from Rea (10% share x $150,000 total div. = $15,000), resulting in a balance of $435,000 (see T-account below).

	Investment in Rea		
1/2/99	$400,000		
Equity in earnings	50,000	$15,000	Dividends
12/31/99	$435,000		

	Investment in Tot	
1/2/99 purchase	50,000	
12/31/99 purchase	150,000	
Equity in earnings	30,000	
	230,000	

31. (d) The investment should have been originally recorded at the $250,000 purchase price. This amount would be increased by Kean's share of Pod's earnings (30% x $100,000 = $30,000), decreased by the amortization of excess of cost over book value, and decreased by dividends received by Kean (none in this case). The book value Kean purchased is $150,000 (30% x $500,000), resulting in an excess of cost over book value of $100,000 ($250,000 – $150,000). This excess must be attributed to the specific assets of Pod which have a fair value greater than their book value; any amount not attributed to specific assets is attributed to goodwill. In this case, the excess would be attributed first to land (30% x $200,000 = $60,000) and the remainder to goodwill ($100,000 – $60,000 = $40,000). The portion attributed to land should not be amortized, while the portion attributed to goodwill should be amortized over 10 years ($40,000 x 1/10 = $4,000). Therefore, Kean's 12/31/98 balance of the investment in subsidiary is $276,000 as computed below.

Original cost	$250,000
Share of income (30% x $100,000)	30,000
Excess amortization ($40,000 x 1/10)	(4,000)
	$276,000

32. (c) APB 18 states that when an investment that has been accounted for using another method qualifies for the use of the equity method due to a change in ownership level (such as from 10% to 30%), the change to the equity method should be reported **retroactively**. At the date of the change (1/2/00), the **investment** account and **retained earnings** are adjusted as if the equity method had been used all along, and the results of operations in prior years are restated to reflect the equity method. In 2000, use of the equity method results in recognition of investment income of $195,000 (30% x $650,000 investee income). 1999 investment income must be restated from the previously reported dividend income (10% x $200,000 = $20,000) to equity method income (10% x $600,000 = $60,000), an adjustment of $40,000 ($60,000 – $20,000 = $40,000).

33. (c) The requirement is to determine the balance in the December 31, 1999, investment account. APB 18 states that when an investment that has been accounted for using another method qualifies for the use of the equity method due to a change in ownership level (in this case, from 10% to 30%), the change to the equity method should be applied retroactively. At the date of the change (12/31/99), the accounts are adjusted as if the equity method had been used all along. If the equity method had been used beginning at 1/2/99, Pare would have recorded its share of Tot's earnings (10% x $300,000 = $30,000) as investment revenue and as an increase in the investment account. Therefore, at 12/31/97, Pare's investment in Tot would be reported at $230,000.

34. (d) Under the equity method, a reciprocal relationship is formed between the investment account on the investor's books and the book values of the net assets on the investee's books. As changes in the investee's net assets occur (earnings, dividends, etc.), the investor will recognize the percentage of ownership share of that change in the investment account. Therefore, cash dividends from the investee will be recorded in the investment account, not the investment income account. The entry includes a debit to cash and a credit to the investment account. Another aspect of the equity method is the amortization of the goodwill related to the purchase. The investment income account and the investment in stock account should include all the income recognitions and amortizations resulting from the investment. The entry to record the goodwill amortization is a debit to Investment income and a credit to Investment in stock. Therefore, answer (d) is correct.

35. (b) When the equity method is used, APB 18 requires the investor to amortize any portion of the excess of fair values over carrying amounts (differential) that relates to depreciable or amortizable assets held by the investee. Amortization of the differential results in a reduction of the investment account and a reduction in the equity of the investee's earnings. For inventory, an excess of FMV over cost, FIFO cost in this case, has the same effect on the investment account and equity in investee earnings in the period in which the goods are sold. Therefore, the portion of the differential that relates to inventory would decrease Park's reported equity in Tun's earnings, and answers (c) and (d) are incorrect. Land is not a depreciable asset, so there would be no amortization of the differential related to land, and answer (a) is incorrect.

36. (d) Dividends received in excess of earnings subsequent to the date of investment are considered a return of investment and are recorded as reductions of cost of the investment. Additionally, per APB 18, para 6b, under the equity method, "dividends received from an investee reduce the carrying amount of the investment." Therefore, answer (d) is correct.

37. (a) The requirement is to determine the effects of a cash dividend on an investors investment account, accounted for both as an available-for-sale security, and under the equity method. Dividends received on available-for-sale securities are to be recognized as income to the investor and the investment account is unaffected. If the dividends received are in excess of earnings to date, then they would be considered a return of the investment and would result in a reduction of the investment account. Under the equity method, the receipt of cash dividends reduces the carrying value of the investment. Therefore, answer (a) is correct as the receipt of a cash dividend would not result in an increase in the investment account under either method.

38. (a) The requirement is to determine the amount of investment income to be reported in the 1999 income statement. APB 18 states that when an investment which has been accounted for using a different method qualifies for the use of the equity method, due to a change in ownership level (such as 10% to 40%), then the change to the equity method should be reported **retroactively**. At the date of the change, the investment account and the retained earnings account are adjusted as if the equity method had been used all along. Therefore answer (a) is correct as Point owned 10% of Iona's stock from January 1 to July 31, 1999, and 40% of Iona's stock from August 1 to December 31, 1999. Answers (b) and (c) are incorrect because income should be recognized under the equity method according to the percentage of ownership existing during each of the periods. Answer (d) is incorrect because when Iona reports its earnings to Point, Point will record its share of the revenue. When Point receives the dividends, (which may be in a different period than Point recognized its share of Iona's income), the carrying amount of the investment will be reduced by the amount received. Therefore, the income recognized does not usually equal the dividends received.

39. (c) APB 18 requires the use of the equity method when accounting for investments in which the investor has the ability to exercise significant influence over the operating and financial policies of the investee. APB 18 generally assumes that ownership of 20% or more of the outstanding common stock demonstrates this ability. In this case, Pulham Corp. owns 30% of Angles and properly uses the equity method. Under the equity method intercompany profits and losses are eliminated. However, receivables and payables are not eliminated as they are in the case of consolidated financial statements. On the December 31, 1999 balance sheet, Pulham should separately disclose the total amount of the receivable. Additionally, this receivable should be shown separately from other receivables. Therefore, answer (c) is correct. Answers (a) and (d) are incorrect because, as stated above, separate disclosure of the related-party receivable is necessary. Answer (b) is incorrect because the entire receivable should be separately disclosed.

E. Stock Dividends and Splits

40. (c) Arlo's annual preferred stock dividend is $120,000 ($2,000,000 x 6%). The $240,000 dividend paid includes $120,000 dividends in arrears from 1998 and $120,000 for 1999. Therefore, Wood would receive **$24,000 of cash dividends** ($200,000 x 6% x 2) which would be reported as **dividend income** in 1999 (preferred dividends in arrears are not recognized as income until declared). No dividend income is recognized when an investor receives a proportional **stock** dividend, because the investor continues to own the same proportion of the investee as before the stock dividend, and the investee has not distributed any assets to the investor.

41. (d) Regardless of the accounting method used, no dividend revenue is recognized when an investor receives a proportional **stock** dividend, because the investor continues to own the same proportion of the investee as before the stock dividend. In addition, the investee has not distributed

any assets to the investor. Therefore, **no entry** is prepared to record the receipt of a stock dividend. The investor simply makes a memo entry to record the additional number of shares owned, while leaving the balance in the investment account unchanged. The balance is then spread over the total number of shares (previous holdings + stock dividend) to determine the new per share cost of the stock.

F. Stock Rights

42. (a) When stock rights are received, the cost of the investment (1,000 x $80 = $80,000) is allocated between the stock and the rights based on the relative fair market value of each, as calculated below.

FMV of stock	1,000 x $95 =	$ 95,000
FMV of rights	1,000 x $ 5 =	5,000
Total FMV		$100,000

The cost allocated to the stock is $76,000 ($80,000 x 95/100) and the cost allocated to the rights is $4,000 ($80,000 x 5/100).

43. (c) When the rights are received, the cost of the investment ($36,000) is allocated between the stock and the rights based on their relative fair market values, calculated below.

FMV of stock	500 x $90	=	$45,000
FMV of rights	500 x $10	=	5,000
Total FMV			$50,000

The cost allocated to the stock is $32,400 ($45,000/ $50,000, or 90%, of $36,000) and to the rights is $3,600 ($5,000/$50,000, or 10%, of $36,000). The net proceeds from the sale of the rights is $5,000 (500 x $10), so the gain on the sale of the rights is $1,400 ($5,000 – $3,600).

G. Cash Surrender Value of Life Insurance

44. (c) The cash surrender value (CSV) of the life insurance policy increased by $21,000 during 1999 ($108,000 – $87,000). Therefore, part of the premium paid is not expense but a payment to increase the CSV. The formula to compute insurance expense is

Cash paid	–	(Ending CSV – Beginning CSV)	–	Cash divs. received		
$40,000	–	($108,000 – $87,000)	–	$0	=	$19,000

The dividends in this problem are **not** cash dividends received. They are dividends which the insurance company applied to increase the CSV. They are not separately considered in the formula above because the effect of the dividends is reflected in the increase in CSV, which is included in the formula. 1999 journal entries are presented below.

Cash surr. value	$15,000	($21,000 – $6,000)
Ins. expense	25,000	
Cash		$40,000
Cash surr. value	$ 6,000	
Ins. expense		$ 6,000

45. (a) When a company insures the lives of employees and names itself the beneficiary, the cash surrender value of the policies is considered an asset. During the first few years of a policy, no cash surrender value may accrue. If no increase in cash surrender value (CSV) occurs, the journal entry to record a premium paid would be

Insurance expense   xxx
    Cash   xxx

However, if cash surrender value increases, part of the cash paid is recorded as an increase in the CSV. The entry is

Insurance expense   xx
Cash surrender value   xx
    Cash   xxx

Therefore, the increase in CSV decreases insurance expense because the same amount of cash paid must be allocated between the two accounts. The increase in CSV does **not** affect investment income [answer (b)] or deferred charges [answer (d)].

46. (b) When a company insures the lives of employees and names itself as the beneficiary, the cash surrender value (CSV) of the policy is considered an asset. Premiums paid are debited to CSV for the increase in CSV that year and to insurance expense for the excess of cash paid over increase in CSV. Upon the death of the insured employee, the company recognizes a gain for the excess of proceeds received over CSV [answer (b)].

Miscellaneous

47. (c) In determining the amount which should be reported in Lake's 1999 income statement as dividend revenue, the first step is to determine what method should be used in accounting for Lake's investments. Per APB 18, para 17, the Board concluded that the equity method of accounting for an investment in common stock should be followed by an investor whose investment in common stock gives it the ability to exercise significant influence over the operating and financial policies of an investee even though the investor may hold 50% or less of the voting stock. Ability to exercise that influence may be indicated in several ways, such as representation on the board of directors. Another important consideration is the extent of ownership by an investor. The Board concluded that an investment of 20% or more of the voting stock of an investee should lead to a presumption, in the absence of evidence to the contrary, that an investor has the ability to exercise significant influence over an investee. Conversely, an investment of less than 20% of the voting stock of an investee should lead to a presumption that an investor does **not** have the ability to exercise significant influence unless such ability can be demonstrated. Lake's 30% ownership of Aub and its representation on Aub's board of directors clearly indicate that the investment in Aub should be accounted for using the equity method. Lake's 1% ownership in Kar and lack of evidence in this problem that Lake has "significant influence" over Kar indicate that this investment should be accounted for using the cost adjusted for fair value method, in accordance with SFAS 115. Per APB 18, para 6b, when the **equity** method is used, dividends received from an investee reduce the carrying amount of the investment (i.e., are **not** reported as dividend revenue). Per APB 18, para 6a, however, the investor recognizes dividends received from investees as **income** under the **cost adjusted for fair value** method. Therefore, the $1,000 of cash dividends from Kar would be reported as dividend revenue by Lake, while the $15,000 of cash dividends from Aub would reduce the car-

rying amount of Lake's investment in Aub. Thus, answer (c) is correct, and answers (a), (b), and (d) are incorrect.

48. (d) Lake's royalty revenue results from the licensing of their trademark to Barr Co. Lake receives royalties of 10% of Barr's sales of trademarked items. To determine royalty revenue for 1999, it must first be realized that the royalty payment on September 1, 1999, is for sales in January through June of 1999. This royalty payment of $7,000 is the first portion of royalty revenue for 1999. The second portion of royalty revenue is for Barr's sales of trademarked items for July through December of 1999. This second portion consists of 10% of Barr's estimated sales of trademarked items for the last half of 1999. Royalty revenue for the second half of 1999 is then $2,000 (10% x $20,000). Therefore, answer (d) is correct because royalty revenue would be $9,000 for 1999 and is comprised of the $7,000 royalty payment received on September 1, 1999, plus 10% of estimated sales for months July through December.

49. (c) Lake receives rental revenue from leasing a parking lot to Day Co. The annual rental payment made by Day Co. to Lake is $48,000. However, Day Co. also paid a nonrefundable deposit of $50,000 on January 1, 1997. This $50,000 deposit, since it is nonrefundable, is considered unearned revenue which must be recognized over the life of the lease on a straight-line basis. Therefore, in addition to the $48,000 annual rental payment, $5,000 ($50,000 ÷ 10 years) of the nonrefundable deposit will be recognized as rental revenue in 1999. Thus, answer (c) is correct because $53,000 will be recognized as rental revenue in 1999. Note that the $8,000 security deposit will not be revenue because it is to be refunded at the end of the lease period. It is deferred in its entirety and recorded as a long-term liability. Only a nonrefundable deposit would be recognized as rental revenue over the life of the lease.

OTHER OBJECTIVE ANSWERS AND ANSWER EXPLANATIONS

Problem 1

Part a.

1. **(H)** SFAS 115 dictates that purchases and sales of trading portfolio securities be classified as operating activities on the statement of cash flows due to the short-term, profit-seeking nature of the investment. In contrast, available-for-sale and held-to-maturity securities are classified as investing activities.

2. **(H)** Unrealized holding gains and losses on trading securities are included in income of the period.

3. **(I)** Unrealized holding gains and losses on securities transferred to held-to-maturity from available-for-sale are reported as a separate component of stockholders' equity (accumulated other comprehensive income) and amortized over the remaining life of the security.

4. **(D)** Held-to-maturity securities are carried at amortized cost.

5. **(A)** Unrealized holding gains and losses on available-for-sale securities are reported as other comprehensive income, whereas those on trading securities are included in income and those on held-to-maturity securities are not reported.

6. **(H)** Trading securities appear on the balance sheet as current assets.

7. **(E)** When a decline in value of a security is deemed to be other than temporary, the impaired security is written down to fair value. Any subsequent recovery may not be recognized in earnings unless realized through sale of the security.

Part b.

8. **(T)** Held-to-maturity securities are classified as current or noncurrent according to how soon they will mature, (i.e., a security maturing within 1 year is classified as current, while one with a more distant maturity date is considered noncurrent).

9. **(T)** Some unrealized holding gains and losses on trading securities could have already been included in income as unrealized components. Thus, to recognize them again upon realization would result in an erroneous doubling of the actual gain/loss.

10. **(F)** Premature sale of held-to-maturity securities are considered at maturity if either (1) the sale occurs so close to maturity that interest rate risk is virtually eliminated, or (2) the sale occurs after at least 85% of the principal has been collected.

Problem 2

1. **(T)** Trading. SFAS 115, para 12a, states that "securities that are bought and held principally for the purpose of selling them in the near term (thus held for only a short period of time) shall be classified as **trading securities**."

2. **(H)** Held-to-maturity. SFAS 114, para 7, states that "investments in debt securities shall be classified as **held-to-maturity** and measured at amortized cost...only if the reporting enterprise has the positive intent and ability to hold those securities to maturity." Both conditions are met in this case.

3. **(A)** Available-for-sale. The company does not have the "positive intent . . .to hold this debt security to maturity," therefore the security cannot be classified as held-to-maturity. Also, since it will be sold beyond the "near term," it cannot be classified as "trading." SFAS 115, para 12b, states that "investments not classified as trading (nor as held-to-maturity securities) shall be classified as **available-for-sale securities**."

4. **(A)** Available-for-sale. Since this security is neither a debt security nor a security that will be sold in the near term, it is classified as available-for-sale.

5. **(G; $100,000)** SFAS 115, para 7, states that held-to-maturity securities "shall be . . .measured at amortized cost." Since this debt security was purchased at par, there is neither a discount nor a premium to amortize, therefore amortized cost equals par or $100,000. Ignore fair value.

6. **(I; $155,000)** SFAS 115, para 12, states "Investments in . . .securities that are not classified as held-to-maturity and that have readily determinable fair values shall be . . .measured at fair value." $155,000 is fair value.

7. **(J; $160,000)** Same answer as question 6. Since security JKL is not a debt security classified as held-to-maturity and since it has a readily determinable fair value it "shall be . . .measured at fair value."

8. **(D, L)** Recognized gains and losses on the sale of available-for-sale securities are measured as the difference between original cost ($190,000) and the selling price of the securities ($175,000). The unrealized loss that existed in accumulated other comprehensive income in the equity section prior to the sale ($25,000) will be reversed as a credit to unrealized loss and that reversal will be reported as other comprehensive income and closed to accumulated other comprehensive income that is reported in the equity section of the balance sheet (see question 10 below). The journal entry to record the sale would be

Cash	$175,000		
Realized loss on sale			
of A-F-S securities	15,000		
A-F-S securities		$165,000	
Unrealized loss on			
A-F-S securities		25,000	

9.   (B, L)   The only unrealized gains or losses on securities reported in the net income relate to value changes in trading securities. In this case the value of the JKL securities has decreased from $160,000 to $155,000.

10.   (C, L)   The 1/1/99 balance of the unrealized gain or loss on A-F-S securities reported in the equity section was $20,000, the difference between the 1/1/99 $25,000 unrealized loss of GHI ($190,000 – $165,000) and the 1/1/99 $5,000 unrealized gain of JKL ($175,000 – $170,000). The changes during the year were (1) the $25,000 reversal (credit) of the unrealized loss of GHI when it was sold and (2) the $15,000 loss ($175,000 – $160,000) in value during the year of JKL. The Other Comprehensive Income account would appear as follows:

Other Comprehensive Income

Beg. bal.	-0-	12/31/99 Reverse GHI	25,000
12/31/99 JKL	15,000		
Close to Accumulated Other Comprehensive Income	10,000		

The Accumulated Other Comprehensive Income account would appear as follows:

Accumulated Other Comprehensive Income

1/1/99	$20,000		
		12/31/99 Close from Other Comprehensive Income	
12/31/99 Balance	10,000		

ANSWER OUTLINE

Problem 1　MES:　Available-for-Sale and Trading Securities Portfolios

a.　Gains or losses should be measured as difference between selling prices and carrying amount of securities sold

　　Differences constitute realized gains and losses

　　　Recognized in income for trading securities net of unrealized gains or losses previously recognized

　　　Recognize in income for available-for-sale securities

b.　Reclassification of trading security to available-for-sale portfolio

　　Unrealized losses up to date of transfer, including those in the current period, were already recognized and are not reversed

　　Basis should be fair value at date of reclassification

c.　BS and IS reporting

　　Each portfolio is reported at fair value

　　Unrealized gains (losses)

　　　Recognize as income for trading securities

　　　Report as component of stockholders' equity (accumulated other comprehensive income) for available-for-sale securities

　　Reasons portfolios are reported this way

　　　Relevance--fair value reflects the effects of management's decision to buy at a certain time and then to hold security for some period of time

　　Matching

　　　Trading securities

　　　　Estimated loss is reported in period it occurred

　　　　Indicates expected cash flow consequences from sale of the securities

　　　Available-for-sale securities

　　　　Realization of gains (losses) from sale is less certain in near term

　　　　Market value decline

　　　　　May not be a reasonable estimate

　　　　　Not useful for cash flow projections

UNOFFICIAL ANSWER

Problem 1　MES:　Available-for-Sale and Trading Securities Portfolios

a.　The differences between the selling prices and the costs of the available-for-sale securities sold should be reported as realized gains and losses in the determination of net income. On the other hand, any realized gains and losses on the trading securities sold are recognized net of unrealized gains or losses previously recognized.

b.　The security in the trading securities portfolio should be reclassified to the available-for-sale portfolio at its fair value on the date of transfer. Unrealized losses up to the date of transfer, including those in the current period, were already recognized in income and should not be reversed.

c.　Each portfolio should be reported on the balance sheet at fair value. Unrealized gains and losses on the trading securities portfolio are recognized in earnings on the income statement. On the other hand, unrealized gains and losses on the available-for-sale securities portfolio are reported as other comprehensive income and as a separate component of stockholders' equity (accumulated other comprehensive income) on the balance sheet.

Reporting the portfolio at fair value reflects the realizable value of the portfolio at the end of the period. For the trading securities portfolio, the estimated loss is reported (matched) in the income statement in the period in which the change in realizable value occurred. Reporting trading securities at fair value indicates the expected cash flow from the sale of the securities. Inclusion of the reduction in fair value in net income assists in cash flow projections by acknowledging the expected impairment in future cash flows as a consequence of the investment. For the available-for-sale portfolio, the decline in market value (loss) is less certain of realization in the near term, and may not be a reasonable estimate of the cash flow consequence of the investment. Therefore, changes in market value of the available-for-sale portfolio are not considered useful for cash flow projections. Accordingly, these losses are not reported in earnings.

ANSWER OUTLINE

Problem 2　Equity Method

a.　Equity method used when investor has ability to exercise significant influence over operating and financial policies of investee

　　Significant influence presumed for 20% or more ownership; not presumed for less than 20% ownership

　　Predominant evidence to the contrary may overcome presumptions:

- Board of directors or policy making participation
- Material intercompany transactions
- Interchange of managerial personnel
- Technological dependency

　　Equity method consistent with accrual accounting; investor recognizes share of investee's earnings/ losses in same period as reflected in investee's accounts

UNOFFICIAL ANSWER

Problem 2　Equity Method

a.　Bing should consider whether it has the ability to exercise significant influence over operating and financial policies of the investee enterprise. That ability is presumed to exist for investments of 20% or more and presumed not to exist for investments of less than 20%. Both presumptions may be overcome by predominant evidence to the contrary, such as board of directors or policy-making participation, material intercompany transactions, interchange of managerial personnel, or technological dependency.

　　The equity method is consistent with accrual accounting, because the investor recognized its share of the earnings and losses of the investee in the periods in which they are reflected in the accounts of the investee.

b.　*Income statement:*

Equity in earnings of Latt	$ 78,000
($400,000 x 19.5% (39,000 ÷ 200,000))	
Amortization of goodwill	
($180,000 ($585,000 – $405,000) ÷10)	(18,000)
	$ 60,000

　　Balance sheet:

Investment in Latt	
($585,000 + $78,000 – $18,000 –	
$19,500 ($100,000 x 19.5%))	$625,500

SOLUTION GUIDE

Problem 3   MES & Equity Method Investment

1. This problem consists of three related requirements concerning a company's investments in marketable equity securities.

1.1 In part a., a schedule of Poe's available-for-sale securities at 12/31/99 must be prepared. This schedule should include columns for cost, market, and unrealized gain or loss.

1.2 A schedule to show the carrying amount of Poe's long-term investments accounted for by the equity method at 12/31/99 is required in part b.

1.3 In part c., a schedule showing all revenues, gains, and losses for 1999 relating to Poe's investments must be prepared.

1.4 The solutions approach for problems of this type in which the requirements are interrelated is to prepare time lines for each security and proceed through the given information making computations and notations on the appropriate time line. Labeling of computations by requirement helps to organize your data. For example, if a computation or number relates to requirement c., it can be labeled "c." Using this approach, the candidate will be solving a part of two to three requirements as each security is covered, but not necessarily in the same order as given on the exam. After working through all the information given, the formal required schedules can be prepared.

2. At 12/31/98, Poe owned 1,000 shares of Axe preferred with a fair value of $42,000 ($42/share). At 10/1/99, Poe converted 500 shares of Axe preferred into 1,500 shares of Axe common. The preferred fair value is allocated to the common since half of the preferred $21,000 was surrendered to acquire it. The remaining preferred is still carried at $21,000 ($42 x 500 shares). At year end, the preferred is reported at $28,000 ($56 FV/sh x 500 sh) and the common stock is reported at $30,000 ($20 FV/sh x 1,500 sh). See time line after 2.1.

2.1 Dividend revenue received on the Axe preferred stock should be included in Poe's income statement. The Axe preferred stock paid a $1.20 dividend on 1,000 shares twice during the year, for a total of $2,400. Note that the second dividend was received on October 5, after 500 shares of preferred were converted. However, the dividend was received for all 1,000 shares, since the date of record was September 9.

3. Poe owned 6,000 shares of Purl common which originally cost $60,000 ($10/sh) and had a fair value of $66,000 ($11/sh) at 12/31/98. 2,500 of these shares were sold. The 3,500 still held have a carrying value of $38,500 (3,500 sh x $11). See time line after 3.2.

3.1 On 1/18/99, Poe sold 2,500 shares of Purl common for $32,500 (2,500 sh x $13) when the carrying value (fair value) was $27,500 (2,500 sh x $11). Since unrealized gains/losses on available-for-sale securities are not recognized in income the gain on the sale is $7,500 ($32,500 – $25,000).

3.2 Dividend income received on the Purl common stock should also be included in Poe's income statement. A $1.00 per share dividend was received on the Purl common stock (3,500 shares x $1.00 per share or $3,500).

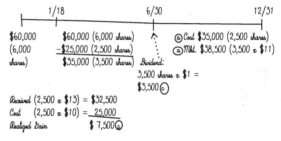

4. At 1/1/99, Poe owned 2,000 shares of Day common which cost $55,000 and had a fair value of $40,000. Day issued a 10% stock dividend on February 14 when the stock's fair value was $44,000 (2,000 x $22), which gave Poe an additional 200 shares (2,000 x 10%) at no additional cost. Therefore, the 2,200 shares had an adjusted cost of $25 per share ($55,000 ÷ 2,200). The adjusted carrying value per share was $18.18 ($40,000 ÷ 2,200 shs). The stock dividend is not reflected in income. Poe sold 500 shares on June 1. The 1,700 still held have a cost of $42,500 (1,700 x $25), a carrying value of $30,900 (1,700 x $18.18) and a fair value of $37,400 (1,700 x $22). See time line after 4.1.

4.1 The Day stock sold for $10,500 (500 x $21) and had a cost of $12,500 (500 x $25). Thus, a $2,000 loss was realized on the sale of Day common and should be included in Poe's income statement.

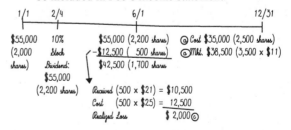

5. Poe intends to hold the Scott stock as a long-term investment. Since Poe owns 30% of the voting stock and can exercise significant influence over Scott, the use of the equity method is appropriate.

5.1 The original cost of the investment was $1,700,000. The excess of investment cost ($1,700,000) over the book value of the net assets purchased ($1,400,000) is $300,000. This amount must be amortized over 40 years ($300,000 ÷ 40 = $7,500) and is a reduction of both investment revenue and the investment account. See time line after 5.3.

Investment revenue   7,500
     Investment in Scott   7,500

5.2   The investment account is also reduced by dividends received when the equity method is used. Scott paid quarterly dividends of $.50 a share, or a total of $50,000 each quarter to Poe (100,000 x $.50). Therefore, Poe received a total of $200,000 in dividends (4 x $50,000) from Scott. See time line after 5.3.

Cash   200,000
     Investment in Scott   200,000

Note that the dividend received from Scott is not recognized as income under the equity method.

5.3   Using the equity method, the investment account is increased by the investor's share of investee earnings (30% x $1,200,000 = $360,000).

Investment in Scott   360,000
     Investment revenue   360,000

UNOFFICIAL ANSWER

Problem 3   MES & Equity Method Investment

a.
Poe Corp.
**SCHEDULE OF AVAILABLE-FOR-SALE
SECURITIES**
December 31, 1999

	Number of shares	Cost	Beginning carrying amount at market	Ending market price per share	Market value	Cumulative gain or (loss)	Unrealized gain or (loss) in 1998
Axe--preferred	500	$ 20,000	$ 21,000	$56	$ 28,000	$ 8,000	$ 7,000
Axe--common	1,500	20,000	21,000	20	30,000	10,000	9,000
Purl--common	3,500	35,000	38,500	11	38,500	3,500	-
Day--common	1,700	42,500	30,900	22	37,400	(5,100)	6,500
		$117,500	$111,400		$133,900	$16,400	$22,500

b.
Poe Corp.
**SCHEDULE OF LONG-TERM MARKETABLE
EQUITY SECURITIES**
December 31, 1999

Scott Corp.--100,000 shares of common stock:

Cost:
  Acquisition price $1,700,000
  Increase in equity during 1999:
    Poe's interest in Scott's income $360,000
    Less:
      Amortization of excess of cost
        over underlying equity $ 7,500   [1]
      Dividends received   200,000   207,500
  Net increase in equity   152,500
Carrying amount of Poe Corp.'s investment in Scott $1,852,500

c.
Poe Corp.
SCHEDULE OF INVESTMENT INCOME
For the Year Ended December 31, 1999

Dividends:			
Axe Corp.--preferred (1,000 shares x $2.40 per share)		$ 2,400	
Purl, Inc.--common (3,500 shares x $1.00 per share)		3,500	
Total dividend revenue			$ 5,900
Gains on marketable equity securities: [2]			
Realized gain/(loss) on sale of securities:			
Purl, Inc.--common ($13 – $10 = $3 x 2,500 shares)		$ 7,500	
Day Co.--common ($55,000/2,000 shares x 110%,			
or cost per share of $25 – $21 selling price			
per share = $4 loss per share x 500 shares sold)		(2,000)	
Net realized gain on sale of securities			5,500
Equity in income of Scott Corp.:			
Poe's 30% interest in Scott's net income of			
$1,200,000		360,000	
Amortization of excess of cost over underlying equity		(7,500) [1]	
Equity in income of Scott Corp.			352,500
Total investment income			$363,900

Explanation of amounts

[1]	Poe's acquisition price for its 30% interest	$1,700,000
	Poe's interest in the underlying equity	1,400,000
	Excess of cost over underlying equity	$ 300,000
	Amortization based on 40 years	$ 7,500

[2]   Unrealized gains (losses) on available-for-sale securities are excluded from investment income and thus are excluded from Poe's schedule of investment income. They are reported as other comprehensive income.

STATEMENT OF CASH FLOWS

A. **Objectives of the Statement of Cash Flows** (See outline of SFAS 95 also)

The primary purposes of this statement are to provide information about an entity's cash receipts and cash payments and to disclose information about the financing and investing activities of an entity. This statement should help the users of the statement assess: (1) an entity's ability to generate positive future cash flows; (2) an entity's ability to meet its obligations and pay dividends; (3) the reasons for differences between income and associated cash receipts and payments; and (4) the cash and noncash aspects of an entity's investing and financing transactions.

In order to facilitate the users in making those assessments, a statement of cash flows shall report cash receipts and cash payments of an entity's operations, its investing transactions, and its financing transactions. A separate schedule accompanying the statement should also report the effects of investing and financing transactions that **do not affect cash**.

The statement of cash flows is required to be prepared based on changes during the period in cash and cash equivalents. Cash equivalents include short-term, highly liquid investments that (1) are readily convertible to known amounts of cash and (2) are so near their maturity (original maturity of 3 months or less from **date of purchase** by the enterprise) that they present negligible risk of changes in value because of changes in interest rates. Treasury bills, commercial paper, and money market funds are all examples of cash equivalents.

B. **Statement of Cash Flows Classification**

Cash receipts and cash payments are to be classified into operating, financing, and investing activities.

Operating activities include delivering or producing goods for sale and providing services. Operating activities include all transactions that are **not** investing and financing activities. More specifically, cash flows from operations should not include cash flows from transactions whose effects are included in income but are investing and financing activities. For example, a gain (loss) on extinguishment of debt should properly be classified as a financing activity, and a gain (loss) from disposal of property should be classified as an investing activity.

Investing activities include the acquisition and disposition of long-term productive assets or securities that are not considered cash equivalents. Investing activities also include the lending of money and collection on loans.

Financing activities include obtaining resources from owners and returning the investment. Also included is obtaining resources from creditors and repaying the amount borrowed.

The FASB has listed the following as examples of classifications of transactions.

	Operating	*Investing*	*Financing*
Cash inflows	• Receipts from sale of goods or services	• Principal collections from loans and sales of other entities' debt instruments*	• Proceeds from issuing stock
	• Sale of loans, debt, or equity instruments carried in trading portfolio	• Sale of equity instruments of other enterprises** and from returns **of** investment in those instruments	• Proceeds from issuing debt (short-term or long-term)
	• Returns on loans (interest)	• Sale of plant & equipment	• Not-for-profits' donor restricted cash that is limited to long-term purposes
	• Returns on equity securities (dividends)		
Cash outflows	• Payments for inventory	• Loans made and acquisition of other entities' debt instruments*	• Payment of dividends
	• Payments to employees and other suppliers	• Purchase of equity instruments** of other enterprises	• Repurchase of entity's stock
	• Payments of taxes	• Purchase of plant & equipment	• Repayment of debt principal, including capital lease obligations
	• Payments of interest		
	• Purchase of loans, debt, or equity instruments carried in trading portfolio		

Held in available-for-sale or held-to-maturity portfolios
**Held in available-for-sale portfolios*

Noncash investing and financing activities

- Acquiring an asset through a capital lease
- Conversion of debt to equity
- Exchange of noncash assets or liabilities for other noncash assets or liabilities
- Issuance of stock to acquire assets

Note that noncash investing and financing activities should be excluded from the statement itself. These transactions involve no cash inflows and outflows, but they have a significant effect on the prospective cash flows of a company. Therefore, they must be distinguished from activities that involved cash receipts and payments and must be reported in a separate schedule or in the footnotes to the financial statements.

In the statement, the inflows and outflows for each category (operating, investing, and financing) should be shown separately, and the **net** cash flows (the difference between the inflows and outflows) should be reported.

C. **Direct or Indirect Presentation in Reporting Operating Activities**

The FASB decided that the preferable method of presenting net cash flows from operating activities is by **directly** showing major classes of operating cash receipts and payments. However, the **indirect (reconciliation) method** is also permitted. When the direct method is used, it is also necessary to present a separate accompanying schedule showing the indirect method. The **direct method** is discussed first followed by a discussion of the **indirect method**.

Under the direct approach, cash flow elements of operating activities are derived from the accrual basis components of net income. In converting to the cash basis, accounts that should be analyzed under operating activities are those which are debited or credited when recording transactions that affect the income statement. These transactions include transactions with outsiders and adjusting entries. For example, these accounts include sales, cost of sales, operating expenses, and tax expense, as well as assets and liabilities which are related to them, such as accounts receivable, inventory, accounts payable, accrued expenses, and prepaid expenses. Note that interest expense and interest revenue are included within operating activities. Formulas for conversion of various income statement amounts from the accrual basis to the cash basis are summarized in the following table:

Accrual basis	*Additions*		*Deductions*		*Cash basis*
Net sales	+ Beginning AR	-	$\left(\begin{array}{l}\text{Ending AR}\\\text{AR written off}\end{array}\right)$	=	Cash received from customers
Cost of goods sold	$+ \left(\begin{array}{l}\text{Ending inventory}\\\text{Beginning AP}\end{array}\right)$	-	$\left(\begin{array}{l}\text{Depreciation and amortization}^*\\\text{Beginning inventory}\\\text{Ending AP}\end{array}\right)$	=	Cash paid to suppliers
Operating expenses	$+ \left(\begin{array}{l}\text{Ending prepaid expenses}\\\text{Beginning accrued}\\\quad\text{expenses payable}\end{array}\right)$	-	$\left(\begin{array}{l}\text{Depreciation and amortization}\\\text{Beginning prepaid expenses}\\\text{Ending accrued expenses}\end{array}\right)$	=	Cash paid for operating expenses

*Applies to a manufacturing entity

A T-account analysis method may be used instead of the above formulas to determine cash received and cash paid. T-account analysis provides a quick, systematic way to accumulate the information needed to prepare the statement.

The direct approach would be presented in the statement of cash flows as follows:

Cash flows from operating activities

Cash received from dividends	$ 500	
Cash received from interest	1,000	
Cash received from sale of goods	9,000	
Cash provided by operating activities		$10,500
Cash paid to suppliers	5,000	
Cash paid for operating expenses	500	
Cash paid for interest	500	
Cash paid for taxes	500	
Cash disbursed from operating activities		6,500
Net cash flows from operating activities		$ 4,000

The other way of reporting net cash flows from operations is known as the **indirect method**. This is done by starting with income from continuing operations and adjusting for changes in operating related accounts (e.g., inventory and accounts payable) and noncash expenses, revenues, losses, and gains.

Noncash items that were subtracted in determining income must be added back in determining net cash flows from operations. Each of these noncash items is a charge against income but does not decrease cash.

Items to be added back include depreciation, amortization of intangibles, amortization of discount on bonds payable, bad debt expense, and any increase in the deferred tax liability. Note each of these items is charged against income but does not decrease cash.

Noncash items that were added in determining income must be subtracted from net income in determining net cash flows from operations. Each of these noncash items is an increase to income but does not increase cash.

Items to be deducted from income include decreases in the deferred tax liability and amortization of the premium on bonds payable.

Finally, gains (losses) on fixed assets require adjustment, since the cash received is not measured by the gain (loss), that is, a fixed asset with a book value of $10, sold for $15 in cash, provides $15 in cash but is reported as only a $5 gain on the income statement. The $15 is shown as a separate item on the cash flow statement under investing activities and the $5 gain is subtracted from income. Losses on asset disposals are added back to income.

When preparing the cash flows from operating activities section of a Statement of Cash Flows under the indirect method, reconstructing journal entries may help in determining if an item should be added or subtracted to net income.

For example, if accounts receivable increased by $20,000 over the year, the journal entry that would result in an increase to accounts receivable would be:

Accounts receivable	xx	
Sales		xx

This entry results in an increase to net income (through sales), but cash is not affected. Therefore, the amount of the increase is deducted from net income in determining cash flows from operating activities.

If accounts payable decreased by $35,000, the entry for a decrease in accounts payable would be:

Accounts payable	xx	
Cash		xx

Since the corresponding credit results in a decrease to cash, the amount of this decrease should be deducted from net income in determining cash flows from operating activities.

When the **indirect** method is used, SFAS 95 permits, but does not require, separate disclosure of cash flows related to extraordinary items and discontinued operations. If an entity chooses to disclose this information, disclosure must be consistent for all periods affected. Extraordinary items, if disclosed, should be added to (or subtracted from) operating activities (adjustment to net income) at the gross amount, not the net-of-tax amount. Under either method the extraordinary item should be included in financing or investing activities, whichever is appropriate.

The direct and indirect approaches will both be illustrated throughout the remainder of this module.

D. **Example of Statement of Cash Flows**

The following information pertains to the Haner Company at December 31, 1999. Comparative balance sheets for 1998 and 1999 are as follows:

	1999	1998	Net change
Cash	$ 9,000	$ 8,000	$ 1,000
Treasury bills	4,000	3,000	1,000
Accounts receivable	4,000	5,000	(1,000)
Inventory	1,000	2,000	(1,000)
Prepaid insurance	2,000	3,000	(1,000)
Investment in Simba Co. (held-for-trading)	18,000	15,000	3,000
Investment in ABC Co. (available-for-sale)	11,900	22,000	(10,100)
Fixed assets	22,000	17,000	5,000
Accumulated depreciation	(5,000)	(4,000)	(1,000)
Deferred tax asset	1,400	-0-	1,400
	$68,300	$71,000	$ (5,500)

	1999	1998	
Accounts payable	$ 4,000	$ 7,000	$ (3,000)
Income tax payable	3,000	1,000	2,000
Deferred tax liability	6,400	3,000	2,000
Bonds payable	5,000	10,000	(5,000)
Common stock	20,000	20,000	-0-
Accumulated other comprehensive income			
Unrealized loss on available-for-sale securities (net of tax)	(2,100)	-0-	(2,100)
Retained earnings	33,400	30,000	3,400
	$68,300	$71,000	$(5,500)

The income statement for 1999 is as follows:

Net sales		$50,000
Cost of goods sold		(20,000)
Gross profit		30,000
Operating expenses		(17,000)
Income from operations		13,000
Other revenue and gains	$5,000	
Other expenses and losses	(2,500)	(2,500)
Income before extraordinary item and income taxes		15,500
Income tax expense:		
Current portion	5,404	
Deferred portion	2,000	7,040
Income before extraordinary item		8,460
Extraordinary loss from early extinguishment of debt, net of income taxes of $40		(60)
Net income		$8,400

The statement of comprehensive income for 1999 is as follows:

Net income		$8,400
Other comprehensive income		
Unrealized loss on available-for-sale securities, net of tax	($3,000)	
Less:		
Realized loss on available-for-sale securities, net of tax	(900)	(2,100)
Comprehensive income		$6,300

Additional information includes:

- Treasury bills have a maturity of less than 3 months from date of purchase
- Fixed assets costing $5,000 with a book value of $2,000 were sold for $4,000
- 3-year insurance policy was purchased in 19X5
- At 12/31/99, available-for-sale investments with a book value of $6,600 at 12/31/98 and $5,100 at 12/31/99 were used to retire $5,000 of bonds outstanding
- The $100 loss on redemption of the bonds ($5,100 FMV of securities – $5,000 BP) was reported on the income statement as an extraordinary item, net of tax of $40
- Other revenue and gains include a $3,000 unrealized gain recognized for trading securities

- Other expenses and losses consist of $1,000 interest paid and $1,500 realized loss on available-for-sale securities
- Changes in investments:
  - No changes in fair value of the investments occurred prior to 1999
  - There were no sales or purchases of trading securities during 1999
  - The tax rate is 40%

1. **Procedural Steps**

   a. The first step is to calculate the change in cash and cash equivalents.

	1999	*1998*	*Change*
Cash	$9,000	$8,000	+$1,000
Treasury bills	4,000	3,000	+ 1,000
Net change in cash and cash equivalents			+$2,000

   b. Calculate net cash flows from operating activities

   (1) Indirect approach

Net income	$ 8,400	
Decrease in accounts receivable	1,000	(a)
Decrease in inventory	1,000	(b)
Decrease in prepaid insurance	1,000	(c)
Decrease in accounts payable	(3,000)	(d)
Increase in income tax payable	2,000	(e)
Increase in deferred tax liability	2,000	(f)
Unrealized gain on trading securities	(3,000)	(g)
Loss on available-for-sale securities	1,500	(h)
Extraordinary loss from early extinguishment of bonds	100	(i)
Gain on sale of fixed assets	(2,000)	(j)
Depreciation expense	4,000	(k)
Net cash flows from operating activities	$13,000	

   Reconstructing journal entries may serve to explain the effect on net income of an increase or decrease of a particular account.

   (a) **Accounts Receivable.** For accounts receivable to decrease, the journal entry must have been

Cash	xx	
Accounts receivable		xx

   Cash increased as a result of the collection of accounts receivable. The amount of the decrease in accounts receivable should be added to net income.

   (b) **Inventory.** For inventory to decrease, the entry must have been

Cost of goods sold	xx	
Inventory		xx

   Expenses (CGS) increased without an additional cash outlay for inventory, so the decrease is added back to net income.

   (c) **Prepaid Insurance.** For prepaid insurance to decrease, the entry must have been

Insurance expense	xx	
Prepaid insurance		xx

   Because expenses increased without a corresponding cash outlay, the amount of the decrease in prepaid insurance should be added to net income.

(d) **Accounts Payable.** For accounts payable to decrease, the entry must have been

| Accounts payable | xx | |
| Cash | | xx |

The entry involves a cash outlay, so the decrease in accounts payable is deducted from net income.

(e) **Income Tax Payable.** For income tax payable to increase, the entry must have been

| Income tax expense | xx | |
| Income tax payable | | xx |

Expenses increased without an actual cash outlay; therefore the amount of the increase in the liability is added back to net income.

(f) **Deferred Tax Liability.** For deferred tax liability to increase, the entry must have been

| Income tax expense | xx | |
| Deferred tax liability | | xx |

Expenses increased without an actual cash outlay; therefore the amount of the increase in the liability is added back to net income.

(g) **Unrealized Gain on Trading Securities.** The entry to record the unrealized gain on trading securities would have been

| Investment in Simba Co.--held-for-trading | 3,000 | |
| Unrealized holding gain | | 3,000 |

Since unrealized gains on trading securities are recognized as income but do not involve a cash inflow, such gains must be subtracted from net income.

(h) **Realized Loss on Available-for-Sale Securities.** When $5,100 stock in ABC Co. was exchanged in redemption of bonds payable, the previously unrealized loss of $1,500 ($5,100 FMV at 12/31/99 – $6,600 FMV at 12/31/98) became realized. The entry to remove this amount from the other comprehensive income account entitled "Unrealized loss on available-for-sale securities account" is

| Realized loss on available-for-sale securities | 1,500 | |
| Unrealized loss on available-for-sale securities | | 1,500 |

Because the realized loss does not involve any cash outflow, it must be added back to net income. Since an unrealized loss on AFS securities of $3,500 was recognized from 1998 to 1999, a $5,000 decline in FMV must have occurred in 1999, as shown below. The deferred tax asset of $1,400 came from recognizing the future benefit of the unrealized loss of $3,500. The entry was

| Deferred tax asset | 1,400 | |
| Deferred tax expense (benefit) | | 1,400 |

	Available-for-Sale Securities				Deferred Tax Asset	
1998 Bal.	22,000			1999 Adj.	1,400	
		5,100	For redemption of BP		**Deferred Tax Expense (Benefit)--Unrealized Loss**	
		5,000	Unreal. loss*			-0-
1998 Bal.	11,900			Closing entry	1,400	1,400	19X6 adj.

	Unrealized G/L on AFS Securities				Accumulated Other Comprehensive Income	
1998 Bal.	-0-	1,500	Realized upon			-0-
Unrel. loss	5,000		redemption of BP	Closing entry	3,500	1,400	Closing entry
		3,500	Closing entry	1999 Bal.	2,100	
1999 Bal.	-0-					

Alternatively, a separate valuation account could be used.

Because unrealized gains/losses on available-for-sale securities are not reflected in income, no adjustment for this change is necessary on the statement of cash flows.

(i) **Loss on Redemption of Bonds Payable.** Since $5,100 worth of ABC stock was exchanged in redemption of $5,000 bonds payable, a loss of $100 was realized. However, because the loss does not involve a cash outflow, it must be added back to net income.

Bonds payable	5,000	
Loss on redemption	100	
Investment in ABC Co.--available-for-sale		5,100

(j) **Gain on Sale of Fixed Assets.** The entry to record the sale would have been

Cash	4,000	
Accumulated depreciation	3,000	
Gain on sale		2,000
Asset		5,000

The total amount of cash received in payment for the asset, not just the amount of the gain, represents the cash inflow. Since cash inflow from the sale (including the amount of the gain) appears in the investing section, the gain should be subtracted from net income.

(k) **Depreciation expense.** The entry to record depreciation is

Depreciation expense	4,000	
Accumulated depreciation		4,000

Because expenses increased without a corresponding cash outlay, the amount recorded for depreciation expense should be added to net income. In this case, the increase in accumulated depreciation must take into consideration the accumulated depreciation removed with the sale of the asset.

	AD		
AD of sold asset	3,000*	4,000	Beg. bal.
		4,000	Depreciation (plug)
		5,000	End. bal.

$5,000 Cost – $2,000 book value

(2) Direct approach

Cash received from customers		$51,000 (a)
Cash provided by operating activities		
Cash paid to suppliers	22,000 (b)	
Cash paid for operating expenses	12,000 (c)	
Cash paid for interest	1,000 (d)	
Cash paid for income taxes	3,000 (e)	
Cash disbursed for operating activities		38,000
Net cash flows from operating activities		$13,000

(a) **Cash Received from Customers.** Net sales + Beginning AR – Ending AR = Cash received from customers ($50,000 + $5,000 – $4,000 = $51,000). Cash received from customers also may be calculated by analyzing T-accounts.

	Accounts Receivable		
Beg. bal.	5,000		
Sales	50,000		
		51,000	Cash collected
End. bal.	4,000		

(b) **Cash Paid to Suppliers.** Cost of goods sold + Beginning AP – Ending AP + Ending inventory – Beginning inventory = Cash paid to suppliers ($20,000 + $7,000 – $4,000 +

$1,000 – $2,000 = $22,000). This is a two-account analysis. The amount for cash paid to suppliers equals the debit to accounts payable, but to solve for that amount, you must first determine purchases. To calculate purchases you must analyze the inventory account.

  Step #1 Calculate purchases

	Inventory		
Beg. bal.	2,000		
		20,000	CGS
Purchases	19,000		
End. bal.	1,000		

  Step #2 Calculate cash payments to suppliers

	Accounts Payable		
		7,000	Beg. bal.
Cash paid to		19,000	Purchases
suppliers	22,000		
		4,000	End. bal.

  Note that the $2,000 difference between the $20,000 CGS (accrual basis amount) and the $22,000 cash payments made to suppliers (cash basis amount) equals the difference between the $1,000 decrease in inventory and the $3,000 decrease in accounts payable when the indirect method is used. However, under the indirect method the difference is deducted from net income. This is because when the direct method is used, expenses such as CGS are examined as **outflows** of cash, whereas when the indirect method is used, net income (revenue-expenses, including CGS) is treated as a net cash **inflow**.

(c) **Cash Paid for Operating Expenses.** Operating expenses + Ending prepaid expenses – Beginning prepaid expenses – Depreciation expense (and other noncash operating expenses) = Cash paid for operating expenses ($17,000 + $2,000 – $3,000 – $4,000 = $12,000). The two accounts in this problem that relate to operating expenses are accumulated depreciation and prepaid insurance.

	Prepaid Insurance					Accumulated Depreciation		
Beg. bal.	3,000						4,000	Beg. bal.
		1,000	Insurance expense	AD of sold asset	3,000			
							4,000	Depreciation expense
End.bal.	2,000						5,000	End. bal.

  Since neither the expiration of prepaid insurance nor depreciation expense required a cash outlay, cash basis operating expenses are accrual expenses of $17,000 less depreciation ($4,000) and insurance expense ($1,000), or $12,000.

(d) **Cash Paid for Interest.** No analysis needed; amount was given in problem

(e) **Cash Paid for Income Taxes.** Current portion of income tax expense + Beginning income tax payable – Ending income tax payable = Cash paid for income taxes ($5,000 + $1,000 – $3,000 = $3,000). The journal entry for income tax expense is

Income tax expense	7,000	
Income tax payable		5,000
(current portion)		
Deferred tax liability		2,000

Therefore, taxes paid are $3,000, as shown in the T-account below.

Income Tax Payable

		1,000	Beg. bal.
Income taxes		5,000	Current portion
paid	3,000		
		3,000	End. bal.

c.   Analyze other accounts and determine whether the change is a cash inflow or outflow and whether it is a financing, an investing, or a noncash investing and financing activity.

(1)   Investments in ABC Co. decreased by $5,100 when this portion was exchanged for bonds outstanding (noncash investing and financing activity). The entry to record the exchange was:

Bonds payable	5,000	
Loss on redemption of bonds	100	
Investment in ABC Co.--		
available-for-sale		5,100

The loss on redemption of bonds is included in operating activities as explained in Section D.1.b.(1)(i) above.

(2)   Fixed assets increased by $5,000 after $5,000 of assets were sold for $4,000 (cash inflow, investing activity). Thus, $10,000 of fixed assets were purchased (cash outflow, investing activity).

Fixed Assets

Beg. bal.	$17,000		
		5,000	Sold asset
Purchase of			
new assets	10,000		
End. bal.	22,000		

(3)   Bonds payable decreased by $5,000 when they were retired as explained in Section c.(1) above (noncash investing and financing activity).

(4)   Common stock had no change.

(5)   Retained earnings increased $3,400 after net income of $8,400, indicating a dividend of $5,000 (cash outflow, financing activity).

Retained Earnings

		30,000	Beg. bal.
		8,400	Net income
Cash			
dividend	5,000		
		33,400	End. bal.

d.   Prepare formal statement

Haner Company
STATEMENT OF CASH FLOWS
For the Year Ended December 31, 1999

Cash flows from operating activities:

Cash received from customers	$51,000	
Cash provided by operating activities		$51,000
Cash paid to suppliers	22,000	
Cash paid for operating expenses	12,000	
Cash paid for income taxes	3,000	
Cash paid for interest expense	1,000	
Cash disbursed for operating activities		38,000
Net cash flows from operating activities		$13,000

Cash flows from investing activities:

Proceeds from sale of fixed assets	4,000	
Acquisition of fixed assets	(10,000)	
Net cash used by investing activities		(6,000)

Cash flows from financing activities:

Dividends paid	(5,000)	
Net cash used by financing activities		(5,000)
Net increase in cash and cash equivalents		$ 2,000
Cash and cash equivalents at beginning of year		11,000
Cash and cash equivalents at end of year		$13,000

Reconciliation of net income to cash provided by operating activities:

[This schedule would include the amounts from D.1.b.(1) (near the beginning of this example) starting with "net income" and ending with Net cash flows from operating activities of $13,000.]

Schedule of noncash investing and financing activities:

Exchange of investments to retire $5,000 bonds payable	$ 5,100

Disclosure of accounting policy:

For purposes of the statement of cash flows, the Company considers all highly liquid debt instruments purchased with a maturity of 3 months or less to be cash equivalents.

Note that if the reconciliation approach for operating activities had been shown in the body of the statement instead of the direct approach, an additional schedule showing interest paid and income taxes paid would be necessary.

E. Accounts Receivable Write-Offs

In the examples we assumed that there were no write-offs of uncollectible receivables. When write-offs occur, the indirect approach is modified only to the extent that the adjustment made to net income is for accounts receivable "net." However, when using the direct approach, the write-offs must be deducted when computing the amount of cash collected and operating expenses must be reduced by the amount of bad debt expense recorded in the period because such expense is a noncash item.

For example, assume a company has the following data available in its records.

Accounts Receivable				Allowance for Bad Debts		
Beg. bal.	15				2	Beg. bal.
Charge		5	Write-off	Write-off 5	4	Est. exp.
Sales	100	98	Cash collected		1	End. bal.
End. bal.	12					

Bad Debts Expense	
Est. exp. 4	

Cash flows would be computed under the indirect and the direct approach as follows:

Indirect approach			*Direct approach*	
Net income	$96		Sales	$100
($100 sales – $4 bad debt			+ Beg. AR	15
expenses)				$115
			- End. AR	12
				103
Add: Decrease in				
AR (net)	2*	-	Less write-offs	5
Cash collected from customers	$98		Cash collected from customers	$ 98
			Operating exp.	$ xx
			Bad debts exp.	– 4
			Cash paid for operating exp.	xx

[AR (net) beg. bal. $13 – end. bal. $11]

Under the **indirect approach**, net income is adjusted for **net** accounts receivable. When an account is written off, both "accounts receivable" and "allowance for doubtful accounts" are reduced, which has no net effect on accounts receivable, and no cash flow effect. Therefore, there is no modification to the calculation for the written-off account.

Under the **direct method**, accounts receivable (net) is not used as in the case of the **indirect method**. Rather the gross accounts receivable are used. The change in gross "accounts receivable" is $3 ($15 beg. bal. – $12 end. bal.) and includes the $5 write-off of the bad debt. Though the accounts receivable is reduced by $3, $5 of this reduction represents a write-off, not a collection. Therefore, the $5 write-off needs to be deducted from $103 ($100 Sales + $3 decrease in AR) to calculate the amount of cash collected of $98 ($103 – $5 write-off).

F. **Capital Leases**

In the period an entity enters into a capital lease, a noncach financing and investing activity in the amount of the present value of the minimum lease payments is reported following the cash flow statement. As payments are made by the lessee, the principal reduction component is reported as a cash outflow under financing activities. The interest component is reported in the operating activities section under the direct method. Under the indirect method, interest paid must be disclosed as supplementary information.

MULTIPLE-CHOICE QUESTIONS (1-37)

1. At December 31, 1999, Kale Co. had the following balances in the accounts it maintains at First State Bank:

Checking account #101	$175,000
Checking account #201	(10,000)
Money market account	25,000
90-day certificate of deposit, due 2/28/00	50,000
180-day certificate of deposit, due 3/15/00	80,000

Kale classifies investments with original maturities of 3 months or less as cash equivalents. In its December 31, 1999 balance sheet, what amount should Kale report as cash and cash equivalents?
   a. $190,000
   b. $200,000
   c. $240,000
   d. $320,000

2. The primary purpose of a statement of cash flows is to provide relevant information about
   a.   Differences between net income and associated cash receipts and disbursements.
   b.   An enterprise's ability to generate future positive net cash flows.
   c.   The cash receipts and cash disbursements of an enterprise during a period.
   d.   An enterprise's ability to meet cash operating needs.

3. Mend Co. purchased a 3-month US Treasury bill. Mend's policy is to treat as cash equivalents all highly liquid investments with an original maturity of 3 months or less when purchased. How should this purchase be reported in Mend's statement of cash flows?
   a.   As an outflow from operating activities.
   b.   As an outflow from investing activities.
   c.   As an outflow from financing activities.
   d.   Not reported.

4. Alp, Inc. had the following activities during 1999:

• Acquired 2,000 shares of stock in Maybel, Inc. for $26,000.

• Sold an investment in Rate Motors for $35,000 when the carrying value was $33,000.

• Acquired a $50,000, 4-year certificate of deposit from a bank. (During the year, interest of $3,750 was paid to Alp.)

• Collected dividends of $1,200 on stock investments.

In Alp's 1999 statement of cash flows, net cash used in investing activities should be
   a. $37,250
   b. $38,050
   c. $39,800
   d. $41,000

5. In 1999, a tornado completely destroyed a building belonging to Holland Corp. The building cost $100,000 and had accumulated depreciation of $48,000 at the time of the loss. Holland received a cash settlement from the insurance company and reported an extraordinary loss of $21,000. In Holland's 1999 cash flow statement, the net change reported in the cash flows from investing activities section should be a
   a. $10,000 increase.
   b. $21,000 decrease.
   c. $31,000 increase.
   d. $52,000 decrease.

6. In a statement of cash flows, if used equipment is sold at a gain, the amount shown as a cash inflow from investing activities equals the carrying amount of the equipment
   a.   Plus the gain.
   b.   Plus the gain and less the amount of tax attributable to the gain.
   c.   Plus both the gain and the amount of tax attributable to the gain.
   d.   With **no** addition or subtraction.

7. On September 1, 1999, Canary Co. sold used equipment for a cash amount equaling its carrying amount for both book and tax purposes. On September 15, 1999, Canary replaced the equipment by paying cash and signing a note payable for new equipment. The cash paid for the new equipment exceeded the cash received for the old equipment. How should these equipment transactions be reported in Canary's 1999 statement of cash flows?
   a.   Cash outflow equal to the cash paid less the cash received.
   b.   Cash outflow equal to the cash paid and note payable less the cash received.
   c.   Cash inflow equal to the cash received and a cash outflow equal to the cash paid and note payable.
   d.   Cash inflow equal to the cash received and a cash outflow equal to the cash paid.

Items 8 and 9 are based on the following:

A company acquired a building, paying a portion of the purchase price in cash and issuing a mortgage note payable to the seller for the balance.

8. In a statement of cash flows, what amount is included in investing activities for the above transaction?
   a.   Cash payment.
   b.   Acquisition price.
   c.   Zero.
   d.   Mortgage amount.

9. In a statement of cash flows, what amount is included in financing activities for the above transaction?
   a.   Cash payment.
   b.   Acquisition price.
   c.   Zero.
   d.   Mortgage amount.

10. Fara Co. reported bonds payable of $47,000 at December 31, 1998, and $50,000 at December 31, 1999. During 1999, Fara issued $20,000 of bonds payable in exchange for equipment. There was no amortization of bond premium or discount during the year. What amount should Fara report in its 1999 statement of cash flows for redemption of bonds payable?

a. $ 3,000
b. $17,000
c. $20,000
d. $23,000

Items 11 and 12 are based on the following:

In preparing its cash flow statement for the year ended December 31, 1999, Reve Co. collected the following data:

Gain on sale of equipment	$ (6,000)
Proceeds from sale of equipment	10,000
Purchase of A.S., Inc. bonds (par value $200,000)	(180,000)
Amortization of bond discount	2,000
Dividends declared	(45,000)
Dividends paid	(38,000)
Proceeds from sale of treasury stock (carrying amount $65,000)	75,000

In its December 31, 1999 statement of cash flows,

11. What amount should Reve report as net cash used in investing activities?
   a. $170,000
   b. $176,000
   c. $188,000
   d. $194,000

12. What amount should Reve report as net cash provided by financing activities?
   a. $20,000
   b. $27,000
   c. $30,000
   d. $37,000

13. On July 1, 1999, Dewey Co. signed a 20-year building lease that it reported as a capital lease. Dewey paid the monthly lease payments when due. How should Dewey report the effect of the lease payments in the financing activities section of its 1999 statement of cash flows?
   a. An inflow equal to the present value of future lease payments at July 1, 1999, less 1999 principal and interest payments.
   b. An outflow equal to the 1999 principal and interest payments on the lease.
   c. An outflow equal to the 1999 principal payments only.
   d. The lease payments should **not** be reported in the financing activities section.

14. Which of the following should be reported when preparing a statement of cash flows?

	Conversion of long-term debt to common stock	*Conversion of preferred stock to common stock*
a.	No	No
b.	No	Yes
c.	Yes	Yes
d.	Yes	No

15. Which of the following information should be disclosed as supplemental information in the statement of cash flows?

	Cash flow per share	*Conversion of debt to equity*
a.	Yes	Yes
b.	Yes	No
c.	No	Yes
d.	No	No

2

16. Which of the following is **not** disclosed on the statement of cash flows when prepared under the direct method, either on the face of the statement or in a separate schedule?
   a. The major classes of gross cash receipts and gross cash payments.
   b. The amount of income taxes paid.
   c. A reconciliation of net income to net cash flow from operations.
   d. A reconciliation of ending retained earnings to net cash flow from operations.

Items 17 through 21 are based on the following:

Flax Corp. uses the direct method to prepare its statement of cash flows. Flax's trial balances at December 31, 2000 and 1999, are as follows:

	December 31	
	2000	**1999**
Debits		
Cash	$ 35,000	$ 32,000
Accounts receivable	33,000	30,000
Inventory	31,000	47,000
Property, plant, & equipment	100,000	95,000
Unamortized bond discount	4,500	5,000
Cost of goods sold	250,000	380,000
Selling expenses	141,500	172,000
General and administrative expenses	137,000	151,300
Interest expense	4,300	2,600
Income tax expense	20,400	61,200
	$756,700	$976,100
Credits		
Allowance for uncollectible accounts	$ 1,300	$ 1,100
Accumulated depreciation	16,500	15,000
Trade accounts payable	25,000	17,500
Income taxes payable	21,000	27,100
Deferred income taxes	5,300	4,600
8% callable bonds payable	45,000	20,000
Common stock	50,000	40,000
Additional paid-in capital	9,100	7,500
Retained earnings	44,700	64,600
Sales	538,800	778,700
	$756,700	$976,100

• Flax purchased $5,000 in equipment during 2000.
• Flax allocated one third of its depreciation expense to selling expenses and the remainder to general and administrative expenses.

What amounts should Flax report in its statement of cash flows for the year ended December 31, 2000, for the following:

17. Cash collected from customers?

a. $541,800
b. $541,600
c. $536,000
d. $535,800

18. Cash paid for goods to be sold?
  a. $258,500
  b. $257,500
  c. $242,500
  d. $226,500

19. Cash paid for interest?
  a. $4,800
  b. $4,300
  c. $3,800
  d. $1,700

20. Cash paid for income taxes?
  a. $25,800
  b. $20,400
  c. $19,700
  d. $15,000

21. Cash paid for selling expenses?
  a. $142,000
  b. $141,500
  c. $141,000
  d. $140,000

22. In a statement of cash flows, which of the following would increase reported cash flows from operating activities using the direct method? (Ignore income tax considerations.)
  a. Dividends received from investments.
  b. Gain on sale of equipment.
  c. Gain on early retirement of bonds.
  d. Change from straight-line to accelerated depreciation.

23. A company's wages payable increased from the beginning to the end of the year. In the company's statement of cash flows in which the operating activities section is prepared under the direct method, the cash paid for wages would be
  a. Salary expense plus wages payable at the beginning of the year.
  b. Salary expense plus the increase in wages payable from the beginning to the end of the year.
  c. Salary expense less the increase in wages payable from the beginning to the end of the year.
  d. The same as salary expense.

24. Metro, Inc. reported net income of $150,000 for 1999. Changes occurred in several balance sheet accounts during 1999 as follows:

Investment in Videogold, Inc. stock, carried on the equity basis	$5,500 increase
Accumulated depreciation, caused by major repair to projection equipment	2,100 decrease
Premium on bonds payable	1,400 decrease
Deferred income tax liability (long-term)	1,800 increase

In Metro's 1999 cash flow statement, the reported net cash provided by operating activities should be

a. $150,400
b. $148,300
c. $144,900
d. $142,800

25. Lino Co.'s worksheet for the preparation of its 1999 statement of cash flows included the following:

	December 31	January 1
Accounts receivable	$29,000	$23,000
Allowance for uncollectible accounts	1,000	800
Prepaid rent expense	8,200	12,400
Accounts payable	22,400	19,400

Lino's 1999 net income is $150,000. What amount should Lino include as net cash provided by operating activities in the statement of cash flows?
  a. $151,400
  b. $151,000
  c. $148,600
  d. $145,400

26. In a statement of cash flows (using indirect approach for operating activities) an increase in inventories should be presented as a(n)
  a. Outflow of cash.
  b. Inflow and outflow of cash.
  c. Addition to net income.
  d. Deduction from net income.

27. How should a gain from the sale of used equipment for cash be reported in a statement of cash flows using the indirect method?
  a. In investment activities as a reduction of the cash inflow from the sale.
  b. In investment activities as a cash outflow.
  c. In operating activities as a deduction from income.
  d. In operating activities as an addition to income.

28. Would the following be added back to net income when reporting operating activities' cash flows by the indirect method?

	Excess of treasury stock acquisition cost over sales proceeds (cost method)	Bond discount amortization
a.	Yes	Yes
b.	No	No
c.	No	Yes
d.	Yes	No

29. Which of the following should **not** be disclosed in an enterprise's statement of cash flows prepared using the indirect method?
  a. Interest paid, net of amounts capitalized.
  b. Income taxes paid.
  c. Cash flow per share.
  d. Dividends paid on preferred stock.

Items 30 through 32 are based on the following:

The differences in Beal Inc.'s balance sheet accounts at December 31, 1999 and 1998, are presented below.

	Increase (Decrease)
Assets	
Cash and cash equivalents	$ 120,000
Short-term investments	300,000
Accounts receivable, net	-
Inventory	80,000
Long-term investments	(100,000)
Plant assets	700,000
Accumulated depreciation	-
	$1,100,000
Liabilities and Stockholders' Equity	
Accounts payable and accrued liabilities	$ (5,000)
Dividends payable	160,000
Short-term bank debt	325,000
Long-term debt	110,000
Common stock, $10 par	100,000
Additional paid-in capital	120,000
Retained earnings	290,000
	$1,100,000

The following additional information relates to 1999:

- Net income was $790,000.
- Cash dividends of $500,000 were declared.
- Building costing $600,000 and having a carrying amount of $350,000 was sold for $350,000.
- Equipment costing $110,000 was acquired through issuance of long-term debt.
- A long-term investment was sold for $135,000. There were no other transactions affecting long-term investments.
- 10,000 shares of common stock were issued for $22 a share.

In Beal's 1999 statement of cash flows,

30. Net cash provided by operating activities was
   a. $1,160,000
   b. $1,040,000
   c. $ 920,000
   d. $ 705,000

31. Net cash used in investing activities was
   a. $1,005,000
   b. $1,190,000
   c. $1,275,000
   d. $1,600,000

32. Net cash provided by financing activities was
   a. $ 20,000
   b. $ 45,000
   c. $150,000
   d. $205,000

Items 33 through 36 relate to data to be reported in the statement of cash flows of Debbie Dress Shops, Inc. based on the following information:

Debbie Dress Shops, Inc.
BALANCE SHEETS

	December 31, 1999	1998
Assets		
Current assets:		
Cash	$ 300,000	$ 200,000
Accounts receivable--net	840,000	580,000
Merchandise inventory	660,000	420,000
Prepaid expenses	100,000	50,000
Total current assets	1,900,000	1,250,000
Long-term investments	80,000	-
Land, buildings, and fixtures	1,130,000	600,000
Less accumulated depreciation	110,000	50,000
	1,020,000	550,000
Total assets	$3,000,000	$1,800,000
Equities		
Current liabilities:		
Accounts payable	$ 530,000	$ 440,000
Accrued expenses	140,000	130,000
Dividends payable	70,000	-
Total current liabilities	740,000	570,000
Note payable--due 2001	500,000	-
Stockholders' equity:		
Common stock	1,200,000	900,000
Retained earnings	560,000	330,000
	1,760,000	1,230,000
Total liabilities and stockholders' equity	$3,000,000	$1,800,000

Debbie Dress Shops, Inc.
INCOME STATEMENTS

	Year ended December 31, 1999	1998
Net credit sales	$6,400,000	$4,000,000
Cost of goods sold	5,000,000	3,200,000
Gross profit	1,400,000	800,000
Expenses (including income taxes)	1,000,000	520,000
Net income	$ 400,000	$ 280,000

Additional information available included the following:

- All accounts receivable and accounts payable related to trade merchandise. Accounts payable are recorded net and always are paid to take all of the discount allowed. The allowance for doubtful accounts at the end of 1999 was the same as at the end of 1998; no receivables were charged against the allowance during 1999.
- The proceeds from the note payable were used to finance a new store building. Capital stock was sold to provide additional working capital.

33. Cash collected during 1999 from accounts receivable amounted to
   a. $5,560,000
   b. $5,840,000
   c. $6,140,000
   d. $6,400,000

34. Cash payments during 1999 on accounts payable to suppliers amounted to

 a. $4,670,000
 b. $4,910,000
 c. $5,000,000
 d. $5,150,000

35. Net cash provided by financing activities for 1999 totaled

 a. $140,000
 b. $300,000
 c. $500,000
 d. $700,000

36. Net cash used in investing activities during 1999 was

 a. $ 80,000
 b. $530,000
 c. $610,000
 d. $660,000

37. Bee Co. uses the direct write-off method to account for uncollectible accounts receivable. During an accounting period, Bee's cash collections from customers equal sales adjusted for the addition or deduction of the following amounts:

	Accounts written off	*Increase in accounts receivable balance*
a.	Deduction	Deduction
b.	Addition	Deduction
c.	Deduction	Addition
d.	Addition	Addition

OTHER OBJECTIVE QUESTIONS

Problem 1   (15 to 25 minutes)

The following condensed trial balance of Probe Co., a publicly held company, has been adjusted except for income tax expense.

Probe Co.
CONDENSED TRIAL BALANCE

	12/31/99 Balances Dr. (Cr.)	12/31/98 Balances Dr. (Cr.)	Net change Dr. (Cr.)
Cash	$ 473,000	$ 817,000	$(344,000)
Accounts receivable, net	670,000	610,000	60,000
Property, plant, and equipment	1,070,000	995,000	75,000
Accumulated depreciation	(345,000)	(280,000)	(65,000)
Dividends payable	(25,000)	(10,000)	(15,000)
Income taxes payable	35,000	(150,000)	185,000
Deferred income tax liability	(42,000)	(42,000)	--
Bonds payable	(500,000)	(1,000,000)	500,000
Unamortized premium on bonds	(71,000)	(150,000)	79,000
Common stock	(350,000)	(150,000)	(200,000)
Additional paid-in capital	(430,000)	(375,000)	(55,000)
Retained earnings	(185,000)	(265,000)	80,000
Sales	(2,420,000)		
Cost of sales	1,863,000		
Selling and administrative expenses	220,000		
Interest income	(14,000)		
Interest expense	46,000		
Depreciation	88,000		
Loss on sale of equipment	7,000		
Gain on extinguishment of bonds	(90,000)		
	$_____0	$_____0	$300,000

Additional information

• During 1999 equipment with an original cost of $50,000 was sold for cash, and equipment costing $125,000 was purchased.

• On January 1, 1999, bonds with a par value of $500,000 and related premium of $75,000 were redeemed. The $1,000 face value, 10% par bonds had been issued on January 1, 1990, to yield 8%. Interest is payable annually every December 31 through 2009.

• Probe's tax payments during 1999 were debited to Income Taxes Payable. Probe recorded a deferred income tax liability of $42,000 based on temporary differences of $120,000 and an enacted tax rate of 35% at December 31, 1998; prior to 1998 there were no temporary differences. Probe's 1999 financial statement income before income taxes was greater than its 1999 taxable income, due entirely to temporary differences, by $60,000. Probe's cumulative net taxable temporary differences at December 31, 1999, were $180,000. Probe's enacted tax rate for the current and future years is 30%.

• 60,000 shares of common stock, $2.50 par, were outstanding on December 31, 1998. Probe issued an additional 80,000 shares on April 1, 1999.

• There were no changes to retained earnings other than dividends declared.

This problem consists of 6 items. Select the **best** answer for each item. Use a No. 2 pencil to blacken the appropriate ovals on the Objective Answer Sheet to indicate your answers. **Answer all items.** Your grade will be based on the total number of correct answers.

Required:

For each transaction in **items 1 through 6**, the following **two** responses are required:

• Determine the amount to be reported in Probe's 1999 statement of cash flows prepared using the indirect method. To record your answer, write the number in the boxes on the Objective Answer Sheet **and** blacken the corresponding oval below each box. Write zeros in any blank boxes preceding your numerical answer, and blacken the zero in the oval below the box. **You cannot receive credit for your answers if you fail to blacken an oval in each column.**

• Select from the list below where the specific item should be separately reported on the statement of cash flows prepared using the indirect method and blacken the corresponding oval on the Objective Answer Sheet.

    O.   Operating.

    I.   Investing.

    F.   Financing.

    S.   Supplementary information.

    N.   Not reported on Probe's statement of cash flows.

1.   Cash paid for income taxes.

2.   Cash paid for interest.

3.   Redemption of bonds payable.

4.   Issuance of common stock.

5.   Cash dividends paid.

6.   Proceeds from sale of equipment.

AUTHOR'S NOTE: Problem 4, income statement preparation, on the same exam asked candidates to use the same trial balance and additional information given above. This problem appears as the "Solution Approach Example for Problems" in Chapter 3.

Problem 2   (25 to 30 minutes)

This question appears in Volume 1, Chapter 3 under Other Objective Questions Solution Approach Example--Fill in the Numbers Example.

PROBLEMS

Problem 1 (20 to 25 minutes)

The statement of cash flows is normally a required basic financial statement for each period for which an earnings statement is presented.

Required:

a. What are the objectives of the statement of cash flows?

b. What are two types of transactions which would be disclosed in a separate schedule in the statement of cash flows although they don't affect cash during the report period?

c. What effect, if any, would each of the following seven items have upon the preparation of a cash flow statement assuming **direct** presentation is used to present cash flows from operations?

1. Accounts receivable--trade.
2. Inventory.
3. Depreciation.
4. Deferred tax liability from interperiod allocation.
5. Issuance of long-term debt in payment for a building.
6. Payoff of current portion of debt.
7. Sale of a fixed asset resulting in a loss.

Problem 2 (45 to 55 minutes)

The following is Omega Corp.'s comparative balance sheet accounts worksheet at December 31, 1999 and 1998, with a column showing the increase (decrease) from 1998 to 1999.

Comparative balance sheet worksheet	*1999*	*1998*	*Increase (Decrease)*
Cash	$ 800,000	$ 700,000	$100,000
Accounts receivable	1,128,000	1,168,000	(40,000)
Inventories	1,850,000	1,715,000	135,000
Property, plant, and equipment	3,307,000	2,967,000	340,000
Accumulated depreciation	(1,165,000)	(1,040,000)	(125,000)
Investment in Belle Co.	305,000	275,000	30,000
Loan receivable	270,000	--	270,000
Total assets	$6,495,000	$5,785,000	$710,000
Accounts payable	$1,015,000	$ 955,000	$ 60,000
Income taxes payable	30,000	50,000	(20,000)
Dividends payable	80,000	90,000	(10,000)
Capital lease obligation	400,000	--	400,000
Capital stock, common, $1 par	500,000	500,000	--
Additional paid-in capital	1,500,000	1,500,000	--
Retained earnings	2,970,000	2,690,000	280,000
Total liabilities and stockholders' equity	$6,495,000	$5,785,000	$710,000

Additional information

• On December 31, 1998, Omega acquired 25% of Belle Co.'s common stock for $275,000. On that date, the carrying value of Belle's assets and liabilities, which approximated their fair values, was $1,100,000. Belle reported income of $120,000 for the year ended December 31, 1999. No dividend was paid on Belle's common stock during the year.

• During 1999, Omega loaned $300,000 to Chase Co., an unrelated company. Chase made the first semiannual principal repayment of $30,000, plus interest at 10%, on October 1, 1999.

• On January 2, 1999, Omega sold equipment costing $60,000, with a carrying amount of $35,000, for $40,000 cash.

• On December 31, 1999, Omega entered into a capital lease for an office building. The present value of the annual rental payments is $400,000, which equals the fair value of the building. Omega made the first rental payment of $60,000 when due on January 2, 2000.

• Net income for 1999 was $360,000.

• Omega declared and paid cash dividends for 1999 and 1998 as follows:

	1999	*1998*
Declared	December 15, 1999	December 15, 1998
Paid	February 28, 2000	February 28, 1999
Amount	$80,000	$90,000

Required:

Prepare a statement of cash flows for Omega, Inc. for the year ended December 31, 1999, using the indirect method. Supplemental schedules and disclosures are **not** required. A worksheet is **not** required.

Problem 3 (30 to 40 minutes)

Presented below are the condensed statements of financial position of Linden Consulting Associates as of December 31, 1999 and 1998, and the condensed statement of income for the year ended December 31, 1999.

Linden Consulting Associates
CONDENSED STATEMENTS OF FINANCIAL POSITION
December 31, 1999 and 1998

	1999	*1998*	*Net change increase (decrease)*
Assets			
Cash	$ 652,000	$ 280,000	$372,000
Accounts receivable, net	446,000	368,000	78,000
Investment in Zach, Inc., at equity	550,000	466,000	84,000
Property and equipment	1,270,000	1,100,000	170,000
Accumulated depreciation	(190,000)	(130,000)	(60,000)
Excess of cost over book value of investment in Zach, Inc. (net)	152,000	156,000	(4,000)
Total assets	$2,880,000	$2,240,000	$640,000
Liabilities and Partners' Equity			
Accounts payable and accrued expenses	$ 320,000	$ 270,000	$ 50,000
Mortgage payable	250,000	270,000	(20,000)
Partners' equity	2,310,000	1,700,000	610,000
Total liabilities and partners' equity	$2,880,000	$2,240,000	$640,000

Linden Consulting Associates
CONDENSED STATEMENT OF INCOME
For the Year Ended December 31, 1999

Fee revenue	$2,664,000
Operating expenses	1,940,000
Operating income	724,000
Equity in earnings of Zach, Inc. (net of $4,000 amortization in excess of cost over book value)	176,000
Net income	$ 900,000

Additional information

- On December 31, 1998, partners' capital and profit sharing percentages were as follows:

	Capital	*Profit sharing %*
Garr	$1,020,000	60%
Pat	680,000	40%
	$1,700,000	

- On January 1, 1999, Garr and Pat admitted Scott to the partnership for a cash payment of $340,000 to Linden Consulting Associates as the agreed amount of Scott's beginning capital account. In addition, Scott paid a $50,000 cash bonus directly to Garr and Pat. This amount was divided $30,000 to Garr and $20,000 to Pat. The new profit sharing arrangement is as follows:

Garr	50%
Pat	30%
Scott	20%

- On October 1, 1999, Linden purchased and paid for an office computer costing $170,000, including $15,000 for sales tax, delivery, and installation. There were no dispositions of property and equipment during 1999.
- Throughout 1999, Linden owned 25% of Zach, Inc.'s common stock. As a result of this ownership interest, Linden can exercise significant influence over Zach's operating and financial policies. During 1999, Zach paid dividends totaling $384,000 and reported net income of $720,000. Linden's 1999 amortization of excess of cost over book value in Zach was $4,000.
- Partners' drawings for 1999 were as follows:

Garr	$280,000
Pat	200,000
Scott	150,000
	$630,000

Required:

a. Using the direct method, prepare Linden's statement of cash flows for the year ended December 31, 1999.

b. Prepare a reconciliation of net income to net cash provided by operating activities.

MULTIPLE-CHOICE ANSWERS

1. c __ __	9. c __ __	17. d __ __	25. a __ __	33. c __ __
2. c __ __	10. b __ __	18. d __ __	26. d __ __	34. d __ __
3. d __ __	11. a __ __	19. c __ __	27. c __ __	35. d __ __
4. d __ __	12. d __ __	20. a __ __	28. c __ __	36. c __ __
5. c __ __	13. c __ __	21. c __ __	29. c __ __	37. a __ __
6. a __ __	14. c __ __	22. a __ __	30. c __ __	
7. d __ __	15. c __ __	23. c __ __	31. a __ __	1st: __/37 = __%
8. a __ __	16. d __ __	24. c __ __	32. d __ __	2nd: __/37 = __%

MULTIPLE-CHOICE ANSWER EXPLANATIONS

A.   Objectives of the Statement of Cash Flows

1.   (c)   The 12/31/99 cash and cash equivalents balance is $240,000, as computed below.

Checking account #101	$175,000
Checking account #201	(10,000)
Money market account	25,000
90-day CD	50,000
Total cash and cash equivalents	$240,000

Bank overdrafts (like account #201) are normally reported as a current liability. However, when available cash is present in another account **in the same bank**, as in this case, offsetting is required. The money market account of $25,000 and the 90-day CD of $50,000 are considered cash equivalents because they had original maturities of 3 months or less. The 180-day CD of $80,000 is excluded because its original maturity was more than 3 months.

2.   (c)   Per SFAS 95, para 4, the **primary** purpose of a statement of cash flows is to provide relevant information about the enterprise's cash receipts and cash payments during a period. Thus, answer (c) is correct. Answers (a), (b), and (d) are incorrect because, although they represent uses of the statement of cash flows, they are not the primary use.

3.   (d)   The statement of cash flows is required to be prepared based on inflows and outflows of cash and cash equivalents during the period. The purchase of a cash equivalent using cash is **not** an outflow of cash and cash equivalents; it is merely a change in the composition of cash and cash equivalents. Cash has decreased and cash equivalents have increased, but total cash and cash equivalents is unchanged. Therefore this purchase is **not** reported in the statement of cash flows.

B.   Statement of Cash Flows Classification

4.   (d)   Investing activities include all cash flows involving **assets**, other than operating items. The investing activities are

Purchase of inv. in stock	$(26,000)
Sale of inv. in stock	35,000
Acquisition of CD	(50,000)
Net cash used	(41,000)

The gain on sale of investment in Rate Motors ($35,000 – $33,000 = $2,000), the interest earned ($3,750), and dividends earned ($1,200) are all operating items. Note that the sale of investment is reported in the investing section at the cash inflow amount ($35,000), not at the carrying value of the investment ($33,000). If the CD had been for 3 months instead of 4 years, it would be part of "Cash and Cash equivalents" and would not be shown under investing activities.

5.   (c)   The building which was destroyed had a book value of $52,000 ($100,000 – $48,000). The cash settlement from the insurance company resulted in a loss of $21,000. Therefore, the cash inflow from this investing activity must be $31,000 as shown below.

Proceeds	–	Book value	=	Loss
?	–	$52,000	=	($21,000)
$31,000	–	$52,000	=	($21,000)

Note that the $21,000 extraordinary loss must be before any income tax effect because SFAS 95 requires that any tax effect be left in operating activities.

6.   (a)   The cash inflow from the sale of equipment is the carrying amount plus the gain and answer (a) is correct. Answers (b) and (c) are incorrect because the tax attributable to the gain is a cash outflow in the operating activities section of the statement of cash flows. Note that when using the indirect method, the gain is deducted from operating activities, as to not double count the gain.

7.   (d)   The requirement is to determine how the equipment transactions should be reported in the statement of cash flows. Per SFAS 95, para 75, companies are required to report the gross amounts of cash receipts and cash payments, rather than net amounts. Therefore, the gross cash inflow from the sale of equipment and the gross outflow for the payment of new equipment should be reported. Thus, answer (d) is the correct answer. Answer (a) is incorrect because both gross inflow and outflow should be reported, rather than reporting the net cash flow from the transaction. Answer (b) is incorrect because gross cash flows, not net, are reported and because a note payable is not reported since the transaction results in no actual inflow or outflow in the period in which the payable occurs. This noncash activity would be reported in a separate schedule or in the footnotes. Noncash transactions commonly recognized in a separate schedule in the financial statements include: conversion of debt to equity and acquisition of assets by assuming liabilities, including lease obligations. Answer (c) is incorrect because the note payable is not reported on the statement of cash flows; rather it is shown in a separate schedule.

8.   **(a)**   Per SFAS 95, para 16, payments at the time of purchase or soon before or after purchase to acquire property, plant, and equipment and other productive assets are categorized as cash outflows for investing activities. Generally, these payments only include advance payments, down payments, or payments made at the time of purchase or soon before or after purchase. Therefore, only the cash payment is considered a cash outflow for investing activities and answer (a) is correct.

9.   **(c)**   Per SFAS 95, para 32, noncash investing and financing activities include acquiring assets by assuming directly related liabilities, such as purchasing a building by incurring a mortgage to the seller. This type of transaction does not involve the flow of cash. Therefore, cash flows for financing activities related to this transaction would be zero and answer (c) is correct. Note that the cash down payment would be reported as a cash outflow for **investing** activities.

10.   **(b)**   To determine the cash paid for redemption of bonds payable, the solutions approach is to set up a T-account for bonds payable.

Bonds Payable

		$47,000	12/31/98
Bonds redeemed	?	20,000	Bonds issued
		50,000	12/31/99

The amount of bonds redeemed can be computed as $17,000. ($47,000 + $20,000 − $50,000 = $17,000)

11.   **(a)**   Investing activities include all cash flows involving **assets** other than operating items. The investing activities are

Proceeds from sale of equipment	$ 10,000
Purchase of A.S., Inc. bonds	(180,000)
Net cash used in investing activities	$(170,000)

The gain on sale of equipment ($6,000) and amortization of bond discount ($2,000) are net income adjustments in the operating section, while dividends paid ($38,000) and proceeds from sale of treasury stock ($75,000) are financing items. The excess of dividends declared over dividends paid is a noncash financing activity.

12.   **(d)**   Financing activities include all cash flows involving **liabilities and owners' equity** other than operating items. The financing activities are

Dividends paid	$(38,000)
Proceeds from sale of treasury stock	75,000
Net cash provided by financing activities	$ 37,000

The excess of dividends declared over dividends paid is a **noncash** financing activity. The gain on sale of equipment ($6,000) and amortization of bond discount ($2,000) are net income adjustments in the operating section, while the proceeds from sale of equipment ($10,000) and purchase of A.S., Inc. bonds ($180,000) are investing items.

13.   **(c)**   Financing activities include the repayment of debt principal or, as in this case, the payment of the capital lease obligation. Thus, the cash outflow is equal to the 1999

principal payments only. The interest on the capital lease is classified as an operating cash outflow.

14.   **(c)**   The requirement is to determine if a conversion of long-term debt and preferred stock to common stock should be reported when preparing a statement of cash flows. Noncash transactions may not involve cash receipts or payments in the period in which they occur but may have a significant effect on prospective cash flows of a company. Therefore, both items should be reported in a separate schedule. Both conversion of long-term debt and conversion of preferred stock to common stock are considered a noncash financing and investing activity and should be disclosed in a separate schedule. Therefore, answers (a), (b), and (d) are incorrect.

15.   **(c)**   Noncash investing and financing activities are reported as supplemental information to the statement of cash flows because while they do not affect cash in the current year, they may have a significant effect on the prospective cash flows of the company. Therefore, conversion of debt to equity is disclosed as supplemental information to the statement of cash flows. However, SFAS 95 specifies that cash flow per share should **not** be reported on the statement of cash flows because it may be misleading and may be incorrectly used as a measure of profitability.

C.   Direct or Indirect Presentation in Reporting Operating Activities

16.   **(d)**   Under either the direct method or indirect method, the major classes of gross cash receipts and gross cash payments [answer (a)] must be reported in the statement of cash flows. Under the direct method, the amount of income taxes paid [answer (b)] is one of the components of net cash flows from operating activities; under the indirect method, it is a required supplemental disclosure. A reconciliation of net income to net cash flow from operations [answer (c)] is a required supplemental disclosure under the direct method, and is included in the body of the statement under the indirect method. Only a reconciliation of ending retained earnings to net cash flow from operations [answer (d)] is **not** required under either method.

17.   **(d)**   Cash collected from customers can be computed using either a formula or a T-account. The formula is

Sales	−	[End AR	−	(Beg AR	− Write-offs)]=	Collections
$538,800	−	[$33,000	−	($30,000	− $0)] =	$535,800

In the formula above, sales is adjusted for the **change in AR, exclusive of write-offs**, because write-offs represent sales (and AR) which will never be collected in cash. In this problem, no mention is made of write-offs, so it must be assumed that the change in the allowance account results solely from bad debt expense (no write-offs). Since there are no write-offs, the increase in AR ($33,000 − $30,000 = $3,000) is subtracted from sales because those sales increased AR instead of cash. The T-account solution is below.

	Accounts Receivable		
12/31/99	30,000		
Sales	538,800	0	Write-offs
		?	Collections = 535,800
12/31/00	33,000		

18.   (d)   Cash paid for goods to be sold can be computed using either a formula or T-accounts. The formula is

CGS	+	(End. inv. – Beg. inv.)	–	(End. AP – Beg AP)	–	Cash paid
$250,000	+	($31,000 – $47,000)	–	($25,000 – $17,500)	–	Cash paid
$250,000	–	$16,000	–	$7,500	–	$226,500

The decrease in inventory ($16,000) is subtracted from CGS because that portion of CGS resulted from a use of inventory purchased in prior years, rather than from a cash payment. The increase in AP is subtracted because that portion of CGS was not paid this year. Using T-accounts, first purchases are computed using the inventory account, then payments are computed using the accounts payable account.

	Inventory		
12/31/99	47,000		
Purchases	?	250,000	CGS
12/31/00	31,000		

1. Purchases = $234,000

	Accounts Payable		
		17,500	12/31/99
Payments	?	234,000	Purchases
		25,000	12/31/00

2. Payments = $226,500

19.   (c)   The trial balance does **not** include prepaid interest or interest payable, both of which would affect the computation of cash paid for interest. In the absence of those accounts, cash paid for interest is equal to interest expense plus (minus) bond premium (discount) amortization.

Interest expense	–	Discount amortization	=	Cash paid
$4,300	–	($5,000 – $4,500)	=	$3,800

Flax's 2000 entry to record interest expense was

Interest expense	4,300	
Cash		3,800
Discount on bonds payable		500

20.   (a)   Cash paid for income taxes can be computed using the following formula:

Inc. tax expense	–	(End. inc. tax payable – Beg. inc. tax payable)	–	(End. def. tax liability – Beg. def. tax liability)	=	Cash paid for inc. tax
$20,400	–	($21,000 – $27,100)	–	($5,300 – $4,600)	=	Cash paid
$20,400	+	$6,100	–	$700	=	$25,800

The decrease in income taxes payable is added to income tax expense because cash was used to decrease the liability as well as to pay tax expense. The increase in the deferred tax liability is deducted from income tax expense because that portion of tax expense was deferred (not paid in cash). Flax's summary journal entry to record income taxes for 2000 is

Inc. tax expense	20,400	
Inc. tax payable	6,100	
Cash		25,800
Deferred taxes		700

21.   (c)   In general, cash paid for selling expenses is affected by prepaid selling expenses, accrued selling expenses, depreciation and/or amortization expense, and possibly bad debts expense. In this case, there are no prepaid or accrued selling expenses in the trial balances, and bad debts expense is apparently included in general and administrative expenses (see discussion below). Therefore, cash paid for selling expenses is $141,000 ($141,500 selling expenses less $500 depreciation expense). Total depreciation expense can be determined from the change in the accumulated depreciation account ($16,500 – $15,000 = $1,500), and 1/3 of that amount is selling expense (1/3 x $1,500 = $500). Note that bad debt expense ($1,300 – $1,100 = $200) must be included in general and administrative expenses, because the answer obtained by assuming it is part of selling expenses ($141,000 – $200 = $140,800) is not given as one of the four choices.

22.   (a)   Per SFAS 95, businesses are encouraged to use the direct method of reporting operating activities under which major classes of cash receipts and cash payments are shown. The minimum cash flows to be disclosed under this method are cash collected from customers, interest and dividends received, cash paid to employees and suppliers, income taxes paid, and interest paid. Therefore, answer (a) is correct.

23.   (c)   In a statement of cash flows in which the operating activities section is prepared using the direct method, the cash paid for wages would be equal to the accrual-basis salary expense, plus/minus any decrease/increase in the wages payable account. (The logic is essentially the same as an accrual-basis to cash-basis adjustment). Therefore, answer (c) is correct and answers (a), (b), and (d) are incorrect.

24.   (c)   Net income was $150,000. Three of the four items given are net income adjustments (the major repair to projection equipment [$2,100] is a cash outflow under investing activities), resulting in net cash provided by operating activities of $144,900.

Net income	$150,000
Equity method income	(5,500)
Premium amortization	(1,400)
Increase in def. tax liability	1,800
Cash provided by operating activities	$144,900

When equity method income is recorded, the offsetting debit is to the investment account, not cash; when premium on bonds payable is amortized, the credit to interest expense is offset by a debit to the premium account, not cash. Therefore, both of these items **increase** income without increasing cash, and must be **deducted** as a net income adjustment. For the deferred tax items, when income tax expense is debited, the offsetting credit is to deferred tax liability, not cash. Therefore, this item **decreases** net income without decreasing cash, and it must be **added back** as a net income adjustment. Note that there should normally be depreciation expense as a net income adjustment, but it is not given.

25. (a) Based only on the items given, net cash provided by operating activities is $151,400, as computed below.

Net income	$150,000
Increase in net AR	
[($29,000 – 1,000) – ($23,000 – 800)]	(5,800)
Decrease in prepaid rent	
($12,400 – $8,200)	4,200
Increase in AP ($22,400 – $19,400)	3,000
Cash provided by ops.	$151,400

The increase in net AR is deducted from net income because it indicates that cash collected is less than sales revenue. The decrease in prepaid rent is added because it reflects rent expense which was **not** a cash payment, but an allocation of previously recorded prepaid rent. Finally, the increase in AP is added because it also represents an expense (cost of goods sold) which was not yet paid.

26. (d) The objective of a statement of cash flows is to explain what caused the change in the cash balance. The first step in this process is to determine cash provided by operations. When presenting cash from operating activities under the indirect approach, net income must be adjusted for changes in current assets other than cash and in current liabilities. These adjustments are required because items which resulted from noncash events must be removed from accrual-based income. For example, when inventory increases during the period, inventory sold is less than inventory purchased. Considering only the increase in the inventory account, cost of goods sold on an accrual basis is less than it would have been if cash basis were being used. In converting to the cash basis, the increase in inventory must be subtracted from net income to arrive at cash from operations [answer (d)]. Answer (a) is incorrect because even though an increase in inventories requires an outflow of cash, inventories are shown as adjustments to net income under the indirect method. Answer (b) is incorrect because it describes how a noncash transaction such as the exchange of land for a note would be handled. Answer (c) is incorrect because an increase in an inventory would be a deduction from net income, not an addition.

27. (c) When using the indirect method for reporting net cash flows from operations, you start with net income from continuing operations and adjust for changes in operating related accounts (i.e., inventory, accounts payable) and noncash expenses, revenues, gains and losses. The proceeds from the sale of equipment is reported as an inflow in the investing section of the statement of cash flows, at its gross amount. This gross amount includes the gain. Therefore, to avoid double counting and to properly classify cash inflows, the gain is subtracted from net income to show the proper cash balance from operating activities. Therefore, answer (c) is correct. Answer (a) is incorrect because the gain from the sale is reported as a cash inflow which increases the cash balance, not as a reduction in cash. Answer (b) is

incorrect because the sale is treated as a cash inflow, not a cash outflow. Answer (d) is incorrect because the gain is treated as a subtraction from income, not an addition.

28. (c) Under the indirect method of reporting cash flows from operations, income from continuing operations is adjusted for changes in operating related accounts and noncash expenses, revenues, losses, and gains. Noncash items that were subtracted in determining income must be added back in. This would include amortization of bond discount, as it is a charge against income but does not decrease cash. The excess of treasury stock acquisition cost over sales proceeds would not be added back to net income. Under the cost method, this loss would not be included in net income but would be charged back to a paid-in capital account or retained earnings. The acquisition and sale of treasury stock, furthermore, would be financing activities. Therefore, answer (c) is correct.

29. (c) SFAS 95 specifies that cash flow per share should **not** be reported on the statement of cash flows because it may be misleading and may be incorrectly used as a measure of profitability. Therefore, answer (c) is correct. Answers (a) and (b) are incorrect because, when the indirect method is used, separate disclosure is required for **interest paid** (net of amounts capitalized) and **income taxes paid**. Answer (d) is incorrect because, regardless of the method used, **dividends paid** on preferred stock are reported as a **financing activity**.

D. Example of Statement of Cash Flows

30. (c) Net cash provided by operating activities can be computed by using either the **direct** or **indirect** approach. In this case, there is not enough information to use the direct approach. In the indirect approach, net income is adjusted for noncash items, as shown below.

Net income	$790,000
Gain on sale of LT investment	(35,000)
Increase in inventory	(80,000)
Depreciation expense	250,000
Decrease in AP and accrued liabs.	(5,000)
	$920,000

The additional information indicates that a LT investment was sold for $135,000. The listing of accounts shows a decrease in LT investments of $100,000. The gain on sale ($135,000 – $100,000 = $35,000) is deducted because the total cash effect of this transaction ($135,000) will be reported as an investing activity. Two of the working capital accounts which changed are related to net income. The increase in inventory ($80,000) is deducted because cash was used to increase inventory. The decrease in accounts payable and accrued liabilities is deducted because cash was used to pay these liabilities. The only other information or account given which affects net income is accumulated depreciation. Although this account did not show any net decrease or increase during 1999, we know it was decreased by $250,000 when the building was sold ($600,000 cost less $350,000 carrying amount equals $250,000 accumulated depreciation). Therefore, depreciation expense of $250,000 must have increased the accumulated depreciation account to result in a net effect for the year of $0. Depreciation expense is added because it is a noncash expense.

An alternative method of computing net cash provided by operating activities is to back into the answer after determining cash used in investing activities and cash provided by financing activities.

Cash provided by Operating	
Activities	$?
Cash used in Investing	
Activities	(1,005,000)
Cash provided by Financing	
Activities	205,000
Net increase in Cash	$ 120,000

The problem tells us that cash and cash equivalents increased by $120,000. Therefore, cash provided by operating activities is $920,000 ($920,000 – $1,005,000 + $205,000 = $120,000).

31. (a) Investing activities include all cash flows involving **assets**, other than operating items. **Financing** activities include all cash flows involving **liabilities and equity**, other than operating items. The common stock issued is a financing activity. In this case, the changes in the inventory and accumulated depreciation accounts are operating items. The cash flows involving the other assets, listed below, are investing activities

Purchase of ST investments	$ (300,000)
Sale of LT investments	135,000
Sale of plant assets	350,000
Purchase of plant assets	(1,190,000)
	$(1,005,000)

The amounts above were given, except for the purchase of plant assets, the amount of which can be determined from the following T-account:

Plant Assets

Cost of equip. acquired	110,000	600,000	Cost of
Cost of plant assets purchased	?		bldg. sold
Net increase	700,000		

The equipment acquired through issuance of LT debt is a **noncash** investing and financing activity so it does not affect net **cash** used in investing activities.

32. (d) Financing activities include all cash flows involving **liabilities and equity**, other than operating items. **Investing** activities include all cash flows involving **assets**, other than operating items. In this case, the change in the **accounts payable and accrued liabilities** account is an operating item. The part of the change in **retained earnings** caused by net income ($790,000) is also an operating item. The cash flows involving the other liability and equity accounts, listed below, are financing activities.

Payment of dividends	
($500,000 – $160,000)	$(340,000)
Issuance of ST debt	325,000
Issuance of common stock	
(10,000 x $22)	220,000
	$205,000

The problem states that $500,000 of dividends were **declared**, and this is confirmed by the change in the retained earnings account ($790,000 net income – $500,000 dividends declared = $290,000 net increase). However, since dividends payable increased by $160,000, only $340,000 of dividends were **paid** ($500,000 – $160,000). The issuance of common stock (10,000 shares x $22 per share = $220,000) is confirmed by the increases in the **common stock** and **additional paid-in capital** accounts ($100,000 + $120,000 = $220,000). The issuance of LT debt for equipment ($110,000) is a **noncash** financing and investing activity, so it does not affect net **cash** provided by financing activities. Note that the answers to the three related questions can be verified by comparing them to the increase in cash and cash equivalents ($120,000) given in the problem.

Cash provided by oper. acts.	$920,000
Cash used in inv. acts,	(1,005,000)
Cash provided by fin. acts.	205,000
Increase in cash and cash	
equivalents	$ 120,000

33. (c) The requirement is to calculate the amount of cash collected during 1999 from accounts receivable. The solutions approach is to prepare a T-account for accounts receivable. The allowance account has no effect on this analysis, because the problem states that the balance in this account has not changed and no accounts receivable were written off. Net credit sales are the only debit to accounts receivable because all accounts receivable relate to trade merchandise. In the T-account below, you must solve for the missing credit to determine that $6,140,000 was collected on account during 1999.

AR--Net

12/31/98 balance	580,000	?	1999
1999 net credit			Collections
sales	6,400,000		
12/31/99 balance	840,000		

AUTHOR'S NOTE: Based on the information given in this problem, no bad debt expense was recorded during 1999. However unrealistic this assumption might be, it is important to simply work with the information as given.

34. (d) The requirement is to calculate the amount of cash payments during 1999 on accounts payable. The solutions approach is to visualize the accounts payable T-account.

Accounts Payable

		440,000	12/31/98
Payments	?	?	Purchases
		530,000	12/31/99

It is apparent that to determine payments to suppliers, purchases of trade merchandise must first be computed. The cost of goods sold statement can be used to compute purchases.

Beginning inventory	$ 420,000	
+ Purchases	+	?
– Ending inventory	–	660,000
Cost of goods sold	$5,000,000	

Purchases   = $5,000,000 – ($420,000 – $660,000)
                    = $5,240,000

Finally, the purchases are entered into the accounts payable T-account, and payments to suppliers of $5,150,000 can be plugged in.

Accounts Payable			
		440,000	12/31/98
Payments	5,150,000	5,240,000	Purchases
		530,000	12/31/99

35.   (d)   The requirement is to determine net cash flows provided by financing activities in 1999. The solutions approach is to work through the comparative balance sheets noting increases and decreases in liability accounts other than those related to operations and increases or decreases in stockholders' equity accounts. The additional information given must be considered in connection with these changes. Cash inflows from financing activities include proceeds from long-term borrowing, and issuance of capital stock.

Proceeds from long-term note	$500,000
Proceeds from issuance of common stock	300,000
	$800,000

To determine the amount of dividends paid, it is necessary to analyze both the retained earnings and the dividends payable accounts.

Dividends Payable				Retained Earnings		
		-0-	12/31/98		330,000	12/31/98
Dividends			Dividends			
paid	?	?	declared	?	400,000	Net income
		70,000	12/31/99		560,000	12/31/99

Dividends declared = $330,000 + 400,000 − 560,000 = $170,000
Dividends paid   = $0 + 170,000 − 70,000 = $100,000

Net cash flows provided by financing activities is $700,000 ($800,000 − $100,000).

36.   (c)   The requirement is to compute the cash used in investing activities during 1999. The two assets other than those related to operations shown on the balance sheet (long-term investments and land, building, and fixtures) have increased from 12/31/98 to 12/31/99, indicating cash purchases since the additional information does not suggest any other means of acquisition. Therefore, cash outflows from investing activities include $80,000 for long-term in-vestments and $530,000 ($1,130,000 − $600,000) for land, building, and fixtures.

E. Accounts Receivable Write-offs

37.   (a)   The solutions approach is to set up T-accounts for the related accounts.

Sales		AR	
	Sales	Beg. Bal.	Collections
		Sales	Write-offs
		End. Bal.	

Sales are debited to AR and credited to sales; collections are debited to cash and credited to AR. Under the direct write-off method, write-offs of customer accounts are debited to bad debts expense, and credited to AR. To adjust sales to cash collections from customers, Bee must subtract the increase in accounts receivable (because Bee has not yet received cash for the sales remaining in AR). Bee must also subtract the accounts written off, because these sales have not resulted in cash receipts (and probably never will).

OTHER OBJECTIVE ANSWERS AND ANSWER EXPLANATIONS

Problem 1

1.   ($185,000, S)   The payments for income taxes during the year were debited to the income taxes payable account. To arrive at the amount of payments, a T-account can be used as follows:

		Income Taxes Payable		
			150,000	12/31/98
Payments		185,000		
12/31/99		35,000		

Note that the taxes payable for 1999 have not yet been recorded. Therefore, the change in the account is comprised entirely of payments. This amount of cash paid for income taxes would be reported separately as supplementary information for a statement of cash flows prepared using the indirect method.

2.   ($ 50,000, S)   Interest paid on the bonds in 1999 would be $50,000 ($500,000 x 10%). Alternatively, the $46,000 plus the $4,000 premium amortization (see explanation for the next item below) also results in $50,000 as the amount paid for interest. This amount of cash paid for interest would be reported separately as supplementary information for a statement of cash flows using the indirect method.

3.   ($485,000, F)   Through the following T-account analyses, a journal entry for the redemption of the bonds payable can be determined:

		Bonds Payable		
		1,000,000	12/31/98	
Redemption	500,000			
		500,000	12/31/99	

	Unamortized Premium on Bonds			
Amortization	4,000	150,000	12/31/98	
Redemption	75,000			
		71,000	12/31/99	

	Gain on Extinguishment of Bonds	
	90,000	12/31/99

	Cash
	?

Journal entry for redemption

Bonds payable	500,000	
Unamortized premium on bonds	75,000	
Gain on extinguishment of bonds		90,000
Cash		485,000

This amount paid for the redemption of the bonds would be separately reported in the financing section on the statement of cash flows prepared using the indirect method. Financing activities include obtaining resources from owners and returning the investment, as well as obtaining resources from creditors and **repaying the amounts borrowed.**

4.   ($255,000, F)   An additional 80,000 shares of $2.50 par value common stock were issued during 1999. The following T-accounts depict the changes in the common stock and additional paid-in capital accounts:

	Common Stock		
	150,000	12/31/98	
	200,000	issuance	(80,000 x $2.50)
	350,000	12/31/99	

	Additional Paid-in Capital	
	375,000	12/31/98
	55,000	issuance
	430,000	12/31/99

The journal entry for the issuance of the stock would have been

Cash	255,000	
Common stock		200,000
Additional paid-in capital		55,000

This amount received for the issuance of the common stock would be reported separately in the financing section of the statement of cash flows prepared using the indirect method. Financing activities include **obtaining resources from owners** and returning the investment, as well as obtaining resources from creditors and repaying the amounts borrowed.

5.   ($ 65,000, F)   The problem states that there were no changes to retained earnings during the year other than dividends declared. Therefore, the following T-account analyses depict the dividend activity during the year:

	Retained Earnings		
		265,000	12/31/98
Dividends declared	80,000		
		185,000	12/31/99

Dividends Payable			Cash	
	10,000	12/31/98	?	
	15,000	Accrual during 1999		
	25,000	12/31/99		

The following journal entry would have been made:

Retained earnings	80,000	
Dividends payable		15,000
Cash		65,000

This amount paid for the dividends would be reported separately in the financing section of the statement of cash flows prepared using the indirect method. Financing activities include obtaining resources from owners and **returning the investment**, as well as obtaining resources from creditors and repaying the amounts borrowed.

6.   ($ 20,000, I)   The following T-account analyses depict the sale of the equipment during 1999:

Property, Plant and Equipment			
12/31/98	995,000		
		50,000	sale
purchase	125,000		
12/31/99	1,070,000		

Accumulated Depreciation			
		280,000	12/31/98
Depreciation on sold asset	23,000	88,000	Depreciation expense
		345,000	12/31/99

Loss on Sale of Equipment			Cash	
12/31/99	7,000		?	

The following journal entry would have been made for the sale of the equipment:

Cash	20,000	
Accumulated depreciation	23,000	
Loss on sale of equipment	7,000	
Property, plant and equipment		50,000

The proceeds from the sale of equipment would be reported separately in the investing section of the statement of cash flows. Included in the investing section are the acquisition and disposition of long-term productive assets or securities (not considered cash equivalents), as well as the lending of money and collection of loans.

ANSWER OUTLINE

Problem 1   Statement of Cash Flows

a.   Objectives of statement
       Information about cash receipts and payments
       Information about investing and financing activities
       Facilitate user assessments

b.   Transactions not affecting cash, but reported in separate
       schedule
       Acquisition of assets with
           Debt
           Other assets
           Equity securities
       Reduction of debt by
           Other debt
           Distribution of assets
           Issuance of equity securities

c.   Effect on statement of cash flows when direct presenta-
       tion used for operating activities
       Change in accounts receivable affects cash received
           from customers
       Change in inventory affects cash used for CGS
       Depreciation is noncash expense
           Deduct from operating expenses
       Change in deferred tax liability is neither inflow nor
           outflow of cash
       Long-term debt issued for building does not affect
           cash
           Noncash financing and investing transaction
              shown on a separate schedule
       Reduction of current debt is outflow of cash--
           financing activity
       Proceeds are an inflow of cash--investing activity

UNOFFICIAL ANSWER

Problem 1   Statement of Cash Flows

a.   The objectives of the statement of cash flows are to
provide information about cash receipts and payments from
operating, investing, and financing activities. This information helps users assess the company's ability to generate
future net cash flows and ability to meet obligations and pay
dividends. The statement also helps users assess the differences between income and associated cash receipts and
payments.

b.   Investing and financing activities that do not involve
cash receipts and payments during the period should be excluded from the cash flow statement and reported in a separate schedule. Transactions that would be classified as noncash financing and investing activities would include the
following:

   1.   Purchase of assets by the issuance of capital stock
or debt, or a reduction in another asset.
   2.   Reduction of a liability by the issuance of capital
stock or the incurrence of another liability, or a reduction in
an asset.

c.   The effects and procedural considerations of the seven
account balances (transactions) upon the preparation of a
statement of cash flows are as follows:

   1.   Accounts receivable--trade are generated as a result
of credit sales. A balance in accounts receivable--trade represents sales (a part of operating earnings) not represented
by cash. An increase in the accounts receivable--trade balance indicates that the actual cash generated is equal to sales
as reported on the earnings statement less the increase in
accounts receivable--trade balance. Conversely, a net decrease in the accounts receivable--trade balance would have
to be added to sales as reported on the earnings statement to
arrive at cash generated from sales. In the preparation of a
statement of cash flows the increase (decrease) in this account balance between two periods is subtracted from (or
added to) net sales to arrive at cash received from customers
for sales.

   2.   Inventory is a component part of cost of goods
sold. The net change in inventory balances affects the cash
used for cost of goods sold. An increase in ending inventory
over beginning inventory reduces the cost of goods sold.
However, cash was presumed to be used to increase the inventory balance. An increase in the inventory balance represents a use of cash. When there is an increase in inventory
balances, the cash used for cost of goods sold is the cost of
goods sold as shown in the current earnings statement plus
the increase in inventory balance.

   A similar analysis leads to the conclusion that a decrease in ending inventory balance with respect to beginning
inventory balance gives rise to a net increase in cost of
goods sold as shown in the current earnings statement but a
reduction in the cash so used.

   3.   Depreciation represents a systematic allocation of
the cost of a fixed asset to the accounting periods benefited
by the asset. The process of recognizing depreciation does
not affect cash. Cash paid for operating expenses is determined by deducting depreciation expense from total operating expenses and adjusting the operating expenses for prepaid expenses.

   4.   Deferred income taxes are the difference between
income taxes matched against earnings and the actual
amount paid or payable for the period. If the balance of the
deferred tax liability account, for example, increases between two periods, the amount of income taxes paid was
less than the indicated income tax expense. Conversely, if
deferred liability tax account decreases, the amount paid was
greater than the correct income tax expense. Although the
change in the deferred tax liability account is included in the
indirect approach, the direct approach is not affected by the
change. To determine the cash paid for taxes under the direct presentation, the **current** portion of income tax expense
is adjusted for the increase or decrease in the income tax
payable account.

   5.   The purchase of a building by issuing long-term
debt obviously does not require a cash outlay. However,
this noncash activity should be reported in a separate
schedule as a noncash financing and investing activity.

   6.   The payment of the current portion of debt represents a cash outflow from financing activities.

   7.   The total proceeds from the sale of the fixed asset
should be shown as an inflow from investing activities. This
transaction would not be reflected under operating activities
when the **direct** presentation is used.

SOLUTION GUIDE

Problem 2   Statement of Cash Flows

1.   The problem requires the preparation of a statement of cash flows. The solutions approach is to analyze the net change in each account, using the additional information where applicable, and to identify the cash inflows, cash outflows, and net income adjustments. Journal entries and T-accounts can be used to facilitate the analysis.

1.1   As each item is analyzed, it can be entered into a "skeleton" statement prepared by listing the heading and main categories, such as cash flows from operating activities, investing activities, and financing activities. The individual descriptions and numbers can be filled in as you go through the problem. The first item under operating activities is net income of $360,000, which was given.

2.   Cash increased by $100,000. This should be the net increase in cash reported in the reconciliation of beginning and ending cash shown at the bottom of the statement.

2.1   Accounts receivable decreased by $40,000. This is **added** as a net income adjustment in the operating section because it indicates that cash collections were greater than the sales reported in the income statement.

2.2   Inventories increased by $135,000. This is **deducted** in the operating section as a net income adjustment. An increase in inventory means that cash was used to purchase not only the goods sold, but also additional inventory to increase the amount on hand.

2.3   Property, plant, and equipment increased by $340,000. This is the net result of two transactions described in the additional information. Equipment (cost, $60,000) with a carrying amount of $35,000 was sold for $40,000 cash.

Cash	40,000	
Accum. depr.	25,000	(60,000 – 35,000)
Equipment		60,000
Gain on sale		5,000 (65,000 – 60,000)

The cash received ($40,000) is a **cash inflow** from investing activities. The gain on sale ($5,000) is **deducted** as a net income adjustment in the operating section because there was no cash inflow other than the $40,000 investing inflow. Therefore, the $5,000 gain increased net income without providing an additional $5,000 of cash. The other transaction affecting property, plant, and equipment is a $400,000 purchase of an office building using a capital lease. This transaction does **not** affect cash in 1999, but it is a significant noncash financing and investing activity reported at the bottom of the statement of cash flows. These two transactions explain the $340,000 net increase in the account, as the T-account below illustrates.

	Prop., Plant, and Equip.		
Purchase	400,000	60,000	Sale
Net increase	340,000		

2.4   Accumulated depreciation increased by $125,000. This net change is the result of the sale of equipment (discussed in 2.3) and depreciation expense. The amount of depreciation expense can be determined through T-account analysis.

	Accumulated Depr.		
Sale	25,000	?	Depr. expense
		125,000	Net increase

The missing amount is depreciation expense of $150,000. Depreciation expense is **added** as a net income adjustment in the operating section because, although it decreased net income, it was not a cash outflow.

2.5   The Investment in Belle Co. account increased by $30,000. The additional information indicates that this is due to the recognition of Omega's share of Belle's income (25% x $120,000 = $30,000). Omega uses the equity method due to its 25% ownership interest and would have prepared the following entry in 1999:

Investment in Belle Co.	30,000	
Income from investment		30,000

This entry increases net income, but does not involve a cash inflow. Therefore, it must be **deducted** as a net income adjustment in the operating section. Note that there is no excess of cash over book value on this investment because 25% of $1,100,000 is $275,000.

2.6   The loan receivable increased by $270,000. This is the net result of two transactions described in the additional information. First, Omega loaned $300,000 cash to Chase Co. This is a **cash outflow** from investing activities. Later, Omega collected the first $30,000 principal installment. This is a **cash inflow** from investing activities. These two transactions explain the net change in the account, as the T-account below illustrates.

	Loan Receivable		
Loan to Chase	300,000	30,000	Collection of loan
Net increase	270,000		

3.   Accounts payable increased by $60,000. This is **added** as a net income adjustment in the operating section because some expenses were incurred on account and therefore did not require the use of cash in 1999.

3.1   Income taxes payable decreased by $20,000. This is **deducted** as a net income adjustment in the operating section because cash was used to pay not only 1999 income tax expense, but also to reduce the payable.

3.2   Dividends payable decreased by $10,000. This is the net result of two transactions described in the additional information. On 2/28/99, a cash dividend declared in 1998 was paid. The journal entry was

Dividends payable   90,000
  Cash   90,000

The $90,000 cash paid is a cash **outflow** from financing activities. On 12/15/97, a cash dividend was declared which will not be paid until 2000. The entry was

Retained earnings   80,000
  Dividends payable   80,000

This transaction does **not** affect cash in 1999, but it is a significant noncash financing activity reported at the bottom of the statement of cash flows. These two transactions explain the $10,000 net decrease in the account, as illustrated below.

	Dividends Payable		
Div. paid	90,000	80,000	Div. declared
Net decr.	10,000		

3.3   The increase in the capital lease obligation ($400,000) was explained in 2.3.

3.4   There was no change in either the capital stock account or the additional paid-in capital account.

3.5   The retained earnings account increased by $280,000. This is the net result of two items described in the additional information: net income of $360,000 (discussed in 1.1) and dividends declared of $80,000 (discussed in 3.2). These two items explain the net increase in retained earnings, as the following T-account illustrates.

	Retained Earnings		
Divs. declared	80,000	360,000	Net income
		280,000	Net incr.

UNOFFICIAL ANSWER

Problem 2   Statement of Cash Flows

Omega Corp.
STATEMENT OF CASH FLOWS
For the Year Ended December 31, 1999

Cash flows from operating activities:

Net Income			$360,000
Adjustments to reconcile net income to net cash provided by operating activities:			
Depreciation	$150,000	[1]	
Gain on sale of equipment	(5,000)	[2]	
Undistributed earnings of Belle Co.	(30,000)	[3]	
Changes in assets and liabilities:			
Decrease in accounts receivable	40,000		
Increase in inventories	(135,000)		
Increase in accounts payable	60,000		
Decrease in income taxes payable	(20,000)		
			60,000
Net cash provided by operating activities			420,000

Cash flows from investing activities:

Proceeds from sale of equipment	40,000	
Loan to Chase Co.	(300,000)	
Principal payment of loan receivable	30,000	
Net cash used in investing activities		(230,000)

Cash flows from financing activities:

Dividends paid	(90,000)	
Net cash used in financing activities		(90,000)
Net increase in cash		100,000
Cash at beginning of year		700,000
Cash at end of year		$800,000

Explanation of Amounts

[1]   Depreciation

Net increase in accumulated depreciation for the year ended December 31, 1999		$125,000
Accumulated depreciation on equipment sold:		
Cost	$60,000	
Carrying value	35,000	25,000
Depreciation for 1999		$150,000

[2]   Gain on sale of equipment

Proceeds	$ 40,000
Carrying value	35,000
Gain	$ 5,000

[3]   Undistributed earnings of Belle Co.

Belle's net income for 1999	$120,000
Omega's ownership	25%
Undistributed earnings of Belle Co.	$ 30,000

SOLUTION GUIDE

Problem 3   SCF

1. This problem consists of three related parts. Part a. requires a statement of cash flows using the **direct** method in the operating activities section of the statement, part b. requires a reconciliation of net income to net cash provided by operating activities (**indirect** method), and part c. requires an analysis of changes in partners' capital accounts. Visualize the format of the statement for part a.: operating activities, investing activities, and financing activities.

2. Cash received from fees is an item that should be included under operating activities. Using the **direct** approach, accrual revenues must be adjusted to revenues on a cash basis. To do this, accrual sales must be increased (decreased) by the decrease (increase) in accounts receivable. Accounts receivable increased by $78,000, implying that some revenue has not yet been collected. Therefore, cash received from fees is $2,586,000 ($2,664,000 fee revenue less $78,000 AR increase).

2.1 Dividends received are also an operating activity. Cash received from dividends, not equity in earnings, must be reported in the statement of cash flows. The investee paid dividends of $384,000, and Linden Consulting Associates (LCA) received 25% of those dividends. This resulted in a cash inflow of $96,000 (25% x $384,000). Note that the equity in earnings ($176,000) is **not** a cash inflow; it results in an increase in the investment account, not in the cash account.

2.2 The last item to include under operating activities is operating expenses. Under the direct approach, cash paid for operating expenses must be computed by adjusting operating expenses for noncash expenses, accrued expenses, and prepaid expenses. In this case, operating expenses are $1,940,000. This amount must be adjusted for a noncash expense, depreciation (indicated by the $60,000 increase in accumulated depreciation) and for the increase in accounts payable and accrued expenses ($50,000). This $50,000 increase implies that operating expenses have been recorded for which the cash payment has not been made. Therefore, cash paid for operating expenses (to suppliers and employees) is $1,830,000 ($1,940,000 − $60,000 − $50,000).

2.3 The net cash flow from operating activities is $852,000. It consists of cash received from fees ($2,586,000) and cash received from dividends ($96,000), less cash paid for operating expenses ($1,830,000).

3. Per SFAS 95, an indirect reconciliation of net income to net cash flow from operating activities is required. When the **direct** approach is used in the body of the statement, this reconciliation should be provided in a separate schedule. If the **indirect** approach is used, this reconciliation is included in the body of the statement under operating activities. In this problem, no reconciliation is included with the SCF in part a., since part b. requires a reconciliation.

3.1 The reconciliation starts with net income. Net income in this case is $900,000. Depreciation expense ($60,000) must be added back because it is a noncash expense which reduced net income but did not reduce cash. The excess of equity in earnings over the dividends received from the investment ($176,000 − $96,000 = $80,000) must be subtracted because $80,000 of equity earnings were not received in cash. The increase in accounts receivable ($78,000) is deducted because it implies that $78,000 of revenue was not collected in cash. The increase in accounts payable and accrued expenses ($50,000) is added back to net income because it implies that some recorded expenses were not paid in cash. Therefore, the net cash flow from operating activities under the indirect approach is $852,000 ($900,000 + $60,000 − $80,000 − $78,000 + $50,000), the same as under the direct approach.

4. The other asset accounts must be analyzed to determine the cash flows from investing activities. All the asset accounts except property and equipment were related to operating activities. Property and equipment increased by $170,000 as the result of a July 1 purchase of an office computer. This cash outflow is reported as an investing activity. Note that the portion of the $170,000 cost which was paid for sales tax, delivery, and installation ($15,000) is considered part of the cost of the asset acquired.

5. The other liability and equity accounts must be analyzed to determine the cash flows from financing activities. Only accounts payable and accrued expenses are solely related to operating activities.

5.1 Mortgage payable decreased by $20,000. The cash outflow to reduce the mortgage is reported as a financing activity.

5.2 Partners' equity increased by $610,000. This increase must be analyzed further to determine the related cash flows. The typical items which affect partners' equity are investments, net income, and drawings. These are summarized below.

Partners' equity, 12/31/98	$1,700,000	
1/1/99 investment by Scott	340,000	Financing
Net income	900,000	Operating
Drawings	(630,000)	Financing
Partners' equity, 12/31/99	$2,310,000	

The investment by the new partner ($340,000) is a cash inflow reported as a financing activity, similar to the issuance of common stock by a corporation. The drawings ($630,000) are a cash outflow reported as a financing activity, similar to the payment of dividends by a corporation. Note that the $50,000 cash payment from the new partner directly to the old partners is **not** a cash flow of the partnership.

5.3 Finally, the amounts within each category can be netted to arrive at net cash inflows or outflows in each of the three main sections of the statement, and the beginning and ending balances of cash can be reconciled at the end of the statement.

UNOFFICIAL ANSWER

Problem 3   SCF

a.

Linden Consulting Associates
STATEMENT OF CASH FLOWS
For the Year Ended December 31, 1999
Increase (Decrease) in Cash

Cash flows from operating activities:

Cash received from customers	$2,586,000 [1]	
Cash paid to suppliers and employees	(1,830,000) [2]	
Dividends received from affiliate	96,000	
Net cash provided by operating activities		$ 852,000

Cash flows from investing activities:

Purchased property and equipment	(170,000)

Cash flows from financing activities:

Principal payment of mortgage payable	(20,000)	
Proceeds for admission of new partner	340,000	
Drawings against partners' capital accounts	(630,000)	
Net cash used in financing activities		(310,000)

Net increase in cash	372,000
Cash at beginning of year	280,000
Cash at end of year	$ 652,000

Explanation of amounts

[1] Fee revenue		$2,664,000
Less ending accounts receivable balance		(446,000)
Add beginning accounts receivable balance		368,000
		$2,586,000
[2] Operating expenses		$1,940,000
Less: Depreciation	$ 60,000	
Ending accounts payable balance	320,000	(380,000)
Add beginning accounts payable balance		270,000
		$1,830,000

b.

Reconciliation of net income to net cash provided by operating activities:

Net income		$900,000
Adjustments to reconcile net income to net cash provided by operating activities:		
Depreciation and amortization	$ 60,000	
Undistributed earnings of affiliate	(80,000) [1]	
Change in assets and liabilities:		
Increase in accounts receivable	(78,000)	
Increase in accounts payable and accrued expenses	50,000	
Total adjustments		(48,000)
Net cash provided by operating activities		$852,000

[1] Linden's share of Zach, Inc.'s:	
Reported net income for 1999 (25% x $720,000) – $4,000	$176,000
Cash dividends paid for 1999 (25% of $384,000)	96,000
Undistributed earnings for 1999	$ 80,000

BUSINESS COMBINATIONS AND CONSOLIDATIONS

Many companies expand their operations by acquiring other businesses. The acquiring company may be seeking diversification of its business, a more stable supply of raw materials for its production, an increase in the range of products or services it offers, or any one of many other business reasons. The accounting issues of business combinations begin with properly recording and reporting the economic events of the date of business combination. Accounting subsequent to the combination is dependent on the alternatives selected at the combination date. Thus, as you study this section, you should fully understand how the combination is first recorded and reported before proceeding to events occurring after the combination date.

From a legal perspective, business combinations are classified into three categories as follows:

1. **Merger**--One company acquires the assets and liabilities of one or more other companies in exchange for stock, cash, or other consideration. The acquiring company continues to exist as a separate legal entity, but the acquired company ceases to exist as a separate legal entity, its stock is cancelled, and its books are closed. The separate assets and liabilities are recorded on the acquiring firm's books. (A Corp. + B Corp. = A Corp.)

2. **Consolidation**--A new firm is formed to issue stock in exchange for the stock of two or more combining or consolidating companies. The acquired firms normally cease to continue as separate legal entities; therefore, the new (acquiring) firm will record the separate assets and liabilities of the acquired firms. (A Corp. + B Corp. = C Corp.)

3. **Acquisition**--A company acquires a majority (> 50%) of the common stock of another company and each company continues its legal existence. The acquiring company (parent) will record an "Investment in Acquired Company's Stock" in the combination entry. (A Corp. + B Corp. = Consolidated Financial Statements of A and B)

Mergers and consolidations require 100% ownership of the acquired company but the acquisition business combination requires only a majority ownership of the outstanding stock. In addition, by maintaining the separate legal existence of the acquired company (B Corp.) and not cancelling its stock, the parent company (A Corp.) can retain greater flexibility in raising additional capital by using B Corp. shares as collateral for a loan or through the issuance of new shares of B Corp.

Financial statements for combinations which are in the legal forms of mergers and consolidations are prepared in the normal accounting process since all assets and liabilities are recorded on just one set of books. Accounting for an **acquisition**, however, results in an investment account on the acquiring company's books while the assets and liabilities are still recorded and shown on the books of the acquired company. Financial reporting for this type of combination generally requires the bringing together, or **accounting consolidation**, of the accounts from these two sets of books to prepare financial reports for the economic entity now formed between the parent and subsidiary companies. This process is explained in detail in Section F of this module.

A.　Accounting for the Combination

Regardless of the legal form (mergers, consolidation, acquisition), there are only two accounting methods applied to any business combination--purchase or pooling. These two methods are mutually exclusive, and the selection of the accounting method is determined by specific aspects of the facts surrounding the combination.

1.　Purchase Accounting

Purchase accounting for a combination is similar to the accounting treatment used in the acquisition of any asset group. The fair market value of the consideration (cash, stock, debt securities, etc.) given by the acquiring firm is used as the valuation basis of the combination. The assets and liabilities of the acquired firm are revalued to their respective fair market values at the combination date. The accounting for a preacquisition contingency of an acquired enterprise under the purchase method is covered by SFAS 38 (see outline). Any difference between the value of the consideration given and the fair market values of the net assets obtained is normally recorded as goodwill. The financial statements of the acquiring company reflect the combined operations from the date of combination.

2.　The Pooling Method

The pooling method assumes a combining of stockholders' interests. The basis of valuation in pooling is the book value of the net assets on the books of the acquired company. Therefore, goodwill may **not** be created at the date of combination in a pooling combination. The financial statements of the acquiring company will include a restatement of all prior years presented to include the operations and financial position of the pooled companies for all years presented.

APB 16 specified 12 criteria which must be met before a combination may be accounted for as a pooling of interests. Failure to meet any one of these 12 criteria will preclude a pooling treatment. A complete list of the criteria is provided in the outline of APB 16. The major criteria are: (a) the combining companies have ownership interests independent of each other and were not recently a subsidiary or division of any other company; (b) the combination is effected by a single transaction or in accord with a plan lasting not more than 1 year; (c) at least 90% of the voting ownership interests of the combinee company are acquired in exchange for the issuance of the combinor company's voting shares, and all shareholders have the same equity rights; and (d) no planned intent exists to segment the operations or acquired stockholders' interests after the combination date.

A recent issue of *Accounting Trends and Techniques* indicates that only 10% of the combinations made by its sample companies used the pooling method. Although its use has been declining, pooling accounting is still an accounting alternative for business combinations and has been tested on recent CPA exams.

B.　A Company and B Company--Date of Combination

A presentation of the date of combination entries for purchase and pooling will be made in the next two sections of this module. We will be using a comprehensive example for these sections and the remaining parts of the discussion on consolidation accounting. The following balance sheets of A Company and B Company provide the foundation for further discussion. As you study the remainder of this module, be sure you understand where the numbers are being derived from.

A Company and B Company
BALANCE SHEETS 1/1/99
(Immediately Before Combination)

Assets	*A Company*	*B Company*
Cash	$ 30,900	$ 37,400
Accounts receivable	34,200	9,100
Inventories	22,900	16,100
Equipment	200,000	50,000
Less: Accumulated depreciation	(21,000)	(10,000)
Patents	-0-	10,000
Total assets	$267,000	$112,600
Liabilities and Equity		
Accounts payable	$ 4,000	$ 6,600
Bonds payable	100,000	-0-
Capital stock ($10 par)	100,000	50,000
Additional paid-in capital	15,000	15,000
Retained earnings	48,000	41,000
Total liabilities and equity	$267,000	$112,600

The concept of book value of the investment is a basic principle of accounting for business combinations and will be used in many different computations. Note that the book value of the net assets of B Company may be computed by two different methods.

1. Subtract the book value of the liabilities from the book values of the assets

$112,600 – $6,600 = $106,000

2. Add the book values of the components of B Company stockholders' equity

$50,000 + $15,000 + $41,000 = $106,000

C. **Date of Combination--Purchase Accounting**

Purchase accounting uses fair market values of the net assets as the valuation basis for the combination. The difference between the value of the consideration given by the acquiring firm and the **book value** of the net assets obtained is the excess of cost over book value, or excess of book value over cost (referred to here as differential) of the net assets obtained. As discussed earlier, this differential has two components, as follows:

1. An amount representing an adjustment of the book values of the net assets up (or down) to their respective fair market values, and

2. An amount representing goodwill

Assume that our Company A purchased **all** the net assets of B Company. At the date of combination, the fair values of all the assets and liabilities were determined by appraisal, as follows:

B Company item	Book value (BV)	Fair market value (FMV)	Difference between BV and FMV
Cash	$ 37,400	$ 37,400	$ -0-
Accounts rec. (net)	9,100	9,100	-0-
Inventories	16,100	17,100	1,000
Equipment (net)	40,000	48,000	8,000
Patents	10,000	13,000	3,000
Accounts payable	(6,600)	(6,600)	-0-
Totals	$106,000	$118,000	$12,000

The $12,000 is the difference between the book value and fair market values of B Company and is one component of the differential. Goodwill, the other component of the differential, is the difference between the cost of the investment and the FMV of the net assets. Goodwill may be positive or negative.

Four different cases displaying a range of total acquisition costs are presented below. The form of consideration paid to B Company by A Company is assumed to be cash but, under purchase accounting, it could be stock, cash, debentures, or any other form of payment.

The allocation of the difference between cost and book value is a two-step process. First, the assets and liabilities must be valued at their respective fair market values and then any remainder is allocated to goodwill. Note that the differential may be positive or negative and that the net assets could have fair market values less than book values.

	Case A	Case B	Case C	Case D
Consideration paid	$134,000	$118,000	$106,000	$100,000
Notes:	(> FMV)	(= FMV)	(< FMV)	(< FMV)
	(> BV)	(> BV)	(= BV)	(< BV)

Step 1. Compute the Differential

	Case A	Case B	Case C	Case D
Book value	$106,000	$106,000	$106,000	$106,000
Investment cost	134,000	118,000	106,000	100,000
Differential	$ 28,000	$ 12,000	-0-	($ 6,000)

Step 2. Allocation of Differential

a. Revaluation of net assets to fair market value

	Case A	Case B	Case C	Case D
FMV, net assets	$118,000	$118,000	$118,000	$118,000
Less BV	106,000	106,000	106,000	106,000
Portion to net assets	$ 12,000	$ 12,000	$ 12,000	$ 12,000

b. Remainder (Excess of cost greater than fair value, or fair value greater than cost)

	Case A	Case B	Case C	Case D
FMV, net assets	$118,000	$118,000	$118,000	$118,000
Less Investment cost	134,000	118,000	106,000	100,000
Goodwill	$ 16,000	-0-	($ 12,000)	($ 18,000)

Step 3. Accounting for Goodwill and the Excess of Fair Value Greater Than Cost.

APB 16 assumes the excess of cost greater than fair value is goodwill (Case A). This would be amortized in accordance with APB 17. If the fair value of the assets is **greater than** the investment cost (Cases C and D), then APB 16 requires this excess to be proportionally applied to reduce the assigned values of the noncurrent assets acquired (except long-term investments in marketable securities). If these assets are reduced to zero value, any remaining excess of fair value over cost shall be established as a deferred credit.

Reallocations are required in Cases C and D because the fair values of the net assets are greater than costs, as follows:

	Item	Assigned values of noncurrent assets acquired	Proportion	Excess of fair value over cost	Reallocation	New assigned value
Case C:	Equipment	$48,000	$48,000/$61,000	($12,000)	($ 9,443)	$38,557
	Patents	$13,000	$13,000/$61,000	($12,000)	($ 2,557)	$10,443
		$61,000			($12,000)	
Case D:	Equipment	$48,000	$48,000/$61,000	($18,000)	($14,164)	$33,836
	Patents	$13,000	$13,000/$61,000	($18,000)	($ 3,836)	$ 9,164
		$61,000			($18,000)	

Date of combination entries on A Company's books for a purchase-merger are

	Case A	Case B	Case C	Case D
Cash	$37,400	$37,400	$37,400	$37,400
A/R	9,100	9,100	9,100	9,100
Inventories	17,100	17,100	17,100	17,100
Equipment (net)	48,000	48,000	38,557	33,836
Patents	13,000	13,000	10,443	9,164
Goodwill	16,000	-0-	-0-	-0-
A/P	$ 6,600	$ 6,600	$ 6,600	$ 6,600
Cash	134,000	118,000	106,000	100,000

B Company would close its books and cease to operate as a separate entity.

If B Company maintained its separate legal status, the combination would be accounted for as a 100% acquisition. The date of combination entries on A Company's books for each of the four cases would be

	Case A	Case B	Case C	Case D
Investment in B Company	$134,000	$118,000	$106,000	$100,000
Cash	$134,000	$118,000	$106,000	$100,000

Consolidated financial statements would normally be prepared when acquisitions of more than 50% of outstanding stock are made. Consolidated statements are discussed later in this module.

Some candidates find that using value lines to display the features of purchase accounting helps to sort out the various concepts. Value lines are provided below for Cases A and D. You might want to do the value lines for Cases B and C.

CASE A

Cost		$134,000

(2b) Remainder (Excess of cost > FMV)
     Goodwill = $16,000

(1) Differential =   FMV $118,000
    $28,000
    (Excess of   (2a) Revalue net assets to FMV
    Cost > BV)   BV $106,000 $12,000

CASE D

                FMV $118,000

                               (2a) Revalue net
                                   assets to FMV   (2b) Remainder
(1) Differential =   BV $106,000 $12,000   (Excess of
    <$6,000>   FMV > Cost)
    (Excess of   ($18,000)
    BV > Cost)   Cost $100,000

D. Date of Combination--Pooling Accounting

Pooling accounting requires a uniting of the stockholders' equities of the combining firms. A comparison of the par or stated value of the surviving company's common stock must be made with the total par or stated value of the common stock capital of the combining companies before combination. This process is often referred to as determining the "mix" of the pooled stockholders' equity and must be performed prior to making the date of combination entries. In determining the "mix" of pooled stockholders' equity, it is necessary to remember that under pooling the book value of the net assets is used to record the combination.

To illustrate this process, we will use the information from our comprehensive example of A Company and B Company. Note that the companies have the following equity accounts immediately before the combination.

	A	B
Capital stock ($10 par)	$100,000	$ 50,000
Additional paid-in capital	15,000	15,000
Retained earnings	48,000	41,000
Totals	$163,000	$106,000

Pooling requires the continuation of at least $65,000 of contributed capital from B Company ($50,000 Capital Stock + $15,000 Additional Paid-in Capital). The "mix" of the contributed capital items in A Company's date of combination entry will be based on the par of the stock given up by A Company.

If the par of the stock issued by the issuer (Company A) is greater than the present par on the books of the combinee company (Company B), the following sequence should be used as each item is fully extinguished.

1. Total par value outstanding of combinee (Company B)
2. Additional paid-in capital of combinee (Company B)
3. Additional paid-in capital of issuer (Company A)
4. Retained earnings of combinee (Company B)
5. Retained earnings of issuer (Company A)

If the par issued is less than the present par on the books of the combinee, the excess of the prior par over the new par is added to Additional Paid-in Capital.

The company name in parentheses provides the company source for determining the amount of the entry.

1. Merger and Consolidation Legal Forms

Case 1: Par value of common stock issued by A Company is $30,000.

	Total SE *before pooling*	*Activity*	*Total SE* *after pooling*
Capital Stock	$150,000	+ 30,000	$130,000
		− 50,000	
APIC	30,000	+ 20,000	50,000
RE	89,000		89,000
Total	$269,000	-0-	$269,000

The entry on A's book would be as follows:

Net assets of B	106,000	
Capital stock (Co. A)		30,000
APIC (Co. B) [15,000 + (50,000 − 30,000)]		35,000
RE (Co. B)		41,000

Explanation:

The book values of B's specific assets and liabilities would be listed separately. To reflect the equity swap, capital stock is credited for the par value of common stock issued by A Company, but **not** for the par value of common stock on B Company books.

The credit to additional paid-in capital consists of two amounts: (1) the carryover of APIC from B Company's books, plus (2) the excess of the par value of common stock on B Company's books over the par value of common stock issued and recorded by A Company. Note that there is a continuation of $65,000 of contributed capital from B Company ($30,000 capital stock plus $35,000 additional paid-in capital).

Finally, the credit to retained earnings is simply a carryover from B Company's books.

Case 2: Par value of common stock issued by A Company is $60,000.

	Total SE *before pooling*	*Activity*	*Total SE* *after pooling*
Capital Stock	$150,000	+ 60,000	$160,000
		− 50,000	
APIC	30,000	− 10,000	20,000
RE	89,000		89,000
Total	$269,000	-0-	$269,000

The entry on A's book would be as follows:

Net assets of B	106,000	
Capital stock (Co. A)		60,000
APIC (Co. B) [15,000 + (50,000 − 60,000)]		5,000
RE (Co. B)		41,000

Explanation:

The credits to capital stock and retained earnings are derived the same way as those in Case 1. However, the credit to APIC is different because in Case 2 the par value of common stock issued and recorded by A Company is $10,000 **greater than** the par value of common stock on B Company's books. This results in a $10,000 decrease in the APIC carried over from B Company's books. Therefore, the total amount credited to APIC on Company A's books is $5,000 ($15,000 – $10,000). Once again there is a continuation of contributed capital from B Company ($60,000 capital stock plus $5,000 additional paid-in capital).

Case 3: Par value of common stock issued by A Company is $75,000.

	Total SE *before pooling*	*Activity*	*Total SE* *after pooling*
Capital Stock	$150,000	+ 75,000	$175,000
		– 50,000	
APIC	30,000	– 25,000	5,000
RE	89,000		89,000
Total	$269,000	-0-	$269,000

The entry on A's book would be as follows:

Net assets of B	106,000	
APIC (Co. A)		
[15,000 + (50,000 – 75,000)]	10,000	
Capital stock (Co. A)		75,000
RE (Co. B)		41,000

Explanation:

The credits to capital stock and retained earnings are derived the same way as in Case 1. However, additional paid-in capital is **debited** in Case 3 because the par of common stock issued by A Company is **greater than** the **total** contributed capital presently on B Company's books.

The difference between the par of common stock issued by A Company and the present par value of B Company's capital stock is $25,000 ($75,000 – $50,000). This amount first extinguishes the $15,000 additional paid-in capital carried over from B Company's books and results in a $10,000 ($25,000 – $15,000) reduction of A Company's additional paid-in capital.

Note that there is a continuation of $65,000 of contributed capital from B Company ($75,000 capital stock minus $10,000 debit to APIC).

2. Acquisition Legal Form

If Company B is maintained as a separate legal entity (i.e., an acquisition), consolidated financial statements will have to be prepared. The combination entries will include an "Investment in B Stock" account rather than the specific net assets of Company B. The combination entry on A's books for Case 1 on the preceding page would be as follows:

Investment in Company B's common stock	106,000	
Capital stock (Co. A)		30,000
Additional paid-in capital (Co. B)		35,000
Retained earnings (Co. B)		41,000

Subsequent cases would be treated similarly based on the par of the stock issued. It is important to note that in 100% acquisitions, all of the final amounts and accounts in the consolidated financial statements would be the same as if the business combination were treated as a merger or consolidation.

APB 16 requires that results of pooled operations be reported from the beginning of the period in which the combination occurred. Thus, if the pooling took place in mid-period, the pooling method will have to be applied retroactively from the point of pooling to the beginning of the period. In addition, if comparative statements are presented, they must be restated on a combined basis to reflect the pooled firms. Intercompany transactions occurring before the date of combination should be eliminated when the pooling method is applied retroactively. Intercompany eliminations are explained later in this module.

E. **Purchase and Pooling Combination Entries Reviewed**

The following matrix provides a review of the combination entries of the surviving or investing firm for the three legal forms of combination (merger, consolidation, and acquisition) for which stock is given. The legal form is primarily dependent on whether the combined company, Company B in our examples, retains a separate, legal existence or transfers its assets and liabilities to Company A and cancels any remaining stock of Company B. The purchase versus pooling choice is independent of the legal form. Accounting for the combination (purchase or pooling) will be determined by the specific aspects of the combination transaction that are specified in APB 16. The items in the parentheses are valuation bases or the company source for determining the dollar amount for the entry.

PURCHASE-POOLING MATRIX

	Accounting method	
Legal form	*Purchase*	*Pooling*

1. Merger
(A Co. + B Co. = A Co.)
	Assets (FMV of B)
	  Liabilities (FMV of B)
	  Capital stock (Co. A)
	  APIC (Co. A)
		Assets (BV of B)
		  Liabilities (BV of B)
		  Capital stock (Co. A)
		  APIC (Co. B)
		  Retained earnings (Co. B)

2. Consolidation
(A Co. + B Co. = C Co.)
	Assets (FMV of both A and B)
	  Liabilities (FMV of A and B)
	  Capital stock (Co. C)
	  APIC (Co. C)
		Assets (BV of both A and B)
		  Liabilities (BV of A and B)
		  Capital stock (Co. C)
		  APIC (both A and B)
		  Retained earnings (both A and B)

3. Acquisition
(A Co. + B Co. =
Consolidated state-
ments of A and B)
	Investment in B (FMV)
	  Capital stock (Co. A)
	
	  APIC (Co. A)
		Investment in B (BV)
		  Capital Stock (Co. A)
		  APIC (Co. B)
		  Retained earnings (Co. B)

F. **Consolidated Financial Statements**

An acquisition of more than 50% of the outstanding voting stock will normally require the preparation of consolidated financial statements. The complete consolidation process is presented in the next section of this module. The investment account will be eliminated in the consolidation working papers and will be replaced with the specific assets and liabilities of the investee corporation. Consolidation is generally required for investments of more than 50% of the outstanding voting stock except when

1. The control is likely to be temporary.
2. Control is not held by the majority owner.

   a. The investee is in legal reorganization or bankruptcy.
   b. The investee operates in a foreign country which has severe restrictions on the financial transactions of its business firms or is subject to material political or economic uncertainty that casts significant doubt on the parent's ability to control the subsidiary.

In these limited cases, the investment will be reported as a long-term investment in an unconsolidated subsidiary on the investor's balance sheet with its balance determined by using the cost method unless the parent can demonstrate that it has significant influence in which case the equity method shall be used.

The concept of consolidated statements is that the resources of two or more companies are under the control of the parent company. Consolidated statements are prepared as if the group of legal entities were one economic entity group. Consolidated statements are presumed to be more meaningful for management, owners, and creditors of the parent company and they are required for fair presentation of the financially-related companies. Individual company statements should continue to be prepared for minority ownership and creditors of the subsidiary companies.

The accounting principles used to record and report events for a single legal entity are also applicable to a consolidated economic entity of two or more companies. The concept of the reporting entity is expanded to include more than one company, but all other accounting principles are applied in the same way as for an individual company. The consolidation process eliminates reciprocal items that are shown on both the parent's and subsidiary's books. These eliminations are necessary to avoid double-counting the same items which would misstate the financials of the combined economic entity.

Consolidated financial statements are prepared from worksheets which begin with the trial balances of the parent and subsidiary companies. Eliminating worksheet entries are made to reflect the two separate companies' results of operations and financial position as one combined economic entity. The entire consolidation process takes place **only on a worksheet**; no consolidation elimination entries are ever recorded on either the parent's or subsidiary's books.

Consolidated balance sheets are typically prepared at the date of combination to determine the initial financial position of the economic entity. Any intercompany accounts between the parent and subsidiary must be eliminated against each other. In addition, the "Investment in subsidiary's stock" account from the parent's books will be eliminated against the reciprocal accounts of the subsidiary's stockholders' equity. The remaining accounts are then combined to prepare the consolidated balance sheet. The preparation of consolidated statements after the date of combination becomes a little more complex because the parent's and subsidiary's income statements may include reciprocal intercompany accounts which must be eliminated. The next section of the module will present an example of the preparation of a consolidated balance sheet at the date of combination for both purchase and pooling accounting. You should carefully review the date of combination consolidation process before proceeding to the preparation of consolidation statements subsequent to combination.

G. **Date of Combination Consolidated Balance Sheet--Purchase Accounting**

This example uses the numbers from the A Company and B Company presented on page 608. The discussion in the preceding sections assumed a 100% combination in which the parent acquired control of all the subsidiary's stock or net assets. For the remainder of the module, we will assume that the parent company (A Company) acquired a 90% interest in the net assets of the subsidiary company (B Company). The remaining 10% of the outstanding stock is held by third-party investors referred to as the **minority**

interest. In the illustrated problem, you will be able to review the determination of how minority interest is computed and disclosed on the consolidated financial statements. Note that only the "acquisition" legal form leads to the preparation of consolidated statements and includes less than 100% business combinations.

The assumptions for this illustration are

1. On January 1, 1999, A Company acquires a 90% interest in B Company in exchange for 5,400 shares of $10 par value stock having a total market value of $120,600.
2. The purchase method of accounting is used for the combination.
3. Any goodwill resulting from the combination will be amortized over a period of 10 years.

The workpaper for a consolidated balance sheet at the date of acquisition is presented below. The first two columns are the trial balances from the books of A Company and B Company immediately following the acquisition.

1. Investment Entry on A Company's books

The entry to record the 90% purchase-acquisition on A Company's books was

Investment in Stock of B Company	120,600	
Capital Stock		54,000
Additional Paid-in Capital		66,600

(To record the issuance of 5,400 shares of $10 par value stock to acquire a 90% interest in B Company.)

Although common stock is used for the consideration in our example, A Company could have used debentures, cash, or any other form of consideration acceptable to B Company's stockholders to make the purchase combination.

A COMPANY AND B COMPANY CONSOLIDATED WORKING PAPERS
For Date of Combination - 1/1/99

Purchase Accounting
90% Interest

	A Company	B Company	Adjustments and eliminations Debit	Adjustments and eliminations Credit	Minority interest	Consolidated balances
Balance sheet 1/1/99						
Cash	30,900	37,400				68,300
Accounts receivable	34,200	9,100				43,300
Inventories	22,900	16,100	(b) 900			39,900
Equipment	200,000	50,000	(b) 9,000			259,000
Accumulated depreciation	(21,000)	(10,000)		(b) 1,800		(32,800)
Investment in stock of B Company	120,600			(a) 120,600		
Difference between cost and book value			(a) 25,200	(b) 25,200		
Excess of cost over fair value (goodwill)			(b) 14,400			14,400
Patents		10,000	(b) 2,700			12,700
Total assets	387,600	112,600				404,800
Accounts payable	4,000	6,600				10,600
Bonds payable	100,000					100,000
Capital stock	154,000	50,000	(a) 45,000		5,000	154,000
Additional paid-in capital	81,600	15,000	(a) 13,500		1,500	81,600
Retained earnings	48,000	41,000	(a) 36,900		4,100	48,000
Minority interest					10,600	10,600 MI
Total liabilities and equity	387,600	112,600	147,600	147,600		404,800

2. Difference Between Investment Cost and Book Value

The difference between the investment cost and the parent company's equity in the net assets of the subsidiary is computed as follows:

Investment cost		$120,600
– Book value % at date of combination		
B Company's:		
Capital stock	$ 50,000	
Additional paid-in capital	15,000	
Retained earnings	41,000	
Total	$106,000	
Parent's share of ownership	x 90%	
Parent's share of book value		95,400
Excess of cost over book value		$ 25,200

This difference is due to several undervalued assets and to unrecorded goodwill. The allocation procedure is similar to that shown on page 798 for a 100% purchase; however, in this case, the parent company obtained a 90% interest and thus will recognize 90% of the difference between the fair market values and book values of the subsidiary's assets, not 100%. The allocation is presented as

Item	Book value (BV)	Fair market value (FMV)	Difference between BV and FMV	Ownership percentage	Percentage share of difference between BV and FMV
Cash	$ 37,400	$ 37,400	$ -0-		
Accounts receivable (net)	9,100	9,100	-0-		
Inventories	16,100	17,100	1,000	90%	$ 900
Equipment	50,000	60,000	10,000	90%	9,000
Accumulated depreciation	(10,000)	(12,000)	(2,000)	90%	(1,800)
Patents	10,000	13,000	3,000	90%	2,700
Accounts payable	(6,600)	(6,600)	-0-		
Total	$106,000	$118,000	$12,000		

Amount of difference between cost and book value share allocated to revaluation of net assets	$10,800
Total differential	25,200
Remainder allocated to goodwill	$14,400

The equipment has a book value of $40,000 ($50,000 less 20% depreciation of $10,000). An appraisal concluded with a judgment that the equipment's replacement cost was $60,000 less 20% accumulated depreciation of $12,000 resulting in a net fair value of $48,000.

3. Elimination Entries on Workpaper

The basic reciprocal accounts are the investment in subsidiary account on the parent's books and the subsidiary's stockholder equity accounts. Only the parent's share of the subsidiary's accounts may be eliminated as reciprocal accounts. The remaining 10% portion is allocated to the minority interest. The entries below include documentation showing the company source for the information. Those aids will help you trace the numbers. The workpaper entry to eliminate the basic reciprocal accounts is

(a) Capital stock--B Co.   45,000
    Additional paid-in capital--B Co.   13,500
    Retained earnings--B Co.   36,900*
    Differential   25,200
       Investment in stock of B Co.--A Co.   120,600

    ($36,900 = 90% x $41,000)

Note that only 90% of B Company's stockholders' equity accounts are eliminated. Also, an account called "Differential" is debited in the workpaper entry. The differential account is a temporary account to record the difference between the cost of the investment in B Company from the parent's books and the book value of the parent's interest (90% in our case) from the subsidiary's books.

The next step is to allocate the differential to the specific accounts by making the following workpaper entry:

(b) Inventories   900
    Equipment   9,000
    Patents   2,700
    Goodwill   14,400
      Accumulated depreciation   1,800
      Differential   25,200

This entry reflects the allocations prepared in Step 2 on the previous page and recognizes the parent's share of the asset revaluations.

The minority interest column is the 10% interest of B Company's net assets owned by outside, third parties. Minority interest must be disclosed because 100% of the book values of B Company are included in the consolidated statements although A Company controls only 90% of the net assets. An alternative method to "prove" minority interest is to multiply the net assets of the subsidiary by the minority interest share, as follows:

Stockholders' equity of B Company		*Minority interest %*		
$106,000	x	10%	=	$10,600

The $10,600 would be reported on the credit side of the consolidated balance sheet between liabilities and stockholders' equity.

The principle used to prepare the consolidated balance sheet is called the **parent company concept**. This is the method used most often on the CPA exam and also used in about 90% of actual cases of consolidations. An alternative approach is known as the **entity concept**. The two differ in the amount of the asset revaluations recognized on the consolidated balance sheet. Under the parent company concept, just the parent's share of the revaluation is shown and the minority interest is reported at its share of the subsidiary's book value. If the entity concept were used, the net assets of B Company would be included in the consolidated balance sheet at 100% of their fair values at the date of acquisition and minority interest would be reported at its share of the fair value of the subsidiary. In our example, minority interest under the entity concept would have been

Total fair market value of net assets of B company		*Minority percentage*		
$118,000	x	10%	=	$11,800

Our example does not include any other intercompany accounts as of the date of combination. If any existed, they would be eliminated to fairly present the consolidated entity. Several examples of other reciprocal accounts will be shown later in this module for the preparation of consolidated financial statements subsequent to the date of acquisition.

H. Date of Combination Consolidated Balance Sheet--Pooling Accounting

The preparation of a consolidated balance sheet for a pooling acquisition follows the basic principles discussed in the section on recording the pooling combination. Book values are reported as the basis of the net assets of the combined companies and the continuity of the acquired stockholders' equity is reflected in the carryforward of the capital "mix" from the values shown on the acquired company's books.

For purposes of this section, the following assumptions will be made.

1. On January 1, 1999, A Company acquired a 90% interest in B Company in exchange for 5,400 shares of $10 par value stock of A Company.
2. All criteria for a pooling have been met and the combination is treated as a pooling of interests.

The workpaper for a consolidated balance sheet at the date of combination is presented below. Note that the first two columns are trial balances of A Company and B Company immediately after the combination was recorded by A Company.

1. Investment Entry Recorded on A Company's Books

The following entry was made by A Company to record its 90% acquisition-pooling of B Company:

Investment in Stock of B Company	95,400	
Capital stock, $10 par		54,000
Additional paid-in capital		4,500
Retained earnings		36,900

A COMPANY AND B COMPANY CONSOLIDATED WORKING PAPERS
For Date of Combination - 1/1/99

Pooling Accounting
90% Interest

	A Company	B Company	Adjustments and eliminations Debit	Adjustments and eliminations Credit	Minority interest	Consolidated balances
Balance sheet 1/1/99						
Cash	30,900	37,400				68,300
Accounts receivable	34,200	9,100				43,300
Inventories	22,900	16,100				39,900
Equipment	200,000	50,000				250,000
Accumulated depreciation	(21,000)	(10,000)				(31,000)
Investment in stock of B Company	95,400			(a) 95,400		
Patents		10,000				10,000
Total assets	362,400	112,600				379,600
Accounts payable	4,000	6,600				10,600
Bonds payable	100,000					100,000
Capital stock	154,000	50,000	(a) 45,000		5,000	154,000
Additional paid-in capital	19,500	15,000	(a) 13,500		1,500	19,500
Retained earnings	84,900	41,000	(a) 36,900		4,100	84,900
Minority interest					10,600	10,600
Total liabilities and equity	362,400	112,600	95,400	95,400		379,600

The investment entry reflects the capital "mix" for a pooling of less than a 100% investment. The following schedule shows the mix for our 90% combination accomplished by the issuance of 5,400 shares of A Company's $10 par value stock:

	B Company	A Company's percentage share	A's share of B's equity
Capital stock	$ 50,000	90%	$45,000
Additional paid-in capital	15,000	90%	13,500
Retained earnings	41,000	90%	36,900
	$106,000		$95,400

The $54,000 (5,400 shares x $10 par) in new capital issued by A Company represents $45,000 from B Company's Capital Stock and $9,000 of the $13,500 share of B Company's Additional Paid-in Capital. Note the remaining $4,500 of capital and $36,900 of B Company's Retained Earnings are carried over to A Company's books in the combination date entry. The $10,600 of B's capital that is not carried over to A will eventually be shown as minority interest on the consolidated balance sheet.

2. Elimination Entry on Workpaper

    Pooling accounting uses book values as a basis of valuation; therefore, no "differential" will ever occur in a pooling. The reciprocal accounts in a pooling consolidated balance sheet are the "Investment in Stock of B Company" account from the parent's books and the stockholders' equity accounts from the subsidiary's books. Again, note that only 90% of the equity of B Company is being eliminated; the 10% remainder will be recognized as minority interest. The workpaper elimination entry is

(a) Capital stock--B Co.   45,000
     Additional paid-in capital--B Co.   13,500
     Retained earnings--B Co.   36,900*
          Investment in stock of B
          Company--A Co.   95,400

     *($36,900 = 90% x $41,000)

The next section of the module will cover the preparation of consolidated financial statements subsequent to the date of acquisition. You should be sure you fully understand date of combination consolidations before proceeding.

I. **Consolidated Financial Statements Subsequent to Acquisition**

    The concepts used to prepare subsequent consolidated statements are essentially the same as used to prepare the consolidated balance sheet at the acquisition date. The income statement and statement of retained earnings are added to reflect the results of operations since the acquisition date for a purchase or from the beginning of the period for a pooling. Furthermore, some additional reciprocal accounts may have to be eliminated because of intercompany transactions between the parent and subsidiary corporations. Please note that the financial statements of a consolidated entity are prepared using the same accounting principles that would be employed by a single, unconsolidated enterprise. The only difference is that some reciprocal accounts appearing on both companies' books must be eliminated against each other before the two corporations may be presented as one consolidated economic entity. Your review should concentrate on the accounts and amounts appearing on the consolidated statements (amounts in the last column of the worksheet). This "end-result" focus will help provide the understanding of why certain elimination entries are necessary.

An expanded version of the consolidated worksheet is necessary if the income statement and retained earnings statement must also be prepared. A comprehensive format often called "the three statement layout" is an integrated vertical array of the income statement, the retained earnings statement, and the balance sheet (see page 617). The net income of the period is carried to the retained earnings statement and the ending retained earnings is carried down to the balance sheet. If you are required to prepare just the consolidated balance sheet, then eliminating entries involving nominal accounts (income statement accounts and "Dividends declared" account) would be made directly against the ending balance of retained earnings presented on the balance sheet.

The following discussion assumes the parent is using the partial equity method to account for the majority investment. Some firms may use the cost method during the period to record investment income because it requires fewer book adjustments to the investment account. In cases where the cost method is used during the period, one approach is to adjust the investment and investment income accounts to the equity method through an entry on the workpaper and the consolidation process may then be continued. Assuming that an income statement and retained earnings statement are being prepared in addition to the balance sheet, the general form of this entry is made on the workpapers.

> Dividend income (for income recognized using cost method)
> Investment in sub (% of undistributed income of sub)
>   Equity in subsidiary's income (for income recognized using equity method)

Additional entries would be required to recognize the equity income in prior periods if the investment were owned for more than one period and to recognize the amortizations of any differential for all periods the investment was held. After these entries are made, the investment and equity in subsidiary's income accounts would be stated at equity and the consolidation process may continue. It is important to note that the formal consolidated statements will be the same regardless of the method used by the parent to account for the investment on its books. The concept of measurement used in the preparation of the consolidated statements is equivalent to the full equity method and the elimination process will result in statements presented under that concept.

J. **Intercompany Transactions and Profit Confirmation**

Three general types of intercompany transactions may occur between the parent and subsidiary companies. Intercompany transactions require special handling because the profit or loss from these events must be properly presented on the consolidated financial statements. The three types of intercompany transactions are: intercompany sales of merchandise, transactions in fixed assets, and intercompany debt/equity transactions. These events may generate "unrealized profit" (also referred to as unconfirmed profit) which is a profit or gain shown in the trial balance from one of the company's books, but should not be shown in the consolidated financial statements. Intercompany bond transactions may require recognition of a gain or loss on the consolidated financials which is not in the trial balances of either the parent or subsidiary companies.

1. Intercompany Inventory Transactions

Unrealized profit in ending inventory arises through intercompany sales above cost that are not resold to third parties prior to year end. Thus, the profit on the selling corporation's books is overstated, because an arm's-length transaction has not yet taken place. The inventory is overstated on the purchaser's books for the amount of the unrealized intercompany profit. An exhibit of the relationships is shown below.

Companies A and B are two separate legal entities and will each record the sale or purchase of goods. From a consolidated or economic entity viewpoint, however, the intercompany transaction is a transfer of assets which cannot result in revenue recognition until these goods are sold to a third party. Assuming a sale from Company A to Company B (a "downstream" intercompany sale), the sale income of Company A cannot be recognized until the goods are sold to third parties by Company B. In addition, the ending inventory of Company B is overstated by the amount of profit in the inventory acquired from Company A. Once intercompany sales have been sold to third parties, the earning process has been verified by an arm's-length transaction with third parties. Thus, recognition of previously unrecognized profit must be made at that time.

2. Intercompany Fixed Asset Transactions

Unrealized profits on fixed assets arise through intercompany sales of fixed assets above undepreciated cost. From a consolidated viewpoint, the transaction represents the internal transfer of assets and no gain (loss) should be recognized. Therefore, any gain (loss) must be eliminated and the carrying value of the transferred asset must be returned to its initial book value basis. In subsequent periods, depreciation expense is overstated, because an overvalued asset is being depreciated on the books of the company showing the asset. This overstatement of depreciation must also be eliminated in the consolidation process.

3. Intercompany Bond Transactions

When one consolidated company buys bonds of another consolidated company, there are several reciprocal items to eliminate: investment in bonds and bonds payable, interest income and interest expense, and interest payable and interest receivable. Intercompany gains and losses **cannot** arise from direct intercompany bond purchases. The book value would be the same on both books and the interest accounts would be reciprocal. Note that APB 21 does not require the use of the effective interest method for debt transactions between parent and subsidiary companies. Straight-line amortizations of premiums or discounts are often used in these instances.

Gains and losses on intercompany bond holdings may occur when

a. Already outstanding bonds are purchased by a parent or subsidiary
b. From a third party
c. For an amount different from the carrying value of the issuer

From a consolidated viewpoint, these bonds are viewed as retired. However, the bonds are still recorded as liabilities on the issuer's separate books and as investment in bonds on the purchasing corporation's books. The eliminating entry is to recognize the gain (loss) on the consolidated "retirement of debt" in the year of intercompany bond purchase. This gain (loss) would normally be an extraordinary item in accordance with SFAS 4.

K. **Example of Subsequent Consolidated Financial Statements**

The following information extends the basic example of A Company and B Company begun earlier in this module. The example illustrates the major consolidation concepts and procedures most likely to appear on the exam.

EXTENDED EXAMPLE

On January 1, 1999, A Company acquired 90% of the stock of B Company in exchange for 5,400 shares of $10 par value stock having a total market value of $120,600.

The purchase method of accounting is used for the combination.

On January 1, 1999, B Company's assets and liabilities had the following book and fair values.

	Book value	Fair value
Cash	$ 37,400	$ 37,400
Accounts receivable (net)	9,100	9,100
Inventories	16,100	17,100
Equipment	50,000	60,000
Accumulated depreciation	(10,000)	(12,000)
Patents	10,000	13,000
Accounts payable	(6,600)	(6,600)
	$106,000	$118,000

Any cost in excess of the fair values of the net assets of B Company was attributable to expected future earnings of B Company and will be amortized over a period of 10 years.

Financial statement data of the two companies as of December 31, 1999 (the end of the first year after combination) are presented below:

During 1999, A Company sold merchandise to B Company that originally cost A Company $15,000 and the sale was made for $20,000. On December 31, 1999, B Company's inventory included merchandise purchased from A Company at a cost to B Company of $12,000.

Also during 1999, A Company acquired $18,000 of merchandise from B Company. B Company uses a normal markup of 25% above its cost. A Company's ending inventory includes $10,000 of the merchandise acquired from B Company.

B Company reduced its intercompany account payable to A Company to a balance of $4,000 as of December 31, 1999, by making a payment of $1,000 on December 30. This $1,000 payment was still in transit on December 31, 1999.

On January 2, 1999, B Company acquired equipment from A Company for $7,000. The equipment was originally purchased by A Company for $5,000 and had a book value of $4,000 at the date of sale to B Company. The equipment had an estimated remaining life of 4 years as of January 2, 1999.

On December 31, 1999, B Company purchased for $44,000, 50% of the outstanding bonds issued by A Company. The bonds mature on December 31, 2006 and were originally issued at par. The bonds pay interest annually on December 31 of each year and the interest was paid to the prior investor immediately before B Company's purchase of the bonds.

The consolidated worksheet for the preparation of consolidated financial statements as of December 31, 1999, is presented on the next page.

The investment account balance at the statement date should be reconciled to ensure the parent company made the proper entries under the method of accounting used to account for the investment. As noted earlier, A Company is using the partial equity method, without amortizations. The amortizations of the excess of cost over book value will be recognized only on the worksheets. This method is the one typically followed on the CPA exam; however, be sure you determine the method used in the exam problem--don't assume! The "proof" of the investment account of A Company is

Investment in Stock of B Company

Original cost	120,600		% of B Company's dividends declared (90% x $4,000)
% of B Company's income (90% x $9,400)	8,460	3,600	
Bal. 12/31/99	125,460		

Any errors will require correcting entries before the consolidation process is continued. Correcting entries will be posted to the books of the appropriate company; eliminating entries are **not** posted to either company's books.

The difference between the investment cost and the book value of the net assets acquired was determined and allocated in the preparation of the date of combination consolidated statements presented on page 617. For purposes of brevity, that process will not be duplicated here since the same computations are used in preparing financial statements for as long as the investment is owned. See outline of SFAS 121 (B.5.) concerning evaluation of assets for impairment.

A COMPANY AND B COMPANY CONSOLIDATED WORKING PAPERS
Year Ended December 31, 1999

Purchase Accounting
90% Owned
Subsequent, partial equity

	A Company	B Company	Adjustments and eliminations Debit	Adjustments and eliminations Credit	Minority interest	Consolidated balances
Income statement for year ended 12/31/99						
Sales	750,000	420,000	(a) 38,000			1,132,000
Cost of sales	581,000	266,000	(b) 5,000	(a) 38,000		814,900
			(i) 900			
Gross margin	169,000	154,000				317,100
Depreciation and interest expense	28,400	16,200	(i) 1,800	(d) 750		45,650
Other operating expenses	117,000	128,400	(i) 1,710			247,110
Net income from operations	23,600	9,400				24,340
Gain on sale of equipment	3,000		(d) 3,000			
Gain on bonds				(e) 6,000		6,000
Equity in subsidiary's income	8,460		(f) 8,460			
Minority income (.10 x $7,400)					740	(740)
Net income	35,060	9,400	58,870	44,750	740	29,600
Statement of retained earnings for year ended 12/31/99						
1/1/99 Retained earnings						
A Company	48,000					48,000
B Company		41,000	(g) 36,900		4,100	
Add net income (from above)	35,060	9,400	58,870	44,750	740	29,600
Total	83,060	50,400			4,840	77,600
Deduct dividends	15,000	4,000		(f) 3,600	400	15,000
Balance December 31, 1999	68,060	46,400	95,770	48,350	4,440	62,600
Balance sheet 12/31/99						
Cash	45,300	6,400	(l) 1,000			52,700
Accounts receivable (net)	43,700	12,100		(l) 1,000		50,800
				(c) 4,000		
Inventories	38,300	20,750	(h) 900	(b) 5,000		54,050
				(i) 900		
Equipment	195,000	57,000	(h) 9,000	(d) 2,000		259,000
Accumulated depreciation	(35,200)	(18,900)		(d) 250		(57,950)
				(h) 1,800		
				(i) 1,800		
Investment in stock of B Company	125,460			(f) 4,860		
				(g) 120,600		
Differential			(g) 25,200	(h) 25,200		
Goodwill			(h) 14,400	(i) 1,440		12,960
Investment in bonds of A Company		44,000		(e) 44,000		
Patents		9,000	(h) 2,700	(i) 270		11,430
Total assets	412,560	130,350				382,990
Accounts payable	8,900	18,950	(c) 4,000			23,850
Bonds payable	100,000		(e) 50,000			50,000
Capital stock	154,000	50,000	(g) 45,000		5,000	154,000
Additional paid-in capital	81,600	15,000	(g) 13,500		1,500	81,600
Retained earnings (from above)	68,060	46,400	95,770	48,350	4,440	62,600
Minority interest					10,940	10,940
Total liabilities and equity	412,560	130,350	261,470	261,470		382,990

The following adjusting and eliminating entries will be required to prepare consolidated financials as of December 31, 1999. Note that a consolidated income statement is required and, therefore, the nominal accounts are still "open." The number or letter in parentheses to the left of the entry corresponds to the key used on the worksheet.

Step 1: Complete the transaction for any intercompany items in transit at the end of the year.

(l) Cash	1,000	
Accounts receivable		1,000

This **adjusting** entry will now properly present the financial positions of both companies and the consolidation process may be continued.

Step 2: Prepare the eliminating entries.

(a) Sales	38,000	
Cost of goods sold		38,000

Total intercompany sales of $38,000 include $20,000 in a downstream transaction from A Company to B Company and $18,000 in an upstream transaction from B Company to A Company.

(b) Cost of goods sold	5,000	
Inventories		5,000

The ending inventories are overstated because of the unrealized profit from the intercompany sales. The debit to cost of goods sold is required because a decrease in ending inventory will increase cost of goods sold to be deducted on the income statement. Supporting computations for the entry are

	In ending inventory of	
	A Company	B Company
Intercompany sales not resold, at selling price	$10,000	$12,000
Cost basis of remaining intercompany merchandise		
From B to A (÷125%)	(8,000)	
From A to B (÷133 1/3%)		(9,000)
Unrealized profit	$ 2,000	$ 3,000

When preparing consolidated workpapers for 2000 (the next fiscal period), an additional eliminating entry will be required if the goods in 1999's ending inventory are sold to outsiders during 2000. The additional entry will recognize the profit for 2000 that was eliminated as unrealized in 1999. This entry is necessary since the entry at the end of 1999 was made only on the worksheet. The 2000 entry will be

Retained earnings--B Comp. (1/1/00)	200	
Retained earnings--A Comp. (1/1/00)	4,800	
Cost of goods sold (2000)		5,000

(c) Accounts payable	4,000	
Accounts receivable		4,000

This eliminates the remaining intercompany receivable/payable owed **by** B Company to A Company. This eliminating entry is necessary to avoid overstating the consolidated entity's balance sheet. The receivable/payable is not extinguished and B Company must still transfer $4,000 to A Company in the future.

(d) Gain on sale of equipment   3,000
      Equipment   2,000
      Accumulated depreciation   250
      Depreciation expense   750

Eliminates the gain on the intercompany sale of the equipment, eliminates the overstatement of equipment, and removes the excess depreciation taken on the gain. Supporting computations for the entry are

	Cost	At date of intercompany sale accum. depr.	1999 depreciation expense	End-of-period accum. depr.
Original basis				
(to seller-A Co.)	$5,000	($1,000)	$1,000	($2,000)
New basis				
(to buyer-B Co.)	7,000	-0-	1,750	(1,750)
Difference	($2,000)		($ 750)	$ 250

If the intercompany sale had not occurred, A Company would have depreciated the remaining book value of $4,000 over the estimated remaining life of 4 years. However, since B Company's acquisition price ($7,000) was more than A Company's basis in the asset ($4,000), the depreciation recorded on the books of B Company will include part of the intercompany unrealized profit. The equipment must be reflected on the consolidated statements at the original cost to the consolidated entity. Therefore, the "write-up" of $2,000 in the equipment, the excess depreciation of $750, and the gain of $3,000 must be eliminated and the ending balance of accumulated depreciation must be shown at what it would have been if the intercompany equipment transaction had not occurred. In future periods, a retained earnings account will be used instead of the gain account; however, the other concepts will be extended to include the additional periods.

(e) Bonds payable   50,000
      Investment in bonds of A Company   44,000
      Gain on extinguishment of debt   6,000

This entry eliminates the book value of A Company's debt against the bond investment account of B Company. To the consolidated entity, this transaction must be shown as a retirement of debt even though A Company has the outstanding intercompany debt to B Company. SFAS 4 specifies gains or losses on debt extinguishment, if material, should be shown as an extraordinary item. In future periods, B Company will amortize the discount, thereby bringing the investment account up to par value and a retained earnings account will be used in the eliminating entry instead of the gain account.

(f) Equity in subsidiary's income--A Co.   8,460
      Dividends declared--B Co.   3,600
      Investment in stock of B Company   4,860

This elimination entry adjusts the investment account back to its balance at the beginning of the period and also eliminates the subsidiary income account.

(g) Capital stock--B Co.   45,000
     Additional paid-in capital--B Co.   13,500
     Retained earnings--B Co.   36,900
     Differential   25,200
      Investment in stock of B Co.--A Co.   120,600

This entry eliminates 90% of B Company's stockholders' equity at the beginning of the year, 1/1/99. Note that the changes **during** the year were eliminated in entry (f) above. The differential account reflects the excess of investment cost greater than the book value of the assets acquired.

(h) Inventories	900	
Equipment	9,000	
Patents	2,700	
Goodwill	14,400	
Accumulated depreciation		1,800
Differential		25,200

This entry allocates the differential (excess of investment cost over the book values of the assets acquired). Note that this entry is the same as the allocation entry made to prepare consolidated financial statements for January 1, 1999, the date of acquisition.

(i) Cost of goods sold	900	
Depreciation expense	1,800	
Other operating expenses--		
Patent amortization	270	
Other operating expenses--		
Goodwill amortization	1,440	
Inventories		900
Accumulated depreciation		1,800
Patents		270
Goodwill		1,440

This elimination entry amortizes the revaluations to fair market value made in entry (h). The inventory has been sold and therefore becomes part of the cost of goods sold. The remaining revaluation will be amortized as follows:

	Amortization revaluation	*Annual period*	*Amortization*
Equipment (net)	$ 7,200	4 years	$1,800
Patents	2,700	10 years	270
Goodwill	14,400	10 years	1,440

The amortizations will continue to be made on future work sheets. For example, at the end of the next year (2000), the amortization entry (i) would be as follows:

Retained earnings--		
A Co. (1/1/00)	4,410	
Depreciation expense	1,800	
Other operating expenses--		
Patent amortization	270	
Other operating expenses--		
Goodwill amortization	1,440	
Inventories		900
Accumulated depreciation		3,600
Patents		540
Goodwill		2,880

The initial debit of $4,410 to retained earnings is an aggregation of the prior period's charges to income statement accounts ($900 + $1,800 + $270 + $1,440). During subsequent years, some authors prefer reducing the allocated amounts in entry (h) for prior period's charges. In this case, the amortization entry in future periods would reflect just that period's amortizations.

This extended example has assumed the purchase method was used to account for the combination of A Company and B Company. As a result, the consolidated financial statements will include the parent company's share of the revaluations to fair market values of the subsidiary's net assets. A pooling, however, is based on book values. No differential exists in pooling accounting and, thus, entry (g) above would be different while entries (h) and (i) would not be made for a pooling. All other eliminating entries would be the same. The basic elimination entry (g) for a pooling, using the equity method of accounting for the investment, would be

Capital stock--B Co.	45,000	
Additional paid-in capital--B Co.	13,500	
Retained earnings--B Co.	36,900	
Investment in stock of B Company		95,400

L. Minority Interest

The parent company often acquires less than 100% (but more than 50%) of the subsidiary's outstanding stock. Under either the purchase or pooling method the consolidated financial statements will include all of the assets, liabilities, revenues, and expenses of these less than wholly-owned subsidiaries. The percentage of the stock not owned by the parent company represents the minority interest's share of the net assets of the subsidiary. Minority interest will be a line item deduction on the income statement for its portion of the subsidiary's income and, under the parent company concept, will be shown on the consolidated balance sheet after long-term debt but before stockholders' equity. The following procedures apply to cases of less than wholly-owned subsidiaries.

1) Only the parent's share of the sub's shareholders' equity is eliminated in the basic eliminating entry. The minority interest's share is presented separately.
2) The entire amount of intercompany reciprocal items is eliminated. For example, all receivables/payables and sales/cost of sales with a 90% subsidiary are eliminated.
3) For intercompany transactions in inventory and fixed assets, the possible effect on minority interest depends on whether the original transaction affected the subsidiary's income statement. Minority interest is adjusted only if the subsidiary is the selling entity. In this case, the minority interest is adjusted for its percentage ownership of the common stock of the subsidiary. The minority interest is **not** adjusted for unrealized profits on downstream sales. The effects of downstream transactions are confined solely to the parent's (i.e., controlling) ownership interests.

The minority interest's share of the subsidiary's income is shown as a deduction on the consolidated income statement since 100% of the subsidiary's revenues and expenses are combined although the parent company owns less than a 100% interest. For our example, the minority interest deduction on the income statement is computed as follows:

B Company's reported income	$ 9,400
Less: unrealized profit on an upstream inventory sale	(2,000)
B Company's income for consolidated financial purposes	$ 7,400
Minority interest share	10%
Minority interest on income statement	$ 740

The minority interest's share of the net assets of B Company is shown on the consolidated balance sheet between liabilities and controlling interest's equity. The computation for the minority interest shown in the balance sheet for our example is

B Company's capital stock, 12/31/99	$50,000	
Minority interest share	10%	$ 5,000
B Company's additional paid-in		
capital, 12/31/99	$15,000	
Minority interest share	10%	1,500
B Company's retained earnings, 1/1/99	$41,000	
Minority interest share	10%	4,100
B Company's 1999 income for		
consolidated purposes	$ 7,400	
Minority interest share	10%	740
B Company's dividends during 1999	$ 4,000	
Minority interest share	10%	(400)
Total minority interest, 12/31/99		$10,940

The remainder of the consolidation process is just worksheet techniques, as follows:

a. Take all income items across horizontally and foot the adjustments, minority interest, and consolidated columns down to the net income line.
b. Take the amounts on the net income line (on income statement) in the adjustments, minority interest, and consolidated balances columns **down to** retained earnings items across the consolidated balances column. Foot and crossfoot the retained earnings statement.
c. Take the amounts of ending retained earnings in each of the four columns down to the ending retained earnings line in the balance sheet. Foot the minority interest column and place its total in the consolidated balances column. Take all the balance sheet items across to consolidated balances column.

M. Subsequent Consolidated Balance Sheet Only

Consolidation exam problems generally require only the consolidated balance sheet. In this case, the effects of all the income statement account balances would have been closed to the retained earnings accounts. You should carefully review the adjustments and eliminations that were made noting that the nominal accounts (income statement accounts and dividends declared account) would be replaced with the account "Retained Earnings." Thus, elimination entry (a) would not be required; entry (b) would be

(b) Retained earnings	5,000	
Inventories		5,000

Retained earnings would be substituted for the nominal accounts in all other eliminating entries. A shortcut alternative to eliminating entries (f) and (g) is to use the ending balance of B Company's retained earnings as follows.

(f & g) Capital stock--B Co.	45,000	
Additional paid-in capital--B Co.	13,500	
*Retained earnings--B Co.	41,760	
Differential	25,200	
Investment in stock of B Co.--A Co.		125,460

($41,760 = 90% x $46,400 ending balance of B Company's Retained earnings)

A worksheet for just the consolidated balance sheet is presented on the next page. The adjusting and eliminating entries are keyed to the entries and entry explanations for the three-statement layout presented earlier. Several elimination entries have been combined and are shown as (f/g) or (h/i). Note that the final consolidated balance sheet amounts are the same when only the balance sheet is being prepared as well as when all three statements are being prepared.

N. Consolidated Net Income and Consolidated Retained Earnings

In some cases, you may be asked just to determine the Consolidated Net Income (CNI) of the parent and subsidiary companies. A shorter, analytical approach may be used instead of the worksheet method. An analytical definition of CNI is exhibited for our example above.

If the "full" equity method had been used to account for the investment, all the adjustments to the parent company's income (see above) would have been reflected in the "Equity in Subsidiary's Income" account on the parent company's books. Under the "partial" equity method, only the equity accrual of $8,460 is shown in the Equity in Subsidiary's Income account. All other adjustments are made only on the consolidated worksheet.

A COMPANY AND B COMPANY CONSOLIDATED WORKING PAPERS
CONSOLIDATED BALANCE SHEET ONLY
December 31, 1999

Purchase accounting
90% Owned
Subsequent, Partial Equity

	A Company	B Company	Debit		Credit		Minority interest	Consolidated balances
Assets								
Cash	45,300	6,400	(l)	1,000				52,700
Accounts receivable (net)	43,700	12,100			(l)	1,000		50,800
					(c)	4,000		
Inventories	38,300	20,750	(h/i)	900	(b)	5,000		54,050
					(h/i)	900		
Equipment	195,000	57,000	(h/i)	9,000	(d)	2,000		259,000
Accumulated depreciation	(35,200)	(18,900)			(d)	250		(57,950)
					(h/i)	3,600		
Investment in stock of B								
Company	125,460				(f/g)	125,460		
Differential			(f/g)	25,200	(h/i)	25,200		
Goodwill			(h/i)	12,960				12,960
Investment in bonds of A								
Company		44,000			(e)	44,000		
Patents		9,000	(h/i)	2,430				11,430
Total	412,560	130,350						382,990
Liabilities and Stock-holders' Equity								
Accounts payable	8,900	18,950	(c)	4,000				23,850
Bonds payable	100,000		(e)	50,000				50,000
Capital stock	154,000	50,000	(f/g)	45,000			5,000	154,000
Additional paid-in capital	81,600	15,000	(f/g)	13,500			1,500	81,600
Retained earnings	68,060	46,400	(b)	5,000	(e)	6,000	4,400	62,600
			(d)	2,250				
			(f/g)	41,760				
			(h/i)	4,410				
Minority interest							10,940	10,940
Total	412,560	130,350		217,410		217,410		382,990

Parent company's net income from **independent** operations		$26,600
+ Parent company's share of subsidiary's equity income (loss) (equity accrual) (90% x $9,400--reported income of B Co.)	+	8,460
+ Period's amortization of difference between cost and book value ($900--inventories; $1,800--equip.; $270--patent; $1,440--goodwill)	–	4,410
–Parent company's share of **unrealized** profit on intercompany transactions ($3,000--merchandise sale of A to B; $1,800--90% of sale of goods from B to A; $3,000--sale of equipment)	–	7,800
+ Parent company's share of **realized** profit on intercompany transactions ($6,000--bonds; $750--from elimination of excessive depr. on equip. sale from A to B)	+	6,750
CNI		$29,600

Consolidated Retained Earnings (CRE) may be determined once CNI is found. An analytical defini-tion of CRE for our example is

Parent company's beginning retained earnings (1/1/99)		$48,000
+ Consolidated net income for period	+	29,600
– Parent company's dividends to its shareholders (NOTE: subsidiary's dividends to outside parties are a component of minority interest, not CRE)	–	15,000
CRE		$62,600

Make special note that under the "full" equity method of accounting, consolidated retained earnings will equal the retained earnings of the parent company. This is true because consolidated retained earnings under the equity method equals beginning of the year consolidated retained earnings plus consolidated net income (which is identical to parent company net income), minus dividends declared during the year by the parent company only.

O. **Changes in Ownership**

Changes in the level of ownership of subsidiaries frequently occur through purchase or sale of the subsidiary's stock by the parent or changes in the sub's shares outstanding. If the subsidiary changes the number of shares outstanding (for example, through treasury stock transactions), the transaction may re-quire an entry on the parent's books to maintain the parent's reciprocity in the net assets of the subsidiary.

For example, if the subsidiary, through treasury stock transactions, increases the relative book value owned by the parent, the increase must be recorded to maintain reciprocity between the investment ac-count on the parent's accounting records and its equivalent stockholders' equity accounts in the subsidi-ary's books.

Investment in subsidiary	xx	
Paid-in capital		xx

On the other hand, if the subsidiary's treasury stock transactions decrease the parent's equity

Paid-in capital	xx	
Investment in subsidiary		xx

When the parent's share of ownership increases through a purchase of additional stock, simply debit investment and credit cash for cost. A problem occurs with consolidated income statements when the change in ownership takes place in mid-period. Consolidated statements should be prepared based on the ending ownership level. For example, assume that A Company increased its ownership of B Company from 90% to 95% on October 1, 1999. The investment was acquired at book value of $5,452.50 [5% x ($50,000 CS + $15,000 APIC + $44,050 RE at 10-1-99)]. If the subsidiary earned its income of $9,400 evenly over the year, the consolidated net income should reflect a net of

	90%	x	$9,400	x	12/12	=	$8,460.00
+	5%	x	$9,400	x	3/12	=	$ 117.50
	95%						$8,577.50

The interim stock purchase will result in a new account being shown on the consolidated income statement. The account is **Purchased Preacquisition Earnings** which represents the percentage of the subsidiary's earnings earned, in this case, on the 5% stock interest from January 1, 1999, to October 1, 1999. The basic eliminating entries would be based on the 95% ownership as follows:

Equity in subsidiary's income--A Co.	8,577.50	
Dividends declared--B Co.		3,600.00
Investment in stock of B Company		4,977.50
Capital stock--B Co.	47,500.00	
Additional paid-in capital--B Co.	14,250.00	
Retained earnings--B Co.	38,750.00*	
Purchased preacquisition earnings	352.50**	
Differential	25,200.00	
Investment in stock of B Co.--A Co.		126,052.50

* [95% x $41,000 beginning 1999 balance	=	$38,950]	
[Less preacquisition dividend of 5% x $4,000	=	($200)]	
[Retained earnings available, as adjusted	=	$38,750]	
** ($352.50 = 5% x $9,400 x 9/12)			

Purchased Preacquisition Earnings is shown as a deduction along with Minority Interest to arrive at Consolidated Net Income. You should note that purchased preacquisition earnings are used only with interim acquisitions under the purchase accounting method; all poolings are assumed to take place at the beginning of the period regardless of when, during the period, the acquisition was actually made.

P. **Combined Financial Statements**

Combined financial statements is the term used to describe financial statements prepared for companies that are owned by the same parent company or individual. These statements are often prepared when several subsidiaries of a common parent are not consolidated. Combined financial statements are prepared by combining all of the separate companies' financial statement classifications. Intercompany transactions, balances, and profit (loss) should be eliminated in the same way as in consolidated statements.

Q. Push-Down Accounting

"Push-down accounting" describes the method used in a purchase-combination whereby a onetime adjustment to revalue the subsidiary's assets and liabilities is made directly on the books of the subsidiary. Use of this method is required by SEC Staff Accounting for all wholly-owned subsidiaries and it is recommended where a controlling interest exists.

Push-down accounting requires the subsidiary to record an entry revaluing all assets and liabilities with a balancing entry to a revaluation capital account. The revaluation capital account will be eliminated in consolidation against the investment in subsidiary account. Push-down accounting will have no effect on the presentation of the consolidated financial statements or the separate financial statements of the parent company. However, the subsidiary's financial statements would be reported at fair value rather than historical cost. Advocates of push-down accounting believe that a change of ownership through a purchase-combination justifies the use of a new basis for the acquired entity. Thus, the new basis should be pushed down or directly recorded on the acquired entity's books.

MULTIPLE-CHOICE QUESTIONS (1-80)

1. On April 1, 1999, Dart Co. paid $620,000 for all the issued and outstanding common stock of Wall Corp. in a transaction properly accounted for as a purchase. The recorded assets and liabilities of Wall Corp. on April 1, 1999, follow:

Cash	$ 60,000
Inventory	180,000
Property and equipment (net of accumulated depreciation of $220,000)	320,000
Goodwill (net of accumulated amortization of $50,000)	100,000
Liabilities	(120,000)
Net assets	$ 540,000

On April 1, 1999, Wall's inventory had a fair value of $150,000, and the property and equipment (net) had a fair value of $380,000. What is the amount of goodwill resulting from the business combination?

- a. $150,000
- b. $120,000
- c. $ 50,000
- d. $ 20,000

2. On August 31, 1999, Wood Corp. issued 100,000 shares of its $20 par value common stock for the net assets of Pine, Inc., in a business combination accounted for by the purchase method. The market value of Wood's common stock on August 31 was $36 per share. Wood paid a fee of $160,000 to the consultant who arranged this acquisition. Costs of registering and issuing the equity securities amounted to $80,000. No goodwill was involved in the purchase. What amount should Wood capitalize as the cost of acquiring Pine's net assets?

- a. $3,600,000
- b. $3,680,000
- c. $3,760,000
- d. $3,840,000

Items 3 and 4 are based on the following:

On December 31, 1999, Saxe Corporation was merged into Poe Corporation. In the business combination, Poe issued 200,000 shares of its $10 par common stock, with a market price of $18 a share, for all of Saxe's common stock. The stockholders' equity section of each company's balance sheet immediately before the combination was

	Poe	*Saxe*
Common stock	$3,000,000	$1,500,000
Additional paid-in capital	1,300,000	150,000
Retained earnings	2,500,000	850,000
	$6,800,000	$2,500,000

3. Assume that the merger qualifies for treatment as a purchase. In the December 31, 1999 consolidated balance sheet, additional paid-in capital should be reported at

- a. $ 950,000
- b. $1,300,000
- c. $1,450,000
- d. $2,900,000

4. Assume that the merger qualifies for treatment as a pooling of interests. In the December 31, 1999 consolidated balance sheet, additional paid-in capital should be reported at

- a. $ 950,000
- b. $1,300,000
- c. $1,450,000
- d. $2,900,000

5. On January 1, 2000, Neal Co. issued 100,000 shares of its $10 par value common stock in exchange for all of Frey Inc.'s outstanding stock. This business combination was accounted for as a pooling of interests. The fair value of Neal's common stock on December 31, 1999, was $19 per share. The carrying amounts and fair values of Frey's assets and liabilities on December 31, 1999, were as follows:

	Carrying amount	*Fair value*
Cash	$ 240,000	$ 240,000
Receivables	270,000	270,000
Inventory	435,000	405,000
Property, plant, and equipment	1,305,000	1,440,000
Liabilities	(525,000)	(525,000)
Net assets	$1,725,000	$1,830,000

What is the amount of goodwill resulting from the business combination?

- a. $175,000
- b. $105,000
- c. $ 70,000
- d. $0

6. Consolidated financial statements are typically prepared when one company has a controlling financial interest in another **unless**

- a. The subsidiary is a finance company.
- b. The fiscal year-ends of the two companies are more than 3 months apart.
- c. Such control is likely to be temporary.
- d. The two companies are in unrelated industries, such as manufacturing and real estate.

7. Which of the following conditions would cause a business combination to be accounted for by the purchase method?

- a. The combined corporation intends to dispose of duplicate facilities within 1 year of the combination.
- b. Cash is to be used to acquire 2% of the outstanding stock of one of the combining companies.
- c. After the combination is consummated, one of the combining companies will be a subsidiary of another combining company.
- d. Before the combination is consummated, one of the combining companies holds 15% of the outstanding stock of another of the combining companies.

8. A business combination is accounted for appropriately as a purchase. Which of the following should be deducted in determining the combined corporation's net income for the current period?

	Direct costs of acquisition	General expenses related to acquisition
a.	Yes	No
b.	Yes	Yes
c.	No	Yes
d.	No	No

9. PDX Corp. acquired 100% of the outstanding common stock of Sea Corp. in a purchase transaction. The cost of the acquisition exceeded the fair value of the identifiable assets and assumed liabilities. The general guidelines for assigning amounts to the inventories acquired provide for
- a. Raw materials to be valued at original cost.
- b. Work in process to be valued at the estimated selling prices of finished goods, less both costs to complete and costs of disposal.
- c. Finished goods to be valued at replacement cost.
- d. Finished goods to be valued at estimated selling prices, less both costs of disposal and a reasonable profit allowance.

10. A supportive argument for the pooling of interests method of accounting for a business combination is that
- a. One company is clearly the dominant and continuing entity.
- b. Goodwill is generally a part of any acquisition.
- c. A portion of the total cost is assigned to individual assets acquired on the basis of their fair value.
- d. It was developed within the boundaries of the historical cost system and is compatible with it.

11. Which of the following statements is supportive of the pooling of interests method in accounting for a business combination?
- a. Bargaining between the parties is based on current values for assets and liabilities.
- b. Stockholder groups remain intact but combine.
- c. Goodwill is generally a part of any acquisition.
- d. A portion of the total cost is assigned to individual assets acquired on the basis of their fair value.

12. A business combination is accounted for as a pooling of interests. Costs of furnishing information to stockholders related to effecting the business combination should be
- a. Deducted directly from retained earnings of the combined corporation.
- b. Deducted in determining net income of the combined corporation for the period in which the costs were incurred.
- c. Capitalized but **not** amortized.
- d. Capitalized and subsequently amortized over a period **not** exceeding 40 years.

13. A business combination is accounted for as a pooling of interests. In the consolidated balance sheet, the following component(s) of stockholders' equity may be less than the sum of those same components of the merging companies

	Retained earnings	Contributed capital
a.	No	No
b.	Yes	No
c.	No	Yes
d.	Yes	Yes

 2

Items 14 through 18 are based on the following:

On January 1, 1999, Polk Corp. and Strass Corp. had condensed balance sheets as follows:

	Polk	Strass
Current assets	$ 70,000	$20,000
Noncurrent assets	90,000	40,000
Total assets	$160,000	$60,000
Current liabilities	$ 30,000	$10,000
Long-term debt	50,000	--
Stockholders' equity	80,000	50,000
Total liabilities and stockholders' equity	$160,000	$60,000

On January 2, 1999, Polk borrowed $60,000 and used the proceeds to purchase 90% of the outstanding common shares of Strass. This debt is payable in 10 equal annual principal payments, plus interest, beginning December 30, 1999. The excess cost of the investment over Strass' book value of acquired net assets should be allocated 60% to inventory and 40% to goodwill.

On Polk's January 2, 1999 consolidated balance sheet,

14. Current assets should be
- a. $99,000
- b. $96,000
- c. $90,000
- d. $79,000

15. Noncurrent assets should be
- a. $130,000
- b. $134,000
- c. $136,000
- d. $140,000

16. Current liabilities should be
- a. $50,000
- b. $46,000
- c. $40,000
- d. $30,000

17. Noncurrent liabilities including minority interests should be
- a. $115,000
- b. $109,000
- c. $104,000
- d. $ 55,000

18. Stockholders' equity should be
- a. $ 80,000
- b. $ 85,000
- c. $ 90,000
- d. $130,000

19. On November 30, 1999, Parlor, Inc. purchased for cash at $15 per share all 250,000 shares of the outstanding common stock of Shaw Co. At November 30, 1999, Shaw's balance sheet showed a carrying amount of net assets of $3,000,000. At that date, the fair value of Shaw's property, plant and equipment exceeded its carrying amount by $400,000. In its November 30, 1999 consolidated balance sheet, what amount should Parlor report as goodwill?
- a. $750,000
- b. $400,000

   c. $350,000

   d. $0

20. A subsidiary, acquired for cash in a business combination, owned inventories with a market value different than the book value as of the date of combination. A consolidated balance sheet prepared immediately after the acquisition would include this difference as part of

   a.   Deferred credits.

   b.   Goodwill.

   c.   Inventories.

   d.   Retained earnings.

21. Company J acquired all of the outstanding common stock of Company K in exchange for cash. The acquisition price exceeds the fair value of net assets acquired. How should Company J determine the amounts to be reported for the plant and equipment and long-term debt acquired from Company K?

	Plant and equipment	*Long-term debt*
a.	K's carrying amount	K's carrying amount
b.	K's carrying amount	Fair value
c.	Fair value	K's carrying amount
d.	Fair value	Fair value

22. In a business combination accounted for as a purchase, the appraised values of the identifiable assets acquired exceeded the acquisition price. How should the excess appraised value be reported?

   a.   As negative goodwill.

   b.   As additional paid-in capital.

   c.   As a reduction of the values assigned to noncurrent assets and a deferred credit for any unallocated portion.

   d.   As positive goodwill.

 3

Items 23 through 27 are based on the following:

On June 30, 1999, Post, Inc. issued 630,000 shares of its $5 par common stock, for which it received 180,000 shares (90%) of Shaw Corp.'s $10 par common stock, in a business combination appropriately accounted for as a pooling of interests. The stockholders' equities immediately before the combination were

	Post	*Shaw*
Common stock	$ 6,500,000	$2,000,000
Additional paid-in capital	4,400,000	1,600,000
Retained earnings	6,100,000	5,400,000
	$17,000,000	$9,000,000

Both corporations continued to operate as separate businesses, maintaining accounting records with years ending December 31. For 1999, net income and dividends paid from separate company operations were

	Post	*Shaw*
Net income		
Six months ended 6/30/99	$1,000,000	$300,000
Six months ended 12/31/99	1,100,000	500,000
Dividends paid		
April 1, 1999	1,300,000	--
October 1, 1999	--	350,000

23. In the June 30, 1999 consolidated balance sheet, common stock should be reported at

   a. $9,650,000

   b. $9,450,000

   c. $8,500,000

   d. $8,300,000

24. In the June 30, 1999 consolidated balance sheet, additional paid-in capital should be reported at

   a. $4,400,000

   b. $4,490,000

   c. $5,840,000

   d. $6,000,000

25. In the June 30, 1999 consolidated balance sheet, retained earnings should be reported at

   a. $ 6,100,000

   b. $ 9,660,000

   c. $10,960,000

   d. $11,500,000

26. In the 1999 consolidated income statement, net income should be reported at

   a. $2,550,000

   b. $2,600,000

   c. $2,820,000

   d. $2,900,000

27. In the December 31, 1999 consolidated balance sheet, total minority interest should be reported at

   a. $950,000

   b. $945,000

   c. $915,000

   d. $900,000

28. How would the retained earnings of a subsidiary acquired in a business combination usually be treated in a consolidated balance sheet prepared immediately after the acquisition?

   a.   Excluded for both a purchase and a pooling of interests.

   b.   Excluded for a pooling of interests but included for a purchase.

   c.   Included for both a purchase and a pooling of interests.

   d.   Included for a pooling of interests but excluded for a purchase.

29. A subsidiary may be acquired by issuing common stock in a pooling of interests transaction or by paying cash in a purchase transaction. Which of the following items would be reported in the consolidated financial statements at the same amount regardless of the accounting method used?

   a.   Minority interest.

   b.   Goodwill.

   c.   Retained earnings.

   d.   Capital stock.

 4

30. Wright Corp. has several subsidiaries that are included in its consolidated financial statements. In its December 31, 1999 trial balance, Wright had the following intercompany balances before eliminations:

	Debit	Credit
Current receivable due from Main Co.	$ 32,000	
Noncurrent receivable from Main	114,000	
Cash advance to Corn Corp.	6,000	
Cash advance from King Co.		$ 15,000
Intercompany payable to King		101,000

In its December 31, 1999 consolidated balance sheet, what amount should Wright report as intercompany receivables?

  a. $152,000
  b. $146,000
  c. $ 36,000
  d. $0

31. Shep Co. has a receivable from its parent, Pep Co. Should this receivable be separately reported in Shep's balance sheet and in Pep's consolidated balance sheet?

	Shep's balance sheet	Pep's consolidated balance sheet
a.	Yes	No
b.	Yes	Yes
c.	No	No
d.	No	Yes

Items 32 through 36 are based on the following:

Selected information from the separate and consolidated balance sheets and income statements of Pard, Inc. and its subsidiary, Spin Co., as of December 31, 1999, and for the year then ended is as follows:

	Pard	Spin	Consolidated
Balance sheet accounts			
Accounts receivable	$ 26,000	$ 19,000	$ 39,000
Inventory	30,000	25,000	52,000
Investment in Spin	67,000	--	
Goodwill	--	--	30,000
Minority interest	--	--	10,000
Stockholders' equity	154,000	50,000	154,000
Income statement accounts			
Revenues	$200,000	$140,000	$308,000
Cost of goods sold	150,000	110,000	231,000
Gross profit	50,000	30,000	77,000
Equity in earnings of Spin	11,000	--	--
Amortization of goodwill	--	--	2,000
Net income	36,000	20,000	40,000

Additional information

  • During 1999, Pard sold goods to Spin at the same markup on cost that Pard uses for all sales. At December 31, 1999, Spin had not paid for all of these goods and still held 37.5% of them in inventory.

  • Pard acquired its interest in Spin on January 2, 1996. Pard's policy is to amortize goodwill by the straight-line method.

32. What was the amount of intercompany sales from Pard to Spin during 1999?

  a. $ 3,000
  b. $ 6,000
  c. $29,000
  d. $32,000

33. At December 31, 1999, what was the amount of Spin's payable to Pard for intercompany sales?

  a. $ 3,000
  b. $ 6,000
  c. $29,000
  d. $32,000

34. In Pard's consolidated balance sheet, what was the carrying amount of the inventory that Spin purchased from Pard?

  a. $ 3,000
  b. $ 6,000
  c. $ 9,000
  d. $12,000

35. What is the percent of minority interest ownership in Spin?

  a. 10%
  b. 20%
  c. 25%
  d. 45%

36. Over how many years has Pard chosen to amortize goodwill?

  a. 15
  b. 19
  c. 23
  d. 40

Items 37 and 38 are based on the following:

On January 1, 1999, Owen Corp. purchased all of Sharp Corp.'s common stock for $1,200,000. On that date, the fair values of Sharp's assets and liabilities equaled their carrying amounts of $1,320,000 and $320,000, respectively. Owen's policy is to amortize intangibles over 10 years. During 1999, Sharp paid cash dividends of $20,000.

Selected information from the separate balance sheets and income statements of Owen and Sharp as of December 31, 1999, and for the year then ended follows:

	Owen	Sharp
Balance sheet accounts		
Investment in subsidiary	$1,300,000	--
Retained earnings	1,240,000	560,000
Total stockholders' equity	2,620,000	1,120,000
Income statement accounts		
Operating income	420,000	200,000
Equity in earnings of Sharp	120,000	--
Net income	400,000	140,000

37. In Owen's 1999 consolidated income statement, what amount should be reported for amortization of goodwill?

  a. $0
  b. $12,000
  c. $18,000
  d. $20,000

38. In Owen's December 31, 1999 consolidated balance sheet, what amount should be reported as total retained earnings?

  a. $1,240,000
  b. $1,360,000
  c. $1,380,000

d. $1,800,000

39. When a parent-subsidiary relationship exists, consolidated financial statements are prepared in recognition of the accounting concept of
   a.   Reliability.
   b.   Materiality.
   c.   Legal entity.
   d.   Economic entity.

40. A subsidiary was acquired for cash in a business combination on January 1, 1999. The purchase price exceeded the fair value of identifiable net assets. The acquired company owned equipment with a market value in excess of the carrying amount as of the date of combination. A consolidated balance sheet prepared on December 31, 1999, would
   a.   Report the unamortized portion of the excess of the market value over the carrying amount of the equipment as part of goodwill.
   b.   Report the unamortized portion of the excess of the market value over the carrying amount of the equipment as part of plant and equipment.
   c.   Report the excess of the market value over the carrying amount of the equipment as part of plant and equipment.
   d.   Not report the excess of the market value over the carrying amount of the equipment because it would be expensed as incurred.

41. Pride, Inc. owns 80% of Simba, Inc.'s outstanding common stock. Simba, in turn, owns 10% of Pride's outstanding common stock. What percentage of the common stock cash dividends declared by the individual companies should be reported as dividends declared in the consolidated financial statements?

	Dividends declared by Pride	Dividends declared by Simba
a.	90%	0%
b.	90%	20%
c.	100%	0%
d.	100%	20%

42. Kiwi, Inc.'s planned combination with Mori Co. on January 1, 1999, can be structured either as a purchase or a pooling of interests. In a purchase, Kiwi would acquire Mori's identifiable net assets for more than their book values. These book values approximate fair values. Mori's assets consist of current assets and depreciable noncurrent assets. Ignoring costs required to effect the combination and income tax expense, how would the combined entity's 1999 net income under purchase accounting compare to that under pooling of interests accounting?
   a.   Less than pooling.
   b.   Equal to pooling.
   c.   Greater than pooling.
   d.   Not determinable from information given.

43. On January 1, 1999, Prim, Inc. acquired all the outstanding common shares of Scarp, Inc. for cash equal to the book value of the stock. The carrying amounts of Scarp's assets and liabilities approximated their fair values, except that the carrying amount of its building was more than fair value. In preparing Prim's 1999 consolidated income statement, which of the following adjustments would be made?
   a.   Depreciation expense would be decreased and goodwill amortization would be recognized.
   b.   Depreciation expense would be increased and goodwill amortization would be recognized.
   c.   Depreciation expense would be decreased and **no** goodwill amortization would be recognized.
   d.   Depreciation expense would be increased and **no** goodwill amortization would be recognized.

44. Matt Co. included a foreign subsidiary in its 1999 consolidated financial statements. The subsidiary was acquired in 1993 and was excluded from previous consolidations. The change was caused by the elimination of foreign exchange controls. Including the subsidiary in the 1999 consolidated financial statements results in an accounting change that should be reported
   a.   By footnote disclosure only.
   b.   Currently and prospectively.
   c.   Currently with footnote disclosure of pro forma effects of retroactive application.
   d.   By restating the financial statements of all prior periods presented.

Items 45 and 46 are based on the following:

On June 30, 1999, Purl Corp. issued 150,000 shares of its $20 par common stock for which it received all of Scott Corp.'s common stock. The fair value of the common stock issued is equal to the book value of Scott Corp.'s net assets. Both corporations continued to operate as separate businesses, maintaining accounting records with years ending December 31. Net income from separate company operations and dividends paid were:

	Purl	Scott
Net income		
Six months ended 6/30/99	$750,000	$225,000
Six months ended 12/31/99	825,000	375,000
Dividends paid		
March 25, 1999	950,000	--
November 15, 1999	--	300,000

On December 31, 1999, Scott held in its inventory merchandise acquired from Purl on December 1, 1999, for $150,000, which included a $45,000 markup.

45. Assume that the business combination qualifies for treatment as a purchase. In the 1999 consolidated income statement, net income should be reported at
   a. $1,650,000
   b. $1,905,000
   c. $1,950,000
   d. $2,130,000

46. Assume that the business combination qualifies for treatment as a pooling of interests. In the 1999 consolidated income statement, net income should be reported at
   a. $1,905,000
   b. $1,950,000
   c. $2,130,000
   d. $2,175,000

Items 47 and 48 are based on the following:

On June 30, 1999, Pane Corp. exchanged 150,000 shares of its $20 par value common stock for all of Sky Corp.'s common stock. At that date, the fair value of Pane's common stock issued was equal to the book value of Sky's net assets. Both corporations continued to operate as separate businesses, maintaining accounting records with years ending December 31. Information from separate company operations follows:

	Pane	Sky
Retained earnings--12/31/98	$3,200,000	$925,000
Net income--6 months ended 6/30/99	800,000	275,000
Dividends paid--3/25/99	750,000	--

47. If the business combination is accounted for as a pooling of interest, what amount of retained earnings would Pane report in its June 30, 1999 consolidated balance sheet?
- a. $5,200,000
- b. $4,450,000
- c. $3,525,000
- d. $3,250,000

48. If the business combination is accounted for as a purchase, what amount of retained earnings would Pane report in its June 30, 1999 consolidated balance sheet?
- a. $5,200,000
- b. $4,450,000
- c. $3,525,000
- d. $3,250,000

49. A business combination occurs in the middle of the year. Results of operations for the year of combination would include the combined results of operations of the separate companies for the entire year if the business combination is a

	Purchase	Pooling of interests
a.	Yes	Yes
b.	Yes	No
c.	No	No
d.	No	Yes

50. In a business combination accounted for as a pooling
- a. Income is combined only from date of combination, **not** for prior periods presented.
- b. Income is combined for all periods presented.
- c. After the combination, balance sheet amounts are carried at fair market value.
- d. Direct acquisition costs are recorded as part of the cost of the investment.

Items 51 and 52 are based on the following:

Scroll, Inc., a wholly owned subsidiary of Pirn, Inc., began operations on January 1, 1999. The following information is from the condensed 1999 income statements of Pirn and Scroll:

	Pirn	Scroll
Sales to Scroll	$100,000	$ --
Sales to others	400,000	300,000
	500,000	300,000
Cost of goods sold:		
Acquired from Pirn	--	80,000
Acquired from others	350,000	190,000
Gross profit	150,000	30,000
Depreciation	40,000	10,000
Other expenses	60,000	15,000
Income from operations	50,000	5,000
Gain on sale of equipment to Scroll	12,000	--
Income before income taxes	$ 62,000	$ 5,000

Additional information
- Sales by Pirn to Scroll are made on the same terms as those made to third parties.
- Equipment purchased by Scroll from Pirn for $36,000 on January 1, 1999, is depreciated using the straight-line method over 4 years.

51. In Pirn's December 31, 1999, consolidating worksheet, how much intercompany profit should be eliminated from Scroll's inventory?
- a. $30,000
- b. $20,000
- c. $10,000
- d. $ 6,000

52. What amount should be reported as depreciation expense in Pirn's 1999 consolidated income statement?
- a. $50,000
- b. $47,000
- c. $44,000
- d. $41,000

53. Clark Co. had the following transactions with affiliated parties during 1999:

- Sales of $60,000 to Dean, Inc., with $20,000 gross profit. Dean had $15,000 of this inventory on hand at year end. Clark owns a 15% interest in Dean and does not exert significant influence.
- Purchases of raw materials totaling $240,000 from Kent Corp., a wholly owned subsidiary. Kent's gross profit on the sale was $48,000. Clark had $60,000 of this inventory remaining on December 31, 1999.

Before eliminating entries, Clark had consolidated current assets of $320,000. What amount should Clark report in its December 31, 1999 consolidated balance sheet for current assets?
- a. $320,000
- b. $317,000
- c. $308,000
- d. $303,000

54. Parker Corp. owns 80% of Smith Inc.'s common stock. During 1999, Parker sold Smith $250,000 of inventory on the same terms as sales made to third parties. Smith sold all of the inventory purchased from Parker in 1999. The following information pertains to Smith and Parker's sales for 1999:

	Parker	Smith
Sales	$1,000,000	$700,000
Cost of sales	400,000	350,000
	$ 600,000	$350,000

What amount should Parker report as cost of sales in its 1999 consolidated income statement?

    a. $750,000
    b. $680,000
    c. $500,000
    d. $430,000

55. Selected information from the separate and consolidated balance sheets and income statements of Pare, Inc. and its subsidiary, Shel Co., as of December 31, 1999, and for the year then ended is as follows:

	Pare	Shel	Consolidated
Balance sheet accounts			
Accounts receivable	$ 52,000	$ 38,000	$ 78,000
Inventory	60,000	50,000	104,000
Income statement accounts			
Revenues	$400,000	$280,000	$616,000
Cost of goods sold	300,000	220,000	462,000
Gross profit	100,000	60,000	154,000

Additional information:

    During 1999, Pare sold goods to Shel at the same markup on cost that Pare uses for all sales.

    In Pare's consolidating worksheet, what amount of unrealized intercompany profit was eliminated?

    a. $ 6,000
    b. $12,000
    c. $58,000
    d. $64,000

56. During 1999, Pard Corp. sold goods to its 80%-owned subsidiary, Seed Corp. At December 31, 1999, one half of these goods were included in Seed's ending inventory. Reported 1999 selling expenses were $1,100,000 and $400,000 for Pard and Seed, respectively. Pard's selling expenses included $50,000 in freight-out costs for goods sold to Seed. What amount of selling expenses should be reported in Pard's 1999 consolidated income statement?

    a. $1,500,000
    b. $1,480,000
    c. $1,475,000
    d. $1,450,000

57. On January 1, 1999, Poe Corp. sold a machine for $900,000 to Saxe Corp., its wholly owned subsidiary. Poe paid $1,100,000 for this machine, which had accumulated depreciation of $250,000. Poe estimated a $100,000 salvage value and depreciated the machine on the straight-line method over 20 years, a policy which Saxe continued. In Poe's December 31, 1999 consolidated balance sheet, this machine should be included in cost and accumulated depreciation as

	Cost	Accumulated depreciation
a.	$1,100,000	$300,000
b.	$1,100,000	$290,000
c.	$ 900,000	$ 40,000
d.	$ 850,000	$ 42,500

58. Wagner, a holder of a $1,000,000 Palmer, Inc. bond, collected the interest due on March 31, 1999, and then sold the bond to Seal, Inc. for $975,000. On that date, Palmer, a 75% owner of Seal, had a $1,075,000 carrying amount for this bond. What was the effect of Seal's purchase of

Palmer's bond on the retained earnings and minority interest amounts reported in Palmer's March 31, 1999 consolidated balance sheet?

	Retained earnings	Minority interest
a.	$100,000 increase	$0
b.	$ 75,000 increase	$ 25,000 increase
c.	$0	$ 25,000 increase
d.	$0	$100,000 increase

59. Sun, Inc. is a wholly owned subsidiary of Patton, Inc. On June 1, 1999, Patton declared and paid a $1 per share cash dividend to stockholders of record on May 15, 1999. On May 1, 1999, Sun bought 10,000 shares of Patton's common stock for $700,000 on the open market, when the book value per share was $30. What amount of gain should Patton report from this transaction in its consolidated income statement for the year ended December 31, 1999?

    a. $0
    b. $390,000
    c. $400,000
    d. $410,000

60. Perez, Inc. owns 80% of Senior, Inc. During 1999, Perez sold goods with a 40% gross profit to Senior. Senior sold all of these goods in 1999. For 1999 consolidated financial statements, how should the summation of Perez and Senior income statement items be adjusted?

    a. Sales and cost of goods sold should be reduced by the intercompany sales.
    b. Sales and cost of goods sold should be reduced by 80% of the intercompany sales.
    c. Net income should be reduced by 80% of the gross profit on intercompany sales.
    d. No adjustment is necessary.

61. Water Co. owns 80% of the outstanding common stock of Fire Co. On December 31, 1999, Fire sold equipment to Water at a price in excess of Fire's carrying amount, but less than its original cost. On a consolidated balance sheet at December 31, 1999, the carrying amount of the equipment should be reported at

    a. Water's original cost.
    b. Fire's original cost.
    c. Water's original cost less Fire's recorded gain.
    d. Water's original cost less 80% of Fire's recorded gain.

62. Port, Inc. owns 100% of Salem, Inc. On January 1, 1999, Port sold Salem delivery equipment at a gain. Port had owned the equipment for 2 years and used a 5-year straight-line depreciation rate with no residual value. Salem is using a 3-year straight-line depreciation rate with no residual value for the equipment. In the consolidated income statement, Salem's recorded depreciation expense on the equipment for 1999 will be decreased by

    a. 20% of the gain on sale.
    b. 33 1/3% of the gain on sale.
    c. 50% of the gain on sale.
    d. 100% of the gain on sale.

63. P Co. purchased term bonds at a premium on the open market. These bonds represented 20% of the outstanding class of bonds issued at a discount by S Co., P's wholly

owned subsidiary. P intends to hold the bonds until maturity. In a consolidated balance sheet, the difference between the bond carrying amounts in the two companies would be
   a. Included as a decrease to retained earnings.
   b. Included as an increase to retained earnings.
   c. Reported as a deferred debit to be amortized over the remaining life of the bonds.
   d. Reported as a deferred credit to be amortized over the remaining life of the bonds.

64. Eltro Company acquired a 70% interest in the Samson Company in 1998. For the years ended December 31, 1999 and 2000, Samson reported net income of $80,000 and $90,000, respectively. During 1999, Samson sold merchandise to Eltro for $10,000 at a profit of $2,000. The merchandise was later resold by Eltro to outsiders for $15,000 during 2000. For consolidation purposes what is the minority interest's share of Samson's net income for 1999 and 2000 respectively?
   a. $23,400 and $27,600.
   b. $24,000 and $27,000.
   c. $24,600 and $26,400.
   d. $26,000 and $25,000.

Items 65 and 66 are based on the following:

   On January 1, 1999, Ritt Corp. purchased 80% of Shaw Corp.'s $10 par common stock for $975,000. On this date, the carrying amount of Shaw's net assets was $1,000,000. The fair values of Shaw's identifiable assets and liabilities were the same as their carrying amounts except for plant assets (net) which were $100,000 in excess of the carrying amount. For the year ended December 31, 1999, Shaw had net income of $190,000 and paid cash dividends totaling $125,000.

65. In the January 1, 1999 consolidated balance sheet, goodwill should be reported at
   a. $0
   b. $ 75,000
   c. $ 95,000
   d. $175,000

66. In the December 31, 1999 consolidated balance sheet, minority interest should be reported at
   a. $200,000
   b. $213,000
   c. $220,000
   d. $233,000

Items 67 through 69 are based on the following:

   On January 2, 2000, Pare Co. purchased 75% of Kidd Co.'s outstanding common stock. Selected balance sheet data at December 31, 2000, is as follows:

	Pare	Kidd
Total assets	$420,000	$180,000
Liabilities	$120,000	$ 60,000
Common stock	100,000	50,000
Retained earnings	200,000	70,000
	$420,000	$180,000

During 2000, Pare and Kidd paid cash dividends of $25,000 and $5,000, respectively, to their shareholders. There were no other intercompany transactions.

67. In its December 31, 2000 consolidated statement of retained earnings, what amount should Pare report as dividends paid?
   a. $ 5,000
   b. $25,000
   c. $26,250
   d. $30,000

68. In Pare's December 31, 2000 consolidated balance sheet, what amount should be reported as minority interest in net assets?
   a. $0
   b. $ 30,000
   c. $ 45,000
   d. $105,000

69. In its December 31, 2000 consolidated balance sheet, what amount should Pare report as common stock?
   a. $ 50,000
   b. $100,000
   c. $137,500
   d. $150,000

70. Poe, Inc. acquired 100% of Shaw Co. in a business combination on September 30, 2000. During 2000, Poe declared quarterly dividends of $25,000 and Shaw declared quarterly dividends of $10,000. Under each of the following methods of accounting for the business combination, what amount should be reported as dividends declared in the December 31, 2000, consolidated statement of retained earnings?

	Purchase	Pooling of interests
a.	$100,000	$130,000
b.	$100,000	$140,000
c.	$130,000	$130,000
d.	$130,000	$140,000

71. On September 1, 1998, Phillips, Inc. issued common stock in exchange for 20% of Sago, Inc.'s outstanding common stock. On July 1, 1999, Phillips issued common stock for an additional 75% of Sago's outstanding common stock. Sago continues in existence as Phillips' subsidiary. How much of Sago's 1999 net income should be reported as accruing to Phillips?
   a. 20% of Sago's net income to June 30 and all of Sago's net income from July 1 to December 31.
   b. 20% of Sago's net income to June 30 and 95% of Sago's net income from July 1 to December 31.
   c. 95% of Sago's net income.
   d. All of Sago's net income.

72. Mr. & Mrs. Dart own a majority of the outstanding capital stock of Wall Corp., Black Co., and West, Inc. During 1999, Wall advanced cash to Black and West in the amount of $50,000 and $80,000, respectively. West advanced $70,000 in cash to Black. At December 31, 1999, none of the advances was repaid. In the combined December 31, 1999 balance sheet of these companies, what amount would be reported as receivables from affiliates?

- a. $200,000
- b. $130,000
- c. $ 60,000
- d. $0

73. Selected data for two subsidiaries of Dunn Corp. taken from December 31, 1999 preclosing trial balances are as follows:

	Banks Co.debit	Lamm Co.credit
Shipments to Banks	$ --	$150,000
Shipments from Lamm	200,000	--
Intercompany inventory profit on total shipments	--	50,000

Additional data relating to the December 31, 1999 inventory are as follows:

Inventory acquired from outside parties	$175,000	$250,000
Inventory acquired from Lamm	60,000	--

At December 31, 1999, the inventory reported on the combined balance sheet of the two subsidiaries should be

- a. $425,000
- b. $435,000
- c. $470,000
- d. $485,000

74. Ahm Corp. owns 90% of Bee Corp.'s common stock and 80% of Cee Corp.'s common stock. The remaining common shares of Bee and Cee are owned by their respective employees. Bee sells exclusively to Cee, Cee buys exclusively from Bee, and Cee sells exclusively to unrelated companies. Selected 1999 information for Bee and Cee follows:

	Bee Corp.	Cee Corp.
Sales	$130,000	$91,000
Cost of sales	100,000	65,000
Beginning inventory	None	None
Ending inventory	None	65,000

What amount should be reported as gross profit in Bee and Cee's combined income statement for the year ended December 31, 1999?

- a. $26,000
- b. $41,000
- c. $47,800
- d. $56,000

75. The following information pertains to shipments of merchandise from Home Office to Branch during 1999:

Home Office's cost of merchandise	$160,000
Intracompany billing	200,000
Sales by Branch	250,000
Unsold merchandise at Branch on December 31, 1999	20,000

In the combined income statement of Home Office and Branch for the year ended December 31, 1999, what amount of the above transactions should be included in sales?

- a. $250,000
- b. $230,000
- c. $200,000
- d. $180,000

76. Mr. and Mrs. Gasson own 100% of the common stock of Able Corp. and 90% of the common stock of Baker Corp. Able previously paid $4,000 for the remaining 10% interest in Baker. The condensed December 31, 1999 balance sheets of Able and Baker are as follows:

	Able	Baker
Assets	$600,000	$60,000
Liabilities	$200,000	$30,000
Common stock	100,000	20,000
Retained earnings	300,000	10,000
	$600,000	$60,000

In a combined balance sheet of the two corporations at December 31, 1999, what amount should be reported as total stockholders' equity?

- a. $430,000
- b. $426,000
- c. $403,000
- d. $400,000

77. Mr. Cord owns four corporations. Combined financial statements are being prepared for these corporations, which have intercompany loans of $200,000 and intercompany profits of $500,000. What amount of these intercompany loans and profits should be included in the combined financial statements?

	Intercompany	
	Loans	Profits
a.	$200,000	$0
b.	$200,000	$500,000
c.	$0	$0
d.	$0	$500,000

78. Combined statements may be used to present the results of operations of

	Companies under common management	Commonly controlled companies
a.	No	Yes
b.	Yes	No
c.	No	No
d.	Yes	Yes

79. Which of the following items should be treated in the same manner in both combined financial statements and consolidated statements?

	Income taxes	Minority interest
a.	No	No
b.	No	Yes
c.	Yes	Yes
d.	Yes	No

80. Which of the following items should be treated in the same manner in both combined financial statements and consolidated statements?

	Different fiscal periods	Foreign operations
a.	No	No
b.	No	Yes
c.	Yes	Yes
d.	Yes	No

OTHER OBJECTIVE QUESTIONS

Problem 1   (45 to 55 minutes)

This question consists of 16 items. Select the **best** answer for each item. Use a No. 2 pencil to blacken the appropriate ovals on the Objective Answer Sheet to indicate your answers. **Answer all items.** Your grade will be based on the total number of correct answers.

Presented below are selected amounts from the separate unconsolidated financial statements of Poe Corp. and its 90%-owned subsidiary, Shaw Co., at December 31, 1999. Additional information follows:

	Poe	Shaw
Selected income statement amounts		
Sales	$710,000	$530,000
Cost of goods sold	490,000	370,000
Gain on sale of equipment	--	21,000
Earnings from investment in subsidiary	61,000	--
Interest expense	--	16,000
Depreciation	25,000	20,000
Selected balance sheet amounts		
Cash	$ 50,000	$ 15,000
Inventories	229,000	150,000
Equipment	440,000	360,000
Accumulated depreciation	(200,000)	(120,000)
Investment in Shaw	189,000	--
Investment in bonds	100,000	--
Discount on bonds	(9,000)	--
Bonds payable	--	(200,000)
Common stock	(100,000)	(10,000)
Additional paid-in capital	(250,000)	(40,000)
Retained earnings	(402,000)	(140,000)
Selected statement of retained earnings amounts		
Beginning balance, December 31, 1998	$272,000	$100,000
Net income	210,000	70,000
Dividends paid	80,000	30,000

Additional information

- On January 2, 1999, Poe, Inc. purchased 90% of Shaw Co.'s 100,000 outstanding common stock for cash of $155,000. On that date, Shaw's stockholders' equity equalled $150,000 and the fair values of Shaw's assets and liabilities equalled their carrying amounts. Poe has accounted for the acquisition as a purchase. Poe's policy is to amortize intangibles over 10 years.

- On September 4, 1999, Shaw paid cash dividends of $30,000.
- On December 31, 1999, Poe recorded its equity in Shaw's earnings.

Required:

a. Items 1 through 3. Items 1 through 3 below represent transactions between Poe and Shaw during 1999. Determine the dollar amount effect of the consolidating adjustment on 1999 consolidated income before considering minority interest. Ignore income tax considerations. To record your answer, write the number in the boxes on the Objective Answer Sheet and blacken the corresponding oval below each box. These items cannot be graded if you fail to blacken the ovals.

Items to be answered

1. On January 3, 1999, Shaw sold equipment with an original cost of $30,000 and a carrying value of $15,000 to Poe for $36,000. The equipment had a remaining life of 3 years and was depreciated using the straight-line method by both companies.

2. During 1999, Shaw sold merchandise to Poe for $60,000, which included a profit of $20,000. At December 31, 1999, half of this merchandise remained in Poe's inventory.

3. On December 31, 1999, Poe paid $91,000 to purchase 50% of the outstanding bonds issued by Shaw. The bonds mature on December 31, 2005, and were originally issued at par. The bonds pay interest annually on December 31 of each year, and the interest was paid to the prior investor immediately before Poe's purchase of the bonds.

b. Item 4. Determine the amount recorded by Poe as amortization of goodwill for 1999. To record your answer, write the number in the boxes on the Objective Answer Sheet and blacken the corresponding oval beneath each box. These items cannot be graded if you fail to blacken the ovals.

c. Items 5 through 16. Items 5 through 16 below refer to accounts that may or may not be included in Poe and Shaw's consolidated financial statements. The list on the right refers to the various possibilities of those amounts to be reported in Poe's consolidated financial statements for the year ended December 31, 1999. Consider all transactions stated in items 1 through 4 in determining your answer. Ignore income tax considerations. For each item, blacken the corresponding oval on the Objective Answer Sheet.

Items to be answered	*Responses to be selected*
5. Cash	A. Sum of amounts on Poe and Shaw's separate unconsolidated financial statements.
6. Equipment	B. Less than the sum of amounts on Poe and Shaw's separate unconsolidated financial statements but not the same as the amount on either.
7. Investment in subsidiary	
8. Bonds payable	
9. Minority interest	C. Same as amount for Poe only.
10. Common stock	D. Same as amount for Shaw only.
11. Beginning retained earnings	E. Eliminated entirely in consolidation.
12. Dividends paid	F. Shown in consolidated financial statements but not in separate unconsolidated financial statements.
13. Gain on retirement of bonds	
14. Cost of goods sold	G. Neither in consolidated nor in separate unconsolidated financial statements.
15. Interest expense	
16. Depreciation expense	

Problem 2   (15 to 25 minutes)

This question consists of 2 parts. Part **a** consists of 5 items and part **b** consists of 10 items. Select the **best** answer for each item. Use a No. 2 pencil to blacken the appropriate ovals on the Objective Answer Sheet to indicate your answers. **Answer all items.** Your grade will be based on the total number of correct answers.

Required:

a. Items 1 through 5, relate to accounting for business combinations. For each item, determine whether the statement is consistent with:

List
(A) Purchase accounting.
(B) Pooling of interests.
(C) Either.
(D) Neither.

Blacken the corresponding oval in the Objective Answer Sheet. An answer may be selected once, more than once, or not at all.

1. When the investment cost is lower than the carrying amounts of the target company's net assets, the target company's assets will be valued on the books of the combined firm at less than their carrying amounts.

2. A combination is finalized within 9 months after the combination plan was initiated.

3. Results of operations for the year of combination include the combined results of the separate companies for the entire year.

4. Costs of furnishing information to stockholders related to effecting the business combination are deducted directly from the combined corporation's retained earnings.

5. When the investment cost is higher than the fair value of the target company's net assets, goodwill may appear in the consolidated financial statements.

Required:

b. On January 2, 1999, Purl Co. purchased 90% of Strand Co.'s outstanding common stock at a purchase price that was in excess of Strand's stockholders' equity. On that date, the fair value of Strand's assets and liabilities equaled their carrying amounts. Purl has accounted for the acquisition as a purchase. Transactions during 1999 were as follows:

• On February 15, 1999, Strand sold equipment to Purl at a price higher than the equipment's carrying amount. The equipment has a remaining life of 3 years and was depreciated using the straight-line method by both companies.

- During 1999, Purl sold merchandise to Strand under the same terms it offered to third parties. At December 31, 1999, one third of this merchandise remained in Strand's inventory.
- On November 15, 1999, both Purl and Strand paid cash dividends to their respective stockholders.
- On December 31, 1999, Purl recorded its equity in Strand's earnings.

Required:

Items 6 through 15 relate to accounts that may or may not be included in Purl and Strand's consolidated financial statements. The list on the right refers to the possible ways those accounts may be reported in Purl's consolidated financial statements for the year ended December 31, 1999. For each item, blacken one corresponding oval on the Objective Answer Sheet. An answer may be selected once, more than once, or not at all.

6. Cash.

7. Equipment.

8. Investment in subsidiary.

9. Minority interest.

10. Common stock.

11. Beginning retained earnings.

12. Dividends paid.

13. Cost of goods sold.

14. Interest expense.

15. Depreciation expense.

	Responses to be selected
A	Sum of the amounts on Purl and Strand's separate unconsolidated financial statements.
B	Less than the sum of the amounts on Purl and Strand's separate unconsolidated financial statements, but not the same as the amount on either separate unconsolidated financial statement.
C	Same as the amount for Purl only.
D	Same as the amount for Strand only.
E	Eliminated entirely in consolidation.
F	Shown in the consolidated financial statements but not in the separate unconsolidated financial statements.

PROBLEMS

Problem 1   (15 to 25 minutes)

On September 1, 1999, Plains Corp. acquired all of Sox Corp.'s outstanding stock for cash. The fair value of Sox's net assets was less than the purchase price but greater than the net carrying amount. During November 1999, Plains sold goods to Sox at a price that included its normal markup. At December 31, 1999, 20% of these goods remained in Sox's inventory. The separate legal entities were maintained and Sox uses push-down accounting for its separate financial statements.

Required:

Ignore income tax considerations when answering all questions.

a. 1. Specify three reasons for preparing consolidated financial statements that present operating results, cash flows, and financial position as if a parent company and its subsidiaries were a single entity.

2. What changes in Plains' September 1, 1999 consolidated balance sheet will result from this acquisition?

3. In preparing Plains' December 31, 1999 consolidated financial statements, what adjustments or eliminations are required as a consequence of the intercompany sales?

b. In preparing separate financial statements immediately after acquisition (September 1, 1999), what is the effect of the purchase on the balance sheet of:

1. Plains?
2. Sox (which uses push-down accounting)?

Problem 2   (15 to 25 minutes)

Flaherty Company entered into a business combination with Steeley Company in the middle of the year. The combination was accounted for as a pooling of interests. Both companies use the same methods of accounting. Registration fees for the equity securities involved in the combination were incurred. There were no intercompany transactions before or after the combination.

Flaherty Company acquired all of the voting common stock of Rubin Company in the middle of the year. This combination was accounted for as a purchase and resulted in goodwill. Both companies use the same methods of accounting. Registration fees for the equity securities involved in the combination were incurred. There were no intercompany transactions before or after the combination.

Required:

a. 1. In the business combination accounted for as a pooling of interests, how should the recorded assets and liabilities of the separate companies be accounted for? What is the rationale for accounting for a business combination as a pooling of interests?

2. In the business combination accounted for as a pooling of interests, how should the registration fees and direct costs related to effecting the business combination be accounted for?

3. In the business combination accounted for as a pooling of interests, how should the results of operations for the year in which the business combination occurred be reported?

b. 1. In the business combination accounted for as a purchase, how should the assets acquired and liabilities assumed be recorded? What is the rationale for accounting for a business combination as a purchase?

2. In the business combination accounted for as a purchase, how should the registration fees and direct costs related to effecting the business combination be accounted for?

3. In the business combination accounted for as a purchase, how should the results of operations of the acquired company for the year in which the business combination occurred be reported?

Problem 3   (40 to 50 minutes)

Pine Corp. issued 200,000 shares of its $10 par common stock on March 31, 1999, to acquire all of the outstanding $25 par value common stock of Strand, Inc. The business combination meets all conditions for a pooling of interests. On March 31, 1999, the market price of Pine's common stock was $35 a share. Both corporations continued to operate as separate businesses, maintaining separate accounting records with years ending December 31.

On March 31, 1999, immediately before the combination, the stockholders' equities were

	Pine	Strand
Common stock	$ 5,500,000	$2,500,000
Additional paid-in capital	4,200,000	470,000
Retained earnings	7,360,000	2,430,000
	$17,060,000	$5,400,000

Additional information

• During March 1999, Pine paid $720,000 for expenditures relating to the business combination with Strand.

• Pine accounts for its investment in Strand using the equity method.

• On March 31, 1999, the fair values of Strand's assets and liabilities equaled their book values, except for its long-term investment in marketable equity securities, for which the aggregate market value exceeded aggregate cost by $600,000.

• On March 10, 1999, Strand paid a cash dividend totaling $250,000 on its common stock.

• On November 15, 1999, Pine paid a cash dividend totaling $1,500,000 on its common stock.

• During August 1999, Pine sold merchandise to Strand at a profit of $800,000. At December 31, 1999, one fourth of this merchandise remained in Strand's inventory.

• For the period April 1 through December 31, 1999, Strand paid Pine management fees totaling $150,000.

• Strand's 1999 net income was $1,450,000. Pine's 1999 income was $2,240,000, before considering equity in Strand's net income.

• The balances in retained earnings at December 31, 1998, were $6,820,000 and $2,290,000 for Pine and Strand, respectively.

Required:

a. Prepare Pine Corp.'s journal entries to record the business combination with Strand, Inc. and the expenditures relating to the business combination.

b. Prepare a schedule to compute the investment in Strand, Inc. at equity, at December 31, 1999.

c. Prepare a formal consolidated statement of changes in retained earnings of Pine Corp. and its subsidiary Strand, Inc. for the year ended December 31, 1999.

MULTIPLE-CHOICE ANSWERS

1. a __ __	18. a __ __	35. b __ __	52. b __ __	69. b __ __
2. c __ __	19. c __ __	36. b __ __	53. c __ __	70. a __ __
3. d __ __	20. c __ __	37. d __ __	54. c __ __	71. b __ __
4. a __ __	21. d __ __	38. a __ __	55. a __ __	72. d __ __
5. d __ __	22. c __ __	39. d __ __	56. d __ __	73. c __ __
6. c __ __	23. a __ __	40. b __ __	57. a __ __	74. b __ __
7. d __ __	24. b __ __	41. a __ __	58. a __ __	75. a __ __
8. c __ __	25. c __ __	42. a __ __	59. a __ __	76. b __ __
9. d __ __	26. c __ __	43. a __ __	60. a __ __	77. c __ __
10. d __ __	27. c __ __	44. d __ __	61. c __ __	78. d __ __
11. b __ __	28. d __ __	45. b __ __	62. b __ __	79. c __ __
12. b __ __	29. a __ __	46. c __ __	63. a __ __	80. c __ __
13. b __ __	30. d __ __	47. b __ __	64. a __ __	
14. a __ __	31. a __ __	48. d __ __	65. c __ __	
15. c __ __	32. d __ __	49. d __ __	66. b __ __	
16. b __ __	33. b __ __	50. b __ __	67. b __ __	1st: __/80 = __%
17. b __ __	34. c __ __	51. d __ __	68. b __ __	2nd: __/80 = __%

MULTIPLE-CHOICE ANSWER EXPLANATIONS

A. Accounting for the Combination, and Sections B. - E.

1. **(a)** In a purchase, the net assets of the acquired firm are recorded at their FMV. The excess of the cost of the investment over the FMV of the net assets acquired is allocated to goodwill. The cost of the investment is $620,000, and the FMV of the net assets acquired, **excluding goodwill**, is $470,000, as computed below.

	FMV
Cash	$ 60,000
Inventory (BV = $180,000)	150,000
Prop. and equip. (BV = $320,000)	380,000
Liabilities	(120,000)
Total FMV	$470,000

Therefore, the amount allocated to goodwill is $150,000 ($620,000 – $470,000).

2. **(c)** In a business combination accounted for as a purchase, the fair market value of the net assets is used as the valuation basis for the combination. In this case, the net assets of the subsidiary have an implied fair market value of $3,600,000 which is the value of the common stock issued to Pine's shareholders (100,000 shares x $36). Also, per APB 16, para 76, the direct cost of acquisition should be included as part of the cost of a company acquired, and the cost of registering equity securities should be a reduction of the issue price of the securities (i.e., additional paid-in capital) in a business combination accounted for by the purchase method. Thus, the $160,000 paid for a consultant who arranged the acquisition should also be capitalized, and the $80,000 cost for registering and issuing the equity securities should be treated as a reduction of additional paid-in capital. The total amount to be capitalized is $3,760,000 ($3,600,000 + $160,000).

3. **(d)** In a business combination accounted for as a purchase, the fair market value of the net assets is used as the valuation basis for the combination. In this case, the net assets of the subsidiary have an implied fair market value of $3,600,000 which is the value of the common stock issued

to Saxe's shareholders (200,000 x $18). Since $3,600,000 is the basis for recording this purchase, the common stock issued is recorded at $2,000,000 (200,000 shares x $10 par value per share) and additional paid-in capital is recorded at $1,600,000 ($3,600,000 – $2,000,000). Therefore, in the 12/31/99 consolidated balance sheet, additional paid-in capital should be reported at $2,900,000 ($1,300,000 + $1,600,000).

4. **(a)** In a pooling of interests, the book values of the previous companies' assets and liabilities are carried forward, so the new company's stockholders' equity must equal the combined stockholders' equity of the preceding companies ($6,800,000 + $2,500,000 = $9,300,000). Common stock must be reported at its par value [$3,000,000 + (200,000 x $10) = $5,000,000]. The retained earnings of the preceding companies are carried forward to the extent possible ($2,500,000 + $850,000 = $3,350,000). Therefore, additional paid-in capital must be recorded at $950,000 [$9,300,000 – ($5,000,000 + $3,350,000)].

5. **(d)** In a pooling of interests, the book values of the previous companies' assets and liabilities are carried forward, and the new company's stockholders' equity equals the combined stockholders' equity of the preceding companies. Therefore, no goodwill is recorded due to a business combination accounted for as a **pooling of interests**. Goodwill can only be recorded in a business combination accounted for as a **purchase**.

6. **(c)** Per ARB 51, para 2, a subsidiary should not be consolidated when control is likely to be temporary. Answers (a) and (d) are incorrect because FASB No. 94, para 13, requires consolidation of all majority-owned subsidiaries regardless of the industry or business of the subsidiary. Answer (b) is incorrect because ARB 51, para 4, states that a difference in fiscal periods of a parent and a subsidiary does not of itself justify the exclusion of the subsidiary from consolidation.

7. **(d)** A business combination which meets **all** of the twelve conditions specified and explained in APB 16, paras 46 - 48, should be accounted for by the pooling of interests method. If any one of these conditions is not met, the combination must be accounted for by the purchase method. Answer (d) is correct because the condition that no more than 10% of any combining company is held by any other combining company is not met. Therefore, the purchase method must be used. Answer (a) is incorrect because the corporation intends to dispose of **duplicate** facilities. Therefore, the condition that the combined corporation does not intend or plan to dispose of a significant part of the assets of the combining companies within 2 years after the combination is still met, and if all other conditions are met, pooling is allowable. Answer (b) is incorrect because all holders of all outstanding shares may be offered cash, and if 10% or less accept the cash payment, then pooling treatment is still allowable if all other conditions are met. Answer (c) is incorrect because the condition that each of the combining companies is autonomous and has not been a subsidiary or division of another corporation within 2 years **before** the plan of combination is initiated is still met. In this case one of the companies is becoming a subsidiary of another company **after** the combination is consummated. Therefore, pooling would still be permitted if all other conditions are met.

8. **(c)** Per APB 16, para 76, the direct costs of acquisition should be included as part of the cost of a company acquired in a business combination accounted for by the purchase method. General expenses related to the acquisition, however, are deducted as incurred in determining the combined corporation's net income for the current period. Therefore, answer (c) is correct.

9. **(d)** The requirement is to select the correct general guideline for assigning amounts to inventories under the purchase method. Answer (d) is correct because per APB 16, para 88, finished goods inventories should be valued at estimated selling prices less the costs of disposal and a reasonable profit allowance for the selling effort of the acquiring corporation. Answer (a) is incorrect because raw materials should be valued at current replacement costs, not original cost. Answer (b) is incorrect because work in process should be valued at the estimated selling prices of finished goods less the costs to complete, the costs of disposal, **and** a reasonable profit allowance. Answer (c) is incorrect because finished goods are valued at estimated selling prices less the costs of disposal and a reasonable profit allowance, not replacement cost.

10. **(d)** Per APB 16, paras 31 and 45, the objective of the pooling of interests method of accounting for business combinations is to present as a single interest two or more common stockholder interests which were previously independent and the combined rights and risks represented by those interests. Pooling demonstrates that stockholder groups neither withdraw nor invest assets, but rather exchange voting common stock in a ratio which reflects their proportionate ownership in the combined entity. No single entity in a pooling of interests is considered to be the "acquirer." The individual assets, liabilities, equity, and income of the individual entities are merely combined. Since a pooling of interests does not involve a "purchase," there is no need to revalue the assets of any of the individual entities to their market value (as would normally take place in a purchase transaction). Proponents of pooling of interests accounting point out that, since no asset revaluation is performed, the pooling concept was developed within the boundaries of the historical cost system and is compatible with it. Therefore, answer (d) is correct. Answer (a) is incorrect because no single entity is considered dominant in a pooling of interests. Answer (b) is incorrect because goodwill cannot result from a combination under pooling of interests accounting. Goodwill cannot be recorded since there is no purchase or asset revaluation and, therefore, there can be no excess of cost over fair market value (which is the "goodwill" portion of the purchase price). Answer (c) is incorrect because no assets are recorded at their fair value in a pooling of interests.

11. **(b)** Per APB 16, paras 31 and 45, the objective of the pooling of interests method of accounting for business combinations is to present as a single interest two or more common stockholder interests which were previously independent and the combined rights and risks represented by those interests. Pooling demonstrates that stockholder groups neither withdraw nor invest assets, but rather exchange voting common stock in a ratio which reflects their proportionate ownership in the combined entity. No single entity in a pooling of interests is considered to be the "acquirer." The individual assets, liabilities, equity, and income of the individual entities are merely combined. Since a pooling of interests does not involve a "purchase," there is no need to revalue the assets of any of the individual entities to their market value (as would normally take place in a purchase transaction). Proponents of pooling of interests accounting point out that, since no asset revaluation is performed, the pooling concept was developed within the boundaries of the historical cost system and is compatible with it. Therefore, answer (b) is correct. Answer (a) is incorrect because, since a pooling of interests does not involve a "purchase," there is no need to revalue the assets of any of the individual entities to their market value. Answer (c) is incorrect because goodwill cannot result from a combination under pooling of interests accounting. Goodwill cannot be recorded since there is no purchase or asset revaluation and, therefore, there can be no excess of cost over fair market value (which is the "goodwill" portion of the purchase price). Answer (d) is incorrect because no assets are recorded at their fair value, and none of the cost is allocated to the assets based on their fair value in a pooling of interests.

12. **(b)** In a business combination accounted for as a pooling of interests, all costs associated with the combination are expensed in the period incurred. Therefore, the costs of furnishing information to stockholders related to effecting the business combination should be deducted in determining net income of the combined corporation in the period in which the costs were incurred. Answers (a), (c), and (d) are therefore incorrect.

13. **(b)** In a pooling of interests, the parent's common stock issued for the acquisition is essentially "swapped" with the subsidiary's common stock. A typical acquisition entry on the parent's books would be as follows:

Investment in sub	xx
Common stock (par value issued)	xx
APIC	xx
Retained earnings	xx

Essentially, the amounts in all of the subsidiary's accounts are brought over to the parent's books, except that if the common stock par values are not equal, then the other equity accounts brought over must be adjusted for the difference. When the par value of the parent's common stock is less than the par value of the subsidiary's common stock, the difference is added to "APIC." When the par value of the parent's common stock is greater than the par value of the subsidiary's common stock, then equity balances are reduced in the following order: APIC – subsidiary, APIC – parent, RE – subsidiary, RE – parent. Contributed capital includes **both** common stock and APIC. It is impossible for contributed capital to decrease after a pooling since any APIC reduction would be negated by the increase to the "common stock" account. It is possible for RE to be reduced, however, as noted above (if all APIC is gone). Therefore, answer (b) is correct.

G. Date of Combination Consolidated Balance Sheet--Purchase Accounting

14.   (a)   In the consolidated balance sheet, the parent company's "investment in subsidiary" account should be eliminated and replaced by the net assets of the subsidiary. Under the purchase method, the assets of the acquired firm are recorded at their FMV. The cost of the investment is $60,000 and the book value of the acquired net assets is $45,000 (90% x $50,000), so the excess of cost over book value is $15,000 ($60,000 – $45,000). 60% of this excess is allocated to inventory because its FMV exceeds its cost (60% x $15,000 = $9,000). Therefore, current assets should be reported at $99,000.

Current assets--Polk	$70,000
Current assets--Strass	20,000
Excess allocated to inventory	9,000
Total	$99,000

15.   (c)   In the consolidated balance sheet, the parent company's "investment in subsidiary" account should be eliminated and replaced by the net assets of the subsidiary. Under the purchase method, the assets of the acquired firm are recorded at their FMV. The cost of the investment is $60,000 and the book value of the acquired net assets is $45,000 (90% x $50,000) the excess of cost over book value is $15,000 ($60,000 – $45,000). 40% of this excess is allocated to goodwill (40% x $15,000 = $6,000). Therefore, noncurrent assets should be reported at $136,000.

Noncurrent assets--Polk	$90,000
Noncurrent assets--Strass	40,000
Excess allocated to goodwill	6,000
Total	$136,000

16.   (b)   In the consolidated balance sheet, the parent company's "investment in subsidiary" account should be eliminated and replaced by the assets and liabilities of the

subsidiary. Therefore, the consolidated balance sheet should include the current liabilities of both companies, plus the current portion of the debt incurred on 1/2/99 ($60,000 ÷ 10 = $6,000). Thus, current liabilities should be reported at $46,000 as computed below.

Current liabs.--Polk	$30,000
Current liabs.--Strass	10,000
Current portion of new debt	6,000
Total	$46,000

17.   (b)   In the consolidated balance sheet, the parent company's "investment in subsidiary" account should be eliminated and replaced by the assets and liabilities of the subsidiary. Therefore, the consolidated balance sheet should include the noncurrent liabilities of both companies, plus the noncurrent portion of the debt incurred on 1/2/99 ($60,000 – $6,000 = $54,000), plus the minority interest in the subsidiary ($50,000 x 10% = $5,000).

Noncurrent liabs.--Polk	$50,000
Noncurrent liabs.--Strass	0
Noncurrent portion of new debt	54,000
Minority interest	5,000
Total	$109,000

18.   (a)   In the consolidated balance sheet, neither the parent company's investment account nor the subsidiary's stockholders' equity is reported. These amounts are eliminated in the same journal entry that records the excess of cost over book value. The portion of the subsidiary's stockholders' equity which is **not** eliminated is reported as minority interest in the noncurrent liabilities section of the consolidated balance sheet. Therefore, the parent's stockholders' equity ($80,000) equals the consolidated stockholders' equity. Note that once the candidate has completed items 1 through 5, the answers can be checked using the balance sheet equation.

$$\left[\begin{array}{c}\text{Current}\\\text{assets}\end{array}\right] + \left[\begin{array}{c}\text{Non-}\\\text{current}\\\text{assets}\end{array}\right] = \left[\begin{array}{c}\text{Current}\\\text{liabilities}\end{array}\right] + \left[\begin{array}{c}\text{Non-}\\\text{current}\\\text{liabilities}\end{array}\right] + \left[\begin{array}{c}\text{Stock-}\\\text{holders'}\\\text{equity}\end{array}\right]$$

$$\$99,000 \quad + \quad \$136,000 \quad = \quad \$46,000 \quad + \quad \$109,000 \quad + \quad \$80,000$$

19.   (c)   In a purchase, the net assets of the acquired firm are recorded at their FMV. The excess of the cost of the investment over the FMV of the net assets acquired is allocated to goodwill. The cost of this investment is $3,750,000 (250,000 shares x $15), and the FMV of the net assets acquired, **excluding goodwill** is $3,400,000 ($3,000,000 + $400,000). Therefore, the amount allocated to goodwill is $350,000 ($3,750,000 – $3,400,000).

20.   (c)   Since the subsidiary was acquired for cash, purchase accounting must be used in preparing the consolidated balance sheet. Therefore, the assets acquired would be revalued to their fair market value. The inventory account would then include the difference between the market value and book value. Answer (a) is incorrect because a deferred credit represents the excess of fair market value over acquisition cost. Answer (b) is incorrect because goodwill represents the excess of cost over fair market value. Answer (d) is incorrect because the retained earnings account is not affected by this transaction when purchase accounting is used.

21. (d) Since Company K was acquired for cash, purchase accounting must be used to account for the acquisition. APB 16, paras 72 and 88, states that, in general, all assets and liabilities (including plant and equipment and long-term debt) should be reported at fair value when the purchase method is used. Answer (a) is incorrect because it describes the treatment accorded to plant and equipment when a combination is accounted for as a pooling of interests. However, since cash is used exclusively in the transaction, a pooling of interests is precluded (APB 16, 47b).

22. (c) When the appraised values of the identifiable assets acquired in a **purchase** combination exceed the acquisition price, the difference is referred to as negative goodwill. APB 16 requires negative goodwill to be allocated against noncurrent assets acquired, excluding marketable securities, in proportion to their fair values. If the noncurrent assets are reduced to zero and some negative goodwill remains unallocated, the excess should be reported on the balance sheet as a deferred credit. Subsequently, this amount is amortized over a period not exceeding 40 years. Answer (a) is incorrect because the excess is not **reported** as negative goodwill. Answer (b) is incorrect because APIC is not affected by this excess. Answer (d) is incorrect because **positive** goodwill results from an excess of acquisition price over appraised value of identifiable assets, not vice versa.

H. Date of Combination Consolidated Balance Sheet -- Pooling

23. (a) In a pooling of interests, the book values of the previous companies' assets and liabilities are carried forward. Therefore, Post will record its investment at $8,100,000 (90% x $9,000,000) and stockholders' equity accounts must be credited at the same amount. The new common stock issued must be recorded at its par value (630,000 x $5 = $3,150,000). Post's share of the subsidiary's retained earnings (90% x $5,400,000 = $4,860,000) is carried forward to the extent possible. Therefore, APIC must be recorded at $90,000 [$8,100,000 – ($3,150,000 + $4,860,000)]. The journal entry is

Investment in stock of Shaw	8,100,000	
Common stock		3,150,000
APIC		90,000
Retained earnings		4,860,000

Thus, common stock should be reported at $9,650,000 ($6,500,000 + $3,150,000). The $900,000 of the subsidiary's equity that is not carried over ($9,000,000 – $8,100,000) will be reported as minority interest.

24. (b) The journal entry to record Post's investment is

Investment in stock of Shaw	8,100,000	
Common stock		3,150,000
APIC		90,000
Retained earnings		4,860,000

For a discussion of this entry, see the explanation for number 23. Therefore, additional paid-in capital will be reported at $4,490,000 ($4,400,000 + $90,000).

25. (c) The journal entry to record Post's investment is

Investment in stock of Shaw	8,100,000	
Common stock		3,150,000
APIC		90,000
Retained earnings		4,860,000

For a discussion of this entry, see the explanation for number 23. Therefore, retained earnings should be reported at $10,960,000 ($6,100,000 + $4,860,000).

26. (c) Per APB 16, para 56, business combinations accounted for by the pooling of interests method should report net income as if the combination took place at the **beginning** of the year. Therefore, the consolidated income would be $2,820,000.

Separate income of Post		
($1,000,000 + 1,100,000)		$2,100,000
Separate income of Shaw		
($300,000 + $500,000)	$800,000	
x Post's % of ownership	x .90	720,000
Consolidated income		$2,820,000

Note that the earnings figures given are for **separate company operations**, so Post's earnings include no income from its investment in Shaw. If Post's earnings had included such income, the amount would have to be calculated and eliminated from Post's earnings before the earnings of the two companies were pooled.

27. (c) The percentage of the subsidiary's stockholders' equity not owned by the parent company represents the minority interest's share of the net assets of the subsidiary. At 12/31/99, the subsidiary's stockholders' equity is $9,150,000.

6/30/99 stockholders' equity	$9,000,000
Income for 6 months	
ended 12/31/99	500,000
Dividends paid on 10/1/99	(350,000)
12/31/99 stockholders' equity	$9,150,000

Since the parent's share is 90%, the minority interest is 10% of $9,150,000 or $915,000.

28. (d) In a consolidated balance sheet prepared immediately after the acquisition, the retained earnings of a subsidiary are included for a pooling of interests (APB 16, para 53) but excluded for a purchase (ARB 51, para 9).

29. (a) The percentage of stock not owned by the parent company represents the minority interest's share of the net assets of the subsidiary. Under both purchase and pooling accounting, minority interest income will be a deduction on the consolidated income statement for its portion of the subsidiary's income. Minority interest will be shown on the consolidated balance sheet in an amount determined by multiplying the owners' equity of the subsidiary by the minority's respective ownership percentage. Answer (b) is incorrect because goodwill is only recorded under the purchase method. Answer (c) is incorrect because under purchase accounting none of the subsidiary's retained earnings is carried over in the consolidated balance sheet whereas under pooling of interest accounting all or some of the subsidiary's retained earnings will be carried over. Answer (d) is incorrect because the additional stock issued by the parent in the pooling transaction will appear in the consolidated balance sheet.

I. Consolidated Financial Statements Subsequent to Acquisition

30. (d)   Consolidated statements are prepared as if the parent and subsidiaries were one economic entity. From the point of view of the consolidated entity, any intercompany receivables or payables from parent to subsidiary or vice versa are **not** payable to or receivable from any **outside** company. In other words, the consolidated entity does not have a receivable or payable. Therefore, all of Wright's intercompany receivables, payables and advances are eliminated. None are reported as intercompany receivables.

31. (a)   When a subsidiary prepares separate financial statements, intercompany receivables (and payables) should be reported in the balance sheet as a separate line item. When consolidated financial statements are prepared by the parent company, all intercompany receivables (and payables) should be eliminated to avoid overstating assets and liabilities. Thus, answer (a) is correct.

32. (d)   Pard's separate revenues are $200,000, and Spin's separate revenues are $140,000, resulting in a total of $340,000 ($200,000 + $140,000). Since the consolidated income statement shows sales of only $308,000, intercompany sales of $32,000 ($340,000 – $308,000) from Pard to Spin must have been eliminated during consolidation.

33. (b)   Pard's separate accounts receivable is $26,000, and Spin's separate accounts receivable is $19,000, resulting in a total of $45,000 ($26,000 + $19,000). Since the consolidated balance sheet shows accounts receivable of only $39,000, intercompany receivables of $6,000 ($45,000 – $39,000) must have been eliminated during consolidation. Since Pard sold goods to Spin which Spin had not fully paid for by 12/31/99, the eliminated receivable must be Pard's receivable from Spin. Therefore, Spin's 12/31/99 payable to Pard is also $6,000.

34. (c)   Pard's intercompany sales to Spin totalled $32,000 during 1999. Therefore, Spin recorded a purchase of inventory of $32,000. At 12/31/99, Spin still held 37.5% of these goods in inventory; in Spin's books, this inventory was carried at $12,000 (37.5% x $32,000). In the consolidated balance sheet, the intercompany profit would be eliminated, and this inventory would be carried at Pard's original cost. Pard's sales to Spin were at the same markup on cost that Pard uses for all sales. In Pard's income statement, cost of sales is 75% of sales ($150,000 ÷ $200,000). Therefore, Pard's original cost for the $12,000 of goods in Spin's inventory is $9,000 (75% x $12,000).

35. (b)   The percentage of the subsidiary's stockholders' equity not owned by the parent company represents the minority interest's share of the net assets of the subsidiary. In the 12/31/99 consolidated balance sheet, minority interest is $10,000. At the same date, Spin's stockholders' equity is $50,000. Therefore, the percent of minority interest ownership is 20% ($10,000 ÷ $50,000).

36. (b)   In the 12/31/99 consolidated financial statements, goodwill is $30,000 and goodwill amortization is $2,000. Since Pard uses straight-line amortization, the goodwill has a remaining useful life of 15 years at 12/31/99 ($30,000 ÷ $2,000). Pard's interest in Spin was acquired on 1/2/96, 4 years prior to 12/31/99. Therefore, Pard must be amortizing the goodwill over 19 years (4 + 15).

37. (d)   The amount of goodwill to be recorded will equal the acquisition cost less the fair value of the identifiable net assets. The problem states that the fair value of net assets equals $1,000,000 ($1,320,000 – $320,000) and that the acquisition cost equals $1,200,000. Thus, the total goodwill will equal $200,000 ($1,200,000 acquisition cost less $1,000,000 fair value of assets). As Owen's amortization policy is 10 years, the annual goodwill amortization will be $20,000 ($200,000/10).

38. (a)   When the equity method of accounting is used the parent company's retained earnings will be equal to the consolidated retained earnings balance. It can be determined that the equity method is being followed because the account "Equity in earnings of Sharp" appears in the parent's income statement. In addition it is important to note that the balance sheet accounts presented are dated as of the end of the year; therefore, the parent company's retained earnings of $1,240,000, should already include **all** income statement balance account adjustments. Thus, no additional income amounts will need to be added to the $1,240,000 retained earnings balance, in order to determine the total retained earnings balance.

39. (d)   The requirement is to determine which accounting concept relates to the preparation of consolidated financial statements. Answer (d) is correct because when a parent-subsidiary relationship exists, the financial statements of each separate entity are brought together, or consolidated. When financial statements represent a consolidated entity, the concept of economic entity applies. Answer (a) is incorrect because reliability is a concept that applies to all financial statements, not just consolidated financial statements. Reliability, as identified in the SFAC 2, is a primary quality that makes accounting information useful for decision making. This quality should be found in all statements. Answer (b) is incorrect because the concept of materiality applies to all financial statements, not just consolidated financial statements. The concept of materiality, as applied to financial statements, deals with the impact an item in the financial statements will have on a users' decision making process, when studying the financial statements. Answer (c) is incorrect because the concept of legal entity refers to the form or type of combination which takes place between entities (i.e., mergers, consolidations or acquisitions), not the basis on which financial statements are prepared.

40. (b)   The purchase method is used to account for this situation because the subsidiary was acquired for cash. APB 16, paras 72 and 88, states that, in general, all assets and liabilities (including equipment) should be reported at market value. The excess of the equipment's market value over its carrying amount is allocated to the equipment and amortized over the equipment's useful life. The unamortized portion of the excess of the market value over the carrying amount of the equipment is then reported as part of plant and equipment. Consequently, answer (b) is correct and answer (c) is incorrect. Answer (a) is incorrect because the unamortized portion of the excess of the market value over the carrying amount of the equipment is reported in plant and equipment, **not** goodwill. Only the unamortized portion of the excess of the acquisition cost over the market value of the net identifiable assets acquired is reported as goodwill. Answer (d) is incorrect because the excess of the market value over the carrying amount of the equipment is capitalized and subsequently amortized over the equipment's useful life, **not** expensed as incurred.

41. **(a)** When two companies own stock in each other, a reciprocal ownership relationship exists. In this case, Pride (the parent) owns 80% of Simba (the sub), and Simba owns 10% of Pride. When Pride declares a cash dividend, 90% of it is distributed to outside parties and 10% goes to Simba. Because Simba is part of the consolidated entity, its 10% share of Pride's dividend is eliminated when determining consolidated dividends declared. Thus, only 90% of dividends declared by Pride will be reported in the consolidated financial statements. When Simba declares a dividend, 80% of the dividend is distributed to Pride (the parent), and 20% is distributed to outside parties (the noncontrolling interest of Simba stock). The 80% share to Pride is eliminated when determining consolidated dividends declared because it represents an intercompany transaction. The remaining 20% to the noncontrolling interest is likewise not included in consolidated dividends declared because, from the parent company's point of view, subsidiary dividends do not represent dividends of the consolidated entity and must be eliminated.

42. **(a)** If purchase accounting is used, the excess of the acquisition cost over the sum of the amounts assigned to identifiable assets acquired less liabilities assumed would be recorded as goodwill [Acquisition cost – (Assets value – Liabilities assumed) = Goodwill]. Conversely, if the pooling of interests method is used, the basis of valuation will be the book value of the net assets on the books of the acquired company. Therefore, no goodwill will be created in a pooling combination. Since goodwill must be amortized, amortization expense will exist under purchase accounting, but no such expense will exist under the pooling method. As all of the other expenses and incomes will be the same, the only difference between purchase and pooling will be due to the additional goodwill amortization expense. This difference will cause the purchase net income to be less than pooling net income. Therefore, answers (b), (c), and (d) are incorrect.

43. **(a)** Since Prim acquired Scarp with cash, the combination of the entities should be accounted for under the purchase method in accordance with APB 16. Under the purchase method, Prim must record all of Scarp's assets and liabilities at their fair market value (FMV) on the date of purchase. Any excess of the purchase price over the net identifiable assets and liabilities will be recorded as goodwill. Since the carrying value (and purchase price) of all assets and liabilities **except the building** approximated their fair values, on the date of purchase Prim will record those assets at Scarp's carrying value. For the building, however,

Prim will not use Scarp's carrying value, but, rather will record the building at its fair value and the excess of the purchase price of the building over its fair value as goodwill. The difference in Prim's and Scarp's carrying values for the building will require Prim to decrease depreciation expense (because the building has a lower depreciable cost on Prim's books) and recognize amortization of goodwill (which only appears on Prim's books).

44. **(d)** APB 20 states that accounting changes that result in financial statements that are, in effect, financial statements of a different reporting entity (such as presenting consolidated statements in place of statements of individual companies) should be reported by restating the financial statements of all prior periods presented so that the resulting restated prior periods' statements on a consolidated basis are the same as if the subsidiary had been consolidated since it was acquired. Therefore, answer (d) is correct.

45. **(b)** In a purchase, the consolidated financial statements reflect the combined operations of the parent and subsidiary **from the date of combination**. Earnings of the subsidiary prior to the combination are **not** included with the parent's income. The parent's 1999 income is $1,575,000 ($750,000 + $825,000), while the subsidiary's income after the combination is $375,000 for a total of $1,950,000 ($1,575,000 + $375,000). The unrealized inventory profit of $45,000 must be eliminated, because from a consolidated viewpoint, revenue cannot be recognized until these goods are sold to a third party (i.e., a sale has not yet occurred). Therefore, 1999 consolidated net income is $1,905,000 ($1,950,000 – $45,000). Note that the net income amounts given are from **separate company operations**, so no elimination of equity earnings or dividend income is necessary.

46. **(c)** Per para 56 of APB 16, business combinations accounted for by the pooling of interests method should report net income **as if the combination took place at the beginning of the year**. The parent's 1999 income is $1,575,000 ($750,000 + $825,000), while the subsidiary's 1999 income (including precombination income) is $600,000 ($225,000 + $375,000), for a total of $2,175,000 ($1,575,000 + $600,000). The unrealized inventory profit of $45,000 must be eliminated, because from a consolidated viewpoint, revenue cannot be recognized until these goods are sold to a third party (i.e., a sale has not yet occurred). Therefore, 1999 consolidated net income is $2,130,000 ($2,175,000 – $45,000). Note that the net income amounts given are from **separate company operations**, so no elimination of equity earnings or dividend income is necessary.

47. **(b)** In a pooling of interests, the new common stock issued must be recorded at its par value (150,000 x $20 = $3,000,000). The subsidiary's retained earnings ($925,000 + $275,000 = $1,200,000) is carried forward to the extent possible. Any credit difference is recorded as APIC. At 6/30, Pane's retained earnings is $3,250,000 ($3,200,000 + $800,000 – $750,000), so consolidated retained earnings is $4,450,000 ($3,250,000 + $1,200,000).

48. **(d)** In a business combination accounted for as a purchase, the FMV of net assets is used as the valuation basis for the combination. The investment is recorded at the fair value of the net assets, common stock is recorded at par value (150,000 x $20 = $3,000,000), and any difference is recorded as APIC. The subsidiary's retained earnings are **not** recorded in a purchase. Therefore, 6/30/99 consolidated retained earnings is equal to Pane's separate 6/30/99 retained earnings $3,250,000 ($3,200,000 + $800,000 – $750,000).

49. (d) Per APB 16, the purchase method treats a business combination as the acquisition of one company by another, and accordingly, only the results of operations of the acquired company subsequent to the combination are included in the reported income of the acquiring corporation. Conversely, the pooling of interests method treats a business combination as the uniting of the ownership interests of the combining companies by an exchange of equity securities. In essence, the companies are treated as if they had always been combined, so results of operations are combined for the entire fiscal period in which the combination occurred (in addition, the reported income of the combined companies for any prior periods presented is combined and restated as income of the combined entity).

50. (b) Per APB 16, para 56, business combinations accounted for by the pooling of interests method should report net income as if the combination took place at the beginning of the year. Financial statements and financial information of the separate companies presented for prior years should be restated on a combined basis to furnish comparative information. Therefore, answer (b) is correct. Answer (a) is incorrect because income should be reported as if the combination took place at the beginning of the year, and the income should also be combined for all prior years presented. Answer (c) is incorrect because, in a pooling of interests, the book values of the previous companies' assets and liabilities are carried forward. Answer (d) is incorrect because APB 16, para 58, states that all expenses relating to effecting a business combination accounted for by the pooling of interests method should be deducted in determining the net income of the resulting combined corporation for the period in which the expenses were incurred.

J. Intercompany Transactions and Profit Confirmation

51. (d) Unrealized profit in ending inventory arises when intercompany sales are made at prices above cost and the merchandise is not resold to third parties prior to year end. The profit is unrealized because the inventory has not yet been sold outside of the consolidated entity. In this case, Pirn sold goods to Scroll for $100,000, which would become Scroll's cost. However, Scroll's cost of goods sold includes only $80,000 of goods acquired from Pirn. Therefore, $20,000 of original $100,000 remains in Scroll's ending inventory. Since Pirn's gross profit rate is 30% ($150,000 ÷ $500,000), the gross profit Pirn recognized on the original $20,000 sale was $6,000 (30% x $20,000). This intercompany profit must be eliminated on the consolidating worksheet.

52. (b) When computing consolidated income, the objective is to restate the accounts as if the intercompany transactions had not occurred. When Scroll recorded depre-

ciation, it included depreciation on the asset purchased from Pirn for $36,000. Since Pirn recorded a $12,000 gain when it sold the asset to Scroll, Pirn's book value at the time of sale must have been $24,000. Therefore, consolidated depreciation expense should be based on $24,000 rather than on $36,000. 1999 depreciation expense must be decreased by $3,000 ($12,000 excess ÷ 4 years). Depreciation expense in Pirn's 1999 consolidated income statement should therefore be $47,000, as computed below.

Pirn's recorded depr.	$40,000
Scroll's recorded depr.	10,000
Less adjustment ($12,000 ÷ 4)	(3,000)
	$47,000

53. (c) Unrealized profit in ending inventory arises when intercompany sales are made at prices above cost and the merchandise is not resold to third parties prior to year end. The profit is unrealized because the inventory has not yet been sold outside of the consolidated entity. In this case, there is no unrealized profit on the sales to Dean because the consolidated statements would not include Dean, and the equity method is not applicable. (Clark owns only 15% of Dean). However, there is unrealized profit on the materials sold by Kent, a wholly owned subsidiary, to Clark. $60,000 of the $240,000 of materials sold by Kent to Clark remains in ending inventory. The gross profit Kent recognized on this $60,000 of materials at the time of sale was $12,000 ($48,000 ÷ $240,000 = 20% gross profit rate; 20% x $60,000 = $12,000). For the consolidated entity, this $12,000 gross profit has not been earned and must be eliminated. Therefore, consolidated current assets should be $308,000 ($320,000 – $12,000).

54. (c) When preparing the consolidated income statement, the objective is to restate the accounts as if the intercompany transactions had not occurred. As a result of the intercompany sale, Parker has recorded $250,000 of sales and Smith has recorded $250,000 cost of sales which should be eliminated (note that Parker's **cost of sales** on the original sale is the amount left in consolidated cost of sales, and Smith's **sales** when the goods were sold to outside parties is the amount left in consolidated sales). Therefore, Parker should report $500,000 as cost of sales in the 1999 consolidated income statement ($400,000 + $350,000 – $250,000).

55. (a) Pare's separate gross profit is $100,000, and Shel's separate gross profit is $60,000, resulting in a total of $160,000. Since the consolidated income statement shows gross profit of only $154,000, unrealized intercompany profit of $6,000 ($160,000 – $154,000) must have been eliminated.

56. (d) The requirement is to determine the amount of **selling** expenses to be reported in Pard's 1999 consolidated income statement. Pard's selling expenses for 1999 include $50,000 in freight-out costs for goods sold to Seed, its subsidiary. This $50,000 becomes part of Seed's inventory because it is a cost directly associated with bringing the goods to a salable condition. One half of the goods sold to Seed by Pard remained in Seed's inventory at the end of 1999. Therefore, one half of the $50,000 ($25,000) flowed out as part of cost of goods sold, and one half remains in ending inventory. Thus, none of the $50,000 represents a selling expense for the consolidated entity, and $1,450,000 ($1,100,000 + $400,000 – $50,000) should be reported as selling expenses in the consolidated income statement.

57. (a) When preparing consolidated financial statements, the objective is to restate the accounts as if the intercompany transactions had not occurred. Therefore, the 1999 gain on sale of machine of $50,000 [$900,000 – ($1,100,000 – $250,000)] must be eliminated, since the consolidated entity has not realized any gain. In effect, the machine must be reflected on the consolidated balance sheet at 1/1/99 at Poe's cost of $1,100,000, and accumulated depreciation of $250,000, instead of at a new "cost" of $900,000. For consolidated statement purposes, 1999 depreciation is based on the original amounts [($1,100,000 – $100,000) x 1/20 = $50,000]. Therefore, in the 12/31/99 **consolidated** balance sheet, the machine is shown at a cost of $1,100,000 less accumulated depreciation of $300,000 ($250,000 + $50,000).

58. (a) When Seal purchased the bonds from Wagner, the bonds were viewed as retired from a consolidated viewpoint since there is no longer any obligation to an outside party. Therefore, the consolidated entity would recognize a $100,000 gain ($1,075,000 carrying amount – $975,000 cash paid), which would increase consolidated retained earnings. This transaction has no effect on minority interest, since the subsidiary (Seal) has merely exchanged one asset for another (cash for investment in bonds).

59. (a) The requirement is to determine the amount of gain to be reported on the consolidated income statement when a wholly owned subsidiary purchases parent company stock. A parent company reports no gain or loss when a wholly owned subsidiary purchases its common stock. In effect, the consolidated entity is purchasing treasury stock when the purchase is made, and gains are not recognized on treasury stock transactions. The dividends paid by the parent to the subsidiary also do not affect income because such intercompany transactions are eliminated when consolidated financial statements are prepared. Therefore, $0 gain should be reported by the consolidated entity and answer (a) is correct.

60. (a) When computing consolidated income, the objective is to restate the accounts as if the intercompany transaction had not occurred. As a result of the intercompany sale, sales and cost of goods sold are overstated and an eliminating entry is needed to reduce these accounts by the intercompany sale. Therefore, answer (a) is correct. Answer (b) is incorrect because sales and cost of goods sold need to be reduced by the entire amount of the intercompany sale in order to arrive at their proper consolidated amounts. Answer (c) is incorrect because net income is not effected by the intercompany sale. Sales and cost of goods sold are overstated by the same amount; thus, net income is correct for consolidated purposes. Answer (d) is incorrect because an adjustment is necessary.

61. (c) The key to this problem is that the equipment must be revalued at Fire's carrying amount (Fire's original

cost less accumulated depreciation) in the consolidation process. Assume the following potential scenario:

Fire buys a piece of equipment on 12/31/98 for $1,000. At 12/31/99, the equipment was depreciated $200, and Fire's carrying value is $800 ($1,000 – $200). On 12/31/99, Fire sells the equipment to Water for $900. Water's original cost is therefore $900, and Fire will record a $100 gain that must be eliminated. After consolidation, the equipment is reported at $800, Fire's carrying value. Fire's carrying value is also equal to Water's original cost ($900) less Fire's recorded gain ($100) and answer (c) is correct. Answer (a) is incorrect because Water's original cost includes an unrealized gain that must be eliminated. Answer (b) is incorrect because revaluing the equipment at Fire's original cost would not take into consideration the depreciation already recorded by Fire. Answer (d) is incorrect because the entire gain, not 80% of the gain, must be eliminated.

62. (b) The requirement is to determine by how much depreciation will be reduced. Use the solutions approach and set up a simple numerical example.

Port's original cost = $1,000
Depreciation per yr = $200
Selling price = $810

If Port sells equipment for $810, they recognize a $210 gain on the sale (selling price of $810 – carrying value of the equipment $600). Salem, Inc. will now depreciate the equipment on their books at $810, the price which they paid. Because the gain was not realized with an entity outside of the consolidated entity, it must be eliminated. In the consolidated financial statements, equipment will be reported at its original carrying value, the gain on the sale will be removed and depreciation expense must be recorded at Port, Inc. original amount ($200), not the amount of depreciation that Salem, Inc. records. Salem would record depreciation of $270 (810/3). Therefore, depreciation must be reduced by $70 on the consolidated financial statements to reflect the original depreciation recorded by Port. Answer (b) is correct because depreciation is reduced by $70, which as shown by the example, is 33 1/3% of the gain ($70/$210). Answers (a), (c), and (d) are incorrect.

63. (a) This question is silent as to which year consolidated financial statements are being prepared. However, answer (a) is correct for either the year of acquisition or a subsequent year. If financial statements were being prepared for the current year the loss would be reported as an extraordinary loss on the income statement. P Co. acquired the 20% interest in S Company bonds and incurred a loss on them. This loss would be carried through to the consolidated balance sheet as a decrease in retained earnings. In subsequent years, the unamortized portion of the loss would also decrease retained earnings.

L. Minority Interest

64. (a) Without the intercompany transaction, the minority interest income from Samson in 1999 would be $24,000 (30% of $80,000). In 2000, the minority interest income would be $27,000 (30% of $90,000). On the consolidated statements in 1999 the $2,000 intercompany profit will be eliminated, because from a consolidated viewpoint an arm's-length transaction has not occurred with third parties. The elimination entry will be to credit inventory (which is in effect on the books of Eltro) for $2,000 and debits will be made of $1,400 to majority interest income and $600 to minority interest income. In 2000 when Eltro sells the inventory to outsiders, the $2,000 profit has effectively been earned. In 2000 an entry will be made on the consolidated books to effectively recognize this profit and allocate it to the majority and minority interest. Thus, the 1999 minority interest income will be reduced by $600 and 2000 minority interest income increased by $600.

	1999		*2000*
MI % of profit	$24,000	MI % of profit	$27,000
Elim. of inter-		Recognition of	
company profit	– 600	profit	+ 600
MI income	$23,400		$27,600

65.   (c)   The cost of this investment is $975,000. Ritt purchased 80% of the identifiable net assets of Shaw, which have a fair value of $1,100,000 ($1,000,000 + $100,000). Thus, Ritt purchased net assets with a fair value of $880,000 (80% x $1,100,000). The excess amount paid ($975,000 – $880,000 = $95,000) is allocated to goodwill.

66.   (b)   The percentage of the subsidiary's stockholders' equity not owned by the parent company represents the minority interest's share of the net assets of the subsidiary. The minority interest is based on **book** value, to remove the minority shareholders' portion of reported equity from the financial statements (parent company concept). At 12/31/99, the subsidiary's stockholders' equity at book value is $1,065,000, as computed below.

1/1/99 net assets (stockholders' equity)	$1,000,000
1999 net income	190,000
1999 dividends	(125,000)
12/31/99 net assets (stockholders' equity)	$1,065,000

Since the parent's share is 80%, the minority interest is 20% of $1,065,000, or $213,000.

67.   (b)   Pare paid cash dividends of $25,000 and Kidd, the 75%-owned subsidiary, paid cash dividends of $5,000. The dividends paid by Pare are all payments to owners of the consolidated company and are reported as dividends paid in the consolidated statement of retained earnings. The $5,000 dividend paid by Kidd is paid 75% to Pare, and 25% to outside parties (the noncontrolling interest in Kidd's stock). The 75% share to Pare is eliminated when determining consolidated dividends declared because it is an intracompany transaction. The remaining 25% to the noncontrolling interest is likewise not included in consolidated dividends declared because, from the parent company's point of view, subsidiary dividends do not represent dividends of the consolidated entity.

68.   (b)   The portion of the subsidiary's stockholders' equity **not** owned by the parent company represents the minority interest's share of the net assets of the subsidiary. At 12/31/00, the subsidiary's stockholders' equity is $120,000 ($50,000 common stock + $70,000 retained earnings). Since the parent's share is 75%, the minority interest is 25% of $120,000, or $30,000.

69.   (b)   In the consolidated balance sheet, neither the parent company's investment account nor the subsidiary's stockholders' equity is reported. These amounts are eliminated in the same journal entry that records the excess of cost over book value. The portion of the subsidiary's stockholders' equity which is **not** eliminated is reported as minority interest. Therefore, the amount reported as common stock in the 12/31/00 consolidated balance sheet consists solely of Pare's common stock ($100,000). Kidd's common stock ($50,000) is eliminated along with the rest of its stockholders' equity.

O.   Changes in Ownership

70.   (a)   In a **purchase,** the consolidated entity is accounted for from the date of acquisition. Poe's consolidated 2000 dividends declared would include three quarterly dividends prior to consolidation (3 x $25,000 = $75,000) and one quarterly dividend after consolidation ($25,000), for a total of **$100,000.** Shaw's fourth quarter dividend declared of $10,000 is not a dividend from the consolidated point of view since the entire amount was paid to Poe. In a **pooling of interests**, the consolidated entity is accounted for on a retroactive basis for all periods presented. Therefore, the consolidated entity paid $130,000 of dividends to unaffiliated entities [$100,000 declared by Poe, and $30,000 declared by Shaw ($10,000 per quarter for the first 3 quarters)]. Shaw's 4th quarter dividend of $10,000 is not a dividend from the consolidated point of view since the entire amount was paid to Poe.

71.   (b)   The requirement is to determine how much of Sago's 1999 net income should be reported as accruing to Phillips. The key to the problem is to determine if the combination of the two entities should be treated as a purchase or pooling. For treatment as a pooling, APB 16 specifies 12 criteria that must be met before a combination may be accounted for as a pooling. If any one of the criteria are not met, the combination will be treated as a purchase, not a pooling. Consolidated net income, under pooling treatment, will reflect net income for both entities for the entire year, as if they had always been a consolidated entity. Under a purchase, consolidated net income reflects the parent's net income to the date of combination and both entities' income after the combination. In this case, the transaction should be treated as purchase because requirements (1) the combining companies have ownership interests independent of each other and were not recently a subsidiary or division of any other company to the extent that one company was not > 10% owned by another prior to the combination; and, (2) the combination is affected by a single transaction or in accord with a plan lasting not more than 1 year; are not met. Therefore, answer (b) is correct. Phillips, Inc. can only recognize the net income of Sago, based on their 20% interest, up to the date of combination. However, after the date of combination they will recognize 95% of Sago's net income, their new ownership interest. Answer (a) is incorrect because Phillips cannot recognize all of Sago's net income after the combination, because they only have a 95% interest in Sago. Answer (c) is incorrect because under the purchase method, Phillips can only recognize 95% of Sago's net income after the date of combination, not for the entire year. Answer (d) is incorrect because Phillips only has a 95% interest in Sago and because the combination should be accounted for as a purchase, not a pooling.

P. Combined Financial Statements

72. (d) **Combined financial statements** are financial statements prepared for companies that are owned by the same parent company or individual. Combined financial statements are prepared by combining all the companies' financial statement classifications. Intercompany transactions and profits should be eliminated in the same way as for consolidated statements (ARB 51, para 23). Therefore, **none** of the intercompany receivables should be included in the combined financial statements.

73. (c) The inventory reported on the 12/31/99 combined balance sheet should reflect the **original cost** to the companies of any inventory on hand (ARB 51, para 23). The inventory on hand which was acquired from outside parties should be reported at its cost ($175,000 + $250,000 = $425,000). The Banks inventory on hand which was acquired from Lamm must be restated back to the cost Lamm originally paid when it was purchased from outside parties. This must be done to eliminate intercompany profits. During 1999, Lamm shipped inventory which originally cost $150,000 to Banks at a billing price of $200,000. Therefore, the original cost is 75% of Banks' carrying amount. Therefore, the correct inventory amount is $470,000 [$175,000 + $250,000 + ($60,000 x 75%)].

74. (b) Combined financial statements are prepared for companies that are owned by the same parent company or individual but are not consolidated. These statements are prepared by combining the separate companies' financial statement classifications. Intercompany transactions, balances, and profit (loss) should be eliminated. Therefore, to determine the gross profit in Bee and Cee's combined income statement, the intercompany profit resulting from Bee's sales to Cee should be eliminated. Cee sold to outsiders 50% ($65,000/$130,000) of the inventory purchased from Bee. The cost of sales to the combined entity is thus 50% of the $100,000 cost of sales reported by Bee. Gross profit of the combined entity amounts to $41,000, equal to $91,000 of sales to unrelated companies less $50,000 cost of sales. Therefore, answer (b) is correct.

75. (a) When computing sales to be reported in the combined income statement, the objective is to restate the accounts as if the intercompany transaction had not occurred. Assuming that there were no sales between Home Office and Branch, the correct amount of sales to be included in the combined income statement is the $250,000 sold by Branch to unrelated customers.

76. (b) Combined financial statements is the term used to describe financial statements prepared for companies that are owned by the same parent company or individual. Combined financial statements are prepared by combining all of the subsidiaries' financial statement classifications. Intercompany transactions should be eliminated in the same way as for consolidated statements. Combining the stockholders' equity accounts of Able and Baker results in a total of

$430,000 ($100,000 + $20,000 + $300,000 + $10,000). The intercompany balances (Investment in Baker, $4,000; and Common Stock, $4,000) must be eliminated, which reduces combined stockholders' equity to $426,000 ($430,000 − $4,000). If these amounts were not eliminated, the combined balance sheet would overstate both assets and equity by $4,000.

77. (c) **Combined financial statements** are financial statements prepared for companies that are owned by the same parent company or individual. Combined financial statements are prepared by combining all the companies' financial statement classifications. Intercompany transactions and profits should be eliminated in the same way as for consolidated statements (ARB 51, para 23). Therefore, **none** of the intercompany loans or profits, answer (c), should be included in the combined financial statements.

78. (d) Per ARB 51, para 22, combined statements may be used to present the financial position and results of operations of commonly controlled companies, companies under common management, and of a group of unconsolidated subsidiaries. Therefore, answer (d) is correct and answers (a), (b), and (c) are incorrect.

79. (c) Per APB 51, para 23, where combined statements are prepared for a group of related companies, intercompany transactions and profit and losses should be eliminated. Matters such as minority interests, income taxes, foreign operations, or different fiscal periods should be treated in the same manner for both combined financial statements and consolidated statements. Therefore, answer (c) is correct.

80. (c) Per ARB 51, para 23, where combined statements are prepared for a group of related companies....if there are any problems in connection with such matters as minority interests, foreign operations, different fiscal periods, or income taxes, they should be treated in the same manner as in consolidated statements. Therefore, answer (c) is correct.

OTHER OBJECTIVE ANSWERS AND ANSWER EXPLANATIONS

Problem 1

1. **($14,000)** When preparing consolidated financial statements, the objective is to restate the accounts as if the intercompany transactions had not occurred. Therefore, the 1999 gain on sale of equipment of $21,000 ($36,000 – $15,000) must be eliminated, since the consolidated entity has not realized any gain. In addition, for consolidated statement purposes, 1999 depreciation is based on the original cost of the equipment to Shaw. Therefore, depreciation expense needs to be adjusted by $7,000 ($12,000 depreciation expense after sale to Poe – $5,000 depreciation expense for Shaw if sale never occurred). The net dollar effect of the consolidating adjustments on 1999 consolidated income before minority interest is $14,000 ($21,000 debit to eliminate gain on sale of equipment – $7,000 credit adjustment to depreciation expense).

2. **($10,000)** Unrealized profit in ending inventory arises when intercompany sales are made at prices above cost and the merchandise is not resold to third parties prior to year end. The profit is unrealized because the inventory has not yet been sold outside the consolidated entity. In this case, one half of the merchandise was left in Poe's inventory at year end. For the consolidated entity, one half of the $20,000 profit has not been earned and must be eliminated.

3. **($9,000)** When Poe purchased the bonds from an investor outside the consolidated entity, the bonds are viewed as retired from a consolidated viewpoint since there is no longer any obligation to an outside party. Therefore, the consolidated entity would recognize an extraordinary gain of $9,000 ($100,000 carrying value of the bonds – $91,000 purchase price) on the retirement of the debt.

4. **($2,000)** The goodwill from Poe's 90% purchase of Shaw can be determined as follows:

$155,000	Purchase price
135,000	Fair value ($150,000 x 90%)
$ 20,000	Goodwill

Since Poe's policy is to amortize intangibles over 10 years, Poe's amortization of goodwill for 1999 is $2,000 ($20,000 ÷ 10).

5. **(A)** Consolidated statements are prepared as if the parent and subsidiaries are one economic entity. Therefore, cash is included in the consolidated balance sheet at their full amounts regardless of the percentage ownership held by the parent.

6. **(B)** When preparing consolidated financial statements, the objective is to restate the accounts as if the intercompany transaction had not occurred. Therefore, on the consolidated balance sheet the equipment needs to be stated at its original cost to Shaw. The three balance sheets would show the sold equipment at December 31, 1999, as follows:

BALANCE SHEET
12/31/99

	Poe	Shaw	Consolidated
Equipment	$36,000	$0	$30,000

7. **(E)** In the consolidated balance sheet, the parent company's "Investment in subsidiary" should be eliminated completely and replaced by the net assets of the subsidiary.

8. **(B)** When Poe purchased the bonds from an investor outside the consolidated entity, the bonds are viewed as retired from a consolidated viewpoint since there is no longer any obligation to an outside party. Therefore, the consolidated balance sheet will show the bonds payable at $100,000.

9. **(F)** The percentage of the subsidiary's stockholders' equity not owned by the parent company represents the minority interest's share of the net assets of the subsidiary. This amount is only reported in the consolidated balance sheet in the noncurrent liabilities.

10. **(C)** In the consolidated balance sheet the subsidiary's common stock is not reported. Therefore, the parent's common stock equals the consolidated common stock.

11. **(C)** In the consolidated balance sheet, the subsidiary's beginning retained earnings is not reported. Therefore, the parent's beginning retained earnings equals the consolidated beginning retained earnings.

12. **(C)** The dividends paid by the subsidiary are eliminated in the consolidated financial statements. Ninety percent of the dividends paid are eliminated along with the "Investment in subsidiary" elimination. The remaining 10% is reflected in "Minority Interest." Therefore, only the parent's dividends paid are included on the consolidated financial statements.

13. **(F)** When Poe purchased the bonds from an investor outside the consolidated entity, the bonds are viewed as retired from a consolidated viewpoint since there is no longer any obligation to an outside party. Therefore, the consolidated entity would recognize a gain of $9,000 ($100,000 carrying value of the bonds – $91,000 purchase price) on the retirement of the debt. Since the bonds are still outstanding in relation to Shaw, no gain would be recognized on Shaw's unconsolidated income statement.

14. **(B)** When preparing the consolidated income statement, the objective is to restate the accounts as if the intercompany transactions had not occurred. As a result of the intercompany sale, Poe has recorded cost of sales of $30,000 and Shaw has recorded cost of sales of $40,000. The actual cost of sales to third parties outside the consolidated entity is $20,000 (1/2 of the merchandise Poe sold to third parties at the original cost of the merchandise purchased by Shaw).

15. **(D)** The requirement is to determine how the interest expense is to be reported in Poe's consolidated financial statements for December 31, 1999. As the Shaw bonds were held by an unaffiliated party for the entire period, the entire interest expense amount recorded by Shaw relates to payments outside the consolidated entity. Thus, the entire portion on Shaw's books should be included in the 12/31/99 consolidated financial statements. Therefore, answer (d) is correct.

16. **(B)** When preparing consolidated financial statements, the objective is to restate the accounts as if the intercompany transactions had not occurred. As a result of the sale of the equipment, Poe recorded depreciation expense of $12,000 ($36,000 ÷ 3 years). For consolidated purposes, depreciation must be computed based on the cost of the asset to the consolidated entity, which is the cost ($30,000) of the asset to Shaw. Therefore, depreciation expense should be $5,000 ($30,000 ÷ 6 yrs.) on the consolidated income statement.

Problem 2

Part a.

1. **(A)** When the investment cost is lower than the book value of the target company's net assets, the situation is referred to as a **bargain purchase**. Pooling of interests is incorrect, because under this method book values are carried forward from the target company in recording the transaction.

2. **(C)** Per APB 16, para 47a, for a business combination accounted for as a pooling, the amount of time permitted if the transaction is carried out under a plan rather than as a single transaction is 1 year. Since there are 12 conditions listed in APB 16, paras 45-48, the transaction could be a purchase if not all of the other 11 criteria were met. Thus, answer (C) is correct.

3. **(B)** Per APB 16, para 56, results for the entire year in which a pooling occurs are combined as if the combination occurred at the beginning of the year. However, in a purchase combination, the results of the acquired company are included with the acquiror's only from the date the transaction was completed.

4. **(D)** Per APB 16, paras 58 and 76, costs of effecting a business combination such as furnishing information to stockholders are recorded as expenses of the combined entity under both methods. Thus, charging such costs to retained earnings is incorrect.

5. **(A)** Under purchase accounting, fair values are reflected for assets and liabilities which would include goodwill if the purchase price exceeds the fair value of identifiable assets and liabilities. Since pooling of interest combinations are reflected at book values, no goodwill results under that method.

Part b.

6. **(A)** The total of cash on each entity's books equals the total for the consolidated entity.

7. **(B)** The amount shown for equipment on the consolidated balance sheet is less than the sum of the amounts on Purl's and Strand's unconsolidated balance sheets because on an upstream intercompany transaction the parent's share (90%) of the gain would be eliminated. The equipment now on the parent's books would be reduced on the worksheet by subtracting 90% of the gain not realized through depreciation from equipment.

8. **(E)** The investment in subsidiary would be eliminated in the process of consolidation in the same entry in which the subsidiary's equity accounts are eliminated.

9. **(F)** Minority interest is presented only in the consolidated balance sheet.

10. **(C)** Only Purl's common stock would be included in the consolidated balance sheet. All of Strand's common stock would be eliminated. Ten percent would be included in minority interest.

11. **(C)** Beginning retained earnings would be the same as Purl's. Under the purchase method none of the acquiree's (Strand's) retained earnings is carried forward in recording the business combination.

12. **(C)** Dividends paid would include only the parent's. The dividends of the subsidiary are all eliminated in consolidation.

13. **(B)** Cost of goods would be less than the sum of that of Purl and Strand because intercompany profit would be eliminated from cost of goods sold. The amount eliminated would be 100% of the intercompany profit on two thirds of the downstream sale from Purl to Strand.

14. **(A)** No information is given to indicate that there is any intercompany interest-bearing debt. Thus, the amount included for interest expense in the consolidated financial statements would be the sum of the two entities.

15. **(B)** Depreciation expense would be less on the consolidated financial statements than the sum of depreciation in each firm's unconsolidated financial statements because the part relating to the intercompany profit on equipment sold upstream would be eliminated in consolidation.

ANSWER OUTLINE

Problem 1   Rationale for and Selected Effects and Adjustments in Preparing Consolidated FS

a. **1.** Consolidated FSs provide information

- Reflecting the status of the companies as a single unit
- Representationally faithful and fair, free of bias
- Comparable with information about other economic entities
- Relevant and complete

2. Changes in consolidated BS upon acquisition

- Include Sox's identifiable assets and liabilities at FV
- Decrease cash by purchase price
- Difference reported as goodwill

3. Effect of intercompany sales is eliminated by reducing the following:

- Sales--intercompany sales
- Ending inventory--markup on goods sold by Plains and held by Sox
- CGS--difference between first two adjustments

b. Effect on BS of
  1. Plains

- Establish investment in Sox at purchase price
- Decrease cash by purchase price

  2. Sox

- Use push-down accounting
- All assets/liabilities, including goodwill, are restated to fair value at 9/1/99
- Retained earnings eliminated
- APIC adjusted for difference

UNOFFICIAL ANSWER

Problem 1   Rationale for and Selected Effects and Adjustments in Preparing Consolidated FS

a. **1.** Consolidated operating results, cash flows, and financial position are prepared, as if a parent company and its subsidiaries are a single entity, to provide information that

- Reflects the operating results, financial status, and central management ties that bind the companies into a single economic and financial unit.
- Is representationally faithful and fair, without the biases caused by exclusions or netting of data.
- Is comparable with information about other economic entities regardless of the companies' legal framework.
- Is relevant and complete for investors and other parties basing decisions on the data.

2. Plains' September 1, 1999 consolidated balance sheet is changed by including all of Sox's identifiable assets and liabilities at their fair values, and cash is decreased by

the purchase price. The excess of purchase price over the fair value of the net assets acquired is reported as goodwill.

3. The effect of the intercompany sales is eliminated from Plains' December 31, 1999 consolidated financial statements by

- Reducing sales by the amount of the intercompany sales.
- Reducing ending inventory by the markup on goods sold by Plains and still held by Sox.
- Reducing cost of goods sold for the difference between the amounts of the two previous adjustments.

b. **1.** The effects on Plains' September 1, 1999 balance sheet, are the establishment of an investment in Sox and a decrease in cash equal to the purchase price.

2. Using push-down accounting, all of Sox's assets and liabilities, including goodwill, are restated to reflect their fair values on September 1, 1999. The retained earnings balance is eliminated. Additional paid-in capital is adjusted for the difference arising from the restatement of the asset and liability balances and the elimination of retained earnings.

ANSWER OUTLINE

Problem 2   Purchase and Pooling of Interests

a. Pooling of interests method
  1. Accounting for assets and liabilities
      Book value recorded
      Existing basis of accounting continues
      Regarded as arrangement among stockholder groups
  2. Accounting for registration fees and direct costs
      Expense in period incurred
  3. Reporting in year of combination
      Report as if combined as of beginning of year

b. Purchase method
  1. Accounting for assets and liabilities
      Allocate cost of acquired company to assets acquired and liabilities assumed
      Identifiable assets acquired and liabilities assumed are recorded at fair values at date of acquisition
      Excess of costs over amounts assigned to identifiable assets less liabilities is recorded as goodwill
      Regarded as a bargained transaction
      Establishes new basis of accounting
  2. Accounting for registration fees and direct cost
      Registration fees are a reduction of determinable fair value of securities
      Direct costs included as part of acquisition cost
  3. Reporting in year of combination
      Include income of acquired company after date of acquisition
      Include revenues and expenses based on cost of acquiring corporation

UNOFFICIAL ANSWER

Problem 2   Purchase and Pooling of Interests

a.   1.   In a pooling of interests, the recorded amounts of the assets and liabilities of the separate companies generally become the recorded amounts of the assets and liabilities of the combined corporation. The existing basis of accounting continues. A pooling of interests transaction is regarded as an arrangement among stockholder groups.

2.   In a pooling of interests, the registration fees and direct costs related to effecting the business combination should be deducted in determining the net income of the resulting combined corporation for the period in which the expenses are incurred.

3.   In a pooling of interests, the results of operations for the year in which the business combination occurred should be reported as though the companies had been combined as of the beginning of the year.

b.   1.   In a purchase, the acquiring corporation should allocate the cost of the acquired company to the assets acquired and liabilities assumed. All identifiable assets acquired and liabilities assumed in the business combination should be recorded at their fair values at date of acquisition. The excess of the cost of the acquired company over the sum of the amounts assigned to identifiable assets acquired less liabilities assumed should be recorded as goodwill. A purchase transaction is regarded as a bargained transaction (i.e., a significant economic event which results from bargaining between independent parties) which establishes a new basis of accounting.

2.   In a purchase, the registration fees related to effecting the business combination are a reduction of the otherwise determinable fair value of the securities (usually as a reduction of paid-in capital). The direct costs related to effecting the business combination are included as part of the acquisition cost of the acquired company.

3.   In a purchase, the results of operations for the year in which the business combination occurred should include income of the acquired company after the date of acquisition by including the revenues and expenses of the acquired company based on the cost to the acquiring corporation.

SOLUTION GUIDE

Problem 3   Pooling of Interests

1.   This problem consists of three related requirements concerning a business combination properly accounted for as a pooling of interests. Part (a) requires journal entries to record the combination, part (b) requires computation of the balance in the investment account at year end, and part (c) requires a formal consolidated statement of changes in retained earnings.

2.   The solutions approach would include studying the problem, labeling the data as to the requirement to which it pertains, and preparing the solution.

3.   The information needed to prepare the entries required in part (a) is given in the introductory paragraph and the first three items of additional information.

3.1   In a pooling of interests, the objective is to combine the net assets and stockholders' equity of the two companies. The specific entry used depends on the facts of the situation.

3.2   The combination could be effected through a merger, a consolidation, or an acquisition. This situation is an acquisition because Strand continues to exist as a separate business. In an acquisition, an investment account is recorded by the acquiring company (Pine) instead of recording the individual assets and liabilities of the acquired company (Strand). Since a pooling of interests is treated as a combination (pooling) of two companies rather than as a purchase-sale transaction, the investment account is recorded at the book value of Strand's net assets (the same amount as Strand's stockholders' equity, $5,400,000). The fact that Strand's long-term investment has a market value which is $600,000 greater than book value, and the fact that the market value of the stock issued by Pine is $7,000,000 (200,000 x $35), is not recorded because a pooling is based on book value.

3.3   On the credit side of the entry, the $5,400,000 debit is offset by credits of $5,400,000 to stockholders' equity accounts. The amounts credited to the various accounts depends on the situation.

3.4   In this case, the par value of the stock issued (200,000 x $10 = $2,000,000) is less than the present par on the books of the combinee ($2,500,000). Since the stock issued must be recorded at **its** par ($2,000,000), the $500,000 difference ($2,500,000 – $2,000,000) is added to additional paid-in capital. Therefore, additional paid-in capital is credited for $970,000 ($500,000 + $470,000 from Strand). Strand's retained earnings ($2,430,000) is carried forward. Therefore the entry is

Investment in Strand	5,400,000	
Common stock		2,000,000
Additional paid-in capital		970,000
Retained earnings		2,430,000

3.5   Pine paid $720,000 for expenditures relating to the business combination. In a purchase, this would be considered part of the cost of the investment acquired, but in a pooling, such costs are expensed. The rationale is that no new capital is raised; only a "pooling" of the existing capital occurs.

4.   Part (b) requires a schedule to compute the investment in Strand, at equity, at 12/31/99. Using the equity method, the 12/31/99 investment balance should be the amount recorded for the investment initially ($5,400,000 as discussed in 3.4 above), plus Pine's share of Strand's income, less Pine's dividends received from Strand.

4.1   Since the investment was acquired on 3/31/99 (and the amount recorded reflects all of Strand's earnings prior to that date), Strand's income for the period 4/1/99 to 12/31/99 must be computed.

4.2   Strand's 1999 income is $1,450,000. The income from 1/1/99 to 3/31/99 must be subtracted to compute the income from 4/1/99 to 12/31/99. The formula below can be used to compute the 1/1-3/31 income.

$$
\begin{array}{ccccc}
\underset{\text{RE}}{12/31/98} + & \text{Net income} - & \text{Dividends} = & \underset{\text{RE}}{3/31/99} \\
\$2,290,000 + & \text{Net income} - & \$250,000 & = \$2,430,000
\end{array}
$$

Therefore, 1/1-3/31 income is $390,000, and the 4/1-12/31 income is $1,060,000 ($1,450,000–$390,000). However, any intercompany profit must be eliminated from this net income figure. Pine sold merchandise to Strand at a profit of $800,000. Since 1/4 of this merchandise remained in Strand's inventory at year end, $200,000 of the profit (1/4 x $800,000) has not been realized by sale to an unaffiliated customer and should therefore be eliminated from Strand's net income to compute Pine's investment in Strand.

4.3 No dividends were paid by Strand after Pine's acquisition on 3/31/99. Therefore, the investment in Strand, at equity, at 12/31/99, is $6,260,000. [$5,400,000 cost + (100% x $1,060,000) – $200,000].

5. Part (c) requires a formal consolidated statement of changes in retained earnings.

5.1 Pine's retained earnings at 12/31/98, as previously reported (before the pooling), was $6,820,000.

5.2 The beginning retained earnings must be retroactively restated to reflect the effects of the pooling as if the companies had been pooled all along. Therefore, Strand's 12/31/98 retained earnings ($2,290,000) is added to compute restated 12/31/98 consolidated retained earnings of $9,110,000 ($6,820,000 + $2,290,000).

5.3 Consolidated net income is added to the restated retained earnings. The separate net incomes of the companies are added ($2,240,000 + $1,450,000 = $3,690,000), and any unrealized intercompany profit is deducted. Pine sold merchandise to Strand at a profit of $800,000. Since 1/4 of this merchandise remained in Strand's inventory at year end, $200,000 of the profit (1/4 x $800,000) has not been realized by sale to an unaffiliated customer. Therefore, 1999 consolidated net income is $3,490,000 ($3,690,000 – $200,000). Note that even though the combination took place on 3/31/99, the 1999 net income includes the entire 12 months, retroactively restated to reflect the pooling.

5.4 The management fees paid by Strand to Pine ($150,000) do not affect the computation of consolidated net income. The transaction resulted in Pine recording revenue of $150,000, and Strand recording expense of $150,000. These two amounts offset each other and would be eliminated.

5.5 Any dividends paid by Strand prior to 3/31/99, or paid by Pine during 1999, must be deducted in the retained earnings statement. Total dividends paid to unaffiliated parties are $1,750,000 ($250,000 by Strand, plus $1,500,000 by Pine).

5.6 Ending consolidated retained earnings is $10,850,000 ($9,110,000 restated beginning retained earnings, plus $3,490,000 net income, less $1,750,000 dividends).

UNOFFICIAL ANSWER

Problem 3   Pooling of Interests

a.

Pine Corp.
JOURNAL ENTRIES
March 31, 1999

Account	Dr.	Cr.
Investment in Strand, Inc.	5,400,000 (1)	
Common stock		2,000,000
Additional paid-in capital		970,000 (2)
Retained earnings of subsidiary		2,430,000

To record issuance of 200,000 shares of common stock for all the outstanding common stock of Strand, Inc., in a business combination accounted for by the pooling-of- interests method.

Expenses of business combination	720,000	
Cash		720,000

To record payment of the expenses relating to the business combination with Strand, Inc.

Explanations of amounts

(1)   Investment in Strand, Inc.

Carrying amount of Strand's stockholders' equity, March 31, 1999	
Capital stock	$2,500,000
Additional paid-in capital	470,000
Retained earnings	2,430,000
Total	$5,400,000

(2) Additional paid-in capital

Strand, Inc. additional paid-in capital, March 31, 1999		$ 470,000
Par value of Strand, Inc. common stock acquired	$2,500,000	
Par value of Pine Corp. common stock issued (200,000 shares x $10)	2,000,000	
Excess added to additional paid-in capital		500,000
Total		$ 970,000

b.

Pine Corp.
INVESTMENT IN STRAND, INC.--AT EQUITY
December 31, 1999

Balance at date of acquisition, 3/31/99		5,400,000
Net income of Strand, Inc. for period 4/1 through 12/31/99	$1,060,000 (3)	
Less: Elimination of intercompany profit in Strand's inventory	200,000	860,000
Balance, 12/31/99		$6,260,000

Explanation of amounts

(3) Net income of Strand, Inc.
       for period 4/1 through 12/31/99

Retained earnings, 12/31/98		$2,290,000
Net income for 1999	$1,450,000	
Less: Dividend paid, 3/10/99	(250,000)	
Net increase in 1999 retained earnings		1,200,000
Retained earnings, 12/31/99		3,490,000
Retained earnings, 3/31/99		(2,430,000)
Net income for period 4/1 through 12/31/99		$1,060,000

c.

Pine Corp. and Subsidiary
**CONSOLIDATED STATEMENT OF CHANGES IN
RETAINED EARNINGS**
For the Year Ended December 31, 1999

Balance, December 31, 1998:		
As originally reported		$ 6,820,000
Adjustment for pooling of interests with Strand, Inc.		2,290,000
As restated		9,110,000
Net income		3,490,000 (4)
		12,600,000
Dividends paid:		
By Strand, Inc., before combination		(250,000)
By Pine Corp., after combination		(1,500,000)
		(1,750,000)
Balance, December 31, 1999		$10,850,000

Explanation of amounts

(4) Consolidated net income for 1999

Pine Corp.'s income before considering equity in Strand's net income		$2,240,000
Strand, Inc.'s separate net income		1,450,000
		3,690,000
Elimination of intercompany profit in Strand's inventory (1/4 x $800,000)		(200,000)
Consolidated net income for 1999		$3,490,000

FOREIGN CURRENCY TRANSLATION AND DERIVATIVES

A. Foreign Currency Translation

1. Objective of Foreign Currency Translation

The rules for the translation of foreign currency into US dollars apply to two major areas.

a. Foreign currency transactions which are denominated in other than a company's functional currency (e.g., exports, imports, loans), and

b. Foreign currency financial statements of branches, divisions, subsidiaries, and other investees which are incorporated with the financial statements of a US company by combination, consolidation, or the equity method

The objectives of translation are

a. To provide information relative to the expected economic effects of rate changes on an enterprise's cash flows and equity, and

b. To provide information in consolidated statements relative to the financial results and relationships of each individual foreign consolidated entity as reflected by the functional currency of each reporting entity

The first objective influences the rules for the translation of foreign currency transactions, while both objectives influence the rules for the translation of foreign currency financial statements. After working through this module, read through the outline of SFAS 52.

2. Translation of Foreign Currency Statements

Assume that a US company has a 100% owned subsidiary in Germany. The subsidiary's operations consist of leasing space in an office building. Its balance sheet at December 31, 1999, and its income statement for 1999 are presented below.

German Company
BALANCE SHEET
December 31, 1999

Assets	*Deutsche Marks*	*Liabilities and owners' equity*	*Deutsche Marks*
Cash	60	Accounts Payable	100
Accounts Receivable (Net)	100	Mortgage Payable	200
Land	200	Common Stock	100
Building	500	Retained Earnings	360
Less Accumulated Depr.	(100)		
Total Assets	DM 760	Total Liabilities and Owners' Equity	DM 760

German Company
INCOME STATEMENT
For Year Ended December 31, 1999

Revenues	DM 260
Operating Expenses (includes depreciation expense of 20 DM)	160
Net Income	DM 100

In addition to the information above, the following data are also needed for the translation process:

1. Transactions involving land, building, mortgage payable, and common stock all occurred in 1994.
2. No dividends were paid during the period 1994-1999.
3. Exchange rates for various dates follow.

> 1DM = $.30 in 1994
> 1DM = $.50 at beginning of 1999
> 1DM = $.55 at end of 1999
> 1DM = $.53 weighted-average for 1999

If the US company wants to present consolidated financial statements which include the results of its German subsidiary, the financial statements of the German company must be translated into US dollars. However, before this can be accomplished, the management of the US company must determine the functional currency of its German subsidiary. SFAS 52 defines an entity's functional currency as ". . .the currency of the primary economic environment in which the entity operates; normally, that is the currency of the environment in which an entity primarily generates and expends cash." The decision concerning the functional currency is important because, once determined, it should be used consistently, unless it is clear that economic facts and circumstances have changed. The selection of the functional currency depends upon an evaluation of several factors. These factors include the following:

1. Cash flows (Do the foreign entity's cash flows directly affect the parent's cash flows and are they immediately available for remittance to the parent?)
2. Sales prices (Are the foreign entity's sales prices responsive to exchange rate changes and to international competition?)
3. Sales markets (Is the foreign entity's sales market the parent's country or are sales denominated in the parent's currency?)
4. Expenses (Are the foreign entity's expenses incurred in the parent's country?)
5. Financing (Is the foreign entity's financing primarily from the parent or is it denominated in the parent's currency?)
6. Intercompany transactions (Is there a high volume of intercompany transactions between the parent and foreign entity?)

If the answers to the questions above are predominantly yes, the functional currency would be the reporting currency of the parent (i.e., the US dollar). On the other hand, if the answers to the questions were predominantly no, the functional currency would be the foreign currency. In the example described previously, the DM would be the functional currency if the answers were no. Note that the functional currency does not necessarily have to be the local currency of the foreign country when the answers to the questions are negative. In other words, it is possible for a foreign currency other than deutsche marks to be the functional currency of our German company. For example, Swiss francs or Italian lira could be the functional currency for the German company if one of these currencies is the currency of the primary economic environment in which the entity operates. However, assume these other possibilities are not alternatives in the example mentioned previously.

If the circumstances indicate the DM to be the functional currency, SFAS 52 mandates that the current rate method be used for translation of the foreign currency financial statements. This technique is illustrated below for the German financial statements shown previously.

<u>Balance Sheet</u>
(Deutsche Mark is Functional Currency)

	DM	Exchange rates	US dollars
Assets			
Cash	60	.55	33
Accounts Receivable (Net)	100	.55	55
Land	200	.55	110
Building (Net)	400	.55	220
Totals	DM 760		$418
Liabilities and Owners' Equity			
Accounts Payable	100	.55	55
Mortgage Payable	200	.55	110
Common Stock	100	.30	30
Retained Earnings	360	see income statement	157
Translation Adjustments	--		66
Totals	DM 760		$418

<u>Combined Income and Retained Earnings Statement</u>

	DM	Exchange rates	US dollars
Revenues	260	.53	$137.80
Operating Expenses (including 20 DM of depreciation expense)	160	.53	84.80
Net Income	100		53.00
Retained Earnings at 1/1/99	260		104.00*
Retained Earnings at 12/31/99	DM 360		$157.00

* The US dollar amount of retained earnings results from applying weighted-average exchange rates to translate revenues and expenses during the period 1994 through 1998. Retained earnings cannot be translated using a single exchange rate.

The following points should be noted from the illustration of the translation process:

1. All assets and liabilities are translated using the current rate at the balance sheet date. All revenues and expenses are translated at the rates in effect when these items are recognized during the period. Due to practical considerations, however, weighted-average rates can be used to translate revenues and expenses which were incurred throughout the year.

2. Owners' equity accounts are translated using historical exchange rates. Common stock was issued in 1994 when the exchange rate was 1DM = $.30. The beginning balance of retained earnings for 1999 was accumulated during the period 1994 through 1998.

3. Translation adjustments result from translating all assets and liabilities at the current rate, while owners' equity is translated using historical rates and income statement items are translated using weighted-average rates. The translation adjustment for the period is reported as other comprehensive income under one of several acceptable reporting alternatives and the accumulated amount is reported as accumulated other comprehensive income in the owners' equity section of the consolidated balance sheet.

This illustration of the current rate technique assumed the DM to be the functional currency. Assume, however, that the circumstances were evaluated by the US company, and the US dollar was chosen as the functional currency. Under this alternative, SFAS 52 requires the foreign currency financial statements to be remeasured into US dollars. According to SFAS 52, the "...remeasurement process is intended to produce the same result as if the entity's books of record had been maintained in the functional currency."

If the US dollar is the functional currency, the remeasurement of foreign currency financial statements into US dollars makes translation adjustments unnecessary. The remeasurement process is illustrated below for the German subsidiary.

Balance Sheet
(US Dollar is Functional Currency)

	DM	Exchange rates	US dollars
Assets:			
Cash	60	.55	33
Accounts Receivable (Net)	100	.55	55
Land	200	.30	60
Building (Net)	400	.30	120
Totals	DM760		$268
Liabilities and			
Owners' Equity:			
Accounts Payable	100	.55	55
Mortgage Payable	200	.55	110
Common Stock	100	.30	30
Retained Earnings	360	see income statement	73
Totals	DM760		$268

Combined Income and Retained Earnings Statement

	DM	Exchange rates	US Dollars
Revenues	260	.53	$137.80
Expenses (exclusive of depreciation)	140	.53	$ 74.20
Depreciation	20	.30	6.00
Total Expenses	160		$ 80.20
Remeasurement Loss	--	--	10.60
Total Expenses and Loss	--	--	$ 90.80
Net Income (Loss)	100		$ 47.00
Retained Earnings at 1/1/99	260		26.00*
Retained Earnings at 12/31/99	DM 360		$ 73.00

*Retained earnings of $26 includes remeasured income from the period 1994 through 1998, which includes remeasurement losses applicable to those years due to the strengthening of the DM compared to the US dollar.

The following observations should be noted about the remeasurement process:

1. Assets and liabilities which have historical cost balances are remeasured using historical exchange rates. Monetary assets and monetary liabilities, on the other hand, are remeasured using the current rate at the balance sheet date.
2. Revenues and expenses that occur during a period are remeasured, for practical purposes, using the weighted-average exchange rate for the period. Revenues and expenses that represent allocations of historical balances (e.g., depreciation) are remeasured using historical exchange rates.
3. The remeasurement loss of $10.60 is reported on the consolidated income statement. The loss is the result of a remeasurement process which assumes that the US dollar is the functional currency.
4. The calculation of the remeasurement loss is the result of the rules employed in the remeasurement process. In mechanical terms, the remeasurement loss is the amount needed to make the debits equal the credits in the German company's US dollar trial balance. Note this technique below.

	DM			US dollars	
	DR	*CR*	*Exchange rates*	*DR*	*CR*
Cash	60		.55	33	
Accounts Rec. (Net)	100		.55	55	
Land	200		.30	60	
Building (Net)	400		.30	120	
Accounts Payable		100	.55		55
Mortgage Payable		200	.55		110
Common Stock		100	.30		30
Retained Earnings (1/1/95)		260			26
Revenues		260	.53		137.80
Expenses	140		.53	74.20	
Depreciation Exp.	20	—	.30	6	
Totals	DM 920	DM 920		$348.20	$358.80
Remeasurement Loss				10.60	
Totals				$358.80	$358.80

The significant points to remember about the German illustration are summarized below.

1. Before foreign currency financial statements can be translated into US dollars, a decision must be made regarding the functional currency.

2. If the functional currency is the foreign currency, the current rate method is used to translate to US dollars. All assets and liabilities are translated using the current rate at the balance sheet date. Owners' equity is translated using historical rates while revenues (and gains) and expenses (and losses) are translated at the rates in existence during the period when the transactions occurred. A weighted-average rate can be used for items occurring numerous times throughout the period. The translation adjustments (debit or credit) which result from the application of these rules are reported as a separate item in owners' equity in the consolidated balance sheet of the US parent.

3. If the functional currency is the reporting currency (the US dollar), the foreign currency financial statements are remeasured into US dollars. All foreign currency balances are restated to US dollars using both historical and current exchange rates. Foreign currency balances which reflect prices from past transactions (e.g., inventories carried at cost, prepaid insurance, property, plant, and equipment, etc.) are remeasured using historical rates while foreign currency balances which reflect prices from current transactions (e.g., inventories and trading and available-for-sale securities carried at market, etc.) are remeasured using the current rate. Monetary assets and liabilities are remeasured using the current rate. (Deferred taxes are remeasured using the current rate.) Remeasurement gains/losses that result from the remeasurement process are reported on the consolidated income statement under "Other Income (Expense)."

The above summary can be arranged in tabular form as shown below.

Functional currency	Functional currency determinants	Translation method	Reporting
Local currency of foreign company	a. Operations not integrated-with parent's operations b. Buying and selling activities primarily in local currency c. Cash flows not immediately available for remittance to parent	Current Rate (All assets/liabilities translated using current rate; revenues/expenses use weighted-average rate; equity accounts use historical rates)	Translation adjustments are reported as other comprehensive income under one of several acceptable reporting alternatives and as accumulated other comprehensive income in the equity section of consolidated balance sheet. Analysis of changes in accumulated translation adjustments disclosed via footnote
US Dollar	a. Operations integrated with parent's operations b. Buying and selling activities primarily in US and/or US dollars c. Cash flows immediately available for remittance to parent	Remeasurement (Monetary assets/liabilities use current rate; historical cost balances use historical rates; revenues/expenses use weighted-average rates and historical rates, the latter for allocations such as depr. exp.).	Remeasurement gain/loss is reported on the consolidated income statement.

Before proceeding to foreign currency transactions, a few comments concerning the translation of foreign currency financial statements in highly inflationary economies should be made. If the cumulative inflation rate is $\geq$ 100% over a 3-year period in a foreign country, the foreign currency statements of a company located in that country are remeasured into the reporting currency (i.e., the US dollar). In other words, it is assumed the US dollar is the functional currency. The following flowchart summarizes the requirements of SFAS 52 with respect to foreign currency financial statements.

FOREIGN CURRENCY FINANCIAL STATEMENTS

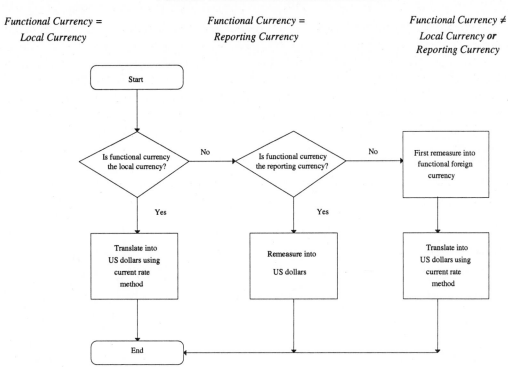

3. **Foreign Currency Transactions**

    a. **Translation**

    A foreign currency transaction, according to SFAS 52, is a transaction ". . .denominated in a currency other than the entity's functional currency." Denominated means that the balance is fixed in terms of the number of units of a foreign currency regardless of changes in the exchange rate. When a US company purchases or sells goods or services (or borrows or lends money) to a foreign entity, and the transaction is denominated in foreign currency units, the US company has a foreign currency transaction in which the US dollar is the functional currency. In these situations, the US company has "crossed currencies" and directly assumes the risk of fluctuating foreign exchange rates of the foreign currency units. This exposed foreign currency risk may lead to recognition of foreign exchange transaction gains or losses in the income statement of the US company, as defined in SFAS 52. If the US company pays or receives US dollars in import and export transactions, the risk resulting from fluctuating foreign exchange rates is borne by the foreign supplier or customer, and there is no need to apply the procedures outlined in SFAS 52 to the transaction reported in US dollars on the US company's books.

    The following example illustrates the terminology and procedures applicable to the translation of foreign currency transactions. Assume that US Company, an exporter, sells merchandise to a customer in Germany on December 1, 1999, for 10,000 Deutsche Marks (DM). Receipt of 10,000 DM is due on January 31, 2000, and US Company prepares financial statements on December 31, 1999. At the transaction date (December 1, 1999), the spot rate for immediate exchange of foreign currencies indicates that 1 DM is equivalent to $.50. This quotation is referred to as a direct quotation since the exchange rate is stated in terms of a direct translation of the currency in which the debt is measured. To find the US dollar equivalent of this transaction, simply multiply the foreign currency amount, 10,000 DM, by $.50 to get $5,000. Occasionally, spot rates are quoted indirectly (e.g., $1 is equivalent to 2 DM). In the example used, since $1 is equivalent to 2 DM, the foreign currency amount would be divided by 2 to get the US dollar amount of $5,000.

    At December 1, 1999, the foreign currency transaction should be recorded by US Company in the following manner:

Accounts receivable-Germany	5,000	
Sales		5,000

    The accounts receivable and sales are measured in US dollars at the transaction date using the spot rate at the time of the transaction. While the accounts receivable is measured and reported in US dollars, the receivable is also denominated or fixed in DM. This characteristic can result in foreign exchange transaction gains or losses if the spot rate for DM changes between the transaction date and the date the transaction is settled.

    If financial statements are prepared between the transaction date and the settlement date, the FASB requires that receivables and liabilities denominated in a currency other than the functional currency be restated to reflect the spot rates in existence at the balance sheet date. Assume that, on December 31, 1999, the spot rate for DM is 1 DM = $.52. This means that 10,000 DM are worth

$5,200, and that the accounts receivable denominated in DM are increased by $200. The following journal entry should be recorded as of December 31, 1999:

Accounts receivable--Germany	200	
Foreign currency transaction gain		200

Note that the sales account, which was credited on the transaction date for $5,000, is not affected by changes in the spot rate. This treatment exemplifies the "two-transaction" viewpoint adopted by the FASB. In other words, making the sale is the result of an operating decision, while bearing the risk of fluctuating spot rates is the result of an investment decision. Therefore, the amount determined as sales revenue at the transaction date should not be altered because of an investment decision to wait until January 31, 2000, for payment of the account. The risk of a foreign exchange transaction loss can be avoided either by demanding immediate payment on December 1 or by entering into a forward exchange contract to hedge the exposed asset (accounts receivable). The fact that US Company in the example did not act in either of these two ways is reflected by the required recognition of foreign currency transaction gains or losses on this type of transaction. These gains or losses are reported on US Company's income statement as financial (nonoperating) items in the period during which the exchange rates changed.

It is also important to note that reporting transaction gains or losses before the transaction is settled results in reporting unrealized gains or losses. This represents an exception to the conventional realization principle which normally applies. This practice also results in a temporary difference between pretax accounting income and taxable income because foreign exchange transaction gains and losses do not enter into the determination of taxable income until the year they are realized. Thus, the recognition of foreign currency transaction gains and losses on unsettled foreign currency transactions results in deferred tax assets/liabilities (depending on whether the temporary differences result in future taxable or future deductible amounts).

To complete the previous illustration, assume that on January 31, 2000, the foreign currency transaction is settled when the spot rate is 1 DM = $.51. Note that the account receivable is valued at $5,200 at this point. The receipt of DM and their conversion into dollars should be journalized as follows:

Foreign currency	5,100	
Foreign currency transaction loss	100	
Accounts receivable--Germany		5,200
Cash	5,100	
Foreign currency		5,100

The net effect of this foreign currency transaction was the receipt of $5,100 from a sale which was measured originally at $5,000. This realized net foreign currency transaction gain of $100 is reported on the income statements of more than one period--a $200 gain in 1999 and a $100 loss in 2000.

The financial statement disclosures required by SFAS 52 consist of the following:

1. Aggregate transaction gain (loss) that is included in the entity's net income
2. Analysis of changes in accumulated translation adjustments which are reported as part of the entity's owners' equity
3. Remeasurement gain (loss) which is reported in an entity's net income

    4.   Significant rate changes subsequent to the date of the financial statements including effects on unsettled foreign currency transactions

4. **Glossary**

Discount or Premium on a Forward Contract

"The foreign currency amount of the contract multiplied by the difference between the contracted forward rate and the spot rate at the date of inception of the contract."

Foreign Currency Statements

"Financial statements that employ as the unit of measure a functional currency that is not the reporting currency of the enterprise."

Foreign Currency Transactions

"Transactions whose terms are denominated in a currency other than the entity's functional currency. Foreign currency transactions arise when an enterprise (a) buys or sells on credit goods or services whose prices are denominated in foreign currency, (b) borrows or lends funds and the amounts payable or receivable are denominated in foreign currency, (c) is a party to an unperformed forward exchange contract, or (d) for other reasons, acquires or disposes of assets, or incurs or settles liabilities denominated in foreign currency."

Foreign Currency Translation

"The process of expressing in the reporting currency of the enterprise those amounts that are denominated or measured in a different currency."

Forward Exchange Contract

"An agreement to exchange at a specified future date currencies of different countries at a specified rate (forward rate)."

Functional Currency

"An entity's functional currency is the currency of the primary economic environment in which the entity operates; normally, that is the currency of the environment in which an entity primarily generates and expends cash."

Local Currency

"The currency of a particular country being referred to."

Remeasurement

"If an entity's books and records are not kept in its functional currency, remeasurement into the functional currency is required. Monetary balances are translated using the current exchange rate and nonmonetary balances are translated using historical exchange rates." If the US dollar is the functional currency, remeasurement into the reporting currency (the US dollar) makes translation unnecessary.

Reporting Currency

"The currency in which an enterprise prepares its financial statements."

Transaction Gain or Loss

"Transaction gains or losses result from a change in exchange rates between the functional currency and the currency in which a foreign currency transaction is denominated. They represent an increase or decrease in (a) the actual functional currency cash flows realized upon settlement of foreign currency transactions, and (b) the expected functional currency cash flows on unsettled foreign currency transactions."

Translation Adjustments

"Translation adjustments result from the process of translating financial statements from the entity's functional currency into the reporting currency."

MULTIPLE-CHOICE QUESTIONS (1-17)

1. Certain balance sheet accounts of a foreign subsidiary of Rowan, Inc., at December 31, 1999 have been translated into US dollars as follows:

	Translated at	
	Current rates	Historical rates
Note receivable, long-term	$240,000	$200,000
Prepaid rent	85,000	80,000
Patent	150,000	170,000
	$475,000	$450,000

The subsidiary's functional currency is the currency of the country in which it is located. What total amount should be included in Rowan's December 31, 1999 consolidated balance sheet for the above accounts?

- a. $450,000
- b. $455,000
- c. $475,000
- d. $495,000

2. A wholly owned subsidiary of Ward, Inc. has certain expense accounts for the year ended December 31, 1999, stated in local currency units (LCU) as follows:

	LCU
Depreciation of equipment (related assets were purchased January 1, 1997)	120,000
Provision for doubtful accounts	80,000
Rent	200,000

The exchange rates at various dates are as follows:

	Dollar equivalent of 1 LCU
December 31, 1999	$.40
Average for year ended 12/31/99	.44
January 1, 1997	.50

Assume that the LCU is the subsidiary's functional currency and that the charges to the expense accounts occurred approximately evenly during the year. What total dollar amount should be included in Ward's 1999 consolidated income statement to reflect these expenses?

- a. $160,000
- b. $168,000
- c. $176,000
- d. $183,200

3. Which of the following should be reported as a stockholders' equity account?

- a. Discount on convertible bonds.
- b. Premium on convertible bonds.
- c. Cumulative foreign exchange translation loss.
- d. Organization costs.

4. A foreign subsidiary's functional currency is its local currency, which has not experienced significant inflation. The weighted-average exchange rate for the current year would be the appropriate exchange rate for translating

	Sales to customers	Wages expense
a.	No	No
b.	Yes	Yes
c.	No	Yes
d.	Yes	No

5. The functional currency of Nash, Inc.'s subsidiary is the French franc. Nash borrowed French francs as a partial hedge of its investment in the subsidiary. In preparing consolidated financial statements, Nash's translation loss on its investment in the subsidiary exceeded its exchange gain on the borrowing. How should the effects of the loss and gain be reported in Nash's consolidated financial statements?

- a. The translation loss less the exchange gain is reported as other comprehensive income.
- b. The translation loss less the exchange gain is reported in net income.
- c. The translation loss is reported as other comprehensive income and the exchange gain is reported in net income.
- d. The translation loss is reported in net income and the exchange gain is reported as other comprehensive income.

6. A balance arising from the translation or remeasurement of a subsidiary's foreign currency financial statements is reported in the consolidated income statement when the subsidiary's functional currency is the

	Foreign currency	US dollar
a.	No	No
b.	No	Yes
c.	Yes	No
d.	Yes	Yes

7. When remeasuring foreign currency financial statements into the functional currency, which of the following items would be remeasured using historical exchange rate?

- a. Inventories carried at cost.
- b. Marketable equity securities reported at market values.
- c. Bonds payable.
- d. Accrued liabilities.

8. Park Co.'s wholly owned subsidiary, Schnell Corp., maintains its accounting records in German marks. Because all of Schnell's branch offices are in Switzerland, its functional currency is the Swiss franc. Remeasurement of Schnell's 1999 financial statements resulted in a $7,600 gain, and translation of its financial statements resulted in an $8,100 gain. What amount should Park report as a foreign exchange gain as net income in its income statement for the year ended December 31, 1999?

- a. $0
- b. $ 7,600
- c. $ 8,100
- d. $15,700

9. On September 1, 1999, Bain Corp. received an order for equipment from a foreign customer for 300,000 local currency units (LCU) when the US dollar equivalent was

$96,000. Bain shipped the equipment on October 15, 1999, and billed the customer for 300,000 LCU when the US dollar equivalent was $100,000. Bain received the customer's remittance in full on November 16, 1999, and sold the 300,000 LCU for $105,000. In its income statement for the year ended December 31, 1999, Bain should report as part of net income a foreign exchange transaction gain of

    a. $0
    b. $4,000
    c. $5,000
    d. $9,000

10. On September 1, 1998, Cano & Co., a US corporation, sold merchandise to a foreign firm for 250,000 francs. Terms of the sale require payment in francs on February 1, 1998. On September 1, 1999, the spot exchange rate was $.20 per franc. At December 31, 1998, Cano's year end, the spot rate was $.19, but the rate increased to $.22 by February 1, 1999, when payment was received. How much should Cano report as foreign exchange transaction gain or loss as part of net income?

    a. $0.
    b. $2,500 loss.
    c. $5,000 gain.
    d. $7,500 gain.

11. Lindy, a US corporation, bought inventory items from a supplier in Germany on November 5, 1998 for 100,000 marks, when the spot rate was $.4295. At Lindy's December 31, 1998 year end, the spot rate was $.4245. On January 15, 1999, Lindy bought 100,000 marks at the spot rate of $.4345 and paid the invoice. How much should Lindy report as part of net income for 1998 and 1999 as foreign exchange transaction gain or loss?

	1998	*1999*
a.	$ 500	($1,000)
b.	$0	($ 500)
c.	($ 500)	$0
d.	($1,000)	$ 500

12. Hunt Co. purchased merchandise for £300,000 from a vendor in London on November 30, 1998. Payment in British pounds was due on January 30, 1999. The exchange rates to purchase one pound were as follows:

	November 30, 1998	*December 31, 1998*
Spot-rate	$1.65	$1.62
30-day rate	1.64	1.59
60-day rate	1.63	1.56

In its December 31, 1998, income statement, what amount should Hunt report as foreign exchange transaction gain as part of net income?

    a. $12,000
    b. $ 9,000
    c. $ 6,000
    d. $0

13. Ball Corp. had the following foreign currency transactions during 1999:

• Merchandise was purchased from a foreign supplier on January 20, 1999, for the US dollar equivalent of $90,000. The invoice was paid on March 20, 1999, at the US dollar equivalent of $96,000.

• On July 1, 1999, Ball borrowed the US dollar equivalent of $500,000 evidenced by a note that was payable in the lender's local currency on July 1, 2001. On December 31, 1999, the US dollar equivalents of the principal amount and accrued interest were $520,000 and $26,000, respectively. Interest on the note is 10% per annum.

In Ball's 1999 income statement, what amount should be included as foreign exchange transaction loss as part of net income?

    a. $0
    b. $ 6,000
    c. $21,000
    d. $27,000

14. On November 30, 1998, Tyrola Publishing Company, located in Colorado, executed a contract with Ernest Blyton, an author from Canada, providing for payment of 10% royalties on Canadian sales of Blyton's book. Payment is to be made in Canadian dollars each January 10 for the previous year's sales. Canadian sales of the book for the year ended December 31, 1998, totalled $50,000 Canadian. Tyrola paid Blyton his 1998 royalties on January 10, 1999. Tyrola's 1998 financial statements were issued on February 1, 1999. Spot rates for Canadian dollars were as follows:

November 30, 1997	$.87
January 1, 1998	$.88
December 31, 1998	$.89
January 10, 1999	$.90

How much should Tyrola accrue for royalties payable at December 31, 1998?

    a. $4,350
    b. $4,425
    c. $4,450
    d. $4,500

15. Shore Co. records its transactions in US dollars. A sale of goods resulted in a receivable denominated in Japanese yen, and a purchase of goods resulted in a payable denominated in French francs. Shore recorded a foreign exchange transaction gain on collection of the receivable and an exchange transaction loss on settlement of the payable. The exchange rates are expressed as so many units of foreign currency to one dollar. Did the number of foreign currency units exchangeable for a dollar increase or decrease between the contract and settlement dates?

	Yen exchangeable for $1	*Francs exchangeable for $1*
a.	Increase	Increase
b.	Decrease	Decrease
c.	Decrease	Increase
d.	Increase	Decrease

16. On October 1, 1998, Mild Co., a US company, purchased machinery from Grund, a German company, with

payment due on April 1, 1999. If Mild's 1998 operating income included no foreign exchange transaction gain or loss, then the transaction could have
    a.   Resulted in an extraordinary gain.
    b.   Been denominated in US dollars.
    c.   Caused a foreign currency gain to be reported as a contra account against machinery.
    d.   Caused a foreign currency translation gain to be reported as other comprehensive income.

17. On October 1, 1999, Velec Co., a US company, contracted to purchase foreign goods requiring payment in francs 1 month after their receipt at Velec's factory. Title to the goods passed on December 15, 1999. The goods were still in transit on December 31, 1999. Exchange rates were one dollar to 22 francs, 20 francs, and 21 francs on October 1, December 15, and December 31, 1999, respectively. Velec should account for the exchange rate fluctuation in 1999 as
    a.   A loss included in net income before extraordinary items.
    b.   A gain included in net income before extraordinary items.
    c.   An extraordinary gain.
    d.   An extraordinary loss.

OTHER OBJECTIVE QUESTIONS

Problem 1   (15 to 25 minutes)

This question consists of 9 items that relate to foreign currency translation. On the CPA Exam, candidates will be instructed to select the best answer for each item. Use a No. 2 pencil to blacken the appropriate ovals on the Objective Answer Sheet to indicate your answers. **Answer all items**. Your grade will be based on the total number of correct answers.

Required:

Items 1 through 9 are based on the following:

A foreign subsidiary's trial balance is translated from its functional currency to the functional currency of the parent.

For each item determine which date the exchange rate from table A should be used for the translation. The subsidiary's functional currency is its **local** currency.

TABLE A

	Event	Date
a.	Company begins	12/31/94
b.	Beginning of current year	1/1/97
c.	1st quarter	4/1/97
d.	2nd quarter	7/1/97
e.	3rd quarter	10/1/97
f.	Year end	12/31/97
g.	1st quarter	4/1/98
h.	Year average	
i.	Average since acquisition	
j.	No translation rate used	

1. Cash

2. Inventory which had been purchased evenly through the year

3. Account payable for equipment purchased on 4/1/97

4. Cost of goods sold

5. Sales

6. Dividends declared on 10/1/97

7. Dividends declared in **6.** above were paid 1/2/98

8. Retained earnings

9. Common stock

PROBLEM

Problem 1   (15 to 25 minutes)

Jay Co.'s 1999 consolidated financial statements include two wholly owned subsidiaries, Jay Co. of Australia (Jay A) and Jay Co. of France (Jay F). Functional currencies are the US dollar for Jay A and the franc for Jay F.

Required:

a.   What are the objectives of translating a foreign subsidiary's financial statements?

b.   How are gains and losses arising from translating or remeasuring of each subsidiary's financial statements measured and reported in Jay's consolidated financial statements?

c.   FASB Statement 52 identifies several economic indicators that are to be considered both individually and collectively in determining the functional currency for a consolidated subsidiary. List three of those indicators.

d.   What exchange rate is used to incorporate each subsidiary's equipment cost, accumulated depreciation, and depreciation expense in Jay's consolidated financial statements?

MULTIPLE-CHOICE ANSWERS

1. c __ __	5. a __ __	9. c __ __	13. d __ __	17. b __ __
2. c __ __	6. b __ __	10. d __ __	14. c __ __	
3. c __ __	7. a __ __	11. a __ __	15. b __ __	1st: __/17 = __%
4. b __ __	8. b __ __	12. b __ __	16. b __ __	2nd: __/17 = __%

MULTIPLE-CHOICE ANSWER EXPLANATIONS

A.2.   Translation of Foreign Currency Statements

1. (c) When the **functional currency** of a foreign subsidiary is the **foreign currency**, asset and liability accounts are **translated** using the **current** exchange rate (the rate of translation in effect at the balance sheet date). Therefore, these accounts should be included in the balance sheet at $475,000. Note that if the **functional currency** was the **US dollar**, balance sheet accounts would be **remeasured** using a combination of **historical and current rates**.

2. (c) The requirement is to determine the total amount of various expenses incurred by a foreign subsidiary which should be reported in the 1999 consolidated income statement. SFAS 52 states that if the foreign currency is the functional currency of the subsidiary, the **current rate** method should be used to translate the financial statements. In this method, revenues and expenses are translated at the rates in effect at the time these items were recognized during the period. Because translation at the date the revenues and expenses were recognized is generally deemed impractical, SFAS 52 allows that an appropriate weighted-average rate may be used to translate these items. This results in a translated expense of $176,000 [($120,000 + $80,000 + $200,000) x .44].

3. (c) The requirement is to determine which item is reported in the stockholders' equity section. According to SFAS 52, para 20, and SFAS 130, accumulated gains and losses on certain foreign currency transactions should be reported as a component of stockholders' equity entitled other comprehensive income. Therefore answer (c) is correct. Answers (a), (b), and (d) are incorrect because these items are reported on the balance sheet in the assets and liabilities sections and are amortized over their respective lives.

4. (b) SFAS 52, para 12, mandates the current rate method for the translation of foreign currency financial statements when a foreign subsidiary's functional currency is its local currency. Using the current rate method, revenue and expenses should be translated into US dollars at the weighted-average rate for the current year. Thus, both sales to customers and wages expense should be translated at the weighted-average rate, and answer (b) is correct.

5. (a) According to SFAS 52, para 13, and SFAS 130, translation adjustments resulting from the translation of foreign currency statements should be reported separately as components of other comprehensive income, accumulated other comprehensive income, and stockholders' equity. Additionally, per para 20, gains and losses on certain foreign currency transactions should also be reported similarly.

Those gains and losses which should be excluded from net income and instead reported as components of other comprehensive income and of accumulated other comprehensive income in stockholders' equity include foreign currency transactions designated as economic hedges of a net investment in a foreign entity. Thus, both the translation loss and the exchange gain are to be reported as other comprehensive income and accumulated other comprehensive income in the stockholders' equity section of the balance sheet. Because the translation loss on the investment exceeds the exchange gain on the borrowing, the translation loss less the exchange gain is the amount to be reported as separate components of other comprehensive income and accumulated other comprehensive income equity in the consolidated financial statements. Therefore, answer (a) is correct.

6. (b) Per SFAS 12, para 13, **translation** adjustments result from translating an entity's financial statements into the reporting currency. Such adjustments, which result when the entity's functional currency is the **foreign currency**, should not be included in net income. Instead, such adjustments should be reported as other comprehensive income and accumulated other comprehensive income in the stockholders' equity section of the balance sheet. If the functional currency is the **reporting currency** (US dollar), a **remeasurement** process takes place, with the resulting gain or loss included in net income. Therefore, answer (b) is correct.

7. (a) The requirement is to determine which item would be remeasured using historical exchange rates when foreign currency financial statements are being remeasured into the functional currency. Per SFAS 52, para 47, when an entity's books are not maintained in the functional currency, it is necessary to use historical exchange rates in the remeasurement process of certain accounts. Among the accounts listed is inventories carried at cost. Therefore, answer (a) is correct. Answer (b) is incorrect as only marketable equity securities reported at **cost** would be remeasured using historical exchange rates. Answers (c) and (d) are incorrect because bonds payable and accrued liabilities would be remeasured at the current rate.

8. (b) Schnell's accounting records are kept in German marks, and its functional currency is the Swiss franc. Before Schnell's financial statements can be consolidated with Park's financial statements, they must be remeasured from German marks to Swiss francs, and then translated from Swiss francs to US dollars. As a result of these restatements, there is a remeasurement gain of $7,600, and a credit translation adjustment of $8,100. SFAS 52 states that a remeasurement gain or loss is included in net income, but a translation adjustment is **not**. Therefore, Park would report a foreign exchange gain of $7,600 in its 1999 income statement.

A.3.a.   Translation

9.   (c)   When the **sale is made** on 10/15/99, Bain would record a receivable and sales at $100,000, the US dollar equivalent on that date.

Accounts receivable	100,000	
Sales		100,000

On 11/16/99, Bain receives foreign currency worth $105,000. Since the receivable was recorded at $100,000, a $5,000 gain must be recorded.

Foreign currency	105,000	
Accounts receivable		100,000
Foreign exchange transaction gain		5,000

The US dollar equivalent when the order was received on 9/1/99 ($96,000) is not used to compute the gain because no entry is recorded on this date. The receipt and acceptance of a purchase order from a customer is an executory commitment which is not generally recorded.

10.   (d)   On 9/1/98, Cano obtained a receivable which will be collected in a foreign currency. Para 15 of SFAS 52 states that a gain (loss) will result if the exchange rate on the settlement date is different from the rate existing on the transaction date. Para 15 further states that a gain (loss) must be recognized at any intervening balance sheet dates, if necessary. Therefore, Cano would recognize a $2,500 foreign exchange transaction loss in its **1998** income statement since a change in the exchange rate reduced the receivable (in US dollars) from $50,000 on 9/1/98 (250,000 x $.20) to $47,500 on 12/31/98 (250,000 x $.19). In **1999**, a foreign exchange transaction gain of $7,500 is recognized because the receivable (in US dollars) increased from $47,500 on 12/31/98 to $55,000 when received (250,000 x $.22).

11.   (a)   A transaction has occurred in which settlement will be made in German marks. Since Lindy's functional currency is the US dollar, a foreign exchange transaction gain (loss) will result if the spot rate on the settlement date is different than the rate on the transaction date (SFAS 52, para 15). Para 15 also states that a provision must be made at any intervening year-end date if there has been a rate change. Thus, in 1998, a $500 foreign exchange transaction gain [100,000 x ($.4295 – $.4245)] would be recognized, while in 1998 a $1,000 foreign exchange transaction loss [100,000 x ($.4245 – $.4345)] would be recognized.

12.   (b)   A purchase has been made for which payment will be made in British pounds. A foreign exchange transaction gain or loss will result if the spot rate on the settlement date is different from the rate used on the transaction date. SFAS 52 states that a gain or loss must also be recorded at any intervening balance sheet date if there has been a rate change. Thus, at 12/31/98, a foreign exchange transaction gain of $9,000 is recognized [300,000 x ($1.65 – $1.62)] as the foreign currency payable is reduced from

$495,000 (300,000 x $1.65) to $486,000 (300,000 x $1.62). The 30-day and 60-day rates would affect Hunt only if the company had entered into forward contracts.

13.   (d)   On 1/20/98, Ball would record purchases and accounts payable at $90,000. When the account was paid, the equivalent of $96,000 was required to liquidate the $90,000 liability, resulting in a foreign exchange transaction loss of $6,000. Para 15 of SFAS 52 requires that foreign exchange transaction gains (losses) also be recognized at intervening balance sheet dates. The note payable originally recorded at $500,000 was equivalent to a liability of $520,000 at the balance sheet date, resulting in a 1998 loss of $20,000. The interest payable of $25,000 ($500,000 x 10% x 6/12) was equivalent to a liability of $26,000 at year end, resulting in an additional 1998 loss of $1,000. Therefore, the total 1998 foreign exchange transaction loss is $27,000 ($6,000 + $20,000 + $1,000).

14.   (c)   The requirement is to determine the amount which Tyrola should accrue for royalties payable, 12/31/98. This situation is a foreign currency transaction in which settlement is denominated in other than a company's functional currency (SFAS 52, paras 5 and 15). In this case the functional currency is the US dollar because it is the currency of the primary economic environment in which the Colorado firm operates. Note that in this royalty agreement, 12/31/98 is the point at which the amount due to the author (50,000 Canadian dollars x 10% = 5,000 Canadian dollars) is determined. Royalty expense is measured and the related liability is denominated at 12/31/98. The year-end accrual would be

.89 (10% x 50,000 Canadian dollars) = $4,450.

On January 10, 1999, Tyrola will have to purchase 5,000 Canadian dollars for payment to the Canadian author. The amount of US dollars required to accomplish this will depend on the spot rate on January 10th ($.90 in this case). The number of US dollars required to satisfy the obligation will be $50 greater [($.90 – .89) x 5,000 Canadian dollars]. This will result in a $50 foreign exchange transaction loss which would be included in 1999 net income.

15.   (b)   In the case of the receivable denominated in Japanese yen, a foreign exchange transaction gain was recorded on the collection of the receivable. This means that more yen was received than was recorded in the receivable account. For that to happen the rate of yen exchangeable for a dollar would have had to decrease, requiring more yen to be paid at the settlement date for the same amount of dollars at the contract date. On the other hand, there was a foreign exchange transaction loss on the payable denominated in French francs. This means that at the settlement date Shore Co. had to pay more francs than were recorded in the payable account. For this to occur the rate of francs exchangeable for a dollar would have had to decrease, requiring more francs to be paid at the settlement date for the same amount of dollars at the contract date. Therefore, answer (b) is correct.

16.   (b)   Per SFAS 52, para 15, a transaction that is denominated in a currency other than the entity's functional currency, which is payable at a fixed amount at a later date, may result in an increased or decreased amount payable, because of a change in the exchange rate. This increase/decrease would be classified as a foreign exchange transaction gain/loss, and would be included as a component of income. Therefore answer (b) is correct. Answer (a) is incorrect because the gain/loss would not be considered extraordinary. Answers (c) and (d) are incorrect because the foreign exchange transaction gain/loss are recognized as net income, not as a contra asset account or in other comprehensive income.

17.   (b)   The requirement is to determine how Velec should account for the exchange rate fluctuation in 1999. A foreign currency transaction, according to SFAS 52, is a transaction denominated in a currency other than the entity's functional currency. Denominated means that the balance is fixed in terms of the number of units of a foreign currency, regardless of changes in the exchange rate. When a US company buys or sells to an unrelated foreign company, and the US company agrees either to pay for goods or receive payment for the goods in foreign currency units, this is a foreign currency transaction from the point of view of the US company (the functional currency is the US dollar). In these situations, the US company has "crossed currencies" and directly assumes the risk of fluctuating foreign exchange rates of the foreign currency units. As exchange rates fluctuate, a company will record an ordinary gain or loss on their income statement, **not** an extraordinary gain or loss. Therefore, answers (c) and (d) are incorrect. Answer (b) is correct because Velec has an accounts payable denominated in a foreign currency (francs) as of December 15, the date the title to the goods passes to Velec. As the value of the franc per dollar rises above 20 francs per dollar, Velec Co. will have to come up with less dollars to pay off the payable, as of December 31, 1999, than they would have on December 15, 1999. This creates a foreign exchange transaction gain. As shown numerically, if 4000 francs are assumed as being payable, on December 15 you would need $200 (4000/20) to pay off the payable. However, on December 31, $190 would be needed (4000/21). The difference between $200 and $190 represents the gain. Answer (a) is incorrect because a foreign exchange transaction gain should be included in net income, not a loss.

OTHER OBJECTIVE ANSWER EXPLANATIONS

Problem 1

1. **(F)**   Assets are valued at the current rate at year end.

2. **(F)**   Assets are valued at the current rate at year end.

3. **(F)**   Liabilities are valued at the current rate at year end.

4. **(H)**   Expense accounts are valued at the average rate for the current year of business.

5. **(H)**   Revenue accounts are valued at the average rate for the current year of business.

6. **(E)**   Dividends are valued at the rate of the date of declaration.

7. **(F)**   Liabilities (dividends payable) are valued at the current rate at year end.

8. **(J)**   The retained earnings are carried over from 1/1/97 with the translated net income added and translated dividends subtracted.

9. **(A)**   Common stock is valued at the historical rate when it was issued.

ANSWER OUTLINE

Problem 1   Foreign Currency Remeasurement and
                Translation

a.   Objectives of translating foreign sub's FS
      Provide information compatible with economic ef-
        fects of rate change on sub's cash flows and equity
      Reflect sub's financial results and relationships in
        consolidated FS
          Measured in its functional currency
            In conformity with GAAP

b.   Gain (loss) is amount required to bring restated FS into
      balance
      Gain (loss) from **remeasuring** Jay A's FS reported in
        consolidated IS
      Gain (loss) from **translating** Jay F's FS reported as
        other comprehensive income and in BS as accumu-
        lated other comprehensive income under SE

c.   Economic indicators used to determine functional cur-
      rency
        Cash flow indicators
        Sales price indicators
        Sales market indicators
        Expense indicators
        Financing indicators
        Intercompany transactions and arrangement indica-
          tors

d.   **Jay A's equipment and related accounts**
        Remeasured by exchange rate prevailing between
          US and Australian dollars on date equipment pur-
          chased
      Jay F's equipment and related accounts
        Translated using current exchange rates prevailing
          between US dollar and French franc
            For equipment cost and AD, use exchange rate at
              12/31/99
            For depreciation expense, use rate on date expense
              recognized or use average rate for 1999

UNOFFICIAL ANSWER

Problem 1   Foreign Currency Remeasurement and
                Translation

a.   The objectives of translating a foreign subsidiary's
financial statements are to

   • Provide information that is generally compatible with
the expected economic effects of a rate change on a
subsidiary's cash flows and equity.

   • Reflect the subsidiary's financial results and relationships in single currency consolidated financial statements, as measured in its functional currency and in conformity with GAAP.

b.   Applying different exchange rates to the various financial statement accounts causes the restated statements to be
unbalanced. The amount required to bring the restated
statements into balance is termed the gain or loss from the
translation or remeasurement. The gain or loss arising from
remeasuring Jay A's financial statements is reported in the
consolidated income statement. The gain or loss arising
from translating Jay F's financial statements is reported as
other comprehensive income and in the balance sheet as
accumulated other comprehensive income under stockholders' equity.

c.   The functional currency is the foreign currency or parent's currency that most closely correlates with the following economic indicators:

   • Cash flow indicators
   • Sales price indicators
   • Sales market indicators
   • Expense indicators
   • Financing indicators
   • Intercompany transactions and arrangement indi-
     cators

d.   All accounts relating to Jay A's equipment are remeasured by the exchange rate prevailing between the US and
Australian dollars at the time equipment was purchased.

   All accounts relating to Jay F's equipment are translated by the current exchange rates prevailing between the
US dollar and French franc. For the equipment cost and
accumulated depreciation this is the current exchange rate at
December 31, 1999. Depreciation expense is translated at
the rate prevailing on the date the depreciation expense was
recognized or an appropriate weighted-average exchange
rate for 1999.

B. Derivative Instruments and Hedging Activities

Hedging activities and the use of derivative instruments has increased dramatically in the past few years. This increase has raised the concern that inconsistent and/or improper accounting treatment could occur, even in the case of identical hedging/derivative activities. As a result, in June 1998 the FASB issued Statement of Financial Accounting Standards 133, *Accounting for Derivative Instruments and Hedging Activities.*

1. **Foundation Principles for SFAS 133**--The basic principles driving the structure of SFAS 133 are

   a. **Fair value measurement.** Derivative instruments meet the definition of assets and liabilities (probable future economic benefits or sacrifices of future economic benefits resulting from past transactions or events). As such they should be reported on an entity's financial statements. The most relevant measure for reporting financial instruments is "fair value." SFAS 133 borrowed the definition for fair value from SFAS 107, *Disclosures About Fair Value of Financial Instruments.* That standard defines fair value as the "current amount at which a financial instrument could be exchanged in a transition between willing parties." As a corollary to this principle, gains and losses that result from the change in the fair value of derivative instruments are **not** assets and liabilities. Therefore, gains and losses should not be reported on the balance sheet but rather should either appear in comprehensive income or be reported in current earnings. The details for reporting gains and losses appear in a subsequent section.

   b. **Hedging.** Certain derivative instruments will qualify under the definition of hedging instruments. Those that qualify will be accounted for using hedge accounting, which generally provides for matching the recognition of gains and losses of the hedging instrument and the hedged asset or liability. (More details about hedge accounting are provided in a later section.) Three kinds of hedges have been defined in the standard.

      (1) Fair value hedge--a hedge of the exposure to changes in the fair value of (a) a recognized asset or liability, or (b) an unrecognized firm commitment.

      (2) Cash flow hedge--a hedge of the exposure to variability in the cash flows of (a) a recognized asset or liability, or (b) a forecasted transaction.

      (3) Foreign currency hedge--a hedge of the foreign currency exposure of (a) an unrecognized firm commitment, (b) an available-for-sale security, (c) a forecasted transaction, or (d) a net investment in a foreign operation.

   If a derivative instrument does not qualify as a hedging instrument under one of the three categories shown above, then its gains or losses must be reported and recognized in current earnings.

2. **Definition of a Derivative Instrument**--SFAS 133 identifies three distinguishing characteristics of a derivative instrument, **all** of which must be present for a financial instrument or other contract to be considered a derivative instrument.

   a. The financial instrument or other contract must contain (a) one or more underlyings, and (b) one or more notional amounts (or payment provisions or both). An underlying is any financial or physical variable that has either observable changes or objectively verifiable changes. Therefore, underlyings would include traditional financial measures such as commodity prices, interest rates, exchange rates, or indexes related to any of these items. More broadly, measures such as an entity's credit rating, rainfall, or temperature changes would also meet the definition of an underlying.

   Notional amounts are the "number of currency or other units" specified in the financial instrument or other contract. In the case of options, this could include bushels of wheat, shares of stock, etc. The settlement amount of a financial instrument or other contract is calculated using the underlying(s) and notional amount(s) in some combination. Computation of the settlement amount may be as simple as multiplying the fair value of a stock times a specified number of shares. On the other hand, calculation of the settlement amount may require a very complex calculation, involving ratios, stepwise variables, and other leveraging techniques.

NOTE: The term "notional amount" is sometimes used interchangeably with "settlement amount." Watch to determine if the context in which the term is used is calling for a number of units, notional amount, or a dollar value settlement amount.)

b. The financial instrument or other contract requires no initial net investment or an initial net investment that is smaller than would be required for other types of contracts that would be expected to have a similar response to changes in market factors. Many derivative instruments require no net investment or simply a premium as compensation for the time value of money. Futures contracts may require the establishment of a margin account with a balance equal to a small percentage (2% - 3%) of the value of the contract. A call option on a foreign currency contract would again only cost a small fraction of the value of the contract. These are typical contracts that would meet this definition and would be included in the definition of derivative instruments.

c. The terms of the financial instrument or other contract do one of the following with regard to settlement:

- Require or permit net settlement, either within the contract or by a means outside the contract. Net settlement means that a contract can be settled through the payment of cash rather than the exchange of the specific assets referenced in the contract. This type of settlement typically occurs with a currency swap or an interest rate swap. This definition may have some unanticipated consequences. For example, a contract with a liquidating damages clause for nonperformance, the amount of which is determined by an underlying, would meet this criterion. This is a prime example of the breadth of the definition of a derivative instrument for the purposes of SFAS 133.
- Provide for the delivery of an asset that puts the recipient in a position not substantially different from net settlement. This might include a futures contract where one party to the contract delivers an asset, but a "market mechanism" exists (such as an exchange) so that the asset can be readily converted to cash.. Convertibility to cash requires an active market and is a determining factor in whether or not a financial instrument or other contract will be treated as a derivative instrument.

3. **Inclusions In and Exclusions From Derivative Instruments**

Included	*Excluded*
• Options to purchase (call) or sell (put) exchange-traded securities	• Normal purchases and sales (does not exclude "take or pay" contracts with little or no initial net investment and products that are readily convertible to cash)
• Futures contracts	
• Interest rate swaps	• Equity securities
• Currency swaps	• Debt securities
• Swaptions (an option on a swap)	• Regular-way (3-day settlement) security trades (this exclusion applies to "to be announced" and "when issued" trades)
• Credit indexed contracts	
• Interest rate caps/floors/collars	• Leases
	• Mortgage-backed securities
	• Employee stock options
	• Royalty agreements and other contracts tied to sales volumes
	• Variable annuity contracts
	• Adjustable rate loans
	• Guaranteed investment contracts
	• Nonexchanged traded contracts tied to physical variables
	• Derivatives that serve as impediments to sales accounting (e.g., guaranteed residual value in a leasing arrangement)

4. **Embedded Derivative Instruments and Bifurcation**

   Financial instruments and other contracts may contain features which, if they stood alone, would meet the definition of a derivative instrument. These financial instruments and other contracts are known as "hybrid instruments." This means that there is a basic contract, known as the "host contract," that has an embedded derivative instrument. In these circumstances, the embedded derivative instrument may have to be separated from the host contract, a process known as bifurcation, and treated as if it were a stand-alone instrument. In this case, the host contract (excluding the embedded derivative) would be accounted for in the normal manner (as if it had never contained the embedded derivative), and the now stand-alone derivative instrument would be accounted for using SFAS 133.

   Three criteria are used to determine if bifurcation must occur. **All** criteria must be met.

   a. The embedded derivative meets the definition of a derivative instrument for the purposes of applying SFAS 133.
   b. The hybrid instrument is **not** regularly recorded at fair value, with changes reported in current earnings as they occur under other GAAP. If this is true, then there is no need to bifurcate the embedded derivative since the same end result is being accomplished already.
   c. The economic characteristics and risks of the embedded derivative instrument are **not** "clearly and closely related" to the economic characteristics and risks of the host contract.

5. **Hedging Instruments--General Criteria**

   Two primary criteria must be met in order for a derivative instrument to qualify as a hedging instrument.

   a. Sufficient documentation must be provided at the beginning of the process to identify at a minimum (1) the objective and strategy of the hedge, (2) the hedging instrument and the hedged item, and (3) how the effectiveness (see below) of the hedge will be assessed on an ongoing basis.
   b. The hedge must be "highly effective" throughout its life. At a minimum, its effectiveness will be measured every 3 months **and** whenever earnings or financial statements are reported. The method used to assess effectiveness must be used throughout the hedge period and must be consistent with the approach used for managing risk. Similar hedges should usually be assessed for effectiveness in a similar manner unless a different method can be justified.

6. **Fair Value Hedges**

   a. **Specific criteria.** The hedged asset/liability must meet certain criteria in order to qualify as a fair value hedge. The hedged item must be either all or a specific portion (e.g., a percentage, a contractual cash flow) of a recognized asset/liability or an unrecognized firm commitment. For an unrecognized firm commitment to qualify, it must be (1) binding on both parties, (2) specific with respect to all significant terms, and (3) contain a nonperformance clause that makes performance probable.
   b. **Accounting for a fair value hedge.** Under SFAS 133, gains and losses on the hedged asset/liability and the hedging instrument will be recognized in current earnings.

   EXAMPLE: On 10/1/99, Dover Corp. purchases 20 shares of Porter, Inc, stock at $40. The securities are classified as available-for-sale. The market price moves to $45 by the end of the year. In order to protect itself from a possible decline in the stock value of its available-for-sale security, Dover purchases an at-the-money put option for $300 on 12/31/99. The put option gives Dover the right, but not the obligation, to sell 200 shares of Porter stock at $45 per share, and the option expires on 12/31/01. Dover designates the hedge as a fair value hedge because it is hedging changes in the security's fair value. The fair value of an option is made up of two components, the time value and the intrinsic value. At the time of purchase, the time value is the purchase price of the options and the intrinsic value is $0 (because the option was pur-

chased at-the-money. Over the life of the option, the time value will drop to $0, and the intrinsic value will vary based on the current stock price vs. the stock price on the date the option was purchased. As is often the case, the intrinsic value of the option is considered to be a "highly effective" hedge against changes in the stock price, while the time value is ineffective and is reflected in current earnings. Additional information is provided below.

Item	1/1/99	12/31/99	12/31/00	12/31/01
Porter stock price	$40	$45	$44	$42
Put option				
Time value		$300	$160	$0
Intrinsic value		$0	$200	$600
			(200 x $1)	(200 x $3)

1/1/99

1. Available-for-sale securities   8,000
         Cash   8,000

    Record the purchase of Porter stock (200 x $40).

12/31/99

2. Available-for-sale securities   1,000
         Other comprehensive income   1,000

    Record the unrealized gain on Porter stock (accounting prior to the hedge in accordance with SFAS 115).
    (200 x $5 valuation increase from holding gain to market value)

3. Put option   300
         Cash   300

    Record the purchase of at-the-money put option.

12/31/00

4. Put option   200
         Gain on hedge activity   200

    Record the increase in the intrinsic value (fair value) of the option.

5. Loss on hedge activity   200
         Available-for-sale securities   200

    Record the decrease in the fair value of the securities (accounting after the hedge is established) $200 = 200 shares x $1 holding loss.
         Note that the $200 gain on hedge activity from the put option is balanced effectively against the $200 loss on hedge activity from the hedged available-for-sale security. SFAS 133 amends SFAS 115 to require that the portion of the unrealized holding gain or loss on an available-for-sale security that is designated as a hedged item in a fair value hedge be recognized in earnings during the period of the hedge. This is why the $200 holding loss on the available-for-sale securities is recognized in the period's earnings.

6. Loss on hedge activity   140
         Put option   140

    Record the loss related to the time value of the option.
    $140 = $300 − $160

12/31/01

7. Put option   400
         Gain on hedge activity   400

    Record the increase in the intrinsic value of the put option.

8. Loss on hedge activity   400
         Available-for-sale securities   400

To record the decrease in the fair value of the securities (accounting after the hedge is established); $400 = 200 Shares x $ holding loss on availabale-for-sale securities.

9. Loss on hedge activity   160
    Put option   160

Record the loss related to the time value of the option.
$140 = $300 − $160

10. Cash   9,000
    Put option   600
    Availablefor-sale securities   8,400

Record the exercise of the put option (sell the 200 shares of stock @ $45) and close out investment activity.

11. Other comprehensive income   1,000
    Gain on Porter stock   1,000

To reclassify the unrealized holding gain recognized in entry 2., from other comprehensive income to earnings, because the securitites were sold.

7. Cash Flow Hedges

a. **Specific criteria.** Additional criteria must be met in order to qualify as a cash flow hedge. The primary criterion is that the hedged asset/liability and the hedging instrument must be "linked." Linking is established if the basis (the specified rate or index) for the change in cash flows is the same for the hedged asset/liability and the hedging instrument. Cash flows do not have to be identical, but they must meet the highly effective threshold discussed above. In addition, if the hedged asset/liability is a **forecasted transaction**, it must be considered **probable**, based on appropriate facts and circumstances (i.e., past history). Also, if the forecasted hedged asset/liability is a series of transactions, they must "share the same risk exposure." Purchases of a particular product from the same supplier over a period of time would meet this requirement.

b. **Accounting for a cash flow hedge.** Under SFAS 133, for the hedging instrument (1) the effective portion is reported in other comprehensive income, and (2) the ineffective portion and/or excluded components are reported on a cumulative basis to reflect the lesser of (1) the cumulative gain/loss on the derivative since the creation of the hedge, or (2) the cumulative gain/loss from the change in expected cash flows from the hedged instrument since the creation of the hedge.

    The above amounts need to be adjusted to reflect any reclassification of other comprehensive income to current earnings. This will occur when the hedged asset/liability affects earnings (e.g., when hedged inventory is sold and the cost of inventory passes through to cost of goods sold).

EXAMPLE: A commercial bakery believes that wheat prices may increase over the next few months. To protect itself against this risk, the bakery purchases call options on wheat futures to hedge the price risk of their forecasted inventory purchases. If wheat prices increase, the profit on the purchased call options will offset the higher price the bakery must pay for the wheat. If wheat prices decline, the bakery will lose the premium it paid for the call options, but can then buy the wheat at the lower price. On June 1, 1999, the bakery pays a premium of $350 to purchase a September 30, 1999 call for 1,000 bushels of wheat at the futures price of $16.60 per bushel. The call option is considered a cash flow hedge because the designated risk that is being hedged is the risk of changes in the cash flows relating to changes in the purchase price of the wheat. On September 30, the bakery settles its call options and purchases wheat on the open market. Pertinent wheat prices are shown below.

Spot price (June 1)	$16.50
Futures price (as of June 1 for September 30)	$16.60
Spot price (September 30)	$17.30

June 1

1. Call option   350
    Cash   350

Record the purchase of the call option.

September 30

2. Loss on hedge activity   350
        Call option   350

    Record the expiration (change in time value) of the call option.

3. Call option   700
        Other comprehensive income   700

    Record the increase in intrinsic value of the call option.
    $700 = [1,000 bushels x ($17.30 – 16.60)]

4. Cash   700
        Call option   700

    Record the cash settlement of the call option.

5. Inventory   17,300
        Cash   17,300

    Record the purchase of the wheat at the spot price.
    $17,000 = 1,000 bushels x $17.30

8. **Foreign Currency Hedges**

    Generally, foreign currency denominated assets/liabilities are required to be translated using current exchange rates. As a result, no special hedge accounting is required to assure that gains and losses are offset throughout the use of hedging instruments. Normal accounting rules (i.e., SFAS 52) will suffice. SFAS 133 permits hedge accounting in four specific areas related to foreign currency hedges. The application of hedge accounting is generally more restrictive under SFAS 133 than it was under SFAS 52, but several exceptions exist. The four foreign currency hedges under SFAS 133 are discussed below.

    a. **Unrecognized firm commitment.** Either a derivative instrument or a nonderivative financial instrument (such as a receivable in a foreign currency) can be designated as a hedge of an unrecognized firm commitment attributable to changes in foreign currency exchange rates. If the requirements for a fair value hedge are met, then this hedging arrangement can be accounted for as a **fair value hedge,** discussed above.

    b. **Available-for-sale securities.** Prior to SFAS 133, a firm commitment to purchase a trading security and several transactions related to held-to-maturity securities were permitted to use hedging accounting under certain conditions. SFAS 133 has eliminated the use of hedge accounting for both trading and held-to-maturity securities (in many cases hedge accounting wasn't required anyway) and limited the use of hedge accounting to transactions for securities designated as available-for-sale. Derivative instruments can be used to hedge debt or equity available-for-sale securities. However, equity securities must meet two additional criteria.

        (1) They cannot be traded on an exchange denominated in the investor's functional currency.
        (2) Dividends must be denominated in the same foreign currency as is expected to be received on the sale of the security.

        If the above criteria are met, hedging instruments related to available-for-sale securities can be accounted for as **fair value hedges,** discussed above.

    c. **Foreign currency denominated forecasted transactions.** This is an expansion in the permitted use of hedge accounting under SFAS 133. Only derivative instruments can be designated as hedges of foreign currency denominated forecasted transactions. Hedge accounting is permissible for transactions between unrelated parties, and under special circumstances (not discussed here) for intercompany transactions. Hedging instruments related to foreign currency denominated forecasted transactions can be accounted for as **cash flow hedges,** discussed above.

    d. **Net investments in foreign operations.** The accounting for net investments in foreign operations has not changed from the SFAS 52 rules, except that the hedging instrument has to meet the new "effective" criterion. The change in the fair value of the hedging derivative is recorded in other comprehensive income which is then closed to the accumulated other comprehensive income account in the equity section of the balance sheet.

9. **Forward Exchange Contracts**

It was stated previously that foreign currency transaction gains and losses on assets and liabilities which are denominated in a currency other than the functional currency can be hedged if US Company enters into a forward exchange contract. In the above example, US Company could enter into a forward exchange contract on December 1 to sell 10,000 DM for a negotiated amount to a foreign exchange broker for future delivery on January 31, 2000. This forward contract is a hedge against the exposed asset position created by having accounts receivable denominated in DM.

The negotiated rate referred to above is called a futures or forward rate. In most cases, this futures rate is not identical to the spot rate at the date of the forward contract. The difference between the futures rate and the spot rate at the date of the forward contract is referred to as a discount or a premium. Any discount or premium must be amortized over the term of the forward contract, generally on a straight-line basis. The amortization of discount or premium is reflected in a separate revenue or expense account, not as an addition or subtraction to the foreign exchange transaction gain or loss amount. Under this treatment it is important to observe that no net foreign exchange gains or losses result if assets and liabilities denominated in foreign currency are completely hedged at the transaction date.

To illustrate the preceding discussion, consider the following additional information for the example previously covered.

> On December 1, 1999, US Company entered into a forward exchange contract to sell 10,000 DM on January 31, 2000, at $.505 per DM. The spot rate on December 1 is $.50 per DM.

The transactions which reflect the sale of goods and the forward exchange contract appear as follows:

Sale transaction entries			*Forward exchange contract entries* (Futures Rate 1 DM = $.505)		
12/01/99 (spot rate 1 DM = $.50)					
Accounts receivable--			Due from exchange broker (US dollars)	5,050	
West Germany	5,000		Due to exchange broker (DM)		5,000
Sales		5,000	Premium on forward contract		50
12/31/99 (spot rate 1 DM = $.52)					
Accounts receivable--			Foreign cur. trans. loss	200	
West Germany	200		Due to exchange broker (DM)		200
Foreign currency			Premium on forward contract	25	
transaction gain		200	Financial revenue		25
			($25 = $50/2 months)		
01/31/00 (spot rate 1 DM = $.51)					
Foreign currency	5,100		Due to exchange broker (DM)	5,200	
Foreign cur. trans. loss	100		Foreign currency		5,100
Accounts receivable--			Foreign cur. trans. gain		100
West Germany		5,200			
			Cash	5,050	
			Due from exchange broker (US dollars)		5,050
			Premium on contract	25	
			Financial revenue		25

The following points should be noted from the entries above:

1. The net foreign currency transaction gain/loss is zero. The account "Due from Exchange Broker" is fixed in terms of US dollars and this amount is not affected by changes in spot rates between the transaction and settlement dates. The account "Due to Exchange Broker" is fixed or denominated in DM. US Company owes the exchange broker 10,000 DM, and these must be delivered on January 31, 2000. Because this liability is denominated in DM, its amount is determined by spot rates. Since spot rates change, this liability changes in an amount equal to the changes in accounts receivable because both amounts are based on the same spot rates. These changes are reflected as foreign currency transaction gains and losses which net to zero.

2. The "Premium on Forward Contract" is fixed in terms of US dollars. This amount is amortized on a straight-line basis to a financial revenue account over the life of the forward contract.

3. The net effect of this transaction is that $5,050 was received on January 31, 2000, for a sale originally recorded at $5,000. The $50 difference was taken into income via amortization of the premium or forward contract.

10. Disclosures

Disclosures related to financial instruments, both derivative and nonderivative, that are used as hedging instruments must include the following information: (1) objectives and the strategies for achieving them, (2) context to understand the instrument, (3) risk management policies, and (4) a list of hedged instruments. These disclosures have to be separated by type of hedge and reported every time a complete set of financial statements is issued. In addition, disclosure requirements exist for derivative instruments that are not designated as hedging instruments.

11. Fair Value and Credit Risk Disclosures of Financial Instruments Other Than Derivatives

SFAS 107, as amended by SFAS 133, requires disclosure of fair values of financial instruments for which it is practicable to estimate fair value (see outline of SFAS 107). This requirement pertains to both asset and liability financial instruments, whether recognized in the balance sheet or not.

A sample footnote is provided below. Additionally a summary of SFAS 107 is presented in the following chart.

Additionally, SFAS 107 requires disclosure of concentrations of credit risk. Credit risk is the risk that a loss will occur because parties to the instrument do not perform as expected. Such concentrations exist when a number of an entity's financial instruments are associated with similar activities and economic characteristics that could be affected by changes in similar conditions (e.g., an entity whose principal activity is to supply parts to one type of industry).

Lenaburg, Inc.
Notes to Financial Statements

FAIR VALUE OF FINANCIAL INSTRUMENTS HELD OR ISSUED FOR PURPOSES OTHER THAN TRADING (in thousands)

	December 31, 1998	
	Carrying amount	*Fair value*
Assets		
Cash and cash equivalents	32,656	32,656
Long-term investments	12,719	14,682
Liabilities		
Short-term debt	3,223	3,223
Long-term debt	150,000	182,500

FAIR VALUE OF FINANCIAL INSTRUMENTS HELD FOR TRADING PURPOSES (in thousands)

	December 31, 1998	
	Carrying amount	*Fair value*
Assets		
Short-term investments	4,074	4,074

Cash and cash equivalents--The carrying amount of cash and cash equivalents approximates fair value due to their short-term maturities.

Long-term investments--The fair value is estimated based on quoted market prices for these or similar investments.

Short-term investments--The Company holds US Treasury notes and highly liquid investments for trading purposes. The carrying value of these instruments approximates fair value.

Short- and long-term debt--The fair value of short- and long-term debt is estimated using quoted market prices for the same or similar instruments or on the current rates offered to the Company for debt of equivalent remaining maturities.

Summary of Disclosure Standards for Financial Instruments Other Than Derivatives

SFAS	Pertains to	Required disclosures
107	Financial Instruments (Assets and Liabilities), Whether on Balance Sheet or Not	• Fair value, when practicable to estimate • Information pertinent to estimating fair value (carrying value, effective interest rate, maturity) if not practicable to estimate, and reasons for impracticability of estimation • Distinguish between instruments held or issued for trading purposes and instruments held or issued for purposes other than trading • Do not net or aggregate fair values of derivative financial instruments with fair values of nonderivative financial instruments or with fair values of other derivative financial instruments
	Financial Instruments With Concentrations of Credit Risk	• Information about similar activity, region, or economic characteristics • Maximum potential accounting loss • Information about collateral or security requirements

Glossary

SFAS 133 defines a number of important terms which are used to describe various derivative instruments and hedging relationships. These include the following:

At the money. An at the money option is one in which the price of the underlying is equal to the strike or exercise price.

Call option. An American call option provides the holder the right to acquire an underlying at an exercise or strike price, anytime during the option term. A premium is paid by the holder for the right to benefit form the appreciation in the underlying.

Derivative instruments. In SFAS 133, derivative instruments are defined by their three distinguishing characteristics. Specifically, derivative instruments are financial instruments or other contracts that have

1. One or more underlyings and one or more notional amounts (or payment provisions or both);

2. No initial net investment or a smaller net investment than required for contracts expected to have a similar response to market changes; and
3. Terms that require or permit

   a. Net settlement
   b. Net settlement by means outside the contract
   c. Delivery of an asset that results in a position substantially the same as net settlement

Fair value. Defined as the amount at which the asset or liability could be bought or settled in an arm's-length transaction; measured by reference to market prices or estimated by net present value of future cash flows, options pricing models, or by other techniques.

Firm commitment. An agreement with an unrelated party, binding on both, usually legally enforceable, specifying all significant terms and including a disincentive for nonperformance sufficient to make performance likely.

Forecasted transaction. A transaction expected to occur for which there is no firm commitment, and thus, which gives the entity no present rights or obligations. Under SFAS 133, forecasted transactions can be hedged and special hedge accounting can be applied.

Forward contract. A forward contract is an agreement between two parties to buy and sell a specific quantity of a commodity, foreign currency, or financial instrument at aan agreed upon price, with delivery and/or settlement at a designated future date. Because a forward contract is not formally regulated by an organized exchange, each party to the contract is subject to the default of the other party.

Futures contract. A futures contract is a forward-based contract to make or take delivery of a designated financial instrument, foreign currency, or commodity during a designated period, at a specified price or yield. The contract frquently has provisions for cash settlement. A futures contract is traded on a regulated exchange and, therefore, involves less credit risk than a forward contract.

Initial net investment. A derivative instrument is one where the initial net investment is zero or is less than the notional amount (possibly plus a premium or minus a discount). This characteristic refers to the relative amount of investment. Derivative instruments allow the opportunity to take part in the rate or price change without owning the asset or owing the liability. If an amount approximating the notional amount must be invested or received, it is not a derivative instrument. The two basic forms of derivative instruments are futures contracts and options. The futures contract involves little or no initial net investment. Settlement is usually near the delivery date. Call options, when purchased, require a premium payment that is less than the cost of purchasing the equivalent number of shares. Even though this distinguishing characteristic is the result of only one of the parties, it determines the application for both.

In the money. A call option is in the money if the price of the underlying is greater than the strike or exercise price of the underlying.

Intrinsic value. With regard to call (put) options, it is the larger of zero or the spread between the stock (exercise) price and the exercise (stock) price.

Libor. London Interbank Offer Rate.

Net settlements. To qualify as a derivative instruments, one of the following settlement criteria must be met:

1. No delivery of an asset equal to the notional amount is required. For example, an interest rate swap does not involve delivery of the instrument in which the notional amount is expressed.
2. Delivery of an asset equal to the notional amount is required of one of the parties, but an exchange (or other market mechanism, institutional arrangement or side agreement) facilitates net settlement. For example, a call option has this attribute.
3. Delivery by one of the parties of an asset equal to the notional amount is required but the asset is either readily convertible to cash (as with a contract for the delivery of a marketable equity security), or is required but that asset is itself a derivative instrument (as is the case for a swaption [an option on a swap]).

This characteristic means that the derivative instrument can be settled by a net delivery of assets (the medium of exchange does not have to be cash). Contract terms based on changes in the price or rate of the notional that implicitly or explicitly require or permit net settlement qualify. Situations where one of the parties can liquidate their net investment or be relieved of the contract rights or obligations without significant transaction costs because of a market arrangement (broadly interpreted) or where the delivered asset can be readily converted to cash also meet the requirements for net settlement. It is assumed that an exchange traded security is readily converted to cash. Thus, commodity-based contracts for gold, oil, wheat, etc. are now included under this standard. The convertible to cash condition requires an active market and consideration of interchangeability and transaction volume. Determining if delivery of a financial asset or liability equal to the notional amount is a derivative instrument may depend upon whether it is readily convertible into cash. Different accounting will result if the notional is not readily converted to cash. Using the notional as collateral does not necessarily mean it is readily convertible to cash.

Notional amount. The notional amount (or payment provision) is the referenced associated asset or liability. A notional amount is commonly a number of units such as shares of stock, principal amount, face value, stated value, basis points, barrels of oil, etc. It may be that amount plus a premium or minus a discount. The interaction of the price or rate (underlying) with the referenced associated asset or liability (notional amount) determines whether settlement is required and, if so, the amount.

Out of the money. A call option is out of the money if the strike or exercise price is greater than the price of the underlying. A put option is out of the money if the price of the underlying is greater than the strike or exercise price.

Put option. An American put option provides the holder the right to sell the underlying at an exercise or strike price, anytime during the option term a gain accrues to the holder as the market price of the underlying falls below the strike price.

Swap. A swap is a forward-based contract or agreement generally between two counterparties to exchange streams of cash flows over a specified period in the future.

Swaption. A swaption is an option on a swap that provides the holder with the right to enter into a swap at a specified future date at specified terms (freestanding option on a swap) or to extend or terminate the life of an existing swap (embedded option on a swap.) These derivatives have characteristics of an option and an interest rate swap.

Time value. The difference between an option's price and its intrinsic value.

Underlyings. An underlying is commonly a specified price or rate such as a stock price, interest rate, currency rate, commodity price, or a related index. However, any variable (financial or physical) with (a) observable changes or (b) objectively verifiable changes such as a credit rating, insurance index, climatic or geological condition (temperature, rainfall) qualifies. Unless it is specifically excluded, a contract based on any qualifying variable is accounted for under SFAS 133 if it has distinguishing characteristics 2 and 3 above.

MULTIPLE-CHOICE QUESTIONS (1-16)

1. Derivatives are financial instruments that derive their value from changes in a benchmark based on any of the following except
   a. Stock prices.
   b. Mortgage and currency rates.
   c. Commodity prices.
   d. Discounts on accounts receivable.

2. Which of the following risks are inherent in an interest rate swap agreement?
   I. The risk of exchanging a lower interest rate for a higher interest rate.
   II. The risk of nonperformance by the counterparty to the agreement.

   a. I only.
   b. II only.
   c. Both I and II.
   d. Neither I nor II.

3. According to SFAS 133, which of the following meet the definition of assets and/or liabilities?

	Derivative instruments	G/L on the fair value of derivatives
a.	Yes	No
b.	No	Yes
c.	Yes	Yes
d.	No	No

4. Which of the following is not an underlying, according to SFAS 133?
   a. A credit rating.
   b. An interest rate index.
   c. A security price.
   d. An average daily temperature.
   e. All of the above could be underlyings.

5. Which of the following financial instruments or other contracts is not specifically excluded from the definition of derivative instruments in SFAS 133?
   a. Leases.
   b. Call (put) option.
   c. Adjustable rate loans.
   d. Equity securities.

6. Gains and losses of the effective portion of a hedging instrument will be recognized in current earnings in each of the reporting period for which of the following?

	Fair value hedge	Cash flow hedge
a.	Yes	No
b.	Yes	Yes
c.	No	No
d.	No	Yes

7. Which of the following foreign currency transactions is not accounted for using hedge accounting?
   a. Available-for-sale securities.
   b. Unrecognized firm commitments.
   c. Net investments in foreign operations.
   d. Foreign currency denominated forecasted transactions.

Items 8 through 10 are based on the following:

On December 12, 1999, Imp Co. entered into three forward exchange contracts, each to purchase 100,000 francs in 90 days. The relevant exchange rates are as follows:

	Spot rate	Forward rate (for March 12, 2000)
December 12, 1999	$.88	$.90
December 31, 1999	.98	.93

8. Imp entered into the first forward contract to hedge a purchase of inventory in November 1999, payable in March 2000. At December 31, 1999, what amount of foreign currency transaction gain from this forward contract should Imp include in net income?
   a. $0
   b. $ 3,000
   c. $ 5,000
   d. $10,000

9. Imp entered into the second forward contract to hedge a commitment to purchase equipment being manufactured to Imp's specifications. The expected delivery date is March 2000 at which time settlement is due to the manufacturer. The hedge qualifies as a fair value hedge. At December 31, 1999, what amount of foreign currency transaction gain from this forward contract should Imp include in net income?
   a. $0
   b. $ 3,000
   c. $ 5,000
   d. $10,000

10. Imp entered into the third forward contract for speculation. At December 31, 1999, what amount of foreign currency transaction gain from this forward contract should Imp include in net income?
   a. $0
   b. $ 3,000
   c. $ 5,000
   d. $10,000

11. On September 1, 1999, Brady Corp. entered into a foreign exchange contract for speculative purposes by purchasing 50,000 deutsche marks for delivery in 60 days. The rates to exchange $1 for one deutsche mark follow:

	9/1/99	9/30/99
Spot rate	.75	.70
30-day forward rate	.73	.72
60-day forward rate	.74	.73

In its September 30, 1999 net income, what amount should Brady report as foreign exchange transaction loss?
   a. $2,500
   b. $1,500
   c. $1,000
   d. $ 500

12. If it is **not** practicable for an entity to estimate the fair value of a financial instrument, which of the following should be disclosed?

I.   Information pertinent to estimating the fair value of the financial instrument.
II. The reasons it is not practicable to estimate fair value.

   a. I only.
   b. II only.
   c. Both I and II.
   d. Neither I nor II.

13. Disclosure requirements for financial instruments include
   a. Method(s) and significant assumptions used in estimating fair value.
   b. Distinction between financial instruments held or issued for trading purposes and purposes other than trading.
   c. A note containing a summary table cross-referencing the location of other financial instruments disclosed in another area of the financial statements.
   d. All of the above should be disclosed.

14. Disclosure of credit risk of financial instruments with off-balance-sheet risk does **not** have to include
   a. The amount of accounting loss the entity would incur should any party to the financial instrument fail to perform.
   b. The entity's policy of requiring collateral or security.
   c. The class of financial instruments held.
   d. The specific names of the parties associated with the financial instrument.

15. Disclosure of information about significant concentrations of credit risk is required for
   a. All financial instruments.
   b. Financial instruments with off-balance-sheet credit risk only.
   c. Financial instruments with off-balance-sheet market risk only.
   d. Financial instruments with off-balance-sheet risk of accounting loss only.

16. Kline Bank has large amounts of notes receivable from companies with high debt-to-equity ratios as a result of buyout transactions. Kline is contemplating the following disclosures for the notes receivable in its year-end financial statements:

I.   Information about shared activity, region, or economic characteristic.
II. A brief description of collateral supporting these financial instruments.

Which of the above disclosures are required under GAAP?
   a. I only.
   b. II only.
   c. Neither I nor II.
   d. Both I and II.

MULTIPLE-CHOICE ANSWERS

1. d __ __	5. b __ __	9. d __ __	13. d __ __	
2. c __ __	6. a __ __	10. b __ __	14. d __ __	
3. a __ __	7. c __ __	11. c __ __	15. a __ __	1st: __/16 = __%
4. e __ __	8. d __ __	12. c __ __	16. d __ __	2nd: __/16 = __%

MULTIPLE-CHOICE ANSWER EXPLANATIONS

B.1.-10. Derivative Financial Instruments

1.   (d)   Derivatives are financial instruments that derive their value from changes in a benchmark based on stock prices, interest rates, mortgage rates, currency rates, commodity prices, or some other agreed-upon base. Discounts on accounts receivable are not the basis of a benchmark for a derivative financial instrument.

2.   (c)   An interest rate swap agreement involves the exchange of cash flows determined by various interest rates. Fluctuations in interest rates after the agreement is entered into may result in the risk of exchanging a lower interest rate for a higher interest rate. Financial instruments, including swaps, also bear credit risk or the risk that a counterparty to the agreement will not perform as expected. Therefore, answer (c) is correct.

3.   (a)   One of the basic principles that supports SFAS 133 is that derivatives do meet the definition of assets/liabilities and, therefore, should be recognized and reported as such on the financial statements. In contrast, gains and losses that result from the change in the fair value of derivatives are not assets/liabilities and should either appear in other comprehensive income or be reported in current earnings.

4.   (e)   All of the above meet the basic definition of an underlying, which is any financial or physical variable that has either observable changes or objectively verifiable changes.

5.   (b)   Only call (put) options are included in the definition of derivative financial instruments. Leases are excluded because they require a payment equal to the value of the right to use the property. Equity securities and adjustable rate loans are excluded because they require an initial net investment equivalent to the fair value.

6.   (a)   Fair value hedges will recognize gains and losses for the effective portion of the hedging instrument in each reporting period. Cash flow hedges will recognize gains and losses for the effect portion of the hedging instrument in other comprehensive income.

7.   (c)   SFAS 52 remains in effect for hedges of net investments in foreign operations. The hedged net investment is viewed as a single asset. The provisions for recognizing the gain or loss on the hedged asset/liability and the hedging instrument in SFAS 133 do not apply to the hedges of net investments in foreign operations.

A.3.b. Forward Exchange Contracts

8.   (d)   In a hedge of a recorded but unsettled foreign currency transaction, the fixed liability/receivable is recorded in dollars using the forward rate, while the foreign currency receivable/payable is recorded in dollars using the spot rate (100,000 x $.88 = $88,000). At an intervening balance sheet date, the foreign currency receivable/payable is adjusted to reflect the current spot rate (100,000 x $.98 = $98,000), and any resulting gain or loss ($98,000 − $88,000 = $10,000 gain) is included in net income. Journal entries are

12/12/99	Foreign currency receivable	88,000	
	Premium on forward contract	2,000	
	Liability to FC dealer		90,000
12/31/99	Foreign currency receivable	10,000	
	FC transaction gain		10,000

The premium would also be amortized to revenue over the life of the contract, but would not affect the FC transaction gain.

9.   (d)   In a hedge of an identifiable foreign currency commitment, the fixed liability/receivable is recorded in dollars using the forward rate, while the foreign currency receivable/payable is recorded in dollars using the spot rate (100,000 x $.88 = $88,000). At an intervening balance sheet date, the foreign currency receivable/payable is adjusted to reflect the current spot rate (100,000 x $.98 = $98,000). Any resulting gain or loss ($98,000 − $88,000 = $10,000 gain) is recognized in net income. Therefore, the gain **included in net income** in this case is $10,000. Journal entries are

12/12/99	Foreign currency receivable	88,000	
	Deferred premium on forward contract	2,000	
	Liability to FC dealer		90,000
12/31/99	Foreign currency receivable	10,000	
	FC transaction gain		10,000

The premium amortization is also deferred. The premium amortization is included in revenue over the life of the contract.

10.   (b)   When speculating in foreign currency, both the fixed liability/receivable and the foreign currency receivable/payable are recorded in dollars using the **forward** rate (100,000 x $.90 = $90,000). At an intervening balance sheet date, the foreign currency receivable/payable is adjusted to reflect the new **forward** rate (100,000 x $.93 = $93,000), and any resulting gain or loss ($93,000 − $90,000 = $3,000 gain) is included in net income. Journal entries are

12/12/99	Foreign currency receivable	90,000	
	Liability to FC dealer		90,000
12/31/99	Foreign currency receivable	3,000	
	FC transaction gain		3,000

11. **(c)** When speculating in foreign currency, both the fixed liability/receivable and the foreign currency receivable/payable are recorded in dollars using the **forward rate** rather than the spot rate. At 9/1/99, the 60-day forward rate is $.74, so the transaction is recorded at $37,000 (50,000 x $.74). At an intervening balance sheet date, the foreign currency receivable/payable is adjusted to reflect the new forward rate and any resulting gain or loss is included in the income statement. At 9/30/99, 30 days have gone by, so the 30-day forward rate is used rather than the 60-day rate, so the foreign currency receivable is adjusted to $36,000 (50,000 x $.72) and a loss of $1,000 is recognized ($37,000 – $36,000). The entries are

9/1	FC receivable	37,000	
	Liability to FC dealer		37,000
9/30	FC transaction loss	1,000	
	FC receivable		1,000

B.11. Fair Value and Credit Risk Disclosures

12. **(c)** According to SFAS 107, para 14, if it is not practicable for an entity to estimate the fair value of a financial instrument, (1) information pertinent to estimating fair value **and** (2) the reasons why it is not practicable to estimate fair value should be disclosed. Therefore answer (c) is correct.

13. **(d)** SFAS 107 requires the following disclosures:

• Method(s) and significant assumptions used in estimating fair value.

• A distinction between financial instruments held or issued for trading purposes and purposes other than trading.

• Information pertinent to estimating the fair value of a financial instrument if it is not practicable for the entity to estimate and the reason why estimation is not practicable.

• Derivative financial instruments may not be combined, aggregated, or netted with nonderivative or other derivative financial instruments.

• If financial instruments are disclosed in more than one area in the financial statements, one note must contain a summary table cross-referencing the location of the other instruments.

14. **(d)** SFAS 107 requires the following disclosures about credit risk for financial instruments with off-balance-sheet credit risk:

• The amount of accounting loss the entity would incur should any party to the financial instrument fail to perform according to the terms of the contract and the collateral, if any, is of no value.

• The class of financial instruments held

• Categorization between instruments held for trading purposes and purposes other than trading.

Therefore, answer (d) is correct.

15. **(a)** Concentrations of credit risk exist when an entity has a business activity, economic characteristic, or location that is common to most of its financial instruments. SFAS 105 requires disclosure of information about significant concentrations of credit risk for **all** financial instruments. Therefore, answer (a) is correct and answers (b), (c), and (d) are incorrect because they each limit such disclosure to certain financial instruments.

16. **(d)** Since many of Kline Bank's debtors have high debt-to-equity ratios, this group of debtors has a similar economic characteristic, and, thus, would be considered a concentration of credit risk to Kline Bank. SFAS 105 **requires** that with concentrations of credit risk, the entity disclose the following:

(1) Information about the shared activity, region, or economic characteristic of the group.

(2) Amount of accounting loss that the entity would incur as a result of the concentrated parties' failure to perform according to the terms of the contracts.

(3) Information regarding entity's policy of requiring collateral.

Therefore, answer (d) is correct.

MISCELLANEOUS

A. Personal Financial Statements*

Personal financial statements may be prepared for an individual, husband and wife, or family. Personal financial statements (PFS) consist of

1. Statement of financial condition--presents estimated current values of assets, estimated current amounts of liabilities, estimated income taxes, and net worth at a specified date

2. Statement of changes in net worth--presents main sources of increases (decreases) in net worth (optional when a statement of financial condition is prepared)

Assets and liabilities, including changes therein, should be recognized using the accrual basis of accounting. Assets and liabilities should be listed by order of liquidity and maturity, not a current/noncurrent basis.

In PFS, **assets** should be presented at their estimated current value. This is an amount at which the item could be exchanged assuming both parties are well informed, neither party is compelled to buy or sell, and material disposal costs are deducted to arrive at current values. **Liabilities** should be presented at the lesser of the discounted amount of cash to be paid or the current cash settlement amount. Income taxes payable should include unpaid income taxes for completed tax years and the estimated amount for the elapsed portion of the current tax year. Also, PFS should include the estimated income tax on the difference between the current value (amount) of assets (liabilities) and their respective tax bases as if they had been realized or liquidated. The table below summarizes the methods of determining "estimated current values" for assets and "estimated current amounts" for liabilities.

Business interests which comprise a large portion of a person's total assets should be shown separately from other investments. An investment in a separate entity which is marketable as a going concern (e.g., closely held corporation) should be presented as one amount. If the investment is a limited business activity, not conducted in a separate business entity, separate asset and liability amounts should be shown (e.g., investment in real estate and related mortgage). Of course, only the person's beneficial interest in the investment is included in their PFS.

---

* *The source of GAAP for personal financial statements is AICPA Statement of Position 82-1 which has been summarized in this module. (These are not outlined in this text.)*

Assets and liabilities	Discounted cash flow	Market price	Appraised value	Other
• Receivables	x			
• Marketable securities		x		
• Options		x		
• Investment in life insurance				Cash value less outstanding loans
• Investment in closely held business	x		x	Liquidation value, multiple of earnings, reproduction value, adjustment of book value or cost
• Real estate	x		x	Sales of similar property
• Intangible assets	x			
• Future interests (nonforfeitable rights)	x			
• Payables and other liabilities	x			Discharge amount if lower than discounted amount
• Noncancelable commitments	x			
• Income taxes payable				Unpaid income tax for completed tax years and estimated income tax for elapsed portion of current tax year to date of financial statements
• Estimated income tax on difference between current values of assets and current amounts of liabilities and their respective tax bases				Computed as if current value of assets and liabilities had been respectively realized or liquidated considering applicable tax laws and regulations, recapture provisions and carryovers

MULTIPLE-CHOICE QUESTIONS (1-16)

1. On December 31, 1999, Shane is a fully-vested partici-pant in a company-sponsored pension plan. According to the plan's administrator, Shane has at that date the nonfor-feitable right to receive a lump sum of $100,000 on Decem-ber 28, 2000. The discounted amount of $100,000 is $90,000 at December 31, 1999. The right is not contingent on Shane's life expectancy and requires no future perform-ance on Shane's part. In Shane's December 31, 1999, per-sonal statement of financial condition, the vested interest in the pension plan should be reported at
   a. $0
   b. $ 90,000
   c. $ 95,000
   d. $100,000

2. The following information pertains to marketable eq-uity securities owned by Kent:

Stock	Fair value at December 31, 2000	1999	Cost in 1998
City Mfg., Inc.	$95,500	$93,000	$89,900
Tri Corp.	3,400	5,600	3,600
Zee, Inc.		10,300	15,000

The Zee stock was sold in January 2000 for $10,200. In Kent's personal statement of financial condition at Decem-ber 31, 2000, what amount should be reported for market-able equity securities?
   a. $93,300
   b. $93,500
   c. $94,100
   d. $98,900

3. Clint owns 50% of Vohl Corp.'s common stock. Clint paid $20,000 for this stock in 1995. At December 31, 1999, Clint's 50% stock ownership in Vohl had a fair value of $180,000. Vohl's cumulative net income and cash divi-dends declared for the 5 years ended December 31, 1999, were $300,000 and $40,000, respectively. In Clint's per-sonal statement of financial condition at December 31, 1999, what amount should be shown as the investment in Vohl?
   a. $ 20,000
   b. $150,000
   c. $170,000
   d. $180,000

4. Jen has been employed by Komp, Inc. since February 1, 1997. Jen is covered by Komp's Section 401(k) deferred compensation plan. Jen's contributions have been 10% of salaries. Komp has made matching contributions of 5%. Jen's salaries were $21,000 in 1997, $23,000 in 1998, and $26,000 in 1999. Employer contributions vest after an em-ployee completes 3 years of continuous employment. The balance in Jen's 401(k) account was $11,900 at Decem-ber 31, 1999, which included earnings of $1,200 on Jen's contributions. What amount should be reported for Jen's vested interest in the 401(k) plan in Jen's December 31, 1999 personal statement of financial condition?
   a. $11,900
   b. $ 8,200

   c. $ 7,000
   d. $ 1,200

5. The following information pertains to an insurance policy that Barton owns on his life:

Face amount	$100,000
Accumulated premiums paid up to December 31, 2000	8,000
Cash value at December 31, 2000	12,000
Policy loan	3,000

In Barton's personal statement of financial condition at De-cember 31, 2000, what amount should be reported for the investment in life insurance?
   a. $97,000
   b. $12,000
   c. $ 9,000
   d. $ 8,000

6. Ely had the following personal investments at Decem-ber 31, 1999:

   • Realty held as a limited business activity not con-ducted in a separate business entity. Mortgage payments were made with funds from sources unrelated to the realty. The cost of this realty was $500,000, and the related mort-gage payable was $100,000 at December 31, 1999.
   • Sole proprietorship marketable as a going concern. Its cost was $900,000, and it had related accounts payable of $80,000 at December 31, 1999.

   The costs of both investments equal estimated current values. The balances of liabilities equal their estimated cur-rent amounts.

   How should the foregoing information be reported in Ely's statement of financial condition at December 31, 1999?

		Assets	Liabilities
a.	Investment in real estate	$ 400,000	
	Investment in sole proprietor-ship	820,000	
b.	Investment in real estate	$ 500,000	
	Investment in sole proprietor-ship	820,000	
	Mortgage payable		$100,000
c.	Investment in real estate	$ 500,000	
	Investment in sole proprietor-ship	900,000	
	Mortgage payable		$100,000
	Accounts payable		80,000
d.	Investments	$1,400,000	
	Accounts and mortgage payable		$180,000

7. At December 31, 1999, Ryan had the following non-cancelable personal commitments:

   • Pledge to be paid to County Welfare Home 30 days after volunteers paint the walls and ceiling of the Home's recreation room $ 5,000
   • Pledge to be paid to City Hospital on the recovery of Ryan's comatose sister   25,000

What amount should be included in liabilities in Ryan's personal statement of financial condition at December 31, 1999?

  a. $0
  b. $ 5,000
  c. $25,000
  d. $30,000

8. The estimated current values of Lane's personal assets at December 31, 1999, totaled $1,000,000, with tax bases aggregating $600,000. Included in these assets was a vested interest in a deferred profit-sharing plan with a current value of $80,000 and a tax basis of $70,000. The estimated current amounts of Lane's personal liabilities equaled their tax bases at December 31, 1999. Lane's 1999 effective income tax rate was 30%. In Lane's personal statement of financial condition at December 31, 1999, what amount should be provided for estimated income taxes relating to the excess of current values over tax bases?

  a. $120,000
  b. $117,000
  c. $ 3,000
  d. $0

9. Shea, a calendar-year taxpayer, is preparing a personal statement of financial condition as of April 30, 1999. Shea's 1998 income tax liability was paid in full on April 15, 1999. Shea's tax on income earned from January through April 1999 is estimated at $30,000. In addition, $25,000 is estimated for income tax on the differences between the estimated current values of Shea's assets and the current amounts of liabilities and their tax bases at April 30, 1999. No withholdings or payments have been made towards the 1999 income tax liability. In Shea's statement of financial condition at April 30, 1999, what is the total of the amount or amounts that should be reported for income taxes?

  a. $0
  b. $25,000
  c. $30,000
  d. $55,000

10. The following information pertains to Smith's personal assets and liabilities at December 31, 1999:

	Historical cost	Estimated current values	Estimated current amounts
Assets	$500,000	$900,000	
Liabilities	100,000		$80,000

Smith's 1999 income tax rate was 30%. In Smith's personal statement of financial condition at December 31, 1999, what amount should be reported as Smith's net worth?

  a. $294,000
  b. $420,000
  c. $694,000
  d. $820,000

11. Personal financial statements usually consist of

  a. A statement of net worth and a statement of changes in net worth.
  b. A statement of net worth, an income statement, and a statement of changes in net worth.

  c. A statement of financial condition and a statement of changes in net worth.
  d. A statement of financial condition, a statement of changes in net worth, and a statement of cash flows.

12. Personal financial statements should report assets and liabilities at

  a. Estimated current values at the date of the financial statements and, as additional information, at historical cost.
  b. Estimated current values at the date of the financial statements.
  c. Historical cost and, as addititonal information, at estimated current values at the date of the financial statements.
  d. Historical cost.

13. A business interest that constitutes a large part of an individual's total assets should be presented in a personal statement of financial condition as

  a. A separate listing of the individual assets and liabilities at cost.
  b. Separate line items of both total assets and total liabilities at cost.
  c. A single amount equal to the proprietorship equity.
  d. A single amount equal to the estimated current value of the business interest.

14. Smith owns several works of art. At what amount should these art works be reported in Smith's personal financial statements?

  a. Original cost.
  b. Insured amount.
  c. Smith's estimate.
  d. Appraised value.

15. For the purpose of estimating income taxes to be reported in personal financial statements, assets and liabilities measured at their tax bases should be compared to assets and liabilities measured at their

	Assets	*Liabilities*
a.	Estimated current value	Estimated current amount
b.	Historical cost	Historical cost
c.	Estimated current value	Historical cost
d.	Historical cost	Estimated current amount

16. In personal financial statements, how should estimated income taxes on the excess of the estimated current values of assets over their tax bases be reported in the statement of financial condition?

  a. As liabilities.
  b. As deductions from the related assets.
  c. Between liabilities and net worth.
  d. In a footnote disclosure only.

1. b __ __	5. c __ __	9. d __ __	13. d __ __	16. c __ __
2. d __ __	6. b __ __	10. c __ __	14. d __ __	
3. d __ __	7. a __ __	11. c __ __	15. a __ __	1st: __/16 = __%
4. b __ __	8. a __ __	12. b __ __		2nd: __/16 = __%

MULTIPLE-CHOICE ANSWER EXPLANATIONS

A. Personal Financial Statements

1.   (b)   In a personal statement of financial condition, assets are generally presented at estimated current values. Depending on the nature of the asset, current value can be estimated using fair market value, net realizable value, discounted cash flow, or appraised value. AICPA Statement of Position 82-1 specifies that a future interest which is nonforfeitable should be valued using discounted cash flow. Therefore, the interest in the pension plan should be valued at $90,000.

2.   (d)   Per SOP 82-1, assets are generally presented at their estimated current values on personal financial statements. For Kent's December 31, 2000, personal statement of financial condition, the current values of the marketable equity securities held as of that date should be used. Thus, Kent should report $98,900 ($95,500 + $3,400) for marketable equity securities.

3.   (d)   Per SOP 82-1, assets are generally presented at their estimated current values. Depending on the nature of the asset, current value can be estimated using fair market value (FMV), net realizable value, discounted cash flow, or appraised value. In this problem, the fair value of the stock ($180,000) is known and should be shown as the investment in Vohl. Note that the net income and dividends have nothing to do with the amount shown as the investment in Vohl, and this information is irrelevant.

4.   (b)   This problem requires that we determine Jen's vested interest in the 401(k) plan to be reported in her December 31, 1999, personal statement of financial condition. The problem states that employer contributions vest after an employee completes 3 years of service. As Jen has not completed 3 years of service as of December 31, 1999, none of the employer's contributions have vested. Thus, the problem is to determine Jen's contributions and the earnings on **her** contributions as follows:

1997 contributions	2,100
1998 contributions	2,300
1999 contributions	2,600
	7,000
Earnings on above contributions	1,200
Jen's vested interest	8,200

5.   (c)   SOP 82-1 states that assets are generally presented at their estimated current values in personal financial statements. Specifically, investments in life insurance are to be valued at their cash surrender value less outstanding loans on the policy. Therefore, the investment should be reported at $9,000 ($12,000 cash value – $3,000 outstanding loan).

6.   (b)   Per SOP 82-1, (Personal Financial Statements), when investments in a limited business activity are not conducted in a separate business entity, separate asset and liability amounts of the investment should be shown on the statement of financial condition. Thus, the realty (asset) and the mortgage (liability) should be reported separately at $500,000 and $100,000, respectively (their estimated current values). An investment in a separate entity which is marketable as a going concern (e.g., closely held corporation) should be presented as one amount. Thus, the $80,000 in accounts payable should be netted against the current value of $900,000 to report a net investment of $820,000.

7.   (a)   Per SOP 82-1, (Personal Financial Statements), noncancelable personal commitments should be reported at their discounted cash flow. A commitment must have all of the following attributes: (1) are for fixed or determinable amounts; (2) are not contingent on others' life expectancies or occurrence of a particular event (e.g., disability/death); and (3) do not require future performance of service by others. As the pledge to County Welfare Home is contingent upon the volunteers painting the walls and ceiling and the pledge to City Hospital is contingent upon the recovery of Ryan's comatose sister, both liabilities should be excluded from Ryan's personal statement of financial condition at December 31, 1999.

8.   (a)   Per SOP 82-1, estimated taxes that would be paid if all the assets were converted to cash and all the liabilities were paid should be included with the liabilities. Thus, $120,000 [($1,000,000 – $600,000) x .30] should be provided for estimated income taxes relating to the excess of current values over tax bases.

9.   (d)   A personal statement of financial condition presents estimated current values of assets and liabilities, estimated income taxes, and estimated net worth at a specified date. Income taxes payable should include unpaid income taxes for completed tax years, the estimated tax for the elapsed portion of the current year, and the estimated income tax on the difference between the current value of assets and the current amounts of liabilities and their respective tax bases. Thus, the amount to be reported on Shea's statement of financial condition for income taxes is $55,000, equal to the sum of $30,000 tax on income earned from January through April and $25,000 estimated income tax on the difference between the current value and tax bases of assets and liabilities. Therefore, answer (d) is correct.

10.   (c)   Per SOP 82-1, assets are generally presented at their estimated current values on personal financial statements. Therefore, the assets should be reported at their fair value of $900,000, rather than at their cost of $500,000. SOP 82-1 also states that liabilities are presented at the lesser of the discounted amount of cash to be paid, or the current cash settlement amount. Therefore, the liabilities should be reported at $80,000. Estimated taxes that would be paid if all the assets were converted to cash and all the liabilities were paid should be included with the liabilities. Thus, 126,000 [(820,000 – 400,000) x .30] should be provided for estimated income taxes relating to the excess of current values over tax bases. Smith's net worth should be reported as $694,000 ($900,000 – $80,000 – $126,000).

11. (c) Per AICPA SOP 82-1, personal financial statements consist of (1) a statement of financial condition and (2) a statement of changes in net worth [answer (c)]. Answers (a), (b), and (d) include financial statements which are not usually included in personal financial statements.

12. (b) Per SOP 82-1, a personal financial statement presents the estimated current values of assets and liabilities. Therefore answer (b) is correct. Answer (a) is incorrect because the additional information at historical cost is not required. Answers (c) and (d) are incorrect because personal financial statements should reflect estimated current values, not historical cost.

13. (d) Per para 10 of SOP 82-1, business interests that constitute a large part of a person's total assets should be shown separately from other investments. The estimated **current value** of an investment in a separate entity, such as a closely held corporation, a partnership, or a sole proprietorship, should be shown in **one amount** as an investment if the entity is marketable as a going concern.

14. (d) Per SOP 82-1, assets are generally presented at their estimated current values in a personal statement of financial condition. Depending on the nature of the asset, current value can be estimated using fair market value, net realizable value, discounted cash flow, or appraised value. The best estimate of the fair value of art is the appraised value, and thus answer (d) is correct.

15. (a) In personal financial statements assets should be stated at their estimated current values and liabilities should be stated at the lower of the discounted value of their future cash payments or their current cash settlement amounts in accordance with SOP 82-1. These current amounts will differ from their tax bases and will give rise to **unrealized** tax gains and losses. A provision for estimated income taxes on these unrealized amounts should be incorporated into personal financial statements because when the unrealized gains and losses are realized, the related income taxes will have to be either paid or received. Answer responses (b), (c), and (d) are incorrect because they refer to historical cost.

16. (c) AICPA SOP 82-1, para 30, specifically addresses the presentation of estimated income taxes on the excess of the estimated current values of assets over their tax bases in the statement of financial condition. This statement requires that the estimated income taxes should be presented between liabilities and net worth in the statement of financial condition. Therefore, answer (c) is correct.

B. Interim Reporting

The term interim reporting is used to describe financial reporting for periods of less than 1 year, generally quarterly financial statements. The primary purposes of interim reporting are to provide information which is more timely than is available in annual reports, and to highlight business turning points which could be "buried" in annual reports.

There are two basic conceptual approaches to interim reporting: the **discrete view** and the **integral view**.

Discrete view--each interim period is a separate accounting period; interim period must stand on its own; same principles and procedures as for annual reports; no special accruals or deferrals.
Integral view--each interim period is an integral part of an annual period; expectations for annual period must be reflected in interim reports; special accruals, deferrals, and allocations utilized.

APB 28 (see outline) adopted the **integral view**.

APB 28 consists of two parts. Part one does not require issuance of interim financial statements, but does prescribe accounting standards to be used in preparing such statements. Part two sets forth minimum disclosures to be included in interim financial reports.

The table below summarizes the accounting standards set forth in part one of APB 28.

Income statement or comprehensive income statement item	*General rule*	*Exceptions*
Revenues	Same basis as annual reports	None
Cost of goods sold	Same basis as annual reports	1. Gross profit method may be used to estimate CGS and ending inventory for each interim period 2. Liquidation of LIFO base-period inventory, if expected to be replaced by year end, should not affect interim CGS 3. Temporary declines in inventory market value need not be recognized 4. Planned manufacturing variances should be deferred if expected to be absorbed by year end
All other costs and expenses	Same basis as annual reports	Expenditures which **clearly benefit** more than one interim period may be allocated among periods benefitted (e.g., annual repairs, property taxes).
Income taxes	(Year-to-date income x Estimated annual tax rate) – (Expense recognized in previous quarters)	None
Discontinued operations	Recognized in interim period as incurred	None

Income statement or comprehensive income statement item	General rule	Exceptions
Extraordinary items	Recognized in interim period as incurred. Materiality is evaluated based on expected annual results	None
Change in accounting principle	Retroactive type--same as annual reports; restate all prior periods including those of previous years presented. Cumulative effect type--if change made in first quarter, report cumulative effect in first quarter's results. If change made in second or third quarter, report cumulative effect in first quarter results, and restate previous interim periods as if changes had been effective as of the first day of the fiscal year	None
Comprehensive income	Report total amount to stockholders in condensed FS of interim periods	None

The disclosures required in part two of APB 28 are summarized in the pronouncement outline. A key disclosure item for interim reporting is the seasonal nature of the firm's operations. This disclosure helps prevent misleading inferences and predictions about annual results.

APB 28 as interpreted by FASB Interpretation 18 requires that income tax expense be estimated each period using an estimated annual effective tax rate (see FASB Interpretation 18). The example below illustrates the application of this requirement.

	(a)	(b)	(c)	(d) = (b) x (c)	(e)	(f) = (d) – (e)
Qtr	Quarterly income before income taxes	Year-to-date income before income taxes	Estimated annual effective tax rate	Year-to-date income tax expense	Previous quarters' expense	Current quarter's expense
1	$100,000	$100,000	30%	$ 30,000	$ 0	$ 30,000
2	150,000	250,000	32%	80,000	30,000	50,000
3	300,000	550,000	36%	198,000	80,000	118,000
4	200,000	750,000	35%	262,500	198,000	64,500

In the above chart, columns (a) and (c) are assumed to be given. Column (b) is obtained by accumulating column (a) figures. Column (e) is either the preceding quarter's entry in column (d) or the **cumulative** total of previous quarters in column (f).

MULTIPLE-CHOICE QUESTIONS (1-15)

1. On January 1, 1999, Builder Associates entered into a $1,000,000 long-term, fixed-price contract to construct a factory building for Manufacturing Company. Builder accounts for this contract under the percentage-of-completion and estimated costs at completion at the end of each quarter for 1999 were as follows:

Quarter	Estimated percentage-of-completion	Estimated costs at completion
1	10%	$750,000
2*	10%	$750,000
3	25%	$960,000
4*	25%	$960,000

No work performed in the 2nd and 4th quarters.

What amounts should be reported by Builder as "Income on Construction Contract" in its quarterly income statements based on the above information?

	Gain (loss) for the 3 months ended			
	3/31/99	6/30/99	9/30/99	12/31/99
a.	$0	$0	$0	$10,000
b.	$25,000	$0	$(15,000)	$0
c.	$25,000	$0	$0	$0
d.	$25,000	$0	$ 6,000	$0

2. Kell Corp.'s $95,000 net income for the quarter ended September 30, 1999, included the following after-tax items:

• A $60,000 extraordinary gain, realized on April 30, 1999, was allocated equally to the second, third, and fourth quarters of 1999.

• A $16,000 cumulative-effect loss resulting from a change in inventory valuation method was recognized on August 2, 1999.

In addition, Kell paid $48,000 on February 1, 1999, for 1999 calendar-year property taxes. Of this amount, $12,000 was allocated to the third quarter of 1999.

For the quarter ended September 30, 1999, Kell should report net income of

    a. $ 91,000
    b. $103,000
    c. $111,000
    d. $115,000

3. Vilo Corp. has estimated that total depreciation expense for the year ending December 31, 1999, will amount to $60,000, and that 1999 year-end bonuses to employees will total $120,000. In Vilo's interim income statement for the 6 months ended June 30, 1999, what is the total amount of expense relating to these two items that should be reported?

    a. $0
    b. $ 30,000
    c. $ 90,000
    d. $180,000

4. On June 30, 1999, Mill Corp. incurred a $100,000 net loss from disposal of a business segment. Also, on June 30, 1999, Mill paid $40,000 for property taxes assessed for the calendar year 1999. What amount of the foregoing items should be included in the determination of Mill's net income or loss for the 6-month interim period ended June 30, 1999?

    a. $140,000
    b. $120,000
    c. $ 90,000
    d. $ 70,000

5. During the first quarter of 1999, Tech Co. had income before taxes of $200,000, and its effective income tax rate was 15%. Tech's 1998 effective annual income tax rate was 30%, but Tech expects its 1999 effective annual income tax rate to be 25%. In its first quarter interim income statement, what amount of income tax expense should Tech report?

    a. $0
    b. $30,000
    c. $50,000
    d. $60,000

6. Bailey Company, a calendar year corporation, has the following income before income tax provision and estimated effective annual income tax rates for the first three quarters of 1999:

Quarter	Income before income tax provision	Estimated effective annual tax rate at end of quarter
First	$60,000	40%
Second	70,000	40%
Third	40,000	45%

Bailey's income tax provision in its interim income statement for the third quarter should be

    a. $18,000
    b. $24,500
    c. $25,500
    d. $76,500

7. Advertising costs may be accrued or deferred to provide an appropriate expense in each period for

	Interim financial reporting	Year-end financial reporting
a.	Yes	No
b.	Yes	Yes
c.	No	No
d.	No	Yes

8. A planned volume variance in the first quarter, which is expected to be absorbed by the end of the fiscal period, ordinarily should be deferred at the end of the first quarter if it is

	Favorable	Unfavorable
a.	Yes	No
b.	No	Yes
c.	No	No
d.	Yes	Yes

9. Due to a decline in market price in the second quarter, Petal Co. incurred an inventory loss. The market price is expected to return to previous levels by the end of the year. At the end of the year the decline had not reversed. When should the loss be reported in Petal's interim income statements?

    a. Ratably over the second, third, and fourth quarters.
    b. Ratably over the third and fourth quarters.
    c. In the second quarter only.
    d. In the fourth quarter only.

10. An inventory loss from a market price decline occurred in the first quarter. The loss was not expected to be restored in the fiscal year. However, in the third quarter the inventory had a market price recovery that exceeded the market decline that occurred in the first quarter. For interim financial reporting, the dollar amount of net inventory should

- a. Decrease in the first quarter by the amount of the market price decline and increase in the third quarter by the amount of the market price recovery.
- b. Decrease in the first quarter by the amount of the market price decline and increase in the third quarter by the amount of decrease in the first quarter.
- c. Not be affected in the first quarter and increase in the third quarter by the amount of the market price recovery that exceeded the amount of the market price decline.
- d. Not be affected in either the first quarter or the third quarter.

11. For external reporting purposes, it is appropriate to use estimated gross profit rates to determine the cost of goods sold for

	Interim financial reporting	*Year-end financial reporting*
a.	Yes	Yes
b.	Yes	No
c.	No	Yes
d.	No	No

12. For interim financial reporting, the computation of a company's second quarter provision for income taxes uses an effective tax rate expected to be applicable for the full fiscal year. The effective tax rate should reflect anticipated

	Foreign tax rates	*Available tax planning alternatives*
a.	No	Yes
b.	No	No
c.	Yes	No
d.	Yes	Yes

13. For interim financial reporting, a company's income tax provision for the second quarter of 1999 should be determined using the

- a. Effective tax rate expected to be applicable for the full year of 1999 as estimated at the end of the first quarter of 1999.
- b. Effective tax rate expected to be applicable for the full year of 1999 as estimated at the end of the second quarter of 1999.
- c. Effective tax rate expected to be applicable for second quarter of 1999.
- d. Statutory tax rate for 1999.

14. APB Opinion No. 28, *Interim Financial Reporting,* concluded that interim financial reporting should be viewed primarily in which of the following ways?

- a. As useful only if activity is spread evenly throughout the year.
- b. As if the interim period were an annual accounting period.
- c. As reporting for an integral part of an annual period.
- d. As reporting under a comprehensive basis of accounting other than GAAP.

15. Conceptually, interim financial statements can be described as emphasizing

- a. Timeliness over reliability.
- b. Reliability over relevance.
- c. Relevance over comparability.
- d. Comparability over neutrality.

MULTIPLE-CHOICE ANSWERS

1. b __ __	5. c __ __	9. d __ __	12. d __ __	15. a __ __
2. a __ __	6. b __ __	10. b __ __	13. b __ __	
3. c __ __	7. b __ __	11. b __ __	14. c __ __	1st: __/15 = __%
4. b __ __	8. d __ __			2nd: __/15 = __%

MULTIPLE-CHOICE ANSWER EXPLANATIONS

B. Interim Reporting

1. (b)   The requirement is to compute the income to be recognized in quarterly (interim) financial statements on a construction contract using the percentage-of-completion method. The solutions approach is to compute the income on the contract at the end of each quarter by (1) applying the estimated percentage-of-completion to the total estimated income to be recognized on the contract, and (2) subtracting the income recognized in preceding quarters to arrive at the income for the latest quarter. In the second and fourth quarters there was no work done on the contract and no change in the total estimated cost of completion. In quarter three the estimated costs of completion are revised upward. Since the cumulative income to date is less than income recognized in the first quarter, it is necessary to recognize a loss in the third quarter. The loss is handled as a change in accounting estimate rather than restating the first quarter.

Quarter 1:
10% ($1,000,000 – $750,000) = $25,000 income recognized

Quarter 2:
-0-

Quarter 3:
25% ($1,000,000 – $960,000) = $10,000 income earned to
date

$10,000 income to date – $25,000 income recognized
  in previous periods = $(15,000) loss for quarter

Quarter 4:
-0-

2. (a)   Per APB 28, para 21, extraordinary items, gains or losses from disposal of a segment of a business, and unusual or infrequently occurring items should not be prorated over the balance of the fiscal year. Thus, the $20,000 ($60,000 ÷ 3) extraordinary gain that was allocated to the third quarter should be subtracted from net income as it actually occurred in the second quarter. Consistent with the view that all accounting changes should be made effective as of the beginning of the fiscal period, the cumulative effect of the accounting change on retained earnings is computed at the beginning of the fiscal year and reported in the first interim period's income statement. If a cumulative-effect type change is made during an interim period subsequent to the first one, the prior interim reports must be restated as if the changes had been effective as of the first day of the fiscal year. Thus, the $16,000 cumulative-effect loss should not be recognized in the third quarter. The prior interim reports should be restated and the $16,000 loss should be added back to income of the third quarter to correct the income to be reported for the quarter. Property taxes should be allocated among the applicable quarters. As Kell Corp. properly allocated their property taxes, no adjustment to

income is needed. Kell should report $91,000 ($95,000 – $20,000 + $16,000) as net income for the quarter ended September 30, 1999.

3. (c)   Per APB 28, para 15a, a cost charged to expense in an annual period should be allocated among the interim periods which clearly benefit from the expense through the use of accruals and/or deferrals. Both yearly bonuses and the use of an asset (depreciation expense) benefit the entire year. The expense for the **6 month** interim statement should be ($60,000 + $120,000) ÷ 2 = $90,000.

4. (b)   APB 28 states that revenues and gains should be recognized in interim reports on the same basis as used in annual reports. At June 30, 1999, Mill Corp. would report the entire $100,000 loss on the disposal of its business segment since the loss was incurred during the interim period. APB 28 also states that a cost charged to an expense in an annual period should be allocated among the interim periods which clearly benefit from the expense through the use of accruals and/or deferrals. Since the $40,000 property tax payment relates to the entire 1999 calendar year, $20,000 of the payment would be reported as an expense at June 30, 1999, while the remaining $20,000 would be reported as a prepaid expense. Therefore, answer (b) is correct.

5. (c)   APB 28, para 19, states that the tax provision for an interim period is the tax for the year to date (estimated effective rate for the year times year-to-date income) less the total tax provisions reported for previous interim periods. In this case, the requirement is to calculate the tax provision for the first quarter interim income statement. The tax expense is $50,000 ($200,000 x 25%).

6. (b)   The requirement is to calculate Bailey's income tax provision (expense) in its interim income statement for the third quarter. APB 28, para 19, states that the tax provision for an interim period is the tax for the year to date (estimated effective rate for the year times year-to-date income) less the total tax provisions reported for previous interim periods.

Year-to-date tax (45%)($170,000)	$76,500
Previously reported tax (40% x $130,000)	52,000
Third quarter tax provision	$24,500

7. (b)   Per APB 28, para 16, advertising costs may be deferred within a fiscal year if the benefits clearly extend beyond the interim period that the expense was paid. Also, advertising costs may be accrued and assigned to interim periods in relation to sales. Year-end accruals and deferrals of costs are also considered appropriate accounting treatment. Note, however, that deferral in year-end reporting is permitted only if the advertising has not been run in the media. Therefore, answer (b) is correct.

8. **(d)** Per APB 28, para 14, a planned volume variance that is expected to be absorbed by the end of the fiscal year should be deferred at interim reporting dates. Therefore, answer (d) is correct and answers (a), (b), and (c) are incorrect.

9. **(d)** The requirement is to determine when the inventory loss should be reported. Per APB 28, para 14, inventory losses from market declines should not be deferred beyond the interim period in which the loss occurs. However, if the market decline is considered to be **temporary** and will be recovered by year end, no loss needs to be recognized. Answer (d) is correct because a loss will be recognized in the fourth quarter only. In the second quarter the loss is considered temporary, therefore no loss is recognized. However, in the fourth quarter, when the decline does not reverse, it is deemed permanent and recognized in the fourth quarter. Answers (a) and (b) are incorrect because losses are recognized in the period in which they occur, not ratably over several periods. Only expenses that benefit several periods (i.e., repairs and maintenance) are recognized ratably. Answer (c) is incorrect because the loss is not recorded in a period of temporary decline, only when the decline is considered to be permanent.

10. **(b)** Per APB 28, a decline in inventory market price, expected to be other than temporary, should be recognized in the period of decline. A subsequent recovery of market value should be recognized as a cost recovery in the period of increase, but **never** above original cost. Thus, answer (b) is correct because the decline should be recognized when it occurs in the first quarter. The subsequent recovery should be recognized when it occurs in the third quarter. Answer (a) is incorrect because the subsequent recovery cannot exceed the amount of decline. Answers (c) and (d) are incorrect because a nontemporary decline should be shown in the quarter of price decrease.

11. **(b)** The requirement is to determine the appropriateness of estimated gross profit rates in determining cost of goods sold for interim and year-end external financial reporting purposes. The use of estimated gross profit rates to determine the cost of goods sold for an interim period is appropriate per APB 28, para 14. The method of estimation used and any significant adjustments that result from reconciliations with the annual physical inventory should be disclosed. An estimation of cost of goods sold is not allowable for year-end financial reporting per APB 43, para 4. (The actual cost of the goods sold must be determined by the use of a cost flow assumption which most clearly reflects periodic income.) Thus, an estimated cost of goods sold figure may be used for interim but not year-end statements.

12. **(d)** Per APB 28, para 19, "the effective tax rate should reflect anticipated investment tax credits, foreign tax rates, percentage depletion, capital gains rates, and other available tax planning alternatives." Therefore, answer (d) is correct.

13. **(b)** The requirement is to determine what tax rate should be used to calculate the income tax provision for interim reporting. Per APB 28, each interim period is considered to be an integral part of the annual period. There-

fore, expectations for the annual period must be reflected in the interim report. The income tax expense should be calculated using the estimated annual effective tax rate. Thus, answer (b) is correct. Answer (a) is incorrect because the estimated tax rate should be updated as of the end of each interim period (here, as of the second quarter). Answer (c) is incorrect because the tax rate should reflect expectations for the full year. Answer (d) is incorrect because the statutory tax rate is only a part of the effective tax. The effective tax rate includes the statutory tax rate and a variety of other items.

14. **(c)** APB 28 adopted the **integral view**, which holds that each interim period is an integral part of an annual period, must reflect expectations for the annual period, and must utilize special accruals, deferrals, and allocations. Answers (a), (b), and (d) do not reflect conclusions found in APB 28; answer (b) describes the other major conceptual approach, the **discrete view**.

15. **(a)** The primary purposes of interim reporting are to provide information which is more **timely** than is available in annual reports and to highlight business turning points which could be "buried" in annual reports. This emphasis on timeliness comes at the expense of **reliability**. Accounting information pertaining to shorter periods may require more arbitrary allocations, and may not be as verifiable or representationally faithful as information contained in annual reports. Answer (b) is wrong because interim reports are generally more relevant and less reliable. Answers (c) and (d) are wrong because interim financial statements should not be any more or less comparable than annual reports.

C. Segment Reporting

SFAS 131 (see outline) sets forth financial reporting standards for segment reporting, the disclosure of information about different components of an enterprise's operations as well as information related to the enterprise's products and services, its geographic areas, and its major customers.

The purpose of segment disclosure is to assist investors and lenders in assessing the future potential of an enterprise. Consolidated statements give the user the overall view (results of operations, financial position, cash flows). However, trends, opportunities, risk factors, etc., can get lost when data for a diversified company are merged into consolidated statements. Additionally, most intersegment transactions that are eliminated from consolidated financial information are included in segment information. Consolidated statements refer to the primary statements of the reporting entity. They are not limited to the statements of parent and subsidiaries (the conventional meaning of the term consolidated statements).

The approach used in SFAS 131 is a "management approach," meaning it is based on the way management organizes segments internally to make operating decisions and assess performance. Companies can segment their financial information by products or services, by geography, by legal entity, or by type of customer. The management approach will facilitate consistent descriptions of an enterprise for both internal and external reporting and in general provides that external financial reporting will more closely conform to internal reporting.

SFAS 131 does not apply to not-for-profit organizations or nonpublic enterprises.

Operating Segments

In SFAS 131, an **operating segment** is defined as

A component of an enterprise engaged in business activity for which it may earn revenues and incur expenses, about which separate financial information is available that is evaluated regularly by the chief operating decision makers in deciding how to allocate resources and in assessing performance.

A segment is significant (reportable) if it satisfies **at least one** of the following three 10% tests:

Revenues--Segment revenue (including intersegment revenue) is 10% or more of combined segment revenue (including intersegment revenue)

Operating profit or loss--The absolute amount of segment profit or loss is 10% or more of the **greater**, in absolute amount, of combined profit of segments reporting profit, or combined loss of segments reporting loss

Identifiable assets--Segment assets are 10% or more of combined segment identifiable assets

Operating profit or loss is unaffiliated revenue and intersegment revenue, less **all** operating expenses. Since segment revenue includes **intersegment sales, transfer pricing** becomes an issue. FASB requires companies to use the same transfer prices for segment reporting purposes as are used internally. Since most segments are **profit centers**, internal transfer prices generally reflect market prices.

Common costs are operating expenses incurred by the enterprise for the benefit of more than one operating segment. These costs should only be allocated to a segment for external reporting purposes if they are included in the measure of the segments profit or loss that is used internally by the chief operating decision maker.

Similarly, only those assets that are included internally in the measure of the segment's assets used to make operating decisions, shall be reported as assets of the segment in external financial reports.

Interperiod comparability must be considered in conjunction with the results of the 10% tests. If a segment fails to meet the tests, but has satisfied the tests in the past and is expected to in the future, it should be considered reportable in the current year for the sake of comparability. Similarly, if a segment which rarely passes the tests does so in the current year as the result of an unusual event, that segment may be excluded to preserve comparability.

There are some limitations to the number of segments which are to be reported. There must be enough segments reported so that at least 75% of unaffiliated revenues is shown by reportable segments (75% test). If the 75% test is not satisfied, additional segments must be designated as reportable until the test is satisfied. Also, the number of reportable segments should not be so large (10 is a rule of thumb) as to make the information less useful. When a reportable segment is excluded or a nonreportable segment included, appropriate disclosure must be made.

The following example illustrates the three 10% tests (revenues, operating profit or loss, and identifiable assets) and the 75% test:

Segment	Unaffiliated revenue	Intersegment revenue	Total revenue	Operating profit (loss)	Identifiable assets
A	$ 90	$ 90	$ 180	$ 20	$ 70
B	120		120	10	50
C	110	20	130	(40)	90
D	200		200	0	140
E	330	110	440	(100)	230
F	380	—	380	60	260
Total	$1,230	$220	$1,450	$ (50)	$840

Revenues test: (10%)($1,450) = $145
    Reportable segments: A, D, E, F

Operating profit or loss test: (10%)($140) = $14
    Reportable segments: A, C, E, F
    [Note: Operating loss ($140) is greater than operating profit, $90]

Identifiable assets test: (10%)($840) = $84
    Reportable segments: C, D, E, F

Reportable segments: Those segments which pass **at least one** of the 10% tests. Segments A, C, D, E, and F are reportable in this example.

75% test: (75%)($1,230) = $922.50
    Segments A, C, D, E, and F have total unaffiliated revenue of $1,110, which is greater than $922.50. The 75% test is satisfied; no additional segments need be reported.

Certain other factors must be considered when identifying reportable segments. An enterprise may consider aggregating two or more operating segments if they have similar economic characteristics and if the segments are similar in each of the following areas:

1. The nature of the products and services

2. The nature of the production processes
3. The type of customer for their products and services
4. The methods used to distribute their products or provide their services
5. The nature of the regulatory environment

Aggregation can occur prior to performing the 10% tests if the enterprise desires.

Additionally, the enterprise may combine information on operating segments that do not meet any of the 10% tests to produce a reportable segment, but only if the segments meet a majority of the aggregation criteria discussed above. It should be noted that information about operating segments that do not meet any of the 10% thresholds may still be disclosed separately.

Segment Disclosures

SFAS 131 requires several disclosures regarding the enterprise's reportable segments. They include

1. **General information**--An explanation of how management identified the enterprise's reportable segments, including whether operating segments have been aggregated. Additionally, a description of the types of products and services from which each reportable segment derives its revenues.

2. **Certain information about reported segment profit and loss, segment assets, and the basis of measurement**--The enterprise shall disclose the following about each reportable segment if the specified amounts are reviewed by the chief operating decision maker:

    a. Revenues from external customers
    b. Intrasegment revenues
    c. Interest revenue and expense (reported separately unless majority of segment's revenues are from interest and management relies primarily on net interest revenue to assess performance)
    d. Depreciation, depletion, and amortization expense
    e. Unusual items, extraordinary items
    f. Equity in the net income of investees accounted for by the equity method
    g. Income tax expense or benefit
    h. Significant noncash items

    Also, the basis of measurement for these items must be disclosed, including differences in measurement practices between a segment and the complete entity and differences in measurement practices in a segment between periods.

3. **Reconciliations**--The enterprise will need to reconcile the segment amounts disclosed to the corresponding enterprise amounts.

4. **Interim period information**--Although the interim disclosures are not as extensive as in the annual financial report, certain segment disclosures are required in interim financial reports.

Restatement of Previously Reported Segment Information

Segment reporting is required on a comparative basis. Therefore, the information must be restated to preserve comparability whenever the enterprise has changed the structure of its internal organization in a manner that causes a change to its reportable segments. The enterprise must explicitly disclose that it has restated the segment information of earlier periods.

Enterprise-Wide Disclosures About Products and Services, Geographic Areas, and Major Customers

The enterprise-wide disclosures are required for all enterprises, even those that have a single reportable segment. Disclosures need to be provided only if not provided as part of the segment information. Disclosures are required regardless of whether the information is used in making operating decisions.

Products and services. Revenue from external customers for each product and service shall be reported by the enterprise, unless it is impractical to do so.

Geographic areas. An enterprise shall report revenues from external customers and long-lived assets attributable to its domestic operations and **foreign operations**, unless it is impractical to do so. If revenues or assets of an individual foreign country are material, then these amounts should be separately disclosed. In addition, the enterprise's basis for attributing revenue to individual countries shall be disclosed.

Major customers. Certain disclosures are made concerning major customers if the following 10% test is met. If 10% or more of **consolidated revenue** comes from a **single** external customer, the enterprise must disclose this fact in addition to the amount of such revenues, and the identity of the segment or segments making the sales. (A group of customers under common control, such as subsidiaries of a parent, is regarded as a single customer. Similarly the various agencies of a government are considered to be a single customer.)

Flowchart for Identifying Reportable Operating Segments*

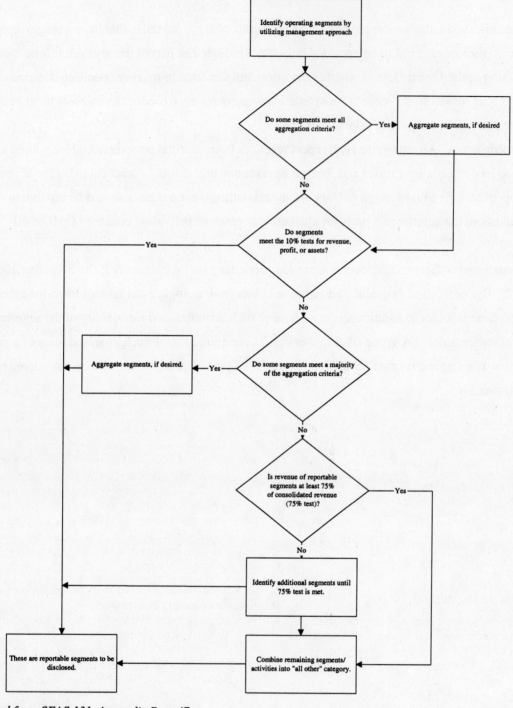

Adapted from SFAS 131, Appendix B, p. 47.

MULTIPLE-CHOICE QUESTIONS (1-11)

1. Correy Corp. and its divisions (each is an operating segment) are engaged solely in manufacturing operations. The following data (consistent with prior years' data) pertain to the operations conducted for the year ended December 31, 1999:

(Industry operating payment)	Total revenue	Operating profit	Identifiable assets at 12/31/98
A	$10,000,000	$1,750,000	$20,000,000
B	8,000,000	1,400,000	17,500,000
C	6,000,000	1,200,000	12,500,000
D	3,000,000	550,000	7,500,000
E	4,250,000	675,000	7,000,000
F	1,500,000	225,000	3,000,000
	$32,750,000	$5,800,000	$67,500,000

In its segment information for 1999, how many reportable segments does Correy have?

   a. Three.
   b. Four.
   c. Five.
   d. Six.

2. The following information pertains to Aria Corp. and its operating segments for the year ended December 31, 1999:

Sales to unaffiliated customers	$2,000,000
Intersegment sales of products similar to those sold to unaffiliated customers	600,000
Interest earned on loans to other industry segments	40,000

Aria and all of its divisions are engaged solely in manufacturing operations and evaluates divisional performance based on controllable contribution. Aria has a reportable segment if that segment's revenue exceeds

   a. $264,000
   b. $260,000
   c. $204,000
   d. $200,000

Items 3 and 4 are based on the following:

Grum Corp., a publicly owned corporation, is subject to the requirements for segment reporting. In its income statement for the year ended December 31, 1999, Grum reported revenues of $50,000,000, operating expenses of $47,000,000, and net income of $3,000,000. Operating expenses include payroll costs of $15,000,000. Grum's combined identifiable assets of all industry segments at December 31, 1999, were $40,000,000. Reported revenues include $30,000,000 of sales to external customers.

3. In its 1999 financial statements, Grum should disclose major customer data if sales to any single customer amount to at least

   a. $ 300,000
   b. $1,500,000
   c. $4,000,000
   d. $5,000,000

4. External revenue reported by operating segments must be at least

   a. $22,500,000
   b. $15,000,000
   c. $12,500,000
   d. $37,500,000

5. Enterprise-wide disclosures include disclosures about

	Geographic areas	Allocated costs
a.	Yes	Yes
b.	Yes	No
c.	No	Yes
d.	No	No

6. Enterprise-wide disclosures are required by publicly held companies with

	Only one reportable segment	More than one reportable segment
a.	Yes	Yes
b.	Yes	No
c.	No	Yes
d.	No	No

7. An enterprise must disclose all of the following about each reportable segment if the amounts are used by the chief operating decision maker, except

   a. Depreciation expense.
   b. Allocated expenses.
   c. Interest expense.
   d. Income tax expense.

8. In financial reporting for segments of a business, an enterprise shall disclose all of the following except

   a. Types of products and services from which each reportable segment derives its revenues.
   b. The title of the chief operating decision maker of each reportable segment.
   c. Factors used to identify the enterprises reportable segments.
   d. The basis of measurement of segment profit or loss and segment assets.

9. In financial reporting for segments of a business enterprise, segment data may be aggregated

   a. Before performing the 10% tests if a majority of the aggregation criteria are met.
   b. If the segments do not meet the 10% tests but meet all of the aggregation criteria.
   c. Before performing the 10% tests if all of the aggregation criteria are met.
   d. If any one of the aggregation criteria are met.

10. The method used to determine what information to report for business segments is referred to as the

   a. Segment approach.
   b. Operating approach.
   c. Enterprise approach.
   d. Management approach.

11. Taylor Corp., a publicly owned corporation, assesses performance and makes operating decisions using the following information for its reportable segments:

Total revenues	$768,000
Total profit and loss	40,600

Included in the total profit and loss are intersegment profits of $6,100. In addition, Taylor has $500 of common costs for its reportable segments that are not allocated in reports used internally. For purposes of segment reporting, Taylor should report segment profit of

a. $35,000
b. $34,500
c. $41,100
d. $40,600

PROBLEM

Problem 1   (15 to 25 minutes)

Barnet Co. has several reportable operating segments that account for 90% of its operations. It has no foreign operations, sales, or major individual customers.

Required:

a. What is the purpose of segment disclosure?

b. Define operating segments and describe the approach used to identify operating segments.

c. What tests should Barnet apply in determining its reportable segments?

MULTIPLE-CHOICE ANSWERS

1. c __ __	4. a __ __	7. b __ __	9. c __ __	11. d __ __
2. b __ __	5. b __ __	8. b __ __	10. d __ __	1st: __/11 = __%
3. d __ __	6. a __ __			2nd: __/11 = __%

MULTIPLE-CHOICE ANSWER EXPLANATIONS

C. Segment Reporting

1. **(c)** A division is a reportable segment if it is significant. A division is significant if it satisfies at least **one** of the three 10% tests:

1. **Revenue** is 10% or more of the combined segment revenue (including intersegment revenue).
2. **Operating profit** (loss) is 10% or more of the greater of the **absolute** combined segment profit or loss.
3. **Identifiable assets** are 10% or more of the combined segment identifiable assets.

Industry A, B, C, and E pass the revenue and operating profit tests, but A, B, C, D, and E all pass the identifiable assets test. Since a division only has to pass one of the three 10% tests to be considered a reportable segment, Corey Corp. has five reportable segments.

2. **(b)** SFAS 131, requires that selected data for a segment be reported separately if one of three criteria is met. One of these criteria is met when a segment's revenue is greater than or equal to 10% of the combined revenues of all industry segments. Para 18 states that combined revenue includes sales to unaffiliated customers and intersegment sales or transfers. Thus, Aria has a reportable segment if that segment's revenues exceed $260,000 [($2,000,000 + $600,000) x 10%]. The $40,000 interest would not be included in combined revenue because it is not controllable at the division level.

3. **(d)** Per SFAS 131, if 10% or more of the revenue of an enterprise is derived from sales to any single customer, that fact and the amount of revenue from each customer shall be disclosed. In this problem, Grum reported revenues of $50,000,000 and thus should disclose major customer data if sales to any single customer amount to $5,000,000 ($50,000,000 x 10%).

4. **(a)** Per SFAS 131, para 20, there must be enough segments reported so that at least 75% of unaffiliated revenues is shown by reportable segments (75% test). Sales to external customers total $30,000,000 so external revenues reported by operating segments must be at least $22,500,000 ($30,000,000 x 75%).

5. **(b)** Per SFAS 131, para 36-39, enterprise-wide disclosures about products and services, geographic areas, and major customers are required for all enterprises.

6. **(a)** Per SFAS 131, para 36, enterprise-wide disclosures are to be reported by all public business enterprises, including those with a single reportable segment because the criteria for splitting the enterprise into reportable segments are not met.

7. **(b)** Per SFAS 131, para 27, the enterprise shall disclose the following about each reportable segment if the specified amounts are reviewed by the chief operating decision maker:

a. Revenues from external customers
b. Intrasegment revenues
c. Interest revenue and expense (reported separately unless majority of segment's revenues are from interest and management relies primarily on net interest revenue to assess performance)
d. Depreciation, depletion, and amortization expense
e. Unusual items, extraordinary items
f. Equity in the net income of investees accounted for by the equity method
g. Income tax expense or benefit
h. Significant noncash items

Allocated expenses are not specifically included as a required disclosure.

8. **(b)** Per SFAS 131, para 25 and 26, an enterprise shall disclose general information, including factors used to identify reportable segments and the types of products and services from which each reportable segment derives its revenues. Para 25 states that an enterprise shall disclose certain information about reported segment profit and loss, assets, and basis of measurement. Para 25 does not require disclosures about the term chief operating decision maker and para 12 specifically states that this term identifies a function, not necessarily a manager with a specific title. Therefore, answer (b) is correct.

9. **(c)** Per SFAS 131, para 17 and 19, two or more operating segments may be aggregated into a single operating segment if all of the aggregation criteria are met or if after performing the 10% test a majority of the aggregation criteria are met. Answer (c) is therefore correct.

10. **(d)** Per SFAS 131, para 4, the method chosen for determining what information to report is referred to as the management approach.

11. **(d)** Per SFAS 131, an enterprise shall report a measure of profit and loss based on the measure reported to the chief operating decision maker for purposes of making decisions. Therefore, answer (d) is correct. The information used by management includes intersegment profits and should be included, but common costs are not allocated to the segments when assessing performance and should not be included.

ANSWER OUTLINE

Problem 1 Segment Reporting: Objectives, Tests, and Discontinued Operations

a. Purposes of segment disclosures
- Assist in analyzing and understanding FS
- Permit better assessment of past performance and future prospects
- Provide more detail with respect to timing and amount of cash flows
- Show variations in rates of profitability, degrees and types of risk, opportunities for growth, and future capital demands among segments

b. An operating segment is a component of an enterprise
- Engaged in business activity for which it may earn revenues and incur expenses
- For which separate financial information is available
- Whose operating results are evaluated regularly by the chief operating decision makers in deciding how to allocate resources and assess performance

Management approach
- Based on the way management organizes segments internally to make operating decisions and assess performance
- Facilitates consistent descriptions of an enterprise for both internal and external reporting
- Provides that external financial reporting will more closely conform to internal reporting

c. Tests applied in determining reportable segments
- Segment revenue (from customers and other segments) is ≥ 10% of combined revenue of all segments
- Segment's absolute operating profit/loss is ≥ 10% of greater in absolute amount of
    - Combined operating profits of all segments with profits, or
    - Combined operating losses of all segments with losses
- Segment's identifiable assets are ≥ 10% of combined identifiable assets of all segments

UNOFFICIAL ANSWER

Problem 1 Segment Reporting: Objectives, Tests, and Discontinued Operations

a. Segment disclosures assist in analyzing and understanding financial statements by permitting better assessment of past performance and future prospects. Disaggregated information provides more precise details of the uncertainties surrounding the timing and the amount of expected cash flows, because the various segments may have different rates of profitability, degrees and types of risk, opportunities for growth, and future capital demands.

b. An operating segment is a component of an enterprise engaged in business activity for which it may earn revenues and incur expenses, about which separate financial informa-

tion is prepared and evaluated by the chief operating decision makers to assess performance and allocate resources.

The approach used to identify segments is referred to as the management approach, meaning it is based on the way management organizes segments internally to make operating decisions and assess performance. The management approach will provide that external descriptions of an enterprise are consistent with internal descriptions and that external reporting will more closely conform to internal reporting used by management.

c. Barnet should have reported a segment that satisfies one or more of the following tests:

- The segment's revenue, including both sales to unaffiliated customers and intersegment sales or transfers, is 10% or more of the combined revenue of all Barnet's segments.

- The segment's absolute amount of operating profit or loss is 10% or more of the greater in absolute amount of

    - The combined operating profits of all segments with operating profits, or
    - The combined operating losses of all segments with operating losses.

- The segment's identifiable assets are 10% or more of the combined identifiable assets of all segments.

D. Partnership Accounting

There are no authoritative pronouncements concerning the accounting for partnerships; thus, all of the principles described below have evolved through accounting practice.

Partnership accounting typically is tested through a few multiple-choice questions on the accounting practice exam. Occasionally, the material is tested through a problem.

1. Partnership Formation

The partnership is a separate **accounting entity** (not to be confused with a separate legal entity), and therefore its assets and liabilities should remain separate and distinct from the individual partner's personal assets and liabilities.

Thus, all assets contributed to the partnership are recorded by the partnership at their **fair market values**. All liabilities assumed by the partnership are recorded at their **present values**.

Upon formation, the amount credited to each partner's capital account is the difference between the fair market value of the assets contributed and the present value of the liabilities assumed from that partner. The capital accounts represent the residual equity of the partnership. The capital account of each partner reflects all of the activity of an individual partner: contributions, withdrawals, and the distributive share of net income (loss). In some cases, a **drawing** account is used as a clearing account for each partner's transactions with only the net effect of each period's activity shown in the capital account.

EXAMPLE: Partnership Formation

A and B form a partnership. A contributes cash of $50,000, while B contributed land with a fair market value of $50,000 and the partnership assumes a liability on the land of $25,000.
The entry to record the formation of the partnership is

Cash	50,000	
Land	50,000	
Liabilities		25,000
A Capital		50,000
B Capital		25,000

2. Allocation of Partnership Income (Loss)

The partners should have a written agreement (articles of copartnership) specifying the manner in which partnership income (loss) is to be distributed. Note that in the absence of a predetermined agreement, the profit and loss (P&L) is divided equally among the partners.

It is important to remember that P&L should **not** be distributed using a ratio based on the partners' capital balances unless this is the ratio specified in the articles of copartnership. A number of issues arise which complicate the allocation of partnership income (loss).

a. Partners may receive interest on their capital balances. If so, it must be determined what will constitute the capital balance (e.g., the year-end amount or some type of weighted-average).
b. Some of the partners may receive a salary.
c. Some of the partners may receive a bonus on distributable net income. If so, you need to determine if the bonus should be computed before or after salary and interest allocations.
d. A formula needs to be determined for allocating the remaining income. The formula agreed upon is usually termed the **residual, remainder**, or **profit (loss) sharing ratio**.
e. Finally, the partners should decide upon how income is to be allocated if net income is insufficient to cover partners' salaries, bonuses, and interest allocations. These allocations are usually

made even if the effect is to create a negative remainder. This remainder is usually allocated in accordance with the profit (loss) ratio. However, it is important to note that partners may choose to allocate losses (or a negative remainder) in a different manner than income.

EXAMPLE: *Partnership P&L Distribution*

> *Partners receive 5% interest on beginning capital balances*
> *Partner B receives a $6,000 salary*
> *Partner C receives a 10% bonus after interest and salaries*
> *The P&L ratios are A -- 50%, B -- 30%, C -- 20%*

Assuming partnership net income of $18,250, the following distribution schedule would be prepared:

		A	B	C
P&L ratio		50%	30%	20%
Beginning capital balance		30,000	10,000	5,000
	Cumulative distribution			
5% interest	2,250	1,500	500	250
Salary	8,250		6,000	
Bonus	9,250			1,000*
Remaining dist.	18,250	4,500	2,700	1,800
P&L dist.		6,000	9,200	3,050
Ending capital balances		36,000	19,200	8,050

*($18,250 - $8,250) x .10 = $1,000

Note that if the interest, salary, and bonus allocation had exceeded net income, the excess would have been deducted on the distribution schedule in the P&L ratio.

3. Partnership Dissolution (Changes in Ownership)

> Partnership dissolution occurs whenever there is a change in ownership (e.g., the addition of a new partner, or the retirement or death of an existing partner). This is not to be confused with partnership liquidation, which is the winding up of partnership affairs and termination of the business. Under dissolution the partnership business continues, but under different ownership.

> When partnership dissolution occurs a new accounting entity results. The partnership should first adjust its records so that all accounts are properly stated at the date of dissolution. After the income (loss) has been properly allocated to the existing partners' capital accounts, all assets and liabilities should be adjusted to their fair market value and their present values, respectively. The latter step is performed because the dissolution results in a new accounting entity.

> After all adjustments have been made, the accounting for dissolution depends on the type of transaction that caused the dissolution. These transactions can be broken down into two types:

- Transactions between the partnership and a partner (e.g., a new partner contributes assets, or a retiring partner withdraws assets)
- Transactions between partners (e.g., a new partner purchases an interest from one or more existing partners, or a retiring partner sells his/her interest to one or more existing partners)

a. **Transactions Between a Partner and the Partnership**

(1) **Admission of a New Partner**

> When a new partner is admitted to the partnership essentially three cases can result. The new partner can invest assets into the partnership and receive a capital balance

(a) Equal to his/her purchase price
(b) Greater than his/her purchase price

(c) Less than his/her purchase price

If the new partner's capital balance is equal to the assets invested, then the entry debits the asset(s) contributed and credits the new partner's capital account for the fair value of the asset(s) contributed.

If the new partner's capital balance is not equal to the assets invested [as in situation (b) and (c) above], then either the bonus or goodwill method must be used to account for the difference.

Bonus method--The old partnership capital plus the new partner's asset contribution is equal to the new partnership capital. The new partner's capital is allocated his purchase share (e.g., 40%) and the old partner's capital accounts are adjusted as if they had been paid (or as if they paid) a bonus. The adjustment to the old partners' capital accounts is made in accordance with their profit (loss) sharing ratio.

The bonus method implies that the old partners either received a bonus from the new partner, or they paid a bonus to the new partner. As a result the old partners' capital accounts are either debited to reflect a bonus paid, or credited to reflect a bonus received. The new partner's capital account is **never** equal to the amount of assets contributed in a case where the bonus method is used.

Goodwill method--The old partnership capital plus the new partner's asset contribution is **not** equal to the new partnership capital. This is because goodwill is recorded on the partnership books for the difference between the total identifiable assets of the partnership (not including goodwill) and the deemed value of the partnership entity (which includes goodwill). An adjustment is made to the capital accounts of the existing partners to reflect the goodwill (whether acquired or given) in their profit (loss) sharing ratio. Under the goodwill method, valuation of the partnership is the objective.

How the value of the partnership is determined depends on whether the book value acquired is greater or less than the asset(s) invested. If the book value acquired is less than the asset(s) invested, the value is determined based upon the new partner's contribution, and goodwill is allocated to the old partners' accounts. If the book value acquired is greater than the asset(s) contributed, the value is based upon the existing capital accounts, and goodwill is attributed to the new partner.

The decision as to whether the bonus or goodwill method should be used rests with the partners involved. In other words, the bonus and goodwill methods are alternative solutions to the same problem.

EXAMPLE: Partnership Dissolution--Bonus Method

Total old capital for ABC Partnership is $60,000

Partner	A	B	C
Capital	*$10,000*	*$20,000*	*$30,000*
P&L Ratio	*40%*	*40%*	*20%*

Case 1

D is admitted to the partnership and is given a 20% interest in the capital in return for a cash contribution of $30,000.

Cash	*30,000*	
D Capital		*18,000*
A Capital		*4,800*
B Capital		*4,800*
C Capital		*2,400*

The total partnership capital to be shown on the books is $90,000 ($60,000 + $30,000) of which D is entitled to a 20% interest, or a capital balance of $18,000. The remaining $12,000 is treated as a bonus to the old partners and is allocated to their capital accounts in accordance with their P&L ratio.

Case 2

D is admitted to the partnership and is given a 20% interest in the capital in return for a cash contribution of $10,000.

Cash	10,000	
A Capital	1,600	
B Capital	1,600	
C Capital	800	
D Capital		14,000

The total partnership capital to be shown on the books is $70,000 ($60,000 + $10,000) of which D is entitled to a 20% interest, or a capital balance of $14,000. The difference of $4,000 ($10,000 – $14,000) is allocated to the old partners' accounts as if they had paid a bonus to the new partner.

EXAMPLE: Partnership Dissolution--Goodwill Method

Use the same original data as given above

Case 1

D is admitted to the partnership and is given a 20% interest in the capital in return for a cash contribution of $20,000. The partners elect to record goodwill. The book value acquired [($60,000 + $20,000) x 20% = $16,000] is less than the asset contributed.

The value of the partnership is determined based upon the contribution of the new partner. In this case it is assumed that the partnership value is $100,000 ($20,000/20%). The resulting goodwill is $20,000 ($100,000 – $80,000). The $80,000 represents the total current capital, exclusive of goodwill, $60,000 of which is attributable to the old partners and $20,000 of which is attributable to the new partner.

Goodwill	20,000	
A Capital		8,000
B Capital		8,000
C Capital		4,000
Cash	20,000	
D Capital		20,000

Goodwill was allocated to the old partners in their P&L ratio. Also note that the capital balance of D represents 20% of the total capital of the partnership.

Case 2

D is admitted to the partnership and is given a 20% interest in the capital in return for a cash contribution of $10,000. The partners elect to record goodwill. The book value acquired [($60,000 + $10,000) x 20% = $14,000] is greater than the asset contributed.

The partnership value is based upon the capital accounts of the existing partners. Because D is entitled to a 20% interest, the $60,000 capital of the old partners must represent 80% of the capital. This means that the total value of the partnership is $75,000 ($60,000/80%). D's total contribution consists of the $10,000 in cash and $5,000 of goodwill. The goodwill is determined as the difference between the cash contribution and the 20% of the partnership capital.

Cash	10,000	
Goodwill	5,000	
D Capital		15,000

Note that in this last case no adjustment is made to the capital accounts of partners A, B, and C.

The table below summarizes the bonus and goodwill situations discussed above:

When to Apply Bonus Method			**When To Apply Goodwill Method**		
New	Old	New Partner's	New	Old	New Partner's
Partnership = Partners' +		Asset	Partnership > Partners' +		Asset
Capital	Capital	Investment	Capital	Capital	Investment

Which Partner(s) Receive Bonus
- **New Partner**

  New Partner's   New Partner's
  Capital Credit $>$ Asset Investment
  (The difference represents the bonus.)

- **Old Partners**

  New Partner's   New Partner's
  Capital Credit $<$ Asset Investment
  (The difference represents the bonus allo-
  cated to old partners in their P&L Ratio.)

Which Partner(s) Goodwill is Recognized
- **New Partner's Goodwill**

  New Partner's   New Partner's
  Capital Credit $>$ Asset Investment
  (The difference represents goodwill.)

- **Old Partner's Goodwill**

  New Partner's   New Partner's
  Capital Credit $=$ Asset Investment
  (Goodwill is allocated to old partners
  in their P&L Ratio.)

(2) Partner Death or Withdrawal

The death or withdrawal of a partner is treated in much the same manner as the admission of a new partner. However, there is no new capital account to be recorded; we are dealing only with the capital accounts of the original partners. Either the bonus or goodwill method may be used. The key thing to remember in regard to a partner's withdrawal from the partnership is that the withdrawing partner's capital account must be adjusted to the amount that the withdrawing partner is expected to receive.

EXAMPLE: Partner Withdrawal

Assume the same partnership data as given for the ABC partnership earlier.

Case 1

Assume that A withdraws from the partnership after reaching an agreement with partners B & C that would pay him $16,000. The remaining partners elect not to record goodwill.

B Capital	4,000	
C Capital	2,000	
A Capital		6,000
A Capital	16,000	
Cash		16,000

The $6,000 bonus is determined as the difference between the current balance of A's capital account and the amount of his buyout agreement. This "bonus" is then allocated between the remaining partners' capital accounts in proportion to their P&L ratios.

Case 2

Assume again that A withdraws from the partnership pursuant to the same agreement except that this time the partners elect to record goodwill.

The first step is to determine the amount of goodwill to be recorded. In this case we know that A's capital account must have a balance of $16,000, the agreed buyout payment he is to receive. In order to accomplish this the total partnership assets must be increased by some amount of which $6,000 represents 40%, A's P&L ratio. Therefore, the amount of goodwill to be recorded is $15,000 ($6,000/40%).

Goodwill	15,000	
A Capital		6,000
B Capital		6,000
C Capital		3,000
A Capital	16,000	
Cash		16,000

Note that in this case all of the partners' capital accounts are adjusted to record the goodwill in accordance with their P&L ratios.

b. Transactions Between Partners

The sale of a partnership interest is a transaction only between the partners. Thus, the treatment accorded the transaction is determined by the partners involved.

There are two means of dealing with such a transaction. The first is to simply transfer a portion of the existing partners' capital to a new capital account for the buying partner.

EXAMPLE: Sale of a Partnership Interest--No Goodwill Recorded

Assume the following for the AB partnership:

Partner	A	B
Capital	$50,000	$50,000
P&L Ratio	60%	40%

Case 1

Assume that C wishes to enter the partnership by buying 50% of the partnership interest from both A and B for a total of $80,000. It is important to note that the $80,000 is being paid to the individual partners and **not** to the partnership. Thus, we are only concerned with the proper adjustment between the capital accounts, **not** the recording of the cash. This approach ignores the price that C paid for the partnership interest.

A Capital	25,000	
B Capital	25,000	
C Capital		50,000

The other method available for recording a transaction between partners involves the recording of implied goodwill.

EXAMPLE: Sale of Partnership Interest--Recording Goodwill

Assume the same facts presented above for the sale of the partnership interest except that in this case the partners elect to record goodwill.

Case 1

Assuming that C paid $80,000 for a 50% interest in the partnership the implied value of the partnership assets is $160,000 ($80,000/50%). Because total capital prior to the purchase is only $100,000, the amount of goodwill that must be recorded is $60,000. The goodwill is allocated to the partners' accounts in proportion to their P&L ratios. Note that this entry is made **before** an adjustment is made to reflect C's admission to the partnership.

Goodwill	60,000	
A Capital		36,000
B Capital		24,000

Now we can record the sale of the partnership interest to C. The capital balance of A is now $86,000 ($50,000 + $36,000) while the capital balance of B is $74,000 ($50,000 + $24,000). Recall that C is to receive 50% of each balance.

A Capital	43,000	
B Capital	37,000	
C Capital		80,000

Notice that in this situation the capital balance of C after the purchase is equal to the amount of the purchase price. Again no entry is made to record the receipt of cash because the cash goes directly to the individual partners, A and B.

4. Partnership Liquidation

A liquidation is the winding up of the partnership business. That is, it sells all of its noncash assets, pays its liabilities, and makes a final liquidating distribution to the remaining partners.

There are four basic steps to a partnership liquidation.

1. Any operating income or loss up to the date of the liquidation should be computed and allocated to the partners' capital accounts on the basis of their P&L ratio.
2. All noncash assets are sold and converted to cash. The gain (loss) realized on the sale of such assets is allocated to the partners' capital accounts on the basis of their P&L ratio.
3. Any creditors' claims, including liquidation expenses or anticipated future claims, are satisfied through the payment or reserve of cash.

4. The remaining unreserved cash is distributed to the remaining partners in accordance with the balance in their capital accounts. Note that this is **not** necessarily the P&L ratio.

Two factors that may complicate the liquidation process are the existence of loans or advances between the partnership and one or more of the partners, or the creation of a deficit in a partner's capital account because of the allocation of a loss. When loans exist between the partnership and a partner, the capital account and the loan(s) are combined to give a net amount. This is often referred to as the right of offset. When a deficit exists, the amount of the deficit is allocated to the remaining solvent partners' capital accounts on the basis of their relative P&L ratio. Note here that if the partner with the capital deficit is personally solvent, he has a liability to the remaining partners for the amount of the deficit.

There are two topics that appear with regularity on the CPA examination in regard to the liquidation of a partnership. They are the statement of partnership liquidation and the determination of a "safe payment" in an installment liquidation.

a. **Statement of Partnership Liquidation**

The statement of partnership liquidation shows in detail all of the transactions associated with the liquidation of the partnership. It should be noted here that the liquidation of a partnership can take one of two forms: simple or installment. A simple liquidation (illustrated below) is one in which all of the assets are sold in bulk and all of the creditors' claims are satisfied before a single liquidating distribution is made to the partners. Because the assets are sold in bulk there is a tendency to realize greater losses than if the assets were sold over a period of time. As a result, many partnerships liquidate on an installment basis. In an installment liquidation the assets are sold over a period of time and the cash is distributed to the partners as it becomes available.

EXAMPLE: Statement of Partnership Liquidation--Simple Liquidation
Assume the following:

The capital balances are as given below.
The P&L ratio is 5:3:2 for A, B, and C, respectively.

STATEMENT OF PARTNERSHIP LIQUIDATION

	Cash	Other assets	Liabilities	Capital A	B	C
Balances	5,000	75,000	45,000	12,000	17,000	6,000
Sale of assets	40,000	(60,000)		(10,000)	(6,000)	(4,000)
	45,000	15,000	45,000	2,000	11,000	2,000
Payment of liabilities	(45,000)		(45,000)			
	0	15,000	0	2,000	11,000	2,000
Sale of assets	10,000	(15,000)		(2,500)	(1,500)	(1,000)
	10,000	0	0	(500)	9,500	1,000
Distribution of A's deficit				500	(300)	(200)
	10,000	0	0	0	9,200	800
Final distribution of cash	(10,000)				(9,200)	(800)

Notice that after the noncash assets have been sold and the creditors satisfied, a $500 deficit remains in A's capital account. The deficit is allocated to the remaining solvent partners on the basis of their relative P&L ratios, in this case, 3:2. A is liable to the partnership for the $500. If A is personally solvent and repays the $500, then $300 will go to B and $200 will go to C.

If in the above example there had been liquidation expenses or loans between the partnership and partners these would have to be recognized in the statement prior to any distribution to partners.

b. **Installment Method of Cash Distribution**

There are two keys to preparing a statement of partnership liquidation under the installment method: the determination of the available cash balance at any given point in time and the determination of which partner(s) is (are) to receive the payment of that cash. The reason that the cash is not distributed in accordance with the P&L ratio is twofold: first, the final cash distribution is based upon the balance in each partner's capital account, **not** the P&L ratio, and second, there will be situations, as illustrated in the previous example, where one or more partners will have deficit balances in their capital accounts. If this is the case, they should **never** receive a cash distribution, even if the deficit does not arise until late in the liquidation process.

The determination of the available cash balance is generally very straightforward. The beginning cash balance (cash on hand at the start of the liquidation process) is adjusted for the cash receipts from receivables, sale of noncash assets, payment to creditors, and liquidation expenses incurred. A situation may occur where a certain amount of cash is to be reserved for payment of future liabilities that may arise. If this is the case, this cash should be treated as a noncash asset which makes it unavailable for current distribution to the partners.

The determination of which partner(s) is (are) to receive the available cash is somewhat more difficult. There are a number of ways to make this computation, all of which are equally correct in the eyes of the examiners. This determination can be made at the beginning of the liquidation process or at the time of each payment. In making this determination there are two key assumptions that must be made: (1) the individual partners are assumed to be personally insolvent, and (2) the remaining noncash assets are deemed to be worthless (thus creating a maximum possible amount of loss).

One method of determining the amount of the "safe payment" is the use of an Installment Cash Distribution Schedule. This schedule is prepared by determining the amount of loss required to eliminate each partner's capital account. As noted above, all of the remaining noncash assets are to be considered worthless at the time a safe payment is determined. Thus, if we determine the amount of loss required to eliminate each partner's capital balance, we can determine the order in which the partners should receive the cash payments.

When preparing this schedule it is important to make sure that the proper capital balance is used. The capital balance used **must** be inclusive of any loans or advances between the partnership and partners. Thus, the capital balance at the beginning of the liquidation process is increased by any amount owed to the partner by the partnership, and decreased by any amount owed to the partnership by the partner.

EXAMPLE: Schedule of Possible Losses and Installment Cash Distribution

Assume the same data as used for the previous example.

SCHEDULE OF POSSIBLE LOSSES

	Total	A	B	C
Capital balances	$35,000	$ 12,000	$ 17,000	$ 6,000
Loss to eliminate A	24,000	(12,000)	(7,200)	(4,800)
		0	$ 9,800	$ 1,200
Additional loss to eliminate C	3,000*		(1,800)	(1,200)
			8,000	0
Additional loss to eliminate B	8,000		(8,000)	
	$35,000		0	

*Allocated 60:40

The total capital balance of $35,000 indicates that if the noncash assets are sold for $35,000 less than their book value, then none of the partners will receive a cash distribution. The purpose of this schedule is to determine how much of a loss each partner's capital account can withstand based on that partner's P&L ratio. In this example A's capital would be eliminated if the partnership incurred a $24,000 ($12,000/50%) loss, B's would be eliminated by a $56,667 ($17,000/30%) loss, and C's by a $30,000 ($6,000/20%) loss. A is assumed to be eliminated first because it would take the smallest amount of loss to eliminate his account. Once A is eliminated as a partner, the P&L ratios change to reflect the relative P&L ratio of the remaining partners, in this case B and C. Based on the remaining capital balances and the relative P&L ratio, it would take a $16,333 ($9,800/60%) loss to eliminate B and a $3,000 ($1,200/40%) loss to eliminate C. Now that C is eliminated B will share all of the profits and losses as a sole partner (i.e., 100%). It will now take an $8,000 loss to eliminate B's capital. The resulting installment cash distribution schedule would appear as follows (this schedule assumes that all creditors have already received full payment; thus, the cash amount represents available cash):

INSTALLMENT CASH DISTRIBUTION SCHEDULE

Partner		A	B	C
First	$ 8,000		100%	
Next	3,000		60%	40%
Next	24,000	50%	30%	20%
Any other		50%	30%	20%

While the example shown in the previous section was not an installment liquidation, the Installment Cash Distribution Schedule shown above could still be used to determine how the available cash of $10,000 is to be distributed. This is illustrated below.

Partner		A	B	C
First	$ 8,000		$8,000	
Next	$ 2,000		$1,200	$800
Total	$10,000	--	$9,200	$800

It is important to note that this method is acceptable for most all purposes; however, a CPA exam problem may require the "safe payment" approach where the amount of the safe payment is computed at a specific point in time.

5. Incorporation of a Partnership

The incorporation of a partnership results in the formation of a new accounting (and legal) entity. This means that the partnership must adjust its records up to the date of incorporation. First, the partnership closes its books and recognizes any income or loss up to the date of incorporation. Second, the books of the partnership are adjusted to reflect the fair market value of the partnership assets and the present value of partnership liabilities. A corresponding adjustment is made to the capital accounts in accordance with the partners' P&L ratio. Third, common stock is distributed to the partners in accordance with the amounts in their capital accounts. Note that the entries to record the receipt of stock by the corporation are different depending upon whether the corporation retains the partnership books or establishes new books.

Retention of the partnership books means that the issuance of common stock results in the closing of the partners' capital accounts with credits going to common stock and additional paid-in capital.

Establishing new books means that the assets and liabilities are closed out and the difference between their net value and the value of the corporate stock is debited to an asset "capital stock from corporation." This account is then credited and the partners' capital accounts debited to record the distribution of stock.

MULTIPLE-CHOICE QUESTIONS (1-23)

1. Roberts and Smith drafted a partnership agreement that lists the following assets contributed at the partnership's formation:

	Contributed by	
	Roberts	*Smith*
Cash	$20,000	$30,000
Inventory	-	15,000
Building	-	40,000
Furniture & equipment	15,000	-

The building is subject to a mortgage of $10,000, which the partnership has assumed. The partnership agreement also specifies that profits and losses are to be distributed evenly. What amounts should be recorded as capital for Roberts and Smith at the formation of the partnership?

	Roberts	*Smith*
a.	$35,000	$85,000
b.	$35,000	$75,000
c.	$55,000	$55,000
d.	$60,000	$60,000

2. On April 30, 1999, Algee, Belger, and Ceda formed a partnership by combining their separate business proprietorships. Algee contributed cash of $50,000. Belger contributed property with a $36,000 carrying amount, a $40,000 original cost, and $80,000 fair value. The partnership accepted responsibility for the $35,000 mortgage attached to the property. Ceda contributed equipment with a $30,000 carrying amount, a $75,000 original cost, and $55,000 fair value. The partnership agreement specifies that profits and losses are to be shared equally but is silent regarding capital contributions. Which partner has the largest April 30, 1999 capital account balance?

a. Algee.
b. Belger.
c. Ceda.
d. All capital account balances are equal.

3. Abel and Carr formed a partnership and agreed to divide initial capital equally, even though Abel contributed $100,000 and Carr contributed $84,000 in identifiable assets. Under the bonus approach to adjust the capital accounts, Carr's unidentifiable asset should be debited for

a. $46,000
b. $16,000
c. $ 8,000
d. $0

4. When property other than cash is invested in a partnership, at what amount should the noncash property be credited to the contributing partner's capital account?

a. Fair value at the date of contribution.
b. Contributing partner's original cost.
c. Assessed valuation for property tax purposes.
d. Contributing partner's tax basis.

5. Red and White formed a partnership in 1999. The partnership agreement provides for annual salary allowances of $55,000 for Red and $45,000 for White. The partners share profits equally and losses in a 60/40 ratio. The partnership had earnings of $80,000 for 2000 before any allowance to partners. What amount of these earnings should be credited to each partner's capital account?

	Red	*White*
a.	$40,000	$40,000
b.	$43,000	$37,000
c.	$44,000	$36,000
d.	$45,000	$35,000

6. Fox, Greg, and Howe are partners with average capital balances during 1999 of $120,000, $60,000, and $40,000, respectively. Partners receive 10% interest on their average capital balances. After deducting salaries of $30,000 to Fox and $20,000 to Howe, the residual profit or loss is divided equally. In 1999 the partnership sustained a $33,000 loss before interest and salaries to partners. By what amount should Fox's capital account change?

a. $ 7,000 increase.
b. $11,000 decrease.
c. $35,000 decrease.
d. $42,000 increase.

7. The partnership agreement of Axel, Berg & Cobb provides for the year-end allocation of net income in the following order:

- First, Axel is to receive 10% of net income up to $100,000 and 20% over $100,000.
- Second, Berg and Cobb each are to receive 5% of the remaining income over $150,000.
- The balance of income is to be allocated equally among the three partners.

The partnership's 1999 net income was $250,000 before any allocations to partners. What amount should be allocated to Axel?

a. $101,000
b. $103,000
c. $108,000
d. $110,000

8. The partnership agreement of Reid and Simm provides that interest at 10% per year is to be credited to each partner on the basis of weighted-average capital balances. A summary of Simm's capital account for the year ended December 31, 2000, is as follows:

Balance, January 1	$140,000
Additional investment, July 1	40,000
Withdrawal, August 1	(15,000)
Balance, December 31	165,000

What amount of interest should be credited to Simm's capital account for 2000?

a. $15,250
b. $15,375
c. $16,500
d. $17,250

9. The Flat and Iron partnership agreement provides for Flat to receive a 20% bonus on profits before the bonus. Remaining profits and losses are divided between Flat and Iron in the ratio of 2 to 3, respectively. Which partner has a greater advantage when the partnership has a profit or when it has a loss?

	Profit	Loss
a.	Flat	Iron
b.	Flat	Flat
c.	Iron	Flat
d.	Iron	Iron

10. Blau and Rubi are partners who share profits and losses in the ratio of 6:4, respectively. On May 1, 1999, their respective capital accounts were as follows:

Blau	$60,000
Rubi	50,000

On that date, Lind was admitted as a partner with a one third interest in capital and profits for an investment of $40,000. The new partnership began with total capital of $150,000. Immediately after Lind's admission, Blau's capital should be

- a. $50,000
- b. $54,000
- c. $56,667
- d. $60,000

11. Kern and Pate are partners with capital balances of $60,000 and $20,000, respectively. Profits and losses are divided in the ratio of 60:40. Kern and Pate decided to form a new partnership with Grant, who invested land valued at $15,000 for a 20% capital interest in the new partnership. Grant's cost of the land was $12,000. The partnership elected to use the bonus method to record the admission of Grant into the partnership. Grant's capital account should be credited for

- a. $12,000
- b. $15,000
- c. $16,000
- d. $19,000

12. Dunn and Grey are partners with capital account balances of $60,000 and $90,000, respectively. They agree to admit Zorn as a partner with a one-third interest in capital and profits, for an investment of $100,000, after revaluing the assets of Dunn and Grey. Goodwill to the original partners should be

- a. $0
- b. $33,333
- c. $50,000
- d. $66,667

Items 13 and 14 are based on the following:

The following condensed balance sheet is presented for the partnership of Alfa and Beda, who share profits and losses in the ratio of 60:40, respectively:

Cash	$ 45,000
Other assets	625,000
Beda, loan	30,000
	$700,000
Accounts payable	$120,000
Alfa, capital	348,000
Beda, capital	232,000
	$700,000

13. The assets and liabilities are fairly valued on the balance sheet. Alfa and Beda decide to admit Capp as a new partner with 20% interest. No goodwill or bonus is to be recorded. What amount should Capp contribute in cash or other assets?

- a. $110,000
- b. $116,000
- c. $140,000
- d. $145,000

14. Instead of admitting a new partner, Alfa and Beda decide to liquidate the partnership. If the other assets are sold for $500,000, what amount of the available cash should be distributed to Alfa?

- a. $255,000
- b. $273,000
- c. $327,000
- d. $348,000

15. In the Adel-Brick partnership, Adel and Brick had a capital ratio of 3:1 and a profit and loss ratio of 2:1, respectively. The bonus method was used to record Colter's admittance as a new partner. What ratio would be used to allocate, to Adel and Brick, the excess of Colter's contribution over the amount credited to Colter's capital account?

- a. Adel and Brick's new relative capital ratio.
- b. Adel and Brick's new relative profit and loss ratio.
- c. Adel and Brick's old capital ratio.
- d. Adel and Brick's old profit and loss ratio.

Items 16 and 17 are based on the following:

On June 30, 1999, the condensed balance sheet for the partnership of Eddy, Fox, and Grimm, together with their respective profit and loss sharing percentages were as follows:

Assets, net of liabilities	$320,000
Eddy, capital (50%)	$160,000
Fox, capital (30%)	96,000
Grimm, capital (20%)	64,000
	$320,000

16. Eddy decided to retire from the partnership and by mutual agreement is to be paid $180,000 out of partnership funds for his interest. Total goodwill implicit in the agreement is to be recorded. After Eddy's retirement, what are the capital balances of the other partners?

	Fox	Grimm
a.	$ 84,000	$56,000
b.	$102,000	$68,000
c.	$108,000	$72,000
d.	$120,000	$80,000

17. Assume instead that Eddy remains in the partnership and that Hamm is admitted as a new partner with a 25% interest in the capital of the new partnership for a cash payment of $140,000. Total goodwill implicit in the transaction is to be recorded. Immediately after admission of Hamm, Eddy's capital account balance should be

- a. $280,000
- b. $210,000
- c. $160,000
- d. $140,000

18. On June 30, 1999, the balance sheet for the partnership of Coll, Maduro, and Prieto, together with their respective profit and loss ratios, were as follows:

Assets, at cost	$180,000
Coll, loan	$ 9,000
Coll, capital (20%)	42,000
Maduro, capital (20%)	39,000
Prieto, capital (60%)	90,000
Total	$180,000

Coll has decided to retire from the partnership. By mutual agreement, the assets are to be adjusted to their fair value of $216,000 at June 30, 1999. It was agreed that the partnership would pay Coll $61,200 cash for Coll's partnership interest, including Coll's loan which is to be repaid in full. No goodwill is to be recorded. After Coll's retirement, what is the balance of Maduro's capital account?

a. $36,450
b. $39,000
c. $45,450
d. $46,200

19. Allen retired from the partnership of Allen, Beck, and Chale. Allen's cash settlement from the partnership was based on new goodwill determined at the date of retirement plus the carrying amount of the other net assets. As a consequence of the settlement, the capital accounts of Beck and Chale were decreased. In accounting for Allen's withdrawal, the partnership could have used the

	Bonus method	Goodwill method
a.	No	Yes
b.	No	No
c.	Yes	Yes
d.	Yes	No

20. When Mill retired from the partnership of Mill, Yale, and Lear, the final settlement of Mill's interest exceeded Mill's capital balance. Under the bonus method, the excess

a. Was recorded as goodwill.
b. Was recorded as an expense.
c. Reduced the capital balances of Yale and Lear.
d. Had **no** effect on the capital balances of Yale and Lear.

 6

21. The following condensed balance sheet is presented for the partnership of Smith and Jones, who share profits and losses in the ratio of 60:40, respectively:

Other assets	$450,000
Smith, loan	20,000
	$470,000
Accounts payable	$120,000
Smith, capital	195,000
Jones, capital	155,000
	$470,000

The partners have decided to liquidate the partnership. If the other assets are sold for $385,000, what amount of the available cash should be distributed to Smith?

a. $136,000
b. $156,000
c. $159,000

d. $195,000

22. On January 1, 1999, the partners of Cobb, Davis, and Eddy, who share profits and losses in the ratio of 5:3:2, respectively, decided to liquidate their partnership. On this date the partnership condensed balance sheet was as follows:

Assets

Cash	$ 50,000
Other assets	250,000
	$300,000

Liabilities and Capital

Liabilities	$ 60,000
Cobb, capital	80,000
Davis, capital	90,000
Eddy, capital	70,000
	$300,000

On January 15, 1999, the first cash sale of other assets with a carrying amount of $150,000 realized $120,000. Safe installment payments to the partners were made the same date. How much cash should be distributed to each partner?

	Cobb	Davis	Eddy
a.	$15,000	$51,000	$44,000
b.	$40,000	$45,000	$35,000
c.	$55,000	$33,000	$22,000
d.	$60,000	$36,000	$24,000

23. Jay & Kay partnership's balance sheet at December 31, 1999, reported the following:

Total assets	$100,000
Total liabilities	20,000
Jay, capital	40,000
Kay, capital	40,000

On January 2, 2000, Jay and Kay dissolved their partnership and transferred all assets and liabilities to a newly-formed corporation. At the date of incorporation, the fair value of the net assets was $12,000 more than the carrying amount on the partnership's books, of which $7,000 was assigned to tangible assets and $5,000 was assigned to goodwill. Jay and Kay were each issued 5,000 shares of the corporation's $1 par value common stock. Immediately following incorporation, additional paid-in capital in excess of par should be credited for

a. $68,000
b. $70,000
c. $77,000
d. $82,000

MULTIPLE-CHOICE ANSWERS

1. b __ __	6. a __ __	11. d __ __	16. c __ __	21. a __ __
2. c __ __	7. c __ __	12. c __ __	17. b __ __	22. a __ __
3. d __ __	8. b __ __	13. d __ __	18. c __ __	23. d __ __
4. a __ __	9. b __ __	14. b __ __	19. d __ __	1st: __/23 = __%
5. b __ __	10. b __ __	15. d __ __	20. c __ __	2nd: __/23 = __%

MULTIPLE-CHOICE ANSWER EXPLANATIONS

D.1. Partnership Formation

1.   (b)   The requirement is to determine the amounts to be recorded as capital for Roberts and Smith at the formation of the partnership. Unless otherwise agreed upon by the partners, individual capital accounts should be credited for the fair market value (on the date of contribution) of the net assets contributed by that partner. It is necessary to assume that the amounts listed are fair market values. The amount of net assets that Roberts contributed is $35,000 ($20,000 + $15,000). The fair market value of the net assets Smith contributed is $75,000 ($30,000 + $15,000 + $40,000 − $10,000). The partners' profit and loss sharing ratio does not affect the initial recording of the capital accounts, thus, answer (b) is correct.

2.   (c)   The requirement is to determine which partner has the largest capital account balance. Use the solutions approach to solve the problem.

	Algee	Belger	Ceda
Partner contribution	50,000	80,000	55,000
Less: Liabilities assumed by the partnership	0	(35,000)	0
Ending capital balance	$50,000	$45,000	$55,000

Each partner values his contribution to the partnership at its fair market value. The fair market value becomes the partner's balance in his capital account and is basis to the partnership under generally accepted accounting principles. Any liabilities assumed by the partnership, reduces the partners' capital balance by the amount assumed. Therefore, answer (c) is correct. Answers (a), (b), and (d) are incorrect.

3.   (d)   Under the bonus method, unidentifiable assets (i.e., Goodwill) are not recognized. The total resulting capital is the FMV of the tangible investments of the partners. Thus, there would be no unidentifiable assets recognized by the creation of this new partnership.

4.   (a)   Noncash assets contributed to an entity should be recorded at fair market value at the date of contribution. The creation of a new entity creates a new accountability for these assets. Answer (b) is incorrect because the partner's original cost relates to a previous accountability. Answers (c) and (d) are incorrect since the assessed valuation and the tax basis may differ from fair market value.

D.2. Allocation of Partnership Income (Loss)

5.   (b)   Credits to partners' capital accounts are based upon earnings after allowance for interest, salary and bonus. The earnings before any allowance of $80,000 is reduced by

the salary allowances of $100,000 and results in a loss of $20,000. The $20,000 loss is then distributed to the partners in relation to their profit and loss ratios as follows:

	Red	White	Total
Profit before allowance			$80,000
Salary allowances	$55,000	$45,000	(100,000)
Loss after allowances 60/40	(12,000)	(8,000)	(20,000)
Earnings credited to partners	$43,000	$37,000	$80,000

It is important to note that the losses are distributed 60/40 while profits are shared equally.

6.   (a)   When dividing the partnership loss of $33,000, first interest and salaries are allocated to the partners, **increasing** their capital balances. This allocation of interest and salaries will also increase the amount of loss. This increased loss amount would then be allocated to the partners, **decreasing** their capital accounts. The computations are shown below.

	Fox	Greg	Howe
Interest allowance (10% of avg. cap. balances)	$12,000	$ 6,000	$ 4,000
Salaries	30,000		20,000
Residual* ($105,000 ÷ 3)	(35,000)	(35,000)	(35,000)
Increase (decrease) in cap. account	$ 7,000	$(29,000)	$(11,000)

Thus, answer (a) is correct; Fox's account increases by $7,000.

The residual loss of $105,000 is the loss resulting after the interest and salary allowances are deducted [$33,000 loss − ($12,000 + $6,000 + $4,000) − ($30,000 + $20,000)].

7.   (c)   The distribution of the partnership net income of $250,000 occurs in three steps as follows:

	Axel	Berg	Cobb
a) Axel: 10% of first $100,000,	$10,000		
20% over $100,000	30,000		
b) Berg & Cobb: 5% of remaining income over $150,000 [($250,000 − $10,000− $30,000 − $150,000) x .05]		$ 3,000	$ 3,000

c) Remaining allocated equally:
 [($250,000 – $10,000–
 $30,000 – $3,000–
 $3,000) x 1/3]   68,000   68,000   68,000
      Totals $108,000 $71,000 $71,000

Thus, $108,000 would be distributed to Axel.

8.   (b)   We must first determine Simm's weighted-average capital balance for 1998 as follows:

Capital bal.	x	# of months/12	=	Weighted-avg.
140,000	x	6/12	=	$ 70,000
180,000	x	1/12	=	15,000
165,000	x	5/12	=	68,750
				$153,750

The problem states that interest of 10% per year is to be credited to each partner's capital account, and 10% of Simm's weighted-average capital balance of $153,750 is $15,375.

9.   (b)   In both the case of a profit or a loss, Flat will have a greater advantage. When there is a profit, Flat will obtain a 20% bonus on profits before the bonus, and also take 40% of the profit after the bonus. Iron on the other hand, will only receive 60% of the profit after the bonus. The following example illustrates this:

	Flat	Iron	Profit
P & L ratio	40%	60%	1,000
20% Bonus	200	0	(200)
			800
Share in profit	320	480	
Total distribution	520	480	

In the case of a loss, it can easily be seen that since Flat has a smaller percentage share in the loss that he has a greater advantage. Therefore, answer (b) is correct.

D.3.a.(1)   Admission of a New Partner

10.   (b)   The requirement is to calculate the balances in the capital accounts of a partnership after the admission of a new partner. In this case, the new partner is investing $40,000 for a 1/3 interest in the new total capital of $150,000. No goodwill is recorded because the new capital ($150,000) equals the total of the old capital ($110,000) and Carter's investment ($40,000). However, a bonus of $10,000 is being credited to the new partner's capital account because his interest (1/3 of $150,000, or $50,000) exceeds his investment ($40,000). The bonus to the new partner is charged to the old partners in their profit and loss ratios as shown below.

Blau [60,000 – 3/5 (10,000)]	$54,000
Rubi [50,000 – 2/5 (10,000)]	46,000
Lind (150,000 ÷ 3)	50,000
	$150,000

11.   (d)   The requirement is to determine the balance in the new partner's capital account after admission using the bonus method. In this case, Grant is investing land with a FMV of $15,000 for a 1/5 interest in the new total capital of $95,000. Using the bonus method, the new capital $95,000 equals the total of the old capital plus Grant's investment ($60,000 + $20,000 + $15,000). Thus, a bonus of $4,000 is

being credited to Grant's capital account because his interest (1/5 of $95,000, or $19,000) exceeds his investment ($15,000). The bonus to the new partner is charged to the old partners' capital accounts in their profit and loss ratios.

12.   (c)   The requirement is to determine the amount of goodwill implied by Zorn's investment. Zorn is investing $100,000 for a 1/3 interest in the partnership. Therefore, $100,000 represents 1/3 of the value of the equity of the new partnership ($100,000 ÷ 1/3 = $300,000). The tangible portion of the equity is $250,000 ($60,000 + $90,000 + $100,000). Thus, the total implied goodwill is $50,000 ($300,000 – $250,000).

13.   (d)   If no goodwill or bonus is to be recorded, the formula to determine the necessary contribution is

$$\begin{array}{c}\text{Partnership} \\ \text{interest of} \\ \text{new partner}\end{array} \times \left(\begin{array}{c}\text{Capital bal.} \\ \text{of existing} \\ \text{partners}\end{array} + \begin{array}{c}\text{Amount} \\ \text{to be} \\ \text{contributed}\end{array}\right) = \begin{array}{c}\text{Amount} \\ \text{to be} \\ \text{contributed}\end{array}$$

20% x ($580,000 + x)	=	x
$116,000 + .2x	=	x
$116,000	=	.8x
$145,000	=	x

An alternative computation is to divide the old partner's capital ($580,000) by their interest after the new partner's admission. The result is the total capital after admission ($580,000 ÷ 80% = $725,000). To compute the new partner's contribution, the old partners' capital can be subtracted from total capital ($725,000 – $580,000 = $145,000), or total capital can be multiplied by 20% (20% x $725,000 = $145,000).

14.   (b)   To determine the amount of cash distributed during liquidation, the solutions approach is to prepare an abbreviated statement of partnership liquidation. In a partnership liquidation, cash is distributed based on the capital balances of the partners **after** adjusting them for any income (loss) to the date of liquidation and any loans or advances between the partners and the partnership. The abbreviated statement follows:

	Alfa	Beda	Total
Beg. capital balance	$348,000	$232,000	$580,000
Adj. for loans		(30,000)	(30,000)
Adj. for loss on sale of assets* (60-40)	(75,000)	(50,000)	(125,000)
Adj. capital balance	$273,000	$152,000	$425,000

*($500,000 – $625,000)

Note that the total cash available also equals $425,000.

Beginning cash	$ 45,000
Proceeds from sale	500,000
Payment of AP	(120,000)
	$425,000

Therefore, Alfa can receive $273,000 in cash in full liquidation of his capital balance.

15.   (d)   The bonus method implies that the old partners either received a bonus from the new partner, or they paid a bonus to the new partner. In this case, Colter, the new partner contributed an amount in excess of the amount credited to Colter's capital account. Accordingly, the excess should be treated as a bonus to Adel and Brick. This bonus should be treated as an adjustment to the old partners' capital accounts and should be allocated by using Adel and Brick's old profit and loss ratio. Therefore, answer (d) is correct.

D.3.a.(2) Partner Death or Withdrawal

16. **(c)** Eddy is to be paid $180,000 for his 50% interest in the partnership. This implies that the net assets of the partnership are worth $360,000 ($180,000 ÷ 50%). Since the net assets are currently reported at $320,000, implied goodwill is $40,000 ($360,000 − $320,000). When goodwill is recorded, the goodwill account is debited and the partners' capital accounts are credited for their share of the goodwill. Therefore, the capital balances of Fox and Grimm are $108,000 and $72,000, as computed below.

	Fox	*Grimm*
Previous capital balance	$96,000	$64,000
Share of goodwill		
Fox (30% x $40,000)	12,000	
Grimm (20% x $40,000)		8,000
New capital balance	$108,000	$72,000

17. **(b)** Hamm will pay $140,000 for a 25% interest in the partnership. This implies that the net assets of the partnership, including the new investment, are worth $560,000 ($140,000 ÷ 25%). Net assets are currently reported at $320,000, and Hamm's cash payment of $140,000 brings that total up to $460,000. Therefore, implied goodwill is $100,000 [$560,000 − ($320,000 + $140,000)]. When goodwill is recorded, the goodwill account is debited and the partners' capital accounts are credited for their share of goodwill. Therefore, Eddy's capital balance ($160,000) is increased by his share of the goodwill (50% x $100,000 = $50,000), to result in a balance of $210,000 ($160,000 + $50,000).

18. **(c)** The requirement is to determine the balance in Maduro's capital account after Coll's retirement. When a partner withdraws from a partnership a determination of the fair market value of the entity must be made. Since it is stated in the problem that the withdrawing partner is selling his interest to the partnership and that no goodwill is to be recorded, the bonus method must be employed after restatement of assets to FMV. The capital accounts after restatement to FMV would be

Coll
  [$42,000 + 20%($216,000 − $180,000)] = $ 49,200

Maduro
  [$39,000 + 20%($216,000 − $180,000)] = $ 46,200

Prieto
  [$90,000 + 60%($216,000 − $180,000)] = $111,600

The bonus paid to Coll is the difference between the cash paid to him for his partnership interest and the balance of that interest plus his loan balance.

Bonus = [$61,200 − ($49,200 + $9,000)] = $3,000

Maduro's capital account would be reduced by his proportionate share of the bonus, based on the profit and loss ratio of the remaining partners [20%/(20% + 60%) = 25%].

Maduro's capital [$46,200 − 25% ($3,000)] = $45,450.

19. **(d)** Under both the bonus and goodwill methods, the assets of the partnership must first be restated to their fair market value. Then, the withdrawing partner's capital account must be adjusted to the amount that the withdrawing partner is expected to receive. When the bonus method is used, no new goodwill is recorded. Instead, the existing partners' capital accounts are reduced by the amount necessary to increase the withdrawing partner's capital to the amount s/he is to be paid. When the goodwill method is used, new goodwill is recorded, and each partner's capital account is increased accordingly. Therefore, answer (d) is correct since the bonus method results in a **decrease** of existing partners' capital accounts, while the goodwill method results in an **increase** of existing partners' capital accounts.

20. **(c)** Answer (c) is correct, because under the bonus method, adjustments are made only among partner's capital accounts (no goodwill is recorded on the partnership books). Since Mill's partnership interest exceeded the amount of Mill's capital balance, the excess interest would reduce the capital balances of Yale and Lear. Answer (a) is incorrect because only under the goodwill method can the excess interest be recorded as goodwill. Answer (b) is incorrect because under no circumstances should the excess partnership interest be recorded as an expense. Answer (d) is incorrect because the remaining partners' capital balances are reduced.

D.4. Partnership Liquidation

21. **(a)** This situation represents a simple liquidation since all assets are distributed at one point in time rather than in installments. In a simple liquidation all of the noncash assets are sold and the proceeds from their sale are compared to their book value to compute the gain or loss. The gain or loss on the assets is then distributed to the partners' accounts before any of the cash is distributed. The partner loan should not be considered a noncash asset for the purpose of determining gain or loss, thus, Smith is responsible to the partnership for the repayment of the entire amount of the loan. The repayment of the loan reduces that partner's (Smith) distribution as follows:

Partner balances before liquidation	*Smith*	*Jones*	*Total*
Loan (debit)	($20,000)		($20,000)
Capital (credit)	195,000	$155,000	350,000
Net balances	$175,000	$155,000	$330,000
Loss on sale of other assets (450 − 385)	39,000	26,000	(65,000)
Cash available for partners	$136,000	$129,000	$265,000
Cash available for credits			120,000
Total cash from sale of noncash assets			$385,000

Therefore, answer (a), $136,000 is the correct response.

22. **(a)** A schedule of safe payments must be prepared to determine the amount of cash to be distributed to each partner at January 15, 1999. The first cash sale of other assets with a total book value of $150,000 realized $120,000 in cash, resulting in a $30,000 loss. This loss is allocated among the partners based upon their profit and loss ratios. The schedule is completed based upon the assumption that the remaining other assets are totally worthless, and their book values are distributed to the partners as losses, based upon the partners' profit and loss ratios. The cash payments to each partner can be found at the bottom of the schedule.

	Cash	*O/A*	*Liab.*
Beginning	$ 50	$250	$ 60
Sale of assets	+120	−150	
	170	100	60
Dist. to creditors	−60		−60
	110	100	-0-
Disposal of other assets		−100	
Dist. to partners	−110		
	-0-	-0-	-0-

	Capital		
	C	*D*	*E*
Beginning	$ 80,000	$ 90,000	$ 70,000
Sale of assets	−15,000	− 9,000	− 6,000
	65,000	81,000	64,000
Disposal of other assets	−50,000	−30,000	−20,000
	15,000	51,000	44,000
Dist. to partners	−15,000	−51,000	−44,000
	-0-	-0-	-0-

Thus, the cash should be distributed as follows: $15,000 to Cobb, $51,000 to Davis, and $44,000 to Eddy.

D.5. Incorporation of a Partnership

23. **(d)** When a partnership incorporates, assets and liabilities must be revalued to their fair market values on the date of incorporation. In this case, the net assets have a fair market value of $92,000 ($80,000 + $12,000) and the amount to be credited to Additional Paid-in Capital is $82,000 ($92,000 − $10,000 par value).

ARB, APB, AND FASB PRONOUNCEMENTS

Study Program for the Accounting Pronouncements

Outlines of the unsuperseded official accounting pronouncements are presented in chronological order in this chapter. Effective dates of pronouncements are omitted unless they are a current implementation problem. You should:

1. Study through the outlines as you are referred to them in the modules in this chapter
   a. On the exam it is not necessary to know the pronouncement numbers
   b. The outlines presume some prior study of the topics covered by the pronouncements
   c. If the outlines are your first contact with the topics
      (1) Read the outline for an overview of the pronouncement
      (2) Refer to an intermediate/advanced financial accounting textbook, if necessary
   d. Note that additional comments have been added to some outlines, relating to the rationale or justification for these standards
2. **Required disclosures.** It is not necessary to memorize all the required disclosures. A good approach is to take the position of a financial analyst: What data would you want to know? Utilizing this approach, you only have to memorize any exceptions (i.e., items you would not normally think a financial analyst would be interested in).

References to FASB Materials

Each of the outlines in the last part of this chapter is referenced to the section where it is found in the FASB *Accounting Standards--Current Texts: General/ Industry Standards*, John Wiley & Sons, Inc. These references appear in parentheses right after the original pronouncement reference in the heading of each pronouncement outlined. When using either the FASB's Current Text or Original Pronouncements to supplement your study, be sure you have a recent edition (not more than 2 years old). If your study of intermediate accounting has been recent (within the last 2 years) or, if longer and you purchase a new intermediate text, it is not likely that you will need them.

In studying the outlines, you might notice that parts of some pronouncements have not been outlined. The reason some sections of the pronouncements are excluded from the outlines is that they have never been tested on the exam. Also, outlines for very specialized pronouncements (e.g., SFAS 50, Financial Reporting in the Record and Music Industry) are not included in this manual. Several others are outlined more generally. Only those FASB Interpretations and Technical Bulletins having widespread applicability are included in this chapter. They are set apart with solid lines **only** to distinguish them from the SFAS.

Accounting Research Bulletins
ARB 43--Chapter 1A (A31, B50, C08, C23, R36, R70, R75)[*] Rules Adopted by Membership

Five rules recommended by the Committee on Cooperation with Stock Exchanges in 1934. The last rule is from another 1934 Institute committee.

1. Profit is realized at the point of sale unless collection is not reasonably assured.
2. Capital (paid-in) surplus should not be charged with losses or expenses, except in quasi reorganizations.
3. Retained earnings of subsidiary created prior to acquisition is not part of consolidated retained earnings. This does not apply to poolings.
4. Receivables from officers, employees, and affiliates must be separately disclosed.
5. Par value of stock issued for assets cannot be used to value the assets if some of the stock is subsequently donated back to the corporation.

---

[*] *The references in parentheses are from the* **FASB Accounting Standards--Current Texts: Volumes I and II**, *John Wiley & Sons, Inc. These are included only for facilitating the use of the Current Texts for candidates who have access to them.*

Chapter 1B (C23) Profits or Losses on Treasury Stock (Revised by APB 6, para 12)

Profits on treasury stock are not income and should be reflected in capital surplus.

Chapter 2A (F43) Comparative Financial Statements (Cross-referenced to APB 20)

Comparative statements enhance the usefulness of financial statements and should be presented.

Chapter 3A (B05, I78) Current Assets and Current Liabilities

(Amended by APB 6, 21 and SFAS 6)

Chapter 3A contains the definitions and examples of current assets and liabilities.

A. **Current assets** are "cash and other assets or resources commonly identified as those which are reasonably expected to be (1) realized in cash, (2) sold, or (3) consumed during the ordinary operating cycle of the business."
   1. Cash available for current operations (para 4)
   2. Inventories
   3. Trade receivables
   4. Other receivables collectible in 1 year
   5. Installment, deferred accounts, and notes receivable
   6. Marketable securities available for current operations
   7. Prepaid expenses

B. **Current liabilities** are "obligations whose liquidation is reasonably expected to require the use of existing resources properly classifiable as current assets or the creation of other current liabilities during the ordinary operating cycle of the business."
   1. Trade payables
   2. Collections received in advance of services
   3. Accruals of expenses
   4. Other liabilities coming due in 1 year
   5. Note that liabilities not using current assets for liquidation are not current liabilities (e.g., bonds being repaid from a sinking fund)

C. **Operating cycle** is "average time intervening between the acquisition of materials or services entering this process and the final cash realization."

Chapter 4 (I78) Inventory Pricing

Contains 10 statements outlining inventory valuation
   1. Inventory consists of tangible personal property
      a. Held for sale in ordinary course of business
      b. In process of production for such sale
      c. To be currently consumed in the production of such goods
   2. Major objective of inventory valuation is proper income determination
      a. Matching of costs and revenues
   3. Primary basis is cost. Cost includes all reasonable and necessary costs of preparing inventory for sale. These costs would include expenditures to bring inventory to existing condition and location.
      a. Direct or variable costing is not acceptable (use absorption costing)
   4. Cost may be determined under any flow assumption. Use method which most clearly reflects income.
   5. Departure from cost to market required when utility of goods, in their disposal in the ordinary course of business, is not as great as cost.
      a. Write-down recognized as a loss of the current period
      b. Use of lower of cost or market method more fairly reflects income of the period than would the cost method
      c. Results in a more realistic estimate of future cash flows to be realized from the assets
      d. Supported by doctrine of conservatism
   6. Market means current replacement cost subject to
      a. Market should not exceed net realizable value (sales price less selling and completion costs)
      b. Market should not be less than net realizable value less normal profit
   7. Lower of cost or market may be applied to individual items or the inventory as a whole. Use method which most clearly reflects income.
   8. Basis for stating inventories and changes therein should be consistent and disclosed.

9. Inventories may be stated above cost in exceptional cases
    a. No basis for cost allocation (e.g., meatpacking)
    b. Disposal assured and price known (e.g., precious metals)
10. Purchase commitment loss should be recognized in the same manner as inventory losses.

Chapter 7A (Q15) Quasi Reorganization

Describes what is permitted before and after quasi reorganization.
A. Procedure in readjustment
    1. A clear report should be made to shareholders to obtain consent for the proposed restatements of assets and shareholders' equity.
    2. Write-down of assets should not go below fair value.
    3. If potential losses exist, provide for maximum probable loss.
    4. When determined, amounts should be written off first to retained earnings and then to capital surplus.
B. Procedure after readjustment
    1. After readjustment, accounting should be similar to that appropriate for a new company
    2. A new, dated retained earnings account should be created
        a. Dated for 10 years to indicate when the reorganization occurred.

Chapter 7B (C20, Q15) Stock Dividends and Stock Splits

A. **Dividend**--evidence given to shareholders of their share of accumulated earnings which are going to be retained in the business
B. **Split**--stock issued to increase number of outstanding shares to reduce market price and/or to obtain a wider distribution of ownership
C. To the recipient, splits and dividends are not income. Dividends and splits take nothing from the property of the corporation and add nothing to the property of the recipient.
    1. Upon receipt of stock dividend or split, recipient should reallocate cost of shares previously held to all shares held.
D. Issuer of a stock dividend (issuance is small in relation to shares outstanding and consequently has no apparent effect on market price) should capitalize retained earnings equal to the fair market value of shares issued.
    1. Unless retained earnings are capitalized, retained earnings thought to be distributed by the recipient will be available for subsequent distribution.
    2. Issuances less than 20-25% of previously outstanding shares are dividends. Issuances greater than 20-25% of previously outstanding shares are splits.
    3. Where stock dividend is so large it may materially affect price (a split effected in the form of a dividend), no capitalization is necessary other than that required by law.
        a. Some jurisdictions require that the par value of splits be capitalized (i.e., changes in par value are not permitted).
    4. For closely held corporations, there is no need to capitalize retained earnings other than to meet legal requirements.

Chapter 10A (T10) Real and Personal Property Taxes

Accounting for personal and real property taxes which vary in time of determination and collection from state to state
A. In practice, the dates below have been used to apportion taxes between accounting periods.
    1. Assessment date
    2. Beginning of fiscal period of taxing authority
    3. End of fiscal period of taxing authority
    4. Lien date
    5. Date of tax levy
    6. Date tax is payable
    7. Date tax is delinquent
    8. Period appearing on tax bill
B. The most acceptable basis is a monthly accrual on the taxpayer's books during the fiscal period of the taxing authority.
    1. At year end, the books will show the appropriate prepayment or accrual.

2. An accrued liability, whether known or estimated, should be shown as a current liability.

3. On income statement, property taxes may be charged to operating expense, deducted separately from income, prorated among accounts to which they apply, or combined with other taxes (but not with income taxes).

Chapter 13B (C47) Stock Option Compensation Plans (Also see APB 25 and SFAS 123)

Cost of services received for compensation paid in stock options should be included in operations.

A. Compensation may arise when the corporation agrees to issue common stock to an employee at a stated price.
   1. Other options may result in employee obligations such as continued employment.
B. Stock options do not result in compensation if
   1. Stock options are offered at a reasonable amount to raise capital
   2. Stock options are offered at a reasonable amount to induce wider holdings by employees
C. Alternative dates of measurement are when
   1. Option plan is adopted
   2. Option is granted
   3. Grantee performs required conditions
   4. Grantee may first exercise option
   5. Grantee exercises option
   6. Grantee disposes of stock
D. Date of grant should be used
   1. Considering the date of grant as a contract, it is the date value is determined
   2. Date of grant is date corporation foregoes alternative use
   3. Adoption date and grantee's disposition date are not relevant
E. Compensation is excess of **fair value over option price**. APB 25 states the quoted market price or best estimate of fair market value is fair value. SFAS 123 uses an option pricing model to determine fair value.
F. Compensation cost should be spread over the period of service covered by the option contract.
   1. Cash and compensation are equal to consideration for the stock when exercised (amount credited to stock and paid-in capital).
G. Disclosure should be made annually of
   1. Number of shares under option
   2. Option price
   3. Number of shares exercisable
   4. Number of shares and price of options exercised

ARB 45 (Co4) Long-Term Construction Contracts

Discusses accounting for multiple period projects

A. The percentage-of-completion method recognizes income as work progresses.
   1. Recognized income based upon a percentage of estimated total income
      a. (Incurred costs to date)/(Total expected costs) known as cost-to-cost measure
      b. Other measure of progress based on work performed (e.g., engineering or architectural estimate)
   2. Costs, for percentage-of-completion estimate, might exclude materials and subcontracts, especially in the early stages of a contract.
      a. Avoids overstating the percentage-of-completion
   3. If a loss is estimated on the contract, the **entire loss** should be recognized currently.
   4. Contracts should be separated into net assets and net liabilities.
      a. Current assets include costs and income (loss) in excess of billings.
      b. Current liabilities include billings in excess of costs and income (loss).
      c. Contracts should not be offset on the balance sheet.
   5. Advantages of percentage-of-completion are periodic recognition of income and reflection of the status of the contract.
      a. Results in appropriate matching of costs and revenues

    b. Avoids distortions in income from year to year and thus provides more relevant information to financial statement users

6. The principal disadvantage is the reliance on estimates.

7. The percentage-of-completion method is required when total costs and percent of completion can be reasonably estimated.

B. The completed-contract method recognizes income when the contract is complete.

    1. General and administrative expenses can be allocated to contracts.

      a. Not necessary if many projects are in process

      b. No excessive deferring of costs

    2. Provision should be made for **entire amount of any expected loss** prior to job completion.

      a. That is, losses are recognized immediately in their entirety--conservative treatment

    3. An excess of accumulated costs over related billings is a current asset. An excess of accumulated billings over related costs is a liability (current in most cases).

      a. Balance sheet accounts are determined as in A.4., except no income is included

      b. Recognized losses in B.2. reduce accumulated costs.

    4. The advantage of the completed-contract method is that it is based on final results, and its primary disadvantage is that it does not reflect current performance.

      a. Overall, the completed-contract method represents a conservative approach.

ARB 51 (B50, C20, C51, R70) Consolidated Financial Statements (Also see APB 16)
(Amended by SFAS 94)

A. Consolidated statements present financial statements of a parent and subsidiaries, as if the group were a single company for the benefit of the parent's stockholders and creditors.

    1. **Substance** (effectively a single entity) takes precedence over **legal form** (legally separate entities).

    2. Consolidated financial statements result in **more meaningful presentation of financial position and operating results** than if separate statements were presented for the parent and subsidiary.

B. The general condition for consolidation is over 50% ownership of subsidiaries.

    1. Theoretical condition is **control** of the subsidiaries.

      a. This is generally implicit in greater than 50% ownership.

    2. Subsidiaries which are a temporary investment (in reorganization, in bankruptcy, etc.) should not be consolidated.

    3. Large indebtedness to bondholders should not preclude consolidation.

C. A difference in fiscal periods should not preclude consolidation.

    1. Differences of 3 months are acceptable if one discloses material intervening events.

    2. Differences in excess of 3 months should be consolidated on the basis of interim statements of the subsidiary.

D. Consolidation policy should be disclosed by headings or footnotes.

E. Intercompany balances and transactions should be eliminated in consolidated statements.

    1. Intercompany gains and losses on assets remaining in the group should be eliminated (eliminate entire gross profit or loss even on transactions with minority interest subsidiaries).

F. Retained earnings of subsidiaries at the acquisition date should not appear in the consolidated statements.

G. When a parent purchases a subsidiary in several blocks of stock, the subsidiary's retained earnings should be determined by the step method (apply equity method to subsidiary retroactively).

H. When a subsidiary is purchased in midyear, subsidiary operations may be included in the consolidated income statement for the year and then the operating results prior to acquisition would be deducted.

    1. As an alternative for a subsidiary purchased in midyear, post acquisition operations can be included in the consolidated income statement.

    2. For midyear disposals, omit operations from the consolidated income statement and include equity in subsidiary's operations up to disposal date as a separate item in the income statement.

NOTE: F. through H. pertain only to acquisitions accounted for as purchases per APB 16.

I. Sometimes combined, as distinguished from consolidated, financial statements are appropriate for commonly owned companies and are prepared when consolidated statements are not appropriate.

Accounting Principles Board Opinions
APB 6 (B05, C23, D40, I60) Status of Accounting Research Bulletins
A.   ARB 43, Chapter 1B   Treasury Stock
   1.   An excess of purchase price of treasury stock, purchased for retirement or constructive retirement, over par or stated value may be allocated between paid-in capital and retained earnings.
      a.   The charge to paid-in capital is limited to all paid-in capital from treasury stock transactions and retirements of the same issue and a pro rata portion of all other paid-in capital of that issue.
      b.   Also, paid-in capital applicable to fully retired issues may be charged.
   2.   Alternatively, losses may be charged entirely to retained earnings.
   3.   All gains on retirement of treasury stock go to paid-in capital.
   4.   When the decision to retire treasury stock has not been made, the cost of such is a contra sharehold-ers' equity item. Losses may only be charged to paid-in capital from treasury transactions and retire-ments of the same issue.
   5.   Some state laws prescribe accounting for treasury stock. The laws are to be followed where they are at variance with this APB. Disclose all statutory requirements concerning treasury stock such as divi-dend restrictions.
B.   ARB 43, Chapter 3A   Current Assets and Liabilities
   Unearned interest, finance charges, etc. included in receivables should be deducted from the related re-ceivable.
C.   ARB 43, Chapter 7B   Stock Dividends and Splits
   States "the shareholder has no income solely as a result of the fact that the corporation has income," but does not preclude use of the equity method.

APB 9 (I17, C08) Reporting the Results of Operations
A.   Designates a new format for income statement in which all normal operating items would be presented at the top of the income statement resulting in "net income before extraordinary items."
   1.   "Net income before extraordinary items" is followed by extraordinary items resulting in "net income."
B.   "Prior period adjustments" are excluded from the income statement and constitute adjustments of begin-ning retained earnings disclosed at the top of the retained earnings statement. (See SFAS 16.)
   1.   Beginning retained earnings are adjusted by "prior period adjustments" resulting in "restated begin-ning retained earnings."
   2.   "Restated retained earnings" is then adjusted for net income and dividends which results in ending re-tained earnings.
C.   Prior period adjustments should be disclosed in the period of adjustment.
   1.   The effect on each prior period presented should be disclosed including restated income taxes.
   2.   Disclosure in subsequent periods is not normally required.
   3.   Historical summary data should also be restated and disclosed in the period of adjustment.
D.   The APB also reaffirmed earlier positions that the following should not affect determination of net in-come:
   1.   Transactions in the company's own stock
   2.   Transfers to or from retained earnings
   3.   Quasi reorganization adjustments

APB 10 (A35, B10, C16, I24, I25, I28, R75) Omnibus Opinion--1966
A.   ARB 43, Chapter 3B   Working Capital
   1.   Offsetting of liabilities and assets in the balance sheet is not acceptable unless a right of offset exists.
   2.   Most government securities are not designed to be prepayment of taxes and thus may not be offset against tax liabilities. Only where an explicit prepayment exists may an offset be used.
B.   Installment method of accounting
   Revenues should be recognized at the point of sale unless receivables are in doubt. The installment or cost recovery method may be used.

APB 12 (C08, C38, D40, I69, V18) Omnibus Opinion--1967

A. Allowance or contra accounts (allowance for bad debts, accumulated depreciation, etc.) should be deducted from assets or groups of assets with appropriate disclosure.

B. Disclosure of depreciable assets should include
1. Depreciation expense for the period
2. Balances of major classes of depreciable assets by nature or function
3. Accumulated depreciation either by major class or in total
4. Description of method(s) of depreciation by major classes of assets

C. Changes in the separate shareholder equity accounts in addition to retained earnings and changes in number of equity securities must be disclosed in the year of change
1. In separate statements
2. Or the financial statements
3. Or the notes

APB 14 (D10, C08) Convertible Debt and Debt Issued With Stock Warrants

A. Convertible debt constitutes securities which are convertible into common stock of the user or affiliate. Terms generally include
1. Lower interest rate than on ordinary debt
2. Initial conversion price greater than the common price at time of issuance
3. A conversion price which does not decrease except to protect against dilution

B. While there are arguments to account for the debt and equity characteristics separately, the APB has concluded no proceeds of a convertible issue should be attributed to the conversion factor.
1. Primary **reasons** are
   a. The inseparability of the debt and conversion features
   b. The practical difficulties of valuing the conversion feature

C. When debt is issued with detachable purchase warrants, the debt and warrants generally trade separately and should be treated separately.
1. The allocation of proceeds should be based on relative market value at date of issuance.
2. Any resulting debt discount or premium should be accounted for as such.

D. Separate valuation of debt and warrants is applicable where the debt may be used as consideration when exercising the warrants. Separate valuation is **not** acceptable where the debt must be tendered to exercise the warrants (i.e., the warrants are, in essence, nondetachable).

APB 16 (B50, I17) Business Combinations

(Para 96 amended by SFAS 79)

Both pooling and purchase accounting are applicable to business combinations but not as alternatives. No part purchase, part pooling

A. A combination meeting all of the following criteria is a pooling; all others are purchases.
1. **Combining companies.** Independent ownerships are combined to continue previously separate operations (para 46).
   a. "Each of the combining companies is autonomous and has not been a subsidiary or division of another corporation within 2 years before the plan of combination is initiated."
   b. "Each of the combining companies is independent of the other combining companies."
      (1) No more than 10% of any combining company is held by any other combining company(ies).
2. **Combining of interest.** Combination by exchange of stock (para 47)
   a. "The combination is effected in a single transaction or is completed in accordance with a specific plan within 1 year after the plan is initiated."
   b. "A corporation offers and issues only common stock with rights identical to those of the majority of its outstanding voting common stock in exchange for substantially all of the voting common stock interest of another company at the date the plan of combination is consummated."
      (1) Cash may be distributed for partial shares but not pro rata to all stockholders.
      (2) 90% of stock outstanding at consummation must be acquired by issuing corporation.
   c. Five of the less significant criteria are not included in this outline.
3. **Absence of planned transactions** (para 48)

a. "The combined corporation does not agree directly or indirectly to retire or reacquire all or part of the common stock issued to effect the combination."

b. "The combined corporation does not enter into other financial arrangements for the benefit of the former stockholders of a combining company, such as a guaranty of loans secured by stock issued in the combination, which in effect negates the exchange of equity securities."

c. "The combined corporation does not intend or plan to dispose of a significant part of the assets of the combining companies within 2 years after the combination other than disposals in the ordinary course of business of the formerly separate companies and to eliminate duplicate facilities or excess capacity."

B. Application of **pooling method**

1. Assets and liabilities are aggregated after adjusting all the accounts to conform to a uniform set of methods. The accounting changes are made retroactively, and prior periods' statements restated.

2. Stockholder equities are also combined. If the par or stated value of the new corporation exceeds that of all the combining companies, the excess should be taken first from combined paid-in capital, and then from retained earnings.

    a. If a combining corporation has a deficit, it should not be eliminated before the combination but rather netted against the combined retained earnings.

    b. An issuing corporation using its treasury stock to effect a combination should account for it first as retired and then reissued.

3. The first combined income statement should be reported as if the pooling had taken place at the beginning of the period (i.e., restate pooling to beginning of period to report a year of combined operations).

    a. The effects of intercompany transactions on current assets and liabilities, revenues, and cost of sales during the interim period prior to the combination should be eliminated.

        (1) Per share effects of nonrecurring transactions on long-term assets and liabilities should be disclosed (they need not be eliminated).

    b. The balance sheet and other statements restated at the beginning of the period should be disclosed as being retroactively combined individual company statements.

    c. Revenue, extraordinary items, and net income of each of the combining companies for the interim period prior to the pooling should be disclosed in the notes to the financial statements.

4. The costs of a pooling are expensed as incurred.

5. The notes of a combined company in the period of pooling should disclose

    a. Name and description of pooled companies

    b. Pooling accounting was used

    c. Description and number of shares issued

    d. Details of operations of separate companies for period prior to pooling included in first year's operation

    e. Accounting adjustments to achieve uniform accounting methods

    f. Explanation of change in retained earnings caused by change in fiscal year

    g. Reconciliation of individual company operating results to combined results

6. The **rationale** for pooling of interests is that it represents a combination of ownership interests in companies that previously were operated separately. It is regarded as an arrangement among stockholder groups. Because of this, under pooling of interests the existing basis of accounting continues.

C. Application of the **purchase method**

1. The standard historical cost principle is applied to purchase accounting.

    a. Use fair value of property given or fair value of property received, whichever is more clearly evident.

2. The cost of a company includes direct costs of acquisition but not indirect general expenses.

3. Additional payments to be made, contingent on future earnings and/or security prices, should be disclosed but not recorded as a liability.

    a. If contingency payments are made because of attainment of specified earnings levels, the additional payment is considered an increase in the cost of the subsidiary (usually results in debit to goodwill).

    b. If contingency payments are made due to attainment of specified security price levels, the cost of the acquired company is not affected. Rather the amount originally recorded as consideration in acquisition should be reduced by the contingency payment (usually results in decreasing paid-in capital).

    c. If the contingency payments are based on both security prices and earnings, the payment should be separated and accounted as in a. and b.

4. The acquiring corporation should allocate the cost of the acquired company to assets and liabilities acquired. Independent appraisals may be used.

    a. Marketable securities--net realizable value

    b. Receivables--present value after allowance and collection costs

    c. Finished goods and work-in-process inventories--net realizable value less normal profit

    d. Raw materials--replacement costs

    e. Plant--replacement cost if to be used and at fair value lest cost to sell if to be sold

    f. Intangible assets (identifiable)--appraisal values

    g. Other assets--appraisal values

    h. Payables--present values

    i. Accruals (warranties, etc.)--present values

5. The acquiring company should recognize the accrual of interest on assets and liabilities recorded at present values.

    a. Previously recorded goodwill of the acquired company should not be recorded by the acquiring company.

    b. The acquiring company should retroactively adjust goodwill for unrecognized tax loss carryforwards of an acquired company as they are recognized.

6. SFAS 109 addresses accounting for deferred tax consequences of differences between assigned values and tax bases of assets and liabilities of enterprise acquired in purchase business combination.

7. The value assigned to net assets should not exceed cost.

    a. If the cost of the net assets acquired exceeds the net revised asset values, the excess should be recorded as goodwill.

    b. If the net revised asset value exceeds cost, the excess should be credited, pro rata, to all noncurrent assets except marketable securities.

        (1) If a credit (negative goodwill) continues to exist after all noncurrent assets except marketable securities are written down to zero, the excess is a deferred credit and should be taken to income systematically and rationally.

        (2) Negative goodwill should not be added directly to shareholders' equity at acquisition.

8. The date of acquisition is the date assets are received and securities issued.

9. The notes of the acquiring company in the year of purchase should include

    a. Name and description of acquired company

    b. Acquisition was a purchase

    c. Period that acquired results of operations are consolidated

    d. Cost of acquired company and shares issued

    e. Plan of amortization and goodwill

    f. Contingent payments

10. Pro forma results of operations of the current and immediate prior period (no other prior periods) should reflect operations of the combination including*

    a. Revenue

    b. Income before extraordinary items

    c. Net income

    d. EPS

11. The **rationale** for purchase accounting is that the business combination represents a bargained or arm's-length transaction. The purchased company is treated as an acquired asset. Because of this, a

---

* *Pro forma results in financial statements no longer required of nonpublic enterprises per SFAS 79.*

new basis of accounting for the net assets of the acquired company is established under purchase accounting.

APB 17 (I60) Intangible Assets
(R&D references amended by SFAS 2)
A. Costs of intangible assets acquired from others should be recorded as assets.
　1. Expenditures to develop or maintain goodwill should be expensed when the intangibles
　　a. Are not specifically identifiable
　　b. Have indeterminate lives
　　c. Are related to the enterprise as a whole
　2. Cost of an unidentifiable intangible is cash or fair value disbursed, or present value of liabilities assumed.
　3. Cost of an unidentifiable intangible (acquired with a group of assets) should be determined per APB 16.
B. Intangibles should be amortized systematically over years benefited in view of the following factors:
　1. Legal, regulatory, or contractual provisions
　2. Provisions for renewal or extension
　3. Obsolescence, demand, competition, etc.
　4. Life expectancies of employees
　5. Expected actions of competitors
　6. Benefits may not be reasonably projected
　7. Composite of many individual factors
C. Straight-line amortization should be used unless another method is more appropriate.
　1. Cost should be amortized over the life of each individual asset.
　2. Period of amortization should not exceed 40 years.
　3. The method and period should be disclosed.
D. Periodic review of amortization policies should be undertaken, and required changes should be made prospectively. Estimated life should not exceed 40 years from the date of acquisition.

APB 18 (I82) The Equity Method for Investments
A. The equity method should be used for corporate joint ventures.
B. The equity method should be applied to investments where less than 50% ownership is held but the investor **can exercise significant influence over operating and financing policies of the investee**.
　1. Twenty percent (20%) or more ownership should lead to presumption of substantial influence, unless there is evidence to the contrary.
　2. Conversely, less than 20% ownership leads to the presumption of no substantial influence unless there is evidence to the contrary.
　3. The 20% test should be based on voting stock outstanding and disregard common stock equivalents.
　4. The following procedures should be used in applying the equity method:
　　a. Intercompany profits should be eliminated.
　　b. Difference between cost and book value of net assets acquired should be accounted for per APB 16 and APB 17.
　　c. The investment account and investor's share of investee income should be presented as single amounts in investor statements with the exception of d. below.
　　d. Investor's share of discontinued operations, extraordinary items, cumulative effects of accounting changes, and prior period adjustments of investee should be so presented in statements of investor.
　　e. Investee capital transactions should be accounted for as are subsidiary capital transactions in consolidated statements.
　　f. Gains on sale of investment are the difference between selling price and carrying value of investment.
　　g. When investee and investor fiscal periods do not coincide, use most recent investee statement and have consistent time lag.
　　h. Losses, not temporary in nature, of investment value should be recognized by investor.

i. Investor's share of investee loss should not be recorded once investment account is written to zero. Subsequent income should be recognized after losses not recognized are made up.

j. Investor's share of investee's earnings should be computed after deducting investee's cumulative preferred dividends whether declared or not.

k. If an investor's holding falls below 20%, discontinue applying the equity method but make no retroactive adjustment.

l. When an investor's holding increases from a level less than 20% to a level equal to or greater than 20%, the investment account and retained earnings of the investor should be adjusted retroactively to reflect balances as if the equity account had been used. This is accounted for like a prior period adjustment.

5. Statements of investors applying the equity method should disclose
    a. Investees and percentages held
        (1) Accounting policies followed
        (2) Treatment of goodwill, if any
    b. Aggregate market value of investment (not for subsidiaries)
    c. When investments are material to investor, summarized information of assets, liabilities, and results of operations of investee may be necessary
    d. Conversion of securities, exercise of warrants, or issuances of investee's common stock which significantly affects investor's share of investee's income

---

FASB INTERPRETATION NO. 35 CRITERIA FOR APPLYING THE EQUITY METHOD OF ACCOUNTING FOR INVESTMENTS IN COMMON STOCK. Interprets APB 18.

Investors owning between 20 and 50 percent of an investee may **not** be able to exercise significant influence over the investee's operating and financial policies. The presumption of significant influence stands until overcome by evidence to the contrary, such as: (1) opposition by the investee, (2) agreements under which the investor surrenders shareholder rights, (3) majority ownership by a small group of shareholders, (4) inability to obtain desired information from the investee, (5) inability to obtain representation on investee board of directors, etc. Whether contrary evidence is sufficient to negate the presumption of significant influence is a matter of judgment requiring a careful evaluation of all pertinent facts and circumstances, in some cases over an extended period of time. Application of this interpretation resulting in changes to or from the equity method shall be treated per APB 18, paras 19l and 19m.

APB 20 (A06, A35) Accounting Changes

Prescribes accounting for three types of accounting changes and correction of an error in prior periods' financial statements. Both should be reported to facilitate analysis and understanding of the financial statements.

A. Changes in principle
    1. Changes of principles should not be made unless to a preferable principle.
        a. When the APB expresses a preference or rejects a principle, this is a justification for change.
        b. Burden of justification for other changes rests on entity proposing change.
    2. Special changes require recognition of cumulative effect on beginning retained earnings as a prior period adjustment, as if new principle had always been followed, and retroactive adjustment of prior period statements.
        a. Special changes include
            (1) **From** LIFO to any other inventory method
            (2) Change in accounting for long-term contracts
            (3) Change to or from full cost method in extractive industries
        b. Nature and justification for change should be disclosed. Also, disclose effect on income before extraordinary items, net income, and per share amounts for all periods presented. The purpose of the disclosure is to avoid misleading financial statement users.
    3. For **all other changes** do not retroactively adjust prior periods.
        a. Apply new method to current year

    b. The cumulative effect of the change on beginning retained earnings, as if the new principle had always been followed, should be presented on the income statement between extraordinary items and net income.

      (1) The cumulative effect should be net of tax effects.

    c. The effect of the change in principle, on income before extraordinary items and net income, should be disclosed for the period of change.

    d. The pro forma effect of retroactive application of the change should be shown on the face of the income statement as a separate section.

    e. If pro forma amounts cannot be calculated, disclose reasons.

    f. If the cumulative effect cannot be computed, disclose reasons and effect of change on current year's income figures.

  4. Exception for a change in amortization (depreciation) method of assets applied to new assets only (existing assets depreciated using old method).

    a. No cumulative effect involved in this exception

    b. Disclose change and effect on income figures in year of change

B. Changes in estimate

  1. A change in estimate should be disclosed in the period of change if it affects that period only.

    a. Disclosure should be made in year of change if it affects future periods (e.g., change in useful life of depreciable assets).

    b. A change in estimate that is recognized by a change in principle should be accounted for as a change in estimate.

      (1) For example, change from capitalizing a cost to immediately expensing it

  2. Disclosure of changes in estimates should include effect on

    a. Income before extraordinary items

    b. Net income

    c. Related per share amounts

C. Change in accounting entity (e.g., a business combination accounted for as a pooling)

  1. Financial statements should be restated for all prior periods.

  2. The nature and reasons of change should be explained in year of change.

  3. Effect of changes on income figures and per share amounts should be disclosed for all periods presented.

D. Correction of an error in prior statements

  1. Prior period adjustment

  2. Nature of error and effect on the income figures and per share amounts should be disclosed in the period the error is discovered.

E. Methods of accounting for and disclosing accounting changes and error correction are designed to facilitate **consistency** in reporting by the entity from period to period, and **comparability** of reporting with that of other entities.

FASB INTERPRETATION NO. 1 ACCOUNTING CHANGES RELATED TO THE COST OF INVENTORY

    Changes in the cost composition of inventory is an accounting change and must conform to APB Opinion 20, including justification for the change. Preferably should be based on financial reporting objectives rather than tax-related benefits.

APB 21 (I69) Interest on Receivables and Payables

Accounting for receivables and payables whose face value does not approximate their present value

A. Applies to receivables and payables except

  1. Normal course of business receivables and payables maturing in less than 1 year

  2. Amounts not requiring repayment in the future (will be applied to future purchases or sales)

  3. Security deposits and retainages

  4. Customary transactions of those whose primary business is lending money

5. Transactions where interest rates are tax affected or legally prescribed (e.g., municipal bonds and tax settlements)
6. Parent-subsidiary transactions
7. Estimates of contractual obligations such as warranties

B. Notes exchanged for cash are recorded at their present value. Present value equals the cash paid/received. If face value of note ≠ cash paid/received, difference is a discount/premium.
1. If **unstated rights or privileges** are exchanged in issuance of note for cash, adjust cash payment to obtain present value of the note and unstated rights.

C. Notes exchanged for **goods or services** in arm's-length transaction are recorded at face amount (presumption that face amount = present value).
1. Presumption not valid if note is
    a. Noninterest-bearing
    b. Stated interest rate is unreasonable
    c. Face amount of the note differs materially from sales price of goods or services
2. When presumption not valid, record note at fair value of goods or services
    a. Compute **implicit** rate (rate that discounts the future value [face of note plus cash interest, if any] to fair value of goods and services) for interest expense/revenue recognition
3. When no established market price for goods and services exists, record note at its fair market value.
    a. Compute **implicit** rate (rate that discounts the future value [face of note plus cash interest, if any] to fair [present] value of note)for interest expense/revenue recognition
4. When no fair market value exists for either the goods and services or the note, record note at approximation of market value.
    a. Use **imputed** rate to compute present value of (and discount on) note.
    b. Imputed rate should approximate the rate an independent borrower and lender would negotiate in a similar transaction. Consider
        (1) Credit standing of issuer
        (2) Restrictive covenants
        (3) Collateral
        (4) Payment and other terms
        (5) Tax consequences to buyer and seller
        (6) Market rate for sale or assignment
        (7) Prime rate
        (8) Published rates of similar bonds
        (9) Current rates charged for mortgages on similar property

D. Discount or premium should be amortized by the interest method (constant rate of interest on the amount outstanding).
1. Other methods (e.g., straight-line) may be used if the results are not materially different from those of the interest method.

E. Discount or premium should be netted with the related asset or liability and **not** shown as separate asset or liability.
1. Issue costs should be reported as deferred charges.

APB 22 (A10) Disclosure of Accounting Policies
A. Accounting policies can affect reported results significantly and the usefulness of the financial statements depends on the user's understanding of the accounting policies adopted by the reporting entity. Disclosure of accounting policies are
1. Essential to users
2. Integral part of financial statements
3. Required for one or more financial statements
4. Required for not-for-profit entities
5. Not required for unaudited interim statements
    a. If no change in accounting policy has occurred

B. Disclosure should include accounting principles and methods of applying them if material to reported amounts.
   1. Generally, disclosure pertinent to principles involving recognition of revenue and expense
   2. Specifically, disclosure pertinent to
      a. Selection from existing alternatives
      b. Principles peculiar to a particular industry
      c. Unusual or innovative applications
   3. Examples
      a. Consolidation method
      b. Depreciation method
      c. Amortization of intangibles
      d. Inventory pricing
      e. R&D references amended by SFAS 2
      f. Translation of foreign currencies
      g. Long-term contract accounting
      h. Franchising and leasing activities
   4. Accounting policy disclosure should not duplicate disclosures elsewhere in the statements.
C. Particularly useful is a separate **Summary of Significant Accounting Policies** either preceding or as the initial note.

APB 23 (I25, I42, and B17) Accounting for Income Taxes--Special Areas
(Amended by SFAS 109)
A. Undistributed earnings of domestic subsidiaries
   1. Inclusion of undistributed earnings in pretax accounting income of parent (either through consolidation or equity method) results in temporary difference.
      a. Tax effect may be based on assumptions such as
         (1) Earnings would be distributed currently as dividends or
         (2) Earnings would be distributed in form of capital gain.
B. Foreign subsidiaries are not required to accrue deferred taxes for undistributed earnings if sufficient evidence exists that subsidiary would reinvest the undistributed earnings indefinitely or remit them tax free.

APB 25 (C47) Accounting for Stock Issued to Employees
Redefines "measure of compensation" in ARB 43, Chapter 13B and prescribes accounting for "variable factor" plans and tax benefits related to stock issue plans (also see SFAS 123)
A. No compensation is recognized for noncompensatory plans. Four noncompensation characteristics must be present.
   1. Substantially all full-time employees may participate.
   2. Stock is offered to employees equally or based on salary.
   3. Time permitted for exercise of option is reasonable.
   4. Discount from market is not greater than would be in an offer to sell stock to shareholders.
B. All other plans are compensatory.
   1. Compensation is the quoted market price less the amount the employee is required to pay.
      a. If unavailable, use best estimate of market value.
   2. The measurement date for determining compensation is the first date on which **both** of the following are known:
      a. Number of shares the individual may receive
      b. Option price, if any
   3. Note that the corporation recognizes compensation cost unless the employee must pay at least the market price (at measurement date).
C. Special rules in applying the measurement principle
   1. Cost of treasury stock distributed in an option plan does not determine compensation cost. Use market value unless
      a. Treasury stock is acquired during period, and
      b. Is awarded to employees shortly thereafter

2. Measurement date is not changed because of provision that termination of employment reduces shares available.
3. Measurement date may be year end rather than date of individual award if
   a. Award is provided by formal plan, and
   b. Plan designates factors to determine award, and
   c. Award pertains to current service
4. Measurement date for convertible securities is date the ratio of conversion is known.
   a. Compensation is based on the higher value of
      (1) Original security, or
      (2) Security into which original is convertible
5. If option plans are combination of more than one plan, compensation should be measured for each of the parts.
   a. If employee has a selection of alternatives, compensation on cost should be measured for the alternative most likely to be chosen.
D. Compensation expense should be recognized as an expense in periods employee performs services.
   1. If an employee performs services for several periods prior to stock issuance, compensation expense should be accrued.
      a. If the measurement date is after the grant date, the compensation should be accrued based on the current market price of stock.
   2. If stock is issued prior to when some of the services are performed, compensation expense should be deferred to those periods as a contra shareholder's equity item.
   3. Any adjustments of estimates regarding option plans should be done currently and prospectively.
      a. If an employee fails to exercise an option, compensation expense recognized in earlier periods should reduce compensation expense of the present period.

FASB INTERPRETATION NO. 28 ACCOUNTING FOR STOCK APPRECIATION RIGHTS AND OTHER VARIABLE STOCK OPTION OR AWARD PLANS

Changes in the market value of stock between the date of the grant and the measurement date (the date both the number of shares and the option price are known) are adjustments to compensation expense in the period the market value of the stock changes.

APB 26 (D14) Early Extinguishment of Debt

(Amended by SFAS 84)
A. Definitions (para 3)
   1. **Extinguishment of debt.** SFAS 76 applies to all extinguishments of debt whether early or not, except for troubled debt restructurings and debt conversions.
   2. **Net carrying amount.** "Amount due at maturity, adjusted for unamortized premium, discount, and cost of issuance."
   3. **Reacquisition price.** "Amount paid on extinguishment, including a call premium and miscellaneous costs of reacquisition."
   4. **Refunding.** Replacement of debt with other debt
B. Retirement is usually achieved by use of liquid assets.
   1. Currently in existence
   2. From sale of equity securities
   3. From sale of debt securities
C. A **difference** between **reacquisition price** and **net carrying amount** of the extinguished debt should be recognized in the year of extinguishment as a separate item.
   1. Gains and losses should not be amortized to future years.
   2. Gains and losses are extraordinary (except on purchases to satisfy sinking fund requirements that an enterprise would have to meet within 1 year of extinguishment date). See SFAS 4 and 64.

APB 28 (I73) Interim Financial Reporting
(Amended by SFAS 3, FASB Interpretation 18)
PART I Application of GAAP to Interim Periods
A. APB faced basic question about interim periods
  1. Are interim periods basic accounting periods?
  2. Are interim periods integral parts of the annual period?
B. The APB decided interim periods are an **integral part of an annual period**.
  1. Certain GAAP must be modified for interim reporting to better relate the interim period to the annual period.
C. Revenue should be recognized on the same basis as for the annual period.
D. Costs directly associated with revenue should be reported as in annual periods with the following **exceptions**:
  1. Estimated gross profit rates may be used to estimate inventory. Disclose method used and significant adjustments to reconcile to later physical inventory.
  2. When LIFO base period inventories are liquidated during the interim period but are expected to be replaced by the end of the annual period, cost of sales should be priced at replacement costs rather than at base period costs.
  3. Declines in inventory market values, unless temporary, should be recognized. Subsequent recovery of market value should be recognized as a cost recovery in the subsequent period.
  4. Unanticipated and unplanned standard cost variances should be recognized in the respective interim period.
E. The objective of reporting all other costs is to obtain fair measure of operations for the annual period. These expenses include
  1. Direct expenditures--salaries
  2. Accruals--vacation pay
  3. Amortization of deferrals--insurance
F. These costs should be applied in interim statements as follows:
  1. Charge to income as incurred, or based on time expiration, benefit received, etc. Follow procedures used in annual reports.
  2. Items not identified with specific period are charged as incurred.
  3. No arbitrary assignment.
  4. Gains and losses of any interim period that would not be deferred at year end cannot be deferred in the interim period.
  5. Costs frequently subjected to year-end adjustments should be anticipated in the interim periods.
    a. Inventory shrinkage
    b. Allowance for uncollectibles, quantity discounts
    c. Discretionary year-end bonuses
G. Seasonal variations in above items require disclosure and one may add 12-month reports ending at the interim date for current and preceding years.
H. The best estimate of the annual tax rate should be used to provide taxes on a year-to-date basis.
  1. The best estimate should take investment credits, capital gains, etc. into account, but not extraordinary items.
  2. Tax effects of losses in early portion of the year should not be recognized unless realization in subsequent interim periods is assured beyond a reasonable doubt (e.g., an established pattern of loss in early periods).
    a. When tax effects of losses in early periods are not recognized, no taxes should be accrued in later periods until loss credit has been used.
I. Extraordinary items should be disclosed separately and recognized in the interim period in which they occur.
  1. The materiality of extraordinary items should be determined in relation to expected annual income.
  2. Effects of disposals of a segment of a business are not extraordinary items, but should be disclosed separately.
  3. Extraordinary items should **not** be prorated over remainder of the year.

    4.   Contingencies should be disclosed in the same manner as required in annual reports.

J. Each interim report should disclose any change in accounting principle from

    1.   Comparable period of prior year

    2.   Preceding periods of current year

    3.   Prior annual report

K. Reporting these changes

    1.   APB 20 should be complied with, including restatement provisions.

    2.   A change in accounting estimate (including effect on estimated tax rate) should be accounted for in period of change and disclosed in subsequent periods of material.

    3.   Changes in principle, requiring cumulative effect, should be calculated for the effect on beginning annual retained earnings.

        a.   The cumulative effect should be reported in the first interim period.

        b.   Previously reported interim information should be restated.

        c.   Changes should be made in first period whenever possible.

        d.   Items not material to annual results, but material to interim results, should be disclosed separately in the interim reports.

PART II Required Interim Disclosures by Publicly Traded Companies

A. Minimum disclosure includes

    1.   Sales, provision for taxes, extraordinary items, cumulative effect of principle changes, and net income

    2.   BEPS and DEPS

    3.   Seasonal revenue, costs, and expenses

    4.   Significant changes in estimates of taxes

    5.   Disposal of a business segment and extraordinary items

    6.   Contingent items

    7.   Changes in accounting principles and estimates

    8.   Significant changes in financial position

    9.   Reportable operating segments

        a.   External revenues

        b.   Intersegment revenues

        c.   Segment profit/loss

        d.   Total assets (if material change from last annual report)

        e.   Description of changes from last annual report in method of determining segments or measurement of segment profit/loss

        f.   Reconciliation of total of reportable segments' profit/loss to corresponding enterprise amount

B. When **summarized interim data** are reported regularly, the above should be reported for the

    1.   Current quarter

    2.   Current year-to-date or last 12 months with comparable data for the preceding year

C. If fourth quarter data are not separately reported, disclose in annual report

    1.   Disposal of business segment

    2.   Extraordinary, unusual, and infrequent items

    3.   Aggregate year-end adjustments

D. The APB encourages interim disclosure of financial position and funds flow data.

    1.   If not disclosed, significant changes therein should be disclosed.

FASB INTERPRETATION NO. 18 ACCOUNTING FOR INCOME TAXES IN INTERIM PERIODS

    Tax on income from continuing operations for an interim period is based on estimated annual effective rate, which reflects anticipated tax planning alternatives. Expense of interim period is (Year-to-date income) x (Estimated rate) less (Expense recognized in prior interim periods). Tax effect of special items (below continuing operations) computed as they occur.

APB 29 (N35, C11) Accounting for Nonmonetary Transactions

A. Definitions (para 3)

1. **Monetary assets and liabilities.** "Assets and liabilities whose amounts are fixed in terms of units of currency by contract or otherwise. Examples are cash, short or long-term accounts and notes receivable in cash, and short or long-term accounts and notes payable in cash."

2. **Nonmonetary assets and liabilities.** "Assets and liabilities other than monetary ones. Examples are inventories; investments in common stocks; property, plant and equipment; and liabilities for rent collected in advance."

3. **Exchange.** "A reciprocal transfer between an enterprise and another entity that results in the enterprise's acquiring assets or services or satisfying liabilities by surrendering other assets or services or incurring other obligations."

4. **Nonreciprocal transfer.** "Transfer of assets or services in one direction, either from an enterprise to its owners (whether or not in exchange for their ownership interests) or another entity or from owners or another entity to enterprise. An entity's reacquisition of its outstanding stock is an example of a nonreciprocal transfer."

5. **Productive assets.** "Assets held for or used in the production of goods or services by the enterprise. Productive assets include an investment in another entity if the investment is accounted for by the equity method but exclude an investment not accounted for by that method. **Similar productive assets** are productive assets that are of the same general type, that perform the same function or that are employed in the same line of business."

B. APB 29 does **not** apply to
  1. Business combinations
  2. Transfer of nonmonetary assets between companies under common control
  3. Acquisition of nonmonetary assets with capital stock of an enterprise
  4. Stock dividends and splits, issued or received

C. APB 29 does apply to
  1. Nonreciprocal transfers with owners. Examples are distributions to stockholders
     a. Dividends
     b. To redeem capital stock
     c. In liquidation
     d. To settle rescission of a business combination
  2. Nonreciprocal transfer with other than owners. Examples are
     a. Contribution to charitable institutions
     b. Contribution of land by governmental unit to a business
  3. Nonmonetary exchange. Examples are exchanges of
     a. Property exchanged for dissimilar property
     b. Property exchanged for similar property

D. Nonmonetary transactions should generally be accounted for as are monetary transactions.
  1. Cost of a nonmonetary asset is the fair value of the asset surrendered to obtain it.
     a. The difference between fair value and book value is a gain or loss.
     b. Fair value of asset received, if clearer than that of asset given, should value transaction.
  2. Fair value should **not** be used to recognize gains unless fair value is determinable within reasonable limits.
  3. Fair value should **not** be used to recognize gains when exchange is not the culmination of an earnings process; for example
     a. Exchange of property held for sale for similar property
     b. Exchange of similar productive assets

E. If a nonmonetary exchange, which is not a culmination of the earnings process, contains boot received, the portion of the gain recognized should be limited to the ratio [Boot ÷ (Boot received + FMV of asset received)] times the gain (Boot + FMV received minus total book value given).
  1. Firm paying boot should **not** recognize any gain.

F. Liquidation distributions to owners should **not** be accounted for at fair value if a gain results (loss may be recognized).
  1. Use historical cost

2. Other nonreciprocal distributions to owners should be accounted for at fair value if fair value
   a. Is objectively measurable
   b. Would be clearly realizable if sold
G. Fair value should be determined in reference to
   1. Estimated realizable values in cash transactions of similar assets
   2. Quoted market prices
   3. Independent appraisals
   4. Estimated fair value of that received in exchange
   5. Other evidence
H. Nonmonetary transaction disclosures should include
   1. Nature of the transactions
   2. Basis of accounting
   3. Gains and losses recognized

FASB INTERPRETATION NO. 30 ACCOUNTING FOR INVOLUNTARY CONVERSIONS OF NONMONETARY ASSETS TO MONETARY ASSETS

When involuntary conversions of nonmonetary assets (e.g., fixed assets) to monetary assets (e.g., insurance proceeds) occur, the difference between the assets' cost and the monetary assets received should be reported as a gain or loss. If an unknown amount of monetary assets are to be received in a later period, gain (loss) is estimated per SFAS 5. Could be extraordinary per APB 30.

APB 30 (E09, I13, I17, I22) Reporting the Results of Operations
(Amended by SFAS 4)
A. Discontinued operations
   1. Definitions
      a. **Segment of a business.** "A component of an entity whose activities represent a separate major line of business or class of customer. A segment may be in the form of a subsidiary, a division or a department, and in some cases a joint venture or other nonsubsidiary investee, provided that its assets, results of operations, and activities can be clearly distinguished, physically and operationally and for financial reporting purposes, from the other assets, results of operations, and activities of the entity." (para 13)
      b. **Measurement date.** "Date on which the management having authority to approve the action commits itself to a formal plan to dispose of a segment of the business, whether by sale or abandonment." (para 14)
      c. **Disposal date.** "Date of closing the sale if the disposal is by sale or the date that operations cease if the disposal is by abandonment." (para 14)
   2. The results of discontinued operations should be disclosed separately after income from continuing operations and before extraordinary items.
      a. Any estimated loss from disposal of discontinued operations should be reported with the results of discontinued operations.
      b. A gain on disposal should be recognized when realized.
      c. An example from APB 30 follows:

Income from continuing operations before income taxes..	$xxxx	
Provision for income taxes....................................	xxx	
Income from continuing operations.................		$xxxx
Discontinued operations (Note ___):		
Income (loss) from operations of discontinued Division X (less applicable income taxes of $___)	$xxxx	
Loss on disposal of Division X, including provision of $___ for operating losses during phase-out period (less applicable income taxes of $___)............	xxxx	xxxx
Net income		$xxxx

3. "Income (loss) from operations" is calculated from beginning of period to measurement date.
4. "Gain (loss) on disposal" is calculated on the measurement date based on
   a. Net realizable value
   b. Less costs directly associated with disposal
      (1) Includes adjustments directly related to the disposal (e.g., severance pay, additional pension expenses, relocation expenses)
      (2) Does not include costs of normal business activities (e.g., write-down of AR or inventories)
   c. Plus (minus) income (loss) from operations subsequent to measurement date (i.e., during phase-out period). If disposal date is in a subsequent period, remaining phase-out income (loss) must be estimated.
      (1) Income limited to amount of loss otherwise recognizable from the disposal
      (2) Limited to those estimates which can be projected with reasonable accuracy
      (3) Limited, in the usual case, to disposals to be completed in less than 1 year
5. Additional disclosures for disposal of a segment
   a. Identity of segment
   b. Expected disposal date
   c. Expected manner of disposal
   d. Description of assets and liabilities remaining at balance sheet date
   e. Income or loss from operations and proceeds

B. Extraordinary items are **both** unusual and infrequent.
1. **Unusual nature.** "The underlying event or transaction should possess a high degree of abnormality and be of a type clearly unrelated to, or only incidentally related to, the ordinary and typical activities of the entity, taking into account the environment in which the entity operates." (para 20)
   a. Special characteristics of the entity
      (1) Type and scope of operations
      (2) Lines of business
      (3) Operating policies
2. **Infrequency of occurrence.** "The underlying event or transaction should be of a type that would not reasonably be expected to recur in the foreseeable future, taking into account the environment in which the entity operates." (para 20)
3. Example of extraordinary presentation (para 11)

Income before extraordinary items..	$xxx
Extraordinary items (less applicable income taxes of $__) (Note __)...	xxx
Net income ....$xxx	

4. Examples of gains and losses that are **not** generally extraordinary
   a. Write-downs or write-offs of receivables, inventories, R&D, etc.
   b. Translation of foreign exchange including major devaluations
   c. Disposal of a segment of a business
   d. Sale of productive assets
   e. Effects of strikes
   f. Accruals on long-term contracts
5. Extraordinary items should be classified separately if material on an individual basis.
6. Gains or losses which are unusual **or** infrequent but not both should be disclosed separately (but not net of tax) in the income statement or notes.
7. Per SFAS 4, gains (losses) on early extinguishment of debt are extraordinary items without regard to whether they meet both of the criteria.

Statements of Financial Accounting Standards
SFAS 2 (Co2, R50) Accounting for Research and Development Costs (R&D)
A. Establishes accounting standards for R&D costs with objective of reducing alternative practices. In summary, all R&D costs are expensed except intangible assets purchased from others and tangible assets that have alternative future uses (which are capitalized and depreciated or amortized as R&D expense).

1. SFAS 2 specifies
   a. R&D activities
   b. Elements of R&D costs
   c. Accounting for R&D costs
   d. Required disclosures for R&D
2. SFAS 2 does not cover
   a. R&D conducted for others under contract
   b. Activities unique to extractive industries

B. R&D activities
1. Research is "planned search or critical investigation aimed at discovery of new knowledge with the hope that such knowledge will be useful in developing a new product or service or a new process or technique in bringing about a significant improvement to an existing product or process."
2. Development is "the translation of research findings or other knowledge into a plan or design for a new product or process or for a significant improvement to an existing product or process whether intended for sale or use."
3. R&D examples
   a. Laboratory research to discover new knowledge
      (1) Seeking applications for new research findings
   b. Formulation and design of product alternatives
      (1) Testing for product alternatives
      (2) Modification of products or processes
   c. Preproduction prototypes and models
      (1) Tools, dies, etc. for new technology
      (2) Pilot plants not capable of commercial production
   d. Engineering activity until product is ready for manufacture
4. Exclusions from R&D
   a. Engineering during an early phase of commercial production
   b. Quality control for commercial production
   c. Troubleshooting during commercial production breakdowns
   d. Routine, ongoing efforts to improve products
   e. Adaptation of existing capability for a specific customer or other requirements
   f. Seasonal design changes to products
   g. Routine design of tools, dies, etc.
   h. Design, construction, startup, etc. of equipment except that used solely for R&D
   i. Legal work for patents or litigation
   j. Items a. - h. above are normally expensed but not as R&D; i. is capitalized

C. Elements of R&D costs
1. Materials, equipment, and facilities
   a. If acquired for a specific R&D project and have no alternative use
   b. If there are alternative uses, costs should be capitalized
      (1) Charge to R&D as these materials, etc., are used
2. Salaries, wages, and related costs
3. Intangibles purchased from others are treated as materials, etc. in 1. above
   a. If capitalized, amortization is covered by APB 17
4. R&D services **performed by others**
5. A reasonable allocation of indirect costs
   a. Exclude general and administrative costs not clearly related to R&D

D. Accounting for R&D
1. Expense R&D as incurred

E. Disclosure required on face of IS or notes
1. Total R&D expensed per period

SFAS 3 (I73) Reporting Accounting Changes in Interim Financial Statements
(Supersedes para 27 of APB 28)
(Amends para 31 of APB 28)
A. For cumulative effect changes made during the first interim period, include the cumulative effect of the change on beginning retained earnings in income of the first interim period.
   1. The new principle is used in the first period.
B. For cumulative effect changes made in other interim periods, restate the previous interim periods using the newly adopted principle.
   1. Also include the cumulative effect on beginning (of the fiscal year) retained earnings in the restated results of the first interim period.
      a. When prechange interim periods are subsequently presented (e.g., for comparative purposes), use restated figures.
C. For changes (principally to LIFO) where the effect on beginning retained earnings and pro forma amounts **cannot** be determined, explain reason for omitting such
   1. If change is made in other than first interim period, restate prior interim periods

SFAS 4 (D14, I17) Reporting Gains and Losses From Extinguishment of Debt
(Amends APB 30)
(Amended by SFAS 64)
A. Gains and losses from debt extinguishment are to be classified as extraordinary items (net of tax effect).
   1. Does not apply to purchases of debt to satisfy sinking fund requirements that an enterprise would have to meet within 1 year of extinguishment date.
   2. Such gains and losses must be disclosed as a separate item.
B. Disclosures required in FS or notes
   1. Description of transaction and source of funds
   2. Tax effect
   3. Per share amount of gain or loss (net of tax)

SFAS 5 (C59, I50, In6, R70) Accounting for Contingencies (Supersedes Chapter 6, ARB 43)
(Supersedes ARB 50)
A. Contingency is "an existing condition, situation, or set of circumstances involving uncertainty as to possible gain (loss) to an enterprise that will ultimately be resolved when one or more future events occur or fail to occur."
   1. Definitions
      a. Probable--future events are likely to occur
      b. Reasonably possible--chance of occurrence is more than remote, but less than likely
      c. Remote--chance of occurrence is slight
   2. Loss contingency examples
      a. Receivable collection
      b. Product warranty obligations
      c. Risk of property losses by fire, explosion, etc.
      d. Asset expropriation threat
      e. Pending, threatened, etc., litigation
      f. Actual or possible claims and assessments
      g. Catastrophe losses faced by insurance companies
      h. Guarantees of indebtedness of others
      i. Banks' obligations under "standby letters of credit"
      j. Agreements to repurchase receivables, related property, etc. that have been sold
B. Estimated loss from contingencies shall be accrued and charged to income when
   1. It is probable (at balance sheet date) that an asset has been impaired or liability incurred
   2. **And** the amount of loss can be reasonably estimated
      a. Difference between estimate recorded and actual amount determined in subsequent period is a change in accounting estimate
C. Loss contingency disclosures

1. Nature and amount of material items
2. Nonaccrued loss contingencies for which a reasonable possibility of loss exists
   a. Disclose nature of contingency
   b. Estimate possible range of loss
      (1) Or state estimate cannot be made
3. If a loss contingency develops after year end, but before statements are issued, disclosure of the nature of the contingency and amount may be necessary.
   a. If a year-end contingency results in a loss before issuance of the statements, disclosure (possibly pro forma amounts) may be necessary.
4. Disclose nature and amount of the following loss contingencies (even if remote)
   a. Guarantees of others' debts
   b. Standby letters of credit by banks
   c. Agreements to repurchase receivables
D. General, unspecified risks are not contingencies.
E. Appropriation of RE for contingencies shown within shareholders' equity is not prohibited.
   1. Cannot be shown outside shareholders' equity
   2. Contingency costs and losses cannot be charged to appropriation.
F. Gain contingency accounting
   1. Normally not reflected in accounts until realized.
   2. Adequate disclosure should be made without misleading implications of likelihood of realization.
G. Rationale for accounting for contingencies per SFAS 5
   1. Reflects **conservatism**--recognize losses immediately (if probable and reasonably estimable), but recognize gains only when realized.
   2. Results in better matching--contingent losses are recognized in time period of origin.

FASB INTERPRETATION NO. 14 REASONABLE ESTIMATION OF THE AMOUNT OF LOSS

A range of the amount of a loss is sufficient to meet the criteria of SFAS 5 that the amount of loss be "subject to reasonable estimate." When one amount in the range is a better estimate, use it; otherwise, use the minimum of the range and disclose range.

STATEMENTS OF POSITION NO. 96-1 ENVIRONMENTAL REMEDIATION LIABILITIES

This SOP includes accounting guidance, preceded by a very detailed description of relevant laws, remediation laws, remediation provisions and other pertinent information, useful to auditors as well as clients. Auditing guidance is limited to recitation of SFAS 5 concerns about reasonable estimation of loss accruals.

Accounting guidance includes the following provisions:
1. Interprets SFAS 5 in the context of environmental obligations (e.g., threshold for accrual of liability, etc.) and sets "benchmarks" for recognition.
2. Benchmarks for accrual and evaluation of estimated liability (stages which are deemed to be important to ascertaining the existence and amount of the liability) are
   a. Identification and verification of an entity as a potentially responsible party (PRP), since the proposal stipulated that accrual should be based on premise that expected costs will be borne by only the "participating potentially responsible parties" and that the "recalcitrant, unproven and unidentified" PRP will not contribute to costs of remediation
   b. Receipt of unilateral administrative order
   c. Participation, as a PRP, in the remedial investigation/feasibility study (RI/FS)
   d. Completion of the feasibility study
   e. Issuance of the Record of Decision (ROD)
   f. Remedial design through operation and maintenance, including postremediation monitoring
3. The amount of liability is affected by
   a. The entity's allocable share of liability for a specified site; and
   b. Its share of the amounts related to the site that will not be paid by the other PRP or the government

4. Costs to be included in the accrued liability are
   a. Incremental direct costs of the remediation effort itself; and
   b. Costs of compensation and benefits for employees directly involved in the remediation effort
   c. Costs are to be estimated based on existing laws and technologies, and not discounted to present value unless timing of cash payments is fixed or reliably determinable
5. Incremental direct costs will include such items as the following:
   a. Fees to outside law firms for work related to the remediation effort
   b. Costs relating to completing the RI/FS
   c. Fees to outside consulting and engineering firms for site investigations and development of remedial action plans and remedial actions
   d. Costs of contractors performing remedial actions
   e. Government oversight costs and past costs
   f. Cost of machinery and equipment dedicated to the remedial actions that do not have an alternative use
   g. Assessments by a PRP group covering costs incurred by the group in dealing with a site
   h. Costs of operation and maintenance of the remedial action, including costs of postremediation monitoring required by the remedial action plan

This SOP emphasizes the EITF 93-5, *Accounting for Environmental Liabilities*, consensus that potential recoveries cannot be offset against estimated liability, and further notes that any recovery recognized as an asset should be reflected at fair value, which implies that only the present value of future recoveries be recorded. It also stipulates that environmental cleanup costs are not unusual in nature, and thus cannot be shown as extraordinary items in the income statement. Furthermore, it is presumed that the costs are operating in nature, and thus cannot normally be included in "other income and expense" category.

Finally, this SOP calls for improved disclosure of accounting policies regarding recognition of a liability and related asset (for recoveries from third parties).

SFAS 6 (B05) Classification of Short-Term Obligations Expected to Be Refinanced
(Modifies para 8 of Chapter 3A, ARB 43)
A. Short-term obligations shall be classified as a current liability unless
   1. Enterprise intends to refinance the obligation on a long-term basis
   2. AND the intent is supported by ability to refinance
      a. Post balance sheet issuance of long-term debt or equity securities, or
      b. Financing agreement that clearly permits refinancing on a long-term basis
         (1) Does not expire or is not callable for 1 year
         (2) No violation of the agreement exists at the balance sheet date or has occurred to date
   3. The amount of the short-term obligation excluded from current liability status should not exceed the
      a. Net proceeds of debt or securities issued
      b. Net amounts available under refinancing agreements
         (1) The enterprise must intend to exercise the financing agreement when the short-term obligation becomes due.
   4. Refinancing of short-term obligations is a FS **classification** issue, **not** a **recognition** and **measurement** issue.

FASB INTERPRETATION NO. 8 CLASSIFICATION OF A SHORT-TERM OBLIGATION REPAID PRIOR TO BEING REPLACED BY A LONG-TERM SECURITY
   Short-term obligations that are repaid after the balance sheet date but **before** funds are obtained from long-term financing are to be classified as current liabilities at the balance sheet date.

EXAMPLES:
   *In situation 1 below, the obligation will be classified as a noncurrent liability at the balance sheet date. Why? Proceeds from refinancing were obtained **prior** to the due date of the obligation.*

Situation 1: Classify obligation due 2/15 as noncurrent liability at balance sheet date.

        *In situation 2 below, the short-term obligation will be classified as a current liability. Why? Proceeds from the issuance of stock or long-term debt were not obtained until **after** the due date of the short-term obligation. Therefore, current assets must have been used to pay the short-term obligation.*

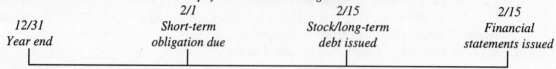

Situation 2: Classify obligation due 2/1 as current liability at balance sheet date

---

SFAS 7 (De4) Accounting and Reporting by Development Stage Companies

A. A company, division, component, etc., is in the development stage if
  1. Substantially all efforts are devoted toward establishing the business, or
  2. Principal operations are underway but have not produced significant revenues
B. Example activities of development stage companies
  1. Financial planning
  2. Raising capital
  3. Exploring or developing natural resources
  4. R&D
  5. Establishing sources of supply
  6. Acquiring property, plant, equipment, etc.
  7. Personnel recruitment and training
  8. Developing markets
  9. Production start-up
C. No special accounting standards apply to development stage companies.
  1. Report revenue in the income statement as in normal operations
  2. Expense costs as one would for a company in normal operations
  3. Capitalize costs as one would for a company in normal operations
    a. Determine cost recoverability within entity for which statements are being prepared
D. Development stage company statements include
  1. A balance sheet with cumulative net losses termed "deficit accumulated during development stage"
  2. An income statement with revenues and expenses for both current period and cumulative expenses and revenues from the inception of the development stage
  3. A statement of cash flows for both current period and cumulative amounts from inception
  4. Statement of owner's investment including
    a. Dates of issuance and number of shares, warrants, etc.
    b. Dollar amounts must be assigned to each issuance
      (1) Dollar amounts must be assigned for noncash consideration
    c. Dollar amounts received for each issuance or basis for valuing noncash consideration
  5. Identification of statements as those of a development stage company
  6. During the first period of normal operations, notes to statements should disclose that company was, but is no longer, in the development stage

SFAS 13 (L10, C51) Accounting for Leases (Supersedes APB 5, 7, 27, 31, and para 15 of APB 18; paras 18 and 23 amended by SFAS 91)

(The outline below is based on the comprehensive restatement as of January 1990 which includes SFAS 17 [rescinded by SFAS 91], 22, 23, 26, 27, 28, and 29 and Interpretations 19, 21, 23, 24, 26, and 27.)

    Applies to agreements for use of property, plant, and equipment, but not natural resources and not for licensing agreements such as patents and copyrights.

The major issue in accounting for leases is whether the benefits and risks incident to ownership have been transferred from lessor to lessee. If so, the lessor treats the lease as a sale or financing transaction and the lessee treats it as a purchase. Otherwise, the lease is accounted for as a rental agreement. These different treatments recognize the **substance** of a transaction rather than its **form**; that is, what is legally a lease may be effectively the same as or similar to an installment purchase by the lessee and a sale or financing transaction by the lessor.

The following terms are given specific definitions for the purpose of SFAS 13:

Bargain purchase option--A provision allowing the lessee the option of purchasing the leased property for an amount which is sufficiently lower than the expected fair value of the property at the date the option becomes exercisable. Exercise of the option must appear reasonably assured at the inception of the lease.

Contingent rentals--Rentals that represent the increases or decreases in lease payments which result from changes in the factors on which the lease payments are based occurring subsequent to the inception of the lease. However, changes due to the pass-through of increases in the construction or acquisition cost of the leased property or for increases in some measure of cost during the construction or preconstruction period should be excluded from contingent rentals. Also, provisions that are dependent only upon the passage of time should be excluded from contingent rentals. A lease payment that is based upon an existing index or rate, such as the consumer price index or the prime rate, is a contingent payment, and the computation of the minimum lease payments should be based upon the index or rate applicable at the inception of the lease.

Estimated economic life of lease property--The estimated remaining time which the property is expected to be economically usable by one or more users, with normal maintenance and repairs, for its intended purpose at the inception of the lease. This estimated time period should not be limited by the lease term.

Estimated residual value of leased property--The estimated fair value of the leased property at the end of the lease term.

Executory costs--Those costs such as insurance, maintenance, and taxes incurred for leased property, whether paid by the lessor or lessee. Amounts paid by a lessee in consideration for a guarantee from an unrelated third party of the residual value are also executory costs. If executory costs are paid by the lessor, any lessor's profit on those costs is considered the same as executory costs.

Fair value of leased property--The property's selling price in an arm's-length transaction between unrelated parties.

When the lessor is a **manufacturer or dealer**, the fair value of the property at the inception of the lease will ordinarily be its normal selling price net of volume or trade discounts.

When the lessor is not a **manufacturer or dealer**, the fair value of the property at the inception of the lease will ordinarily be its costs net of volume or trade discounts. However, if a significant amount of time has lapsed between the acquisition of the property by the lessor and the inception of the lease, fair value should be determined in light of market conditions prevailing at the inception of the lease. Thus, fair value may be greater or less than the cost or carrying amount of the property.

Implicit interest rate--The discount rate that, when applied to the minimum lease payments, excluding that portion of the payments representing executory costs to be paid by the lessor, together with any profit thereon, and the unguaranteed residual value accruing to the benefit of the lessor, causes the aggregate present value at the beginning of the lease term to be equal to the fair value of the leased property to the lessor at the inception of the lease, minus any investment tax credit retained and expected to be realized by the lessor (and plus initial direct costs in the case of direct financing leases)

Inception of the lease--The date of the written lease agreement or commitment (if earlier) wherein all principal provisions are fixed and no principal provisions remain to be negotiated

Incremental borrowing rate--The rate that, at the inception of the lease, the lessee would have incurred to borrow over a similar term (i.e., a loan term equal to the lease term) the funds necessary to purchase the leased asset

Initial direct costs--(See outline of SFAS 91 Section E.2.)

Lease term--The fixed, noncancelable term of the lease plus all renewal terms when renewal is reasonably assured. *NOTE: The lease term should not extend beyond the date of a bargain purchase option.* (See expanded definition in the outline of SFAS 98.)

Minimum lease payments--For the **lessee**: The payments that the lessee is or can be required to make in connection with the leased property. Contingent rental guarantees by the lessee of the lessor's debt, and the lessee's obligation to pay executory costs are excluded from minimum lease payments. If the lease contains a bargain purchase option, only the minimum rental payments over the lease term and the payment called for in the bargain purchase option are included in minimum lease payments. Otherwise, minimum lease payments include the following:

1. The minimum rental payments called for by the lease over the lease term
2. Any guarantee of residual value at the expiration of the lease term made by the lessee (or any party related to the lessee), whether or not the guarantee payment constitutes a purchase of the leased property. When the lessor has the right to require the lessee to purchase the property at termination of the lease for a certain or determinable amount, that amount shall be considered a lessee guarantee. When the lessee agrees to make up any deficiency below a stated amount in the lessor's realization of the residual value, the guarantee to be included in the MLP is the stated amount rather than an estimate of the deficiency to be made up.
3. Any payment that the lessee must or can be required to make upon **failure to renew or extend** the lease at the expiration of the lease term, whether or not the payment would constitute a purchase of the leased property

For the **lessor**: The payments described above plus any guarantee of the residual value or of the rental payments beyond the lease term by a third party unrelated to either the lessee or lessor (provided the third party is financially capable of discharging the guaranteed obligation).

Unguaranteed residual value--the estimated residual value of the leased property exclusive of any portion guaranteed by the lessee, by any party related to the lessee, or any party unrelated to the lessee. If the guarantor is related to the lessor, the residual value shall be considered as unguaranteed.

A. Classification of leases by lessees. Leases that meet one or more of the following criteria are accounted for as capital leases; all other leases are accounted for as operating leases:
   1. Lease transfers ownership (title) to lessee during lease term.
   2. Lease contains a bargain purchase option.
   3. Lease term is 75% or more of economic useful life of property.
   4. Present value of minimum lease payments equals 90% or more of FMV of the leased property.
      a. Present value is computed with lessee's incremental borrowing rate, unless lessor's implicit rate is known and is less than lessee's incremental rate (then use lessor's implicit rate).
      b. FMV is cash selling price for sales-type lease; lessor's cost for direct financing of lease. (If not recently purchased, estimate FMV)
      NOTE: 3. and 4. do not apply if lease begins in last 25% of asset's life.

B. Classification of leases by lessors
   1. Sales-type leases provide for a manufacturer or dealer profit (i.e., FMV of leased property is greater than lessor cost or carrying value).
      a. Sales-type leases must meet one of the four criteria for lessee capital leases (A.1. to A.4. above) and **both** of the following two criteria:
         (1) Collectibility is reasonably predictable, and
         (2) No important uncertainties regarding costs to be incurred by lessor exist, such as unusual guarantees of performance. Note estimation of executory expense such as insurance, maintenance, etc., is not considered.
   2. Direct financing leases must meet same criteria as sales-type leases (just above) but do not include a manufacturer's or dealer's profit.
   3. Operating leases are all other leases which have not been classified as sales-type, direct financing, or leveraged.

C. Lease classification is determined at the inception of the lease.
   1. If changes in the lease are subsequently made which change the classification, the lease should be considered a new agreement and reclassified and accounted for as a new lease. Exercise of renewal options, etc., are not changes in the lease.
   2. Changes in estimates (e.g., economic life or residual value) or other circumstances (e.g., default) do not result in a new agreement but accounts should be adjusted and gains or losses recognized.

3. At the time of inception, sales-type leases involving real estate are subject to the additional requirements that a sale of the same property would have to meet for full and immediate profit recognition under the AICPA Industry Accounting Guide applicable to sales of real estate. If these additional requirements are not satisfied, the lease that would otherwise have been accounted for as a sales-type lease will be classified as an operating lease.

4. Lease classification shall not be changed as a result of a business combination.

5. An important goal of SFAS 13 was to achieve **symmetry** in lease accounting (i.e., an operating lease for the lessee will be an operating lease for the lessor) and likewise for capital leases.

D. Accounting and reporting by lessees

1. Record capital leases as an asset and liability

   a. Leased asset shall not be recorded in excess of FMV. If the present value of the lease payments is greater than the FMV, the leased asset and related liability are recorded at FMV and the effective interest rate is thereby increased.

   b. Recognize interest expense using the effective interest method

   c. If there is a transfer of ownership or a bargain purchase option, the asset's depreciation/amortization period is its economic life. Otherwise, depreciate/amortize assets to the expected residual value at the end of the lease term

2. Rent on operating leases should be expensed on a straight-line basis unless another method is better suited to the particular benefits and costs associated with the lease.

3. When a lessee purchases a leased asset that has been capitalized, any difference between the purchase price and the lease obligation is an adjustment to the asset carrying value but **immediate recognition of a loss** is not prohibited.

4. Contingent rentals are reported as rent expense in the period incurred.

5. Disclosures by lessees include

   a. General description of leasing arrangement including

      (1) Basis of computing contingent payments

      (2) Existence and terms of renewal or purchase options and escalation clauses

      (3) Restrictions imposed by the lease agreement such as limitations on dividends and further leasing arrangements

   b. Capital lease requirements

      (1) Usual current/noncurrent classifications

      (2) Depreciation/amortization should be separately disclosed

      (3) Future minimum lease payments in the aggregate and for each of the 5 succeeding fiscal years with separate deductions being made to show the amounts representing executory cost and interest

      (4) Total minimum sublease rentals to be received in the future under noncancelable subleases

      (5) Total contingent rental actually incurred for each period for which an income statement is presented

   c. Operating leases which have initial or remaining noncancelable term > 1 year

      (1) Future minimum lease payments in the aggregate and for each of the 5 succeeding fiscal years

      (2) Total minimum sublease rentals to be received in the future under noncancelable subleases

      (3) All operating leases--rent expense of each IS period

         (a) Present separate amounts for minimum rentals, contingent rentals, and sublease rentals

         (b) Rental payments for leases with a term of a month or less may be excluded

E. Accounting and reporting by lessors

1. Sales-type leases

   a. Lease receivable is charged for the gross investment in the lease (the total net minimum lease payments plus the unguaranteed residual value). Sales is credited for the present value of the minimum lease payments.

   b. Cost of sales is the carrying value of the leased asset plus any initial direct costs less the present value of the unguaranteed residual value. Note that in a sales-type lease, initial direct costs are deducted in full in the period when the sale is recorded. Unearned Interest Income is credited for the difference between the gross investment and the sales price.

    c. Recognize interest revenue using the effective interest method

    d. At the end of the lease term, the balance in the receivable account should equal the amount of residual value guaranteed, if any.

    e. Contingent rental payments are reported as income in the period earned.

2. Direct financing leases

    a. Accounting is similar to sales-type lease except that no manufacturer's or dealer's profit is recognized.

    b. Lease receivable is charged for the gross investment in the lease, the asset account is credited for the net investment in the lease (cost to be acquired for purpose of leasing) and the difference is recorded as unearned income.

    c. Initial direct costs are recorded in a separate account. A new effective interest rate is computed that equates the minimum lease payments and any unguaranteed residual value with the combined outlay for the leased asset and initial direct costs. The initial direct costs and unearned lease revenue are both amortized so as to produce a constant rate of return over the life of the lease.

    d. The remaining requirements are the same as those for the sales-type lease.

3. Operating leases

    a. Leased property is to be included with or near PP&E on the BS, and lessor's normal depreciation policies should be applied.

    b. Rental revenue should be reported on a straight-line basis unless another method is better suited to the particular benefits and costs associated with the lease.

    c. Initial direct costs should be deferred and allocated over the lease term in proportion to the recognition of rental revenue.

F. Related-party leases shall be accounted for as unrelated-party leases except when terms have been significantly affected by relationship.

  1. Nature and extent of related-party leasing must be disclosed.

  2. See ARB 51 and APB 18 for consolidated or investor-investee transactions.

  3. Leasing subsidiaries must be consolidated.

G. Sale-leasebacks

  1. Legally two separate transactions

  2. Lessee (seller) accounts for the gain (loss) as follows:

    a. Loss (when FMV < Book value) on the sale should be recognized immediately.

    b. Gain treatment

      (1) Seller relinquishes the right to substantially all of the remaining use of the property sold (PV of reasonable rentals $\leq$ 10% of fair value of asset sold)--then separate transactions, and entire gain is recognized.

      (2) Seller retains more than a minor part, but less than substantially all of the remaining use (PV of reasonable rentals are > 10% but < 90% of fair value of asset sold)--then gain on sale is recognized to the extent of the excess of gain over the present value of minimum lease payments (operating) or the recorded amount of the leased asset (capital).

      (3) Seller retains right to substantially all of the remaining use--then entire gain on sale is deferred.

    c. If the gain is deferred and lease is accounted for as

      (1) Capital lease--defer and amortize gain over lease term using same method and life used for depreciating/amortizing cost of leased asset

        (a) Deferral and amortization of the gain are required because the sale and leaseback are components of a single transaction and are interdependent.

      (2) Operating lease--recognize gain on straight-line basis

        (a) Treat as a reduction of rent expense.

  3. Lessor records as a purchase of asset to be leased and as a direct financing or operating lease

---

FASB TECHNICAL BULLETIN 85-3 ACCOUNTING FOR OPERATING LEASES WITH SCHED-ULED RENT INCREASES

SFAS 13 requires lessees or lessors to recognize rent expense or rental income for an operating lease on a straight-line basis. Certain operating lease agreements specify scheduled rent increases over the lease term. The effects of these scheduled rent increases, which are included in minimum lease payments under SFAS 13, should also be recognized by lessors and lessees on a straight-line basis over the lease term.

SFAS 15 (D22) Accounting by Debtors and Creditors for Troubled Debt Restructurings
(Superseded by SFAS 114 with regard to creditors)
A. Troubled debt restructurings occur when a creditor is compelled to grant relief to a debtor due to the debtor's inability to service the debt. This SFAS prescribes accounting for such debt restructurings if
  1. By creditor-debtor agreement
  2. Imposed by a court
  3. Result of repossessions and foreclosures
  4. But not changes in lease agreements
    a. Nor legal actions to collect receivables
    b. Nor quasi reorganizations
B. If a **debtor** transfers assets to settle fully a payable, recognize a gain on restructuring equal to the book value of the payable less FMV of assets transferred.
  1. Estimate asset value by cash flows and risk if FMV cannot be determined.
  2. The difference between set FMV and carrying value of the assets transferred is a gain or loss in disposition of assets per APB 30.
C. If a **debtor** issues an equity interest to settle fully a payable, account for equity issued at FMV.
  1. Excess of carrying value of payable over equity FMV is a gain on restructuring.
D. A **debtor** having the terms of troubled debt modified should account for the restructure prospectively (i.e., no adjustment of the payable).
  1. Recompute the new effective rate of interest based on the new terms
    a. Total cash payments to be paid, less carrying value of payable is the interest
    b. Amortize the payable by the interest method (APB 21) using the new interest rate
  2. Exception is if restructured terms require total cash payments (including interest) which are less than the carrying value of the payable, write down the payable to the total cash to be paid
    a. Include contingent payments in calculation; this precludes recognizing a gain currently and interest expense later
    b. Recognize gain on the write-down
    c. All future cash payments reduce the payable (i.e., no interest expense is recognized)
E. If restructured by partial settlement (assets and/or equity issuance) and modified terms
  1. First account for asset and/or equity issuance per above
  2. Then account for modified terms per above
F. Related matters
  1. A repossession or foreclosure is accounted for per the above.
  2. Gains from restructuring debt are aggregated and, if material, are an extraordinary item (see SFAS 4).
  3. Contingent payments on restructured debt shall be recognized per SFAS 5 (i.e., its payment is probable and subject to reasonable estimate).
  4. Legal fees on debt restructuring involving equity issuance reduce the amounts credited to the equity accounts.
    a. All other direct costs of debt restructuring reduce gain or are expenses of the period if there is no gain.
G. Disclosures by **debtors**
  1. Description of major changes in debt of each restructuring
  2. Aggregate gain on debt restructuring and related tax effect

3. Aggregate net gain (loss) on asset transfers due to restructuring
4. EPS amount of aggregate gain on restructuring net of tax effect

SFAS 16 (A35, C59, I16, I17, and I73) Prior Period Adjustments (Supersedes paras 23 and 24 of APB 9) (Amends inconsistent references to APB 9 in APB 20, 30, and SFAS 5)

A. All P&L items are included in the determination of net income except the correction of an error in statements of a prior period.
   1. Account for and report as a prior period adjustment to beginning retained earnings
B. An exception exists for interim reporting regarding certain adjustments relating to prior interim periods of the current year.
   1. These "adjustments" (affecting prior interim periods of the current fiscal year) are settlements or adjustments of
      a. Litigation or similar claims
      b. Income taxes
      c. Renegotiation proceedings
      d. Utility revenue per the rate-making process
   2. These "adjustments" must also
      a. Be material to operating income, trends in income, etc.
      b. All or part of the adjustment is specifically identified with specified prior interim periods of the current fiscal year.
      c. Not subject to reasonable estimation prior to the current interim period (e.g, new retroactive tax legislation)

SFAS 34 (I67, I69) Capitalization of Interest Cost
(Paras 8 and 9 amended by SFAS 42)
(Paras 9, 10, and 20 amended by SFAS 58)

A. Interest costs, when material, incurred in acquiring the following types of assets, shall be capitalized:
   1. Assets constructed or produced for a firm's own use
      a. Including construction by others requiring progress payments
   2. Assets intended for lease or sale that are produced as discrete projects
      a. For example, ships and real estate developments
   3. But not on
      a. Routinely produced inventories
      b. Assets ready for their intended use
      c. Assets not being used nor being readied for use
      d. Land, unless it is being developed (e.g., as a plant site, real estate development, etc.)
   4. The objective of interest capitalization is to
      a. Reflect the acquisition cost of assets
      b. Match costs to revenues in the period benefited
   5. Capitalized interest shall be treated as any other asset cost for depreciation and other purposes.
   6. Required interest cost disclosures
      a. Total interest cost incurred
      b. Interest capitalized, if any
B. Amount of interest to be capitalized
   1. Conceptually, the interest that would have been avoided if the expenditures had not been made
   2. Based on the average accumulated expenditures on the asset for the period
      a. Includes payment of cash, transfer of other assets, and incurring interest-bearing liabilities
      b. Reasonable approximations are permitted
   3. Use the interest rates incurred during period
      a. First, the rates on specific new borrowings for the asset
      b. Second, a weighted-average of other borrowings
         (1) Use judgment to identify borrowings
   4. Interest cost capitalized in any period cannot exceed interest cost incurred in that period.
      a. On a consolidated basis for consolidated statements

     b.   On an individual company basis for individual company statements

    5. Capitalized interest should be compounded.

C. Interest capitalization period

    1. Begins when all the following three conditions are present:

       a.   Asset expenditures have been made

       b.   Activities to ready asset for intended use are in progress

          (1) Includes planning stages

       c.   Interest cost is being incurred

    2. If activities to ready asset for intended use cease, interest capitalization ceases

       a.   Not for brief interruptions that are externally imposed

    3. Capitalization period ends when asset is substantially complete

       a.   For assets completed in parts, interest capitalization on a part of the asset ends when that part is complete

       b.   Capitalize all interest on assets required to be completed in entirety until entire project is finished

    4. Interest capitalization continues if capitalized interest raises cost above market values

       a.   Reduction of asset cost to market value is a separate accounting transaction

SFAS 38 (B50, C59) Accounting for Preacquisition Contingencies of Purchased Enterprises
(Amends para 88 of APB 16)

A. This statement describes accounting for contingencies of an acquired enterprise that existed **prior** to the date on which a business combination accounted for as a **purchase** was consummated.

    1. In essence, the acquiring entity may assign final valuations to the acquired assets and liabilities up to 1 year after the combination occurs.

B. Definitions

    1. **Preacquisition contingency**--Contingency (asset, asset impairment, or liability) which is acquired from another enterprise in a business combination accounted for by the purchase method

    2. **Allocation period**--Period of time necessary to identify and measure the assets purchased and liabilities assumed. This period ends when the acquirer has secured all known and available information. Typically, this period should not extend beyond 1 year of the date the combination was consummated.

C. Portion of total purchase price allocated to a preacquisition contingency other than the potential tax benefit arising from temporary differences, carryforwards, and other income tax uncertainties related to the acquisition is measured as follows:

    1. If fair value is determinable during the "allocation period," use fair value as the basis of allocation.

    2. If fair value is **not** determinable during the "allocation period," use criteria of SFAS 5 and FASB Interpretation 14.

D. Adjustment resulting from a preacquisition contingency made subsequent to the "allocation period" is a determinant of net income in the later period.

SFAS 43 (C44) Accounting for Compensated Absences

A. This statement addresses the accounting for future sick pay benefits, holidays, vacation benefits, and other like compensated absences.

B. Accrual of a liability for future compensated absences is required if **all** of the conditions listed below exist.

    1. Obligation of employer to compensate employees arises from services already performed

    2. Obligation arises from vesting or accumulation of rights

    3. Probable payment of compensation

    4. Amount can be reasonably estimated

C. Above criteria require accrual of a liability for vacation benefits; however, other compensated absences typically may not require accrual of a liability.

    1. In spite of the above criteria, accrual of a liability is not required for accumulating nonvesting rights to receive sick pay benefits because amounts are typically not large enough to justify cost.

SFAS 45 (Fr3) Accounting for Franchise Fee Revenue

A. Definitions

1. **Franchisee**--Party who has been granted business rights
2. **Franchisor**--Party who grants business rights
3. **Area franchise**--Agreement transferring franchise rights within a geographical area permitting the opening of a number of franchise outlets
4. **Continuing franchise fee**--Consideration for continuing rights granted by the agreement (general or specific) during its life
5. **Franchise agreement**--Essential criteria
    a. Contractual relation between franchisee and franchisor
    b. Purpose is distribution of a product, service, or entire business concept
    c. Resources contributed by both franchisor and franchisee in establishing and maintaining the franchise
    d. Outline of specific marketing practices to be followed
    e. Creation of an establishment that will require and support the full-time business activity of the franchisee
    f. Both franchisee and franchisor have a common public identity
6. **Initial franchise fee**--Consideration for establishing the relationship and providing some initial services
7. **Initial services**--Variety of services and advice (e.g., site selection, financing and engineering services, advertising assistance, training of personnel, manuals for operations, administration and recordkeeping, bookkeeping and advisory services, quality control programs)

B. Franchise fee revenue from individual sales shall be recognized when all material services or conditions relating to the sale have been substantially performed or satisfied by the franchisor.
  1. Substantial performance means
      a. Franchisor has no remaining obligation or intent to refund money or forgive unpaid debt
      b. Substantially all initial services have been performed
      c. No other material conditions or obligations exist
  2. If large initial franchise fee is required and continuing franchise fees are small in relation to future services, then portion of initial franchise fee shall be deferred and amortized over life of franchise.
C. Continuing franchise fees shall be reported as revenue as fees are earned and become receivable from the franchise. Related costs shall be expensed as incurred.
D. Direct franchise costs shall be deferred until related revenue is recognized.
  1. These costs should not exceed anticipated revenue less estimated additional related costs.
E. Disclosure of all significant commitments and obligations that have not yet been substantially performed are required
  1. Notes to the FS should disclose whether the installment or cost recovery method is used.
  2. Initial franchise fees shall be segregated from other franchise fee revenue if significant.

SFAS 47 (C32) Disclosure of Long-Term Obligations

A. This statement requires that firm disclose
  1. Commitments under unconditional purchase obligations that are associated with suppliers (financing arrangements)
  2. Future payments on long-term borrowings
B. **Unconditional purchase obligations** are obligations to transfer funds in the future for fixed or minimum amounts of goods or services at fixed or minimum prices.
C. Unconditional purchase obligations that have all the following characteristics must be disclosed; they are not recorded on the balance sheet.
  1. Is noncancelable or cancelable only
      a. Upon occurrence of a remote contingency, or
      b. With permission of another party, or
      c. If a replacement agreement is signed between same parties, or
      d. Upon penalty payment such that continuation appears reasonably assured
  2. Was negotiated as part of arranging financing for the facilities that will provide the contracted goods
  3. Has a remaining term greater than 1 year

D. Disclosure of those unconditional purchase obligations **not recorded** on the balance sheet shall include
1. Nature and term of obligation
2. Amount of fixed and determinable portion of obligation as of most recent BS in aggregate and if determinable for each of next 5 years
3. Description of any variable elements of the obligation
4. Amounts purchased under the obligation(s) for each year an income statement is presented
5. Encourages disclosing imputed interest to reduce the obligation to present value using
   a. Effective interest rate, or if unknown
   b. Purchaser's incremental borrowing rate at date obligation was entered into
E. This statement **does not change** the accounting for obligations that **are recorded on the balance sheet**, nor does it suggest that disclosure is a substitute for accounting recognition. For **recorded** obligations, the following information should be disclosed for each of the next 5 years:
1. Aggregate amount of payments for unconditional obligations that meet criteria for balance sheet recognition
2. Combined aggregate amount of maturities and sinking fund requirements for all long-term borrowings

SFAS 48 (R75) Revenue Recognition When Right of Return Exists

(Extracts from AICPA Statement of Position [SOP] 75-1)
A. Specifies accounting for sales in which a product may be returned for refund, credit applied to amounts owed, or in exchange for other products.
1. Right is specified by contract or is a matter of existing practice.
2. Right may be exercised by ultimate customer or party who resells product to others.
3. Not applicable to service revenue, real estate or lease transactions, or return of defective goods
B. Recognize revenue from right of return sales only if all of the following conditions are met:
1. Price is substantially fixed or determinable at date of sale.
2. Buyer has paid or is unconditionally obligated to pay.
3. Obligation is not changed by theft, destruction, or damage of product.
4. Buyer has "economic substance" apart from seller (i.e., sale is not with a party established mainly for purpose of recognizing sales revenue).
5. Seller has no significant obligation for performance to directly cause resale of product.
6. Amount of future returns can be reasonably estimated.
C. If all of the conditions in B. above are met, record sales and cost of sales **and**
1. Reduce sales revenue and cost of sales to reflect estimated returns
2. Accrue expected costs or losses in accordance with SFAS 5
D. If any condition in B. above is not met, do not recognize sales and cost of sales until either
1. All conditions are subsequently met, or
2. Return privilege has substantially expired
E. Factors which may impair ability to make a reasonable estimate of returns include
1. Susceptibility of product to significant external factors (e.g., obsolescence or changes in demand)
2. Long period of return privilege
3. Absence of experience with similar products or inability to apply such experience due to changing circumstances (e.g., marketing policies or customer relationships)
4. Absence of large volume of similar transactions

SFAS 52 (F60) Foreign Currency Translation (Supersedes SFAS 8, SFAS 20, and SFAS Interpretations 15 and 17)

A. Primary objectives of foreign currency translation
1. Should provide information disclosing effects of rate changes on enterprise cash flows and equity
2. Should also provide information in consolidated statements as to financial results and relationships of individual consolidated entities measured in their respective functional currencies in accordance with US GAAP
B. **Functional currency** is the currency of the primary economic environment in which a foreign entity operates (i.e., the environment in which the entity generates and spends cash).

1. A foreign entity's assets, liabilities, revenues, expenses, gains, and losses shall be measured in that entity's functional currency.
2. The functional currency could be the currency of the country in which the entity operates if the entity is a self-contained unit operating in a foreign country.
    EXAMPLE: An entity (1) whose operations are not integrated with those of the parent, (2) whose buying and selling activities are primarily local, and (3) whose cash flows are primarily in the foreign currency.
3. There may be several functional currencies if there are many self-contained entities operating in different countries.
4. The functional currency might be the US dollar if the foreign entity's operations are considered to be a direct and integral part of the US parent's operations.
    EXAMPLE: An entity (1) whose operations are integrated with those of the parent, (2) whose buying and selling activities are primarily in the parent's country and/or the parent's currency, and (3) whose cash flows are available for remittance to the parent.
5. Functional currency for a foreign entity, once determined, shall be used consistently unless it is clear that economic facts and circumstances have changed.
    a. If a change is made, do not restate previously issued financial statements
6. If a foreign entity's bookkeeping is not done in the functional currency, the process of converting from the currency used for the books and records to the functional currency is called remeasurement.
    a. Remeasurement is intended to produce the same result (e.g., balances for assets, expenses, liabilities, etc.) as if the functional currency had been used for bookkeeping purposes.
    b. In highly inflationary economies (cumulative inflation over a 3-year period is $\geq 100\%$), the remeasurement of a foreign entity's financial statements shall be done as if the functional currency were the reporting currency (i.e., the US dollar).
7. The functional currency (if not the US dollar) is translated to the reporting currency (assumed to be the US dollar) by using appropriate exchange rates (see item C. below).
    a. If the functional currency is the US dollar, there is no need to translate (if the books and records are maintained in US dollars).

C. The translation of foreign currency FS (those incorporated in the FS of a reporting enterprise by consolidation, combination, or the equity method of accounting) should use a current exchange rate if the foreign currency is the functional currency.
    1. Assets and liabilities--exchange rate at the balance sheet date is used to translate the functional currency to the reporting currency
    2. Revenues (expenses) and gains (losses)--exchange rates when the transactions were recorded shall be used to translate from the functional currency to the reporting currency
        a. Weighted averages for exchange rates may be used for items occurring numerous times during the period.
    3. Translation adjustments will result from the translation process if the functional currency is a foreign currency.
        a. Translation adjustments are not an element of net income of the reporting entity.
        b. Effects of current translation adjustments are reported in other comprehensive income for the period with the accumulated amount reported as part of the reporting entity's owners' equity and labeled accumulated other comprehensive income.
        c. Accumulated translation adjustments remain part of the owners' equity until the reporting entity disposes of the foreign entity.
            (1) In period of disposal, these adjustments are reported as part of the gain (loss) on sale or liquidation.

D. **Foreign currency transactions** are those which are denominated (fixed) in other than the entity's functional currency.
    1. Receivables and/or payables, which are fixed in a currency other than the functional currency, may result in transaction gains (losses) due to changes in exchange rates after the transaction date.
    2. Transaction gains or losses generally are reported on the income statement in the period during which the exchange rates change.

3. Deferred taxes may have to be provided for transaction gains or losses which are realized for income tax purposes in a time period different than that for financial reporting.
E. **A forward exchange contract** represents an agreement to exchange different currencies at a specified future rate and at a specified future date.
   1. A forward exchange contract is accounted for like a foreign currency transaction.
   2. Gains (losses) on forward contracts (except those noted in 4. below) are disclosed on the income statement during the period in which the spot rates change.
      a. **Spot rate** is the rate for immediate delivery of the currencies exchanged.
   3. Discounts (premiums) on forward contracts are accounted for separately from the gains or losses noted in 2. above.
      a. Discounts (premiums) generally are amortized and charged to income during the life of the forward contract.
   4. Gains (losses) on a forward contract that is intended to hedge an identifiable foreign currency commitment should be deferred until the transaction date.
      a. Losses should not be deferred if deferral leads to the recognition of losses in later periods.
F. FS disclosures required
   1. Aggregate transaction gain (loss) that is included in the entity's net income
   2. Analysis of changes in accumulated translation adjustments which are reported as part of other comprehensive income
   3. Significant rate changes subsequent to the date of the financial statements including effects on unsettled foreign currency transactions

---

FASB INTERPRETATION NO. 37 ACCOUNTING FOR TRANSLATION ADJUSTMENTS UPON SALE OF PART OF AN INVESTMENT IN A FOREIGN ENTITY

If an enterprise sells part of its ownership interest in a foreign entity, a pro rata portion of the accumulated translation adjustment component of equity attributable to that investment shall be recognized in measuring the gain (loss) on the sale.

SFAS 57 (R36) Related-Party Disclosures
A. Definitions
   1. **Affiliate**--Party is controlled by another enterprise that controls, or is under common control with another enterprise, directly or indirectly
   2. **Control**--Power to direct or cause direction of management through ownerships contract, or other means
   3. **Immediate family**--Family members whom principal owners or management might control/ influence or be controlled/influenced by
   4. **Management**--Persons responsible for enterprise objectives who have policy-making and decision-making authority
      a. For example, board of directors, chief executive and operating officers, and vice-presidents
      b. Includes persons without formal titles
   5. **Principal owners**--Owners of more than 10% of a firm's voting interests
      a. Includes known beneficial owners
   6. **Related parties**--Affiliates, equity method investees, employee benefit trusts, principal owners, management or any party that can significantly influence a transaction
B. FS shall include disclosures of material transactions between related parties except
   1. Compensation agreements, expense allowances, and other similar items in the ordinary course of business
   2. Transactions which are eliminated in the preparation of consolidated/combined FS
C. Disclosures of material transactions shall include
   1. Nature of relationship(s)
   2. Description of transaction(s), including those assigned zero or nominal amounts

3. Dollar amounts of transactions for each income statement period and effect of any change in method of establishing terms
4. Amounts due to/from related parties, including terms and manner of settlement

D. Representations concerning related party transactions shall not imply that terms were equivalent to those resulting in arm's-length bargaining unless such statement can be substantiated.

E. When a **control** relationship exists, disclose such relationship even though no transactions have occurred.

SFAS 64 (D14, I17) Extinguishments of Debt Made to Satisfy Sinking Fund Requirements
(Amends para 8 and footnote 2 of SFAS 4)

A. Gains (losses) on extinguishment of debt made to satisfy sinking fund requirements which would need to be met within 1 year of extinguishment date do **not** require extraordinary item classification.

B. Means used to achieve the extinguishment (cash, noncash) does not affect the resultant classification of gains (losses).

SFAS 66 (Re1, R10) Accounting for Sales of Real Estate

A. Other than retail land sales
   1. Use the full accrual method if the following criteria are satisfied:
      a. Sale is consummated
      b. Buyer's initial and continuing investments demonstrate a commitment to pay for the property
      c. Seller's receivable is not subject to future subordination
      d. Risks and rewards of ownership have been transferred
   2. When the criteria are not met and dependent upon the particular circumstance, use one of the following methods:
      a. Installment method
      b. Cost recovery method
      c. Deposit method
      d. Reduced profit method
      e. Percentage-of-completion

B. Retail land sales (not outlined due to specialized nature)

SFAS 68 (R55) Research and Development Arrangements

A. Establishes accounting for enterprise's obligation under arrangement in which R&D is funded by others

B. Obligation to repay any of the funds provided by other parties **regardless of the outcome** of the R&D is a liability which shall be estimated and recognized.
   1. Obligation may be written, contractual, or presumed (because of surrounding conditions)
   2. Charge R&D costs to expense as incurred

C. Obligation for contract to perform R&D for others arises (no liability recorded) when financial risk associated with R&D has been transferred because repayment of any funds provided by other parties depends **solely** on the results.

D. Loan or advance made by enterprise to other parties should be expensed if repayment depends solely on R&D results having future economic benefits.
   1. Classify as R&D expense unless related to some other function (advertising, marketing, etc.)

SFAS 78 (B05) Classification of Obligations That Are Callable by the Creditor
(Amends ARB 43, Chapter 3A)

A. Statement specifies that the current liability classification is also intended to include
   1. Obligations that, by their terms, are due on demand or will be due on demand within 1 year (or operating cycle, if longer) from balance sheet date, even though liquidation may not be expected within that period
   2. Long-term obligations that are or will be callable by creditor either because
      a. Debtor's violation of debt agreement provision at balance sheet date makes obligation callable **or**
      b. Violation, if not cured within grace period, will make obligation callable

B. Callable obligations in A.2. should be classified current unless one of the following conditions is met:
   1. Creditor has waived or subsequently lost the right to demand repayment for more than 1 year (or operating cycle, if longer) from balance sheet date
   2. For long-term obligations containing grace period within which debtor may cure violation, it is probable violation will be cured within that period
      a. If obligation meets this condition, the circumstances shall be disclosed
C. This statement does **not** modify SFAS 6 or 47

SFAS 84 (D10, D14) Induced Conversions of Convertible Debt
(Amends APB 26, para 2)
A. Establishes accounting and reporting standards for conversion of convertible debt to equity securities when debtor induces conversion of the debt
   1. Applies only to conversions that both
      a. Occur pursuant to changed conversion privileges exercisable only for limited period of time
      b. Include issuance of all of the equity securities issuable pursuant to the original conversion privileges for each instrument that is converted
   2. Examples of changed terms to induce conversion
      a. Reduction of original conversion price
      b. Issuance of warrants or other securities not included in original conversion terms
      c. Payment of cash or other consideration to debt holders who convert during the specified time period
B. Debtor enterprise shall recognize expense equal to excess of fair value of all securities and other consideration transferred in the transaction over fair value of securities issuable pursuant to the original conversion terms.
   1. Expense is not an extraordinary item.
   2. Fair value of securities/other consideration measured as of inducement date
      a. Typically date converted by debt holder or binding agreement entered into

SFAS 86 (Co2) Accounting for the Costs of Computer Software to Be Sold, Leased, or Otherwise Marketed
A. Establishes standards of financial accounting and reporting for the costs of computer software to be sold, leased, or otherwise marketed as a separate product or as part of a product or process, whether internally developed and produced or purchased.
B. Research and development costs consist of all costs to establish technological feasibility.
   1. Evidence of technological feasibility:
      a. Process of creating the computer software product includes a detail program design **or**
      b. Process of creating the computer software product includes a product design and a completed working model.
C. Capitalization costs include costs incurred subsequent to establishing technological feasibility.
   1. Capitalization shall cease when product is available for general release to customers.
D. Amortization of capitalized software costs is performed on a product-by-product basis.
   1. Annual amortization is the greater of
      a. The amount computed using the ratio current gross product revenues to total current and anticipated future gross product revenues **or**
      b. S-L method using the estimated economic life of the software product
   2. Amortization begins when product is available for general release to customers.
   3. Unamortized capitalized costs cannot exceed the net realizable value (NRV) of that software product. Any excess shall be written off at the end of the year.
E. Inventory costs include costs incurred for duplicating software materials and for physically packaging the product.
   1. Costs of maintenance and customer support are charged to expense.
F. FS disclosures shall include
   1. Unamortized computer software costs
   2. Total amount charged to amortization expense and amounts written down to NRV

SFAS 87 (C59, I67, P16, Re6) Employers' Accounting for Pensions
(Supersedes ARB 8 and SFAS 36, Amended by SFAS 132)

Applies to any arrangement that is similar in substance to pension plan regardless of form or means of financing. Applies to written plan and to plan whose existence may be implied from well-defined, although perhaps unwritten, practice of paying postretirement benefits. Does not apply to plan that provides only life insurance benefits or health insurance benefits, or both, to retirees. Does not apply to postemployment health care benefits.

The following terms are given specific definitions for the purposes of SFAS 87:

Accumulated benefit obligation--Actuarial present value of benefits (whether vested or nonvested) attributed by the pension benefit formula to employee service rendered before a specified date and based on employee service and compensation (if applicable) prior to that date. The accumulated benefit obligation differs from the projected benefit obligation in that it includes no assumption about future compensation levels. For plans with flat-benefit or non-pay-related pension benefit formulas, the accumulated benefit obligation and the projected benefit obligation are the same.

Actual return on plan assets component (of net periodic pension cost)--Difference between fair value of plan assets at the end of the period and the fair value at the beginning of the period, adjusted for contributions and payments of benefits during the period.

Actuarial present value--Value, as of a specified date, of an amount or series of amounts payable or receivable thereafter, with each amount adjusted to reflect (a) the time value of money (through discounts for interest) and (b) the probability of payment (by means of decrements for events such as death, disability, withdrawal, or retirement) between the specified date and the expected date of payment.

Amortization--Usually refers to the process of reducing a recognized liability systematically by recognizing revenues or reducing a recognized asset systematically by recognizing expenses or costs. In pension accounting, amortization is also used to refer to the systematic recognition in net pension cost over several periods of previously **unrecognized** amounts, including unrecognized prior service cost and unrecognized net gain or loss.

Defined contribution pension plan--Plan that provides pension benefits in return for services rendered, provides an individual account for each participant, and specifies how contributions to the individual's account are to be determined instead of specifying the amount of benefits the individual is to receive. Under a defined contribution pension plan, the benefits a participant will receive depend solely on the amount contributed to the participant's account, the returns earned on investments of those contributions, and forfeitures of other participants' benefits that may be allocated to such participant's account.

Gain or loss--Change in the value of either the projected benefit obligation or the plan assets resulting from experience different from that assumed or from a change in an actuarial assumption. See also "Unrecognized net gain or loss."

Gain or loss component (of net periodic pension cost)--Sum of (a) the difference between the actual return on plan assets and the expected return on plan assets and (b) the amortization of the unrecognized net gain or loss from previous periods. The gain or loss component is the net effect of delayed recognition of gains and losses (the net change in the unrecognized net gain or loss) except that it does not include changes in the projected benefit obligation occurring during the period and deferred for later recognition.

Interest cost component (of net periodic pension cost)--Increase in the projected benefit obligation due to passage of time.

Market-related value of plan assets--Balance used to calculate the expected return on plan assets. Market-related value can be either fair market value or a calculated value that recognizes changes in fair value in a systematic and rational manner over not more than 5 years. Different ways of calculating market-related value may be used for different classes of assets, but the manner of determining market-related value shall be applied consistently from year to year for each asset class.

Net periodic pension cost--Amount recognized in an employer's financial statements as the cost of a pension plan for a period. Components of net periodic pension cost are service cost, interest cost, actual return on plan assets, gain or loss, amortization of unrecognized prior service cost, and amortization of the unrecognized net obligation or asset existing at the date of initial application of SFAS 87. SFAS 87 uses the term **net peri-**

odic pension cost instead of **net pension expense** because part of the cost recognized in a period may be capitalized along with other costs as part of an asset such as inventory.

Prepaid pension cost--Cumulative employer contributions in excess of accrued net pension cost.

Prior service cost--Cost of retroactive benefits granted in a plan amendment. See also "Unrecognized prior service cost."

Projected benefit obligation--Actuarial present value as of a date of all benefits attributed by the pension benefit formula to employee service rendered prior to that date. The projected benefit obligation is measured using assumptions as to future compensation levels if the pension benefit formula is based on those future compensation levels (pay-related, final-pay, final-average-pay, or career-average-pay plans).

Service cost component (of net periodic pension cost)--Actuarial present value of benefits attributed by the pension benefit formula to services rendered by employees during the period. The service cost component is a portion of the projected benefit obligation and is unaffected by the funded status of the plan.

Unfunded accrued pension cost--Cumulative net pension cost accrued in excess of the employer's contributions (usually used without word "unfunded").

Unfunded accumulated benefit obligation--Excess of the accumulated benefit obligation over plan assets.

Unrecognized net gain or loss--Cumulative net gain (loss) that has not been recognized as a part of net periodic pension cost. See "Gain or loss."

Unrecognized prior service cost--Portion of prior service cost that has not been recognized as a part of net periodic pension cost.

A. Single-Employer Defined Benefit Plans
  1. Pension benefits are part of compensation paid to employees for services
     a. Amount of benefits to be paid depends on a number of future events specified in the **plan's benefit formula**.
  2. Any method of pension accounting that recognizes cost before payment of benefits to retirees must deal with two problems:
     a. Assumptions must be made concerning future events that will determine amount and timing of benefits
     b. Approach to attributing cost of pension benefits to individual years of service must be selected
B. Basic Elements of Pension Accounting
  1. Prior service cost
     a. Except as specified otherwise, prior service cost shall be amortized by assigning an equal amount to each future service period of each employee active at the date of a plan amendment who is expected to receive benefits under plan.
     b. If all/almost all of plan's participants are inactive, cost of retroactive plan benefits should be amortized over remaining life expectancy of those participants.
     c. Consistent use of alternative amortization approach that more rapidly reduces unrecognized cost of retroactive amendments is acceptable.
        (1) Alternative method used should be disclosed.
     d. When period during which employer expects to realize economic benefits from amendment granting retroactive benefits is shorter than entire remaining service period of active employees, amortization of prior service cost should be accelerated.
     e. Plan amendment can reduce, rather than increase, the projected benefit obligation.
        (1) Reduction should be used to reduce any existing unrecognized prior service cost.
        (2) Excess should be amortized on same basis as cost of benefit increases.
  2. Gains and losses
     a. Gains (losses)
        (1) Result from changes in amount of either projected benefit obligation or plan assets due to experience different than assumed and changes in assumptions
        (2) Include both **realized** and **unrealized** amounts
     b. Asset gains (losses) include both (a) changes reflected in the market-related value of assets and (b) changes not yet reflected in the market-related value.

(1) Asset gains (losses) not yet reflected in market-related value are not required to be amortized as B.2.c. below.

  c. As a minimum, amortization of unrecognized net gain (loss) should be included as a component of net pension cost for a year if, as of the beginning of the year, that unrecognized net gain (loss) $\geq .10$ of the larger of the projected benefit obligation or the market-related value of plan assets.

    (1) Minimum amortization should be the excess divided by the average remaining service period of active employees expected to receive benefits under the plan.

      (a) Amortization must always reduce beginning-of-the-year balance.

      (b) Amortization of a net unrecognized gain (loss) results in a decrease (increase) in net periodic pension cost.

    (2) If all/or almost all of plan's participants are inactive, average remaining life expectancy of inactive participants should be used instead of average remaining service.

  d. Any systematic method of amortization of unrecognized gains (losses) may be used in lieu of the minimum specified above provided that

    (1) Minimum is used in any period in which minimum amortization is greater (reduces the net balance by more)

    (2) Method is applied consistently and disclosed

  3. Recognition of liabilities and assets

    a. Liability (asset) is recognized if net periodic pension cost recognized exceeds (is less than) amounts the employer has contributed to the plan.

    b. Recognition of "additional minimum liability" is required if accumulated benefit obligation is greater than the fair market value of plan assets and

      (1) An asset has been recognized as prepaid pension cost,

      (2) The liability already recognized as unfunded accrued pension cost is less than the unfunded accumulated benefit obligation, or

      (3) No accrued or prepaid pension cost has been recognized

    c. If "additional minimum liability" must be recognized, recognize an equal amount as an "intangible asset," provided that asset recognized should not exceed amount of unrecognized prior service cost.

      (1) If "additional liability" required to be recognized exceeds unrecognized prior service cost, excess should be reported as other comprehensive income and a separate component (a reduction) of equity labeled accumulated other comprehensive income.

      (2) Each time a new determination of required additional liability is made, related intangible asset and accumulated other comprehensive income should be eliminated or adjusted as necessary.

C. Attribution

  1. Pension benefits should be attributed to periods of employee service based on plan's benefit formula.

  2. When employer has a present commitment to make future amendments, and substance of plan is to provide benefits attributable to prior service that are greater than benefits defined by written terms of the plan.

    a. The substantive commitment should be basis for accounting, and

    b. Existence and nature of the commitment to make future amendments should be disclosed

  3. Assumptions

    a. Assumed discount rates reflect rates at which pension benefits could be effectively settled

      (1) Used in measurements of projected and accumulated benefit obligations and the service and interest cost components of net periodic pension cost

    b. Assumed compensation levels (when measuring service cost and the projected benefit obligation) should reflect an estimate of the actual future compensation levels of employees involved, including future changes attributed to general price levels, productivity, seniority, promotion, and other factors.

    c. Accumulated benefit obligation shall be measured based on employees' history of service and compensation without estimate of future compensation levels.

    d. Automatic benefit increases specified by plan that are expected to occur should be included in measurements of projected and accumulated benefit obligations and the service cost component.

e. Retroactive plan amendments should be included in computations of projected and accumulated benefit obligations.
(1) Once they have been contractually agreed to
(2) Even if some provisions take effect only in future periods

D. Measurement of Plan Assets
1. For purposes of measuring minimum liability and required disclosures, plan investments, whether equity or debt securities, real estate, or other, should be measured at their fair value as of measurement date.
2. Market-related asset value is used for purposes of determining the expected return on plan assets and accounting for asset gains and losses.

E. Acceptable Measurement Dates
1. As of date of financial statements, or
2. If used consistently from year to year, as of a date $\leq$ 3 months prior to that date
3. Measurement date is not intended to require that all procedures be performed after that date.
4. Information for items requiring estimates can be prepared as of an earlier date and projected forward to account for subsequent events (e.g., employee service).
5. The "additional minimum liability" reported in interim financial statements should be the same "additional minimum liability" recognized in previous year-end balance sheet.
a. Adjusted for subsequent accruals and contributions unless measures of both the obligation and plan assets are available as of a current date or a significant event occurs, such as plan amendment, that would call for such measurements
6. Measurements of net periodic pension cost for both interim and annual financial statements should be based on assumptions used for previous year-end measurements.
a. If more recent measurements are available or a significant event occurs, use these more recent measurements.

F. Disclosures (Amended by SFAS 132)

SFAS 88 (P16) Employers' Accounting for Settlements and Curtailments of Defined Benefit Pension Plans and for Termination Benefits (Supersedes SFAS 74, Amended by SFAS 132)

Statement applies to an employer that sponsors a defined benefit pension plan accounted for under the provisions of SFAS 87 if all or part of the plan's pension benefit obligation is settled or the plan is curtailed. It also applies to an employer that offers benefits to employees in connection with their termination of employment.

The following terms are given specific definitions for the purposes of SFAS 88:

Settlement--Transaction that (a) is an irrevocable action, (b) relieves the employer (or the plan) of primary responsibility for a pension benefit obligation, and (c) eliminates significant risks related to the obligation and the assets used to effect the settlement. Examples include making lump sum cash payments to plan participants in exchange for their rights to receive specified pension benefits and purchasing nonparticipating annuity contracts to cover vested benefits. A transaction must meet all of the above three criteria to constitute a settlement for purposes of this statement.

Annuity contract--Irrevocable contract in which an insurance company* unconditionally undertakes a legal obligation to provide specified benefits to specific individuals in return for a fixed consideration or premium. It involves the transfer of significant risk from the employer to the insurance company. Participating annuity contracts provide that the purchaser (either the plan or the employer) may participate in the experience of the insurance company. The insurance company ordinarily pays dividends to the purchaser. If the substance of a participating annuity contract is such that the employer remains subject to all or most of the risks and rewards associated with the benefit obligation covered or the assets transferred to the insurance company, the purchase of the contract does not constitute a settlement.

---

* *If the insurance company is controlled by the employer or there is any reasonable doubt that the insurance company will meet its obligation under the contract, the purchase of the contract does not constitute a settlement for purposes of this statement.*

Curtailment--Event that significantly reduces the expected years of future service of present employees or eliminates for a significant number of employees the accrual of defined benefits for some or all of their future services. Curtailments include (a) termination of employee's services earlier than expected, which may or may not involve closing a facility or discontinuing a segment of a business and (b) termination or suspension of a plan so that employees do not earn additional defined benefits for future services. In the latter situation, future service may be counted toward vesting of benefits accumulated based on past services.

A. Relationship of Settlements and Curtailments to Other Events
   1. Settlement and curtailment may occur separately or together.
      a. If benefits to be accumulated in future periods are reduced but the plan remains in existence and continues to pay benefits, to invest assets, and to receive contributions, a curtailment has occurred but not a settlement.
      b. If employer purchases nonparticipating annuity contracts for vested benefits and continues to provide defined benefits for future services, either in the same plan or in a successor plan, a settlement has occurred but not a curtailment.
      c. If a plan is terminated (i.e., the obligation is settled and the plan ceases to exist) and not replaced by a successor defined benefit plan, both a settlement and a curtailment have occurred.

B. Accounting for Settlement of Pension Obligation
   1. For purposes of this statement, when a pension obligation is settled, the maximum gain or loss subject to recognition is the unrecognized gain or loss defined in SFAS 87 plus any remaining unrecognized net asset existing at the date of initial application of SFAS 87. (See definition of gains and losses in the outline of SFAS 87.)
      a. Maximum amount includes any gain or loss first measured at the time of settlement.
      b. Maximum amount should be recognized if the entire projected benefit is settled.
         (1) If only part of the projected benefit is settled, recognize a pro rata portion of the maximum amount equal to the percentage reduction in the projected benefit obligation.
   2. If the purchase of a participating annuity contract constitutes a settlement, the maximum gain (but not the maximum loss) should be reduced by the cost of the participation right before determining the amount to be recognized in earnings.
   3. If the cost of all settlements in a year is less than or equal to the sum of the service cost and interest cost components of net periodic pension cost for the plan for the year, gain or loss recognition is permitted but not required for those settlements.
      a. Accounting policy adopted should be consistently applied.
      b. For the following types of settlements, the cost of the settlement is
         (1) Cash settlement: amount of cash paid to employees
         (2) Settlement using nonparticipating annuity contracts: cost of the contracts
         (3) Settlement using participating annuity contracts: cost of the contracts less amount attributed to participation rights

C. Accounting for Plan Curtailment
   1. Unrecognized prior service cost is a loss.
      a. Cost must be associated with years of service no longer expected to be rendered as result of curtailment.
      b. Costs include cost of retroactive plan amendments (refer to outline of SFAS 87) and any remaining unrecognized net obligation existing at the date of initial application of SFAS 87 (refer to outline of SFAS 87).
   2. The projected benefit obligation may be decreased (a gain) or increased (a loss) by a curtailment*
      a. To the extent that such a gain exceeds any unrecognized net loss (or entire gain, if unrecognized net gain exists), it is a **curtailment gain**.
      b. To the extent that such a loss exceeds any unrecognized net gain (or the entire loss, if an unrecognized net loss exists), it is a **curtailment loss**.

---

* *Increases in the projected benefit obligation that reflect termination benefits are excluded from the scope of this paragraph.*

      c.   Any remaining unrecognized net asset existing at the date of initial application of SFAS 87 should be treated as an unrecognized net gain and should be combined with the unrecognized net gain or loss arising subsequent to the transition to SFAS 87.
   3. If the sum of the effects identified in C.1. and C.2. is a net loss
      a.   Recognize in earnings when it is probable that a curtailment will occur and
      b.   Effects are reasonably estimable
   4. If the sum of those effects identified in C.1. and C.2. is a net gain
      a.   Recognize in earnings when related employees terminate or plan suspension or amendment is adopted
D. Termination Benefits
   1. Employer may provide benefits to employees in connection with their termination of employment.
      a.   Special termination benefits--offered for a short period of time or
         (1) Recognize a liability and a loss when the employee accepts the offer and the amount can be reasonably estimable
      b.   Contractual termination benefits--required by terms of plan only if specified event occurs
         (1) Recognize a liability and a loss when it is probable that employees will be entitled to benefits and amount can be reasonably estimable
   2. Termination benefits may take many forms consisting of
      a.   Lump sum payments
      b.   Periodic future payments
   3. The cost of termination benefits recognized as a liability and a loss shall include the amount of any lump sum payments and present value of any expected future payments.
E. Disposal of a Segment
   1. If gain (loss) measured in accordance with B., C., and D. above is directly related to a disposal of a segment of a business, include it in determining gain (loss) with that event and recognize per APB 30.
F. Disclosure and Presentation (Amended by SFAS 132)

SFAS 89 (C28) Financial Reporting and Changing Prices

This statement **encourages** but does not require a business enterprise that prepares its financial statements in US dollars and in accordance with US generally accepted accounting principles to disclose supplementary information on changing prices.
A. Measurement
   1. Inventory
      a.   Current cost is the current cost of purchasing or manufacturing, whichever is applicable
         (1) Or recoverable amount if lower
   2. Property, plant, and equipment
      a.   Current cost is current cost of acquiring same service potential (or recoverable amount if lower)
         (1) That is, the same operating costs and output
         (2) Three valuation methods
            (a) Current cost of new asset less depreciation
            (b) Cost of comparable used asset
            (c) Adjusting new asset cost for differences in
               1] Useful life
               2] Output capacity
               3] Nature of service
               4] Operating costs
   3. In summary, there are several approaches to determine current costs.
      a.   Indexation (application of price indices to original cost)
         (1) Externally generated by class of goods
         (2) Internally generated by class of goods
      b.   Direct pricing
         (1) Current invoices
         (2) Vendor's price quotations

(3) Current standard manufacturing costs
4. Recoverable amount
   a. Current worth of net amount of cash expected to be recoverable from the use or sale of an asset

SFAS 91 (Bt7, D22, Fi4, In6, I89, L10, L20, Mo4) Accounting for Nonrefundable Fees and Costs Associated With Originating or Acquiring Loans and Initial Direct Costs of Leases (Rescinds SFAS 17, Amends SFAS 13, 60, and 65)

Establishes the accounting for nonrefundable fees and costs associated with lending, committing to lend, or purchasing a loan or group of loans. Applies to all types of loans.

A. Loan origination fees shall be recognized over life of related loan as adjustment of yield.
B. Certain direct loan origination costs shall be deferred over the life of the related loan as a reduction of the loan's yield.
C. All loan commitment fees shall be deferred except for certain retrospectively determined fees.
   1. Those commitment fees meeting specified criteria shall be recognized over the loan commitment period.
   2. All other commitment fees shall be recognized as an adjustment of yield over the related loan's life.
   3. If commitment expires unexercised, then recognize in income upon expiration of the commitment.
D. Loan fees, certain direct loan origination costs, and purchase premiums and discounts on loans shall be recognized as an adjustment of yield generally by the interest method based on contractual terms of the loan.
   1. Prepayments by debtors may be anticipated in certain specified circumstances.
E. Application to Leasing Activities
   1. Lessors shall account for initial direct costs as part of the net investment in a direct financing lease.
   2. Initial direct costs are those costs incurred by the lessor that are
      a. Costs to originate a lease incurred in transactions with independent third parties that
         (1) Result directly from and are essential to acquire that lease, and
         (2) Would not have been incurred had that leasing transaction not occurred, and
      b. Certain costs directly related to specified activities performed by the lessor for that lease including
         (1) Evaluating the prospective lessee's financial condition
         (2) Evaluating and recording guarantees, collateral, and other security arrangements
         (3) Negotiating lease terms
         (4) Preparing and processing lease documents
         (5) Closing the transaction
         (6) Costs directly related to those activities shall include only that portion of the employees' total compensation and payroll-related fringe benefits directly related to time spent performing those activities for that lease and other costs related to those activities that would not have been incurred but for that lease

SFAS 94 (C51) Consolidation of All Majority-Owned Subsidiaries (Amends ARB 51 With related amendment of ARB 43, Chapter 12)

A. Precludes use of parent company FS prepared for issuance to stockholders as FS of primary reporting entity
B. Requires consolidation of all majority-owned (ownerships, directly or indirectly, of more than 50% of outstanding voting shares of another company) subsidiaries
   1. Unless control
      a. Temporary
      b. Not held by majority owner (e.g., subsidiary)
         (1) Is in legal reorganization or bankruptcy
         (2) Operates under foreign exchange restrictions, controls, or other governmentally imposed uncertainties
   2. Even if
      a. Subsidiary's operations nonhomogeneous
      b. Large minority interest exists

c. Subsidiary located in foreign country

SFAS 95 (C25) Statement of Cash Flows
A. Statement of Cash Flows in General
 1. Required for each period results of operation (income statement) are provided
 2. Objectives
   a. Provide information about cash receipts and cash payments
   b. Provide information about operating, investing, and financing activities
   c. Helps users to assess
    (1) Ability to generate future net cash flows
    (2) Ability to meet obligations and pay dividends
    (3) Reasons for differences between income and associated cash receipts and payments
    (4) Both cash and noncash aspects of entity's investing and financing activities
 3. Shall report
   a. Cash effects during a period from
    (1) Operating activities
    (2) Investing activities
    (3) Financing activities
   b. Noncash financing and investing activities in supplemental schedule
B. Gross and Net Cash Flows
 1. Gross amount of cash receipts and payments is relevant.
   a. For example, must show issuance of bonds and retirement of bonds separately
 2. Statement should explain change during the period in **cash and cash equivalents**.
   a. Cash equivalents
    (1) Short-term, highly liquid investments that are
     (a) Readily convertible into known amounts of cash
     (b) Near maturity (original maturity of 3 months or less from **date of purchase** by the enterprise) and present negligible risk of changes in value
    (2) Examples
     (a) Treasury bills
     (b) Commercial paper
     (c) Money market funds
C. Classification
 1. Investing activities
   a. Include
    (1) Lending money and collecting on those loans
    (2) Acquiring and selling, or disposing
     (a) Securities that are neither cash equivalents nor held in a trading portfolio
     (b) Productive assets expected to generate revenue over long periods of time
    (3) Cash inflows
     (a) Receipts from loans by
      1] Principal repayments
      2] Sale of loans made by the entity
     (b) Receipts from sale of
      1] Securities of other entities carried in held-to-maturity (debt only) or available-for-sale portfolios (debt or equity)
      2] Property, plant, and equipment
    (4) Cash outflows
     (a) Loans made or purchased by the entity
     (b) Payments to acquire assets
      1] Securities of other entities carried in held-to-maturity (debt only) or available-for-sale portfolios (debt or equity)
      2] Property, plant, and equipment

2.   Financing activities
    a.   Include
        (1) Obtaining resources from owners and providing them with a return on, and a return of, their investment
        (2) Obtaining resources from creditors and repaying the amounts borrowed
    b.   Cash inflows
        (1) Proceeds from the issuance of
            (a) Equity securities
            (b) Bonds
            (c) Mortgages
            (d) Notes
            (e) Other short- or long-term borrowing
    c.   Cash outflows
        (1) Payments of dividends
        (2) Outlays to repurchase entity's shares
        (3) Repayments of amounts borrowed
3.   Operating activities
    a.   Include
        (1) All transactions and other events that are not investing and financing
        (2) Delivering or producing goods for sale and providing services
        (3) Cash effects of transactions and other events that enter into the determination of income
    b.   Cash inflows
        (1) Cash receipts from sale of goods or services
        (2) Interest and dividends received
        (3) Other operating cash receipts
        (4) Sales of "trading portfolio" securities
    c.   Cash outflows
        (1) Payments to employees and other suppliers of goods or services
        (2) Income taxes paid
        (3) Interest paid
        (4) Other operating cash payments
        (5) Purchases of "trading portfolio" securities
D. Exchange Rate Effects
    1.   Report the reporting currency equivalent of foreign currency cash flows using exchange rates in effect at time of cash flows
    a.   Weighted-average exchange rate may be used, if result substantially same.
E. Content and Form
    1.   Report net cash provided or used by operating, investing, and financing activities
    2.   At end of statement, reconcile beginning and ending cash and cash equivalents by showing net increase or decrease for period as addition to beginning balance to obtain ending balance
    3.   Cash flow from operating activities
    a.   Direct presentation (encouraged by FASB)
        (1) Report major classes of operating receipts and payments (C.3.b.-c. above)
        (2) Difference between cash receipts and payments--net cash flow from operating activities
        (3) Supplemental schedule using indirect presentation must be presented when direct method used in body of statement
    b.   Indirect presentation (acceptable format)
        (1) Shall separately report all major classes of reconciling items
            (a) Deferrals of past operating cash receipts and cash payments such as depreciation and changes during the period in inventory and unearned revenue
            (b) Accruals of expected future operating cash receipts and cash payments such as changes during the period in receivables and payables

(2) Interest paid (net of amounts capitalized) and income taxes paid must appear in related disclosures

   c. Does not include cash flows from transactions or events whose effects are included in income, but which are not operating activities; for example,

     (1) Gain or loss on extinguishment of debt--financing activities

     (2) Gain or loss on sale of assets or from disposal of discontinued operations--investing activities

4. Inflows and outflows of cash from investing and financing activities

   a. Noncash aspects should be clearly identified in separate schedule; for example,

     (1) Conversion of debt to equity

     (2) Acquisition of assets by assuming liabilities

        (a) Includes capital lease obligations

     (3) Exchanges of assets or of liabilities

5. Enterprise shall disclose policy for determining items included in cash equivalent.

   a. Change in policy is change in accounting principle requiring restatement of comparative FS.

F. Cash flow per share shall not be reported.

SFAS 98 (L10) Accounting for Leases (Amends SFAS 13, 66, and 91. Rescinds SFAS 26 and Technical Bulletin 79-11)

AUTHOR'S NOTE: The outline below includes those changes that relate to all leases. The remainder of SFAS 98 deals with real estate leases which are not outlined since they are not expected to be tested on the exam.

A. Lease term, as redefined, includes

1. All periods covered by bargain renewal options

2. All periods for which failure to renew the lease imposes a penalty

3. All periods during which a loan, directly or indirectly related to the leased property, is outstanding

4. All periods covered by ordinary renewal options preceding the exercisable date of a bargain purchase option

5. All periods representing renewals or extensions of the lease at the lessor's option

B. Definition of penalty

1. Any requirement that can be imposed on lessee that would cause lessee to forego economic benefit or suffer economic detriment

2. Requirement can be imposed by lease agreement or by factors outside lease agreement

SFAS 106 (P40) Employers' Accounting for Postretirement Benefits Other Than Pensions
(Supersedes SFAS 81; amends APB 12, SFAS 87, APB 16; Amended by SFAS 132)

Standard applies to all forms of postretirement benefits, particularly postretirement health care benefits. Applies to written plan and to a plan whose existence may be implied from well-defined, although perhaps unwritten, practice of paying postretirement benefits (called the substantive plan). Does not apply to pensions.

The following terms are given specific definitions for purposes of SFAS 106:

Attribution period--The period of an employee's service to which the expected postretirement benefit obligation for that employee is assigned. The beginning of the attribution period is the employee's date of hire unless the plan's benefit formula grants credit only for service from a later date, in which case the beginning of the attribution period is generally the beginning of that credited service period. The end of the attribution period is the full eligibility date.

Benefit formula--The basis for determining benefits to which participants may be entitled under a postretirement benefit plan. A plan's benefit formula specifies the years of service to be rendered, age to be attained while in service, or a combination of both that must be met for an employee to be eligible to receive benefits under the plan.

Full eligibility date--The date at which an employee has rendered all of the service necessary to have earned the right to receive all of the benefits expected to be received by that employee (including any beneficiaries and dependents expected to receive benefits).

Health care cost trend rates--An assumption about the annual rate(s) of change in the cost of health care benefits currently provided by the postretirement benefit plan, due to factors other than changes in the composition of the plan population by age and dependency status, for each year from the measurement date until the end of the period in which benefits are expected to be paid.

Incurred claims cost (by age)--The cost of providing the postretirement health care benefits covered by the plan to a plan participant, after adjusting for reimbursements from Medicare and other providers of health care benefits and for deductibles, coinsurance provisions, and other specific claims costs borne by the retiree.

Net periodic postretirement benefit cost--The amount recognized in an employer's financial statements as the cost of a postretirement benefit plan for a period. Components of net periodic postretirement benefit cost include service cost, interest cost, actual return on plan assets, gain or loss, amortization of unrecognized prior service cost, and amortization of the unrecognized transition obligation or asset.

Plan amendment--A change in the existing terms of a plan. A plan amendment may increase or decrease benefits, including those attributed to years of service already rendered.

Transition asset--The unrecognized amount, as of the date this statement is initially applied, of (a) the fair value of plan assets plus any recognized accrued postretirement benefit cost or less any recognized prepaid postretirement benefit cost in excess of (b) the accumulated postretirement benefit obligation.

Transition obligation--The unrecognized amount, as of the date this statement is initially applied, of (a) the accumulated postretirement benefit obligation in excess of (b) the fair value of plan assets plus any recognized accrued postretirement benefit cost or less any recognized prepaid postretirement benefit cost.

Unrecognized transition asset--The portion of the transition asset that has not been recognized either immediately as the effect of a change in accounting or on a delayed basis as a part of net periodic postretirement benefit cost, as an offset to certain losses, or as a part of accounting for the effects of a settlement or a curtailment.

Unrecognized transition obligation--The portion of the transition obligation that has not been recognized either immediately as the effect of a change in accounting or on a delayed basis as a part of net periodic postretirement benefit cost, as an offset to certain gains, or as a part of accounting for the effects of a settlement or a curtailment.

A. Single Employer Defined Benefit Plans
1. Postretirement benefits are part of compensation paid to employees for services
   a. Amount of benefits to be paid depends on future events specified in plan's benefit formula
2. Postretirement benefits formerly were accounted for on a pay-as-you-go (cash) basis. SFAS 106 changes this practice by requiring accrual, during the years that the employee renders necessary service, of **expected** cost of providing those benefits to an employee. Any method of postretirement benefits accounting that recognizes cost before payment of benefits to retirees must deal with two problems.
   a. Assumptions must be made concerning future events that will determine amount and timing of benefits.
   b. Approach to attributing cost of postretirement benefits to individual years of service must be selected.

B. Basic Elements of Postretirement Benefits Accounting
1. Prior service cost
   a. Except as specified otherwise, prior service cost shall be amortized by assigning an equal amount to each future service period of each employee active at the date of a plan amendment who was not yet fully eligible for benefits at that date.
   b. If all or almost all of a plan's participants are fully eligible for benefits, prior service cost shall be amortized over remaining life expectancy of those participants.
   c. Consistent use of alternative amortization approach that more rapidly reduces unrecognized cost of retroactive amendments is acceptable.
      (1) Alternative method used should be disclosed.
   d. When period during which employer expects to realize economic benefits from amendment granting increased benefits is shorter than entire remaining service period of active employees, amortization of prior service cost shall be accelerated.
   e. Plan amendment can reduce, rather than increase, accumulated postretirement benefit obligation
      (1) Reduction should be used to reduce any existing unrecognized prior service cost

(2) Then to reduce any remaining unrecognized transition obligation

(3) Excess, if any, shall be amortized on same basis as specified for prior service cost

2. Gains and losses
    a. Gains (losses)
       (1) Result from changes in amount of either accumulated postretirement benefit obligation or plan assets due to experience different than assumed and changes in assumptions
       (2) Include both **realized** and **unrealized** amounts
    b. Asset gains (losses) include both (a) changes reflected in market-related value of assets and (b) changes not yet reflected in market-related value.
       (1) Asset gains (losses) not yet reflected in market-related value are not required to be amortized as c. below.
    c. As a minimum, amortization of unrecognized net gain (loss) should be included as a component of net postretirement benefit cost for a year if, as of the beginning of the year, that unrecognized net gain (loss) > .10 of the larger of the accumulated postretirement benefit obligation or the market-related value of plan assets.
       (1) Minimum amortization should be the excess divided by the average remaining service period of active employees expected to receive benefits under the plan
          (a) Amortization must always reduce beginning of the year balance
          (b) Amortization of a net unrecognized gain (loss) results in a decrease (increase) in net periodic pension cost
       (2) If all or almost all of plan's participants are inactive, average remaining life expectancy of inactive participants should be used instead of average remaining service.
    d. Any systematic method of amortization of unrecognized gains (losses) may be used in lieu of the minimum specified above provided that
       (1) Minimum is used in any period in which minimum amortization is greater (reduces the net balance by more)
       (2) Method is applied consistently and disclosed

3. Recognition of liabilities and assets
    a. SFAS 106 requires an employer's obligation for postretirement benefits expected to be provided to an employee be **fully** accrued by the full eligibility date of employee, even if employee is to render additional service beyond that date
    b. Transition obligations
       (1) SFAS 106 measures the transition obligation as the unfunded and unrecognized accumulated postretirement benefit obligation for all plan participants. Two options are provided for recognizing that transition obligation.
          (a) **Immediate** recognition of the transition obligation as the effect of an accounting change (i.e., include all of the obligation as part of the net periodic postretirement benefit cost)
          (b) Recognize the transition obligation in the balance sheet and income statement on a delayed basis over the plan participants' future service periods, with proper disclosure of the remaining unrecognized amount. Note that delayed recognition **cannot** result in less rapid recognition than accounting for the transition obligation on a pay-as-you-go basis

C. Attribution
    1. The expected postretirement benefit obligation shall be attributed, in equal amounts, to each year of service in the attribution period.
    2. However, if a benefit plan contains a benefit formula that attributes a disproportionate share of the expected postretirement benefit obligation to employees' early years of service, the postretirement benefits should be attributed based on the plan's benefit formula.
    3. Assumptions
       a. Assumed discount rates shall reflect time value of money in determining present value of future cash outflows currently expected to be required to satisfy postretirement benefit obligation
          (1) Used in measurements of expected and accumulated postretirement benefit obligations and service and interest cost components of net periodic postretirement benefit cost

    b. Assumed compensation levels (when measuring service cost and expected and accumulated post-retirement benefit obligations) shall reflect estimate of actual future compensation levels of employees involved, including future changes attributed to general price levels, productivity, seniority, promotion, and other factors.

    c. Accumulated postretirement benefit obligation shall be measured based on employees' history of service and compensation without estimate of future compensation levels.

    d. Automatic benefit changes specified by plan that are expected to occur should be included in measurements of projected and accumulated benefit obligations and the service cost component.

    e. Plan amendments should be included in computations of projected and accumulated benefit obligations.

      (1) Once they have been contractually agreed to

      (2) Even if some provisions take effect only in future periods

D. Measurement of Plan Assets

  1. For purposes of required disclosures, plan investments, whether equity or debt securities, real estate, or other, shall be measured at FMV as of measurement date.

  2. Market-related asset value is used for purposes of determining the expected return on plan assets and accounting for asset gains and losses.

E. Acceptable Measurement Dates

  1. As of date of financial statements, or

  2. If used consistently from year to year, as of a date $\leq$ 3 months prior to that date

  3. Measurement date is not intended to require that all procedures be performed after that date

  4. Information for items requiring estimates can be prepared as of an earlier date and projected forward to account for subsequent events (e.g., employee service)

  5. Measurements of net periodic postretirement benefit cost for both interim and annual financial statements shall be based on assumptions used for previous year-end measurements

    a. If more recent measurements are available or a significant event occurs, use more recent measurements

F. Disclosures (amended by SFAS 132)

SFAS 107 (F25) Disclosures About Fair Value of Financial Instruments

A. Statement requires entities to disclose the fair value of financial instruments, both assets and liabilities whether recognized or not recognized in the statement of financial position, for which it is practicable to estimate fair value.

  1. Applies to all entities

  2. Does not change any recognition, measurement, or classification requirements for financial instruments in financial statements

  3. Fair value disclosures of financial instruments previously prescribed by GAAP meet the requirements of this statement.

B. Financial Instruments include

  1. Cash

  2. Evidence of ownership interest in an entity, or

  3. A contract that both

    a. Imposes contractual obligation on one entity to deliver cash or another financial instrument to second entity or to exchange financial instruments on potentially unfavorable terms with second entity, and

    b. Conveys contractual right to second entity to receive cash or another financial instrument from first entity or to exchange financial instruments on potentially favorable terms with first entity

C. Fair value of a financial instrument is the current amount at which a financial instrument could be exchanged in a transaction between willing parties.

D. Standard lists a number of areas for which the disclosure requirements are not applicable, including pensions and other deferred compensation arrangements and leases.

E. Disclosure Requirements

1. When practicable (i.e., without incurring excessive costs), an entity must disclose the fair value of financial instruments in either the body of the financial statements or in the accompanying notes.
   a. Disclosure must include the method(s) and significant assumptions used in estimating fair value
      (1) Quoted market price is generally the best estimate of fair value.
      (2) If quoted market price is not available, management must estimate fair value based upon similar financial instruments or valuation techniques.
      (3) No disclosure is required for trade receivables and payables when carrying amount approximates fair value.
   b. Disclosure must distinguish between financial instruments held or issued for
      (1) Trading purposes
      (2) Purposes other than trading
2. If estimation of the fair value of financial instruments is not practicable, entity must disclose
   a. Information pertinent to estimating the fair value (i.e., the carrying amount, effective interest rate, and maturity), and
   b. The reason why estimation of fair value is not practicable.
3. Derivative financial instruments may not be combined, aggregated or netted with nonderivative or other derivative financial instruments.
4. If financial instruments disclosed in more than one area in FS, one note must contain a summary table cross-referencing the location of the other instruments.
5. Disclosure of concentrations of credit risk of all financial instruments
   a. Disclose all significant concentrations of credit risk from **all** financial instruments, whether from an individual counterparty or groups of counterparties.
   b. Group concentrations exist if a number of counterparties are engaged in similar activities and have similar economic characteristics such that they would be similarly affected by changes in conditions.
   c. Disclose for each significant concentration
      (1) Information about the (shared) activity, region, or economic characteristics
      (2) The amount of accounting loss the entity would incur should any party to the financial instrument fail to perform according to the terms of the contract and the collateral or security, if any, is of no value.
      (3) The entity's policy of requiring collateral or security, the entity's access to that collateral or security, and the nature and brief description of the collateral or security.

SFAS 109 (I27) Accounting for Income Taxes
(Supercedes SFAS 96, SFAS 100, SFAS 103, and SFAS 108)
A. Establishes financial accounting and reporting requirements for income taxes resulting from an entity's activities during the current and preceding years.
   1. Continues BS oriented asset and liability approach consistent with SFAC 6.
   2. Objectives
      a. Recognize taxes payable or refundable for current year.
      b. Recognize deferred tax liabilities and assets for future tax consequences of events previously recognized in financial statements or tax returns.
B. Basic principles
   1. Recognize current tax liability or asset for estimated taxes payable or refundable on tax returns for current year
   2. Measure and recognize deferred tax liability or asset using enacted tax rate(s) expected to apply to taxable income in periods in which the deferred tax assets and liabilities are expected to be realized or settled
   3. Adjust measurement of deferred tax assets so as to not recognize tax benefits not expected to be realized
   4. Deferred tax assets and liabilities are **not** discounted to reflect their present value
C. Measurement of Deferred Taxes
   1. Temporary differences

    a. Difference between tax basis of asset or liability and its reported amount for financial accounting which results in taxable or deductible amounts in future years

        (1) Includes all timing differences

        (2) Includes tax-book differences in asset's bases

    b. Future effects

        (1) **Taxable amounts** are from temporary differences that will result in lower amounts of expense or higher amounts of revenue being reported on the tax return than are reported on the books in the future period.

        (2) **Deductible amounts** are from temporary differences that will result in higher amounts of expense or lower amounts of revenue being reported on the tax return than are reported on the books in the future period.

  2. Deferred tax liability or asset measured each BS date

    a. Identify types and amounts of existing temporary differences **and** nature of each type of operating loss and tax credit carryforward and the remaining length of the carryforward period

    b. Measure total deferred tax liability for taxable temporary differences using the enacted applicable tax rate

    c. Measure total deferred tax asset for deductible temporary differences and operating loss carryforwards using the enacted applicable tax rate

    d. Measure deferred tax assets for each type of tax credit carryforward

    e. Reduce deferred tax assets by a valuation allowance, **if more likely than not** (a likelihood of more than 50%) that some or all of deferred tax asset will not be realized

        (1) All available evidence (positive and negative) should be considered to determine whether valuation allowance is needed.

D. Changes in Tax Rates or Status

  1. Change in rates

    a. Change previously recorded amounts of deferred tax liabilities or assets

    b. Net adjustments shall be reflected in tax expense on continuing operations in period that includes enactment date.

E. Business Combinations

  1. Recognize deferred tax asset or liability for differences between assigned values and tax basis of assets and liabilities recognized in a purchase combination

F. Intraperiod Tax Allocation

  1. Allocate income tax expense or benefit for the period among continuing operations, extraordinary items, other comprehensive income, and items charged or credited to stockholders' equity

    a. In cases where there is only one item after continuing operations, portion of income tax expense (benefit) remaining after allocation to continuing operations is amount allocated to that item.

    b. In cases where there are two or more items after continuing operations, portion left after allocation to continuing operations is allocated among other items in proportion to their individual effects on income tax expense (benefit).

G. Financial Statement Presentation and Disclosure

  1. Balance sheet

    a. Report deferred tax liabilities and assets as current or noncurrent based on classification of related asset or liability

    b. Classify deferred tax liabilities or assets not related to an asset or liability (i.e., one related to a carryforward) according to the expected reversal date of the temporary difference

    c. For a tax paying component of an enterprise and within a particular tax jurisdiction

        (1) All current deferred tax liabilities and assets should be offset and reported as a single amount

        (2) All noncurrent deferred tax liabilities and assets should be offset and reported as a single amount

  2. Must disclose the following components of the net deferred tax liability or asset:

    a. The total of all deferred tax liabilities

    b. The total of all deferred tax assets

    c. The total valuation allowance for deferred tax assets

3. Additional disclosures
    a. Disclose any net change in the total valuation allowance
    b. Disclose the types of temporary differences, carryforwards, and carrybacks
4. Income statement
    a. Components of tax expense attributable to continuing operations shall be disclosed in financial statements or notes. For example
        (1) Current tax expense or benefit
        (2) Deferred tax expense or benefit (exclusive of other components listed below)
        (3) Investment tax credits
        (4) Government grants (to the extent recognized as a reduction of income tax expense)
        (5) Benefits of operating loss carryforwards
        (6) Tax expense resulting from allocation of certain tax benefits either directly to contributed capital or to reduce goodwill or other noncurrent intangible assets of an acquired entity
        (7) Adjustments of a deferred tax liability or asset resulting from enacted changes in tax laws, rates, or status
    b. Variances between statutory and effective tax rates must be disclosed.
        (1) Public entities should disclose reconciliation using percentages or dollar amounts.
        (2) Nonpublic entities must disclose nature of significant reconciling items.
    c. Disclose amounts and expiration dates of operating loss and tax credit carryforwards **and** any portion of the deferred tax asset valuation allowance for which subsequently recognized tax benefits will be allocated to reduce intangible assets or directly reduce accumulated other comprehensive income.

SFAS 112 (C44) Employers' Accounting for Postemployment Benefits

A. Statement sets forth accounting standards for employers providing post**employment** benefits to former/inactive employees, **after employment but before** retirement.
    1. Applies to any postemployment benefits provided to former employers and their beneficiaries and dependents except
        a. Special or contractual termination benefits addressed by SFAS 88 and 106.
        b. Postemployment benefits derived from post**retirement** benefit or pension plans.
        c. Stock compensation plans covered by APB 25.
        d. Deferred compensation plans for individual employees which are covered by APB 12.
    2. Postemployment benefits may
        a. Result from death, disability, layoff, etc.
        b. Be paid in cash or in kind
        c. Be paid upon assumption of inactive status or over a period of time
B. Applicable postemployment benefits must be accounted for according to SFAS 43, para. 6, which states:
    1. Liability for future compensated absences must be accrued if
        a. Obligation relates to services already provided by the employee,
        b. Rights to compensation vest or accumulate,
        c. Payment of obligation is probable, **and**
        d. Amount to be paid is reasonably estimable.
C. If conditions listed above are not met but the benefits are within scope of SFAS 43, they are accounted for according to SFAS 5, para 8, which states:
    1. Estimated loss contingency accrued if
        a. It is known before FS are issued that it is probable that asset has been impaired or a liability incurred and that future events will probably confirm the loss, **and**
        b. Amount of loss is reasonably estimable.
D. Disclosure required if liability for postemployment benefits not accrued solely because amount not reasonably estimable.

SFAS 114 (D22) Accounting by Creditors for Impairment of a Loan (Amends SFAS 5 and 15; amended by SFAS 118)

A. Scope of SFAS 114

1. Applies to all creditors and to all loans except for those specified in A.3 (a.-d.)
2. Applies to all loans (including A.3.a.) that are restructured in a troubled debt restructuring involving a modification of terms
3. Exceptions
   a. Large groups of smaller-balance homogeneous loans collectively evaluated for impairment
   b. Loans that are measured at fair value or at the lower of cost or fair value
   c. Leases
   d. Debt securities
4. Does not specify how a creditor should identify loans that are to be evaluated for collectibility

B. Recognition of Impairment
1. A loan is impaired when it is probable that a creditor will be unable to collect all amounts due according to the contractual terms.
   a. Probable--future event or events are likely to occur
   b. All amounts due according to the contractual terms include both interest and principal payments collected as scheduled in loan agreement.
2. If a loan qualifies as exception A.3.a., the creditor may not apply the provisions of SFAS 114 until the debt is restructured.
3. Instances when a loan is not impaired
   a. Insignificant delays or shortfalls
   b. A delay in which creditor expects to collect all amounts due including interest accrued for the period of delay

C. Measurement of Impairment
1. Creditor measures impairment based on present value of expected future cash flows discounted at the loan's effective interest rate
   a. Effective interest rate--rate implicit in loan at time of origination
   b. If effective interest rate varies (based on an independent index or rate)
      (1) May be calculated based on the index or rate as it changes over life of loan
      (2) Or may be fixed at rate in effect at date the loan meets impairment criterion
   c. Expected future cash flows determined as creditor's best estimate based on reasonable and supportable assumptions and projections (including estimated costs to sell)
2. Loans with common risk characteristics may be aggregated and impairment measured using historical statistics and a composite effective interest rate.
3. Alternative measures of impairment
   a. Loan's observable market price
   b. Fair value of collateral if loan is collateral dependent
      (1) Collateral dependent means repayment provided solely by the underlying collateral
      (2) This method must be used when foreclosure is probable (and loan is collateral dependent)
4. When measure of impaired loan is less than recorded investment in loan
   a. Create valuation allowance with charge to bad debt expense
   b. Or adjust existing valuation allowance with charge to bad debt expense
5. Significant changes (increases or decreases) subsequent to initial measure of impairment
   a. Recalculate impairment
   b. Adjust valuation allowance
   c. Net carrying amount of loan may never exceed recorded investment in loan

D. Income Recognition
1. The present value of an impaired loan changes over time and also changes because of revised estimates in the amount or timing of cash flows.
2. Recognition and measurement methods to reflect changes in present value are not specified in this statement as amended.

E. Disclosures
1. The recorded investment in impaired loans, total allowance for credit losses related to impaired loans, and amount for which no allowance for credit losses
2. The creditor's income recognition method, including cash receipts

3. For each period presented which relates to the impaired loans
   a. Average recorded investment
   b. Interest revenue recognized
   c. If practicable, interest revenue recognized on a cash basis

SFAS 115 (I80) Accounting for Certain Investments in Debt and Equity Securities
(Supersedes SFAS 12)

A. Establishes financial accounting and reporting requirements for all investments in debt securities and for small investments in equity securities with readily determinable fair values
   1. "Small" investments are those not accounted for by the equity method or involving consolidated subsidiaries
B. Segregates debt and equity securities into three categories
   1. Held-to-maturity securities
      a. Applies only to debt securities
      b. Requires intent and ability to hold to maturity
         (1) Will **not** sell in response to changes in
            (a) Funding terms and sources
            (b) Interest rates and prepayment risk
            (c) Foreign currency risk
            (d) Attractiveness of alternative investments
            (e) Liquidity needs
         (2) In rare cases, intent may change due to nonrecurring and unforeseeable circumstances.
            (a) Continuing deterioration of issuer's credit
            (b) Elimination of tax-exempt status of interest
            (c) Business combination or disposition that increases interest rate risk or credit risk
            (d) Regulatory change in permissible investments
            (e) Downsizing to meet industry capital requirements
            (f) Increased risk weight of debt securities held as regulatory risk-based capital
         (3) Considered maturity if
            (a) Sale occurs so close to maturity that interest rate risk is virtually eliminated
            (b) Sale occurs after at least 85% of the principal has been collected
      c. Balance sheet
         (1) Report at amortized cost
         (2) Classify as current or noncurrent on an individual basis
      d. Income statement
         (1) Do not report unrealized holding gains and losses
         (2) Include realized G(L) in earnings
         (3) Include interest income and premium/discount amortization in earnings
      e. Statement of cash flows
         (1) Classify cash inflows from sales and outflows from purchases gross (not netted) as investing activities
   2. Trading securities
      a. Applies to debt and equity securities held for current resale
      b. Balance sheet
         (1) Report at fair value
         (2) Classify as current assets
      c. Income statement
         (1) Include unrealized holding G(L) in earnings
         (2) Exclude previously recognized realized G(L) from earnings
         (3) Include dividend and interest revenue
      d. Statement of cash flows
         (1) Classify purchases and sales as operating activity
   3. Available-for-sale securities

    a.   Applies to debt and equity securities not categorized as held-to-maturity or trading securities

    b.   Balance sheet

        (1) Report at fair value

        (2) Classify as current or noncurrent on an individual basis

        (3) Report net unrealized holding G(L) in other comprehensive income and accumulated other comprehensive income as separate component of stockholders' equity

    c.   Income statement

        (1) Include realized G(L) in earnings

        (2) Include dividend and interest revenue and premium/discount amortization in earnings

    d.   Statement of cash flows

        (1) Classify sales and purchases gross (not netted) as investing activity

C. Transfers between categories are accounted for at fair value

   1. From trading

     a.   Do not reverse recognized unrealized holding G(L) at date of transfer.

   2. To trading

     a.   Recognize unrealized holding G(L) immediately

   3. To available-for-sale from held-to-maturity

     a.   Report unrealized holding G(L) as other comprehensive income

     b.   Transfers from held-to-maturity should be rare

   4. To held-to-maturity from available-for-sale

     a.   Report unrealized holding G(L) as other comprehensive income

     b.   Amortize G(L) over remaining life of security as adjustment to yield

D. Impairment of securities

   1. Applies to held-to-maturity and available-for-sale securities

   2. If permanent decline

     a.   Write down to fair value

     b.   Include realized loss in earnings

   3. No write-up for subsequent recoveries

E. Disclosures

   1. Only held-to-maturity and available-for-sale securities

   2. By major security type

     a.   Aggregate fair value

     b.   Gross unrealized holding gains and losses

     c.   Amortized cost basis

   3. By maturity of debt securities

     a.   All enterprises disclose contractual information.

     b.   Financial institutions disclose fair value and amortized cost for 4 or more groups of maturities

       (1) Up to 1 year

       (2) Over 1 through 5 years

       (3) Over 5 through 10 years

       (4) Over 10 years

     c.   Securities maturing at multiple dates

       (1) May disclose separately

       (2) May allocate over groupings

   4. Available-for-sale securities

     a.   Proceeds from sales

     b.   Gross realized G(L)

     c.   Cost basis for determining G(L)

     d.   Change in net unrealized holding G(L) reported as comprehensive income in stockholders' equity

   5. Trading securities

     a.   Change in net unrealized holding G(L) reported in earnings

   6. Transfers

     a.   Gross G(L) on transfer from available-for-sale to trading

    b. Of held-to-maturity securities
       (1) Amortized cost
       (2) Realized or unrealized G(L)
       (3) Reason for sale

SFAS 116 (C67) Accounting for Contributions Received and Contributions Made*

Establishes accounting standards for contributions received or made for all types of entities, not-for-profit, and business enterprises.

A. Contributions-defined

Contributions can be defined as an unconditional promise to give cash or other assets to an entity. A cancellation of a liability is also considered a contribution.

B. Contributions received (donee accounting)

   1. Shall be capitalized by the donee at FMV of the item and recognized as revenue in period received.

C. Contributions made (donor accounting) shall be recognized at FMV as expense in period the item is donated

   1. Donation expense should be classified under other expense on the income statement.

   2. If difference exists between the FMV and book value of the item, then gain or loss on disposal will be recognized.

SFAS 118 (D22) Accounting by Creditors for Impairment of a Loan-Income Recognition and Disclosures (Amends SFAS 114)

(This statement is not outlined separately; instead the SFAS 114 outline has been changed accordingly.)

SFAS 121 (I08) Accounting for the Impairment of Long-Lived Assets and for Long-Lived Assets to Be Disposed of

A. Establishes financial accounting and reporting requirements for long-lived assets, certain identifiable intangibles, goodwill related to those assets to be held and used, and long-lived assets and certain identifiable intangibles to be disposed of.

B. Assets to be held and used

   1. Reviewed for impairment when circumstances indicate that the carrying amount of long-lived assets or identifiable intangibles is not recoverable

     a. Significant decrease in market value

     b. Change in way asset used or physical change in asset

     c. Legal factors or change in business climate that might affect asset's fair value or adverse action or assessment by regulator

     d. Asset costs incurred greater than planned

     e. Operating or cash flow losses from the asset

   2. Impaired if the expected total future cash flows are less than the carrying amount of the assets

     a. Assets should be grouped at lowest level for which there are identifiable cash flows independent of other groupings

     b. Expected future cash flows are future cash inflows to be generated by the assets less the future cash outflows expected to be necessary to obtain those inflows

     c. Expected future cash flows are **not** discounted and do not consider interest charges

   3. Written down to fair value and loss recognized upon impairment

     a. Fair value is the amount at which the asset can be bought or sold in a current transaction between willing parties

     b. If quoted market price in active market is not available, the estimate of fair value should be based on best information available

   4. Fair value increases on assets previously written down for impairment losses may not be recognized.

   5. When testing for recoverability, goodwill arising in purchase business combinations that includes long-lived assets and identifiable intangible assets is allocated to each grouping of assets.

---

* This standard and SFAS 117 are discussed in more detail in Module 39, Not-for-Profit Accounting, because most of the exam questions from this standard are likely to appear on the Accounting and Reporting Exam.

     a. Allocate all unamortized goodwill to the asset groupings using the relative fair values of long-lived tangible and identifiable intangible assets.

     b. If only some assets being tested, allocate all unamortized goodwill to only those assets using relative fair values at acquisition date.

     c. In recognizing losses, first eliminate goodwill allocated to each asset grouping, then write down impaired long-lived assets and identifiable intangibles.

  6. Disclosures

     a. Description of impaired assets and circumstances which led to impairment

     b. Amount of impairment and manner in which fair value was determined

     c. Caption in income statement in which impairment loss is aggregated, if it is not presented separately thereon

     d. Business segment(s) affected (if applicable)

C. Assets to be disposed of

  1. Defined as all long-lived assets and certain identifiable intangibles to be disposed of which are not part of a disposal of a segment of a business per APB 30 and for which management has adopted a plan of disposal

  2. Reported at lesser of carrying amount or fair value less cost to sell

     a. Cost to sell includes broker commissions, legal and title transfer fees, and closing costs prior to legal title transfer

  3. In future periods, adjusted carrying amount of asset shall be revised to extent of changes in estimate of fair value less cost to sell, provided that the adjusted carrying amount does not exceed the carrying amount of the asset prior to the adjustment reflecting the decision to dispose of the asset

     a. Thus, recoveries may be recognized when assets are to be **disposed of** but not on impaired assets that continue to be used.

  4. Disclosures

     a. Description of assets to be disposed of, reasons for disposal, expected disposal date, and carrying amount of those assets

     b. Business segments affected, if applicable

     c. Loss, if any, recognized

     d. Gain or loss, if any, resulting from changes in carrying amount due to further changes in market value

     e. Caption in income statement in which gains and losses (from c. and d.) are aggregated if they are not presented separately thereon

SFAS 123 (C36) Accounting for Stock-Based Compensation

A. Provides a fair value based method of accounting for stock-based compensation plans

  1. Encourages entities to adopt provisions of this standard rather than those of APB 25

  2. Applies to all transactions between an entity and its "suppliers" (whether employees or nonemployees) in which the entity acquires goods or services through issuance of equity instruments or incurrence of liabilities based on fair value of the entity's common stock or other equity instruments

  3. Examples include stock purchase plans, stock options, restricted stock, and stock appreciation rights

B. Transactions with Nonemployees--Accounted for based on fair value of consideration received or fair value of equity instruments given, whichever is more readily determinable.

C. Transactions with Employees--Utilize the intrinsic value based method (i.e., difference between market price and exercise price) outlined in APB 25 or the fair value based method (use of estimates to value compensation cost) per SFAS 123; however, both require disclosures as specified in SFAS 123.

D. Measurement Methods

  1. Settlement by equity instrument

     a. Nonvested stock is measured at market price of a share of the same stock as if it were vested and issued at grant date.

     b. Stock options are measured via use of an option pricing model which considers, as of grant date, exercise price and expected life of the option, current price of underlying stock and its anticipated volatility, expected dividends on the stock, and risk-free interest rate for expected term of the option.

    c. If fair value cannot be determined as of grant date, final measure shall be based on stock price and any other pertinent factors when it becomes reasonably possible to estimate that value. Current intrinsic value shall be used as a measure until a final determination of fair value can be made.

  2. Settlement by cash requires the recording of liability based on current stock price at end of each period. Changes in stock price during service period are recognized as compensation cost over service period. A change in stock price subsequent to service period is recognized as compensation cost of that period.

E. Recognition of Compensation Cost
  1. Total compensation cost is based on the number of instruments that eventually vest
    a. Vesting is defined as moment when employee's right to receive or retain such instruments or cash is no longer contingent on performance of additional services
    b. No compensation cost shall be recognized for employees that forfeit eligibility due to failure either to achieve service requirement or performance condition
    c. Compensation cost shall not be reversed if vested employee's stock option expires unexercised
  2. Acceptable accrual methods
    a. As of grant date, base accruals of compensation cost on best available estimate of the number of options or instruments expected to vest, with necessary adjustments made if additional information indicates that actual forfeitures vary from initial estimates made.
    b. As of grant date, accrue compensation cost as if all options or instruments that are subject only to a service requirement will vest. Recognize actual forfeitures as they occur.

F. Tax consequences of stock-based compensation transactions shall be accounted for pursuant to SFAS 109.

G. Disclosures
  1. APB 25 and SFAS 123 require disclosures listed under 3-7 below
  2. Additionally, when APB 25 used for recognition and measurement SFAS 123 requires that pro forma net income and earnings per share shall be presented for the intrinsic value based method as if fair value based method had been used. Pro forma amounts should reflect
    a. Difference in compensation cost under APB 25 and SFAS 123
    b. Related tax effect of using SFAS 123 vs. APB 25
  3. Vesting requirements, maximum term of options granted, and number of shares authorized for grants of options or other equity instruments
  4. The number and weighted-average exercise prices of each group of options
  5. The weighted-average grant-date fair value of options granted during the year, classified according to whether exercise price equals, exceeds, or is less than fair value of stock at date of grant
  6. A description of methods used and assumptions made in determining fair values of the options
  7. Total compensation cost recognized for the year
  8. For options still outstanding, range of exercise prices and weighted-average remaining contractual life

SFAS 124 (I80) Accounting for Certain Investments Held by Not-for-Profit Organizations
(This statement deals with a topic covered on the Accounting and Reporting Examination; it is included in Module 39.)

SFAS 125 (L10 and R20) Accounting for Transfers and Servicing of Financial Assets and Extinguishment of Liabilities*

A. Provides accounting and reporting standards for transfers and servicing of financial assets and extinguishment of liabilities

B. Sale or Transfer of Assets
  1. Necessary conditions to qualify
    a. Transferred assets have been isolated from the transferor or its creditors,
    b. Transferee has the unconstrained right to pledge or exchange the transferred assets, and
    c. Transferor does not maintain effective control over the transferred assets through

---

* *AUTHOR'S NOTE: Refer to the flowchart on p. 282 as you study this outline.*

      (1) An agreement that obligates the transferor to repurchase or redeem them before their maturity, or

      (2) An agreement that entitles transferor to repurchase transferred assets that are not obtainable elsewhere

  2. Upon any transfer of assets the transferor shall

    a. Continue to carry in its balance sheet any retained interest in the transferred assets

    b. Allocate the previous carrying amount between the assets sold and the retained interest based on their relative fair values

  3. Upon any completion of a transfer of assets which satisfies the conditions of a sale

    a. Derecognize all assets sold

    b. Recognize all assets obtained and liabilities incurred in consideration as sale proceeds

    c. Initially measure at fair value assets obtained and liabilities incurred in a sale

    d. Recognize in earnings any gain (loss) on sale

C. Servicing Assets and Liabilities

  1. Under an obligation to service financial assets, an entity recognizes a service asset or service liability unless it

    a. Securitizes the assets.

    b. Retains all of the resulting securities

    c. Classifies them as held-to-maturity debt securities

  2. Servicing asset purchased or assumed

    a. Measured at FMV

    b. Amortized in proportion over the period of estimated net service income or net service cost

    c. Assessed for asset impairment or increased obligation

  3. Duties included in servicing assets and liabilities

    a. Collecting interest, principal, and escrow payments from borrowers

    b. Paying taxes and insurance from escrowed funds

    c. Monitoring delinquencies

D. Secured Borrowing and Collateral

  1. Pledge

    a. Debtor grants a security interest in certain assets

    b. Collateral transferred to the secured party

  2. Accounting for secured borrowings

    a. Debtor to separate the asset on balance sheet into an encumbered assets section if

      (1) Secured party permitted to sell or repledge asset

      (2) Debtor does not have the right to reclaim asset on short notice

    b. The secured party shall recognize the collateral as its asset

      (1) Initially measure it at fair value

      (2) Recognize its obligation to return it

  3. Debtor defaults under the terms of the agreement

    a. Debtor derecognizes the collateral

    b. Secured party recognizes the collateral as its asset at fair market value

E. Extinguishment of Liabilities

  1. Debtor shall derecognize a liability when it has been extinguished

    a. Debtor pays the creditor and is relieved of its obligation for the liability.

    b. Debtor is legally released from being obligor under the liability, either judicially or by the creditor.

F. Required Disclosures

  1. Repurchase agreements or securities lending transactions

  2. Extinguished debt

    a. General description of transaction

    b. Amount of debt that was considered extinguished at end of period

  3. Description of assets set aside for satisfying scheduled payments of a specific obligation

  4. Nonestimable fair value of assets

    a. Description of the assets or liabilities

    b. The reasons why it is not practicable to estimate the assets or liabilities

  5. For all servicing assets and servicing liabilities

    a. Amounts of servicing assets or liabilities recognized and amortized during the period

    b. Fair value on recognized servicing assets and liabilities and the method used to estimate the fair value

    c. Risk characteristics of the underlying financial assets used to stratify recognized servicing assets

    d. Activity in any valuation allowance for impairment of recognized servicing assets

SFAS 126 (F25) Exemption From Certain Required Disclosures About Financial Instruments for Certain Nonpublic Entities (an amendment of FASB Statement No. 107)

(This pronouncement is not outlined because the authors believe that it is too specialized for the CPA Exam)

SFAS 127 (F38) Deferral of the Effective Date of Certain Provisions of FASB Statement No. 125 (an amendment of FASB Statement No. 125)

(This pronouncement is not outlined because the authors believe that it is too specialized for the CPA Exam)

SFAS 128 (E11) Earnings per Share

A. Presentation on Financial Statements

  1. Entities with publicly held common stock and simple capital structures (no potential common shares) need only present basic per-share amounts. All other entities must present basic and diluted per share amounts with equal prominence.

  2. Must present EPS on face of income statement for

    a. Income from continuing operations

    b. Net income

  3. May present on face of income statement or in notes

    a. Discontinued operations

    b. Extraordinary items

    c. Cumulative effect of change in accounting principle

B. Basic EPS--Measures entity performance over a period of time

  1. Computed as net income minus preferred dividends divided by the weighted-average number of common shares outstanding. The claims of senior securities (nonconvertible preferred dividends) should be deducted from income prior to computing EPS to properly determine net income available to **common** shareholders. Therefore, dividends on cumulative preferred are deducted whether or not declared, while dividends on noncumulative preferred are deducted only if declared.

  2. EPS figures should be based upon consolidated income figures after consolidating adjustments and eliminations.

  3. To compute the weighted-average of common shares outstanding, treasury shares should be excluded as of date of repurchase.

  4. EPS data for all periods presented should be retroactively adjusted for all splits and dividends, even those subsequent to the period being presented.

  5. For stock issued in purchase combinations, use weighted-average from date of combination. For pooling combination, shares assumed outstanding the entire period regardless of when issued.

C. For Diluted EPS, these additional procedures apply

  1. The "if converted" method is used to adjust EPS on outstanding common shares for dilutive convertible securities.

    a. The convertible securities are considered to have been converted at the beginning of the period (or at issuance if later) increasing the denominator of EPS.

    b. For convertible bonds, the interest savings net of tax is added to the numerator of EPS.

    c. For convertible preferred, the preferred dividends deducted in arriving at EPS are not deducted, thereby increasing the numerator. There is no tax effect because dividends are not an expense.

2. The "treasury stock" method is used to adjust EPS on outstanding common shares for dilutive options and warrants (i.e., those for which the exercise price is below the market price).
   a. The options and warrants are assumed to be exercised at the beginning of the period (or the date the options and warrants were issued if later). The shares assumed issued increase the denominator of EPS.
   b. The hypothetical proceeds are used to purchase treasury stock at the average price over the year.
   c. No retroactive adjustment should be made to EPS figures for options and warrants as a result of market price changes.
3. When convertible securities require payment of cash at conversion, they are considered the equivalent of warrants. The "if converted" method is used for the conversion and the "treasury stock" method is applied to the cash proceeds.
4. Fixed awards and nonvested stock to be issued to an employee under a stock-based compensation arrangement are considered options and are considered to be outstanding as of the grant date even though their exercise may be contingent upon vesting.
5. Contingently issuable shares are shares whose issuance is contingent upon the satisfaction of certain conditions and shall be considered outstanding and included in the diluted EPS computation as follows:
   a. If all necessary conditions have been satisfied by the end of the period, the shares should be included as of the beginning of the period in which the conditions were satisfied (or as of the date of the contingent stock agreement, if later).
   b. If all necessary conditions have not been satisfied, the number of contingently issuable shares shall be based on the number of shares (if any) that would be issuable if the end of the reporting period were the end of the contingency period and if the result would be dilutive. These shares shall be included in the diluted EPS denominator as of the beginning of the period (or as of the date of the contingent stock agreement if later).
6. Antidilutive securities shall not be included in diluted EPS computations.

D. Additional Disclosure Requirements
1. A reconciliation of the numerators and denominators of the basic and diluted per-share computations for income from continuing operations, including the individual income and share amount effects of all securities that affect earnings per share.
2. The effect that has been given to preferred dividends in arriving at income available to common shareholders in computing basic EPS.
3. Securities that are antidilutive for the period(s) presented but could potentially dilute basic EPS in the future.
4. A description of any transaction that occurs after the end of the most recent period but before issuance of the financial statements that would materially change the number of shares outstanding at the end of the period if the transaction had occurred before the end of the period.

SFAS 129 (C24) Disclosure of Information About Capital Structure

A. Information to be Disclosed about Securities Within the Financial Statements
1. The rights and privileges of the various securities outstanding; for example
   a. Dividend and liquidation preferences
   b. Participation rights
   c. Call prices and dates
   d. Conversion/exercise prices/rates and dates
   e. Sinking fund requirements
   f. Unusual voting rights
   g. Significant terms of contracts to issue additional shares
2. The number of shares issued upon conversion, exercise, or satisfaction of required conditions during at least the most recent annual fiscal period and any subsequent interim period presented.
B. Disclosure of Liquidation Preference of Preferred Stock Within the Financial Statements
1. Relationship between the preference in liquidation and the par/stated value of the shares when preferred stock (or other senior stock) has a preference in involuntary liquidation considerably in excess

of the par/stated value of the shares. This disclosure should be made in the equity section of the balance sheet in the aggregate, either parenthetically or "in short."
   2. Aggregate or per share amounts at which preferred stock may be called or is subject to redemption through sinking fund operations or otherwise.
   3. Aggregate and per share amount of arrearages in cumulative preferred dividends.
C. Disclosure of Redeemable Stock Within the Financial Statements
   1. The amount of redemption requirements, separately by issue or combined, for all issues of capital stock that are redeemable at fixed or determinable prices on fixed or determinable dates in each of the 5 years following the date of the latest balance sheet presented.

SFAS 130 (C49) Reporting Comprehensive Income
A. Establishes standards for reporting and display of comprehensive income (net income plus **other comprehensive income**) in a full set of general-purpose FS
B. Items, and changes therein, to be included as part of and separately classified in **other comprehensive income**
   1. Foreign currency items
   2. Unrealized gains (losses) on certain investments in debt and equity securities
   3. Minimum pension liability adjustments
C. Presentation of comprehensive income
   1. Alternative display options
      a. At the bottom of IS, continue from net income to arrive at a **comprehensive income** figure (equals net income plus other comprehensive income), or
      b. In a separate statement that starts with net income, or
      c. In the statement of changes in stockholders' equity; FASB prefers a. or b.
   2. Components of other comprehensive income may be displayed net of related tax effects or before related tax effects with one amount shown for the aggregate income tax effect (with detail shown in notes)
   3. Reclassification (recycling) adjustments
      a. Made to avoid double counting of other comprehensive income items included in net income (earnings) for the period
      b. Display separately from the balance of each item adjusted (B.1. and B.2. above) (gross display)
         (1) For reclassification adjustments related to the minimum pension liability, a single amount shall be displayed (net display)
D. Separate EPS numbers are not required for other comprehensive income or comprehensive income

SFAS 131 (S30) Disclosures About Segments of an Enterprise and Related Information*
A. Requires disclosures about
   Operating segments of an enterprise, products and services, geographic areas, major customers
   1. Disclosures are required for **public** companies in complete annual FS per GAAP and in condensed FS of interim periods including comparative presentations
   2. Purpose of disclosures is to better assist statement users in appraising past and future performance of the enterprise and assessing prospects for future net cash flows.
B. Definitions
   1. **Management approach.** Method chosen by the FASB to determine what information should be reported; it is based on the way that management organizes segments internally for making operating decisions and assessing performance.
   2. **Operating segment.** Component of an enterprise which may earn revenues and incur expenses, about which separate financial information is available that is evaluated regularly by the chief operating decision maker in deciding how to allocate resources and in assessing performance.
   3. **Chief operating decision maker.** Person whose general function (not specific title) is to allocate resources to, and assess the performance of, the segments of an enterprise.

---

* *AUTHOR'S NOTE: Refer to the flowchart on p. 716 as you study this outline.*

4. **Segment revenue.** Includes revenue from unaffiliated customers and intersegment sales (use company transfer prices to determine intersegment sales).
5. **Segment operating profit (loss).** Segment revenue less all operating expenses, including any allocated revenues or expenses.
6. **Segment assets.** Tangible and intangible assets directly associable or used by the segment, including any allocated portion of assets used jointly by more than one segment

C. To determine reportable segments
  1. Identify operating segments under management approach
  2. Determine if aggregation of operating segments is appropriate.
  3. Perform quantitative threshold tests (10% tests).

D. Operating segments may be aggregated by management if they have similar economic characteristics and if segments are similar in each of the following areas:
  1. Nature of products and services
  2. Nature of production processes
  3. Type of customer for their products and services
  4. Methods used to distribute their products or provide their services
  5. Nature of regulatory environment; for example, banking

E. Operating segments which meet any of the three quantitative thresholds (10% tests) are immediately deemed reportable segments.
  1. Segment revenue is ≥ 10% of combined revenue (revenue includes intersegment revenue).
  2. Segment operating profit or loss is ≥ 10% of the greater of, in absolute amount
    a. Combined operating profit of all operating segments with profit, or
    b. Combined operating loss of all operating segments with loss
  3. Segment assets are ≥ 10% of combined assets of all segments.

F. Additional considerations when determining reportable segments.
  1. Management may combine information about operating segments that do not meet the 10% tests with information on other operating segments that do meet the 10% tests to produce reportable segment only if majority of the aggregation criteria exists.
  2. Segment which was reported previously should continue to be reported if judged to be of continuing significance by management even if it does not meet the 10% tests in current period.
  3. Combined sales to nonaffiliated customers of segments reporting separately must be at least 75% of total consolidated sales
    a. If not, additional segments must be identified as reportable segments
  4. All other operating segments which are not reportable shall be combined with any other business activities (e.g., corporate headquarters) and disclosed in "all other" category.
  5. Number of reportable segments probably should not exceed 10.
    a. Combine closely related segments if number of segments becomes impracticable

G. Information is to be presented for each reportable segment and in aggregate for remaining segments not reported separately
  1. General information, including
    a. Explanation of factors used to identify the enterprise's reportable segments
    b. Types of products and services from which revenue is derived
  2. An enterprise shall report a measure of profit or loss and total assets for each reportable segment. To the extent the following is included in the measure of profit or loss or assets it shall also be disclosed:
    a. Revenues from external customers
    b. Revenues from transactions with other operating segments of the same enterprise
    c. Interest revenue
    d. Interest expense
    e. Depreciation, depletion, and amortization expense
    f. Unusual items not qualifying as X-O items
    g. Equity in net income of investees accounted for by equity method
    h. Income tax expense or benefit
    i. Extraordinary items

   j.   Significant noncash items other than depreciation, depletion, and amortization expense
3. For segment assets
   a.   Total expenditures for additions to long-lived assets
   b.   Amount of investment in equity method investees
4. Enterprise shall provide an explanation of the measurements of segment profit or loss and assets, including
   a.   Basis of accounting
   b.   Nature of any differences between measurement of profit and loss or assets for the segment and that of the consolidated enterprise
   c.   Nature of any changes from prior periods
   d.   Nature and effect of asymmetrical allocations (e.g., allocating depreciation, but not related assets to segment)
5. Enterprise will need to provide reconciliations for the segment amounts disclosed to the corresponding enterprise amounts.
6. Although not as extensive as in the annual report, certain disclosures are required in the interim reports.

H. Previously issued segment information must be restated (unless impractical to do so) if any enterprise changes structure of internal organization that causes composition of reportable segments to change

I. Information about products and services
   1.   Enterprise-wide disclosure required even if only one and segment disclosures required.
   2.   Revenue from external customers for each product and service shall be reported by the enterprise.

J. Information about geographic areas (individual countries)
   1.   Enterprise-wide disclosure required even if only one and segment disclosures required.
   2.   Enterprise shall report revenues from external customers and long-lived assets attributable to its domestic operations and foreign operations.
   3.   If enterprise functions in two or more foreign geographic areas, to the extent revenues or assets of an individual foreign geographic area are material, then these amounts should be separately disclosed.

K. Major Customers
   1.   Enterprise-wide disclosure required even if segment disclosures are not required
   2.   Disclose amount of revenue to each customer accounting for $\geq$ 10% of revenue
   3.   Disclose similarly if $\geq$ 10% of revenue derived from sales to domestic government agencies or foreign governments
   4.   Identify segment making sales

SFAS 132 (Not available) Employers' Disclosures About Pensions and Other Postretirement Benefits
(Amends SFAS 87, 88, and 106)
A. Disclosures for defined benefit pensions plans and defined benefit postretirement plans
   1.   A reconciliation of beginning and ending balances of the benefit obligation with the effects of the following shown separately:
      a.   Service cost
      b.   Interest cost
      c.   Contributions by plan participants
      d.   Actuarial gains and losses
      e.   Foreign currency exchange rate changes
      f.   Benefits paid
      g.   Plan amendments
      h.   Business combinations
      i.   Divestitures
      j.   Curtailments
      k.   Settlements
      l.   Special termination benefits
   2.   A reconciliation of beginning and ending balances of the fair value of plan assets with the effects of the following shown separately:

       a.   Actual return on plan assets
       b.   Foreign currency exchange rate changes
       c.   Contributions by the employer
       d.   Contributions by plan participants
       e.   Benefits paid
       f.   Business combinations
       g.   Divestitures
       h.   Settlements

3. The funded status of the plans
4. The amounts recognized and the amounts not recognized in the statement of financial position such as
   a. Any unamortized service cost
   b. Any unrecognized net gain or loss
   c. Any unamortized net obligation or net asset existing at the initial date of prior Statement 87 or 106 that are still unrecognized
   d. Prepaid assets or accrued liabilities of the net pension or other postretirement benefits
   e. Any intangible asset
   f. The amount of other comprehensive income recognized
5. The recognized amount of the net periodic benefit cost with the components shown separately
6. The amount caused from a change in the additional minimum pension liability that was included in other comprehensive income
7. Rates for
   a. Assumed discount rate
   b. Rate of compensation increase
   c. Expected long-term rate of return on plan assets
8. Trend rates assumed for health care cost for the next year and thereafter
9. The effects of a one-percentage point increase or decrease of the trend rates for health care costs on
   a. The aggregate of the service and interest cost components
   b. The accumulated postretirement benefit obligation
10. If applicable
    a. The amounts and types of securities of the employer or a related party in plan assets
    b. The amount of future benefits covered by insurance contracts issued by the employer or a related party
    c. Any significant transactions between the plan and the employer or a related party
    d. An amortization method used not pursuant to prior standards
    e. Any substantive commitment used as the basis for accounting for the benefit obligation
    f. The cost of special or contractual termination benefits recognized during the period with a description of the event
11. An explanation of significant changes in the benefit obligation or plan assets that is not apparent in the other disclosures required

B. Disclosures for employers with more than one plan
1. Disclosures required in this statement may be disclosed in aggregate for an employer's defined benefit pension plans and in aggregate for an employer's defined benefit postretirement plans but must still present separately prepaid benefit costs and accrued benefit liabilities recognized in the statement of financial position.
2. An employer may not combine the disclosures of plans outside the US and plans in the US if the benefit obligation of the plans outside the US represent a significant portion of the total benefit obligation and significant differences exist in the assumptions used.

C. Disclosure requirements for nonpublic entities
1. Nonpublic entities may choose to disclose the following instead of the disclosures stated in A.:
   a. Benefit obligation
   b. Fair value of plan assets
   c. Funded status of the plan
   d. Contributions by the employer and the participant

     e.   Amounts recognized in the statement of financial position of
        (1) Prepaid assets or accrued liabilities
        (2) Any intangible asset
     f.   Amount of accumulated other comprehensive income recognized and the amount resulting from a change in the minimum pension liability recognized
     g.   Net periodic benefit cost recognized
     h.   Rates for
        (1) Assumed discount rate
        (2) Rate of compensation increase
        (3) Expected long-term rate of return on plan assets
     i.   Trend rates assumed for health care cost for the next year and thereafter
     j.   If applicable
        (1) Amounts and types of securities of the employer or a related party
        (2) Future annual benefits covered by insurance contracts issued by the employer or a related party
        (3) Any significant transactions between the plan and the employer or a related party
     k.   Nature and effect of significant nonroutine events
  D. Disclosures for defined contribution plans
     1.   Amount of cost recognized for pension or postretirement benefit plans must be separate from the cost recognized for defined benefit plans
     2.   Nature and effect of any significant changes that affect comparability must be disclosed
  E. Disclosures for multiemployer plans
     1.   Amount of contributions to multiemployer plans
     2.   Nature and effect of changes which affect comparability
     3.   If withdrawals made by an employer from a multiemployer plan will result in an obligation for a portion of the unfunded benefit obligation or the unfunded accumulated postretirement benefit obligation, follow the provision of SFAS 5, *Accounting for Contingencies*

SFAS 133 Accounting for Derivative Instruments and Hedging Activities

Because of the complexity of this pronouncement we are not including an outline of this standard. Detailed coverage of it appears in Module 32B.

Statements of Financial Accounting Concepts (SFAC)

Statements of Financial Accounting Concepts (SFAC set forth financial accounting and reporting objectives and fundamentals that will be used by the FASB in developing standards. Practitioners may also use SFAC in areas where promulgated GAAP does not exist (see SAS 43). SFAC do not establish GAAP as indicated by Rule 203 of the AICPA Code of Professional Ethics.

SFAC 1 Objectives of Financial Reporting by Business Enterprises

A. Financial accounting concepts are fundamentals on which standards of financial accounting and reporting are based.
     1.   That is, do not establish GAAP
        a.   And do not come under AICPA Ethics Rule 203
     2.   Defines financial accounting concepts broader than financial statements and other data
B. Environmental context of objectives
     1.   Financial reporting provides information for making business and economic decisions.
     2.   The United States is a market economy
        a.   Dominated by investor owned enterprises
        b.   Even though the government generates economic statistics
C. Characteristics and limitations of information
     1.   Primarily financial (quantitative) in nature
     2.   Limited to individual business enterprises

3.   Based on approximated measures (i.e., estimates)
4.   Largely limited to past transactions (i.e., historically based)
5.   Just one source of users' data base
6.   Must conform to cost-benefit rationale

D.   Potential users and their interests
   1.   "Owners, lenders, potential investors, suppliers, creditors, employees, management, directors, customers, financial analysts and advisors, brokers, underwriters, stock exchanges, lawyers, economists, taxing authorities, regulatory authorities, legislators, financial press and reporting agencies, labor unions, trade associations, business researchers, teachers and students, and the public."
   2.   Users are generally interested in cash flow generation.
      a.   Amounts, timing, and uncertainties
   3.   Many external users lack authority to prescribe information.
      a.   For example, absentee owners, customers, etc.

E.   General purpose external financial reporting
   1.   To satisfy informational needs of external users who lack authority to prescribe data they desire
   2.   Focuses on external users
      a.   Management may prescribe data for their needs
   3.   Directed primarily at investors and creditors
      a.   Which results in data of likely usefulness to others

F.   Objectives of financial reporting
   1.   "Financial reporting should provide information that is useful to present and potential investors and creditors and other users in making rational investment, credit, and similar decisions."
   2.   "Financial reporting should provide information to help present and potential investors and creditors and other users in assessing the amounts, timing, and uncertainty of prospective cash receipts from dividends or interest and the proceeds from the sale, redemption, or maturity of securities or loans."
   3.   "Financial reporting should provide information about the economic resources of an enterprise, the claims to those resources (obligations of the enterprise to transfer resources to other entities and owner's equity), and the effects of transactions, events, and circumstances that change resources and claims to those resources."
      a.   Economic resource, obligation, and owners' equity data permit assessment of
         (1) Liquidity and solvency
         (2) Financial strength
      b.   Funds flow data is important
      c.   Earnings performance data permit assessment of future performance
         (1) Thus, primary focus of reporting is on earnings
      d.   Management stewardship and performance are reported on
      e.   Management explanation and interpretation are important

SFAC 2 Qualitative Characteristics of Accounting Information
(Para 4 superseded by SFAC 6)

A.   Purpose is to examine the characteristics that make accounting information useful and establish criteria for selecting and evaluating accounting alternatives.
   1.   Guidance needed by both FASB and individual accountants
   2.   The usefulness of accounting information must be evaluated in relation to decision making.
   3.   Based on objectives of financial reporting (SFAC 1)
   4.   Applies to financial information reported by business enterprises and not-for-profit organizations

B.   The hierarchy of accounting qualities
   1.   User-specific qualities (not inherent in information)
      a.   Understandability
      b.   Decision usefulness
   2.   Decision-specific qualities (necessary for usefulness)
      a.   **Relevance**--"capacity" of information to "make a difference" in a decision
         (1) **Timeliness**--being available while able to influence decisions

        (2) **Predictive value**--improves decision makers' capacity to predict

        (3) **Feedback value**--enables users to confirm or correct prior expectations

    b. **Reliability**--freedom from error and bias and faithful representation of what is claimed to be represented

        (1) **Verifiability**--secures a high degree of consensus among independent measurers

        (2) **Representative faithfulness**--agreement between data and resources or events represented (validity)

        (3) **Neutrality**--freedom from bias toward a predetermined result

3. Secondary and interactive qualities
   a. Comparability between enterprises
   b. Consistency in application over time
4. Constraints
   a. **Materiality**--information should not be provided if below the user's threshold for recognition
   b. **Costs and benefits**--benefits derived from disclosure must exceed associated costs

SFAC 5 Recognition and Measurement in Financial Statements of Business Enterprises

A. Statement addresses principal items that a full set of FS should show and provides fundamental recognition criteria to use in deciding which items to include in FS.
   1. Recognition criteria presented are not radical change from current practice
   2. Only applies to business enterprises
B. FS
   1. A principal means of communicating financial information to those outside an entity
   2. Some useful information is better provided by other means of financial reporting, such as notes to the statements or supplementary information (SFAC 1).
   3. Objectives of financial reporting (which encompasses FS) are detailed in SFAC 1.
   4. Full set of FS should show
      a. Financial position at end of period
      b. Earnings for period
      c. Comprehensive income for period
      d. Cash flows for period
      e. Investments by and distributions to owners during period
   5. Are intended as "general purpose" statements and, therefore, do not necessarily satisfy all users equally well
   6. Simplifications, condensations, and aggregations are necessary and useful, but focusing on one figure (i.e., "the bottom line") exclusively should be avoided.
   7. FS interrelate and complement each other.
   8. Information detailed in 4. above is provided by the following individual financial statements:
      a. **Statement of Financial Position**
         (1) Provides information about entity's assets, liabilities, and equity and their relationships to each other at a particular point in time
         (2) Does not purport to show the value of an entity
      b. **Statement of Earnings and Comprehensive Income**
         (1) Shows how the equity of an entity increased or decreased from all sources (other than from transactions with owners) during period
         (2) Item "earnings" is similar to present net income term but does not include certain accounting adjustments recognized in current period (i.e., change in accounting principle).
         (3) Earnings is a performance measure concerned primarily with cash-to-cash cycles.
         (4) Comprehensive income includes all recognized changes in equity except those from transactions with owners (SFAC 6).
         (5) The terms "gains" and "losses" are used for those items included in earnings.
         (6) The terms "cumulative accounting adjustments" and "other nonowner changes in equity" are used for those items excluded from earnings but included in comprehensive income.
      c. **Statement of Cash Flows**

        (1) Shows entity's cash flows from operating, investing, and financing activities during a period

   d. **Statement of Investments by and Distributions to Owners**

        (1) Shows capital transactions of entity which are increases and decreases in equity from transactions with owners during period

  9. FS help users assess entity's liquidity, financial flexibility, profitability, and risk.

  10. Full set of FS based on concept of financial capital maintenance--a return is achieved only after capital has been maintained or recovered.

C. Recognition criteria

  1. Recognition is presentation of item in both words and numbers that is included in the totals of the financial statements (SFAC 6).

  2. Item should meet four fundamental recognition criteria to be recognized

    a. **Definitions**--item is element of FS as defined by SFAC 6

    b. **Measurability**--item has a relevant attribute that is measurable with sufficient reliability

        (1) Five measurement attributes are used in current practice

          (a) Historical cost (historical proceeds)

          (b) Current (replacement) cost

          (c) Current market value

          (d) Net realizable (settlement) value

          (e) Present (discounted) value of future cash flows

        (2) Statement suggests that use of different attributes will continue

        (3) The monetary unit of measurement of nominal units of money is expected to continue to be used

    c. **Relevance**--item has capacity to make a difference in users' decisions (SFAC 2)

    d. **Reliability**--item is representationally faithful, verifiable, and neutral (SFAC 2)

        (1) Reliability may affect timing of recognition due to excessive uncertainties

        (2) A trade-off may sometimes be needed between relevance and reliability because waiting for complete reliability may make information untimely

D. Guidance in applying recognition criteria

  1. Need to identify which cash-to-cash cycles are substantially complete

  2. Degree of skepticism is needed (SFAC 2, para 97)

  3. **Revenues and gains**

    a. Generally not recognized until realizable (SFAC 6, para 83)

        (1) Realizable means assets received or held are readily convertible to known amounts of cash or claims to cash

    b. Not recognized until earned (APB Statement 4, para 149 or SFAC 6, para 64)

  4. **Expenses and losses**

    a. Generally recognized when economic benefits are consumed or assets lose future benefits

    b. Some expenses are recognized when associated revenues are recognized (e.g., cost of goods sold).

    c. Some expenses are recognized when cash is spent or liability incurred (e.g., selling and administrative salaries).

    d. Some expenses are allocated by systematic and rational procedures to periods benefited (e.g., depreciation and insurance).

E. Recognition of changes in assets and liabilities

  1. Initial recognition generally based on current exchange prices at date of recognition

  2. Changes can result from two types of events

    a. Inflows and outflows

    b. Changes in amounts which can be a change in utility or substance (e.g., depreciation) or changes in price

  3. Current price information may only be used if it is reliable, cost justified, and more relevant than alternative information.

SFAC 6 Elements of Financial Statements
(Replaces SFAC 3)

A. Statement contains definitions of FS elements
1. Definitions provide a significant first screen in determining content of FS.
   a. Possessing characteristics of a definition of an element is necessary but not sufficient condition for including an item in FS
   b. To qualify for inclusion in FS an item must
      (1) Meet recognition criteria (e.g., revenue recognition tests)
      (2) Possess a relevant attribute which can be measured reliably (e.g., historical cost/historical proceeds)

B. Elements of FS of both business enterprises and not-for-profit organizations
1. **Assets** are probable future economic benefits controlled by a particular entity as a result of past transactions or events.
   a. Characteristics of assets
      (1) Probable future benefit by contribution to future net cash inflows
      (2) Entity can obtain and control access to benefit
      (3) Transaction or event leading to control has already occurred
   b. Asset continues as an asset until collected, transferred, used, or destroyed.
   c. Valuation accounts are part of related asset.
2. **Liabilities** are probable future sacrifices of economic benefits, arising from present obligations of a particular entity which result from past transactions or events.
   a. Characteristics of liabilities
      (1) Legal, equitable, or constructive duty to transfer assets in future
      (2) Little or no discretion to avoid future sacrifice
      (3) Transaction or event obligating enterprise has already occurred
   b. Liability remains a liability until settled or discharged.
   c. Valuation accounts are part of related liability.
3. Equity (net assets) is the owner's residual interest in the assets of an entity that remains after deducting liabilities.
   a. Business enterprises
      (1) Characteristics of equity
         (a) The source of distributions by enterprise to its owners
         (b) No unconditional right to receive future transfer of assets; depends on future profitability
         (c) Inevitably affected by enterprise's operations and circumstances affecting enterprise
      (2) Transactions or events that change owners' equity include revenues and expenses; gains and losses; investments by owners; distributions to owners; and changes within owners' equity (does not change total amount)
   b. Not-for-profit organizations
      (1) Characteristics of net assets (equity)
         (a) Absence of ownership interest
         (b) Operating purposes not centered on profit
         (c) Significant receipt of contributions, many involving donor-imposed restrictions
      (2) Classes of net assets
         (a) **Permanently restricted net assets** is the part of net assets of a not-for-profit organization resulting from
            1] Contributions and other inflows of assets whose use by the organization is limited by donor-imposed stipulations that neither expire by passage of time nor can be fulfilled or otherwise removed by actions of the organization
            2] Other asset enhancements and diminishments subject to same kinds of stipulations
            3] Reclassifications from (or to) other classes of net assets as a consequence of donor-imposed stipulations
         (b) **Temporarily restricted net assets** is the part of net assets of a not-for-profit organization resulting from

1] Contribution and other inflows of assets whose use by the organization is limited by donor-imposed stipulations that either expire by passage of time or can be fulfilled and removed by actions of the organization pursuant to those stipulations

2] Other asset enhancements and diminishments subject to same kinds of stipulations

3] Reclassifications to (or from) other classes of net assets as a consequence of donor-imposed stipulations, their expiration by passage of time, or their fulfillment and removal by actions of the organization pursuant to those stipulations

(c) **Unrestricted net assets** is the part of net assets of a not-for-profit organization that is neither permanently restricted nor temporarily restricted by donor-imposed stipulations. They result from

1] All revenues, expenses, gains, and losses that are not changes in permanently or temporarily restricted net assets and

2] Reclassifications from (or to) other classes of net assets as a consequence of donor-imposed stipulations, their expiration by passage of time, or their fulfillment and removal by actions of the organization pursuant to those stipulations

(3) Transactions and events that change net assets include revenues and expenses, gains and losses, and changes within net assets that do not affect assets or liabilities (including reclassifications between classes of net assets).

(4) Changes in classes of net assets of not-for-profit organizations may be significant because donor-imposed restrictions may affect the types and levels of services that a not-for-profit organization can provide.

(a) Characteristics of change in permanently restricted net assets

1] Most increases in permanently restricted net assets are from accepting contributions of assets that donors stipulate must be maintained in perpetuity. Only assets that are not by their nature used up in carrying out the organization's activities are capable of providing economic benefits indefinitely. Gifts of cash, securities, and nonexhaustible property are examples.

(b) Characteristics of change in temporarily restricted net assets

1] Most increases in temporarily restricted net assets are from accepting contributions of assets that donors limit to use after specified future time or for specified purpose. Temporary restrictions pertain to contributions with donor stipulations that expire or can be fulfilled and removed by using assets as specified.

(c) Characteristics of change in unrestricted net assets

1] Change in unrestricted net assets for a period indicates whether organization has maintained the part of its net assets that is fully available (free of donor-imposed restrictions) to support the organization's services to beneficiaries in the next period.

4. **Revenues** are increases in assets or decreases in liabilities during a period from delivering goods, rendering services, or other activities constituting the entity's major or central operations.

a. Characteristics of revenues

(1) Accomplishments of the earning process

(2) Actual or expected cash inflows resulting from central operations

(3) Inflows reported gross

5. **Expenses** are decreases in assets or increases in liabilities during a period from delivery of goods, rendering of services, or other activities constituting the entity's major or central operations.

a. Characteristics of expenses

(1) Sacrifices involved in carrying out earnings process

(2) Actual or expected cash outflows resulting from central operations

(3) Outflows reported gross

6. **Gains (losses)** are increases (decreases) in equity from peripheral transactions of entity excluding revenues (expenses) and investment by owners (distribution to owners).

a. Characteristics of gains and losses

(1) Result from peripheral transactions and circumstances which may be beyond control

(2) May be classified according to sources or as operating and nonoperating

(3) Change in equity reported net

7. **Accrual accounting** and **related concepts** include
   a. **Transaction**--external event involving transfer of something of value between two or more entities
   b. **Event**--a happening of consequence to an entity (internal or external)
   c. **Circumstances**--a set of conditions developed from events which may occur imperceptibly and create possibly unanticipated situations
   d. **Accrual accounting**--recording "cash consequence" transactions as they occur rather than with movement of cash; deals with process of cash movement instead of beginning or end of process (per para 44 of SFAC 1)
      (1) Based on cash and credit transactions, exchanges, price changes, changes in form of assets and liabilities
   e. **Accrual**--recognizing revenues and related asset increases and expenses and related liability increases as they occur; expected future cash receipt or payment follows recognition of revenue (expense)
   f. **Deferral**--recognizing liability for cash receipt with expected future revenue or recognizing asset for cash payment with expected future expense; cash receipt (payment) precedes recognition of revenues (expenses)
   g. **Allocation**--process of assigning or distributing an amount according to a plan or formula
      (1) Includes amortization
   h. **Amortization**--process of systematically reducing an amount by periodic payments or write-downs
   i. **Realization**--process of converting noncash resources and rights into money; refers to sales of assets for cash or claims to cash
      (1) Realized--identifies revenues or gains or losses on assets sold
      (2) Unrealized--identifies revenues or gains or losses on assets unsold
   j. **Recognition**--process of formally recording an item in financial statements
      (1) Major differences between accrual and cash basis accounting is timing of recognition of income items
   k. **Matching**--simultaneous recognition of revenues with expenses which are related directly or jointly to the same transaction or events

C. Elements of FS exclusive to business enterprises
   1. **Investments by owners** are increases in net assets resulting from transfers by other entities of something of value to obtain ownership.
   2. **Distributions to owners** are decreases in net assets resulting from transferring assets, rendering services, or incurring liabilities by the enterprise to owners.
   3. **Comprehensive income** is the change in equity of an entity during a period from transactions and other events of nonowner sources (i.e., all equity amount changes except investment and distributions).
      a. Term "comprehensive" income is used instead of net earnings (net income) because the board is reserving "earnings" for a component part of comprehensive income yet to be determined.*
      b. Concept of capital maintenance or recovery of cost is needed in order to separate return **on** capital from return **of** capital.
      c. Financial capital maintenance concept vs. physical capital maintenance concept
         (1) Financial capital maintenance--objective is to maintain purchasing power
         (2) Physical capital maintenance--objective is to maintain operating capacity
      d. Comprehensive income is return on financial capital.
      e. Characteristics, sources, and components of comprehensive income include

---

* *Although SFAS 130 has defined comprehensive income as including net income plus other comprehensive income, it has not yet changed the components that comprise net income. Additionally, prior period adjustments are still reported in the retained earnings statement, not as comprehensive income.*

(1) Cash receipts (excluding owner investments) less cash outlays (excluding distributions to owners) over life of enterprise
   (a) Recognition criteria and choice of attributes to be measured affect timing, not amount.
(2) Specific sources of income are
   (a) Transactions between enterprise and nonowners
   (b) Enterprise's productive efforts
   (c) Price changes, casualties, and other interactions with environment
(3) **Earnings process** is the production and distribution of goods or services so firm can pay for goods and services it uses and provide return to owners.
(4) Peripheral activities may also provide income.
(5) Components of comprehensive income
   (a) Basic components--revenues, expenses, gains and losses
   (b) Intermediate components result from combining basic components
(6) Display considerations (e.g., items included in operating income) are the subject of another SFAC.

EXAMINATION IN FINANCIAL ACCOUNTING AND REPORTING
(BUSINESS ENTERPRISES)

NOTE TO CANDIDATES: *Information for Uniform CPA Examination Candidates*, published by the AICPA, states that candidates should allocate the total time for each examination section to the questions for that section in proportion to the point value given for the question. Thus, candidates should begin each examination session by calculating the estimated time to be spent on each question.

All questions are required:	Point Value
No. 1	60
No. 2	20
No. 3	10
No. 4	10
Total	100

Number 1

Select the **best** answer for each of the following items.

1. Under Statement of Financial Accounting Concepts 2, which of the following is an ingredient of the primary quality of relevance?
   a. Predictive value.
   b. Materiality.
   c. Understandability.
   d. Verifiability.

2. When valuing raw materials inventory at lower of cost or market, what is the meaning of the term "market"?
   a. Net realizable value.
   b. Net realizable value less a normal profit margin.
   c. Current replacement cost.
   d. Discounted present value.

3. When the cash proceeds from a bond issued with detachable stock purchase warrants exceeds the sum of the par value of the bonds and the fair value of the warrants, the excess should be credited to
   a. Additional paid-in capital.
   b. Retained earnings.
   c. Premium on bonds payable.
   d. Detachable stock warrants outstanding.

4. A company reacquires shares of its own stock and reports the transaction in the theoretically correct manner. What effect will this transaction have on stockholders' equity and earnings per share respectively?
   a. Decrease and decrease.
   b. Increase and no effect.
   c. Decrease and increase.
   d. Increase and decrease.

5. When the allowance method of recognizing bad debt expense is used, the typical write-off of a specific customer's account
   a. Has **no** effect on net income.
   b. Decreases net income.
   c. Decreases current assets.
   d. Decreases working capital.

6. A businessman wants to withdraw $3,000 (including principal) from an investment fund at the end of each year for 5 years. How should he compute his required initial investment at the beginning of the first year if the fund earns 6% compounded annually?
   a. $3,000 times the amount of annuity of $1 at 6% at the end of each year for 5 years.
   b. $3,000 divided by the amount of an annuity of $1 at 6% at the end of each year for 5 years.
   c. $3,000 times the present value of an annuity of $1 at 6% at the end of each year for 5 years.
   d. $3,000 divided by the present value of an annuity of $1 at 6% at the end of each year for 5 years.

7. The effect of a change in enacted tax rates on deferred tax assets/liabilities should be reflected as a(n)
   a. Extraordinary item.
   b. Component of income tax expense on continuing operations.
   c. Cumulative effect of change in accounting principle.
   d. Prior period adjustment.

8. Why is a reclassification adjustment used when reporting other comprehensive income?
   a. Adjustment made to reclassify an item of comprehensive income as another item of comprehensive income.
   b. Adjustment made to avoid double counting of items.
   c. Adjustment made to make net income equal to comprehensive income.
   d. Adjustment made to adjust for the income tax effect of reporting comprehensive income.

9. The market price of a bond is the
   a. Present value of its maturity amount plus the present value of all future interest payments.
   b. Maturity amount plus the present value of all future interest payments.
   c. Maturity amount plus all future interest payments.
   d. Present value of its maturity amount only.

10. In a periodic inventory system which uses the FIFO cost flow method, the cost of goods available for sale is net purchases
   a. Plus the ending inventory.
   b. Plus the beginning inventory.
   c. Minus the ending inventory.
   d. Minus the beginning inventory.

11. On July 1, 1999, a company received a 1-year note receivable bearing interest at the market rate. The face amount of the note receivable and the entire amount of the interest are due on June 30, 2000. When the note receivable was recorded on July 1, 1999, which of the following were debited?

	Interest receivable	*Unearned discount on note receivable*
a.	Yes	No
b.	Yes	Yes
c.	No	No
d.	No	Yes

12. For a compensatory stock option plan for which the date of grant and the measurement date are different, under APB 25, compensation cost should be recognized in the income statement
   a. At the later of grant or measurement date.
   b. At the exercise date.
   c. Of each period in which the services are rendered.
   d. At the adoption date of the plan.

13. Which of the following situations would result in a temporary difference in accounting for income taxes?
   a. Research and development costs are deducted for income tax purposes in the year incurred.
   b. A material gain on a sale-leaseback transaction in which the seller-lessee retains only a minor portion of the rights to use the property is taxed in the year of sale.
   c. Unamortized discount and call premium on an early extinguishment of debt are deducted for income tax purposes in the year of extinguishment.
   d. Goodwill amortization for tax return in excess of goodwill for financial (pretax accounting) income.

14. Which of the following should be disclosed in the summary of significant accounting policies?

	Basis of consolidation	*Composition of plant assets*
a.	No	No
b.	No	Yes
c.	Yes	No
d.	Yes	Yes

15. A parent corporation which uses the equity method of accounting for its investment in a 40% owned subsidiary, which earned $20,000 and paid $5,000 in dividends, made the following entries:

Investment in subsidiary	8,000	
Equity in earnings of		
subsidiary		8,000
Cash	2,000	
Dividend revenue		2,000

What effect will these entries have on the parent's statement of financial position?
   a. Investment in subsidiary understated, retained earnings understated.
   b. Investment in subsidiary overstated, retained earnings overstated.
   c. Investment in subsidiary overstated, retained earnings understated.

   d. Financial position will be fairly stated.

16. The possible amount of loss from an instrument that has not been recognized as an asset or liability is known as
   a. Credit risk.
   b. Investment risk.
   c. Market risk.
   d. Off-balance-sheet risk.

17. If a unit of inventory has declined in value below original cost, but the market value exceeds net realizable value, the amount to be used for purposes of inventory valuation is
   a. Net realizable value.
   b. Original cost.
   c. Market value.
   d. Net realizable value less a normal profit margin.

18. In an arm's-length transaction, Company A and Company B exchanged nonmonetary assets with no monetary consideration involved. The exchange did culminate an earning process for both Company A and Company B, and the fair values of the nonmonetary assets were both clearly evident. The accounting for the exchange should be based on the
   a. Fair value of the asset surrendered.
   b. Fair value of the asset received.
   c. Recorded amount of the asset surrendered.
   d. Recorded amount of the asset received.

19. In financial reporting for segments of a business enterprise, segment data may be aggregated
   a. Before performing the 10% tests if a majority of the aggregation criteria are met.
   b. If the segments do not meet the 10% tests but meet all of the aggregation criteria.
   c. Before performing the 10% tests if all of the aggregation criteria are met.
   d. If any one of the aggregation criteria are met.

20. On January 1, 1999, Whalen, Inc. had 120,000 shares of common stock outstanding. A 10% stock dividend was issued on April 1, 1999. Whalen issued 40,000 shares of common stock for cash on July 1, 1999. What is the number of shares that should be used in computing basic earnings per share for the year ended December 31, 1999?
   a. 146,000
   b. 149,000
   c. 152,000
   d. 172,000

21. Information relating to the capital structure of the Galaxy Company is as follows:

	December 31	
	1998	*1999*
Outstanding shares of:		
Common stock	90,000	90,000
Convertible preferred stock	10,000	10,000
9% convertible bonds	$1,000,000	$1,000,000

During 1999, Galaxy paid dividends of $2.50 per share on its preferred stock. The preferred stock is convertible into

20,000 shares of common stock. The 9% convertible bonds are convertible into 30,000 shares of common stock. The net income for the year ended December 31, 1999, is $485,000. Assume that the income tax rate is 50%. What should be the diluted earnings per share, rounded to the nearest penny, for the year ended December 31, 1999?

a. $3.79
b. $3.96
c. $4.11
d. $4.51

22. On January 1, 1996, Cabal Company bought a machine for $1,500,000. At January 1, 1996, this machine had an estimated useful life of 6 years, with no salvage value. Cabal uses straight-line depreciation. As a result of additional information, Cabal determined on January 1, 1999, that the machine had an estimated useful life of 8 years from the date it was acquired, with no salvage value. Accordingly, the appropriate accounting change was made in 1999. How much depreciation expense for this machine should Cabal record for the year ended December 31, 1999?

a. $125,000
b. $150,000
c. $187,500
d. $250,000

23. At December 31, 1999, the following information is provided by the J.O. Corporation after the corporation amends its pension plan giving retroactive benefits to its employees:

Unrecognized prior service cost	$ 1,700,000
Plan assets (at fair value)	6,000,000
Accrued pension cost	300,000
Market-related asset value	5,800,000
Accumulated benefit obligation	9,000,000
Projected benefit obligation	10,000,000

What is the amount of the additional liability that must be recorded as of December 31, 1999, so that the books will reflect the components of the required pension liability to be reported on the balance sheet?

a. $3,000,000
b. $2,700,000
c. $3,300,000
d. $0

24. Company N donated computer equipment to a university (a nonreciprocal transfer). The fair value of the computer equipment was determinable. The difference between the fair value of the nonmonetary asset transferred and its recorded amount at the date of donation should be recognized in Company N's income statement when the difference results in a

	Gain	*Loss*
a.	Yes	No
b.	Yes	Yes
c.	No	Yes
d.	No	No

25. Theodore Corporation's stockholders' equity section of its December 31, 1998 balance sheet was as follows:

Common stock, authorized 1,000,000 shares; issued 900,000 shares; outstanding 800,000 shares; $10 par value	$ 9,000,000
Capital in excess of par	2,200,000
Retained earnings	5,600,000
Less shares held in treasury, 100,000 shares at cost	(800,000)
Total stockholders' equity	$16,000,000

During 1999, Theodore reissued 50,000 shares of the treasury stock at $12 per share. No other treasury stock transactions occurred during 1999. What amount and type of income should be reported on this transaction on the financial statements for the year ended December 31, 1999?

a. $0.
b. $100,000 ordinary income.
c. $200,000 ordinary income.
d. $200,000 extraordinary income.

26. The following items were among those that were reported on Lee Co.'s income statement for the year ended December 31, 1999:

Legal and audit fees	$170,000
Rent for office space	240,000
Interest on inventory floor plan	210,000
Loss on abandoned data processing equipment used in operations	35,000

The office space is used equally by Lee's sales and accounting departments. What amount of the above listed items should be classified as general and administrative expenses in Lee's multiple-step income statement?

a. $290,000
b. $325,000
c. $410,000
d. $500,000

27. Gei Co. determined that equipment with an original cost of $900,000 and accumulated depreciation at January 1, 1999, of $420,000 had suffered impairment because the undiscounted future cash flows from this equipment were less than its carrying amount. The fair value of the equipment as of the beginning of the year is $300,000. As a result the equipment should be written down. In addition, the remaining useful life of the equipment was reduced from 8 years to 3. In its December 31, 1999 balance sheet, what amount should Gei report as accumulated depreciation?

a. $100,000
b. $520,000
c. $600,000
d. $700,000

28. In 1998, Orlando, Inc. issued for $105 per share, 8,000 shares of $100 par value convertible preferred stock. One share of preferred stock can be converted into three shares of Orlando's $25 par value common stock at the option of the preferred shareholder. In August 1999, all of the preferred stock was converted into common stock. The market value of the common stock at the date of the conversion was $30 per share. What total amount should be credited to additional paid-in capital as a result of the issuance of the preferred stock and its subsequent conversion into common stock?

    a. $ 80,000
    b. $120,000
    c. $200,000
    d. $240,000

29. Selected information from the accounting records for the Code Company is as follows:

Cost of goods sold for 1999	$1,200,000
Inventories at December 31, 1998	350,000
Inventories at December 31, 1999	310,000

Assuming a business year consisting of 300 days, what was the number of days' sales in average inventories for 1999?

    a. 36.5
    b. 77.5
    c. 82.5
    d. 87.5

30. On January 1, 1999, the Ben Company formed a foreign subsidiary. On February 15, 1999, Ben's subsidiary purchased 100,000 local currency units (LCU) of inventory. 25,000 LCU of the original inventory purchased on February 15, 1999, made up the entire inventory on December 31, 1999. The exchange rates were 2.2 LCU to $1 from January 1, 1999, to June 30, 1999, and 2 LCU to $1 from July 1, 1999, to December 31, 1999. Assume the foreign currency is the functional currency. The December 31, 1999 inventory balance for Ben's foreign subsidiary should be translated into United States dollars of

    a. $10,500
    b. $11,364
    c. $11,905
    d. $12,500

31. On January 1, 1999, Liberty Company sold a machine to Bell Corporation in an "arm's-length" transaction. Bell signed a noninterest-bearing note requiring payment of $20,000 annually for 10 years. The first payment was made on January 1, 1999. The prevailing rate of interest for this type of note at date of issuance was 12%. Information on present value factors is as follows:

Period	Present value of $1 at 12%	Present value of ordinary annuity of $1 at 12%
9	0.361	5.328
10	0.322	5.650

Liberty should record the above sale in January 1999 at

    a. $ 64,400
    b. $ 84,980
    c. $113,000
    d. $126,560

32. On July 1, 1993, Belmont Corporation issued for $960,000, one thousand of its 9%, $1,000 callable bonds. The bonds are dated July 1, 1993, and mature on July 1, 2003. Interest is payable semiannually on January 1 and July 1. Belmont uses the straight-line method of amortizing bond discount. The bonds can be called by the issuer at 101 at any time after June 30, 1998.

On July 1, 1999, Belmont called in all of the bonds and retired them. Ignoring income taxes, how much loss should Belmont report on this early extinguishment of debt for the year ended December 31, 1999?

    a. $50,000
    b. $34,000
    c. $26,000
    d. $10,000

33. On September 1, 1999, the Consul Company acquired $10,000 face value 8% bonds of Envoy Corporation at 104. The bonds were dated May 1, 1999, and mature on April 30, 2004, with interest payable each October 31 and April 30. Consul intends to hold the bonds to maturity.

What entry should Consul make to record the purchase of the bonds on September 1, 1999?

a.	Investment in bonds	10,400	
	Interest receivable	266	
	Cash		10,666
b.	Investment in bonds	10,666	
	Cash		10,666
c.	Investment in bonds	10,666	
	Accrued interest receivable		266
	Cash		10,400
d.	Investment in bonds	10,000	
	Premium on bonds	666	
	Cash		10,666

34. Adam Corp. had the following infrequent transactions during 1999:

• A $190,000 gain on reacquisition and retirement of bonds.

• A $260,000 gain on the disposal of a segment of a business. Adam continues similar operations at another location.

• A $90,000 loss on the abandonment of equipment.

In its 1999 income statement, what amount should Adam report as total infrequent net gains that are **not** considered extraordinary?

    a. $100,000
    b. $170,000
    c. $360,000
    d. $450,000

35. On January 1, 1999, Huff Company owned a machine having a carrying amount of $240,000. The machine was purchased 4 years earlier for $400,000. Huff uses straight-line depreciation. The machine was used in 1999. In December, management decided to dispose of the machine. Huff sold the machine for $65,000 (net of disposal costs) on January 5, 2000. In its income statement for the year ended December 31, 1999, Huff should recognize a loss of

    a. $200,000
    b. $175,000
    c. $135,000
    d. $0

36. During 1999, Trencher, Inc. incurred research and development costs as follows:

Experimental and development cost of a new process patented in December 1999	$250,000
Testing for evaluation of new products	300,000
Modification of the formulation of a chemical product	150,000
Research and development costs reimbursable under a contract with Quality Chemicals Corporation	500,000

What amount should Trencher report as research and development expense in its income statement for the year ended December 31, 1999?

    a. $0
    b. $450,000
    c. $700,000
    d. $950,000

37. Chip Company has four reportable segments. Total sales for 1999 for all the segments combined were $1,500,000. Sales for Segment No. 2 were $600,000 and traceable costs were $225,000. Total common costs for all the segments combined were $750,000. Chip measures operating profit as sales less both traceable and allocated common costs. Chip allocates common costs based on the ratio of a segment's sales to total sales. The operating profit presented for Segment No. 2 for 1999 should be

    a. $ 75,000
    b. $210,000
    c. $300,000
    d. $375,000

38. Dell Company sells its products in reusable, expensive containers. The customer is charged a deposit for each container delivered and receives a refund for each container returned within 2 years after the year of delivery. Dell accounts for the containers not returned within the time limit as being retired by sale at the deposit amount. Information for 1999 is as follows:

Containers held by customers at December 31, 1998, from deliveries in:		
1997	$ 50,000	
1998	145,000	$195,000
Containers delivered in 1999		260,000
Containers returned in 1999 from deliveries in:		
1997	30,000	
1998	85,000	
1999	95,000	210,000

What amount should Dell report as a liability for returnable containers at December 31, 1999?

    a. $165,000
    b. $215,000
    c. $225,000
    d. $245,000

39. The Kirby Construction Company has consistently used the percentage-of-completion method of recognizing income. In 1998, it began a construction project to erect a building for $3,000,000. The project was completed during 1999. Under this method, the accounting records disclosed the following:

	1998	*1999*
Progress billings during year	$1,100,000	$1,900,000
Cost incurred during year	900,000	1,800,000
Collections on billings during year	700,000	2,300,000
Estimated cost to complete	1,800,000	--

What amount of income should Kirby have recognized in 1998?

    a. $100,000
    b. $110,000
    c. $150,000
    d. $200,000

40. On January 10, 1999, an explosion and fire occurred at Staren Chemical Corporation's plant, causing extensive property damage to neighboring buildings. On March 1, 1999, Staren's management and attorneys concluded that $2,000,000 would be a reasonable estimate of liability for damages, although no claims had yet been asserted against Staren in connection with the accident. Of the $2,000,000 potential liability, only $500,000 was covered by insurance. In Staren's December 31, 1998 financial statements, which were issued on April 1, 1999, how should this item be reported?

    a. As a footnote disclosure indicating the possible loss of $1,500,000.
    b. As an accrued liability of $1,500,000, with a corresponding direct charge to retained earnings.
    c. As an accrued liability of $2,000,000, with a corresponding charge to income.
    d. As an accrued liability of $1,500,000, with a corresponding charge to income.

41. On January 1, 1999, when the market rate for bond interest was 14%, Luba Corporation issued bonds in the face amount of $500,000, with interest at 12% payable semiannually. The bonds mature on December 31, 2008 and were issued at a discount of $53,180. How much of the discount should be amortized by the interest method at July 1, 1999?

    a. $1,277
    b. $2,659
    c. $3,191
    d. $3,723

42. The following information was abstracted from the accounts of the Oar Corporation at December 31, 1999:

Total income since incorporation	$840,000
Total cash dividends paid	260,000
Gain on sale of donated X Co. stock	90,000
Total value of stock dividends distributed	60,000
Excess of proceeds over cost of treasury stock sold	140,000

What should be the current balance of retained earnings?

a. $520,000
b. $580,000
c. $610,000
d. $670,000

43. Baker, Inc. owns 35% of the outstanding stock of Cable, Inc. During the calendar year 1999, Baker's "Investment in Cable" account appeared as follows:

Balance, January 1, 1999	$650,000
Equity in 1999 earnings of Cable	100,000
Dividends received from Cable--	
1999	(20,000)
Balance, December 31, 1999	$730,000

Baker feels that its equity in Cable's undistributed earnings will be realized in the form of future dividends. Assuming a 40% income tax rate for all affected years, by how much should the deferred tax liability increase because of these facts?

a. $6,400
b. $6,000
c. $7,200
d. $9,000

44. In single period statements, which of the following should be reflected as an adjustment to the opening balance of retained earnings?

a. Effect of a failure to provide for uncollectible accounts in the previous period.
b. Effect of a decrease in the estimated useful life of depreciable equipment.
c. Cumulative effect of a change of income recognition from the installment sale method to recognition at point of sale.
d. Cumulative effect of a change from an accelerated method to straight-line depreciation.

45. In January 1997, Cameron Corporation established a sinking fund in connection with its issue of bonds due in 2007. A bank was appointed as independent trustee of the fund. At December 31, 1999, the trustee held $364,000 cash in the sinking fund account, representing $300,000 in annual deposits to the fund, and $64,000 of interest earned on those deposits. How should the sinking fund be reported in Cameron's balance sheet at December 31, 1999?

a. No part of the sinking fund should appear in Cameron's balance sheet.
b. $64,000 should appear as a current asset.
c. $364,000 should appear as a current asset.
d. $364,000 should appear as a noncurrent asset.

46. On January 1, 1999, Richmond, Inc. signed a fixed-price contract to have Builder Associates construct a major plant facility at a cost of $4,000,000. It was estimated that it would take 3 years to complete the project. Also on January 1, 1999, to finance the construction cost, Richmond borrowed $4,000,000 payable in 10 annual installments of $400,000 plus interest at the rate of 11%. During 1999, Richmond made deposit and progress payments totaling $1,500,000 under the contract; the average amount of accumulated expenditures was $650,000 for the year. The excess borrowed funds were invested in short-term securities from which Richmond realized investment income of $250,000.

What amount should Richmond report as capitalized interest at December 31, 1999?

a. $ 71,500
b. $165,000
c. $190,000
d. $440,000

47. Taft Corp., which began business on January 1, 1998, appropriately uses the installment sales method of accounting. The following data are available for December 31, 1998 and 1999:

	1998	*1999*
Balance of deferred gross profit on sales account:		
1998	$300,000	$120,000
1999	--	440,000
Gross profit on sales	30%	40%

The installment accounts receivable balance at December 31, 1999, is

a. $1,000,000
b. $1,100,000
c. $1,400,000
d. $1,500,000

48. An inventory loss from market decline of $900,000 occurred in May 1999. Kerr Company recorded this loss in May 1999, after its March 31, 1999 quarterly income statement was issued. None of this loss was recovered by the end of 1999. How much of the inventory loss should be recognized in Kerr's quarterly income statement for the 3 months ended December 31, 1999?

a. $0
b. $225,000
c. $300,000
d. $900,000

49. John Tracey, M.D., keeps his accounting records on the cash basis. During 1999, Dr. Tracey collected $150,000 in fees from his patients. At December 31, 1998, Dr. Tracey had accounts receivable of $20,000. At December 31, 1999, Dr. Tracey had accounts receivable of $35,000 and unearned fees of $5,000. On the accrual basis, how much was Dr. Tracey's patient service revenue for 1999?

a. $130,000
b. $160,000
c. $165,000
d. $170,000

50. On July 1, 1999, Glendora Corporation issued $1,000,000 of 10% nonconvertible bonds at 103, due June 30, 2019. Each $1,000 bond was issued with 30 detachable stock warrants, each of which entitled the bondholder to buy one share of Glendora's $10 par value common stock for $25. On July 1, 1999, the market values of Glendora's common stock and warrants were $30 and $4, respectively. How much should Glendora record on July 1, 1999, as paid-in capital from stock warrants?

a. $ 30,000
b. $120,000
c. $150,000
d. $300,000

Items 51 through 53 are based on the following:

Dice Corp.'s balance sheet accounts as of December 31, 1999 and 1998, and information relating to 1999 activities are presented below.

	December 31	
	1999	*1998*
Assets		
Cash	$ 230,000	$ 100,000
Available-for-sale securities	300,000	--
Accounts receivable (net)	510,000	510,000
Inventory	680,000	600,000
Held-to-maturity securities	200,000	300,000
Plant assets	1,700,000	1,000,000
Accumulated depreciation	(450,000)	(450,000)
Goodwill	90,000	100,000
Total Assets	$3,260,000	$2,160,000

Liabilities and Stockholders' Equity		
Accounts payable and accrued liabilities	$ 825,000	$ 720,000
Short-term debt	325,000	--
Common stock, $10 par	800,000	700,000
Additional paid-in capital	370,000	250,000
Retained earnings	940,000	490,000
Total liabilities and stockholders' equity	$3,260,000	$2,160,000

Information relating to 1999 activities

- Net income for 1999 was $690,000.
- Cash dividends of $240,000 were declared and paid in 1999.
- Equipment costing $400,000 and having a carrying amount of $150,000 was sold in 1999 for $150,000.
- A held-to-maturity security was sold in 1999 for $135,000. There were no other transactions affecting held-to-maturity securities in 1999.
- 10,000 shares of common stock were issued in 1999 for $22 a share.
- Available-for-sale securities consist of treasury bills maturing on 6/30/00.

51. Net cash provided by Dice's 1999 operating activities was
  - a. $690,000
  - b. $915,000
  - c. $940,000
  - d. $950,000

52. Net cash used in Dice's 1999 investing activities was
  - a. $1,115,000
  - b. $ 895,000
  - c. $ 865,000
  - d. $ 815,000

53. Net cash provided by Dice's 1999 financing activities was
  - a. $305,000
  - b. $440,000
  - c. $455,000
  - d. $545,000

54. Dodd Corp. is preparing its December 31, 1999 financial statements and must determine the proper accounting treatment for the following situations:

- For the year ended December 31, 1999, Dodd has a loss carryback of $120,000 and a carryforward of $60,000 available to offset future taxable income. There is little doubt concerning the realizability of the $60,000 carryforward. There are no temporary differences.

- On December 30, 1999, Dodd received a $200,000 offer for its patent. Dodd's management is considering whether to sell the patent. The offer expires on February 28, 2000. The patent has a carrying amount of $100,000 at December 31, 1999.

Assume a current and future income tax rate of 30%. In its 1999 income statement, Dodd should recognize an increase in net income of
  - a. $0
  - b. $ 54,000
  - c. $ 70,000
  - d. $124,000

55. Nolan Co. began operations in 1995. It had been computing depreciation by an accelerated method until January 1, 1999, when a change to straight-line method was made. Assume the change is justified.

Depreciation computed by the accelerated method was reported as follows:

1995	*1996*	*1997*	*1998*
$9,000	$8,000	$8,000	$7,000

Had the straight-line method been used, depreciation would have been as follows:

1995	*1996*	*1997*	*1998*
$5,200	$5,200	$5,800	$5,800

The change to straight-line depreciation is effective January 1, 1999, and the new method will be applied both to assets acquired prior to that date and to those subsequently acquired.

Nolan's 1999 income tax rate has been 40% throughout the years 1995-1998.

Nolan's 1999 income before taxes and before the cumulative effect of the accounting change is $50,000. What is Nolan's 1999 net income?
  - a. $16,000
  - b. $24,000
  - c. $36,000
  - d. $60,000

56. On May 15, 1999, Munn, Inc. approved a plan to dispose of a segment of its business. It is expected that the sale will occur on February 1, 2000, at a selling price of $500,000. During 1999, disposal costs incurred by Munn totaled $75,000. The segment had actual or estimated operating losses as follows:

1/1/99 to 5/14/99	$130,000
5/15/99 to 12/31/99	50,000
1/1/00 to 1/31/00	15,000

The carrying amount of the segment at the date of sale was expected to be $850,000. Before income taxes, what amount should Munn report as a loss on disposal of the segment in its 1999 income statement?

a. $490,000
b. $475,000
c. $440,000
d. $425,000

57. The following balance sheet is for the partnership of Able, Boyer, and Cain:

Cash	$ 20,000
Other assets	180,000
	$200,000
Liabilities	$ 50,000
Able, Capital (40%)	37,000
Boyer, Capital (40%)	65,000
Cain, Capital (20%)	48,000
	$200,000

Figures shown parenthetically reflect agreed profit and loss sharing percentages.

If the firm, as shown on the original balance sheet, is dissolved and liquidated by selling assets in installments, the first sale of noncash assets having a book value of $90,000 realizes $50,000 and all cash available after settlement with creditors is distributed; the respective partners would receive (to the nearest dollar)

a. Able, $8,000; Boyer, $8,000; Cain, $4,000.
b. Able, $6,667; Boyer, $6,667; Cain, $6,666.
c. Able, $0; Boyer, $13,333; Cain, $6,667.
d. Able, $0,; Boyer, $3,000; Cain, $17,000.

58. For financial statement reporting, the Lexington Corporation recognizes royalty income in the period earned. For income tax reporting, royalties are taxed when collected. At December 31, 1999, unearned royalties of $400,000 were included in Lexington's balance sheet. All of these royalties had been collected in 1999. During 2000, royalties of $600,000 were collected. Unearned royalties in Lexington's December 31, 2000 balance sheet amounted to $350,000. Assume that the income tax rate is 30% for all affected years and that Lexington appropriately reported deferred tax assets of $120,000 and $105,000 in its December 31, 1999 and 2000 balance sheets, respectively. The amount reported in the provision for deferred income taxes (i.e., the deferred portion of income tax expense) in Lexington's income statement for the year ended December 31, 2000, should be a

a. $ 15,000 debit.
b. $105,000 credit.
c. $120,000 debit.
d. $180,000 credit.

Items 59 and 60 are based on the following:

Assume that Operating Corporation purchases a 10% common stock interest in Service Corporation for $10,000 on January 1, 1998, and an additional 20% interest for

$22,000 on January 1, 1999. The balance sheets of Service Corporation, which pays no dividends, follow:

	December 31, 1999	December 31, 1998	January 1, 1998
Cash	$130,000	$110,000	$100,000
Total assets	$130,000	$110,000	$100,000
Common stock	$100,000	$100,000	$100,000
Retained earnings	30,000	10,000	-0-
Total owners' equity	$130,000	$110,000	$100,000

59. During 1998, Operating Corporation carries this investment under the cost adjusted for fair value method and on January 1, 1999, adopts the equity method. For 1999, Operating Corporation should report as income from this 30% investment the single amount of

a. $9,000
b. $7,000
c. $6,000
d. $5,950

60. The investment described in item **59.** should be reported as a long-term investment in Operating Corporation's balance sheet at December 31, 1999, as a single amount of

a. $41,000
b. $39,000
c. $38,000
d. $37,900

Number 2

Rand, Inc., a nonpublic enterprise, is negotiating a loan for expansion purposes and the bank requires audited financial statements. Before closing the accounting records for the year ended December 31, 1999, Rand's controller prepared the following comparative financial statements for 1999 and 1998:

Rand, Inc.
BALANCE SHEETS
December 31, 1999 and 1998

	1999	*1998*
Assets		
Cash	$ 275,000	$150,000
Marketable securities	67,000	81,000
Accounts receivable	487,000	392,000
Allowance for doubtful accounts	(50,800)	(32,000)
Inventories	425,000	307,000
Property and equipment	310,000	217,000
Accumulated depreciation	(150,000)	(121,000)
Total assets	$1,363,200	$994,000
Liabilities & Stockholders' Equity		
Accounts payable & accrued liabilities	$ 420,000	$347,000
Estimated liability from lawsuit	100,000	--
Common stock, $10 par	260,000	260,000
Additional paid-in capital	130,000	130,000
Retained earnings	464,200	254,000
Unrealized gain (loss) on marketable securities	(11,000)	3,000
Total liabilities & stockholders' equity	$1,363,200	$994,000

Rand, Inc.
INCOME STATEMENTS
For the Years Ended December 31, 1999 and 1998

	1999	*1998*
Net sales	$1,580,000	$1,250,000
Operating expenses:		
Cost of sales	755,000	690,000
Selling & administrative	485,800	365,000
Depreciation	29,000	18,000
Estimated loss from lawsuit	100,000	--
	1,369,000	1,073,000
Net income	$ 210,200	$ 177,000

During the course of the audit, the following additional information was obtained:

• The investment portfolio consists of available-for-sale securities with a total cost of $78,000. No marketable securities were purchased or sold in either 1998 or 1999.

• In discussion with company officials, it was determined that the doubtful accounts expense rate based on net sales should be reduced to 2% from 3%, effective January 1, 1999.

• As a result of errors in physical count, inventories were overstated by $12,000 at December 31, 1998, and by $18,000 at December 31, 1999.

• On January 1, 1998, the cost of equipment purchased for $30,000 was debited to repairs and maintenance. Rand depreciates machines of this type by the straight-line method over a 5-year life, with no residual value.

• On July 1, 1999, fully depreciated equipment purchased for $21,000 was sold as scrap for $3,000. The only entry Rand made was to debit cash and credit property and equipment for the scrap proceeds. The property and equipment (net) had a current cost of $250,000 at December 31, 1999.

• Advertising and promotion expense for the year ended December 31, 1998, includes the $25,000 cost of printing sales catalogs for a special promotional campaign in January 1999.

• Rand was named as a defendant in a lawsuit in October 1999. Rand's counsel is of the opinion that Rand has a good defense and does not anticipate any impairment of Rand's assets or that any significant liability will be incurred. Nevertheless, Rand's management wished to be conservative and established a loss contingency of $100,000 at December 31, 1999.

Required:

Items 61 through 74 require the computation of numerical answers. On the CPA exam, candidates are instructed to write the computed amount in the boxes of the Objective Question Answer Sheet corresponding to the numbered item and blacken the appropriate oval below each box. For Rand Inc.'s 1999 financial statements, determine the amount for each item listed below.

Balance sheet items:
61. Adjustment to the investment account
62. Allowance for doubtful accounts
63. Inventories
64. Property and equipment
65. Accumulated depreciation
66. Estimated liability from lawsuit
67. Total increase in retained earnings excluding net income
68. Total decrease in retained earnings (no dividends were declared)

Income statement items:
69. Cost of sales
70. Selling and administrative expense
71. Depreciation expense
72. Estimated loss from lawsuit
73. Amount of loss on marketable equity securities charged to 1999 income
74. Other income

Number 3

On July 1, 1999, Marie Company sold special-order merchandise on credit and received in return an interest-bearing note receivable from the customer. Marie will receive interest at the prevailing rate for a note of this type. Both the principal and interest are due in one lump sum on June 30, 2000.

On September 1, 1999, Marie sold special-order merchandise on credit and received in return a noninterest-bearing note receivable from the customer. The prevailing rate of interest for a note of this type is determinable. The note receivable is due in one lump sum on August 31, 2001.

On November 1, 1999, other trade accounts receivable were transferred. Control over the receivables was surrendered. However, the transaction resulted in a recourse liability which can be estimated. The factor withheld 5% of the trade accounts receivable factored as protection against sales returns and allowances and charged a finance charge of 3%.

Required:

a.   How should Marie determine the interest income for 1999 on the
    1.   Interest-bearing note receivable? Why?
    2.   Noninterest-bearing note receivable? Why?

b.   How should Marie report the interest-bearing note receivable and the noninterest-bearing note receivable on its balance sheet at December 31, 1999?

c.   How should Marie account for the trade accounts receivable transferred on November 1, 1999? Why?

Number 4

On January 2, 1999, Cody Inc. sold equipment to Griff Co. for cash of $864,000 and immediately leased it back under a capital lease for 9 years. The carrying amount of the equipment was $540,000, and its estimated remaining eco-

nomic life is 10 years. Annual year-end payments of $153,000, which include executory costs of $3,000 are based on an implicit interest rate of 10%, which is known to Cody. Cody's incremental borrowing rate is 13%. Cody uses the straight-line method of depreciation. The rounded present value factors of an ordinary annuity for 9 years are 5.76 at 10% and 5.2 at 13%.

Required:

a.   What is the theoretical basis for requiring lessees to capitalize certain long-term leases? **Do not discuss the specific criteria for classifying a lease as a capital lease.**

b.   Prepare the journal entries that Cody must make to record the sale and the leaseback on January 2, 1999.

c.   Prepare the journal entries, including any adjusting entries, that Cody must make at December 31, 1999.

ANSWERS TO SAMPLE EXAMINATION
FINANCIAL ACCOUNTING AND REPORTING (BUSINESS ENTERPRISES)

Answer 1

1. a ___	11. c ___	21. a ___	31. d ___	41. a ___	51. c ___
2. c ___	12. c ___	22. b ___	32. c ___	42. a ___	52. a ___
3. c ___	13. d ___	23. b ___	33. a ___	43. a ___	53. a ___
4. c ___	14. c ___	24. b ___	34. b ___	44. a ___	54. b ___
5. a ___	15. b ___	25. a ___	35. c ___	45. d ___	55. c ___
6. c ___	16. d ___	26. a ___	36. c ___	46. a ___	56. a ___
7. b ___	17. a ___	27. d ___	37. a ___	47. d ___	57. d ___
8. b ___	18. a ___	28. d ___	38. c ___	48. a ___	58. a ___
9. a ___	19. c ___	29. c ___	39. a ___	49. b ___	59. c ___
10. b ___	20. c ___	30. d ___	40. a ___	50. b ___	60. b ___
					___/60 = ___%

Hints for Multiple-Choice Questions

1. Information makes a difference if it provides feedback on past events or indicates possible future events.

2. Market is limited to a ceiling (NRV) and a floor (NRV less normal profit).

3. The proceeds are allocated between the bonds and the warrants based on relative FMV; bond premium/discount is based on the proceeds assigned.

4. The acquisition of treasury stock reduces the amount of contributed capital and the number of shares outstanding.

5. The entry to write off a bad debt consists of a debit to the allowance and a credit to the receivable.

6. The present value of an ordinary annuity is the value today, given a discount rate (6%), of a series of future payments (each $3,000).

7. The effect of changing tax rates is recognized currently.

8. Unrealized items become realized.

9. All future cash inflows must be discounted to the present to determine the value of the bond.

10. The cost flow assumption may affect the dollar amount but not the method of computing the cost of goods available for sale.

11. Face rate = Market rate (Note: "unearned discount" is a senseless term).

12. An employee earns compensation as services are rendered to the employer.

13. Under GAAP, the entire gain on a sale-leaseback is recognized when a minor portion of rights to the property are retained.

14. Composition of plant assets is disclosed as part of the financial statements.

15. "Investment in subsidiary" should have been credited instead of "dividend revenue."

16. Asset or liability not recognized.

17. Recall upper and lower limits and prepare a diagram showing the placement of the variables.

18. The fair value of the asset received should only be used if it is more clearly evident.

19. Segments may be aggregated if similar economic characteristics and certain other criteria are met.

20. For EPS purposes, share of stock issued as a result of stock dividends or splits should be considered outstanding for the entire year.

21. No tricks here.

22. A change in estimate should be handled prospectively.

23. The amount of unfunded ABO must be adjusted for any accrued/prepaid pension cost in determining additional liability.

24. Earnings process is culminated.

25. "Paid-in capital--treasury stock" would be credited.

26. Not all of the rent is allocable to one department.

27. How are impairment losses accounted for? What account is the credit to?

28. APIC = Cash received – Par value of common.

29. How is inventory turnover related to days?

30. All assets and liabilities are translated at the current exchange rate at the balance sheet date.

31. In an annuity due, the PV factor used is the n-1 factor with 1.00 added to that factor.

32. Carrying value at 7/1/99 is $960,000 + ($40,000 discount x 6/10 amortized).

33. The investor must account for accrued interest paid so that, when the interest payment is received, interest income will be offset by the amount of interest not earned by the investor.

34. The effects of discontinued operations are never extraordinary items.

35. When should a loss be recognized?

36. R&D done under contract for others is matched with revenue using the completed-contract or percentage-of-completion method.

37. No tricks here.

38. The 1997 containers would be retired (no liability) because they are more than 2 years old.

39. $\dfrac{\$900,000 \text{ costs incurred}}{\$900,000 + \$1,800,000 \text{ estimated total costs}} = 1/3$ complete at 12/31/98.

40. Since no claims have yet been asserted, the contingent loss is regarded as reasonably possible.

41. Interest expense = (Carrying amount x Market rate) x 6/12 .

42. Per SFAS 116, donated assets are recorded as assets and as revenue at FMV. However, the $90,000 is included in income.

43. Remember that companies are allowed to exclude 80% of the dividend income from domestic investees.

44. How are errors in previous periods reported?

45. The assets of a sinking fund do not relate to current operations and thus are in the nature of long-term investments.

46. Interest capitalized is the lesser of actual interest cost or avoidable interest (i.e., purchase of an existing facility would eliminate construction expenditures).

47. The 1998 gross profit rate was 30%, so the balance of installment AR in 1999 that is left over from 1998 still only earns 30%.

48. The loss was already recognized in the interim period in which it was incurred (and will be recognized at 12/31/99 in the **annual** report).

49. AR from 1998 and unearned fees should be subtracted from cash receipts because they represent revenues earned in another period or not at all.

50. The incremental method, used when the FV of either the bonds or the warrants is not determinable, allocates FV to the determinable security and the remaining proceeds to the other.

51. Upon sale of equipment, $250,000 would have been removed from AD; thus, since the balance of AD did not change, depreciation was $250,000 in 1999.

52. Equipment costing $400,000 was sold, so $1,100,000 of equipment must have been purchased during 1999 ($1,000,000 12/31/98 – $400,000 + $1,100,000 = $1,700,000 12/31/99).

53. Financing activities include borrowing from creditors and repaying these amounts, and obtaining capital and providing owners with a ROI.

54. A deferred tax asset reduces income tax expense.

55. If Nolan had always used the straight-line method, prior years' income would have been higher.

56. Results before the measurement date comprise income (loss) from **operations**.

57. Under the installment method, the amount of "safe payment" to each partner must be determined using a Schedule of Possible Losses.

58. Income tax expense (on income statement) = Income tax payable (from tax return) $\pm$ Change in deferred taxes (net).

59. When an investor changes from the cost adjusted for fair value method to the equity method, prior years' income must be **retroactively** restated.

60. Balance in investment account = Original interest + Interest purchased 1/1/99 (for 30% total) + Retroactive income for 1998 + Share of 1999 income.

Answer 2

61.	$ 14,000	66.	$0	71.	$35,000
62.	$ 35,000	67.	$ 49,000	72.	$0
63.	$407,000	68.	$ 12,000	73.	$0
64.	$322,000	69.	$761,000	74.	$ 3,000
65.	$141,000	70.	$495,000		

Hints for Other Objective Questions

61.   Available-for-sale securities must be "marked-to-market."

62.   Find the difference between doubtful accounts expense at each rate.

63.   Prior period adjustment affects cost of sales.

64.   The **cost** of equipment should be removed from PP&E upon sale.

65.   Examine PP&E corrections.

66.   Accrue only if probable and reasonably estimable.

67.   What prior period adjustments are credited to retained earnings?

68.   What prior period adjustments are debited to retained earnings?

69.   Adjust for inventory errors.

70.   Adjust for doubtful accounts.

71.   Equipment purchased must be depreciated.

72.   Accrue only if probable and reasonably estimable.

73.   Available-for-sale MES are valued with an unrealized gain (loss) account.

74.   Examine PP&E transactions.

Answer Explanations

61. ($14,000) At 12/31/98, the marketable securities are carried at $81,000. However, as of 12/31/99, the market value of the securities had dropped to $67,000. Therefore, the investment account must be reduced by $14,000 ($81,000 – $67,000):

Unrealized gain (loss) on marketable securities	14,000	
Marketable securities		14,000

This entry also leaves a balance of ($11,000) in the contra stockholders' equity account--accumulated other comprehensive income corresponding to available-for-sale securities.

62. ($35,000) Decline in doubtful accounts expense rate effective 1/1/99

Doubtful accounts expense charged at 3% at net sales for 1999 (3% x $1,580,000)	$47,400
Doubtful accounts expense stated at 2% of net sales for 1999 (2% x $1,580,000)	31,600
Decrease in allowance and expense	$15,800

Allow. for doubtful accounts	15,800	
Selling and administrative exp. (Doubtful accounts expense)		15,800

12/31/99 allowance account bal. = $50,800 – $15,800 = $35,000

63. ($407,000)

$425,000 Beg. Bal – $18,000 overstatement = $407,000
(See item #69 for treatment of the 12/31/98 overstatement)

64. ($322,000)
Entries made:

	1998	
Repairs and maintenance	30,000	
Cash		30,000

	1999	
Cash	3,000	
Property and equipment		3,000

Correcting entries (1999):

Property and equipment	30,000	
Depreciation expense	6,000	
Accumulated depreciation		12,000
Retained earnings		24,000
Accumulated depreciation	21,000	
Property and equipment		18,000
Other income (gain on sale)		3,000

Ending balance = $310,000 before adjustment + $30,000 purchase – $18,000 sale ($21,000 cost – $3,000 credited to PP&E at sale date) = $322,000

65. ($141,000)

	Accumulated Depreciation		
		121,000	1/1/99
		29,000	1999 deprec.
		150,000	12/31/99 before corrections
To correct sale entry	21,000	12,000	To correct for asset expensed in 1998
		141,000	12/31/99 per audit

66. ($0) Loss is not probable per SFAS 5.

67. ($49,000)
Total credits to retained earnings

	Retained Earnings		
		254,000	1/1/99
To correct 1998 inv. overstatement	12,000		
		24,000	To correct for equip. expensed (See #64)
		25,000	To correct for 1999 promotion exp. over-statement (See #70)

68. ($12,000) Only debit to retained earnings (see #67).

69. ($761,000)

Correcting entries (1999):

Retained earnings	12,000	
Cost of sales		12,000
Cost of sales	18,000	
Inventory		18,000

	Cost of Sales		
12/31/99 before adjust.	755,000	12,000	To correct overstated beginning
To correct overstated ending inventory	18,000		inventory
12/31/99	761,000		

70. ($495,000)

Per preliminary income statement	$485,800
Change in doubtful accounts expense estimate (See #62)	(15,800)
Understatement of 1999 promotion expense	25,000
	$495,000

71. ($35,000)

Depreciation expense:
$29,000 per 1999 preliminary IS + $6,000 (see first correcting entry in #64)

72. ($0) Same as #66

73. ($0) Any fluctuation in the market value of available-for-sale securities is reported in "other comprehensive" income, not net income. Thus, this amount may not be charged to income as long as it remains unrealized and Rand recognizes **no** loss on marketable securities for 1999.

74. ($3,000) See second correcting entry under #64.

Answer 3

a. **1.** For the interest-bearing note receivable, the interest income for 1999 should be determined by multiplying the principal (face) amount of the note by the note's rate of interest by one-half (July 1, 1999, to December 31, 1999). Interest accrues with the passage of time, and it should be accounted for as an element of income over the life of the note receivable.

2. For the noninterest-bearing note receivable, the interest income for 1999 should be determined by multiplying the carrying value of the note by the prevailing rate of interest at the date of the note by one-third (September 1, 1999, to December 31, 1999). The carrying value of the note at September 1, 1999, is the maturity amount discounted for 2 years at the prevailing interest rate from the maturity date of August 31, 2000, back to the issuance date of September 1, 1999. Interest, even if unstated, accrues with the passage of time, and it should be accounted for as an element of income over the life of the note receivable.

b. The interest-bearing note receivable should be reported at December 31, 1999, as a current asset at its principle (face) amount.

The noninterest-bearing note receivable should be reported at December 31, 1999, as a noncurrent asset at its face amount less the unamortized discount on the note at December 31, 1999.

c. Because the trade accounts receivable were transferred with control surrendered, the transfer is recorded as a sale. On November 1, 1999, Marie should credit accounts receivable for the amount of trade accounts receivable transferred and credit a recourse liability. Marie should debit cash for the amount received from the factor, debit a receivable from the factor for 5% of the trade accounts receivable factored, and debit a loss for 3% of the trade accounts receivable transferred plus the amount of the recourse liability.

Answer 4

a. The theoretical basis for capitalizing certain long-term leases is that the economic effect or substance of such leases on the lessee is that of an installment purchase. Such a lease transfers substantially all the risks and benefits incident to the ownership of property to the lessee, and obligates the lessee in a manner similar to that created when funds are borrowed.

b.

Cash	864,000	
Deferred gain		324,000
Equipment		540,000
Leased equipment	864,000	
Capital lease obligation		864,000

c.

Interest expense	86,400	[1]	
Capital lease obligation	63,600		
Executory costs	3,000		
Cash			153,000
Depreciation	96,000	[2]	
Accumulated depreciation			96,000
Deferred gain	36,000	[3]	
Depreciation			36,000

[1] 864,000 x 10% implicit rate
[2] 864,000 ÷ 9-year lease period
[3] 324,000 ÷ 9-year lease period

APPENDIX B

AICPA Summary of Exam Coverage (Last 5 Exams) and Released Questions From the Financial Accounting and Reporting (FARE) Section of November 1997 and May 1998 Uniform CPA Examinations*

Summary of Exam Coverage--May 1996 through May 1998 Uniform CPA Examinations

The following summary of coverage provides an analysis of the Content Specification Outline coverage for the May 1996 through May 1998 FARE section of the Uniform CPA Examinations. This summary is intended only as a study aid and should not be used to predict the content of future Examinations.

How to interpret this table

The percentages on the third line of the table indicate the percentage points allocated to each type of question on these Examinations. For example, on the May 1998 Financial Accounting and Reporting section (FARE), 60% of the examination points were allocated to multiple-choice questions, 20% of the points were allocated to other objective answer format (OOAF), and 20% of the points were allocated to the essays.

The AICPA has also provided the **actual number** of multiple-choice questions asked for each area (identified with a roman numeral) and topic (identified with an uppercase letter) of the content specification outlines; (e.g., for the May 1998 Examination, there were 11 multiple-choice questions asked in Area I that were distributed among topics A-D). In addition, the AICPA has indicated the **percentage** of OOAF and essay questions asked by area and topic.

The number of questions released for the Financial Accounting and Reporting Section is as follows:

Multiple-Choice	_Other Objective Answer Format_	_Essay/Problem_
11	1	2

---

* These Content Specification Outlines and questions were published in _Selected Questions and Unofficial Answers Indexed to Content Specification Outlines_ (1999 Edition); reprinted with permission of the AICPA.

Financial Accounting and Reporting

	Multiple-Choice					OOAFs					Essays				
	M98 (60%)	N97 (60%)	M97 (60%)	N96 (60%)	M96 (60%)	M98 (20%)	N97 (20%)	M97 (20%)	N96 (20%)	M96 (20%)	M98 (20%)	N97 (20%)	M97 (20%)	N96 (20%)	M96 (20%)
I. Concepts and Standards for Financial Statements	11	14	0	4	7	2%	1%	5%	5%	10%	7%	5%	15%	11%	3%
A. Financial Accounting Concepts	0	0	0	2	0	2%	1%					2%	5%		3%
B. Financial Accounting Standards for Presentation and Disclosure in General Purpose Financial Statements	8	12	0	1	6			5%	5%	10%	7%	3%	10%	11%	
C. Other Presentations of Financial Data	3	2	0	1	1										
D. Financial Statement Analysis	0	0	0	0	0										
II. Recognition, Measurement, Valuation, and Presentation of Typical Items in Financial Statements in Conformity With Generally Accepted Accounting Principles	19	24	28	22	30	18%	0%	0%	10%	10%	4%	12%	5%	6%	0%
A. Cash, Cash Equivalents, and Marketable Securities	2	0	3	3	2										
B. Receivables	2	1	2	1	0							7%			
C. Inventories	2	2	2	0	3				10%	10%					
D. Property, Plant, and Equipment	0	3	3	0	2	5%									
E. Investments	1	0	1	2	2							2%		4%	
F. Intangibles and Other Assets	1	1	1	2	1										
G. Payables and Accruals	2	2	2	1	2										
H. Deferred Revenues	0	1	1	1	1										
I. Notes and Bonds Payable	0	3	2	2	1	4%									
J. Other Liabilities	0	1	2	0	1										
K. Equity Accounts	3	2	3	4	4										
L. Revenue, Cost, and Expense Accounts	6	8	5	6	11	9%					3%	3%	2%	2%	
III. Recognition, Measurement, Valuation, and Presentation of Typical Items in Financial Statements in Conformity With Generally Accepted Accounting Principles	30	22	32	34	23	0%	19%	15%	5%	0%	9%	3%	0%	3%	17%
A. Accounting Changes and Corrections of Errors	2	0	2	0	0										6%
B. Business Combinations	2	1	3	0	2		4%		5%						
C. Cash Flow Components--Financing, Investing, and Operating	2	3	0	2	2			5%			4%				
D. Contingent Liabilities and Commitments	0	1	2	2	0									4%	
E. Discontinued Operations	2	2	2	2	0										
F. Earnings per Share	2	0	2	1	1		2%								
G. Employee Benefits	3	1	4	6	2			5%						3%	
H. Extraordinary Items	2	3	3	2	2							3%			9%
I. Financial Instruments	1	1	0	3	2									2%	
J. Foreign Currency Transactions and Translation	1	1	2	1	1						2%				
K. Income Taxes	2	2	0	4	2			5%							
L. Interest Costs	2	0	2	2	1										2%

Financial Accounting and Reporting (cont.)

	Multiple-Choice					OOAFs					Essays				
	M98	N97	M97	N96	M96	M98	N97	M97	N96	M96	M98	N97	M97	N96	M96
M. Interim Financial Reporting	2	0	2	1	2		3%								
N. Leases	0	0	2	2	1		10%				3%				
O. Nonmonetary Transactions	1	2	2	2	2										
P. Quasi Reorganizations, Reorganizations, and Changes in Entity	1	1	0	1	0										
Q. Related Parties	2	2	2	1	2										
R. Research and Development Costs	2	2	1	1	1										
S. Segment Reporting	1	0	1	1	0										

I. Concepts and Standards for Financial Statements
B. Financial Accounting Standards for Presentation and Disclosure in General Purpose Financial Statements

1.   During 1995, Beck Co. purchased equipment for cash of $47,000, and sold equipment with a $10,000 carrying value for a gain of $5,000. How should these transactions be reported in Beck's 1995 statement of cash flows?
  a.   Cash outflow of $32,000.
  b.   Cash outflow of $42,000.
  c.   Cash inflow of $5,000 and cash outflow of $47,000.
  d.   Cash inflow of $15,000 and cash outflow of $47,000.

1.   (R1197,FARE,7)   **(d)**   The correct answer is (d). The purchase of equipment for $47,000 represents a cash outflow of $47,000 in the investing section of the statement of cash flows. Selling equipment for a gain of $5,000 that had a book value of $10,000 represents a cash inflow of $15,000 in the investing section. The money received would have to equal the book value plus the gain, $10,000 + $5,000, which is $15,000. Per SFAS 95, the inflows and the outflows must be shown separately, not netted in each section of the statement of cash flows.

B.2. Balance Sheet

2.   According to the FASB conceptual framework, comprehensive income includes which of the following?

	Loss on discontinued operations	*Investments by owners*
a.	Yes	Yes
b.	Yes	No
c.	No	Yes
d.	No	No

2.   (R598,FARE,1)   **(b)**   According to the FASB conceptual framework, comprehensive income includes all changes in equity during a period from nonowner transactions. Therefore, loss on discontinued operations is part of comprehensive income, while investments by owners is not. Therefore, answers (a), (c), and (d) are incorrect.

C.2. Personal Financial Statements

3.   Which statements are usually included in a set of personal financial statements?
  a.   A statement of net worth and an income statement.
  b.   A statement of financial condition and a statement of changes in net worth.
  c.   A statement of net worth, an income statement, and a statement of cash flows.
  d.   A statement of financial condition, a statement of changes in net worth, and a statement of cash flows.

3.   (R598,FARE,2)   **(b)**   Personal financial statements prepared for an individual, husband and wife, or a family consist of two financial statements: statement of financial condition and statement of changes in net worth. The statement of financial condition presents estimated amounts of assets, liabilities, income taxes, and net worth at a specified date. The statement of changes in net worth shows the main sources of increases (decreases) in net worth. Therefore, answers (a), (c), and (d) are incorrect.

4.   At May 31, 1997, Quay owned a $10,000 whole-life insurance policy with a cash-surrender value of $4,500, net of loans of $2,500. In Quay's May 31, 1997 personal statement of financial condition, what amount should be reported as investment in life insurance?
  a. $ 4,500
  b. $ 7,000
  c. $ 7,500
  d. $10,000

4.   (R598,FARE,3)   **(a)**   In a statement of financial condition, assets are estimated at their current values. The current value of the life insurance policy is its cash-surrender value, which is $4,500. The loans of $2,500 would be classified in the liabilities section of the statement.

II. Recognition, Measurement, Valuation, and Presentation of Typical Items in Financial Statements in Conformity With Generally Accepted Accounting Principles
D. Property, Plant, and Equipment

5. During January 1995, Yana Co. incurred landscaping costs of $120,000 to improve leased property. The estimated useful life of the landscaping is 15 years. The remaining term of the lease is 8 years, with an option to renew for an additional 4 years. However, Yana has not reached a decision with regard to the renewal option. In Yana's December 31, 1995 balance sheet, what should be the net carrying amount of landscaping costs?

    a. $0
    b. $105,000
    c. $110,000
    d. $112,000

5. (R1197,FARE,8) **(b)**   The correct answer is (b). When leasehold improvements are made, the improvements are depreciated using the useful life of the asset or the term of the lease, whichever is shorter. If the lessee expects to renew the lease, the depreciation period could be extended up to the end of the new lease term and compared with the useful life of the landscaping costs. In this case 12 years (8 years original term + 4 years extension) would be shorter than 15 years. However, Yana Co. has not made a decision about renewing the lease, so the depreciation should be calculated only based on the original term of the lease, 8 years.

$$ \$120,000 / 8 \text{ yrs.} = \$15,000 \text{ per year} $$

After 1 year of recognizing depreciation, the net carrying amount of the improvements is $120,000 − 15,000 = $105,000.

I. Notes and Bonds Payable

6. The market price of a bond issued at a premium is equal to the present value of its principal amount

    a.   Only, at the stated interest rate.
    b.   And the present value of all future interest payments, at the stated interest rate.
    c.   Only, at the market (effective) interest rate.
    d.   And the present value of all future interest payments, at the market (effective) interest rate.

6. (R1197,FARE,9) **(d)**   The correct answer is (d). The market price of a bond is equal to the future cash flows discounted back to present value. Two types of cash flows exist with a bond, payment of principal and interest. To determine the present value, the market rate must be used for both the payment of the principal and the interest payments. Answer (a) is incorrect because both the present value of the principal and interest payments must be determined using the market rate of interest. Answer (b) is incorrect because the present value is calculated using the market rate of interest, not the stated rate. The stated rate of interest is multiplied by the par or principal amount to determine the cash interest payments to be made. Answer (c) is incorrect because the present value of the interest payments must also be determined to calculate the market price of a bond.

K. Equity Accounts

7. Eagle and Falk are partners with capital balances of $45,000 and $25,000, respectively. They agree to admit Robb as a partner. After the assets of the partnership are revalued, Robb will have a 25% interest in capital and profits, for an investment of $30,000. What amount should be recorded as goodwill to the original partners?

    a. $0
    b. $ 5,000
    c. $ 7,500
    d. $20,000

7. (R598,FARE,4) **(d)**   With the addition of a new partner, the old partnership has dissolved and a new partnership has been created. The partnership is in essence buying the goodwill of the old partnership. The goodwill to be recorded is calculated as follows:

25% x New total capital	=	$ 30,000
New total capital	=	$120,000

$30,000 of capital belongs to Robb, and $90,000 belongs to Eagle and Falk. They have capital balances totaling $70,000 ($45,000 + $25,000) in the old partnership. The difference of $20,000 is goodwill which would be shared by them in their P&L ratio in the old partnership which was where the goodwill originated.

L. Revenue, Cost, and Expense Accounts

8. Ichor Co. reported equipment with an original cost of $379,000 and $344,000, and accumulated depreciation of $153,000 and $128,000, respectively, in its comparative financial statements for the years ended December 31, 1995 and 1994. During 1995, Ichor purchased equipment costing $50,000, and sold equipment with a carrying value of $9,000. What amount should Ichor report as depreciation expense for 1995?
  a. $19,000
  b. $25,000
  c. $31,000
  d. $34,000

8. (R1197,FARE,10) **(c)**   The correct answer is (c). To determine the depreciation expense for the year, set up T-accounts for property, plant, and equipment and accumulated depreciation.

PP&E			
Bal. 1/1/95	$344,000		
Purchased equipment	50,000	?	Sold equipment
Bal. 12/31/95	$379,000		

The cost of the equipment sold was $15,000. Now, the accumulated depreciation T-account can be completed.

Acc. Depr.			
		$128,000	1/1/95 bal.
Equipment sold	$6,000		
		?	Depreciation expense for 1995
		$153,000	12/31/95 bal.

The $6,000 [cost minus accumulated depreciation is equal to carrying value ($15,000 – X = 9,000)] is the accumulated depreciation of the asset sold, which reduces the accumulated depreciation account. Thus, depreciation expense for the year is equal to $31,000 ($25,000, the net increase in the account plus $6,000, the gross decrease in the account from the sale of equipment).

III. Recognition, Measurement, Valuation, and Presentation of Specific Types of Transactions and Events in Financial Statements in Conformity With Generally Accepted Accounting Principles
F. Earnings per Share

9. In computing the weighted-average number of shares outstanding during the year, which of the following midyear events must be treated as if it had occurred at the beginning of the year?
  a. Declaration and distribution of stock dividend.
  b. Purchase of treasury stock.
  c. Sale of additional common stock.
  d. Sale of preferred convertible stock.

9. (R598,FARE,5)   **(a)**   To compute the weighted-average number of shares outstanding for the year, midyear events of a stock dividend or a stock split must be treated as if the events had occurred at the beginning of the year. The purchase of treasury stock, sale of additional common stock, and sale of preferred convertible stock are calculated from the date of the occurrence, not the beginning of the year. Therefore, answers (b), (c), and (d) are incorrect.

K. Income Taxes

10. Hut Co. has temporary taxable differences that will reverse during the next year and add to taxable income. These differences relate to noncurrent assets. Deferred income taxes based on these temporary differences should be classified in Hut's balance sheet as a
  a. Current asset.
  b. Noncurrent asset.
  c. Current liability.
  d. Noncurrent liability.

10. (R1197,FARE,11) **(d)**   The correct answer is (d). Temporary differences can result in either deferred tax assets or deferred tax liabilities and as either current or noncurrent. For Hut Co. the difference will add to taxable income in the next year, which will increase taxable income. Thus, the company will have to use more of its resources in the next year because of the temporary difference, so it is a liability. It is classified as a noncurrent liability because the asset that the difference relates to is a noncurrent asset. If the difference does not relate to a specific asset or liability, it should be classified based on the timing of the reversal or utilization date (e.g., the deferred tax asset resulting from a net operating loss carryforward).

Q. Related Parties

11. Lemu Co. and Young Co. are under the common management of Ego Co. Ego can significantly influence the operating results of both Lemu and Young. While Lemu had no transactions with Ego during the year, Young sold merchandise to Ego under the same terms given to unrelated parties. In the notes to their respective financial statements, should Lemu and Young disclose their relationship with Ego?

	Lemu	*Young*
a.	Yes	Yes
b.	Yes	No
c.	No	Yes
d.	No	No

11. (R598,FARE,6)   **(a)**   SFAS 57, *Related-Party Disclosures*, requires disclosures of any material transactions between related parties. When a control relationship exists, the relationship should be disclosed even if no transactions occurred. Lemu Co. and Young Co. are both in a control relationship with Ego Co. and therefore, the relationship must be disclosed in both cases. Answers (b), (c), and (d) are incorrect.

I. Concepts and Standards for Financial Statements
A. Financial Accounting Concepts

III. Recognition, Measurement, Valuation, and Presentation of Specific Types of Transactions and Events in Financial Statements in Conformity With Generally Accepted Accounting Principles
A. Accounting Changes and Corrections

OTHER OBJECTIVE QUESTIONS

Problem 1   (R1197,FARE2)

This problem consists of 4 items. Select the **best** answer for each item. Use a No. 2 pencil to blacken the appropriate ovals on the Objective Answer Sheet to indicate your answers. **Answer all items.** Your grade will be based on the total number of correct answers.

On January 2, 1996, Falk Co. hired a new controller. During the year, the controller, working closely with Falk's president and outside accountants, made changes in existing accounting policies, instituted new accounting policies, and corrected several errors dating from prior to 1996.

Falk's financial statements for the year ended December 31, 1996, will not be presented in comparative form with its 1995 financial statements.

Required:

Items 1 through 4 represent Falk's transactions.

List A represents possible classifications of these transactions as a change in accounting principle, a change in accounting estimate, correction of an error in previously presented financial statements, or neither an accounting change nor an error correction.

List B represents the general accounting treatment required for these transactions. These treatments are:

- Cumulative effect approach--Include the cumulative effect of the adjustment resulting from the accounting change or error correction in the 1996 financial statements.
- Retroactive restatement approach--Adjust 1996 beginning retained earnings if the error or change affects a period prior to 1996.
- Prospective approach--Report 1996 and future financial statements on the new basis, but do not adjust beginning retained earnings or include the cumulative effect of the change in the 1996 income statements.

List A (Select one)		List B (Select one)	
Type of change		*General accounting treatment*	
(A)	Change in accounting principle.	(X)	Cumulative effect approach.
(B)	Change in accounting estimate.	(Y)	Retroactive restatement approach.
(C)	Correction of an error in previously presented in financial statements.	(Z)	Prospective approach.
(D)	Neither an accounting change nor an error correction.		

For **Items 1 and 2**, select a classification for each transaction from List A and the general accounting treatment required to report the change from List B, and blacken the corresponding ovals on the Objective Answer Sheet.

1. Falk manufactures customized equipment to customer specifications on a contract basis. Falk changed its method of accounting for these long-term contracts from the completed-contract method to the percentage-of-completion method because Falk is now able to make reasonable estimates of future construction costs.

2. Based on improved collection procedures, Falk changed the percentage of credit sales used to determine the allowance for uncollectible accounts from 2% to 1%.

For **Items 3 and 4**, in addition to selecting a classification for each transaction from List A **and** the general accounting treatment required to report the change from List B, a third response is required. For these items, determine the amount, if any, of the cumulative change or prior period adjustment, ignoring income tax effects, and record the amount by blackening the corresponding ovals on the Objective Answer Sheet. To record a **zero** answer for an item, you must blacken all the **zero ovals** for that particular item. If zeros precede your numerical answer, blacken the zeros in the ovals preceding your answer. **You can-**

not receive credit for your answers if you fail to blacken an oval in each column. You may write the numbers in the boxes provided to facilitate blackening the ovals; however, the numbers written in the boxes will **not** be graded.

3. Effective January 1, 1996, Falk changed from average cost to FIFO to account for its inventory. Cost of goods sold under each method was as follows:

Year	Average cost	FIFO
Years prior to 1995	$71,000	$77,000
1995	79,000	82,000

4. In January 1995, Falk purchased a machine with a 5-year life and no salvage value for $40,000. The machine was depreciated using the straight-line method. On December 30, 1996, Falk discovered that depreciation on the machine had been calculated using a 25% rate.

I. Concepts and Standards for Financial Statements
A. Financial Accounting Concepts

III. Recognition, Measurement, Valuation, and Presentation of Specific Types of Transactions and Events in Financial Statements in Conformity With Generally Accepted Accounting Principles
A. Accounting Changes and Corrections

OTHER OBJECTIVE ANSWERS AND ANSWER EXPLANATIONS

Problem 1   (R1197,FARE2)

1. (A,Y) Changing from using the completed-contract method to the percentage-of-completion method is a change in accounting principle per APB 20. Five situations require retroactive restatement of all periods presented as if the new method had been used in all prior periods. Per APB 20, a change in the method of accounting for long-term contracts requires a retroactive restatement.

1. Change from LIFO to another inventory method
2. Change in method of accounting for long-term contracts
3. Change to or from the full cost method of accounting for exploration costs in the extractive industries
4. Any change made by a company first issuing financial statements to the public for the purpose of obtaining additional equity capital or effecting a business combination or registering securities
5. Change that is mandated by an authoritative pronouncement to use the retroactive approach

2. (B,Z) The percentage of net credit sales used in determining the amount to be added to the allowance for uncollectible accounts is an estimate made by management. Changing the percentage is a change in accounting estimate, which is treated prospectively.

3. (A,X, $9,000) Changing from average cost to FIFO is a change in accounting principle. Most changes in accounting principle are treated as a cumulative effect approach. However, the five special situations above require retroactive restatement. This situation does not fit any of the five scenarios in number 1. above, so the change in accounting principle should be treated using the cumulative effect approach. To determine the amount, the prior years' effect of the change on the beginning retained earnings needs to be computed and displayed net of tax after extraordinary items and before net income. Because the change is effective in 1996, all prior years, including 1995, need to be included. The cost of goods sold would have been $6,000 higher in years prior to 1995 and $3,000 higher in 1995 under the FIFO method. The total cumulative effect ignoring income taxes is $6,000 + $3,000 = $9,000. The entry to record the cumulative effect is as follows:

Cumulative effect of a change in accounting principle	9,000	
Inventory		9,000

Note that this situation represents a situation where prices have been decreasing causing FIFO inventory (latest prices) to be less than average cost inventory and cost of goods sold to be greater under FIFO.

4. (C,Y, $2,000) An error has occurred because using the straight-line method for a 5-year-life asset should compute depreciation using a 20% rate (100%/5 years). A correction of an error in previously presented financial statements is treated as a prior period adjustment with retroactive restatement and should be reported as adjustments to beginning retained earnings of each year presented. The amount of the adjustment is the difference in the amount of depreciation taken and what should have been taken in 1995 only. Because the error was found in 1996, depreciation expense for 1996 could be corrected. Depreciation in 1995 was $10,000 ($40,000 x 25%). It should have been $8,000 ($40,000 x 20%) or [($40,000 – 0) /5]. The difference of $2,000 is the adjustment necessary.

Accumulated depreciation	2,000	
Retained earnings		2,000

I. Concepts and Standards for Financial Statements
A. Financial Accounting Concepts *and*
B. Financial Accounting Standards for Presentation and Disclosure in General Purpose Financial Statements

II. Recognition, Measurement, Valuation, and Presentation of Typical Items in Financial Statements in Conformity With Generally Accepted Accounting Principles
K. Equity Accounts

III. Recognition, Measurement, Valuation, and Presentation of Specific Types of Transactions and Events in Financial Statements in Conformity With Generally Accepted Accounting Principles
G. Employee Benefits

ESSAY

Problem 1   (R1197,FARE2)

Field Co.'s stockholders' equity account balances at December 31, 1995, were as follows:

Common stock	$ 800,000
Additional paid-in capital	1,600,000
Retained earnings	1,845,000

The following 1996 transactions and other information relate to the stockholders' equity accounts:

- Field had 400,000 authorized shares of $5 par common stock, of which 160,000 shares were issued and outstanding.
- On March 5, 1996, Field acquired 5,000 shares of its common stock for $10 per share to hold as treasury stock. The shares were originally issued at $15 per share. Field uses the cost method to account for treasury stock. Treasury stock is permitted in Field's state of incorporation.
- On July 15, 1996, Field declared and distributed a property dividend of inventory. The inventory had a $75,000 carrying value and a $60,000 fair market value.
- On January 2, 1994, Field granted stock options to employees to purchase 20,000 shares of Field's common stock at $18 per share, which was the market price on that date. The options may be exercised within a 3-year period beginning January 2, 1996. The measurement date is the same as the grant date. On October 1, 1996, employees exercised all 20,000 options when the market value of the stock was $25 per share. Field issued new shares to settle the transaction.
- Field's net income for 1996 was $240,000.
- Field intends to issue new stock options to key employees in 1997. Field's management is aware that SFAS 123, *Accounting for Stock-Based Compensation*, which was issued in 1995, discusses both the "intrinsic value" method and the "fair value" method of accounting for stock options. Field's management is unsure of the difference between the two methods.

Required:

a.   Prepare the stockholders' equity section of Field's December 31, 1996 balance sheet. Support all computations.

b.   In a brief memo to Field's management, explain how compensation cost is measured under both the "fair value" method and the "intrinsic value" method of accounting for stock options, and when the measured cost is recognized.

I. Concepts and Standards for Financial Statements
A. Financial Accounting Concepts *and*
B. Financial Accounting Standards for Presentation and Disclosure in General Purpose Financial Statements

II. Recognition, Measurement, Valuation, and Presentation of Typical Items in Financial Statements in Conformity With Generally Accepted Accounting Principles
K. Equity Accounts

III. Recognition, Measurement, Valuation, and Presentation of Specific Types of Transactions and Events in Financial Statements in Conformity With Generally Accepted Accounting Principles
G. Employee Benefits

SOLUTION GUIDE AND ANSWER OUTLINE

Problem 1   (R1197,FARE2)

a. To prepare the stockholders' equity section of Field's December 31, 1996 balance sheet, certain computations need to be made first.

1. The common stock authorized does not change throughout the problem; it is 400,000 shares. The number of shares outstanding increases by the 20,000 shares issued when the stock options were exercised. The balance in the common stock account is the number of shares issued times the par value of the common stock (180,000 x $5 = $900,000).

2. The treasury stock is accounted for by the cost method, which means the treasury stock is recorded at cost (5,000 shares x $10 = $50,000). The journal entry for the treasury stock is

Treasury stock	50,000	
Cash		50,000

3. The information given indicates that the intrinsic value method of APB 25 is used because no fair value is given for these options which would be needed to use the fair value method of SFAS 123. Compensation cost is zero and no entry is made until the options are recognized. Additional paid-in capital is the amount of money received for stock above the par value. The exercise or option price of the stock options exercised was $18 per share. The $13 per share paid above the par value of the stock needs to be added to the additional paid-in capital account, so $260,000 ($13 x 20,000 shares) should be added to the beginning balance of $1,600,000 for a total of $1,860,000 in the additional paid-in capital account.

4. The formula for retained earnings is

    > Beginning balance
    > Add: Net income
    > <u>Less: Dividends</u>
    > Ending balance

    The amount of the dividends is the fair market value of the property distributed, which is $60,000

in this case. A $15,000 loss is recognized from the property dividend for the difference between the $75,000 carrying value and market value of the inventory. However, this loss would already be included in 1996 net income. Retained earnings is

Beginning balance	$1,845,000
Add: Net income	240,000
Less: Dividend	(60,000)
Ending balance	$2,025,000

b. Fair value method

- Cost measured at grant date at value of award
- Value based on option-pricing model

Intrinsic value method

- Measured at grant date (or other measurement date)
- Difference between market price at grant date over employee exercise price

Recognize expense methods over service period for both

UNOFFICIAL ANSWER

Problem 1   (R1197,FARE2)

a.

Field Co.
STOCKHOLDERS' EQUITY SECTION OF BALANCE SHEET
December 31, 1996

Common stock, $5 par value, 400,000 shares authorized,		
180,000 shares issued, 175,000 shares outstanding		$ 900,000 [1]
Additional paid-in capital		1,860,000 [2]
Retained earnings:		
Beginning balance	$1,845,000	
Add: Net income	240,000	
Less: Property dividend distributed	(60,000)	2,025,000
		4,785,000
Less common stock in treasury, 5,000 shares at cost		(50,000)
Total stockholders' equity		$4,735,000

[1]   Shares issued: 160,000 + 20,000 = 180,000 x $5 = $900,000
[2]   Additional paid-in capital $1,600,000 + [20,000 x ($18 – 5)] = $1,860,000 (1,600,000 + 260,000)

b.   To: Management, Field Co.
Re: Accounting for Stock-Based Compensation

As you are aware, SFAS 123 discusses both the "intrinsic value" method and the "fair value" method of accounting for stock options. The purpose of this memo is to inform you of the difference between the two methods and of when the company should record compensation cost associated with 1997 stock option issuances.

Under the "fair value" method of accounting for stock options, compensation cost is measured at the grant date based on the value of the award. This value is computed using an option-pricing model. Under the "intrinsic value" method, compensation cost is the excess, if any, of the quoted market price of the stock at the grant date (or other measurement date) over the amount an employee must pay to acquire the stock.

Under both methods, compensation cost, if any, is recognized over the service period, which is usually the vesting period.

I. Concepts and Standards for Financial Statements
B.2. Balance Sheet

ESSAY

Problem 2 (R598,FARE1)

The following information relates to the obligations of Villa Watch Co. as of December 31, 1997:

- Accounts payable for goods and services purchased on open account amounted to $35,000 at December 31, 1997.
- On December 15, 1997, Villa declared a cash dividend of $.05 per common share, payable on January 12, 1998, to shareholders of record as of December 31, 1997. Villa had 1,000,000 shares of common stock issued and outstanding throughout 1997.
- On December 31, 1997, Villa entered into a 6-year capital lease on a warehouse and made the first annual lease payment of $100,000. Villa's incremental borrowing rate was 12%, and the interest rate implicit in the lease, which was known to Villa, was 10%. The rounded present value factors for an annuity due for 6 years are 4.6 at 12% and 4.8 at 10%.
- On July 1, 1997, Villa issued $500,000, 8% bonds for $440,000 to yield 10%. The bonds mature on June 30, 2003, and pay interest annually every June 30. At December 31, 1997, the bonds were trading on the open market at 86 to yield 12%. Villa uses the effective interest method.
- Villa's 1997 pretax financial income was $850,000 and its taxable income was $600,000. The difference is due to $100,000 of permanent differences and $150,000 of temporary differences related to noncurrent assets. At December 31, 1997, Villa had cumulative taxable differences of $300,000 related to noncurrent assets. Villa's effective tax rate is 30%. Villa made no estimated tax payments during the year.
- Contingency information

  - Villa has been named a liable party for toxic waste cleanup on its land, and must pay an as-yet undetermined amount for environmental remediation activities.
  - An adjoining landowner, Clear Toothpaste Co., sold its property because of possible toxic contamination of the water supply and resulting potential adverse public reaction toward its product. Clear sued Villa for damages. There is a reasonable possibility that Clear will prevail and be awarded between $250,000 and $600,000.
  - As a result of comprehensive risk assessment, Villa has discontinued rockslide insurance for its warehouse, which is located at the base of a mountain. The warehouse has never sustained rockslide damage, and the probability of sustaining future damage is only slight.

Required:

Begin the answer to each requirement (i.e., a., b., and c.) on the top of a new page.

a. Prepare the liabilities section of Villa's December 31, 1997 balance sheet.

b. Discuss the information Villa is required to disclose, either in the body of the financial statements or the notes thereto, related to bonds payable and capital leases included in the liabilities presented above.

c. Explain how Villa should account for each contingency in its 1997 financial statements. Discuss the theoretical justification for each accounting treatment.

I. Concepts and Standards for Financial Statements
B.2. Balance Sheet

SOLUTION GUIDE AND ANSWER OUTLINE

Problem 1   (R598,FARE1)

a. 1. Accounts payable are current because these amounts are typically due in less than 1 year

2. Cash dividends payable are current because they will be paid in the following January. The amount is $50,000 ($.05 x 1,000,000 shares)

3. The lease obligation must be separated into a current and noncurrent portion. The current portion is the amount by which the lease obligation's principal will be reduced in the next year. The carrying value of the lease obligation at 12/31/97 is $380,000 [(4.8 x $100,000) – $100,000]. The amount of principal reduction (current liability) for 1998 is $62,000 [$100,000 – ($380,000 x 10%)]. The noncurrent liability is $318,000 ($380,000 – $62,000). Because the lessor's implicit rate of 10% is lower than Villa's incremental borrowing rate and Villa is aware of the lessor's implicit rate, it shall be used per SFAS 13.

4. Accrued interest on the bonds is a current liability. The amount is $20,000 ($500,000 x 8% x 1/2) for the 6 months they are outstanding in 1997.

5. The bonds payable are all noncurrent because they do not mature until 2003. The carrying amount is the issue amount plus the amortization of the bond discount for 6 months or $442,000 [$440,000 + (10% x $440,000 x 1/2) – (8% x $500,000 x 1/2)]. The information about the current market price and yield rate is not relevant because under the historical cost model per GAAP, the bonds market price and yield rate at the issue date are used throughout the life of the bond issue.

6. Income taxes payable is a current liability of $180,000 ($600,000 x 30%).

7. Deferred income tax liability is a long-term liability because it relates to noncurrent assets. Only temporary differences have future taxable or deductible amounts that result in deferred tax liabilities or deferred tax assets. Current pretax financial income was reduced by the $150,000 temporary difference, a current deductible amount that will result in a future taxable amount(s). The cumulative temporary differences including the $150,000 that arose this period are $300,000. Therefore, the deferred tax liability is $90,000 ($300,000 x 30%).

b. Capital lease disclosures on face of BS or in notes
- Gross amount of assets
  - Major classes
- Future minimum lease payments
- General description of arrangement
  - Existence and terms or renewal

- Escalation clauses
- Restrictions

Bonds payable disclosures on face of
- BS or in notes
- Face amount
- Nature and terms
  - Credit and market risk
  - Cash requirements
  - Related accounting policies

c. Toxic waste
- Loss incurred
- Disclose nature and cannot be estimated

Clear's claim
- Not probable, so do not accrue
- Disclose existence, nature, and estimate

Rockslide insurance
- No impairment
- No liability incurred
- Do not accrue
- Remote, disclosure not needed

UNOFFICIAL ANSWER

Problem 1   (R598,FARE1)

a.

Villa Co.
BALANCE SHEET--LIABILITIES SECTION
December 31, 1997

Accounts payable	$ 35,000	
Accrued interest payable	20,000	[2]
Income taxes payable	180,000	[3]
Dividends payable	50,000	
Current portion, long-term debt	62,000	[1]
Total current liabilities	347,000	
Capital lease payable, less		
$62,000 current portion	318,000	[1]
Bonds payable	442,000	[2]
Deferred tax liability	90,000	[3]
Total liabilities	$1,197,000	

[1] $100,000 x 4.8 = $480,000
$480,000 – $100,000 = $380,000
$380,000 x 10% = $ 38,000
$100,000 – $38,000 = $ 62,000
$380,000 – $62,000 = $318,000

[2] 500K x 8% x 1/2 = 20K
440K x 10% x 1/2 = 22K
440 K + (22K – 20K) = 442,000

[3] 600K x 30% = 180K
300K x 30% = 90K

b. Villa should disclose the following information about the capital leases, either in the body of the financial statements or in the notes thereto:

- The gross amount of assets recorded under the capital leases, presented by major classes. This information may be combined with owned assets.

- Future minimum lease payments as of the balance sheet date, in the aggregate and for each of the 5 succeeding years.
- A general description of the leasing arrangement, including the existence and terms of renewal, escalation clauses, and restrictions imposed by the lease agreements.

Villa should disclose the following information about the bonds payable, either in the body of the financial statements or in the notes thereto:

- The face amount.
- The nature and terms of the bonds and a discussion of their credit and market risk, cash requirements, and related accounting policies.
- The fair value of the bonds and the method used to estimate their fair value. The price at which the bonds are trading is the most reasonable estimate of their fair value at December 31, 1997.

c. Villa should account for each contingency in a slightly different way because the likelihood of Villa's incurring a loss differs in each situation.

For the toxic waste cleanup, a loss has been incurred. In the notes to its financial statements, Villa should disclose the nature of the loss on cleanup and indicate that an estimate of the loss, or range of the loss, cannot be made. No accrual should be made because the loss cannot be reasonably estimated and accrual of an uncertain amount would impair the integrity of the financial statements.

With regard to Clear's claim it is only reasonably possible, and not probable, that Villa will have to pay. Accordingly, Villa should not accrue the loss. Villa should disclose the existence and nature of Clear's claim in the notes to its financial statements. Disclosure should include an estimate of the potential range of loss.

Regarding the lack of rockslide insurance, no asset has been impaired and no liability has been incurred. Accordingly, Villa should not accrue a loss. Since the likelihood of a rockslide is remote, disclosure of the uninsured risk, while permitted, is not required.